MANAGEMENT

McGRAW-HILL SERIES IN MANAGEMENT

FRED LUTHANS
AND KEITH DAVIS,
CONSULTING EDITORS

Arnold and Feldman: Organizational Behavior

Bartol and Martin: Management

Cascio: Managing Human Resources: Productivity, Quality of Work Life, Profits

Certo and Peter: Selected Cases in Strategic Management

Certo and Peter: Strategic Management: A Focus on Process

Certo and Peter: Strategic Management: Concepts and Applications

Daughtrey and Ricks: Contemporary Supervision: Managing People and Technology

Davis and Newstrom: Human Behavior at Work: Organizational Behavior

Dobler, Burt and Lee: Purchasing and Materials Management: Text and Cases

Dunn and Rachel: Wage and Salary Administration: Total Compensation Systems

Feldman and Arnold: Managing Individual and Group Behavior in Organizations

Frederick, Davis, Post: Business and Society: Management, Public Policy, Ethics

Gerloff: Organizational Theory and Design: A Strategic Approach for Management

Hampton: Management

Hampton: Inside Management: Readings from *Business Week*

Hodgetts: Effective Supervision: A Practical Approach

Jauch and Glueck: Business Policy and Strategic Management

Jauch and Glueck: Strategic Management and Business Policy

Jauch and Townsend: Cases in Strategic Management and Business Policy

Karlins: The Human Use of Human Resources

Kast and Rosenzweig: Experiential Exercises and Cases in Management

Knudson, Woodworth, and Bell: Management: An Experiential Approach

Koontz and Weihrich: Essentials of Management

Koontz and Weihrich: Management

Kopelman: Managing Productivity in Organizations: A Practical, People-Oriented Perspective

Levin, Rubin, Stinson, and Gardner: Quantitive Approaches to Management

Luthans: Organizational Behavior

Luthans and Thompson: Contemporary Readings in Organizational Behavior

Miles: Theories of Management: Implications for Organizational Behavior and Development

Miles and Snow: Organizational Strategy, Structure, and Process

Mills: Labor-Management Relations

Mitchell and Larson: People in Organizations: An Introduction to Organizational Behavior

Molander: Responsive Capitalism: Case Studies in Corporate Social Conduct

Monks: Operations Management: Theory and Problems

Newstrom and Davis: Organizational Behavior: Readings and Exercises

Pearce and Robinson: Corporate Strategies: Readings from *Business Week*

Porter and McKibbin: Management Education and Development: Drift or Thrust into the 21st Century?

Prasow and Peters: Arbitration and Collective Bargaining: Conflict Resolution in Labor Relations

Quick and Quick: Organizational Stress and Preventive Management

Rue and Holland: Strategic Management: Concepts and Experiences

Rugman, Lecraw, and Booth: International Business: Firm and Environment

Sayles: Leadership: Managing in Real Organizations

Schlesinger, Eccles, and Gabarro: Managing Behavior in Organizations: Text, Cases and Readings

Schroeder: Operations Management: Decision Making in the Operations Function

Sharplin: Strategic Management

Steers and Porter: Motivation and Work Behavior

Steiner and Steiner: Business, Government, and Society: A Managerial Perspective, Text and Cases

Steinhoff and Burgess: Small Business Management Fundamentals

Sutermeister: People and Productivity

Walker: Human Resource Planning

Weihrich: Management Excellence: Productivity through MBO

Werther and Davis: Human Resources and Personnel Management

Wofford, Gerloff, and Cummins: Organizational Communications: The Keystone to Managerial Effectiveness

MANAGEMENT

Kathryn M. Bartol
University of Maryland, College Park

David C. Martin
American University

McGRAW-HILL, INC.

New York
St. Louis
San Francisco
Auckland
Bogotá
Caracas
Lisbon
London
Madrid
Mexico

Milan
Montreal
New Delhi
Paris
San Juan
Singapore
Sydney
Tokyo
Toronto

MANAGEMENT

34567890 VNH VNH 95432

ISBN 0-07-100255-5

This book was set in Palatino by York Graphic Services, Inc. The editors were Alan Sachs, Rhona Robbin, and Peggy Rehberger; the designer was Joan E. O'Connor; the production supervisor was Diane Renda. The photo editor was Inge King. Von Hoffmann Press, Inc., was printer and binder.

Acknowledgments and photo credits appear at the back of this book, and on this page by reference.

Library of Congress Cataloging-in-Publication Data

Bartol, Kathryn M.
　　Management/Kathryn M. Bartol, David C. Martin. p.　　cm.—
　　(McGraw-Hill series in management)
　　Includes bibliographical references and index.
　　ISBN 0-07-003926-7
　　1. Management.
　　I. Martin, David Clarke.
　　II. Title.
　　III. Series.
HD31.B36942　　　1991
658—dc20　　　　　90-48498

9 780071 007559

ABOUT THE AUTHORS

Kathryn M. Bartol is Professor of Organizational Behavior and Human Resource Management in the College of Business and Management at the University of Maryland, College Park. She is a past president of the Academy of Management and is a Fellow of the Academy of Management, the American Psychological Association, and the American Psychological Society. She holds a Ph.D. in Management from Michigan State University, has published articles in numerous scholarly journals and professional publications, and is currently Associate Editor of the *Academy of Management Executive*. She has received the Allen Krowe Award for Excellence in Teaching from the College of Business and Management and was recently named a Distinguished Scholar-Teacher at the University of Maryland for excellence in both research and teaching.

David C. Martin is an Associate Professor of Management and Human Resource Management at Kogod College of Business Administration at The American University. He received his Ph.D. degree in Management from the University of Maryland. He is the author of many publications in both academic and professional journals. Professor Martin has been recognized as the Kogod College of Business Administration Teacher of the Year, Faculty Administrator of the Year, Teacher-Scholar of the Year, and the Scholarship/Researcher of the Year.

To my husband, Robert A. Bartol, and my father, Walter R. Ottinger. Thank you for your constant love and support.

To Jan and Kathy, whose love, support, understanding, and willingness to wait made this book possible.

CONTENTS IN BRIEF

Preface   xix
Academic Reviewers   xxiv
A Guided Tour to *Management*   xxv

PART ONE   INTRODUCTION   2

1 THE CHALLENGE OF MANAGEMENT   3
2 PIONEERING IDEAS IN MANAGEMENT   38
3 UNDERSTANDING EXTERNAL AND INTERNAL ENVIRONMENTS   75
4 SOCIAL RESPONSIBILITY AND ETHICS IN MANAGEMENT   112

PART TWO   PLANNING AND DECISION MAKING   152

5 ESTABLISHING ORGANIZATIONAL GOALS AND PLANS   153
6 STRATEGIC MANAGEMENT   187
7 MANAGING INNOVATION AND CHANGE   223
8 MANAGERIAL DECISION MAKING   258
9 PLANNING AND DECISION AIDS   293

PART THREE   ORGANIZING   332

10 BASIC ELEMENTS OF ORGANIZATION STRUCTURE   333
11 STRATEGIC ORGANIZATION DESIGN   367
12 HUMAN RESOURCE MANAGEMENT   402

PART FOUR   LEADING   442

13 MOTIVATION   443
14 LEADERSHIP   478
15 MANAGERIAL COMMUNICATION   515
16 MANAGING GROUPS   549

PART FIVE   CONTROLLING   590

17 CONTROLLING THE ORGANIZATION   591
18 MANAGERIAL CONTROL METHODS   625
19 OPERATIONS MANAGEMENT   660
20 INFORMATION SYSTEMS FOR MANAGEMENT   696

PART SIX   ACROSS ALL FUNCTIONS   734

21 INTERNATIONAL MANAGEMENT   735
22 ENTREPRENEURSHIP AND SMALL BUSINESS   770

APPENDIX: MANAGING YOUR CAREER   807

Indexes   I-1

CONTENTS

Preface   xix
Academic Reviewers   xxiv
A Guided Tour to Management   xxv

PART ONE   INTRODUCTION   2

1   THE CHALLENGE OF MANAGEMENT   3
Chapter Outline 3   Learning Objectives 3
MANAGEMENT: AN OVERVIEW   6
What Is Management? 6   The Management Process 9
WHAT MANAGERS ACTUALLY DO   10
Work Methods 10   Managerial Roles 10   Managerial Work Agendas 11
MANAGERIAL KNOWLEDGE, SKILLS, AND PERFORMANCE   18
Knowledge Base 18   Key Management Skills 18   Performance 20
MANAGERIAL JOB TYPES   21
Vertical Dimension: Hierarchical Levels 21   Differences among Hierarchical
Levels 23   Promoting Innovation: The Entrepreneurial Role 26   Horizontal
Dimension: Responsibility Areas 29   Differences According to
Responsibility Area 29
LEARNING TO BE AN EFFECTIVE MANAGER   30
Managerial Education 30   Management Experience 31   Understanding
Future Trends 32

CHAPTER SUMMARY / MANAGERIAL TERMINOLOGY / QUESTIONS FOR
DISCUSSION AND REVIEW / DISCUSSION QUESTIONS FOR CHAPTER
OPENING CASE / MANAGEMENT EXERCISE: PRODUCING THE NEW
BINDING MACHINE

Gaining the Edge:
Quality Stands Out at
Corning and Steuben   4
Practically Speaking:
How to Build Networks   12
Case in Point:
Behind-the-Scenes Skills at
Carnegie Hall   19
Case in Point:
JVC Persists with the
Videocassette Recorder   27
Concluding Case:
A Day in the Life of a Bank
Manager   36

2   PIONEERING IDEAS IN MANAGEMENT   38
Chapter Outline 38   Learning Objectives 38
THE BIRTH OF MANAGEMENT IDEAS   41
Early Innovative Practices 41   The Evolution of Management Theories 41
PRECLASSICAL CONTRIBUTORS   42
Major Contributors 42   Assessing the Preclassical Contributors 44
CLASSICAL VIEWPOINT   45
Scientific Management 45   Bureaucratic Management 49   Administrative
Management 51
BEHAVIORAL VIEWPOINT   53
Early Behaviorists 54   Hawthorne Studies 55   Human Relations
Movement 58   Behavioral Science Approach 61
QUANTITATIVE MANAGEMENT VIEWPOINT   61
Management Science 62   Operations Management 62   Management
Information Systems 62
CONTEMPORARY VIEWPOINTS   63
Systems Theory 63   Contingency Theory 67   Emerging Views 68
PROMOTING INNOVATION: CONTRIBUTIONS OF THE MAJOR
VIEWPOINTS   69

CHAPTER SUMMARY / MANAGERIAL TERMINOLOGY / QUESTIONS FOR
DISCUSSION AND REVIEW / DISCUSSION QUESTIONS FOR CHAPTER
OPENING CASE / MANAGEMENT EXERCISE: PROBLEMS AT THE ICE CREAM
PLANT

Gaining the Edge:
Henry Ford Puts Pioneering
Ideas to Work   39
Case in Point:
Robert's Rules Bring Order
44
Case in Point:
Ford's Edsel Flops   64
Concluding Case:
Ford Motor Charges Ahead
and into Globalization   73

Note: The cases set in red type indicate international organizations.

Gaining the Edge:
Liz Claiborne's Empire
Grows 76
Case in Point:
IKEA Chooses
U.S. Beachhead 85
Practically Speaking:
Keeping Tabs
on Competitors 89
Case in Point:
Champion Loses Its
Spark 96
Case in Point:
Harley-Davidson on the
Road Again 101
Concluding Case:
Xerox Works to Meet
Environmental
Challenges 110

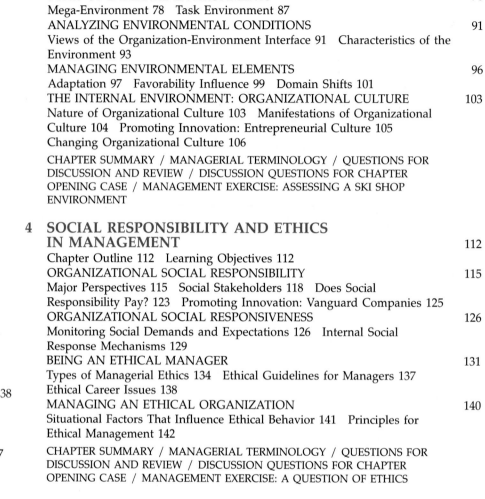

**3 UNDERSTANDING EXTERNAL AND INTERNAL
ENVIRONMENTS** 75

Chapter Outline 75   Learning Objectives 75
TYPES OF EXTERNAL ENVIRONMENTS 78
Mega-Environment 78   Task Environment 87
ANALYZING ENVIRONMENTAL CONDITIONS 91
Views of the Organization-Environment Interface 91   Characteristics of the
Environment 93
MANAGING ENVIRONMENTAL ELEMENTS 96
Adaptation 97   Favorability Influence 99   Domain Shifts 101
THE INTERNAL ENVIRONMENT: ORGANIZATIONAL CULTURE 103
Nature of Organizational Culture 103   Manifestations of Organizational
Culture 104   Promoting Innovation: Entrepreneurial Culture 105
Changing Organizational Culture 106

CHAPTER SUMMARY / MANAGERIAL TERMINOLOGY / QUESTIONS FOR
DISCUSSION AND REVIEW / DISCUSSION QUESTIONS FOR CHAPTER
OPENING CASE / MANAGEMENT EXERCISE: ASSESSING A SKI SHOP
ENVIRONMENT

**4 SOCIAL RESPONSIBILITY AND ETHICS
IN MANAGEMENT** 112

Chapter Outline 112   Learning Objectives 112
ORGANIZATIONAL SOCIAL RESPONSIBILITY 115
Major Perspectives 115   Social Stakeholders 118   Does Social
Responsibility Pay? 123   Promoting Innovation: Vanguard Companies 125
ORGANIZATIONAL SOCIAL RESPONSIVENESS 126
Monitoring Social Demands and Expectations 126   Internal Social
Response Mechanisms 129
BEING AN ETHICAL MANAGER 131
Types of Managerial Ethics 134   Ethical Guidelines for Managers 137
Ethical Career Issues 138
MANAGING AN ETHICAL ORGANIZATION 140
Situational Factors That Influence Ethical Behavior 141   Principles for
Ethical Management 142

CHAPTER SUMMARY / MANAGERIAL TERMINOLOGY / QUESTIONS FOR
DISCUSSION AND REVIEW / DISCUSSION QUESTIONS FOR CHAPTER
OPENING CASE / MANAGEMENT EXERCISE: A QUESTION OF ETHICS

Gaining the Edge:
Johnson & Johnson   113
Case in Point:
NYSEG   124
Case in Point:
Minolta Chief Urges Greater
Giving   128
Case in Point:
Levi Strauss   131
Practically Speaking:
Ethical Business Decisions   138
Case in Point:
Caught in a Trap of His
Own Making   139
Concluding Case:
Tony Santino's Dilemma   147
Part Ending Case:
Marriott   148

PART TWO PLANNING AND DECISION MAKING 152

**5 ESTABLISHING ORGANIZATIONAL GOALS
AND PLANS** 153

Chapter Outline 153   Learning Objectives 153
THE OVERALL PLANNING PROCESS 156
Major Components of Planning 156   Organizational Mission 157
THE NATURE OF ORGANIZATIONAL GOALS 158
Benefits of Goals 158   Levels of Goals 161
HOW GOALS FACILITATE PERFORMANCE 164
Goal Content 164   Goal Commitment 166   Work Behavior 168   Other
Process Components 169   Potential Problems with Goals 171
LINKING GOALS AND PLANS 172
Levels of Plans 172   Plans According to Extent of Recurring Use 173
Time Horizons of Goals and Plans 175   Promoting Innovation: The Role of
the Planning Process 175   Potential Obstacles to Planning 178

Gaining the Edge:
Cypress Semiconductor
Thrives on "Turbo MBO"
154
Practically Speaking:
How to Set Goals 167

MANAGEMENT BY OBJECTIVES 179
Steps in the MBO Process 179   Strengths and Weaknesses of MBO 181
Assessing MBO 183

CHAPTER SUMMARY / MANAGERIAL TERMINOLOGY / QUESTIONS FOR
DISCUSSION AND REVIEW / DISCUSSION QUESTIONS FOR CHAPTER
OPENING CASE / MANAGEMENT EXERCISE: WORKING WITH MBO

Case in Point:
Matsushita 170
Case in Point:
3M 176
Concluding Case:
Wal-Mart 185

6   STRATEGIC MANAGEMENT 187
Chapter Outline 187   Learning Objectives 187
THE CONCEPT OF STRATEGIC MANAGEMENT 190
The Strategic Management Process 190   Importance of Strategic
Management 191   Levels of Strategy 192   Promoting Innovation: Modes
of Strategic Management 194
THE ROLE OF COMPETITIVE ANALYSIS IN STRATEGY FORMULATION 196
Environmental Assessment 196   Organizational Assessment 200
FORMULATING CORPORATE-LEVEL STRATEGY 201
Grand Strategies 201   Portfolio Strategy Approaches 205
FORMULATING BUSINESS-LEVEL STRATEGY 211
Porter's Competitive Strategies 211   Assessing Porter's Strategies 215
FORMULATING FUNCTIONAL-LEVEL STRATEGY 215
STRATEGY IMPLEMENTATION 216
Carrying Out Strategic Plans 216   Maintaining Strategic Control 218

CHAPTER SUMMARY / MANAGERIAL TERMINOLOGY / QUESTIONS FOR
DISCUSSION AND REVIEW / DISCUSSION QUESTIONS FOR CHAPTER
OPENING CASE / MANAGEMENT EXERCISE: DEVELOPING A STRATEGY FOR
PMB

Gaining the Edge:
The Magic Returns to Disney
188
Case in Point:
The Unlimited Limited 203
Case in Point:
Baxter's of Speyside Focuses
on Specialty Foods 213
Concluding Case:
Cray Research, Inc., Faces
Stiff Competition 221

7   MANAGING INNOVATION AND CHANGE 223
Chapter Outline 223   Learning Objectives 223
THE NATURE OF CHANGE AND INNOVATION 225
Distinguishing between Change and Innovation 226   Forces for Change
and Innovation 227
ORGANIZATIONAL LIFE CYCLES 228
Four Life-Cycle Stages 228   Organizational Termination 233   Promoting
Innovation: The Change and Innovation Process 234   A Six-Step Model 235
Managing Resistance to Change 239   Intrapreneurship 243
KEY ORGANIZATIONAL CHANGE COMPONENTS 246
Structural Components 246   Technological Components 247   Human
Resources Components 247   Cultural Components 247   Interrelationship
among Components 248
ORGANIZATIONAL DEVELOPMENT 249
Diagnosis 251   Intervention 251

CHAPTER SUMMARY / MANAGERIAL TERMINOLOGY / QUESTIONS FOR
DISCUSSION AND REVIEW / DISCUSSION QUESTIONS FOR CHAPTER
OPENING CASE / MANAGEMENT EXERCISE: FORCE-FIELD ANALYSIS

Gaining the Edge:
Merck Produces Biotech Stars
224
Case in Point:
Wang Fights to Revitalize
231
Case in Point:
Pepperidge Farm Freshens Up
237
Practically Speaking:
Checklist for Choosing
Intrapreneurial Ideas 245
Case in Point:
Cultural Revolution at
Europe's Philips 248
Concluding Case:
BankAmerica Struggles to
Fulfill Its Founder's Dreams
256

8   MANAGERIAL DECISION MAKING 258
Chapter Outline 258   Learning Objectives 258
THE NATURE OF MANAGERIAL DECISION MAKING 261
Types of Problems Decision Makers Face 262   Differences in Decision-
Making Situations 262
MANAGERS AS DECISION MAKERS 265
The Rational Model 265   Nonrational Models 265
STEPS IN AN EFFECTIVE DECISION-MAKING PROCESS 268

Gaining the Edge:
Coke Gets Back Its Kick
259

Case in Point:
Gould's Adventurous Spirit
Runs into Trouble 267

Case in Point:
Expo 86 Escalates 278

Practically Speaking:
How to Be More Creative
284

Case in Point:
The CAT Scanner Greets an
Astonished World 285

Concluding Case:
Profits Finally Come to *USA
Today* 291

Identifying the Problem 268   Generating Alternative Solutions 269
Evaluating and Choosing an Alternative 270   Implementing and
Monitoring the Chosen Solution 271
OVERCOMING BARRIERS TO EFFECTIVE DECISION MAKING   272
Accepting the Problem Challenge 272   Searching for Sufficient
Alternatives 273   Recognizing Common Decision-Making Biases 275
Avoiding the Decision Escalation Phenomenon 277
GROUP DECISION MAKING   279
Advantages of Group Decision Making 279   Disadvantages of Group
Decision Making 280   Enhancing Group Decision-Making Processes 281
PROMOTING INNOVATION: THE CREATIVITY FACTOR IN DECISION
MAKING   281
Basic Ingredients 282   Stages of Creativity 285   Techniques for Enhancing
Group Creativity 286

CHAPTER SUMMARY / MANAGERIAL TERMINOLOGY / QUESTIONS FOR
DISCUSSION AND REVIEW / DISCUSSION QUESTIONS FOR CHAPTER
OPENING CASE / MANAGEMENT EXERCISE: BRAINSTORMING

Gaining the Edge:
United Airlines Develops a
Sophisticated Work-Force
Planning System 294

Case in Point:
The Delphi Method at BHEL
302

Case in Point:
Expanding Canadian
National Railway's Line
Capacity 314

Case in Point:
Insurers Race to Develop
Expert Systems 322

Concluding Case:
Management Science
Transforms Citgo Petroleum
326

Part Ending Case:
Sears Charts New Strategies
328

9 **PLANNING AND DECISION AIDS**   293
Chapter Outline 293   Learning Objectives 293
FORECASTING   296
Quantitative Forecasting 297   Promoting Innovation: Technological, or
Qualitative, Forecasting 301   Judgmental Forecasting 304   Choosing a
Forecasting Method 304
PROJECT PLANNING AND CONTROL MODELS   305
Gantt Charts 305   PERT 306
OTHER PLANNING TECHNIQUES   308
Linear Programming 309   Queuing, or Waiting-Line, Models 311
Inventory Models 312   Routing, or Distribution, Models 313   Simulation
Models 313
QUANTITATIVE AIDS FOR DECISION MAKING   316
Payoff Tables 316   Decision Trees 317   Break-Even Analysis 319   Game
Theory 320
DECISION SUPPORT AND EXPERT SYSTEMS   321
Decision Support Systems 321   Expert Systems 321

CHAPTER SUMMARY / MANAGERIAL TERMINOLOGY / QUESTIONS FOR
DISCUSSION AND REVIEW / DISCUSSION QUESTIONS FOR CHAPTER
OPENING CASE / MANAGEMENT EXERCISE: USING PERT

Gaining the Edge:
America's Most Successful
Entrepreneur 334

Case in Point:
Job Enrichment at First
National Bank of Chicago
342

PART THREE   ORGANIZING   332

10 **BASIC ELEMENTS OF ORGANIZATION STRUCTURE**   333
Chapter Outline 333   Learning Objectives 333
THE NATURE OF ORGANIZATION STRUCTURE   335
Organization Structure Defined 336   The Organization Chart 336   Chain
of Command 337
JOB DESIGN   338
Approaches to Job Design 339   Alternative Work Schedules 343
TYPES OF DEPARTMENTALIZATION   345
METHODS OF VERTICAL COORDINATION   345
The Role of Formalization 346   Span of Management 348

Centralization versus Decentralization 352   Delegation 353
Line and Staff Positions 354
PROMOTING INNOVATION: METHODS OF HORIZONTAL
COORDINATION   357
Slack Resources 358   Information Systems 359   Lateral Relations 359
CHAPTER SUMMARY / MANAGERIAL TERMINOLOGY / QUESTIONS FOR
DISCUSSION AND REVIEW / DISCUSSION QUESTIONS FOR CHAPTER
OPENING CASE / MANAGEMENT EXERCISE: DESIGNING AN INNOVATING
ORGANIZATION

Case in Point:
Celestial Seasonings Retains
Its Innovative Flair   347
Case in Point:
Toyota Sheds Management
Levels   350
Practically Speaking:
Guidelines for Effective
Delegating   355
Concluding Case:
GM Reorganizes   365

11   STRATEGIC ORGANIZATION DESIGN   367
Chapter Outline 367   Learning Objectives 367
DESIGNING ORGANIZATION STRUCTURES: AN OVERVIEW   369
Which Comes First—Strategy or Structure? 369   Factors Influencing
Organization Design 370
ASSESSING STRUCTURAL ALTERNATIVES   370
Functional Structure 370   Divisional Structure 373   Hybrid Structure 377
Matrix Structure 379
WEIGHING CONTINGENCY FACTORS   383
Technology 383   Size 386   Environment 387   Mintzberg's Five Structural
Configurations 389
MATCHING STRATEGY AND STRUCTURE   391
PROMOTING INNOVATION: USING STRUCTURAL MEANS TO
ENHANCE PROSPECTS   393
Vital Roles 394   Differentiation Paradox 394   Reservations 394   Transfer
Process 394
CHAPTER SUMMARY / MANAGERIAL TERMINOLOGY / QUESTIONS FOR
DISCUSSION AND REVIEW / DISCUSSION QUESTIONS FOR CHAPTER
OPENING CASE / MANAGEMENT EXERCISE: DEVELOPING AN
ORGANIZATION STRUCTURE

Gaining the Edge:
Post-It Notes Win Out at 3M
368
Case in Point:
Brand Management at
Procter & Gamble   381
Case in Point:
Perstorp Excels at Innovation
397
Concluding Case:
The Lowering of the Pirate's
Flag at Apple   401

12   HUMAN RESOURCE MANAGEMENT   402
Chapter Outline 402   Learning Objectives 402
STRATEGIC HUMAN RESOURCE MANAGEMENT   405
The HRM Process: An Overview 405   The Strategic Importance of
HRM 406
HUMAN RESOURCE PLANNING   406
Job Analysis 407   Demand for Human Resources 408   Supply of Human
Resources 408   Reconciling Demand and Supply 410
STAFFING   411
Recruitment 412   Selection 413
DEVELOPMENT AND EVALUATION   418
Training and Development 419   Performance Appraisal 421
COMPENSATION   424
Types of Equity 424   Designing the Pay Structure 425   Promoting
Innovation: Nontraditional Compensation Approaches 427   Employee
Benefits 428
MAINTAINING EFFECTIVE WORK-FORCE RELATIONSHIPS   429
Labor-Management Relations 429   Current Employee Issues 431
CHAPTER SUMMARY / MANAGERIAL TERMINOLOGY / QUESTIONS FOR
DISCUSSION AND REVIEW / DISCUSSION QUESTIONS FOR CHAPTER
OPENING CASE / MANAGEMENT EXERCISE: MANAGING HUMAN
RESOURCES IN RETAIL HARDWARE

Gaining the Edge:
Changes in Human Resource
Management Boost CARE
403
Practically Speaking:
How to Conduct an Effective
Interview   416
Case in Point:
Training Makes a Difference
at First Service Bank   420
Case in Point:
The UAW versus Nissan
430
Concluding Case:
Nucor Prospers in Tough
Steel Industry   436
Part Ending Case:
Daimler-Benz Diversifies
438

Gaining the Edge:
A Motivational Balancing
Act at Genentech   444
Case in Point:
Original Ways of Motivating
Behavior   451
Case in Point:
Soviet Factory Implements
Revolutionary Idea   459
Case in Point:
Learning the Domino Theory
471
Concluding Case:
Making Visible Changes
477

PART FOUR   LEADING   442

13   MOTIVATION   443
Chapter Outline 443   Learning Objectives 443
THE NATURE OF MOTIVATION   445
Early Approaches to Motivation 446   A Simplified Model of
Motivation 447
NEED THEORIES   448
Hierarchy of Needs Theory 448   ERG Theory 449   Two-Factor Theory 452
Acquired-Needs Theory 453   Assessing Need Theories 455
COGNITIVE THEORIES   456
Expectancy Theory 456   Equity Theory 461   Goal-Setting Theory 463
Assessing Cognitive Theories 464
REINFORCEMENT THEORY   464
Types of Reinforcement 464   Schedules of Reinforcement 467   Using
Reinforcement Theory 468
SOCIAL LEARNING THEORY   469
Major Components 469   Using Social Learning Theory 471   Promoting
Innovation: A Social Learning Perspective 472

CHAPTER SUMMARY / MANAGERIAL TERMINOLOGY / QUESTIONS FOR
DISCUSSION AND REVIEW / DISCUSSION QUESTIONS FOR CHAPTER
OPENING CASE / MANAGEMENT EXERCISE: MARKETEER OR
ENTREPRENEUR

Gaining the Edge:
Leadership Helps Apple
Shine   479
Case in Point:
Successful Leaders at Joyce
and Crain   487
Case in Point:
Company Founder Chung
Ju-Yung Builds Hyundai
495
Case in Point:
Leading Embassy Suites to
an Enviable Reputation   505
Concluding Case:
GE's Controversial Leader
513

14   LEADERSHIP   478
Chapter Outline 478   Learning Objectives 478
HOW LEADERS INFLUENCE OTHERS   480
Sources of Leader Power 481   Effective Use of Leader Power 481
SEARCHING FOR LEADERSHIP TRAITS   483
IDENTIFYING LEADER BEHAVIORS   484
Iowa Studies 484   Michigan Studies 486   Ohio State Studies 487
The Managerial Grid 489   Female versus Male Leader Behaviors 489
DEVELOPING SITUATIONAL THEORIES   490
Fiedler's Leadership Theories 490   Situational Leadership Theory 496
Revised Normative Leadership Model 498   Path-Goal Theory 502
PROMOTING INNOVATION: TRANSFORMATIONAL LEADERSHIP   506
ARE LEADERS NECESSARY?   508
The Romance of Leadership 508   Substitutes for Leadership 509
Leadership and the Organizational Life Cycle 510

CHAPTER SUMMARY / MANAGERIAL TERMINOLOGY / QUESTIONS FOR
DISCUSSION AND REVIEW / DISCUSSION QUESTIONS FOR CHAPTER
OPENING CASE / MANAGEMENT EXERCISE: THE QUESTION OF
SUBORDINATE INVOLVEMENT

Gaining the Edge:
Stew Leonard's Brand of
Communicating   516
Case in Point:
Communication Helps SAS
Stage Turnaround   522
Case in Point:
Ashland Oil   526
Case in Point:
At Many Firms, Employees
Speak a Language of Their
Own   530

15   MANAGERIAL COMMUNICATION   515
Chapter Outline 515   Learning Objectives 515
THE NATURE OF MANAGERIAL COMMUNICATION   518
Types of Communication 519   Managerial Communication Preferences 520
Basic Components of the Communication Process 523
FACTORS THAT IMPEDE OR ENHANCE INDIVIDUAL
COMMUNICATION   527
Perceptual Processes 527   Semantics 529   Verbal and Nonverbal
Consistency 531   Communication Skills 532
GROUP COMMUNICATION NETWORKS   535

ORGANIZATIONAL COMMUNICATION CHANNELS   536
Vertical Communication 536   Horizontal Communication 539   Informal
Communication: The Grapevine 539   Promoting Innovation: Multiple
Communication Channels 541   The Growing Potential of Electronics 543
CHAPTER SUMMARY / MANAGERIAL TERMINOLOGY / QUESTIONS FOR
DISCUSSION AND REVIEW / DISCUSSION QUESTIONS FOR CHAPTER
OPENING CASE / MANAGEMENT EXERCISE: A QUESTION OF INFERENCES

Practically Speaking:
How to Listen Effectively
533
Concluding Case:
Chairman's Cost-Cutting
Humor at Bear, Stearns
547

16 MANAGING GROUPS   549
Chapter Outline 549   Learning Objectives 549
FOUNDATIONS OF WORK GROUPS   552
What Is a Group? 552   Types of Work Groups 552   How Informal Groups
Develop 556   How Work Groups Operate 557
WORK GROUP INPUTS   558
Work Group Composition 558   Member Roles 559   Group Size 561
WORK GROUP PROCESSES   563
Group Norms 564   Group Cohesiveness 565   Group Development 567
PROMOTING INNOVATION: SPECIAL WORK GROUP APPLICATIONS   569
Task Forces 571   Teams 571
NORMATIVE MODEL OF GROUP EFFECTIVENESS   574
Components of the Model 575   Using the Model 576
MANAGING CONFLICT   578
Causes of Conflict 579   Reducing and Resolving Conflict 579   Stimulating
Conflict 580
CHAPTER SUMMARY / MANAGERIAL TERMINOLOGY / QUESTIONS FOR
DISCUSSION AND REVIEW / DISCUSSION QUESTIONS FOR CHAPTER
OPENING CASE / MANAGEMENT EXERCISE: LOST AT SEA

Gaining the Edge:
Compaq Succeeds with
Teams 550
Practically Speaking:
How to Lead a Meeting
570
Case in Point:
Team Taurus Scores Big
572
Case in Point:
Groups Make a Difference
at Brazil's Semco 577
Concluding Case:
Ben and Jerry's Thrives on
Company Spirit 585
Part Ending Case:
Herman Miller: Where
Innovation and Participation
Are Gospel 587

PART FIVE   CONTROLLING   590

17 CONTROLLING THE ORGANIZATION   591
Chapter Outline 591   Learning Objectives 591
CONTROL AS A MANAGEMENT PROCESS   594
Significance of the Control Process 594   Role of Controls 594
Levels of Control 598
THE CONTROL PROCESS   600
Steps in the Control Process 600   Deciding What to Control:
A Closer Look 604
TYPES OF CONTROLS   606
Major Control Types by Timing 606   Multiple Controls 609
Cybernetic and Noncybernetic Control 610
MANAGERIAL APPROACHES TO IMPLEMENTING CONTROLS   611
Market Control 611   Bureaucratic Control 612   Clan Control 613
Blending the Approaches 613   Choosing a Managerial Control Style 615
Promoting Innovation: Control and the Innovation Process 617
ASSESSING CONTROL SYSTEMS   619
Potential Dysfunctional Aspects of Control Systems 619   Overcontrol
versus Undercontrol 620   Characteristics of an Effective Control
System 620
CHAPTER SUMMARY / MANAGERIAL TERMINOLOGY / QUESTIONS FOR
DISCUSSION AND REVIEW / DISCUSSION QUESTIONS FOR CHAPTER
OPENING CASE / MANAGEMENT EXERCISE: OPPORTUNITY KNOCKS

Gaining the Edge:
Controlling Success at
McDonald's 592
Case in Point:
Marks & Spencer Struggles
in North America 596
Case in Point:
Developing Better Controls
at Lotus 609
Case in Point:
UPS Runs a Tight Ship 614
Concluding Case:
Loose Controls Lead to the
Demise of E. F. Hutton 624

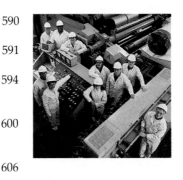

18 MANAGERIAL CONTROL METHODS   625
Chapter Outline 625   Learning Objectives 625
MAJOR CONTROL SYSTEMS   627
Managerial Level 628   Timing Emphasis 629
FINANCIAL CONTROL   629
Financial Statements 629   Ratio Analysis 632   Comparative Financial
Analysis 636   Financial Audits 636   Avoiding Financial Control Pitfalls 637
BUDGETARY CONTROL   638
Responsibility Centers 639   Types of Budgets 642   The Budgetary
Process 644   Zero-Base Budgeting 645   Impacts of the Budgeting
Process 646
QUALITY CONTROL   646
Strategic Implications of Quality 647   Total Quality Control 648
Promoting Innovation: Quality Circles and Beyond 651   Statistical Aids to
Quality Control 652
INVENTORY CONTROL   653
Significance of Inventory 653   Costs of Inventory 653   Economic Order
Quantity 654   Just-in-Time Inventory Control 655
CHAPTER SUMMARY / MANAGERIAL TERMINOLOGY / QUESTIONS FOR
DISCUSSION AND REVIEW / DISCUSSION QUESTIONS FOR CHAPTER
OPENING CASE / MANAGEMENT EXERCISE: MEETING WATER BED DEMAND

Gaining the Edge:
Controls Make Food Lion a
Roaring Success   626
Case in Point:
Giant RJR Nabisco Goes by
the Numbers   635
Case in Point:
Budgets Are Sacred at
Hanson PLC   641
Practically Speaking:
Deming's 14 Points on How
to Improve Quality   649
Case in Point:
Upgrading Quality at
Spectrum Control, Inc.   650
Concluding Case:
Poor Quality Leads to
Financial Problems for Regina
659

19 OPERATIONS MANAGEMENT   660
Chapter Outline 660   Learning Objectives 660
DEFINING OPERATIONS MANAGEMENT   663
The Productivity-Operations Management Linkage 663   Manufacturing
versus Service Organizations 664   The Operations Management
Process 666
FORMULATING OPERATIONS STRATEGY   666
Strategic Role Stages 667   Types of Operations Strategies 669
DEVELOPING AND IMPLEMENTING OPERATING SYSTEMS   671
Forecasting 672   Capacity Planning 672   Aggregate Production
Planning 673   Scheduling 675   Materials Requirements Planning 676
Purchasing 679
DESIGNING AND UTILIZING FACILITIES   680
Expansion and Contraction Decisions 680   Facilities Location 681
Facilities Layout 682
PROMOTING INNOVATION: PROCESS TECHNOLOGY   687
Computer-Integrated Manufacturing 687   Implementing CIM Systems 688
Services Applications 689
IMPROVING PRODUCTIVITY   690
CHAPTER SUMMARY / MANAGERIAL TERMINOLOGY / QUESTIONS FOR
DISCUSSION AND REVIEW / DISCUSSION QUESTIONS FOR CHAPTER
OPENING CASE / MANAGEMENT EXERCISE: OPERATION LANDSCAPING

Gaining the Edge:
Fanuc Leads the World in
Electronic Factory Help   661
Case in Point:
Motorola's Bandit Line
Makes 29 Million Variations
668
Case in Point:
ServiceMaster Cleans,
Repairs, and Maintains   670
Case in Point:
Winnebago's Production
Lines Go Awry   685
Concluding Case:
Caterpillar Uses Operations
Management to Become
Competitive Again   694

20 INFORMATION SYSTEMS FOR MANAGEMENT   696
Chapter Outline 696   Learning Objectives 696
COMPUTER-BASED INFORMATION SYSTEMS: AN OVERVIEW   699
The Nature of Information Systems 699   Computer Components of
Information Systems 701   Characteristics of Useful Information 703
Information Needs by Managerial Level 705   Information Needs by
Specialized Area 706
TYPES OF INFORMATION SYSTEMS   707

Transaction-Processing Systems 707   Office Automation Systems 708
Management Information Systems 709   Decision Support Systems 709
Executive Support Systems 712
PROMOTING INNOVATION: STRATEGIC IMPLICATIONS OF
INFORMATION SYSTEMS   713
Strategic Targets 714   Strategic Thrusts 715
DEVELOPING COMPUTER-BASED INFORMATION SYSTEMS   717
The Systems Development Life Cycle 717   Alternative Means of Systems
Development 719   Selecting a Development Approach 720
MANAGING INFORMATION SYSTEM RESOURCES   721
Factors Favoring Centralization 721   Factors Favoring Decentralization 721
Trends in Centralization and Decentralization 722   Managing End-User
Computing 722
IMPACTS OF INFORMATION TECHNOLOGY ON ORGANIZATIONS   723
Organization Structure 723   Individual Jobs 723   Organizational Risk 725
CHAPTER SUMMARY / MANAGERIAL TERMINOLOGY / QUESTIONS FOR
DISCUSSION AND REVIEW / DISCUSSION QUESTIONS FOR CHAPTER
OPENING CASE / MANAGEMENT EXERCISE: SOXSPORT, INC.

Gaining the Edge:
Mrs. Fields's Secret
Ingredient 697
Practically Speaking:
A Guide to Major Types
of Computers   704
Case in Point:
Decision Support at
Hidroeléctrica Española   710
Case in Point:
McKesson Forges Strong
Computer Links with
Customers   716
Concluding Case:
Du Pont's Edge in Managing
Information Technology
730
Part Ending Case:
Milliken & Company Sets
the Pace for Quality   731

PART SIX   ACROSS ALL FUNCTIONS   734

21   INTERNATIONAL MANAGEMENT   735
Chapter Outline 735   Learning Objectives 735
THE NATURE OF INTERNATIONAL MANAGEMENT   738
Changing Character of International Business 738   Organizations Engaging
in International Management 739   Orientations toward International
Management 741
ASSESSING THE INTERNATIONAL ENVIRONMENT   742
Environmental Elements 743   Promoting Innovation: The Competitive
Advantage of Nations 748
GAUGING INTERNATIONAL STRATEGIC ISSUES   750
Methods of International Entry 751   Multinational Corporation
Strategies 754
ORGANIZING INTERNATIONAL BUSINESS   756
Worldwide Functional Divisions 756   Worldwide Product Divisions 757
International Division 758   Geographic Regions 759   Global Matrix 759
ADAPTING TO CULTURAL DIFFERENCES   761
Managing International Human Resources 761   Selection and Training 762
Adjusting Leadership Styles 763
HANDLING SOCIAL RESPONSIBILITY AND ETHICAL ISSUES   764
International Social Responsibility 764   International Value Conflicts 765
Questionable-Payments Issue 765
CHAPTER SUMMARY / MANAGERIAL TERMINOLOGY / QUESTIONS FOR
DISCUSSION AND REVIEW / DISCUSSION QUESTIONS FOR CHAPTER
OPENING CASE / MANAGEMENT EXERCISE: GOING INTERNATIONAL

Gaining the Edge:
Unilever: One of the World's
Largest Multinational
Corporations   736
Case in Point:
Benetton Makes Unique
Ideas Work Worldwide   753
Case in Point:
Texas Instruments Strives for
a Multifocal Perspective
755
Concluding Case:
Loctite Creates International
Cohesion   769

22   ENTREPRENEURSHIP AND SMALL BUSINESS   770
Chapter Outline 770   Learning Objectives 770
THE NATURE OF ENTREPRENEURSHIP   773
Defining Entrepreneurship 773   Promoting Innovation: Assessing
Entrepreneurial Opportunities 774   Economic and Social Contributions
of Entrepreneurship 775

Gaining the Edge:
Phil Romano Keeps Scoring
Entrepreneurial Successes
771

Case in Point:
Katha Diddel Launches Her
Home Collection   781
Case in Point:
Europe's Most Successful
New Entrepreneur   784
Practically Speaking:
Steps in Developing a
Business Plan   789
Case in Point:
James Bildner's Spectacular
Rise and Fall   796
Concluding Case:
Barbara Grogan Beats out
Big-Name Competition   801
Part Ending Case:
Soho Natural Soda: From
the Kitchen to the World
803

FACTORS INFLUENCING ENTREPRENEURSHIP   776
Personal Characteristics 777   Life-Path Circumstances 779   Favorable
Environmental Conditions 780   Perceptions of Desirability and
Feasibility 781
DECIDING WHAT TYPE OF BUSINESS TO PURSUE   782
Starting a New Firm 782   Buying an Existing Business 785   Purchasing a
Franchise 785
PREPARING TO OPERATE A SMALL BUSINESS   786
Developing a Business Plan 786   Obtaining Resources 790   Selecting an
Appropriate Site 792
MANAGING A SMALL BUSINESS   793
Stages of Small-Business Growth 793   Entrepreneurship versus
Intrapreneurship 797   Major Issues and Problems 797

CHAPTER SUMMARY / MANAGERIAL TERMINOLOGY / QUESTIONS FOR
DISCUSSION AND REVIEW / DISCUSSION QUESTIONS FOR CHAPTER
OPENING CASE / MANAGEMENT EXERCISE: AN ENTREPRENEURIAL
OPPORTUNITY

APPENDIX   MANAGING YOUR CAREER   807
THE NATURE OF CAREER MANAGEMENT   807
ENGAGING IN CAREER MANAGEMENT   808
Steps in the Career Management Process 808   Stages in Career
Development 810   Linkages into Organizational Development
Programs 811
SPECIAL CAREER ISSUES   812
Dual-Career Couples 812   Mentors and Mentoring 813   Career Plateaus
and Lateral Moves 813

GLOSSARY   G-1
REFERENCES   R-1
ACKNOWLEDGMENTS   A-1
PICTURE CREDITS   P-1
NAME INDEX   I-1
SUBJECT INDEX   I-5
ORGANIZATIONS INDEX   I-15
INTERNATIONAL ORGANIZATIONS INDEX   I-19

We live in an era of accelerating global competition. Pressures from foreign companies are causing many managers to reassess their approaches as they strive to deal effectively with a formidable competitive environment. More than ever, managers operating both globally and domestically require the best ideas that the field of management has to offer in order to gain a competitive edge. One important means of gaining an edge is through *innovation*, the major and minor improvements that ultimately add up to outstanding performance. How do managers promote such innovations within organizations? How do they apply the wealth of ideas that flow from research on management? How can they adapt the practices of successful organizations to their own situation? Such are the exciting challenges that managers face in today's competitive world.

Introducing *Management*

This book has been uniquely geared to address the needs of individuals learning how to manage effectively in the contemporary competitive environment. Although the wide variety of means used to meet such needs are delineated more fully later in this Preface, several major mechanisms are worthy of particular attention at this point. Specifically, the text highlights methods for promoting innovation, provides integrated international coverage, features chapters on ethics and entrepreneurship, and reflects current research and major trends.

Highlights Methods for Promoting Innovation. Given the requirement that organizations must continuously improve their performance, the text highlights means of promoting innovation in today's organizations. Each chapter incorporates a special section that explains methods of promoting innovation that mesh appropriately with the relevant subject matter. For example, the chapter on decision making contains a special section on fostering innovation by encouraging creativity, while the chapter on strategic organization design includes a section on structural means of enhancing innovative prospects. At the same time, a separate chapter on innovation and change integrates coverage of the management of innovation with the more traditional treatment

of change issues in order to better address the challenges of operating in today's world.

In addition, each chapter begins with a substantive and lively opening case entitled "Gaining the Edge," which features an organization with a reputation for being innovative (e.g., Corning, Merck, 3M, and DEC). In this way, readers gain insights into how successful organizations actually operate and, more specifically, how they go about encouraging innovation. The opening case is then mentioned several times in the chapter to reinforce its applicability to the subject at hand. The case provides sufficient detail to enable students to obtain useful insights into how real organizations function. The text also incorporates numerous carefully integrated short examples of innovative and other practices in real organizations that clearly illustrate the concepts being explained.

Provides Integrated International Coverage. Given the increasing need to be aware of organizational practices in other parts of the world, the text offers integrated international coverage through five main means. For one thing, an entire chapter is devoted to international management. For another, each chapter contains either an opening or concluding case or a Case in Point, a minicase that features an international organization. In this way students can become familiar with organizations in vastly different global settings. Yet another mechanism is the use of numerous short in-text examples that mention practices in international organizations, as well as the presentation of topics relating to international issues in various chapters. The frequent appearance of photographs reflecting international settings, accompanied by meaningful captions offers yet another means of providing international coverage. Finally, a separate index of international organizations mentioned in the text helps students and professors locate international examples throughout the book.

Features Ethics and Entrepreneurship. Another special aspect of the book is the presence of full chapters on social responsibility and ethics and on entrepreneurship and small business. The chapter on social responsibility and ethics offers solid theoretical concepts from the management literature, yet imparts practical advice in a nonpedantic way. The chapter also provides students with a sense of the dilemmas involved in effectively dealing with organizational social responsibilities and managerial ethics questions. The placement of the chapter in an early part of the book reflects the growing concern over ethics in business.

The chapter on entrepreneurship and small business addresses current issues involved in starting new ventures and running small businesses. These topics are particularly germane since many students who read this text are likely to obtain positions working in or managing small businesses. At the same time, many business schools are emphasizing entrepreneurship, and students typically are extremely interested in materials addressing the prospects of starting new ventures.

Reflects Current Research and Major Trends. The heavy reliance on the research literature as a basis for text content provides strong, up-to-date academic coverage in all areas and particularly reflects recent developments in organizational behavior and organizational theory. The content of the text also addresses the major curriculum recommendations of the Lyman W. Porter and Lawrence E. McKibbin study, *Management Education and Development: Drift or Thrust into the 21st Century?* (published by McGraw-Hill, 1988), sponsored by the American Association of Collegiate Schools of Business. This is achieved particularly through coverage of the external environment, information systems, international management, entrepreneurship, and behavioral issues.

The Content of *Management*

Management uses the four major managerial functions of planning, organizing, leading, and controlling as the underlying structure for presenting materials. In total, the text consists of six main parts.

Part One introduces the reader to the topic of management. This section of four chapters presents an overview of the managerial process, delves into the roots of current management thought, and explores aspects of the outside environment and internal culture of organizations. The final chapter in this section examines the nature of organizational social responsibility and managerial ethics.

Part Two investigates the managerial function of planning. In doing so, this segment of the text includes two chapters that examine the overall planning process, the setting of goals, and the important aspects of strategic management. A chapter on innovation and change also is included in this part of the text because of the importance of planning in ultimately bringing about needed changes and innovations. Two chapters then deal with managerial decision making and review planning and decision aids.

Part Three analyzes the organizing function. Basic elements of organizational structure and strategic issues related to structure receive coverage in two chapters. A third chapter addresses the effective management of an organization's human resources.

Part Four probes the leading function. The topic of motivation opens this section, followed by discussions of leadership and managerial communication. The section ends with a consideration of group dynamics, an increasingly important topic as more organizations seek to harness the potential power of work in teams.

Part Five explores the managerial function of controlling. This segment of the text includes discussions of various aspects of the control process, as well as consideration of specific control systems, such as financial control, budgetary control, quality control, inventory control, operations management, and computer-based information systems. Separate chapters address the latter two types of control systems.

Part Six is devoted to two important topics that draw on all four management functions—international management, and entrepreneurship and small business. Although international coverage pervades the text, the international chapter takes a particularly close look at several major issues that are especially relevant to international management. The final chapter examines important aspects of creating one's own business or managing an existing small business, both fascinating prospects that readers typically enjoy exploring. The appendix, appearing after Part Six, provides helpful materials on effectively managing one's career.

In developing the chapters and sections, considerable effort has been made to provide some flexibility in the order of chapters so that professors can adapt the text to their own preferred sequence of teaching the course. The flexibility has been provided by including cross-references to relevant materials in other chapters that students can consult, as well as by generally presenting explanations that do not rely on student recall of earlier materials. In this way, a professor can make adjustments, such as assigning the communication chapter before the chapter on leadership or covering the managerial decision-making chapter before other planning chapters.

Learning Aids and Special Features of *Management*

Management has been developed with the ultimate consumer—the student—constantly in mind. Accordingly, a wide array of educational features has been included to help facilitate the learning process and make the book as enticing to read and study as possible. A summary of the main features follows:

Innovation Content. A special section in each chapter, as well as a chapter on innovation and change, provide substantial content on major methods of promoting innovation.

Opening Cases. Each chapter opens with an introductory case entitled Gaining the Edge, which illustrates successful innovative practices in a real organization and other aspects of theory and research subsequently discussed in the chapter.

International Management Coverage. Integrated coverage of international management is achieved through the inclusion of an entire chapter devoted to the subject, frequent use of international examples, many international cases and minicases, discussions of related issues, and a separate index of international organizations.

Cases in Point. Each chapter contains two or three Case in Point, or minicase, discussions. These cases, which are fully integrated into the text presentation, provide students with extended examples of how the concepts in the text apply to real organizations. The organizations featured in these minicases range from Celestial Seasonings, the Colorado-based maker of herbal tea, to not-for-profit Carnegie Hall, the famous cultural center located in New York City. For the most part, at least one Case in Point in each chapter depicts managerial practices in an international organization.

Ethics and Entrepreneurship Chapters. Coverage includes a full chapter on social responsibility and ethics, as well as on entrepreneurship and small business—topics of particular current importance and interest to individuals studying management.

Practically Speaking Discussions. Special Practically Speaking sections in many chapters provide readers with practical advice on how to implement certain concepts discussed in the text. For example, Practically Speaking discussions offer guidance on how to conduct an interview, how to run a meeting, and how to set goals.

Real-World Examples. The text includes numerous carefully integrated examples of practices in real organizations that clearly illustrate the concepts being explained. The examples include a wide variety of organizations ranging from France-based Groupe Michelin, the world's largest tire maker, to the mail order operations of venerable L. L. Bean.

Concluding Cases. Each chapter features a concluding case that further illustrates the major points made. The concluding case and accompanying questions provide students with an opportunity to relate the concepts discussed to practical situations found in the real world.

Part Cases. Each of the six major parts of *Management* is followed by a case that addresses many of the major aspects covered in the chapters within that particular segment of the text. The part cases and the accompanying questions provide an opportunity to review and integrate major concepts, as well as apply them to real organizations.

Management Exercises. Each chapter contains a management exercise that incorporates the need to use major concepts that were covered within the chapter. The exercises give students an opportunity to apply the concepts in the chapter in an experiential way.

Discussion Questions for Chapter Opening Cases. Discussion questions for the chapter opening case appear at the end of each chapter to facilitate further discussion if an instructor so desires.

Exceptionally Readable Writing Style. One consistent and exceptionally readable writing style is used throughout the book to capture and hold the interests of readers.

Chapter Outlines and Objectives. Each chapter begins with a topical outline and related objectives that highlight the major points to be covered. The outline and objectives help orient the reader to the chapter content.

Glossaries. A marginal running glossary highlights and defines significant terms in the margin near their first appearance in the book. The extensive Glossary at the back of the text repeats the marginal definitions of key terms in order to provide a ready reference source for the reader.

Chapter Summaries of Key Points and Managerial Terminology. At the end of each chapter, there is a summary of the main points covered within the chapter. Following the summary is a list of managerial terminology, a compilation of the major terms that are highlighted in the chapter along with page numbers indicating where each term is defined.

State-of-the-Art Illustrations. Since an illustration is often worth a thousand words, many of the points in the text are underscored visually through carefully selected drawings, graphs, and photographs. Frameworks that are frequently used to delineate interrelationships among concepts are typically depicted in illustrations that help the reader visualize these interrelationships. The extensive use of color further serves to enhance the impact of the illustrations. Moreover, the captions accompanying the photographs clearly tie the subject matter to concepts in the text, making the photographs a particularly effective learning tool.

Indexes. Several indexes located at the back of the text facilitate easy access to various types of information. These are separate name, subject, organization, and international organization indexes.

Supplementary Materials for Instructors

Management has an extensive set of supplementary materials available for users. The materials are geared to meet the varying needs of professors teaching under different conditions and are oriented toward increasing the value of the text as a teaching and learning tool.

Instructor's Manual. The two-color Instructor's Manual includes a number of features designed to facilitate effective teaching. A course planning guide helps instructors develop an overall plan for the course. Lecture outlines then provide frameworks for presentations. Special Lecture Enrichment Modules, included after each chapter outline, provide supplementary minilectures on topics of current interest. The Instructor's Manual also includes detailed Teaching Notes for all text cases and exercises, as well as 22 Supplementary Management Exercises with accompanying instructor's notes. The Instructor's Manual was prepared by Mary Coulter, Southwest Missouri State University, Terence C. Krell, California State University, Northridge, and L. Allen Slade, University of Delaware. The Enrichment Modules were written by Helen Deresky, State University of New York at Plattsburgh; Robert Lussier, Springfield College, and Karen Marquis, The Wharton School. The Supplementary Management Exercises were developed by Daniel J. Rowley, University of Northern Colorado.

Test Bank. The Test Bank prepared by E. Leroy Plumlee, Western Washington University, features approximately 3,000 high-quality multiple choice and true-false test items. Each item is coded to show the correct solution, the text page reference, whether the item is factual or applied, and the level of difficulty. A computerized version of the Test Bank is also available, as is classroom management software. In addition, McGraw-Hill provides a phone-in test service for ordering customized tests.

Transparency Acetates and Masters. The transparency program includes 150 full-color overheads with very large type that can be easily read, even in large lecture halls. This set of overheads comprises figures taken from the text as well as new illustrations intended to augment the text presentation. Each overhead is keyed to the relevant section in the lecture outline of the Instructor's Manual. There is also a set of transparency masters that features reproductions of key text graphics.

Integrated Videotape Series. The series features a range of high quality programs and is designed to supplement major topic areas of the text. Teaching notes accompany each video. Trudy Verser, Western Michigan University, served as a consultant in coordinating this series.

The McGraw-Hill/University of Illinois Film Library. Free rental of videos and films also are available under a program for adopters.

Supplementary Materials for Students

Student Study Guide. The Study Guide prepared by Terence C. Krell, California State University, Northridge, assists students in gaining a firm grasp of text materials.

Threshold: A Competitive Management Simulation (IBM). Through this interactive simulation, students can apply management concepts to decisions and problems they would face as managers of a small manufacturing company.

Planning Your Career in Business Today. This 59-page manual by Les R. Dlabay, Lake Forest College, is FREE to adopters of *Management*. Adopters may obtain the manual in quantity for class use through their McGraw-Hill representative.

Acknowledgments

In developing *Management*, we have been greatly aided by many individuals to whom we owe a great debt of gratitude. We appreciate the ongoing support of Dean Rudolph P. Lamone, College of Business and Management, University of Maryland, College Park, and Dean William H. Peters and Acting Dean Thomas J. O'Connor, Kogod College of Business Administration, American University, as well as our colleagues in management at both of these institutions.

We also thank the members of a focus group that helped us launch this project, as well as the many reviewers who have commented on the various stages of the manuscript. These individuals are listed on page xxiv, and this text is a much better product as a result of their candor and many helpful contributions.

We deeply appreciate the wonderful support that we have received from many individuals associated with our publisher, McGraw-Hill. Seibert Adams, editor in chief, maintained continual interest in the project and provided the necessary resources. June Smith, publisher, took the time from her busy schedule to offer innovative ideas based on her extensive experience in publishing and provided ongoing enthusiastic support. Sponsoring editor Kathleen Loy originally outlined a vision for this book that intrigued us, while her successor, Alan Sachs, adopted the vision and helped us immeasurably in bringing it to fruition.

Rhona Robbin, senior developmental editor, has been a constant colleague, friend, and advocate. She provided continuity of direction, offered invaluable feedback, and raised the penetrating questions on behalf of our future readers that caused us to continually improve our presentations. Her high professional standards meshed well with our own, and her valuable ideas and insights are reflected throughout this text. Our supplements editor, Dan Alpert, brought together a team of unusually qualified professionals who not only produced the arguably best set of supplemental materials ever prepared for a management text but also had them completed when the book was ready for distribution.

Senior editing supervisor Peggy C. Rehberger painstakingly oversaw the editing and production of the text, and contributed many helpful ideas as well. Joan O'Connor produced the striking book design that fueled our enthusiasm during the final stages of the project. Susan Gottfried, with her skillful and consistent editing, greatly aided our presentations while preserving our ideas. Diane Renda, production supervisor, coordinated the production process so that all the production elements were of high quality and handled in a timely manner.

Our photo editor, Inge King, assembled a collection of captivating photographs that provide a valuable additional learning dimension. Elsa Peterson and Frederick T. Courtright obtained the many necessary permissions. Peitr Bohen and others at McGraw-Hill aided us in numerous ways, both large and small.

This list certainly would not be complete without acknowledging the valuable clipping service provided by Walter R. Ottinger, the father of Kathryn Bartol. We also want to highlight the continuing encouragement of our spouses, Robert Bartol and Jan Martin. In deference to our deadlines, they postponed activities they wanted to pursue and took on tasks that needed to be done. They listened to our frustrations and continued to express faith in our efforts. Throughout, they were there when we needed them, and this book certainly is better as a result.

Thank you, to all who have helped us. We could not have produced this text without you!

Kathryn M. Bartol
David C. Martin

ACADEMIC REVIEWERS

We would like to express our sincere thanks to the following people who have reviewed all or various portions of the manuscript.

Kathryn M. Bartol
David C. Martin

Alie, Raymond
Western Michigan University

Armenakis, Achilles
Auburn University

Blakeney, Roger
University of Houston

Bluedorn, Allen
University of Missouri—Columbia

Bockley, W. R.
University of New Haven

Calvasina, Gerald E.
University of North Carolina—
Charlotte

Cavaleri, Steven A.
Central Connecticut State
University

Cook, Raymond L.
University of Texas—Austin

Coulter, Mary
Southwest Missouri State
University

Darrow, Arthur
Bowling Green University

Daruty, Kathy
Los Angeles Pierce College

DeFillippi, Robert
Suffolk University

Deresky, Helen
SUNY-Plattsburgh

Elsea, Stan
Kansas State University

Farrell, Dan
Western Michigan University

Gartner, Bill
Georgetown University

Goldberg, Robert
Northeastern University

Hughes, John
Texas Tech University

Hulpke, John
California State University—
Bakersfield

Hunt, Eugene
Virginia Commonwealth
University

Johnson, Dewey
California State University—
Fresno

Krell, Terence
California State University—
Northridge

Lewis, Pamela
University of Central Florida

Liverpool, Patrick
Virginia State University

Loveland, John
New Mexico State University

Luthans, Fred
University of Nebraska—Lincoln

McCaul, Harriette S.
North Dakota State University

McElroy, James
Iowa State University

Morrison, Edward J.
University of Colorado—Boulder

Neider, Linda
University of Miami

O'Clock, George
Mankato State University

Parker, Gerald
St. Louis University

Patrick, Floyd
Eastern Michigan University

Paul, Robert J.
Kansas State University

Rowley, Daniel James
University of Northern Colorado

Saavedra, Richard
University of Minnesota—
Minneapolis

Scott, Theresa
Community College of
Philadelphia

Siegel, Sidney
Drexel University

Slade, L. Allen
University of Delaware

Terpening, Willbann D.
Gonzaga University

Thibodeaux, Mary
University of North Texas

Thompson, Kenneth
DePaul University

Verser, Trudy
Western Michigan University

Wicander, Linda
Central Michigan University

A GUIDED TOUR TO *MANAGEMENT*

CHAPTER EIGHT

MANAGERIAL
DECISION MAKING

CHAPTER OUTLINE

The Nature of Managerial Decision Making
Types of Problems Decision Makers Face
Differences in Decision-Making Situations

Managers as Decision Makers
The Rational Model
Nonrational Models

Steps in an Effective Decision-Making Process
Identifying the Problem
Generating Alternative Solutions
Evaluating and Choosing an Alternative
Implementing and Monitoring the Chosen Solution

Overcoming Barriers to Effective Decision Making
Accepting the Problem Challenge
Searching for Sufficient Alternatives
Recognizing Common Decision-Making Biases
Avoiding the Decision Escalation Phenomenon

Group Decision Making
Advantages of Group Decision Making
Disadvantages of Group Decision Making
Enhancing Group Decision-Making Processes

Promoting Innovation: The Creativity Factor in Decision Making
Basic Ingredients
Stages of Creativity
Techniques for Enhancing Group Creativity

LEARNING OBJECTIVES

After studying this chapter, you should be able to:

■ Explain the major types of problems facing decision makers and describe the difference between programmed and non-programmed decisions.

■ Contrast the rational and non-rational models of managers as decision makers.

■ Describe each of the steps in an effective decision-making process.

■ Explain how to overcome the barriers associated with accepting the problem challenge and searching for sufficient alternatives.

■ Describe how to recognize common decision-making biases and avoid the decision escalation phenomenon.

■ Assess the advantages and disadvantages of group decision making.

■ Explain the basic ingredients and stages of creativity.

■ Describe the major techniques for enhancing group creativity.

Chapter Outline

An outline at the front of each chapter provides an orientation to the main points that will be covered.

Learning Objectives

Learning objectives at the beginning of each chapter chart the main points that the reader should retain after studying the material.

Opening Case

A case that opens each chapter illustrates how a real organization goes about "gaining the edge." The case is geared to capturing reader interest and depicting many of the concepts to be covered, including methods of promoting innovation.

---

4   PART ONE ■ INTRODUCTION

GAINING THE EDGE

QUALITY STANDS OUT AT CORNING AND STEUBEN

Corning, Inc., is rapidly earning a reputation as one of the most quality-oriented companies in the world. The company is probably best known for its popular consumer products, such as its Corning, Corelle, and Pyrex brands of housewares and its fine Steuben crystal. Although the company has long been considered a producer of high-quality products, James R. Houghton, the founder's great-great-grandson who took over as chairman and chief executive officer of the company in 1983, recognized that some of Corning's competitors were catching up with and even surpassing Corning in terms of the overall quality of their products and operations. Japanese companies posed a particular threat.

After studying quality programs in both Japan and the United States, Houghton found that the very best programs defined quality much more broadly than was typically the case. Quality, according to such programs, referred not only to the product itself but to every aspect of the work, such as designing a product, handling a customer, writing a memo, holding a meeting, making a sales call—in short, everything. By stressing quality in every phase of their operations, companies with serious quality programs were avoiding the rework and waste that undermine profit levels. At the same time, they were pleasing customers.

As a result of these findings, Houghton announced a major commitment to total quality and set up a program called the Total Quality Management System in all of Corning's 49 plants and laboratories in the United States and six other countries. Under the system, all 28,000 employees take courses on quality, including an introductory course on quality awareness that emphasizes such factors as understanding the requirements of the customer and meeting those requirements on time, every time. An integral part of the quality thrust is innovation, the development of new ideas to improve processes, services, or product offerings.

Nowhere is the broad quality and innovation effort more evident than at Steuben (pronounced Stoo-BEN, with the accent on the last syllable), a Corning division that has long been the symbol of company excellence. Since 1933, Steuben has produced only clear lead crystal, developing the material into an art form. Every U.S. president since President Truman has chosen Steuben for gifts of state. Steuben glass can be found in museum collections all over the world.

Yet even Steuben found that it could change for the better. "We are very much committed to the quality program," says Susan B. King, who took over as president of Steuben in January 1987. One part of the program involved conducting new research on customer requirements. Steuben found that while traditional customers valued the design, quality, and craftsmanship of the glassware, the newer, younger customers wanted products that also had functional value. In addition, the research indicated that the prime outlet for Steuben glass, located on Manhattan's Fifth Avenue, was viewed almost as a museum, making the pieces themselves seem more suitable for exhibits than for use in the home.

These research findings prompted Steuben management, headed by King, to make major changes. For instance, new Steuben ads use color for the first time and try to combine sophistication, humor, and a human touch in order to highlight the appropriate use of the glass pieces in homes. The ads are so intriguing that one of them won *Advertising Age*'s Best Magazine Ad of 1988 award. The product mix has been changed from an equal balance to 30 percent

Steuben glass products have always been known for their fine quality, but now the emphasis on quality extends from the shop to the management office to the retail sales staff. The institution of the Total Quality Management System at Steuben has led to innovative advertising, a different product mix, a rejuvenated sales staff, and a team approach to the making of the glass.

Part of Rubbermaid's success is due to the careful planning that is reflected in all of its activities. Before any new product goes out to the stores, Rubbermaid employee conduct hours of consumer research. For instance, researchers observed children at play on Rubbermaid's line of indoor gym equipment before that product went on the market. Rubbermaid's Chairman Stanley Gault notes that "We absolutely watch the market, and we work at it 24 hours a day." Such careful planning pays off, for the success rate of new Rubbermaid products is 90 percent.

agement can foster innovation. Finally, we investigate what it takes to become an effective manager, taking into account education, experience, and a suitable understanding of future trends and issues.

MANAGEMENT: AN OVERVIEW

Organization Two or more persons engaged in a systematic effort to produce goods or services

For most of us, organizations are an important part of our daily lives. By **organization,** we mean two or more persons engaged in a systematic effort to produce goods or services. We all deal with organizations when we attend classes, deposit money at the bank, buy clothing, and attend a movie. We are also influenced by organizations more indirectly through the products that we use. For example, if you have handled a dustpan lately, chances are that it was made by Rubbermaid, Inc., the company based in Wooster, Ohio, that makes plastic household and commercial items. The dustpan was a drastic departure from the company's original product line of balloons when it was first added to company offerings in 1934. Since then, the lowly dustpan has spawned more than 2000 additional products, giving the company a reputation for innovation and steady growth. What makes Rubbermaid so successful?

Like Corning and Steuben, Rubbermaid began to experience greatly accelerated success after a new chief executive officer (CEO), Stanley C. Gault, took over the helm in 1981. Gault had previously been a vice-chairman of General Electric. By the late 1980s, once-staid Rubbermaid even began appearing in *Fortune* magazine's annual survey of the 10 most admired companies in America. In contrast, over an 11-year period, William H. Bricker, CEO of Diamond Shamrock, transformed the company from a profitable chemical company with modest oil holdings into a debt-ridden energy company and was forced to resign.[2] To understand how management can make such a difference in an organization, we need to explore the nature of management further.

Management The process of achieving organizational goals through engaging in the four major functions of planning, organizing, leading, and controlling

What Is Management?

Management is the process of achieving organizational goals throug in the four major functions of planning, organizing, leading, and This definition recognizes that management is an ongoing activity, e

distance that the ball travels relative to targets or goals. Not surprisingly, strong evidence suggests that neither goals nor knowledge of results *alone* is sufficient for performance improvement. Instead, *both* goals and knowledge of results are necessary (imagine the difficulty of learning to play golf if one attempted to practice in the dark).[36] One company that has benefited from using goals to influence performance in a positive way is the Matsushita Electric Industrial Company (see the following Case in Point discussion).

 CASE IN POINT: Quality and Productivity Increase at Matsushita

The Matsushita Electric Industrial Company (MEIC) employs more than 1200 people at a former Motorola plant in Franklin Park, Illinois, that produces television receivers and microwave ovens. Within 5 years after this Japanese company acquired the plant from Motorola, quality had improved significantly. In-process defects had dropped from 1.4 to .07 defects per television set or microwave oven. In addition, productivity (the ratio of inputs, such as materials and labor, to outputs) had increased 30 percent. For example, the labor required to produce a color television receiver had been cut in half. These gains were achieved through a combination of managerial practices designed to revitalize an already skilled labor force and improvements in equipment, technology, and training.

In the area of managerial practice, manufacturing and quality control personnel meet every 6 months to set quality goals for the products manufactured. The group considers such issues as the number of defects allowed and the time allotted to complete the assembly of each item produced. Bar charts are then kept that indicate which areas are above, near, or below their targets. Once a week, all operations in the plant cease for 10 or 15 minutes while supervisors meet with their crews to consider progress relative to goals in such areas as quality, productivity, absenteeism, and scrap.

Special effort is made to improve performance on a particularly designated assembly line, called the "model line." Workers on that line and various support personnel, such as quality experts and engineers, meet once a week to gauge progress and consider new ideas. New practices that have proved successful on the model line are then adapted to fit other lines.

A quality-emphasis month is declared twice a year. Slogan and poster competitions, crossword puzzles with quality terms, suggestion contests, and other methods are used to boost awareness. Winners are entertained at a restaurant and given a modest reward.

The underlying purpose of these activities is to improve quality and productivity by creating an environment that will be conducive to cooperation and problem solving. The various activities also serve to emphasize the goals, encourage commitment, and provide knowledge about results, all important elements in making the goal-setting process effective.

Matsushita Electric also attempts to provide the equipment and technology that are necessary to meet the goals. For example, automated equipment developed in Japan was brought in to facilitate chassis assembly. Product design changes reduced the number of required workers by 26 percent, as equipment and design engineers worked together to make quality products easier to manufacture. Newly developed assembly lines allow workers to control their own work flow individually. In place of a continuous, conveyor-paced line, operators can use foot levers to detour work to their station and to forward finished pieces to the next workstations. Closed-circuit television systems were installed to

---

Interesting Photos and Captions

Each chapter contains a number of interesting photographs that help enhance the major points covered and make them memorable. The captions provide substantive information about the subject matter depicted and reinforce the linkage to text concepts.

Running Glossary

Significant terms are boldfaced, and each is printed with their definition in the margin near the first mention of the term. This arrangement facilitates easy access and review by readers.

Cases in Point

Two to three Cases in Point, or minicases, in each chapter provide detailed descriptions of how the concepts apply in real organizations. Most chapters have at least one internationally related Case in Point, which is designated with a globe insignia.

Promoting Innovation Section

A section addressing how organizations can promote innovation also is included in each chapter. The section is closely tied to the subject matter of the particular chapter and is highlighted by the symbol shown here.

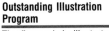

Outstanding Illustration Program

The figures help illustrate major points in ways that enhance clarity and also are pleasing to the eye.

---

cause they specify detailed desired actions in recurring circumstances, SOPs frequently are good tools for training new employees. Of course, if they are allowed to become outdated, SOPs may cause employees to learn, and continue to do, things that are no longer appropriate or needed.

A **rule** is a statement that spells out specific actions to be taken or not taken in a given situation. Unlike procedures, rules do not normally specify a series of steps. Instead, they specify exactly what must be or must not be done, leaving little flexibility or room for deviation. For example, most colleges and universities have rules specifying the circumstances under which a course may be dropped after a certain date.

Rule A statement that spells out specific actions to be taken or not taken in a given situation

Time Horizons of Goals and Plans

The different levels of goals and plans are related to different time horizons (see Figure 5-6). Strategic goals and plans usually address long-range issues involving time periods of 5 years or more. The period varies somewhat depending on the industry. When the environment changes rapidly, long-range planning may focus on periods that are even less than 5 years; when the environment is relatively stable (such as that of the utility industry), long-range planning may extend to periods of 10 to 20 years. Tactical goals and plans typically address intermediate-range issues involving periods that usually vary from 1 to 5 years. Operational goals and plans are mainly oriented toward short-range issues spanning periods of 1 year or less.

Promoting Innovation: The Role of the Planning Process

Research evidence suggests that the overall planning process can play a vital role in innovation in organizations through the mission, goals, and plans components. Creativity expert Teresa M. Amabile argues that the basic orientation of an organization toward innovation must stem primarily from the highest levels.[46] Ideally, the CEO envisions a future for the organization that is based on innovation and then attempts to communicate that vision to organization mem-

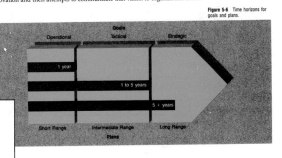

Figure 5-6 Time horizons for goals and plans.

P R A C T I C A L L Y   S P E A K I N G

KEEPING TABS ON COMPETITORS

Here are 10 legal ways to track what your competitors are doing:

1. Commercial data bases are an easy and fast means of obtaining information. Data bases contain published articles from newspapers, magazines, and trade publications, as well as reports from stock analysts, patent filings, biographical information, etc. This information can be accessed by computer. Information about various data bases is contained in the *Directory of Online Data Bases,* published by Cuandra/Elsevier (New York).
2. Specialty trade publications that deal with industries and product areas provide very current information about major personnel changes, product advertising, new product announcements, trade show notices, and the like. The *Standard Periodical Directory* and the *Oxbridge Directory of Newsletters,* both published by Oxbridge Communications (New York), may help you locate trade publications applicable to your area of interest.
3. News clippings from local newspapers often provide specific information not available in national publications. You can either subscribe to the newspapers themselves or hire a clipping service. Clipping services charge a basic fee, as well as a fee for each clipping.

Check your telephone directory for clipping services.
4. Help-wanted advertisements give clues about expansion plans, new technologies competitors are pursuing, and even financial status information that may be embedded in ads, especially those for high-level managers. Since clipping services usually will clip ads for certain types of jobs, but generally will not clip ads for only a particular company, you may want to subscribe to your competitor's hometown papers and check the Sunday edition, in particular.
5. Published market research reports can often be helpful. To learn about these reports, consult *Findex,* published by the National Standards Association (Gaithersburg, Maryland). *Findex* appears annually with midyear supplements and also is available in a computerized data base that is updated on a more frequent basis.
6. Wall Street reports give information about public companies (stock is publicly traded) and their various subsidiaries through analysis by securities analysts at brokerage firms. These reports often are available through a data base called Investext, which is offered by several data-base services. Another source of information is the *Wall Street Transcript,* which is a weekly newsletter that covers roundtable discussions about particular industries, including private as well as public companies.
7. Trade shows and the product literature that can be obtained

at such shows are good sources of information about new product innovations, price changes, and methods of marketing. Speeches and presentations given at trade shows often are helpful as well.
8. Public filings (federal, state, and local) often provide information about financial data and future plans. The filings include reports that public companies must submit to the SEC, records of bankruptcy cases and other court cases, state-required annual reports, Uniform Commercial Code (UCC) filings (required by most states when a company obtains a commercial loan from a bank), and franchise filings (often required by states when a franchise is sold).
9. Advertisements give clues about competitors' marketing strategies. Advertising or clipping services often can obtain copies of advertisements for you. Information about competitors' advertising expenditures by product in various media (TV, magazine, etc.) can be obtained from services like Leading National Advertisers in New York.
10. Personal contacts can provide many tidbits of useful information about competitor movements. A contact base may include university professors who have knowledge about technological advances, suppliers, customers, purchasing agents, service technicians, and Wall Street analysts. Trade shows and professional conferences are particularly good places to develop contacts.[24]

Practically Speaking Discussion

Many chapters contain a special section that provides practical advice on how to apply important concepts to real-world situations.

Chapter Summary

Each chapter contains a summary that reviews the major points made within the chapter.

Managerial Terminology

The major terms are listed at the end of each chapter with page numbers indicating where each term is first introduced and defined.

Questions for Discussion and Review

Questions that both help review the major concepts and encourage discussion are located at the end of each chapter.

CHAPTER SUMMARY

Work groups are becoming an increasingly important competitive factor in organizations. There are two major types of work groups, formal and informal. Formal groups include command, or functional, groups and task groups. Informal groups include interest and friendship groups. Required aspects of formal groups lead to the emergent behaviors, interactions, and sentiments associated with informal groups.

A useful way to analyze groups is to view them as systems that use inputs, engage in various processes or transformations, and produce outcomes. Important group inputs are group composition, particularly member characteristics and reasons for attraction to the group; member roles, including group task roles, group maintenance roles, and individual roles; and group size.

Hopefully, work group processes result in positive synergy. Important factors influencing group processes are group norms, group cohesiveness, and group development. Group norms stem from explicit statements by supervisors and coworkers, critical events in a group's history, primacy, and carryover behaviors. A number of factors contribute to group cohesiveness, which in turn has important consequences for group communication, satisfaction, performance, hostility and aggression toward other groups, and a group's willingness to innovate and change. New groups typically go through five stages of development: forming, storming, norming, performing, and adjourning. Because of the widespread presence of groups, managers spend a considerable amount of their time in meetings. Therefore, it is important for managers to know how to lead a meeting effectively. Important outcomes to consider in evaluating the effectiveness of groups are group performance, member need satisfaction, and future work group compatibility.

Some of the major mechanisms that organizations use to tap the creativity and innovative capacity of groups include task forces, or ad hoc committees, and teams, particularly entrepreneurial and self-managing teams.

The normative model of group effectiveness focuses specifically on those aspects of work groups that a manager has the best chance of influencing. It is particularly useful for designing work teams. Major elements of the model include organizational context, group design, group synergy, process criteria of effectiveness, and material resources leading to group effectiveness.

Managing conflict is also an important managerial skill related to groups. Causes of conflict include task interdependence, scarce resources, goal incompatibility, communication failures, individual differences, and poorly designed reward systems. Methods of reducing or resolving conflict include changing situational factors, appealing to superordinate goals, and using interpersonal conflict-handling modes. In addition, managers may need to simulate conflict in order to encourage creativity and innovation.

MANAGERIAL TERMINOLOGY

accommodation (580)
ad hoc committee (571)
adjourning (569)
autonomous work group (573)
avoidance (580)
collaboration (580)
command, or functional, group (553)
competition (580)
compromise (580)
conflict (578)

entrepreneurial team (571)
formal group (552)
forming (567)
free riders (563)
friendship group (555)
group (552)
group cohesiveness (565)
group maintenance roles (560)
group task roles (560)

informal group (554)
informal leader (561)
interest group (554)
linking pin (553)
negative synergy (563)
norming (568)
norms (564)
performing (569)
positive synergy (563)
role (560)
self-managing team (573)

self-oriented roles (560)
social loafing (563)
standing committee (553)
storming (568)
superordinate goals (581)
task force (571)
task group (553)
team (571)

QUESTIONS FOR DISCUSSION AND REVIEW

1. Outline the major types of work groups. Identify several work groups at your college or university. Classify them according to work group type.
2. Explain how informal groups develop in organiza-

tions. Choose an organization with which you are familiar and identify two informal groups. Trace how the informal groups came about.

3. Using a systems perspective, identify the main fac-

CHAPTER THREE ■ UNDERSTANDING EXTERNAL AND INTERNAL ENVIRONM

DISCUSSION QUESTIONS FOR CHAPTER OPENING CASE

1. Identify the major elements of the task environment at Liz Claiborne, Inc. Assess the company's handling of these major elements.
2. At various times, retailer orders for Liz Claiborne clothing have exceeded available supplies, and the company has been forced to cut back orders. Iden-

tify the environmental adaptation method used. Evaluate the pros and cons of other forms of environmental adaptation in this situation.

3. What avenues exist for Liz Claiborne, Inc., to further manage environmental elements that have the potential of affecting the company?

MANAGEMENT EXERCISE: ASSESSING A SKI SHOP ENVIRONMENT

Your best friend's sister and brother-in-law run the local ski shop near campus in your college town, but they have recently bought another type of business in another town. They want you and your friend to take over managing the ski shop. If you run it successfully, you and your friend will gradually be given substantial equity in the shop and eventually would own the whole thing.

So far, the shop has been only marginally profitable. Although the shop carries ski equipment, as well as ski clothing, it has habitually run out of both during the peak of the skiing season. At the same time, hastily ordered extra merchandise to meet the demand has often arrived late and then could not be sold until the next season, if at all. In addition, the shop does very little business from March through August.

Due to a dispute over the size and prominence of the outside sign displaying the shop's name, the relationship with local government officials is extremely poor. Tact and diplomacy are not a major strength of your friend's brother-in-law. As a result, the shop gets more than its share of inspections by the fire marshal, and a recent effort to gain permission to expand the parking lot was turned down by the zoning board.

So far, beyond some minimal advertising, little effort has been expended making inroads on campus. Yet

it would seem that the campus, with its 12,000 students, would be a lucrative market. The remainder of the town of 120,000 also contains a large number of avid skiers, since good skiing is only about 1½ hours away by car. Unfortunately, many of these skiers make their purchases of ski equipment and clothing at the various ski lodges that they frequent. One reason is that these lodges tend to have better arrangements for repairing and maintaining ski equipment.

Your initial assessment is that, so far, the ski shop has not attempted to deal adequately with its environment. There have been persistent rumors that another ski shop may open in the next year, creating a local competitor. You and your friend (and possibly some of your other friends who are willing to give you advice) are about to meet to try to develop some approaches that will help the ski shop manage its environment better. This analysis is crucial to your ultimate decision about whether to take on managing the ski shop. Also, your friend's sister and brother-in-law want to hear your ideas.

First, outline the major elements in the ski shop's task environment. Then prepare a proposal indicating how you would attempt to better manage the environmental impacts on the ski shop.

Discussion Questions for Chapter Opening Case

Discussion questions that address issues in the chapter opening case are included at the end of each chapter to facilitate using the opening case for discussion purposes.

Management Exercise

A management exercise that promotes experiential learning of major chapter concepts is included at the end of each chapter.

Concluding Case

In each chapter, a concluding case with accompanying questions depicts another real organization in considerable detail, so that students can obtain realistic views of the ways in which various organizations operate and also apply the concepts discussed in the chapter.

CONCLUDING CASE

WAL-MART LEAPFROGS THE COMPETITION

He stands on the nearest box, table, or platform and shouts to the crowd: "Give me a W!" The enthusiastic, resounding "W" from the associates gathered for the Saturday morning meeting all but shakes the building. So it goes for all the letters in Wal-Mart, before everyone joins in the chorus, "Wal-Mart, we're number 1!" The energy and enthusiasm displayed on this Saturday morning has played a major role in the phenomenal growth of Wal-Mart Stores, Inc. Today Wal-Mart is in the process of passing K-Mart and becoming second only to Sears, Roebuck and Company, which still holds the title as America's leading retailer.

The success of the company can be traced directly to founder Samuel Moore Walton, who grew up in the four-state area of Arkansas, Missouri, Oklahoma, and Kansas. After graduating from the University of Missouri in 1940 with a degree in economics, he immediately accepted a position with J. C. Penney as a management trainee; but that career was interrupted by Army service in World War II. Soon after returning from military duty, he opened the first Walton's Ben Franklin store (a five-and-dime type of store) in Versailles, Missouri. After losing his lease in 1950, Walton moved his business to Bentonville, Arkansas, where he opened a Walton 5 & 10. He also continued to establish Ben Franklin franchises and had 15 by 1962, when he opened the first Wal-Mart [...] ity. By 1969, when the [...] as incorporated as Wal-[...], Inc., there were 18 [...] and 15 Ben Franklin [...] rating throughout Ar-[...] issouri, Kansas, and

Wal-Mart Stores, the discount store chain that includes Sam's Wholesale Club outlets, blankets the southern and central states with 1355 stores. Founder Samuel Walton built up his booming business by servicing small communities bypassed by the big retailers; now the company is poised to spread into the larger metropolitan areas. In this picture cashiers at a new Sam's Wholesale Club in Flint, Michigan, cheer at the opening day ceremonies. Walton treats employees as partners in the organization and gives them important roles to play in achieving both corporate and individual store goals.

Oklahoma. From 1970 to 1979, annual sales grew from $44 million to $1.248 billion, and there were 276 Wal-Mart stores in 11 states. The steady expansion since that time has resulted in sales of more than $20 billion and 1355 stores (including 120 Sam's Wholesale Clubs and 14 DOT Discount Drug stores) in the 27 central and southern states of the nation. The west, northwest, and northeast are considered prime target areas for the future.

Wal-Mart has followed a strategy of building and expanding in areas where the local population is under 50,000. One or two stores are built, and then a distribution center is constructed nearby that will support further expansion in the geographic area. Other stores are then built within a day's drive of the distribution center. Wal-Mart currently has 19 distribution centers, which are widely considered to be major factors in the company's spectacular success.

Wal-Mart's mission stresses three major elements, or principles: value and aggressive service for

customers, partnership with associates (employees), and strong relationships with the communities in which stores are located. As part of the effort toward aggressive customer service, a "greeter" welcomes customers at the door with a smile and offers them directions, if needed. Associates throughout the stores are trained to look customers in the eye, greet them, and ask them if they would like help. In the area of value, the prices are probably lower than at any other store in the area.

The Wal-Mart relationship with associates is based on the premise that they are partners in

185

PART ENDING CASE

MARRIOTT GROWS FROM ROOT BEER STAND TO CORPORATE EMPIRE

Following in his late father's footsteps, J. Willard "Bill" Marriott, Jr., makes a habit of periodically visiting one or more of the hotels, contract food service operations, retirement centers, and other facilities that make up the vast Marriott empire founded by his parents. For instance, on one recent day, after a brief tour of company facilities in Maine, Wisconsin, and California, the Marriott chairman and president flew into Miami, attended a testimonial dinner, and then put in an extra hour of "homework" before turning in. The next day, after several meetings he traveled to Cleveland to tour the company's airport hotel before proceeding to Palm Desert, California, to inspect a new hotel and participate in another series of meetings. Two more cities were next on his agenda, with a quick trip scheduled for London a few days later.

With his busy travel schedule, Marriott typically logs about 200,000 miles per year, yet he describes his activities as "fun." He explains that "it's work, of course, but it's necessary. I go to check on our properties, to meet with employees, and make sure things are running smoothly. If I sit back and relax. If I sit back and relax. After all, if you're going to be a star performer, you can't sit back and relax. A star performer has to work hard and make sacrifices, and at Marriott Corp., we do both."

Such dedication helps to explain Marriott's spectacular success. The company's sales exceed $7.5 billion per year. Over 230,000 employees work for Marriott Cor-

poration, making it the eighth-largest employer in the United States. It conducts business in all 50 states, and in 26 countries around the world. Annual growth has averaged 20 percent for more than 3 decades and current plans call for the corporation to grow at a rate of 15 to 20 percent each year during the 1990s. The Marriott family owns about 25 percent of the public stock of the company, currently worth about $1 billion.

When the corporation's great success is mentioned, though, Bill Marriott is quick to give credit to the guidance of his father, J. Willard Marriott, Sr., and his mother, Alice, who together started the company by opening a nine-seat A&W root beer stand in Washington, D.C., in 1927. During the first summer, business at the stand was brisk but sales dwindled as the weather turned cooler in the fall. The Marriotts then began offering food such as chili, barbecue, and hot tamales, items that were then in vogue in the western part of the United States. As sales increased, they renamed their enterprise, which had now been transformed into a restaurant, the "Hot Shoppe." The company still owns a small group of Hot Shoppes in the Washington, D.C. area.

The senior Marriott understood the potential advantages of a chain of food establishments compared with a single restaurant, namely that a chain could have much better purchasing power, develop a more flexible pool of labor, and build a solid reputation with customers in a wider geographical area. He also recognized the prospects associated with the rapidly expanding ownership of cars. Accordingly, within a year of establishing his root beer stand, he opened the first drive-in restaurant on the east coast. Despite the De-

What started as a nine-seat root beer stand in Washington, D.C. in 1927 has grown into a billion dollar, worldwide food service and lodging industry. One of the most recent additions to the Marriott corporate empire is the Warsaw Marriott, completed in the fall of 1989, just in time for the opening of eastern Europe. Attention to the needs of customers and employees and a keen sense of innovative business opportunities account for the company's spectacular success.

pression, people still needed to eat and the fledgling restaurant chain prospered and grew. Within 3 years of starting the company, the Marriotts were millionaires.

By 1937, they saw another opportunity when a manager of a Hot Shoppe near Washington's old Hoover Field (where the Pentagon now stands) reported that people often purchased food to eat during airplane flights. Marriott, Sr., negotiated contracts to supply meals during Eastern and American airlines flights, launching the company into the field of airline catering. By the time the first offering of stock was made to the public in 1953, the company had such a positive reputation that the offering sold out within 2 hours.

148

Part Case

An extensive case at the end of each major part of the book focuses heavily on issues related to the chapters in that particular part. The case, and its accompanying questions, helps students integrate the material from the various chapters within each respective part.

MANAGEMENT

PART ONE

INTRODUCTION

M anagement is at one of its most significant stages in history. Global competition has become a way of life. Changes in areas like technology, international affairs, business practices, and ideas of organizational social responsibility are causing managers to reexamine their methods and goals, as well as place increased emphasis on innovation. In this section we will consider how some of the basic principles of management apply in today's rapidly changing environment.

Chapter 1 provides an overview of the management process, focusing on what managers actually do and on the skills and knowledge they need to be effective and innovative managers.

Yet, innovative practices do not emerge in a vacuum; they build on the best ideas about management that have been developed over a period of time. **Chapter 2** analyzes the roots of current approaches growing out of the scientific, behavioral, quantitative, and contemporary management perspectives.

As **Chapter 3** makes clear, effective management requires a knowledge of the outside environment in which an organization operates, as well as the nature of the organization's internal culture. Successful managers are able to deal with external and internal factors in ways that support the achievement of organizational goals.

A broad perspective also encompasses the ongoing debate concerning how much social responsibility an organization should assume relative to shareholders, employees, customers, the community, and society at large. **Chapter 4** explores the nature and extent of organizational social responsibility and examines managerial ethics.

CHAPTER ONE

THE CHALLENGE OF MANAGEMENT

CHAPTER OUTLINE

Management: An Overview
What Is Management?
The Management Process

What Managers Actually Do
Work Methods
Managerial Roles
Managerial Work Agendas

Managerial Knowledge, Skills, and Performance
Knowledge Base
Key Management Skills
Performance

Managerial Job Types
Vertical Dimension: Hierarchical Levels
Differences among Hierarchical Levels
Promoting Innovation: The Entrepreneurial Role
Horizontal Dimension: Responsibility Areas
Differences According to Responsibility Area

Learning to Be an Effective Manager
Managerial Education
Management Experience
Understanding Future Trends

LEARNING OBJECTIVES

After studying this chapter, you should be able to:

■ Explain the four functions of management and identify the other major elements in the management process.

■ Describe three common work methods that managers use and ten major roles that managers play.

■ Explain the main factors influencing work agendas and how managers use such agendas to channel their efforts.

■ Delineate the three major types of skills needed by managers.

■ Distinguish between effectiveness and efficiency as they relate to organizational performance.

■ Describe how managerial jobs differ according to hierarchical level and responsibility area.

■ Explain how managers at different hierarchical levels can use the entrepreneurial role to foster innovation.

■ Describe the role of management education and experience in preparing managers.

GAINING THE EDGE

QUALITY STANDS OUT AT CORNING AND STEUBEN

Corning, Inc., is rapidly earning a reputation as one of the most quality-oriented companies in the world. The company is probably best known for its popular consumer products, such as its Corning, Corelle, and Pyrex brands of housewares and its fine Steuben crystal. Although the company has long been considered a producer of high-quality products, James R. Houghton, the founder's great-great-grandson who took over as chairman and chief executive officer of the company in 1983, recognized that some of Corning's competitors were catching up with and even surpassing Corning in terms of the overall quality of their products and operations. Japanese companies posed a particular threat.

After studying quality programs in both Japan and the United States, Houghton found that the very best programs defined quality much more broadly than was typically the case. Quality, according to such programs, referred not only to the product itself but to every aspect of the work, such as designing a product, handling a customer, writing a memo, holding a meeting, making a sales call—in short, everything. By stressing quality in every phase of their operations, companies with serious quality programs were avoiding the rework and waste that undermine profit levels. At the same time, they were pleasing customers.

As a result of these findings, Houghton announced a major commitment to total quality and set up a program called the Total Quality Management System in all of Corning's 49 plants and laboratories in the United States and six other countries. Under the system, all 28,000 employees take courses on quality, including an introductory course on quality awareness that emphasizes such factors as understanding the requirements of the customer and meeting those requirements on time, every time. An integral part of the quality thrust is innovation, the development of new ideas to improve processes, services, or product offerings.

Nowhere is the broad quality and innovation effort more evident than at Steuben (pronounced Stoo-BEN, with the accent on the last syllable), a Corning division that has long been the symbol of company excellence. Since 1933, Steuben has produced only clear lead crystal, developing the material into an art form. Every U.S. president since President Truman has chosen Steuben for gifts of state. Steuben glass can be found in museum collections all over the world.

Yet even Steuben found that it could change for the better. "We are very much committed to the quality program," says Susan B. King, who took over as president of Steuben in January 1987. One part of the program involved conducting new research on customer requirements. Steuben found that while traditional customers valued the design, quality, and craftmanship of the glassware, the newer, younger customers wanted products that also had functional value. In addition, the research indicated that the prime outlet for Steuben glass, located on Manhattan's Fifth Avenue, was viewed almost as a museum, making the pieces themselves seem more suitable for exhibits than for use in the home.

These research findings prompted Steuben management, headed by King, to make major changes. For instance, new Steuben ads use color for the first time and try to combine sophistication, humor, and a human touch in order to highlight the appropriate use of the glass pieces in homes. The ads are so intriguing that one of them won *Advertising Age*'s Best Magazine Ad of 1988 award. The product mix has been changed from an equal balance to 30 percent

Steuben glass products have always been known for their fine quality, but now the emphasis on quality extends from the shop to the management office to the retail sales staff. The institution of the Total Quality Management System at Steuben has led to innovative advertising, a different product mix, a rejuvenated sales staff, and a team approach to the making of the glass.

ornamental and 70 percent functional (vases, bowls, candlesticks, and the like). The Fifth Avenue store has been refurbished to provide a much friendlier atmosphere, and the sales staff has gone through extensive training aimed at helping employees provide the best possible service to match the quality of the product. For the first time, pieces are also sold through a Corning store, catalogs, and select department stores for prices ranging from $150 to more than $300,000.

While Steuben has traditionally had a very strong commitment to product quality, in the past there was not very much emphasis on being efficient in the sense of using resources carefully to make a profit. That culture is changing. "We want to do the *right* things right," King says.

As part of the effort, King has been taking steps to encourage openness and the sharing of ideas among workers and managers. For example, each month three or four workers from different parts of the Steuben factory at Corning, in upstate New York, participate in a senior staff meeting at Steuben's New York City headquarters. While in Manhattan, the workers spend an hour on the sales floor learning more about the customers and also visit luxury stores that carry the glassware of competitors. The process provides both managers and workers with a broader perspective of the business.

At the factory, a new management and labor "partnership" steering committee meets all day every Monday to plan improvements in the production process. Recent changes include instituting a team approach to making the glassware. Teams of workers follow the whole process of glassmaking from start to finish: from forming the glass through to finishing and inspecting the items and finally signing the Steuben name on each piece. The change from an assembly-line type of approach to a team approach has reduced defects by 25 percent, largely because problems that could cause difficulties later in the process are more likely to be identified and rectified by a team of persons working together. One current challenge facing management is the need to expand capacity. The company now sells all that it can make.

In addition to its consumer-sector operations, of which Steuben is a part, Corning also has businesses in three other global market sectors: specialty glass and ceramics, telecommunications, and laboratory sciences. To help everyone in the company appreciate the importance of the quality effort, "Jamie" (as he likes to be called by everyone at Corning, including employees at the lowest levels) Houghton annually visits about 50 separate Corning facilities around the world and stresses the importance of the quality program.[1]

The innovations and quality improvements at Corning and Steuben are indicative of the kinds of efforts that are being made by organizations intent on gaining the competitive edge. This book will examine many such organizations as we consider the management approaches that are critical to organizational success. In the process, we will highlight management techniques that are especially effective at promoting innovation. We will see why even companies like Corning, with an established reputation for quality products and a strong tradition of success, must be receptive to improvements through innovative approaches if they are to continue to compete effectively in today's global marketplace.

We begin the current chapter by providing an overview of the nature of management and the basic processes involved. We then consider what managers actually do by describing the work methods that they use, the different roles that they play, and the work agendas that guide their actions. We also examine the knowledge base and skills that managers need in order to achieve high performance. We explore two major dimensions along which managerial jobs differ, and we consider how the entrepreneurial role at different levels of man-

Part of Rubbermaid's success is due to the careful planning that is reflected in all of its activities. Before any new product goes out to the stores, Rubbermaid employee conduct hours of consumer research. For instance, researchers observed children at play on Rubbermaid's line of indoor gym equipment before that product went on the market. Rubbermaid's Chairman Stanley Gault notes that "We absolutely watch the market, and we work at it 24 hours a day." Such careful planning pays off, for the success rate of new Rubbermaid products is 90 percent.

agement can foster innovation. Finally, we investigate what it takes to become an effective manager, taking into account education, experience, and a suitable understanding of future trends and issues.

MANAGEMENT: AN OVERVIEW

Organization Two or more persons engaged in a systematic effort to produce goods or services

For most of us, organizations are an important part of our daily lives. By **organization,** we mean two or more persons engaged in a systematic effort to produce goods or services. We all deal with organizations when we attend classes, deposit money at the bank, buy clothing, and attend a movie. We are also influenced by organizations more indirectly through the products that we use. For example, if you have handled a dustpan lately, chances are that it was made by Rubbermaid, Inc., the company based in Wooster, Ohio, that makes plastic household and commercial items. The dustpan was a drastic departure from the company's original product line of balloons when it was first added to company offerings in 1934. Since then, the lowly dustpan has spawned more than 2000 additional products, giving the company a reputation for innovation and steady growth. What makes Rubbermaid so successful?

Like Corning and Steuben, Rubbermaid began to experience greatly accelerated success after a new chief executive officer (CEO), Stanley C. Gault, took over the helm in 1981. Gault had previously been a vice-chairman of General Electric. By the late 1980s, once-staid Rubbermaid even began appearing on *Fortune* magazine's annual survey of the 10 most admired companies in America. In contrast, over an 11-year period, William H. Bricker, CEO of Diamond Shamrock, transformed the company from a profitable chemical company with modest oil holdings into a debt-ridden energy company and was forced to resign.[2] To understand how management can make such a difference in an organization, we need to explore the nature of management further.

Management The process of achieving organizational goals through engaging in the four major functions of planning, organizing, leading, and controlling

What Is Management?

Management is the process of achieving organizational goals through engaging in the four major functions of planning, organizing, leading, and controlling. This definition recognizes that management is an ongoing activity, entails reaching important goals, and involves knowing how to perform the four major functions of management. Since the four major functions are crucial to effective management, we use them as the basic framework for this book.[3] Accordingly, you will find that we devote a major unit to each of these management functions—planning, organizing, leading, and controlling. For now, though, we provide a brief overview of these major functions (see Figure 1-1) before considering how they relate to other major aspects of managerial work.

Planning. **Planning** is the management function that involves setting goals and deciding how best to achieve them. This function also includes considering what must be done to encourage necessary levels of change and innovation. For example, Rubbermaid typically sets an annual goal of increasing sales by at least 15 percent. In addition, though, the company aims to reap 30 percent of those sales from products that are no more than 5 years old—a powerful signal that innovation is important. One result is that the company typically launches 100 or more new products per year. The success rate for the new products is an enviable 90 percent, largely because of the careful planning that also goes into new product development and product launches. Rubbermaid's recent successful products include an imaginatively designed indoor gym for kids and a new line of inexpensive office workstations.[4]

> **Planning** The process of setting goals and deciding how best to achieve them

At Diamond Shamrock, the major goal was to change the chemical company into a major energy company; this was based on Bricker's view in the late 1970s (later proven to be faulty) that energy prices would continue their upward trend. Even so, progress toward the goal was somewhat erratic and reflected poor planning. Diamond Shamrock sold its gas stations to Sigmor Corporation and then bought them back 5 years later; overpaid by $600 million when purchasing San Francisco–based Natomas, an oil and gas producer, for $1.3 billion; and even, at one point, purchased a stake in a prize bull (partially owned by Bricker).[5]

> **Organizing** The process of allocating and arranging human and nonhuman resources so that plans can be carried out successfully

Organizing. **Organizing** is the management function that focuses on allocating and arranging human and nonhuman resources so that plans can be carried out

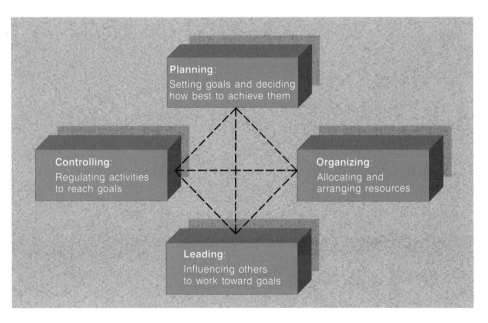

Figure 1-1 The functions of management.

successfully. It is through the organizing function that managers determine which tasks are to be done, how tasks can best be combined into specific jobs, and how jobs can be grouped into various units that make up the structure of the organization. Staffing jobs with individuals who can successfully carry out plans is also part of the organizing function. For example, Rubbermaid recently reorganized to serve customers better by creating five divisions aimed at different customer needs: housewares, office products, commercial products, international operations, and the Little Tikes Company toy subsidiary. In addition, recruiting is done with a careful eye toward bringing in individuals with the potential to take on leadership positions as the company continues to expand. Resources are allocated on the basis of major company goals.[6]

In contrast, at Diamond Shamrock considerable organizing effort was channeled toward developing luxurious facilities for use by top management and the board of directors. Despite the company's difficulties, resources were allocated for such amenities as a lavish 12,000-acre Texas ranch worth $9 million that was used for corporate meetings and entertainment, a $1 million box at the Dallas Cowboys' home stadium, and a fleet of airplanes to transport the CEO and various directors around the world. One frequent visitor to the ranch was Sir Richard Musgrave, a professional shoot manager whom the company flew in from Ireland to organize pheasant hunts for Diamond Shamrock's customers and executives.[7]

Leading The process of influencing others to engage in the work behaviors necessary to reach organizational goals

Leading. **Leading** is the management function that involves influencing others to engage in the work behaviors necessary to reach organizational goals. Leading includes communicating with others, helping to outline a vision of what can be accomplished, providing direction, and motivating organization members to put forth the substantial effort required. At Rubbermaid the number-one rule of products is clearly articulated to everyone: They're to be useful, long-lasting, and inexpensive. Translating this vision into practical terms, CEO Gault let organizational members know from the start that he was aiming for $1.2 billion in sales by 1990 (compared with about $300 million when he took over), a performance level that the company reached ahead of time.[8] To help motivate organization members, Rubbermaid offers an incentive plan that enables eligible Rubbermaid managers to receive bonuses based partially on profit levels. In addition, many hourly workers participate in a retirement plan based on profits. One result of these practices is that, in the housewares division alone, employees recently contributed 12,600 suggestions for improvements during a 12-month period, thereby demonstrating their strong commitment to Gault's vision.[9]

Chosen partially for his support of Diamond Shamrock's tradition of participatory management, Bricker assumed an autocratic style after becoming CEO. Many executives who had been with the company for some time concluded that it was useless to fight with Bricker over his high-risk ideas. According to Raymond F. Evans, Bricker's former mentor and predecessor as CEO, Bricker "changed 180 degrees when he became CEO. He just became a different guy. I guess his ego got him."[10]

Controlling The process of regulating organizational activities so that actual performance conforms to expected organizational standards and goals

Controlling. **Controlling** is the management function that is aimed at regulating organizational activities so that actual performance conforms to expected organizational standards and goals.[11] To do the necessary regulating, managers need to monitor ongoing activities, compare the results with expected standards or progress toward goals, and take corrective action as needed. For example, in order to reach earnings goals, Rubbermaid must keep a careful eye on costs. Recently the costs of certain resins that were a key ingredient in a newly launched plastic desk product suddenly increased 52 percent. Managers moved quickly to take corrective action by changing to a less expensive combination of petrochemicals. At Rubbermaid, considerable effort also goes into monitoring the product quality that has become almost synonymous with the company name. In fact, the Rubbermaid name has such a solid reputation with customers that some stores even label their housewares department the "Rubbermaid section."[12]

As oil prices and earnings began to drop, Diamond Shamrock began to sell assets and cut expenses. Still, the $9 million ranch was retained. The original fleet of five company planes was cut back to three, but then the company leased extra planes for various trips. News of various potential conflicts of interest involving company dealings with Bricker's friends began to emerge.[13]

The Management Process

Although the four major functions of management form the basis for the managerial process, several additional elements are considered key ingredients of this process as well. The additional elements were identified by management scholars Steven J. Carroll and Dennis J. Gillen, on the basis of their review of major studies on managerial work. An extended model of the management process is shown in Figure 1-2.[14] As indicated, the functions of management form the central part of the process. However, the model also shows that work methods and managerial roles, as well as work agendas, feed into the management functions. A manager's working knowledge and key management skills also are important factors that contribute to high performance (achieving goals). We consider each of these elements in greater detail in the next several sections of this chapter. As we examine these variables, it is useful to keep in mind that the management process applies not only to profit-making organizations, like Corning and Rubbermaid, but also to not-for-profit organizations.[15] A **not-for-profit organization** (sometimes called a *nonprofit organization*) is an organization whose main purposes center on issues other than making profits. Common examples of

Not-for-profit organization
An organization whose main purposes center on issues other than making profits

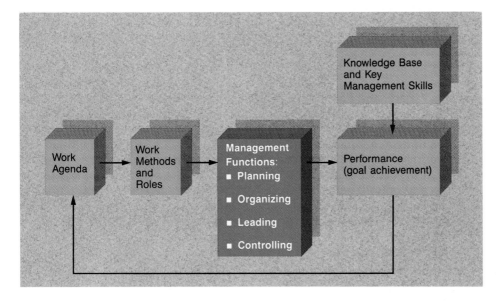

Figure 1-2 An extended model of the management process. (Adapted from Stephen J. Carroll and Dennis J. Gillen, "Are the Classical Management Functions Useful in Describing Managerial Work?" *Academy of Management Review*, vol. 12, 1987, pp. 38–51.)

not-for-profit organizations are government organizations (e.g., the federal government), educational institutions (your college or university), cultural institutions (New York's Carnegie Hall), charitable institutions (United Way), and many health-care facilities (Mayo Clinic). Of course, environmental factors (such as the state of the economy and actions by competitors) also have a bearing on ultimate goal achievement.[16] We discuss these issues further in Chapter 3.

WHAT MANAGERS ACTUALLY DO

One of the most famous studies of managers was conducted by management scholar Henry Mintzberg, who followed several top managers around for 1 week each and recorded everything that they did.[17] Mintzberg was interested in documenting what managers actually do on the job. After following the senior managers around for days, he came to some interesting conclusions about their work methods and about several major roles that managers play.

Work Methods

Mintzberg found that the actual work methods of the managers differed quite drastically from popular images of managers as reflective, systematic planners who spend considerable quiet time in their offices pouring over formal reports. Three of his findings provide particularly intriguing glimpses into the world of high-level managers.

Unrelenting Pace. The managers in Mintzberg's study worked at an unrelenting pace. They began working from the moment they arrived at the office in the morning and kept working until they left at night. Rather than taking coffee breaks, the managers usually drank their coffee while they attended meetings, which averaged eight each day. Similarly, lunches were almost always eaten in the course of formal or informal meetings. When the managers were not in meetings, they had to handle their average of 36 pieces of mail per day as well as other matters that landed on their desk or were communicated by telephone. If they happened to have a free minute or two, the time was usually quickly usurped by subordinates anxious to have a word with the boss. Donald Schuenke, head of Northwestern Mutual Life Insurance, estimates that he would have to work no less than 24 hours per day if he were to honor all the requests for just a small amount of his time.[18]

Brevity, Variety, and Fragmentation. Another of Mintzberg's findings was that the managers' work was characterized by brevity, variety, and fragmentation. The managers handled a wide variety of issues throughout the day, ranging from awarding a retirement plaque to discussing the bidding on a multi-million-dollar contract. Many of their activities were surprisingly brief. For example, about half the activities that Mintzberg recorded were completed in less than 9 minutes, and only 10 percent took more than 1 hour. Telephone calls tended to be short, lasting an average of 6 minutes; work sessions at the manager's desk and informal meetings averaged 15 and 10 minutes, respectively. The managers experienced continual interruptions from telephone calls and subordinates. They often stopped their own desk work to place calls or request that subordinates drop in. Leaving meetings before the end was common. As a result of the fragmentation and interruptions, a number of top managers save their major thinking about planning and important issues for times outside the normal workday. For example, Susan King of Steuben does much of her major reading, thinking, and planning at the office after 6 p.m. when the workday pace slows. In the process, she puts in a total of about 60 to 70 hours of work per week. Stan Pace of General Dynamics does his reflecting on big issues when he is outside the office—for example, in his car while driving to and from work, on long plane trips, and at home over the weekend.[19]

Verbal Contacts and Networks. The managers in Mintzberg's study also showed a strong preference for verbal communication, preferring to communicate through phone conversations and informal and formal meetings rather than depending on more formal written memos and reports. For obtaining and transmitting information, they relied heavily on networks. A **network** is a set of cooperative relationships with individuals whose help is needed in order for a manager to function effectively. The network of contacts in Mintzberg's study included superiors, subordinates, peers, and other individuals inside the organization, as well as numerous outside individuals. Some of the contacts were personal, such as friends and peers. Others were experts, such as consultants, lawyers, and insurance underwriters. Still others were trade association contacts, customers, and suppliers. Because of their position, managers also tended to receive unsolicited information that was sometimes helpful.

Network A set of cooperative relationships with individuals whose help is needed in order for a manager to function effectively

Implications of Mintzberg's Findings on Work Methods. Although Mintzberg's study focused on top-level managers, other research supports Mintzberg's contention that these findings apply to a wide variety of managers.[20] For example, one study of factory supervisors found that they engaged in between 237 and 1073 activities within a given workday—or more than one activity every 2 minutes. This same study indicated that during a typical day the average supervisor talked with many different individuals, ranging from about 25 to more than 50 persons.[21] Such research also strongly supports the notion that managers need to develop a major network of contacts in order to have influence and to operate effectively. For some ideas on how managers develop such contacts, see the Practically Speaking discussion, "How to Build Networks," which appears on the following page.

Managerial Roles

As he chronicled how managers work, Mintzberg also collected reams of data about what they did. To make sense of his voluminous data, Mintzberg attempted to categorize the managers' various activities into three general types of roles. A **role** is an organized set of behaviors that is associated with a particular office or position.[22] Positions usually entail multiple roles. For example, roles for a salesperson position in a retail store might include information giver, stock handler, and cashier.

Role An organized set of behaviors that is associated with a particular office or position

In the activities of the managers that he observed, Mintzberg saw three general types of roles: interpersonal, informational, and decisional. Within these three types of roles, Mintzberg outlined 10 more specific roles that managers play. These roles are summarized in Table 1-1.

Interpersonal Roles. Interpersonal roles grow directly out of the authority of a manager's position and involve developing and maintaining positive relationships with significant others. More specifically, the *figurehead* role entails sym-

P R A C T I C A L L Y   S P E A K I N G

HOW TO BUILD NETWORKS

Experts agree that building networks of influence with others involves the principle of reciprocity. Reciprocity means that people generally feel that they should be paid back for the various things they do and that one good (or bad) turn deserves another. For the most part, individuals do not expect to be paid back right away or in specific amounts; approximations will usually do. Because individuals anticipate that their actions will be reimbursed in one way or another, influence and networking are possible.

One way to think about using the reciprocity principle in networking is to think of oneself as a "trader" and to use the metaphor of "currencies" as a means of approaching the process of exchange. Just as there are many types of currencies used in the world, there are many different kinds of currencies that are used in organizational life. Too often individuals think only in terms of money, promotions, and status, but there are actually many possibilities.

SOME POSSIBLE CURRENCIES
Some possible currencies that you might be able to trade include the following:

Resources: giving budget increases, personnel, space, etc.

Assistance: helping with projects or taking on unwanted tasks

Information: furnishing organizational and/or technical knowledge

Recognition: acknowledging effort, accomplishment, or abilities

Visibility: providing the chance to be known by higher-ups

Advancement: giving tasks that can aid in promotion

Personal support: providing personal and emotional backing

Understanding: listening to others' concerns

HOW TO USE CURRENCIES
In using currencies, it helps to consider these four steps:

1. *Think of each individual whom you need to deal with as a potential ally or network member.* If you want to have influence with an organization and get the job done, you will need to create internal network members or allies. Assuming that even a difficult person is a potential network member makes it easier to try to understand that person's world and the things that person values and needs.
2. *Get to know the world of the potential network member, including the pressures that the person is under, as well as the person's needs and goals.* An important factor influencing behavior is how performance is measured and rewarded. If you ask an individual to do things that will be perceived as poor performance within that individual's work unit, you are likely to encounter resistance.
3. *Be aware of your own strengths and potential weaknesses as a networker.* Sometimes net-

workers underestimate the range of currencies that they have available to exchange. Make a list of potential currencies and resources that you have to offer. Then do some introspection about your own preferred style of interaction with others. Would-be networkers often fail to understand how their preferred style of interaction fits or doesn't fit with the potential ally's preferred style. For instance, does the potential ally like to socialize first and work later? If that's the case, the person may find it difficult to deal with someone who likes to solve the problem first and only then talk about the weather, the family, or office politics. Skilled networkers learn to adapt their own style to that of others in dealing with potential allies.
4. *Gear your exchange transactions so that both parties can come out winners.* For the most part, transactions in organizations are not one-time occurrences. Usually the parties will need to deal with one another again, perhaps frequently. In fact, that is the idea of networks—to have contacts to call on as needed. The implication here is that in most exchange relationships there are two outcomes that ultimately make a difference. One is success in achieving the task goals at hand. The other is maintaining and improving the relationship so that the contact remains a viable one. With networking, it is better to lose the battle than to lose the war.[23]

Table 1-1   Mintzberg's 10 Managerial Roles

Role	Description
INTERPERSONAL	
Figurehead	Performs symbolic duties of a legal or social nature
Leader	Builds relationships with subordinates and communicates with, motivates, and coaches them
Liaison	Maintains networks of contacts outside work unit who provide help and information
INFORMATIONAL	
Monitor	Seeks internal and external information about issues that can affect organization
Disseminator	Transmits information internally that is obtained from either internal or external sources
Spokesperson	Transmits information about the organization to outsiders
DECISIONAL	
Entrepreneur	Acts as initiator, designer, and encourager of change and innovation
Disturbance handler	Takes corrective action when organization faces important, unexpected difficulties
Resource allocator	Distributes resources of all types, including time, funding, equipment, and human resources
Negotiator	Represents the organization in major negotiations affecting the manager's areas of responsibility

Source: Adapted from Henry Mintzberg, *The Nature of Managerial Work,* Harper & Row, New York, 1980.

bolic duties that are associated with the manager's formal organizational position and authority (such as presiding over an employee awards banquet, officially signing a contract, or meeting briefly with an important customer). The *leader* role involves building relationships with subordinates and includes communicating with, motivating, and coaching subordinates. The *liaison* role focuses on maintaining a network of relationships outside a manager's own work unit, including outside the organization. Managers' interpersonal relationships make it possible for them to build the networks necessary to carry out the next set of roles, the informational roles.

Informational Roles. Informational roles pertain to receiving and transmitting information so that managers can serve as the nerve centers of their organizational units. One informational role, the *monitor* role, focuses on seeking information both internally and externally about issues that can affect the organization. For example, *USA Today* executive Nancy Woodhull noticed that radio stations were big users of the company's fledgling videotex service, which brings news to consumers via home-computer screens.[24] After finding out that the stations were using the service for on-air scripts early in the morning, she hatched the idea for a radio-script service. In contrast, the *disseminator* role is aimed at transmitting information internally. The disseminator role operates in two ways. First, the manager conveys information received from outsiders to individuals inside the organization who can use the information. Second, the manager helps transfer information from one subordinate to another subordinate or among other internal members who can benefit from the information. While the disseminator role involves internal information needs, the *spokesperson* role addresses the transmission of information to outsiders (including the board of directors) on such matters as the organization's plans, policies, actions, and results. Thus the manager seeks information in the monitor role, communicates it internally in the disseminator role, and transmits it externally in the spokesperson role. The three information roles, then, combine to provide important information required in the decisional roles.

Decisional Roles. Decisional roles involve making significant decisions that affect the organization. Four roles describe the manager as a decision maker. The *entrepreneur* role involves acting as an initiator, designer, and encourager of change, particularly in exploiting new opportunities and solving nonpressing problems. For instance, after Woodhull recognized that a radio-script service might be a profitable idea, she initiated the creation of the service. The ABC radio network soon bought exclusive rights to the service, thereby ensuring the profitability of the service and providing the bonus of a constant source of on-the-air mentions of *USA Today*.[25] Due to increasing domestic and foreign competition, the entrepreneur role has been gaining in importance as a means of encouraging innovation. We discuss the entrepreneur role in further detail later in this chapter. The *disturbance handler* role is associated with taking corrective action when the organization faces important, unexpected difficulties. The *resource allocator* role addresses distributing resources of all types, including time, funding, equipment, and human resources. Finally, the *negotiator* role focuses on representing the organization in major negotiations affecting the manager's areas of responsibility.

Implications of Roles. When Mintzberg developed the three categories of general roles and the ten specific roles, he acknowledged that his delineation was somewhat arbitrary. He divided the various managerial activities into roles that made sense to him after observing the various managers. Since that time, a few researchers have attempted to verify the usefulness of Mintzberg's categories with somewhat mixed results. In one case, for example, the activities associated with four of the roles (figurehead, disseminator, disturbance handler, and negotiator) were found to overlap to a considerable degree with the activities of other roles.[26] Still, the notion of roles, even with overlap, provides some insight into what managers actually do during their workday. The roles also give us clues about the kinds of skills that managers are likely to need in order to carry out their work effectively.

Mintzberg's role approach provides a somewhat different perspective on management than do the four major functions of management. At first glance, it might seem that Mintzberg's findings are incompatible with the view that the major functions of planning, organizing, leading, and controlling are an important part of the management process. Recently, though, researchers have pointed out that Mintzberg's study did not consider *why* managers were engaging in the different roles that he chronicled. When the *why* is taken into consideration, it becomes clear that the functions of management provide an important blueprint that helps managers channel their role behaviors in ways that will ultimately lead to goal achievement.[27] For example, transmitting information through the disseminator role or representing the organization through the negotiator role in itself has little meaning unless it is linked to a purpose such as planning, organizing, leading, or controlling. But how do managers tie their various activities and roles into the planning, organizing, leading, and controlling necessary to achieve goals? Part of the answer is suggested by another well-known study, conducted by management researcher John Kotter.

Managerial Work Agendas

Kotter's study focused on fifteen general managers in nine different corporations representing a broad range of industries.[28] General managers typically have responsibility for a major business sector of the corporation and, in that capacity, have multiple specialties (such as marketing, manufacturing, and engineering) reporting to them. The study was based on business documents, observations of each manager for about 35 hours, and extensive interviews with the managers themselves and a number of associates. On the basis of his findings, Kotter suggested that managers focus their various efforts productively through the use of work agendas.

Nature of Work Agendas. A **work agenda** is a loosely connected set of tentative goals and tasks that a manager is attempting to accomplish. Managers usually develop work agendas during their first 6 months on a new job, although the agendas are continually subject to reassessment in the face of changing circumstances and emerging opportunities. Typically, such agendas address immediate, as well as more long-run, job responsibilities and are used in addition to more formal organizational plans.

Kotter found that to put their work agendas into practice, the general managers work hard to establish the extensive networks of relationships identified by Mintzberg. Thus Kotter's work serves to reemphasize the importance of networks for managers.

By making use of work agendas and networking strategies, the managers in Kotter's study were able to engage in short, seemingly disjointed conversations and still accomplish their missions. For example, the following set of short discussions, taken from a day in the life of John Thompson, a division manager in a financial services corporation, was documented by Kotter to illustrate the typical way in which the managers in his study worked.[29] The conversation began one morning in Thompson's office when two of his subordinates, Phil Dodge and Jud Smith, were present:

> **Work agenda** A loosely connected set of tentative goals and tasks that a manager is attempting to accomplish

Thompson:	"What about Potter?"
Dodge:	"He's OK."
Smith:	"Don't forget about Chicago."
Dodge:	"Oh yeah." *(Makes a note to himself)*
Thompson:	"OK. Then what about next week."
Dodge:	"We're set."
Thompson:	"Good. By the way, how is Ted doing?"
Smith:	"Better. He got back from the hospital on Tuesday. Phyllis says he looks good."
Thompson:	"That's good to hear. I hope he doesn't have a relapse."
Dodge:	"I'll see you this afternoon." *(Leaves the room)*
Thompson:	"OK. *(To Smith)* Are we all set for now?"
Smith:	"Yeah." *(Gets up and starts to leave)*
Lawrence:	*(Steps into the doorway from the hall and speaks to Thompson)* "Have you seen the April numbers yet?"
Thompson:	"No, have you?"
Lawrence:	"Yes, 5 minutes ago. They're good except for CD, which is off by 5 percent."
Thompson:	"That's better than I expected."
Smith:	"I bet George is happy."
Thompson:	*(Laughing)* "If he is, he won't be after I talk to him." *(Turner,*

Thompson's secretary, sticks her head through the doorway and tells him Bill Larson is on the phone.)

Thompson: "I'll take it. Will you ask George to stop by later? (*Others leave and Thompson picks up the phone.*) Bill, good morning, how are you? . . . Yeah. . . . Is that right? . . . No, don't worry about it. . . . I think about a million and a half. . . . Yeah. . . . OK. . . . Yeah, Sally enjoyed the other night, too. Thanks again. . . . OK. . . . Bye."

Lawrence: (*Steps back into the office*) "What do you think of the Gerald proposal?"

Thompson: "I don't like it. It doesn't fit with what we've promised Corporate or Hines."

Lawrence: "Yeah, that's what I thought, too. What is Jerry going to do about it?"

Thompson: "I haven't talked to him yet. (*Turns to the phone and dials*) Let's see if he's in."

Although the dialogue would probably seem somewhat chaotic to an outsider, that perception stems from not having the specific business and organizational knowledge shared by the managers. For example, an outsider would not be able to readily identify Potter, Ted, Phyllis, Bill Larson, Sally, Hines, or Jerry. Nor would an outside observer understand the full meaning of the references to "Chicago," "April numbers," "CD," or the "Gerald proposal" or, more importantly, know Thompson's agenda and where these various pieces fit in that agenda.

Yet these conversations actually accomplished a great deal. Among other things, Thompson learned the following facts:

■ Mike Potter agreed to help with a problem loan that could otherwise thwart Thompson's business expansion plans in a certain area.
■ Plans for the loan for the following week were moving along as intended.
■ Ted Jenkins, one of his subordinates and a central figure in Thompson's plans for the division over the next 2 years, is feeling better after an operation.
■ Division income for April met budget except for one area, saving him from having to divert attention away from other plans to take remedial action.

In addition, Thompson initiated several actions:

■ He set up a meeting with George Masolia about the one area in the April budget report that is off target to see what can be done to get things on target again.
■ He passed on some useful information to Bill Larson, a peer who has done him favors in the past and who could help him in the future.
■ He placed a call to Jerry Wilkins, one of his subordinates, to find out his reaction to a proposal that could impact Thompson's division, especially the division's 5-year revenue goals.

Thompson's discourse shows the fast pace, brevity, variety, and fragmentation that are characteristic of a manager's workday, and it illustrates the use of verbal contacts and networks that were identified in Mintzberg's study. One can also discern the use of some of the roles outlined by Mintzberg. For example, Thompson used the monitor role in seeking information about a number of items, the disseminator role in providing information to both Larson and Lawrence, and the entrepreneur role in following up on issues (such as the loan) that could affect his business expansion plans. Still, Thompson's actions were not just fulfilling roles per se—indeed, he probably gave no thought to the notion of roles. His actions had purposes that ultimately related to reaching his goals. Many of Thompson's remarks (until he began to speak about the Gerald proposal) reflect mainly the controlling function—checking to be sure that various important activities are moving along as expected. The discussion about the Gerald proposal reflects the planning function. When he talks with George about the budget problem, he will engage in leading and planning.

Without a work agenda (the manager's own working plan), of course, similar discussions could actually be fairly random and far from efficient. Even with an agenda, managers need to be careful that they work within its guidelines. Within a year after he became chief executive officer at First Chicago, a major bank holding company, Barry Sullivan had a solid idea about his priorities. Still, he had a vague sense that in the course of relentless day-to-day activity, he was not spending his time in ways that adequately matched his priorities. He hired some consultants to assess how he was spending his time, and after their evaluation he stated, "I was responding to demands on my time in more of an ad hoc manner rather than against some broad idea of how much time I really wanted to allocate to different things." Now he decides how much time he wants to assign to certain activities and tentatively blocks out parts of his calendar up to a year in advance to help him match his time with his priorities.

Work agendas provide rough guidelines within which managers operate in determining how to orient their various activities and roles. But what factors influence the content of work agendas?

Factors Influencing Work Agendas. Rosemary Stewart, a British expert on managerial work, sheds light on the factors that are likely to have an impact on a manager's work agenda. According to the model there are three main factors: demands, constraints, and choices.[30]

Job demands are the activities a manager *must* do in a job. For example, managers usually have responsibilities related to the major goals and plans of the organization (such as achieving a 10 percent increase in sales) that are difficult to ignore.

Job constraints are the factors, both inside and outside the organization, that limit what a manager holding a certain job can do. Constraints include such variables as resource limitations, legal restrictions, union contract provisions, technological limitations, and the degree to which the work of a manager's unit is defined.

Job choices are work activities that the managerial jobholder can do but does not have to do. Even given the demands and constraints imposed upon them, managers usually have at least some choices. For one thing, managers often have some latitude in regard to *how* the work is done. For another, they usually have at least some options about *which* work is done. For example, a manager may be able to emphasize some parts of the job and downplay others, delegate some parts of the job to subordinates, take on additional work in new areas, negotiate some changes in current areas of responsibility, volunteer for committees, or participate in public activities on behalf of the organization. Thus, in most cases, there is at least some latitude in setting one's work agenda. One implication is that work agendas tend to reflect, at least to some extent, the personal preferences and career objectives of individual managers (as well as the demands and constraints of the job).

MANAGERIAL KNOWLEDGE, SKILLS, AND PERFORMANCE

For managers to develop work agendas, act out roles, and engage in planning, organizing, leading, and controlling, they need a sound knowledge base and key management skills. In this section, we discuss these essential elements in the management process and explain how they relate to the issue of performance.

Knowledge Base

Although managers often switch companies and work in different industries, they are apt to run into difficulties if they don't have a reasonably extensive knowledge base relevant to their particular managerial job. A *knowledge base* can include information about an industry and its technology, company policies and practices, company goals and plans, company culture, the personalities of key organization members, and important suppliers and customers. For example, Kotter found that one of the reasons why the general managers in his study were able to accomplish so much within short periods of time was that they could take action with only very small bits of information at their disposal at a given time. They could do so because their extensive knowledge base enabled them to attach the appropriate meaning to the information fragments they obtained.[31]

Key Management Skills

In addition to having a knowledge base, managers need three key types of skills to carry out the various functions of management. A *skill* is the ability to engage in a set of behaviors that are functionally related to one another and that lead to a desired performance level in a given area.[32] For managers, the three key skill types are technical, human, and conceptual.

Technical skills Skills that reflect both an understanding of and a proficiency in a specialized field

Technical Skills. **Technical skills** are skills that reflect both an understanding of and a proficiency in a specialized field. For example, a manager may have technical skills in a specialized field such as accounting, finance, engineering, manufacturing, or computer science.

Human skills Skills associated with a manager's ability to work well with others both as a member of a group and as a leader who gets things done through others

Human Skills. **Human skills** are skills associated with a manager's ability to work well with others both as a member of a group and as a leader who gets things done through others. Managers with effective human skills typically are particularly adept at communicating with others and motivating them to develop themselves and perform well in pursuit of organizational goals.

Conceptual skills Skills related to the ability to visualize the organization as a whole, discern interrelationships among organizational parts, and understand how the organization fits into the wider context of the industry, community, and world

Conceptual Skills. **Conceptual skills** are skills related to the ability to visualize the organization as a whole, discern interrelationships among organizational parts, and understand how the organization fits into the wider context of the industry, community, and world. Managers need to recognize these various elements and understand the complex relationships among them so that they can take actions that advance the goals of the organization. Conceptual skills, coupled with technical skills, human skills, and a knowledge base, are important ingredients in organizational performance, as can be seen in the case of Carnegie Hall, a not-for-profit organization (see the following Case in Point discussion).

A major concert, such as this one at New York City's Carnegie Hall, involves far more than just the collective musical talents on stage. Behind the scenes are stagehands, electricians, light operators, sound technicians, piano tuners, guards, ticket sellers, public relations personnel, and many others. Conducting the performance of all these individuals is a tour de force in itself. Carnegie Hall is fortunate to have a general manager who has the managerial skills to coordinate the efforts of these diverse groups.

CASE IN POINT: Behind-the-Scenes Skills at Carnegie Hall

As they enjoy performances at New York's Carnegie Hall, few members of the audience likely give any thought to the management knowledge and skills at work behind the scenes of the nation's most celebrated cultural center. Since 1986, Carnegie Hall has been run by Judith Arron, general manager and artistic director of the concert landmark. Although she has a university degree in cello and piano, she decided to make concert management her career. Among her previous managerial positions, she served for 17 years as general manager of the Cincinnati Symphony Orchestra before winning the Carnegie Hall position over a field of 30 candidates from all over the United States.

She arrived at Carnegie Hall in the midst of a $50 million renovation project, the most extensive in the concert center's history. When concerts resumed in December 1986, Arron's responsibilities included season planning, artist procurement, marketing and promotion, overall supervision of hall operations, and development of community outreach programs. The budget for the concert season typically runs close to $20 million, of which about one-third is earmarked for the approximately 175 events scheduled in the main hall and the Weill Recital Hall and for the outreach programs.

Her outreach work in Cincinnati has made Arron a strong advocate of the programs that Carnegie Hall sponsors in the New York City area in local communities, in shelters, and particularly in elementary schools. In the school program, either musicians are hired and sent to a school or the children are brought to Carnegie Hall for concerts. "We've got to make an enormous effort to develop audiences on an ongoing basis," Arron says. "It's an investment we make today and hope there will be a return on that investment 10, 20, 30 years from now, even if we can't put a dollar value on it in terms of tickets sold."

In addition, Arron often plans major special events like the 1990 to 1991 centennial celebration. Well-known contemporary composers such as Alfred Schnittke, Steven Stucky, and Pulitzer prize winner William Bolcom are among the artists who provided commissioned works. Preview events for the celebration included a one-hundredth birthday tribute to composer Berlin, which was attended by an array of celebrities, and a televised ceremony at which a time capsule was laid in the cornerstone of a new building going up on land next door, owned by Carnegie Hall.

Arron's workday typically begins when she leaves home about 7:30. She is usually at her desk by 9 a.m., and a major part of her day is consumed by meetings with such groups as senior staff members, department heads, the board of directors, orchestra representatives, artists, conductors, and staff members. Although her workday tends to end about 6:30 p.m., she may stay for a weeknight concert and frequently comes in for concerts or special events on weekends. "We may have an established superstar or a newcomer I want to hear, or a new orchestra that needs special care." She generally plans to "work 6 days a week and go to two or three concerts."

She is known for being particularly skilled at handling people, including some of the temperamental, but talented, artists who play on Carnegie's stage. Indeed, the cast of artists has been stellar, including such luminaries as Leonard Bernstein, Itzhak Perlman, Mistislav Rostropovich, Alicia de Larrocha, Joan Sutherland, and Benita Valente, to name a few.[33] ▬▬▬▬

Arron came to her job at Carnegie Hall with an extensive knowledge base about the concert field, gleaned from her years as orchestra manager of the Cincinnati Symphony and several previous jobs. In addition, her strong technical skills in music, human skills in handling people, and conceptual skills in seeing the big picture have been important factors in her high performance and that of Carnegie Hall.

Performance

What constitutes high performance in an organization? Peter Drucker, the noted management writer and consultant, points out that performance actually is made up of two important dimensions: effectiveness and efficiency.[34]

Effectiveness The ability to choose appropriate goals and achieve them

Effectiveness. **Effectiveness** is the ability to choose appropriate goals and achieve them. Effectiveness, then, has two parts. First, goals must be appropriate. Second, goals must be reached. For example, Nordstrom, Inc., a Seattle-based apparel, shoe, and soft-goods retailer, is carving out an admirable niche for itself by providing legendary good customer service at its 55 department stores (mainly on the West Coast). Sales associates (many of whom are college graduates) gift-wrap packages for no extra cost and have even been known to drop them off at customers' homes in a pinch. Piano players serenade customers while they shop. According to one story, which the store has not denied, a customer got his money back on a tire. Given that the company does not sell tires, the story illustrates the store's dedication to a return policy based on "no questions asked." Bill Baer, a men's clothing salesman in the Palo Alto store, says, "Nordstrom tells me to do whatever I need to do to make you happy. Period."[35] This stance has enabled the upscale chain to expand into new areas of the country such as Washington, D.C., and New Jersey. Nordstrom illustrates what Drucker means when he points out that effectiveness is essentially doing (accomplishing) the right things.

Efficiency The ability to make the best use of available resources in the process of achieving goals

Efficiency. In contrast, **efficiency** is the ability to make the best use of available resources in the process of achieving goals. In the case of Nordstrom, the store enjoys the highest sales per square foot of any department store: $310. That figure is $160 more than average and $55 more than the next highest figure, that of Parisian, Inc., a store based in Birmingham, Alabama, that also has a reputation for exceptional service.[36] In this respect, Nordstrom illustrates what Drucker has in mind when he speaks of efficiency as doing things right.

In essence, organizations need to exhibit both effectiveness (doing the right things) and efficiency (doing things right) in order to be good performers. Although we highlight the importance of efficiency at this point, we will typically use the term "effectiveness" throughout the book to include both effectiveness and efficiency. We do this for the sake of simplicity and readability.

MANAGERIAL JOB TYPES

Although we have been exploring the nature of managerial work in general, managerial jobs do vary somewhat on the basis of two important dimensions. One is a vertical dimension, focusing on different hierarchical levels in the organization. The other is a horizontal dimension, addressing variations according to the area for which managers have major responsibility. We explore these dimensions and their implications in this section. In the process, we give special attention to differences in the entrepreneurial role at various hierarchical levels as a means of fostering innovation.

Vertical Dimension: Hierarchical Levels

Along the vertical dimension, managerial jobs in organizations fall into three categories: first-line, middle, and top management. These categories can be viewed as vertical differentiation among managers because they involve three different levels of the organization, as shown in Figure 1-3.

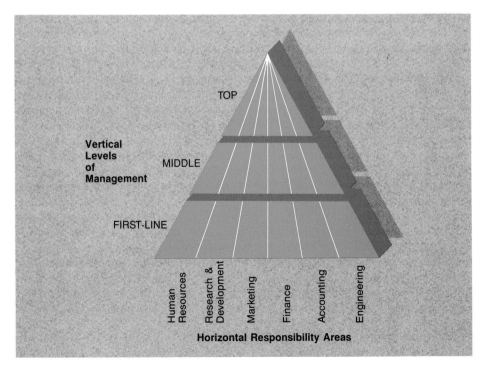

Figure 1-3 Types of managers by level and responsibility area.

**First-line managers/
supervisors** Managers at
the lowest level in the
hierarchy who are directly
responsible for the work of
operating (nonmanagerial)
employees

First-Line Managers. **First-line managers** (or **first-line supervisors**) are managers at the lowest level in the hierarchy who are directly responsible for the work of operating (nonmanagerial) employees. They often have titles that include the word "supervisor." First-line managers are extremely important to the success of an organization because they have the major responsibility of seeing that day-to-day operations run smoothly in pursuit of organizational goals.

Because they operate at the interface between management and the rest of the work force, first-line supervisors can easily find themselves in the middle of conflicting demands. At the same time, the power of first-line supervisors has been gradually eroding because of such factors as union influence and the increasing educational level of workers.[37]

According to one recent review of research literature on first-line supervisors, the autonomy and influence of first-line managers is likely to ebb still further in the future. One reason is the increasing attempts by organizations to emulate the Japanese emphasis on worker participation in managing the workplace. Another is the trend toward work teams, such as those at the Steuben factory. Still another is the use of computers to keep track of many activities formerly regulated by first-line managers. Finally, a growing number of specialists, particularly in fields involving sophisticated technology, provide advice and direction to work areas. One implication of these developments is that the job of the first-line supervisor is likely to change toward a greater emphasis on dealing with internal human relations and on representing the unit externally.[38]

Middle managers
Managers beneath the top
levels of the hierarchy who
are directly responsible for
the work of other managers
below them

Middle Managers. **Middle managers** are managers beneath the top levels of the hierarchy who are directly responsible for the work of other managers below them. The managers for whom they have direct responsibility may be other middle managers or first-line managers. Middle managers also sometimes supervise operating personnel, such as administrative assistants and several specialists (such as engineers or financial analysts). Many different titles are used for middle managers. Some typical titles include such words as "manager," "director of," "chief," "department head," and "division head." Middle managers are mainly responsible for implementing overall organizational plans so that organizational goals are achieved as expected.

Organizations, particularly very large ones, often have several layers of middle managers. For example, in recent years, giant General Motors has generally had about 14 or 15 management levels. That number reflects a post-World War II trend aimed at adding layers of middle management to help coordinate expanding activities. By the early 1980s, however, that trend began to reverse. At that point, many companies began cutting the number of levels of management hierarchy in an attempt to lower costs, reduce the layers involved in decision making, and facilitate communication. In fact, one observer speculates that General Motors may have only five or six management layers by the mid-1990s.[39]

One common result of having fewer layers is that the remaining middle-management levels gain greater autonomy and responsibility. For instance, when Xerox reduced some headquarters managerial layers, district sales managers acquired greater latitude in such areas as adjusting prices and extending credit to important customers. Now, as long as the district managers meet their goals, the upper-level managers do not generally interfere with their efforts. As one Xerox senior vice president notes, "Your reward for doing well is that you don't have to see your boss."[40]

Not surprisingly, pressure on middle managers appears to be increasing in the face of these changes. More than half the respondents in one survey report that the middle managers in their organization are working longer hours than they did 5 years ago, and one-fourth said that they are spending more weekends in the office.[41] Critics argue that many middle managers are being asked to carry an unreasonable burden. Defenders retort that reducing layers enables middle managers to do their work with less bureaucratic interference.[42]

Although there may be fewer middle managers in the future, management researcher Rosabeth Moss Kanter, who has studied trends in managerial work, argues that the distinction between managers and those managed also is declining. She predicts that there will be less emphasis on hierarchical level and, instead, more weight on horizontal influence, increased reliance on peer networks, greater access to information, and more control over assignments at lower levels.[43] Thus it appears that many of the responsibilities of middle managers will be increasingly distributed to lower levels in the organization, thereby raising the importance of positions at those levels.

Top Managers. **Top managers** are managers at the very top levels of the hierarchy who are ultimately responsible for the entire organization. Top-level managers are few in number; their typical titles include "chief executive officer" (CEO), "president," "executive vice president," "executive director," "senior vice president," and sometimes "vice president." Top-level managers are often referred to as executives, although the term "executive" also is sometimes used to include the upper layers of middle managers as well. Top managers have direct responsibility for the upper layer of middle managers. They typically oversee the overall planning for the organization, work to some degree with middle managers in implementing that planning, and maintain overall control over the progress of the organization.

Top managers Managers at the very top levels of the hierarchy who are ultimately responsible for the entire organization

Differences among Hierarchical Levels

Although the same basic managerial process that we have been discussing in this chapter applies to all three hierarchical levels of management, there are some differences in the emphasis that is placed on various aspects of the management process. Major differences stem mainly from the importance of the four functions of management, the skills necessary to perform effectively, the emphasis on managerial roles at each level, and the use of the entrepreneurial role.

Functions of Management. Studies of managers at various levels indicate that the relative importance of planning, organizing, leading, and controlling differs somewhat depending on managerial level.[44] As indicated in Figure 1-4, planning tends to be more important for top managers than for middle or first-line managers. The main reason is that top managers are responsible for determining the overall direction of the organization, a charge that requires extensive planning.

At the same time, organizing is somewhat more important for both top and middle-level managers than for first-level managers. This difference stems from the fact that it is the top and middle levels of management that are mainly responsible for allocating and arranging resources, even though this function also is performed to some extent by first-line supervisors.

In contrast, leading is substantially more important for first-line supervisors than for managers at higher levels. Since first-line supervisors are charged with the ongoing production of goods or services, they must engage in substantially

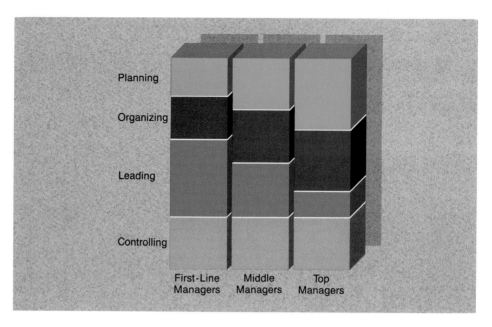

Figure 1-4 Use of management functions at different hierarchical levels.

higher amounts of the communicating, motivating, directing, and supporting that are associated with leading.

Finally, the management function that is most similar at all three hierarchical levels of management is controlling. This similarity reflects a common degree of emphasis at all levels on monitoring activities and taking corrective action as needed.

Management Skills. The three levels of management also differ in the importance attached to the three key management skills discussed earlier: technical, human, and conceptual (see Figure 1-5).[45] Generally, conceptual skills are most important at the top management level. The reason is that top managers have the greatest need to see the organization as a whole, understand how the various parts of the organization relate to one another, and associate the organization to the world outside.

In contrast, first-line managers have the greatest need for technical skills. The logic here is that it is the first-line managers who directly supervise most of the technical and professional employees who are not managers. On the other hand, middle managers often may need to have technical skills that are at least sufficient to assist in communicating with subordinates and recognizing major problems.[46] Even top managers must have some technical skills, particularly when technology is an important part of the products or services their organizations produce. Otherwise, upper-level managers will have difficulty fostering innovation, allocating resources efficiently, or devising strategies to stay ahead of the competition.

For example, when Chairman John Sculley joined Apple Computer, most of his experience was in marketing with PepsiCo and he knew little about computers. He realized immediately that he was not going to be able to function well without more technical knowledge. "I'm essentially an intuitive leader, and you can only be intuitive about something you understand." As a result, he quickly initiated an extensive effort to boost his knowledge of computer technology through such steps as arranging for tutors, reading books, and talking with knowledgeable staff members.[47]

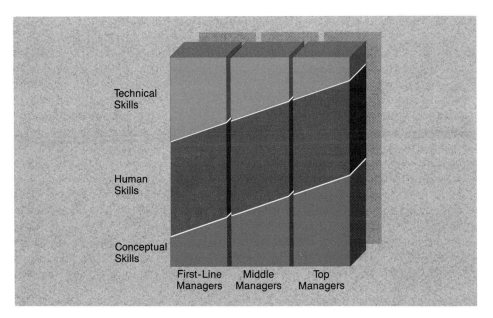

Figure 1-5 Use of key management skills at different hierarchical levels.

Interestingly, all three levels of management must have strong human skills because they all must get things done through people. In fact, in one recent study, managers at all levels rated human skills as most important for good job performance.[48] Ironically, individuals often are promoted into first-level management because they have good technical skills, without adequate consideration being given to the adequacy of their human skills. Individuals who lack sufficient human skills usually run into serious difficulties attempting to deal with individuals inside and outside their work units.

Reinforcing the importance of human skills for managers, the Center for Creative Leadership, a not-for-profit research and educational institution in Greensboro, North Carolina, conducted a study that compared 21 executives who were derailed from their career paths with 20 similarly situated executives who made it all the way to the top. The derailed executives were individuals who had generally done well and expected to be promoted to even higher levels in their organizations, but who late in their careers were plateaued, fired, or forced to retire early. In interviews with a number of people who were in a position to know why the particular individual in each case derailed, the reason most frequently cited was insensitivity to others—a human skill. The top 10 reasons for derailment found by the study are shown in Table 1-2. While no derailed executive exhibited all the flaws on the list, the individuals studied typically possessed two of them. Almost all the traits listed involve human skills, at least to some degree. In most cases, the derailed executives ran into trouble due to a combination of personal qualities and situational factors. The executives generally found themselves in changed situations in which weaknesses that had not been critical in the past suddenly became lethal liabilities.[49]

Managerial Roles. Although Mintzberg argued that the 10 managerial roles he identified apply to all levels of management, he did note that there may be some differences in emphasis at various levels. He particularly felt that the figurehead role would be most important at higher levels, because managers at the top are more involved in formal occasions at which they must officially represent the organization (such as awards ceremonies and brief visits with customers).[50] Sub-

This leadership development seminar at Pacific Bell helps build human skills in various levels of management. Such skills greatly enhance communication among organizational levels.

Table 1-2   The Top 10 Reasons for Executive Derailment

1. Insensitive to others: abrasive, intimidating, bullying style
2. Cold, aloof, arrogant
3. Betrayal of trust
4. Overly ambitious: thinking of next job, playing politics
5. Specific performance problems with the business
6. Overmanaging: unable to delegate or build a team
7. Unable to staff effectively
8. Unable to think strategically
9. Unable to adapt to boss with different style
10. Overdependent on advocate or mentor

Source: From Morgan W. McCall, Jr., and Michael M. Lombardo, "What Makes a Top Executive?" *Psychology Today,* February 1983, p. 28.

sequent research by others also suggests that the figurehead role and several others such as liaison and spokesperson may become more important as a manager moves up the hierarchy. On the other hand, there is evidence that the leader role is more critical at the lower levels, a finding that supports the idea that the leading function itself has greater importance for lower-level managers than for those higher up.[51]

In the most recent study of the importance of the various roles, managers at all levels gave particularly high ratings to the entrepreneurial role.[52] Several experts on innovation, however, argue that the entrepreneurial role differs in some important ways depending on a manager's level in the hierarchy.[53] Because of the particular importance of innovation to the success of organizations, we explore these differences further.

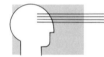

Promoting Innovation: The Entrepreneurial Role

An **innovation** is a new idea applied to initiating or improving a process, product, or service.[54] The process of innovation is closely allied with the entrepreneurial role in organizations, particularly as that role relates to exploiting new opportunities. In fact, innovative activities in organizations, especially major ones, frequently are referred to as entrepreneurship within organizations. More recently, individuals who engage in entrepreneurial roles inside organizations often are called **intrapreneurs.** The term is used to differentiate innovators working inside existing organizations from individuals who innovate by creating new organizations (the latter are often called *entrepreneurs;* see Chapter 22). Similarly, the process of innovating within an existing organization is sometimes referred to as **intrapreneurship.**

Encouraging innovation in organizations takes special effort. Furthermore, successful innovations are rarely the product of only one person's work. Rather, research shows that the innovative process is much more likely to occur in a situation in which individuals at various levels fulfill three different types of entrepreneurial roles: idea generator or champion, sponsor, and orchestrator.[55]

Idea Champion. An **idea champion** is an individual who generates a new idea or believes in the value of a new idea and supports it in the face of numerous potential obstacles. We often think of these individuals as entrepreneurs, inventors, creative individuals, or risk takers. They are usually individuals at lower

Innovation   A new idea applied to initiating or improving a process, product, or service

Intrapreneurs   Individuals who engage in entrepreneurial roles inside organizations

Intrapreneurship   The process of innovating within an existing organization

Idea champion   An individual who generates a new idea or believes in the value of a new idea and supports it in the face of numerous potential obstacles

levels in the organization who recognize a problem and help develop a solution. First-line supervisors can be idea champions in the sense of coming up with innovative ideas, nurturing ideas in others, and fighting tenaciously to help make the ideas a reality. Exactly because idea champions are relatively far down in the hierarchy, they often do not have the power and status to get their innovations accepted by the organization. This situation creates the need for the next type of role.

Sponsor. A **sponsor** is a middle manager who recognizes the organizational significance of an idea, helps obtain the necessary funding for development of the innovation, and facilitates its actual implementation. For the most part, sponsors tend to be middle managers because their higher-level position in the organization makes it more feasible for them to provide the strong backing necessary for new innovations to survive. Innovations in organizations are not likely to occur without a sponsor, but their occurrence also depends on an individual who fills a third role.

Orchestrator. An **orchestrator** is a high-level manager who articulates the need for innovation, provides funding for innovating activities, creates incentives for middle managers to sponsor new ideas, and protects idea people. Because innovations often constitute a challenge to the current ways of doing things, they frequently are resisted by those who are comfortable with or have a particular stake in the status quo. (For example, an expert in a process may resist a change that will cause it to be outmoded.) An orchestrator maintains the balance of power so that new ideas have a chance to be tested in the face of possible negative reactions. Otherwise, new ideas may be blocked. By filling the role of orchestrator, top management encourages innovation.

Without all three roles, major innovations are much less likely to occur. The development of the VHS videocassette recorder at JVC illustrates the importance of entrepreneurial or innovative roles at the various levels of the organization (see the following Case in Point discussion).

> **Sponsor** A middle manager who recognizes the organizational significance of an idea, helps obtain the necessary funding for development of the innovation, and facilitates its actual implementation

> **Orchestrator** A high-level manager who articulates the need for innovation, provides funding for innovating activities, creates incentives for middle managers to sponsor new ideas, and protects idea people

CASE IN POINT: JVC Persists with the Videocassette Recorder

An early pioneer of television technology, inventor Kenjiro Takayanagi had a vision that he shared in the 1950s with some of the younger engineers at Japan-based JVC. JVC (from Victor Company of Japan, Ltd.) is an independent subsidiary of the giant Matsushita Electric Industrial Company, Ltd., and had mainly produced phonograph records and hi-fi sets. Takayanagi envisioned finding a way that ordinary people could develop their own images to put on their TVs, perhaps through some sort of magnetic tape. Although the engineers, Yuma Shiraishi and Shizuo Takano, were intrigued by the idea, JVC had largely missed out on the television boom and seemed to be an unlikely company to ultimately develop a video tape recorder (VTR) for use in homes.

The first concrete evidence that Takayanagi's vision could become a technological reality came in 1964 when six American engineers at Ampex Corporation built the first magnetic tape recorder that captured pictures as well as sound. The Ampex machine was very large (about the size of an old-fashioned jukebox), used 2-inch-wide reel-to-reel tape, and was extremely expensive. The machine was readily adopted by TV networks and affiliates, which could now broadcast prerecorded shows when they best fit audience schedules rather than having to

Persistence among the champions of a video cassette recorder at JVC paid off. Despite lack of sponsor support for several years, the designers of the VHS (video home system) clung to the idea of a video cassette that could record for 2 hours—the length of most movies. When the parent company's chairman gave an indirect go-ahead for the project, resistance to the system gave way. Today most video cassette recorders found in U.S. homes use the VHS format.

broadcast live. JVC quickly set out to develop its own VTR, while Sony built a machine that conformed to the industry standards established by Ampex. By the time JVC introduced its own machine, which was technologically superior to but incompatible with Ampex and Sony recorders, it was out of step with the industry and failed to sell.

By 1970, Sony produced a prototype ¾-inch tape in a cassette. Sony shared the prototype with Matsushita and JVC in return for help on perfecting the tape technology. The resulting improved ¾-inch-tape cassette was a major breakthrough in technology. Although each of the companies then went on independently to produce its own first videocassette recorder (VCR), the recorders they developed were still too big, bulky, complex, and expensive for home use. Sony, with inroads into major businesses and schools, made a modest profit, while Matsushita and JVC lost money on their ventures. At this point, JVC's top management canceled most of its support, leaving only a small team headed by Shiraishi and supported by Takano, both of whom continued to be obsessed with the idea of a VCR for home use.

Frustrated, Shiraishi and three other engineers decided to start from scratch in thinking about what should go into a machine that could be used in the home. One of the specifications on their final list was that the minimum recording time should be 2 *hours* so that consumers would be able to videotape movies for later viewing. By now Takano was senior managing director of JVC's video products division, and he continued to ignore suggestions from upper management that he drop work on the home VCR. Keeping the work at a low profile, Takano and his team developed a fairly advanced ½-inch VCR prototype using a format that they called VHS (video home system), which would run for 2 hours.

Then one day the chairman of JVC's parent company, Konosuke Matsushita, visited the video products division's research and development (R&D) facility in Yokohama and happened upon the prototype. Matsushita had already seen a new competing Sony prototype VCR based on a ½-inch-tape format called Betamax. After the technical aspects of the JVC prototype were explained to him, he smiled, leaned over, pressed his cheek to the recorder, and said, "It's marvelous. You have made something very nice." Although Matsushita made no official statements of support and issued no directives, the story quickly ran through the grapevine and from then on the development team found it much easier to operate internally.

Even though Sony brought its Betamax VCR to market first, Sony was not able to persuade Matsushita or JVC to adopt its machine standards because its tape would run for only 1 hour. Several months later, the JVC project group completed its work on the VCR with the VHS format. JVC was then able to get several other manufacturers, including Matsushita, to use its format. JVC needed others to join in so that consumers would feel that they were buying a machine that would play standard tapes. Also, the company was too small to produce enough machines for the market by itself if the product was successful. The VHS videocassette pioneered by JVC was formally introduced in September 1976. Although the VHS machines took some time to catch on, Takayanagi's dream finally became a reality.[56] ■■■■■

In the JVC situation, the company would never have been successful with the VHS videocassette recorder without Takayanagi, Shiraishi, and Takano as original idea champions. Top managers at JVC operated as orchestrators early on, but they withdrew much of their support later. Still, Takano was able to act as a sponsor and allow the project to continue despite some negative pressure from above. Ultimately, the indirect intervention of Matsushita as an orchestrator became crucial. These three types of entrepreneurial roles constitute another vertical difference among managers.

Horizontal Dimension: Responsibility Areas

In addition to their vertical differences, managerial jobs differ on a horizontal dimension that relates to the nature of the area of responsibility involved (see Figure 1-3). The three major types of horizontal differentiation among managerial jobs on the basis of responsibility area are functional, general, and project managers.

   Functional managers are managers who have responsibility for a specific, specialized area (often called a *functional area*) of the organization and supervise mainly individuals with expertise and training in that specialized area. Common specialized, or functional, areas include finance, manufacturing or operations, marketing, human resources management, accounting, quality assurance, and engineering.

   General managers are managers who have responsibility for a whole organization or a substantial subunit that includes most of the common specialized areas within it. In other words, a general manager presides over a number of specialties or functional areas (hence the term "general"). General managers have a variety of titles, such as "division manager" and "president," depending on the circumstances. A small company usually will have only one general manager, who is the head of the entire organization. Depending on how it is organized, a large company may have several general managers (in addition to the chief executive officer). Each of these additional general managers usually presides over a major division that includes a number of important specialized, or functional, areas within it. For example, Corning's Susan King would be considered a general manager because she presides over a major division, Steuben, which includes within it most of its own main functions, such as production, marketing, and human resources. At the same time, Jamie Houghton, Corning's CEO, would also be considered a general manager because he is responsible for the entire corporation. Sometimes plant managers with major responsibilities who have some accounting, human resources, and other staff members reporting to them are also called general managers.[57]

   Project managers are managers who have responsibility for coordinating efforts involving individuals in several different organizational units who are all working on a particular project. Because the individuals report not only to managers in their specific work units but also to project managers, project managers usually must have extremely strong interpersonal skills to keep things moving smoothly (we discuss this issue further in Chapter 11). Project managers are frequently used in aerospace and other high-technology firms to coordinate projects, such as airplane or computer project development. They also are used in some consumer-oriented companies to launch or stay on top of market development for specific products such as cookies or margarine.[58]

Functional managers Managers who have responsibility for a specific, specialized area of the organization and supervise mainly individuals with expertise and training in that specialized area

General managers Managers who have responsibility for a whole organization or a substantial subunit that includes most of the common specialized areas within it

Project managers Managers who have responsibility for coordinating efforts involving individuals in several different organizational units who are all working on a particular project

Differences According to Responsibility Area

Only a limited amount of research has focused on differences in managerial jobs on the basis of responsibility area. Some evidence indicates that the specialized, or functional, areas in which managers operate influence their use of planning, organizing, leading, and controlling. One recent study involving 600 managers in a large corporation with plants in multiple locations showed that human resources managers tended to engage in considerable amounts of long-range planning and leading in the sense of working closely with individuals from other units to coordinate efforts across departments. Accounting managers also engaged in considerable long-range planning but, as might be expected given that they must maintain the integrity of financial data, placed even greater emphasis on controlling. On the other hand, manufacturing managers reported engaging in considerable leading and controlling, functions particularly necessary in managing ongoing manufacturing activities.[59] These examples serve to illustrate that the extent to which managers engage in planning, organizing, leading, and controlling is likely to vary somewhat across functional areas and must be tailored to the specific needs of jobs.

Another separate study of managers from a wide variety of service and manufacturing firms in southern California suggests that the importance of managerial skills also may vary by responsibility area.[60] Since all the managers from the responsibility areas in the study gave fairly high ratings to all three skills (human, conceptual, and technical), would-be managers would do well to develop the three types of managerial skills regardless of their responsibility area.

LEARNING TO BE AN EFFECTIVE MANAGER

How can one learn to be an effective manager? Some clues can be gleaned from several recent studies of CEOs, individuals who made it to the top levels of organizations. Most observers agree that it takes a combination of education and experience.

Managerial Education

Recent surveys of CEOs indicate the growing importance of formal education in preparing managers. One survey cataloged responses from almost 250 CEOs representing 800 of the largest industrial and service firms in the United States. Respondents included well-known executives like David Roderick of USX Corporation, Rand Araskog of ITT, and Robert Galvin of Motorola.[61] Among the CEOs, 99 percent had attended college and 91 percent were college graduates. These figures contrast with the fact that only about 33 percent of U.S. adults attend college and only about half that number actually graduate.

Business was by far the most popular major, followed by engineering and liberal arts (see Figure 1-6). Furthermore, 47 percent of the CEOs held advanced degrees, with an MBA being the most common and a law degree the next most common. The CEOs also tended to maintain good grades in college. A total of 38 percent reported having an overall grade average of A, while 53 percent said that they had an overall B grade average. Another study of CEOs from major countries around the world supports the trend toward companies being led by college graduates, with business increasingly the undergraduate major of choice and graduate degrees growing in prevalence.[62]

For most managers, education does not end with college and graduate school degrees. Instead, managers usually take additional management-related courses as part of special programs on college campuses, organizational training programs offered in-house, or commercial programs offered by a variety of trade associations and commercial vendors. One recent survey of management train-

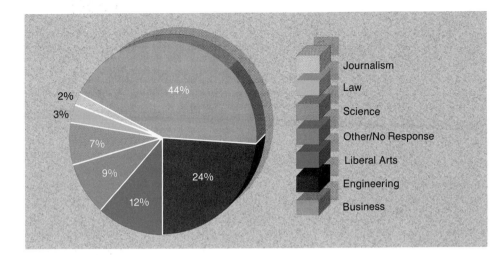

Figure 1-6 College majors of chief executive officers. (Reprinted from Louis E. Boone, David L. Kurtz, and C. Patrick Fleenor, "CEOs: Early Signs of a Business Career," *Business Horizons*, September–October 1988, p. 21.)

ing and education practices among private companies with at least 1000 employees showed that 89 percent use formal training and educational programs as part of their training of managers.[63] In essence, effective managers think of management education as a process to be continued throughout their careers.

Management Experience

Not surprisingly, experience also is a major factor in learning to be an effective manager. For the CEO respondents in the survey of 800 large U.S. companies, work experience started in high school (79 percent had jobs) and largely continued in college (56 percent had jobs). Another early source of management experience was holding office in college clubs. Approximately 70 percent of the respondent CEOs held at least one office in a campus club, fraternity, or other campus organization while in college.

A number of the CEOs (38 percent) participated in intercollegiate sports. Those who engaged in college athletics noted that this experience helped them learn teamwork and interpersonal skills that served them well in managerial positions. For example, C. J. Silas, CEO of Phillips Petroleum and winner of a gold medal for basketball at the 1955 Pan American Games, notes that engaging in sports helped him recognize that "you can't do it all yourself."[64]

Although one sometimes gets the impression from reading business newspapers and magazines that managers, particularly top ones, change jobs frequently, the reverse is more true. Almost 75 percent of the CEOs reported that previous experience with their organization was a major factor in their being selected for the top job. In fact, almost half the CEOs indicated that they had been working for their firm for at least 20 years. Furthermore, most of the corporate leaders reported that they had been employed by two or fewer other companies. Still, the situation may be growing more fluid. One recent study showed that the number of CEOs who had been promoted to the top slot after being with their present company for less than a year grew to 17 percent from 9 percent a decade ago.[65] The researchers speculated that part of the reason was the recent wave of mergers and takeovers. For example, Ross Johnson, who was CEO of Nabisco when it was acquired by R. J. Reynolds in 1985, accepted a second-in-command position in the new company, RJR Nabisco. Within 18 months, the board of directors selected Johnson as CEO. Then, when Johnson joined with

Table 1-3 CEO Working Hours and Frequency of Travel

WORKING HOURS

Average hours per weekday:

Fewer than 8	1%
8–9	14
10–11	65
12 or more	18

Average hours per weekend:

None	6%
1–5	60
6–10	28
11–15	4
16 or more	1

BUSINESS TRAVEL

Days per month:

Fewer than 4	8%
4–6	35
7–10	43
11 or more	13

Source: Reprinted from *The Wall Street Journal,* Mar. 20, 1987, p. 22D.

other members of his management team and several Wall Street partners to make an offer to buy the company in 1988, the board of directors accepted a rival bid from the investment firm Kohlberg Kravis Roberts & Company. At that point, Johnson was ousted and the investment firm brought in Louis V. Gerstner, Jr., president of American Express, to be CEO of RJR Nabisco.[66]

The large number of hours put in by CEOs also tends to accelerate the experience factor. According to a survey by *The Wall Street Journal,* most CEOs work 10 hours or more on weekdays and more than one-third said that they put in 6 hours or more on weekends (see Table 1-3). Furthermore, most travel at least 4 days per month. Yet the CEOs generally seem to like their busy schedules. For Beverly F. Doland, chairperson, president, and chief executive of Textron, Inc., a typical workday is 10½ hours long, but she says, "Work isn't work as a negative. Being able to work is a pleasure. I truly enjoy what I do."[67]

The age at which managers tend to be promoted to CEO positions also supports the notion that experience plays an important role. One study showed that 75 percent of CEOs were at least 45 before they were promoted to their position, with more than half being 50 or over at the time of promotion.[68] Management expert Fred Luthans has found that managers who use networking are more likely to be successful in terms of getting promoted to higher levels. Ironically, he also found that these same managers were not necessarily the most effective in getting the job done.[69] Effective managers were particularly likely to be strong in the areas that fit mainly into the category of the leading functions. Perhaps the best strategy for individuals wanting to move up in organizations is to engage in both networking and the functions of management, including leading. That way, hopefully, they can be both effective and successful (see the earlier Practically Speaking discussion, "How to Build Networks").

Understanding Future Trends

Although it is always difficult to predict the future, several informal and formal surveys suggest three particular trends that are likely to impact managerial work in the future. A good understanding of these trends is important to those preparing for a career in management. One trend, the growing degree to which organizations must assume an international perspective in conducting their business, stems from two factors. One factor is that businesses increasingly face global competition. As Louis Gerstner, CEO of RJR Nabisco, points out, "The world is going to become more competitive in an industrial, commercial sense. More competitive perhaps than we've seen in the history of modern economic society."[70] The second factor is that more and more companies are likely to be doing business in other countries. Corning, Inc., for example, frequently engages in joint ventures with companies in other countries, such as its recent partnership with the Japan-based Asahi Glass Company to manufacture television-bulb glass.[71] The implication of this trend is that managers will need to have greater knowledge of international business. Accordingly, we devote an entire chapter to the issue of international management (see Chapter 21). In addition, you will find that we frequently use international companies as examples to help you increase your knowledge of them and of the way they do business.

A second trend, the increasing use of sophisticated information technology and computers to assist managers, is capable of greatly changing the way managers obtain and use information, as well as the way they interact with others. For instance, William McGowan, chief executive of MCI Communications Corporation, used to hold a breakfast meeting every Monday morning at 7:30 with his 25 top executives so that they could keep one another informed about significant issues. Now the information is transmitted to each executive electronically in the form of a computerized memo called "breakfast." The memo is compiled every Friday afternoon from information furnished by the executives, making the breakfast meeting unnecessary.[72] With computers and telecommunications, managers can transmit and share information with their counterparts literally all over the world in minutes. We discuss these issues further in Chapter 15, on communications, and Chapter 20, on information systems for management.

Finally, there also is a trend toward greater concern with managerial ethics.[73] Such concerns have emerged out of recent Wall Street scandals, the Beech-Nut case involving alleged substitution of artificial for natural apple juice, and the growing number of white-collar crimes. We consider ethical issues and their influence on managers in greater depth in Chapter 4, on social responsibility and ethics in management.

Although the three trends outlined are likely to have particularly important future impacts on managerial work, these trends are not the only emerging developments of consequence. In Chapter 3, on understanding external and internal environments, we consider other issues of future importance to managers and their organizations.

In this chapter, we have provided an overview of the basic challenge of management, including a forward glance at three trends that are likely to influence the way managers work in the future. In the next chapter, we take a look back at the pioneering ideas that have helped shape our knowledge of management today.

CHAPTER SUMMARY

Management is the process of achieving organizational goals through engaging in the four major functions of planning, organizing, leading, and controlling. Although these four functions form the basis of the managerial process, several other elements contribute to an understanding of how managers actually operate. For instance, work methods and managerial roles, as well as work agendas, feed into the management functions aimed at performance. A manager's knowledge base and management skills also are important factors in reaching targeted performance.

Mintzberg's famous study of top managers found that their work methods were characterized by an unrelenting pace, brevity, variety, fragmentation, and heavy use of verbal contacts and networks. In order to make sense of the voluminous data that he collected while observing the managers, Mintzberg isolated three major categories of roles: interpersonal, informational, and decisional. Within these categories, he identified 10 specific roles: figurehead, leader, liaison, monitor, disseminator, spokesperson, entrepreneur, disturbance handler, resource allocator, and negotiator. To a large extent, these work methods and roles are also characteristic of managers at other levels of organizations.

On the basis of his research on general managers, Kotter found that managers channel their various efforts through the use of work agendas, which are loosely connected sets of tentative goals and tasks that a manager is attempting to accomplish. Work agendas usually develop from the demands, constraints, and choices associated with a manager's job. As a result, work agendas tend to reflect, at least to some extent, the personal preferences and career objectives of managers.

For managers to develop work agendas, act out roles, and engage in planning, organizing, leading, and controlling, they also need a knowledge base and key management skills. The key management skills fit into three categories: technical, human, and conceptual. These skills, as well as the other elements in the management process, impact performance. Performance is made up of two important dimensions: effectiveness and efficiency. Effectiveness is the ability to choose appropriate goals and achieve them, while efficiency is the ability to make the best use of available resources in the process of achieving goals.

Managerial jobs differ according to hierarchical level (a vertical dimension) and responsibility areas (a horizontal dimension). Managerial jobs generally are divided into three hierarchical levels: first-line, middle, and top. Managers at these levels vary in the emphasis they place on planning, organizing, leading, and controlling. They also differ in the importance that they place on the key management skills and in the degree to which they use the different types of managerial roles. Although managers at all levels rate the entrepreneurial role as highly important, the way that they use this role to encourage innovation depends on their hierarchical level, as follows: idea champion (first-line), sponsor (middle), and orchestrator (top). In contrast, horizontal managerial job differences focus on responsibility area and involve three major types of managers: functional, general, and project. The limited evidence suggests that managers who have different responsibility areas also vary in the degree to which they engage in the four functions of management, as well as in the importance that they attach to the key skills. Overall, the primary implication of these findings is that managers need to be prepared to tailor somewhat the use of the management functions and skills to meet the particular requirements of their job.

Studies of CEOs provide clues about what prepara-tion is necessary to be an effective manager. The consensus is that it takes a combination of education and experience. In the educational arena, CEOs for the most part are college graduates, tend to have a graduate degree, and are likely to have participated in formal training and educational programs sponsored or supported by their organization. On the experience side, they typically have held some type of job in high school or college, been in at least one officer position in a campus organization, and worked for two or fewer companies other than the one they head. In addition, they tend to put in long hours.

According to several recent informal surveys, managerial work in the future is particularly likely to be affected by the growing internationalization of business, the increasing use of sophisticated information technology to facilitate managerial work, and the expanding public concern with managerial ethics.

MANAGERIAL TERMINOLOGY

conceptual skills (18)	general managers (29)	management (6)	planning (7)
controlling (8)	human skills (18)	middle managers (22)	project managers (29)
effectiveness (20)	idea champion (26)	network (11)	role (11)
efficiency (20)	innovation (26)	not-for-profit organization (9)	sponsor (27)
first-line managers/	intrapreneurs (26)	orchestrator (27)	technical skills (18)
supervisors (22)	intrapreneurship (26)	organization (6)	top managers (23)
functional managers (29)	leading (8)	organizing (7)	work agenda (15)

QUESTIONS FOR DISCUSSION AND REVIEW

1. Describe each of the major functions of management: planning, organizing, leading, and controlling. For a campus or other organization to which you belong, give an example of a manager engaging in each one of these functions. If one or more of the functions are lacking, what are the implications?

2. Identify three common managerial work methods identified by Mintzberg. To what extent could a manager misuse these work methods to the point that they would lead to poor performance?

3. Explain the three general types of roles and the ten specific roles that managers play. Suppose that you opened a ski-and-surf shop near campus that carries clothing, skis, and other accessories for recreation at ski resorts and beaches. Assume that you have six employees. How might you use the ten roles in managing your shop?

4. Outline three major sources of managerial work

agendas. How do work agendas help managers channel their efforts toward the appropriate level of performance?

5. Explain why a knowledge base and the key management skills are important to managers. What might be some ways that managers can acquire an appropriate knowledge base and the key skills?

6. Contrast effectiveness and efficiency as they apply to organizational performance. What happens when you have one without the other?

7. Describe how managerial jobs differ according to hierarchical level. What are the implications for managers?

8. Outline how managers at different hierarchical levels use the entrepreneurial role. What do you think is likely to happen if the entrepreneurial role is missing from the middle or top levels of the organization?

9. Indicate how managerial jobs differ according to

responsibility area? What are the implications for managers?

10. Describe what major studies have revealed about the management education and experience of CEOs. How can this information be helpful to beginning managers?

DISCUSSION QUESTIONS FOR CHAPTER OPENING CASE

1. What evidence of planning, organizing, leading, and controlling can you find at Corning, Inc., and its Steuben unit?

2. What entrepreneurial roles do Houghton and King play? What has been the impact?

3. Assess the degree to which technical, human, and conceptual skills would be important in a position like King's. What evidence exists that she uses these skills?

MANAGEMENT EXERCISE: PRODUCING THE NEW BINDING MACHINE

You are a first-line supervisor in the production department of a local concern that manufactures a variety of office products, such as staplers, binders, and cellophane-tape holders. Recently, the research department has developed an innovative small machine that binds reports in one easy operation. According to market research and early sales figures, the demand for the new machine (on which the company holds the patent) is expected to be strong because the machine produces good-looking reports at a very reasonable price. Because sales of the machine are already brisk, the company has decided to add a new production unit. The creation of the new unit will require the hiring of a new first-line supervisor to head the unit.

You, your boss (who heads the production department), and a few other first-line supervisors who also work for your boss are having a working lunch in a small room off the company cafeteria. The purpose of the meeting is to discuss the basic requirements of the new job and the details that the group should be prepared to explain to job candidates. It is likely that many of the candidates will not have management experience and, hence, may be somewhat unfamiliar with the nature of managerial jobs.

Use your knowledge of the management process and managerial job types to prepare a list of the information that the group might provide to candidates.

A DAY IN THE LIFE OF A BANK MANAGER*

It is 7:15 a.m. in Hayward, California, and Marjorie Wong-Gillmore, a 32-year-old bank manager and mother of two, is driving down Highway 17 toward the Milpitas branch of Security Pacific National Bank, where she usually arrives by 8 a.m. To help her plan her typically hectic day, Wong-Gillmore already has a three-page list of things to do that she prepared the night before.

Deregulation of banks has increased the competitive pressures and made it much more necessary for bank managers to be proactive in attracting new business. As a result, Wong-Gillmore says that her number-one priority is customer service—keeping current customers satisfied and signing up new ones. In attempting to bring in new customers, she tries to make visits each day to potential business customers. Unless she finds the time to make such visits, she is unlikely to meet her goal of building her business customer base. In fact, she already has scheduled several appointments for the afternoon. One visit will be to a Chinese restaurant whose proprietor is installing a new credit card imprinter that will deposit the credit slips into a Security Pacific acceptance account. She needs to provide bank supplies for use with the imprinter and to make sure that the operation runs smoothly for the new customer.

Author's note: Since this case was written, Wong-Gillmore accepted a position in the commercial lending area of Security Pacific National Bank, where she gained considerable expertise in credit analysis. She has recently become Vice President and Commercial Lending Officer for Plaza Bank in San Jose.

Near the top of her list is a new-customer campaign that has most recently been aimed at certified public accountants. She has already sent letters to CPAs in the area attempting to interest them in a special type of account that lets the account holder write himself or herself a loan as needed. Now, as she fights the traffic moving toward the heart of the Silicon Valley, Wong-Gillmore is trying to figure out when she can allocate time for follow-up phone calls.

Wong-Gillmore also is thinking about a personnel problem that weighs heavily. One of her assistant managers, Yvonne Frechette, was recently promoted to a better job at a larger branch in nearby Sunnyvale. While she is happy for Frechette, the promotion has made it difficult for Wong-Gillmore because her branch now has only one assistant manager instead of the usual two. The situation makes Wong-Gillmore's job much more difficult because she must absorb some of the extra work load. Hopefully, she will have a replacement soon.

As Wong-Gillmore arrives at her office at 8 a.m., she is quickly immersed in a flurry of activities. First, she goes to her desk to take care of the most immediate task of the day, reviewing her circulation file. The file contains new procedures she is to initiate at the branch, as well as information about new special promotions (such as discounts on traveler's checks or incentives to open checking accounts) that must be implemented immediately.

Next, Wong-Gillmore reviews reports from the previous day's activities. One report shows rejected debits, indicating insufficient funds. On the basis of a customer's account history, Wong-Gillmore

Since holding her position as Bank Manager, Marjorie Wong-Gillmore has been promoted to Vice President and Commercial Lending Officer for Plaza Bank. In her new position, she uses technical skills to give good credit advice, human skills to enlist new clients for the bank, and conceptual skills to understand the overall needs of the bank and her clients.

must decide whether to cover a check or let it bounce, a task that would usually be handled by an assistant manager if the branch were not shorthanded because of Frechette's promotion.

The remaining assistant manager is busy coordinating the counting of the cash deposits from the bank's night depository. Since this is a Monday, there are large numbers of deposits that were made by business owners over the weekend. The counting of the deposits involves several people, since each locked canvas deposit bag must be opened and simultaneously counted by two people, a time-consuming process called "dual control." As a result, Mondays are usually especially busy.

On other days, Wong-Gillmore holds various staff meetings at 9 a.m., often to go over the bank's various products. For example, there are at least seven different kinds of checking accounts. "It's gotten so diverse that you can get a customer in the door and spend 15 or 20 minutes just explaining all the options," she says. Wong-Gillmore has to expend considerable time and effort to ensure that the staff is well versed in the varied and constantly changing products of the bank.

At 10 a.m. the branch opens, and customers begin pouring in. During the peak time in the middle of the day, Wong-Gillmore becomes what she calls a "utility player," pitching in wherever needed. She might review loan applications, talk with customers, and deal with the constant problems that arise, such as a breakdown of an automated teller machine. Sometimes she works at a teller window if customer lines get particularly long. She also must sometimes deal with irate customers who get upset if lines are long or a mistake is made.

Still, as much as possible, she likes to leave the operations of the branch to her assistant managers. Otherwise, she might easily get completely caught up in the day-to-day problems and lose sight of the fact that her main task is getting more customers for the bank. Nevertheless, when things are not running smoothly at the branch, Wong-Gillmore must juggle her time schedule to help resolve major problems. As a result, Wong-Gillmore is under constant time pressures.

An added pressure is the fact that the teller lines close at 3 p.m. each day and all paper records of the day's transactions must be ready to be picked up by courier at 3:30 to be transferred to the bank's regional office. "From 3:00 to 3:30, it's basically a madhouse around here," Wong-Gillmore says. In addition to overseeing the transactions paperwork, Wong-Gillmore must have any of her own memos about interdepartmental dealings ready to go at 3:30 as well.

Often Wong-Gillmore is visiting customers in the afternoon, but if she happens to be in the bank instead, she might analyze customer credit requests, check current levels of supplies, and try to catch up on the things that have fallen behind due to unforeseen interruptions and problems. Requests for credit from businesses often take a great deal of complex analysis in order to come up with the right solution to a business's credit needs, another time-consuming job in her already hectic day. Nevertheless, Wong-Gillmore enjoys the many contacts she makes in the business community, and she likes "dealing with different companies and learning how they operate."

Wong-Gillmore also likes working with her staff. She says that when people do well, as Frechette did in getting promoted, "that's not only a reflection of their achievement, but a reflection of my achievement as well." Conversely, she states that when an employee does not do well, "you feel like you're failing, too. This year we've had to let go of two or three people. That's not easy, especially when you know they're good people, and they were trying their best, but they just weren't careful enough." Generally, people are fired for having shortages in their cash drawer. Regardless of the reason for the shortages, she must lay off employees who have chronic shortages—a less than pleasant task. She also dislikes the paperwork and the constant changes in procedures. "We're constantly getting reviews of regulations, and we might get an indication of things that change one way, and then see them go the other way two months later."[74]

QUESTIONS FOR CHAPTER CONCLUDING CASE
1. To what extent does Wong-Gillmore's day coincide with the managerial work methods identified by Mintzberg? What roles are evident in her activities?
2. Identify the planning, organizing, leading, and controlling functions performed by Wong-Gillmore.
3. What work agendas does Wong-Gillmore seem to have? How do technical, human, and conceptual skills come into play in Wong-Gillmore's job?

CHAPTER TWO

PIONEERING IDEAS IN MANAGEMENT

CHAPTER OUTLINE

The Birth of Management Ideas
Early Innovative Practices
The Evolution of Management
   Theories

Preclassical Contributors
Major Contributors
Assessing the Preclassical Contributors

Classical Viewpoint
Scientific Management
Bureaucratic Management
Administrative Management

Behavioral Viewpoint
Early Behaviorists
Hawthorne Studies
Human Relations Movement
Behavioral Science Approach

Quantitative Management Viewpoint
Management Science
Operations Management
Management Information Systems

Contemporary Viewpoints
Systems Theory
Contingency Theory
Emerging Views

**Promoting Innovation: Contributions
   of the Major Viewpoints**

LEARNING OBJECTIVES

*After studying this chapter, you
should be able to:*

■ Identify several early innovative
management practices and explain the basic evolution of
management theories.

■ Trace the preclassical conribu-
tions to the field of management.

■ Explain the major approaches
within the classical viewpoint
of management.

■ Describe the major developments contributing to the establishment of the behavioral
viewpoint.

■ Explain the major approaches
within the quantitative management viewpoint.

■ Discuss the relevance of systems theory and contingency
theory to the field of management.

■ Explain how management in
Japan has influenced the
emerging Theory Z viewpoint
of management.

■ Explain how current knowledge
about management is the result
of innovative processes involving many management pio-
neers.

HENRY FORD PUTS PIONEERING IDEAS TO WORK

Henry Ford, founder of the Ford Motor Company, was born to successful Michigan farmers, Mary and William Ford, on July 30, 1863. His father had important connections with merchants running the agricultural markets in Detroit and was a friend of the mayor, alliances that would later help Henry in raising money to start a company.

The young Ford showed an early penchant for mechanical things and was repairing watches by the age of 7. At age 16, Henry left the farm to complete an apprenticeship as a mechanic. The following year, he went to work for the Detroit Dry Dock Company, maker of iron ships, and returned to the farm just before turning 21 years old.

Through helping a neighbor repair a small portable steam engine, Henry landed a job with Westinghouse as area demonstrator and repairman for the southern Michigan territory. Henry then returned to farming, but supplemented his income with various mechanics jobs. Then, in 1891, Henry took a job as a mechanic with the Detroit Illuminating Company (which later became Detroit Edison) and soon became head engineer, a job that gave him some time to think about building an automobile.

When he was not working at his job, he was building his first car, which was completed in 1896. It was called a Quadricycle and looked like two bicycles held together by an engine. The car demonstrated that his gasoline engine could be used successfully to power a multipurpose vehicle. An improved Quadricycle, produced 3 years later, brought financial backers. His first company, the Detroit Automobile Company, was formed on August 5, 1899. Unfortunately, the company was dissolved in November 1900 after disputes between Henry, who wanted to perfect his car, and the backers, who were interested in mass production.

During the next year, Henry produced another improved car, which won a major U.S. auto race. A new group of backers provided money for a new company, the Henry Ford Company, in November 1901. Within 4 months, Henry was ousted, again because he preferred working on his racing cars to producing automobiles for public consumption. As his part of the settlement, he received $900, the blueprints for his next racing car, and the agreement that the firm could no longer use his name. However, unlike his first company, this organization remained in business with a new name, Cadillac. Eight years later, the Cadillac Company joined with the Buick and Olds companies to become the fledgling General Motors Corporation. Thus Henry had a direct hand in the birth of Cadillac automobiles and a major competitor, General Motors.

Henry's next racing car won another major race in October 1902. When reports of the race mentioned that he planned to introduce yet another car, a new wave of investors came forth with money to found the Ford Motor Company. Henry received 25.5 percent of the stock and within 3½ years would buy out the other stockholders. This time, Henry was more attentive to the business of producing automobiles. In 1903, the company introduced the Model A Ford into a receptive market. Several other models soon followed, perhaps the most famous being the Model T Ford, introduced in 1908. The Model T, priced at $825, generated a demand for thousands of the cars, but the manufacturing process was not geared to producing such large numbers.

New manufacturing methods were needed, and Ford became a student of the modern management methods that were emerging at the time. For example, Ford was familiar with the work of Frederick Taylor, who was gaining his own notoriety as the driving force behind the new principles of scientific manage-

Henry Ford is shown here with his first car, the Quadricycle, and the 10 millionth Model T car off the production line. Ford Motor Company was able to produce cars in such great numbers because Henry Ford had made a thorough study of scientific management techniques and implemented these ideas in developing the mechanized assembly line at his plant.

ment and the use of time-and-motion studies to increase job efficiency. Legend has it that Henry Ford also visited the Sears mail-order plant in Chicago, where he witnessed a mass-production facility with an assembly line, a conveyor belt, standardized and interchangeable parts, and plantwide production scheduling. Henry believed that production efficiency could be increased both through the use of scientific management methods and through the judicious use of machines.

By combining these pioneering ideas, Ford established his famous mechanized assembly line in the Highland Park plant in 1913. The average time for assembling a motor and chassis dropped from 12½ hours to 93 minutes. The number of workers required to assemble a car also dropped dramatically. World transportation, manufacturing, and management were never the same. Henry's innovative use of the latest management ideas of his time set the stage for the Ford Motor Company to become one of America's largest corporations.[1]

Imagine inventing a highly desirable product but having difficulty producing it in the quantities required. In devising a solution to this problem, Ford made use of scientific management, the most advanced management approach of his day. Throughout this book, we discuss the most current, leading-edge approaches to management available today. Still, as the case of Henry Ford illustrates, new ideas about management do not typically arise in a vacuum. More frequently, they emerge from a foundation of the best available ideas that have been developed over a period of time. As a result, managers need to understand the roots of the major current ideas about management. An understanding of major contributions to current management approaches also helps managers assess why some approaches are likely to be successful and others unsuccessful, at least in given situations.

Thus, in this chapter, we explore the birth of management ideas, including some of the earliest innovative practices. We briefly examine the pioneering ideas of several preclassical contributors, individuals who predated modern management thinking but helped lay some initial groundwork. We consider the tenets of scientific management, the management approach that heavily influenced Henry Ford, and also take a look at other important perspectives that fit under the umbrella of the classical management viewpoint. Next, we analyze each of the three other major management viewpoints—the behavioral, quantitative, and contemporary perspectives. Finally, we summarize the main innovative contributions of the major viewpoints as they relate to modern management.

THE BIRTH OF MANAGEMENT IDEAS

Knowledge about management today can itself be considered to be the result of a long and continuing innovative process. In this section, we first take a short excursion back into recorded history to trace some famous ground-breaking management practices of early times. We then take an overall look at the evolution of management theories as we know them today before exploring each of the major viewpoints in greater detail in later sections.

Early Innovative Practices

The actual practice of management can be traced back to early recorded history. In fact, ancient history contains a number of monumental examples of management in practice. For instance, the Sumerians ran ancient Mesopotamia with the help of temple corporations, communities in which priests and scribes kept track of legal and economic transactions through an elaborate system of records written on clay tablets. The Egyptians built an extensive irrigation system and major buildings, as well as the famous pyramids. Hammurabi developed a sophisticated legal system, the Code of 282 Laws, to help him rule Babylonia. The Romans controlled their extensive empire through a carefully devised system of four geographic divisions, which were further subdivided into dioceses and then provinces. These achievements represent early examples of innovative practices in management.[2]

While these management accomplishments were so significant that they are remembered today, they provided very limited information about how to actually manage. For example, noted management consultant and writer Peter Drucker has argued that the best managers in history are the ones who managed the building of the pyramids. Although these managers had major time constraints, limited transportation facilities, and few scientific resources, they still managed to build one of the great wonders of the world.[3] Yet the Egyptians told us very little about their management methods.[4] Thus there is a major difference between practicing management well and adding to knowledge about the field of management so that others also can learn to manage.

The Evolution of Management Theories

Although examples of management practice go back several thousand years, the development of management as a field of knowledge is much more recent. Much of the impetus for developing management theories and principles grew out of the industrial revolution, which spawned the growth of factories in the early 1800s. With the proliferation of factories came the widespread need to coordinate the efforts of large numbers of people in the continual production of goods.

The challenge posed by the factories brought forth a number of individuals who began to think in terms of innovative ways to run factories more effectively.

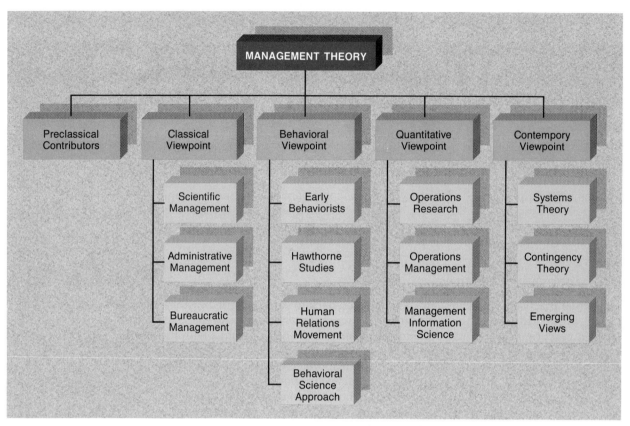

Figure 2-1   Major viewpoints in the development of modern management.

Robert Owen, a cotton mill owner in Scotland in the early 19th century, pioneered ideas about better treatment of workers. Owen argued that improving working conditions would not only improve the workers' quality of life but would lead to a 50 to 100 percent increase in productivity.

This group, known as the preclassical contributors to management (see Figure 2-1), focused largely on particular techniques that might be applied to solve specific problems. They were followed by individuals who began to develop broader principles and theories that make up major viewpoints, or schools, of management: classical, behavioral, quantitative, and contemporary. Each of these major viewpoints encompasses several approaches that have contributed to the development of the particular viewpoint (see Figure 2-1). In the remaining sections of this chapter, we explore the major ideas of the preclassical contributors, as well as those associated with the classical, behavioral, quantitative, and contemporary viewpoints that make up modern management thinking.

PRECLASSICAL CONTRIBUTORS

Major Contributors

A number of individuals in the preclassical period of the middle and late 1800s began to offer ideas that laid the groundwork for broader inquiries into the nature of management that followed. Among the principle preclassical contributors are Robert Owen, Charles Babbage, and Henry P. Towne (see Table 2-1).

Robert Owen. A successful British entrepreneur, Robert Owen (1771–1858) was well ahead of his time in recognizing the importance of human resources. He became particularly interested in the working and living conditions of his em-

Table 2-1 The Preclassical Contributors and Their Pioneering Ideas

Contributor	Pioneering Ideas
Robert Owen	Advocated concern for the working and living conditions of workers
Charles Babbage	Built the first practical mechanical calculator and a prototype of modern computers; predicted the specialization of mental work; suggested profit sharing
Henry P. Towne	Outlined the importance of management as a science and called for the development of management principles

ployees while he was running a cotton mill in New Lanark, Scotland. As was common, the mill employed 400 to 500 young children, who worked 13-hour days that included 1½ hours off for meals. Although his business partners resisted some of his ideas, Owen tried to improve the living conditions of the employees by upgrading streets, houses, sanitation, and the educational system in New Lanark.

Owen tried to convince other factory owners to treat workers better by arguing that such steps often lead to between 50 and 100 percent returns on productivity. When his efforts to influence other owners failed, Owen proposed a bill limiting employment in factories to workers over age 10, reducing the workday to 10½ hours, and prohibiting night work for children. The bill encountered strong opposition from manufacturers and politicians. When it was finally passed in 1819, the bill was relatively weak; it applied exclusively to cotton mills, set the age limit at 9 instead of 10, and included no provision for inspections. Although his views are widely accepted today, Owen was considered to be a radical at the time. His ideas laid the groundwork for the human relations movement, which is discussed later in this chapter.[5]

Charles Babbage. Although English mathematician Charles Babbage (1792–1871) is widely known as "the father of modern computing," he also made direct contributions to thinking about management. The son of a wealthy banker, Babbage used his inheritance to delve into projects that piqued his curiosity. In areas related to computing, his projects produced the world's first practical mechanical calculator (the main principles of which were later incorporated into the Burroughs accounting machines) and an "analytical engine" that had the basic elements of a modern-day computer. His management interests stemmed from his difficulties with directing his various projects. As a result, he visited a number of factories to glean ideas about manufacturing and management.[6]

Like the eighteenth-century economist Adam Smith, Babbage was particularly enthralled with the idea of work specialization. *Work specialization* is the degree to which work is divided into various jobs. (The notion of work specialization is discussed further in Chapter 10.) Smith had concentrated mainly on ways to divide jobs involving physical labor into more specialized tasks, but Babbage carried the specialization idea a step further by recognizing that not only physical work but also mental work could be specialized.[7] In this sense, he foresaw the prospect of specialists, such as accountants who specialize in either personal or corporate taxes. In fact, part of the impetus behind developing the mechanical calculator and other machines was the desire to mechanize some of the work of mathematicians so that they could specialize in more important functions.[8]

Babbage also had some innovative ideas in the area of reward systems. He

Henry Towne was an engineer who realized the importance of good business skills in running a company. He called for studying management as a science and developing a set of principles that could be put to use in all types of management situations.

devised a profit-sharing plan that had two parts, a bonus that was awarded for useful suggestions and a portion of wages that was dependent on factory profits. His ideas foreshadowed some modern-day group incentive plans, such as the Scanlon Plan, in which workers actively participate in offering suggestions to improve productivity and then share in the profits from resulting gains.

Babbage was viewed by his contemporaries as a genius, even if a somewhat irascible one. For example, he disliked the organ-grinders of the day because they disturbed his concentration. He was known to blow bugles and create loud scenes to scare them away from his house. Not surprisingly, his neighbors thought of the genius as somewhat of a crackpot.[9]

Henry R. Towne. President of the Yale and Towne Manufacturing Company and a mechanical engineer, Henry R. Towne (1844–1924) stands out as the person who articulated the need to consider management as a separate field of *systematic* inquiry on a par with engineering. He outlined his views in a landmark paper titled "The Engineer as an Economist," which was delivered in 1886 to the American Society of Mechanical Engineers in Chicago. He observed that although good engineering skills and good business skills were rarely combined in the same individual, both skills were needed to run an organization effectively. Accordingly, the paper called for the establishment of a science of management and the development of principles that could be applied across management situations. Although the engineering society itself did not become a major force in developing knowledge about management, Towne's presentation was attended by Frederick Taylor, who subsequently was instrumental in building the management field.[10]

Assessing the Preclassical Contributors

Although the early pioneers explored several different avenues relating to management, their efforts were somewhat fragmentary. They were largely oriented toward developing specific techniques, often to solve visible problems. For example, you have probably heard of *Robert's Rules of Order*, a publication that originated in the preclassical era and is still used today to run many large, formal meetings (see the following Case in Point discussion).

CASE IN POINT: Robert's Rules Bring Order

During the late 1800s, when Henry Martyn Robert, a brigadier general in the U.S. Army, was pursuing his military career as a civil engineer, he frequently attended meetings with people from many backgrounds. In fact, because he was an engineer in the civil works division, he often had to preside at these meetings.

He quickly learned about the challenge of running meetings when the first meeting over which he presided ended in total chaos. He was perplexed because he had prepared his subject well and had even gathered advice on how to conduct a meeting. Still, the attendees, a collection of ministers who made up the Baptist Board of New Bedford, Massachusetts, behaved in a very unruly manner, almost came to blows, and finally broke up the meeting with nothing being resolved or settled. After witnessing this debacle, Robert decided that he would never again participate in such a disastrous encounter.

For the next 7 years, he collected information concerning how to conduct a meeting, and he subsequently produced a 176-page book titled *Pocket Manual of*

Rules of Order for Deliberative Assemblies. The book provided a set of parliamentary rules for conducting meetings. Unfortunately, his publisher backed out of sponsoring the book at the last minute. Undaunted, Robert used his own money to publish 4000 copies of the book.

He promoted the book by sending 1000 copies to the best parliamentarians in the United States, including governors, legislators, the vice president, and a few attorneys, and he asked the recipients for their comments. After receiving many enthusiastic responses and several very good suggestions, he modified the original text, adding 16 pages and changing the title to *Robert's Rules of Order.* The book has become a classic source of guidance for running large, formal meetings and is used by many legislative bodies, government councils, associations, and other organizations where decisions are made by member vote. It was first published in 1876 and has not been out of print since. More than 4 million copies have been sold throughout the English-speaking world. It has also been published in Braille.[11] ■

Since they generally came from technical backgrounds, the early pioneers did not tend to think in terms of management as a separate field—that is, until Towne presented his influential paper. Still, they were important innovators who laid the groundwork for other major management thinkers who came after them. Their forward-looking ideas have endured the test of time.

CLASSICAL VIEWPOINT

Henry Towne's call for establishing management as a separate field of inquiry helped usher in a major approach to management called the classical viewpoint. The **classical viewpoint** is a perspective on management that emphasizes finding ways to manage work and organizations more efficiently. It is made up of three different approaches: scientific management, administrative management, and bureaucratic management. This viewpoint is labeled "classical" because it encompasses early works and related contributions that have formed the main roots of the field of management.[12]

Classical viewpoint A perspective on management that emphasizes finding ways to manage work and organizations more effectively

Scientific Management

Scientific management is an approach within classical management theory that emphasizes the scientific study of work methods in order to improve worker efficiency. Major representatives of the scientific management approach include Frederick Winslow Taylor, Frank and Lillian Gilbreth, and Henry Gantt.

Scientific management An approach that emphasizes the scientific study of work methods in order to improve worker efficiency

Frederick Winslow Taylor. Frederick Winslow Taylor (1856–1915) is known as "the father of scientific management." Born to a relatively wealthy Philadelphia family, Taylor became an apprentice pattern maker and machinist for a local firm before moving on to Midvale Steel. At Midvale, his meteoric rise from laborer to chief engineer in 6 years gave him an opportunity to tackle a serious problem that he had observed—soldiering by workers.[13] **Soldiering** is deliberately working at less than full capacity. Taylor believed that workers engaged in soldiering for three main reasons. First, they feared that increasing their productivity would cause them or other workers to lose their jobs. Second, faulty wage systems set up by management encouraged workers to operate at a slow pace. For

Soldiering Deliberately working at less than full capacity

Frederick Taylor took up Henry Towne's challenge and developed specific principles of scientific management, such as time and motion studies and wage incentives. These principles, but into practice, did result in greater productivity and worker efficiency, but some observers criticized Taylor for "exploiting" workers to get them to produce more.

example, pay by the hour or the day mainly encouraged attendance rather than output. On the other hand, companies that cut incentive pay when workers began to exceed standards also made workers reluctant to excel. Third, general methods of working and rules of thumb handed down from generation to generation often were very inefficient. These factors led Taylor to conclude that managers, not workers, were responsible for the soldiering because it was up to management to design jobs and wage systems that would encourage productivity.

Taylor believed that managers could resolve the soldiering problem by developing a *science* of management based on the four principles summarized in Table 2-2. Central to the approach was the concept of using scientific means to determine how tasks should be done rather than relying on the past experience of each individual worker. Taylor felt that scientific methods represented a "mental revolution" in managing work. Specifically, Taylor pioneered a method now known as the *time-and-motion study* (Taylor called it a time study). This type of study involves breaking down the work task into its various elements, or motions, eliminating unnecessary motions, determining the best way to do the job, and then timing each motion to determine the amount of production that could be expected per day (with allowances for delays and rest periods).[14]

In addition to advocating the use of scientific means to develop the best way to do a task, Taylor argued that several other principles were important. For one thing, workers with appropriate abilities had to be selected and trained in the appropriate task method. For another, supervisors needed to build cooperation among the workers to ensure that they followed the designated method of work. Building such cooperation included soliciting workers' suggestions and being willing to discuss ideas for improved work methods.[15] Finally, there needed to be a clear division of work responsibilities. Previously, the workers planned how to approach a task, and then they executed it. Under the Taylor scheme, it was management's job to do the task planning, using scientific methods.[16]

In order to solve the problem of wage systems that encouraged soldiering, Taylor also advocated the use of wage incentive plans. He argued that workers should be paid from 30 to 100 percent higher wages for using the scientifically developed work methods and for attaining daily standards.[17]

After leaving Midvale, Taylor held a succession of jobs and consulting assignments, including consulting with Bethlehem Steel, where he conducted two of his most famous studies. His pig-iron handling study involved workers whose task consisted of picking up a "pig" of iron weighing 92 pounds, carrying it up a plank, loading it into a railroad car, and walking back to get another pig in order to repeat the process. When Taylor began his work, the pig handlers were loading an average of 12½ tons per worker per day. By selecting workers most suited to the task, making changes in the way the work was done, adding care-

Table 2-2   Taylor's Four Principles of Scientific Management

1. Scientifically study each part of a task and develop the best method for performing the task.
2. Carefully select workers and train them to perform the task by using the scientifically developed method.
3. Cooperate fully with workers to ensure that they use the proper method.
4. Divide work and responsibility so that management is responsible for planning work methods using scientific principles and workers are responsible for executing the work accordingly.

fully spaced rest periods, and offering incentive pay ($1.85 per day for reaching standard versus a previous $1.15), Taylor had workers loading the new expected standard of 47½ tons per day.[18]

His second famous study at Bethlehem Steel focused on shoveling. Until Taylor introduced scientific management, workers typically brought their own tools to the job. Taylor noted that a worker might use the same shovel for both iron ore and ashes, even though the relative weights of the materials were very different. On the basis of his studies, Taylor determined that the optimum weight for shoveling was 21 pounds. Therefore, he argued that it made sense to have shovels of different sizes for different classes of materials so that the weight of what was being shoveled would be about 21 pounds. Results of implementing his plan with company-owned shovels demonstrated that the average number of tons shoveled per worker per day increased from 16 to 59; the average earnings per worker per day increased from $1.15 to $1.88; and the average cost of handling a long ton (2240 pounds) decreased from $0.072 to $0.033. Again, Taylor's plan included additional incentive pay for workers and was beneficial for the company.[19]

Taylor, who had a tendency to become rather dogmatic when any aspect of his approach was questioned, ran into opposition from some members of management, citizens of Bethlehem, and others who argued that he was exploiting workers by getting them to produce more and causing large reductions in the work force at Bethlehem Steel. After being forced out of the company, he began to devote more attention to writing. He achieved great notoriety through his testimony in a case before the Interstate Commerce Commission in which the Eastern railroads sought to raise freight rates. Taylor's assertions that railroads could reduce their costs through the use of his scientific principles made newspaper headlines throughout the country in 1910 and raised scientific management to a high level of visibility.[20] A strike at the Watertown (Massachusetts) Army Arsenal, where some of Taylor's ideas were being tested, led to a congressional investigation (1911–1912) that was not able to find any concrete evidence that workers were being abused by "Taylorism." Still, the negative publicity slowed the momentum of scientific management to some degree.[21] Nonetheless, by the end of World War I scientific management, aided by several French management experts was spreading throughout Europe and was being used in such diverse places as English chocolate factories, Icelandic fisheries, German paper mills, and Swedish typewriter factories.[22]

Critics argue that Taylor failed to acknowledge some previous work by others on the issue of shoveling and that data related to his pig-iron handling study were reported inconsistently and may even have been fabricated to some extent.[23] On the other hand, supporters state that the issues raised by critics either are misguided or involve minor issues.[24] Despite the controversy, there is little doubt that the innovative ideas that Taylor popularized remain in use today. This is particularly true of his strong support of science and its important role in management, but it applies to his methods of studying work as well.[25] As we will see in Chapter 10, the use of scientific management can sometimes make jobs overspecialized, often resulting in worker resentment, monotony, poor quality, absenteeism, and turnover.

The Gilbreths. Other major advocates of scientific management were the husband and wife team of Frank (1868–1924) and Lillian (1878–1972) Gilbreth. Although Frank had qualified for admission to the Massachusetts Institute of Technology, he decided to become a bricklayer because of the importance of the profession at the time. As Frank became involved in training young bricklayers,

Frank and Lillian Gilbreth and eleven of their dozen children gather outside the lighthouse that was their home in Nantucket, Massachusetts. Frank and Lillian worked as a team developing scientific management techniques (some of which they tried out in their household).

This time-exposure photograph taken by Frank Gilbreth shows the motions necessary to move and file 16 boxes full of glass. Such time and motion studies were used to increase efficiency in the workplace.

he noticed the inefficiencies that were handed down from experienced workers.

To remedy the situation, he proposed using motion studies to streamline the bricklaying process. Frank also designed special scaffolding for different types of jobs and devised precise directions for mortar consistency. On the basis of these and other ideas, Frank was able to reduce the motions involved in bricklaying from 18½ to 4. Using his approach, workers increased the number of bricks laid per day from 1000 to 2700 with no increase in physical exertion.[26] As he conducted his studies, Frank became familiar with the work of Frederick Taylor and was a staunch supporter of scientific management.[27]

Meanwhile, Frank married Lillian Moller, who began working with him on projects while she completed her doctorate in psychology. The two continued their studies aimed at eliminating unnecessary motions and expanded their interests to exploring ways of reducing task fatigue. Part of their work involved the isolation of 17 basic motions, each called a *therblig* ("Gilbreth" spelled backward, with the "t" and "h" reversed). Therbligs included such motions as select, position, and hold—motions that were used to study tasks in a number of industries. The Gilbreths used the therblig concept to study jobs and also pioneered the use of motion picture technology in studying jobs.[28]

Lillian's doctoral thesis was published as a book, *The Psychology of Management,* making it one of the early works applying the findings of psychology to the workplace.[29] At the insistence of the publisher, the author was listed as L. M. Gilbreth to disguise the fact that the book was written by a woman.

Lillian helped define scientific management by arguing that scientific studies of management must focus on both analysis and synthesis. With analysis, a task is broken down into its essential parts, or elements. With synthesis, the task is reconstituted to include only those elements necessary for efficient work.[30]

She also had a particular interest in the human implications of scientific management, arguing that the purpose of scientific management is to help people reach their maximum potential by developing their skills and abilities.[31]

The Gilbreth family eventually numbered 12 children, two of whom wrote a book, *Cheaper by the Dozen,* describing life with their efficiency-minded parents.[32] For example, they report that their father learned to use two shaving brushes simultaneously to put shaving cream on his face, thereby saving 17 seconds. When he tried shaving with two razors, he found that the process took 44 seconds less than it did with one razor. Unfortunately, it took 2 minutes to apply each bandage to the resulting cuts. His children reported that it was the loss of 2 minutes, not the cuts, that made him abandon the use of two razors.[33]

In 1924, Frank died suddenly of a heart attack, leaving Lillian with their dozen children, ranging from age 2 to 19. She then continued their innovative studies and consulting, finally becoming a professor of management at Purdue University.[34] Lillian Gilbreth ranks as the first woman to gain prominence as a major contributor to the development of management as a science.

Henry L. Gantt. One of Taylor's closest associates was Henry Gantt (1861–1919), who worked with Taylor in several companies, including Midvale Steel and Bethlehem Steel.[35] Gantt later became an independent consultant and made several contributions of his own. The most well known is the *Gantt chart,* a graphic aid to planning, scheduling, and control that is still in use today. (An example of a Gantt chart is given in Chapter 9.) He also devised a unique pay incentive system that not only paid workers extra for reaching standard in the allotted time but also awarded bonuses to supervisors when workers reached standard. He wanted to encourage supervisors to coach workers who were having difficulties.

Later in his life, Gantt began to devote more attention to the social responsibilities of business and management. Writing around the time of the Russian Revolution (1917), Gantt expressed concern that business could run into severe difficulties if it did not find a reasonable balance between seeking profits and serving the welfare of society. He was especially concerned that large businesses might attempt to exert monopolistic power in the form of less customer responsiveness and excess profits. Thus Gantt joins Owen as an early writer on the subject of the social responsibilities of business.

Bureaucratic Management

Another branch of the classical viewpoint is **bureaucratic management,** an approach that emphasizes the need for organizations to operate in a rational manner rather than relying on the arbitrary whims of owners and managers. The bureaucratic management approach is based mainly on the work of prominent German sociologist Max Weber.

Weber (1864–1920) was the son of an affluent family with strong political and social connections.[36] He pursued a career as a consultant, professor, and author. Because he was so well read, he was able to make contributions that cross a number of academic disciplines, such as management, sociology, economics, and philosophy. Among his most important contributions to the discipline of management are his ideas on the need for organizations to operate on a more rational basis.

In formulating his ideas, Weber was reacting to the prevailing norms of class consciousness and nepotism. For example, it was customary practice to allow only individuals of aristocratic birth to become officers in the Prussian Army or

Bureaucratic management An approach that emphasizes the need for organizations to operate in a rational manner rather than relying on the arbitrary whims of owners and managers

Max Weber coined the term "bureaucracy" and theorized about its ideal characteristics: specialization, formal rules and regulations, hierarchy, promotion on the basis of merit, and authority that derives from position, not personal status. Weber's ideas have had great influence on how people view large organizations.

to attain high-level positions in government and industry. Weber felt that the situation not only was unfair but also led to a significant waste of human resources. He also believed that running organizations on the basis of *whom* one knows rather than *what* one knows and engaging in nepotism, the hiring of relatives regardless of their competence, tended to interfere with organizational effectiveness.

In an effort to visualize how the large organizations evolving out of the industrial revolution might ideally operate, Weber formulated characteristics of the "ideal bureaucracy." He coined the term "bureaucracy" (based on the German *büro*, meaning office) to identify large organizations that operated on a rational basis. Weber understood clearly that his ideal bureaucracy did not actually exist. In fact, he never intended that his ideas be used as guidelines for managers. Rather, his purpose was to develop some ideas that could be used as a starting point in understanding such organizations.[37] However, when his work was translated into English in the late 1940s, many U.S. management scholars found his ideas useful in considering how organizations could be more effectively managed.

Several major characteristics of Weber's bureaucracy are shown in Table 2-3. For instance, Weber believed that large organizations would operate on a more rational, systematic basis if tasks were specialized, rules and regulations were formalized and uniformly applied to let people know what was expected, reporting relationships were established through a well-defined hierarchy, career advancement was based on merit, and authority was based on the official position one holds rather than on personal status.

Because of the possibility of carrying Weber's ideas to excess, the term "bureaucracy" is sometimes used in a pejorative sense to denote red tape and excessive rules. Yet there clearly are advantages to the bureaucratic characteristics

Table 2-3   Major Characteristics of Weber's Ideal Bureaucracy

Characteristic	Description
Specialization of labor	Jobs are broken down into routine, well-defined tasks so that members know what is expected of them and can become extremely competent at their particular subset of tasks.
Formal rules and procedures	Written rules and procedures specify the behaviors desired from members, facilitate coordination, and ensure uniformity.
Impersonality	Rules, procedures, and sanctions are applied uniformly regardless of individual personalities and personal considerations.
Well-defined hierarchy	Multiple levels of positions, with carefully determined reporting relationships among levels, provide supervision of lower offices by higher ones, a means of handling exceptions, and the ability to establish accountability of actions.
Career advancement based on merit	Selection and promotion is based on the qualifications and performance of members.

outlined by Weber. For example, recent troubles at family-owned U-Haul can be traced to confusion over roles, clandestine meetings of the board of directors, secret rule changes, and advancement determined by family ties—all violations of Weber's ideal. The resulting feuds and court battles among family members are seriously threatening the viability of the national renter of trucks, trailers, and other equipment.[38]

Administrative Management

While the advocates of scientific management concentrated on developing principles that could be used to help organize individual worker tasks more effectively and Weber struggled with the concept of bureaucracy, another branch within the classical viewpoint was also developing. The **administrative management** approach focuses on principles that can be used by managers to coordinate the internal activities of organizations. Major contributors include Henri Fayol and Chester Barnard, both of whom were executives of large enterprises.

Henri Fayol. French industrialist Henri Fayol (1841–1925), a well-known contributor to the administrative management approach, was born into a middle-class family near Lyon, France.[39] Trained as a mining engineer, he joined the French coal-and-iron combine Commentary-Fourchambault Company as an apprentice and rose to the top position of managing director in 1888. He accomplished the difficult task of moving the company out of severe financial difficulties and into a strong position by the time of his retirement at age 77. The company survives today as part of LeCreusot-Loire, a large mining and metallurgical group in central France.

On the basis of his experiences as a top-level manager, Fayol was convinced that it should be possible to develop theories about management that could then be taught to individuals with administrative responsibilities. His efforts toward developing such theories were published in *General and Industrial Management*, which originally appeared in monograph form in 1916 but attained prominence in the United States after a second English translation appeared in 1949.[40]

In one part of his work, Fayol attempted to isolate the major types of activities involved in industry or business. Of particular importance is his delineation of the major functions that are included within the category of "managerial activities": planning, organizing, commanding, coordinating, and controlling. Thinking of management as encompassing these functions is known as the *functional* approach to management. You probably have noticed the similarity between Fayol's functions and the four functions of management (planning, organizing, leading, and controlling) used as an organizing framework in this book. Many contemporary books on management use a form of the functional approach that has roots in Fayol's work.

Fayol also outlined a number of principles that he found useful in running his large coal-and-iron concern. These principles are outlined in Table 2-4. Fayol provided the principles as a starting point, envisioning that others would be added as knowledge about management expanded. Although contemporary research has found exceptions to his principles under some conditions that will be discussed in later chapters, the principles are generally in widespread use today.

Chester Barnard. Another major contributor to administrative management was Chester Barnard (1886–1961). Born in Massachusetts, he attended Harvard but did not complete his degree work.[41] After joining AT&T as a statistician, he rose

Administrative management
An approach that focuses on principles that can be used by managers to coordinate the internal activities of organizations

The functional approach to management—focusing on major managerial activities—owes much to the pioneering theoretical work of Henri Fayol. Many of the principles of managing that Fayol outlined are still used today.

Table 2-4 Fayol's General Principles of Management

1. *Division of work.* Work specialization can result in efficiencies and is applicable to both managerial and technical functions. Yet there are limitations to how much that work should be divided.
2. *Authority.* Authority is the right to give orders and the power to exact obedience. It derives from the formal authority of the office and from personal authority based on factors like intelligence and experience. With authority comes responsibility.
3. *Discipline.* Discipline is absolutely necessary for the smooth running of an organization, but the state of discipline depends essentially on the worthiness of its leaders.
4. *Unity of command.* An employee should receive orders from one superior only.
5. *Unity of direction.* Activities aimed at the same objective should be organized so that there is one plan and one person in charge.
6. *Subordination of individual interest to general interest.* The interests of one employee or group should not prevail over the interests and goals of the organization.
7. *Remuneration.* Compensation should be fair to both the employee and the employer.
8. *Centralization.* The proper amount of centralization or decentralization depends on the situation. The objective is the optimum use of the capabilities of personnel.
9. *Scalar chain.* A scalar (hierarchical) chain of authority extends from the top to the bottom of an organization and defines the communication path. However, horizontal communication also is encouraged as long as the managers in the chain are kept informed.
10. *Order.* Materials should be kept in well-chosen places that facilitate activities. Similarly, due to good organization and selection, the right person should be in the right place.
11. *Equity.* Employees should be treated with kindness and justice.
12. *Stability of personnel tenure.* Because time is required to become effective in new jobs, high turnover should be prevented.
13. *Initiative.* Managers should encourage and develop subordinate initiative to the fullest.
14. *Esprit de Corps.* Since union is strength, harmony and teamwork are essential.

Source: Adapted from Henri Fayol, *General and Industrial Management,* Constance Storrs (trans.), Pitman & Sons, Ltd., London, 1949, pp. 19–42.

rapidly and was named president of the New Jersey Bell Telephone Company in 1927. Both while and after he presided over New Jersey Bell, he also held a number of prestigious public service positions, such as head of the Rockefeller Foundation.[42] Barnard recorded his observations about effective administration in a single classic book, *The Functions of the Executive,* published in 1938. The book was developed from a series of lectures, given by Barnard in 1937 at the Lowell Institute in Boston, that were intended to help stimulate the development of a theory of organizations.[43]

Written just as the first notions of viewing organizations as systems were emerging, Barnard's work shows some influences of the systems viewpoint, which we will consider later in the chapter. He viewed organizations as cooperative systems of consciously coordinated activities. In his own view, though, Barnard felt that an organizational system required three universal elements in order to operate: communication, a willingness to serve, and a common purpose. Therefore, according to Barnard, executives need to pay particular attention to arranging for a system of communication, nurturing a willingness to cooperate, and ensuring that there is a clearly articulated common purpose. Barnard saw the common purpose as helping to rally a willingness to cooperate and also as essential to giving meaning to the environment. Otherwise, he argued, the environment becomes ''a mere mass of things'' that have little meaning to managers.[44] His emphasis on organizational purpose endures in the continuing contemporary concern with this concept. For example, a number of major companies, such as Dayton-Hudson and Intel, have official statements that outline their basic purposes as organizations.[45] We consider the role of organizational purpose or mission in depth in Chapter 5.

One of Barnard's best-known contributions is his acceptance theory of authority. The **acceptance theory of authority** argues that authority does not depend as much on "persons of authority" who *give* orders as on the willingness of those who *receive* the orders to comply. Thus, in Barnard's view, it is really the employees who decide whether or not to accept orders and directions from above. From a practical point of view, Barnard felt that managers generally are able to exert authority on a day-to-day basis because each individual possesses a "zone of indifference" within which the individual is willing to accept orders and directions without much question.

On the basis of his view that authority flows from the bottom to the top, Barnard argued that employees are more willing to accept directions from a manager if they (1) understand the communication, (2) see the communication as consistent with the purposes of the organization, (3) feel the actions indicated are in line with their needs and those of other employees, and (4) view themselves as mentally and physically able to comply. Barnard's acceptance theory has been somewhat controversial because of the degree of emphasis placed on subordinate acceptance. Still, it has helped emphasize that individuals do not necessarily comply with orders and directions from managers, making it important that managers give some thought to the way in which they attempt to exert power and authority. For example, James Dutt, one-time chairman of the Beatrice Company, earned a reputation for being a "fiery-tempered autocrat" who was prone to firing individuals who disagreed with him. Unfortunately, many of the executives left the firm or were fired, the company subsequently performed poorly, and Dutt was ultimately ousted during a takeover backed by the investment firm of Kohlberg Kravis Roberts & Company.[46]

In considering worker reactions to orders and directions, Barnard helped bridge the concern with authority growing out of the administrative and bureaucratic approaches with the emphasis on worker needs that was simultaneously developing within the behavioral viewpoint. Barnard was familiar with the work of Max Weber and with that of Mary Parker Follett, an early behaviorist.[47] He also knew of the Hawthorne studies, which were a primary force in the development of the behavioral viewpoint, to which we turn next.[48]

> **Acceptance theory of authority** A theory that argues that authority does not depend as much on "persons of authority" who *give* orders as on the willingness of those who *receive* the orders to comply

BEHAVIORAL VIEWPOINT

The classical theorists generally viewed individuals as mechanisms of production. As a result, their efforts were largely geared to finding ways for organizations to use these productive mechanisms more efficiently. The prospect that an employee's behavior might be influenced by internal reactions to various aspects of the job situation was generally not seen as particularly germane to the quest for greater efficiency. In contrast, the **behavioral viewpoint** is a perspective on management that emphasizes the importance of attempting to understand the various factors that affect human behavior in organizations.

Why did the behavioral viewpoint emerge? The main reason was that although the classical viewpoint made some major contributions to management, the approach did not seem to be the whole answer to the problem of what constituted effective management. Other ideas started to surface as management began to develop as a separate field of knowledge. One of these ideas came

> **Behavioral viewpoint** A perspective on management that emphasizes the importance of attempting to understand the various factors that affect human behavior in organizations

Hugo Münsterberg, a German psychologist, pioneered the field of industrial psychology. He was especially interested in identifying the conditions that would promote an individual's best work and in finding ways to influence workers to act in accord with management interests.

Mary Parker Follett, an early behaviorist, focused on group dynamics in her work and writings. Her ideas on power sharing, conflict resolution, and the integration of organizational systems were far in advance of their time.

from a study that sought to apply the scientific approach to the question of whether brighter lighting would improve worker productivity. Researchers uncovered inexplicable results, which then led to a further search to explain the productivity increases found. In exploring the behavioral viewpoint, we examine four aspects of its development: the contributions of the early behaviorists, the Hawthorne studies, the human relations movement, and the more contemporary behavioral science approach.

Early Behaviorists

Some inklings that scientific management might not hold the entire answer to the management question began to appear even as scientific management was rising to prominence. With the growing interest in the subject of management, individuals from other backgrounds began to offer alternative perspectives to the emphasis on engineering that characterized the scientific management approach. Two early behaviorists, psychologist Hugo Münsterberg and political scientist Mary Parker Follett, offered pioneering ideas that contributed to the growth of the behavioral perspective into a major viewpoint.

Hugo Münsterberg. Born and educated in Germany, Hugo Münsterberg (1863–1916) earned both a Ph.D. in psychology and a medical degree. In 1892, he set up a psychological laboratory at Harvard and began seeking practical applications of psychology. Before long, his attention turned to industrial applications, leading him to publish an important book, *Psychology and Industrial Efficiency*, which appeared in 1913. The book argued that psychologists could help industry in three major areas. The first, closely allied to scientific management, focused on studying jobs and finding ways of identifying the individuals who are best suited to the particular jobs. The other two provided some recognition of the idea that factors besides those recognized by the classical theorists might influence behavior at work. For example, Münsterberg argued that the second area in which psychologists could help industry involved identifying the psychological conditions under which individuals are likely to do their best work. The third area centered on finding ways to influence individuals to behave in manners that are congruent with management interests. The ideas and examples he provided ignited the imagination of others and led to the establishment of the field of *industrial psychology*, the study of human behavior in a work setting. Thus, Münsterberg is considered to be "the father of industrial psychology."[49]

Mary Parker Follett. Another well-known early behaviorist was Mary Parker Follett (1868–1933). Born in Boston and educated in political science at what is now Radcliffe College, Follett was a social worker who became interested in employment and workplace issues. Her experience in dealing with work issues, as well as her speaking and writing abilities, eventually led to consulting assignments with many large corporations. Although she lived mainly during the era of classical management, her thinking was more in line with the behavioral and, to some extent, the systems viewpoints of management.[50]

Despite the fact that Frederick Taylor had recognized the importance of groups in conjunction with the soldiering problem, groups did not figure prominently in his scientific management approach. Instead, he focused mainly on efficient methods for completing individual tasks. In contrast, Follett attributed much greater significance to the functioning of groups in organizations. She argued that members of organizations are continually influenced by the groups within which they operate. In fact, she held that groups have the capacity to exercise control over themselves and their own activities, a concept that is congruent with the recent interest in self-managing teams in American business (see Chapter 16). For example, at General Motor's new Saturn plant, most of the work is done by teams that have no traditional boss.[51]

Another of Follett's forward-looking ideas was her contention that organizations should operate on the principle of "power with" rather than "power over." Power, to her, was the general ability to influence and bring about change. She argued that power should be a jointly developed, cooperative concept involving employees and managers working together rather than a coercive concept based on hierarchical pressure. Although her views likely influenced Barnard's acceptance theory of authority, she had in mind sharing power, rather than Barnard's emphasis on engendering the appropriate response from below.[52]

One of the important means she suggested for bringing about the "power with" concept was resolving conflict through *integration*. By integration she meant finding a solution to a conflict that would satisfy both parties. Giving an example of integration, she cited a situation in which a dairy cooperative almost disbanded because of a controversy over the pecking order in unloading milk cans at a creamery located on the downgrade of a hill. Members who came downhill and those who came uphill both thought they should be given precedence in unloading. The situation was at an impasse until an outsider pointed out that the position of the loading dock could be changed so that both groups could unload their cans at the same time. Follett noted, "Integration involves invention, and the clever thing is to recognize this, and not to let one's thinking stay within the boundaries of two alternatives that are mutually exclusive."[53] Her ideas on integration heralded modern methods of conflict resolution (see Chapter 16).

Follett placed great importance on achieving what she called *integrative unity*, whereby the organization would operate as a functional whole, with the various interrelated parts working together effectively to achieve organizational goals. Yet she saw the process of working together as a dynamic process because environmental factors would necessitate change. Her notion of integrative unity also likely influenced Barnard. As we will see, her ideas anticipated the systems viewpoint of management.[54] One recent reviewer of her work has argued that its overall significance "rivals the long-standing influence of such giants as Taylor and Fayol."[55]

Hawthorne Studies

While Follett was doing her speaking and writing, a number of researchers were involved in the Hawthorne studies. The **Hawthorne studies** are a group of studies conducted at the Hawthorne plant of the Western Electric Company during the late 1920s and early 1930s whose results ultimately led to the human relations view of management, a behavioral approach that emphasized concern for the worker. To understand their significance, we need to trace the studies from the beginning.

When they started, the Hawthorne studies were right in the scientific management tradition of seeking greater efficiency through improving the tools and methods of work—in this case, lighting. The studies came about because the General Electric Company wanted to sell more light bulbs and, along with other electric companies, supported studies on the relationship between lighting and productivity that were to be conducted by a research group called the National

Hawthorne studies A group of studies conducted at the Hawthorne plant of the Western Electric Company during the late 1920s and early 1930s whose results ultimately led to the human relations view of management

The productivity of the five women assembling electrical relays was monitored over several years in the Hawthorne studies. Researchers found that regardless of what working conditions they manipulated the women still increased their output over the period of the study. Later researchers have concluded that it was a change in supervisory arrangement, not the experimental manipulations, that accounted for the rise in their productivity.

Research Council. The tests were to be held at the Hawthorne Works (Chicago) of the Western Electric Company, an equipment-producing subsidiary of AT&T.[56] Ultimately, three sets of studies were done.

First Set of Studies. The first set of studies, called the Illumination Studies, took place between 1924 and 1927 under the direction of several engineers. In one of these studies, light was decreased over successive periods for the experimental group (the group for whom the lighting was altered), while light was held at a constant level for the control group (a comparison group working in a separate area). In both groups, performance rose steadily, even though the lighting in the experimental group finally reached a point at which workers in the group complained that they could hardly see. At that point, performance in the experimental group finally began to decline (see Figure 2-2). The researchers concluded that factors other than lighting were at work (since performance rose in both groups) and the Committee on Industrial Lighting discontinued the project.[57] In retrospect, one possibility based on the records of the studies is that the experimental and control groups were in contact and may have begun competing with one another.

Second Set of Studies. Intrigued with the positive changes in productivity, some of the engineers and company officials decided to attempt to determine the causes through further studies. Accordingly, a second set of experiments took place between 1927 and 1933. The most famous study involved five women assembling electrical relays in the Relay Assembly Test Room, a special room away from other workers where the researchers could alter work conditions and evaluate the results. Apparently, the researchers were concerned about possible negative reactions and resistance from the workers who would be included in the experiment. To lessen potential resistance, the researchers changed the usual supervisory arrangement so that there would be no official supervisor; rather, the workers would operate under the general direction of the experimenter. The workers also were given special privileges such as being able to leave their workstation without permission, and they received considerable attention from the experimenters and company officials.[58] The study was aimed at exploring the best combination of work and rest periods, but a number of other factors were also varied (sometimes simultaneously), such as pay, length of the workday, and provisions for free lunches. Generally, productivity increased over the period of the study, regardless of how the factors under consideration were manipulated.[59]

A Harvard University group (who first became involved in assessing the results when a representative visited the plant in 1928) ultimately concluded that the change in the supervisory arrangement was the major reason for the increase in productivity in the Relay Assembly Test Room study and in two related studies involving different work groups. The researchers felt that the physical changes, such as rest periods, free lunches, and shortened hours, as well as the group incentive pay plans, were factors of lesser importance (largely because adverse changes in some of these factors did not seem to decrease performance).

Since the supervisory arrangement by the researchers had been set up before the study began, this change was not actually part of the study manipulations and was not intended to affect the results. One outcome of the studies was the identification of a famous concept that ultimately came to be known as the Hawthorne effect. The **Hawthorne effect** refers to the possibility that individuals singled out for a study may improve their performance simply because of the added attention they receive from the researchers, rather than because of any specific factors being tested in the study.[60]

More contemporary investigations now suggest that the Hawthorne effect concept is too simplistic to explain what happened during the Hawthorne studies and that the Hawthorne effect concept itself is defective. It now appears likely that the results obtained at the Hawthorne plant stemmed from the fact that the workers interpreted what was going on around them differently than did the researchers (rather than from the idea that the workers reacted positively

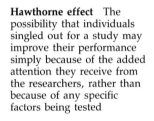

Hawthorne effect The possibility that individuals singled out for a study may improve their performance simply because of the added attention they receive from the researchers, rather than because of any specific factors being tested

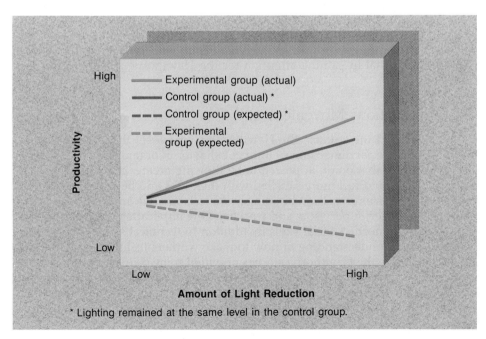

Figure 2-2 Actual versus expected results for the experimental and control groups in one of the Hawthorne Illumination Studies.

simply because of attention from the researchers). In the Hawthorne situation, the workers likely viewed the altered supervision as an important positive change in their work environment, even though that was not what the researchers intended.[61]

Third Set of Studies. The third group of Hawthorne studies built on the emerging findings of the second set. It included the famous Bank Wiring Observation Room study (1931–1932), in which studying a group of male workers provided knowledge about informal social relations within groups and about group norms that restrict output when such steps seem advantageous to the group. It also included a massive interviewing program (1928–1931) that was initially aimed at improving supervision but evolved into a means of learning what workers had on their minds and allowing them to let off steam.[62]

Assessing the Hawthorne Studies. The Hawthorne studies have been severely criticized mainly because the studies often had major flaws (such as changing several factors at the same time) and because important data were sometimes ignored in drawing conclusions (especially in discounting the potential importance of pay).[63] In their defense, the studies were conducted at a time when knowledge about how to conduct such studies was fairly embryonic.

Yet, despite their shortcomings, the effects of these pioneering studies were far-reaching. In strong contrast to the impersonality that characterized the classical approach, the Hawthorne studies pointed to the impact that social aspects of the job had on productivity, particularly the effect of personal attention from supervisors and relationships among group members. As a result, the focus of the field of management was drastically altered. As one writer has pointed out, "No other theory or set of experiments has stimulated more research and controversy nor contributed more to a change in management thinking than the Hawthorne studies and the human relations movement they spawned."[64]

One reason that the studies achieved such a high level of visibility can be attributed in part to the Harvard group, particularly George Elton Mayo (1880–1949) and Fritz J. Roethlisberger (1898–1974), who became associated as consultants in the later years of the studies. They were more heavily involved in assessing and popularizing the results than in actually conducting the studies.[65] Still, their various writings, sometimes in collaboration with Hawthorne executives, were instrumental in gaining attention for the Hawthorne study results.

Human Relations Movement

However flawed the studies, the Hawthorne research set the stage for intense interest in the social dimension of human behavior in organizations. The key to productivity, at that point, appeared to be showing greater concern for workers so that they would feel more satisfied with their jobs and be willing to produce more. There was emphasis on building more collaborative and cooperative relationships between supervisors and workers. One implication, though, was that managers now needed social skills in addition to technical skills. They also required a better understanding of how to make workers feel more satisfied with their jobs. While the Hawthorne studies provided some clues, managers needed more definitive help. Two major theorists, Abraham Maslow and Douglas McGregor, were among those who came forward with ideas that managers found helpful.

Abraham Maslow, a psychologist, contributed to the human relations movement with his theory of motivation. Maslow concluded that humans have various needs that go beyond the most basic ones of food and shelter. The discovery of the need for self-actualization, (developing one's full potential) has provided managers with new insights on how to motivate workers.

Abraham Maslow. Abraham Maslow (1908–1970) was born in Brooklyn, received his doctorate in psychology at the University of Wisconsin, and eventually became chairman of the psychology department at Brandeis University. Maslow developed a theory of motivation that was based on three assumptions about human nature. First, human beings have needs that are never completely satisfied. Second, human action is aimed at fulfilling the needs that are unsatisfied at a given point in time. Third, needs fit into a somewhat predictable hierarchy ranging from basic, lower-level needs at the bottom to higher-level needs at the top.[66] The hierarchy outlined by Maslow has five levels of needs: physiological (lowest), safety, belongingness, esteem, and self-actualization (highest). Self-actualization needs refer to the requirement to develop our capabilities and reach our full potential.[67]

We discuss this hierarchy more thoroughly in Chapter 13. For now, it is sufficient to note that Maslow's work was particularly important for two reasons. For one thing, it dramatized to managers that workers have needs beyond the basics of earning money to put a roof over their heads. This concept conflicted with the views of scientific management, which emphasized the importance of pay. Second, it provided managers with some specific insights about other needs workers might have. Maslow's hierarchy of needs theory is probably the management-related theory that is best known to managers even today.

Douglas MacGregor has influenced how managers deal with workers. His Theory X and Theory Y focused on employer assumptions about employees. Basically he held that their expectations led managers to behave in ways that engendered the employee behaviors that they expected.

Douglas McGregor. The movement toward having managers think of workers in a new light also was given impetus by the work of Douglas McGregor (1906–1964). McGregor was born in Detroit, Michigan, earned a doctorate at Harvard, and spent most of his career as a professor of industrial management at the Massachusetts Institute of Technology. A 6-year stint as president of Antioch College brought him to the realization that the notion of trying to have everyone like the boss (i.e., maintaining good human relations) offered inadequate guidance to managers.

To fill the void, he developed a well-known dichotomy, Theory X versus

Theory Y, dealing with the possible assumptions that managers make about workers. McGregor felt that such assumptions exert a heavy influence on how managers operate. Theory X managers (see Table 2-5) tend to assume that workers are lazy, need to be coerced, have little ambition, and are mainly focused on security needs. In contrast, Theory Y managers (see Table 2-5) assume that workers do not inherently dislike work, are capable of self-control, have the capacity to be creative and innovative, and generally have higher-level needs that are often unmet on the job.

McGregor believed that managers who hold Theory X assumptions are likely to treat workers accordingly by means of such measures as setting up elaborate controls and attempting to motivate strictly through economic incentives. As a result, workers are likely to respond in a manner that reinforces the manager's original assumptions.

In contrast, managers with Theory Y assumptions have the potential for integrating individual goals with organizational goals. McGregor believed this integration could occur when managers give workers latitude in performing their tasks, encourage creativity and innovation, minimize the use of controls, and attempt to make the work more interesting and satisfying in regard to higher-level needs. Under such conditions, workers are likely to exhibit greater commitment to organizational goals, because the goals coincide more closely with their own. McGregor understood that there could be some relatively immature and dependent workers who might need greater controls at first in order to develop the maturity needed for the Theory Y approach.[68]

Like Maslow's hierarchy, McGregor's Theory X and Theory Y approach helped managers develop a broader perspective on the likely nature of workers and new alternatives for interacting with them. The innovative ideas of both men had an intuitive appeal to managers searching for ways of operating more effectively; their theories became extremely popular and are still widely applied today.

Table 2-5 Theory X and Theory Y Managerial Assumptions

THEORY X ASSUMPTIONS
1. The average person dislikes work and will try to avoid it.
2. Most people need to be coerced, controlled, directed, and threatened with punishment to get them to work toward organizational goals.
3. The average person wants to be directed, shuns responsibility, has little ambition, and seeks security above all.

THEORY Y ASSUMPTIONS
1. Most people do not inherently dislike work; the physical and mental effort involved is as natural as play or rest.
2. People will exercise self-direction and self-control to reach goals to which they are committed; external control and threat of punishment are not the only means for ensuring effort toward goals.
3. Commitment to goals is a function of the rewards available, particularly rewards that satisfy esteem and self-actualization needs.
4. When conditions are favorable, the average person learns not only to accept but also to seek responsibility.
5. Many people have the capacity to exercise a high degree of creativity and innovation in solving organizational problems.
6. The intellectual potential of most individuals is only partially utilized in most organizations.

Behavioral Science Approach

Maslow, McGregor, and others who helped develop the human relations viewpoint tried to show that there was an alternative to the rational economic perspective of workers held by the classical school. They brought into focus a view of workers as social creatures, who had a variety of needs to be met on the job. Still, the picture that they drew was fairly general, somewhat simplistic, and often left managers uncertain about the specific actions that they should take and the implications of such actions. The need to take a more complex view of the work situation led to the rise of the behavioral science perspective.

The **behavioral science** approach emphasizes *scientific research* as the basis for developing theories about human behavior in organizations that can be used to develop practical guidelines for managers. The approach draws on findings from a variety of disciplines, including management, psychology, sociology, anthropology, and economics. Concepts are thoroughly tested in business organizations, and sometimes also in laboratory settings, before they are heralded as viable approaches for managers. The ultimate aim of the behavioral science approach is to develop theories that managers can use as guides in assessing various situations and deciding on appropriate actions. Since humans themselves are complex and their interactions with others are even more so, the quest for an understanding of organizations and their members is an ongoing activity of considerable challenge.

One example of an outcome of behavioral science research that is helpful to managers is the idea that individuals perform better with challenging, but attainable, goals than they do without goals. Of course, the goals must be specific and measurable ("I want to get an A in my management course this semester"), rather than vague ("I want to do well in my courses this semester"). This idea that goal setting leads to better performance grew out of extensive research by management researcher Edwin A. Locke and others.[69] We consider the motivational aspects of goal setting more extensively in Chapter 5.

Behavioral science An approach that emphasizes *scientific research* as the basis for developing theories about human behavior in organizations that can be used to develop practical guidelines for managers

QUANTITATIVE MANAGEMENT VIEWPOINT

The quantitative management viewpoint emerged as a major force during World War II. The sheer magnitude of the war effort caused the British and then the U.S. military services to turn to quantitative methods for help in deploying resources in the most effective way. For example, one set of quantitative studies by the U.S. Navy led to eliminating the "catch-as-catch-can" method that airplanes had used in searches for enemy vessels. Instead, quantitative analysis produced a pattern for such airplane searches that not only reduced the number of search planes needed for a given area but also increased the coverage. Aside from conserving scarce resources, the new search pattern in the South Atlantic led to the seizure of enemy ships carrying valuable cargo that significantly aided the Allied effort.[70] This and other important applications of quantitative methods gained the attention of business organizations, particularly as quantitative specialists found jobs in non-military-related organizations after the war.

The quantitative management viewpoint focuses on the use of mathematics, statistics, and information aids to support managerial decision making and organizational effectiveness.[71] Three main branches have evolved: management science, operations management, and management information systems.

Management Science

Management science An approach aimed at increasing decision effectiveness through the use of sophisticated mathematical models and statistical methods

Operations research Another name commonly used for management science

Management science is an approach aimed at increasing decision effectiveness through the use of sophisticated mathematical models and statistical methods. (*Caution:* This term is *not* used synonymously with the term "scientific management," discussed earlier.) Another name commonly used for management science is **operations research.** The increasing power of computers has greatly expanded the possibilities for using the mathematical and statistical tools of management science in organizations. Computers make it possible to quickly do the extensive calculations that are often required. For example, at Avon, the well-known maker of beauty, health-care, and fashion jewelry products, Group Vice President for Planning and Development Robert W. Pratt used statistical methods to analyze the implications of changing the company's common practice of offering heavy product discounts to generate larger orders. His results indicated that the ailing company could improve profits significantly with lesser discounts, even if it meant smaller average orders per salesperson.[72] In Chapter 9, we take a closer look at some operations research tools, such as linear programming; queuing, or waiting-line, models; and routing, or distribution, models.

Operations Management

Operations management The function or field of expertise that is primarily responsible for managing the production and delivery of an organization's products and services

Operations management is the function, or field of expertise, that is primarily responsible for managing the production and delivery of an organization's products and services.[73] It includes such areas as inventory management, work scheduling, production planning, facilities location and design, and quality assurance. Operations management specialists use such quantitatively oriented tools as forecasting, inventory analysis, materials requirements planning systems, networking models, statistical quality control methods, and project planning and control techniques. Operations management is often applied to manufacturing settings in which various aspects of product production need to be managed, including designing the production process, purchasing raw materials, scheduling employees to work, and storing and shipping the final products. For example, Seeq Technology, a Silicon Valley maker of microchips, relied heavily on operations management when a sudden market glut of its main 128K EPROM chip caused the price to plummet from $15 to $2 in a period of a few months. Since the per-chip costs at that point were $5, the company had to take such steps as rethinking its production process, improving inventory management, and lowering machine maintenance costs in order to stay in business while it completed proprietary new technology.[74] Operations management applies to delivering services as well. We consider some of these techniques in Chapter 9 and explore the area of operations management at considerable length in Chapter 19.

Management Information Systems

Management information systems The field of management that focuses on designing and implementing computer-based information systems for use by management

Management information systems is the name often given to the field of management that focuses on designing and implementing computer-based information systems for use by management. Such systems turn raw data into information that is useful to various levels of management. In many industries, computer-based information systems are becoming a powerful competitive weapon because organizations are able to handle large amounts of information in new and better ways. For example, the creation of *USA Today,* the national

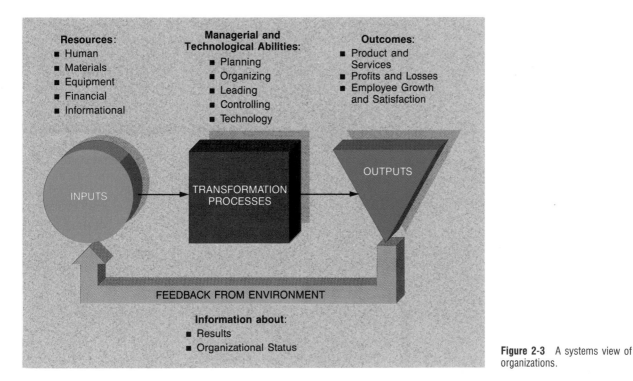

Figure 2-3   A systems view of organizations.

newspaper, was made feasible by advances in computer-based telecommunication systems. We discuss computer-based information systems more thoroughly in Chapter 20, on information systems for management.

CONTEMPORARY VIEWPOINTS

While the classical, behavioral, and quantitative approaches continue to make contributions to management, other viewpoints also have emerged. These are contemporary in the sense that they represent recent major innovations in thinking about management. Two of the most important contemporary viewpoints are the systems and contingency theories. In addition, at any given point in time, there are emerging views that influence the development of the management field even though they have not reached the status of enduring viewpoints.

Systems Theory

The **systems theory** approach is based on the notion that organizations can be visualized as systems.[75] A **system** is a set of interrelated parts that operate as a whole in pursuit of common goals. The systems approach as applied to organizations is based largely on work in biology and the physical sciences.[76] In this section, we consider major systems components, open versus closed systems, and the characteristics of open systems.

Major Components. According to the systems approach, an organizational system has four major components (see Figure 2-3). **Inputs** are the various human,

Systems theory An approach based on the notion that organizations can be visualized as systems

System A set of interrelated parts that operate as a whole in pursuit of common goals

Inputs The various human, material, financial, equipment, and informational resources required to produce goods and services

Transformation processes
The organization's managerial and technological abilities that are applied to convert inputs into outputs

Outputs The products, services, and other outcomes produced by the organization

Feedback Information about results and organizational status relative to the environment

material, financial, equipment, and informational resources required to produce goods and services. **Transformation processes** are the organization's managerial and technological abilities that are applied to convert inputs into outputs. **Outputs** are the products, services, and other outcomes produced by the organization. **Feedback** is information about results and organizational status relative to the environment.[77]

One advantage of the systems approach is that it can be used to analyze systems at different levels.[78] For example, systems expert J. Miller has outlined a typology of hierarchical levels of living systems, ranging from an individual human cell, including atoms and molecules, up to a supranational system consisting of two or more societies.[79] For the most part, managers consider the organism (individual), group, organization, and society levels, although the growing global emphasis has brought the supranational level into increasing play. Another advantage of the systems view is that it provides a framework for assessing how well the various parts of an organization interact to achieve a common purpose. Still another advantage is that it emphasizes that a change in one part of the system may affect other parts. In thinking about the interrelationships among parts in an organization, you might visualize that the parts are interconnected by rubber bands. A pull on one subpart may well affect the position of other subparts. Finally, another advantage of the systems approach is that it considers how an organization interacts with its environment—the factors outside the organization that can affect its operations. In order to consider the environment adequately, an organization needs to operate as an open system.

Open system A system that operates in continual interaction with its environment

Closed system A system that does little or no interacting with its environment and receives little feedback

Open versus Closed Systems. Systems can be open or closed. An **open system** is one that operates in continual interaction with its environment. The open system engages in such interactions in order to take in new inputs and learn about how its outputs are received by various important outside elements. In contrast, a **closed system** does little or no interacting with its environment and receives little feedback. From a practical point of view, all organizations are open systems to some extent, since it is virtually impossible for organizations to operate for a significant period of time without some interaction with the environment. Still, organizations can vary tremendously in the degree to which they operate along the open-closed continuum. If an organization operates too closely to the closed end, it might not find out about important environmental factors that can affect it until problems are major.[80] Consider what happened when the Ford Motor Company attempted to launch a new automobile called the Edsel (see the following Case in Point discussion).

CASE IN POINT: Ford's Edsel Flops

During the late 1940s, managers at Ford realized that they had a problem. According to studies, 1 out of 5 car buyers each year was moving from a low-priced to a medium-priced car. Furthermore, among the owners of General Motors (GM) cars, about 87 percent of those trading up stayed with GM, choosing either a Pontiac, Oldsmobile, or Buick. Almost 47 percent of the Plymouth owners moving to a medium-priced car picked a Dodge or DeSoto—which, like the Plymouth, were within the Chrysler family. Ford, however, had only one medium-priced car, the Mercury, and only 26 percent of the Ford owners trading up selected a Mercury. Accordingly, the company began a decade of elaborate

the **EDSEL**

"Mile by mile, your   satisfaction grows"

The Edsel car, introduced by the Ford Motor Company with great fanfare in 1957, was a dud. Production was closed out 2 years later. Ford managers had perceived the need for the mid-priced car but paid insufficient attention to negative feedback and events outside the company that combined to make sales sluggish.

planning and preparation aimed at creating a successful new midpriced car geared to young executives and professionals.

The endeavor proved to be quite a challenge. For one thing, finding the right name turned out to be difficult. After extensive marketing research, 10 names were sent to the executive committee; but the committee chose a name that was not on the list—Edsel, the name of Henry Ford's only son. The name "Edsel" was picked despite the fact that market research had shown that it engendered mixed customer reactions. Furthermore, Edsel's three sons in active management at the company (Henry II, Benson, and William Clay) were not particularly enthused about their father's name turning "on a million hubcaps."

Another major issue was styling. The search for a distinctive, yet discreet, style involved 800 stylists, all of whom finally agreed on a vertical front grille shaped like a horse collar. Other features of the car included a body that was 2 inches longer than the largest Oldsmobile, extensive use of push buttons (including the transmission), and an extremely powerful engine—all characteristics determined by market research in the early 1950s to appeal to midrange car buyers.

To build and distribute the car, Ford set up a separate division at headquarters and separate Edsel dealers, rather than selling the car through one of the established Ford, Mercury, Lincoln, and Continental divisions and chains of experienced dealerships. While it was felt that this would allow the division and dealers to concentrate totally on the Edsel, the system also added greatly to the overhead associated with the car. This meant that it was necessary to sell large numbers of cars in order to make a profit. The executives felt that they were being conservative in estimating that 200,000 cars (or about 650 per day) would be sold the first year.

Although advertising was launched on July 22, 1957, the actual style of the car was kept a closely guarded secret until introduction day on September 4, about a month before competitors would be introducing their 1958 models. Sales of the Edsel on the first day were somewhat promising, but they quickly dwindled. In 1958, only about 35,000 Edsels were sold, far short of the conservative target. The 1959 Edsel models were shorter, lighter, less powerful, and less costly, and they were handled through a merged Lincoln-Mercury-Edsel division. Sales that year were about double those of the first year. When the 1960 models failed to generate additional excitement after they were introduced in the fall of 1959, production of the Edsel was scrapped. Losses reached about $200 million.

What went wrong? First, there was a stock market collapse in August 1957 that had a severe negative impact on purchases of medium-sized cars that year. Second, Ford relied heavily on initial marketing data to plan the car and failed to alter the plans in the face of the growing impact of smaller, more fuel-efficient foreign cars, which were beginning to capture portions of the U.S. car market. Third, the first Edsels were prone to oil leaks, mysterious rattles, faulty brakes, and starting difficulties—problems that should have been detected before they reached the newspapers and national visibility. Because of these maladies the car was quickly labeled a "lemon" and became the source of jokes. Fourth, Ford relied on a network of inexperienced new dealers to woo prospective customers. Fifth, the car was introduced while other carmakers were offering discounts on their previous year's models, making the new Edsel seem expensive. Finally, top management ignored negative marketing information from potential customers when it selected the name "Edsel."

Perhaps the Edsel could have survived one of these difficulties, but in combination, the problems were lethal. The situation illustrates the need to pay close attention to things going on outside that can affect system functioning and success. ■

Characteristics of Open Systems. Organizations that operate closer to the open end of the system share certain characteristics that help them survive and prosper. Three major characteristics of open systems are negative entropy, differentiation, and synergy.[81]

Entropy refers to the tendency of systems to decay over time. In contrast, **negative entropy** is the ability of open systems to bring in new energy in the form of inputs and feedback from the environment in order to delay or arrest entropy, the decaying process. One reason the Edsel ran into trouble was that the company relied on market research conducted in the early 1950s and ignored the newer signs indicating that consumers were turning to more fuel-efficient foreign cars.

Differentiation is the tendency of open systems to become more complex. The increased complexity usually stems from the addition of specialized units to handle particularly troublesome or challenging parts of the environment. Specialized units or positions are also added in response to new organizational tasks or in an attempt to increase controls over existing tasks (e.g., a quality assurance unit may be created). Closed systems are less likely to recognize the need for differentiation or may differentiate in inappropriate ways. For example, Ford engaged in unwarranted differentiation when it ignored the risks inherent in the environment and set up a separate division, along with a network of new dealers, to sell the Edsel. These moves raised the overhead so high that the car had little chance of surviving unless it was a stupendous instant success.

The third major characteristic of open systems is **synergy,** the ability of the whole to equal more than the sum of its parts. This means that an organization ought to be able to achieve its goals more effectively and efficiently than would be possible if the parts operated separately. The parts of the organization were not operating in synchronization when the top management committee ignored the market research on the name of the car and chose the ill-fated "Edsel" tag.

According to the systems viewpoint, managers are likely to be more suc-

Negative entropy The ability of open systems to bring in new energy in the form of inputs and feedback from the environment in order to delay or arrest entropy

Differentiation The tendency of open systems to become more complex

Synergy The ability of the whole to equal more than the sum of its parts

cessful if they attempt to operate their units and organizations as open systems that are carefully attuned to the factors in the environment that could significantly affect them. We discuss these environmental factors more specifically in Chapter 3.

Contingency Theory

The classical theorists, like Taylor and Fayol, were attempting to identify "the one best way" for managers to operate in a variety of situations. If universal principles could be found, then becoming a good manager would essentially involve learning the principles and how to apply them. Unfortunately, things were not to be that simple. Researchers soon found that some classical principles, such as Fayol's unity of command (each person should report to only one boss), could sometimes be violated with positive results. Consequently, contingency theory began to develop. **Contingency theory** is a viewpoint that argues that appropriate managerial action depends on the particular parameters of the situation. Hence, rather than seeking *universal* principles that apply to every situation, contingency theory attempts to identify *contingency* principles that prescribe actions to take depending on the characteristics of the situation (see Figure 2-4).[82]

Contingency theory A viewpoint that argues that appropriate managerial action depends on the particular parameters of the situation

One of the major pioneering studies that helped establish the contingency viewpoint was conducted in the 1950s by a research team headed by Joan Woodward, an industrial sociologist at the South Essex College of Technology in Great Britain.[83] The study of 100 British firms, which differed in size and product lines, was aimed at determining whether the better-performing companies adhered more closely to classical principles, such as unity of command, than did companies with average and below-average performances. When the comparisons revealed no major differences in how classical principles were being used by the companies in the three performance categories, the researchers began to look elsewhere in their data for an explanation of the performance differences.

In analyzing their data, the researchers decided to explore the type of technology used by the companies. They divided the companies into three categories: unit or small-batch (products custom-made to customers' specifications), large-batch and mass-production (products produced in large amounts, mainly by assembly lines), and continuous-process (products produced in a noninter-

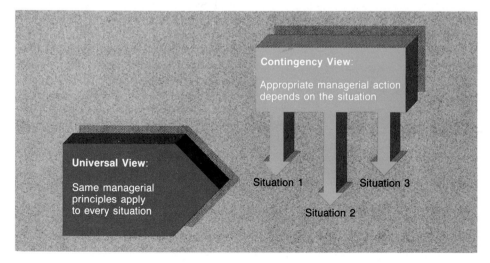

Figure 2-4 The contingency managerial viewpoint.

rupted flow, as in oil refining or chemical production). When they considered these differences in technology, patterns related to performance began to emerge. The researchers found that successful companies operated somewhat differently depending on their technology category. (For example, depending on their technology category, the companies had a different number of layers in their hierarchy and different numbers of subordinates reporting to managers at the various levels.) We discuss this study further in Chapter 11, but the point being stressed here is that the contingency approach argues that appropriate actions by managers often depend on (are contingent on) the situation.

To be fair, Fayol and most of the other classical theorists recognized that some judgment was needed in applying their various principles. Still, they emphasized universal principles and were rather vague about when the principles might not apply. In contrast, the contingency viewpoint attempts to nail down the specific situational factors that managers need to consider in deciding what management steps to take.[84]

Throughout this book you will encounter theories and concepts related to the contingency viewpoint—that is, areas in which applications of management ideas depend on situational factors. The contingency approach applies particularly well in such areas as environmental factors, strategy, organizational design, technology, and leadership.

Emerging Views

Given that management is a complex endeavor, innovative approaches are constantly needed to help advance the knowledge base. Sometimes the new approaches develop into major viewpoints when research and managerial practice show that they are effective. In other cases, new ideas whither after investigations indicate that they are not living up to their promise.

One recent perspective that has gained attention can best be termed the **Japanese management** approach, since it focuses on aspects of management in Japan that may be appropriate for adoption in the United States. The interest in Japanese management has arisen because of the recent admirable success of Japanese companies, particularly in manufacturing such items as televisions, videocassette recorders, and computer printers.

On the basis of his research of both American and Japanese management approaches, management expert William Ouchi has outlined Theory Z. **Theory Z** combines positive aspects of American and Japanese management into a modified approach aimed at increasing U.S. managerial effectiveness while remaining compatible with the norms and values of American society and culture (see

Japanese management An approach that focuses on aspects of management in Japan that may be appropriate for adoption in the United States

Theory Z A concept that combines positive aspects of American and Japanese management into a modified approach aimed at increasing U.S. managerial effectiveness while remaining compatible with the norms and values of American society and culture

Figure 2-5 Characteristics of Theory Z management. (Adapted from William G. Ouchi and Alfred M. Jaeger, ''Theory Z Organizations: Stability in the Midst of Mobility,'' *Academy of Management Review*, vol. 3, 1978, pp. 308, 311.)

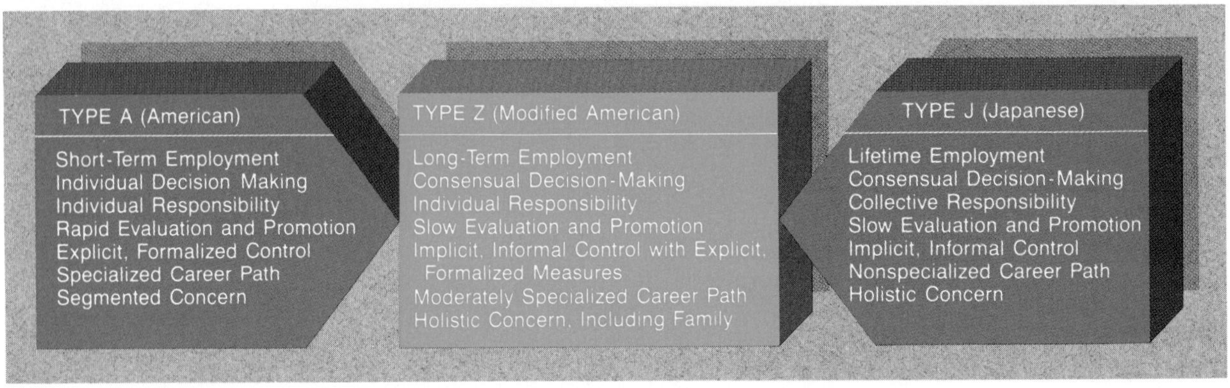

TYPE A (American)	TYPE Z (Modified American)	TYPE J (Japanese)
Short-Term Employment	Long-Term Employment	Lifetime Employment
Individual Decision Making	Consensual Decision-Making	Consensual Decision-Making
Individual Responsibility	Individual Responsibility	Collective Responsibility
Rapid Evaluation and Promotion	Slow Evaluation and Promotion	Slow Evaluation and Promotion
Explicit, Formalized Control	Implicit, Informal Control with Explicit, Formalized Measures	Implicit, Informal Control
Specialized Career Path	Moderately Specialized Career Path	Nonspecialized Career Path
Segmented Concern	Holistic Concern, Including Family	Holistic Concern

Figure 2-5). The Theory Z approach involves giving workers job security; including them in some decision making; emphasizing group responsibility; increasing quality; establishing gradual-advancement policies, more informal controls, and broader career paths; and showing greater concern for employees' work and nonwork well-being. A number of U.S. companies, such as General Motors, the Ford Motor Company, Hewlett-Packard, and Intel, have adopted aspects of Theory Z, particularly the concepts of involving workers in decision making, instituting more informal controls, and encouraging group members to accept responsibility for work in their unit.

PROMOTING INNOVATION: CONTRIBUTIONS OF THE MAJOR VIEWPOINTS

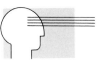

Each major viewpoint has added important ideas to current knowledge about management and, in the process, has changed the way that managers think about and behave in organizations. The main contributions of each major viewpoint are summarized in Table 2-6.

Table 2-6   Main Innovative Contributions of Major Viewpoints

Viewpoint	Innovative Contributions
Classical	Highlights the need for a scientific approach to management Points out that work methods often can be improved through study Identifies a number of important principles that are useful in running organizations efficiently Emphasizes the potential importance of pay as a motivator
Behavioral	Spotlights the managerial importance of such factors as communication, group dynamics, motivation, and leadership Articulates practical applications of behavioral studies Draws on the findings of a number of disciplines such as management, psychology, sociology, anthropology, and economics Highlights the importance of organization members as active human resources rather than passive tools
Quantitative	Provides quantitative aids to decision making Develops quantitative tools to assist in providing products and services Pioneers new computer-based information systems for management
Contemporary (systems and contingency)	Emphasizes that organizations can be visualized as systems of interrelated parts Points out the potential importance of the environment and feedback to organizational success Argues that there is no one best way to manage and identifies the circumstances or contingencies that influence which particular approach will be effective in a given situation

The classical viewpoint emphasizes the importance of scientific studies of management, offers basic administrative principles that continue to be useful today, prods managers to consider the effectiveness of work methods, and recognizes the potential importance of pay as a motivator. The behavioral viewpoint emphasizes the importance of organizational members as human resources; articulates practical implications of behavioral studies; points to the importance of such factors as communication, group dynamics, motivation, and leadership; and also provides more sophisticated means for studying behavior in organizations.

The quantitative viewpoint offers quantitative methods to help with making decisions, producing products and services, and handling information systems for management. The contemporary viewpoints, including the systems and contingency approaches, add a systems view of organizations, spotlight the importance of the environment and feedback, and help build contingency theories that managers can use to adapt to changing situations.

The concepts within each viewpoint have served as catalysts in spawning additional new ideas that not only enhanced the particular viewpoint but also led to the development of other innovative approaches to management. For example, the Hawthorne studies began in the context of scientific management, but they helped give birth to the behavioral approach. Difficulties in universally applying the contributions of the classical and behavioral approaches led to the contingency view. Although we will be highlighting methods of managing innovations throughout this book, it is useful to recognize that the field of management is itself the result of innovative processes involving many pioneers who championed ground-breaking ideas. These ideas and the viewpoints they developed are reflected in various ways in the chapters that follow. For example, the systems approach helped highlight the influence of the external environment on organizations, a topic we explore in the next chapter.

CHAPTER SUMMARY

Although management practices can be traced back to ancient times, much of the impetus for developing management theories and principles grew out of the industrial revolution and the need for better ways to run the resulting factory systems. Preclassical contributors such as Robert Owen, Charles Babbage, and Henry P. Towne provided some initial ideas that eventually led to the identification of management as an important field of inquiry. From this base, four major management viewpoints have developed: classical, behavioral, quantitative, and contemporary.

The classical viewpoint, which emphasizes finding ways to manage work and organizations more efficiently, includes three different approaches. The scientific management approach, represented by the work of Frederick Winslow Taylor, Frank and Lillian Gilbreth, and Henry Gantt, emphasizes the scientific study of work methods in order to improve worker efficiency. The bureaucratic approach, pioneered by Max Weber, focuses on the need for organizations to operate in a rational manner rather than relying on the arbitrary whims of owners and managers. The administrative

management approach, supported by Henri Fayol and Chester Barnard, explores principles that can be used by managers to coordinate the internal activities of organizations.

The behavioral viewpoint is a major management perspective that seeks to understand the various factors that affect human behavior in organizations. As the notion of management as a science was being popularized by representatives of the classical view, early behaviorists such as Hugo Münsterberg and Mary Parker Follett began offering ideas that fit more within the behavioral framework. It was the Hawthorne studies, though, that dramatically demonstrated that workers were more than mere tools of production. Although the studies had major flaws, they produced insights that led to the establishment of the human relations movement, with its emphasis on concern for the worker. Abraham Maslow's hierarchy of needs theory and Douglas McGregor's Theory X and Theory Y provided some guidance for managers but were still fairly general. The behavioral science approach, with its emphasis on scientific research, emerged to build more specific theories about behavior in organizations that can be used to provide practical guidelines for managers.

The quantitative viewpoint, with its focus on the use of mathematics, statistics, and information aids to support managerial decision making and effectiveness, has three main branches. Operations research is an approach aimed at increasing decision effectiveness through the use of sophisticated mathematical models and statistical methods. Operations management is the field of expertise that is primarily responsible for managing the production and delivery of an organization's products and services. Management information systems is the name often given to the field of management that focuses on designing and implementing computer-based information systems for use by management.

The contemporary viewpoints represent recent major innovations in thinking about management and include the systems and contingency theories, as well as emerging views. The systems theory approach is based on the notion that organizations can be visualized as systems, including inputs, transformation processes, outputs, and feedback. Contingency theory argues that appropriate managerial action depends on the particular parameters of a given situation. Emerging viewpoints include new promising approaches that may develop into major viewpoints if research supports their relevance. One important emerging view is Japanese management, represented by Theory Z, a theory that combines the positive aspects of American and Japanese management into a modified approach appropriate to business in the United States.

All the major viewpoints contribute significantly to innovation in the field of management. Other viewpoints will likely develop as the field progresses.

MANAGERIAL TERMINOLOGY

acceptance theory of
  authority (53)
administrative
  management (51)
behavioral science (61)
behavioral viewpoint (53)
bureaucratic management
  (49)
classical viewpoint (45)

closed system (64)
contingency theory (67)
differentiation (66)
feedback (64)
Hawthorne effect (57)
Hawthorne studies (55)
inputs (63)
Japanese management
  (68)

management information
  systems (62)
management science (62)
negative entropy (66)
open system (64)
operations management
  (62)
operations research (62)
outputs (64)

scientific management
  (45)
soldiering (45)
synergy (66)
system (63)
systems theory (63)
Theory Z (68)
transformation processes
  (64)

QUESTIONS FOR DISCUSSION AND REVIEW

1. Trace two early innovative management practices. Explain how these practices illustrate the difference between practicing management and developing theories about management.

2. Explain how the preclassical contributors helped set the stage for the development of management as a science. Identify a time when you have used the guidelines in *Robert's Rules of Order* or seen them used. Why have the rules been so popular over a considerable period of time?

3. Contrast the three major approaches within the classical viewpoint: scientific management, bureaucratic management, and administrative management. Give some examples of how these approaches are reflected in an organization with which you are familiar.

4. Review the scientific management principles advocated by Frederick Taylor. How effective do you think these principles would be in eliminating sol-

diering? What might be some disadvantages of his approach? What did Frank and Lillian Gilbreth add to Taylor's approach?

5. Explain the development of the behavioral viewpoint. How is it possible that a flawed set of studies—the Hawthorne studies—helped bring about the behavioral viewpoint of management?

6. Differentiate among the three major approaches within the quantitative management viewpoint. How have computers aided the development of this viewpoint?

7. Explain the major ideas underlying the systems viewpoint. Use the systems viewpoint to analyze your college or university. To what extent would you consider it to be an open system? Give reasons for your view.

8. Describe the reasoning behind the contingency viewpoint. Why did it emerge? How does the work that Joan Woodward and her research group did

on technology illustrate the contingency theory concept?

9. Explain the Theory Z approach to management. Under which system would you prefer to work: American (Type A), Japanese (Type J), or modified American (Type Z)? Why? Which approach do you think would work best in the following work environments: research, production, mining, agriculture, service?

10. Trace how current management knowledge is the result of innovative processes involving many management pioneers. What can we learn about the process of innovation from studying these pioneering ideas in management?

DISCUSSION QUESTIONS FOR CHAPTER OPENING CASE

1. How did scientific management help Henry Ford build the Ford Motor Company?

2. Use the systems view to analyze the reasons for the failure of Ford's first two companies and the success of his third attempt with the Ford Motor Company.

3. If the Hawthorne studies had already been conducted and the human relations movement had been emerging at that time, how might they have influenced Henry Ford's approach?

MANAGEMENT EXERCISE: PROBLEMS AT THE ICE CREAM PLANT

You are the manager of a plant that produces a special type of extra creamy ice cream. Sales have been increasing every quarter for the past 4 years, until last quarter. During the last quarter sales slipped 17 percent, production was about 15 percent short of projections, absenteeism was about 20 percent higher than the previous quarter, and tardiness increased steadily. You believe that the problems are probably management-related, but you are not sure about the causes or the steps you should take to correct them. You decide to call in a consultant to help you determine what to do next. The consultant tells you that she wholeheartedly supports scientific management and usually looks at problems from that point of view. She mentions that there are other consultants in the area who tend to take other views. In order to get the most complete idea of what should be done at your plant, you also call in five other consultants, each of whom supports one of the following additional approaches: administrative management, bureaucracy, human relations, quantitative management, and systems theory.

Form a triad (group of three) with two of your classmates. Have each member of the triad play the role of a consultant for two (one at a time) of the six management approaches mentioned in the paragraph above. Be sure that each of the six approaches is assigned. In the role of a consultant, the triad member will analyze the likely problems at the ice cream plant and offer solutions from the point of view of the particular management approach that the member is representing. Each triad member should play the role of a consultant for one of the approaches that he or she has been assigned and then repeat the process for his or her second consultant role. The other two members of the triad will critique the explanations presented by their classmates.

FORD MOTOR CHARGES AHEAD AND INTO GLOBALIZATION

Amidst the auto industry turn-down of the early 1980s, Henry Ford's motor company was hemor-rhaging. Henry Ford II had just retired from his position as chairman of the company that his grandfather had built. Between 1979 and 1982, the company lost $3 billion. The company was plagued by a reputation for producing cars designed for yesterday's consumers, and—worse—quality was poor. Wall Street analysts predicted that the car company was forever doomed to be an "also-ran" in world car competition.

Faced with a dire situation, the new leaders, Philip Caldwell as chairman and Donald Petersen as president, began a corporate soul-searching that covered everything from how cars were designed and produced to whether so many finance staffers were needed at headquarters. By the time that Petersen took over as chairman and CEO in 1985, massive changes were under way.

Cutting costs and raising quality were clear priorities. By the mid-1980s, the company had reduced its hourly work force from 190,000 to 110,000, cut back on white-collar workers by 30 percent, and shut down 8 U.S. plants. The remaining 81 plants were revamped and upgraded technologically to make the work as efficient as possible. Computerized robots and upgraded inventory control were part of the massive changes. At the same time, Ford tied its efficiency and cost-cutting efforts to its quality quest. It has adopted the Japanese manage-ment view that higher quality ulti-mately means lower costs. According to one manufacturing manager, "If you don't make bad parts, you won't have bad parts—and if you do, you have to scrap them. This is how cost-conscious plant managers become quality conscious." Such changes reduced costs by $5 billion by the mid-1980s, with another $5 billion in savings expected by the early 1990s.

Then there was the issue of the style of Ford cars, which even Caldwell had characterized as looking like "cold, alligator-shoe cars." To change the approach to design, Petersen, who was president at the time, gave Ford's design head for North America the now-famous order to "design the kind of cars *you* would like to drive." The resulting Taurus and Sable, both introduced in December 1985, have been runaway successes. In fact, customer orders for the cars had topped 100,000 by the time the cars reached the showrooms. The drastically redesigned Lincoln Continental, introduced in December 1988 as the first big U.S. luxury car with soft lines, has been a sellout. The 1989 Thunderbird, redesigned with a new aerodynamic look, made the July cover of *Car and Driver* and won the coveted *Motor Trend* magazine's "Car of the Year" designation. The Thunderbird also was introduced in December, a tradition since the Taurus and Sable debut. Petersen recently recalled, "We had made so many mistakes in the past by following this or that trend, this or that competitor. Finally, we realized that we should not be driven by other people's choices, but by our customers. We've been going our own way ever since."

These successes have taxed the capacity of Ford plants in their attempt to keep up with the demand

As part of its attempt to resuscitate an outmoded company, Ford management took some of its operations overseas, aiming for the global market. This plant in Valencia, Spain, is one of 22 Ford plants in Europe.

and have caused customers to wait months for their cars, but Petersen has resisted building new plants. Instead, some 18 to 20 percent of Ford's cars are built on overtime, a situation that has made it more difficult to keep up the massive improvements aimed at equaling the quality of Japanese cars. Petersen was reluctant to add capacity because he believes that various automotive companies are expanding at a rate that will cause a 9-million-unit overcapacity worldwide by the early 1990s. As he sees it, for decades Ford was an erratic company with a banner year one year and a disaster the next. He wants to keep the company on a more even keel so that it is better able to deal with the future. "It's a new world with an overtone of uncertainty," he says.

Some of the less visible changes at Ford relate to the new approach to internal management. Once considered to have the most

LIZ CLAIBORNE'S EMPIRE GROWS

I n the early 1970s when she was chief designer of Youth Guild, the junior-dress division of Jonathan Logan, Inc., Liz Claiborne noted an important sociocultural trend, the increasing numbers of professional women in the work force. But when she tried to persuade her bosses to get out of selling junior dresses and into serving the needs of the growing class of highly paid career women, she got nowhere. Frustrated, Liz and her husband, textile industry executive Arthur Ortenberg, decided to risk starting their own company. They put up their life savings of about $50,000 and collected more than $200,000 from family and friends to start Liz Claiborne, Inc., in January 1976. By September, the company was solidly in the black, no small feat in the fiercely competitive women's apparel market. Five years later, the company went public; by 1986, it had moved onto *Fortune* magazine's list of the 500 largest industrial companies in the United States, one of the youngest companies to do so.

The company, with Claiborne as president until 1989, has been consumer-oriented from the start. Adopting the commandment "Satisfy Thy Consumer," Claiborne was one of the first designers to offer executive and professional women alternatives to the navy blue suit and bow tie. Her colorful, comfortable clothes are up to date but not faddish or avant-garde. With clothing priced just above the moderate range, she has successfully bucked the conventional belief that professional and executive women would wear only expensive designer garments. Further, she has been a pacesetter in producing clothes to fit real people, not the ultrathin models often featured in fashion shows. Claiborne once described the company's clothing designs as "businesslike, but not too pinstripe, more casual, more imaginative, less uptight."

Liz Claiborne, Inc., offers a constant flow of new merchandise, providing for six seasons instead of the usual four. This major extra effort has made it possible for the customer to find a summer outfit in July and a winter one in January. Other labels force the consumer to make purchases months ahead of the time when the clothing is actually to be worn.

Using the latest in computer technology, the company also has developed a system called Systematic Updated Retail Feedback (SURF) that helps it shorten the feedback loop on consumer trends. The system analyzes weekly information on actual customer purchases, provided by a cross section of retail stores. Traditionally, apparel makers have relied on retail orders from buyers to track consumer trends, but this information can be misleading because what a buyer orders may not be what customers ultimately purchase.

While serving the consumer is the first commandment of the company, a close second is "Support Thy Retailer." Upholding this commandment was originally the responsibility of the cochairmen: Ortenberg, who headed operations until 1989, and his college roommate, Jerome Chazen, who took charge of marketing. Ortenberg says that he particularly enjoyed the logistical end of the business, equating getting the proper garments to the right place at the right time to "three-dimensional chess." One result is that the company enjoys a reputation among retailers as an unusually dependable, well-run operation.

As part of the focus on supporting retailers, Liz Claiborne, Inc., has "travelers," or "fashion specialists," who spend their time visiting stores, talking with customers, helping with displays, and giving training programs to salespeople. The travelers have been instrumental in encouraging retail stores to set up special areas for displaying and selling Claiborne garments. Results have been im-

Clothing designer Liz Claiborne paid attention to an important trend in the business environment—the increase in professional women—and positioned her fledgling company in 1976 to take advantage of the market with clothes that were "businesslike, but not too pinstripe." Claiborne's consumer-oriented approach landed her company in the Fortune 500 within ten years.

pressive. Annual sales per square foot of floor space are typically double the average generated by other women's apparel makers.

In another departure from industry custom, the company has no sales force. Instead, buyers must come to showrooms in New York to see merchandise. This policy not only has cut costs but has been advantageous in other ways as well. The company can display its merchandise much more effectively in its own showrooms. Furthermore, the showroom format has attracted visits by high-level retailing executives, who often come to New York. Their visits to the showrooms have enabled the company to build important linkages beyond those possible with traveling salespeople.

Liz Claiborne, Inc., has made some missteps. In the spring of 1987, for example, the company followed the industry in producing thigh-high miniskirts and midriff-baring tops that were rejected by usually loyal customers. It also had difficulty, at first, with its new menswear line when the initial offerings were too stylized and carefully matched for male tastes, but it has since revamped the line. Moreover, the company has been affected somewhat by the general retailing slump in the late 1980s. According to one industry analyst, "Liz Claiborne is a good company, but there's very little it could do with the industry environment so bad."

In describing the corporate culture of Liz Claiborne, Inc., Ortenberg uses a sports analogy. "We turn to the great New York Knicks team of 1969–79," he says. "No one was a superstar, but it was probably one of the most glorious teams that ever existed. When someone asked Walt Frazier what made the team so great, he thought for a while and said, 'Well, we always passed the ball to the open person.' That's what we try to do here." Everyone at Liz Claiborne, Inc., operates on a first-name basis, including "Liz" and "Art." The company directory lists the more than 3000 employees alphabetically by first name. According to one former corporate marketing director, "It's run like a Japanese company. People feel part of it." Recently, the company took the unusual move of giving one of the most promising designers, Dana Buchman, her own label (for a line of more expensive sportswear).

Now that the company controls about one-third of the market for women's better sportswear, growth will be more difficult. The company has been branching into other areas, such as a new Liz Claiborne fragrance that has been a major success, a line of clothing for women who wear size 14 and up, and a chain of retail stores called First Issue that sell less expensive sportswear. In 1989, Claiborne and Ortenberg retired from day-to-day participation in the company, although they remain active participants on the board of directors. They say that they have a strong management group in place to preside over the future of the company.[1]

A major factor in the success of Liz Claiborne, Inc., was Claiborne's recognition of an important shift in the educational and working patterns of women. This shift portended changing clothing needs among working women, a change that Claiborne's company squarely positioned itself to meet. As the Liz Claiborne situation illustrates, an organization's effectiveness is influenced by its **external environment,** the major forces outside the organization that have the potential of significantly impacting on the likely success of products or services. At the same time, Liz Claiborne might not have achieved its spectacular success without a compatible **internal environment,** the general conditions that exist within an organization. Although the internal environment can encompass such factors as organization members, the nature of their interactions, and the physical setting within which they operate, the notion of organizational culture often is used as a summary description of the general conditions, or internal environ-

External environment The major forces outside the organization that have the potential of significantly impacting on the likely success of products or services

Internal environment The general conditions that exist within an organization

Organizational culture A
system of shared values,
assumptions, beliefs, and
norms that unite the
members of an organization

ment, of an organization. Accordingly, we use the organizational culture concept to describe the general nature of an organization's internal environment. **Organizational culture** is a system of shared values, assumptions, beliefs, and norms that unite the members of an organization.[2] For example, emphasizing teamwork and nurturing the talents of others helped Liz Claiborne, Inc., remain innovative as it grew.

In this chapter, we examine the external environment of organizations, considering both the general environment, or mega-environment, within which an organization functions and the more specific, immediate elements that make up an organization's task environment. We also explore differing views about the relationship between an organization and its environment and consider important environmental characteristics. Next, we investigate the possibilities for managing environmental elements. Finally, we examine the internal environment through the use of the organizational culture concept and consider the prospects for promoting innovation through developing an entrepreneurial culture.

TYPES OF EXTERNAL ENVIRONMENTS

While Liz Claiborne, Inc., was successful in catching the wave of a new trend, the Warren Featherbone Company had the opposite problem—recognizing the ebbing of a lucrative market. The Warren Featherbone Company built a thriving business about 100 years ago around its patented product, the featherbone. Made of finely split turkey quills combined to form a cord, the product was used to stiffen corsets, collars, bustles, and gowns. Although the company made it through the Great Depression in fairly good shape, technological change in the form of plastic was emerging. The company saw the trend and, in 1938, started making plastic baby pants to go over diapers, just as the demand for featherbone was sinking badly. The company also made a rocky expansion into baby clothing. Fortunately, its baby clothing developed into a solid business in the mid-1960s, just about the time that the emergence of the disposable diaper destroyed much of the demand for the plastic pants.[3] As the history of the Warren Featherbone Company makes clear, organizations can be drastically affected by the environment within which they operate.

Systems theory helps highlight the importance of the environment to organizations. According to the systems view, an organization is likely to be more successful if it operates as an open system that continually interacts with and receives feedback from its external environment (see Chapter 2). The implication is that organizations need to have managers who expend considerable effort understanding the nature of the external environment that their organizations face. The external environment of an organization can be divided into two major segments: the general environment, or mega-environment, and the task environment. These two segments of the environment are depicted in Figure 3-1. (The internal environment, as reflected in the notion of organizational culture, also is shown. Organizational culture will be discussed later in this chapter.)

Mega-Environment

Mega-environment The
broad conditions and trends
in the societies within which
an organization operates

The **mega-environment,** or general environment, is the segment of the external environment that reflects the broad conditions and trends in the societies within which an organization operates. The mega-environment consists of five major

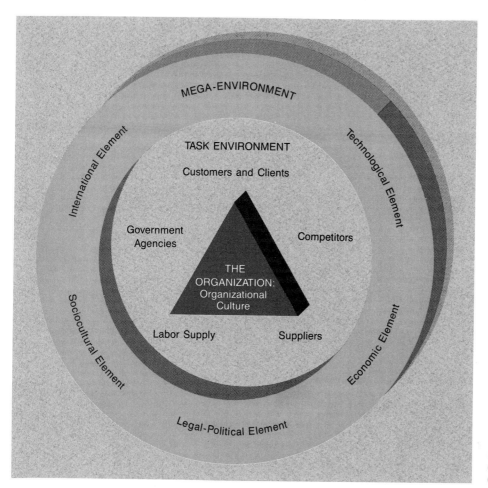

Figure 3-1 The internal and external environments of the organization.

elements: technological, economic, legal-political, sociocultural, and international (see Figure 3-1).[4] Because these elements reflect major trends and conditions existing outside the organization, they tend to be beyond the ability of a single organization to affect or alter directly, at least in the short run. The mega-environment of the Xerox Corporation is shown in Figure 3-2.

Technological Element. The **technological element** is the part of the mega-environment that reflects the current state of knowledge regarding the production of products and services. Although specific organizations may have technical knowledge and patents that give them a competitive edge for some period of time, most organizations can be greatly affected, either positively or negatively, by technological progress.

 Research in the minicomputer, cement, and airline industries indicates that technology tends to evolve through periods of incremental change punctuated by technological breakthroughs that either enhance or destroy the competence of firms in an industry.[5] For example, Nobel prize–winning Bell Laboratory physicists pioneered the computer age with the invention of the transistor in 1947. Subsequent developments with microchips have affected businesses and their products in a wide range of industries, from automobile and small-appliance manufacturing to home building. Recent breakthroughs in the ability to understand the structures of atoms and genes are raising the prospect of greatly

Technological element The current state of knowledge regarding the production of products and services

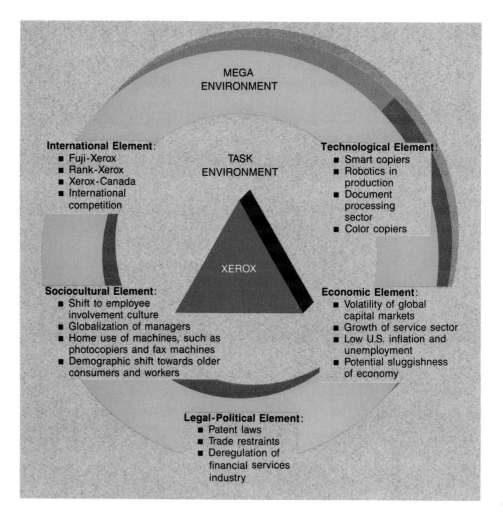

International Element:
- Fuji-Xerox
- Rank-Xerox
- Xerox-Canada
- International competition

Technological Element:
- Smart copiers
- Robotics in production
- Document processing sector
- Color copiers

Sociocultural Element:
- Shift to employee involvement culture
- Globalization of managers
- Home use of machines, such as photocopiers and fax machines
- Demographic shift towards older consumers and workers

Economic Element:
- Volatility of global capital markets
- Growth of service sector
- Low U.S. inflation and unemployment
- Potential sluggishness of economy

Legal-Political Element:
- Patent laws
- Trade restraints
- Deregulation of financial services industry

MEGA ENVIRONMENT

TASK ENVIRONMENT

XEROX

Figure 3-2 Elements of the mega-environment at the Xerox Corporation.

accelerated changes in products and services. For example, scientists are at least talking about the possibility of such new products as aircraft made of materials that will allow speeds of more than 1000 miles per hour, genetically engineered plants that will make their own fertilizer, and "designer" catalysts created through molecular engineering that will cheaply convert natural gas into gasoline.[6]

After holding technological supremacy for several decades, U.S. companies have increasingly found that technological competition is global. Research and development spending as a percent of gross national product in countries such as Japan, West Germany, and the Soviet Union has been steadily rising, while such spending in the United States is on the rise again after a slump during the 1970s.[7] In order to remain competitive, organizations must, at a minimum, stay abreast of current technological developments that may affect their ability to offer desirable products and services. For example, some observers of the U.S. steel industry argue that low expenditures for R&D are threatening to put American companies technologically far behind their Japanese and European rivals.[8] Key published sources that provide information regarding technological and other environmental elements are identified in Table 3-1.

Table 3-1   Key Sources of External Information

Source	Brief Description
Statistical Abstract of the United States (published annually)	Provides social, demographic, geographic, political, and economic information about the United States.
United States Industrial Outlook (published annually)	Provides industry forecasts, profiles, data, trends, and projections. Industries are classified by type of business and by SIC Code.
Survey of Business (published quarterly)	Provides information concerning the economic outlook of specific industries. Many graphs are given.
Business Conditions Digest (published monthly)	Provides charts and graphs of past, present, and forecasted unemployment rates, productivity and income data, consumption patterns, and prices of products and services.
Survey of Manufacturers (published annually)	Provides manufacturing data for many industries, including the value of inventories, plant and equipment expenditures, book values of assets, rental payments, etc.
Predicasts (published quarterly)	A guide to corporate organization developments, including liquidations, name changes, new companies, joint ventures, bankruptcies, and divestitures.
Survey of Buying Power (published annually)	Provides information on households, population shifts, disposable income, and retail sales by geographic area.
Federal Reserve Bulletin (published monthly)	Includes congressional reports, staff studies, announcements, legal developments in the monetary and banking systems.
Forbes (published weekly)	A magazine that focuses on current business issues and topics.
Business Week (published weekly)	A magazine that contains current business news, including corporate strategy articles.
Fortune (published biweekly)	A popular magazine that reports news and events in the business world.
Federal Register (published daily)	Gives all public regulations and legal notices issued by federal agencies.
Trade journals	Provide news, forecasts, changes, and developments in particular industries. Examples are *Hardware Ace* and *The Underwriter*.
Securities and Exchange Commission's *10K Reports* (published annually)	Gives detailed descriptive and financial information on a specific company.
Annual reports (published annually)	Published by corporations for shareholders and interested parties. Reveal company plans, organization, and financial condition.

(continued)

Source	Brief Description
Moody's Industrial Manual (published annually)	Provides information on firms' capital structure, history, financial condition, and bond ratings.
The Dun & Bradstreet Corporation, Three Century Drive, Parsippany, N.J. 07054	Publishes many reference indexes, including *Market Profile Analysis, Dun's Business Rankings, The Billion Dollar Directory, Who Owns Whom,* and *Principal International Business.*
United States Census of Manufacturers (published annually)	Presents manufacturing data by state and area within states. Includes data on employment, payroll, number of workers, hours, wages, capital expenditures, and the like.
Value Line (published weekly)	Provides investment information on companies and industries. Evaluates companies and industries on financial criteria.
Guide to Consumer Markets (published annually)	Provides detailed consumer information on the distribution and prices of goods and services, labor force changes, and other key areas.
Chambers of commerce	Provide valuable local business information such as traffic patterns, location of particular businesses, household income levels, etc.
Facts on File (published weekly)	Weekly summaries of world business news are provided.

Source: Reprinted from Fred R. David, *Concepts of Strategic Management, 2d ed.,* Merrill, Columbus, Ohio, 1989, pp. 144–145.

Economic element The systems of producing, distributing, and consuming wealth

Capitalist economy An economy in which economic activity is governed by market forces and the means of production are privately owned by individuals

Socialist economy An economy in which the means of production are owned by the state and economic activity is coordinated by plan

Economic Element. The **economic element** is the part of the mega-environment that encompasses the systems of producing, distributing, and consuming wealth. Companies that are based in the United States function primarily within a capitalist economy, although they may do business with and/or operate in countries that have socialist economies. In a **capitalist economy,** economic activity is governed by market forces and the means of production are privately owned by individuals, either directly or through corporations. In a **socialist economy,** the means of production are owned by the state and economic activity is coordinated by plan.

In practice, countries tend to have hybrid economies. Although the United States operates close to the capitalist end of the continuum, there is considerable government regulation in such areas as utilities and communications. Conversely, in the Soviet Union, which operates close to the socialist end of the continuum, there are aspects of capitalism at work. For example, recent reforms include a law encouraging private businesses, such as family-run shops, cafés, and even gypsy taxis, as long as they register to be taxed by the government.[9] The economies of most countries, such as Sweden, France, and Yugoslavia, fall somewhere between the prevailing types in the United States and the Soviet Union. Third world countries (mainly poorer countries of the world with very low per capita income, little industry, and high birthrates) also provide many variations in patterns as they struggle to decide whether to emulate the capitalist or socialist economic model. The result is that organizations that do business in a variety of different countries can be confronted with quite different sets of economic ground rules within which they must operate.

Within economic systems, organizations are influenced by a variety of economic factors over which they have little independent control, such as inflation and interest rates. For example, the inflation that ran rampant in the United States during the 1970s and early 1980s had a major impact on organizational costs, but it also allowed managers to raise prices to cover mistakes such as producing excess inventory. High interest rates can drive up organizational costs, particularly for expansion, and reduce the amount of disposable income available to consumers. High interest rates during the early 1980s made it particularly difficult for companies to make capital investments. Since then, the recessions of 1980 and 1982, coupled with disinflation and mounting competition, have launched an era in which managers are under heavy pressure both to control and to cut costs in order to be competitive.

Legal-Political Element. The **legal-political element** is the part of the mega-environment that includes the legal and governmental systems within which an organization must function. Trends in the areas of legislation, court decisions, politics, and government regulation are particularly important aspects of the legal-political environment.

Legal-political element The legal and governmental systems within which an organization must function

For example, organizations must operate within the general legal framework of the countries in which they do business. They also are governed by a variety of laws that specifically address the manner in which they function. Such laws in the United States include the Clean Air and Clean Water acts, which are aimed at controlling pollution; the Occupational Safety and Health Act, which specifies safety regulations; and the Employee Retirement Income Security Act, which regulates organizational pension funds.

At the same time, organizations are subject to an increasing number of lawsuits filed in courts by a growing variety of interest groups, ranging from employees to clients. The increase has been spurred in part by the large sums of money awarded by juries, and possibly by the recent increase in the number of lawyers. Product liability suits, in particular, have been on the rise, forcing companies like the Manville Corporation and the A. H. Robins Company into the bankruptcy courts.[10] There also have been a growing number of suits against corporate directors from disgruntled shareholders, sending directors and officers scurrying for insurance coverage at rates that have skyrocketed. The number of cases against directors has been rising, particularly since the Delaware Supreme Court found that the directors of the Trans Union Corporation had accepted a takeover bid without checking other alternatives. The court found the directors personally liable, forcing them to pay $13.5 million of the $23.5 million settlement (insurance covered only $10 million).[11] Employees and former employees are increasingly likely to sue employers for reasons ranging from age discrimination to defamation of character.[12] Legal issues are causing companies to review procedures in areas likely to be involved in litigation, as well as to seek increased legal advice.

Various political processes also influence the legal system. The political party of the incumbent President, as well as the relative numbers of Democrats and Republicans in the Senate and House of Representatives, often have a bearing on the types of laws passed. Political issues also may influence the extent of government regulation of various laws. For instance, recent Wall Street scandals have increased political pressure on the Securities and Exchange Commission (SEC) to step up computerized tracking and criminal prosecutions of illegal stock trading by "insiders." Insider trading involves stock transactions by individuals, such as company officers or investment bankers for a company, who are privy to company information that is likely to affect stock prices when it becomes public.

Sociocultural element The attitudes, values, norms, beliefs, behaviors, and associated demographic trends that are characteristic of a given geographic area

Sociocultural Element. The **sociocultural element** is the element of the mega-environment that includes the attitudes, values, norms, beliefs, behaviors, and associated demographic trends that are characteristic of a given geographic area. Sociocultural variables often are discussed in comparisons of different countries, such as the United States and Japan or Great Britain and Germany.[13] Multinational companies face the challenge of understanding various sociocultural differences among countries that may influence competitive success. In recognition of such differences, McDonald's requires that its foreign franchisees stick closely to operating procedures, but it allows room for different marketing methods and even a few menu modifications. For example, in Brazil, McDonald's sells a soft drink made from an Amazonian berry, and in Malaysia the menu features milk shakes flavored with durian, a foul-smelling southeast Asian fruit considered locally to be an aphrodisiac.[14]

Because sociocultural aspects are subject to change, it is important for managers to monitor trends that might offer new opportunities or pose significant threats. Among the current changes affecting Americans are the delay of marriage until a later age, the emergence of the single head of household as a growing consumer element, the aging of the large baby-boomer group, the growing shortage of workers in the 18- to 24-year-old group, and the increasing influence of minorities in business, politics, and community life.[15]

As we saw with Liz Claiborne, Inc., sociocultural trends can result in important shifts in the demands for certain types of products. Because of recent concerns for fitness, Americans are eating less bacon and fewer eggs, consuming more chicken and less pork, smoking fewer cigarettes, and increasingly passing up alcoholic beverages in favor of bottled water and diet soft drinks. Yet the trends are not always consistent. Although typically high in cholesterol, cheese is selling briskly, and candy sales are booming despite concerns about calories.[16] Such shifting trends point out the need for organizations to carefully monitor sociocultural factors in areas related to their products and services, including regional differences within a given country.

International element The developments in countries outside an organization's home country that have the potential of impacting on the organization

International Element. The **international element** is the element of the mega-environment that includes the developments in countries outside an organization's home country that have the potential of impacting on the organization. Although we have discussed international aspects in conjunction with the other elements of the mega-environment, we single out the international element as a separate aspect of the mega-environment because of its growing importance. The international element can have a major impact on organizations.

For one thing, international developments can greatly affect the ability of an organization to conduct business abroad. For example, fluctuations of the dollar against foreign currencies influence the ability of an organization to compete in international markets. When the price of the dollar is high against foreign currencies, U.S. companies find it more difficult to compete in the world market. Conversely, when the dollar falls against foreign currencies, new business opportunities open up.

For example, when the Japanese yen rose 89 percent against the dollar between 1985 and 1987, the Campbell Soup Company took advantage of the situation by lowering prices on its soups by 16 percent, from 220 yen to 185 yen, while retaining retailers' profit margins at their same level. Arguing that the

Table 3-2   U.S.-Pioneered Technology for Which Market Share of U.S. Companies Is Declining

U.S.-Invented Technology	1987 Market Size (millions $)	U.S. Producers' Share of Domestic Market (%)			
		1970	1975	1980	1987
Phonographs	630	90	40	30	1
Color TVs	14,050	90	80	60	10
Audiotape recorders	500	40	10	10	0
Videotape recorders	2,895	10	10	1	1
Machine tool centers	485	99	97	79	35
Telephones	2,000	99	95	88	25
Semiconductors	19,100	89	71	65	64
Computers	53,500	N.A.	97	96	74

*Data: Council on Competitiveness, Commerce Dept.
Source: Reprinted from Otis Port, "Back to Basics," *Business Week, Innovation 1989,* p. 17.

lower price would increase volume, the Campbell Soup representative was able to double the number of stores in Japan that were handling the soup. Because of the falling dollar, however, Campbell Soup was able to reduce prices and increase profits at the same time. With the dollar worth 240 yen in 1985, a can of Campbell's soup sold for the equivalent of 91 cents. By 1987, even with the price cut, a can of Campbell's soup sold for the equivalent of about $1.30 because of the rise in the value of the yen relative to the dollar.[17] Thus international factors largely beyond the direct manipulation of a particular organization can have profound effects on the ability of managers to operate successfully.

Another way that the international element influences organizations is by producing new global competitors. For example, a number of technological advances pioneered in the United States have led to successful products. Yet, in regard to such items as phonographs, color televisions, tape recorders (audio and video), telephones, semiconductors, and computers, U.S. producers have gradually lost a significant share of the domestic market to foreign competitors who took the basic technology and successfully built upon it (see Table 3-2).[18]

A major Swedish furniture retailer, which conducted business in 18 countries, considered many potential environmental factors in selecting its first business site in the United States (see the following Case in Point discussion).

CASE IN POINT: IKEA Chooses U.S. Beachhead

When IKEA (pronounced eye-KEY-ah), the big, Swedish home-furnishings retailer, wanted to enter the U.S. market, its first choice for a store site was California. The retailer already was operating in eighteen countries, including nine stores in Canada, and had annual revenues approaching $2 billion. A closer look at California, though, revealed problems. For one thing, California has a standard for flammability in upholstered furniture that would have forced the company to perform a battery of time-consuming tests before opening a store in California, or else produce special goods for that California market. Either option would have required that the company raise prices significantly, or delay their estimated opening date substantially. Another obstacle was California's unitary tax system, which taxes multinational corporations like IKEA on their global profits rather than on the earnings of their local operations. The company,

IKEA, a Swedish-based home furnishings company, won over its American market with such in-store facilities as a "ballroom" for children to play in while their parents shop. The company now has six U.S. stores, with more to come. Such environmental factors as availability of inexpensive land near highways, the right demographics (families with moderate incomes), and state regulations on furniture standards help determine where the stores are located.

which is privately owned, was reluctant to provide California with the information on its worldwide operations that the paperwork would have required. As a result, company executives began to explore possibilities on the East Coast.

IKEA has been successful internationally by orienting itself toward providing well-designed furniture at an affordable price. To meet this goal, the company offers furniture that is unassembled and packaged in cartons that are easy to transport. The ready-to-assemble (RTA) furniture is easily assembled at home and sells for 30 to 50 percent less than competing, fully assembled furniture. To keep costs down, founder Ingvar Kamprad preaches that employees must be "cost-conscious almost to the point of stinginess."

Another reason for the company's success is its showrooms. The IKEA stores are usually two-story and are typically situated on undeveloped suburban land that is inexpensive and located near major highways. At the entrance is a "ballroom," a supervised playroom for small children that has a slide and is filled to knee level with softball-size colorful plastic balls. A video room located nearby offers amusement for older children while parents shop. Plenty of strollers are available. A cafeteria with good food at reasonable prices also enables customers to remain in the store longer and buy more.

In looking for an East Coast site for its first store, IKEA first went to Boston, where economic development officials gave the company representatives the usual briefing and supplied them with maps. "We drove around Boston for 2 or 3 days and really didn't get a feel for the place," says Bjorn Bayley, the president of the North American operations of IKEA. The reception around Washington, D.C., the second East Coast site of interest, was similarly cool.

In Philadelphia, the third choice, IKEA received substantial help from the Greater Philadelphia International Network, Inc., a small, business-backed group that helps attract foreign companies to the area. "For 3 days we didn't have 1 minute to ourselves," Mr. Bayley says. "They booked us into hotels, introduced us to bankers and real estate brokers. We had helicopter tours of the city. Cocktail parties every evening. These people never gave up."

The Philadelphia area (including Delaware and southern New Jersey) provided other advantages, including plenty of young, middle-income families and relatively inexpensive commercial real estate. With the network's help, the company found suitable space in a mall located next to a turnpike exit, in the suburb of Plymouth Meeting.

The store opened in 1985 and attracted close to 130,000 shoppers. Since then the store averages about 30,000 visitors per week, about 40 percent of whom are from outside Pennsylvania. More recently, IKEA has opened stores in the Virginia suburbs of Washington, D.C., in Baltimore, and in Pittsburgh. IKEA plans to have 10 stores operating in the United States by 1992.[19] ■■■■■■■■

The success of IKEA was aided greatly by its careful attention to broad environmental factors that would boost the odds in its favor. The managers recognized clearly that although there were many aspects of the environment that they could not directly alter, they did have some discretion in selecting certain of the environmental conditions within which they would subsequently function. They considered particularly the economic and sociocultural aspects of the Philadelphia location. The legal environment nixed the California location.

Task Environment

In the case of IKEA, attention to the broad environmental conditions that make for success was coupled with more specific concerns, such as providing a baby-sitting service and a cafeteria to make individuals feel at home and want to stay and shop. Similarly, in the case of Liz Claiborne, Inc., Claiborne's initial insight into broad, general trends affecting the clothing industry was only part of the reason for her namesake company's outstanding success. Once they started their company, she and Ortenberg devised innovative ways of getting feedback from more immediate outside elements, such as customers and retailers. Rather than just following the same paths as the competition, they carefully analyzed these important elements and often took bold new steps such as the "travelers" program, to respond to identified needs. These moves addressed the **task environment,** the segment of the external environment made up of the specific outside elements with which an organization interfaces in the course of conducting its business.

Task environment The specific outside elements with which an organization interfaces in the course of conducting its business

The task environment depends largely on the specific products and services that an organization decides to offer and the locations where it chooses to conduct its business. A single organization usually has difficulty exerting a direct influence on the mega-environment, but it may be more successful in affecting its task environment. Major elements in the task environment of an organization typically include customers and clients, competitors, suppliers, labor supply, and government agencies.[20] Each organization must assess its own situation in order to determine its specific task environment. Elements of the task environment for the Xerox Corporation are shown in Figure 3-3.

Customers and Clients. An organization's **customers and clients** are those individuals and organizations that purchase its products and/or services. A number of organizations have recently been making greater efforts to stay close to the customer by paying particular attention to service and quality, looking for niches where they can serve the customer better than anyone else, and listening to customers about their needs—particularly customers that are themselves leaders in their industry.[21] Staying close to the customer paid off well for Penny Wise Budoff, who guessed right when she figured that women were ready for a

Customers and clients Those individuals and organizations that purchase an organization's products and/or services

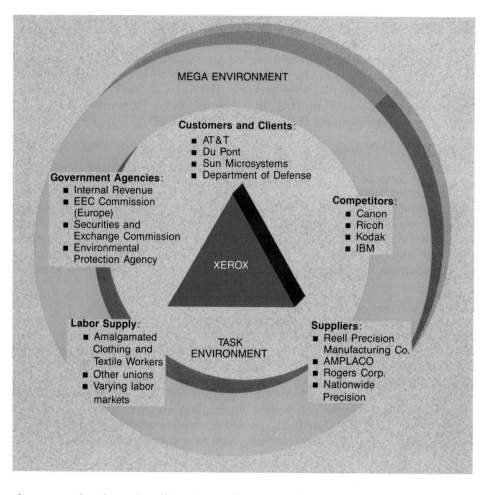

Figure 3-3 Elements of the task environment at the Xerox Corporation.

change at the doctor's office. As a physician, she was sensitive to women's accusations that doctors rushed them through appointments, told them little, and often were patronizing. So, in 1985, she raised $3 million to open a full-service clinic for women in Bethpage, New York. Within a year, the clinic had 7000 patients.[22]

Competitors Other organizations that either offer or have a high potential of offering rival products or services

Competitors. An organization's **competitors** are other organizations that either offer or have a high potential of offering rival products or services. Organizations need to be concerned with known competitors, as well as to monitor the competitive scene for potential newcomers. For example, the office supply store market is currently being invaded by three major discount merchants—Staples, Office Depot, and Office Club. The discounters run large stores that look almost like warehouses and offer discounts ranging from 20 to 75 percent off retail prices on a huge selection of office supplies. Customers use grocery store carts to gather their purchases and take them to checkout counters. Telephone orders can be delivered for a small fee. The pioneer, Staples, opened its first store in 1986. The discounters appear likely to make a major impact on the $100-billion-per-year office supply market.[23]

While organizations need to concern themselves with who their competitors are, they also need to keep abreast of what their competitors are doing. For

KEEPING TABS ON COMPETITORS

Here are 10 legal ways to track what your competitors are doing:

1. Commercial data bases are an easy and fast means of obtaining information. Data bases contain published articles from newspapers, magazines, and trade publications, as well as reports from stock analysts, patent filings, biographical information, etc. This information can be accessed by computer. Information about various data bases is contained in the *Directory of Online Data Bases,* published by Cuandra/Elsevier (New York).

2. Specialty trade publications that deal with industries and product areas provide very current information about major personnel changes, product advertising, new product announcements, trade show notices, and the like. The *Standard Periodical Directory* and the *Oxbridge Directory of Newsletters,* both published by Oxbridge Communications (New York), may help you locate trade publications applicable to your area of interest.

3. News clippings from local newspapers often provide specific information not available in national publications. You can either subscribe to the newspapers themselves or hire a clipping service. Clipping services charge a basic fee, as well as a fee for each clipping.

Check your telephone directory for clipping services.

4. Help-wanted advertisements give clues about expansion plans, new technologies competitors are pursuing, and even financial status information that may be embedded in ads, especially those for high-level managers. Since clipping services usually will clip ads for certain types of jobs, but generally will not clip ads for only a particular company, you may want to subscribe to your competitor's hometown papers and check the Sunday edition, in particular.

5. Published market research reports can often be helpful. To learn about these reports, consult *Findex,* published by the National Standards Association (Gaithersburg, Maryland). *Findex* appears annually with midyear supplements and also is available in a computerized data base that is updated on a more frequent basis.

6. Wall Street reports give information about public companies (stock is publicly traded) and their various subsidiaries through analysis by securities analysts at brokerage firms. These reports often are available through a data base called Investext, which is offered by several data-base services. Another source of information is the *Wall Street Transcript,* which is a weekly newsletter that covers roundtable discussions about particular industries, including private as well as public companies.

7. Trade shows and the product literature that can be obtained

at such shows are good sources of information about new product innovations, price changes, and methods of marketing. Speeches and presentations given at trade shows often are helpful as well.

8. Public filings (federal, state, and local) often provide information about financial data and future plans. The filings include reports that public companies must submit to the SEC, records of bankruptcy cases and other court cases, state-required annual reports, Uniform Commercial Code (UCC) filings (required by most states when a company obtains a commercial loan from a bank), and franchise filings (often required by states when a franchise is sold).

9. Advertisements give clues about competitors' marketing strategies. Advertising or clipping services often can obtain copies of advertisements for you. Information about competitors' advertising expenditures by product in various media (TV, magazine, etc.) can be obtained from services like Leading National Advertisers in New York.

10. Personal contacts can provide many tidbits of useful information about competitor movements. A contact base may include university professors who have knowledge about technological advances, suppliers, customers, purchasing agents, service technicians, and Wall Street analysts. Trade shows and professional conferences are particularly good places to develop contacts.[24]

example, Xerox uses a technique called benchmarking to estimate what the competitor does and how much it costs. To get a fix on Kodak's distribution and handling costs, for instance, Xerox managers ordered some Kodak copiers and then traced where and how they were shipped, including how they were packed.[25] For some ideas about how organizations obtain information about competitors, see the Practically Speaking discussion, "Keeping Tabs on Competitors."

Suppliers Those organizations and individuals that supply the resources an organization needs to conduct its operations

Suppliers. An organization's **suppliers** are those organizations and individuals that supply the resources (such as raw materials, products, or services) the organization needs to conduct its operations. Traditionally, the conventional belief in the United States has been that it is best to have multiple suppliers in order to reduce dependence on any one source. World competition is changing that view. Companies are finding that they are better able to cut costs by reducing the number of suppliers they deal with and negotiating contracts with them. In 1980, Xerox ordered parts and components from 5000 vendors worldwide. Since then, by using fewer vendors, Xerox has been able to enforce tougher quality standards, get better prices, and build more cooperative working relationships with suppliers. One concrete outgrowth of the new Xerox policy is that 99.2 percent of the parts the company orders arrive defect-free, compared with 92 percent previously.[26] In an attempt to increase its competitive position, General Motors, which traditionally made 70 percent of the component parts used in its cars, recently announced that it will continue to produce only those component parts that are "world-class competitive." Parts that do not meet that standard will be purchased from outside suppliers.[27]

Labor supply Those individuals who are potentially employable by an organization

Labor Supply. An organization's **labor supply** consists of those individuals who are potentially employable by the organization. The ability to attract, motivate, and retain the human resources necessary to provide competitive products and services is a crucial variable for most organizations. The recent economic boom in New England, for example, has caused a serious shortage of workers for employers in the region, particularly those operating in the area's urban centers, such as Boston, Hartford, and Providence. Unemployment in the area has been running 3 percentage points below the national average, making workers harder to recruit, more difficult to retain, and more expensive. Indicative of the difficulties, the tight labor market caused Boston's Shawmut Bank to offer a $1000 signing bonus to qualified applicants who accepted secretarial positions. At the same time, high housing costs discourage workers from migrating to the area. Economic planners worry, with good reason, that the severe worker shortage will encourage employers to head south, where workers are more readily available.[28] The Automobile Association of America (AAA) recently moved its headquarters from a Washington, D.C., suburb to Orlando, Florida, primarily because of consultant reports projecting severe labor shortages in the D.C. area over the next several decades.[29]

Similarly, the declining number of workers in the 18- to 24-year-old age group (mentioned earlier) is causing severe labor shortages in industries that rely on a large supply of entry-level workers. Employers are reacting with creative efforts to obtain the necessary help. A McDonald's franchisee in affluent Darien, Connecticut, buses teenage workers from the Bronx, 28 miles away, while TWA diverts some of the overflow calls from its telephone reservation system to young prisoners in Camarillo, California.[30] Labor supply issues are discussed further in Chapter 12.

Government Agencies. Various **government agencies** provide services and monitor compliance with laws and regulations at local, state or regional, and national levels. For the most part, the task environment of a particular organization involves interactions with representatives of specific government agencies. Interactions at the local level may involve representatives from such organizations as zoning commissions, local tax agencies, consumer affairs offices, and police departments. Agencies at the state level may include health departments, state tax agencies, and worker's compensation commissions. At the national level, interfaces may be necessary with such diverse agencies as the Equal Employment Opportunities Commission, Department of Labor, Internal Revenue Service, U.S. Customs Service, and Federal Communications Commission.

The particular product or service offered largely determines the agencies with which an organization is likely to interact on a routine basis. For example, a business that sells directly to consumers is more likely to have dealings with a local consumer affairs office than is a business that sells at the wholesale level. A company that sells food is more likely to have frequent visits from health officials than is a software company that runs a small cafeteria for employees only. On the other hand, most businesses are likely to interact with agencies such as the Internal Revenue Service. Even not-for-profit organizations must obtain clearances of their tax-exempt status from various tax agencies.

Government agencies
Agencies that provide services and monitor compliance with laws and regulations at local, state or regional, and national levels

ANALYZING ENVIRONMENTAL CONDITIONS

Although most organizational researchers view the environment as an important element affecting organizations, perspectives differ on the exact nature of the relationship between organizations and their environments. In this section, we examine two major views of the organization-environment interface, and we explore major characteristics of the environment.

Views of the Organization-Environment Interface

Researchers have expended considerable effort attempting to understand how organizations and their environments are related. Among the most prominent approaches to explaining the nature of the interface are the population ecology and resource dependence models.[31]

Population Ecology Model. The **population ecology model** is a view of the organization-environment interface that focuses on populations or groups of organizations and argues that environmental factors cause organizations with appropriate characteristics to survive and others to fail. The model is sometimes referred to as the **natural selection model.**

The population ecology model has three stages. In the first stage, *variations* occur in the forms of organizations in the environment. The notion of forms of organizations refers to various aspects of organizations, like structure, technology, and human resources, that can change. The variations in forms can come from a variety of sources, such as new firms initiated by entrepreneurs, changes in existing organizations due to perceptions of the environment, or unplanned alterations that are made in the course of operating. The second stage is *selection.* Selection occurs because some variations are more suited to the environment than others. In this stage, organizations attempt to locate a niche, a combination

Population ecology model
A model that focuses on populations or groups of organizations and argues that environmental factors cause organizations with appropriate characteristics to survive and others to fail

Natural selection model A term sometimes used for the population ecology model

The idea of a five and dime store met with great success earlier in this century, but Woolworth's was slow in experimenting with new formats. As a result its Woolco discount retailing chain failed to compete with K mart and Wal-mart. Today the five and dime stores comprise only about 25 percent of Woolworth's outlets. Company growth has accelerated over the past decade since it began operating shopping-mall specialty stores, such as Foot Locker, which sells athletic shoes, and Afterthoughts, which offers costume jewelry, handbags, and accessories.

of resources and other conditions that allow them to support their existence. If they cannot find a suitable niche, they will not be able to survive. Even if they do find a supportive niche, organizations often suffer from inertia (due to such factors as existing plants and equipment, insufficient information, and/or legal constraints) and may not change rapidly enough to keep up with changes in environmental conditions. The third stage is *retention*, in which organizational forms that survive tend to be preserved and often are reproduced or copied by others. Still, even at this stage, environmental conditions may shift, making particular organizational forms obsolete. Thus, in the population ecology view, organizational survival is largely due to fortuitous circumstances in which particular organizational forms happen to fit particular environmental conditions. Since organizations generally do not change rapidly, according to this view, managers have very limited capacity to affect the fates of their organizations.[32]

The potential ramifications of the environment are illustrated by a study conducted by *Forbes* magazine on its seventieth anniversary in 1987. *Forbes* wanted to determine how many of the 100 largest companies (in terms of assets) in 1917 were still among the 100 largest 70 years later. Only 11 of the companies that made the list in 1987 had the same company name as they had in 1917 (American Telephone & Telegraph; Eastman Kodak; E. I. Du Pont de Nemours; Ford Motor; General Electric; General Motors; Pacific Gas & Electric; Procter & Gamble; Sears, Roebuck; Southern California Edison; and Westinghouse Electric). Another 11 were still in the top 100 but had changed their name. The other 78 companies had met a variety of fates. Some had grown, but too slowly to retain their top position; others had been acquired; still others had faltered badly and faded from sight. At now-defunct Baldwin Locomotive, for example, executives had insisted that new technology could never replace the steam locomotive. Similarly, Frank Woolworth's concept for the five-and-dime store propelled the company to the top 100, but successors didn't adjust the concept to the changing needs of customers. On the other hand, Atlantic Gulf & West Indies Steam Ship Lines presumably ran into a string of bad luck associated with the loss of ships on high seas.[33] Could something have been done to keep these major companies prospering? Proponents of the population ecology model do not think so. The resource dependence model, however, presents a different perspective on the situation.

Resource dependence model
A model that highlights organizational dependence on the environment for resources and argues that organizations attempt to manipulate the environment to reduce that dependence

Resource Dependence Model. The **resource dependence model** is a view of the organization-environment interface that highlights organizational dependence on the environment for resources and argues that organizations attempt to manipulate the environment to reduce that dependence.[34] In the resource dependence view, no organization can generate internally all the various resources (such as financing, materials, and services) it needs to operate effectively. For example, even giant General Motors purchases many of its parts from outside the organization, rather than making them internally. By forming relationships with other organizations, an organization can solve many of its resource problems. At the same time, such interorganizational relationships create dependence on other organizations and reduce the flexibility that organizations have in making their own decisions and taking their own actions. Hence, organizations attempt to be as independent as possible by controlling as many of their critical resources as feasible or developing alternative sources.

For example, when it was developing the new PS/2 personal computer, IBM contracted with the Microsoft Corporation of Redmond, Washington, for the preparation of a new software operations system called OS/2. Microsoft had been the creator of MS-DOS, the operating system that ran IBM's first entry into the personal computer market. The new OS/2 software would include "windows," an innovative way of displaying information on a computer screen that makes the PS/2 easier to use than IBM's earlier personal computers and those of many other manufacturers. While this arrangement speeded IBM's movements in the highly competitive PC market, it also virtually ensured that millions of copies of the Microsoft software would be sold. In the process, the contract also increased the dependence of the two organizations on one another.

Meanwhile, Microsoft also proceeded to market a software program called Windows, which runs with the old PC operating systems, MS-DOS—a software package that the OS/2 supposedly would replace. By making the old operating system easier to use, the Windows program slowed sales of OS/2 and in the process helped corporate users avoid upgrading their old machines to the new IBM PS/2. It also reduced the dependence of Microsoft on the success of IBM's new PS/2 computer. Several major software producers, such as the Lotus Development Corporation, which has been spending millions of dollars preparing its popular spreadsheet package (Lotus 1-2-3) to run with OS/2 (but not with MS-DOS plus Windows), accused Microsoft of manipulating the situation to come out a winner no matter which operating system—MS-DOS plus Windows or OS/2—wins the most favor with computer users.[35] Meanwhile, IBM signed an agreement with Microsoft Corporation's rival, Steven Jobs (founder of Apple Computers and presently head of Next, Inc.), to help with personal computer development, thus perhaps developing options to its dependence on Microsoft for software.[36] Hence, this situation helps illustrate how resource needs and dependence intertwine as organizations seek to deal with their environments.

In contrast to the population ecology approach, which holds that managerial actions are of limited consequence in dealing with the environment, the resource dependence model argues that managers do have strategic choices, or options, and that these choices impact organizational success. Managers not only have choices about the way in which they react to environmental change, but they also have options in attempting to influence the nature of the environment itself.[37] Hence, in regard to the *Forbes* study mentioned previously, perhaps Baldwin Locomotive and Woolworth's would have fared better had their managers paid closer attention to the changing environment. Even in the case of Atlantic Gulf & West Indies Steam Ship Lines, possibly the company could have had some part of the business oriented to less risk.

Reconciling the Differing Models. Both the population ecology and the resource dependence models offer perspectives that are useful to managers.[38] The population ecology model helps highlight the fact that organizations have little control over a number of environmental factors that may impact them.

On the other hand, the resource dependence approach points out that managers likely do have options in influencing many aspects of the environment, including relationships with other organizations. Hence, there are reasons for managers to attempt to monitor, understand, and potentially influence environmental elements, recognizing that unforeseen environmental factors still can have major impacts on organizations.

Characteristics of the Environment

Accurately assessing the environment is a difficult, if not impossible, task. From one point of view, an organization's environment is an *objective* reality—a set of concrete conditions that theoretically could be measured perfectly to give managers complete information. Yet, from a practical point of view, managers are more likely to take action on the environment as they see it. Thus, operationally, the environment may be more realistically thought of as a *subjective* reality in the minds of managers.[39] Since managers are likely to act on their own perceptions, they need to verify those perceptions, if possible, with alternative sources of information (perhaps the opinions of others, as well as objective data).

One valuable way of analyzing the overall environmental situation faced by an organization is to consider two key concepts, environmental uncertainty and environmental munificence, or capacity. Although the main focus is on the task environment, major trends in the mega-environment that are likely to have a strong direct or indirect impact on the organization and its industry also should be considered.

Environmental uncertainty
A condition of the environment in which future conditions affecting an organization cannot be accurately assessed and predicted

Environmental Uncertainty. **Environmental uncertainty** is a condition of the environment in which future conditions affecting an organization cannot be accurately assessed and predicted.[40] The more uncertain an organization's environment, the more time and effort managers must expend monitoring the environment, assessing the implications for the organization, and deciding what present and future actions to take.[41] The degree of environmental uncertainty is a function of two major factors, complexity and dynamism.[42]

Environmental complexity
The number of elements in an organization's environment and their degree of similarity

Complexity. **Environmental complexity** refers to the number of elements in an organization's environment and their degree of similarity.[43] Environments in which there are a relatively small number of similar items are said to be homogeneous. In contrast, environments in which there are a large number of dissimilar items are considered to be heterogeneous. As the elements in the environment become more heterogeneous, managers have more variables with which they must contend.

Environmental dynamism
The rate and predictability of change in the elements of an organization's environment

Dynamism. **Environmental dynamism** refers to the rate and predictability of change in the elements of an organization's environment.[44] Environments in which the rate of change is slow and relatively predictable are considered to be stable. Conversely, environments in which the rate of change is fast and relatively unpredictable are said to be unstable. As elements in the environment become more unstable, they present greater challenges to managers.

Assessing Environmental Uncertainty. The concepts of complexity and dynamism can be used to make an overall assessment of the degree of environmental uncertainty. Such an assessment can be done by analyzing the important elements in the task environment and the major potential influences in the mega-environment (see Figure 3-4). As Cell 1 in Figure 3-4 suggests, uncertainty is relatively low when both dynamism and complexity are low. Such a situation is likely to prevail in the case of the funeral industry, in which there is slow change and a relatively steady stream of customers with similar needs. In Cell 2, dynamism is low but complexity is high, creating a situation of moderately low uncertainty. An example of this type of situation is the insurance industry, in which companies serve a diverse set of customer needs but competitive elements change fairly slowly. In Cell 3, dynamism is high but complexity is low, leading to moderately high uncertainty. This situation is characteristic of the women's apparel industry, in which the customers and retailers constitute fairly homogeneous market segments but fashion trends change rapidly. Finally, Cell 4 represents both high dynamism and high complexity, resulting in a condition of high uncertainty. High environmental uncertainty is currently found in the computer software industry, in which conditions change rapidly and a large number of

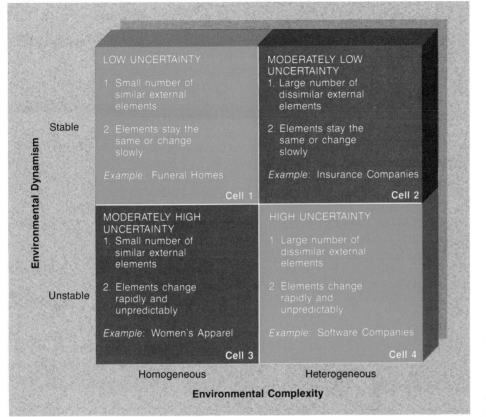

Figure 3-4 Assessing the degree of environmental uncertainty. (Adapted from Robert Duncan, "What Is the Right Organization Structure? Decision Tree Analysis Provides the Answer." *Organizational Dynamics*, Winter 1979, p. 63.)

environmental factors such as technological change, vast numbers of diverse customers, and strenuous competition exert strong heterogeneous pressures.

Conditions of uncertainty may change over a period of time. For example, an environment can be relatively homogeneous and stable at one point in time and change (perhaps even gradually) to a condition of greater uncertainty. As a result, it is necessary for managers to make periodic reassessments of their situations. Otherwise, important environmental changes can occur that are not perceived by managers, or even if they are perceived, their potential impact is not recognized.[45]

Environmental Munificence. Another important characteristic of the environment is **environmental munificence,** or capacity, the extent to which the environment can support sustained growth and stability.[46] Environmental munificence can range from relatively rich to relatively lean, depending on the level of resources available to the organization within the environment. Unfortunately, rich environments eventually tend to attract other organizations. Munificence is important because when organizations operate in rich environments, they are able to build up a cushion of internal resources, such as capital, equipment, and experience. At the same time, a high level of internal resources can subsequently fund the innovations and expansions that may help an organization sustain its position, as well as weather leaner times. Unfortunately, at the Champion Spark Plug Company, managers did not perceive the impact of some of the major changes taking place in their environment, including the declining munificence (see the following Case in Point discussion).

Environmental munificence
The extent to which the environment can support sustained growth and stability

CASE IN POINT: Champion Loses Its Spark

Almost since 1910, when it was founded by the Stranahan brothers in Toledo, Ohio, the Champion Spark Plug Company has been the leading U.S. maker of spark plugs. In the mid-1980s, the company had 38 percent of the market, compared with its two closest competitors, General Motor's AC brand (32 percent) and Allied Signal's Autolite (24 percent).

Unfortunately, market share was not the only issue. Since the early 1970s, when the oil shortage spurred efforts to make cars more fuel-efficient, there has been a steady decline in the proportion of eight-cylinder cars. By the mid-1980s, at least 45 percent of the new cars built in North America had four-cylinder engines, compared with about 3 percent in the mid-1970s. The fewer the cylinders, the fewer the spark plugs that are needed. In addition, the introduction of electronic ignitions and unleaded fuel has meant that a spark plug can now last for 30,000 miles, rather than 10,000 miles, as in the past. Another development affecting the demand for spark plugs is the fact that most Japanese cars sold in the United States have spark plugs made by Japanese companies. The cumulative effect of these factors has been a seriously declining market for spark plugs. Not surprisingly, Champion has been experiencing sinking profit levels.

Although the downward trend in spark plug use has been apparent for some time, Champion, led by a son of one of the founders, was slow to respond. During the 1970s, the company did buy the Anderson Company, the leading maker of windshield wipers, and DeVilbiss, a maker of a variety of products ranging from spray-painting robots to health-care equipment. Yet while competitors began taking such actions as expanding their product lines and setting up motor tune-up franchises, Champion kept its brand name attached to a single product. "If you're a gardener of roses and grow championship roses, you don't introduce new strains," says Duane Stranahan, Jr., grandson of one of the company's founders and a member of the board.

Finally, in 1986, the Stranahan clan brought in a new chief executive, O. Lee Henry, who began to bring about needed major changes, such as putting the Champion name on a new line of products, including air filters, ignition cables, and fuel additives. Progress was slow, however, because the limited shelf space in auto supply stores meant that many retailers were reluctant to stock the new Champion products. Despite efforts by the Stranahan family, which controlled 31 percent of the stock, to keep the company independent, Champion was acquired by Cooper Industries, a Houston-based industrial-products maker, in 1989.[47]   ■

MANAGING ENVIRONMENTAL ELEMENTS

Perhaps the problems at the Champion Spark Plug Company could have been avoided. While recognizing that there are limitations on the ability of organizations to manage environmental factors, a number of organizational theorists (e.g., those advocating the resource dependence model) view environmental elements as somewhat malleable to action by managers and advocate proactive action. As organizational theorist James D. Thompson has pointed out, managers essentially have three major options in attempting to manage environmental uncertainty and its potential impact: adapt to the existing environmental elements, attempt to influence environmental favorability, and/or shift the domain of operations away from threatening environmental elements toward more beneficial ones.[48] These three approaches, or options, are shown in Table 3-3, along

Table 3-3   Approaches to Managing Environmental Impacts

Approaches	Methods
Adaptation	Buffering, smoothing, forecasting, and rationing
Favorability influence	Advertising and engaging in public relations, boundary spanning, recruiting, negotiating contracts, co-opting, establishing joint ventures, joining trade associations, and engaging in political activity
Domain shifts	Changing domain completely or diversifying into some new areas

with major methods of implementing the approaches. The feasibility of any or all of these approaches depends on the situation, but maneuverability is enhanced if the environment offers high munificence or the organization has been able to build up a cushion of resources in the past. In Champion Spark Plug's situation, the company was able to survive and maintain a profit for a number of years, even though the company's long-term prospects were declining.

Adaptation

The adaptation approach involves changing internal operations and activities to make the organization more compatible with its environment. This strategy essentially accepts the existing environment as a given and seeks to develop some rational process for adjusting to it. Four common approaches used by organizations to adapt to environmental fluctuations are buffering, smoothing, forecasting, and rationing.[49]

Buffering. The use of **buffering** involves stockpiling either inputs into or outputs from a production or service process in order to cope with environmental fluctuations. Buffering by stockpiling inputs is used when it is difficult to line up reliable sources of inputs, such as supplies. Conversely, buffering by maintaining inventories of finished products is used when wide fluctuations in market demand make it difficult to produce outputs efficiently as they are ordered. Buffering is not always feasible because of high expense, perishability of materials, or the difficulty of stockpiling services, such as customer service in a restaurant. Furthermore, substantial buffering of inputs and finished products can pose serious risks of obsolescence before they are used or sold.

Buffering Stockpiling either inputs into or outputs from a production or service process in order to cope with environmental fluctuations

Smoothing. While buffering seeks to accommodate market fluctuations, **smoothing** involves taking actions aimed at reducing the impact of fluctuations, given the market. For example, utilities often discount their rates during certain time periods to encourage use of energy in designated slow-demand periods. Department stores may run sales during slow months. Restaurants often offer coupons that can be used only on certain weekday nights when business is typically slow. Such actions may avoid the inefficiencies associated with expanding to meet peak demands and then having resources underutilized during non-peak times.

Smoothing Taking actions aimed at reducing the impact of fluctuations, given the market

Forecasting. Another approach to dealing with environmental fluctuations is *forecasting,* the systematic effort to estimate future conditions. To the extent that it is possible to predict future conditions with a reasonable level of accuracy, it

These staff economists at Data Resources in Boston are trained to look at economic trends and make predictions about future conditions. The use of forecasting techniques is one way that a company tries to adapt to environmental fluctuations.

may be possible to prepare in advance to meet the fluctuations. For example, grocery stores frequently hire part-time cashiers to supplement regular staff during probable busy periods. Campus police departments schedule extra personnel to direct traffic and take care of emergencies when athletic events are being held. These types of actions are based on experience with customer patterns, and such forecasts may be reasonably accurate. When environmental fluctuations are related to more complex and dynamic factors, such as trends in the economy, more sophisticated forecasting techniques may be required. Many companies have staff economists and/or subscribe to services that provide economic forecasts based on elaborate econometric models. For example, Marina vonNeumann Whitman, economist and vice president of General Motors, oversees the company's economic forecasting efforts, as well as environmental, lobbying, and public-affairs staffs.[50]

Rationing Providing limited access to a product or service that is in high demand

Rationing. Environmental fluctuations are sometimes also handled by **rationing,** providing limited access to a product or service that is in high demand. For example, automobile companies frequently ration the number of popular cars available to dealers when the demand exceeds the ability to produce. Many colleges and universities ration slots for popular majors by establishing program prerequisites, such as the achievement of a certain grade point average by the end of the sophomore year. Rationing has the advantage of allowing the organization to avoid the expense of expanding capacity to meet a temporary upward swing in demand, since many costs associated with capacity expansion (e.g., extra plants, equipment, or classroom buildings) continue during downward demand swings. Rationing also is used when demand exceeds forecasts or when managers expand new production slowly because of heavy costs and considerable risk if forecasted demand does not materialize. On the other hand, rationing has the disadvantage of denying a consumer a product or service, while the organization is forced to turn away potential business. For example, after IKEA, the Swedish furniture retailer, opened stores in the United States, shortages of the most popular items cost the company an estimated $500 million in annual sales.[51]

Favorability Influence

In contrast to adaptation strategies, the favorability influence approach involves attempting to alter environmental elements in order to make them more compatible with the needs of the organization. Rather than accepting environmental elements as givens, this approach views at least some aspects of the environment as potentially being within the capacity of the organization to change in advantageous ways.

Major methods that organizations use in attempting to influence significant elements in the environment are advertising and engaging in public relations, boundary spanning, recruiting, negotiating contracts, co-opting, establishing joint ventures, joining trade associations, and engaging in political activities. Influence methods such as advertising and public relations involve high cost but relatively little increased dependence on environmental elements. Conversely, negotiating a contract might involve little cost (other than paying for the contractual services) but may increase organizational dependence on the contractor.[52]

Advertising and Public Relations. One means of influencing the environment is through **advertising,** the use of communications media to gain favorable publicity for particular products and services, and **public relations,** the use of communications media and related activities to create a favorable overall impression of the organization among the public. In combination, advertising and public relations can help engender a positive feeling toward an organization among environmental elements. For example, in addition to regular advertising, many major companies sponsor such events as U.S. participation in the Olympics, participate in charitable endeavors such as the United Way, and donate time and money to a variety of groups including colleges and universities.

Advertising The use of communications media to gain favorable publicity for particular products and services

Public relations The use of communications media and related activities to create a favorable overall impression of the organization among the public

Boundary Spanning. Another means of influence is **boundary spanning,** creating roles within the organization that interface with important elements in the environment. Boundary spanners can fulfill two different functions.[53] First, they can serve an information processing function by collecting information from the environment, filtering out what is important, and transmitting the relevant information to those inside the organization who can act on the information. Second, they can perform an external representation function by presenting information about the organization to those outside. Although this latter function is most directly related to environmental influence, the information processing function greatly enhances the knowledge base on which influence strategies are built. Examples of boundary-spanning roles include salespersons, purchasing specialists, personnel recruiters, admissions officers, shipping and receiving agents, receptionists, lawyers, and scientists who maintain close ties with developments in their fields.

Boundary spanning Creating roles within the organization that interface with important elements in the environment

Recruiting. A further potential means of environmental influence is *recruiting,* attracting job candidates who meet the needs of the organization. This tool can be used for environmental influence when organizations seek job candidates who have a knowledge of and close ties to a significant element of the environment. For example, companies often hire executives from specific companies or in particular industries because of their environmental knowledge and connections. Many executives in rival computer firms began their careers at IBM. Companies and associations often recruit former members of Congress and congressional aides as lobbyists because of their knowledge of and connections with Congress.

Negotiating contracts
Seeking favorable agreements on matters of importance to the organization

Negotiating Contracts. In some cases, influence attempts are made by **negotiating contracts,** which means seeking favorable agreements on matters of importance to the organization. Specific agreements with customers and suppliers are one common means of creating environmental favorability.

Co-opting   Absorbing key members of important environmental elements into the leadership or policy-making structure of an organization

Co-opting. Another means of influence is **co-opting,** the process of absorbing key members of important environmental elements into the leadership or policy-making structure of an organization. A common example of co-optation is the addition of key members of the environment to boards of directors. For instance, most universities have prominent individuals on their boards of directors or regents. These individuals often help the universities deal more effectively with environmental elements, particularly in the area of raising funds from business and/or legislatures.

Interlocking directorates   A situation in which organizations have board members in common either directly or indirectly

Direct interlock   A situation in which two companies have a director in common

Indirect interlock   A situation in which two companies each have a director on the board of a third company

A related influence approach is the use of **interlocking directorates,** a situation in which organizations have board members in common either directly or indirectly. In a **direct interlock,** two companies have a director in common. The Clayton Act specifically forbids the same individual from holding a directorship in two companies that directly compete. In an **indirect interlock,** two companies each have a director on the board of a third company. One study of 130 large U.S. companies showed 530 direct and 12,193 indirect board interlocks among the firms.[54] Through interlocking directorates, organizations can obtain valuable information and build favorable connections with other organizations.[55] The addition of powerful and influential outside directors does pose the risk that such directors may raise serious questions about organizational practices and, thereby, constitute a threat to current management.[56] When General Motors purchased the Electronic Data Systems Corporation, the computer software company built by Ross Perot, part of the deal was a seat on the GM board of directors for Perot. However, Perot's loud and continual criticisms of the automotive giant led the company to pay him a premium $700 million to give up his stock, get off the board, and keep quiet.[57]

Joint venture   An agreement involving two or more organizations that arrange to produce a product or service jointly

Joint Ventures. An increasing phenomenon, a **joint venture** is an agreement involving two or more organizations that arrange to produce a product or service jointly. Joint ventures usually occur because there is some mutual advantage for the organizations involved that would be difficult to duplicate if each acted alone. Joint ventures are not new. In 1879, General Electric founder Thomas A. Edison teamed up with Corning Glass Works to make his experimental incandescent light bulb. However, such alliances are becoming more common largely for cost, market, and technological reasons. For example, Toys 'R' Us and McDonald's recently announced a joint venture to open a chain of toy stores in Japan, sometimes with McDonald's food outlets on the premises.[58] Unfortunately, many joint ventures fail. Independent studies by McKinsey & Company and Coopers & Lybrand reveal that some 7 out of 10 joint ventures fall short of expectations or are disbanded. Prime reasons are that the technology or market doesn't materialize, a partner's objectives change, or managers in the two organizations find it difficult to work together.[59]

Trade associations
Organizations composed of individuals or firms with common business concerns

Trade Associations. Trade associations are organizations composed of individuals or firms with common business concerns. Individuals or organizations joining associations include manufacturers, distributors, importers, brokers, and retailers of a product or group of products. They may also be individuals or organizations concerned with supplying, transporting, or using goods or services of a particular industry. Examples of trade associations are the National

Coffee Service Association, a group of 700 companies that supply coffee, snacks, and vending equipment to America's offices; the National Tire Dealers and Retreaders Association, consisting of 5000 tire dealers and retreaders; and the Third Class Mail Association, representing 500 companies who depend on the less costly third-class postal rate.[60] Because they represent the pooled resources of many individuals or organizations, trade associations are frequently in an enhanced position for conducting public relations campaigns, influencing legislation through lobbying efforts, and otherwise positively affecting the favorability of the environment within which their members operate.

Political Activity. The use of political activity involves attempts by organizations to enhance their competitive situation through influencing legislation and/or the behavior of government regulatory agencies. Political activities may be carried out by single organizations in their own behalf or by several organizations or associations for the collective well-being of the group. When the Dayton Hudson Corporation, a Minnesota-based retailer, was threatened by a takeover attempt from Washington's Haft family, the company swung into political action. Although it had a good reputation in Minnesota, the company hired the top five lobbying firms in the state, got its employees to engage in a massive letter-writing campaign, and called in favors from Minnesota charities that it had supported for years. As a result, emergency legislation giving Minnesota one of the toughest antitakeover laws in the country was passed and signed by the governor just 7 days after the company asked the state to tighten its takeover laws.[61]

Domain Shifts

Another method of managing environmental elements is to make **domain shifts,** changes in the mix of products and services offered so that an organization will interface with more favorable environmental elements. One major approach is to move entirely out of a current product, service, or geographic area into a more favorable domain. A second domain-shift approach is to expand current domains through diversification, the expansion of products and services offered. For example, when the Acmat Corporation, a leading asbestos removal company, ran into severe difficulties renewing its liability insurance, the company invested in the insurance business. The result was United Coastal Insurance, which specializes in writing asbestos liability policies.[62] Diversification can occur through geographic expansion of existing products or services or through the development of new and different products or services. One well-known company that has used both domain shifts and favorability influence approaches in order to deal with environmental threats is Harley-Davidson (see the following Case in Point discussion).

Domain shifts Changes in the mix of products and services offered so that an organization will interface with more favorable environmental elements

CASE IN POINT: Harley-Davidson on the Road Again

Harley-Davidson, Inc., the Milwaukee-based maker of large, heavy motorcycles called "hogs" by owners, has staged a major comeback after almost being driven out of business by imports. Harley's troubles began in the mid-1970s, when the company was owned by AMF, Inc., and had a reputation for uneven quality and a slow rate of innovation. The engine used on the Harley cycles was known for leaking oil and vibrating excessively. Moreover, Japanese cycles of much better quality were invading the market.

Elizabeth Taylor (shown here with the late Malcolm Forbes) was given a purple Harley-Davidson motorcycle as part of a promotion of her new perfume called Passion. Not so incidentally, the gift from Forbes also promoted Harleys. Harley-Davidson has managed a complete turnaround since the mid-1970s by clever advertising and public relations, by pressure on politicians to impose a temporary tariff on Japanese cycles, and by broadening the product mix of the company.

By 1975, AMF hired Vaughn Beals to run Harley. Beals quickly set up a quality control and inspection program that helped reduce some of the most major problems. The company then set out to improve its engines and develop new product lines to compete better with Japanese bikes. Although Harley's sales stayed fairly strong, the company's market share began to decline as Japanese entries into the heavyweight bike category continued to flood the market. By 1980, AMF lost interest in the company and sold it to Beals and 12 other Harley executives for $81.5 million.

Over the next 18 months, the company lost close to $30 million as the executives struggled to cut costs, install a new inventory system, and encourage worker involvement in making improvements. In 1983, the company managed to make a small profit. A major break came that same year when Harley convinced President Reagan and the U.S. International Trade Commission that Japanese competitors were selling excess inventory in the United States at below cost. The commission set a 5-year tariff on heavy motorcycles that would gradually decline from 45 percent to 10 percent by 1988. Harley says that some competitors (such as the Honda Motor Company and Kawasaki Heavy Industries, Ltd.) got around the tariff by making their heavy bikes in the United States. Still, the tariff helped ease the competitive threat.

By 1984, quality had improved significantly, and Harley launched a major advertising campaign to get the word to potential customers. A series of television ads invited bikers to visit any of more than 600 dealers for a free ride on a new Harley. Within 3 weeks, dealers had given 90,000 rides to 40,000 people (about 50 percent owned bikes made by other manufacturers). The initial promotion did not sell enough Harley cycles to cover the costs, but apparently it got the point across. Many who rode the new bikes came back during the following year or two to make purchases. The SuperRide, as the program is called, has become the only ongoing program of its kind in the industry and has been such a major source of sales that Harley now has fleets of demonstration cycles that it sends to various motorcycle rallies. The company also created the Harley Owners Group (HOG), which currently has close to 100,000 members and a bimonthly newsletter.

By 1986, Harley was making enough profits to sell stock to the public. The company used the funds to help accelerate new product development and to purchase a motor-home maker, Holiday Rambler. Harley also began to land defense and commercial contracts that amounted to about 12 percent of sales. Meanwhile, the company asked to have the Japanese tariffs removed in 1987, a year early.

When the company celebrated its eighty-fifth anniversary, in 1988, every motorcyclist in the United States was invited to the event, including those who rode other brands. To attend, a cyclist had to contribute $10 to the Muscular Dystrophy Association. Groups led by Harley-Davidson executives biked from as far away as California and Florida to Milwaukee for a day of activities. As they gathered to watch video tapes of their ride into Milwaukee, the crowd rose in a tumultuous demonstration—a tribute to the rebirth of the Harley-Davidson legend.[63] ▬▬▬

Thus Harley-Davidson is attempting to deal with environmental difficulties partially through expanding its domain to other areas where company officials feel prospects look promising. At the same time, the company's survival to this point is partially due to its efforts to influence the favorability of the environment by convincing President Reagan and the International Trade Commission to impose tariff restrictions on big foreign motorcycles during a crucial period for the company. Advertising and public relations were other means of influencing the environment that Harley-Davidson used. The survival of Harley-Davidson highlights the fact that organizations can be proactive in managing parts of their environment through adaptation, favorability influence, and domain shifts.

THE INTERNAL ENVIRONMENT: ORGANIZATIONAL CULTURE

Harley-Davidson both influenced the favorability of and adapted to its environment. Part of the transformation of the company also involved changes in its organizational culture, a major aspect of the internal environment of an organization. For example, in the process of making various changes, the company got workers involved in suggesting improvements and in supporting the needed emphasis on quality. This stance was a major departure from the policy of the past, in which engineers would figure out what to do and then managers would tell the employees what should be done.[64] In this section, we examine the concept of culture more closely, considering the nature and manifestations of culture, as well as how culture can be used as a means of promoting innovation.

Nature of Organizational Culture

As mentioned earlier in this chapter, organizational culture is a system of shared values, assumptions, beliefs, and norms that unite the members of an organization.[65] Culture reflects common views about "the way things are done around here."[66] Organizational culture is sometimes referred to as **corporate culture** because the culture concept is frequently used to describe the internal environment of major corporations. Yet the culture notion can also be used to describe internal conditions in not-for-profit organizations, such as government agencies, charitable organizations, museums, and the like. Culture is important to organizations because as individuals act on shared values and other aspects of organizational culture, their behaviors can have a significant impact on organizational effectiveness.[67]

Corporate culture A term sometimes used for organizational culture

Organizational cultures develop from a variety of sources.[68] As new organizations are formed, cultures often develop that reflect the drive and imagination of the individuals involved. Strong founders, too, may have a major impact on the culture that forms. For example, Ray Kroc, the founder of McDonald's, espoused "quality, service, cleanliness, and value," still the corporate creed.[69] As reward systems, policies, and procedures are instituted, they impact culture by further specifying notions of appropriate behavior. Moreover, critical incidents, such as an employee's being rewarded or fired for pushing a major innovation, may add to individuals' perceptions of internal norms over time.

Three aspects of organizational culture are particularly important in analyzing the likely impact of culture on a given organization: direction, pervasiveness, and strength.[70] *Direction* refers to the degree to which a culture supports, rather than interferes with, reaching organizational goals. *Pervasiveness* addresses the extent to which a culture is widespread among members, as opposed to being unevenly distributed. *Strength* refers to the degree to which members accept the values and other aspects of a culture.

A culture can have a *positive* impact on organizational effectiveness when the culture supports organizational goals, is widely shared, and is deeply internalized by organizational members.[71] For example, a consistent and shared emphasis on innovation has helped 3M produce a steady stream of new products, as well as make continual improvements in existing ones.[72] In contrast, a culture can have a *negative* impact when the culture is widely shared and well internalized but influences behaviors in directions that do not further (and possibly interfere with) organizational goals. More mixed situations tend to have less impact. For example, a culture that is unevenly distributed and weakly held is unlikely to have much impact (either positively or negatively), regardless of its direction.

Manifestations of Organizational Culture

An interesting feature of organizational culture is that the values, assumptions, beliefs, and norms that constitute a particular culture generally are not directly observable. Rather, we often infer the nature of a particular culture through the organization's use of concrete manifestations, such as symbols, stories, and rites and ceremonials.[73]

Symbol An object, act, event, or quality that serves as a vehicle for conveying meaning

Symbols. A **symbol** is an object, act, event, or quality that serves as a vehicle for conveying meaning.[74] For example, a very explicit symbol used to support an organizational value is Corning, Inc.'s use of a "quapple," a pin that is shaped like a combination of the letter "Q" and an apple. Organizational members receive the quapple after successfully completing their initial training course in quality improvement and then wear the quapple to signify their own commitment to quality.[75]

Symbols often are more subtle than the quapple, however. For example, at a recent gathering of General Motor's top 900 executives, David A. Hansen, a midlevel executive, stood up to comment from Table 37. "We would really appreciate it if you could lick the temperature problem in this corner of the room," he said. Roger B. Smith, who was GM Chairman at the time, replied, "I've got a sweater on. One of the things we've got to do in this corporation is find 15-cent solutions to million-dollar problems." Without hesitating, Hansen asked, "Could I please borrow your sweater?" A nervous laughter went through the crowd, but Smith calmly stepped off the stage, walked back to Table 37, took off his brown sweater, and gave it to Hansen. As Smith returned to the podium, the crowd applauded enthusiastically. GM officials insist the incident was not staged, but they cite the giving of the sweater as symbolic of a recent shift in emphasis toward listening more to employees and trusting them.[76]

Story A narrative based on true events, which sometimes may be embellished to highlight the intended value

Stories. A **story** is a narrative based on true events, which sometimes (but not always) may be embellished to highlight the intended value.[77] According to one story told at 3M, a worker was fired because he continued to work on a new product idea even after his boss had told him to stop. Despite being fired and taken off the payroll, the individual continued to come to work, pursuing his idea in an unused office. Eventually, he was rehired, developed the idea into a huge success, and was made a vice president. In this case, the story conveys an important value in the innovative 3M culture—persisting when you believe in an idea.[78]

Rite A relatively elaborate, dramatic, planned set of activities intended to convey cultural values to participants and, usually, an audience

Ceremonial A system of rites performed in conjunction with a single occasion or event

Rites and Ceremonials. A **rite** is a relatively elaborate, dramatic, planned set of activities intended to convey cultural values to participants and, usually, an audience. A **ceremonial** is a system of rites performed in conjunction with a single occasion or event. One company that is well known for its ceremonial activities is Mary Kay Cosmetics, which holds "seminars" that involve extrava-

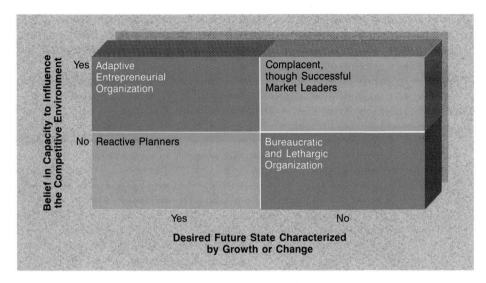

Figure 3-5 Organization opportunity matrix. (Adapted from Howard H. Stevenson and David E. Gumpert, "The Heart of Entrepreneurship," *Harvard Business Review*, March–April 1985, p. 93.)

gant events presented at the Dallas Convention Center. Hundreds of Mary Kay salespeople attend training sessions during the day, and at night they partici- pate in lavish activities that company founder Mary Kay Ash describes as "a combination of the Academy Awards, the Miss America Pageant, and a Broad- way opening!" The highlight is a 5-hour extravaganza at which Mary Kay crowns the very best salespersons in various categories. The crowned individu- als receive expensive gifts as they are surrounded by a court of other outstand- ing salespeople. The message conveys the critical importance of sales to com- pany and personal success.[79]

Promoting Innovation: Entrepreneurial Culture

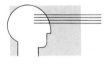

Culture can be an important part of the innovation orientation of an organiza- tion. Entrepreneurial specialists Howard H. Stevenson and David E. Gumpert argue that organizations can be classified into a corporate opportunity matrix.[80] The matrix is based on the extent to which the culture supports both a desire for change and a belief in its capacity to influence the competitive environment (see Figure 3-5).

For example, adaptive, entrepreneurial organizations tend to have cultures in which members view growth and change as desirable and also believe that they can affect the competitive environment to their advantage. In the opposite vein, bureaucratic and lethargic organizations are more likely to have members who prefer the status quo and have little faith in their ability to influence the competitive environment. In more mixed situations, cultures that support a de- sire for change but have little belief in their ability to influence competitive situa- tions are likely to produce reactive planner organizations. Reactive planners try to plan for environmental change but are not proactive in attempting to influ- ence the environment. Cultures oriented to very slow change, coupled with a belief in their ability to affect the competitive environment, are likely to produce organizations that are complacent, though perhaps successful, market leaders (at least as long as the environment changes only slowly).

In assessing how to achieve a more innovative organizational culture, Ste- venson and Gumpert outlined an organizational culture continuum with an en- trepreneurial focus at one end and an administrative focus at the opposite end

Table 3-4   Characteristics of Entrepreneurial versus Administrative Cultures

Dimensions	Entrepreneurial Characteristics	⟷	Administrative Characteristics
Strategic orientation	Driven by perceptions of opportunity		Driven by controlled resources
Commitment to seize opportunities	Revolutionary change within short period		Evolutionary change over long period
Commitment of resources	Many stages, with minimal exposure at each stage		A single stage, with complete commitment based on one decision
Control of resources	Use of free-lance help and rental of required resources		Employment or ownership of required resources
Management structure	Few levels, with emphasis on informal communication patterns		Many levels, with emphasis on communication through formal hierarchy

Source: Adapted from Howard H. Stevenson and David E. Gumpert, "The Heart of Entrepreneurship," *Harvard Business Review,* March–April 1985, p. 89.

(see Table 3-4). The continuum considers several dimensions. For instance, at the entrepreneurial end, organizations are more likely to have a strategic orientation aimed at identifying outside opportunities brought about by environmental change; make revolutionary changes within short periods of time; commit resources in many smaller stages to minimize exposure at each stage; use freelance help and rented resources in order to maintain flexibility; and create organizations that have few levels of management and emphasize informal communication. In contrast, organizations at the administrative end are more apt to have a strategic orientation toward defensively protecting the resources under their control against threats; want every aspect of the situation planned in advance, leading to evolutionary change over a long period of time; make large major commitments at one time; want to employ or own their own resources; and have many levels of management, with emphasis on communicating through the official hierarchy.

Changing Organizational Culture

Because organizational cultures involve fairly stable values, assumptions, beliefs, and norms, such cultures can be difficult to change.[81] According to organizational culture expert Ralph H. Kilmann, one way to change organizational culture is to follow five main steps.[82]

The first step, *surfacing actual norms,* involves having organization members list the actual norms (expected behaviors in the organization) that they believe currently influence their attitudes and actions. This process typically takes place in a workshop setting and may include a representative group of employees or many groups of employees, depending on how many can be handled in a single setting. For organizations in which the impact of organizational culture on organizational effectiveness is negative, such sessions often reveal norms such as "Don't rock the boat," "Don't enjoy your work," and "Don't share information with other groups."

In the second step, *articulating new directions,* group members discuss the current direction of the organization and the behaviors that are necessary for organizational success. In the third step, *establishing new norms*, group members develop a list of new norms that would have a positive impact on organizational effectiveness. The fourth step, *identifying culture gaps*, involves identifying the areas in which there is a major difference (culture gap) between actual norms and those that would positively impact organizational effectiveness. The fifth step, *closing culture gaps*, entails agreeing on new norms and designing means of reinforcing them, such as developing reward systems that encourage members to follow the new cultural norms. We discuss approaches for bringing about change in organizations in Chapter 7.

Meanwhile, the issue of values, beliefs, and norms in organizations also is important to the topic of the next chapter. In that chapter, we explore questions of organizational social responsibility and managerial ethics.

CHAPTER SUMMARY

Organizations are affected by the external environment, the major outside forces that have the potential of significantly impacting on the likely success of products or services. Broad conditions and trends in the societies within which an organization operates constitute an organization's mega-environment. The mega-environment consists of five major elements: technological, economic, legal-political, sociocultural, and international. Generally, elements of the mega-environment tend to be beyond the ability of a single organization to alter directly, at least in the short run.

The task, or operational, environment identifies specific outside elements with which an organization interfaces in the course of conducting its business. The task environment depends largely on the specific products and services that an organization decides to offer and the locations where it chooses to conduct its business. A single organization may be more successful in affecting its task environment than the mega-environment. Major elements in the task environment of an organization typically include customers and clients, competitors, suppliers, labor supply, and government agencies.

Two important, but differing, perspectives on the nature of the relationship between organizations and their environments are the population ecology model and the resource dependence model. Managers can analyze their organization's environmental situation in terms of two key concepts, environmental uncertainty and environmental munificence, or capacity. The concept of environmental uncertainty refers to the extent to which future conditions affecting an organization cannot be accurately assessed and predicted, while environmental munificence refers to the extent to which the environment can support sustained growth and stability. The degree of environmental uncertainty is a function of two major factors, complexity and dynamism.

Three major options that managers have in attempting to manage environmental elements are adaptation, favorability influence, and domain shifts. Adaptation involves changing internal operations and activities to make the organization more compatible with its environment. Methods of adaptation include buffering, smoothing, forecasting, and rationing. Favorability influence focuses on attempting to alter environmental elements in order to make them more compatible with the needs of the organization. The resource dependence perspective argues that the environmental areas that organizations are most likely to attempt to influence are those on which they are most dependent. Major methods of favorability influence include advertising and engaging in public relations, boundary spanning, recruiting, negotiating contracts, co-opting, establishing joint ventures, joining trade associations, and engaging in political activities. Domain shifts involve changes in the mix of products and services offered so that an organization will interface with more favorable environmental elements. One method is to move entirely out of a current product, service, or geographic area into a more favorable domain. The second domain-shift method is diversification through the geographic expansion of existing products or services or the development of new products or services.

Organizational culture is a system of shared values, assumptions, beliefs, and norms that unite members of an organization. The nature of a particular organization's culture is typically inferred through the organization's use of concrete manifestations, such as symbols, stories, and rites and ceremonials. In entrepreneurial cultures that encourage innovation, members tend to view growth and change as desirable and also believe that they can affect the competitive environment. Changing organizational culture can be difficult and is likely to involve a multistep process.

MANAGERIAL TERMINOLOGY

advertising 99
boundary spanning 99
buffering 97
capitalist economy 82
ceremonial 104
competitors 88
co-opting 100
corporate culture 103
customers and clients 87
direct interlock 100
domain shifts 101
economic element 82
environmental complexity 94

environmental dynamism 94
environmental munificence 95
environmental uncertainty 94
external environment 77
government agencies 91
indirect interlock 100
interlocking directorates 100
internal environment 77
international element 84

joint venture 100
labor supply 90
legal-political element 83
mega-environment 78
natural selection model 91
negotiating contracts 100
organizational culture 78
population ecology model 91
public relations 99
rationing 98

resource dependence model 92
rite 104
smoothing 97
socialist economy 82
sociocultural element 84
story 104
suppliers 90
symbol 104
task environment 87
technological element 79
trade associations 100

QUESTIONS FOR DISCUSSION AND REVIEW

1. Outline the major elements that make up the mega-environment. Identify a major trend in each element of the mega-environment that could impact the organization in which you or some member of your family works.

2. Identify the major elements that typically make up the task environment of an organization. Use these major elements to develop an outline of the task environment for an organization in which you or some member of your family works.

3. Contrast the population ecology and resource dependence views of the organization-environment interface. Identify a situation in which environmental change caused an organization to go out of existence. What possible actions, if any, might management have taken to avoid the organization's demise?

4. Explain how environmental uncertainty impacts organizations. How would you assess environmental uncertainty for Harley-Davidson, the maker of heavy motorcycles?

5. Describe how environmental munificence impacts organizations. How would you assess environmental munificence for Harley-Davidson?

6. Outline the major methods that can be used to help organizations adapt to their environmental elements. For each method, give an example based on an organization with which you are familiar.

7. Enumerate the major methods that can be used to help organizations favorably influence their environments. For five of these methods, give an example based on an organization with which you are familiar.

8. Explain how domain shifts can help organizations cope with their environments. Give an example of an organization that made a major domain shift. Was the shift beneficial to the organization? Why, or why not?

9. Explain the nature of organizational culture and its major manifestations. Give an example of each of the major manifestations of culture at your college or university. Briefly describe your perception of the culture at your college or university.

10. Explain the difference between an entrepreneurial and an administrative culture. Contrast the organizational culture of IKEA with that of Champion Spark Plug.

DISCUSSION QUESTIONS FOR CHAPTER OPENING CASE

1. Identify the major elements of the task environment at Liz Claiborne, Inc. Assess the company's handling of these major elements.
2. At various times, retailer orders for Liz Claiborne clothing have exceeded available supplies, and the company has been forced to cut back orders. Iden-

tify the environmental adaptation method used. Evaluate the pros and cons of other forms of environmental adaptation in this situation.

3. What avenues exist for Liz Claiborne, Inc., to further manage environmental elements that have the potential of affecting the company?

MANAGEMENT EXERCISE: ASSESSING A SKI SHOP ENVIRONMENT

Your best friend's sister and brother-in-law run the local ski shop near campus in your college town, but they have recently bought another type of business in another town. They want you and your friend to take over managing the ski shop. If you run it successfully, you and your friend will gradually be given substantial equity in the shop and eventually would own the whole thing.

So far, the shop has been only marginally profitable. Although the shop carries ski equipment, as well as ski clothing, it has habitually run out of both during the peak of the skiing season. At the same time, hastily ordered extra merchandise to meet the demand has often arrived late and then could not be sold until the next season, if at all. In addition, the shop does very little business from March through August.

Due to a dispute over the size and prominence of the outside sign displaying the shop's name, the relationship with local government officials is extremely poor. Tact and diplomacy are not a major strength of your friend's brother-in-law. As a result, the shop gets more than its share of inspections by the fire marshal, and a recent effort to gain permission to expand the parking lot was turned down by the zoning board.

So far, beyond some minimal advertising, little effort has been expended making inroads on campus. Yet

it would seem that the campus, with its 12,000 students, would be a lucrative market. The remainder of the town of 120,000 also contains a large number of avid skiers, since good skiing is only about 1½ hours away by car. Unfortunately, many of these skiers make their purchases of ski equipment and clothing at the various ski lodges that they frequent. One reason is that these lodges tend to have better arrangements for repairing and maintaining ski equipment.

Your initial assessment is that, so far, the ski shop has not attempted to deal adequately with its environment. There have been persistent rumors that another ski shop may open in the next year, creating a local competitor. You and your friend (and possibly some of your other friends who are willing to give you advice) are about to meet to try to develop some approaches that will help the ski shop manage its environment better. This analysis is crucial to your ultimate decision about whether to take on managing the ski shop. Also, your friend's sister and brother-in-law want to hear your ideas.

First, outline the major elements in the ski shop's task environment. Then prepare a proposal indicating how you would attempt to better manage the environmental impacts on the ski shop.

XEROX WORKS TO MEET ENVIRONMENTAL CHALLENGES

After once holding a near monopoly in the photocopier business, the Xerox Corporation has been making major changes to retain its position as a major player. CEO David T. Kearns, who took over in 1982, has been emphasizing cost cutting, a renewed dedication to customer service, and 100 percent quality (no defects) in manufacturing. In addition, the company has been making major efforts to develop innovative new copiers and related products.

Xerox's saga begins with founder and entrepreneur Joseph C. Wilson, who turned his tiny company, originally called Haloid, into a giant by purchasing exclusive world rights to inventor Chester F. Carlson's xerographic process in 1947. The company launched the first commercial plain-paper copier in 1959, and by 1972, Xerox's annual sales reached $2.4 billion.

Meanwhile, Wilson had named a successor, C. Peter McColough, who took over as CEO in 1968. In order to cope with the burgeoning growth, McColough began instituting a variety of controls and procedures, coupled with increasing layers of management. Unfortunately, these efforts were somewhat excessive and turned the company into a slow-moving bureaucracy, in which product development was subject to long delays. Nevertheless, the company continued its massive growth. Its sales and service groups were among the best.

Under McColough, the company made a crucial decision in 1972 not to import a low-volume copy machine from Fuji Xerox, a Japanese affiliate. Instead, McColough wanted to develop a similar machine in the United States. Seven years later, after several product development failures, Xerox finally imported the machine from its Fuji affiliate. By then, Japanese competitors, such as Canon, had gained strong footholds that enabled them to capture most of the low-end market. McColough emphasized development of mid- and high-volume copiers, focusing on potential threats from IBM and Kodak. Those efforts have helped Xerox retain close to 40 percent of the market at the mid- and high-volume ends.

Meanwhile, McColough began to acquire a variety of high-technology companies, particularly those in the computer industry, but most of them were not especially successful. Still, they did produce a number of innovations. Xerox's Palo Alto research center developed much of the basic technology used in personal computers, yet Xerox did not capitalize on this and other new technology. Instead, a "cold war" developed between the East Coast copier faction at Xerox headquarters in Rochester, New York, and the West Coast computer specialists. The cultures of these two groups were very different, because the headquarters culture was very bureaucratic and the West Coast group was more entrepreneurial. According to one former Xerox executive, the cultural differences "led to infighting and paralysis. It was pathetic to watch."

By the time Kearns came in as CEO, Xerox had discovered that its Japanese competitors' costs per machine were 40 to 50 percent less than those of Xerox, making it easy for competitors to undercut Xerox prices. Furthermore, Xerox's net income had declined almost 50 per-

Xerox CEO David T. Kearns has transformed his company from an excessively bureaucratic culture to a more open and entrepreneurial culture. Profits have gone up as Kearns has focused on improving quality and satisfying customers. Here Kearns is shown practicing what he preaches: he is chatting with William A. Garrett, information officer at AT&T, one of Xerox's biggest customers.

cent as the company gave up market share and had to lower prices in order to compete. Kearns has attempted to restore the entrepreneurial culture that existed under founder Wilson. Under the Leadership Through Quality program, begun in 1980, more than 100,000 employees have become dedicated to quality and have learned the importance of meeting customers' requirements. Defects in manufacturing at the main manufacturing plant in Rochester have dropped 50 percent, coming very close to the quality level of Japanese competitors. The number of suppliers has been decreased from 5000 to 350, and by working closely with the remaining suppliers, Xerox has reduced the number of defective incoming parts from 100,000 per million to 300. There are fewer management levels, greater authority has been delegated to lower levels, and employees are much more involved in major decisions and activities. In recognition of its great strides in quality, Xerox received the prestigious Malcolm Baldrige National Quality award in 1989. The award, named for the late commerce secretary, is presented by the Commerce Department in recognition of companies that attain "preeminent quality leadership." Moreover, Xerox's market share in copiers has been rising.

The company also decided to move into a nonmanufacturing business—one that would not require effort from its manufacturing experts and related resources and that had little foreign competition. It created Xerox Financial Services, which has been doing well and providing some needed revenue for Xerox's extensive research and development. The company is getting ready for a new onslaught of Japanese machines aimed at the mid- and high-volume market. In addition, it is keeping an eye on Kodak, which has purchased IBM's copy business and is attempting to become a larger market force, particularly in high-volume copiers.[83]

QUESTIONS FOR CHAPTER CONCLUDING CASE

1. How have major elements of the mega-environment and task environment impacted Xerox?
2. What major methods has Xerox used to attempt to manage environmental impacts?
3. Compare and contrast the organizational cultures at Xerox during the McColough and Kearns eras.

CHAPTER FOUR

SOCIAL RESPONSIBILITY AND ETHICS IN MANAGEMENT

CHAPTER OUTLINE

Organizational Social Responsibility
Major Perspectives
Social Stakeholders
Does Social Responsibility Pay?
Promoting Innovation: Vanguard
 Companies

Organizational Social Responsiveness
Monitoring Social Demands and
 Expectations
Internal Social Response Mechanisms

Being an Ethical Manager
Types of Managerial Ethics
Ethical Guidelines for Managers
Ethical Career Issues

Managing an Ethical Organization
Situational Factors That Influence
 Ethical Behavior
Principles for Ethical Management

LEARNING OBJECTIVES

After studying this chapter, you should be able to:

■ Explain three major perspectives on corporate social responsibility and identify the five major stakeholder groups frequently mentioned in conjunction with social responsibility.

■ Assess the extent to which organizational social responsibility pays.

■ Explain the characteristics of vanguard companies.

■ Outline approaches that can be used to monitor social demands and expectations.

■ Describe internal social response mechanisms available to organizations.

■ Contrast the three major types of managerial ethics.

■ Outline ethical guidelines for managers and explain actions managers can take to handle ethical situations and avoid ethical conflicts.

■ Describe situational factors that influence ethical behavior and outline principles for ethical management.

JOHNSON & JOHNSON TURNS TO CREDO IN CRISIS

In the fall of 1982, a crisis confronted Johnson & Johnson (J&J) managers when seven Chicago-area residents died after taking Extra-Strength Tylenol capsules contaminated with cyanide. Not only was Tylenol the best-selling U.S. drug, but it was a product that symbolized the Johnson & Johnson reputation for quality, gentleness, and fine health care. A $400-million-per-year product and the reputation of one of the nation's most respected drug companies was at risk.

Despite the pressures of dealing with national media coverage, J&J executives took decisive action. They immediately opened their doors to the press and took great pains to keep the public informed of the facts surrounding the situation. A major issue that quickly emerged was what to do about the 31 million bottles of Extra-Strength Tylenol that were on drug store shelves throughout the country. As information was pieced together, it soon became apparent that the cyanide had been put into the capsules after they had left J&J factories and that the problem appeared to be isolated in the Chicago area. Nevertheless, Tylenol sales sank to 20 percent of their previous level, and an opinion poll showed that 61 percent of Tylenol users said that they would discontinue using the product. It seemed that Tylenol was doomed and that years of effort in building loyal customers for the product and goodwill for the company were about to go down the drain.

Nevertheless, the FBI and the Food and Drug Administration advised J&J managers not to take any drastic action. Even so, J&J managers promptly took the unprecedented step of recalling the 31 million bottles of Tylenol at a cost of $100 million. A few weeks later they made a second major decision, the decision to reintroduce Tylenol capsules in a triple-sealed, tamper-resistant package. In the months following the tragedy, the company established a consumer hotline, continued extensive cooperation with the media, made a widely advertised refund offer for any precrisis capsules still in the possession of consumers, and had then Chairman James E. Burke appear on the Donahue show. One opinion poll taken 3 months after the tragedy showed that 93 percent of the public felt that Johnson & Johnson had done a good job of handling its responsibilities.

In considering these events, David R. Claire, J&J's president, said, "Crisis planning did not see us through this tragedy nearly as much as the sound business management philosophy that is embodied in our 'Credo.' It was the Credo that enabled us to make the right early decisions that eventually led to the comeback phase." Chairman Burke also noted that "the guidance of the Credo played the most important role" in the company's decision process.

The J&J Credo was originally drafted by General Robert Wood Johnson in the 1940s and has as its first line: "We believe our first responsibility is to the doctors, nurses and patients, to mothers and all others who use our products and services." The Credo outlines the belief that businesses have social responsibilities, but it also reflects the J&J view that paying attention to social responsibilities is important to business survival and growth. A copy of the document (see Figure 4-5 near the end of this chapter) is given to every new employee, and copies adorn walls throughout the company.

During the 1970s Chairman Burke arranged for "Credo challenge meetings" to test the document's current relevance. The result of the meetings was that the Credo, with very slight revisions, received the endorsement of J&J managers and was reemphasized throughout the company. As a result, the Credo served as a guideline to decision making in the Tylenol situation. Burke pointed out, "We had spent a lot of time committing this corporation to a set of principles that

"The public comes first" is the essence of the Johnson & Johnson Credo, a set of principles that governs the company's actions. It was this Credo that led Johnson & Johnson to remove all boxes of Extra-Strength Tylenol from retail shelves across the country after cyanide-laced Tylenol capsules caused seven deaths in the Chicago area. The overwhelmingly favorable response from the public proved that this socially responsible action was also a sound business decision.

clearly said that the public comes first. If we had decided to violate that, every single employee in the world would have known what we were doing. So not only did we box ourselves in to a set of firm beliefs, but we were given in this horrible situation an opportunity to institutionalize them for a long time to come.''

Unfortunately, another opportunity soon presented itself. In early 1986, a second Tylenol crisis occurred when a 23-year-old woman died after taking a cyanide-laced Tylenol capsule. The company quickly offered to replace all capsules with caplets, a tablet in the shape of a capsule. The replacement effort cost J&J $150 million. In addition, J&J announced that it would no longer offer Tylenol in capsules, another bold and costly move in keeping with its Credo. The actions of J&J in the two Tylenol incidents earned the company widespread praise.[1] Among 300 large companies included in the 1987 *Fortune* magazine survey of America's most admired corporations, J&J was rated number one on community and environmental responsibility, and the company has often been on the magazine's most admired list.[2]

Johnson & Johnson's actions in the Tylenol situation were unusually swift, decisive, and costly. A contrasting approach was taken by the managers of the A. H. Robins Company, manufacturer of the Dalkon Shield, an intrauterine contraceptive device. The shield has engendered close to 9000 claims related to serious injury and, in a few cases, death from infections related to the product's use. When approving one $4.6 million liability suit against the company, Judge Miles Lord of the federal district court chided top management for failing to withdraw the product from the market when difficulties began to appear. The judge noted that, instead, the managers had concentrated their efforts on legal maneuvers and congressional lobbying to absolve the company of any responsibility.[3] Eventually, the company filed for bankruptcy protection in an attempt to limit its mounting liabilities associated with the shield and was acquired by American Home Products Corp.

As the Johnson & Johnson and A. H. Robins cases illustrate, managers can take very different stances with regard to their responsibilities to others. Furthermore, many of the situations confronting managers are less clear-cut, often falling into murky, gray areas involving responsibilities. While the J&J and Robins situations involved specific products, product-related problems constitute only one type of social issue likely to confront managers and their organizations. The news of late has reported a variety of other events that are indicative of issues surrounding the social responsibilities of organizations. Some of these events are as follows:

This oil-drenched bird was one of thousands of wildlife victims of the Exxon *Valdez* oil spill in Alaska in 1989. Many people have faulted the Exxon corporation for negligence in the operation of its oil tanker and in the clean-up of the spill.

■ Several executives departed from the Anheuser-Busch Company after allegations of kickbacks to three Anheuser executives were made during the bankruptcy-court proceedings of a defunct advertising agency.[4]
■ A high-level official of Kidder, Peabody & Company, a securities firm acquired by General Electric, pleaded guilty to insider trading and described a system whereby Kidder had earned millions of dollars by trading on information allegedly received from another Wall Street firm.[5]
■ The former chief executive officer of Intelsat, the international communications satellite agency, and two business associates pleaded guilty to criminal fraud and conspiracy charges stemming from $4.8 million that was siphoned from the agency during construction of its Washington, D.C., headquarters.[6]
■ A tanker operated by Exxon, the world's largest oil company, hit an underwater reef off the coast of Alaska. The resulting spill of 250,000 barrels of oil into Prince William Sound triggered widespread protests.[7]

■ Goodwill Industries, Inc., of Chicago found itself potentially liable for a multi-million-dollar cleanup of an 8-acre site on Chicago's west side that was found to be contaminated after it had been donated by Howard Conant, a director of the Valspar Corporation. Valspar had operated a paint factory on the site, which it had leased from Conant.[8]

Issues like these focus attention on questions of the social responsibility of organizations and the ethics of their managers. For example, in a recent Louis Harris & Associates national poll for *Business Week,* 58 percent of the respondents rated the ethical standards of business executives as only fair or poor.[9] *Ethics* are standards of conduct and moral judgment that differentiate right from wrong.[10] **Managerial ethics,** then, are standards of conduct and moral judgment used by managers of organizations in carrying out their business. In this chapter, we explore the nature and extent of the social responsibilities of organizations, including those that are both socially responsible and innovative. We consider various methods by which organizations can be responsive to social responsibilities. We also address the issue of the individual ethics of managers. Finally, we examine the challenge of managing an ethical organization.

Managerial ethics
Standards of conduct and moral judgment used by managers or organizations in carrying out their business

ORGANIZATIONAL SOCIAL RESPONSIBILITY

Organizational social responsibility refers to the obligation of an organization to seek actions that protect and improve the welfare of society along with its own interests. Organizational social responsibility often is referred to as **corporate social responsibility** because the concept is most often applied to business firms. Views differ on the degree to which businesses and other organizations should consider social responsibilities in conducting their affairs.

Organizational social responsibility The obligation of an organization to seek actions that protect and improve the welfare of society along with its own interests

Corporate social responsibility A term often used to refer to the concept of organizational social responsibility as applied to business organizations

Major Perspectives

Major concerns about organizational social responsibility are a relatively recent phenomenon. Such responsibilities began to emerge as an issue during the late 1800s when large organizations arose, commanded by such captains of industry as Cornelius Vanderbilt, John D. Rockefeller, and Andrew Carnegie. Anticompetitive practices, such as kickbacks and price-fixing, eventually led to government regulations and labor movement pressures for reform. A few important figures, such as Andrew Carnegie, became major donors to various social causes. The movement toward greater concern for social responsibilities gained momentum during the Great Depression, when the stock market crash served as a backdrop for the creation of the Securities and Exchange Commission and the enactment of additional laws regulating business. By 1936, General Robert E. Wood, CEO of Sears, had become one of the first top managers to argue for managerial, rather than just governmental, actions in behalf of social concerns. The various social movements of the 1960s (e.g., civil rights, women's liberation, and environmentalism) highlighted still further the public notion that organizations have social responsibilities.[11]

These historical developments have led to three major contrasting perspectives on corporate social responsibility: the invisible hand, the hand of government, and hand of management.[12]

The Invisible Hand. The chief spokesperson for the invisible-hand, or classical, perspective of corporate social responsibility is economist Milton Friedman, but

Invisible hand   A view that holds that the entire social responsibility of a corporation can be summed up as "make profits and obey the law"

its roots can be traced back to Adam Smith. The **invisible-hand** view holds that the entire social responsibility of a corporation can be summed up as "make profits and obey the law." According to this view, each corporation should actively pursue increasing profits through legal means. In this way, corporate responsibility will be guided by the invisible hand of free market forces to ultimately see that resources are allocated efficiently for the betterment of society. Otherwise, business executives will be taking on the right to allocate resources, giving them excessive power with little accountability to society for allocation decisions. Further, Friedman argues that charitable activities by corporations are not socially responsible because, in making such contributions, the corporation prevents individual stockholders from making their own decisions about how to dispose of their funds.[13]

The Hand of Government.   Under the hand-of-government perspective of corporate responsibility, the role of corporations also is to seek profits within existing laws. However, the **hand-of-government** view argues that the interests of society are best served by having the regulatory hands of the law and the political process, rather than the invisible hand, guide the results of corporations' endeavors. Thus, undesirable side effects of business functioning can be overcome by passing laws such as the Equal Pay Act of 1963, the Toxic Substances Control Act of 1976, and the Plant Closing Act of 1988, and by expanding the purview of regulatory agencies as necessary. This perspective agrees that a system provides for corporate social responsibility. Rather than the market, however, it is a system of laws and regulations guided by political managers, such as members of Congress and government officials, who act as the custodians of public purpose.[14] Neither the invisible-hand nor the hand-of-government approach is willing to afford corporate leaders latitude in the area of social issues.

Hand of government   A view that argues that the interests of society are best served by having the regulatory hands of the law and the political process, rather than the invisible hand, guide the results of corporations' endeavors

Hand of management   A view that states that corporations and their managers are expected to act in ways that protect and improve the welfare of society as a whole, as well as advance corporate economic interests

The Hand of Management.   The **hand-of-management** perspective states that corporations and their managers are expected to act in ways that protect and improve the welfare of society as a whole, as well as advance corporate economic interests.[15] One of the arguments in favor of viewing business leaders as having social responsibilities is the notion that the growing interdependencies of present times have inexorably woven a web of common interests between corporations and the communities in which they exist.[16] This broader view of the

Figure 4-1   Social responsibilities of management. (Adapted from Archie B. Carroll, "A Three-Dimensional Conceptual Model of Corporate Performance," *Academy of Management Review*, vol. 4, 1979, p. 499.)

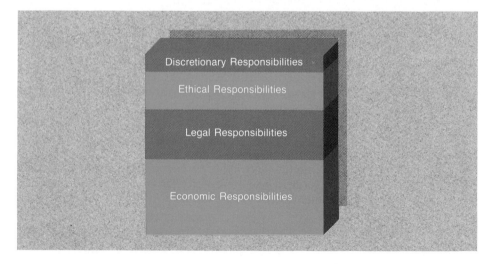

Discretionary Responsibilities

Ethical Responsibilities

Legal Responsibilities

Economic Responsibilities

social responsibilities of management encompasses economic, legal, ethical, and discretionary responsibilities, as depicted in Figure 4.1.[17] The proportions shown in the figure suggest the magnitude of each responsibility for corporate leaders.

The hand-of-management perspective recognizes ethical and possible discretionary responsibilities beyond the economic and legal responsibilities dictated by the invisible-hand and hand-of-government views. The ethical responsibilities include additional behaviors and activities that are not required by laws but still are expected of business by society's members. For example, mounting public pressure, as well as managerial concerns about apartheid, have led many organizations to discontinue doing business in South Africa even though they are not legally obligated to take such action.[18] Responsibilities in the ethical category tend to be somewhat ill-defined, frequently controversial, and subject to change over time. As a result, it often is difficult for business leaders to clearly identify such responsibilities.

On the other hand, discretionary responsibilities include beneficial activities that are not strongly expected of business by society's members. Discretionary activities are voluntary in the sense that they are not required by any laws and an organization would not generally be viewed as unethical per se if it declined to participate in them. Elements of society may, however, view such activities by corporations as highly desirable. Examples of voluntary activities are making philanthropic contributions, sponsoring a clinic for AIDS victims, and training the economically disadvantaged. For instance, Merck decided to provide free supplies of its new drug, Ivermectin, to millions of individuals in Africa, South America, and the Middle East who are in danger of contracting a serious disease called river blindness. One or two tablets taken per year prevents the parasitic disease that is responsible for disfiguring, debilitating, and blinding up to 15 percent of the population in some areas. The program will cause the drug company to forgo millions of dollars in profits.[19]

Meeting the expectations of society regarding ethical and discretionary responsibilities can be especially difficult for corporations, particularly because of diverse views regarding the nature of these responsibilities. For example, in 1987 the Council on Economic Priorities, a New York–based research organization that monitors corporate social behavior, instituted the America's Corporate Conscience awards. The 10 award winners included the Sara Lee Corporation, the Polaroid Corporation, and General Mills, Inc., for their charitable contributions; the International Business Machines Corporation and the Amoco Corporation for their community action; the Procter & Gamble Company for its practice of supporting the family concerns of employees; Avon Products, Inc. for its policy of promoting minorities and women into management; and Johnson & Johnson and the Ford Motor Company for their corporate disclosure, particularly their participation in the council's study of current business practices. Earlier, the council had published a related book, *Rating America's Corporate Conscience,* a shopping guide for socially conscious consumers.[20]

Shortly after the council's book was published, *New Republic* editor Michael Kinsley severely criticized, in a *Wall Street Journal* "Viewpoint" column, the standards used in determining corporate responsibility. As you might guess from the nature of the corporate award program, the standards included share of profits donated to charity; number of women and minorities among top officers and on boards of directors; and willingness to disclose "social information, involvement in South Africa, and conventional- and nuclear-weapons contracting." Kinsley argued that "corporations should keep to their own sphere and not attempt to become all-embracing social-service agencies."[21]

A microscopic worm transmitted by the bite of a fly that breeds along rivers in tropical climates causes a progressive disease that results in blindness. In many African villages children act as guides for their blind elders. In a discretionary action that has won widespread applause, the Merck Company has offered medically qualified programs in affected areas free supplies of a drug that counteracts the disease.

These differing views illustrate the conflicting pressures that confront managers, especially with regard to social responsibilities in the ethical and discretionary categories. Generally, society's expectations appear to be expanding regarding the social responsibilities of business firms, again particularly in the ethical and discretionary areas.[22] The result is the increasing relevance of the hand of management as the basis for corporate action.

Social Stakeholders

If corporations and their managers are to be socially responsible, then one important issue is: To whom are they to be responsible? Five major, somewhat overlapping groups are frequently mentioned: shareholders, employees, customers, the community, and general society.[23] These groups are considered social stakeholders because they can be affected for better or worse by the business activities of corporations.

Shareholders. Despite increasing social perceptions that business has obligations to a number of constituencies, there is still general agreement that the primary role of management in publicly held corporations is to earn profits and dividends for shareholders.[24] The shareholders have fulfilled a crucial role by providing the capital that allows the corporation to survive and grow. As a result, shareholders may expect management to operate the business in such a way that the shareholders are provided with the largest possible return on their investment, both through dividends and increasing stock value.

On the other hand, managers tend to view themselves as being responsible for the survival of the firm, perpetuating the firm through development and expansion, and balancing the demands of all stakeholders so that multiple demands do not jeopardize achievement of company objectives. The somewhat different perspectives held by shareholders and management can sometimes lead to conflict, particularly over such matters as the amount of dividends (versus reinvestment allocations) or the size of expenditures for executive perquisites such as stock options, country club memberships, and other fringe benefits. From a practical point of view, most shareholders will probably be reasonably satisfied as long as the company makes efficient use of their money and the stock provides a good return on their investment while consideration is given to the company's social impacts. In actuality, there is evidence that managers at various levels do not necessarily place shareholder desires ahead of those of other stakeholders. For example, one survey asked 1460 managers representing the supervisory, middle, and top levels to rate the importance of various organizational stakeholders (such as customers, myself, employees, the general public, and shareholders). The results indicated that top management gave higher ratings than the other two groups to customers and shareholders but still rated shareholders at about the same level of importance as the general public. Interestingly, all three levels of managers in the study gave relatively high importance ratings to themselves.[25]

Shareholders sometimes use their position to pressure for change in the social stance of management. For example, many individuals and institutions sold or threatened to sell their stock in corporations continuing to conduct business in South Africa, a factor in the decisions of some companies to discontinue their business dealings there.[26]

Employees. At a minimum, business firms and other organizations need to honor specific agreements made with employees and obey laws relating to employee-employer relationships. Recent years have witnessed a growing number of laws and government regulations that specify employer responsibilities in such areas as equal employment, pensions and benefits, and health and safety. The increasing number of laws relating to employment reflects public displeasure regarding abuses on the part of some employers.

Although it has become fashionable for top managers to speak of the employees of an organization as "family," actual treatment of employees can vary considerably. For example, one area of much recent concern is the treatment of employees during **plant closings,** a generic term that refers to shutting down operations at a factory or nonfactory site either permanently or for an extended period of time. As shown in Table 4-1, plant closings can occur with various degrees of social concern for employees. Such variations led to the passage of a plant-closing act in 1988, which requires that employees be notified at least 60 days in advance of the closing of business operations.[27]

> **Plant closings** A generic term that refers to shutting down operations at a factory or nonfactory site either permanently or for an extended period of time

Table 4-1   Plant Closings: A Continuum of Social Responsibility

Degree of Social Responsibility		
Low ←——————————————————————————————————→ High		
REACTIVE	MIXED	PROACTIVE
Penntech Papers Notified employees on same day closing took effect.	*Warner-Lambert* Gave 1-month advance notice of closing; provided outplacement counseling; did not conduct retraining programs; provided retirement planning.	*Brown & Williamson* Gave 18-month advance notice and phased out closing over a 3-year period; relocated employees; provided separation pay plus continued medical and life insurance coverage for 6 months after termination; provided vocational training.
Borg Warner Notified employees 2 days in advance of closing.		
National Car Rental Notified employees 3 weeks in advance of an indefinite closing; did not inform employees of permanent closing until 13 months later; did not coordinate efforts with union; sent employees to a state agency for retraining and job development programs.	*American Hospital Supply* Gave no advance warning to one-third of work force; other affected employees got 1-month advance notice; provided outplacement counseling; provided a 3-month extension of basic benefit coverage.	*Union Carbide* Gave 1-year advance notice; provided vocational training; provided outplacement counseling and retirement planning. *Ford Motor Co.* Gave 6-month advance notice; provided outplacement counseling and personal counseling; provided vocational training and cooperated and coordinated with the union. *Electrolux* Gave six-month advance notice; involved state and local agencies in outplacement program; provided retirement planning; offered transfers and moving assistance; gave paid time off for job interviews.

Source: Adapted from Angelo Kinicki, Jeffrey Bracker, Robert Kreitner, Chris Lockwood, and David Lemak, "Socially Responsible Plant Closings," *Personnel Administrator*, June 1987, p. 118.

Treatment of employees can vary on other issues as well. An extreme lack of social concern for employees is illustrated by a case in which officials from the suburban Chicago plant of Film Recovery Systems, Inc., were found guilty of murder in the death of an employee from cyanide poisoning. The death occurred because the workers, mostly non-English-speaking immigrants, had not been warned that cyanide was being used to extract silver from film scraps and had been provided with only minimal safety equipment.[28]

At the other end of the continuum of social concern for employees, some employers treat employees well enough to warrant being listed in the annual publication *The Best 100 Companies to Work for in America*.[29] Examples of specific benefits at these companies are listed in Table 4-2. One general listing of employee practices at major companies that are highly successful and take social responsibilities very seriously included the following: stakeholder status for unions, employee stock ownership, a fair measure of job security, lifelong training, benefits tailored to individual needs, participation in decision making, freedom of expression, and incentive pay.[30]

Customers. Although *caveat emptor* ("let the buyer beware") was once the motto of many businesses, consumers have come to expect more. Two areas of current social concern regarding consumers are health and safety issues and false and/or misleading advertising.[31]

Table 4-2 Selected Benefits at Some of the "Best Companies to Work For"

Company	Benefit
Reader's Digest	Workers have a 4-week paid vacation after their first year on the job.
Northwestern Mutual Life Insurance Co. (Milwaukee)	Lunch is free—everyday—for all employees.
Moog, Inc. (a small aerospace company in upstate New York)	Employees receive a 7-week paid vacation on their tenth anniversary—on top of their regular 3 weeks—and the 7-week treat is awarded every 5 years thereafter.
Time Warner, Inc. (New York)	If an employee works past 8 p.m., the company picks up the tab for the taxi home—even if the worker lives in New Jersey.
Nissan plant	Every employee with a year's service is eligible for a leasing deal that in Detroit is available only to top managers. For a reasonable monthly fee, the employee can lease a new Nissan car. The lease covers maintenance, taxes, license, and insurance. The employee just has to pay for gas.
Procter & Gamble	If an employee wants to adopt a child, the company will help out with the financing.
Intel Corp.	Under the company sabbatical program, after 7 years on the job each employee is eligible for 8 weeks off with pay.
Polaroid	A democratically elected employee committee represents the workers in negotiations with management.

Source: Abridged from Milton Moskowitz, "Lessons from the Best Companies to Work For," *California Management Review*, vol. 27, 1985, pp. 42–46.

In the area of health and safety, product liability suits are becoming everyday occurrences and can drastically affect business prospects. For example, the value of the stock of the Bic Corporation dropped when the company revealed a number of suits claiming that Bic lighters exploded, causing severe injuries and even death.[32] Due to the growing number of product liability cases, many organizations are experiencing difficulties in obtaining liability insurance. One result is that questions have been raised about the social responsibilities of businesses, and some wonder whether the pendulum has swung too far in favor of the consumer. One argument is that a manufacturer should be held liable for a product's safety only if the manufacturer "knew, or should have known, about its dangers." However, even this approach has perils since it is difficult to determine the extent to which a manufacturer should do research to ensure that every possible product safety contingency is considered. A stringent 100 percent requirement may mean that most products would take years to get to market—if they make it at all—and would be extremely expensive. One approach taken by businesses that care about consumers involves a compromise: attempting to be 99 percent certain that the product is safe, taking out large insurance policies, and hoping for the best.

In the area of advertising, blatant lies have been on the decline because of strong regulatory activity by the Federal Trade Commission. In a 1978 milestone case, the Supreme Court required that Warner-Lambert run "corrective advertisements" to rescind the long-term claim that Listerine "kills the germs" that cause sore throats and colds. While actual lying in advertising is less common, four other advertising problem areas remain as social responsibility issues: the selective ad, the preemptive ad, the statistical proof ad, and the suggestive ad. The *selective ad* emphasizes the good points of a product and downplays the bad points. For example, some fast-food chains have been severely criticized for running ads that tout the nutritional value of some aspects of their offerings, such as the bun, but fail to mention fat-content issues related to what is inside the bun.[33] The *preemptive ad* suggests that the claims being made apply to the advertised product but not to competing brands. Such ads often mention secret ingredients or special formulas that may or may not constitute exclusive product characteristics, but give that impression. The *statistical proof ad* uses statistics to make vague and unattributed assertions about a product. For example, an ad may state that a certain detergent contains "8 percent whitener," a claim that on close inspection is difficult to interpret, must less verify. The *suggestive ad* implies that the benefits of a product go beyond its basic purpose. Cologne ads, for instance, frequently imply that the product not only will make the user smell good but also will attract desirable members of the opposite sex. In judging the fairness of advertising, the Federal Trade Commission uses a "reasonable-person" test. If the majority of reasonable people are likely to be misled, then the advertising is considered improper. Alternatively, one scholar in the area of social responsibility, Thaddeus Tuleja, argues that when your product meets an actual customer need, "you don't need tricks to make your case."[34]

Community. In reference to social responsibility, an organization's community is its area of local business influence.[35] Most communities have social needs that extend beyond the available resources. As a result, businesses are likely to receive more requests for assistance than it is reasonable to honor, necessitating priorities in giving. A sampling of major requests for funds made to a large manufacturer in the midwest during a single year included support for air and water pollution control, funds for artistic and cultural activities, assistance in urban planning and development, support of local health-care programs, a do-

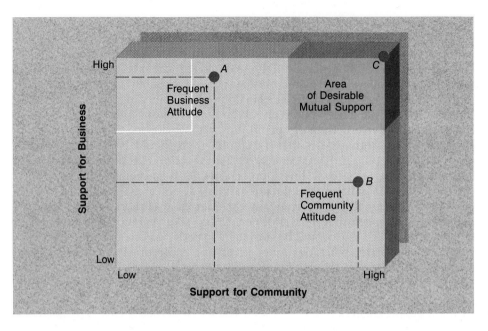

Figure 4-2 Possible levels of business and community mutual support. (Reprinted from William C. Frederick, Keith Davis, and James E. Post, *Business and Society*, 6th ed., McGraw-Hill, New York, 1988, p. 342.)

nation of equipment to a local school system, and executive aid for the local United Way drive.

At the same time, businesses need various forms of support from communities, including an adequate transportation system, taxes that are equitable and do not discriminate for or against business, adequate school and recreational facilities, and complete public services, such as police and fire protection and sewage, water, gas, and electric services. Because of these complementary needs, businesses and the communities in which they operate are somewhat interdependent, and both often can function more effectively with a high level of mutual support (see Figure 4-2). For example, when the H. B. Fuller Company, based in St. Paul, Minnesota, recently decided to build a glue factory in Minneapolis, company managers invited nearby homeowners and city officials to offer their suggestions about how the company could be a good neighbor. As a result, Fuller agreed to pay for expensive street lighting in the neighborhood, build a jogging track, and preserve a wooded area.[36]

Companies often are particularly generous to the areas in which their headquarters are based. Hence takeovers by more distant "parents" can reduce company donations for community purposes. For example, Syracuse, New York, had a long and beneficial relationship with two Fortune 500 companies that were taken over by nonlocal parents. Carrier, an air-conditioner manufacturer, was raided in 1979 by United Technologies, a conglomerate based in Hartford, Connecticut. Crouse-Hinds, an electrical equipment and cable maker, was saved from a hostile takeover in 1981 by Cooper Industries, a Houston-based conglomerate. While the city of Syracuse is generally prospering, there is great local concern that past major donations, such as the Carrier and the Crouse-Hinds theaters in the civic center, the Crouse-Hinds School of Management, and the Carrier dome over the football stadium at Syracuse University, might not be repeated.[37] One recent study suggests that companies tend to be less generous in making contributions to community charities when either the CEO or some other individual owns a significant percentage of stock in the company. In contrast, when managers are not owners, companies give more money to charity.

Apparently, a single individual with a significant stake keeps a more watchful eye on the purse strings.[38]

Society. Social responsibility at the societal level encompasses issues at regional and national levels.[39] Multinational corporations are likely to face differing expectations regarding their social responsibilities in the various nations in which they do business. At the same time, the further that corporate resource expenditures in the name of social responsibility stray from a tie to concrete business-related results, the more proponents of the invisible-hand view of social responsibility are likely to object. Conversely, the hand-of-government view would favor government regulation of social expenditures, possibly through higher taxes on corporations to allow governmental allocation of funding.

Three major counterarguments are typically advanced in favor of social responsibility to society. The **antifreeloader argument** indicates that since businesses benefit from a better society, they should bear part of the costs by actively working to bring about solutions to social problems. The **capacity argument** states that the private sector, because of its considerable economic and human resources, must make up for recent government cutbacks in social programs. The **enlightened self-interest argument** holds that businesses exist at society's pleasure and that, for their own legitimacy and survival, businesses should meet the expectations of the public regarding social responsibility. Otherwise, they are likely to eventually suffer financially and go out of business. This latter argument is related to the **iron law of responsibility,** which states that "in the long run, those who do not use power in a manner that society considers responsible will tend to lose it."[40] One Harris poll during the Reagan administration indicated that Americans by almost a 3-to-1 margin felt that businesses were not doing as much as they should in the areas of unemployment, education, and aid to the handicapped, elderly, and poor.[41]

Antifreeloader argument An argument that indicates that since businesses benefit from a better society, they should bear part of the costs by actively working to bring about solutions to social problems

Capacity argument An argument that states that the private sector, because of its considerable economic and human resources, must make up for recent government cutbacks in social programs

Enlightened self-interest argument An argument that holds that businesses exist at society's pleasure and that, for their own legitimacy and survival, businesses should meet the expectations of the public regarding social responsibility

Iron law of responsibility A law that states that "in the long run, those who do not use power in a manner that society considers responsible will tend to lose it"

Does Social Responsibility Pay?

One intriguing question is whether companies that are socially responsible are more successful financially. Several research studies have attempted to address this question, with largely mixed results. One of the problems in studying this issue is the difficulty of accurately measuring the social responsibility of one firm as compared with that of another. While these measurement difficulties preclude a definitive answer, the cumulative research, using the best measurement techniques currently available, indicates that no clear relationship exists between a corporation's degree of social responsibility and its financial success—at least in the short run.[42]

One interesting recent study linked the ratings of company social responsibility obtained in *Fortune*'s annual survey of the most admired companies with measures of both presurvey and postsurvey financial performance. The results suggested a firm's financial performance may predict social responsibility, rather than the reverse. One possibility is that organizations which are doing well financially feel more able to engage in activities related to social responsibility. Other results of the study indicated that firms may engage in social responsibility to bring about more stable relationships with major stakeholders and to help reduce the risk of lawsuits and governmental fines that could pose major threats to organizational well-being.[43] Thus there may be some reduced risk associated with social responsibility.

Other researchers have found that announcements of corporate illegal actions tend to have an adverse effect on a firm's stock price on the date the stories

Corporate philanthropy
Corporate contributions for charitable and social responsibility purposes

are released, although the long-term impact is unclear.[44] Ironically, generous charitable contributions may be one factor contributing to perceptions of companies as socially responsible, even if they behave illegally. One recent study tracked legal records indicating company trade crimes and also obtained data on **corporate philanthropy,** corporate contributions for charitable and social responsibility purposes. Companies that obeyed the law and were generous with corporate contributions, the "saints," tended to be rated highly on social responsibility in the annual *Fortune* magazine study of corporate reputations. However, companies that committed crimes but also were high contributors were seen as more socially responsible than companies that committed no crimes but were low contributors.[45] Unfortunately, this study suggests that public perceptions of a company's social responsibility may be linked more closely to the visibility of its philanthropic activities than to the degree to which its managers actually obey the law.

Top managers frequently find themselves caught between the expectations of various stakeholders who favor socially responsible behavior and the complaints of other sectors that favor a concentration on profit making. One result is that many corporations are attempting to orient philanthropic and other socially responsible activities toward areas that can affect their bottom line and ultimately give them a competitive edge. For example, Dayton Hudson, a midwest-based department store chain which contributes 5 percent of its taxable income to social causes, has recently been concentrating the funds in two areas, social action and the arts. Social action is considered important because by helping the poor become more prosperous, the company is increasing the potential pool of shoppers. The arts are considered to be compatible with the fashion business.[46] Another approach to social responsibility and profits has been instituted by the New York State Electric & Gas Corporation (see the following Case in Point discussion).

The contestant gets a kiss and Project SHARE gets a donation. The New York State Electric & Gas Corporation (NYSEG) sponsored this 10 kilometer run including a wheel chair division, to raise funds for an emergency assistance program for the elderly or disabled. NYSEG also has hired 13 former social workers to help its needy customers find their way around the social welfare system and obtain benefits for which they are qualified. One hoped-for result of these charitable actions is that the utility bills also will get paid.

CASE IN POINT: Utility Aids Customer's Welfare Needs

At the kitchen table of her threadbare Adirondack Mountains trailer home, Alzada Pulsifer pours out her problems to the understanding woman.

"You name it, I've had it," the 65-year-old grandmother says sadly, ticking off cancer, heart attacks, and cataracts. Now emphysema ties her to an oxygen machine several hours each day. Of her gaunt husband, Chet, she says: "I almost lost him the other day. They had to shock his heart back to beating." Then there's the dog, who's sick, and the past-due electric bill, and . . .

Ah, the electric bill.

The sympathetic stranger at the table, Paula Ross, is really a bill collector from the New York Electric & Gas (E&G) Corporation's nearby Plattsburgh office. But Ross isn't here to badger the Pulsifers. Rather, she wants to tell them about public-assistance programs for which they may qualify. While she emphasizes programs that pay a poor person's utility bill, the 40-year-old Ross also imparts information about medical, educational, and other plans. She will even fill out the forms and go to the agencies.

A trained social worker, Ross is part of an unusual corporate responsibility program that contains as much pragmatism as altruism. While other companies may contribute to worthy causes or divest themselves of their South African subsidiaries, New York State E&G helps people navigate the byzantine social-welfare system. In the process, it keeps thousands of customers with potential payment problems off its bad-debt rolls. For example, Ross and the 12 other

New York State E&G consumer representatives, all former social workers, helped about 200 families obtain roughly $90,000 in April, or about $450 per family. That included about 160 families who received about $45,000 to pay utility bills.[47] ▬▬▬

Although New York State E&G's program has been a public relations and financial success, it does have detractors who argue that the utility is really only interested in serving itself. Yet, increasingly, corporations are seeking to channel their philanthropy toward programs from which they can obtain at least some tangible returns. When American Express donated 2 cents to the San Francisco Arts Festival every time customers used the company's credit card during a 3-month period, American Express exceeded its marketing goals and the festival received $100,000.[48]

Promoting Innovation: Vanguard Companies

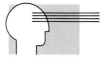

Although there might not be a direct relationship between social responsibility and financial performance (at least in the short run), researchers in the area of social responsibility are able to point to a number of examples of firms that score highly on *both* social responsibility and success. In his book *Vanguard Management: Redesigning the Corporate Future,* social responsibility scholar James O'Toole has termed such organizations "Vanguard" corporations. Some of his examples are Atlantic Richfield, Control Data, Dayton Hudson, John Deere, Honeywell, Levi Strauss, Motorola, and Weyerhaeuser. Vanguard organizations have the following four characteristics in common:

1. *They try to satisfy all their stakeholders*. The basic idea is that the interests of the shareholders are best served in the long run when corporations attempt to satisfy the legitimate concerns of all stakeholders. Such organizations work particularly hard at resolving conflicts and finding ways to simultaneously serve all their constituencies.
2. *They are committed to a higher purpose*. These corporations see their role as providing society with necessary goods and services, furnishing employment, and creating surplus wealth in the form of profits that can ultimately increase the general standard of living and quality of life. In this sense, profit is the means, rather than the end, of corporate efforts.
3. *They value continuous learning*. These companies recognize that flexibility, change, and responsiveness are vital to organizational survival. As a result, they monitor changes in the environment and assess the applicability of the strategies and practices of their companies.
4. *They aim high*. They are dedicated to being the best at everything they do. Because they strive for the best, they place a heavy emphasis on innovation as a vehicle that will help them reach high goals.

O'Toole argues that these four orientations do not depend on visionary, charismatic leaders. Rather, they depend on leadership with moral courage, including the courage to change things even when they are going well, to share authority and power, to hire subordinates who are likely to outperform oneself, to stick to one's values in hard times, to resist pressures for short-run gains, to take unpopular positions when necessary, and to be a subordinate who offers innovative ideas.[49] Thus there are companies that have succeeded in achieving a fairly high level of social responsibility and have been very successful financially as well. For example, since the early 1960s, Motorola has transformed its consumer electronics business into a leading producer of semiconductors while continuing to build its communications business (such as pagers and data terminals). In the process, the company has gained a reputation for innovative technology, as well as good treatment of employees and high ethical standards. According to one manager, "We could make a potful of dough selling technology to the Russians that isn't *quite* restricted by our government. But no one would dare broach the subject with Bob Galvin. He adamantly puts principles before profit."[50]

ORGANIZATIONAL SOCIAL RESPONSIVENESS

Organizational social responsiveness A term that refers to the development of organizational decision processes whereby managers anticipate, respond to, and manage areas of social responsibility

Corporate social responsiveness A term used to refer to the concept of organizational social responsiveness as applied to business organizations

While managers may have a particular concept of their organization's social responsibilities, the concept takes on practical meaning only when managers actually respond to those social responsibilities. **Organizational social responsiveness** refers to the development of organizational decision processes whereby managers anticipate, respond to, and manage areas of social responsibility. Organizational social responsiveness often is referred to as **corporate social responsiveness** because the idea is most frequently applied to business organizations. In fact, in this section, we address mainly social responsiveness in business settings. Keep in mind, though, that social responsiveness also is important for other types of organizations. For example, not-for-profit schools and hospitals also are expected to monitor the changing expectations of their various stakeholders and attempt to be responsive to them.

Two processes usually are essential in developing organizational social responsiveness. First, it is necessary to establish methods of monitoring social demands and expectations in the external environment. Second, it is important to develop internal social response mechanisms, such as committees and departments that handle issues related to social responsibility.

Monitoring Social Demands and Expectations

Major means of assessing social demands and expectations relative to organizations include social forecasting, opinion surveys, social audits, issues management, and executive scanning. Each of these is discussed in turn.

Social forecasting The systematic process of identifying social trends, evaluating the organizational importance of those trends, and integrating these assessments into the organization's forecasting program

Futurists Individuals who track significant social and other trends in the environment and attempt to predict their impact on the organization

Social Forecasting. **Social forecasting** is the systematic process of identifying social trends, evaluating the organizational importance of those trends, and integrating these assessments into the organization's forecasting program. One approach to social forecasting is the use of **futurists,** individuals who track significant social and other trends in the environment and attempt to predict their impact on the organization, usually 10 or more years into the future. Many organizations also use consultants and research institutes that specialize in social forecasting.

Opinion Surveys. Associations and major business publications often conduct surveys of public opinion on various issues of social concern. These surveys frequently provide useful feedback to businesses regarding the perceptions of social responsibility among various groups. See, for example, Figure 4-3, which presents partial results of a recent Harris poll commissioned by *Business Week;* the poll is discussed later on in this chapter.

**BUSINESS WEEK/HARRIS POLL:
IS AN ANTIBUSINESS BACKLASH BUILDING?**

Q How would you describe your own attitude toward business in this country... very favorable, somewhat favorable, somewhat unfavorable, or very unfavorable?

A Very favorable....................................18%
Somewhat favorable.........................54%
Somewhat unfavorable......................18%
Very unfavorable................................6%
Not sure...4%

Q How would you rate the ethical standards of business executives... excellent, pretty good, only fair, or poor?

A Excellent...2%
Pretty good......................................38%
Only fair...46%
Poor...12%
Not sure...2%

Q Do you think white-collar crime is very common, somewhat common, not very common, or not common at all?

A Very common...................................49%
Somewhat common..........................41%
Not very common................................7%
Not common at all..............................2%
Not sure...1%

Figure 4-3 Feedback provided by an opinion survey. (Adapted from *Business Week*, July 20, 1987, p. 71.)

Social Audits. A **social audit** is a systematic study and evaluation of the social, rather than the economic, performance of an organization. The audit includes an assessment of the social impact of various activities of the firm, an evaluation of programs specifically aimed at achieving social goals, and a determination of areas in need of organizational action. Social audits are difficult to carry out because there can be disagreements regarding what should be included, results can be somewhat intangible and/or difficult to measure, and differing interpretations of what is adequate or good social performance are likely. Nevertheless, companies are increasingly assessing their social performance through social audits.

Social audit A systematic study and evaluation of the social, rather than the economic, performance of an organization

Despite the costs associated with conducting them, social audits have five major advantages. First, they provide an opportunity to evaluate the extent to which the organization is meeting its social objectives. Second, they foster a greater concern for social issues among organization members. Third, they provide data for comparing the effectiveness of various programs. Fourth, they provide cost data for budgetary purposes. Finally, social audits illuminate areas in which the organization is vulnerable to public pressure and those in which the organization's social performance is strong. Although the data are gathered for internal use, more and more companies are mentioning aspects of their social performance in their annual reports to shareholders.[51] Some companies, such as Atlantic Richfield, prepare special reports on social performance for release to the public. Ben & Jerry's Homemade, Inc., the ice cream maker, recently included a four-page social audit in its annual report.[52]

Issues Management. As it applies to social responsiveness, **issues management** is the process of identifying a relatively small number of emerging social issues of particular relevance to the organization, analyzing their potential impact, and preparing an effective response. Typically, 10 to 15 issues are identified, but the number can vary somewhat depending on organizational circumstances. Issues management attempts to minimize "surprises" resulting from environmental forces and to facilitate a proactive stance toward environmental change. Otherwise, managers may find themselves continually reacting to changing circum-

Issues management The process of identifying a relatively small number of emerging social issues of particular relevance to the organization, analyzing their potential impact, and preparing an effective response

stances with little time for planning appropriate actions.[53] The Monsanto Company is an example of an organization that has used issues management to assess areas of potential concern to the public. During the mid-1980s, the top-level Executive Management Committee, chaired by the company president, Richard Mahoney, worked with various parts of the organization to identify 170 different relevant social issues. Ultimately, the list was narrowed to five issues of critical importance related to the Monsanto business environment: fair trade, biotechnology regulation, intellectual property rights, agricultural policy, and hazardous waste and public compensation. One result was that the company became a leader in the increasing cooperation between industry and environmental groups. Among other things, Monsanto was instrumental in the creation of Clean Sites, Inc., a partnership formed between environmental groups and industry to help accelerate the cleanup of hazardous waste sites.[54]

Social scanning The general surveillance of various elements in the task environment to detect evidence of impending changes that will affect the organization's social responsibilities

Social Scanning. Social scanning is the general surveillance of various elements in the task environment to detect evidence of impending changes that will affect the organization's social responsibilities. Scanning environmental elements is usually done by executives on an informal and somewhat unsystematic basis, according to their own experiences of factors that are likely to have important organizational implications. There is some evidence that executives of successful firms are more likely than their less successful counterparts to focus on areas of the environment that are potentially the most uncertain.[55] Managers may also rely on the more systematic means of monitoring social demands and expectations, discussed above. On the basis of his assessment of social expectations in the United States, the president and CEO of Minolta recently urged U.S. subsidiaries of Japanese companies to pay greater attention to U.S. standards of corporate social responsibility (see the following Case in Point discussion).

CASE IN POINT: Minolta Chief Urges Greater Giving

Speaking at a seminar on Japanese citizenship in the United States, Sadahei Kusumoto, president and CEO of the Minolta Corporation, the Japan-based maker of cameras, recalled a scene from the *Wizard of Oz*. In the scene, Dorothy and her dog, Toto, are swept by a tornado to the kingdom of Oz. Dorothy then exclaims to her dog, "Toto, I have a feeling we're not in Kansas anymore." Kusumoto drew an analogy between Dorothy's feelings and those of the Japanese who come to live in the United States amidst major differences in language, social structure, and customs. Kusumoto believes that the Japanese managers need to recognize clearly that they're "not in Honshu [Japan's largest island] anymore."

One area that is very different, according to Kusumoto, is the American notion of corporate social responsibility. In Japan, corporate social responsibility means taking care of your employees. The American idea that the public and private sectors have a shared responsibility for the community at large is an alien notion to the Japanese. Furthermore, U.S. businesses have a tax incentive to make charitable contributions, because such contributions are usually tax deductible. There is no comparable tax incentive in Japan. As a result, Japanese managers at U.S. subsidiaries of Japanese firms tend not to think in terms of corporate philanthropy. Another impediment to corporate giving is the fact that Japanese executives in the United States have difficulty taking action because they feel that they are not very familiar with community concerns. Finally, U.S. subsidiaries are often distributors with low profit margins, rather than manufacturers that have more opportunity for higher profit levels. As a result, they may not have enough leverage with corporate headquarters in Japan to get larger budgets for discretionary spending.

Kusumoto stated:

> Those are all good reasons why Japanese companies haven't been more active in U.S. philanthropy in the past. Now let me offer a good reason why they should be more involved: In the long run, failure to play an active role in the community will brand these companies as irresponsible outsiders and dim their prospects for the future.

> The singer Bob Dylan is well known for a lyric that says: "You don't need a weatherman to know which way the wind blows." Likewise, I don't need a graduate degree in sociology to understand that there is an immense and growing amount of resentment in the United States about Japan's economic success here. At this point, it wouldn't take much for these vague feelings of ill will to solidify into something really frightening—namely, hard-core protectionism that could trigger a global trade war.

Recalling the Japanese adaptability in changing the poor post-World War II image of Japanese products in the United States through constant efforts toward improvement, Kusumoto believes that changes are needed in the realm of social responsibility as well: "I have every hope that this same dedication and open-mindedness can help Japanese businesses in a new era of challenges. By applying hard work to American concepts of private- and public-sector partnership, I'm confident Japanese businesses here will acquit themselves with honor and fully prove themselves worthy corporate citizens in the United States."[56] ▬▬▬

Thus executives often play an important role in scanning the environment and noting important trends that can impact organizations. In Kusumoto's case, he was assessing major social trends that could adversely impact many Japanese companies operating in the United States. American executives must do the same, not only in the United States but also in the other countries of the world in which they do business. While monitoring social demands and expectations is important, organizations also must have social response mechanisms.

Internal Social Response Mechanisms

While social responsiveness depends on developing methods of identifying important social issues, it also requires that an internal means of responding be instituted. The internal social response mechanisms of an organization include the departments, committees, and human resources that affect its responsiveness to changes in the social environment.[57] Common means used by organizations to facilitate effective social responses include individual executives, temporary task forces, permanent committees, permanent departments, or combinations of these elements.[58]

Individual Executives. The use of individual executives as a social response mechanism involves either appointing or allowing certain executives to handle critical social issues as they occur. This type of approach is more often used in relatively small organizations, but it can be found in large organizations as well.

Temporary Task Forces. This mechanism involves appointing several persons to serve on a committee for a limited period of time to deal with a current critical

Charles Tyler, shown here visiting a school on Halloween, is an employee of ARCO Transportation Company, which honored him as Volunteer of the Year in 1989. Not only does he counsel students on the value of a diploma, but he also coaches two soccer teams and officiates at games, and volunteers his time and effort at an agency serving battered women and children.

social issue. When the necessary action is taken, the committee or task force is disbanded. Temporary task forces can be particularly effective when an important social issue arises suddenly and requires input from various parts of the organization.

Permanent Committees. There are many variations in the use of permanent committees. Almost 100 of the Fortune 500 companies have special committees on the board of directors that deal with social issues. These committees are often called public policy, public issues, social responsibility, and corporate responsibility committees.[59] Other committee arrangements include permanent committees made up of individuals at the executive level, committees composed of members from all layers of management, and division-level committees that channel critical issues to higher-level committees.

Permanent Departments. Many companies have a permanent department that coordinates various ongoing social responsibilities and identifies and recommends policies for new social issues. Although there are many alternative names, this department often is referred to as the **public affairs department.** It may be responsible for coordinating government relations, community relations, and other external relations activities. One study of large and medium-size U.S. business firms found that 361 of the 400 respondents had some type of public affairs unit, with one-third of them established since 1975.[60]

Public affairs department
A permanent department that coordinates various ongoing social responsibilities and identifies and recommends policies for new social issues

Combination Approaches. In practice, organizations may use a combination of these mechanisms to enhance their social performance.[61] For example, division-level committees may make recommendations to an executive-level committee, or a public affairs department may make recommendations to certain key executives. One unique use of permanent committees involving employees from throughout the organization has been pioneered by Levi Strauss, a company with a strong positive reputation in the area of social responsiveness. The approach is coordinated through regional and corporate community affairs departments (see the following Case in Point discussion).

CASE IN POINT: Levi Strauss's Community Involvement Teams

An important element in the success of Levi Strauss's philanthropic programs is the idea that merely giving *money* is not enough—time and effort are the greatest gifts one can give. To further employee involvement in community projects, the company established community involvement teams (CITs) at each company site in the United States. The program went international in 1977, when it was introduced to plants in Canada, Asia, Europe, Brazil, and Mexico. Today, there are CITs in 15 countries, and the company estimates that about one-quarter of all employees volunteer their time to participate.

As a company brochure explains, "The CITs are comprised of employees who elect their own officers, identify the needs of their communities, and develop a variety of projects to meet those needs. The projects are directed by the employees themselves through volunteer time." When a local team has decided where it wants to expend its energy and time, the members meet with the staff person at the regional community affairs office, who in turn reports to a division of the Levi Strauss corporate community affairs department. If the projects suggested by the local team are approved by the regional and national offices, the Levi Strauss Foundation donates some of the required funds. The community affairs staff helps arrange other funding sources, such as government grants, and advises CIT members as they work on their projects.

The CIT projects are as varied as the communities they serve. The teams establish volunteer fire departments in small American towns. They dig wells or build water treatment plants in Pacific Basin villages. They take senior citizens on holiday outings and hold Special Olympics for retarded and disabled youngsters. They have found and furnished a shelter for abused women and children, and they have donated equipment to local schools as well.[62]   ▬▬▬

BEING AN ETHICAL MANAGER

Ultimately, questions of organizational social responsibility and responsiveness depend on the ethical standards of managers who run businesses and other types of organizations. Lately, business ethics has not been receiving good press. In a recent cover story, *Time* magazine posed the question: "What's wrong?"[63] Citing a number of ethical issues ranging from the ouster of televangelist Jim Bakker for an affair with a church secretary to Ivan Boesky's plea of guilty to trading on inside information, the article proclaimed that "hypocrisy, betrayal and greed unsettle the nation's soul." Public concern with ethics also is reflected in the fact that Milton Bradley's hot-selling game "A Question of Scruples" sold 1.6 million copies in its first year. The game's 252 "dilemma" cards offer tough, but realistic, issues that an individual might face in such areas as friendship, family, marriage, sex, romance, business, and politics. The objective is to guess what other players will say they would do about the dilemmas.[64] Some business-related examples from the game are shown in Table 4-3. These examples illustrate just how difficult resolving ethical dilemmas can be. Citicorp has developed a similar game, called "The Work Ethic," tailored to situations and issues that its own employees are likely to confront.[65]

An article accompanying *Time*'s cover story on ethics focused on business ethics. In big, bold type it stated: "Not since the reckless 1920s has the business

Table 4-3 Business Ethical Dilemmas from Milton Bradley's "A Question of Scruples"

Situation	Dilemma
You're not physically ill, but you're exhausted emotionally.	Do you call in sick to work?
In a meeting with the department head, your superior takes credit for the work of a friend who is not present.	Do you set the record straight?
The taxi driver offers to leave the amount of the fare blank on your receipt. You can claim expenses.	Do you take it?
You are applying for a job requiring experience you don't have.	Do you claim you do?

Source: Reprinted from "Test Your Principles," *USA Today,* July 15, 1987, p. 4D.

world seen such searing scandals. White-collar scams abound: insider trading, money laundering, greenmail. Greed combined with technology has made stealing more tempting than ever. Result: what began as the decade of the entrepreneur is becoming the age of the pinstriped outlaw."[66] The magazine also cited a recent poll, conducted for *Time* by Yankelovich Clancy Shulman, in which 76 percent of the respondents saw lack of ethics in businessmen as contributing to tumbling moral standards.

Noting in particular the rising rate of *white-collar crime* (usually a crime committed against an organization or client for an individual's own benefit),[67] the article on business ethics estimated that, while common street crime costs the nation approximately $4 billion a year, white-collar crime drains at least $40 billion from corporations and governments—and ultimately from consumers and taxpayers. Major reasons given for the rise are the current heavy emphasis on materialism and competitive pressures to perform.[68] Women, long a stronghold against business crime, increasingly are appearing in white-collar criminal ranks.[69]

In March 1988, partially in reaction to these alarming trends, Arthur Andersen & Company, a major accounting firm, announced a 5-year, $5 million program to encourage and support the teaching of business ethics in U.S. business schools. Part of the program involves the company's Conference on Teaching Business Ethics, which provides a means for business school faculty from various disciplines to assess how to integrate ethics into the business courses that they teach. Hundreds of faculty members representing more than 150 colleges and universities have attended the conference and received related materials.[70]

A recent *Business Week* Harris poll (see Figure 4-3) collaborates public perceptions regarding the ethical standards of managers and particularly the prevalence of white-collar crime. In one study commissioned by *The Wall Street Journal* and run by the Gallup Organization, middle-level managers and members of the general public were asked to react to several ethical dilemmas. You might try your own hand at the six dilemmas, which are presented in Table 4-4. A profile of the responses from the participants appears after the six dilemmas. The current difficulties and public concerns with business ethics raise three particularly important issues regarding being an ethical manager: the types of managerial ethics existing in organizations, the kinds of ethical guidelines a manager might consider adopting, and the ethical career issues that one is likely to face.

Table 4-4   Compare Your Ethical Decisions to Those of Executives and the General Public

In a Gallup Organization poll conducted for *The Wall Street Journal*, 396 executives and 1558 adult members of the general public were asked to respond to a number of business-related ethical dilemmas. As you read the dilemmas below, decide how you would respond. Then compare your answers with those of the executives and public.

THE INFLATED SALARY
An employer finds that the candidate who is by far the best qualified for a job really earned only $18,000 a year in his last job and not the $28,000 he claimed. Should the employer hire the candidate anyway, or should he choose someone else even though that person will be considerably less qualified? What would you say if the real salary were $25,000, only $3000 less than the amount claimed?

FAMILY VS. ETHICS
Jim, a 56-year-old middle manager with children in college, discovers that the owners of his company are cheating the government out of several thousand dollars a year in taxes. Jim is the only employee who would be in a position to know this. Should Jim report the owners to the Internal Revenue Service at the risk of endangering his own livelihood, or should he disregard the discovery in order to protect his family's livelihood?

THE ROUNDABOUT RAISE
When Joe asks for a raise, his boss praises his work but says the company's rigid budget won't allow any further merit raises for the time being. Instead, the boss suggests that the company "won't look too closely at your expense accounts for a while." Should Joe take this as an authorization to pad his expense account on grounds that he is simply getting the same money he deserves through a different route, or should he refuse this roundabout "raise"?

THE FAKED DEGREE
Bill has done a sound job for over a year. Bill's boss learns that he got the job by claiming to have a college degree, although in reality he never graduated. Should his boss dismiss him for submitting a fraudulent résumé or overlook the false claim since Bill has otherwise proved to be conscientious and honorable, and since making an issue of the degree might ruin Bill's career?

SNEAKING PHONE CALLS
Helen discovers that another employee regularly makes about $100 a month worth of personal long-distance telephone calls from an office telephone. Should Helen report the employee to the company, or disregard the calls on the grounds that many people make personal calls at the office? What should Helen do if the calls totaled only $10 a month?

COVER-UP TEMPTATION
Bill discovers that the chemical plant he manages is creating slightly more water pollution in a nearby lake than is legally permitted. Revealing the problem will bring considerable unfavorable publicity to the plant, hurt the lakeside town's resort business, and create a scare in the community. Solving the problem will cost the company well over $100,000. It is unlikely that outsiders will discover the problem. The violation poses no danger whatever to people. At most, it will endanger a small number of fish. Should Bill reveal the problem despite the cost to the company, or consider the problem as little more than a technicality and disregard it?

Responses of the Managers and General Public

The results of the Gallup poll indicated that general citizens are considerably more inclined than executives to condone wrongdoing if there are mitigating circumstances.

The Inflated Salary: When the applicant's real previous salary was inflated by $10,000, some 63 percent of the general public surveyed recommended hiring the applicant, compared with

(continued)

Table 4-4 *(Continued)*

47 percent of the executives. When the salary was inflated by only $3000, 68 percent of the general public and 60 percent of the executives would hire the able but errant applicant.

Family vs. Ethics: Roughly half, 49 percent of the general citizens and 52 percent of the executives, think Jim should disregard his discovery in order to protect his family. About 34 percent of both the executives and the public think Jim should report the owners.

The Roundabout Raise: The public decisively (65 percent) rejected the roundabout raise, with the executives (91 percent) rejecting it even more overwhelmingly.

The Faked Degree: Half of the executives recommended dismissing Bill. The general public was more lenient, with 66 percent recommending overlooking the claim.

Sneaking Phone Calls: The difference in the dollar worth of the phone calls matters. When the employee is sneaking $100 a month worth of calls, 64 percent of the public and 76 percent of executives think that Helen should report him. But when the amount involved is $10 a month, only 47 percent of the public and 48 percent of the executives favor reporting him.

Cover-Up Temptation: Some 63 percent of the general public and 70 percent of the executives think Bill should reveal the problem.

Source: Reprinted from *The Wall Street Journal*, Nov. 3, 1983, p. 33.

Types of Managerial Ethics

Managerial ethics, as explained earlier in this chapter, are standards of conduct or moral judgment used by managers of organizations in carrying out their business. Such standards arise from the general norms and values of society; from an individual's experiences within family, religious, educational, and other types of institutions; and from interpersonal interactions with others. Therefore, managerial ethics may differ among individuals.[71] An eminent researcher in the area of social responsibility, Archie B. Carroll, notes that three major levels of moral, or ethical, judgment characterize managers: immoral management, amoral management, and moral management (see Figure 4-4).[72] Characteristics of the three types are summarized in Table 4-5.

Immoral management An approach that not only lacks ethical principles but is actively opposed to ethical behavior

Immoral Management. "Immoral" and "unethical" can be considered synonymous in business. Thus **immoral management** not only lacks ethical principles but is actively opposed to ethical behavior. This perspective is characterized by principal or exclusive concern for company gains, emphasis on profits and company success at virtually any price, lack of concern about the desires of others to

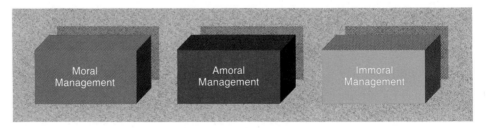

Figure 4-4 Types of managerial ethics. (Reprinted from Archie B. Carroll, "In Search of the Moral Manager," *Business Horizons*, March–April 1987, p. 8.)

Table 4-5   Characteristics of Managerial Ethics Types

Organizational Characteristics	Immoral Management	Amoral Management	Moral Management
Ethical Norms	Management decisions, actions, and behavior imply a positive and active opposition to what is moral (ethical). Decisions are discordant with accepted ethical principles. An active negation of what is moral is implied.	Management is neither moral nor immoral, but decisions lie outside the sphere to which moral judgments apply. Management activity is outside or beyond the moral order of a particular code. May imply a lack of ethical perception and moral awareness.	Management activity conforms to a standard of ethical, or right, behavior. Conforms to accepted professional standards of conduct. Ethical leadership is commonplace on the part of management.
Motives	Selfish. Management cares only about its or the company's gains.	Well-intentioned but selfish in the sense that impact on others is not considered.	Good. Management wants to succeed but only within the confines of sound ethical precepts (fairness, justice, due process).
Goals	Profitability and organizational success at any price.	Profitability. Other goals are not considered.	Profitability within the confines of legal obedience and ethical standards.
Orientation toward Law	Legal standards are barriers that management must overcome to accomplish what it wants.	Law is the ethical guide, preferably the letter of the law. The central question is what we can do legally.	Obedience toward letter and spirit of the law. Law is a minimal ethical behavior. Prefer to operate well above what law mandates.
Strategy	Exploit opportunities for corporate gain. Cut corners when it appears useful.	Give managers free rein. Personal ethics may apply but only if managers choose. Respond to legal mandates if caught and required to do so.	Live by sound ethical standards. Assume leadership position when ethical dilemmas arise. Enlightened self-interest.

Source: Reprinted from Archie B. Carroll, "In Search of the Moral Manager," *Business Horizons,* March–April 1987, p. 12.

be treated fairly, views of laws as obstacles to be overcome, and a willingness to "cut corners." The key operating principle of immoral management is: "Can we make money with this action, decision, or behavior?" Implied in this approach is the view that other considerations matter little, if at all.

One example of immoral management cited by Carroll involved three plant managers at a GM Chevrolet truck plant in Flint, Michigan, who secretly installed a control box in a supervisor's office. In a flagrant violation of the company contract with the United Auto Workers, they then used the control box to override a control panel that normally set the speed of the assembly line. The managers, under heavy pressure from higher-level executives because of missed deadlines, soon began meeting production goals and receiving praise from their

Chain brakes on saws significantly reduce the risk of accidents. McCulloch Corporation took a moral stand by making the chain brakes standard equipment on its saws and withdrawing from the Chain Saw Manufacturers Association, which fought adopting the higher safety standards.

Moral management An approach that strives to follow ethical principles and precepts

Amoral management An approach that is neither immoral nor moral but, rather, ignores or is oblivious to ethical considerations

bosses. When the scheme was discovered, workers won a $1 million settlement because of the extra work they had been forced to do.

Moral Management. In contrast to immoral management, **moral management** strives to follow ethical principles and precepts. While moral managers also desire to succeed, they seek to do so only within the parameters of ethical standards and the ideals of fairness, justice, and due process. As a result, moral managers pursue business objectives that involve simultaneously making a profit and engaging in legal and ethical behaviors. They follow not only the letter but also the spirit of the law and recognize that moral management generally requires operating well above what the law mandates. The central guiding principle is: "Is this action, decision, or behavior fair to us and all parties involved?"

One example of moral management in which an organization assumed ethical leadership involved the McCulloch Corporation, a manufacturer of chain saws. The acute potential dangers of chain saws were highlighted in Consumer Product Safety Commission statistics showing that chain saws were involved in 123,000 medically attended injuries in 1981, up from 71,000 in 1976. Despite this alarming data, the Chain Saw Manufacturers Association fought mandatory safety standards, arguing that the statistics were inflated and did not provide sufficient justification for mandatory standards. Further, the association argued that when chain brakes, an important safety device, were offered as options, there were few purchases. Displaying moral leadership, McCulloch decided to make chain brakes standard equipment on its saws in 1975; later, the company withdrew from the association after its repeated attempts to persuade the association to adopt higher safety standards failed.

Amoral Management. The **amoral management** approach is neither immoral nor moral but, rather, ignores or is oblivious to ethical considerations. There are two types of amoral management: intentional and unintentional. *Intentional* amoral managers do not include ethical concerns in their decision making, actions, or behavior, because they basically think that general ethical standards are more appropriate to other areas of life than to business. *Unintentional* amoral managers also do not think about ethical issues in their business dealings, but the reason is different. These managers are basically inattentive or insensitive to the moral implications of their decision making, actions, and behavior. Overall, amoral managers pursue profitability as a goal and may be generally well-meaning, but intentionally or unintentionally they pay little attention to the impacts of their behaviors on others. They generally leave other managers free to behave as they wish unless their behavior leads to outside notoriety or pressure. The basic question governing their behavior is: "Within the letter of the law, can we make money with this action, decision, or behavior?"

One example of amoral management is Swiss-based Nestlé's decision to market baby formula in third world countries. The company did not anticipate the negative effects on mothers and babies of marketing formula in areas with impure water, poverty, and illiteracy. Its indifference eventually escalated into the famous worldwide activist boycott of all Nestlé products. Similarly, when Pepsico used the "Frito-Bandito" theme to promote its corn chips, it did not foresee the concept's offensiveness to a group of Mexican-Americans who ultimately pressured the company into withdrawing the advertising.

Carroll believes that the amoral management style predominates in organizations today, but he argues that a moral management stance is more likely to be in the long-run best interests of organizations.

Ethical Guidelines for Managers

As the study presented in Table 4-4 illustrates, not everyone has the same ethical standards. In addition, it is difficult to write hard-and-fast rules for every possible condition, because situations differ from one another. Also, some situations seem ambiguous and fall into gray areas (e.g., at what point does a "token gift" from a supplier constitute a bribe?).[73] Yet there are a few common sense guidelines that can be helpful in thinking about the ethical implications of managerial decisions and behaviors. The guidelines discussed below, offered by James O'Toole, are basically consistent with the principle of enlightened self-interest.[74]

Obey the Law. A basic tenet of social responsibility and managerial ethics is obedience to the law, preferably both the letter and the spirit of the law. The Wedtech Corporation, a Bronx-based defense contractor, was once famous as the first major employer of unemployed minorities from the South Bronx slums. But the company collapsed amidst a scandal involving political payoffs that Wedtech executives admit they made to get lucrative government contracts.[75]

Tell the Truth. Telling the truth is important in building trust with relevant stakeholders. One company with a stellar reputation as a good company for which to work is the Digital Equipment Corporation (DEC). When a group of employees asked the company to look into an apparent high rate of miscarriages among women working on the semiconductor assembly lines, DEC swiftly commissioned a study. The study, which cost several hundred thousand dollars, confirmed that the miscarriage rate was 39 percent in the semiconductor area but only 18 percent in other parts of the company and in the general population. DEC quickly informed employees of the results and shared them with the Semiconductor Industry Association.[76]

Show Respect for People. The notion of treating people with respect has deep roots in the study of ethics. "Respect for the individual" has been a guiding principle at IBM since the concept was first articulated by founder Thomas Watson. The principle has translated into a reputation for treating employees well and a tradition of no layoffs. Instead, the company has recently reduced staffing levels several times through offers of early retirement.[77]

Stick to the Golden Rule. The Golden Rule, "Do unto others as you would have them do unto you," provides a benchmark for evaluating the ethical dimensions of business decisions. Translated into business terms, it means treating individuals fairly, just as the managers would want the business treated if it were an individual.[78] When Cummins Engine announced the closure of a components plant in Darlington, England, British trade union leaders went to Columbus, Indiana, to try to get the company to reverse its position. Although the company felt it had to stand by its decision, it did offer funding for a program to help the 500 displaced workers find new jobs. The union leaders praised the company for its sympathetic concern.[79]

Above All, Do no Harm *(Primum non nocere)***.** This principle—the first rule of medical ethics—is considered by some writers to be the bottom-line ethical consideration and one easily adaptable to business. H. J. Heinz recently told growers supplying fruit and vegetables for its baby foods that products cannot be treated with chemicals that are being studied by federal agencies as possible

QUESTIONS TO FACILITATE ETHICAL BUSINESS DECISIONS

When you face an ethical dilemma, you may find it useful to work through the following list of questions. The questions will help you clarify your thinking and decide what to do.

1. Have you defined the problem accurately?
2. How would you define the problem if you stood on the other side of the fence?
3. How did this situation occur in the first place?
4. To whom and to what do you give your loyalty as a person and as a member of the corporation?
5. What is your intention in making this decision?
6. How does this intention compare with the probable results?
7. Whom could your decision or action injure?
8. Can you discuss the problem with the affected parties before you make your decision?
9. Are you confident that your position will be as valid over a long period of time as it seems now?
10. Could you disclose without qualm your decision or action to your boss, your CEO, the board of directors, your family, or society as a whole?
11. What is the symbolic potential of your action if understood? If misunderstood?
12. Under what conditions would you allow exceptions to your stand?[81]

Reprinted by permission of *Harvard Business Review*. See references at back of book.

---

threats to health. This unprecedented step was taken even though the chemicals are legal to use.[80]

Practice Participation, not Paternalism. This principle is aimed at learning about the needs of relevant stakeholders, rather than deciding what is best for them. Weyerhaeuser, a forest-products company, has built a good reputation among environmentalists by eliciting their views before finalizing any plans for land or facility development.

Always Act When You Have Responsibility. Managers have the responsibility of taking action whenever they have the capacity or resources to do so or whenever those nearby are in need and a manager is the only one who can help.

For a set of questions that can help you, as a manager, utilize these principles in making ethical business decisions, see the Practically Speaking discussion, "Questions to Facilitate Ethical Business Decisions."

Ethical Career Issues

Like most managers, you are likely to experience some ethical dilemmas during the course of your career. Typically, these dilemmas arise from gray areas, where different interpretations of a situation are possible. In addition to considering the social responsibilities involved, managers need to think carefully about personal values and self-protection in determining how they will handle such situations. They also need to consider what actions they can take to anticipate and avoid ethical conflicts.[82]

Assessing Values and Protecting Yourself. When you are faced with an ethical dilemma, three steps are important in career terms. First, seek expertise and support from a wide network of people whom you trust. There may be times when others in the workplace accept a questionable practice as ethical that you may see as falling into the gray area. That is the time to check with trusted friends, former schoolmates, peers, and/or experts. This step helps you clarify your own values on the issue and decide whether further action is necessary. Second, if necessary, take internal actions to bring about change. Managers have an obligation to their company and colleagues to make sure that they have their facts straight before suggesting that the behaviors of others may be inappropriate or illegal. Then they need to bring the matter to the attention of superiors and attempt to persuade them to take a different course of action. If the ethical dilemma persists, it may be necessary to move to the third step, which is to take internal actions to protect yourself. Managers who are in the chain of command are in danger of becoming the scapegoat for actions that were implicitly or explicitly condoned by those above. Attempting to argue that one was only following orders will not get a manager off the hook in an illegal action. Instead, it often is a good idea to write a memo for the file, outlining objections and conversations with others. Talk with other employees about your concerns. Actively seeking another job is a further step that one should seriously consider. Above all, *do not engage in illegal activities*. Together these actions build a strong case supporting the fact that a manager has attempted to halt the ethical difficulty.

Anticipating Ethical Conflicts. Although it often is difficult to accurately predict the likelihood of ethical conflicts, there are some steps that you can take to do so. First, when seeking employment, look for organizational signals that indicate conflicts are likely. Ask your family, friends, and teachers about the organization. Check the library for recent articles and background information. Use job interviews to learn about how the organization operates. If possible, it often is helpful to meet with some of the people whom you would be working with. Try to detect signs of serious dissatisfaction and dissension in the ranks that may signal ethical conflicts. Second, check on industry practices. Industries that have been stable for a sizable period of time may have developed informal networks that encourage collusion among competitors. Industries at the other end of the spectrum, where there is easy entry and a highly competitive environment, may also be particularly susceptible to ethical difficulties because of the severe market pressures. Third, avoid making even small ethical compromises—they have a way of escalating out of control. Managers can help themselves avoid such compromises, according to some experts, by assigning a high priority to setting aside backup money in a bank account so that they can walk out of an unbearable situation. Otherwise, managers could find themselves caught up a trap like the one José L. Gomez fashioned for himself (see the following Case in Point discussion).

CASE IN POINT: Caught in a Trap of His Own Making

José L. Gomez, a former managing partner of the Grant Thornton accounting firm, is currently serving the first leg of a 12-year prison term.

In 1986, 39-year-old Gomez pleaded guilty to charges, in two federal courts and an Ohio state court, involving his role in the fraud at E.S.M. Government Securities, Inc., the once-obscure Fort Lauderdale, Florida, firm that collapsed in 1985 and triggered one of the biggest financial scandals of the decade. An E.S.M.'s auditor, Gomez knowingly approved the firm's false financial statements for 5 years, thus allowing the massive fraud to continue. He must serve at least 4 years.

In these days, when white-collar crime is rocking Wall Street, Gomez's story is a particularly telling one. In some regards, he was almost a cliché: an ambitious young man who rose too fast and wound up in the worst sort of trouble. He says he crossed the line into criminality without even realizing it.

When Gomez's activities came to light, many people were stunned, for he had seemed to be the model of success. He was one of the youngest people ever to be made a partner at his Chicago-based firm, which then was called Alexander Grant & Company. He was active in community affairs.

But he was also a fraud. Investors initially lost some $320 million in the scheme Gomez helped perpetrate, and the scandal was even blamed for a brief decline in the dollar on international markets.

In a recent interview, Gomez talked of his rise and fall. He says he never intended to do anything wrong. In August 1979, however, just days after being told of his promotion to the position of partner at Grant, two officers of E.S.M. told him of a crude accounting ruse that was hiding millions of dollars in losses; they had to bring Gomez in on the scheme to keep it from unraveling.

Gomez says he had missed the ruse in two previous annual audits, signing bogus financial statements that showed E.S.M. to be in robust condition. He says one of the E.S.M. officers used that error to draw him into the fraud.

In Chicago, Burt K. Fischer, executive partner of Grant Thornton, says Gomez's fears about his blunder were misplaced. "I can't think of a partner who made an honest mistake who has been hung out to dry," he says. The firm also contends that Gomez learned of the fraud before 1979.

Gomez says he decided to go along with the scheme at E.S.M., convinced that the firm's managers could make up the losses. E.S.M.'s losses continued to mount, and Gomez continued to approve phony financial statements. In late 1980, E.S.M. officers began arranging loans for Gomez, who was having personal financial problems. The loans, which weren't repaid, totaled $200,000.[83]

The aftershocks of the E.S.M. collapse led to the 1985 Ohio savings and loan crisis. The crisis began when it became clear that the Cincinnati-based Home State Savings Bank, whose loans were secured by a deposit insurance fund that was considered to be inadequate, was likely to suffer severe losses from the E.S.M. troubles. Ultimately, the Grant Thornton accounting firm paid $80 million to settle suits filed against it. Still pending are potential liabilities that approach $200 million.[84]   ▬▬▬

MANAGING AN ETHICAL ORGANIZATION

In an interview with *The Wall Street Journal*, Gomez argued that in hindsight he thinks that he was too inexperienced to be handling an audit and that there was too much emphasis on the ability to produce new clients, charges that the Grant Thornton accounting firm vigorously denies. Although it is easy in retrospect to blame everyone else, and although individuals are ultimately responsible for their actions, Gomez's allegations do have some relevance for managers. One important challenge of management is operating an organization in which members conduct their business in an ethical manner. One aspect of this challenge is having a knowledge of environmental and organizational conditions that increase the likelihood of unethical behavior. A second aspect is providing ethical leadership to the rest of the organization. In this section, we explore some of the major situational factors that influence ethical behavior. We conclude by reviewing four principles for ethical management suggested by a prominent CEO.

Situational Factors That Influence Ethical Behavior

Much of the research on ethical versus unethical behavior in organizations has focused on actually breaking the law, although factors influencing crimes also are likely to have a bearing on other types of unethical behaviors. Several factors in the environment of an organization can be conducive to unethical behavior (see Table 4-6).[85] Of course, the values of managers themselves will also have a bearing on whether an individual manager actually engages in unethical behavior, even though some types of situations make it more likely.

For example, *environmental competitiveness* tends to encourage unethical behavior. Some industries in which price-fixing has been common, such as those producing automobiles, paper cartons, plumbing fixtures, and heavy electrical equipment, tend to have strong competition, products that are fairly similar, and frequent price changes and negotiations. Competition can foster unethical behavior in not-for-profit organizations, as well. Such behavior is manifested in illegal payments to college athletes, illegal campaign contributions to candidates, and misrepresentations of the amount of charitable contributions actually going to those being helped.

Low *environmental munificence* also may be conducive to unethical behavior, as organizations struggle for financial performance in an environment in which the opportunities for success are limited. For example, executives at the Beech-Nut Nutrition Corporation, the second-largest U.S. baby food manufacturer, ignored warnings from chemists that the apple concentrate that the company was buying at below-market prices was probably extensively altered. Ultimately, two top executives each received prison terms of 1 year and 1 day and fines of $100,000 for their role in selling the completely synthetic juice, which had been labeled "100 percent fruit juice." The scandal also adversely affected sales of the company's baby food products. Executives had ignored the warnings of Beech-Nut chemists because the company was bordering on insolvency.[86]

A third important external factor that can influence unethical behavior is *extreme dependency* of one organization on another. Such dependencies can create pressures for bribes and payoffs. For example, before various drugs can be offered to the public, they must be approved by the Food and Drug Administration (FDA). Efforts by some generic-drug makers to expedite the approvals led to a scandal in which at least three FDA employees pleaded guilty to taking illegal gratuities from generic-drug makers and two generic-drug makers admitted submitting false data to the agency.[87]

Factors internal to the organization also can increase the likelihood of unethical behavior. Heavy *pressure for higher performance* and output may induce individuals to take "shortcuts" such as fixing prices, secretly speeding up the assembly line, or releasing unsafe products. At E. F. Hutton, the pressure from above to engage in good cash management eventually led a number of managers to draw against bank funds that were not covered by deposits, thus taking short-

Table 4-6 Situational Factors Influencing Ethical Behavior

External Factors	Internal Factors
Environmental competitiveness	Pressure for high performance
Environmental munificence	Poor internal financial performance
Extreme dependency	Labor dissatisfaction
	Delegation
	Encouragement of innovation

term unauthorized loans from the 400 banks with whom they did business. When the scheme was discovered, it precipitated a scandal that led to fines, indictments, firings of executives, and a tarnished reputation for the brokerage firm. Similarly, *poor internal financial performance,* such as falling profits or indebtedness, may influence organizational members to commit unethical acts. *Labor dissatisfaction* may result in unethical behavior as anger replaces more constrained and rational behavior. Ironically, *delegation* of authority and encouragement of *innovation* may increase the likelihood of unethical behavior because of the greater latitude and the encouragement of creativity involved. Innovation involves a departure from usual ways of doing things and may, in the process, raise major ethical questions. For example, American Express found itself in the embarrassing position of having to publicly apologize to a competitor, international banker Edmond J. Safra, after it was found that some American Express employees had been planting malicious rumors about Safra in European publications in an effort to discredit him. The employees thought that they were engaging in a creative approach to undermining a competitor. As a result of the incident, American Express also donated $8 million to Safra's favorite charities in an effort to make amends for the unauthorized actions.[88]

Although these various environmental and internal factors may increase the likelihood of unethical behavior, the factors themselves are not necessarily unethical. On the contrary, at least in the short run, many environmental factors are facts of life for an organization. While some of the internal factors, such as poor financial performance or labor dissatisfaction, may be undesirable, they may be phases in efforts to improve. Some internal factors, such as performance pressure, delegation, and innovation, can be positive forces. Hence the issue here is that since external factors and internal pressures may increase the likelihood of unethical acts, managers need to monitor such conditions. When the conditions exist, managers must expend even greater effort in conveying the importance of ethical behavior on the part of organization members.

One recent study suggests that upper-level managers may not feel as much ethical pressure as do managers at the middle and lower levels. The study, which polled 6000 executives and managers in a survey sponsored by the American Management Association, asked participants to respond to the statement "I find that sometimes I must compromise my personal principles to conform to my organization's expectations." The results indicated that supervisory or first-level managers were more than twice as likely to agree than executive or top-level managers (37.1 percent versus 17.2 percent), with middle managers falling in between (22.8 percent).[89] One possible implication is that upper-level managers may not be sufficiently aware of the pressures on middle and lower levels and, as a result, may not take sufficient action to counter such pressures.

Principles for Ethical Management

An important issue, then, is: What can managers do to foster ethical behavior in others in the organization? Vernon R. Loucks, Jr., president and CEO of Baxer Travenol Laboratories, Inc., offers the following four practical principles.

Hire the right people. It is easier to have ethical behavior in an organization if you hire people with principles. Look for such people, and let them know that their principles are one of the main reasons that they are being hired.

Set standards more than rules. A code of conduct cannot cover every eventuality. People who are inclined to be unethical may not be deterred by signing a heavy code of conduct. Instead of spending a great deal of time on extensive

Our Credo

We believe our first responsibility is to the doctors, nurses and patients,
to mothers and fathers and all others who use our products and services.
In meeting their needs everything we do must be of high quality.
We must constantly strive to reduce our costs
in order to maintain reasonable prices.
Customers' orders must be serviced promptly and accurately.
Our suppliers and distributors must have an opportunity
to make a fair profit.

We are responsible to our employees,
the men and women who work with us throughout the world.
Everyone must be considered as an individual.
We must respect their dignity and recognize their merit.
They must have a sense of security in their jobs.
Compensation must be fair and adequate,
and working conditions clean, orderly and safe.
We must be mindful of ways to help our employees fulfill
their family responsibilities.
Employees must feel free to make suggestions and complaints.
There must be equal opportunity for employment, development
and advancement for those qualified.
We must provide competent management,
and their actions must be just and ethical.

We are responsible to the communities in which we live and work
and to the world community as well.
We must be good citizens — support good works and charities
and bear our fair share of taxes.
We must encourage civic improvements and better health and education.
We must maintain in good order
the property we are privileged to use,
protecting the environment and natural resources.

Our final responsibility is to our stockholders.
Business must make a sound profit.
We must experiment with new ideas.
Research must be carried on, innovative programs developed
and mistakes paid for.
New equipment must be purchased, new facilities provided
and new products launched.
Reserves must be created to provide for adverse times.
When we operate according to these principles,
the stockholders should realize a fair return.

Johnson & Johnson

Figure 4-5 The Johnson &
Johnson Credo.

regulations, concentrate on clarifying standards. Let people know what level of
performance is expected, and explain that ethical behavior is a must.

According to a survey conducted by the Opinion Research Corporation and
sponsored by the Ethics Resource Center in Washington, D.C., nearly three-
quarters of the major U.S. corporations have written codes of ethics. While almost all the companies say that the codes are helpful in maintaining ethical
behavior among employees, only 36 percent distribute the code to all employees
and only 20 percent display the code throughout the organization. An example
of a code that is given to every new employee and is displayed throughout the
organization is the Johnson & Johnson Credo, shown in Figure 4-5. As another

aid in setting standards, company training programs on ethics are on the increase.[90]

Don't let yourself get isolated. Managers can become isolated not only from markets and competitors but from what is going on in their own operations. Nevertheless, managers are still responsible for what goes on, whether they know about it or not. When a subsidiary of the Toshiba Corporation sold $19 million of secret defense equipment to the Soviet Union, the public outrage, particularly in the United States, caused both the chairman and the president of Toshiba to resign even though the sale was consummated without their knowledge.

Ombudsperson Usually an executive operating outside the normal chain of command whose job is to handle issues involving hot-line-communicated employee grievances and warnings about serious ethical problems

Whistle-blower An employee who reports a real or perceived wrongdoing under the control of his or her employer to those who may be able to take appropriate action

One recent method of providing an extra measure of upward communication is the use of an organizational ombudsperson. An **ombudsperson** is usually an executive operating outside the normal chain of command who handles issues involving hot-line-communicated employee grievances and warnings about serious ethical problems. One objective is to handle problems internally and avoid having employees become external whistle-blowers. A **whistle-blower** is an employee who reports a real or perceived wrongdoing under the control of his or her employer to those who may be able to take appropriate action. When a whistle-blower goes to an outside person or organization, often unfavorable publicity, legal investigations, and lawsuits result.[91]

Most important, make sure your ethical example is absolutely impeccable at all times. It is important to operate ethically in dealing with various stakeholders and with the competition. Subordinates are likely to pay more attention to what you do than to what you say. Also watch the indirect signals that you send. If a manager continuously focuses on profits, subordinates may interpret the singular emphasis as a message that any method, as long as it brings in profits, is acceptable.

CHAPTER SUMMARY

Organizational, or corporate, social responsibility refers to the obligation of a business firm to seek actions that protect and improve the welfare of society along with its own interests. Three major contrasting perspectives on the nature of corporate social responsibility are the invisible hand, the hand of government, and the hand of management. Due to expanding societal expectations regarding the social responsibility of businesses and other organizations, the hand-of-management view is increasingly relevant to managers.

The social responsibilities of management focus mainly on five major stakeholders: shareholders, employees, customers, the community, and general society. Although the measurement difficulties associated with comparing organizations on social responsibility preclude a definite answer, studies to date indicate that there is no clear relationship between a corporation's degree of social responsibility and its short-run financial success. Nevertheless, it is possible to be both socially responsible and financially successful. The iron law of

responsibility suggests that socially responsible behavior may have a positive long-run effect on organizational success. Increasingly, organizations are attempting to orient philanthropic and other socially responsible activities toward areas that also can affect their bottom line and ultimately give them a competitive edge.

Corporate social responsiveness refers to the development of organizational decision processes whereby managers anticipate, respond to, and manage areas of social responsibility. Two processes usually are essential. First, it is necessary to establish methods of monitoring social demands and expectations through such means as social forecasting, opinion surveys, social audits, and issues management. Second, it is important to develop internal social response mechanisms, such as the use of individual executives, temporary task forces, permanent committees, permanent departments, or combinations of these elements.

Ultimately, questions of corporate social responsibility and corporate social responsiveness depend on the ethical standards of managers. Three types of managerial ethics are immoral, amoral, and moral. While amoral behavior tends to prevail, moral management is likely to be in the long-run best interests of organizations. Ethical guidelines for managers include obey the law; tell the truth; show respect for people; stick to the Golden Rule; above all, do no harm; practice participation, not paternalism; and always act when you have responsibility. Ethical career issues for managers may involve assessing their own values and protecting themselves, as well as considering what actions they can take to anticipate and avoid ethical conflicts.

One important challenge is managing an organization in which members conduct their business in an ethical manner. One aspect of this challenge is having a knowledge of environmental and organizational conditions that increase the likelihood of unethical behavior. A second aspect for top managers is providing ethical leadership to the rest of the organization through such methods as hiring the right people, setting standards more than rules, not letting themselves get isolated, and making sure that their ethical example is impeccable at all times.

MANAGERIAL TERMINOLOGY

amoral management (136)
antifreeloader argument (123)
capacity argument (123)
corporate philanthropy (124)
corporate social responsibility (115)
corporate social responsiveness (126)

enlightened self-interest argument (123)
futurists (126)
hand of government (116)
hand of management (116)
immoral management (134)
invisible hand (116)

iron law of responsibility (123)
issues management (127)
managerial ethics (115)
moral management (136)
ombudsperson (144)
organizational social responsibility (115)

organizational social responsiveness (126)
plant closings (119)
public affairs department (130)
social audit (127)
social forecasting (126)
social scanning (128)
whistle-blower (144)

QUESTIONS FOR DISCUSSION AND REVIEW

1. Explain the three major perspectives on corporate social responsibility. What evidence might you use to determine whether an organization's management subscribes most closely to the invisible-hand, hand-of-government, or hand-of-management view of social responsibility?

2. Identify the five major stakeholder groups frequently mentioned in conjunction with social responsibility. To what extent do these stakeholder groups apply to your college or university? What others might you add?

3. Evaluate the extent to which organizational social responsibility is likely to pay off financially. Colleges and universities often are the recipients of corporate philanthropy. Identify two ways in which such philanthropy has helped your college or university. In what ways might contributors benefit from such donations?

4. Identify major approaches that can be used to monitor social demands and expectations. Choose an organization with which you are familiar and sug-

gest how it might use these methods to monitor relevant social demands and expectations.

5. Explain several internal social response mechanisms available to organizations. Identify two internal social response mechanisms used by your college or university.

6. Distinguish among the three major types of managerial ethics. Use *Business Week* or *The Wall Street Journal* to identify an example of one of these types of managerial ethics.

7. Enumerate the ethical guidelines for managers that are suggested by O'Toole. How might the ethical guidelines have helped José Gomez, the former managing partner of the Grant Thornton accounting firm, avoid his ethical problems?

8. Suggest some steps you could take when seeking employment that might help you detect potential ethical problems. To what extent do students whom you know consider these issues when seeking jobs?

9. Describe situational factors that are likely to influ-

ence ethical behavior. Analyze José Gomez's situation in terms of these situational factors.

10. Outline the basic principles for ethical management. Suppose that you have just been appointed to a top-level executive position with a major defense contractor. How might you use these principles to help prevent some of the ethical difficulties, such as misrepresenting costs on defense contracts, that have plagued some other major contractors?

DISCUSSION QUESTIONS FOR CHAPTER OPENING CASE

1. Identify the major stakeholders in the two Tylenol crises. To what extent were the interests of the various stakeholders satisfied by J&J's actions?

2. What evidence of corporate social responsiveness is apparent from the information given about J&J?

3. Would you characterize the type of managerial ethics evidenced at J&J during the Tylenol crises as immoral, amoral, or moral? Explain the reasoning behind your assessment.

MANAGEMENT EXERCISE: A QUESTION OF ETHICS

After earning an undergraduate degree in history and an M.B.A. in finance, Roberta was offered a position with a medium-size real estate development firm in her hometown. Much to her liking, the job involved working in the firm's "community projects" area, where she would oversee the books for the company's construction of low-cost housing projects.

The opportunity to work in finance while also aiding the public good appealed to Roberta. While interviewing for other jobs in finance and real estate, she didn't like the competitive atmosphere at larger firms, where the size of salaries and bonuses seemed to be the overriding concern of most new hires.

After a few weeks in her position, Roberta discovered a discrepancy in the books of one of her firms's housing projects. Six separate checks for $10,000 each had been written by Roberta's boss over the past year, and each was made payable to cash with no further explanation. When Roberta approached her boss, she was told that they were just another cost of doing business and that she should inflate the cost of other items to cover the payments.

Through further investigation, Roberta learned that the checks were being paid to building inspectors to overlook the use of certain substandard materials. Roberta again protested to her boss, who responded with obvious irritation. He said such payments were common and the use of substandard materials wouldn't affect safety.

The boss implied that significant cost savings on materials were necessary if the firm was to build low-income housing on a profitable basis. He noted that the cost of each unit would increase by only $2000 to cover the payments and that the eventual owners probably expect that they'll have to upgrade their units from time to time anyway.

Roberta knows that, at the least, replacement or repairs would be needed after only 2 or 3 years because of the substandard materials. Concerned that a wrong was committed and fearful that she might personally become entangled in the mess, Roberta protested to her boss's supervisor. The supervisor told Roberta that he "would look into it." Roberta hasn't heard anything in the 3 weeks since and has just discovered that a seventh $10,000 check payable to cash has come through. What should Roberta do now?[92]

TONY SANTINO'S DILEMMA

Tony Santino was a 39-year-old manager facing an ethical dilemma. Three years earlier he had received his M.B.A. from a leading business school, but he had not yet established a stable work history. He lost his first job after graduate school when he, along with a small band of fellow M.B.A. "hotshots," got caught in the cross fire between two warring executives in an aerospace firm. Tony's mentor left the company as a result of the battle and, shortly after, Tony did too. He had hoped to find a job with another large firm in the same industry, but at 37 his lack of a private-sector track record seemed to be a liability.

After a prolonged and disappointing job search, Tony was appointed director of marketing for a small firm that manufactured undifferentiated, inexpensive—but critical—parts for industrial equipment. Once again Tony discovered he was trapped between two warring executives. The company was displeased with the performance of the current vice president of marketing; during Tony's job interview, the president said Tony could hope to replace that vice president, who meanwhile was Tony's direct boss.

One of Tony's first assignments from the vice president was to acquire information about a competitor by pretending to be an executive recruiter. Tony at first protested, but remembering his recent job search and the fact that the assignment came after only 1 month on the job, he reluctantly performed the task.

The president and the marketing vice president were both strong-willed individuals and frequently did not see eye to eye, but they joined forces when Tony expressed reluctance to sign and distribute what he believed to be an illegal and unethical price list. Tony's employer, as it turned out, had been illegally setting prices in collusion with its major competitor for years, yielding a handsome profit.

One of the competing firms had invested this monopoly profit back into R&D and developed a process for manufacturing the same product line at 40 percent of the current cost. The competitor was passing on the savings to customers and devouring the market, especially for new customers. Tony's firm, anxious to maintain its market share with less competitive goods, developed a fictitious product line that would sell at the competitor's price.

The lower-priced items were exactly the same as the higher-priced products, but they were labeled differently and made available only to new customers. The purchasing engineers of old customers were too loyal and lazy to run the certification tests necessary to switch to a new product line or supplies. The deception in Tony's company would involve lab technicians, phone order clerks, and the company sales force.

Tony believed this practice to be a violation of the Robinson-Patman and Sherman Antitrust laws, an opinion he conveyed to his superiors. He suggested that the only way to compete effectively in an industry with an undifferentiated product was by being a cost leader. Tony's bosses, however, defended their proposed action as common industry practice and asked Tony not to be so "negative."

Tony consulted with a local lawyer, a friend who confirmed the illegality of the proposed pricing scheme but also emphasized that "small companies were known for this kind of stuff." The probability of apprehension and any kind of legal action was negligible, the lawyer said.

In addition, Tony hired an outside marketing consultant to advise the company on broad strategic issues. In a meeting attended by the consultant, Tony, and his superiors, Tony asked about the Robinson-Patman violation. His bosses looked on in horror as he described the pricing decision, but they were relieved as the consultant said, "The jails are not big enough to hold all the people who do this sort of thing."

Tony had to obtain forged lab test results from the company's R&D engineers to implement the pricing scheme. Although they complied promptly, one of the engineers commented, "Tony, I know you're just caught in the middle, but I've been around here 39 years and have never been able to like these things any better." . . .

The dilemma was exacerbated when Tony's bosses asked him to sign the cover sheet of the new price list. He confided to a friend: "I still think I know what's right, but with all these other voices telling me to sign the price list, maybe I'm just making a mountain out of a molehill. Then again, maybe I compromised myself through the executive headhunter intrigue. I already feel like a bit of a prostitute. And if I leave, how do I explain my short job tenure to any potential employer?"[93]

QUESTIONS FOR CHAPTER CONCLUDING CASE

1. What ethical guidelines for managers are relevant to this situation?
2. What steps would you recommend that Tony take to clarify his own values and protect himself in this situation?
3. How might Tony try to avoid getting into a similar situation if he seeks a new job?

MARRIOTT GROWS FROM ROOT BEER STAND TO CORPORATE EMPIRE

Following in his late father's footsteps, J. Willard "Bill" Marriott, Jr., makes a habit of periodically visiting one or more of the hotels, contract food service operations, retirement centers, and other facilities that make up the vast Marriott empire founded by his parents. For instance, on one recent day, after a brief tour of company facilities in Maine, Wisconsin, and California, the Marriott chairman and president flew into Miami, attended a testimonial dinner, and then put in an extra hour of "homework" before turning in. The next day, after several meetings he traveled to Cleveland to tour the company's airport hotel before proceeding to Palm Desert, California, to inspect a new hotel and participate in another series of meetings. Two more cities were next on his agenda, with a quick trip scheduled for London a few days later.

With his busy travel schedule, Marriott typically logs about 200,000 miles per year, yet he describes his activities as "fun." He explains that "it's work, of course, but it's necessary. I go to check on our properties, to meet with employees, and make sure things are running smoothly. If I sit back and relax, a lot of other people will sit back and relax. After all, if you're going to be a star performer, you can't sit back and relax. A star performer has to work hard and make sacrifices, and at Marriott Corp., we do both."

Such dedication helps to explain Marriott's spectacular success. The company's sales exceed $7.5 billion per year. Over 230,000 employees work for Marriott Cor-

poration, making it the eighth-largest employer in the United States. It conducts business in all 50 states, and in 26 countries around the world. Annual growth has averaged 20 percent for more than 3 decades and current plans call for the corporation to grow at a rate of 15 to 20 percent each year during the 1990s. The Marriott family owns about 25 percent of the public stock of the company, currently worth about $1 billion.

When the corporation's great success is mentioned, though, Bill Marriott is quick to give credit to the guidance of his father, J. Willard Marriott, Sr., and his mother, Alice, who together started the company by opening a nine-seat A&W root beer stand in Washington, D.C., in 1927. During the first summer, business at the stand was brisk but sales dwindled as the weather turned cooler in the fall. The Marriotts then began offering food such as chili, barbecue, and hot tamales, items that were then in vogue in the western part of the United States. As sales increased, they renamed their enterprise, which had now been transformed into a restaurant, the "Hot Shoppe." The company still owns a small group of Hot Shoppes in the Washington, D.C. area.

The senior Marriott understood the potential advantages of a chain of food establishments compared with a single restaurant, namely that a chain could have much better purchasing power, develop a more flexible pool of labor, and build a solid reputation with customers in a wider geographical area. He also recognized the prospects associated with the rapidly expanding ownership of cars. Accordingly, within a year of establishing his root beer stand, he opened the first drive-in restaurant on the east coast. Despite the De-

What started as a nine-seat root beer stand in Washington, D.C. in 1927 has grown into a billion dollar, worldwide food service and lodging industry. One of the most recent additions to the Marriott corporate empire is the Warsaw Marriott, completed in the fall of 1989, just in time for the opening of eastern Europe. Attention to the needs of customers and employees and a keen sense of innovative business opportunities account for the company's spectacular success.

pression, people still needed to eat and the fledgling restaurant chain prospered and grew. Within 3 years of starting the company, the Marriotts were millionaires.

By 1937, they saw another opportunity when a manager of a Hot Shoppe near Washington's old Hoover Field (where the Pentagon now stands) reported that people often purchased food to eat during airplane flights. Marriott, Sr., negotiated contracts to supply meals during Eastern and American airlines flights, launching the company into the field of airline catering. By the time the first offering of stock was made to the public in 1953, the company had such a positive reputation that the offering sold out within 2 hours.

The expanded highway system and growing use of automobiles created another opportunity for the company when, in 1957, it opened the largest motel in the United States, the Twin Bridges Marriott Motor Hotel in Arlington, Virginia, just across the Potomac River from Washington, D.C. The motel was managed by the Marriott's oldest son, Bill, who by now, at 25 years of age, had joined the company full time. Bill Marriott actually had been involved in the business since he was a child, often accompanying his father on his inspection tours of various company enterprises. One result is that the younger Marriott has adopted many of the business approaches of his father and has followed them as he has risen to the top of the corporation. For instance, the elder Marriott was noted for rummaging through garbage bags for signs of waste in Marriott restaurants. Similarly, his son checks company kitchens for left over portions of food that indicate failure to adequately adjust food preparation to demand levels. The father personally read every single complaint card submitted by customers, a practice that was extremely effective in focusing the attention of Marriott managers on areas of complaint. His son still answers about 10 percent of the complaint letters himself. Bill Marriott also keeps extensive notes of comments made to managers during his visits about problems such as worn carpets, lack of cleanliness, or poorly polished floors. The managers know that the notebook will be reviewed on the next return visit.

Like his father, Bill also uses his various trips to operate as a morale-booster. He shakes employees' hands, praises good work, and poses for pictures. "'Take care of employees and customers,' my fa-

ther emphasized," says Bill Marriott. "My father knew if he had happy employees, he would have happy customers, and then that would result in a good bottom line." Not surprisingly, there is considerable emphasis on actively seeking employee input. "If you don't listen to your people, you lose your greatest resource," says Marriott, who tends to speak in terms of "we," not I. "Bill has built an incredible degree of loyalty and purpose among his people," says the head of a major rival hotel chain.

Such careful attention to various aspects of the business, and employees as well, has paid off in strong customer satisfaction. Occupancy rates in Marriott hotels habitually run 10 percentage points above those of competitors. The company generally receives widespread praise for its excellent performance. For instance, a recent survey by *Business Travel News* ranked Marriott hotels and resorts first in eleven service related categories. Bill Marriott himself also has been recognized for his vision and managerial skills. For example, he has been honored by *Chief Executive* magazine as Chief Executive of the Year, and was featured in a recent *Fortune* article designating the "star" (highest performing) companies in the *Fortune* Service 500.

One reason for the praise is the company's spectacular growth. During the late 1960s, Marriott Corporation greatly expanded its restaurant business by acquiring the Big Boy restaurant chain and launching the Roy Rogers fast food chain. It also made its first move into the international realm by purchasing an airline catering kitchen in Caracas, Venezuela. Meanwhile, Bill Marriott had risen to the post of CEO, and by the mid-1970s, he began to explore the possibility of

expanding through borrowing. His father was reluctant to see the company assume significant debt because during the Depression he had seen hotels that were in debt go bankrupt. "We wore him down," says Bill Marriott. "He went along because the management and the board supported the plan. But he never believed in it."

In addition to expanding its restaurant chains, catering operations and hotel chains, by 1982 Marriott Corporation had purchased Host International, making Marriott the largest operator of airport terminal food, beverage, and merchandise facilities in the United States. The company also acquired the Gino restaurant chain and converted most of the outlets to Roy Rogers restaurants. By 1985, the year that Marriott, Sr., died, Marriott, Jr., had more than realized his own dream of having Marriott Corporation be as large as the Howard Johnson organization when he purchased the Howard Johnson chain for a bargain price of $300 million. In comparison with Marriott Corporation, the Howard Johnson organization had experienced relatively stagnant growth over the previous 20 years because of an extremely conservative management approach and a disdain for debt. For example, in 1965, Marriott's annual sales were $350 million compared to $500 million for Howard Johnson's. By 1985, though, Marriott's annual sales had grown to $3.3 billion, while Howard Johnson's were just above the $500 million mark. That year, Bill Marriott became chairman of the board of Marriott Corporation.

Other bold moves for Marriott Corporation since 1980 include entering into the moderately-priced hotel market with Courtyard hotels, designed to resemble modern country inns. The chain competes directly with Holiday Inn and Ramada Inn by offering prices in the $45–$70 range in the suburbs and under $100 a night in downtown areas. There are currently more than 150 Courtyard hotels, and more than 300 are scheduled to be in operation by the mid-1990s, including 12 to 15 in Great Britain. The company also has achieved a leadership position in institutional food service by acquiring three companies (Gladieux Corporation, Service System Corp., and Saga Corp.) that have added to Marriott's capacity to supply meals to various businesses, health-care facilities, and educational institutions.

Recognizing a niche in the economy-priced lodging market, Marriott opened its first Fairfield Inn in 1987. Forty-nine more Fairfield Inns and 2 years later, Marriott sold the chain for $235.5 million, a considerable profit. The Residence Inns, an all-suite hotel chain targeted to travelers staying a longer period of time, originally acquired in 1987, is being expanded to more than 300 hotels in the early 1990s.

In another major move, the company has built an upscale Marriott Marquis hotel in New York's Times Square. The key to the success of the Marriott Marquis is not theatergoers who pay $220 per night to stay there, but the income derived from its close proximity to the Jacob Javits Convention Center, the largest convention facility in the world. The 1,877-room hotel is the flagship of Marriott's new convention hotels, which also have been built in such cities as Atlanta, San Francisco, and Orlando. When it opened in 1985, the Marquis, which is 50 percent owned and totally managed by the Marriott Corporation, had $178 million in advance bookings, including a room for a New Year's Eve party on December 31, 1999.

Building on its expertise in running hotels and food services, Marriott Corporation has recently entered the life-care market aimed at the elderly. Demographics indicate that the elderly will comprise a growing significant proportion of the population in the 1990s and beyond. One such effort is a retirement center concept, featuring a high-rise building with almost 400 apartments, and also offering a variety of amenities, including a swimming pool, maid service, a health club, a dining room for communal meals, 24-hour emergency call buttons, a floor with rooms for skilled nursing care, and another floor of assisted living rooms for those who do not need nursing care, but need some help to function (for example, aid with dressing). The first two such facilities, one just outside of Philadelphia and the other near Fort Belvoir, Va., had 80 percent of the units sold the day they opened. One hundred-and-fifty of these retirement centers are scheduled for completion by the mid-1990s. Two other types of facilities offering progressively greater assisted living and nursing care are also being implemented.

A major reason for the overall spectacular record of success is the exhaustive research and planning that precedes the entrance into new markets and the introduction of new products. At one point, for example, Marriott developed 28 model hotel rooms and had 1000 individuals assess them. Reactions indicated that the rooms were too bright, guidance that Marriott has taken into consideration in future room decoration. After surveys indicated that customers disliked waiting in line to check out, the company pioneered an automatic check-out system, where the bill is slipped under the door at night,

making it possible for guests to check out by just dropping off billing materials and the key at a counter. The company also offers a "breakfast free if not delivered on time program," to make ordering room service breakfast more attractive to customers. Such efforts have earned Marriott a reputation for innovation.

"We do our homework here," Bill Marriott says. "We always want to know what we're getting into." As part of the planning process each year top managers (including Bill Marriott's younger brother, Richard, who is vice-chairman and executive vice president) consider several new business opportunities. They limit the risk of entering new businesses by carefully controlling the amount of their initial investment. In addition, they are willing to get out of businesses that do not subsequently live up to profit expectations. For example, Marriott retains only a percentage of one of the three Sun Line cruise ships that it originally acquired in 1971. Two Great American theme parks, located in Gurnee, Illinois, and Santa Clara, California, were sold after about 10 years of operation. Efforts during the 1980s to enter the travel agent business and initiate home and business security operations were later either sold or shut down. In all cases, observers speculated that Marriott retreated from these businesses because they ultimately did not provide the type of growth potential and return on investment commensurate with Marriott expectations.

In a recent significant strategic move, the corporation announced that it is abandoning a plan to convert its restaurant chains (Roy Rogers, Howard Johnson, Wags, and Bickford's) into a national home style restaurant chain called Allie's. Instead, the company unveiled plans to sell its free standing restaurants (for example, the Roy Rogers chain was subsequently sold to Hardees Food Systems) and also its airline catering operations. The airport and travel plaza operations, food and service management operations, such as those at many universities, and about a dozen Hot Shoppes in the Washington, D.C., area were scheduled to be retained. The reasons for this dramatic move, selling profitable operations, was reported to be threefold. First, Marriott Corporation wanted to sharpen its focus on markets in the lodging, contract services, and elderly care areas of operations in the 1990s. Second, more people are staying at home to eat and watch their television sets rather than going to restaurants. And last, Marriott has indicated that because of competition and changing conditions it would be difficult for a new brand name (such as Allie's) to become number one in the family restaurant business.

Despite careful analysis of the environment and prudent planning, some major mistakes have been made. For example, Bill Marriott acknowledges what was "probably the biggest mistake of the company." The Marriott Corporation was approached by Atlanta architect John C. Portman, Jr., in the 1960s when he was seeking clients for a new dramatic concept of hotel design featuring huge atriums, glass elevators, and dazzling entrance lobbies. The concept was rejected by Marriott at the time, because lavish style was not a priority. Instead, Marriott was attempting to keep cost relatively low and obtain good value for its investments in hotel buildings, most of which are later sold, but continue to be managed by Marriott.

Unfortunately for Marriott, the rival Hyatt hotel organization adopted Portman's revolutionary designs. Bill Marriott indicated years later that this type of architecture, which has become a trademark of the Hyatt chain, was largely responsible for the major inroads in the hotel business that have made the Hyatt organization Marriott's biggest competitor.

In an effort to enhance the way the corporation is managed, it was recently divided into two major groups. The Marriott Service Group includes all contract services and life-care retirement communities. The Marriott Lodging Group includes all of Marriott's hotels and resorts, which increasingly are located throughout the world.

In addition to a work week that has frequently encompassed 80 hours, Bill Marriott typically devotes another 20 hours per week to the Mormon Church and has served as president of its Washington, D.C., stake (a group of 8 to 10 congregations). In addition, he serves as director of the Chamber of Commerce of the United States and on the boards of a number of not-for-profit organizations, such as the Boy Scouts of America. He also is a member of the Conference Board, The Business Council, The Business Roundtable and the advisory council of the Stanford University Graduate School of Business. A dedicated family person, he never misses Sunday dinner and goes out with his wife Donna for dinner at least once a week (at a Marriott facility, of course, so that he can check the food and service).

When asked what he does best as a manager, Bill Marriott says, "maybe setting an example of hard work and concern for both the customer and the employee, while also

driving hard to make money. People say you can't balance the two, but my father believed you could, and I do, too." After suffering a mild heart attack in late 1989, Bill Marriott has decided that he will only attempt to visit about 100 properties a year, down from his usual 200. Also he plans to work 10 to 12 hours per day instead of the usual 14. His brother, Richard, and other high level managers will take on more of the traveling and speaking.*

QUESTIONS FOR DISCUSSION
1. Trace evidence of the use of the four functions of management (planning, organizing, leading, and controlling) at Marriott Corporation.
2. In what ways do J. W. "Bill" Marriott, Jr.'s actions as chairman and president of Marriott Corporation reflect the work methods and managerial roles that are typically part of the management process?
3. Explain how the development of Marriott Corporation over the years has taken into consideration various environmental factors. Would you consider Marriott Corporation to be an open system? Why or why not?
4. How would you describe the organizational culture at Marriott? What evidence can you cite to support your assessment?
5. To what extent does Marriott Corporation appear to subscribe to the hand of management view of social responsibility?

*Sources: See References at back of book.

PART TWO

PLANNING AND DECISION MAKING

An organization without planning is like a sailboat minus its rudder. Without planning, organizations are subject to the winds of environmental change, yet have little means to take advantage of the prevailing currents in determining their own direction. Planning is the management function that involves setting goals and deciding how best to achieve them. The function also includes considering what must be done to encourage necessary levels of change and innovation. Planning provides a basis for the other major functions of management—organizing, leading, and controlling—by charting the course and providing the steering mechanism. This section, then, is geared to helping you acquire a basic knowledge of the planning function.

Chapter 5 examines the overall planning process and explores how setting goals can facilitate organizational performance. As you will learn, goals and the related plans necessary to carry them out vary in important ways according to organizational level.

One of the most important aspects of planning is strategic management. *Chapter 6* explores how managers formulate and implement large-scale action plans called strategies that help the organization attain a competitive edge.

Most experts agree that requirements for innovation in organizations must be an integral part of the planning process. *Chapter 7* probes ways that managers can effectively facilitate needed innovation and change.

The kinds of problems that managers attempt to resolve through decision making, as well as the appropriate steps to take in the decision process are the focus of *Chapter 8.* The chapter also addresses creativity, an important ingredient in innovation.

As *Chapter 9* shows, managers have recourse to many aids in their planning and related decision making, such as forecasting techniques, various planning models, quantitative analysis, and computer-based expert systems.

CHAPTER FIVE

ESTABLISHING ORGANIZATIONAL GOALS AND PLANS

CHAPTER OUTLINE

The Overall Planning Process
Major Components of Planning
Organizational Mission

The Nature of Organizational Goals
Benefits of Goals
Levels of Goals

How Goals Facilitate Performance
Goal Content
Goal Commitment
Work Behavior
Other Process Components
Potential Problems with Goals

Linking Goals and Plans
Levels of Plans
Plans According to Extent of
    Recurring Use
Time Horizons of Goals and Plans
Promoting Innovation: The Role of the
    Planning Process
Potential Obstacles to Planning

Management by Objectives
Steps in the MBO Process
Strengths and Weaknesses of MBO
Assessing MBO

LEARNING OBJECTIVES

*After studying this chapter, you
should be able to:*

■ Describe the major components
  in the overall planning process.

■ Explain the concept of organizational mission and the purposes of a mission statement.

■ Outline the major benefits of
  goals and explain how goals
  differ according to organizational level.

■ Describe the various components that help explain how
  goals facilitate performance.

■ Explain how plans differ by
  organizational level and extent
  of recurring use.

■ Assess the role of goals and
  plans in promoting innovation.

■ Outline the major steps in
  management by objectives and
  assess the strengths and weaknesses of the approach.

CYPRESS SEMICONDUCTOR THRIVES ON "TURBO MBO"

When the Cypress Semiconductor Corporation was founded in 1983, the president and CEO, Dr. Thurman John Rodgers (more commonly known as "T. J.") instituted a management by objectives (MBO) program that obtains positive results. Starting from scratch, the organization now has an annual income in excess of $200 million, more than 1300 employees, and 4 subsidiaries.

Cypress's basic mission is to be a profitable $1 billion semiconductor company that ships quickly, operates efficiently, and is a technological leader. The company competes by producing more than 130 complex, state-of-the-art computer chips for specialized markets. The management by objectives system, which Rodgers likes to call "Turbo MBO," helps the company manage its intricate operations by having employees set goals each week that are then tracked by computer. "Producing a semiconductor is a very unforgiving entity," says Rodgers. "If it takes 1000 tasks to make one and you do 999 right but then you forget one or do one wrong, the semiconductor will not work. The [MBO] system forces management to stick its nose in a big book every single week and find out what is going on. We can't afford surprises."

As part of the overall system, senior management and the board of directors develop broad corporate goals for a 5-year period and engage in strategic planning to determine how best to reach the goals. The process involves a review of the projected sales, marketing, and manufacturing plans, and it also considers other important variables such as the number of employees and the amount of capital involved relative to expected outcomes. The 5-year plan is updated annually, and the results are passed to middle managers, who then develop goals and related plans (often called tactical goals and plans) at their level to be accomplished during the coming year. The tactical goals and plans are given to project and program leaders at the next lower level, who develop goals and plans (often called operational goals and plans) that are oriented to the current year and frequently to an even shorter period, such as the immediate quarter. Within the goals and plans developed at the strategic, tactical, and operational levels, the Turbo MBO system operates on a weekly basis.

In addition to establishing five-year and annual goals, Cypress Semiconductor Corporation sets and monitors weekly goals through a computerized management by objectives (MBO) program. Employees map out their goals at weekly meetings (as shown here), which are conducted by project leaders. The goals are entered into a central computer system and reviewed by higher levels of management. The MBO program has paid off in high employee morale, market success, and good financial management of the company.

The weekly goal cycle starts on Monday, when every project leader holds a meeting with members of the project group to review the status of various goals that are due and map out what each group member will do that week. Individuals may attend more than one project group meeting if they work on multiple projects, agreeing to specific goals at each meeting. Each employee normally has three to ten goals he or she is expected to achieve. The goals may be as simple as ordering a new filing cabinet or as complex as making a critical change in the circuitry of a new chip. All the new goals for the week are put into a computer system so that more than 40 managers have access to the data through their personal computers. The system is designed to report goals that are delinquent (past due) and identify individuals who are delinquent on three or more goals.

On Tuesdays, managers review the goals put into the computer the previous day; they consider such issues as priorities, timeliness, equity of work loads, and appropriate progress on projects. Adjustments are made to ensure that the necessary goals for the week can be accomplished. On Wednesday afternoons, Rodgers and his seven vice presidents review the status of various goals. The computer system allows a review from two viewpoints: the manager responsible and the project or program.

If a manager is more than 35 percent behind in the accomplishment of goals, the appropriate vice president must explain why and discuss what will be or is being done to remedy the situation. If the problem is an aberration that occurs during one week and will be rectified the following week, the matter is dropped. If the shortfall persists, however, the vice president must assist the manager in rectifying the problem. Subsequently, the vice presidents review their own goals with the group, explaining any shortfalls of 20 percent or more. Rodgers himself monitors shortfalls at the vice presidential level; if there is no improvement in a month or so, he will determine the reasons for the continuing problem and take corrective action. Such actions could include devoting more resources to the project, revising time schedules, or possibly altering goals.

The remainder of the Wednesday afternoon meeting is devoted to reviewing the status of goals for significant projects, as well as considering critical management ratios, such as revenue per employee, revenue to gross capital, performance to original schedule, sales and administration as a percent of revenue, and other measures for which goals have been set for the company as a whole. By the end of this weekly meeting, goals have been reviewed and revised where appropriate. At this point, a printout of everyone's weekly goals is distributed to each employee.

A permanent record of each employee's goal accomplishments is made monthly. These records are accumulated and used as input for each employee's annual performance evaluation, which is the basis for annual merit increases.

Each manager spends about 6 hours per week working on the Turbo MBO system, which is generally liked by organization members even though it does take some time to learn how to use the system. Employees tend to favor the system because it is largely "bottom-up" in the sense that they are able to set their own goals within the overall-goals framework. Managers are enthusiastic because the system keeps communications at a high level between themselves and the employees who have goals in their areas. Cypress's financial backers laud it because it keeps the company performing according to plan.

Like all systems, the Cypress MBO system is not flawless. Managers indicate that it is sometimes possible to cheat the system by developing elaborate-sounding goals that actually take little time to accomplish. Also, since there are no assigned priorities, it can be difficult for employees to know which goals should have priority until a project leader or manager indicates that a particular

Planning is at the heart of the success of Steve Bostic, the founder of American Photo Group. Bostic developed his multimillion dollar business with a simple approach: systematically buy up struggling regional photo processors to create a national photo processing company that would produce quality work while cutting costs through economies of scale. Bostic was so successful in his endeavor that Eastman Kodak bought him out. Now Bostic has started a new company built around an automated photo machine. His goal: blanket the country with the machines and create a $1 billion business.

goal is important. Rodgers points out also that managers can acquire a false sense of security by thinking they are doing their best by constantly meeting their goals, even though they are not extending themselves. Furthermore, some employees can use their goals as excuses for not doing unexpected jobs, by claiming that they are fully committed.

Despite these limitations, Turbo MBO has been very effective for Cypress Semiconductor. Employee turnover is about 18 percent in an industry whose turnover rate averages about 40 percent. Cypress itself has been valued at 2.25 × sales, whereas other major companies in the field are valued at less than 1 × sales. The company has received numerous awards, including the Wall Street Transcript Silver award, for being among the best financially managed companies in the industry. Thus goal setting and planning through its MBO system has paid off handsomely for Cypress.[1]

Rodgers learned the value of goals and planning while he was a project manager at American Microsystems (another high-technology firm), where he filled blackboards with lists of "several hundred things to get done, who would do it, and when." Turbo MBO at Cypress is essentially a computerized refinement of that system, an innovation that has helped Cypress succeed in a very competitive industry. While few organizations have MBO systems in which goals are set as often as weekly, there is strong support in the management literature for the importance of goals and the related planning, which jointly form the heart of the planning function. In this chapter, we examine the overall planning process, including the development of the mission of the organization. We also consider the nature of organizational goals and examine a model that helps explain how goals facilitate performance. We next probe the link between goals and plans, considering how plans differ according to level, extent of recurring use, and time horizon, as well as examining the role of goals and plans in promoting innovation. Finally, we explore the steps in the management by objectives process and review the major strengths and weaknesses of MBO.

THE OVERALL PLANNING PROCESS

How was Steve Bostic, head of the American Photo Group, able to build the company from $149,000 to $78 million in annual sales before selling the high-technology photography group to Eastman Kodak for a reported $45 million? Bostic attributes his success to having a vision, being able to put specifics down on paper, and having things "well planned and well thought out."[2] As Bostic's experience suggests, a good idea of the overall mission of the organization, accompanied by more specific goals on paper and carefully configured plans, can be important to the success of an organization. In this section, we briefly explore these major components of the planning process before examining them more closely here and in various other sections of this chapter.

Major Components of Planning

Goal A future target or end result that an organization wishes to achieve

One could argue that it is virtually impossible for organizations to function without at least some goals and plans. A **goal** is a future target or end result that an organization wishes to achieve. Many managers and researchers use the term "goal" interchangeably with "objective." Others consider "goal" to be a broader term, encompassing a longer time horizon, and use "objective" to refer to more narrow targets and shorter time frames.[3] We use both terms interchangeably in

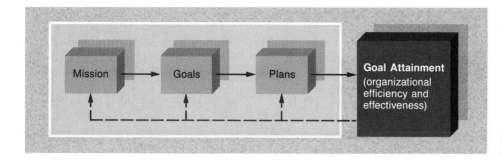

Figure 5-1 The overall planning process.

this text for the sake of simplicity and because it is clear from the context whether a broad or narrow scope or a long or short time frame is involved (at least when the distinction is important to the concepts being examined).

Whereas a goal is a future end result that an organization wants to achieve, a **plan** is the means devised for attempting to reach a goal. The planning function encompasses both goals and plans. *Planning* is the management function that involves setting goals and deciding how best to achieve them. An overall view of the planning process is shown in Figure 5-1. Hopefully, the setting of goals and developing of plans leads to goal attainment and, ultimately, to organizational efficiency and effectiveness. As the diagram indicates, the planning process also involves the mission of the organization.

Plan The means devised for attempting to reach a goal

Organizational Mission

Essentially, the planning process builds on the **mission** of the organization, the organization's purpose or fundamental reason for existence. A **mission statement** is a broad declaration of the basic, unique purpose and scope of operations that distinguishes the organization from others of its type.[4] A mission statement serves several purposes. For managers, it can be a benchmark against which to evaluate success. For employees, a mission statement defines a common purpose, nurtures organizational loyalty, and fosters a sense of community among members. For external agencies, such as investors, governmental agencies, and the public at large, mission statements help provide unique insight into an organization's values and future directions.[5] In highlighting the importance of mission statements, noted management consultant Peter Drucker argues that the mission statement defines the organization. He points out, "Only a clear definition of the mission and purpose of the organization makes possible clear and realistic business objectives."[6] In some organizations, the mission statement is explicit in the sense that it is a formal written document; in others, the mission may be more implicitly understood. Of course, in the latter case, there is the danger that various organization members may have different perceptions of the organization's mission, perhaps without realizing it.[7]

One study estimates that about 60 percent of the Fortune 500 companies have written mission statements.[8] A related study of the mission statements of 75 firms from the Business Week 1000 indicates that mission statements tend to be made up of some or all of the following nine components:[9]

Mission The organization's purpose or fundamental reason for existence

Mission statement A broad declaration of the basic, unique purpose and scope of operations that distinguishes the organization from others of its type

1. *Customers.* Who are the organization's customers?
2. *Products or services.* What are the organization's major products or services?
3. *Location.* Where does the organization compete?
4. *Technology.* What is the firm's basic technology?

5. *Concern for survival*. What is the organization's commitment to economic objectives?
6. *Philosophy*. What are the basic beliefs, values, aspirations, and philosophical priorities of the organization?
7. *Self-concept*. What are the organization's major strengths and competitive advantages?
8. *Concern for public image*. What are the organization's public responsibilities, and what image is desired?
9. *Concern for employees*. What is the organization's attitude toward its employees?

Excerpts from mission statements that match each of these components are shown in Table 5-1. Laura Nash, a management researcher who has studied mission statements, reports that her favorite mission statement hangs, yellow with age, on the wall of a Boston shoe repair shop. It reads: "We are dedicated to the saving of soles, heeling, and administering to the dyeing."[10]

If mission statements are so important, then why don't more organizations have them written down? One reason is that explicitly developing such statements causes managers to confront directly such fundamental issues as "What is our business?" Thus it is very possible that considerable controversy may arise in attempting to develop a mission statement. Another reason is that managers may be so busy with day-to-day matters that they neglect developing the long-term vision that a mission statement entails.[11] Finally, a lack of knowledge about what should go into a mission statement may be part of the reason why more organizations do not have mission statements. In the study of Fortune 500 firms mentioned earlier, about 10 percent of the CEOs responding requested help from the researchers on how to develop a mission statement.[12]

THE NATURE OF ORGANIZATIONAL GOALS

As we have seen, organizational goals form one of the important elements in the overall planning process. Research on the potential usefulness of goals over several decades has highlighted the importance of goals in enhancing organizational efficiency and effectiveness.[13] In this section, we assess the major benefits of goals and examine how goals differ according to organizational level.

Benefits of Goals

The use of goals has several major benefits.[14] For one thing, goals can increase performance. Increases in performance due to setting challenging goals frequently range from 10 to 25 percent, and they are sometimes even higher. Furthermore, such increases have occurred with a variety of employee groups, including clerical personnel, maintenance workers, production workers, salespeople, managers, engineers, and scientists.[15]

Another benefit of goals is that they help clarify expectations. When goals are set, organization members are more likely to have a clear idea of the major outcomes that they are expected to achieve. Without goals, organization members can all be working very hard but may collectively accomplish very little—as if they were rowers independently rowing the same boat in different directions and together making very little progress.

Goals also facilitate the controlling function, because goals provide benchmarks against which progress can be assessed so that corrective action can be taken as needed. Thus goals help individuals gauge their progress, as well as

Table 5-1 Major Components of Mission Statements and Sample Excerpts

Major Components	Sample Excerpts
Customers	The purpose of Motorola is to honourably serve the needs of the community by providing products and services of superior quality at a fair price to our customers. (Motorola)
Products or services	We provide our customers with retail banking, real estate finance, and corporate banking products which will meet their credit, investment, security, and liquidity needs. (Carteret Savings and Loan Association)
Location	Sara Lee Corporation's mission is to be a leading consumer marketing company in the United States and internationally. (Sara Lee Corporation)
Technology	Du Pont is a diversified chemical, energy, and specialty products company with a strong tradition of discovery. Our global businesses are constantly evolving and continually searching for new and better ways to use our human, technological, and financial resources to improve the quality of life of people around the world. (Du Pont)
Concern for survival	To serve the worldwide need for knowledge at a fair profit by gathering, evaluating, producing, and distributing valuable information in a way that benefits our customers, employees, authors, investors, and our society. (McGraw-Hill)
Philosophy	It's all part of the Mary Kay philosophy—a philosophy based on the golden rule. A spirit of sharing and caring where people give cheerfully of their time, knowledge, and experience. (Mary Kay Cosmetics)
Self-concept	Crown Zellerbach is committed to leapfrogging competition within 1000 days by unleashing the constructive and creative abilities and energies of each of its employees. (Crown Zellerbach)
Concern for public image	The company feels an obligation to be a good corporate citizen wherever it operates. (Eli Lilly and Company)
Concern for employees	To compensate its employees with remuneration and fringe benefits competitive with other employment opportunities in its geographical area and commensurate with their contributions toward efficient corporate operations. (Public Service Electric and Gas Company)

Source: Adapted from Fred David, "How Companies Define Their Mission," *Long Range Planning,* February 1989, pp. 92–93.

assist managers in maintaining control over organizational activities. The situation at W. W. Grainger, Inc., based in Skokie, Illinois, serves as an example. The company sells equipment such as sump pumps, industrial staplers, warehouse fans, and commercial air conditioners to contractors, small manufacturers, and distributors. During the 1970s, Grainger charged premium prices but also provided premium service. Unfortunately, the emphasis on service gradually took a back seat to other priorities and by the early 1980s, earnings began to slow. The

Recognizing the contributions that employees make in meeting company goals can increase the motivation of workers. Each year W. W. Grainger, an Illinois-based company specializing in industrial and commercial equipment, sponsors a Service Recognition Dinner to show appreciation for employee accomplishments.

company reacted by placing major displays within reach of its customers in its branches, which now number more than 300, and renewing its emphasis on service. With half its sales stemming from its 24,000-item catalog, the company has put considerable effort into training its rows of telephone operators, who wear headsets and take orders from customers. A board at the front of the room keeps a tally on progress. On one day in fall, 1989, for example, 1.6 percent of the 367 callers had to listen to a recording while waiting to order. The goal is 0 percent. "Three years earlier, 25 percent was the norm," says one branch manager.[16]

Yet another benefit of goals is increased motivation. The added motivation develops from meeting goals, feeling a sense of accomplishment, and receiving recognition and other rewards for reaching targeted outcomes.

An intriguing study conducted by goal-setting researchers Gary P. Latham and Edwin A. Locke demonstrates the benefits of goal setting. The situation involved drivers of logging trucks for a forestry-products company in the western United States. The unionized drivers were concerned that if their trucks were overloaded, they could be fined by the highway department and subsequently lose their jobs, so they seldom loaded their trucks to more than 63 percent of capacity. Interestingly, the company had not provided any goals concerning the level at which the company expected drivers to load their trucks.

In an experiment aimed at improving the situation, the company coordinated a plan with the union that included a goal of loading to 94 percent of each truck's legal capacity and an agreement that no driver would be reprimanded if the goal was not met. No monetary reward or fringe benefits were offered. However, verbal praise was given when drivers loaded their trucks to greater levels than they had previously. Results for the first month of the experiment showed that the trucks were hauling 80 percent of their capacity, more than they ever had before. In the second month, however, performance decreased to 70 percent of capacity. Interviews with the drivers revealed that they were testing management to determine whether action would be taken against drivers who did not reach the goal. When the drivers realized that no action was going to be taken, they increased their performance. Overall performance reached over 90 percent in the third month and remained there for more than the following 7 years. The savings to the company were more than $250,000 in the 9-month period during which the study was conducted.[17] Thus the goals clarified expectations, helped increase motivation, provided standards against which progress could be gauged, and led to significant increases in performance. The experiment is one of many studies that support the importance of goal setting throughout the organization.[18]

Levels of Goals

Organizations typically have three levels of goals: strategic, tactical, and operational, as shown in Figure 5-2. (Also shown are three parallel levels of plans, which will be discussed later in this chapter.)

Strategic Goals. **Strategic goals** are broadly defined targets or future end results set by top management. Such goals typically address issues relating to the organization as a whole and may sometimes be stated in fairly general terms. Strategic goals are sometimes called *official goals* because they are formally stated by top management.[19] At Cypress Semiconductor, for example, one official goal related to productivity is to provide the very highest quality product coupled with on-time delivery. One outcome has been that the company recently was

Strategic goals Broadly defined targets or future end results set by top management

Figure 5-2 Levels of goals and plans.

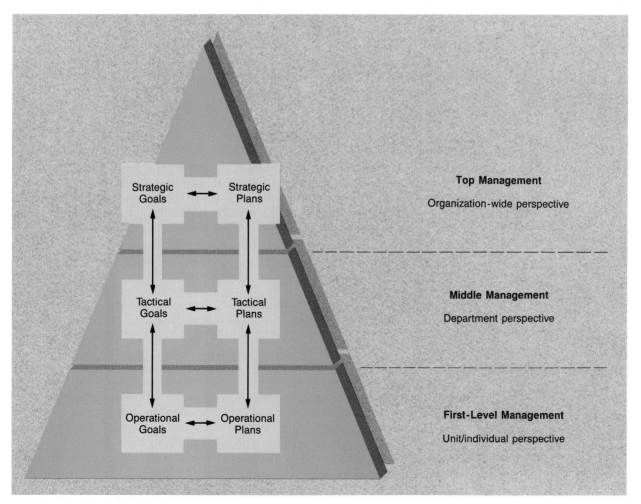

Table 5-2   Eight Major Areas for Strategic Goals

Major Area	Description
Market standing	Desired share of present and new markets, including areas in which new products are needed, and service goals aimed at building customer loyalty
Innovation	Innovations in products or services, as well as innovations in skills and activities required to supply them
Human resources	Supply, development, and performance of managers and other organization members; employee attitudes and development of skills; relations with labor unions, if any
Financial resources	Sources of capital supply and how it will be utilized
Physical resources	Physical facilities and how they will be used in the production of goods and services
Productivity	Efficient use of resources relative to outcomes
Social responsibility	Responsibilities in such areas as concern for the community and maintenance of ethical behavior
Profit requirements	Level of profitability and other indicators of financial well-being

Source: Based on Peter F. Drucker, *Management: Tasks, Responsibilities, Practices,* Harper & Row, 1974, pp. 100–117.

recognized by Hughes (a subsidiary of General Motors) as one of only three suppliers to achieve a zero-defect, 100 percent on-time delivery record.[20]

Management consultant Peter Drucker suggests that business organizations need to set goals in at least the eight major areas shown in Table 5-2. The eight areas encompass a number of aspects that are important to the health and survival of most profit-making organizations.

Tactical goals Targets or future end results usually set by middle management for specific departments or units

Tactical Goals. Tactical goals are targets or future end results usually set by middle management for specific departments or units. Goals at this level spell out what must be done by various departments to achieve the results outlined in the strategic goals. Tactical goals tend to be stated in more measurable terms than is sometimes true of strategic goals. For example, at Cypress Semiconductor, a tactical goal for the Static Random-Access Memories (SRAM) Group, the largest of Cypress's product divisions, might be to achieve preferred supplier status with specified customers. For instance, Cypress recently received preferred SRAM supplier status from AT&T, a designation earned by only four other semiconductor suppliers (Motorola, Hitachi, Fujitsu, and Toshiba).[21] The preferred status makes it easier to do business with a firm and usually leads to increased future orders.

Operational goals Targets or future end results set by lower management that address specific measurable outcomes required from the lower levels

Operational Goals. Operational goals are targets or future end results set by lower management that address specific, measurable outcomes required from the lower levels. For example, in order to achieve the tactical and strategic goals related to product quality and on-time delivery, manufacturing units within divisions such as the SRAM Group must set stringent operational goals aimed at zero defects and 100 percent on-time delivery. Reflecting such operational goals, the computerized MBO system at Cypress keeps close track of unscheduled orders (orders on backlog for which more than 3 days are required to schedule production) and performance on the quality dimension.[22]

Hierarchy of Goals. The three levels of goals can be thought of as forming a *hierarchy of goals*. With a hierarchy, goals at each level need to be synchronized so that efforts at the various levels are channeled ultimately toward achieving the major goals of the organization. In this way, the various levels of goals form a *means-end chain*, in which the goals at the operational level (means) must be achieved in order to reach the goals at the tactical level (end). Likewise, the goals at the tactical level (means) must be reached in order to achieve the goals at the strategic level (end). In the case of Cypress Semiconductor, the company cannot meet its strategic goal of high quality and on-time delivery without reaching related goals at the tactical and operational levels. Similarly, the partial hierarchy of goals presented in Figure 5-3, based on the mission and several strategic objectives of JC Penney, illustrates how goals at various levels fit together to support a united effort geared to ultimately accomplishing organizational goals.

Figure 5-3 Hypothetical hierarchy of goals. (Mission and strategic goals are based on the JC Penney publication *Managing in the Tradition of Partnership*.)

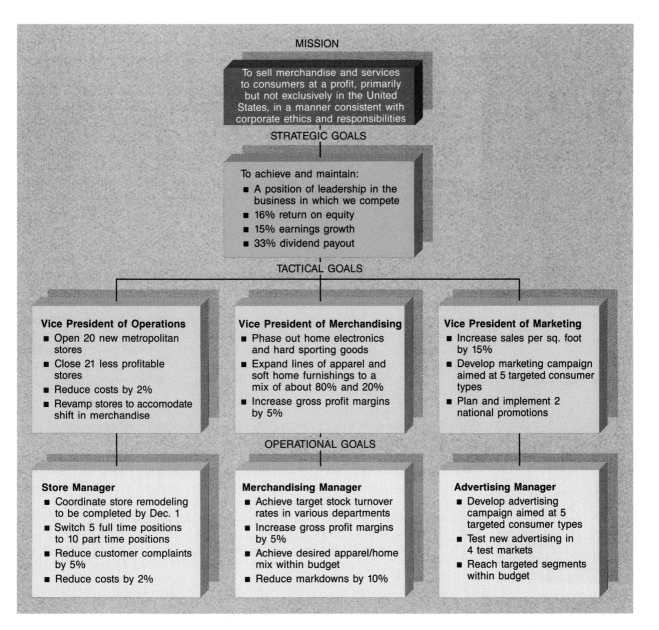

MISSION

To sell merchandise and services to consumers at a profit, primarily but not exclusively in the United States, in a manner consistent with corporate ethics and responsibilities

STRATEGIC GOALS

To achieve and maintain:
■ A position of leadership in the business in which we compete
■ 16% return on equity
■ 15% earnings growth
■ 33% dividend payout

TACTICAL GOALS

Vice President of Operations
■ Open 20 new metropolitan stores
■ Close 21 less profitable stores
■ Reduce costs by 2%
■ Revamp stores to accomodate shift in merchandise

Vice President of Merchandising
■ Phase out home electronics and hard sporting goods
■ Expand lines of apparel and soft home furnishings to a mix of about 80% and 20%
■ Increase gross profit margins by 5%

Vice President of Marketing
■ Increase sales per sq. foot by 15%
■ Develop marketing campaign aimed at 5 targeted consumer types
■ Plan and implement 2 national promotions

OPERATIONAL GOALS

Store Manager
■ Coordinate store remodeling to be completed by Dec. 1
■ Switch 5 full time positions to 10 part time positions
■ Reduce customer complaints by 5%
■ Reduce costs by 2%

Merchandising Manager
■ Achieve target stock turnover rates in various departments
■ Increase gross profit margins by 5%
■ Achieve desired apparel/home mix within budget
■ Reduce markdowns by 10%

Advertising Manager
■ Develop advertising campaign aimed at 5 targeted consumer types
■ Test new advertising in 4 test markets
■ Reach targeted segments within budget

HOW GOALS FACILITATE PERFORMANCE

In order to make effective use of goals, managers need to understand just how goals can facilitate performance. A model reflecting major research on using goals, much of it conducted by goals expert Edwin A. Locke and his associates, is shown in Figure 5-4 on the facing page. The model has several major components.[23] In this section, we consider the various components, highlighting particularly the goal content, goal commitment, work behavior, and feedback aspects.

Goal Content

Goals that are effective in channeling effort toward achievement at the strategic, tactical, and operational levels have a content that reflects five major characteristics. Goals should be challenging, attainable, specific and measurable, time-limited, and relevant.

Challenging. Extensive research indicates that, within reasonable limits, challenging, difficult goals lead to higher performance. Assuming that the goals are accepted, people tend to try harder when faced with a challenge. For example, Kronus, Inc., a Waltham, Massachusetts, maker of innovative electronic time clocks with software that ties into computerized company payroll systems, was losing money with founder and inventor Mark Ain at the helm. One of the first actions taken by an outsider brought in to manage the company was raising sales quotas by 60 percent, a goal that was easily met by the 94 sales and service offices. Back to developing new products, Ain mused, "I'm a bad manager."[24] Interestingly, when individuals are asked to do their "best," they typically do not perform nearly as well as when they have specific, challenging goals.

This bootmaker at L. L. Bean is working under a new company motto: "Get it right the first time." The mail order company's reputation for quality and service had suffered in recent years under the pressure of unrealistic sales goals. In one year customers returned almost $80 million worth of purchases. Now management has scaled back its goals for growth and reemphasized product quality and customer service.

Attainable. Although goals need to be challenging, they usually work best when they are attainable. At some point, individuals are making maximum use of their skills and abilities and cannot achieve higher performance levels. Developing goals that are almost impossible to achieve may discourage rather than energize workers and may make them feel inadequate. Even with extremely difficult goals, though, individuals usually attempt to achieve as much of the goal as possible—*if* they are given credit for what they do achieve. Still, asking workers to achieve difficult, but attainable, goals is more likely to engender sustained performance over a period of time than is continually asking them to do the impossible.[25]

Recognizing the need to have realistic, attainable goals, L. L. Bean, the venerable mail-order source for clothing and outdoor gear, recently scaled back its goal of reaching $1 billion in sales by 1992. The decision was made in order to protect Bean's reputation for service. One symptom indicating that customers were not satisfied was the $80 million worth of goods that they had returned during 1987, an amount accounting for 14 percent of Bean's sales. The returns cost the company $18 million in postage and handling costs. As a result, the company has launched a new service campaign with the theme "Get it right the first time." "We don't mind fewer new customers as long as we do it right," says Leon Gorman, Bean's president. Accordingly, the company plans to grow at a rate of about 5 to 8 percent, compared with growth of about 23 percent over the past 10 years.[26]

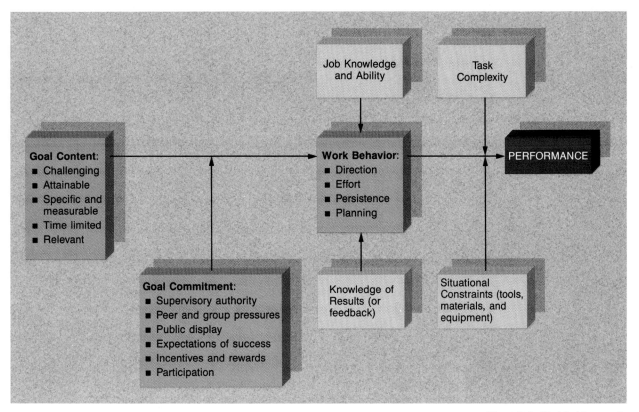

Figure 5-4 Model of how goals facilitate performance. (Adapted from Thomas W. Lee, Edwin A. Locke, and Gary P. Latham, "Goal Setting Theory and Job Performance," in Lawrence A. Pervin, ed., *Goal Concepts in Personality and Social Psychology*, Lawrence Erlbaum, Hillsdale, N.J., 1989.)

Specific and Measurable. To be effective, goals need to be specific and measurable so that it is clear what is expected and when the goal has been achieved. When possible, goals should be stated in quantitative terms. *Quantitative goals* encompass objective numerical standards that are relatively easy to verify. At Rubbermaid, Inc., a company with a reputation for innovative products, a quantitative goal is to derive 30 percent of its sales from products that are less than 5 years old. For some purposes, though, qualitative goals are more appropriate. *Qualitative goals* involve subjective judgment about whether or not a goal is reached. An example of a qualitative goal for Rubbermaid is to develop an idea and prototype for a new plastic desk accessory that is useful, long-lasting, and inexpensive.[27]

Time-Limited. Goals also need to be time-limited; that is, there should be a defined period of time within which the goals must be accomplished. Otherwise, goals have little meaning, since individuals can keep putting off achieving them. At Cypress Semiconductor, the weekly goals (which are reviewed at the project level every Monday and at other levels on Tuesdays and Wednesdays) keep attention focused on achieving goals within the desired time frame. In many organizations, goals are set annually but may be reviewed at various times during the year, such as quarterly.[28]

Relevant. Goals are more likely to engender support when they are clearly *relevant* to the major work of the organization and the particular department or work unit. For example, Jack Stack, head of the Springfield Remanufacturing Corporation in Springfield, Missouri, learned an important lesson about goals and relevancy after he took the helm of the ailing equipment manufacturing plant. The company had contracted to ship 800 tractors to the Soviet Union, but there was a shortage of some parts that were needed to complete the tractors, which were due to be shipped in less than a month. In desperation, Stack put up a huge sign that read, "Our Goal: 800 Tractors." The workers responded by coming in at night to figure out what parts were missing from which tractors; they then got the parts through every means they could think of. As a result, the very difficult goal was met.[29]

For guidelines on how to go about actually setting goals, see the Practically Speaking discussion, "How to Set Goals."

Goal Commitment

Goal commitment   One's attachment to, or determination to reach, a goal

A critical element in using goals effectively is getting individuals and/or work groups to be committed to the goals they must carry out. **Goal commitment** is one's attachment to, or determination to reach, a goal.[30] Without commitment, setting specific, challenging goals will have little impact on performance. If you are like most people, you probably have had the experience of having someone attempt to interest you in a difficult goal to which you felt no commitment. Perhaps it was a relative wanting you to achieve a college degree in a major that you believed did not match your capabilities and/or interests. Chances are that you felt little commitment to the goal. Similarly, in work situations, appropriate goals can be set, but such goals are not likely to enhance performance without the goal commitment of organization members. How, then, can a manager gain commitment to important organizational goals? Research indicates that five major factors positively influence goal commitment: supervisory authority, peer and group pressure, public display of commitment, expectations of success, and incentives and rewards. We also discuss a potential sixth factor, participation.

Supervisory Authority. Individuals and groups are often willing to accept a goal and become committed to it when the goal and reasons for it are explained by a person with supervisory authority, usually one's boss. With this approach, goals are essentially assigned by the supervisor, who provides an explanation of the need for the goals and any necessary instructions to his or her employees. The explanation and instructions are likely to be more effective when the supervisor is supportive in the sense of providing encouragement and offering opportunities for individuals to ask questions, rather than just telling subordinates to meet the goals. Trust in the supervisor also may facilitate the commitment process.

Peer and Group Pressure. Pressure from peers and work group members can enhance goal commitment when everyone's efforts are channeled in the same direction. This is because enthusiasm about potential accomplishments becomes infectious. In addition, successful individuals can serve as role models to others who observe their efforts. On the other hand, peer and group pressure can detract from goal commitment, particularly if the goals are perceived as unfair.

Public Display. Recent evidence suggests that commitment to difficult goals is higher when the commitment is public (made in front of others) than when it is

HOW TO SET GOALS

There are six main steps in setting goals to obtain optimal results:

1. *Specify the goal to be reached or tasks to be done.* What do you want to accomplish? Do you want to increase sales? Reduce costs? Improve quality? Boost customer service? Maybe, at the moment, you are thinking that you would like to obtain an A in a particular course this semester (perhaps the one involving this textbook).

2. *Specify how the performance will be measured.* Some outcomes can be measured more easily than others. For example, some outcomes, such as number of units sold and dollar volume of sales, can be measured fairly easily. Work outcomes (the results achieved) typically are measured according to one of three parameters:

Physical units: For example, quantity of production, market share, number of errors, number of rejects (quality control)

Time: For example, meeting deadlines, servicing customers, completing a project, coming to work each day, being punctual

Money: For example, profits, sales, costs, budgets, debts, income

Similarly, many course-of-study outcomes can be measured in terms of physical units (such as number of questions answered correctly on examinations and grades received on papers and assignments) and in terms of time (such as meeting deadlines for assignments and attending classes).

Sometimes, outcomes are difficult to measure, perhaps because the measurement process would be too costly or because the outcomes are affected by factors beyond an individual's control. In such cases, it may be necessary to measure behaviors or actions rather than outcomes. For example, if a manager's goal of overcoming worker resistance to certain impending changes is likely to be significantly affected by the actions of others, it may be possible to measure crucial activities instead of outcomes. Such activities might include whether the manager clearly explains why the change is needed, outlines how the change will affect others, and listens to employee's concerns. When possible, though, the goal-setting process should focus on outcomes.

3. *Specify the standard or target to be reached.* This step builds on the type of measure chosen in step 2 by spelling out the *degree* of performance to be included in the goal. For example, the target might be producing 40 units per hour, reducing errors by 2 percent, completing a project by Dec. 15, answering the telephone within three rings, or increasing sales by 10 percent.

In pursuit of the general objective of attaining an A in a particular course, one might set targets of answering correctly at least 90 percent of the questions on the midterm and final exams, offering one knowledgeable point during the discussion part of each class, and fulfilling written assignments at a level of quality likely to earn high grades. Setting subgoals, such as the number of textbook pages to be read and outlined each day, also can help goal achievement.

4. *Specify the time span involved.* To have a positive impact on performance, goals need to have a time span within which they are to be completed. In a production situation, the goal may be stated in terms of production per hour or day. In a service situation, the time frame may be oriented toward delivering the service. For example, a photocopier repair service may have the goal of responding to customer calls within 2 hours. Other goals, such as major projects, may have time spans involving several months or even years.

For instance, your goals for the semester may involve a few months, while goals associated with obtaining your degree and further building your career may span several years.

5. *Prioritize the goals.* When multiple goals are present, as is likely with most jobs, goals need to be prioritized so that effort and action can be directed in proportion to the importance of each goal. Otherwise, individual effort can be focused improperly.

For example, suppose that in the course in which you wish to obtain an A, examinations count 70 percent, a paper counts 20 percent, and discussion in class counts 10 percent. In this case, a goal related to the examinations should be given first priority, while goals related to the paper and the class discussion should receive second and third priority, respectively.

6. *Determine coordination requirements.* Before a set of goals is finalized, it is important to investigate whether achieving the goals depends on the cooperation and contributions of other individuals. If so, coordination with the other individuals may be necessary. In organizations, such coordination vertically is usually relatively easy. It may be more difficult, but nevertheless important, to achieve coordination horizontally, particularly if some of the individuals report to other managers outside your work unit.

In the case of the course in which you are attempting to excel, your efforts may require coordination with your boss (if you are employed) so that your work schedule allows you sufficient study time before exams. If you plan ahead, you also may be able to get parents, a spouse, or friends to help you out with other duties at crucial times during the semester, such as right before exams, so that you have plenty of time to review.[31]

private. At Nordstrom's, the Seattle-based apparel, shoe, and soft-goods retailer known for excellent customer service, store managers must publicly state their sales goals at regional meetings. Once a manager has declared store sales goals, a top executive shows goals for the same store developed by a "secret committee." Managers whose goals fall below those of the secret committee are booed, while those with goals above the secret committee level are cheered.[32]

Expectations of Success. Goal commitment is more likely when individuals or groups perceive that they have high expectations of success—that is, they perceive that they have high probabilities of performing well on the tasks involved in reaching the goal. Managers can foster such expectations through instruction and coaching in the areas in which an individual needs assistance in order to be successful. If goals involve tasks that individuals believe they cannot accomplish, they are unlikely to be committed to them.

Incentives and Rewards. Goal commitment is also enhanced by incentives and rewards. Incentives are offered during the goal-setting process, while rewards occur upon goal achievement. Some incentives may be tangible, such as money, while others may be intangible, such as challenge of the job, anticipation or positive feelings about accomplishment, feedback, competition (as long as it is constructive), and recognition for goal attainment. At Nordstrom's, salespeople with especially good results are honored monthly as "All-Stars" and receive $100 and large discounts on store merchandise. The salespeople who achieve the most are inducted annually into the Pace Setters Club, which also makes them eligible for major discounts. The names of managers who excel at reaching their goals are engraved on a plaque in the executive headquarters of the company.[33] On the other hand, if workers fear that producing more will lead to negative outcomes, such as layoffs, commitment to high production goals will be low.

Participation. Although research indicates that participation is not usually needed to gain goal commitment, having individuals participate in the goal-setting process can be an effective means of engendering goal commitment. Participation can be particularly helpful in developing plans for implementing goals. As a result, managers often include subordinates in goal setting and the subsequent planning of how to achieve the goals. Still, it is useful to know that participation is not a necessary ingredient in goal commitment, because complete participation of all affected persons often is not feasible.[34]

For instance, tactical and operational goals often must be set to achieve strategic goals that have been developed at the upper levels of management. While there may be some negotiation possible with upper management to alter goals that are unfeasible, middle and lower levels often must find ways of implementing goals that are necessary for the achievement of strategic objectives, rather than altering the goals themselves. Fortunately, goal-setting research suggests that organization members will usually attempt to support goals when they understand why the goals are important for the organization, regardless of whether they have participated in setting them.

Work Behavior

Given goals and commitment, how does the goal-setting process ultimately influence behavior? Research so far suggests that goal content and goal commitment affect an individual's actual work behavior by influencing four work behavior factors: direction, effort, persistence, and planning.

Direction. Goals provide direction by channeling attention and action toward activities related to those goals, rather than to other activities. Thus goals to which we are committed can help us make better choices about the activities that we will undertake.

Effort. In addition to channeling activities, goals to which we are committed boost effort by mobilizing energy. As indicated by the research on goal setting, individuals are likely to put forth more effort when goals are difficult than when they are easy.

Persistence. Persistence involves maintaining direction and effort in behalf of a goal until it is reached, a requirement that may involve an extended period of time. Commitment to goals makes it more likely that we will persist in attempting to reach them.

Planning. In addition to the relatively direct effects on direction, effort, and persistence, goals also have an important indirect effect on work behavior by influencing planning. Goal setting affects planning because individuals who have committed themselves to achieving difficult goals are likely to develop plans or methods that can be used to attain those goals. With easy goals, however, little planning may be necessary.

Other Process Components

Several other components ultimately influence the impact of goals on job performance. For one thing, *job knowledge and ability* are likely to affect an individual's work behavior and prospects for reaching goals, even when there is strong commitment. For another, the *complexity of the task* may affect the degree to which goal-directed work behaviors influence job performance. According to related studies, the impact of goals on performance is greater with relatively simple tasks (such as basic arithmetic, toy assembly tasks, or basic typing) than with more complex ones (such as supervision or engineering projects).[35] The reason seems to be that the effect of goals on the direction, effort, and persistence of work behavior, as well as on planning, is dissipated somewhat into different aspects of a complex task. In contrast, with a simple task, direction, effort, persistence, and planning can focus in one direction only. Regardless of whether tasks are simple or complex, as noted earlier, goals need to be challenging in order to have a significantly positive impact on performance. Goals can be set at a challenging level even for relatively simple tasks (such as reaching a typing proficiency of 60 words per minute while making no more than 1 error per minute—a likely challenging, but attainable, goal for a reasonably good typist).

Situational constraints constitute still another element that influences the impact of goals on performance. Having the proper tools, materials, and equipment is important for achieving difficult goals. Finally, *knowledge of results* or feedback about progress toward goals is a particularly important aspect of using goals effectively in organizations. While goals set the target, knowledge of results ultimately impacts goal achievement by enabling individuals to gauge their progress toward goal attainment. For example, an individual learning to play golf can gauge the adequacy of his or her golf swing by observing the path and distance that the ball travels relative to targets or goals. Not surprisingly, strong evidence suggests that neither goals nor knowledge of results *alone* is sufficient for performance improvement. Instead, *both* goals and knowledge of results are necessary (imagine the difficulty of learning to play golf if one attempted to practice in the dark).[36] One company that has benefited from using goals to influence performance in a positive way is the Matsushita Electric Industrial Company (see the following Case in Point discussion).

CASE IN POINT: Quality and Productivity Increase at Matsushita

The Matsushita Electric Industrial Company (MEIC) employs more than 1200 people at a former Motorola plant in Franklin Park, Illinois, that produces television receivers and microwave ovens. Within 5 years after this Japanese company acquired the plant from Motorola, quality had improved significantly. In-process defects had dropped from 1.4 to .07 defects per television set or microwave oven. In addition, productivity (the ratio of inputs, such as materials and labor, to outputs) had increased 30 percent. For example, the labor required to produce a color television receiver had been cut in half. These gains were achieved through a combination of managerial practices designed to revitalize an already skilled labor force and improvements in equipment, technology, and training.

In the area of managerial practice, manufacturing and quality control personnel meet every 6 months to set quality goals for the products manufactured. The group considers such issues as the number of defects allowed and the time allotted to complete the assembly of each item produced. Bar charts are then kept that indicate which areas are above, near, or below their targets. Once a week, all operations in the plant cease for 10 or 15 minutes while supervisors meet with their crews to consider progress relative to goals in such areas as quality, productivity, absenteeism, and scrap.

Special effort is made to improve performance on a particularly designated assembly line, called the "model line." Workers on that line and various support personnel, such as quality experts and engineers, meet once a week to gauge progress and consider new ideas. New practices that have proved successful on the model line are then adapted to fit other lines.

A quality-emphasis month is declared twice a year. Slogan and poster competitions, crossword puzzles with quality terms, suggestion contests, and other methods are used to boost awareness. Winners are entertained at a restaurant and given a modest reward.

The underlying purpose of these activities is to improve quality and productivity by creating an environment that will be conducive to cooperation and problem solving. The various activities also serve to emphasize the goals, encourage commitment, and provide knowledge about results, all important elements in making the goal-setting process effective.

Matsushita Electric also attempts to provide the equipment and technology that are necessary to meet the goals. For example, automated equipment developed in Japan was brought in to facilitate chassis assembly. Product design changes reduced the number of required workers by 26 percent, as equipment and design engineers worked together to make quality products easier to manufacture. Newly developed assembly lines allow workers to control their own work flow individually. In place of a continuous, conveyor-paced line, operators can use foot levers to detour work to their station and to forward finished pieces to the next workstations. Closed-circuit television systems were installed to broadcast information about quality, such as particular defect types and how to prevent them, as well as information on progress toward quality goals.

Training also is an important part of the Matsushita Electric approach. New employees receive up to 5 days of classroom training, as well as on-the-job training, to increase their job knowledge and improve their skill levels. The training also provides a forum in which managers can assess whether new workers have the ability to perform adequately and can determine whether they like the working conditions.[37] ▬▬

Thus, goal setting has been an important tool in increasing productivity and quality at Matsushita Electric. Still, care must be taken to use goal setting properly, lest problems arise.

Potential Problems with Goals

Although there are many positive features associated with using goals in organizations, there also are some potential pitfalls to be avoided.[38] These potential problems and possible solutions are summarized in Table 5-3.

For one thing, setting difficult goals increases the risk that they will not be reached. Failure to reach anticipated goals can have serious business implications, hence only calculated risks (rather than goals with only a small prospect of success) should be considered. For another, high goals often increase the stress levels of organization members. Up to a point, some increased stress is likely to be beneficial. Beyond a certain point, excessive stress may have a detrimental effect on performance, suggesting that it would be wise to lower goals or provide additional help, such as added staff or further training, to make reaching the goals more feasible. Still another danger is that failure to meet high goals may lead individuals to experience feelings of self-doubt and inadequacy, as well as anger toward those perceived as thwarting goal achievement. Such feel-

Table 5-3   Potential Goal-Setting Problems and Possible Solutions

Potential Problems	Possible Remedies
Excessive risk taking	Analyze risk; avoid careless or foolish risks.
Increased stress	Eliminate unnecessary stress by adjusting goal difficulty, adding staff, and offering training in necessary skills.
Undermined self-confidence (due to failure)	Treat failure as a problem to be solved rather than a signal to punish.
Ignored nongoal areas	Make sure goals encompass key areas.
Excessive short-run thinking	Include some long-term goals.
Dishonesty and cheating	Set example of honesty, avoid using goals punitively, offer help in overcoming difficulties, give frequent feedback, and be open to information indicating goals are inappropriate.

Source: Based on Edwin A. Locke and Gary P. Latham, *Goal Setting: A Motivational Technique That Works*, Prentice-Hall, Englewood Cliffs, N.J., 1984, pp. 171–172.

ings are less likely when goals are used as guidelines, rather than as tools to punish those who do not quite reach their targets. When goals are not met, the supervisor and subordinate should meet and consider the problems and how they can be corrected. Of course, continual failure to meet reasonable goals may require further training, transfer, or some other action to resolve the problem.

Yet another potential pitfall is that there may be a tendency to ignore non-goal areas. A major advantage of goals is that they focus attention on the behaviors that are most important (causing less attention to be given to less important aspects). At the same time, managers need to make sure that the major key areas involved are included in the goal setting. Another potential danger is that goals will encourage excessive short-range thinking, an accusation sometimes made against U.S. managers. However, goals can encourage a focus on the long term if they are set for 2, 3, or 5 years or even longer periods of time (perhaps with subgoals that apply to shorter time periods). Finally, goal setting may encourage dishonesty and cheating. This tendency can be minimized by deemphasizing punishment for shortfalls in meeting goals, providing frequent feedback about progress, offering help in overcoming difficulties, and being open to information that suggests that the goals are inappropriate, perhaps because the situation has changed. Of course, goals should be changed only when there is sufficient evidence that they are inappropriate.

LINKING GOALS AND PLANS

Goals and plans are closely related. Even though an organization may establish goals at the strategic, tactical, and operating levels, these goals will have little meaning unless careful consideration is given to how the goals will actually be achieved. While goals are the desired ends, plans are the means that will be used to bring about the desired ends. The importance of developing plans becomes apparent when one considers that there may be more than one means of reaching a particular goal. Plans differ by level in the organization and also by extent of recurring use.

Levels of Plans

In much the same way that there are levels of goals, plans also differ according to level in the organization (see Figure 5-2). Thus there are strategic, tactical, and operational plans.[39]

Strategic plans Detailed action steps mapped out to reach strategic goals

Strategic Plans. Strategic plans are detailed action steps mapped out to reach strategic goals. Strategic plans address such issues as how to respond to changing conditions, how to allocate resources, and what actions should be taken to create a unified and powerful organizationwide effort ultimately aimed at strategic goals.[40] Strategic plans generally are developed by top management in consultation with the board of directors and with middle management. Strategic plans typically cover a relatively long time horizon that may extend 3 to 5 years or more into the future. At Cypress Semiconductor, for example, strategic planning considers the future 5 years ahead. Comprehensive statements of strategic plans in organizations often include the mission and goals because these form the basis for strategic action steps. We discuss issues related to strategic planning at considerable length in the next chapter.

Tactical Plans. Tactical plans are the means charted to support implementation of the strategic plan and achievement of tactical goals. Tactical plans tend to focus on intermediate time frames, usually encompassing 1 to 3 years. For the most part, tactical plans are developed by middle managers, who may consult lower-level managers before making commitments to top-level management. Tactical plans outline the major steps that particular departments will take to reach their tactical goals. Generally, tactical plans are more specific and concrete than strategic plans. In developing tactical plans, managers may consider a number of possibilities before settling on a final plan (the plan is, of course, subject to change, should things not progress as expected). Tactical plans are important to the success of strategic plans. For example, middle-level managers at Cypress Semiconductor develop tactical plans that support top-level strategic plans.

> **Tactical plans** The means charted to support implementation of the strategic plan and achievement of tactical goals

Operational Plans. Operational plans are the means devised to support implementation of tactical plans and achievement of operational goals. Operational plans generally consider relatively short time frames of less than 1 year, such as requirements for a few months, weeks, or even days. Plans at this level are usually developed by lower-level managers in conjunction with the middle management levels. Operational plans spell out specifically what must be accomplished over short time periods in order to achieve operational goals. For example, at Cypress Semiconductor, considerable emphasis is placed on operational plans covering 1 week. Unless operational goals are achieved in organizations, tactical and strategic plans will not be successful and goals at those levels will not be achieved.

> **Operational plans** The means devised to support implementation of tactical plans and achievement of operational goals

Plans According to Extent of Recurring Use

Plans can also be categorized according to the extent to which they will be used on a recurring or ongoing basis. There are two types of plans: single-use plans and standing plans (see Figure 5-5).

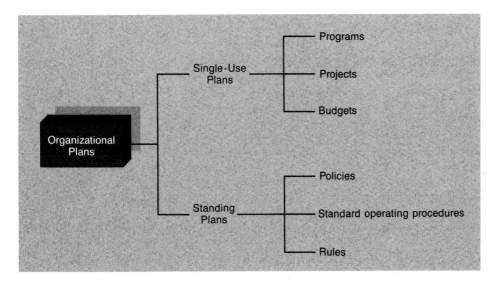

Figure 5-5 Plans according to extent of recurring use.

After studying the customer service operations of 12 other companies, Rosemarie Greco, president of Fidelity Bank in Philadelphia, has developed a standing plan for dealing with complaints from customers. She established one telephone line to deal with the complaints of 14 different business segments in the bank. She personally handles the major problems of clients and reviews all other complaints and inquiries. As a result of her complaint policy and procedures, customer satisfaction increased from 57 percent to 87 percent within 2 years.

Single-use plans Plans aimed at achieving a specific goal that, once reached, will most likely not recur in the future

Program A comprehensive plan that coordinates a complex set of activities related to a major nonrecurring goal

Project A plan that coordinates a set of limited-scope activities that do not need to be divided into several major projects in order to reach a major nonrecurring goal

Standing plans Plans that provide ongoing guidance for performing recurring activities

Policy A general guide that specifies the broad parameters within which organization members are expected to operate in pursuit of organizational goals

Procedure A prescribed series of related steps to be taken under certain recurring circumstances

Single-Use Plans. **Single-use plans** are plans aimed at achieving a specific goal that, once reached, will most likely not recur in the future. There are two major types of single-use plans: programs and projects.

A **program** is a comprehensive plan that coordinates a complex set of activities related to a major nonrecurring goal. Programs typically involve several different departments or units of the organization, are composed of several different projects, and may take more than 1 year to complete. Programs usually include six basic steps: (1) dividing what is to be done into major parts, or projects, (2) determining the relationships among the parts and developing a sequence, (3) deciding who will take responsibility for each part, (4) determining how each part will be completed and what resources will be necessary, (5) estimating the time required for completion of each part, and (6) developing a schedule for implementing each step.[41] Programs frequently have their own budgets. A *budget* is a statement that outlines the financial resources needed to support the various activities included in the program. An example of a program is the 20,000-mile optical-fiber network recently built by U.S. Sprint at a cost of several billion dollars. Stretching from coast to coast, each pair of fiber strands within the cable can handle 16,000 simultaneous conversations.[42] Installing the Sprint network was a nonrecurring goal, because once the network was completed, there was no need to be concerned with redoing it for a considerable period of time.

A **project** is a plan that coordinates a set of limited-scope activities that do not need to be divided into several major projects in order to reach a major nonrecurring goal. Projects also often have their own budgets. A project may be one of several related to a particular program. For example, the fiber-optic program of Sprint consisted of many smaller projects involving laying the fiber-optic cable in various locations. Conversely, a project may be a separate, self-contained set of activities sufficient to reach a particular goal. For instance, at U.S. Sprint, work continues on a project to develop a voice card that would allow a caller to speak into a phone and have a Sprint computer recognize the voice and automatically bill the call.[43] The voice-card project is a self-contained activity that will not need to be repeated once the project is completed.

Standing Plans. **Standing plans** are plans that provide ongoing guidance for performing recurring activities. The three main types of standing plans are policies, procedures, and rules.[44]

A **policy** is a general guide that specifies the broad parameters within which organization members are expected to operate in pursuit of organizational goals. Policies do not normally dictate exactly what actions should be taken. Rather, they provide general boundaries for action. For example, policies frequently spell out important constraints. Many retail stores, for instance, have a policy requiring that returned merchandise be accompanied by a sales receipt. Similarly, policies also often outline desirable actions. At the Hechinger Company, a Maryland-based retailer of hardware and home and garden products, returns are accepted even when the customer has obviously abused the item. In fact, a Hechinger manager can have a dozen roses sent to customers who are particularly upset.[45]

A **procedure** is a prescribed series of related steps to be taken under certain recurring circumstances. Well-established and formalized procedures often are called *standard operating procedures* (SOPs). Unlike policies, which tend to be fairly general, procedures provide detailed step-by-step instructions as to what should be done. As such, they do not allow much flexibility or deviation. For example, banks typically have SOPs governing how tellers handle deposits. Because they specify detailed desired actions in recurring circumstances, SOPs frequently are good tools for training new employees. Of course, if they are allowed to become outdated, SOPs may cause employees to learn, and continue to do, things that are no longer appropriate or needed.

A **rule** is a statement that spells out specific actions to be taken or not taken in a given situation. Unlike procedures, rules do not normally specify a series of steps. Instead, they specify exactly what must be or must not be done, leaving little flexibility or room for deviation. For example, most colleges and universities have rules specifying the circumstances under which a course may be dropped after a certain date.

Rule A statement that spells out specific actions to be taken or not taken in a given situation

Time Horizons of Goals and Plans

The different levels of goals and plans are related to different time horizons (see Figure 5-6). Strategic goals and plans usually address long-range issues involving time periods of 5 years or more. The period varies somewhat depending on the industry. When the environment changes rapidly, long-range planning may focus on periods that are even less than 5 years; when the environment is relatively stable (such as that of the utility industry), long-range planning may extend to periods of 10 to 20 years. Tactical goals and plans typically address intermediate-range issues involving periods that usually vary from 1 to 5 years. Operational goals and plans are mainly oriented toward short-range issues spanning periods of 1 year or less.

Promoting Innovation: The Role of the Planning Process

Research evidence suggests that the overall planning process can play a vital role in innovation in organizations through the mission, goals, and plans components. Creativity expert Teresa M. Amabile argues that the basic orientation of an organization toward innovation must stem primarily from the highest levels.[46] Ideally, the CEO envisions a future for the organization that is based on innovation and then attempts to communicate that vision to organization mem-

Figure 5-6 Time horizons for goals and plans.

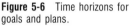

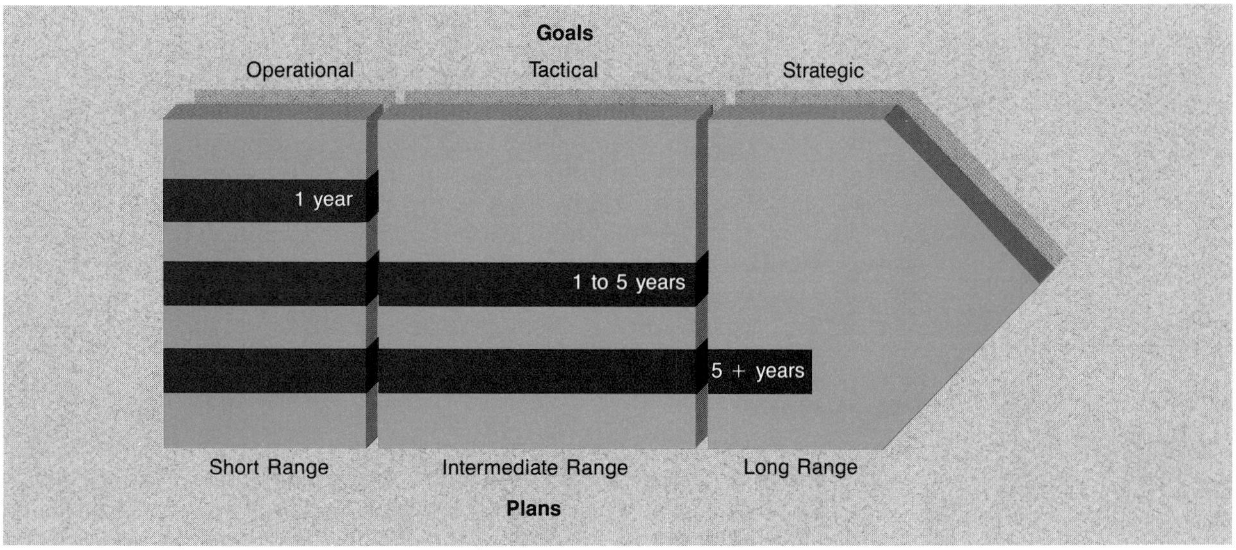

bers. One primary means of signaling the importance of innovation is the organizational mission statement, which can also address the general areas in which innovation is to be emphasized. For example, the mission statement for Cypress Semiconductor designates the major types of "leading-edge process technologies" that will be emphasized, and it specifies, "Cypress's products are strategic components for next-generation computation, instrumentation, telecommunication, military, and aerospace systems." Thus Cypress has clearly committed itself to innovation in attempting to provide those "next-generation" components, and its mission statement also provides some general information about the major areas of innovation.[47] The vision incorporated in such mission statements helps highlight the importance of innovation and motivate organization members to innovate.

The goals component of the planning process can also support innovation. For example, translating a mission into strategic goals might lead to the following specification: "Within 5 years, the organization will be the number-one provider of state-of-the-art semiconductor chips in a [specified broad] area." The "state-of-the-art" designation signals the need for product innovation. A corresponding goal at the tactical level might be: "Within 2 years, the programmable logic devices division will introduce 20 new products." Finally, at the operational level, a goal for a particular work unit might be: "Within 1 year, the unit will have a working prototype that meets the following general specifications. . . ." Thus goals at each level can be used to encourage innovation.

The plans component of the planning process also plays a role in innovation. While goals calling for innovative outcomes can be stated in at least general terms, actual plans for achieving innovative outcomes, such as new products, often are somewhat looser than might be the case with situations in which exactly what must be done to reach a goal is relatively predictable. The use of general plans for achieving innovative outcomes reflects the difficulty of specifying exactly what should be done when seeking innovative breakthroughs and nurturing new ideas, particularly in product or service development. Of course, managers can take a number of steps to increase the possibilities that innovative goals will be met by making sure that organizational conditions foster innovation. We discuss several of these conditions, such as organizational structure, resource levels, communication patterns, and leadership in subsequent chapters.

Plans can also be used to help achieve goals that do not themselves represent innovative outcomes but, rather, rely on innovative means. For example, a goal might focus on a desired end result, such as cost cutting or quality improvement, yet the development of plans can encourage finding innovative means of reaching the target. In this way, the focus is on developing innovative ways to reach goals that are not themselves stated in terms of innovative outcomes. For example, 3M, a company that is well known for encouraging the development of innovative products (we discuss this aspect of 3M in Chapter 11), recently used goals as a vehicle to encourage the search for innovative means of supporting necessary cost-cutting efforts (see the following Case in Point discussion).

CASE IN POINT: 3M Mines the Work Force for Ideas

A company with a strong reputation for innovative products, 3M has a vast catalog of 60,000 items ranging from Scotch brand transparent tape to floppy disks. Nearly one-third of the company's $12 billion in annual sales comes from products developed during the past 5 years. While the company has excelled at

Slitting tape is now a more efficient operation at 3M's tape factory. By moving the tape coating and slitting machines next to each other and giving the operators responsibility in quality control, the factory has been able to coordinate output and cut down on both inventory and manufacturing time.

churning out new product offerings, innovation in its factories has not always kept stride. The relative lack of innovation at the factory level did not matter greatly until recently, when global rivals began developing their own new products, often at costs lower than 3M's. In reacting to the threat, 3M instituted a major cost-cutting effort aimed at reducing costs in its manufacturing sector. Rather than laying off workers and closing plants, as companies often do, 3M asked each of its over 40 divisions to develop ideas aimed at streamlining operations and boosting productivity.

In dealing with the need for cost cutting, CEO Allen F. Jacobson used an approach that is similar to that used for product innovation. "What we had to do was put people to work on some clear objectives," he says. Jacobson had determined that by 1990 3M needed to improve productivity, speed manufacturing cycles, and cut expenses caused by poor quality. The amount of change for the better that was needed in each area was 35 percent. The initiative came to be called the J-35 program (the "J" is for Jake, Jacobson's nickname).

To meet the overall objective of 35 percent, each division and each individual factory set up specific goals. Instead of implementing companywide policies on where costs were to be cut, Jacobson left it up to the various managers to determine how to meet the goals. Jacobson reasoned that each division might face different challenges in meeting the goals, while plant managers would be in the best position to know where to make necessary changes.

Results have been encouraging. At an Aberdeen, South Dakota, plant that assembles workplace respirators, workers decided that the plant setup was inefficient. After each of seven steps in the manufacturing process, filter materials were placed into a warehouse to await the next step. The result was that the filters made seven different trips back to the warehouse.

To remedy the situation, teams of factory workers helped untangle the flow of materials and components throughout the plant. Their recommendations were relatively radical in that the workers decided to eliminate the traditional assembly line. Instead, the new work flow design called for organizing the machinery into work cells, where all the steps necessary to produce a respirator could be done quickly in a logical sequence. The new setup eliminated the need to send unfinished filters to the warehouse between manufacturing steps. These changes and a new inventory control system helped improve quality and reduce wasted materials by 54 percent.

To encourage such innovative ideas, 3M has worked at rewarding good ideas. At Aberdeen, pizza parties were staged for workers when they reached their goals, and they also received trophies. In order to encourage the workers to coordinate their efforts, individual bonuses were tied to the innovative solutions of the team. The J-35 program has helped the company greatly reduce the costs of its goods sold at the same time that the company has increased research spending.[48]

Potential Obstacles to Planning

Several potential obstacles threaten the ability of organizations to develop effective plans. One barrier is a rapidly changing environment, which makes planning more difficult because plans must be altered frequently. Another obstacle to effective planning is a view among some managers that planning is unnecessary, a stance that may arise when managers have at least a general idea in their heads about future directions and means of reaching organizational goals. Steve Bostic, whose American Photo Group tallied a 52,244 percent increase in sales over a 5-year period before he sold the company to Kodak, argues that plans must be put on paper: "I want people to buy into the plan, so it isn't just my plan anymore. It becomes theirs as well. That way, I know everybody is following the same road map when we go out into the real world." Bostic argues that unless the plan is specific enough to be put on paper, communications with others about the plan will be vague, and they will not be able to give the plan their full support. Meanwhile, Bostic has started another company, the R. Stevens Corporation, built around the idea of an automated photo machine, which is something like an automated teller machine for photo processing.[49] Another potential barrier to planning is the day-to-day work pressures on managers that may channel managerial attention away from doing planning even when they believe that planning is beneficial.[50] Yet another barrier is poor preparation of line managers in terms of their planning knowledge and skills. Finally, effective planning can sometimes be thwarted if staff specialists are allowed to dominate the planning process, leading to low involvement by managers who must ultimately implement the plans.[51]

Organizations can take several steps to reduce the obstacles to planning. One step is encouraging strong top-management support for the planning process. Top-level managers can signal their commitment by being personally involved in the planning process and by maintaining an ongoing interest in how the plans are being implemented. Such commitment encourages managers at lower levels to engage in and support planning. Another step is making sure that planning staffs, often known as corporate planners, maintain a helping role, rather than do the actual planning. A **planning staff** is a small group of individuals who assist top-level managers in developing the various components of the planning process. Such staffs typically help monitor both internal and external environments in order to generate data for strategic decisions by top management. They also suggest possible changes in organizational missions, goals, and plans.[52] From the 1960s through the early 1980s, the influence of corporate planners grew to the point where they often dominated the planning process, leaving line managers with minor roles. By the mid-1980s, many organizations reacted by reducing the role of planning staffs.[53] For instance, when John F.

Planning staff A small group of individuals who assist top-level managers in developing the various components of the planning process

Welch, Jr., took over as chairman at General Electric, he cut the corporate planning group from 58 to 33. Other corporate planners were cut in various divisions and units throughout the company. For example, in GE's major appliance group, the planning staff was cut from 25 to 0 so that managers in the group could be directly involved in the planning process.[54]

The moves at GE reflect another step that organizations can take to reduce the obstacles to planning. Top management can actively involve the managers who will be primarily responsible for carrying out the plans. One part of that involvement entails providing such managers with training in the planning process. Yet another step managers can take in surmounting obstacles is reviewing plans frequently, particularly when the environment tends to change rapidly. To cope with a rapidly changing environment, managers can also engage in contingency planning. **Contingency planning** is the development of alternative plans for use in the event that environmental conditions evolve differently than anticipated, rendering original plans unwise or unfeasible.[55]

Contingency planning The development of alternative plans for use in the event that environmental conditions evolve differently than anticipated, rendering original plans unwise or unfeasible

MANAGEMENT BY OBJECTIVES

One method used by a number of organizations to facilitate the linking of goals and plans is management by objectives. **Management by objectives (MBO)** is a process through which specific goals are set collaboratively for the organization as a whole and every unit and individual within it; the goals then are used as a basis for planning, managing organizational activities, and assessing and rewarding contributions.[56] MBO usually incorporates considerable participation among managers and subordinates in setting goals at various levels.

Although the origins of MBO are not completely clear, General Electric appears to be the first organization that implemented the process and noted management consultant Peter Drucker is generally credited with being the first individual who wrote about it.[57] Since then, MBO has been used by a wide variety of organizations to help coordinate the goal-setting and planning processes at various levels so that the collective efforts of organization members ultimately support organizational goals.[58] Organizations that have used MBO include Purex, Black and Decker, Tenneco, Texas Instruments, Wells Fargo Bank, Boeing, and Westinghouse.[59] The term "management by objectives" also is sometimes used to describe the more limited application of goal setting to a particular organizational subunit and its members.

Management by objectives (MBO) A process through which specific goals are set collaboratively for the organization as a whole and every unit and individual within it; the goals are then used as a basis for planning, managing organizational activities, and assessing and rewarding contributions

Steps in the MBO Process

There can be considerable variation in the way that MBO is practiced across organizations.[60] Most viable MBO processes include the following six steps (see Figure 5-7):[61]

1. *Develop overall organizational goals.* Goals at this stage are based on the overall mission of the organization and address targets to be achieved by the organization as a whole (e.g., a certain rate of return for a given period or a specific increase in market share). These goals are essentially strategic goals set by top management.

2. *Establish specific goals (or objectives) for various department, subunits, and individuals.* In this step, goals are set for various levels in the organization so that the cumulative effect leads to reaching the overall organizational goals set in

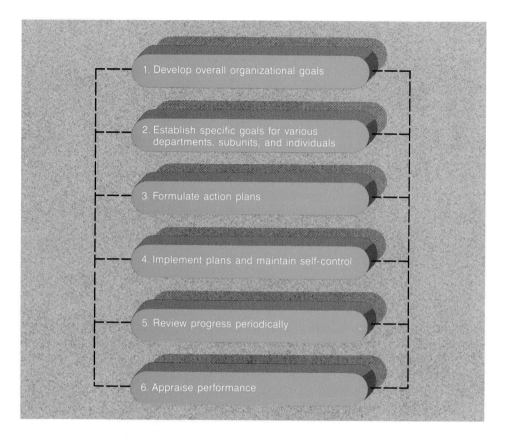

Figure 5-7 Steps in the MBO process.

the previous step. This stage of the process begins when upper-level managers formulate specific objectives that they plan to accomplish, usually related to their own departments or areas of responsibility (such as marketing or production). These goals are usually developed in collaboration with managers at the next level. For example, the head of the marketing department may set a goal of increasing sales volume to 100,000 for a certain product during the coming year, a goal set in collaboration with the regional sales managers. Then the regional sales managers confer with their district managers in setting goals at the regional levels. For example, the eastern sales manager may set a goal of increasing sales volume to 25,000 for the particular product as the eastern region's contribution toward the 100,000 goal of the marketing department at the national level. The process, which is sometimes referred to as the cascading of goals, continues until all units at various levels have specific goals for the coming year. At each level, goals are typically set in key areas, where results are critical to the success of the organization.

Although many organizations follow the top-down process just described, some organizations pursue a more bottom-up approach, in which goals are proposed by lower levels on the basis of what they believe they can achieve. Goals are then developed at the tactical level that are based on the proposed goals provided by the operational level. These tactical goals are then proposed to the strategic level. Usually, though, a bottom-up approach is conducted following at least some general guidelines developed at the strategic level. In any event, with MBO, there typically is some give-and-take among levels before goals at the various levels are finalized.

3. *Formulate action plans.* Once goals are set, there is a need to develop action plans that focus on the methods or activities necessary to reach particular goals. In essence, an *action plan* is a description of what is to be done, how, when, where, and by whom in order to achieve a goal. Action plans help access the feasibility of reaching goals, aid identifying problem areas, assist in spelling out areas in which resources and assistance will be needed, and facilitate the search for more efficient and effective ways to achieve objectives. Such plans usually are developed by subordinates in conjunction with their supervisors.

4. *Implement and maintain self-control.* A basic notion underlying MBO is that once goals are set and action plans determined, individuals should be given considerable latitude in carrying out their activities. The rationale is that individuals know what they are supposed to achieve, have plans mapped out, and can gauge their progress against set goals. Therefore, it should not be necessary for the supervisor to become as involved in the individual's day-to-day activities as might be the case without goals and action plans. The notion of self-control is particularly true with respect to managerial positions. Of course, supervisors still need to be kept informed about progress and any unanticipated difficulties that arise. Supervisors also may need to provide coaching and support if subordinates are having difficulties.

5. *Review progress periodically.* Periodic reviews are important to ensure that plans are being implemented as expected and that goals ultimately will be met. Such reviews provide a good opportunity for checking performance to date, identifying and removing obstacles, solving problems, and altering action plans that are not achieving the expected results. Reviews also make it possible to assess the continuing appropriateness of the goals and to change them if necessary or to add new goals if required by changing conditions. How frequently progress reviews are held will depend on how quickly situations change, but quarterly reviews are common.

6. *Appraise performance.* At the end of the goal-setting cycle, which usually runs for a period of 1 year, managers meet with each of their subordinates to conduct an appraisal of performance over the cycle. The appraisal typically focuses on the extent to which goals were met, as well as on shortfalls, the reasons for them, and actions that can be taken to prevent the same difficulties in the future. The appraisal session includes praise and recognition for areas in which the subordinate has performed effectively, as well as discussion of areas in which the subordinate could benefit from future development of knowledge and skills. Goals and plans for the next cycle may also be discussed at this point.

As Figure 5-7 indicates, feedback from each step may lead to the revision of prior goals or the setting of future ones. While constant revision of prior goals tends to defeat the purpose of MBO, some revisions may be necessary to accommodate major changes in circumstances. The purpose of the goal-setting and planning processes is essentially to coordinate efforts toward important organizational goals. If those goals need changing, then efforts probably require redirecting as well; hence corresponding goals at various levels should be changed also.

Strengths and Weaknesses of MBO

As suggested by the successful use of MBO at Cypress Semiconductor, management by objectives has a number of major strengths (see Table 5-4).[62] For one thing, MBO aids the coordination of goals and plans and, thereby, increases the prospects for ultimately achieving long-term organizational goals. For another, it

Table 5-4 Strengths and Weaknesses of MBO

Strengths	Weaknesses
1. Aids coordination of goals and plans	1. Tends to falter without strong, continual commitment from top management
2. Helps clarify priorities and expectations	2. Necessitates considerable training of managers
3. Facilitates vertical and horizontal communication	3. Can be misused as a punitive device
4. Fosters employee motivation	4. May cause overemphasis of quantitative goals

helps clarify priorities and spell out what outcomes are needed at each level so that individuals know what is expected of them. For example, Illinois Health Care Associations experienced declining membership, lower credibility with members, and reduced revenues before instituting an MBO system that helped members collaborate on future directions and coordinate activities.[63] Yet another strength is that MBO facilitates communication among the various levels and among peers at the same level when coordination is needed to achieve mutual goals. MBO also aids controlling by providing benchmarks against which progress can be evaluated. Finally, MBO can increase motivation by providing employees with feedback about their progress and recognition for accomplishments.

On the other hand, MBO also has several potential weaknesses (see Table 5-4). One potential weakness is that successful operation of an MBO system tends to falter without strong, continual commitment from top management. The necessary commitment includes the willingness to set top-level goals, communicate the goals to other organizational levels, participate with immediate subordinates in establishing individual goals, provide the resources necessary to achieve goals at various levels, and offer feedback regarding goal accomplishment. Another weakness is that managers may not be adequately trained to set appropriate goals and coach employees when necessary. Still another weakness is that MBO can be misused as a punitive device for failure to meet goals, rather than as a means of encouraging employee motivation and development. Finally, MBO systems may overemphasize quantitative goals and production.

The possible implications of these latter two potential weaknesses can be seen in the case of MiniScribe, a computer disk-drive company. The Colorado-based company had been doing poorly before Q. T. Wiles, who had a reputation for resuscitating ill companies, took over the helm. The company's stock quintupled within 2 years on the basis of strong financial reports before it was finally revealed that the data were bogus. Interviews with current and former executives, employees, competitors, suppliers, and others familiar with the company revealed major internal difficulties. Wiles set unrealistic sales goals and used an abusive management style that created such pressure that managers began to falsify data through such steps as booking shipments as sales and simply fabricating figures.[64] At Nordstrom's, the Seattle-based retailer, some present and former employees have complained of extreme pressure to meet sales goals. A recent investigation by the Washington State Department of Labor and Industries found that the company systematically violated state law by failing to pay employees for the time spent doing such duties as delivering merchandise to customers or working on inventory.[65]

Assessing MBO

Because of the possible weaknesses, MBO has not always reached its potential. Although it has been successful in some organizations, MBO has failed in others.[66] According to one estimate, MBO has been used in almost half the Fortune 500 companies, yet it has been successful only about 20 to 25 percent of the time. Failures of MBO systems seem to stem from a lack of adequate support from top management and poor goal-setting and communication skills among managers who must implement the system.[67] Hence the way in which MBO is operated by managers may undermine its effectiveness. While overall organizational or strategic goals are important to the MBO process, they are also a critical element in strategic management, a subject that we explore in the next chapter.

CHAPTER SUMMARY

Major components of the overall planning process are the mission, goals, and plans of the organization. The mission is the organization's purpose or fundamental reason for existence. The mission statement, a broad declaration of the basic, unique purpose and scope of operation that distinguishes the organization from others of its type, has several purposes. The statement can be a benchmark against which to evaluate success; a means of defining a common purpose, nurturing loyalty, and fostering a sense of community among members; and a signal about values and future directions. A goal is a future target or end result that an organization wishes to achieve. A plan is a means devised for attempting to reach the goal.

Goals have several potential benefits. They can increase performance, clarify expectations, facilitate the controlling function, and help increase motivation. Organizations typically have three levels of goals: strategic, tactical, and operational. These three levels of goals can be conceptualized as a hierarchy of goals.

A number of key components help explain how goals facilitate performance. Goal content is one component; goals should be challenging, attainable, specific and measurable, time-limited, and relevant. Goal commitment is another key component and can usually be positively influenced through supervisory authority, peer and group pressure, public display of commitment, expectations of success, and incentives and rewards. Participation also may engender goal commitment. Work behavior is also a major component; goal content and goal commitment influence the direction, effort, persistence, and planning aspects of work behavior. Other major components are job knowledge and ability, complexity of task, and situational constraints. Care must be taken to avoid a number of potential problems with goal setting.

In much the same way that there are levels of goals, plans also differ according to level in the organization. Thus there are strategic, tactical, and operational plans. Plans also can be categorized according to the extent to which they will be used on a recurring basis. Single-use plans usually will not need to be repeated in the future and include programs and projects. Standing plans are used on a recurring basis and include policies, procedures, and rules. The different levels of goals and plans are related to different time horizons, with strategic goals and plans usually focused on long-range issues 5 years or more in the future, tactical goals and plans aimed at intermediate-range issues 1 to 5 years in the future, and operational goals and plans oriented toward 1 year or less. Research suggests that the planning process can help promote innovation through a mission statement that signals the importance of innovation, goals aimed at innovative outcomes, and loose plans that allow latitude in the innovation process or focus on innovative means of reaching goals. Managers must take steps to reduce or avoid several potential obstacles to developing plans.

Management by objectives includes the following steps: develop overall organizational goals; establish specific goals for various departments, subunits, and individuals; formulate action plans; implement and maintain self-control; review progress periodically; and appraise performance. MBO has several strengths and weaknesses. Failures of MBO systems seem to stem from a lack of adequate support from top management and poor goal-setting and communication skills among managers who must implement the system.

MANAGERIAL TERMINOLOGY

contingency planning (179)
goal (156)
goal commitment (166)
management by objectives (MBO) (179)

mission (157)
mission statement (157)
operational goals (162)
operational plans (173)
plan (157)
planning staff (178)

policy (174)
procedure (174)
program (174)
project (174)
rule (175)
single-use plans (174)

standing plans (174)
strategic goals (161)
strategic plans (172)
tactical goals (162)
tactical plans (173)

QUESTIONS FOR DISCUSSION AND REVIEW

1. Outline the major components in the overall planning process. Trace these components for an organization with which you are familiar.
2. Define the concept of organizational mission, and explain the purposes of a mission statement. Think of an organization that you would like to establish. What type of mission would you develop?
3. Outline the major benefits of goals. Describe a situation in which you have observed the major benefits of goals.
4. Explain how goals and plans differ according to organizational level. Describe how goals and plans may be different at the various levels of management at your college or university.
5. Describe the major components in the model indicating how goals facilitate performance. Give an example of a situation in which you have seen goals work well and an example of a situation in which goals did not seem to work. Use the model to explain the successful situation and the failure situation.
6. Explain how to set goals. Give four examples of goals that you might set for yourself during the coming semester.
7. Delineate several potential problems with goal setting. Give an example of how two of these potential problems might apply in an organization with which you are familiar (perhaps an organization on campus). What steps might you take to avoid such problems?
8. Explain the various types of single-use and standing plans. Give an example of each type of plan at your college or university.
9. Assess the role of goals and plans in promoting innovation. Explain how goals and plans helped 3M reduce costs in its manufacturing sector.
10. Explain the steps in the management by objectives process and assess the strengths and weaknesses of MBO.

DISCUSSION QUESTIONS FOR CHAPTER OPENING CASE

1. Trace the overall planning process at Cypress Semiconductor.
2. Assess the benefits of the use of goals at Cypress, and explain how the goal-setting process works.
3. Evaluate the strengths and weaknesses of MBO as practiced by Cypress.

MANAGEMENT EXERCISE: WORKING WITH MBO

You have recently received your degree and have accepted a position as a department head at a local hardware store that is part of a small, but growing, chain. The chain uses an MBO system. Some of the strategic goals are reaching $400 million in annual sales within 5 years, building a reputation for excellent customer service, and having a double-digit return on investment throughout the period. Some of the tactical goals include opening six new stores each year for the next 3 years,

opening one new store in your district this year, reaching annual sales of $1 million, earning a return on investment of 14 percent, increasing customer satisfaction by 5 percentage points on the annual survey, and having departmental sales of $40,000 for each employee in the department.

On the basis of these strategic and tactical goals, draft some goals for the operational level of your sales department.

WAL-MART LEAPFROGS THE COMPETITION

He stands on the nearest box, table, or platform and shouts to the crowd: "Give me a W!" The enthusiastic, resounding "W" from the associates gathered for the Saturday morning meeting all but shakes the building. So it goes for all the letters in Wal-Mart, before everyone joins in the chorus, "Wal-Mart, we're number 1!" The energy and enthusiasm displayed on this Saturday morning has played a major role in the phenomenal growth of Wal-Mart Stores, Inc. Today Wal-Mart is in the process of passing K-Mart and becoming second only to Sears, Roebuck and Company, which still holds the title as America's leading retailer.

The success of the company can be traced directly to founder Samuel Moore Walton, who grew up in the four-state area of Arkansas, Missouri, Oklahoma, and Kansas. After graduating from the University of Missouri in 1940 with a degree in economics, he immediately accepted a position with J. C. Penney as a management trainee; but that career was interrupted by Army service in World War II. Soon after returning from military duty, he opened the first Walton's Ben Franklin store (a five-and-dime type of store) in Versailles, Missouri. After losing his lease in 1950, Walton moved his business to Bentonville, Arkansas, where he opened a Walton 5 & 10. He also continued to establish Ben Franklin franchises and had 15 by 1962, when he opened the first Wal-Mart Discount City. By 1969, when the company was incorporated as Wal-Mart Stores, Inc., there were 18 Wal-Mart and 15 Ben Franklin stores operating throughout Arkansas, Missouri, Kansas, and

Oklahoma. From 1970 to 1979, annual sales grew from $44 million to $1.248 billion, and there were 276 Wal-Mart stores in 11 states. The steady expansion since that time has resulted in sales of more than $20 billion and 1355 stores (including 120 Sam's Wholesale Clubs and 14 DOT Discount Drug stores) in the 27 central and southern states of the nation. The west, northwest, and northeast are considered prime target areas for the future.

Wal-Mart has followed a strategy of building and expanding in areas where the local population is under 50,000. One or two stores are built, and then a distribution center is constructed nearby that will support further expansion in the geographic area. Other stores are then built within a day's drive of the distribution center. Wal-Mart currently has 19 distribution centers, which are widely considered to be major factors in the company's spectacular success.

Wal-Mart's mission stresses three major elements, or principles: value and aggressive service for

Wal-Mart Stores, the discount store chain that includes Sam's Wholesale Club outlets, blankets the southern and central states with 1355 stores. Founder Samuel Walton built up his booming business by servicing small communities bypassed by the big retailers; now the company is poised to spread into the larger metropolitan areas. In this picture cashiers at a new Sam's Wholesale Club in Flint, Michigan, cheer at the opening day ceremonies. Walton treats employees as partners in the organization and gives them important roles to play in achieving both corporate and individual store goals.

customers, partnership with associates (employees), and strong relationships with the communities in which stores are located. As part of the effort toward aggressive customer service, a "greeter" welcomes customers at the door with a smile and offers them directions, if needed. Associates throughout the stores are trained to look customers in the eye, greet them, and ask them if they would like help. In the area of value, the prices are probably lower than at any other store in the area.

The Wal-Mart relationship with associates is based on the premise that they are partners in the organization. Associates have access to information about their stores, such as costs, freight charges, and profit margins, that many other organizations show only to general managers. Associates play a major role in achieving various overall Wal-Mart and individual store goals.

In building relationships with the community, each store participates in one fund-raising project each year in its local community. The funds raised are then matched by funds from the Wal-Mart Foundation. Each store also awards a $1000 scholarship to a deserving student each year. Annually, Wal-Mart contributes several million dollars to both the Children's Miracle Network and the United Way.

Goals play an important part in the way that Wal-Mart is managed. Goals are developed using MBO as part of the planning process. At Wal-Mart, the top level of management provides some guidelines in areas such as profits and growth; these are then used as a basis for setting goals at the division and store levels. Most of the more specific tactical goals are developed at the division level and then are forwarded to the corporate or top level, where they are reviewed and are used to formulate the final goals at the strategic level. Stores also have some input into the goals that are ultimately set and have annual operational goals of their own to achieve. Some of the specific goals set at Wal-Mart during a recent annual goal-setting effort included the following:

■ Adding 20 percent more floor space by opening 115 new stores and expanding 60 existing stores

(Another 30 stores were scheduled for remodeling.)
■ Opening 10 to 12 new Sam's Wholesale Clubs and doubling the sales of this division
■ Opening one new DOT Discount Drug store
■ Adding three more distribution centers
■ Trying out 25,000- to 35,000-square-foot store prototypes in small communities (The regular Discount City store has 60,000 to 90,000 square feet of sales space.)
■ Pursuing a "Buy American" plan to give preference to stocking merchandise manufactured in the United States.

Wal-Mart usually sets some goals aimed at innovation, such as testing the 25,000- to 35,000-square-foot store prototypes. Wal-Mart also has recently been experimenting with Hypermart USA stores; each one is basically a huge combination Wal-Mart and grocery store.

Individual stores generally are expected to achieve at least a 10 percent increase in sales over the previous year. Stores also have profit goals. Associates receive a share of the profits above the goals set for each store. In addition, associates play a major role in reducing "shrinkage," the losses experienced by each store from theft and damage. Each store has a goal for shrinkage; if that goal is surpassed, every associate in the store receives an annual bonus of up to $200. Through its system of rewards for exceeding store goals, Wal-Mart has kept its shrinkage to just over 1 percent (which amounts to about $200 million annually), compared with an industry average of 2 percent. Once goals are set, the various levels engage in action plan-

ning to determine the specific means that will be used to achieve the goals.

Goals are monitored throughout the fiscal year to ensure that they are being achieved as intended. Rarely are they not met, but on some occasions Wal-Mart has not been pleased with the performance of some stores and has sold them. For example, the Ben Franklin stores were phased out in 1976 to make room for more Wal-Mart stores. A line of Helen's Arts and Crafts stores was sold. Wal-Mart also tried a do-it-yourself building concept that failed. It is reported that some executives would like to sell the DOT Discount Drug chain. Thus not all of Wal-Mart's ventures have been successful from the company's point of view.

On balance, however, Wal-Mart has been extremely successful. A $1000 investment in Wal-Mart's initial stock offering in 1970 would be worth more than half a million dollars today. Wal-Mart is frequently among the leaders in *Fortune*'s survey of the most admired corporations in America. It was named one of the five best-managed U.S. companies by *Business Month* in December 1988. The company is still growing at a rate of more than 20 percent a year.[68]

QUESTIONS FOR CHAPTER CONCLUDING CASE
1. Trace the overall planning process at Wal-Mart.
2. Use the goal-setting process to explain why the use of goals at Wal-Mart enhances performance.
3. Describe the MBO process at Wal-Mart.

CHAPTER SIX

STRATEGIC MANAGEMENT

CHAPTER OUTLINE

The Concept of Strategic Management
The Strategic Management Process
Importance of Strategic Management
Levels of Strategy
Promoting Innovation: Modes of
   Strategic Management

**The Role of Competitive Analysis in
   Strategy Formulation**
Environmental Assessment
Organizational Assessment

Formulating Corporate-Level Strategy
Grand Strategies
Portfolio Strategy Approaches

Formulating Business-Level Strategy
Porter's Competitive Strategies
Assessing Porter's Strategies

Formulating Functional-Level Strategy

Strategy Implementation
Carrying Out Strategic Plans
Maintaining Strategic Control

LEARNING OBJECTIVES

*After studying this chapter, you
should be able to:*

■ Explain the concept of strategic
management and differentiate
among the three main levels of
strategy.

■ Outline the major components
of the strategic management
process.

■ Distinguish among three major
modes of strategy formulation
and explain how each can be
used to promote innovation.

■ Describe the role of competitive
analysis in strategy formulation
and the major approaches to
such analysis.

■ Enumerate the main generic
strategies available at the corporate level.

■ Explain the three major portfolio strategy approaches for use
at the corporate level.

■ Describe Porter's competitive
strategies for the business level.

■ Explain the role of strategies at
the functional level.

■ Outline the process of strategy
implementation.

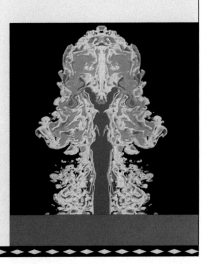

◆◆

GAINING THE EDGE

THE MAGIC RETURNS TO DISNEY

By the early 1980s, the magical kingdom of Walt Disney Productions had lost its sparkle. It seemed that the creative juices in the company had slowly ebbed after the death in 1966 of Walt Disney, creator of such luminaries as Mickey Mouse, Minnie Mouse, and Donald Duck. Walt Disney's immediate successors were wary of tampering with what had been a successful formula and, thus, made changes only slowly. As a result, attendance at the Disney theme parks in California and Florida began to level off, Tomorrowland began to lose its forward look, and, for the first time in almost three decades, no Disney-produced show was appearing on television. With few exceptions, Disney movies were dismal failures at the box office.

Rumors began to circulate that outside investors might acquire the company, sell off many of its valuable assets (such as its film library, movie studio, and real estate), and leave only the declining theme parks. Alarmed at the potential demise of the magical empire, Roy Disney, Walt Disney's nephew and the company's largest shareholder, resigned from the board of directors and joined with other major investors in insisting on a new regime at the top.

The dire situation reversed dramatically after the board brought in Michael D. Eisner as chairman and chief executive officer and Frank G. Wells as president and chief operating officer. Eisner, who has a creative bent, had been an extremely successful president of Paramount Pictures while Frank Wells, a lawyer with a strong financial background, had been a noteworthy vice-chairman of Warner Brothers. When the two took charge at Disney in September 1984, they quickly began to infuse the company with a renewed entrepreneurial spirit. "We saved Disney from the enemy and kept Disney together," says Eisner. "What's more, we discovered that our major assets were the Disney name, the Disney culture, its movies and library. So we began our management of these assets by revitalizing them, and intertwining them with new assets. We have introduced new movies, new ideas, new theme parks, and new executives."

One major move was revamping Disney World and Disneyland to such an extent that the number of visitors to the parks has increased dramatically. Others included opening Tokyo Disneyland; introducing the *Mickey and Donald* cartoon series to China Central Television, where it is the most popular children's program; signing an agreement with the French goverment to build and operate a $2 billion theme park near Paris called Euro Disneyland (scheduled to open in 1992); and returning Disney to network television with the *Disney Sunday Night Movie* on ABC, hosted by Eisner himself.

The company, now called the Walt Disney Company, has three main operating divisions: filmed entertainment, consumer products, and theme parks and resorts. In the filmed entertainment division, the new management team has converted Walt Disney Studios from a lackluster performer that had only 3 percent of the movie market to a studio that has been leading the pack with such hits as *Honey, I Shrunk the Kids*, *Dead Poets Society*, and *Dick Tracy*, as well as sequels to its earlier huge successes, *Three Men and a Baby* and *Good Morning, Vietnam*. Many such films are adult fare, released under Touchstone and other labels.

The consumer-products division ensures that Disney products, such as Mickey Mouse watches, sweatshirts, stuffed animals, and crib linen, are available throughout the world. The items are all manufactured under license. Annual sales in Japan alone commonly are in the $1 billion range. Disney also has a new chain of U.S. retail stores that has performed well beyond expectations, so much so that premier malls are vying for the 100 stores that will be open by 1992. The Disney label dominates the charts in children's records.

In May 1989, the theme parks and resorts division opened a new $500 million movie studio theme park at Disney World in Orlando. Drawing record crowds, the studio park, a joint venture with MGM, has been so successful that plans are under way to double its size by 1992. The previous regime at Disney was so cautious that top management allowed investors to build and own Tokyo Disneyland, which opened in Tokyo in 1983, with Disney receiving only 10 percent of all admission receipts and 5 percent of all sales at the facility. Nevertheless, Disney World, Disneyland, and Tokyo Disneyland together account for about 56 percent of Disney's revenues and 64 percent of operating profits. The U.S. parks provide operating margins of 30 percent. Recently, Disney has been adding hotels on Disney World property and has spent more than $1 billion on new attractions such as Typhoon Lagoon water rides and the Pleasure Island area, which provides nightlife, including comedy and dance acts, as well as beer, wine, and liquor. The company also is planning a major expansion of Disneyland, which perhaps will include another site in California.

Many of the ideas for films, consumer products, and park attractions originate with Eisner himself, who counts on Wells to squelch his more impractical suggestions, such as his vision of a 43-story hotel in the shape of Mickey Mouse. Other ideas begin with the famous Disney Imagineering division, an innovative group that is mainly responsible for dreaming up new ideas and figuring out how they can be engineered to work. It is the Imagineering group, for example, that envisions and ultimately builds new attractions, such as the new ride at Disney World that simulates zipping along the path of the human bloodstream, including visits to the heart and brain.

While Imagineering is the company's think tank, financial aspects of projects also are important. Accordingly, after Imagineering develops design and engineering requirements for a project, the project is then submitted to a six-person strategic planning group, which reviews the project's compatibility with strategic directions and checks to make sure that the financial aspects make sense. Then, together, the two groups outline a budget and a schedule before the package goes to Wells and Eisner, who quickly make the final decision about whether or not to proceed.

In providing strategic directions, Eisner and Wells encourage synergy among various divisions, so the efforts of one division often help those of others. For example, suppose the animation studio creates a cartoon character like Roger Rabbit to appear in films. The consumer-products division then often can license the character to merchandisers who manufacture stuffed animals and other products, such as T-shirts, which can be sold in Disney retail stores and in the theme parks. The character also may become the basis for a costumed figure in the parks and possibly the subject of new rides or attractions.

In Eisner's view, his chief duty at Disney is leading creatively and being an orchestrator, thinker, inventor, and cheerleader for new ideas. Wells keeps close tabs on financial aspects. So far their efforts have returned the magic to Disney and pleased investors as well. Revenues have climbed at an average annual rate of 23 percent, while net income has grown at an annual rate of almost 50 percent since the duo took the helm.[1]

How were Eisner and Wells able to take a languishing company and make it so visibly prosperous again? Their success stems in part from their strong commitment to Disney's growth and their ability to map out important strategic

Mickey and Minnie Mouse draw huge crowds to Tokyo Disneyland, but the Disney company earns only 10 percent of the operating receipts. That is because the cautious management team that took over after Walt Disney's death in 1966 sold the rights to build and own Tokyo's theme park. Reluctance to take the bold measures that would match the founder's vision sent the Disney company into a decline. In 1984, however, power passed to a new management team whose creative strategies have turned the company around in all three of its divisions—filmed entertainment, consumer products, and theme parks and resorts.

directions for the company. To make sure that the company and its various parts stay on track, the six-person strategic planning group reviews each project for compatibility with the strategic plan before the project is sent to Eisner and Wells for final approval. In Chapter 5, we consider various levels of goals and plans, including those at the strategic level. Strategic goals and plans are a particularly important part of the managerial planning function because they ultimately determine the overall direction of the organization. Accordingly, in this chapter, we take a more thorough look at strategic-level planning issues, exploring in depth how companies like Disney are managed strategically. We begin by examining the concept of strategic management, including how modes of strategic management can influence innovation. We then consider how competitive analysis can form the basis for developing effective strategies aimed at gaining an edge over competitors. We next analyze policy formulation at the corporate, business, and functional levels. Finally, we probe the process of strategy implementation.

THE CONCEPT OF STRATEGIC MANAGEMENT

Strategies Large-scale action plans for interacting with the environment in order to achieve long-term goals

Most well-run organizations attempt to develop and follow **strategies,** large-scale action plans for interacting with the environment in order to achieve long-term goals.[2] A comprehensive statement of an organization's strategies, along with its mission and goals, constitutes an organization's strategic plan.[3] To learn where such strategies originate and how they are put into action, we need to examine carefully an aspect of the planning function called strategic management. **Strategic management** is a process through which managers formulate and implement strategies geared to optimizing strategic goal achievement, given available environmental and internal conditions.[4] This definition recognizes that strategic management is oriented toward reaching long-term goals, weighs important environmental elements, considers major internal characteristics of the organization, and involves developing specific strategies. Thus the strategic management process encompasses a major part of the planning process introduced in Chapter 5.

Strategic management A process through which managers formulate and implement strategies geared to optimizing strategic goal achievement, given available environmental and internal conditions

The Strategic Management Process

The strategic management process is made up of several major components, as shown in Figure 6-1. The process begins with identifying the organization's mission and strategic goals, concepts that are discussed in depth in Chapter 5. The process also includes analyzing the competitive situation, taking into consideration both the external environment and relevant organizational factors. Once the situation has been carefully analyzed, managers can begin to develop, or formulate, various strategies that can be used to reach strategic goals. The part of the strategic management process that includes identifying the mission and strategic goals, conducting competitive analysis, and developing specific strategies is often referred to as **strategy formulation.** In contrast, the part of the strategic management process that focuses on carrying out strategic plans and maintaining control over how those plans are carried out is known as **strategy implementation.**[5] Strategy implementation is increasingly highlighted as a distinct part of the strategic management process because even the most brilliantly formulated strategies must be implemented effectively in order to reach strategic goals.

Strategy formulation The process of identifying the mission and strategic goals, conducting competitive analysis, and developing specific strategies

Strategy implementation The process of carrying out strategic plans and maintaining control over how those plans are carried out

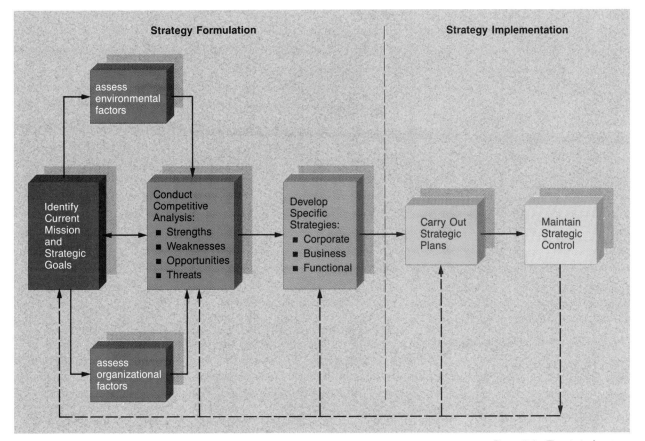

Figure 6-1 The strategic management process.

Importance of Strategic Management

Strategic management is important to organizations for several reasons.[6] For one thing, the process helps organizations identify and develop a **competitive advantage,** which is a significant edge over the competition in dealing with competitive forces.[7] For example, Disney has been able to gain a competitive advantage in the family entertainment industry by creating amusement parks, movies, and products based on the renowned Disney characters. We discuss strategies aimed at gaining a competitive advantage in greater detail in later sections of this chapter.

Another reason for the importance of strategic management is that it provides a sense of direction so that organization members know where to expend their efforts. Without a strategic plan, managers throughout the organization may concentrate on day-to-day activities only to find that a competitor has maneuvered itself into a favorable competitive position by taking a more comprehensive, long-term view of strategic directions. For example, the Rayovac Corporation, a battery and flashlight maker based in Madison, Wisconsin, had fallen behind competitors in the early 1980s because of its aging product line, outdated packaging, and slowness in entering the market for alkaline batteries (which became the industry standard). Since that time, a new chairman and vice-chairman, the husband-and-wife team of Thomas and Judith Pyle, have rejuvenated the company partially through a variety of innovative new products, such as the Luma 2, a sleek flashlight with an extremely bright krypton

Competitive advantage
A significant edge over the competition in dealing with competitive forces

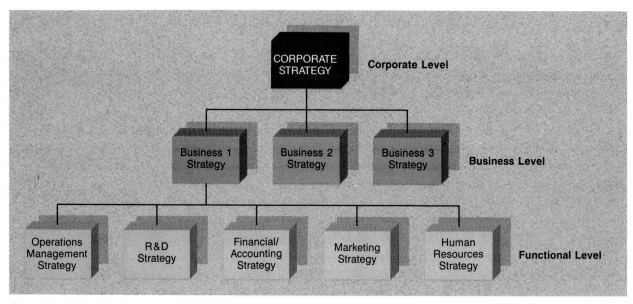

Figure 6-2 Levels of strategy. (Adapted from John A. Pearce II and Richard B. Robinson, Jr., *Strategic Management: Strategy Formulation and Implementation*, 3d ed., Irwin, Homewood, Ill., 1988, p. 9.)

light and a lithium-powered, long-lasting backup bulb. Rayovac says that with the backup system, the flashlight should work for about 10 years.[8]

Yet another reason for the importance of strategic management is that it can help highlight the need for innovation and provide an organized approach for encouraging new ideas related to strategies.[9] For instance, Disney has a special procedure for handling major innovations, whereby new ideas and accompanying financial considerations are forwarded to the strategic planning group, which evaluates them for compatibility with the firm's overall strategy. In addition, the process can be used to involve managers at various levels in planning, thus making it more likely that the managers will understand the resulting plans and be committed to their implementation.[10]

Finally, studies support the existence of a link between strategic management and organizational financial performance, although results have not always been consistent.[11] Of course, assessments of strategic management should also consider other important outcomes, such as the satisfaction of various organizational stakeholders (see Chapter 4) and the extent to which the organization adequately deals with relevant factors in the environment (see Chapter 3).

Levels of Strategy

Many organizations develop strategies at three different levels: corporate, business, and functional. The three levels are shown in Figure 6-2.[12]

Corporate-level strategy
A type of strategy that addresses what businesses the organization will operate, how the strategies of those businesses will be coordinated to strengthen the organization's competitive position, and how resources will be allocated among the businesses

Corporate-Level Strategy. **Corporate-level strategy** addresses what businesses the organization will operate, how the strategies of those businesses will be coordinated to strengthen the organization's competitive position, and how resources will be allocated among the businesses. Strategy at this level is typically developed by top management, often with the assistance of strategic planning personnel, at least in large organizations.[13]

The board of directors also is involved in developing corporate-level strategy, although the degree of board participation varies (see Table 6-1). The three areas in which boards of directors can typically be most helpful within the strate-

Table 6-1   Degree of Involvement in Strategic Management by Board of Directors

Degree of Involvement	Board Actions
Low	Approves mission, strategic goals, and strategies; conducts limited competitive analysis
Moderate	Helps develop mission and strategic goals; conducts limited analysis of competitive situation; approves strategies
High	Helps develop mission and strategic goals; conducts extensive analysis of competitive situation, as well as proposed strategies

Source: Adapted from Frank T. Paine and Carl R. Anderson, *Strategic Management,* Dryden, Chicago, 1983, p. 370.

gic management process are advising on new directions for growth, suggesting when major changes are needed in strategy, and providing input on the timing of major investments.[14]

Business-Level Strategy. **Business-level strategy** concentrates on the best means of competing within a particular business while also supporting the corporate-level strategy. Strategies at this level are aimed at deciding the type of competitive advantage to build, determining responses to changing environmental and competitive conditions, allocating resources within the business unit, and coordinating functional-level strategies. Business-level strategies are usually established for each strategic business unit. A **strategic business unit (SBU)** is a distinct business, with its own set of competitors, that can be managed reasonably independently of other businesses within the organization.[15] Most often, the heads of the respective business units develop business strategies, although such strategies are typically subject to the approval of top management. When an organization comprises only a single business, corporate-level and business-level strategies essentially are the same. Thus the corporate-level and business-level distinction applies only to organizations with separate divisions that compete in different industries.[16]

Business-level strategy
A type of strategy that concentrates on the best means of competing within a particular business while also supporting the corporate-level strategy

Strategic business unit (SBU)
A distinct business, with its own set of competitors, that can be managed reasonably independently of other businesses within the organization

Functional-Level Strategy. **Functional-level strategy** focuses on action plans for managing a particular functional area within a business in a way that supports the business-level strategy. Strategies at this level address main directions for each of the major functional areas within a business, such as manufacturing or operations, marketing, finance, human resources management, accounting, research and development, and engineering. Functional-level strategies are important because they often reflect strong functional competencies that can be used to competitive advantage. Functional strategies usually are developed by functional managers and are typically reviewed by business unit heads.

Functional-level strategy
A type of strategy that focuses on action plans for managing a particular functional area within a business in a way that supports the business-level strategy

Coordinating Levels of Strategy. Coordinating strategies across the three levels is critical in maximizing strategic impact. The strength of the business-level strategy is enhanced when functional-level strategies support its basic thrust. Similarly, the corporate level is likely to have greater impact when business-level strategies complement one another in bolstering the corporate-level strategy.[17] Thus the three levels must be closely coordinated as part of the strategic management process.

In the next several sections, we examine more thoroughly strategy formulation at the three major levels, and we consider aspects of the strategic management process beyond the identification of the organization's mission and strategic goals. (These latter topics are discussed in Chapter 5.) First, though, we look at three overall modes of strategy formulation and examine their potential for influencing the degree of innovation in organizations.

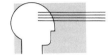

Promoting Innovation: Modes of Strategic Management

Modes of strategic management are the actual kinds of approaches taken by managers in formulating and implementing strategies. They address the issues of who has the major influence in the strategic management process and how the process is carried out.[18] Research indicates that managers tend to use one of three major approaches to, or modes of, strategic management: entrepreneurial, adaptive, and planning.[19] The mode selected is likely to influence the degree of innovation that occurs within the organization. Innovation is particularly important in the context of strategic management, because organizations that do not continually incorporate new ideas are likely to fall behind competitively, particularly when the environment is changing rapidly.[20] As we saw in the Disney situation, the failure to innovate adequately after Walt Disney's death almost led to the company's demise. Although innovation can be associated with all three modes, it frequently plays a major role in the entrepreneurial mode.

Entrepreneurial mode An approach in which strategy is formulated mainly by a strong visionary chief executive who actively searches for new opportunities, is heavily oriented toward growth, and is willing to make bold decisions or to shift strategies rapidly

Entrepreneurial Mode. In the **entrepreneurial mode,** strategy is developed mainly by a strong visionary chief executive who actively searches for new opportunities, is heavily oriented toward growth, and is willing to make bold decisions or to shift strategies rapidly when deemed desirable. The entrepreneurial mode is most likely to be found in organizations that are young or small, have a strong leader, or are in such serious trouble that bold moves are their only hope.[21] Not surprisingly, in the entrepreneurial mode, the extent to which the strategic management process encourages innovation depends largely on the orientation of top leaders. Their personalities, power, and information enable them to overcome obstacles and push for change. Conversely, strong leaders also are in a position to thwart innovative activities, should they be so inclined.[22] For example, J. Mitchell Boyd, the chairman and chief executive of Shoney's, Inc., a Nashville-based company that operates or franchises more than 1500 chain restaurants in 30 states, spent only 6 months in his position before resigning under pressure from the company's founder and major stockholder, Raymond L. Danner. Danner, who had previously retired from the top spot, clashed with Boyd over strategic directions and other matters. Danner believed emphasis should be placed on day-to-day operations and on efforts to minimalize costs. In contrast, Boyd wanted to increase spending on marketing, advertising, and promoting the company's image. He also began experimenting with menu changes rather than following the traditional Shoney's menu. Ironically, profits had risen significantly after Boyd took charge.[23]

Adaptive mode An approach to strategy formulation that emphasizes taking small incremental steps, reacting to problems rather than seeking opportunities, and attempting to satisfy a number of organizational power groups

Adaptive Mode. The **adaptive mode** of strategy formulation, which is mainly a "muddling through" approach, emphasizes taking small incremental steps, reacting to problems rather than seeking opportunities, and attempting to satisfy a number of organizational power groups. The adaptive mode is most likely to be used by managers in established organizations that face a rapidly changing environment and yet have several coalitions, or power blocks, that make it difficult to obtain agreement on clear strategic goals and associated long-term plans.[24] For example, before London-based Grand Metropolitan PLC purchased Pillsbury, including the Burger King chain, the chain was plagued by constant turnover, marketing problems, inconsistent service, and angry franchisees who frequently told Pillsbury what to do. Grand Met is now working to put the chain back on track through a strategy that emphasizes doing "whatever it takes to create a positive, memorable experience." Concrete measures include increasing the number of field representatives who visit Burger King stores, highlighting cleanliness, and rewarding employees who take the initiative in improving service by doing things differently.[25] With the adaptive approach, the degree of innovation fostered by the strategic management process is likely to depend on the ability of managers to agree on at least some major goals and basic strategies that set essential directions. In addition, lower-level managers must have some flexibility in carrying out the basic strategy rather than being given extremely detailed plans to follow; this approach might be effective in a more stable environment or one in which agreement among coalitions is easy to obtain.[26] Without at least some agreement among high-level managers on major goals and directions, however, the adaptive mode may be ineffective in moving the organization in viable strategic directions.

Planning Mode. The **planning mode** of strategy formulation involves systematic, comprehensive analysis, along with integration of various decisions and strategies. With the planning mode, executives often utilize planning specialists to help with the strategic management process. The ultimate aim of the planning mode is to understand the environment well enough to influence it. The planning mode is most likely to be used in large organizations that have enough resources to conduct comprehensive analysis, have an internal situation in which agreement is possible on major goals, and face an environment that has enough stability to enable the formulation and implementation of carefully conceived strategies. For example, the managers at Disney are able to engage in considerable planning because of its relatively stable environment. Disney's recent plans include entry into the convention hotel business with its Dolphin Hotel, operated by the Sheraton Corporation, and Swan Hotel, run by the Westin Hotel Company. Combined, the two hotels offer 2350 rooms and more than 200,000 square feet of convention space inside Disney World. The hotels were heavily booked well in advance of their opening in 1990.[27] With the planning mode, innovation is most likely to occur when strategies explicitly articulate needs for product and service innovation and when top-level managers, such as those at Disney, help integrate efforts in the direction of encouraging innovation.[28]

Planning mode An approach to strategy formulation that involves systematic, comprehensive analysis, along with integration of various decisions and strategies

Assessing the Modes. Each mode can be relatively successful as long as it is matched to an appropriate situation. In fact, it may be possible to use different modes within the same organization. For example, a top-level manager may adopt an entrepreneurial mode for a new business that is just starting and use the planning mode for strategic management of the rest of the organization.[29] Each of these modes can either promote organizational innovation or stifle it, depending on how the mode is used.

Still, operating effectively in any of the three modes requires a knowledge of the strategic management process. In carrying out the process, once the mission and strategic goals are determined, managers engage in competitive analysis.

THE ROLE OF COMPETITIVE ANALYSIS IN STRATEGY FORMULATION

SWOT analysis   A method of analyzing an organization's competitive situation that involves assessing organizational strengths (S) and weaknesses (W), as well as environmental opportunities (O) and threats (T)

Before managers can devise an effective strategy for gaining a competitive edge, they need to analyze carefully the organization's competitive situation. This involves assessing both the environmental and the organizational factors that influence an organization's ability to compete effectively. Such an assessment can be made with SWOT analysis.[30] **SWOT analysis** is a method of analyzing an organization's competitive situation that involves assessing organizational strengths (S) and weaknesses (W), as well as environmental opportunities (O) and threats (T). Identifying opportunities and threats entails an assessment of relevant environmental factors.

For SWOT analysis purposes, an *opportunity* is an environmental condition that offers significant prospects for improving an organization's situation relative to competitors. Conversely, a *threat* is an environmental condition that offers significant prospects for undermining an organization's competitive situation. On the other hand, strengths and weaknesses apply to internal characteristics. A *strength* is an internal characteristic that has the potential of improving the organization's competitive situation. In contrast, a *weakness* is an internal characteristic that leaves the organization potentially vulnerable to strategic moves by competitors. Some of the types of issues that might be considered in SWOT analysis are shown in Table 6-2. Note that both environmental and organizational factors must be assessed.

Environmental Assessment

In analyzing opportunities and threats, managers need to consider elements in the general environment, or mega-environment, that have the potential of positively or adversely influencing an organization's ability to reach its strategic goals. Such elements are broad factors, including technological, economic, legal-political, sociocultural, and international influences. Managers also need to assess major elements in the organization's task environment, which includes the more specific outside elements with which the organization interfaces in conducting its business. Such elements include customers, competitors, and suppliers. Elements of the general, as well as the task, environment are discussed in greater detail in Chapter 3.

Five competitive forces model   Porter's approach to analyzing the nature and intensity of competition in a given industry in terms of five major forces

Porter's Five Competitive Forces Model. One particularly helpful means of addressing the strategic implications of certain aspects of an organization's task environment is a model developed by strategy expert Michael E. Porter. The **five competitive forces model,** as it is called, is an approach to analyzing the nature and intensity of competition in a given industry in terms of five major forces. The collective strength of these forces directly affects the profit potential, or long-term return on investment, available to businesses operating in the particular industry. The five competitive forces are rivalry, bargaining power of customers, bargaining power of suppliers, threat of new entrants, and threat of substitute products or services. The major reasons for lower profit potential are summarized in Table 6-3.

Rivalry is the extent to which competitors continually jockey for position by using such tactics as price competition, advertising battles, product introductions, and increased customer service or warranties. All these tactics have the ability to lower profits for the various competitors in the industry either by

Table 6-2 Major Issues to Consider in SWOT Analysis

POTENTIAL INTERNAL STRENGTHS	POTENTIAL INTERNAL WEAKNESSES
A distinctive competence	No clear strategic direction
Adequate financial resources	Obsolete facilities
Good competitive skill	Subpar profitability because . . .
Well thought of by buyers	Lack of managerial depth and talent
An acknowledged market leader	Missing some key skills or competence
Well-conceived functional area strategies	Poor track record in implementing
Access to economies of scale	strategy
Insulated (at least somewhat) from strong	Plagued with internal operating
competitive pressures	problems
Proprietary technology	Falling behind in R&D
Cost advantages	Too narrow a product line
Better advertising campaigns	Weak market image
Product innovation skills	Weaker distribution network
Proven management	Below-average marketing skills
Ahead on experience curve	Unable to finance needed changes in
Better manufacturing capability	strategy
Superior technological skills	Higher overall unit costs relative to
Other?	key competitors
	Other?
POTENTIAL EXTERNAL OPPORTUNITIES	**POTENTIAL EXTERNAL THREATS**
Serve additional customer groups	Entry of lower-cost foreign competitors
Enter new markets or segments	Rising sales of substitute products
Expand product line to meet broader range	Slower market growth
of customer needs	Adverse shifts in foreign exchange
Diversify into related products	rates and trade policies of foreign
Vertical integration	governments
Falling trade barriers in attractive foreign	Costly regulatory requirements
markets	Vulnerability to recession and business
Complacency among rival firms	cycle
Faster market growth	Growing bargaining power of
Other?	customers or suppliers
	Changing buyer needs and tastes
	Adverse demographic changes
	Other?

Source: Reprinted from Arthur A. Thompson, Jr., and A. J. Strickland III, *Strategic Management: Concepts and Cases,* 5th ed., BPI/Irwin, Homewood, Ill., 1990, p. 91.

Table 6-3 Porter's Five Competitive Forces Model

Competitive Forces	Reasons for Lower Profit Potential
Rivalry	Various competitive tactics among rivals lower prices that can be charged or raise costs of doing business.
Bargaining power of customers	Customers force price reductions or negotiate increases in product quality and service at the same price.
Bargaining power of suppliers	Suppliers threaten price increases and/or reductions in the quality of goods or services.
Threat of new entrants	New entrants bid prices down or cause incumbents to increase costs in order to maintain market position.
Threat of substitute products or services	Availability of substitutes limits the prices that can be charged.

Source: Based on Michael E. Porter, *Competitive Strategy,* Free Press, New York, 1980, pp. 3–28.

Strong rivalry among competitors poses a threat to a company's plans and goals. For example, as major record companies have increased their artistic offerings on compact disc (CD), the intensified competition has caused prices of CDs to fall. One result is that profit margins in the industry have been shrinking.

lowering the prices that can be charged or raising the costs of doing business. For example, the magazine industry has become so competitive that a number of magazines are being forced out of business. The News Corporation recently discontinued its *In Fashion* magazine, which was aimed at young women. After Diamandis Communications acquired ABC Publishing's *High Fidelity* and *Modern Photography*, it took them out of circulation and used their circulation lists to boost its own *Stereo Review* and *Popular Photography*. At the same time, several publishers have been reporting lower profit margins because they are selling subscriptions at a discount, offering bargain cover prices at newsstands, and accommodating advertiser pressures for special rates (rather than running the risk of losing advertisers to rival publications.)[31] Thus the magazine industry illustrates Porter's premise that the greater the rivalry, the lower the profit potential for businesses operating in the industry.

The *bargaining power of customers* is the extent to which customers are able to force down prices, bargain for higher quality or more service at the same price, and play competitors against each other. Customers tend to be powerful when the quantities they purchase are large in proportion to a seller's total sales, when the products or services represent a significant portion of a customer's costs, or when the items needed are standard in the supplier industry. For instance, U.S. suppliers in the auto parts industry have found that they must offer better quality at lower prices than they did in the past in order to gain orders from Japanese automakers operating plants in the United States. Such measures are necessary particularly because many Japan-based auto parts suppliers have built U.S. plants, providing alternative sources of supplies.[32] The greater the bargaining power of customers, the lower the profit potential in the industry.

The *bargaining power of suppliers* is the extent to which suppliers can exert power over businesses in an industry by threatening to raise prices or reduce the quality of goods and services provided to those businesses. Suppliers tend to be powerful when there are only a few suppliers selling to many businesses in an industry, when there are no substitutes for the products or services provided by the suppliers, or when the suppliers' products or services are critical inputs to the buyer's business. The greater the bargaining power of suppliers, the lower the profit potential for businesses operating in the industry.

For example, French makers of champagne are running into difficulties because of a shortage of land for growing grapes in the Champagne region of France, famous for producing ideal grapes that have made the sparkling wine increasingly popular throughout the world. One result is that Moët & Chandon, France's biggest champagne producer, pays $1.75 a pound for grapes compared with $0.14 in Spain. Given that a bottle of champagne requires 3.3 pounds of grapes, production costs are $5 per bottle less in Spain. To remedy the supply shortage, Moët and various other French champagne makers, such as Pommery et Greno and Laurent-Perrier, are purchasing wineries and land suitable for growing grapes in the United States (mainly in California and Oregon), as well as in Australia, Spain, Latin America, and elsewhere. Still, a debate rages over the comparative virtues of grapes grown in France versus those grown in other locations. Executives of a premier champagne producer, Veuve Clicquot, for instance, argue that top-quality champagne requires grapes from France's Champagne region, affording area growers considerable power as suppliers.[33]

The *threat of new entrants* is the extent to which new competitors can enter the same product or service markets. New entrants bring added capacity and possibly substantial resources. The results are price wars and/or increases in costs for existing businesses, which frequently must increase expenditures (for adding advertising, a larger sales force, better service, etc.) in order to maintain market position. The threat of entry depends on the barriers to entry that exist and the likely reaction against the new entrant from existing competitors. High barriers to entry exist when large capital investments are required to enter a business (as is the case in the steel industry), when established competitors have products or services that are perceived as unique by loyal customers (e.g., a brand-name perfume), or when economies of scale make it difficult for a new entrant to start small and gradually build up volume (e.g., television manufacturing).

When barriers to entry are high and new entrants can expect vigorous reaction from existing competitors, the threat of new entrants is low. For example, Anheuser-Busch, the nation's largest brewer, recently announced that it would start matching the steep discounts that smaller competitors were offering to invade some of the brewer's markets. Because of economies of scale, Anheuser-Busch's costs per barrel of beer are substantially lower than those of competitors, giving it heavy ammunition in a price war. With the handwriting on the wall, the smaller brewers quickly discontinued much of their heavy price-cutting.[34] In contrast, when barriers are low and new entrants can expect mild reactions from incumbent competitors, the threat of new entrants is high and, consequently, the profit potential for the industry is low.

The *threat of substitute products or services* is the extent to which businesses in other industries offer substitute products. For example, artificial sweeteners can be substituted for sugar, electricity can often be substituted for gas in producing energy, and wallpaper can be substituted for paint as an indoor wall covering. The Coca-Cola Company has been attempting to get workers in small offices to switch from coffee to Coke by providing a compact new machine, called the BreakMate, which chills water, carbonates it, and mixes it with Coca-Cola syrup before dispensing the soft drink into 6½-ounce cups.[35] The availability of substitutes constrains the prices that firms in an industry (such as the coffee industry) can charge because of the danger that customers will be encouraged to switch to the substitutes (such as Coca-Cola) as prices rise. As a result, the availability of substitute products or services reduces the profit potential for the industry.

Assessing Porter's Model. Porter argues that organizations need to give special consideration to the nature of a particular industry in determining new areas in which to do business and in formulating strategies. The greater the competitive forces, the greater the threat that the organization's strategic goals may not be reached because of reduced profit potential. On the other hand, the weaker the competitive forces, the greater the opportunities for operating successfully. Hence, in an analysis of potential environmental threats and opportunities, the competitive forces model is a particularly useful tool.

Organizational Assessment

In conducting a competitive analysis, managers also need to give considerable attention to how organizational factors affect the competitive situation. More specifically, managers need to assess major internal strengths and weaknesses as they influence the ability of the organization to compete.

Strengths are important because they are potential sources of competitive advantage. A strength that is unique and that competitors cannot easily match or imitate is known as a **distinctive competence.** Distinctive competences can be exploited in gaining a competitive advantage precisely because competitors will have difficulty following suit.[36] Of course, the distinctive competence must be able to provide results that are important to customers or clients. For example, by taking advantage of its distinctive competence in research and development, 3M has produced a broad range of useful product innovations over a sustained period of time.[37]

Such strengths often make it possible to develop organizational *synergy,* in which two or more units working together have greater impact than is possible with the units operating independently (see Chapter 2). In a strategy-related sense, synergy occurs mainly when the distinctive competencies of some departments or businesses make significant differences in the ability of other departments or businesses to operate effectively.[38] For example, at Hewlett-Packard, a major centralized R&D unit called Hewlett-Packard Laboratories conducts high-risk, long-term research that frequently benefits product development at the company's more than 50 divisions. The centralized R&D unit receives 15 percent of the Hewlett-Packard R&D budget and conducts research that is too costly for individual divisions to undertake.[39]

On the other hand, organizational weaknesses are important if they leave the organization vulnerable to competitor actions that will have an adverse effect on the organization. For instance, the Kerr-McGee Corporation, an Oklahoma City–based energy company, ran into trouble with its oil and gas explorations during the 1970s and early 1980s when its salary levels failed to keep up with those offered by competitors, causing most of its exploration and production talent to defect. Since that time, the company has been rebuilding its staff, with the result that the exploration staff recently made two significant oil reserve finds in the North Sea.[40]

One common aid in assessing internal organizational strengths and weaknesses is a functional audit. A **functional audit** is an exhaustive appraisal of an organization and/or its individual businesses conducted by assessing the important positive and negative attributes of each major functional area.[41] For instance, a functional audit might assess such aspects as the appropriate segmentation and targeting of markets by the marketing department, the currency of equipment in the operations department, and the availability of working capital from the finance department. Of course, a functional audit would address many more aspects of each department and consider other departments as well.[42]

Distinctive competence
A strength that is unique and that competitors cannot easily match or imitate

Functional audit An exhaustive appraisal of an organization and/or its individual businesses conducted by assessing the important positive and negative attributes of each major functional area

In determining which aspects to consider in conducting a functional audit, managers might find it useful to compile a list of the internal characteristics that appear to be the *key success factors* in the industry.[43] The list can then be used as the basis for the organizational assessment of the relevant functional areas. (In compiling the list, managers will need to have information about competitors. Some ideas about obtaining such data are given in Chapter 3 in the Practically Speaking discussion, "Keeping Tabs on Competitors.") Analysis of environmental opportunities and threats, as well as organizational strengths and weaknesses, then sets the stage for developing corporate-level strategies.

FORMULATING CORPORATE-LEVEL STRATEGY

Corporate-level strategy addresses the overall strategy that an organization will follow. Corporate strategy development generally involves selecting a grand strategy and using portfolio strategy approaches to determine the various businesses that will make up the organization.

Grand Strategies

A **grand strategy** (sometimes called a *master strategy*) provides the basic strategic direction at the corporate level.[44] There are several generic types, which can be grouped into three basic categories: growth, stability, and defensive grand strategies.[45] These strategies and their major subcategories are shown in Figure 6-3.

Grand strategy A master strategy that provides the basic strategic direction at the corporate level

Growth. Growth strategies are grand strategies that involve organizational expansion along some major dimension. In business organizations, growth typically means increasing sales and earnings, although other criteria (such as number of geographic locations) are possible. Similarly, not-for-profit organizations can grow in terms of revenue, clients served, or other criteria. Three major growth strategies are concentration, vertical integration, and diversification.

Growth strategies Grand strategies that involve organizational expansion along some major dimension

Concentration focuses on effecting the growth of a single product or service or a small number of closely related products or services. Concentration usually takes place through *market development* (gaining a larger share of a current market or expanding into new ones), *product development* (improving a basic product or service or expanding into closely related products or services), or *horizontal integration* (adding one or more businesses that are similar, usually by purchasing such businesses). For example, France-based Groupe Michelin recently engaged in horizontal integration when it took over the Uniroyal Goodrich Tire Company, making Michelin the world's largest tire manufacturer. Indicative of its strategy of high concentration, more than 90 percent of Michelin's annual sales are based on tires.[46]

Concentration An approach that focuses on effecting the growth of a single product or service or a small number of closely related products or services

Vertical integration involves effecting growth through the production of inputs previously provided by suppliers or through the replacement of a customer role (such as that of a distributor) by disposing of one's own outputs. When a business grows by becoming its own supplier, the process is known as *backward integration*.[47] One interesting organization that is prospering partially through backward integration is PGA Tour, Inc., the professional golf association headed by Commissioner Deane Beman. When Beman took over the organization in 1973, its annual revenues from professional golfing events were $3.1 million. Today, annual revenues top $100 million. This is partly because Tour

Vertical integration An approach that involves effecting growth through the production of inputs previously provided by suppliers or through the replacement of a customer role by disposing of one's own outputs

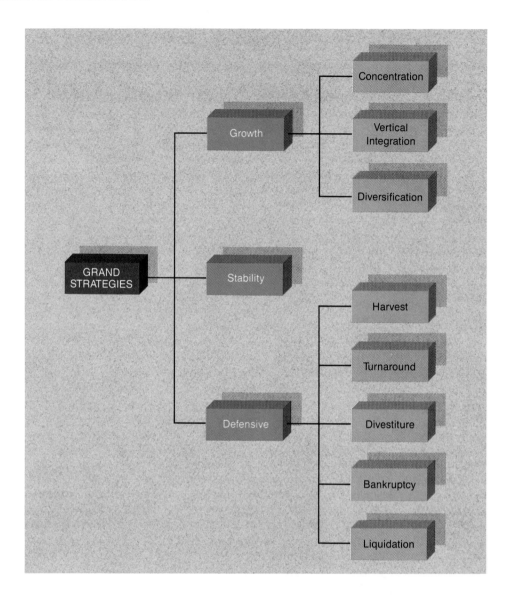

Figure 6-3 Types of grand strategies.

now owns, operates, or licenses more than 13 courses and clubs used each year for Tour events; the remainder of the time, the courses and clubs are available to members, who pay dues. Thus Tour has not only become its own supplier of sites for tournaments but also receives dues revenues; in addition, it often gets close to 20 percent of the gains from residential development on certain properties next to courses. In another move toward vertical integration, Tour has been working on producing its own telecasts of games for national television, rather than having relatively high-cost network personnel supply the production services.[48] When organizational growth encompasses a role previously fulfilled by a customer, the process is known as *forward integration*. Liz Claiborne, Inc., has recently engaged in forward integration by opening Liz Claiborne and First Issue retail stores to sell directly to individuals, rather than selling exclusively through department stores and outlets owned by others. According to one study, organizations are more likely to use a vertical integration strategy when product or service demand is reasonably certain, rather than highly uncertain.[49]

Diversification entails effecting growth through the development of new areas that are clearly distinct from current businesses. In addition to diversifying for growth reasons, organizations often diversify to reduce the risk that can be associated with single-product or -industry operations.[50] *Conglomerate diversification* takes place when an organization diversifies into areas that are unrelated to its current business. Organizations that adopt a conglomerate diversification strategy often are referred to as *conglomerates.* For example, Textron, Inc., a conglomerate, has an aerospace business that is being adversely affected by the current downturn in defense spending. However, its two other major businesses, commercial products (auto parts, lawn mowers, fasteners, etc.) and financial services (Paul Revere Insurance and other financial and leasing services) have helped cushion the effects.[51] Because of the diversity of businesses involved, conglomerates can be difficult for top management to administrate effectively.[52] *Concentric diversification* occurs when an organization diversifies into a related, but distinct, business. With concentric diversification, businesses can be related through products, markets, or technology. In the case of The Limited, Inc., the concentric diversification was through related products, mainly women's clothing (see the following Case in Point discussion).

Diversification An approach that entails effecting growth through the development of new areas that are clearly distinct from current businesses

CASE IN POINT: The Unlimited Limited

When Leslie Wexner opened his first women's clothing store in Columbus, Ohio, in 1963 with a $5000 stake, few would have predicted that the shop was the beginning of a major women's clothing empire. Wexner called his first shop "The Limited" because it offered only women's sportswear. He got the idea of specializing after working in his parent's clothing store and noticing that office garments and fancy dresses did not sell nearly as fast as sportswear. When he attempted to persuade his parents to concentrate on sportswear and eliminate the other merchandise, they insisted that the shop needed a wide variety of clothing to attract customers. In fact, his father told him: "You'll never be a merchant." Within a year, the son's new shop proved to be so successful that the parents closed up their store and joined forces with their "merchant" son. By 1969, when The Limited, Inc., made a public stock offering, Wexner had opened six stores. Seven years later, there were 100 The Limited stores; that number had increased more than sevenfold by the end of the 1980s.

Along with the growth of The Limited stores, there have been shifts in emphasis. While The Limited originally targeted women between 15 and 25, Wexner found that he was losing these customers as they grew older. Accordingly, he repositioned The Limited to appeal to women in the 20-to-35 age bracket and started a new chain, the Limited Express, to appeal to teenagers and women in their early twenties.

In order to keep the company growing at a fast pace, Wexner also has expanded into other areas related to women's clothing. For example, in 1981, he bought a small chain of lingerie stores, called Victoria's Secret, and expanded it to more than 300 stores within 7 years. He also purchased the Lane Bryant stores in 1982 and eliminated the tall and largest sizes because of the relatively small market. Instead, he expanded offerings in sizes 14 through 20, noting that 40 percent of women are size 14 or larger. The acquisition of the Lane Bryant chain marked the first time that Wexner had entered the size 14 and above market.

Next, Wexner bought the Lerner chain, which he called the "McDonald's of the clothing business" because it was the largest women's clothing chain when he purchased it in 1985. It was also close to bankruptcy, owing largely to poor management, including abysmal inventory control. Lerner now carries the same type of merchandise found in The Limited stores, but the items are geared to a lower-priced market.

More recently, according to The Limited chain's president, Verna K. Gibson, the chain has developed a larger version of its The Limited stores. The new International Fashion stores, with about 12,500 square feet of floor space (compared with 3700 at regular The Limited stores), can accommodate the usual The Limited fare along with career clothing, lingerie, and children's apparel. Thus The Limited and its various related chains, now numbering more than 3000 outlets, continue to experiment with creative ways to keep the company growing, mainly in women's clothing or closely related areas, such as men's and children's clothing.[53] ▬▬▬▬▬

All three growth strategies, including the diversification approach used by The Limited, can be implemented through internal growth or through acquisition, merger, or joint venture. With internal growth the organization expands by building on its own internal resources. An **acquisition** is the purchase of all or part of one organization by another; while a **merger** is the combining of two or more companies into one organization. (We discuss mergers and acquisitions further in Chapter 7.) Finally, a joint venture occurs when two or more organizations provide resources to support a given project or product offering (see Chapter 3.) Thus there are several alternative routes to implementing particular growth strategies.

Acquisition The purchase of all or part of one organization by another

Merger The combining of two or more companies into one organization

Stability strategy A strategy that involves maintaining the status quo or growing in a methodical, but slow, manner

Stability. A **stability strategy** involves maintaining the status quo or growing in a methodical, but slow, manner. Organizations might choose a stability strategy for a number of reasons. For instance, if a company is doing reasonably well, managers may not want the risks or hassles associated with more aggressive growth. This is often the case in small, privately owned businesses, which constitute the largest group likely to adopt a strategy of stability. For example, Bob Sidell started California Cosmetics after formulating special cosmetics to cope with the skin problems of teenage actors appearing in the TV show *The Waltons*. Within 3 years, Sidell and his partner, Paula Levey, had developed their mail-order operation into a company with annual sales of $10 million. Such fast growth, though, brought botched orders, rising complaints, and returns and nondeliveries in the 17 percent range. After some initial cutbacks to gain stability, the company plans to grow much more slowly. "We'll probably never be the richest folks on the block," says Levey. "But we're going to be around years from now."[54] Another major reason for choosing stability is that it provides a chance to recover. An organization that stretched its resources during a period of accelerated growth may need to attain stability before it attempts further accelerated growth. On the other hand, if managers believe that growth prospects are low, they may choose a stability strategy in an attempt to hold on to current market share. (Worsening situations, however, may call for defensive strategies.) Finally, a stability strategy may even occur through default if managers are unconcerned with their strategic direction.

Defensive strategies Strategies that focus on the desire or need to reduce organizational operations usually through cost and/or asset reductions

Defensive. **Defensive strategies** (sometimes called *retrenchment strategies*) focus on the desire or need to reduce organizational operations usually through cost reductions (such as cutting back on nonessential expenditures and instituting hiring freezes) and/or asset reductions (such as selling land, equipment, and businesses).[55] Defensive strategies include harvest, turnaround, divestiture, bankruptcy, and liquidation.

Harvest entails minimizing investments while attempting to maximize short-run profits and cash flow, with the long-run intention of exiting the market.[56] A harvest strategy is often used when future growth in the market is doubtful or will require investments that do not appear to be cost-effective. For example, when vacuum tubes became obsolete because of the late 1940s' invention of the transistor and subsequent advanced solid-state circuitry, many large producers of vacuum tubes (e.g., Western Electric, General Electric, and Westinghouse) gradually phased out their production.[57] With a harvest strategy, the resulting short-run profits often are then used to build other businesses with better future prospects.

A **turnaround** is designed to reverse a negative trend and restore the organization to appropriate levels of profitability. Such efforts often require at least temporary reductions in order to conserve funds. (The term "turnaround" is sometimes used more loosely to denote a major shift from a negative direction to a positive one.) A **divestiture** involves an organization's selling or divesting of a business or part of a business. One study found that when divestitures are congruent with corporate or business strategies outlined in company publications, they have a positive effect on the price of the firm's stock; conversely, when divestitures are conducted in the absence of clear strategic goals, they generally have a negative market effect.[58]

Under Chapter 11 of the Federal Bankruptcy Act, **bankruptcy** is a means whereby an organization that is unable to pay its debts can seek court protection from creditors and from certain contract obligations while it attempts to regain financial stability. For example, two U.S. subsidiaries of the Canada-based Campeau Corporation, the Allied Stores Corporation and Federated Department Stores, Inc., filed for bankruptcy in January 1990, constituting the largest retailing bankruptcy in U.S. history. The chains include such well-known stores as Bloomingdale's, Abraham & Straus in New York, Rich's in Atlanta, and Burdines in Florida. The Campeau empire ran into a cash-flow problem when sales were slower than expected, and the company experienced difficulty in paying debts associated with its recent acquisitions.[59] **Liquidation** entails selling or dissolving an entire organization. Liquidation usually occurs when serious difficulties, such as bankruptcy, cannot be resolved.

Portfolio Strategy Approaches

While grand strategies address an organization's overall direction, portfolio strategy approaches help managers determine the types of businesses in which the organization should be engaged. More specifically, a **portfolio strategy approach** is a method of analyzing an organization's mix of businesses in terms of both individual and collective contributions to strategic goals. The concept is analogous to that of an individual attempting to assemble a group, or portfolio, of stocks that provide balance in terms of risk, long-term growth, and other factors that may be important to the individual. Three of the most frequently used major portfolio approaches are the BCG growth-share matrix, the GE business screen, and the product/market evolution matrix. Each uses a two-dimensional matrix, which measures one variable along one dimension and another along a second dimension to form four or more cells. Portfolio approaches apply to analyzing existing or potential strategic business units.

Harvest A strategy that entails minimizing investments while attempting to maximize short-run profits and cash flow, with the long-run intention of exiting the market

Turnaround A strategy designed to reverse a negative trend and restore the organization to appropriate levels of profitability

Divestiture A strategy that involves an organization's selling or divesting of a business or part of a business

Bankruptcy A strategy in which an organization that is unable to pay its debts can seek court protection from creditors and from certain contract obligations while it attempts to regain financial stability

Liquidation A strategy that entails selling or dissolving an entire organization

Portfolio strategy approach A method of analyzing an organization's mix of businesses in terms of both individual and collective contributions to strategic goals

BCG growth-share matrix
A four-cell matrix (developed by the Boston Consulting Group) that compares various businesses in an organization's portfolio on the basis of relative market share and market growth rate

BCG Growth-Share Matrix. One of the earliest portfolio approaches to gain extensive use is the four-cell matrix developed by the Boston Consulting Group (BCG), a prominent management consulting firm. The **BCG growth-share matrix,** shown in Figure 6-4, compares various businesses in an organization's portfolio on the basis of relative market share and market growth rate. Relative market share is determined by the ratio of a business's market share (in terms of unit volume) compared to the market share of its largest rival. Market growth rate is the growth in the market during the previous year relative to growth in the economy as a whole.[60] In the BCG matrix shown in Figure 6-4, each business is plotted on the matrix and then illustrated by a circle, with the size of the circle indicating the particular business's percent revenue relative to the revenues generated by other businesses in the portfolio. The resulting matrix divides the businesses into four categories.

The *star* has a high market share in a rapidly growing market. Because of the high growth potential, stars often require substantial investment capital beyond what they are able to earn themselves. For example, General Electric recently spent $2.3 billion to acquire a chemical business that was part of the Borg-Warner Corporation. Combined with GE's own chemical operations, the chemical business previously owned by Borg-Warner (and now operating under the GE name) gives GE a larger presence and a star in the fast-growing plastics business.[61]

A *question mark* (often also called a *problem child*) has a low market share in a rapidly growing market. Question marks present somewhat of a dilemma for their organizations: they require substantial investment to take advantage of the rapidly growing market, yet their low market share usually means that they have limited ability to generate substantial amounts of cash themselves; thus,

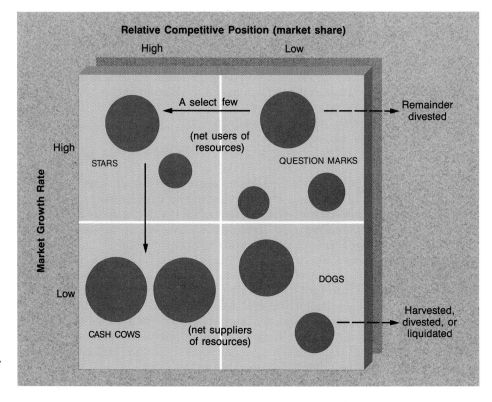

Figure 6-4 BCG growth-share matrix. (Adapted from John A. Pearce II and Richard B. Robinson, Jr., *Strategic Management: Strategy Formulation and Implementation,* 3d ed., Irwin, Homewood, Ill., 1988, p. 280.)

IBM's System/370 mainframe has been a cash cow for the company for many years. Its market share is close to 70 percent, and it pulls in about 50 percent of IBM's total revenues and 65 percent of its profits. But now the 370's market is under siege from technologically advanced computers that can do the same kinds of jobs for less cost. The 370's "milking" days may be drawing to a close.

they are "cash hogs." For example, Cincinnati-headquartered Roto-Rooter, Inc., is best known as a service that uses a motor-driven auger to snake through drains and clogged sewer lines to drill out obstructions. Since acquiring Roto-Rooter in the early 1980s, the Chemed Corporation has attempted to expand the company into residential plumbing repair work and industrial pipe cleaning. So far, Roto-Rooter has about 1 percent of the plumbing market, but it will take considerable further funding to build up what might be the first large national plumbing company.[62] With question marks, managers usually must either provide substantial cash to fuel growth or divest the business.

The *cash cow* has a high market share in a slowly growing market; as a result, it tends to generate more cash than is necessary to maintain its market position. Cash cows often are former stars and can be valuable in a portfolio because they can be "milked" to provide cash for stars and question marks. For instance, the drain-cleaning business of Roto-Rooter provides excess cash that has been used to open new company outlets and buy back old franchises to facilitate the buildup of the plumbing business.[63]

A *dog* has a low market share in an area of low growth and usually generates only a modest cash flow or may even have a small negative cash flow. Usually, dogs are harvested, divested, or liquidated. For example, General Electric sold a consumer electronics division that was only marginally profitable to the French electronics giant Thompson S.A. in 1988. Thompson was interested in the acquisition as a means of acquiring operations in the United States.[64]

Overall, the BCG matrix suggests using revenues from cash cows to fund the growth of stars, as well as to build the market share of those question marks with the best prospects. Dogs and the remaining question marks are usually divested unless they provide sufficient positive cash flow to justify retaining them, at least in the short run. One recent study suggests that dogs may generate more cash than they are generally given credit for and that managers, therefore, should evaluate them carefully before taking the divestiture step.[65]

The BCG matrix is useful in providing a means of viewing a set of businesses as a portfolio with differing cash flows and cash requirements.[66] The matrix also helps develop a rationale for prioritizing resource allocations across businesses, thereby assisting managers in formulating strategies for building some businesses and divesting others.

Still, the BCG matrix does have a number of shortcomings.[67] Among the most important is that the matrix does not directly address the majority of businesses that have average market shares in markets of average growth (note that the matrix has only two categories, high and low, for each dimension). Generalizations based on the matrix also may be misleading, since organizations with low market shares may not necessarily be question marks. For example, at West Germany–based Daimler-Benz, managers raise car production only after careful debate, lest the Mercedes lose its exclusive image.[68] Similarly, businesses with large market shares in slow growth markets may not necessarily be cash cows because they may actually need substantial investments to retain their market position. For example, Nabisco Brands (a division of RJR Nabisco) has about 30 percent of the cookie market (e.g., Oreos) and about half the cracker market (e.g., Ritz), both markets that are growing relatively slowly. Still, RJR Nabisco had planned to spend $4 billion in capital investments to retain the division's position as a low-cost producer. The expenditures were placed on hold in 1989 because Nabisco had to pay off massive debts associated with its takeover by the investment firm of Kohlberg Kravis Roberts & Company.[69] Another shortcoming of the matrix is that it provides little guidance regarding which question marks to support and which dogs to salvage. Finally, one survey suggests that executives dislike the BCG terminology. According to one executive, "We try to avoid the use of words such as 'cash cow' or 'dog' like the plague. If you call a business a dog, it'll respond like one. It's one thing to know that you are an ugly duckling—much worse to be told explicitly that you are."[70] Despite these shortcomings, the BCG matrix does have research support in terms of its ability to differentiate among businesses for purposes of thinking about strategy.[71]

GE Business Screen. Another popular portfolio matrix is the GE business screen, developed by General Electric with the help of McKinsey & Company.[72] The **GE business screen** (also often called the GE planning grid) is a nine-cell matrix that is based on long-term industry attractiveness and on business strength (see Figure 6-5). The major factors to consider in assessing these two dimensions are summarized in Figure 6-5. On the screen, or grid, each business is represented by a circle, with the size of the circle proportional to the size of the industry (measured by total industry sales) in which the business competes. (Note that the meaning of the circle differs from that in the BCG matrix, in which the circle represents the particular business's percent revenue relative to the revenues generated by other portfolio businesses). The pie slice within the circle shows the business's market share within the industry.

GE business screen A nine-cell matrix (developed by General Electric with McKinsey & Company) that is based on long-term industry attractiveness and on business strength

In the GE screen, the three cells at the upper left of the matrix represent situations of long-term industry attractiveness and business strength; the strategic prescription for businesses in these cells is *grow and build*. The three cells at the opposite end of the matrix (lower right) represent situations of relatively low industry attractiveness and weak business strength, indicating that the strategy generally should be *harvest and/or divest*. The remaining cells depict mixed situations in which the strategy usually is *hold and maintain*.

The GE business screen has three main advantages over the BCG matrix.[73] For one thing, the terminology is potentially more palatable to managers, particularly in the harvest and/or divest section of the grid. In addition, multiple factors are considered in determining where a business fits on the two dimensions; thus the GE screen includes more information about businesses. Finally, the three categories for industry attractiveness and business strength result in

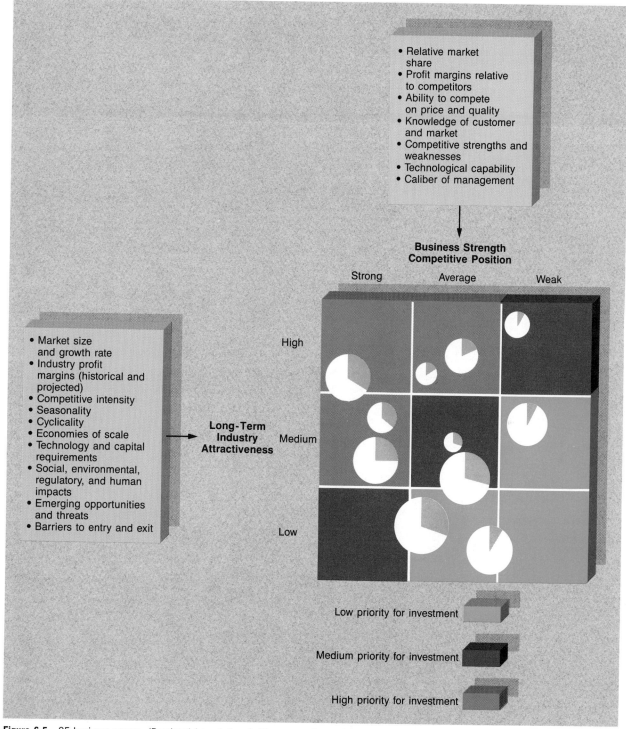

Figure 6-5 GE business screen. (Reprinted from Arthur A. Thompson, Jr., and A. J. Strickland III, *Strategic Management: Concepts and Cases,* 5th ed., BPI/Irwin, Homewood, Ill., 1990, p. 201.)

finer distinctions among businesses, particularly those that are average. Still, the screen does not specify the strategies that should be followed by various businesses, nor does it provide a means for identifying businesses that are just about to move into a period of high growth.[74]

Product/Market Evolution Matrix. To help resolve the issue of identifying companies, particularly new businesses, that are about to accelerate their growth, strategy researcher Charles W. Hofer has suggested a further refinement.[75] The **product/market evolution matrix** (sometimes called the *life-cycle portfolio matrix*) is a 15-cell matrix in which businesses are plotted according to the business unit's business strength, or competitive position, and the industry's stage in the evolutionary product/market life cycle (see Figure 6-6). The first dimension, the business unit's competitive position, is similar to the business strength, or competitive position, dimension in the GE screen. On the second dimension, the product/market evolution matrix uses the product/market evolution stage, rather than long-term industry attractiveness (as did the GE business screen). The new second dimension shows the industry's stage in the evolutionary life cycle, starting with initial development and proceeding through the growth, competitive shakeout, maturity and saturation, and decline stages. The maturity and saturation stage is particularly important because it often lasts for an ex-

Product/market evolution matrix A 15-cell matrix (developed by Hofer) in which businesses are plotted according to the business unit's business strength, or competitive position, and the industry's stage in the evolutionary product/market life cycle

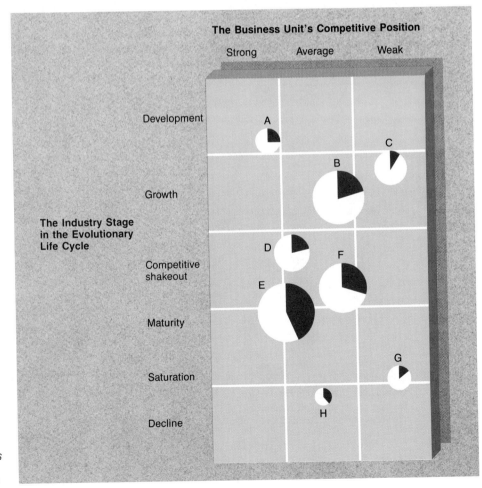

Figure 6-6 Product/market evolution matrix. (Reprinted from Arthur A. Thompson, Jr., and A. J. Strickland III, *Strategic Management: Concepts and Cases*, 5th ed., BPI/Irwin, Homewood, Ill., 1990, p. 204.)

tended period of time. An industry is said to have reached *maturity* when growth slows and the market moves toward the saturation point, where demand is limited to replacement of the product or service.[76] The challenge in the maturity and saturation stage is preserving or slowly expanding market share while avoiding the decline stage.[77] As in the GE screen, the size of the circle representing each business is proportional to the size of the industry in which the business competes, while the pie slice within the circle shows the business's market share within the industry.

The data shown in Figure 6-6 suggest that business A has good prospects for growth and should be developed. Business E is a well-established business that would be considered a star in BCG matrix terminology, although it is moving toward maturity. Business F is gradually losing its competitive position but is a probable cash cow. Business G is most likely a candidate for divesting or liquidating and would be considered a dog.

Assessing the Portfolio Matrixes. Each portfolio matrix offers a somewhat different perspective that is likely to be useful in the strategy formulation process. Therefore, it is possible to use one or more. Regardless of the number of matrixes used, they are basically tools to enhance thinking in terms of the mix of businesses in an organization's portfolio. For example, the Westinghouse Electric Corporation recently has been using a portfolio approach to divest many of its traditional businesses (e.g., light bulbs, electric motors, and transformers) in favor of more than 70 small new businesses, mainly in high-growth service sectors (such as broadcasting, financial services, truck refrigeration, and waste disposal). The new configuration of businesses, which makes the company less vulnerable to an economic downturn, has led to a significant boost in profits for Westinghouse.[78] Portfolio matrixes, however, do not provide advice about specific strategies for various businesses. Such specifics are addressed by strategies at the business level.

FORMULATING BUSINESS-LEVEL STRATEGY

Business-level strategy is concerned with how a particular business competes. Considerable research has been conducted on strategic alternatives for individual businesses within an organization (or for organizations that operate a single business). The best-known approach for developing strategy at the SBU level is based on the research of strategy expert Michael E. Porter.

Porter's Competitive Strategies

Porter has outlined three generic business-level strategies that can be used to gain competitive advantage over other firms operating in the same industry.[79] The strategies are termed "generic" because they are widely applicable to a variety of situations. Still, they are more specific than the generic strategies reviewed earlier that apply to the corporate level. Porter's three strategies are cost leadership, differentiation, and focus. Common requirements for successfully pursuing Porter's competitive strategies are summarized in Table 6-4.

Cost Leadership. A **cost leadership strategy** involves emphasizing organizational efficiency so that the overall costs of providing products and services are lower than those of competitors. This low-cost approach entails careful attention

Cost leadership strategy A strategy outlined by Porter that involves emphasizing organizational efficiency so that the overall costs of providing products and services are lower than those of competitors

Table 6-4 Common Requirements for Successfully Pursuing Porter's Competitive Strategies

Generic Strategy	Commonly Required Skills and Resources	Common Organizational Requirements
Overall cost leadership	Substained capital investment and access to capital Process engineering skills Intense supervision of labor Products designed for ease in manufacture Low-cost distribution system	Tight cost control Frequent, detailed control reports Structured organization and responsibilities Incentives based on meeting strict quantitative targets
Differentiation	Strong marketing abilities Product engineering Creative flair Strong capability in basic research Corporate reputation for quality or technological leadership Long tradition in the industry or unique combination of skills drawn from other businesses Strong cooperation from channels	Strong coordination among functions in R&D, product development, and marketing Subjective measurement and incentives instead of quantitative measures Amenities to attract highly skilled labor, scientists, or creative people
Focus	Combination of the above policies directed at the particular strategic target	Combination of the above policies directed at the particular strategic target

Source: Reprinted from Michael E. Porter, *Competitive Strategy,* Free Press, New York, 1980, pp. 40–41.

A low-cost strategy has to be balanced against product quality. H. J. Heinz installed high-speed dicing machines to cut production costs of Tater Tots at its Ore-Ida plant, but the machines diced the potatoes too thin, resulting in mushy Tots. Company managers decided to slow down the machines in order to put the crisp back into their product. Increased sales have more than paid for the increased production costs.

to minimizing necessary costs in every aspect of the business, such as developing efficient production methods, keeping tight controls on overhead and administrative costs, seeking savings by procuring supplies at low prices, and monitoring costs in other areas (such as promotion, distribution, and service). Lower costs enable an organization to gain an edge over competitors by offering lower prices and potentially earning above-average profits because of higher profit margins or large sales volumes. For instance, Louisville-based Humana, Inc., a publicly owned health-care company, claims that the reason why it recently has been achieving a significantly higher return on equity than others in the industry and has been realizing pretax profit margins of around 10 percent is that it is the lowest-cost producer of health care in the United States.[80]

Of course, for a cost leadership strategy to be effective, achieving lower costs cannot be done at the expense of necessary quality. For example, the H. J. Heinz Company ran into difficulties at its Ore-Ida division when cost-cutting efforts related to Heinz's low-cost strategy caused changes in manufacturing methods for popular Tater Tots frozen spuds. Sales began to decline because, as a result of the changes, the Tater Tot insides were mushy and the outsides had lost their light and crispy coating. With the changes reversed, Tater Tots now have more than 55 percent of the market for frozen fried potatoes.[81]

A low-cost strategy is not without risks. To be effective, the strategy usually requires that a business be *the* cost leader, not just one of several. Otherwise, two or more businesses vying for cost leadership can engage in a rivalry that drives profits down to extremely low levels. thus the business must have a cost advantage that is not easily or inexpensively imitated, and it must stay abreast of new technologies that can alter the cost curve. In addition, managers still must consider making at least those product or service innovations that are very important to customers, lest competitors, using a differentiation strategy, lure customers away with significant product or service improvements.

Differentiation. A **differentiation strategy** involves attempting to develop products and services that are viewed as unique in the industry. Successful differentiation allows the business to charge premium prices, leading to above-average profits. Differentiation can take many forms—for example, design or brand image (Baker in furniture, Coach in handbags, Ralph Lauren in menswear), technology (Hewlett-Packard in laser printers, Coleman in camping equipment, Hyster in lift trucks), customer service (IBM in computers, Crown Cork and Seal in metal cans, and Nordstrom's in apparel retailing), features (Jenn-Air in electric ranges), quality (Xerox in copiers, Milliken in textiles, Swarovski in rhinestones), and selection (Echlin in auto parts). With differentiation, a company still cannot afford to ignore costs, but costs are not as important as perceptions of product or service uniqueness.

> **Differentiation strategy** A strategy outlined by Porter that involves attempting to develop products and services that are viewed as unique in the industry

Still, there are vulnerabilities associated with a differentiation strategy. If costs are too high, customers may choose less costly alternatives, even though they forgo some desirable features. Also, customer tastes and needs can change, so businesses following a differentiation strategy must carefully assess customers' shifting requirements. Differentiation, of course, works best when the differentiating factor is both important to customers and difficult for competitors to imitate. While differentiation usually is aimed at a fairly broad market, a focus strategy concentrates on a narrow niche.

Focus. A **focus strategy** entails specializing by establishing a position of overall cost leadership, differentiation, or both, but only within a particular portion, or segment, of an entire market. The segment may be a particular group of customers, a specific geographic area, or a certain part of the product or service line. The rationale is that by specializing the organization can serve the market segment more effectively than can competitors who attempt to cover the entire market. The focus strategy still relies on a low-cost or a differentiation approach, or perhaps both, to establish a strong position within the particular market segment, or niche. The differentiation within a focus strategy can occur by tailoring products to the specialized needs of the market segment. A cost advantage may be simultaneously possible because a firm may be able to offer better prices on custom orders even though another firm may have the cost leadership in serving the larger-volume needs of the broader market. An example of a company that has successfully used a focus strategy is Baxters of Speyside (see the following Case in Point discussion).

> **Focus strategy** A strategy outlined by Porter that entails specializing by establishing a position of overall cost leadership, differentiation, or both, but only within a particular portion, or segment, of an entire market

CASE IN POINT: Baxters of Speyside Focuses on Specialty Foods

"We take the produce of the hills and glens of Bonnie Scotland and make beautiful things," says Gordon Baxter, chairman, summing up the basic approach that has made Scotland's specialty food producer, Baxters of Speyside, a major success. Baxters of Speyside has become a popular brand name in Britain and increasingly elsewhere, with premium soups, jams, and other specialties. For example, the company offers soups with such intriguing names as Cream of Pheasant, Cream of Scampi, Cock-a-Leekie, and Royal Game. These innovative

It started in 1868 as a grocery store in a tiny town of the Scottish highlands; today Baxters of Speyside sells about $33 million worth of soups, jams, and specialty foods in the British Isles each year. Baxters has been so successful because the firm never lost sight of its special segment of the market—premium foods. Baxters' family proprietorship and exotic recipes help to differentiate the firm and are an important part of the company's focus strategy.

products have helped establish the company's reputation in Britain's premium-food market, where overseas customers are willing to pay as much as twice the price of competing brands for Baxters of Speyside specialties. Baxter's wife, Ena, developed most of the exotic recipes; now, a team of chefs and food technologists help her.

The family-run company, with annual sales topping $40 million, has evolved from a grocery store founded in 1868 by Baxter's grandfather in Fochabers, a remote location along the River Spey in Morayshire, 65 miles northeast of Aberdeen, Scotland. Baxter's father added a jam factory and began selling items to two of Britain's best-known department stores, Harrods and Fortnum & Mason, during the 1920s and 1930s. After the company was almost destroyed during World War II, Baxter and his brother rebuilt and expanded it. Since then, several of Baxter's children have joined the company, adding a fourth generation of involvement.

Capitalizing on its unusual products and location, Baxter and his entourage often wear kilts and even bring along bagpipes on sales trips to the United States. "Scotland is very projectable," he says. According to one salesperson at Harrods in London, Baxters of Speyside products sell partly because customers visualize the product being carefully stirred by hand in a pot, even though the foods are made in a modern factory. They also imagine that the Baxters themselves actually stalk the game and gather the ingredients. Still, most of the ingredients do come from local suppliers, giving some credence to the vision.

Sales began to grow significantly when Baxter was able to persuade some of Britain's chain retailers, such as Tesco Stores, J. Sainsbury, and Waitrose Supermarkets, to carry the premium brand. As a result, the company has about 77 percent of Britain's premium soup market. "Supermarkets today in America and Britain are all trading up," he says happily. Based on a suggestion from a Hilton Hotel executive, the company moved quickly to package its premium jams in special 1½-ounce jars that are now sold to such customers as Hilton and Trusthouse Forste hotels and BA airlines.

With only about 4 percent of its total sales in the United States, the potential for growth is great. Not surprisingly, Baxter's files contain letters from many

U.S. companies, such as General Foods, General Mills, Libby's, Carnation, RJR Nabisco, Colgate-Palmolive, Campbell, and Heinz, expressing interest in purchasing Baxters of Speyside. Baxters operates within its cash flow. The company has no debt; the Baxter family owns 96.5 percent of the shares. Profit margins are above the industry average.[82] ▬▬▬▬

Despite the success of Baxters of Speyside, there are some areas that a business adopting a focus strategy needs to monitor. The major risks are possibilities that costs for the focused firm will become too great relative to those of less focused competitors, differentiation will become less of an advantage as competitors serving broader markets embellish their products, and competitors will begin focusing on a group *within* the customer population being served by the firm with the focus strategy. For example, Roadway Package Systems (RPS) is attempting to invade the market for door-to-door ground delivery of packages, currently dominated by United Parcel Service (UPS). RPS contracts with 2500 independent individuals to lease or buy distinctive white RPS delivery trucks. The individuals then pick up and deliver packages in a particular territory for RPS. The independents are paid for work performed, rather than receiving the higher unionized wages and generous benefits typical of UPS. While UPS limits packages to 70 pounds and also delivers to residents, RPS has set a 100-pound limit and restricts delivery to businesses. With about 150 terminals so far, RPS can deliver to about 75 percent of the United States, and another 80 terminals are planned by the mid-1900s.[83]

Assessing Porter's Strategies

Studies of Porter's generic strategies have mainly supported the view that companies pursuing one of these strategies are likely to be more profitable than those not adopting one of these generic types.[84] Still, some studies have produced evidence showing that a minority of firms have successfully pursued broad markets by simultaneously using both differentiation and low-cost strategies.[85] Porter has argued that such an effort aimed at broad markets (as opposed to narrow ones, which are the domain of a focus strategy) will leave an organization stuck in the middle. A major reason is that attempting to pursue a differentiation strategy requires an expenditure of funds that makes it difficult to achieve cost leadership. While debate continues on the issue, one researcher notes that an example of a situation in which differentiation might be compatible with low cost is one in which a differentiated product achieves high growth, leading to sufficient volume to enable economies of scale (and, therefore, lower costs).[86]

Regardless of which generic strategy is used, the ability to carry it out successfully depends on distinctive competencies. Such distinctive competencies typically develop at the functional level.

FORMULATING FUNCTIONAL-LEVEL STRATEGY

Functional-level strategies support the basic thrust of strategy at the business level. The role of functional strategies is spelling out the specific ways that functional areas can be used to bolster the business-level strategy. For example, under a product differentiation strategy, the R&D department might be called upon to accelerate the innovation process in order to provide new products in advance of the competition. Along similar lines, marketing might develop a plan to support the new product lines using premium prices, distribution through prestigious locations, and a special promotion scheme aimed at targeted market segments. For its part, operations, the function that is responsible for actually producing the product, might devise a functional strategy based on using excellent raw materials, incorporating the latest technology, and having some components subcontracted in order to produce a premium product.

In contrast, under a strategy of low cost, the R&D department might be called upon to develop innovations in the manufacturing process so that costs can be lowered. Marketing might develop a functional strategy that emphasizes selling large quantities of relatively standardized products, marketing by telephone, developing computerized ordering systems that save money, and building promotions around good quality for a low price. Operations might, then, develop a functional strategy aimed at producing high volumes at low prices, an approach that may entail new, cost-efficient machinery.

In essence, strategies at the functional level can be extremely important in supporting a business-level strategy. Typically, the functional areas develop the distinctive competencies that lead to potential competitive advantages. Such competencies do not usually occur by chance; instead, they need to be carefully conceived and may take several years to develop. For example, the talent that Disney has built in its Imagineering group provides a distinctive competence that helps the company continually innovate.

STRATEGY IMPLEMENTATION

While strategy formulation is an important part of the strategic management process, strategies are unlikely to have the intended impact unless they are implemented effectively. Strategic implementation includes the various management activities that are necessary to put the strategy in motion, institute strategic controls that monitor progress, and ultimately achieve organizational goals. The strategic implementation phase of the strategic management process is shown in Figure 6-7.

Carrying Out Strategic Plans

Strategy implementation experts Jay R. Galbraith and Robert K. Kazanjian suggest that several major internal aspects of the organization may need to be synchronized in order to put a chosen strategy into action. Major factors (shown in Figure 6-7) are technology, human resources, reward systems, decision pro-

Figure 6-7 The strategy implementation phase of the strategic management process.

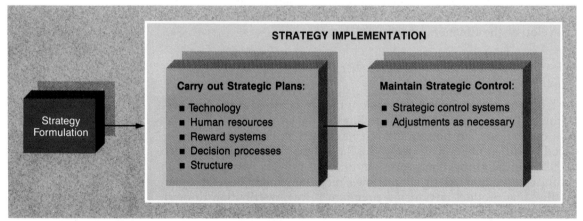

STRATEGY IMPLEMENTATION

Strategy Formulation

Carry out Strategic Plans:
- Technology
- Human resources
- Reward systems
- Decision processes
- Structure

Maintain Strategic Control:
- Strategic control systems
- Adjustments as necessary

cesses, and structure.[87] The factors tend to be interconnected, so a change in one may necessitate changes in one or more others.

Technology. Technology is the knowledge, tools, equipment, and work techniques used by an organization in delivering its product or service. Technology is often an important factor in strategy implementation because the technological emphasis must fit the strategic thrust. For example, if an organization pursues a low-cost strategy, changes in technology may be necessary to reduce costs. On the other hand, following a strategy of differentiation may entail technological change in order to develop and/or produce the enhanced products or services.

Human Resources. Human resources are the individuals who are members of the organization. Having the individuals with the necessary skills in the appropriate positions is a prerequisite for effective strategy implementation.[88] This is accomplished by conducting strategic human resources planning, which links the human resources needs with the strategies to be pursued. Research has indicated that different strategies require unique skills and backgrounds among the general managers who carry out each designated strategy.[89] Furthermore, the skills and experience of an organization's human resources often are a source of competitive advantage. For example, a skilled work force usually has a greater ability to find ways to reduce costs or produce the new product or service idea that constitutes a source of differentiation. We discuss human resources more thoroughly in Chapter 12.

Reward Systems. Reward systems include bonuses, awards, or promotions provided by others, as well as rewards related to internal experiences, such as feelings of achievement and challenge. Carefully considered reward systems are likely to constitute an important source of motivation to support a given strategy. For example, at Albertson's, Inc., a major food and drug retail chain with stores in 17 Sunbelt and western states, employees receive bonuses based on profits as a means of encouraging productivity and better service.[90] Specific rewards may be matched to the type of strategy being pursued. For example, a manager in an organization following a stability strategy might receive a bonus for a job well done, whereas a manager following a growth strategy may be given stock in the expanded venture as a reward for meeting organizational goals.[91] We discuss motivational issues further in Chapter 13.

Decision Processes. Decision processes include the means of resolving questions and problems that occur in organizations. Issues of resource allocation are particularly important to strategy implementation because strategic plans are more likely to be successful when resources are channeled to provide strong support for such plans. Decision-making processes also can help resolve specific problems and issues that arise during the course of implementing the plan. We discuss managerial decision making at greater length in Chapters 8 and 9.

Structure. Organization structure is the formal pattern of interactions and coordination designed by management to link the tasks of individuals and groups in achieving organizational goals. Such patterns help various parts of the organization coordinate their efforts. The broad outlines of an organization's structure are often depicted through the use of organization charts. Current research suggests that strategies may be more successful when the structure supports the strategic direction. We discuss this issue further in Chapter 11.

Maintaining Strategic Control

While there are a variety of factors that must be considered in carrying out strategic plans, managers also need to be able to monitor progress through strategic control. Strategic control involves monitoring critical environmental factors that could affect the viability of strategic plans, assessing the effects of organizational strategic actions, and ensuring that strategic plans are implemented as intended. Instituting strategic control includes designing information systems that provide feedback regarding how strategic plans are being implemented, as well as their apparent effects. Such strategic control systems allow managers to make adjustments in the carrying out of strategic plans, as necessary. Issues related to strategic control are considered extensively in Chapters 17 and 18. Chapter 20 investigates various management information systems that can be used for strategic control purposes.

The strategy implementation process, of which strategic control is a part, essentially entails bringing about change and innovation. In the next chapter, we give special attention to the critical issues that are involved in managing change and innovation processes in organizations.

CHAPTER SUMMARY

Strategic management is a process through which managers formulate and implement strategies geared to optimizing strategic goal achievement. One reason for the importance of the process is that it helps organizations identify and develop a competitive advantage, a significant edge over the competition in dealing with competitive forces. Many organizations develop strategies at three different levels: corporate, business, and functional. Corporate-level strategy addresses what businesses the organization will operate, how the strategies of those businesses will be coordinated to strengthen the organization's competitive position, and how resources will be allocated among the businesses. Business-level strategy concentrates on the best means of competing within a particular business while also supporting the corporate-level strategy. Functional-level strategy focuses on action plans for managing a particular functional area within a business in a way that supports the business-level strategy.

The part of the strategic management process that includes identifying the mission and strategic goals, conducting competitive analysis, and developing specific strategies is often referred to as strategy formulation. The part of the strategic management process that focuses on carrying out strategic plans and maintaining control over how those plans are carried out is known as strategy implementation. The three major strategic management modes, which address the issue of who has the major influence in the strategic management process and how the process is conducted, are entrepreneurial, adaptive, and planning. Each mode can have a positive

influence on innovation, depending on how it is used.

Before attempting to devise an effective strategy, managers need to make an assessment of both the environmental and the organizational factors that influence an organization's ability to compete effectively. One general method is SWOT analysis, which involves assessing organizational strengths (S) and weaknesses (W), as well as environmental opportunities (O) and threats (T). Porter's five competitive forces model helps analyze the nature and intensity of competition in a given industry in terms of five major forces: rivalry, bargaining power of customers, bargaining power of suppliers, threat of new entrants, and threat of substitute products or services. A common aid in assessing internal organizational strengths and weaknesses is the functional audit.

Corporate strategy development generally involves selecting a grand strategy and using portfolio strategy approaches to determine the various businesses that will make up the organization. The three basic types of grand strategies are growth (which includes concentration, vertical integration, and diversification), stability, and defensive (which includes harvest, turnaround, divestiture, bankruptcy, and liquidation). Three of the most frequently used portfolio approaches are the BCG growth-share matrix, the GE business screen, and the product/market evolution matrix.

At the business level, use of Porter's competitive strategies, which include cost leadership, differentiation, and focus strategies, constitutes the best-known approach. Functional-level strategies support the basic thrust of strategy at the business level and help specify major ways that functional areas can be used to bolster the business-level strategy.

In carrying out strategic plans during strategy implementation, managers need to consider major internal aspects of the organization that may need to be synchronized. Such aspects include technology, human resources, reward systems, decision processes, and structure. Strategy implementation also includes maintaining strategic control; this involves monitoring critical environmental factors that could affect the viability of strategic plans, assessing the effects of organizational strategic actions, and ensuring that strategic plans are implemented as intended.

MANAGERIAL TERMINOLOGY

acquisition (204)
adaptive mode (194)
bankruptcy (205)
BCG growth-share matrix (206)
business-level strategy (193)
competitive advantage (191)
concentration (201)
corporate-level strategy (192)
cost leadership strategy (211)

defensive strategies (204)
differentiation strategy (213)
distinctive competence (200)
diversification (203)
divestiture (205)
entrepreneurial mode (194)
five competitive forces model (196)
focus strategy (213)
functional audit (200)

functional-level strategy (193)
GE business screen (208)
grand strategy (201)
growth strategies (201)
harvest (205)
liquidation (205)
merger (204)
planning mode (195)
portfolio strategy approach (205)
product/market evolution matrix (210)

stability strategy (204)
strategic business unit (SBU) (193)
strategic management (190)
strategies (190)
strategy formulation (190)
strategy implementation (190)
SWOT analysis (196)
turnaround (205)
vertical integration (201)

QUESTIONS FOR DISCUSSION AND REVIEW

1. Explain the concept of strategic management and the notion of competitive advantage. Identify an organization that you think has a competitive advantage in its industry, and describe the nature of the competitive advantage.

2. Outline the major components of the strategic management process. Explain why engaging in strategic management is likely to be beneficial for an organization.

3. Distinguish among the three major modes of strategy formulation. Explain how each can be used to promote innovation.

4. Explain SWOT analysis. Conduct a brief SWOT analysis of your college or university by developing two items for each of the four SWOT categories.

5. Outline Porter's five competitive forces model. Use the model to assess the nature and intensity of competition in an industry with which you are familiar.

6. Describe the three major generic strategies available at the corporate level, and explain the subcategories within each. For each generic strategy, give

an example of an organization that appears to be pursuing that particular strategy.

7. Contrast the three major approaches to portfolio strategy at the corporate level. If you were on the strategic planning staff of a major company with 35 different businesses, which approach would you recommend and why?

8. Describe Porter's competitive strategies for the business level. Assess the competitive strategy of an organization with which you are familiar, and explain its usefulness in dealing with Porter's five competitive forces.

9. Explain the role of strategies at the functional level. Describe the connection between functional strategies and distinctive competence. What distinctive competencies exist at Baxters of Speyside?

10. Outline the process of strategy implementation. Which corporate-level generic strategy do you believe is being pursued by your college or university? Evaluate the effectiveness of strategy implementation at your college or university.

DISCUSSION QUESTIONS FOR CHAPTER OPENING CASE

1. What type of grand strategy does the Walt Disney Company appear to be pursuing? Cite evidence to support your conclusion.
2. Use Porter's five competitive forces model to analyze the competitive situation facing the Walt Disney Company.
3. Which of Porter's competitive strategies best charac-terizes the strategy being used by the various Disney businesses, such as the theme parks and resorts, consumer-products, and filmed entertainment divisions? Assess the appropriateness of the strategy. To what extent would each of Porter's competitive strategies be appropriate for each of the divisions?

MANAGEMENT EXERCISE: DEVELOPING A STRATEGY FOR PMB

You have been an extremely successful entrepreneur. Your Pedal More Bicycle (PMB) Company has more than doubled its sales each year for the past 10 years. PMB manufactures various types of bicycles, including racing and mountain bikes. PMB also makes accessories, such as seat covers, travel packs, and reflectors, and does a brisk business in bicycle parts. Your company has been successful by offering better quality and more innovative designs and features than can be obtained from competitors. Last year, your firm went public and was an instant hit on the market, making the controlling interest that you retained worth a great deal of money. PMB still has considerable growth potential. Nevertheless, you are now ready to take on new challenges. PMB has a sound reputation, which will be an asset if you want to borrow money to expand your business. You are aware of several current business opportunities:

1. The Winston Roller Bearing Company, a manufacturer of fabricated steel products and roller bearings, can be purchased for a fair price. The company is currently family-owned.
2. The Roxborough Leather Company, which produces leather goods for automobiles and shoes, can be acquired or leased on a long-term basis.
3. A Harley-Davidson motorcycle sales franchise is available in your area.
4. A very good location for an auto parts outlet is going to be available within the next year. The information you have at this time indicates that an auto parts outlet would be received very well in the area.
5. A small chain of three retail bicycle outlets will soon be offered for sale because the owners want to move back to their home town, about 800 miles away, in order to be closer to their families. The outlets have done reasonably well, but improvements could be made that would probably increase sales dramatically.
6. The XYZ computer outlet, a retailer of home computers and software, is looking for a buyer. The current owners, who have been very successful, want to retire and move to the family farm in southern California.

You believe that sufficient funds could be raised to acquire two of these businesses. However, there are probably other considerations. Assume that PMB has strong manufacturing and marketing capabilities and no glaring internal weaknesses relative to competitors in the bicycle business. Develop a grand strategy for PMB, and use a portfolio strategy approach to analyze the various business alternatives. Use Porter's generic strategies to choose a strategy for each business that you select. Be prepared to explain the reasoning behind your choices.

CRAY RESEARCH, INC., FACES STIFF COMPETITION

In the field of supercomputers, one name stands out: Cray. The company, Cray Research, Inc., was founded by Seymour Cray in 1972 to build the world's fastest computers. Seymour Cray had previously worked for Sperry-Univac and then for Control Data, in each case designing computers that were, at the time, the world's most powerful. He ultimately left Control Data to start his own company because he believed that Control Data had lost its focus on designing fast computers for the scientific community. When Cray Research finally produced its first computer in 1976, it was 10 times faster than the most powerful computer that Seymour Cray had designed for Control Data. Since that time, the scientist has continued to produce computers that are so much faster than the computers available from most vendors that they form a separate category called supercomputers.

When Cray Research began, the founders estimated that there was a world market for about 80 to 100 of the ultraspeed computers, which today can cost as much as $25 million each. Since then, the market has grown to $1 billion in sales and leases as more potential uses for supercomputers have emerged. About 45 percent of Cray's revenue comes from sales to U.S. government agencies, and a significant portion is based on supplying computers to government-supported universities. Increasingly, businesses are using supercomputers, although sales to businesses are more susceptible to downturns in the economy. Supercomputers are now used for such business applications as analyzing billions of pieces of data to determine which stocks to buy and sell on the stock market, allowing automakers to assess how new car designs will fare on the road without building expensive prototypes, and testing supersonic aircraft designs to determine how aircraft will perform at speeds that are difficult to simulate even with the use of elaborate wind tunnels. Cray's chairman, John A. Rollwagen, says that the market is "just way beyond anything we ever thought about. And it's a very profitable business, so it attracts flies."

Indeed, the growing market for supercomputers has brought competitors who would like to overtake the premier firm. For example, three giant Japanese companies, NEC, Hitachi, and Fujitsu, have already entered the field with supercomputers that are technologically about 2 years behind those available from Cray. Each of the Japanese companies is spending an estimated $100 million on developing new generations of supercomputers that will be available in the 1990s. Because the three companies earn profits from diverse product lines, they can use profits from those other businesses to fund the long-term development of supercomputers. In contrast, Cray must use profits from its computers and funds from investors to fuel its extensive R&D efforts. Cray invests about 15 percent of its revenues in R&D, a figure that is high even for high-technology companies. About half the R&D funds are channeled into creating software; this is a Cray strength compared to the policies of competitors.

In the United States, ETA Systems, Inc., a subsidiary of the Control Data Corporation, gave up its quest to become a significant player in the supercomputer market in 1989, after sustaining continuing

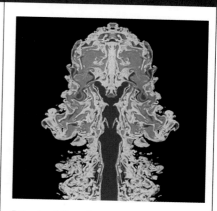

This simulation of two gases colliding with great force is made possible by the Cray X-MP, a supercomputer using multiple processors that enable the machine to work on many parts of a problem at the same time and at lightning speed. Cray Research, Inc., one of the first companies to develop the supercomputer, still dominates the world market. But the ever-increasing uses for the machines, ranging from weather forecasting to geological exploration to missile guidance, have attracted other entries into the market. Cray has been forced to develop new competitive strategies, including formation of a separate company to develop an advanced high speed supercomputer and entry into the low end of the market with mini-supercomputers.

losses. Most industry analysts say that ETA built good machines but could not furnish software comparable to the more than 500 programs available for Cray supercomputers. At the same time, Supercomputer Systems, Inc., of Eau Claire, Wisconsin, looms as a potential competitor. The company was founded by Steve Chen, an eminent computer designer, who left Cray in 1987 after Cray Research canceled his computer project. The project was aimed at developing a computer 100 times faster than existing supercomputers. Revised estimates for the project, which was originally expected to be completed in the early 1990s, indicated that it would take about twice as long as expected and cost double the planned $50 million. As a result, Cray Research believed that the risks were too great to continue the project. Chen's new company soon received financial backing from IBM, which had previously stayed out of the supercomputer realm. Its first products are scheduled to appear in the early 1990s, much earlier than the original Cray estimates.

In 1989, faced with another major decision about which projects to fund, Cray Research created a separate company, called the Cray Computer Corporation, to support a supercomputer design effort headed by Seymour Cray. Slower-than-expected sales, due to a sluggish economy and delayed orders from government agencies, had forced Cray Research to make a choice between two rival projects. One project was the C-90 machine under development by the group that had been working with Steve Chen before he left the company. The C-90, expected to be completed in the early 1990s, is based on known technology and is compatible with a popular Y-MP line that the company began selling in 1988. The other project was the innovative Cray 3 machine being developed by a group working with Seymour Cray. The Cray 3 is based on a new technology involving gallium-arsenide semiconductors. The new semiconductors are difficult to work with but have the potential of being significantly faster at handling data than are the silicon chips that are now in use. Thus knowledge gained from pursuing the new technology could provide a competitive advantage in producing future generations of supercomputers. Nevertheless, top management at Cray Research believed that the Cray 3 was too experimental and too different from the company's existing products to retain it over the C-90 project.

As a separate company, the Cray 3 project could attract additional funding without adversely affecting the balance sheet of Cray Research itself. Rollwagen says that the new company, in which Cray Research has a stake, was formed in order to avoid the internal conflict that would have ensued at Cray Research if the project headed by Seymour Cray had been discontinued in favor of the C-90 project. "A traditional company would have chosen just one design and shut down the other project," he says. Yet, when Cray Research announced that Seymour Cray was leaving in May 1989, the company's stock dropped 6 points.

On the international scene, U.S. trade negotiators have vigorously protested the exclusion of Cray's computers from Japanese government laboratories. They point out that only about 10 percent of the more than 100 supercomputers installed in Japan are Crays.

Meanwhile, the low end of Cray Research's market has been invaded by rivals, particularly Convex Computer, based in Richardson, Texas. The Convex minisupercomputers, as they are sometimes called, use simpler technology to perform calculations at about one-quarter of the speed of supercomputers, and they sell for about one-tenth of the price. When Northwest Airlines, Inc., recently needed a computer for crew and maintenance scheduling, it purchased a Convex computer. "The Cray was faster than Convex, but the cost was prohibitive," says Elroy Olson, Northwest's director of crew utilization. In an apparent move to keep other companies from seriously invading the supercomputer market, Cray recently announced its own low-end entry. "We've always defined the high end, but nobody's defined the low end," Rollwagen says. "But we can do it now with our technology."[92]

QUESTIONS FOR CHAPTER CONCLUDING CASE

1. Using SWOT analysis, how would you characterize the competitive situation facing Cray Research?

2. Which of Porter's competitive strategies best matches the strategy being used by Cray Research?

3. What major alterations in distinctive competence have occurred at Cray? How might these changes affect the firm's competitive advantage?

CHAPTER SEVEN

MANAGING INNOVATION AND CHANGE

CHAPTER OUTLINE

The Nature of Change and Innovation
Distinguishing between Change and Innovation
Forces for Change and Innovation

Organizational Life Cycles
Four Life-Cycle Stages
Organizational Termination

Promoting Innovation: The Change and Innovation Process
A Six-Step Model
Managing Resistance to Change
Intrapreneurship

Key Organizational Change Components
Structural Components
Technological Components
Human Resources Components
Cultural Components
Interrelationship among Components

Organizational Development
Diagnosis
Intervention
Evaluation

LEARNING OBJECTIVES

After studying this chapter, you should be able to:

■ Distinguish change from innovation and identify the major forces for change and innovation.

■ Enumerate the four life-cycle stages of organizations and discuss organizational revitalization and termination.

■ Explain the six-step model of the change and innovation process.

■ Indicate why employees resist change.

■ Explain how to overcome resistance to change, including the use of force-field analysis.

■ Describe the common characteristics of intrapreneurs and the major factors that induce them to pursue new ideas within existing organizations.

■ Outline the key organizational components that usually must be altered in the process of implementing major changes and innovations.

■ Explain the meaning of organizational development, the major steps involved, and the major techniques used in interventions.

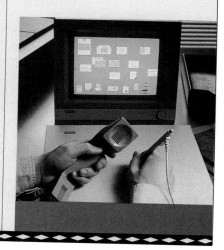

MERCK PRODUCES BIOTECH STARS

Many companies place pictures of their founders and past top managers in reception areas and corridors. But the stars at the Rahway, New Jersey, headquarters of Merck & Company are molecules. Microscope photographs of molecules, representing the firm's best-selling drugs, line office corridors and provide a visible manifestation of what counts at Merck. Sales from these famous drugs provide the funds for the company's high-powered research efforts aimed at discovering even more molecules of star-studded quality. Lately, a stellar cast of new molecules has been the envy of the biotechnology industry.

The onslaught of innovative prescription drugs from Merck's labs is unusual in an industry that produces important new drugs about as often as the Navy launches new aircraft carriers. Recently, Merck introduced five innovative drugs within a 12-month period: treatments for hypertension, ulcers, and urinary tract infections, a powerful multipurpose antibiotic, and a genetically engineered hepatitis B vaccine. Other starlets under development include a widely praised family of compounds that lower cholesterol in the blood.

A large part of the company's surging success can be traced to the management efforts of its chief executive, P. Roy Vagelos, a 57-year-old physician and biochemist. Since taking charge of Merck's research labs in 1976, he has led the company to a front position in the mushrooming biotechnology field. Indicative of its recent preeminence, Merck has appeared frequently on *Fortune*'s list of America's most admired companies.

The son of Greek immigrants, Vagelos grew up six blocks from Merck's headquarters. As a boy, he worked in his family's luncheonette, which was frequented by Merck personnel. Although these customers helped inspire him to choose a career in medicine, he was not thinking of working for a drug company. Instead, after working his way through the University of Pennsylvania and Columbia's medical school, he landed prestigious research jobs. He was a senior surgeon at the National Institutes of Health and later headed the biochemistry department at Washington University in St. Louis. His career path changed when Merck offered the local kid a job that he found difficult to refuse: senior vice president in the research division.

Although much had changed in his hometown and the family luncheonette was gone by the time Vagelos returned to Rahway, the way in which chemists conducted research had remained pretty much the same. Lab technicians developed thousands of different compounds and then tested them for promising medical developments. It was a time-consuming, trial-and-error approach that was typical of the industry. Unfortunately, this painstaking process of discovery often resulted in long periods of time when no new drugs were forthcoming. When Vagelos arrived, Merck had been experiencing a particularly long drought in the production of new drugs, and the drug giant's reputation was sinking. It was up to Vagelos to change the situation.

Demonstrating both his aggressive determination and calm bedside manner, Vagelos outlined a bold new approach to developing innovative drugs. He saw unique opportunities for drug research in new discoveries in medical science. He argued that the best path to drug innovations was studying how diseases affect the body's chemistry. On the basis of his vision, he persuaded researchers to begin studying the biochemical reactions that a disease triggers and then to develop a chemical that could arrest these reactions.

As researchers adopted the new approach, Merck supported them by annually pouring hundreds of millions of dollars into research. The company also spent heavily to build plant capacity for drugs under development. Increasing its commitment to innovative research still further, Merck sold its consumer-products business, which marketed over-the-counter items such as Sucrets throat lozenges and Calgon bubble bath.

Meanwhile, Merck worked harder than ever to recruit and retain research scientists working at the leading edge in such areas as biochemistry, neurology, immunology, and molecular biology. They were attracted not only by the high pay but also by the lavishly equipped facilities, which some likened to "a college campus in heaven." Merck scientists are encouraged to publish papers, and about 450 of their papers appear each year in scientific journals. At the same time, Merck has put together the largest and most intensively trained sales force in the industry, right down to its representatives' portable lap-top computers full of summaries of articles with the latest research on Merck drugs.

It took some time to put together all the pieces necessary for Merck's change in direction. Even in the early 1980s, Wall Street analysts claimed that Merck was throwing all its money down a deep, black hole. By the time Vagelos become CEO in 1985, however, drug innovations were pouring out of Merck's labs, and they have continued to do so. Recently, Merck has hired an additional 800 sales-people to help handle the large number of new drugs that have been released within the last 3 years or so. Merck's drug stars have been shining brightly.[1]

Imagine how excited Vagelos must have felt upon taking over the research helm at a major company that had featured so prominently in his youth. Yet he faced a severe challenge, because Merck was not doing very well at that point. Fortunately, Vagelos recognized the importance of managing the process of change and innovation. As management consultant Peter Drucker has pointed out, innovation does not just occur automatically. Instead, requirements for innovation and change must be an integral part of the planning process. Only then will there be a common understanding throughout the organization that innovation and change are necessary both for organizational survival and for individual job security and success. Vagelos's ability to incorporate the need for innovation and change into Merck's strategic management process was a key factor in his success as senior vice president in charge of research and his later selection as chief executive officer.[2]

In this chapter, we consider the nature of change and innovation, including major forces that pressure organizations to alter their ways. We examine how organizational life cycles affect the need for the management of change and innovation. We also consider the process that is involved in bringing about change and innovation, as well as examine why people resist change and how to overcome that resistance. We then outline the key organizational components that can be used to help implement change, and we explore an approach to long-term organizational change called organizational development.

"What's more exciting than trying to do something that's never been done before?" asks Merck & Co. CEO P. Roy Vagelos. This innovative spirit is a key to the success of the New Jersey pharmaceutical firm. Vagelos plows 11 percent of Merck revenues into research and development and fosters competition in the laboratory in order to come up with new wonder drugs. Many of these are still in the developing and testing stages, but those that have reached the market have produced high revenues for Merck.

THE NATURE OF CHANGE AND INNOVATION

The fierce domestic and foreign competition during the past decade has brought about a new emphasis on innovation and change in organizations. General Electric's Major Appliance Business Group discovered the hazards of failing to innovate when Whirlpool quietly introduced a number of new features that virtually wiped out GE's lead in side-by-side refrigerator-freezers. The GE appliance had remained essentially unchanged for almost 15 years.[3] Similarly, although the videocassette recorder was an American invention, originally conceived by Ampex and RCA in the 1960s, U.S. manufacturers failed to persist in developing the technology into a successful product. As a result, Japanese manufacturers succeeded in monopolizing the entire U.S. market for VCRs.[4] Events like these have caused managers to become increasingly interested in issues of change and innovation. In this section, we provide a closer look at change and innovation, and we briefly consider the major forces that exert pressure on organizations to change and innovate.

Distinguishing between Change and Innovation

Change Any alteration of the status quo

Innovation A new idea applied to initiating or improving a process, product, or service

In considering more closely the concepts of change and innovation, it is useful to distinguish between the two terms. **Change** refers to any alteration of the status quo, whereas innovation is a more specialized kind of change. **Innovation** is a new idea applied to initiating or improving a process, product, or service.[5] All innovations imply change; but not all changes are innovations, since changes may not involve new ideas or lead to significant improvements. For example, a recent Illinois Supreme Court ruling involving asbestos removal in Chicago schools has raised the specter of property-damage liabilities for major asbestos manufacturers, such as W. R. Grace, Union Carbide, and GAF. The ruling forced the asbestos makers to make a change by expanding their legal defenses.[6] This situation required an alteration of the status quo, but not one that would generally be considered an innovation. In fact, the problems resulting from the court ruling illustrate that changes not only may fail to result in improvements but can cause significant difficulties as well.

In contrast, the McCord gasket division of J. P. Industries, Inc., based in Ann Arbor, Michigan, has recently acquired computer-controlled machine tools. The use of the tools has resulted in major improvements in the work processes of the division. In the McCord case, the application of the computer-controlled machines to the gasket-making process represents a significant innovation aimed at moving ahead of the competition technologically.[7] In other situations, enhancements may have less importance. As long as an idea for bringing about an improvement is perceived as new by the individuals involved, it generally is considered to be an innovation even though outside observers may view it as an imitation of something already existing elsewhere.[8] Of course, organizations must exercise care that in adapting ideas they do not engage in illegal borrowings, such as violations of copyright laws or infringements of patents held by others.

A team of 100 employees of Japan's Matsushita Electric Industrial Company spent 8 years to produce this improved and less costly glass lens, used in compact disk players and related products. The lens is an example of how a small, incremental change can greatly expand market share for a product.

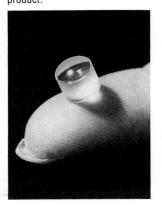

Innovations in organizations can range from radical new breakthroughs (such as laser technology) to small, incremental improvements (such as an improved paper tray on a computer printer). Although radical advances are important to many organizations, incremental improvements also can be advantageous.[9] Japanese companies, in particular, have become known for their ability to enhance products and services through a variety of small, incremental improvements. For example, at the Japan-based Matsushita Electric Industrial Company a team of 100 technicians, Ph.D scientists, and factory engineers persisted for 8 years before developing an improved glass lens for use in projection televisions and several laser-based products, such as videodisc systems and compact disc players. Furthermore, the new lenses can be made for 90 percent less than the cost of existing lenses. Thus a relatively modest goal—improving a component in successful products—led to a rapidly expanding market share for the Matsushita lens, particularly for use in compact disc players.[10]

As management researcher Rosabeth Moss Kanter, who has studied innovation in a number of different organizations, points out, the innovation process encompasses a distinctive combination of characteristics. For one thing, innovation involves considerable *uncertainty*, since progress and successful outcomes may be difficult to predict. For another, the process tends to be *knowledge-intensive* in the sense that those close to the development of the innovation may possess most of the knowledge about the situation, at least during the development stages. As a result, innovation efforts can be particularly vulnerable to employee turnover. Still another characteristic is that the innovation process often is *controversial*, because resources aimed at a particular innovation effort could presumably be used to pursue alternative courses of action. Finally, the innovation process often *crosses organizational boundaries*, because development and implementation frequently involve more than one unit, increasing the complexity of the effort.

Hence there is a need for managers not only to understand the major aspects of change but also to plan for the special needs of the innovation process. Throughout this chapter, we use the term "change" to connote any type of alteration in the status quo, including an innovation, in an organization. We use the term "innovation" in the more narrow sense of a new idea associated with an improvement. At times, we may use both terms to highlight the particular importance of the discussion for both change and innovation.

Forces for Change and Innovation

A variety of forces influence change and innovation in organizations. Some of these forces stem from external factors, while others arise from factors that are mainly internal to organizations.

External Forces. External forces on organizations develop in the external environment, which is made up of both the general, or mega-environment, and the task environment (see Chapter 3). The mega-environment reflects broad social conditions and trends related to technological, economic, political, sociocultural, and international environmental elements. Since such trends tend to be beyond the ability of a single organization to influence, organizations typically must attempt to adapt to such changes. On the other hand, organizations may have at least some prospects for affecting task environments, which typically include customers, competitors, suppliers, labor supply, and government agencies. The task environment depends largely on the specific products and services that an organization decides to offer and on the locations where it chooses to conduct its business.

For example, many restaurants have been experiencing declines in business due largely to factors in the mega-environment, such as technological advances (microwave ovens and VCRs) and sociocultural developments (baby-boomers who now have children)—factors that have made it more convenient and economical to eat at home.[11] To cope with such trends, Marty's Wine and Food Emporium in the Oak Lawn section of Dallas has located its take-out operation near major office buildings, allowing it to do a booming lunch business. Yet the emporium also has managed to attract a sizable evening business by providing microwaveable fare such as spinach-stuffed chicken or beef tenderloin that workers can purchase to take home for dinner.[12] Thus, while some external forces may pressure organizations to change in ways that are less than desirable, such forces often open up opportunities for applications of innovative ideas.

Internal Forces. Internal forces for change and innovation in organizations de-

How does a restaurant adapt to changes in eating habits that keep more and more people at home? By offering take-out and take-home specialties. Marty's Food and Wine Emporium in Dallas, Texas, caters to the singles and working couples who pick up their microwavable dinners on the way home from the office. While forced to adapt to changes in the mega-environment, Marty's was also able to shape the behavior of one aspect of its task environment—its customers.

velop from a variety of sources. Some of these forces include alterations of strategies and plans, ethical difficulties that arise because of employee behaviors, decisions that require changes and innovations, organizational culture shifts, reorganizations, technological advances, and leadership changes. For instance, after acquiring the Zayre Corporation discount chain in 1988, Peter B. Hollis, president and CEO of Ames Department Stores, Inc., quickly orchestrated a number of internal changes geared to improving the profitability of the chain. Changes included cutting the Zayre's administrative staff by half, putting the Ames name on the stores, and allocating $100 million for the major remodeling of stores to give them wider aisles and more space for higher-margin products.[13] Of course, as in the Ames situation, many internal changes have origins in factors that can be traced ultimately to the environment. Some of the needs for internal change that confront organizations are predictable to some extent because organizations tend to follow certain life cycles.

ORGANIZATIONAL LIFE CYCLES

Life cycles Predictable stages of development

Organizational termination The process of ceasing to exist as an identifiable organization

One way of viewing the need for continual management of innovation and change is to recognize that organizations have **life cycles,** or predictable stages of development. The evolution through each stage requires certain changes in order for organizations to survive and grow. Otherwise, **organizational termination,** the process of ceasing to exist as an identifiable organization, may occur. Organizational terminations are common events. Many new businesses fail within their first 5 years. If you think about your local shopping center or business district, you can probably name several businesses that you have seen get started but then not survive.

Four Life-Cycle Stages

Although management scholars differ somewhat on the precise number of stages in organizational life cycles and the specific details of each stage, general patterns are emerging. Organizations tend to evolve through four major stages of development.[14] The four stages and their common characteristics are presented in Table 7-1. Each of these stages requires that changes be made in the

Table 7-1   Characteristics Associated with the Four Life-Cycle Stages

Characteristics	Entrepreneurial Stage	Collectivity Stage	Formalization and Control Stage	Elaboration of Structure Stage
Structure	Little or none	Informal	Functional; centralization	Self-contained; decentralization
Focus	Survival; seeking resources	Growth	Efficiency; coordination	Restructuring
Innovation	Invention	Enhancement	Implementation	Renewal
Planning	Little or none	Short range	Long range	Long range; opportunistic
Commitment	Individual sense	Group sense	Complacency	Recommitment
Managers	Entrepreneurs	Entrepreneurs and early joiners	Professional managers	Professional managers and orchestrators

Source: Based on Larry E. Greiner, "Evolution and Revolution as Organizations Grow," *Harvard Business Review,* July–August 1972, pp. 37–46; and Robert E. Quinn and Kim Cameron, "Organizational Life Cycles and Shifting Criteria of Effectiveness: Some Preliminary Evidence," *Management Science,* vol. 29, 1983, pp. 33–51.

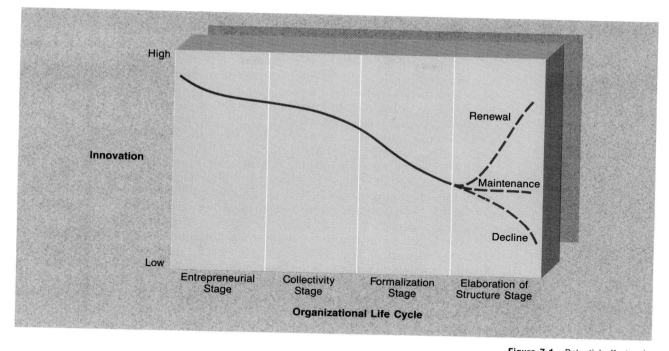

Figure 7-1 Potential effects of the four life-cycle stages on innovation.

methods of operating if the organization is to survive and prosper. Paradoxically, unless managers take steps to plan for and encourage innovation, these same changes may inhibit the ability of the organization to make further innovations. The potential effects of the four life cycle stages on innovation are shown in Figure 7-1.

Entrepreneurial Stage. At the *entrepreneurial stage,* there is usually an invention or major innovation around which a new organization is created. Frequently, the organization is formed on the basis of the initiative of a single individual and is a one-person show, although a few others may be involved initially as well. The entrepreneur is excited about the new idea, and the creative juices are flowing. Since the organization is still in its infancy, there is little planning and coordination. The prime inventor, or entrepreneur, makes the decisions. Work progresses, but the continuing need for resources eventually causes a crisis. At this point, the entrepreneurial enterprise usually either fails or moves to the next stage.

For example, Howard Head, a metals expert, ski enthusiast, and inventor of the famous Head skis, persisted for more than 3 years in his efforts to develop a metal ski to replace wooden ones. His various attempts at metal skis met with acute skepticism from ski pros, and he frequently returned from the ski slopes with broken and twisted skis. Having started his company with only $8000, his fledgling company began to run out of money and he faced a resource crisis. The company was saved by an influx of $60,000 from investors in return for 40 percent ownership of his company. It was still several years before Head was able to perfect his design. The resulting product was so good that the skis were called "cheaters."[15] The need to involve others as investors and helpers, however, had taken the Head company to the next stage of development.

Collectivity Stage. At the *collectivity stage,* the entrepreneur is joined by a few dedicated others who believe in the idea. The organization is in its youth. There are strong feelings of group identification and a real sense of mission. Members of the organization put in many long hours and demonstrate a high level of commitment. The structure and communication patterns are informal; major decisions may involve the group. Innovation continues to be relatively high. Members frequently work for comparatively low pay and often receive company stock that is relatively worthless at that point in time, but the vision is the grander days to come. A number of long-term employees at Digital Equipment Corporation, who received stock early in the company's development, are now millionaires because of a rise in the stock value from $22 in 1965 to more than $2800 today, adjusted for splits.[16]

The crisis at this stage usually occurs when growth accelerates and the informal management systems characteristic of this stage provide inadequate leadership direction and control. Often the entrepreneurs who began the organization are not particularly well suited in either temperament or ability for managing a larger organization, so they bring in a professional manager. For example, when Apple cofounder Steven Jobs lured John Sculley from Pepsi-Cola USA to serve as president of the computer maker, Apple was experiencing serious coordination difficulties that Jobs believed could be handled more effectively by a seasoned manager such as Sculley. Within 2 years, though, Jobs had resigned after Sculley stripped him of his job as executive vice president of the Macintosh division because of schedule delays and other problems involving Macintosh development.[17]

Formalization and Control Stage. At the *formalization and control stage,* the organization has reached the point where it has taken on a more formalized structure, with departments that usually are organized according to major specialized areas, such as finance, manufacturing, or marketing. Emphasis at this stage tends to shift toward efficiency and maintenance of market share. To help provide coordination, rules and procedures become more commonplace and there is greater centralization of control. With the organization reaching adulthood, this stage helps it consolidate its position, achieve better direction, and continue to grow.

As growth continues, eventually the organization becomes larger and more difficult to coordinate. Frequently, innovation is replaced by a more conservative stance that may unwittingly discourage risk taking and future innovation. During this stage, competitive challenges, technological change, and other factors may increase the information-processing needs of the hierarchy, making it slow to respond. A crisis occurs when members of the organization are hampered by the detrimental effects of red tape and centralized control. For example, after years of operating in a market in which it could not keep up with the demand, Levi Strauss, the jeans giant, found itself unable to react quickly to a slowdown in the jeans market and the move to more fashionable apparel. One former employee observed that the company had "enough staff and organization to run General Motors. It was a thin line, with everyone being a manager to everyone else."[18] At this point in the life cycle, an organization is ready for the next stage.

Elaboration-of-Structure Stage. At the *elaboration-of-structure stage,* managers begin to seek ways to streamline the excess bureaucratization that has cropped up at the formalization and control stage. Decision making is decentralized, often through the adoption of departments organized around specific products or services. This stage also frequently involves considerable emphasis on coordination among individuals at similar levels in different work units, often through temporary or ongoing groups formed to address interdepartmental issues. (We

Table 7-2   Dysfunctional Consequences of Organizational Stabilization and Decline

Consequences	Explanations
Curtailed innovation	No experimentation is conducted; risk aversion is prevalent, and skepticism exists about activities that are not related specifically to current major directions.
Scapegoating	Leaders are blamed for the pain and uncertainty.
Resistance to change	Conservatism and turf protection lead to rejection of new alternatives.
Turnover	The most competent leaders tend to leave first, causing leadership anemia.
Conflict	Competition and infighting for control predominate when resources are scarce.

Source: Adapted from Kim S. Cameron, David A. Whetten, and Myung U. Kim, "Organizational Dysfunctions of Decline," *Academy of Management Journal*, vol. 30, 1987, p. 128.

discuss these groups further in Chapters 10 and 16). In addition to the changes in organizational structure that are commonplace at this stage, managers often engage in considerable cost cutting and reemphasize promising strategic directions.

Essentially, the chief aim of efforts at the elaboration-of-structure stage is **revitalization,** the renewal of the innovative vigor of organizations.[19] For example, when Celanese began to experience competitive difficulties, managers and employees formed special groups to study where cost cuts could be made. One result was a dramatic reduction in the number of financial reports that operating managers were required to furnish to headquarters. A 15 percent cut in the R&D budget, however, got bad reviews from both employees and Wall Street because of fears that such cuts would slow down new technological innovations. Most of the R&D budget was soon restored, but with a new emphasis. Now more than 80 percent of the budget, compared with about 35 percent earlier, is spent on developing new products rather than improving existing ones.[20]

Revitalization The renewal of the innovative vigor of organizations

Not all organizations attempt or are successful at revitalization. Some organizations stabilize and manage to maintain themselves at least for some period of time. Others decline, despite revitalization efforts, and may eventually fail.[21] Unfortunately, organizations that stabilize over a significant period of time or decline to a serious degree are particularly susceptible to several major dysfunctions that make them more difficult to manage.[22] These dysfunctions are summarized in Table 7-2. Note in particular that innovation tends to be curtailed and that resistance to change becomes more pronounced, factors that make renewal and revitalization all the more difficult. The experience of Wang Laboratories, producer of word-processing and data-processing equipment, illustrates the organizational life cycle and the particular difficulties inherent in making the transition from the formalization and control stage to the elaboration-of-structure stage (see the following Case in Point discussion).

CASE IN POINT: Wang Fights to Revitalize

When Wang Laboratories experienced a rapid decline in profits in the mid-1980s, the usually reclusive Dr. An Wang, founder and chief executive of Wang Laboratories, a leading producer of word-processing and data-processing equipment,

Wang Laboratories, long a leading producer of word processing and data processing equipment, is now in the position of having to revitalize its organization. One of its strategies is to push new products. Shown above is the Freestyle/Light electronic desk, which allows personal computer users to create and annotate pages by typing, drawing, writing, or making voice comments (using the handset shown in the photo). (Freestyle is a trademark of Wang Laboratories, Inc.)

suddenly became very visible. He allocated a good portion of his time to traveling around the United States, visiting with customers and delivering inspirational speeches to the Wang sales staff. He spent the rest of his time at the company headquarters in Lowell, Massachusetts, working feverishly to reverse the company's sagging fortunes.

A native of Shanghai, Wang had been part of a group of young, talented men sent by Chiang Kai-shek to learn the technology of the West. After Wang received his doctorate from Harvard in 1948, he stayed in the United States because of the civil war taking place in China at that time. Working at Harvard's Computation Laboratory, he quickly invented a version of the magnetic core memory, an invention that produced a steady income until he sold the patent to IBM for $400,000 in 1956. With his wife, Lorraine, and a patent attorney, Wang started Wang Laboratories in 1951 above a store in Boston's South End. Support staff consisted of one part-time assistant. The company achieved its first major product success in 1964 when An Wang invented an electronic desktop calculator, the first that could compute logarithmic functions. It quickly became a mainstay for engineers, scientists, bankers, corporate financial officers, and others who needed to make complex calculations. Sales had risen to more than $39 million by 1972, but shortly thereafter sales declined abruptly. Competitors had begun to use semiconductors to make small, inexpensive calculators, causing Wang to retreat from the market that he had created.

Fortunately, Wang had continued his innovative efforts, and the company had begun producing word processors and small computers in 1971. Wang competed successfully against competitors such as IBM and the Digital Equipment Corporation by offering relatively low prices, a wide array of peripheral equipment, and programs tailored to customers' needs. Growth skyrocketed; within a decade, the small group of early employees of the company had expanded dramatically as Wang Laboratories became a $2 billion company.

Just as the future had begun to look particularly bright and Wang had withdrawn somewhat from active management of the company in the early 1980s, serious problems began to emerge with the sudden popularity of personal computers. Because they could be used for both word processing and computing, the PCs were more flexible than Wang products. As a result, Wang introduced 14 new products and promised delivery in 8 months, but the company was a year late in producing the products, which ultimately fell far short of customer needs. The situation made some customers wary of further Wang purchases. Generally, the company experienced difficulty in moving quickly enough in a rapidly changing market.

Meanwhile, both the current president and his immediate successor left the company, mainly because their career paths were blocked by Wang's plan to have his eldest son succeed him as chairman. The son, Fred Wang, who had joined the company in 1972, had a bachelor's degree in mathematics from Brown University. Detractors argued that he did not have his father's scientific credentials and that he was difficult to please. Perceptions improved, however, when Fred took over as president in 1987, and An Wang again reduced his active participation in managing the company. Unfortunately, after a slight improvement in profit levels, the company reported a $424.3 million loss in 1989, prompting Fred Wang's resignation and causing serious financial difficulties for the company. An Wang then began working half-time as chairman and chief executive officer while recovering from surgery for cancer of the esophagus. The company also hired an outsider, Richard W. Miller, who was a veteran of the RCA Corporation and General Electric but who had little experience in the computer field, as president and chief operating officer. Revitalization became even more crucial to Wang's ability to remain an independent company. When the senior Wang died of cancer in 1990, Miller assumed the posts of chairman and chief executive officer.[23] ▬▬▬▬▬

Organizational Termination

Although the problems at Wang probably will not put the company completely out of business, the 1980s have witnessed a large number of organizational terminations, situations in which organizations run into difficulties and cease to exist as known entities. There are several important reasons why an organization may be terminated. One reason, frequently related to such factors as environmental changes, deficient management, and/or technological obsolescence, is bankruptcy. Under Chapter 11 of the Federal Bankruptcy Act, *bankruptcy* is a means whereby an organization that is unable to pay its debts can seek court protection from creditors and from certain contract obligations while the organization attempts to regain financial stability (see Chapter 6). A. H. Robins declared bankruptcy in order to stem liability in suits emanating from its ill-fated Dalkon Shield contraceptive device and still remain in business. However, managers subsequently found that it was cumbersome to operate in that status since it was necessary to obtain court permission for major expenditures and actions.[24] When organizations seek legal protection from creditors but continue to experience problems, their assets are usually eventually sold in order to settle debts with creditors. At that point, the organization goes out of business.

A second cause of organizational termination is *liquidation*, in which, for reasons usually associated with serious business difficulties and seemingly insurmountable obstacles, an entire organization is either sold or dissolved.[25] For instance, liquidation occurred when Rich's Shoe Store, the longest-operating retail establishment in downtown Washington, D.C., recently went out of business. After operating as a family business for four generations, the store found it could no longer survive the constant upheaval caused by downtown redevelopment and the competition from specialty shoe stores and large chains that import cheap shoes from abroad.[26]

Other reasons for organizational termination are mergers and acquisitions (see Chapter 6). A *merger* occurs when two or more organizations combine into one organization. For instance, when the Burroughs Corporation and the Sperry Corporation merged in 1986, they sorted through 31,000 suggestions from employees before choosing the new name "Unisys."[27] An *acquisition* is the purchase of all or part of one organization by another. (Sometimes the terms "acquisition" and "merger" are used interchangeably when an entire organization is sold to another.) Acquisitions and mergers can occur for reasons other than business difficulties, such as the desire to move into new markets, expand existing markets, or boost technological expertise. In some acquisition situations, the acquired organization may continue as an identifiable entity. This is particularly likely when the organization is being acquired because it has been successful. General Motors acquired its Electronic Data Systems unit to obtain both diversification and technological expertise; however, the unit was allowed to operate as an independent subsidiary. On the other hand, an organization that is experiencing difficulty is more likely to lose its prior identification and, in that sense, be terminated. For example, when the American Home Products Corporation acquired bankrupt A. H. Robins in 1989, the latter company ceased to exist as an identifiable entity.[28]

One form of acquisition, about which you have probably been reading in

Table 7-3 Recent Large Acquisitions in the United States

Transaction	Value (billions $)
Gulf by Standard Oil California (now Chevron)	13.3
Getty by Texaco	10.1
Chesebrough-Pond's by Unilever	3.1
Conoco by Du Pont	7.4
Marathon Oil by U.S. Steel (now USX)	6.5
RCA by General Electric	6.4
Superior Oil by Mobil	5.7
Shell by Royal Dutch–Shell	5.7
General Foods by Philip Morris	5.6
Southern Pacific by Santa Fe (now Santa Fe Southern Pacific)	5.2
Hughes Aircraft by General Motors	5.0
Signal by Allied (now Allied-Signal)	4.9
Sperry by Burroughs (now Unisys)	4.8
Connecticut General by INA (now Cigna)	4.3
Texasgulf by Aquitaine	4.2

Source: Based on *The Washington Post*, Mar. 27, 1987, p. F2, and *Business Week*, Jan. 15, 1990, p. 57.

Takeover The purchase of a controlling share of voting stock in a publicly traded company

the newspaper, is the **takeover,** the purchase of a controlling share of voting stock in a publicly traded company. Takeovers are considered hostile when the current management and board of directors do not wish to be taken over by the group attempting to purchase the stock; they are considered friendly when the organization is amenable to the takeover. Organizations are more likely to become takeover targets when their performance lags below potential, negatively affecting the price of their stock but making them attractive targets for acquisition. Table 7-3 lists some of the largest companies that have been acquired by other organizations during the 1980s.

Most frequently, organizations face termination because they have not been able to innovate and change fast enough to compete. Termination can occur at any stage in the life cycle. Therefore, managers need to do some thinking about where their organization currently fits in the life cycle. This analysis helps them determine the types of changes that may be necessary to move the organization to the next stage of development. Considering the organization life cycle also assists managers in assessing potential declines in innovation that often occur as the life cycle matures. On the basis of their diagnosis, managers may want to take additional steps to promote innovation. Therefore, at this point, it is useful to explore further how the process of change and innovation works.

PROMOTING INNOVATION: THE CHANGE AND INNOVATION PROCESS

Reactive change Change that occurs when one takes action in response to perceived problems, threats, or opportunities

The processes of change and innovation are similar, although innovation—a special type of change—tends to be more difficult because it moves beyond the more traditional changes and relies on incorporating significant new ideas. Managers are typically involved with two types of change. **Reactive change** occurs when one takes action in response to perceived problems, threats, or opportunities. Since one is reacting to events, there often is not sufficient time to analyze the situation carefully and prepare a well-conceived response. For example, Johnson & Johnson faced a crisis in 1982 when seven people died after taking

Extra-Strength Tylenol capsules laced with cyanide. (Additional details about the Tylenol situation are given in the opening case in Chapter 4.) The company moved quickly to recall 31 million bottles of the pain reliever at a cost of $100 million. Then, when its market share plummeted from 35.3 to 7 percent, J&J boosted advertising by more than 30 percent to $58.6 million. The company's subsequent regaining of all but a fraction of its former market share was termed "one of the greatest marketing feats in our industry" by one drugstore executive.[29] The Tylenol situation illustrates that it is not possible for managers to anticipate every problem that will arise and that sometimes managers are forced by events to react.

However, there are many situations in which it is possible to engage in **planned change,** which involves actions based on a carefully thought-out process for change that anticipates future difficulties, threats, and opportunities. For example, although everyone hoped that the Tylenol crisis was an isolated incident, J&J took steps to place the product in a tamper-resistant container. Furthermore, when the second Tylenol crisis hit in early 1986 (when a 23-year-old woman died after taking a cyanide-laced Tylenol capsule), it was clear that the company had done some planning in anticipation of a possible future threat. Chairman James E. Burke appeared on television almost immediately and announced that J&J was eliminating the use of the capsule in favor of a capsule-shaped tablet that he called a "caplet." He had with him an enlarged model of the caplet. The company offered to replace all capsules with the caplets, a move that cost $150 million. Furthermore, the decision to stop using the capsule cost the company millions of dollars. It was clear from the speed and forthrightness with which the company took such major steps that the managers had done considerable planning in anticipation of the potential threat and were ready with a carefully conceived course of action, including a plan for implementation.[30]

When managers habitually operate in a reactive mode, they dramatically increase their chances of making serious mistakes because they are continually making changes without proper planning. As a result, most effective managers engage in planned, or managed, change and innovation whenever possible.

> **Planned change** Change that involves actions based on a carefully thought-out process for change that anticipates future difficulties, threats, and opportunities

A Six-Step Model

When managers engage in planned innovation and change, they typically follow a process such as the one illustrated in Figure 7-2.[31] There are six basic steps in the process.

Perceiving an Opportunity or a Problem. The first step in the process is perceiving an opportunity or a problem. Noted management consultant Peter Drucker convincingly argues that one reason why managers are not more innovative is that there is a tendency to focus on immediate problems and to ignore opportunities. Yet organizations that want to maintain a competitive edge clearly need to look ahead to opportunities, as well as to solve current and anticipated difficulties or problems. Drucker offers several suggestions for increasing the focus on opportunities. He notes that management in most companies requires a report on operating performance each month. Typically, the first page lists areas in which performance is not going as well as expected. Drucker suggests the addition of a second "first page" that would list things that are going better than expected, calling attention to possible unexploited opportunities. Another of Drucker's ideas is holding meetings every 6 months or so in which three or four executives would report on entrepreneurial activities that have gone exceptionally well; included would be explanations of the practices others might adopt to

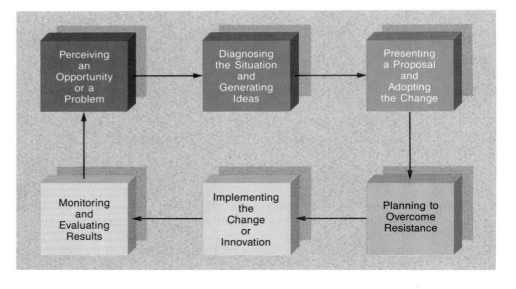

Figure 7-2 Model of planned innovation and change process. (Adapted from Richard L. Daft and Richard M. Steers, *Organizations: A Micro/Macro Approach*, Scott, Foresman, Glenview, Ill., 1986, p. 569.)

achieve similar successes. Finally, he suggests holding periodic sessions at which senior managers would ask junior managers to indicate areas in which they see opportunities for or threats to the organization and any new things they think should be done.[32]

Diagnosing the Situation and Generating Ideas. The second step in the process of planned innovation and change consists of diagnosing the situation and generating some new ideas. Without both these factors, it is very difficult to fix problems or take advantage of opportunities. Upon becoming CEO of Campbell Soup, Gordon McGovern studied the current position of the company and came to the conclusion that Campbell Soup was missing important opportunities related to the fact that consumers had become more health-conscious and sophisticated. Armed with this diagnosis, he encouraged new ideas targeted at this emerging consumer group. One eventual outcome was a reformulation of the Swanson's TV dinners line to incorporate such trendy dishes as fettuccine Alfredo; the change spurred new growth in the somewhat stagnant product line. While the company pursued new ideas in some areas, though, it paid insufficient attention to its mainstream soup line, allowing several Japanese and Korean companies to capture 9 percent of the U.S. soup market with inexpensive dry soups based on long, thin ramen noodles. Such missteps eventually led McGovern to resign.[33] Thus, in pursuing new ideas, it is important not to overlook the status of ongoing activities relative to the competition.

Presenting a Proposal and Adopting the Change. The third step is presenting a proposal and deciding to adopt the change. Unless managers work hard to establish the fact that innovation and change are important to the organization, most good ideas will be rejected when they are proposed. Large companies that are well known for their innovative ways, such as 3M and Hewlett-Packard, typically ask that managers and employees who are petitioning for money prepare a written business plan outlining how the new idea will be developed. The main purpose of this request is to make sure that the ideas are well thought out. However, employees in such companies do not need permission from above to use limited amounts of resources for initially exploring ideas.[34] At Merck, for example, scientist Donald J. Hupe spends 10 to 20 percent of his time working with the National Cancer Institute on potential anticancer agents, but he did not need to obtain official permission to do so.[35] In smaller companies, ideas are proposed more informally. When B. Thomas Golisano was a sales manager at Electronic Account Systems, Inc., a small computerized payroll-processing organization in Rochester, New York, that catered to larger companies, he recognized that there might be a market in going after business from smaller companies. He presented the idea to his bosses, but no one would listen. So he started his own company, Paychex, which is now the second-largest payroll-processing company in the United States. Says his former employer, "He was right and we were wrong."[36]

An important step in the process of promoting innovation is listening to proposals for promising new ideas. Not listening can be costly. When a computerized payroll processing company that catered to large organizations showed no interest in an employee's proposal to service small companies as well, the employee left to form his own company, Paychex, which has been very successful.

Planning to Overcome Resistance. The fourth step involves planning to overcome resistance in implementing the change. The fact that one group, even top management, decides to adopt a change does not mean that others will readily go along with it. Later in the chapter, we describe at some length the reasons why employees resist change and the means of overcoming such resistance, since such issues are critical to managing change and innovation effectively. Thus, even if a change is a popular one, a poorly planned implementation may end up scuttling the whole idea.

Implementing the Change or Innovation. The fifth step is actually implementing the change or innovation. This is the moment of truth when the change is put into operation. How smoothly this step goes depends on how well thought out the change was to begin with and how carefully the planning step was carried out. For example, the Kellogg Company, a leader in breakfast cereals, has not experienced the difficulties of many other large companies in implementing factory automation. One reason is that Kellogg carefully tests new equipment and production techniques in an experimental plant in London, Ontario. As a result, implementations of new innovations tend to run smoothly.[37]

Monitoring the Results. The sixth step in the innovation and change process is monitoring the results. It is foolhardy to implement a significant change without monitoring and evaluating what happens after the change has been implemented. For example, in order to make sure that its new automation systems are working properly, Kellogg monitors quality by sampling cereal at mathematically determined intervals.[38]

Successful innovations and changes usually follow these six basic steps. You might think about how these six steps could be used to revitalize a good company that has leveled off. A new chief executive officer at Pepperidge Farm faced exactly that situation (see the following Case in Point discussion).

CASE IN POINT:　Pepperidge Farm Freshens Up

When he took over as CEO of Pepperidge Farm, a subsidiary of the Campbell Soup Company, Richard Shea saw both difficulties and opportunities. The three previous CEOs had emphasized frozen foods, a market experiencing tremendous growth, but there was a significant problem. Unlike its competitors, Pepperidge Farm had missed the mark by failing to package frozen foods so that they could be used directly in a microwave oven. At the same time, the company

Herbert Tolmich (on the left) is the man behind the cookies that account for a third of Pepperidge Farm's sales. As manager of product development, Tolmich did the careful planning and testing that led to the production of the popular American Collection, lumpy cookies that look homemade and not cranked out of a machine. Pepperidge Farm keeps careful computerized records of inventory so stores will not run out of the product and the cookies will be delivered in close to 72 hours after baking.

had grown complacent about its biscuit and bread business. For example, Pepperidge sat it out during the "great cookie war" in which Procter & Gamble introduced the highly successful Duncan Hines cookies and other major competitors, such as Keebler, marketed competing products. Finally, Pepperidge introduced a *Star Wars* cookie, just as the *Star Wars* craze was ending. As a result, the cookie was a flop.

In assessing the situation, Shea and his managers decided that they needed some attractive new products with a quality emphasis befitting the Pepperidge Farm image. Their diagnosis also indicated, however, that to get good shelf space in supermarkets, Pepperidge had to be a low-cost manufacturer so that it could offer retailers prospects of high margins and, therefore, high profits. They also found that to compete effectively with cookie stores and other cookie companies, Pepperidge products had to get fresher. Finally, they concluded that they needed more advertising. Without careful diagnosis, Pepperidge might have designed new products doomed to failure because of high costs, low freshness, or insufficient advertising. Instead, armed with a good notion of what they wanted to accomplish, the managers began to generate ideas. The idea generation was aimed not only at creating new products but also at finding ways to lower costs and get products to customers in the freshest condition possible.

Among the proposals that were adopted were plans for a new line of lumpy, bumpy cookies—the American Collection—that were so chunky that manufacturing engineers had to design new production methods to get them to hold together. The cookies, in five variations, have broken all previous Pepperidge Farm sales records, becoming the fastest-growing and most popular products the company has ever introduced. Another popular new line, Distinctive Cookies, was patterned after the butter cookies with molded chocolate tops created by Delacre, a Belgian affiliate of Campbell Soup. Pepperidge also designed a computerized feedback system to obtain inventory information from the marketplace.

In considering the changes and making plans for implementation, Pepperidge managers studied all the reasons why they might not be able to accomplish what they wanted to and then planned how they would overcome each change-resistant element. Implementation included replacing 16 top executives and selling 4 plants. Because of the manager's efforts, many of the planned new products reached market shelves. In the battle for freshness, hundreds of the company's 2200 franchised drivers began using hand-held computers to record inventories on their routes and periodically relay the information by modem to Pepperidge computers. Advertising also was stepped up.

Pepperidge closely monitored these changes. For example, Pepperidge has claimed that it could not even keep up with the initial heavy demand for its lumpy, bumpy cookies. While the national oven-to-market average is 5 to 10 days for cookies and 5 days for bread, Pepperidge edged closer to its goal of 72 hours. Pepperidge has continued to work on changes and innovations, knowing that at least some of its competitors are certain to react.[39] ▆▆▆▆▆

Managing Resistance to Change

As mentioned earlier, one of the reasons why it takes concerted managerial planning and skill to bring about innovation and change is that people often resist change. Sometimes people resist change even when it appears to an observer or implementer of the change that the change is in the best interest of those affected. In this section, we consider why individuals resist change, and we examine ways of overcoming that resistance.

Why Individuals Resist Change. Why do people—including ourselves—sometimes resist change? Although there are a number of reasons why a given individual might feel resistant to a particular change, several major reasons stand out.[40]

One reason is *self-interest*. When people hear about a change, they have a natural tendency to ask, "How will this change affect me?" If an individual perceives the answer to be "adversely," there may be some effort made to resist the change. How much resistance is mounted will usually be a function of how strongly the individual feels his or her self-interests are affected. Sometimes things that might appear to be minor issues to one individual or group will seriously affect another person. For example, a change in office space that results in moving an individual's desk away from a window may be perceived by one person as a loss of status, causing resistance, while another person might see the same change as a move away from a draft and be pleased. Other times changes may be good for one part of an organization but somewhat detrimental to another section. This mixed situation can lead to overt and/or covert political struggles between the factions favoring and opposing the change. Citicorp lost a number of its top investment banking experts in Europe when it took steps to integrate its international commercial and investment banking businesses. The departing investment experts perceived the change as an undesirable intrusion on their turf.[41]

Another common reason for resisting change is *misunderstanding and lack of trust*. People frequently resist change when they misunderstand the nature of the change. In addition, low levels of trust between managers and employees are common in many organizations, contributing to the possibility that misunderstandings will occur. As you may have discovered in your own work experience, it is not always the employees who resist change. Efforts to involve employees in decision making about their work often are resisted by managers who mistrust employees and fear loss of power.[42]

Resistance also often results from *different assessments* of the virtues of the change. Differential assessment is a prime reason for lack of support for innovations. Because innovations involve new concepts, their value is not always obvious to others. Hence individuals may not see a change as useful and may even view it as detrimental to the organization. Of course, not every change is for the better. There are times when an impending change is actually a poor decision that fortunately is resisted by those who were supposed to implement it. In order to allow employees to appeal decisions that they feel miss the mark, IBM has long had a policy whereby any employee can appeal a supervisor's decision without fear of retaliation.

Finally, individuals differ in their ability to adjust to change, with some individuals having a *low tolerance for change*. As a result, they sometimes resist change because they fear that they will not be able to learn the new skills and behaviors necessitated by the change. In this case, individuals may even perceive that the change is a good one but still may have difficulty implementing the change. In addition, it is possible that individuals may see suggestions for changes as indirect criticisms of the status quo, for which they may feel responsible. Therefore, they may interpret a suggestion for change as a personal attack.

Part of a manager's job is to diagnose the potential reasons why individuals who must be involved in a change might resist it. This assessment helps managers choose a means of overcoming resistance. Otherwise, their efforts to foster innovation and change may be unexpectedly broadsided.

Overcoming Resistance to Change. One well-known general approach to the notion of overcoming resistance to change has been offered by organizational researcher Kurt Lewin, who has visualized the change process as being composed of three steps.[43] The first step, *unfreezing*, involves developing an initial awareness of the need for change. The second step, *changing*, focuses on learning the new required behaviors. The third step, *refreezing*, centers on reinforcing the new behaviors, usually by positive results, feelings of accomplishment, and/or rewards from others. Lewin's approach is important because it helps managers recognize that an unfreezing process is usually necessary before individuals are willing to change. Furthermore, the refreezing step is important for reinforcing and maintaining desired changes.

There are several methods that managers can adopt to help overcome initial resistance to change and facilitate unfreezing.[44] These alternatives, the situations in which they are commonly used, and the advantages and disadvantages of each method are summarized in Table 7-4.

One strategy for overcoming resistance to change is *education and communication*, providing adequate information and making sure that the change is clearly communicated to those involved. In one variation of this approach, which has proved to be particularly effective, management provides information showing that comparable organizations are performing better. Such information also should illustrate how existing methods could be changed to enhance performance and make it comparable to or better than that of the competition. With this approach, management also sets up means of appraising future performance so that progress can be gauged.[45] At Zebco, a unit of the Brunswick Corporation that makes fishing reels, the union work force was resistive of efforts by management to increase productivity, so management took a busload of employees to a trade show in Dallas. The show was dominated by Japanese and Korean competitors that had doubled their imports over the previous 5 years. The increasing competition had forced Zebco to limit price increases over that time period to a meager 4 percent. Subsequent worker efforts and pressure on suppliers to provide better parts resulted in a doubling of productivity over a

Table 7-4   Methods of Overcoming Resistance to Change

Approach	Commonly Used in Situations	Advantages	Drawbacks
Education + communication	Where there is a lack of information or inaccurate information and analysis	Once persuaded, people will often help with the implementation of the change	Can be very time-consuming if lots of people are involved
Participation + involvement	Where the initiators do not have all the information they need to design the change, and where others have considerable power to resist	People who participate will be committed to implementing change, and any relevant information they have will be integrated into the change plan	Can be very time-consuming if participators design an inappropriate change
Facilitation + support	Where people are resisting because of adjustment problems	No other approach works as well with adjustment problems	Can be time-consuming and expensive and still fail
Negotiation + agreement	Where someone or some group will clearly lose out in a change, and where that group has considerable power to resist	Sometimes it is a relatively easy way to avoid major resistance	Can be too expensive in many cases if it alerts others to negotiate for compliance
Manipulation + co-optation	Where other tactics will not work or are too expensive	It can be a relatively quick and inexpensive solution to resistance problems	Can lead to future problems if people feel manipulated
Explicit + implicit coercion	Where speed is essential and the change initiators possess considerable power	It is speedy and can overcome any kind of resistance	Can be risky if it leaves people mad at the initiators

Source: Reprinted from John P. Kotter and Leonard A. Schlesinger, "Choosing Strategies for Change," *Harvard Business Review,* March–April 1979, p. 111.

4-year period. As one worker sagely commented, "They got to keep the company, and we got to keep our jobs."[46]

Another means of overcoming resistance to change is *participation and involvement*. Resistance tends to be less pronounced when the individuals who will be affected by a change are allowed to participate in planning and implementing it. Participation increases understanding of the change, allows employees to offer their own ideas in making it successful, and frequently improves the final outcome. At Corning Glass Works, worker involvement has been a key factor in the success of a cost-saving effort. One suggestion came from a maintenance employee who recommended substituting one flexible tin mold for a number of different fixed molds used to shape the wet ceramic material for baking into catalytic converters for automobiles. The result was a savings of $99,000 per year.[47] There is evidence that managers tend to underutilize participation as a means of overcoming resistance to change. One study involving 91 change situations showed that using participation brought about a successful change 75 percent of the time but was only used in 17 percent of the cases.[48]

The use of *facilitation and support* is yet another means of overcoming resistance. When individuals react to impending changes with fear and anxiety, encouragement and help from the manager often reduces resistance to change. For example, training may be useful in preparing individuals for new behaviors required by a change. Providing the proper equipment and materials also can be important in making implementation of a change go smoothly. In addition, moral support from the manager can help ease anxiety levels, particularly if employees lack confidence about their ability to perform effectively under the new conditions.

An approach involving *negotiation and agreement* can also be useful in lessening resistance to change. Negotiation can be an important strategy when one group perceives that it will be hurt by the change and is in a position to cause the change effort to fail. When other strategies, such as education and participation, fail, it may be necessary to negotiate in order to gain cooperation with the change effort. After a 12-day strike at the Chrysler Corporation in October 1985, the company agreed to return to annual guaranteed wage increases for union members. The following year, Chrysler was able to negotiate "modern operating agreements" at 5 of its 31 factories. The changes, aimed at improving flexibility in job assignments and making operations more efficient, increased net income some $28 million to $35 million.[49]

Another means of overcoming resistance to change is *manipulation and co-optation*. The manipulation aspect usually involves selectively providing information about a change so that it appears more attractive or necessary to potential resisters. Ethical questions arise when the selective use of information involves a misrepresentation of the potential negative aspects of the change. The co-optation aspect of this strategy typically is aimed at giving a leader or influential person among the potential resisters a seemingly desirable role in the change process in order to gain cooperation. Usually, the role is somewhat symbolic, in the sense that the individual is given very little real input into the change process. However, the role may be advantageous enough to the influential person to obtain his or her support. For example, an individual might be given a position on a prestigious implementation task force but actually be afforded very little power because of being greatly outnumbered by individuals in favor of the change. The danger with manipulation and co-optation is that this strategy can easily backfire if the person recognizes what is being done and feels manipulated.

Finally, *explicit and implicit coercion* can also be used to overcome resistance to change. This strategy involves the direct or indirect use of power to pressure change resisters to conform. Tactics usually focus on direct or veiled threats regarding loss of jobs, promotions, pay, recommendations, and similar areas. Individuals may be fired or transferred. With coercion, there is a strong probability that the recipients of the pressure will be resentful even if they succumb. Furthermore, there is a danger that the coercion may escalate the resistance. When Kaiser Cement imposed its final contract offer on the work force at its Cushbury plant at Lucerne Valley, California, the offer included a sizable cut in seniority rights, a loosening of work rules, a loss of 5 paid sick days, and a lower pay tier for new employees. As a result, the union filed 4000 grievances over a 3-month period, and the company began to experience serious sabotage problems, such as having metal tools end up in cement-grinding mills. Although the union denied that its members were engaging in sabotage, it did say that its members were adhering to the exact specifications of the company-imposed settlement—a move admittedly aimed at driving labor costs up.[50] If a change is relatively unpopular but must be implemented quickly, managers may be forced by circumstances to use this strategy. At the same time, evidence indicates that managers resort to coercion more often than necessary, causing them to foster negative feelings among subordinates that may impede future changes.[51]

Sometimes managers find it helpful to analyze the situation and consider appropriate options for overcoming resistance to change through the use of **force-field analysis.** Developed by psychologist Kurt Lewin, the method involves analyzing the two types of forces, driving forces and restraining forces, that influence any proposed change and then assessing how best to overcome resistance. **Driving forces** are those factors that pressure *for* a particular change, whereas **restraining forces** are those factors that pressure *against* a change. At any given point in time, the two types of forces pushing in opposite directions lead to an equilibrium that defines current conditions, or the status quo. As a result, in order to change the status quo to the desired condition, it is necessary either to increase the driving forces, to decrease the restraining forces, or to do both. Although there is a tendency for managers to think in terms of increasing the driving forces, according to Lewin, such increases are highly likely to engender a corresponding increase in the resistant forces. As a result, managers have a better chance of bringing about a successful change if they work on reducing the restraining forces.[52]

Faced with serious competition from abroad, Xerox set a goal of cutting manufacturing costs by one-half at its copier manufacturing operation near Rochester. The company had worked over the years to build a climate of communication and trust with the union, the Amalgamated Clothing and Textile Workers Union, but this relationship was being strained by periodic layoffs. The situation grew potentially worse when Xerox announced plans to have wiring harnesses made by a subcontractor; the move, aimed at lowering costs, would eliminate about 150 jobs. Because there was a high desire among union leaders to save jobs and because company-union relations had been historically good, union leaders asked to meet with managers to consider ways to keep the wiring harness work in the plant.

Figure 7-3 shows a force-field analysis of the major driving and restraining forces maintaining the status quo—costs that were too high for Xerox to compete effectively. The wider the arrow, the stronger the force. In discussing possible solutions, the union leaders suggested relaxing some work rules so that workers could do such things as make minor repairs on machines instead of having to wait for machine maintenance workers to fix the equipment. Union leaders and management also studied other ways to save money that finally led to eliminating 6 paid days off, cutting medical insurance, and developing better ways to control absenteeism. In return, the company promised no layoffs for the next 3 years. By working mainly on some of the restraining forces, the company and the union were able to come to an agreement that resulted in lower cost levels in the plant without contracting out the wire harnessing work.[53]

Intrapreneurship

A number of organizations have been fostering innovation by encouraging individuals to take on entrepreneurial roles, such as idea generator or champion, sponsor, and orchestrator (see Chapter 1). Such roles are sometimes referred to as *intrapreneurial roles* when they are engaged in by individuals inside existing organizations. (We consider the entrepreneurial role as it relates to creating new organizations in Chapter 22.)

Although individuals fulfilling any of the three roles fit into the category of intrapreneurial, the idea champion is most often referred to as an intrapreneur. The reason is that the idea champion has the actual hands-on responsibility of turning the idea into a reality.[54] The *idea champion* is the individual who either generates a new idea or recognizes its value and then supports it despite numerous obstacles.

Force-field analysis A method that involves analyzing the two types of forces that influence any proposed change: driving forces and restraining forces

Driving forces Factors that pressure *for* a particular change

Restraining forces Factors that pressure *against* a change

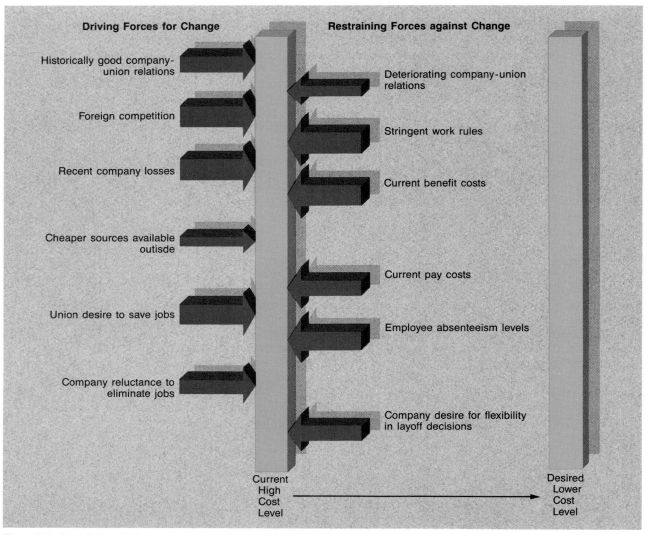

Driving Forces for Change

Historically good company-union relations

Foreign competition

Recent company losses

Cheaper sources available outisde

Union desire to save jobs

Company reluctance to eliminate jobs

Restraining Forces against Change

Deteriorating company-union relations

Stringent work rules

Current benefit costs

Current pay costs

Employee absenteeism levels

Company desire for flexibility in layoff decisions

Current High Cost Level

Desired Lower Cost Level

Figure 7-3 Force-field-analysis diagram of forces maintaining high cost level at Xerox plant.

According to Gifford Pinchot III, who has studied intrapreneuring, intrapreneurs tend to have certain characteristics that can be learned at least to some extent if one wishes to become more intrapreneurial. For one thing, intrapreneurs tend to be visionary in the sense of being able to visualize what they wish to create. Their vision comes from spending a great deal of time thinking about an idea. For example, Hulki Aldikacti, who was the intrapreneur responsible for Pontiac's successful Fiero model, had a solid notion of the sports car that he wanted to build before the project ever started. When a wooden model of the car was developed, he used to sit in it during his coffee breaks attempting to build on his vision still further. Intrapreneurs also tend to be action-oriented, extremely dedicated, and willing to do mundane tasks in order to avoid project delays. They also are likely to set goals for themselves beyond those asked of them, maintain high internal standards about their work, and rebound from mistakes and failures. For example, intrapreneur Phil Palmquist continued to work on reflective coatings at 3M even though his bosses told him to stop because it was not his job. Working 4 nights a week from 7 to 10 p.m., he finally produced the reflective coating now used on most highways. It is 100 times brighter than white paint.[55] Of course, part of the secret of being a good intrapreneur is choosing a good idea to pursue. For some guidelines on how to recognize a good intrapreneurial idea and what to do if it is rejected, see the Practically Speaking discussion, "Checklist for Choosing Intrapreneurial Ideas."

Why would individuals want to pursue an entrepreneurial idea within a company (i.e., be intrapreneurs) rather than starting their own company? Existing companies, particularly large ones, often can offer a strong technological base (such as proprietary knowledge and scientific resources), marketing resources (such as a known name, sales staff, and advertising funds), a network of individuals who can help, established production facilities, and in-house financing. Intrapreneur Art Fry, who championed the development of 3M's famous Post-it note pads (see the opening case in Chapter 11), views it this way: "I have only so much time in my life and I want to do as much as I can. I can do things faster here as part of 3M and so I get to do more things."[56] In the process of helping ideas become realities, intrapreneurs typically take on official or unoffi-

---

PRACTICALLY SPEAKING

CHECKLIST FOR CHOOSING INTRAPRENEURIAL IDEAS

Good intrapreneurial ideas that you can pursue need to meet three kinds of needs: yours, the customer's, and the company's. Otherwise, the intrapreneurial endeavor is unlikely to be successful. To help test an idea, you can use the following checklist.

Fit with Your Skills and Experience:
■ Do you believe in the product or service?
■ Does the need it fits mean something to you personally?
■ Do you like and understand the potential customers?
■ Do you have experience in this type of business?
■ Do the basic success factors of this business fit your skills?
■ Are the tasks of the intrapreneurial project ones you could enjoy doing yourself?
■ Are the people who would work on the project ones you will enjoy working with and supervising?

■ Has the idea begun to take over your imagination and spare time?

Fit with Customers and the Market:
■ Is there a real customer need?
■ Can you get a price that gives you good margins?
■ Would customers believe in the product coming from your company?
■ Does the product or service you propose produce a clearly perceivable customer benefit which is significantly better than that provided by competing means of satisfying the same basic need?
■ Is there a cost-effective way to get the message and the product to the customer?

Fit with the Company:
■ Is there a reason to believe that your company could be very good at the business?
■ Does it fit the company culture?
■ Can you imagine who might sponsor it?
■ Does it look profitable (high margin, low investment)?

■ Will it lead to larger markets and growth?

WHAT TO DO IF YOUR IDEA IS REJECTED
Frequently, as an intrapreneur, you will find that your idea has been rejected. There are a few things you can do:

1. Give up and select a new idea.
2. Listen carefully, understand what is wrong, improve your idea and your presentation, and try again.
3. Find someone else to whom you can present your idea by considering:
   a. Who will benefit most if it works, and can that person be a sponsor?
   b. Who are the potential customers, and will they demand the product?
   c. How can you get to the people who really care about intrapreneurial ideas?[57]

cial management duties and, like managers, must have a good understanding of how to bring about change in organizations.

KEY ORGANIZATIONAL CHANGE COMPONENTS

Significant changes or innovations usually involve making alterations in one or more of these key components: structure, technology, human resources, and culture (see Figure 7-4).[58] As a result, it is useful for managers to consider directly the possibility of facilitating necessary change through shifts in any or all of these key change areas. Since these elements are somewhat interrelated, a change in one component may create the need for adjustments in other components.

Structural Components

Organizational structure is the pattern of interactions and coordination designed by management to link the tasks of individuals and groups in achieving organizational goals. Structure includes such factors as the way jobs are defined and clustered into work units and the various mechanisms used to facilitate vertical and horizontal communication (e.g., delegation and the use of interdepartmental teams).[59] Because structures must be adapted as circumstances change, reorganizations are common. Reorganizations influence change by altering the pattern of interactions and coordination. (Specific structural alternatives are discussed in depth in Chapters 10 and 11.) According to one estimate, well over half the companies on *Fortune*'s list of the 1000 largest U.S. corporations have undergone a major reorganization during the 1980s.[60] Minor structural changes also occur frequently in most large organizations, although many of these changes may fit into the category of "fine-tuning" a previous reorganization. One recent research study indicated that reorganizations representing a *quantum*

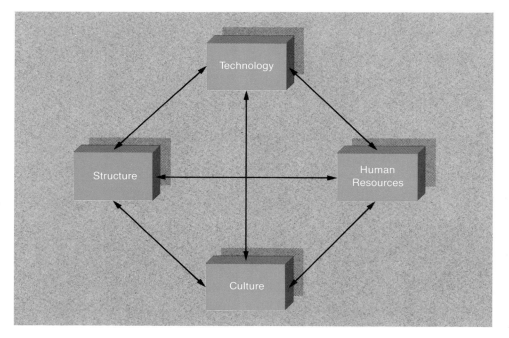

Figure 7-4 Key components for implementing change. (Adapted from Harold J. Leavitt, "Applied Organization Change in Industry: Structural, Technical, and Human Approaches," in W. W. Cooper, H. J. Leavitt, M. W. Shelly II, eds., *New Perspectives in Organization Research*, Wiley, New York, 1964, p. 56.)

change—a change that is both concerted and dramatic—tend to be more frequently associated with subsequent high performance than do piecemeal and incremental reorganizations.[61]

Technological Components

Technology involves the knowledge, tools, equipment, and work techniques used by an organization in delivering its products or services. Technological change is reflected both in major new products and services (such as videocassette recorders and automated teller machines) and in frequent improvements in current products and services. Technological change is an important factor in current international competition. When two Japanese companies, Yamaha Motor and Honda Motor, were competing for the Japanese motorcycle market in the early 1980s, Yamaha declared that it would surpass Honda. Unfortunately for Yamaha, Honda reacted by flooding the Japanese market with new models, sometimes at a rate of one per week. Continually forced to discount obsolete models, Yamaha Motor lost $300 million in 2 years.[62] The need to produce technological innovations for competitive reasons has resulted in a strong focus on technological change at Yamaha, Honda, and similar organizations.

Technological innovations also are altering the ways in which work is done in organizations. For example, the advent of word-processing equipment and personal computers has eliminated the necessity of retyping whole documents when corrections are needed. Access to computerized data banks is providing more and better information to various specialists, such as doctors, engineers, educators, and research scientists. Robot apprentices are helping scientists in the field of biotechnology study deoxyribonucleic acid (DNA), the raw material of genes, by performing in hours tests that it used to take a trained chemist weeks or months to do.[63] Technological changes often affect the number of employees required and the types of skills that they need.

Human Resources Components

Bringing about change in individuals in the workplace is typically aimed at altering the knowledge, skills, perceptions, and behaviors needed to do the job. Changing individuals generally relies on training and development activities, supplemented by performance appraisal and reward systems that reinforce the needed behaviors. Frequently, recruitment and selection systems also must be adjusted to reflect the varied needs of individuals with differing skills. Having individuals who possess appropriate knowledge and skills for handling changing circumstances takes careful planning. For example, at IBM, which has a corporate policy against laying off employees, a variety of training and placement efforts are used to ensure that employee skills keep pace with current needs. During the recent efforts to cut costs and streamline operations, IBM has used attractive early retirement programs to maintain its policy against layoffs.[64] Characteristics of effective human resources systems are discussed more extensively in Chapter 12. Changes in such systems often are necessary in order to support the effectiveness of alterations made in other organizational components, such as structure and technology.

Cultural Components

Organizational culture is a system of shared values, assumptions, beliefs, and norms that unite the organization's members.[65] A number of organizations, such as IBM, J. C. Penney, Digital Equipment Corporation, and Hewlett-Packard, attribute some measure of their success to strong cultures that are rooted in values articulated by strong founders and reinforced by subsequent top executives.[66] As a result, other organizations have been attempting to alter their cultures to fit more closely with new strategic directions. For example, AT&T and independent regional companies such as Southwestern Bell have been striving to change their cultures to reflect more adequately the need for greater innovation, market competitiveness, and a profit-making orientation, while Westinghouse has been attempting to place greater emphasis on the development of people, concern for productivity, and quality of work.[67] Thus major organizational changes often require alterations in organizational culture. Issues related to organizational culture are discussed further in Chapter 3.

Interrelationship among Components

Although minor changes may be focused on only one of these components, major changes are likely to encompass all four organizational components of change. This is largely because major changes in one component tend to have implications for other components. You might think of the components as being connected by rubber bands. As you move one component, it creates tensions on the others until they are adjusted accordingly. These interrelationships are illustrated by a large-scale change effort initiated by one of Europe's largest companies, N. V. Philips (see the following Case in Point discussion).

CASE IN POINT: Cultural Revolution at Europe's Philips

N. V. Philips, an electronics company headquartered in Eindhoven, Netherlands, and one of *Fortune*'s 50 largest industrial corporations in the world, has undergone massive changes during the past 20 years. After a quarter of a century of dynamic growth both in volume and profits, Philips found itself facing new challenges in the 1970s. Sales growth was no longer keeping up with the 10 percent annual increase in labor productivity that the company had enjoyed since 1945. At the same time, the company's top executives were surprised by the sudden success of Japanese products in the United States. Preoccupied with burgeoning growth in Europe, Philips found itself with U.S. sales accounting for only 3 percent of total sales. Furthermore, international Japanese companies such as Hitachi and Sony represented a serious threat to Philips's aspirations in the rest of the world.

In studying its Japanese competitors, Philips found several major differences between its methods of operating and those of its Japanese counterparts. Historically, Philips had based its industrial structure on countries, not continents, and had concentrated on products that catered to local needs. As a result, Philips had small factories in a variety of countries and produced many different products geared to local markets. For example, radios sold in Italy differed from those sold in France. The Japanese strategy of producing relatively few products in large factories at low cost was a serious potential threat to the way in which Philips did business. The Japanese companies' lower labor costs, due primarily to the fact that the average Japanese worker works 3000 hours per year, compared with 1600 to 2000 for the average European worker, added a significant dimension to the challenge.

It took Philips almost 3 years to begin a massive revitalization effort aimed at making the company more competitive. At first, little was done. "We were just looking with big eyes at our problems," said one of Philips's senior corporate planners. Since then, however, Philips has taken major steps to revamp the company. After reorganizing the structure and centralizing product decision making, the Philips executives began to study the current level of technology in their products. New emphasis was placed on encouraging innovation, improving research and development, and focusing research efforts on areas likely to yield product breakthroughs. Efforts also were made to upgrade methods of production, and 40 plants whose costs could not be lowered significantly were closed. Training for managers was increased, and developmental assignments were geared to moving managers into responsible positions at a much faster pace. Recruiting was widened to attract the best scientific talent available, and human resources systems were designed to reinforce the need for innovations that could be turned into marketable products. At the same time, Philips took steps to abandon its paternalistic culture, which in 1970 included such benefits as delivery of employees' babies by company midwives, use of company nursery schools, and visits from company doctors if employees or their parents became sick. In place of complacency and self-satisfaction, the top executives have tried to instill a new corporate culture based on the belief that it is necessary to strive continuously to improve the quality of the total organization if it is to compete effectively.

Such efforts are beginning to produce positive results. In several key product areas, such as compact disc players (sold under the Magnovox label in the United States) and ultra-advanced memory chips, Philips has been gaining in market share against Japanese companies. Philips is the number-one world producer of light bulbs, has a significant share of the global color television market, and is expected to be a major power in high-definition TV in the 1990s. The company has been engaged in a joint effort with Siemens AG, a Germany-based electronics giant, to compete with the Japanese in developing and producing certain types of memory chips; but, so far, it is experiencing difficulty catching up to and surpassing Japanese competitors. In computers, Philips faces stiff competition in Europe from IBM and the Digital Equipment Corporation, who dominate the market.[68] ▬▬▬▬

In the Philips situation, when the managers began to make major changes in the company, they found it necessary to alter all four major targets of change: structure, technology, human resources, and culture. The Philips managers were reacting largely to external forces. A more proactive means of bringing about change is through the use of organizational development.

ORGANIZATIONAL DEVELOPMENT

When we think about our own personal development, it is clear that there are a number of things we can do to enhance our future prospects. For example, we would probably benefit from eating meals that are nutritionally balanced, avoiding too many sweets, and making sure that we get enough exercise. Other developmental activities may be less obvious, and we may need to do some diagnosing of our strengths and weaknesses in order to decide where we want to put our efforts. We may read books about career planning, take tests at our college or university career center to help us focus our interests, and study our performance in various classes to figure out what we do particularly well. Conversely, because we have a number of things that we can do with our time, we might not spend much time and effort on our own personal development. In the latter case, unless we are lucky, we probably will not be as successful as we could be at whatever occupation we choose.

Organizations face similar developmental choices. In particular, organizations must be ready to cope with changing environments. However, like individuals, they do not always make adequate preparations. One way organizations can increase their long-term prospects is by using organizational development. **Organizational development (OD)** can be defined as a change effort that is (1) planned, (2) focused on an entire organization or a large subsystem, (3) managed from the top, (4) aimed at enhancing organizational health and effectiveness, and (5) based on planned interventions made with the help of a change agent or third party who is well versed in the behavioral sciences.[69]

An elaboration of this definition is helpful in understanding the major characteristics of organizational development. First, the change effort is planned and proactive, rather than reactive. Second, the changes are aimed either at a whole organization or a major part of one, such as a large division or department, rather than one small group or narrow aspect, such as an inventory system or a compensation system. Third, the effort is managed from the top in the sense that upper management recognizes the need for change, but the change effort itself typically involves the collaboration of organization members at other levels as well. Fourth, although immediate problems may be solved through the OD approach, the major focus is on increasing the capacity for long-run effectiveness.[70] In the process, OD attempts to help the organization develop its own self-renewing capacity, including its ability to create new and innovative solutions to its problems.[71] Fifth, OD relies on the use of **interventions,** OD change strategies developed and initiated with the help of a change agent. The **change agent,** or consultant, is an individual with a fresh perspective and a knowledge of the behavioral sciences who acts as a catalyst in helping the organization approach old problems in new or innovative ways. The change agent role can be filled by an outside consultant, an OD specialist who is an employee of the organization, a new manager, or an enlightened manager who is able to look beyond traditional approaches. The advantages and disadvantages of outside and inside change agents are summarized in Table 7-5.

Organizational development (OD) A change effort that is planned, focused on an entire organization or a large subsystem, managed from the top, aimed at enhancing organizational health and effectiveness, and based on planned interventions

Interventions OD change strategies developed and initiated with the help of a change agent

Change agent An individual with a fresh perspective and a knowledge of the behavioral sciences who acts as a catalyst in helping the organization approach old problems in new or innovative ways

Table 7-5 Advantages and Disadvantages of Internal and External Change Agents

Internal Agents	External Agents
ADVANTAGES	
Possess better knowledge of the organization	Have more objective views of the organization
Are more quickly available	Have more experience in dealing with diverse problems
Require lower out-of-pocket costs	Can call on more individuals with diverse expertise
Are a known quantity	Have more technical knowledge, competence, and skills available
Have more control and authority	
DISADVANTAGES	
May be too close to the problem	Have less knowledge of the organization
May hold biased views	Require higher out-of-pocket costs
May create additional resistance if viewed as part of the problem	Are an unknown quantity
Must be reassigned; not available for other work	Have longer start-up time
	Reflect unfavorably on the image of management

Source: Reprinted from Judith R. Gordon, *A Diagnostic Approach to Organizational Behavior,* Allyn and Bacon, Boston, 1987, p. 695.

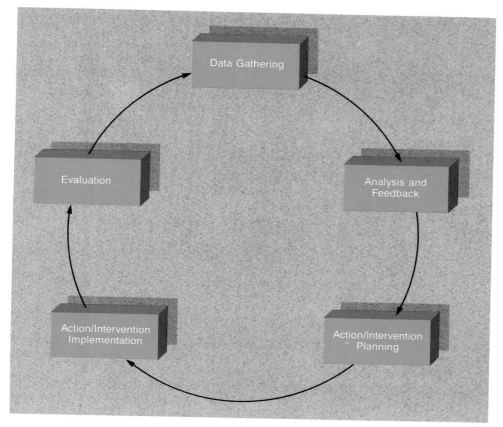

Figure 7-5   The action-research process.

The organizational development process itself consists of three major steps: diagnosis, intervention, and evaluation.[72] These steps are compatible with the planned innovation and change process discussed earlier, since organizational development is actually a specialized type of change effort. An OD process is most likely to be initiated when top management or a key person in the organization believes that there are deficiencies in the way in which the overall organization is functioning.

Diagnosis

Organizational development efforts usually begin with a diagnosis of the current situation. The diagnosis often focuses particular attention on the widely shared beliefs, values, and norms of organization members that may be interfering with maximum effectiveness. One popular OD method that places heavy emphasis on data gathering and collaborative diagnosis before action is taken is known as **action research.** The general process of action research is depicted in Figure 7-5. In action research, data is gathered under the direction of the change agent, who does a preliminary analysis. The data is then fed back to those involved in the change effort, joint action and intervention planning is conducted, planned actions and interventions are implemented, and an initial evaluation is made. If necessary, the process is repeated until the organization is operating to the satisfaction of top management and the key persons involved in the change.

During the diagnostic phase multiple means of gathering data usually are used, such as interviews, questionnaires, observations of employee behaviors,

Action research A method that places heavy emphasis on data gathering and collaborative diagnosis before action is taken

and various internal documents and reports. Questionnaires are becoming a particularly popular means of diagnosis, because they can easily be repeated in order to monitor changes over a period of time. Companies such as IBM, Sears, and Ford Motor have long histories of conducting surveys to keep abreast of employee thinking on a variety of issues. When the Hartmarx Corporation, a Chicago-based clothing maker and retailer, recently began a questionnaire survey of its 25,000 employees, the data were compiled and then fed back to employees in small groups to elicit further data for use in diagnosis.[73]

Intervention

Once the situation has been properly diagnosed, OD interventions, or change strategies, can be designed and implemented with the help of the change agent. Although there are numerous OD change strategies, five of the major techniques used by OD specialists are described briefly below.[74]

Process consultation is concerned with the interpersonal relations and dynamics operating in work groups. The OD change agent or consultant observes the group and provides feedback regarding dysfunctions in such areas as communication patterns, handling of conflicts, and decision making. The goal is to help group members gain the skills they need to identify and resolve group dynamics issues on their own.

Team building is aimed at helping work groups become effective at task accomplishment. Like process consultation, it typically includes OD consultant feedback in such areas as communication and conflict resolution. However, it also includes OD consultant help in assessing group tasks, member roles, and strategies for accomplishing work tasks.

Third-party intervention is concerned with helping individuals, groups, or departments resolve serious conflicts that may relate to specific work issues or may be caused by suboptimal interpersonal relations. The OD consultant helps the parties resolve their differences through such techniques as problem solving, bargaining, and conciliation.

Technostructural activities are intended to improve work technology and/or organizational structure. Through this approach, the OD consultant helps organization members learn to enhance their own work effectiveness by evaluating and making appropriate changes in work methods, task design, and organizational structure.

Organizational culture change involves the development of a corporate culture that is in synchronization with organizational strategies and other factors, such as structure (see also Chapter 3). The OD consultant assists in developing methods of determining the current corporate culture, assessing its appropriateness, and planning necessary changes.

Notice that these intervention techniques have one principle in common. They all are geared toward not only solving current problems but also helping individuals and groups acquire the skills necessary to solve future problems. For example, process consultation assists groups in operating more effectively immediately, but its main focus is on helping group members acquire the skills they will need to diagnose group problems in the future. The emphasis on skill building and long-term development is characteristic of OD efforts.

One recurring criticism of organizational development is that it places too much emphasis on interpersonal skills while ignoring other issues, such as organizational structure and technology. Increasingly, OD specialists have expanded the types of interventions they manage to include a wide range of approaches in

---

Process consultation   A technique concerned with the interpersonal relations and dynamics operating in work groups

Team building   A technique aimed at helping work groups become effective at task accomplishment

Third-party intervention   A technique concerned with helping individuals, groups, or departments resolve serious conflicts that may relate to specific work issues or may be caused by suboptimal interpersonal relations

Technostructural activities   Activities intended to improve work technology and/or organizational structure

Organizational culture change   The development of a corporate culture that is in synchronization with organizational strategies and other factors, such as structure

such areas as technostructural activities and cultural change. Most successful OD efforts are likely to involve multiple intervention techniques.[75]

Evaluation

As with any change effort, it is important to monitor the effectiveness of OD efforts. Because OD is oriented toward long-term change, it can take several years to achieve significant results. The ability to evaluate the effects of OD interventions depends heavily on how well the diagnosis stage pinpointed the areas in need of change and specified the desired results. In order to facilitate the evaluation process, it usually is advantageous to collect data on the target areas for change before the OD effort begins. These data can then be used as benchmarks to make at least some assessment of the effectiveness of various interventions after they have been implemented. One review of 65 studies of the effects of OD interventions on "hard" criteria, such as quantitative measures of job behavior and system performance, concluded that no one OD technique works in all situations. Furthermore, even successful interventions have not necessarily produced results in all the targeted areas.[76] These findings reinforce the need to monitor and evaluate results. Definitive studies of the effectiveness of organizational development are difficult because OD efforts are usually conducted in situations in which many factors, such as economic conditions and the competitive environment, are changing rapidly.

Of course, organizational development and other major efforts involving innovation and change also require considerable decision making on the part of managers, particularly about the nature of future directions. In the next chapter, we explore the managerial decision-making process and examine how managers can become effective decision makers.

CHAPTER SUMMARY

Largely because of increasing competition, the management of change and innovation has become increasingly important to the survival and prosperity of organizations. Change refers to any alteration in the status quo, while innovation involves applying a new idea to significantly improve a process, product, or service. Forces for change can be external or internal. As they grow, organizations tend to go through four life cycles, or predictable stages of development: entrepreneurial, collectivity, formalization and control, and elaboration of structure. Movement through these stages requires changes in methods of operating, but these same changes may inhibit innovation unless managers plan and encourage innovation. Failure to adapt to changing conditions may lead to organizational termination through such means as bankruptcy, voluntary liquidation, and merger, acquisition, or takeover.

Although managers may sometimes be forced to react to unpredictable situations, effective managers attempt to plan for major changes and innovations whenever possible through the use of a six-step model that includes perceiving an opportunity or a problem, diagnosing the situation and generating ideas, presenting a proposal and adopting the change, planning to overcome resistance, implementing the change, and monitoring the results. Planning to overcome resistance to implementing a change necessitates an understanding of the reasons why people resist change. Major reasons are self-interest, misunderstanding and lack of trust, different assessments, and low tolerance for change. Managers must also have a knowledge of methods for overcoming resistance to change, including education and communication, participation and involvement, facilitation and support, negotiation and agreement, manipulation and co-optation, and explicit and implicit coercion. The use of force-field analysis is helpful in understanding the driving forces and restraining forces that account for the status quo. It frequently is more effective to try to reduce the restraining forces than to attempt to increase the driving forces for change. Intrapreneurship is growing in importance in organizations, and intrapreneurs have certain characteristics that are somewhat learnable, such as being visionary, action-oriented, and willing to set goals associated with new ideas.

Major changes usually involve adjustments to one or more of the following key organizational change components: structure, technology, human resources, and culture. Since the components are somewhat interrelated, changes in one component frequently require adjustments in other components to carry out successful change and innovation efforts.

Organizational development is a change effort that is planned, focused on an entire organization or a large subsystem, managed from the top, aimed at enhancing organizational health and effectiveness, and based on planned interventions made with the help of a change agent or third party who is well versed in the behavioral sciences. Organizational development involves three major stages: diagnosis, intervention, and evaluation. Five intervention techniques used by OD specialists include process consultation, team building, third-party intervention, technostructural activities, and organizational culture change.

MANAGERIAL TERMINOLOGY

action research   (251)
change   (226)
change agent   (250)
driving forces   (243)
force-field analysis   (243)
innovation   (226)
interventions   (250)
life cycles   (228)

organizational culture
  change   (252)
organizational
  development (OD)
  (250)
organizational
  termination   (228)

planned change   (235)
process consultation
  (252)
reactive change   (234)
restraining forces   (243)
revitalization   (231)

takeover   (234)
team building   (252)
technostructural activities
  (252)
third-party intervention
  (252)

QUESTIONS FOR DISCUSSION AND REVIEW

1. Explain the difference between change and innovation. Think of some changes that you have noticed on campus in the past year. In each case, explain the extent to which the forces for change were external or internal. Which changes would you classify as innovations? Why?

2. Describe the four life-cycle stages of organizations. Choose an organization with which you are familiar and determine its stage in the organizational life cycle. On the basis of your analysis, what changes are likely to be needed in the future?

3. Explain the six-step model of the change and innovation process. Use this model to develop a plan for getting a student group to which you belong to take advantage of an unexploited opportunity.

4. Outline the main reasons why employees resist change. When the new Pepperidge Farm CEO attempted to make changes, he encountered resistance among some upper-level managers who had been with the company for a period of time. Analyze why these managers may have resisted the changes.

5. Explain the major approaches for overcoming resistance to change. Suppose you are a manager in a small manufacturing plant that is facing increased competition from foreign-made products and needs to increase productivity. Design a plan for overcoming the resistance of your employees to changes and innovations necessary to increase productivity. What is your most preferred strategy? What is your least preferred strategy?

6. Explain force-field analysis. Suggest three situations in which it might be useful in helping you analyze a change situation.

7. Describe some common characteristics of intrapreneurs. Assuming, as Gifford Pinchot suggests, that these characteristics are learnable, how might you go about acquiring them?

8. Enumerate the key organizational components that usually must be adjusted in implementing major changes and innovations. Identify a recent change at your college or university that was aimed mainly at one of these components. To what extent did the change in that component alter the others?

9. Explain the concept of organizational development. Suppose that you are helping with an OD project at your college or university. What major steps or phases will be involved? What data-collection methods might you suggest for the diagnosis step?

10. Delineate the major intervention techniques used by OD specialists. On the basis of the information that you have regarding the cultural revolution at Philips, what types of OD interventions might have helped the company make appropriate changes?

DISCUSSION QUESTIONS FOR CHAPTER OPENING CASE

1. Would you characterize the approach to change and innovation at Merck as reactive or planned? What evidence exists to support your view?

2. At what stage in the organizational life cycle would you place Merck? Why? What changes are likely to be needed in the future?

3. How would you describe the organizational culture at Merck? What other sources of information would help you make such an assessment?

MANAGEMENT EXERCISE: FORCE-FIELD ANALYSIS[77]

Specification

Think about a situation in which you would like to make a change or institute an innovation, but one in which you face resistance. (The situation might involve getting a better grade in a course, instituting an innovative project in a student organization, overcoming a challenge at work, or improving a relationship with a peer or friend.) Write a sentence or two describing the status quo. Then write a brief description of the situation as you would like it to be if you could change it.

Analysis

List the major driving forces, the factors that pressure *for* change, and then list the major restraining forces, the factors that pressure *against* change. Draw a force-field-analysis diagram like the one shown in Figure 7-3 on page 244. Remember, the wider the arrow, the stronger the force.

Solution

Select two or three restraining forces on your diagram and develop means for reducing the degree of resistance. Be prepared to explain your diagram and your solutions to another class member who will act as your consultant.

BANKAMERICA STRUGGLES TO FULFILL ITS FOUNDER'S DREAMS

The BankAmerica Corporation's roots are unusual for a major bank. Shortly after the turn of the century, its founder, a successful young executive named A. P. Giannini, became a member of the board of directors of a savings and loan in the North Beach area of San Francisco. A. P. soon ran into difficulty when he tried to convince the other directors to extend banking services to everyone, not just the relatively rich. Rebuffed, he left the board and started his own bank, the Bank of America, which Giannini referred to as the "Bank of the Little People."

When it began, the bank served mainly individuals in the lower economic levels, particularly Italian immigrants in North Beach. Giannini's idea of banking included many innovations. He introduced advertising, then considered by other banks to be professionally unethical. One of many slogans he developed was "Let's take the 'ice' out of service." He eliminated private offices and smoky back rooms in favor of having officers sit in the lobby, a practice common today. A risk taker and a believer in improving the quality of life through bank services, he financed bonds to build the Golden Gate Bridge during the Depression, pioneered time-plan loans, and financed Walt Disney in a project considered foolhardy at the time—the production of the first full-length cartoon movie, *Snow White and the Seven Dwarfs*. By 1940, 1 out of every 3 Californians was a Bank of America customer. When Giannini died in 1949, he left behind a legacy of visionary leadership and human concern.

The next few decades were characterized by heavy regulation in the banking industry, and the organizational culture at the Bank of America gradually changed. During the 1970s the Bank of America emerged as the BankAmerica Corporation; it became the most profitable banking company in the country under a CEO, A. W. "Tom" Clausen, whose authoritarian ways with subordinates earned him the title "the dictator." When Clausen left in 1981 to head the World Bank, BankAmerica looked great on paper but critics argued that Clausen had made too many high-risk loans, spent virtually nothing on new technology such as automated teller machines, and allowed BankAmerica to become the most undercapitalized major bank in the country.

Clausen left behind his hand-picked successor, Samuel H. Armacost, a 42-year-old banking wonder whose rise at BankAmerica had

Innovation and risk taking enabled founder A. P. Giannini to make Bank of America the foremost bank in California. By the 1980s, however, the bank seemed to have left Giannini's vision behind: it was conservative in attitude and slow to make use of technology. The current management is attempting to turn the company around by using aggressive advertising and promotions, removing 33,000 employees from the payroll, introducing automated tellers, and requiring branch banks to meet specified targets.

been meteoric. As Armacost took the helm, however, the banking industry environment was becoming increasingly deregulated and troubles stemming from the previous regime began to show up in the form of earnings declines. As a result, the bank's top management began to engage in some serious introspection. With the help of consultants, the managers assessed the current corporate culture.

Interviews with employees regarding their beliefs about what the bank expected of them revealed a very different bank than Giannini had envisioned. One belief that emerged was that everyone was expected to "be nice" to everyone else. This belief had gradually become translated into a norm that said, "Keep any concerns and objections to a course of action to yourself, even if you have serious reservations and information that would suggest that another course of action would be better." Another concept that came out of the interviews was "Don't worry about performance." Over the years, the attitude had developed that a job with BankAmerica was a job for life and that employees, therefore, didn't have to be concerned with performance. This view was reinforced by a pay system that gave lip service to performance but in actuality dispensed equal pay. Another belief that surfaced strongly was "Don't risk failure." As a result, BankAmerica began to lag behind its competition in technology and innovation. To add to the bank's troubles, increasing numbers of high-risk loans made during the previous decade began to sour.

With Armacost at the helm, earnings declined steadily, largely due to the actions of his predecessor. Armacost did build a major automated teller network that helped the bank catch up technologically. Still, critics argue that he was hesitant about firing anyone, including incompetent executives, and was not able to influence the large BankAmerica bureaucracy to support the necessary strategic directions. Finally, when the bank experienced an unexpected $640 million loss in the second quarter of 1986, the bank's board reluctantly asked for Armacost's resignation. The bank's status had changed from the largest and most profitable banking company in the United States, when Armacost became its head, to the bank losing the most money.

In attempting to turn around the seriously wounded institution, the board took the unusual move of bringing back the former CEO, Clausen. The move was criticized by some because it was Clausen who had allowed the bank to grant many of the shaky foreign loans that had soured and who also apparently had kept profits high partially by postponing needed technological improvements, such as automated teller machines.

Clausen immediately took major steps. He brought in several top managers from the bank's aggressive archrival, Wells Fargo & Company. The bank became extremely aggressive in pushing retail banking through a variety of new services, massive advertising, and promotions. For example, recently on the bank's Founder's Day, honoring A. P. Giannini, the bank offered checking accounts that are free for the first 3 years. The promotion attracted 40,000 new accounts and, since it was held on a Saturday, helped dramatize the bank's new Saturday hours. Another winning idea was the institution of "Alpha" accounts, checking accounts with a line of credit that takes over (at 16.8 percent interest) if the accounts are overdrawn. Costs were cut by trimming 33,000 employees from the payroll. Branches were given quotas for selling new bank products and services, such as various types of accounts. Throughout the corporation, listings were made available of each branch's results, as well as results by individuals. Branch managers who did not meet targets were fired. As a result, the bank returned to profitability, although the potential for more shaky loan defaults continues to exist.

Although these various actions placed the bank on much firmer ground, friends say that Clausen continued to envision BankAmerica as a global bank and was concerned that the necessary emphasis on retail banking oriented to local consumers would jeopardize that vision. He also worried that the cost cutting could be carried too far with such steps as shifting tellers to part-time positions and eliminating some of their benefits. Nevertheless, apparently feeling that his reputation as an effective bank chief executive had been restored, Clausen announced his retirement in 1990. He named as his successor Richard M. Rosenberg, the marketing specialist who joined BankAmerica in 1987 and spearheaded the successful effort in retail banking.[78]

QUESTIONS FOR CHAPTER CONCLUDING CASE

1. Where would you place BankAmerica on the organizational life cycle? What changes does your analysis suggest?
2. How would you characterize top management's approach to change and innovation up to this point? How might the bank improve the change and innovation process?
3. How useful would organizational development be in this situation? How might one proceed with such a program?

CHAPTER EIGHT

MANAGERIAL DECISION MAKING

CHAPTER OUTLINE

The Nature of Managerial Decision Making
Types of Problems Decision Makers Face
Differences in Decision-Making Situations

Managers as Decision Makers
The Rational Model
Nonrational Models

Steps in an Effective Decision-Making Process
Identifying the Problem
Generating Alternative Solutions
Evaluating and Choosing an Alternative
Implementing and Monitoring the Chosen Solution

Overcoming Barriers to Effective Decision Making
Accepting the Problem Challenge
Searching for Sufficient Alternatives
Recognizing Common Decision-Making Biases
Avoiding the Decision Escalation Phenomenon

Group Decision Making
Advantages of Group Decision Making
Disadvantages of Group Decision Making
Enhancing Group Decision-Making Processes

Promoting Innovation: The Creativity Factor in Decision Making
Basic Ingredients
Stages of Creativity
Techniques for Enhancing Group Creativity

LEARNING OBJECTIVES

After studying this chapter, you should be able to:

■ Explain the major types of problems facing decision makers and describe the difference between programmed and nonprogrammed decisions.

■ Contrast the rational and nonrational models of managers as decision makers.

■ Describe each of the steps in an effective decision-making process.

■ Explain how to overcome the barriers associated with accepting the problem challenge and searching for sufficient alternatives.

■ Describe how to recognize common decision-making biases and avoid the decision escalation phenomenon.

■ Assess the advantages and disadvantages of group decision making.

■ Explain the basic ingredients and stages of creativity.

■ Describe the major techniques for enhancing group creativity.

COKE GETS BACK ITS KICK

Several times per day, Roberto C. Goizueta (pronounced Goy-SWET-ah), the chief executive officer of the Coca-Cola Company, walks from his oak-floored office in Atlanta down the hall to a Quotron machine in order to check Coke's stock price. The price check is one of the small pleasures of his day, akin to the enjoyment that millions of people throughout the world derive from popping open a can of one of the company's soft drinks. Since he was awarded the top slot at Coca-Cola in 1981, the news from the Quotron has usually, but not always, been good.

Goizueta, a bright chemical engineer from Havana, Cuba, who fled the Castro regime, had made major changes in the once-sleepy company and its southern traditions. For one thing, he began emphasizing that management's chief job is maximizing shareholder value so that shareholders receive good returns on their investments in the company's stock. To help boost company growth and returns, Goizueta and Coke's Iowa-bred president, Donald Keough, began finding new ways to make money by more effectively utilizing the company's most prized possession: the world's most valuable trademark.

Although it seems amazing now, the name "Coca-Cola" was attached to only one product when Goizueta and Keough took over management of the company. They proceeded to put the famous brand name on a diet cola and five other soft-drink variations. Despite the problems the company encountered when it introduced the sweeter-tasting New Coke in 1985, the extended set of products with Coke's name on them bypassed the number of Pepsi-named products carried by food stores in 1986.

Already a leading soft-drink company in 155 countries, the company has between 50 and 60 percent of the market share in most of the countries in which it does business. The challenge now is to increase consumption levels. Coke has been waging a major campaign to persuade individuals who live in the various countries in which it does business to drink Coke instead of tea, coffee, and other beverages. According to one marketing manager for the central Pacific, "We want a major share of stomach."

Goizueta and his top management team have also become innovative deal makers. When Goizueta took command, Coke's long-term debt (less than 2 percent) was unusually low for a company of its size, largely due to the conservative financial policies of his predecessors. Since then, Goizueta has increased long-term debt to around 18 percent and also used the company's huge cash flow to make some substantial acquisitions in order to enhance growth and boost investment returns. For example, the company invested $2 billion to enter the bottling business, rather than continuing the traditional arrangement of relying almost solely on independent franchisees. The bottling operation has been set up as an independent business, Coca-Cola Enterprises, Inc. Initial earnings of the bottling entity have been disappointing because of price wars that have necessitated cutting wholesale prices in order to win shelf space in retail stores. There have been signs, though, that the price wars may be easing somewhat.

Coke also spent another $1.5 billion to expand into movies and television by purchasing Columbia Pictures and related businesses, a move that did not yield returns as high as the company had hoped. As a result, Coke sold its stake in these businesses to the Sony Corporation in 1989 at what Goizueta says was a "very attractive price." Since that time, Goizueta has been rethinking the notion of diversifying into types of businesses that are largely unrelated to the soft-drink industry, and has recently said that, in the future, Coke will concentrate mainly on being a soft drink company. A major reason for the shift toward a

When Coca-Cola came out with a new sweeter-tasting Coke in 1985, the outraged public response (such as that shown here) was totally unexpected. Extensive consumer research had indicated that customers would prefer the new Coke to the old. Sometimes following all the proper decision-making procedures still does not result in the right decision. Within 3 months the company had the old Coke, renamed Coca-Cola Classic, back on the shelves along with the new product.

one-product company is that Coke has been able to achieve an exceptionally high return on assets in its soft drink business and sees considerable room for growth in international markets. Presently, on average, Americans annually consume about 18 gallons of soft drink products made by Coke; whereas consumption is only about 40 percent of that figure in Europe, about 10 percent of that amount in Asia and the Pacific region, and roughly 5 percent of the U.S. figure in Africa. In addition, Coke is generally able to charge relatively high prices in international markets where competition is generally less than the company faces domestically.

By encouraging risk taking, Goizueta has nurtured a new entrepreneurial spirit among managers in the company, in contrast to its traditional, rather conservative, decision-making orientation. He has worked hard to create an atmosphere in which new ideas can flourish. Yet, to encourage teamwork, he insists that he and his three top officers agree before any major corporate decision is made. Goizueta once vetoed a major acquisition because one member of the team opposed the move.

Perhaps his biggest gamble was putting Coke's name on a diet coke. Although the decision seems simple in retrospect, Goizueta and Keough say that it was the most difficult one that they have made. They saw horrendous risk in putting the venerable Coke name on a product that could fail. Nevertheless, they took the gamble in 1982. Within 5 years, Diet Coke became the third-largest-selling soft drink in the United States, and it accounts for most of Coke's growth in total market share.

Then there is the issue of New Coke. Goizueta continues to argue strongly that Coke was correct in offering the new, sweeter-tasting formula in 1985 because of Pepsi's increasing popularity, particularly with children. Looking back, though, he wishes that he had brought old Coke back in 1 month, rather than waiting for 3 months before announcing that the old formula would be reintroduced as Coca-Cola Classic. He says that he will never forget having to appear on television telling the American people that he had made a mistake.

Few errors produce such good results. Coca-Cola Classic outsells the new formula (now simply called Coke) by a margin of 10 to 1 and is now the top-selling cola drink in the United States. Goizueta wants to keep the new formula on the shelves, though, because he believes, "It's more important that Coke's name is on its best-tasting product than its best-selling product." In his view, the new formula may still be successful over the long term because many baby-boomers and later generations have been raised on relatively sweet-tasting soft drinks. PepsiCo, Inc., and Coke continue to wage major battles for market share across their various products.

Before introducing New Coke, the company conducted extensive market tests in over 30 U.S. cities. In obtaining the opinions of more than 40,000 people, Coke sampled eight times the usual number of consumers. With the brand name hidden, 55 percent of the people chose the new Coke formula over the old formula, while 52 percent placed it ahead of Pepsi. The general consensus is that the company did everything right in terms of following the best market research procedures. Nevertheless, no one predicted the vehemence of customer reactions.

Thus, even though Coke did extensive market research, these efforts did not lead to the best final decision. Still, the managers did follow an appropriate decision-making process, including generating alternative formulas and evaluating them carefully. Fortunately, in this case, the decision was reversible. By following effective decision-making procedures, though, managers at Coke increase the likelihood of making good decisions. So far, their track record has been good, and the company's stock has been rising significantly.[1]

As the Coca-Cola situation graphically illustrates, gaining and maintaining a competitive edge requires extensive managerial decision making. **Decision making** is the process through which managers identify organizational problems and attempt to resolve them. In Goizueta's situation, he recognized that Coke was in danger of losing its preeminence in the soft-drink industry. He also saw that the company was not using its tremendous assets to their full capacity. Hence he took steps to solve these problems. Managers may not always make the right decision, but they can use their knowledge of appropriate decision-making processes to increase the odds.

In this chapter we explore the nature of managerial decision making, including the types of problems and decision-making situations that managers are likely to face. We also evaluate managers as decision makers and consider the steps in an effective decision-making process. We examine how major barriers to effective decision making can be overcome, and we weigh the advantages and disadvantages of group decision making. Finally, we show how managers can promote innovation through the use of the creativity factor in decision making.

Decision making The process through which managers identify organizational problems and attempt to resolve them

THE NATURE OF MANAGERIAL DECISION MAKING

Like Goizueta, managers make many different decisions in the course of their work. While managers at lower levels in organizations might not make such monumental decisions as changing the formula for a revered product, many smaller decisions at lower levels have a cumulative effect on organizational effectiveness. For example, Motorola has built its reputation for high quality and innovation (particularly in semiconductors, electronic pagers, and cellular telephones) partially by encouraging individuals from design, manufacturing, and marketing departments to involve themselves early in decision making for new projects.[2] Good decision-making processes are important at all levels.

An effective decision-making process generally includes the four steps shown in Figure 8-1.[3] Some authors refer to these four steps as problem solving and reserve the term "decision making" for the first three steps—the process up to, but not including, implementation and follow-up.[4] Here we use "decision making" and "problem solving" interchangeably to refer to the broad process depicted in Figure 8-1. We do this because "decision making" is the term more commonly used in business, and we believe that it will be clear when we are using this term in its more narrow sense. We analyze the four steps in the decision-making process in greater detail in a later section of this chapter. First, though, it is useful to examine the major types of problems that managers usu-

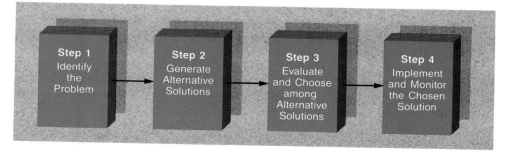

Figure 8-1 Model of the decision-making process. (Adapted from George P. Huber, *Managerial Decision Making*, Scott, Foresman, Glenview, Ill., 1980, p. 8.)

ally encounter and to consider the important differences in managerial decision-making situations.

Types of Problems Decision Makers Face

Managerial decision making typically centers on three types of problems: crisis, noncrisis, and opportunity problems.[5]

Crisis problem A serious difficulty requiring immediate action

Crisis. A **crisis problem** is a serious difficulty requiring immediate action. An example of a crisis is the discovery of a severe cash-flow deficiency that has a high potential of quickly evolving into serious losses. Coca-Cola faced a crisis when loyal customers protested the demise of the classic coke formula.

Noncrisis problem An issue that requires resolution but does not simultaneously have the importance and immediacy characteristics of a crisis

Noncrisis. A **noncrisis problem** is an issue that requires resolution but does not simultaneously have the importance and immediacy characteristics of a crisis. Many of the decisions that managers make center on noncrisis problems. Examples of such problems are a factory that needs to be brought into conformity with new state antipollution standards during the next 3 years and an employee who frequently is late for work. The flat earnings in Coke's troubled food division represent a noncrisis problem, and Goizueta's appointing of a new president and CEO of the division is a first step toward addressing this issue.[6]

Opportunity problem A situation that offers a strong potential for significant organizational gain if appropriate actions are taken

Opportunity. An **opportunity problem** is a situation that offers a strong potential for significant organizational gain if appropriate actions are taken. Opportunities typically involve new ideas and novel directions and, therefore, are major vehicles for organizational innovation. Top management at Coca-Cola saw opportunity in the possibility of placing the Coke name on a more extensive line of soft drinks. Opportunities involve ideas that *could* be used, rather than difficulties that *must* be resolved. Noninnovative managers sometimes fall prey to focusing on various crisis and noncrisis problems, and in the process, they may neglect opportunities. In one study of 78 managerial decision-making situations, 13 percent of the situations were crisis problems, 62 percent were noncrisis problems, and 25 percent involved taking advantage of opportunities.[7] In addition to facing three types of decision problems, managers also typically deal with different types of decision-making situations.

Differences in Decision-Making Situations

Managers would be overwhelmed with decision making if they had to handle each and every problem as if it were a completely new situation. Fortunately, that is not the case. Generally, managerial decision situations fall into two categories: programmed and nonprogrammed. Examples of these two categories of decisions are shown in Table 8-1.

Table 8-1   Types of Managerial Decision-Making Situations

Type of Organization	Programmed Decision	Nonprogrammed Decision
Fast-food restaurant	Determine supplies to be reordered.	Identify location for new franchise.
University	Decide if students meet graduation requirements.	Choose new academic programs.
Automaker	Determine union employee pay rates.	Select new car design.

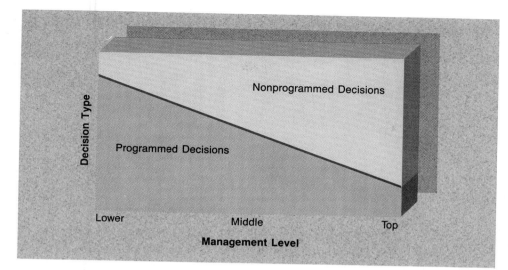

Figure 8-2 Relationship of decision-making situation to management level in organizations. (Adapted from Richard L. Daft and Richard M. Steers, *Organizations: A Micro/ Macro Approach*, Scott, Foresman, Glenview, Ill., 1986, p. 440.)

Programmed Decisions. **Programmed decisions** are those made in routine, repetitive, well-structured situations through the use of predetermined decision rules. The decision rules may be based on habit, computational techniques, or established policies and procedures. Such rules usually stem from prior experience or technical knowledge about what works in the particular type of situation. For example, most organizations have established policies and procedures for handling basic employee disciplinary problems.

Although programmed decisions are applicable to routine, well-structured situations, they can be quite complex. The proliferation of computers has greatly enhanced the possibilities for making sophisticated programmed decisions, because computers can collect and analyze vast amounts of information that can facilitate programmed managerial decision making. For example, managers at San Diego Gas & Electric switch gas and oil suppliers on the basis of decisions made hourly in the utility's vast computerized "mission control" room.[8] When we shop with a credit card, a programmed decision often is made by computer regarding the authorization of our purchase. However, if we wish to charge an unusually large dollar amount or one that exceeds the ceiling for our account, the transaction may require that a supervisor engage in further programmed decision making based on policies and procedures governing such situations.

Most of the decisions made by first-line managers and many of those made by middle managers are the programmed type, but very few of the decisions made by top-level managers are the programmed type (see Figure 8-2). Managers must continually assess the appropriateness of the programmed decision approach. Inappropriate use of programmed decisions can lead to undesirable outcomes. For example, the new owners of a Seattle-based retail chain called Pay 'n Save ran into trouble when they tried to apply the same merchandise-buying and inventory rules they had used in another company. The type of merchandise didn't appeal to the new customer base. In addition, the new owners didn't alter the old ordering rules to account for the decreased amount of available floor space in the new operation.[9]

Nonprogrammed Decisions. In contrast, **nonprogrammed decisions** are those for which predetermined decision rules are impractical because the situations are novel and/or ill-structured.[10] Most of the highly significant decisions that managers make fall into the nonprogrammed category. Because of their nature,

Programmed decisions
Decisions made in routine, repetitive, well-structured situations through the use of predetermined decision rules

Nonprogrammed decisions
Decisions for which predetermined decision rules are impractical because the situations are novel and/or ill-structured

A French boat manufacturer, Chantiers Bénéteau, opened a plant in Marion, South Carolina. This was a nonprogrammed decision necessitated by rapid changes in the economy, including a declining U.S. dollar.

Uncertainty A condition in which the decision maker must choose a course of action without complete knowledge of the consequences that will follow implementation

Risk The possibility that a chosen action could lead to losses rather than the intended results

nonprogrammed decisions usually involve significant amounts of **uncertainty,** a condition in which the decision maker must choose a course of action without complete knowledge of the consequences that will follow implementation.

For example, during the early 1980s, Edward Cooley, chairman of the Precision Castparts Corporation, and his top managers had to decide whether or not to invest heavily in plants and technology. Based in Portland, Oregon, the company casts large and small complex parts, such as turbine blades and vanes, from highly specialized alloys of titanium, nickel, and other metals. Since the parts are used mainly in jet engines, the recession in the airline industry at the time made the future extremely uncertain. Management chose to expand, figuring correctly that the recession would ultimately lead to increased demand, since the airlines would expand and also would need to replace and upgrade current airplanes.[11]

Decisions made under uncertainty involve **risk,** the possibility that a chosen action could lead to losses rather than the intended results. Experts on decision making used to differentiate between uncertainty and risk, but they now view uncertainty as the reason why a situation is risky.[12] Uncertainty can stem from a variety of sources. For example, elements in the environment that are difficult to predict or control can affect the success of a decision. Cost and time constraints can limit the information that can realistically be collected. Social and political factors in the organization, such as poor communication across units, can make relevant information gathering difficult. Finally, situations can change rapidly, causing current information to quickly become obsolete.[13] Partially to cope with rapid change and the declining U.S. dollar, Annette Roux, head of France-based Chantiers Bénéteau, recently decided to open a U.S. manufacturing plant in South Carolina to manufacture the company's line of pleasure craft, including sailboats.[14]

The proportion of nonprogrammed decisions that managers must make increases at each level of the hierarchy (see Figure 8-2). Because nonprogrammed decisions require effective decision-making skills—and, frequently, creativity—nonprogrammed decisions provide the biggest decision-making challenges to managers. As a result, organizations often expend considerable effort through formal training programs and job experience to develop managers who can effectively handle nonprogrammed decision situations. This chapter focuses mainly on issues related to nonprogrammed decisions.

MANAGERS AS DECISION MAKERS

Because the decisions that managers make have a profound impact on the success of the organization, managerial approaches to decision making have been the subject of considerable curiosity and research. In this section, we describe two major types of models regarding how managers make decisions: rational and nonrational.

The Rational Model

The rational model of managerial decision making, a view that was in vogue during the first half of this century, has roots in the economic theory of the firm. In developing theories about the economic behavior of business firms, economists tended to make the simplifying assumption that managers would always make decisions that were in the best economic interests of their firms. This same assumption about managerial decision making was accepted by many management theorists. According to the **rational model,** managers engage in completely rational decision processes, ultimately make optimal decisions, and possess and understand all information relevant to their decisions at the time they make them (including all possible alternatives and all potential outcomes and ramifications). If you have purchased a major competitive item such as a personal computer or an automobile lately, you have probably experienced the difficulties of obtaining perfect information and making "optimal" decisions in complex situations. As a result, you will probably not be surprised to find that there are serious flaws in the rational view of how managers make decisions.[15] Managers, like most decision makers, also are influenced by their own values about what is important, as well as by personality factors such as propensity for risk taking. Nevertheless, the rational view is useful in providing a benchmark against which to compare actual managerial decision-making patterns.

Rational model A model that suggests that managers engage in completely rational decision processes, ultimately make optimal decisions, and possess and understand all information relevant to their decisions at the time they make them

Nonrational Models

In contrast to the rational view, several **nonrational models** of managerial decision making suggest that information-gathering and -processing limitations make it difficult for managers to make optimal decisions. Within the nonrational framework, researchers have identified alternative strategies, or approaches, that managers may adopt in making decisions. Three major nonrational models of managerial decision making are the satisficing, incremental, and garbage-can models.

Nonrational models Models that suggest that information-gathering and -processing limitations make it difficult for managers to make optimal decisions

Satisficing Model. During the 1950s economist Herbert Simon (who later won a Nobel prize for his work in this area) began to study the actual behaviors of managerial decision makers. On the basis of his studies, Simon offered the concept of bounded rationality as a framework through which actual managerial decision making can be better understood.[16] **Bounded rationality** means that the ability of managers to be perfectly rational in making decisions is limited by such factors as cognitive capacity and time constraints. The concept of bounded ra-

Bounded rationality A concept that suggests that the ability of managers to be perfectly rational in making decisions is limited by such factors as cognitive capacity and time constraints

tionality suggests that the following factors commonly limit the degree to which managers are perfectly rational in making decisions:

■ Decision makers may have inadequate information, not only about the nature of the issue to be decided but also about possible alternatives and their strengths and limitations.

■ Time and cost factors often constrain the amount of information that can be gathered in regard to a particular decision.

■ Decision makers' perceptions about the relative importance of various pieces of data may cause critical information to be overlooked or ignored.

■ The part of human memory that is used in making decisions can retain only a relatively small amount of information at one time.

■ The calculating capacities associated with intelligence limit the degree to which decision makers can determine optimal decisions, even assuming that perfect information has been gathered.[17]

Satisficing model A model stating that managers seek alternatives only until they find one that looks *satisfactory*, rather than seeking the optimal decision

According to the bounded rationality view, executives do not optimize their decisions. In other words, they do not have complete information and do not weigh every factor precisely in order to make the very best decisions possible. Rather, Simon argued, they tend to follow the **satisficing model,** which holds that managers seek alternatives only until they find one that looks *satisfactory*, rather than seeking the optimal decision. Satisficing can be an appropriate decision-making approach when the cost of delaying a decision or searching for a better alternative outweighs the likely payoff from such a course. For example, if one is driving on an unfamiliar highway with only a little bit of gas left, it might be better to choose a gas station within sight than to hold out for one's favorite brand. On the other hand, managers sometimes make a habit of using the simplistic satisficing approach even in situations in which the cost of searching for further alternatives is justified given the potential gain.[18]

For instance, Sant Singh Chatwal, founder of Bombay Palace Restaurants, Inc., a New York–based chain, wanted to expand in Manhattan but found that leasing property there was extremely expensive. To solve his problem, he quickly merged with another chain, Lifestyle Restaurants, Inc., a publicly owned chain that owned, operated, or franchised close to 50 Beefsteak Charlie's restaurants. The attraction was that Lifestyle owned a number of cheap leases, particularly in very expensive parts of Manhattan. Chatwal says that he had heard about the Lifestyle chairman's "reputation for rough business practices" and troubles with liquor boards in New York and Maryland. Still, Chatwal retained him as president and chief executive of Lifestyle, guaranteeing him a generous $400,000-per-year salary and a 5-year contract, in addition to other attractive financial concessions involving stock. Within 4 months, Chatwal was involved in an ongoing major court battle in an attempt to break the contract because of allegedly undisclosed Lifestyle tax liabilities and other problems involving the previous Lifestyle chairman. With Chatwal distracted by these problems, the Bombay Palace chain began to experience losses.[19] Thus Chatwal's haste in selecting what seemed to be a quick solution to his leasing problems illustrates the potential pitfalls of satisficing.

Incremental model A model stating that managers make the smallest response possible that will reduce the problem to at least a tolerable level

Incremental Model. Another approach to decision making is the **incremental model,** which holds that managers make the smallest response possible that will reduce the problem to at least a tolerable level.[20] This approach is geared more toward achieving short-run alleviation of a problem rather than toward making decisions that will facilitate future goal attainment. Like the satisficing model, the incremental model does not require that managers process a great deal of information in order to take action. As a result, incremental strategies are usually more effective in the short run than in the long run. One researcher likened incrementalizing to the actions of a homeowner who deals with the problem of insufficient electric outlets by using various multioutlet adapters, such as extension cords. In the long run, the homeowner's incremental decisions may prove to be unworkable, since additional pieces of electrical equipment (e.g., VCRs and personal computers) may cause fuses to blow.[21]

Garbage-Can Model. The **garbage-can model** of decision making holds that managers behave in virtually a random pattern in making nonprogrammed decisions. Typically, decision outcomes occur by chance, depending on such factors as the participants who happen to be involved, the problems about which they happen to be concerned at the moment, the opportunities that they happen to stumble upon, and the pet solutions that happen to be looking for a problem to solve. The garbage-can strategy is most likely to be used when managers have no goal preferences, the means of achieving goals are unclear, and decision-making participants change rapidly.[22] Desirable outcomes can sometimes be achieved with a garbage-can strategy, but this approach can also lead to serious difficulties. Witness the difficulties encountered by Gould, Inc., when its former "iron-willed" CEO, William Ylvisaker, decided to remake the company (see the following Case in Point discussion).[23]

Garbage-can model A model stating that managers behave in virtually a random pattern in making nonprogrammed decisions

CASE IN POINT: Gould's Adventurous Spirit Runs into Trouble

According to company lore, gambling can be traced far back in the history of Gould, Inc., the Rolling Meadows, Illinois, maker of computers, silicon chips, automation systems, and other electric gear, whose annual sales once were in the $2 billion range. Founder Lytton J. Shields, company members say, flipped a coin to decide whether to rebuild his battery factory after it was gutted by fire in 1920. More recently, William T. Ylvisaker, former chairman and CEO, earned a reputation for taking excessive amounts of risk based on personal whims.

For example, Gould bought into a Florida real estate development in the late 1970s. The company then invested more than $80 million to improve the properties, including building a polo club (Ylvisaker was a polo buff). The idea was that the new development would produce between $30 and $50 million per year to help finance new electronics ventures. Unfortunately, interest rates rose and land values dropped, causing Gould to lose $49.2 million.

Similarly, Gould proceeded to bid on a fixed-price contract to provide a new field radio for the Navy and Marines, despite the fact that designs for the product were still undergoing development. More than 3 years later, the company had not produced any of the radios or even finalized the design.

Most observers agree that during his 18 years as head of the company, Ylvisaker transformed Gould from a small battery maker into a major electronics company. At its peak, the company was a leader in factory automation, a noted maker of specialty computers for use in such devices as flight simulators, and a well-known defense contractor.

Unfortunately, while Ylvisaker liked to acquire businesses, he had no well-defined plan for Gould and he lacked the management skills needed to run the multifaceted large enterprise that Gould had become. The lack of central focus caused the company to falter from both an organizational and a financial point of view. By the time Ylvisaker was ousted in 1986, the company was in grave difficulty and the new chairman, former IBM executive James F. McDonald, was not able to reverse the situation quickly enough. The company was taken over by Japan-based Nippon Mining in August 1988, after Nippon made a $1.1 billion offer for what was left of Gould.[24] ▬▬▬

Thus, while the garbage-can approach can sometimes lead managers to take advantage of unforeseen opportunities, it can also lead to severe problems from which it may be difficult to recover. The garbage-can approach often is used in the absence of solid strategic management. (See Chapter 6 for a discussion of strategic management.)

STEPS IN AN EFFECTIVE DECISION-MAKING PROCESS

Descriptive decision-making models Models of decision making that attempt to document how managers actually *do* make decisions

Normative decision-making models Models of decision making that attempt to prescribe how managers *should* make decisions

The models of managerial decision making just outlined are sometimes referred to as **descriptive decision-making models** because they attempt to document how managers actually *do* make decisions. In contrast, models such as the decision-making approach outlined in Table 8-2 are sometimes referred to as **normative decision-making models** because they attempt to prescribe how managers *should* make decisions. According to decision-making experts, managers are more likely to be effective decision makers if they follow the general approach outlined in Table 8-2. Although following such steps does not guarantee that all decisions will have the desired outcomes, it does increase the likelihood of success.[25] While managers frequently do not have control over many factors affecting the success of their decisions, they do have substantial control over the process that they use to make decisions. In this section, we discuss the four-step decision-making process in greater detail.

Identifying the Problem

Organizational problems Discrepancies between a current state or condition and what is desired

The first step in the decision-making process is identifying the problem. **Organizational problems** are discrepancies between a current state or condition and

Table 8-2 Steps in an Effective Decision-Making Process

Step	Activities
Identify the problem.	Scan the environment for changing circumstances. Categorize the situation as a problem (or nonproblem). Diagnose the problem's nature and causes.
Generate alternative solutions.	Restrict criticism of alternatives. Freewheel to stimulate thinking. Offer as many ideas as possible. Combine and improve on ideas.
Evaluate and choose an alternative.	Evaluate feasibility. Evaluate quality. Evaluate acceptability. Evaluate costs. Evaluate reversibility.
Implement and monitor the chosen solution.	Plan the implementation of the solution. Be sensitive to the decision's effects on others. Develop follow-up mechanisms.

what is desired. This step has three general stages: scanning, categorization, and diagnosis.[26]

Scanning Stage. The *scanning stage* involves monitoring the work situation for changing circumstances that may signal the emergence of a problem. At this point, a manager may be only vaguely aware that an environmental change could lead to a problem or that an existing situation is constituting a problem. For example, since the 1960s, the managers at the American Can Company had watched the can business slowly decline as customers began to turn to new containers, particularly plastic ones. As a result, management had been steadily diverting money from the can business and slowly acquiring new businesses. However, in the late 1970s, high interest rates, inflation, and overcapacity in both the company's can and paper operations began to suggest more serious difficulties.[27]

Categorization Stage. The *categorization stage* entails attempting to understand and verify signs that there is some type of discrepancy between a current state and what is desired. At this point, the manager attempts to categorize the situation as a problem or a nonproblem, even though it may be difficult to specify the exact nature of the problem, if one exists. For example, the managers at the American Can Company found that their core businesses suddenly were not generating much cash.

Diagnosis Stage. The *diagnosis stage* involves gathering additional information and specifying both the nature and the causes of the problem. Without appropriate diagnosis, it is difficult to experience success in the rest of the decision process. At the diagnosis stage, the problem should be stated in terms of the discrepancy between current conditions and what is desired, and causes of the discrepancy should be specified. For example, American Can's chief, William Woodside, and the other top executives began to recognize that they were "going downhill." The problem was that they could no longer slowly shift to new businesses as desired because their current businesses were no longer generating sufficient cash to allow new acquisitions.

Generating Alternative Solutions

The second step in the decision-making process is developing alternatives. This practice usually leads to higher-quality solutions,[28] particularly when the situation calls for creative and innovative ones. The development of alternatives can be facilitated through the use of four principles frequently associated with brainstorming:

1. *Don't criticize ideas while generating possible solutions.* Criticism during the idea-generation stage inhibits thinking. Also, because discussion tends to get bogged down in criticizing early ideas, only a few ideas are generated.
2. *Freewheel.* Offer even seemingly wild and outrageous ideas. Although they may never be used, they may trigger some usable ideas from others.
3. *Offer as many ideas as possible.* Pushing for a high volume of ideas increases the probability that some of them will be effective solutions.
4. *Combine and improve on ideas that have been offered.* Often the best ideas come from combinations of the ideas of others.[29]

Although brainstorming is typically done in a group, the principles also can be used by individuals, in the sense of jotting down a number of possible solutions, including farfetched ideas, trying to generate a high idea volume, and combining or building on ideas as one proceeds. Brainstorming and other methods of generating ideas will be considered further when we discuss creativity in a later section of this chapter.

At this point, it is important to emphasize the need to generate a number of alternatives for consideration during this phase of the decision-making process. For example, at American Can, Woodside found that he had to push to get a variety of alternatives because there was a tendency for his managers to pose alternatives that were only small incremental changes from the status quo. (Such a tendency is common; see the incremental model discussion earlier in this chapter.) One early plan proposed by the paper division, which made up a quarter of the company, involved selling one mill and entering into a joint venture with another paper mill. Yet this scenario would still leave the division with a need for $1 billion of investment over the next 5 years just to stay competitive. Woodside told the managers to go back and consider every possible alternative, even drastic ones like selling the business.

Evaluating and Choosing an Alternative

This step involves carefully considering the advantages and disadvantages of each alternative before choosing one of them. Each alternative should be evaluated systematically according to five general criteria: feasibility, quality, acceptability, cost, and reversibility.

Feasibility. The feasibility criterion refers to the extent to which an alternative can be accomplished within related organizational constraints, such as time, budgets, technology, and policies. Alternatives that do not meet the criterion of feasibility should be eliminated from further consideration.

Quality. The quality criterion refers to the extent to which an alternative effectively solves the problem under consideration. Alternatives that only partially solve the problem or represent a questionable solution are eliminated at this stage.

Acceptability. This criterion refers to the degree to which the decision makers and others who will be affected by the implementation of the alternative are willing to support it. Acceptability has long been recognized as an important criterion against which to judge decisions.[30]

Costs. The costs criterion refers to both the resource levels required and the extent to which the alternative is likely to have undesirable side effects. Thus the term "costs" is used here in the broad sense to include not only direct monetary expenditures but also more intangible issues such as possible vigorous competitor retaliation.

Reversibility. This criterion refers to the extent to which the alternative can be reversed, if at all. Peter Drucker has argued that the importance of a decision is not measured by the amount of money involved but, rather, by how easily the decision can be reversed. For example, when the Coca-Cola Company ran into difficulties in introducing its new formula for Coke in 1985, it was able to reverse the decision by reintroducing its old formula as Coke Classic. The company

Customers who lose their American Express Travelers Cheques will not have them personally delivered by American Express spokesperson Karl Malden, who has been frequently shown on television holding replacement checks in faraway places. Nevertheless, extensive preparations including special employee training have been key to the successful implementation of the new American Express service whereby replacement checks can be hand delivered to customers in nearly 570 million locations around the world.

could do this because it still had its old formula. Other types of decisions, such as introducing computerized production facilities, may be much more difficult to reverse.[31] Many times, however, the best alternative may be one that is difficult to reverse. In such cases, the alternative should be reconsidered very carefully before it is selected to be sure that it meets the other criteria. Several of the chosen alternatives at American Can fit the category of irreversible. For example, the company decided to sell its paper and can divisions altogether and buy into such businesses as insurance, financial services, and specialty retail operations. The name of the company was eventually changed to Primerica Corporation.

Implementing and Monitoring the Chosen Solution

For the entire decision-making process to be successful, considerable thought must be given to *implementing* and *monitoring* the chosen solution. It is possible to make a "good" decision in terms of the first three steps and still have the process fail because of difficulties at this final step.

Implementing the Solution. Successful implementation usually depends on two major factors: careful planning and sensitivity to those involved in the implementation and/or affected by it.

In the planning area, minor changes may require only a small amount of planning, while major changes may call for extensive planning efforts, such as written plans, careful coordination with units inside and outside the organization, and special funding arrangements. In general, the more difficult it is to reverse a solution, the more important it is to plan for effective implementation. For example, in a *Wall Street Journal* article, Harvey Gittler, a materials manager for a manufacturer of heating and air-conditioning equipment, discussed his involvement in the installation of a new assembly line. The decision to install the new assembly line was based heavily on the enormous projected cost savings over present methods of production. Because of the size of the potential savings, the decision makers began to push for a speedy implementation. Finally, Gittler asked his boss, "What happens if the new method does not work?" That question caused a slowdown of 4 months while the new process was carefully tested, extensive planning was done, and people were properly trained. The implementation, which had been heading for disaster, ultimately was a huge success.[32]

Implementation also tends to occur more smoothly when decision makers show sensitivity in considering the possible reactions of those the decision will affect. In general, affected individuals are more likely to support a decision when they are able to participate in its implementation. If a large number of individuals will be affected, direct participation may not be feasible. At the very least, it is important to keep affected individuals informed of the changes and to ensure that they receive any training necessary to implement the decision effectively. For instance, when Pacific Southwest Cable in San Diego, California, decided to place heavy emphasis on service, both to internal (individuals inside the company) and external customers, the company spent considerable time orienting and training workers. Part of the change involved giving employees more latitude in taking service actions, such as allowing service representatives to make billing adjustments without prior management approval. As a result of the careful orientation and training, workers were able to implement the changes smoothly, leading to considerable increases in market penetration and profits.[33]

Monitoring the Solution. Managers need to monitor decision implementation to be sure that things are progressing as planned and that the problem that triggered the decision-making process has been resolved. The more important the problem, the greater the effort that needs to be expended on appropriate follow-up mechanisms.

OVERCOMING BARRIERS TO EFFECTIVE DECISION MAKING

Unfortunately, as the nonrational models of managerial decision making suggest, managers often do not follow the four-step decision-making process just outlined. Despite the fact that this general approach is endorsed by a number of decision experts, managers may deviate from an effective decision-making process because they are not aware of the experts' recommendations. However, deviations also occur because of several barriers to effective decision making that managers face. In this section, we discuss means of overcoming four key decision-making barriers: accepting the problem challenge in the first place, searching for sufficient alternatives, recognizing common decision-making biases, and avoiding the decision escalation phenomenon.

Accepting the Problem Challenge

Decision researchers David Wheeler and Irving Janis have identified four basic reaction patterns that characterize the behavior of individuals when they are faced with a legitimate problem in the form of a difficulty or an opportunity. The first three, complacency, defensive avoidance, and panic, represent barriers to effective decision making. The fourth, deciding to decide, constitutes a more viable approach for decision makers to follow.[34]

Complacency A condition in which individuals either do not see the signs of danger or opportunity or ignore them

Complacency. The **complacency** reaction occurs when individuals either do not see the signs of danger or opportunity or ignore them. With complacency, the failure to detect the signs usually stems from a lack of adequate scanning of the environment. Ignoring the signs altogether is more akin to the "ostrich" effect—putting one's head in the sand and hoping that the danger or opportunity will resolve itself. Complacency can be present even when an individual appears to be responding to the situation. For example, complacency occurs when an individual immediately accepts a job offer that looks like a good opportunity without expending any time or effort on attempting to assess the situation thoroughly.

Defensive Avoidance. With **defensive avoidance,** individuals either deny the importance of a danger or an opportunity or deny any responsibility for taking action. Defensive avoidance can take three different forms: rationalization ("It can't happen to me"), procrastination ("It can be taken care of later"), or buck-passing ("It's someone else's problem").

> **Defensive avoidance** A condition in which individuals either deny the importance of a danger or an opportunity or deny any responsibility for taking action

Panic. With **panic** or paniclike reactions, individuals become so upset that they frantically seek a way to solve a problem. In their haste, they often seize upon a quickly formulated alternative without noticing its severe disadvantages and without considering other, potentially better alternatives. Panic is particularly likely to occur with crisis problems.[35]

> **Panic** A reaction in which individuals become so upset that they frantically seek a way to solve a problem

Deciding to Decide. With the **deciding-to-decide** response, decision makers accept the challenge of deciding what to do about a problem and follow an effective decision-making process. Deciding to decide is an important reaction to a legitimate problem situation. Of course, managers cannot attend to every potential problem, no matter how minor and remote, that appears on the horizon. Some guidelines for deciding to decide are presented in Table 8-3.

> **Deciding to decide** A response in which decision makers accept the challenge of deciding what to do about a problem and follow an effective decision-making process

Searching for Sufficient Alternatives

For many decision situations, particularly nonprogrammed decisions, it is unrealistic for decision makers to collect enough information to identify *all* potential alternatives and assess *all* possible pluses and minuses. A major reason is that information acquisition typically requires time and money. Such costs accrue even when information gathering is confined to checking with knowledgeable

Table 8-3   Guidelines for Deciding to Decide

APPRAISE CREDIBILITY OF INFORMATION
Is the source in a position to know the truth?
If so, is the source likely to be honest?
Is there any evidence, and how good is it?

ASCERTAIN IMPORTANCE OF THREAT OR OPPORTUNITY
How likely is a real danger or opportunity?
If a threat, how severe might the losses be?
If an opportunity, how great might the gains be?

DETERMINE THE NEED FOR URGENCY
Is the threat or opportunity likely to occur soon?
Will it develop gradually, or is sudden change likely?
If some action is urgent, can part be done now and the rest later?

Source: Adapted from Daniel D. Wheeler and Irving L. Janis, *A Practical Guide for Making Decisions,* Macmillan, New York, 1980, pp. 34–35.

organizational members or holding a meeting. As a result, decision makers must evaluate how much time, effort, and money should be expended in gathering information that will help in making a particular decision.

This information-gathering dilemma is depicted in Figure 8-3. The horizontal axis indicates potential information about the decision, spanning from 0 to 100 percent. The vertical axis depicts the value and cost of additional information. As indicated by line a, as the decision maker collects more and more information, the value of the additional information in many situations begins to level off. At the same time, as shown by line b, the cost of additional information during the initial search is usually not very high but tends to get much higher as one moves toward obtaining perfect information. As a result, the marginal, or incremental, value of additional pieces of information (line c) rises at first to a point of optimality and then begins to decline at the point at which cost begins to exceed the value of additional pieces of information. The area of optimal information gathering also is shown.

A prime area in which decision makers' efforts tend to fall seriously *below* the zone of cost effectiveness is the process of identifying a sufficient number of potential alternatives. For example, one study of 78 decision-making situations found that in 85 percent of the cases, there was little or no search for viable alternatives. Instead, decision makers tended to engage in such practices as quickly copying a solution used by others, accepting an off-the-shelf solution offered by a consultant, or seizing upon an idea of unknown or debatable value and trying to find support for it. Even in the 15 percent of the cases in which a deliberate effort was made to develop viable alternatives, there was a tendency to cut off the search process after identifying only a few possibilities.[36] Managers frequently find it more expedient to do a quick search, find an adequate solution, and then take action. Unfortunately, as mentioned previously, such behavior often becomes a habit that is then applied inappropriately.

Unless countered, the tendency to skip or cut short the search for alternatives is likely to have a stifling effect on innovation. Of course, for rather trivial decisions, managers may correctly feel that the time and effort involved in identifying multiple alternatives are not warranted. However, for more important decisions, managers need to place particular emphasis on identifying alterna-

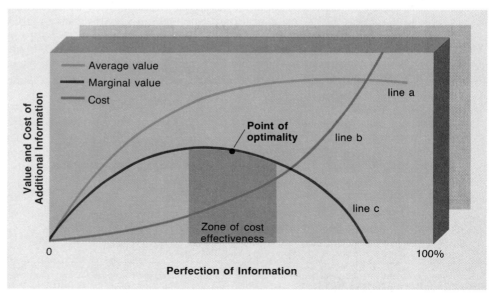

Figure 8-3 The cost of additional information. (Adapted from E. Frank Harrison, *The Managerial Decision-Making Process*, 2d ed., Houghton Mifflin, Boston, 1981, p. 34.)

tives if the decision-making process is to be truly effective. Some approaches that may be helpful in generating decision alternatives will be discussed later in this chapter in the section on creativity.

Recognizing Common Decision-Making Biases

Psychologists Daniel Kahneman and Amos Tversky, who for years have been investigating how decision makers operate, have pointed out several biases that tend to characterize the way that decision makers process information.[37] These biases, which are explained below, are framing, representativeness, availability, and anchoring and adjustment. A related issue is the decision makers' tendency toward overconfidence under some conditions. These biases are most likely to affect the way in which decision makers evaluate alternative solutions, but they may also influence the way in which they identify difficulties and opportunities. Consider the following situation:

> Threatened by a superior enemy force, the general faces a dilemma. His intelligence officers say his soldiers will be caught in an ambush in which 600 of them will die unless he leads them to safety by one of two available routes. If he takes the first route, 200 soldiers will be saved. If he takes the second, there's a one-third chance that 600 soldiers will be saved and a two-thirds chance that none will be saved. Which route should he take?

If you are like most people, you chose the first alternative, reasoning that the general should save the 200 rather than risk the possibility of even higher losses. Suppose, however, that the situation is as follows:

> The general again has to choose between two escape routes. But this time his aides tell him that if he takes the first, 400 soldiers will die. If he takes the second, there's a one-third chance that no soldiers will die and a two-thirds chance that 600 soldiers will die. Which route should he take?

In this situation, most people argue that the general should take the second route. Their rationale is that with the first route 400 will certainly be dead. With the second route there is at least a one-third chance that no one will die, and casualties will only be 50 percent higher if the scheme fails.

Interestingly, most people draw the opposite conclusion from these two problems. In the first problem, people favor the first alternative 3 to 1; in the second problem, they choose the second alternative 4 to 1. Yet a close look will reveal that the problems in both cases are exactly the same—they are just stated differently. The first problem is stated in terms of lives lost, the second in terms of lives saved. The tendency to make different decisions depending on how a problem is presented is called **framing.**

To explain the paradoxical decision pattern exhibited in the general's dilemmas, Kahneman and Tversky have developed the prospect theory. Based on the belief that decision makers tend to be "loss averse," the **prospect theory** posits that they find the prospect of an actual loss more painful than giving up the possibility of a gain.[38] The credit card industry seems to have an intuitive understanding of prospect theory, as evidenced by a common arrangement whereby customers receive "discounts for cash" at gas stations rather than being charged "credit surcharges" for using their credit cards. Prospect theory suggests that customers are less willing to pay an *extra* charge for using credit cards (an actual loss) than they are to forgo a discount for paying cash (a potential gain).

Prospect theory at work: those who use credit cards instead of cash to pay for gasoline would prefer to think that they are giving up a discount than that they are paying a surcharge.

Framing The tendency to make different decisions depending on how a problem is presented

Prospect theory A theory positing that decision makers find the prospect of an actual loss more painful than giving up the possibility of a gain

Linda is 31, single, outspoken, and very bright. She majored in philosophy in college. As a student, she was deeply concerned with discrimination and other social issues and participated in antinuclear demonstrations. Which of the following statements is more likely?

   a. Linda is a bank teller.
   b. Linda is a bank teller and active in the feminist movement.

Most people choose the alternative that says that Linda is both a bank teller and a feminist. Actually, however, the laws of probability suggest that an occurrence (bank teller) is more likely to happen on its own than in conjunction with another occurrence (bank teller *and* feminist). The Linda problem illustrates a common decision shortcut called **representativeness,** the tendency to be overly influenced by stereotypes in making judgments about the likelihood of occurrences. We increase the odds of decision-making difficulties when our judgments run counter to the laws of probability.

> In a typical English text, does the letter "K" appear more often as the first letter in a word or the third letter?

People generally judge that the letter "K" is more likely to be the first letter in a word even though the letter is almost twice as likely to appear in the third position. We tend to do this because of a bias called **availability,** the tendency to judge the likelihood of an occurrence on the basis of the extent to which other like instances or occurrences can easily be recalled. In this case, it is usually easier to recall words beginning with the letter "K" than words in which "K" is the third letter. Availability also shows up in tendencies to overestimate the likelihood of deaths due to vividly imaginable causes such as airplane accidents, fires, and murder and to underestimate more common, but less spectacular, causes such as emphysema and stroke.[39] Examples of instances in which managers may fall victim to the availability bias include basing annual performance appraisals on the most recent and easily recalled performance of subordinates, judging how well competitors' products are doing by the extent to which the managers have seen them in use, and gauging employee morale by relying on the views of immediate subordinates.

> A newly hired engineer for a computer firm in the Boston metropolitan area has 4 years' experience and good all-around qualifications. When asked to estimate the starting salary for this employee, a chemist who had very little knowledge about the profession or industry guessed an annual salary of $17,000. What is your estimate?[40]

Most people do not think that the chemist's guess influenced their own estimate. Yet people tend to give higher salary estimates when the chemist's estimate is stated as $60,000 than when it is $17,000. This tendency to be influenced by an initial figure, even when the information is largely irrelevant, is known as **anchoring and adjustment.** For example, employers often ask job candidates about their current salary and then use the figure as a basis for extending an offer, even though the candidate may currently be underpaid or overpaid.

These information-processing biases suggest that decision makers should be cautious about the accuracy of their estimates regarding the likelihood of events. At the same time, evidence suggests that decision makers tend toward **overconfidence,** the tendency to be more certain of judgments regarding the

Representativeness The tendency to be overly influenced by stereotypes in making judgments about the likelihood of occurrences

Availability The tendency to judge the likelihood of an occurrence on the basis of the extent to which other like instances or occurrences can easily be recalled

Anchoring and adjustment The tendency to be influenced by an initial figure, even when the information is largely irrelevant

Overconfidence The tendency to be more certain of judgments regarding the likelihood of a future event than one's actual predictive accuracy warrants

likelihood of a future event than one's actual predictive accuracy warrants.[41] Ironically, overconfidence appears most likely to occur when decision makers are working in areas with which they are unfamiliar.[42] The overconfidence stems from a failure to fully understand the potential pitfalls involved. Thus managers may be particularly susceptible to overconfidence when they are planning moves into new, unfamiliar areas of business.

For example, the Allied Chemical Corporation ran into acute difficulties when the company and two partners, Gulf Oil and Royal Dutch/Shell, began building a plant to turn years of radioactive waste accumulated from U.S. nuclear power plants into reusable nuclear fuel. Believing it could triumph where others had failed, Allied plunged into the project in the early 1970s without fully assaying the multitude of technological questions and the complex political issues involved. In 1971, Allied and its partners began building the Barnwell nuclear fuel plant on a 1587-acre tract next to the federal government's immense Savannah River reserve, a South Carolina nuclear-waste dump. By 1977, the Carter administration had banned plutonium processing, and by 1981, the partners had abandoned the project after spending over $200 million, conceding that the politics, costs, and technological challenges of the effort were unsurmountable—at least for a private enterprise. Nevertheless, Du Pont is now building an $870 million nuclear-waste plant in the same area. However, Du Pont is operating as a contractor; the Department of Energy is the owner and financier of the project.[43]

Managers can avoid some of the ill effects of information-processing biases by being aware of how such biases are likely to affect their judgments. Gathering enough information to be fairly well versed about the issues associated with important decisions also should help. Another suggestion is to get decision makers to think about why their judgments might be wrong or far off the target. Such thinking may help reveal contradictions and inaccuracies.[44] Some quantitative methods that can help decision makers make more accurate judgments are covered in Chapter 9.

Avoiding the Decision Escalation Phenomenon

When a manager makes a decision, it often is only one decision in a series of decisions about a particular issue. Further decisions may be necessary depending on the results of a previous decision. For example, suppose that you decide to hire a new employee because you expect that the person will be an excellent performer. However, after several months on the job it is apparent that the person is not performing at an acceptable level. Should you take steps to terminate the worker? Of course, at this point you have invested considerable time and money in training the individual, and it is possible that the individual is still learning the job. So you decide to spend more time helping the worker, and you line up some further training. Even with these additional inputs, 2 months later the worker still is not performing at the necessary level. What do you decide now? Although you have more reason to "cut your losses," you also have even more invested in making the individual productive. When do you discontinue your "investment"?[45]

Decision situations like this one present difficult dilemmas for managers. Substantial costs have already been incurred because of an earlier decision. On the other hand, future actions have the potential of either reversing the situation or compounding the initial losses. Such situations are sometimes referred to as **escalation situations,** because they signal the strong possibility of escalating commitment and accelerating losses.[46]

Escalation situations Situations that signal the strong possibility of escalating commitment and accelerating losses

Nonrational escalation The tendency to increase commitment to a previously selected course of action beyond the level that would be expected if the manager followed an effective decision-making process; also called *escalation phenomenon*

Sunk costs Costs that, once incurred, are not recoverable and should not enter into considerations of future courses of action

Research studies indicate that when managers incur costs associated with an initial decision, they often react by allocating more resources to the situation even when the prospects for turning the situation around are dim. Such situations can develop into what decision expert Max H. Bazerman has called nonrational escalation. **Nonrational escalation,** or the escalation phenomenon, is the tendency to increase commitment to a previously selected course of action beyond the level that would be expected if the manager followed an effective decision-making process.[47] As experts in the fields of economics and accounting have pointed out, costs that have already been incurred (e.g., time and money) should be considered **sunk costs.** Such costs, once incurred, are not recoverable and should not enter into considerations of future courses of action. Yet decision makers often are heavily influenced by prior costs when they themselves have made the initial decisions and, hence, are highly susceptible to nonrational escalation.

Part of the reason for the escalation phenomenon is that decision makers tend to be loss averse and may be reluctant to write off the prior costs. Thus the tendency may be related to prospect theory, discussed earlier. In addition, the decision maker may be concerned that a change in the course of action may cause others to regard the original decision as a mistake or failure. Methods of avoiding nonrational escalation include setting advance limits on how far to extend the commitment, asking tough questions about why the commitment is being continued, reviewing the costs involved, and watching for escalation situations that may constitute commitment traps.[48] Otherwise, decision makers may find themselves in a situation similar to that which plagued Expo 86 (see the following Case in Point discussion).

CASE IN POINT: Expo 86 Escalates

Since the late 1970s, British Columbia, Canada, had been planning to host a world's fair, to be held in Vancouver during 1986. The idea for the fair was originally proposed by William Bennett, the provincial premier, and it initially appeared to be something that would bring both visibility and financial benefits to the province. Unfortunately, as the planning progressed, the original estimates of attendance, costs of construction, and projected earnings all proved to be overly optimistic. It became apparent that the city did not have the infrastructure of hotels, parking, and transportation that was needed to host the planned number of visitors. Additionally, the projected cost of the exposition ballooned from $78 million to $1.5 billion, while more realistic revenue projections indicated that the fair would not be a break-even proposition but could be expected to lose over $300 million. In short, what started out as a great idea turned into a fiscal and procedural quagmire.

Expo 86 began with positive expectations for most aspects of the project. There were to be large revenues coming in not only from the fair's concessions and gate receipts but from gains associated with many other sectors of the city (e.g., hotels, restaurants, and general tourist trade). These project considerations turned negative, however, as financial planners realized that revenues were overstated and costs underestimated. Yet, as this negative news grew in magnitude, the premier of British Columbia became even more committed to the project. Estimates of attendance were raised to justify the project (at one point they were well beyond the city's physical capacity to host the fair's visitors), and the major problems of housing and transportation were minimized. Premier Bennett not only argued strenuously for the fair's continuance but staked his

Expo 86, the world's fair held in Vancouver, British Columbia, went ahead as planned despite the growing realization of overestimated revenues and underestimated costs. To have canceled the fair would have entailed a loss of $80 million, not to mention a loss of pride and prestige.

career on the project to the point at which withdrawal might cost him his political office.

As the time of the fair approached, the estimated costs of canceling the event were projected to exceed $80 million, making a reversal of the initial decision extremely difficult. Various interest groups became so dependent on the fair that they argued for its completion at nearly any price. In addition, the fair eventually became central to more abstract goals and purposes of the region, such as signifying Vancouver's view of itself as a first-class city, the equal of Toronto and Montreal. Finally, the province instituted a lottery that raised the necessary funds to cover the expected deficit of $300 million, and the fair was held as scheduled.[49] ▪

GROUP DECISION MAKING

Major decisions in organizations are most often made by more than one person. For example, at Coca-Cola, Goizueta and the other three top executives must agree on any major decision. Even at nonsupervisory levels, groups increasingly are involved in making operational decisions. For instance, Gencorp Automotive has geared its new $65 million reinforced plastics plant near Indianapolis to run with just three levels: plant manager, team leaders, and 25 teams of 5 to 15 production workers. The teams will make most of the decisions involving their work area.[50] In this section, we consider the advantages and disadvantages of group decision making, as well as means of enhancing group decision-making processes.[51]

Advantages of Group Decision Making

Compared with individual decision making, group decision making has several advantages (see Table 8-4). One advantage is that multiple individuals bring more information and knowledge to bear on the question under consideration. Another is that individuals as a group usually can generate more alternative

Table 8-4 Advantages and Disadvantages of Group Decision Making

Advantages	Disadvantages
1. More information and knowledge is focused on the issue.	1. It is usually more time-consuming.
2. An increased number of alternatives can be developed.	2. Disagreements may delay decisions and cause hard feelings.
3. Greater understanding and acceptance of the final decision are likely.	3. The discussion may be dominated by one or a few group members.
4. Members develop knowledge and skills for future use.	4. Groupthink may cause members to overemphasize gaining agreement.

solutions for evaluation. Yet another advantage is that group members are more likely to both understand and support the final decision when they have participated in the decision-making process. Finally, group decision making helps members develop the knowledge base and decision-making skills needed in the future. One recent study of more than 200 project teams, who were involved in educational courses related to management, indicates that the groups outperformed their most proficient group member 97 percent of the time.[52]

Disadvantages of Group Decision Making

Despite its advantages, group decision making also has several disadvantages when contrasted with individual decision making (see Table 8-4). For one thing, decision making in groups is usually fairly time-consuming because various members must be given the opportunity to communicate their ideas as part of the group discussion. For another, disagreements in the group may result in delayed decisions and may cause hard feelings among group members. Yet another disadvantage is that the group discussion may be dominated by one or a few group members, thus canceling some of the advantages of making a decision in groups. Finally, groupthink may cause members to place too much emphasis on gaining agreement.

Groupthink The tendency in cohesive groups to seek agreement about an issue at the expense of realistically appraising the situation

Groupthink is the tendency in cohesive groups to seek agreement about an issue at the expense of realistically appraising the situation.[53] With groupthink, group members are so concerned about preserving the cohesion of the group that they are reluctant to bring up issues that may cause disagreements or to provide information that may prove unsettling to the discussion. Such tendencies can have disastrous consequences when major issues are being considered. For example, the *Challenger* tragedy has been attributed to groupthink. Despite some contrary information, the decision was made to go ahead with the mission by top managers at the National Aeronautics and Space Administration (NASA) and at Morton Thiokol, the company that manufactures the solid rocket boosters. The upper-level officials tended to ignore information from engineers at Morton Thiokol and from others about possible malfunctions due to unusually cold weather conditions. Faced with a desire to secure continued funding and intense public interest in the Teacher in Space program, the decision makers became a cohesive group that was largely unwilling to seriously consider contrary facts.[54] Recent research suggests that groupthink may occur even when groups are not highly cohesive. One major factor may be a directive leader who states a particular preference early in the discussion. Apparently, when that happens, groups often willingly comply, perhaps partially because their search for alternatives is inhibited by the suggested preference.[55]

Enhancing Group Decision-Making Processes

Managers can take a number of steps to avoid the major pitfalls involved in group decision making, while reaping the advantages of the group decision-making process. One step is involving the group in decisions when the information and knowledge of the group have an important bearing on the decision outcome. That way, the time consumed by group decision making can probably be justified. The group should also be involved when their understanding and acceptance of the decision is important to successful implementation of the decision. Here, too, the time involved in group interaction is likely to be justified. In Chapter 14, we further discuss the issue of when managers should make the decision themselves and when they should involve the group.

Another step in facilitating the group decision-making process is considering carefully the composition of the group. For example, including individuals who are likely to consider major organizational goals helps overcome any tendency toward self-interest. Problems caused by one or more individuals dominating the group can often be minimized by including an individual who is skilled at encouraging the ideas of others.

Yet another step that can be taken to facilitate group decision making is setting up mechanisms that help avoid groupthink. One such mechanism is designating one or more **devil's advocates,** individuals who are assigned the role of making sure that the negative aspects of any attractive decision alternatives are considered.[56] Another mechanism is engaging in **dialectical inquiry,** a procedure in which a decision situation is approached from two opposite points of view.[57] With this approach, one decision possibility is developed and the underlying assumptions are identified; then another group is asked to develop a feasible decision possibility that operates on opposite assumptions. The approach forces the group to confront the implications of their assumptions in the decision process.

Group decision-making processes can also be improved through the use of techniques that enhance creativity. Creativity is an essential part of the decision-making process because it helps generate novel alternatives that lead to innovation and also fosters the development of unique perspectives on the nature of problems. In the next section, we discuss several approaches for encouraging greater creativity in individuals and groups.

Devil's advocates Individuals who are assigned the role of making sure that the negative aspects of any attractive decision alternatives are considered

Dialectical inquiry A procedure in which a decision situation is approached from two opposite points of view

PROMOTING INNOVATION: THE CREATIVITY FACTOR IN DECISION MAKING

Creativity is the cognitive process of developing an idea, concept, commodity, or discovery that is viewed as novel by its creator or a target audience.[58] Hence creativity usually is identified by assessing outcomes.[59] In fact, creativity researcher Teresa M. Amabile argues, "Creativity is not a quality of a person; it is a quality of ideas, of behaviors, or products."[60]

Creativity is crucial to solving problems in ways that result in important organizational innovations. It provides the novel approaches that the innovation process translates into new methods, products, or services. As worldwide competition heats up, greater emphasis is being placed on creativity. Japan, in particular, is trying to overcome its reputation as a copycat of the technology of other countries through increased efforts at creativity. For example, Matsushita Electronics Corporation's semiconductor executives wear badges stating "Create." At the Nippon Electric Company (NEC), posters and placards encourage

Creativity The cognitive process of developing an idea, concept, commodity, or discovery that is viewed as novel by its creator or a target audience

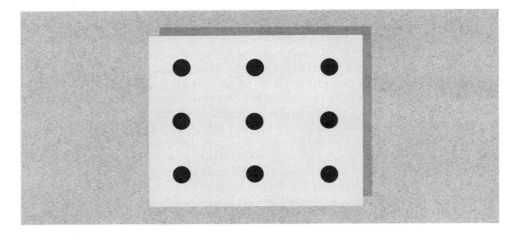

Figure 8-4 The nine-dot problem. Without lifting your pencil from the paper, draw no more than four lines that will cross through all nine dots.

workers to "invent the new VCR" and offer $100 awards for creative ideas.[61]

Try your hand at the classic creativity problem shown in Figure 8-4. Then look at Figure 8-5, which presents some possible solutions to the problem. Many individuals are unable to solve the nine-dot problem because they make the assumption that the lines cannot go outside the nine dots. As this problem illustrates, creativity requires both convergent and divergent thinking. **Convergent thinking** is the effort to solve problems by beginning with a problem and attempting to move logically to a solution. One might liken convergent thinking to searching for oil by digging an ever bigger and deeper hole.[62] **Divergent thinking,** on the other hand, is the effort to solve problems by generating new ways of viewing a problem and seeking novel alternatives. Rather than digging in the same hole, a divergent thinker digs in many different places to generate new perspectives. In the creative process, convergent thinking helps define a problem and evaluate proposed solutions. Divergent thinking helps develop alternative views of the problem, as well as seek novel ways of dealing with problems. For example, in the nine-dot problem, divergent thinking is needed to help overcome the assumption that the lines cannot go outside the dots. Convergent thinking can then logically move toward a solution. Divergent thinking may again be used to help formulate some of the more novel solutions shown in Figure 8-5. In this section, we examine the basic ingredients of creativity, describe the stages of the creative process, and offer some major techniques for enhancing group creativity that can be used by managers.

Convergent thinking The effort to solve problems by beginning with a problem and attempting to move logically to a solution

Divergent thinking The effort to solve problems by generating new ways of viewing the problem and seeking novel alternatives

Basic Ingredients

According to creativity expert Amabile, the following three basic ingredients are necessary for creativity.

Domain-Relevant Skills. These skills are associated with expertise in the relevant field. They include related technical skills or artistic ability, talent in the area, and factual knowledge.

Figure 8-5 Some possible solutions to the nine-dot problem. (Based on J. L. Adams, *Conceptual Blockbusting: A Guide to Better Ideas,* 2d ed., Norton, New York, pp. 25–30, and reprinted from Diane E. Papalia and Sally Wendkos Olds, *Psychology,* McGraw-Hill, New York, 1985, p. 297.)

This puzzle is difficult to solve if the imaginary boundary (limit) enclosing the nine dots is not exceeded. A surprising number of people will not exceed the imaginary boundary, for often this constraint is unconsciously in the mind of the problem-solver, even though it is not in the definition of the problem at all. The overly strict limits are a block in the mind of the solver. The widespread nature of this block is what makes this puzzle classic. (Adams, 1980, p. 24)

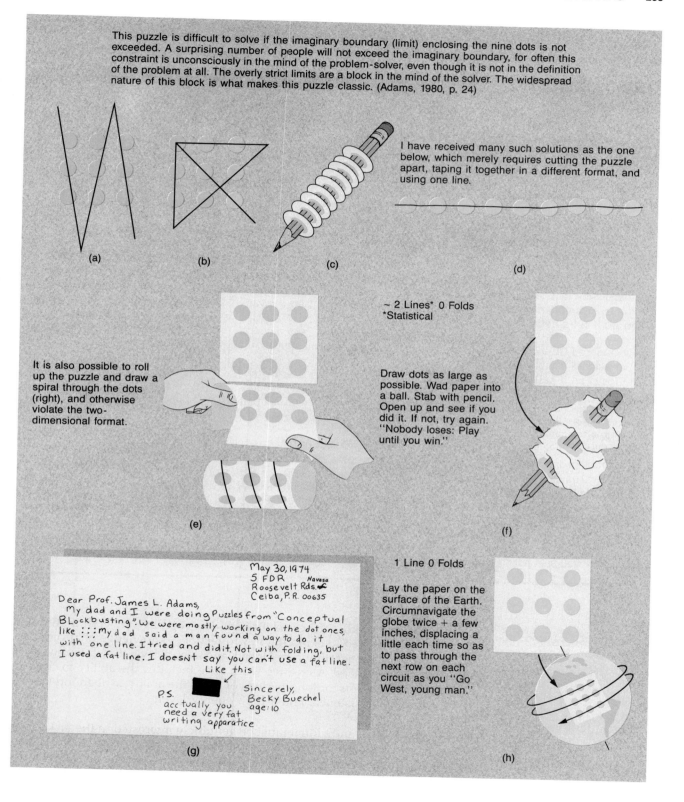

(a)

(b)

(c)

I have received many such solutions as the one below, which merely requires cutting the puzzle apart, taping it together in a different format, and using one line.

(d)

It is also possible to roll up the puzzle and draw a spiral through the dots (right), and otherwise violate the two-dimensional format.

~ 2 Lines* 0 Folds
*Statistical

Draw dots as large as possible. Wad paper into a ball. Stab with pencil. Open up and see if you did it. If not, try again. "Nobody loses: Play until you win."

(e)

(f)

May 30, 1974
5 FDR   Navasa
Roosevelt Rds.
Ceiba, P.R. 00635

Dear Prof. James L. Adams,
   My dad and I were doing puzzles from "Conceptual Blockbusting". We were mostly working on the dot ones, like ::: my dad said a man found a way to do it with one line. I tried and did it. Not with folding, but I used a fat line. I doesn't say you can't use a fat line.
         Like this

P.S.   Sincerely,
acctually you   Becky Buechel
need a very fat   age: 10
writing apparatice

(g)

1 Line 0 Folds

Lay the paper on the surface of the Earth. Circumnavigate the globe twice + a few inches, displacing a little each time so as to pass through the next row on each circuit as you "Go West, young man."

(h)

HOW TO BE MORE CREATIVE

Some of the following suggestions, which are based on research and thinking on creativity, may help you be more creative in your work and your daily life.

What Do You Want to Do?
■ Take time to understand a problem before you begin trying to solve it.
■ Get all the facts clearly in mind.
■ Identify the facts that seem to be the most important before you try to work out a detailed solution.

How Can You Do It?
■ Set aside a sizable block of time to focus on a particular problem, rather than attending to it in scattered sessions.
■ Work out a plan for attacking the problem.
■ Establish subgoals. Solve part of the problem and go on from there. You don't have to do everything at once. Write out your thoughts. This allows you to capture important points and to come back to them later. It also allows you to look for patterns.
■ Imagine yourself acting out the

problem. *Actually* act out the problem.
■ Think of a similar problem you've solved in the past and build on the strategy you used then.
■ Use analogies whenever possible. See whether you can generalize from a similar situation to your current problem.
■ Use several different problem-solving strategies—verbal, visual, mathematical, acting. Draw a diagram to help you visualize the problem, or talk to yourself out loud, or "walk through" a situation.
■ Look for relationships among various facts.
■ Trust your intuition. Take a guess and see whether you can back it up.
■ Play with ideas and possible approaches. Try looking at the same situation in a number of different ways.

How Can You Do It Better?
■ Try consciously to be original, to come up with new ideas.
■ Don't worry about looking foolish if you say or suggest something unusual or if you come up with the wrong answer.
■ Eliminate cultural taboos in your thinking (such as gender stereo-

typing) that might interfere with your ability to come up with a novel solution.
■ Try to be right the first time, but if you're not, explore as many alternatives as you need to.
■ Keep an open mind. If your initial approach doesn't work, ask whether you made assumptions that might not be true.
■ If you get stuck on one approach, try to get to the solution by another route.
■ Be alert to odd or puzzling facts. If you can explain them, your solution may be at hand.
■ Think of unconventional ways to use objects and the environment. Look at familiar things as if you've never seen them before.
■ Consider taking a detour that delays your goal but eventually leads to it.
■ Discard habitual ways of doing things, and force yourself to figure out new ways.
■ Do some brainstorming with one or more other people. This involves trying to produce as many new and original ideas as possible, without evaluating any of them until the end of the session.
■ Strive for objectivity. Evaluate your own ideas as you would those of a stranger.[63]

Creativity-Relevant Skills. These skills include a cognitive style, or method, of thinking that is oriented to exploring new directions, knowledge of approaches that can be used for generating novel ideas, and a work style that is conducive to developing creative ideas. A creative work style includes the ability to concentrate effort and attention for long periods of time, the ability to abandon unproductive avenues, persistence, and a high energy level.

Task Motivation. The individual must be genuinely interested in the task for its own sake, rather than because of some external reward possibility, such as money. Recent evidence suggests that primary concern with external rewards tends to inhibit the creative process. For example, a scientist attempting to develop a new drug in order to obtain a bonus or prize is not likely to be as creative as a scientist whose primary interest is learning more about a promising new

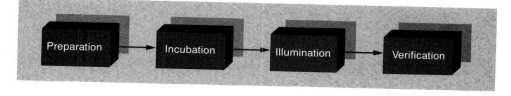

Figure 8-6 Stages of creativity.

direction.[64] For some ideas on how to boost your creativity, see the Practically Speaking discussion, "How to Be More Creative."

Stages of Creativity

The creativity process involves several stages. One commonly used model of creativity has four stages,[65] which are shown in Figure 8-6 and described below.

Preparation. This stage involves gathering initial information, defining the problem or task requiring creativity, generating alternatives, and seeking and carefully analyzing further data relating to the problem. At this stage, the individual becomes thoroughly immersed in every relevant aspect of the problem. For complex technical problems, this stage may take months or even years.

Incubation. This stage of the creativity process involves mainly subconscious mental activity and divergent thinking to explore unusual alternatives. During this stage, the individual generally does not consciously focus on the problem; this allows the subconscious to work on a solution.

Illumination. At this stage, a new level of insight is achieved, often through a sudden breakthrough in "eureka" fashion.

Verification. This stage involves testing the ideas to determine the validity of the insight. At this point, convergent, logical thinking is needed to evaluate the solution. If the solution does not prove feasible, it may be necessary to cycle back through all or some of the previous steps.

The invention of the computerized tomographic scanner (often referred to as the CAT scanner), a revolutionary device that allows radiologists to take three-dimensional pictures of the inside of the body with much greater clarity than conventional X rays, illustrates the creativity process. Inventor Godfrey Hounsfield received a Nobel prize for his work (see the following Case in Point discussion).

CASE IN POINT: The CAT Scanner Greets an Astonished World

CAT scanner inventor Godfrey Hounsfield worked as an electrical engineer for EMI, Ltd., a British pioneer in entertainment and electronic technologies, which is located in Hayes, England. Although Hounsfield had made some major breakthroughs in computer memory storage in the 1960s, EMI elected not to pursue the technology because the company did not want to take on IBM. So Hounsfield's boss told him to find another idea to work on. Armed with computer knowledge from his previous work, Hounsfield was comparing notes with a colleague when they made an interesting observation. If one were able to take readings that could detect the presence of materials from all angles through a box, in three dimensions, it would be possible to determine what was in the box

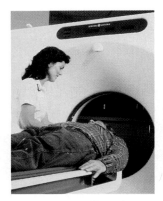

The CAT scanner allows doctors to make diagnoses without the need for exploratory surgery. This technological miracle emerged as a brainstorm in the mind of an electrical engineer who also had an extensive computer background.

without opening it. The notion was related to the field of pattern recognition, a highly theoretical field that was gaining attention from scientists in engineering and mathematics. Scientists were trying to find ways that computers could recognize images as swiftly as the eye and brain and take appropriate action.

For some reason, Hounsfield's mind leaped to a different vision—a mathematical puzzle so vast that solving it by conventional means would be impossible. He also kept thinking about the box. He speculated that if the object was reduced to "picture points" like the tiny dots that make the picture on a TV screen, then all the picture points could be assigned a mathematical value. The picture points could be recorded through the use of X rays, and each point could be viewed as the result of a mathematical equation. Then, if one assembled all the relevant mathematical equations outside the box and had a computer reassemble them, one could show the object inside the box on a computer screen. The idea was definitely in the realm of science fiction.

Hounsfield mulled over his notion for some time. Then, suddenly, his thoughts joined two unrelated planes, linking his knowledge of computerized pattern recognition with that of medical radiology. What if one could make pictures of what is inside the human body? As he thought about it, he realized that the pictures could be three-dimensional, giving the medical profession vastly improved information about a patient's condition. Formidable obstacles still lay ahead in developing a practical means of implementing his ideas. Hounsfield worked with an enormous dedication, often until midnight each night, to develop a practical prototype.

Finally, in 1972, a demonstration of the first head scanner was made in Chicago to an enraptured audience at a meeting of the Radiological Society of North America. Hounsfield had found a way to take pictures inside the human body with greater clarity than the medical profession had thought possible. His scanner could record soft tissue and see behind dense materials such as bones to areas that are obscured in conventional X rays. Through Hounsfield's efforts in the central research laboratories of EMI between 1968 and 1975, the science of "medical imaging" made a transition from the basic technology of photographic film to the vast possibilities inherent in computer science.[66] ▬▬▬

Hounsfield's preparation involved his new computer knowledge, his ability to visualize the problem of seeing inside the box, and his ideas about solving huge mathematical puzzles with computers. As he mulled over these various pieces during the incubation period, he suddenly achieved a breakthrough in the illumination stage when he realized that his idea might be used to see inside the human body. His verification period was long and arduous as he struggled with the practical aspects of making a prototype. The rest is history. Many major hospitals now have a CAT scanner. The device has eliminated much exploratory surgery and greatly enhanced effective treatment prospects for many patients throughout the world.

Techniques for Enhancing Group Creativity

This section examines techniques for enhancing creativity in group settings, whereas the preceding discussion focused on an individual's creative efforts. Among the techniques that have been developed to help facilitate creativity in group settings, three major ones are brainstorming, the nominal group technique, and synectics.

Brainstorming. The **brainstorming** technique is a means of enhancing creativity that encourages group members to generate as many novel ideas as possible on a given topic without evaluating them. The four basic rules—do not criticize during idea generation, freewheel, offer many ideas, and improve on already offered ideas—have been discussed previously.

> **Brainstorming** A technique that encourages group members to generate as many novel ideas as possible on a given topic without evaluating them

The idea for the brainstorming technique came from advertising executive Alex F. Osborn, a principal in the New York advertising agency Batten, Barton, Durstine & Osborn. In trying to figure out why some people in the agency were so much more creative than others, Osborn came to the conclusion that fear of ridicule was a major factor inhibiting the creative efforts of some employees. Accordingly, he developed the brainstorming technique in an effort to preclude the evaluation of ideas while ideas were being generated. That way, individuals who were concerned about being ridiculed could feel more free to offer truly novel ideas. Osborn soon found that it was not easy to keep people from wanting to criticize an idea as soon as it was generated. His solution? When anyone began to offer critical remarks, Osborn would loudly ring a bell that he kept close at hand.[67]

Brainstorming is often coupled with other approaches, such as choosing a word in the dictionary and brainstorming associations between the word and aspects of the problem. This approach worked for Current, Inc., a Colorado Springs greeting-card company. Focusing on the word "shrink" led artists and writers to develop Wee Greetings, a line of business-size cards that fit well in lunch boxes and shirt pockets. Using the word "enlarge," they envisioned Greeting Gifts, cards that come with balloons or confetti.[68] Brainstorming to find new uses of aluminum was encouraged in a recent contest, "The Great American Aluminum Challenge," sponsored by the Aluminum Association. Ideas included a plan for an aluminum sail, a proposal to use aluminum in place of plastic for credit cards, a grenade-resistant armor plate made of aluminum, and various construction suggestions, ranging from roof coverings to tiles for inside the home.[69]

Nominal Group Technique. The **nominal group technique (NGT)** is a means of enhancing creativity and decision making that integrates both individual work and group interaction within certain ground rules. The technique was developed to foster individual, as well as group, creativity and further overcome the tendency in groups for members to criticize ideas when they are offered. The ground rules, or steps, involved in NGT are as follows:

> **Nominal group technique (NGT)** A technique that integrates both individual work and group interaction within certain ground rules

1. The individual members independently prepare a list of their ideas on a problem.
2. Each group member presents his or her ideas in a round-robin session (one idea at a time from each group member in turn) without discussion. The ideas are recorded on a blackboard or flip chart so that everyone can see the ideas. If an idea offered by someone else triggers a new idea, members are encouraged to add the new idea to their individual list for presentation on one of their future round-robin turns.
3. When all the individual ideas are recorded on the group list, the members discuss the ideas for clarification and evaluation purposes.
4. Individuals silently and independently vote on the ideas, using a rank-ordering or rating procedure. The final outcome is determined by the pooled outcome of the individual votes.[70]

Evidence generally supports the effectiveness of NGT in developing large numbers of creative alternatives while maintaining group satisfaction.[71]

Synectics A technique that relies on analogies to help group members look at problems from new perspectives

Synectics. The **synectics** technique is a means of enhancing creativity that relies on analogies to help group members look at problems from new perspectives. The approach was developed by William J. Gordon when he was an executive for the consulting firm Arthur D. Little. Through studying tape recordings of creative teams, Gordon noticed that when someone came up with a significant new idea, it was usually stated in terms of an analogy with something in nature or another aspect of life. Accordingly, Gordon developed an approach whereby problem solvers assimilate background information, pare the problem down to its barest essentials, and use four types of analogies to try to look at the problem in new ways. *Personal analogies* involve placing oneself in the role of the persons or objects in the problem (e.g., "If I were a telephone, how would I behave?"). *Direct analogies* are aimed at making direct comparisons with objects or processes that have some similar characteristics (e.g., after someone thought of a machine-gun belt, a seed company came up with dissolvable tape packaging to ensure that seeds are evenly spaced in the field). *Symbolic analogies* require expressing the problem in terms of symbols or images (e.g., the use of mathematics to express a relationship). Finally, *fantasy analogies* require imagining the most ideal solution, no matter how farfetched, and then adjusting the fantasy so that it is more feasible (e.g., "What would be the ideal sports car?"). One limitation of the synectics approach is that the assistance of an expert is usually required to lead the group through the process.[72]

Gordon and several associates later formed Synectics, Inc., a company specializing in the concept. In one application, Synectics was asked by a small company to find a way to compress potato chips into a small space. The problem was solved when group members discovered an analogy in leaves. Although leaves are fragile, they often are found compressed and undamaged when they are moist. Hence the idea arose to shape potato chips while they are moist. The idea was subsequently sold to Procter & Gamble and eventually resulted in Pringle's potato chips in a can.[73] Similarly, several years ago GE's appliance operations in Louisville asked Synectics, Inc., to help it find ways to integrate electronics technology into its products. The session produced a number of creative ideas—including the self-diagnostic systems that have recently been incorporated into GE dishwashers and refrigerators.[74]

Thus there are a number of means that managers can use to encourage creativity and innovation in work settings. While this chapter has focused on understanding various aspects of decision processes in organizations, the next chapter highlights a variety of specific tools that can assist organization members in both planning and decision making.

CHAPTER SUMMARY

Decision making is the process through which managers identify organizational problems and attempt to resolve them. Managers deal with three types of problems: crisis, noncrisis, and opportunity. Opportunity problems provide a major vehicle for organizational innovation. Because opportunities involve ideas that could be used, rather than difficulties that must be resolved, opportunities sometimes receive insufficient attention.

Generally, managerial decision situations fall into two categories: programmed and nonprogrammed. Because of their nature, nonprogrammed decisions usually involve significant amounts of uncertainty and risk.

Two types of models have been developed to better understand the way in which managers make decisions. The rational model suggests that managers are almost perfect information handlers and, therefore, make optimal decisions. In contrast, several nonrational models of managerial decision making, including the satisficing, incremental, and garbage-can models, suggest that information-gathering and -processing limitations make it difficult for managers to make optimal decisions.

An effective decision-making process includes four major steps. The first step, identifying the problem, involves the scanning, categorization, and diagnosis stages. The second step, generating alternative solutions, emphasizes the importance of alternatives in achieving a high-quality solution. The third step, evaluating and selecting an alternative, requires consideration of feasibility, quality, acceptability, costs, and reversibility. The fourth step, implementing and following up on the solution, focuses on careful planning, sensitivity to those involved in the implementation and/or affected by it, and the design of follow-up mechanisms.

As the nonrational models of managerial decision making suggest, managers sometimes do not follow an effective decision-making process. This is largely because of four major decision barriers that must be overcome. The first, accepting the problem challenge, requires deciding to decide, rather than reacting with complacency, defensive avoidance, or panic. The second involves searching for sufficient alternatives. The third focuses on recognizing common decision-making biases, such as framing, representativeness, availability, anchoring and adjustment, and overconfidence. Finally, recent research indicates that under certain conditions managers lean toward nonrational escalation, or the escalation phenomenon, the tendency to increase commitment to a previously selected course of action beyond

the level that would be expected if the manager followed an effective decision-making process.

Group decision making has several advantages and disadvantages. The advantages are that more information and knowledge is focused on the issue, an increased number of alternatives potentially can be developed, greater understanding and acceptance of the final decision are likely, and members develop knowledge and skills for future use. Disadvantages are that group decisions are usually more time-consuming, disagreement may delay decision making and cause hard feelings, the discussion may be dominated by one or a few group members, and groupthink may cause members to overemphasize gaining agreement. Managers can take a number of steps to help minimize the disadvantages.

A major aspect of promoting innovation is the creativity factor. Creativity involves both convergent and divergent thinking. Basic ingredients of the creative process are domain-relevant skills, creativity-relevant skills, and task motivation. The creativity process comprises four stages: preparation, incubation, illumination, and verification. Techniques for enhancing creativity include brainstorming, the nominal group technique, and synectics.

MANAGERIAL TERMINOLOGY

anchoring and
   adjustment (276)
availability (276)
bounded rationality
   (265)
brainstorming (287)
complacency (272)
convergent thinking
   (282)
creativity (281)
crisis problem (262)
deciding to decide (273)
decision making (261)
defensive avoidance (273)

descriptive decision-
   making models (268)
devil's advocates (281)
dialectical inquiry (281)
divergent thinking (282)
escalation situations
   (277)
framing (275)
garbage-can model (267)
groupthink (280)
incremental model (266)
nominal group technique
   (NGT) (287)
noncrisis problem (262)

nonprogrammed
   decisions (263)
nonrational escalation
   (278)
nonrational models
   (265)
normative decision-
   making models (268)
opportunity problem
   (262)
organizational problems
   (268)
overconfidence (276)
panic (273)

programmed decisions
   (263)
prospect theory (275)
rational model (265)
representativeness (276)
risk (264)
satisficing model (266)
sunk costs (278)
synectics (288)
uncertainty (264)

QUESTIONS FOR DISCUSSION AND REVIEW

1. Outline the major types of problems that managers are likely to confront. Give an example of each type of problem as it has occurred or could occur at your college or university.
2. Explain the difference between programmed and nonprogrammed decision situations. Choose an organization with which you are familiar and identify two programmed and two nonprogrammed decision situations.

3. Contrast the rational and nonrational models of managers as decision makers. Think of a recent nonprogrammed decision situation that you have seen handled in an organization (perhaps a student group or association to which you belong). Which of the following decision models best describes the decision process involved: rational, satisficing, incremental, or garbage can? Explain why.
4. Describe each of the steps in an effective decision-

making process. We sometimes witness serious organizational problems, such as disorganization and/or poor service, that have not been resolved. What are some potential managerial reactions to problem situations that might account for why such problems persist?

5. Explain the main decision barriers involved with accepting the problem challenge and searching for sufficient alternatives. How can these barriers be overcome?

6. Give an example of each of the common decision-making biases. Explain how these biases might influence evaluations of alternative solutions.

7. Explain the conditions under which the escalation phenomenon is most likely to occur. What steps can a manager take to minimize the possibilities of falling prey to nonrational escalation?

8. Assess the advantages and disadvantages of group decision making. Give an example of a situation in which you felt the advantages outweighed the disadvantages and vice versa. In the latter case, what could have been done to prevent the decision-making difficulty?

9. Explain the main ingredients necessary for creativity. Identify evidence indicating that the basic ingredients for creativity were present in Godfrey Hounsfield's inventing of the CAT scanner.

10. Suppose that you are the chairperson of a bank task force charged with coming up with new ideas for enhancing customer service. What approaches might be used to facilitate the flow of creative ideas? Which one would you pick, and why?

DISCUSSION QUESTIONS FOR CHAPTER OPENING CASE

1. Would you characterize the various decisions made in the case as programmed or nonprogrammed? Why?

2. To what extent does it appear that Goizueta and the top management at Coca-Cola generally follow an effective decision-making process?

3. Assess the manner in which Goizueta and Coke's top management appear to react to problem challenges.

MANAGEMENT EXERCISE: BRAINSTORMING

Objectives

■ To learn how the brainstorming technique for stimulating creativity operates
■ To gain experience in generating ideas in a brainstorming session

Instructions

1. Select a problem of common interest to the members of the group. If the group has difficulty selecting a problem, try one of these:
   a. How can students be more involved in developing the policies of your college or university (e.g., new programs, admissions and transfers, and electives)?
   b. What kind of game could be developed to help learn how to make better decisions?
   c. What features would you like cars to have 10 years from now?
   d. What new approaches could seniors use in developing job leads?

2. Spend 30 minutes brainstorming alternative solutions. Someone in the group should record all the ideas. Even if the group runs out of steam after 15 minutes or so, keep brainstorming. Usually, the best ideas occur later in the brainstorming session. Freewheel. Offer ideas even if they seem wild and impractical. Remember, no criticizing is allowed during the brainstorming phase.

3. Go over the list and select the 10 best ideas. Evaluation is allowed in this phase of the process.

4. Narrow the list to the five best ideas, and then select the best idea.

5. Be prepared to discuss your top five ideas with the class as a whole.

PROFITS FINALLY COME TO *USA TODAY*

Allen H. Neuharth, Gannett Company's chairman, threw a little champagne party in June 1987 at company headquarters in Arlington, Virginia, to celebrate the first profitable month for Gannett's national newspaper, *USA Today*. Buoyed by advertising and circulation gains, Neuharth savored the triumph. He told his staff to expect a long and successful future for the venture they had launched in the fall of 1982.

But as glasses clicked and trays of oysters and pâté made the rounds, many people in the room knew that *USA Today*'s success had come at a high price. The project, which had become Neuharth's obsession, had made and broken careers at Gannett. It bruised big egos. Meanwhile, 5 years of heavy operating losses had severely pinched the media chain's 90 other newspapers and disheartened their staffs.

Recently, fresh discord has been stirred up by *The Making of McPaper*, a Neuharth-authorized book about the obstacles and sacrifices involved in creating and expanding *USA Today*. Prior to publication, a few draft copies of the book were circulated. Reactions within the Gannett organization have been strong, renewing the clash between Neuharth's backers and the financial and production executives who had early doubts. Many of those who were reluctant to jump on the Neuharth bandwagon now take offense at being portrayed as naysayers and foot-draggers.

Such discord is one price Gannett has had to pay while Neuharth has been building his oft-maligned entrepreneurial venture into what is now widely regarded as a valuable corporate asset. But the company has managed to swallow the paper's heavy operating losses, as Gannett's earnings and the stock price have been steadily rising. Now the question is whether Neuharth can bring profitability to *USA Today* and reduce the human costs as well.

The book airs plenty of dirty linen. It describes the bitter infighting at Gannett and reveals tales of those who suffered breakdowns in the anxious, early days of *USA Today*'s publication. Even the book's title causes resentment among staffers, dredging up the derogatory nickname assigned to the paper by critics who viewed it as "fast-food" journalism.

"I wanted to write an honest account," explains Peter Prichard, the book's author and the managing editor for *USA Today*'s cover stories. "If this book proves anything, there really is free speech at the Gannett company."

Other Gannett executives believe that the book unfairly casts as villains people who Neuharth apparently felt had plotted to thwart his project. Douglas H. McCorkindale, the company's chief financial officer, for instance, is described by Neuharth as one of the "enemies within" who "planned for failure" instead of success. According to Prichard, the questions McCorkindale raised about the project cost him the chief executive's job, now held by John J. Curley.

Though a supporter now, McCorkindale says he did oppose the way the *USA Today* project was carried out. Neuharth and Curley abandoned Gannett's usually careful procedures for planning major capital expenditures, such as new printing plants, McCorkindale says. In addition, the management

Allen Neuharth, the now retired chairman of Gannett Company, is shown here with his successor, John J. Curley, in the *USA Today* newsroom. Neuharth has come under fire for scrapping conventional decision-making procedures in allocating major resources to support *USA Today*, which has been in the red most years. Time will tell if Neuharth's decision will ultimately pay off or simply serve as an example of a classic escalation situation.

and staff of *USA Today* in Arlington were allowed to spend large sums of money, while Gannett's other daily newspapers were forced to pinch pennies.

"There's a lackadaisical attitude toward a lot of things now because of what many in the company saw as the inordinate waste involved in the project," states McCorkindale in the book. "They say, 'Why should we kill ourselves in Gitchagumee, Idaho, (to make money) when they'll just waste it over there (at *USA Today*) anyway.'"

McCorkindale is sticking to his guns. "*USA Today* should have been playing by the same rules" as Gannett's other papers, he says. "The planning wasn't complete. It was full of holes. They didn't want questions raised because it would raise more questions, and people don't like that."

Indeed, *USA Today*'s financial cost to Gannett exceeded even McCorkindale's forecasts. Excluding capital expenditures and the costs of employees that *USA Today* continues to borrow from other newspapers, *USA Today* has amassed operating losses of more than $230 million since its launch in 1982.

The *USA Today* staff has itself experienced heavy turnover. According to Prichard, the paper has "ground up and spit out" four circulation managers. Within a year of its start-up, about 70 news staffers departed or were fired, according to staff estimates. Only 280 of the original 413 who worked on *USA Today* remain with Gannett today, according to Prichard. The newspaper is on its seventh president and third publisher in 5 years, though some predecessors have remained at Gannett.

The departed and those still with Gannett cite the organization's disarray, the new rules that were made up daily, and the intense pressure that resulted from Neuharth's direct involvement in the project. For many staffers, the pressure was intense. Neuharth made it clear that the venture would be a test of everyone's character, according to Prichard. During a low point for *USA Today* in 1984, Neuharth held a meeting at Pumpkin Center, his home in Cocoa Beach, Florida. He told the top managers that they had to cut costs and improve circulation and advertising or else the paper wouldn't make it.

After the meeting, the executives were treated to a "last supper." The table was laid out with Manischewitz wine and unleavened bread, and Neuharth stepped from behind a curtain wearing a crown of thorns and standing in front of a wooden cross. He told the executives, "I am the crucified one." And he warned that they would be the "passed over" if the newspaper failed.[75] Since becoming marginally profitable, the paper has slipped back into the red ink to some degree because its circulation has slowed and advertising has declined throughout the newspaper industry.[76]

QUESTIONS FOR CHAPTER CONCLUDING CASE

1. Which model of managers as decision makers appears to best match the situation involving the birth of *USA Today*?

2. Evaluate the extent to which Gannett top executives used an effective decision-making approach in deciding to launch *USA Today* and in dealing with subsequent problems. What was the impact?

3. Evaluate the extent to which the *USA Today* situation represented an escalation situation (between the time the paper was launched and the time it began to make money).

CHAPTER NINE

PLANNING AND DECISION AIDS

CHAPTER OUTLINE

Forecasting
Quantitative Forecasting
Promoting Innovation: Technological,
   or Qualitative, Forecasting
Judgmental Forecasting
Choosing a Forecasting Method

Project Planning and Control Models
Gantt Charts
PERT

Other Planning Techniques
Linear Programming
Queuing, or Waiting-Line, Models
Inventory Models
Routing, or Distribution, Models
Simulation Models

**Quantitative Aids for Decision
   Making**
Payoff Tables
Decision Trees
Break-Even Analysis
Game Theory

Decision Support and Expert Systems
Decision Support Systems
Expert Systems

LEARNING OBJECTIVES

*After studying this chapter, you
should be able to:*

■ Identify the three major categories of forecasting methods and
explain the main factors to consider when choosing among
them.

■ Describe the main approaches
included within the quantitative
and judgmental forecasting
categories.

■ Enumerate the main ap-
proaches that fit under the
technological, or qualitative,
forecasting category and explain how they can be used to
promote innovation.

■ Differentiate between Gantt
charts and PERT as means
for planning and controlling
projects.

■ Explain the purpose of linear
programming and describe, in
general, how it works.

■ Differentiate among the following planning models: queuing,
or waiting-line; inventory;
routing, or distribution; and
simulation.

■ Describe payoff tables, decision
trees, break-even analysis, and
game theory as decision-
making tools.

■ Explain the role of decision
support systems and expert
systems as aids to decision
making.

UNITED AIRLINES DEVELOPS A SOPHISTICATED WORK-FORCE PLANNING SYSTEM

During the early 1980s, United Airlines embarked on a significant expansion of flight schedules. The expansion was part of its competitive response to increased rivalry among major competitors: American, Delta, Northwest, Texas Air, and United. During a single month, for example, United added 67 departures to its operations at Chicago's O'Hare Airport. It soon became the first airline with service to cities in all 50 states. While the expansion brought the desired major increases in passenger volumes, it also began to strain the current work-force scheduling and planning systems. Increases in staffing levels were necessary. Because of airline-ticket price pressures and heavy discounting from Texas Air, it was imperative for United to control labor costs while attempting to maintain desired customer service levels.

To meet the challenge of providing good reservation and airport service while controlling costs, the airline turned to management science. *Management science* (also often called *operations research*) is a management perspective aimed at increasing decision effectiveness through the use of sophisticated mathematical models and sophisticated statistical methods. (Background information about management science is provided in Chapter 2.) Management science offers a variety of quantitative techniques that can greatly help managers in planning and making decisions about complex situations such as those facing United.

In the United situation, the airline had 11 reservation offices that employed over 4000 reservation sales representatives (RSRs) and support personnel. The RSRs mainly used on-line computer terminals tied into United's central Apollo reservations system. The representatives booked reservations, processed special requests for meals, handled advance seat assignments, maintained waiting lists, and notified passengers of schedule changes.

At its 10 largest airports, United employed 1000 customer service agents (CSAs). The CSAs ticketed passengers, checked them in at the gates, and handled passenger services such as lost and found. Both the RSRs and CSAs included full-time and part-time workers with shifts ranging from 2 to 8 hours. Employees were allowed 30 minutes for lunch and were given breaks about every 2 hours.

In the past, shift schedules at reservation offices and airports had been prepared by hand. The number of employees scheduled for each half-hour period was based either on the shift's peak requirement during the week or on its average requirement over the course of the week. Schedules based on the peak requirement were costly because employees were underutilized on nonpeak workdays. Conversely, schedules based on the average requirement over the week did not provide adequate coverage during peak periods. Because of the coverage problem, scheduling using the peak-based strategy tended to be used most often, even though it resulted in the most expensive staffing costs. Although actual work-load patterns differed according to the particular day of the week, the hand-scheduling process was largely confined to considering a "representative" day. Not surprisingly, this approach became more costly with the expansion of service.

In response to these scheduling problems, a planning group was established, under United's senior vice president for corporate services, to develop a better system that could also be computerized. Because the need for the new system was urgent, the planning group that was appointed quickly developed a prototype, or preliminary, system. The group fully expected that the prototype system would need considerable refinement before it could be implemented, because it represented only a rough estimate of what was needed. Tests of the system then began at a few reservation offices. The first work schedules developed by the prototype system did not receive enthusiastic acceptance. Although the schedules were economically optimum, the reservation managers did not feel that the system incorporated some of the considerations that they felt were essential. The development group also found that because they had not involved the managers who would be using the system in the system's development, the reservation managers did not accept the system. The development group then substantially increased the participation of the managers, who convinced the planners that the system did, in fact, need to be made more flexible. The final result was a better system and one that was accepted by the managers.

Because of the size and complexity of the scheduling problems, the new computer-based system, the Station Manpower Planning System (SMPS), involves several integral parts. For the reservation sales representatives, forecasting models predict call volumes on the basis of historical trends. As part of the forecasting procedure, a quantitative queuing (waiting-line) model considers probable waiting times (i.e., lengths of time customers are waiting in the telephone queue for a sales representative to answer) and determines the number of employees that will be needed to provide the desired level of service.

At United Airlines computers are not just tools that these reservation representatives use to book customers on flights. A sophisticated computer system devises employee work schedules, a planning aid that has yielded United many benefits: more flexible work force scheduling, improved customer service, labor cost savings, and greater employee satisfaction.

The system uses a similar approach to forecasting necessary staffing levels for customer service agents at airports. For the service agents, passenger loads and arrival trends are used as a basis for determining likely passenger volume. A queuing model then helps determine the staffing level that will be needed to keep the number of passengers waiting in line to the desired low levels. The forecasting procedures, including the queuing models, make up the first part, or module, of the SMPS.

The next two modules in the SMPS make use of a management science technique called linear programming. This technique helps managers determine possible shift start times and potential monthly shift schedules that minimize labor costs while meeting employee preferences and service needs.

The fourth module in the SMPS is a report module that produces monthly shift schedules for the various offices. The schedules are set up so that supervisors and/or schedulers can access them by computer, test out the feasibility and costs of various changes, and make a final determination of the overall schedule for a given month. Thus, in addition to allowing for considerable customized input from the particular location being scheduled, the system enables supervisors to do some fine-tuning on a monthly shift schedule.

The fifth and final module in the SMPS, the days-off module, uses a management science technique called a distribution model to coordinate the monthly schedules from one month to the next for a given office and to translate the monthly shift schedules into specific tours of duty for individuals. It considers such issues as ensuring that individuals do not work more than 6 days consecutively and contains an option to maximize the spreading of weekend days off among employees. This module replaced manual functions that were extremely time-consuming, and it has produced a more credible pattern of schedules for individuals.

The SMPS has been an overwhelming success at United. Benefits have included significant labor cost savings, improved customer service, and greater satisfaction among employees with their work schedules. The system has reduced the work-force coverage requirements at United's reservation offices and larger airports by an average of 6 percent. The realized savings in direct salary and benefit costs have reached $6 million annually. Other less easily quantifiable benefits have included additional revenue generated by improved service and savings from reduced manual scheduling efforts. Many of United's key managers believe that the intangible benefits have been even greater than the tangible ones. They are particularly pleased with the improved service possible through the SMPS. One manager described the system as "magical, . . . just as the [customer] lines begin to build, someone shows up for work; and just as you begin to think you're overstaffed, people start going home." While initially used to schedule about 4000 employees, the system will eventually be expanded to schedule up to 10,000 employees in reservation and airport offices.[1]

The success of the SMPS at United is one example of the growing number of aids available to help managers gain the competitive edge through innovations in the areas of planning and decision making. Many, but not all, of these aids rely heavily on quantitative techniques associated with the field of management science. The increased availability of computers also has helped expand the number of planning and decision-making techniques that are readily available for managerial use. The planners at United, though, made the SMPS system easy to use so that the managers would not need to have sophisticated knowledge of computers or mathematics to operate it. Yet the system actually incorporates many of the latest quantitative management science techniques.

Generally, managers do not necessarily require in-depth knowledge of mathematics and computers to utilize management science tools. Rather, managers need to have a basic knowledge of the major tools available so that they can visualize possible applications of such tools. Managers also need to be able to communicate with management science experts who can develop applications of such tools for specific situations. With the growing availability of packaged software that can be adapted to many work settings, many of the techniques in this chapter are more accessible than in the past to various organizations at reasonable prices. As a result, the importance of many of these planning and decision-making aids is likely to increase in the future. As illustrated by the United Airlines scheduling issue, such aids help managers effectively carry out the planning function by facilitating the setting of goals and the process of deciding how best to achieve them. Of course, managers still need to assume ultimate responsibility for planning and decision making because the various aids are merely tools that facilitate these processes.

In this chapter, we describe many of the major aids to planning and decision making that are available to innovative managers. In doing so, we consider several forecasting methods, including a forecasting approach that is useful for promoting innovation. We also examine tools that are widely used for planning and controlling projects and explore a variety of other useful quantitative planning techniques. We next investigate several quantitative aids for decision making. Finally, we briefly explore the recent trend toward computer-based decision support and expert systems.

FORECASTING

Forecasting is a process aimed at predicting changing conditions and future events that may significantly affect the business of an organization.[2] The forecasting process is important to both planning and decision making because each depends heavily on assessments of future conditions. Forecasting is used in a variety of areas, such as production planning, budgeting, strategic planning, sales analysis, inventory control, marketing planning, logistics planning, purchasing, material requirements planning, and product planning.[3] Forecasting methods fall into three major categories: quantitative; technological, or qualitative; and judgmental.[4]

Quantitative Forecasting

Quantitative forecasting relies on numerical data and mathematical models to predict future conditions. The three main methods of quantitative forecasting are the time-series, explanatory, and monitoring methods.

Time-Series Methods. **Time-series methods** use historical data to develop forecasts of the future. The assumption underlying time-series models is that there are patterns or combinations of patterns that repeat over time. Time-series models use extensive amounts of historical data, such as weekly sales figures, to identify such patterns and then base future projections on those patterns.

Examples of the types of patterns that may be identified by time-series methods are shown in Figure 9-1. A *trend* reflects a long-range general movement in either an upward or a downward direction. For example, after identifying a general decline in coffee consumption, Hillside Coffee, Inc., of Carmel, California, began to try out coffees with chocolate and nut flavorings. The experiments with the new flavored coffees began after the company learned that many of its restaurant customers were adding sweet liquors to coffee to make appealing hot drinks. The company wanted to create similar types of flavors without alcohol for use in the home. Free samples and recommendations from customers have helped the company gain a strong group of consumers, particularly teenagers and individuals in their early twenties. "Near the college campuses we're selling flavors like Chocolate Macadamia, Swiss Chocolate Almond, and Vanilla Nut," says Hillside's president, Steve Schulman.[5] A *seasonal* pattern indicates upward or downward changes that coincide with particular points within a given year, such as particular seasons of the year. For example, because the major season for soft-drink sales is the summer, Coca-Cola chief executive Roberto C. Goizueta strongly discourages company top executives from taking summer vacations. The executives are needed to help with major decisions that may be required because of the fiercely competitive situation. Price wars and other competitive challenges in the soft-drink industry also are common during

Quantitative forecasting A type of forecasting that relies on numerical data and mathematical models to predict future conditions

Time-series methods Methods that use historical data to develop forecasts of the future

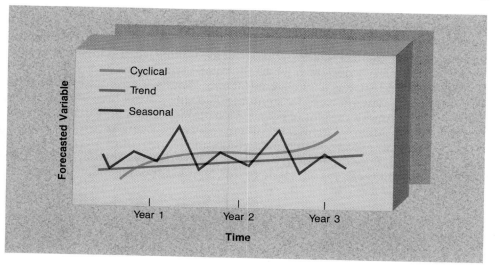

Figure 9-1 Examples of patterns that may be identified through time-series methods. (Adapted from Charles A. Gallagher and Hugh J. Watson, *Quantitative Methods for Business Decisions*, McGraw-Hill, New York, 1980, p. 116.)

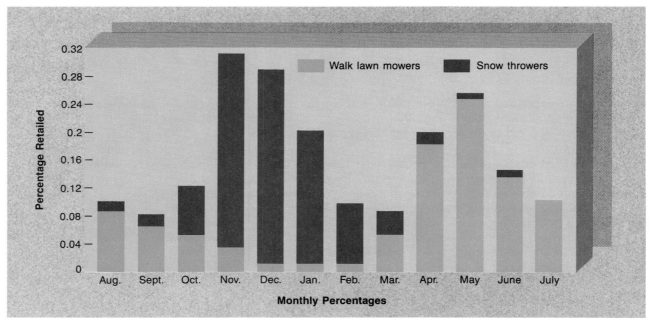

Figure 9-2   Toro Consumer Division retail sales percentage by two major product lines. (Courtesy of The Toro Company)

major holiday seasons.[6] The Toro Company sells both lawn mowers and snow throwers as a means of handling seasonal differences in customer demand patterns (see Figure 9-2). A *cyclical* pattern involves changes at particular points in time that span longer than a year. For example, sunspot intensity varies over an 11-year cycle and has an effect on the agriculture industry.[7]

Because time-series methods rely strictly on historical data, they are not very useful in predicting the impact of present or future actions that managers might take to bring about change. Time-series approaches are more suited to predicting broad environmental factors, such as general economic prospects, employment levels, general sales levels, or cost trends, that may be heavily influenced by past events. There are a wide variety of methods for analyzing time series, many of them quite sophisticated and requiring the use of computers. Although time-series methods attempt to predict the future by identifying patterns, they do not concern themselves with the causes of such patterns.

While time-series approaches can be useful, there are dangers in relying too heavily on past trends. Miller Brewing learned about such dangers the hard way. On the basis of a decade in which the company grew at a hefty 640 percent, while the beer industry as a whole grew at only about 40 percent, Miller decided to build a huge new brewery in Trenton, Ohio. Just as the brewery was completed in 1982, American sales of beer leveled off for the first time in 25 years. At the same time, Miller's archrival, Anheuser-Busch, began an expensive, but highly successful, expansion and marketing campaign. Within 5 years, sales of Miller High Life, once the number-two beer in America, declined by 50 percent. The new Trenton brewery, which never opened, led to a $280 million write-off for Miller.[8]

Explanatory, or causal, models Models that attempt to identify the major variables that are related to or have caused particular past conditions and then use current measures of those variables (predictors) to predict future conditions

Explanatory, or Causal, Models. Explanatory, or **causal, models** attempt to identify the major variables that are related to or have caused particular past conditions and then use current measures of those variables (predictors) to predict future conditions. Developing such models often leads to a better under-standing of the situations being forecasted than time-series models offer. Explanatory models also allow managers to assess the probable impact of changes in the predictors. For example, a manager may be able to assess the impact on future sales of adding more sales personnel or expanding shelf space. Thus explanatory models are generally more amenable than time-series models to assessing the probable impact of managerial actions relative to the variables.

Three major types of explanatory models are regression models, econometric models, and leading indicators. The first type, **regression models,** are equations that express the fluctuations in the variable being forecasted in terms of fluctuations among one or more other variables. An example of simple regression, in which one variable (a predictor) is used to predict the future level of another (forecasted) variable, is shown in Figure 9-3.[9] Here, a company that sells burglar alarm systems for homes is attempting to predict the demand for alarm systems (forecasted variable) on the basis of the number of information leaflets (predictor variable) requested by the public. The leaflets are offered in an advertisement run in newspapers in a major metropolitan area. The various data points plotted in Figure 9-3 represent leaflets requested and sales within 1 month of the leaflet request. In a simple regression, the relationship between the predictor and forecasted variables is stated in mathematical form. The form is $y = a + bx$, where y is the forecasted variable, x is the predictor variable, a is a constant representing the point where the regression line crosses the vertical axis, and b indicates how much the value of y changes when the value of x changes one unit. A statistical technique is used to develop the straight line that best fits the data points and to provide the values for a and b. Then future projections can be made by substituting different values for x in the equation and determining the impact on y. For example, if our equation came out to be $y = 1.5 + .085x$, then substituting 350 leaflets for x would predict sales of 27 alarm systems.

More complex multiple regression models incorporating multiple predictor variables also are used for forecasting. For example, Elaine Garzarelli, executive vice president for research at Shearson Lehman, was one of the rare Wall Street

Regression models
Equations that express the fluctuations in the variable being forecasted in terms of fluctuations among one or more other variables (predictors)

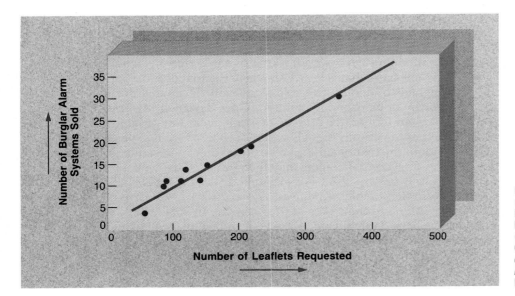

Figure 9-3 Data points and regression line for number of leaflets requested and number of burglar alarm systems sold. (Adapted from Charles A. Gallagher and Hugh J. Watson, *Quantitative Methods for Business Decisions*, McGraw-Hill, New York, 1980, p. 134.)

figures who predicted "black Monday." In predicting the market crash that occurred on October 19, 1987, she used quantitative analysis of thirteen pieces of data, three relating to economic cycles, several pertaining to monetary issues, and three concerning market valuation.[10]

Econometric models
Systems of simultaneous multiple regression equations involving several predictor variables that are used to identify and measure relationships or interrelationships that exist in the economy

The second major category of explanatory models is **econometric models.** The term "econometric model" most often is used to refer to systems of simultaneous multiple regression equations involving several predictor variables that are used to identify and measure relationships or interrelationships that exist in the economy. Such models attempt to predict the likely future directions of the economy and, often, the impact of changes such as proposed tax legislation on various segments of the economy. The development of econometric models is quite complex and expensive. As a result, such models are beyond the scope of most managerial jobs and all but very large organizations. However, a number of econometric forecasting services, such as the Wharton School, Chase Econometric Associates, and Mapcast (GE), allow companies to subscribe and obtain many of the benefits of econometric forecasting at a cost that is substantially less than the cost of developing one's own econometric model.

Leading indicators
Variables that tend to be correlated with the phenomenon of major interest but also tend to occur in advance of that phenomenon

The third major category of explanatory models is **leading indicators,** variables that tend to be correlated with the phenomenon of major interest but also tend to occur in advance of that phenomenon. In general, the use of leading indicators tends to be a fairly simple method of forecasting, although the methods of analysis used on leading indicators can be quite sophisticated. For example, the growth of the gross national product (GNP) works very well as a leading indicator for Pitney Bowes's Data Documents, Inc., division. For a number of years, sales of the division's business forms have generally trailed changes in GNP growth by about 6 months. However, locating appropriate leading indicators is not always a simple task. To predict outboard-motor sales, the Brunswick Corporation's Mercury Marine division uses the monthly consumer confidence index published by the Conference Board, a research group. Unfortunately, so far Brunswick has not been able to find a good leading indicator for sales of the inboard-outboard units that are typically found in middle-of-the-market boats.[11] Thus it can be difficult to identify a useful leading indicator that provides reasonably accurate predictions.

Monitoring methods
Methods that provide early warning signals of significant changes in established patterns and relationships so that managers can assess the likely impact and plan responses if necessary

Monitoring Methods. **Monitoring methods** provide early warning signals of significant changes in established patterns and relationships so that managers can assess the likely impact and plan responses if necessary. Quantitative approaches to monitoring rely on a tracking signal. A *tracking signal* is a mathematically derived measure that is based on recent fluctuations in a variable of interest and is designed to identify possible significant deviations presently occurring that are worthy of managerial attention. Once designed, the tracking signal, or measure, is used to monitor present movements in the variable of interest; it is set so that it automatically signals when deviations from expected patterns are merely random fluctuations that can be ignored or represent a possible nonrandom shift in direction. Managers may then be asked to evaluate the significance of the apparent pattern shift. For example, Dillard's, a $2.7 billion department store based in Bentonville, Arkansas, is noted for its extensive use of computer technology. Many of the stores in the chain are in small cities, such as Council Bluffs, Iowa, and Hutchinson, Kansas. If top management in the family-run company wants to know how much business was done by noon in each of the nine St. Louis stores, the managers can quickly bring the information up on an oversize computer monitor. Within seconds, they can also retrieve such detailed information as the morning's sales of Estée Lauder cosmetics in the Santa Fe store. With so much data available, top managers cannot check all the various aspects personally. Instead, data can be monitored by computer for significant deviations, which then can be called to the attention of management through special reports. One outgrowth of monitoring methods is a program called Quick Response, which electronically reorders certain basic items, such as men's dress shirts or ladies' lingerie, each week on the basis of historical records.[12] Monitoring methods constitute a relatively new aid to forecasting and typically are computerized to facilitate the tracking process. Such methods are likely to be used more extensively in the future as researchers develop increasingly sophisticated quantitative approaches.

Promoting Innovation: Technological, or Qualitative, Forecasting

Technological, or **qualitative, forecasting** is aimed primarily at predicting long-term trends in technology and other important aspects of the environment. Particular emphasis is placed on technology, since the ability of organizations to innovate and remain competitive often is related to being able to take advantage of opportunities evolving from technological change. Technological, or qualitative, forecasting differs from quantitative approaches in that it focuses more heavily on longer-term issues that are less amenable to numerical analysis. Therefore, rather than relying on quantitative methods, technological forecasting depends on such qualitative factors as expert knowledge, creativity, and judgment. This type of forecasting provides an excellent opportunity to generate innovative thinking among participants because the emphasis is on future possibilities. The difficulties of accurately predicting the future are obvious, and predictors often have missed major shifts, such as the magnitude and speed of the increase in global competition. Although a number of approaches have been developed to facilitate technological, or qualitative, forecasting, three of the most prominent are the Delphi method, morphological analysis, and the La Prospective approach.

The Delphi Method. The **Delphi method** is a structured approach to gaining the judgments of a number of experts on a specific issue relating to the future. One unique aspect of the Delphi method, which was originally developed at the Rand Corporation, is that the experts are not brought together to discuss their views. On the contrary, the experts are intentionally kept apart so that their initial judgments will not be influenced by other experts involved in the process. Other characteristic features of the Delphi method are anonymity for participants, the opportunity for experts to revise their original forecasts as the process progresses, and summary feedback regarding the opinions of the other experts involved.[13] The Delphi method has been used in a variety of organizations, including TRW, IBM, AT&T, Corning Glass Works, Goodyear, and ICL in Britain. Although experts participating in the Delphi method can come from inside or outside the organization, many organizations prefer to use internal experts in order to retain better internal control over the results.[14] One recent study, which used both an external and an internal group of experts to predict future events in the sociopolitical environment of business, showed that both groups produced similar estimates.[15] The Delphi method can be used to seek creative solutions to problems; however, its most frequent function is forecasting, particularly predicting technological change.

There are three basic steps in the Delphi method. First, a panel of experts is asked to identify likely scientific breakthroughs in a given area within a specific long-term period (e.g., over the next 50 years). The experts also are asked to estimate when, within the specified period, they expect the breakthroughs to occur. On the basis of the information received, a list of potential breakthroughs

Technological, or **qualitative, forecasting** A type of forecasting aimed primarily at predicting long-term trends in technology and other important aspects of the environment

Delphi method A structured approach to gaining the judgments of a number of experts on a specific issue relating to the future

An employee of Dillard's, a midwestern department store chain, clocks in by entering her social security number into a computer terminal. This is just one example of the many ways that Dillard's uses computer technology at its stores—including the monitoring of selling trends.

is compiled, along with information regarding the estimated time frame within which each is likely to occur. Second, the list and the average time frame for each item are sent back to the experts, and they are asked to estimate (often on the basis of a 50-50 probability) whether each breakthrough is likely to occur earlier or later than the average estimated time frame. They also may be permitted to specify that they do not believe the breakthrough will occur during the time period (e.g., the 50 years) under consideration. Third, the experts are provided with a new list that represents the information gathered in step 2. If there is general consensus, those who disagree with the majority are asked to explain why they do. If there are major differences among the experts, the participants may be asked to furnish reasons for their views. Experts can, and often do, alter their estimates at this point. If there continues to be a wide divergence of opinion, step 3 may be repeated and may include the various explanations that have been given thus far.

Although these steps outline the basic approach used in the Delphi method, organizations frequently make minor alterations to suit their particular needs. The Delphi method was recently used by the Alaska Department of Commerce and Economic Development to assess Alaska's energy, economy, and resource development future.[16] It was also used in technological forecasting for power generation by Bharat Heavy Electricals, Ltd. (BHEL), a billion-dollar company in India (see the following Case in Point discussion).[17]

CASE IN POINT   The Delphi Method at BHEL

Bharat Heavy Electricals, Ltd., the largest heavy electrical equipment company in India, has used the Delphi process to explore the future direction of power development, especially in the areas of electric energy and electric transportation. The company's products form systems for the generation of electric power through thermal, nuclear, and hydro sources, as well as for the transmission of power to the industrial and transportation sectors. The Delphi process involved 286 company members from a variety of engineering disciplines.

In the first step, or round, an open-ended questionnaire was sent to prospective respondents. The purpose of the first round was to gather as many ideas as possible regarding major technological breakthroughs that could conceivably be developed within the next 30 to 40 years. Participants also estimated when they expected the technological breakthroughs to occur.

In the second round, the list of technological breakthroughs and basic statistical information about the estimated timings of the breakthroughs were fed back to the participants. With this information, the participants were requested to reconsider their earlier timing estimates and give fresh ones, provide reasons if their estimates were outside the general range of timings provided by the participants in the first round, and supply a priority ranking for each technological development in terms of the urgency of each requirement. The replies from the second round led to an emerging trend toward consensus on most issues.

In the third round, participants were given the collated comments and the new basic statistical information about estimated timings that had been collected in round 2. In this round, participants were asked to give their final estimates and indicate the basis for their final forecasts.

The end results included estimates for technological developments such as computerized power stations and wind power in the 1990 to 1995 range and ocean tidal power and magnetic levitation and propulsion by 1995 to 2000. Not only did the process identify the likely developments of 19 different forms of energy sources, but it also provided "refined guesstimates" regarding when such new energy sources would appear. Bharat felt that these and other estimates would be useful in corporate planning. In addition, the results were extremely useful in formulating R&D projects related to corporate plans.[18] ■■■■

Morphological Analysis. Based on the work of Swiss mathematician Frank Zwicky, **morphological analysis** is a system of forecasting potential technological breakthroughs by breaking the possibilities into component attributes and evaluating various attribute combinations. For example, suppose that you want to develop a new means of transportation. You might identify some component attributes, such as the driving force or source of energy, the mode of movement, the material used in construction, and the primary purpose. For each component attribute, you could list a number of alternatives. For example, the driving force might be diesel, gas turbine, steam, and so on (see Table 9-1). You could then generate a number of technological possibilities by combining an alternative source of energy with an alternative form of each of the other components. Using the lists in Table 9-1, you can see that one possibility is pedal, rollers, glass, and foods, while another is squirrels in a cage, water, plastic, and plants.[19] Some attribute combinations may trigger new ideas, while others may be fairly ridiculous and can be discarded quickly. However, the process can be helpful in exploring possible new technological alternatives. Two organizations that have used morphological analysis in research are General Electric and the Stanford Research Institute.[20]

Morphological analysis A system of forecasting potential technological breakthroughs by breaking the possibilities into component attributes and evaluating various attribute combinations

La Prospective. Developed in France and widely used in Europe, the La Prospective view (sometimes also called the futuristics or futuribles view) argues that there are many different possible futures depending on such factors as confrontations among actors, the continuation of current trends, regulatory and other constraints, and the relative power of the actors involved. As a result, organizations need to consider a number of futures and attempt to make decisions and take actions that do not greatly inhibit further freedom of choice. Otherwise, taking inflexible and irreversible actions may lead to severe difficulties if forecasts turn out to be grossly off the mark. The **La Prospective** approach addresses a variety of possible futures by evaluating major environmental variables, assessing the likely strategies of other significant actors (e.g., other organizations), devising possible counterstrategies, developing ranked hypotheses about the variables, and formulating alternative scenarios. **Scenarios** are outlines of possible future conditions, including possible paths the organization could take that would likely lead to these conditions.[21]

La Prospective An approach that addresses a variety of possible futures by evaluating major environmental variables, assessing the likely strategies of other significant actors, devising possible counterstrategies, developing ranked hypotheses about the variables, and formulating alternative scenarios that do not greatly inhibit freedom of choice

Scenarios Outlines of possible future conditions, including possible paths the organization could take that would likely lead to these conditions

Table 9-1 Morphological Analysis for Developing a New Means of Transportation

Driving Force	Mode of Movement	Material	Purpose
diesel	rail	plastic	people
gas turbine	wheel	metals	animals
steam	rollers	wood	heavy freight
pedal	coasters	stone	baggage
electric	air cushion	cloth	foods and spices
squirrels in a cage	water	glass	plants
horse			
wind			

Source: Reprinted from William C. Miller, *The Creative Edge: Fostering Innovation Where You Work,* Addison-Wesley, Reading, Mass., 1987, p. 69.

Table 9-2 Criteria for Choosing a Forecasting Method

		Quantitative	Technological	Judgmental
CRITERIA	FORECASTING METHOD			
Time horizon*		Short to medium	Medium to long	Short to long
Time required		Short if method developed; long otherwise	Medium to long	Short
Development costs		Often high	Medium	Low
Accuracy in identifying patterns		High	Medium	Medium to high
Accuracy in predicting turning points		Low for time series; medium for other methods	Medium	Low
East of understanding		Low to medium	High	High

*Short term = 1 to 3 months; medium term = 3 months to 2 years; long term = 2 years or more.
Source: Adapted from Spyrous Makridakis and Steven C. Wheelwright, "Forecasting an Organization's Futures," in Paul C. Nystrom and William H. Starbuck (eds.), *Handbook of Organizational Design,* Oxford University Press, 1981, NY, p. 132.

Judgmental Forecasting

Judgmental forecasting A type of forecasting that relies mainly on individual judgments or committee agreements regarding future conditions

Judgmental forecasting relies mainly on individual judgments or committee agreements regarding future conditions. Although judgmental forecasting is the most widely used forecasting method in industry, the judgmental approach typically relies on informal opinion gathering and is the least systematic of the forecasting methods. As a result, judgmental forecasting methods are highly susceptible to the common decision-making biases discussed in Chapter 8.[22] Two major means of judgmental forecasting are the jury of executive opinion and sales-force composites.

Jury of executive opinion A means of forecasting in which organization executives hold a meeting and estimate, as a group, a forecast for a particular item

The Jury of Executive Opinion. The **jury of executive opinion** is a means of forecasting in which organization executives hold a meeting and estimate, as a group, a forecast for a particular item. However, since the estimators are in direct contact with one another, the outcome may be heavily weighted by power and personality factors within the group. The process can be improved by providing relevant background information to the executives before the meeting.

Sales-force composite A means of forecasting that is used mainly to predict future sales and typically involves obtaining the views of various salespeople, sales managers, and/or distributors regarding the sales outlook

Sales-Force Composites. The **sales-force composite** is a means of forecasting that is used mainly to predict future sales and typically involves obtaining the views of various salespeople, sales managers, and/or distributors regarding the sales outlook. While salespeople and distributors tend to be relatively close to the customer, they often do not have information about broad economic factors that may affect future sales. On the other hand, when sales management makes the forecasts, the process begins to mirror the difficulties encountered in a jury of executive opinion. Some companies have improved the process by providing salespeople and distributors with economic trend information before having them make their estimates.

Choosing a Forecasting Method

Various criteria that can be used in selecting a forecasting method are summarized in Table 9-2, which also presents the general characteristics of the forecasting methods.[23] As the information in this table suggests, managers need to consider such factors as the desired time horizon for the forecast, type of accuracy needed, ease of understanding, and development costs. Each method has advantages and disadvantages, depending on the needs of the particular forecasting situation.

PROJECT PLANNING AND CONTROL MODELS

Managers frequently are responsible for *projects,* one-time sets of activities that have a clear beginning and a clear ending. For example, a manager may be responsible for a project to design and implement a new computer system, a project to build a new manufacturing plant, or a project to develop a new product. Such projects are unique, one-time sets of activities, although the manager may have been responsible for similar types of projects in the past. When projects are large and complex, it may be necessary for the manager to utilize some type of planning and control model to help manage the project effectively. Two well-known types of planning and control models are Gantt charts and PERT.

Gantt Charts

One of the earliest and most flexible project planning tools is the **Gantt chart,** a specialized bar chart developed by Henry L. Gantt (a prominent member of the scientific management school; see Chapter 2), that shows the current progress on each major project activity relative to necessary completion dates. A simple example of a Gantt chart is shown in Figure 9-4. A project, in this case completing a management course, is broken down into separate major activities that are then listed on the left side of the chart. The time frame for the entire project is indicated at the top or on the bottom of the chart. The duration and scheduling

Gantt chart A specialized bar chart developed by Henry L. Gantt that shows the current progress on each major project activity relative to necessary completion dates

Figure 9-4 Partial Gantt chart for completing a management course.

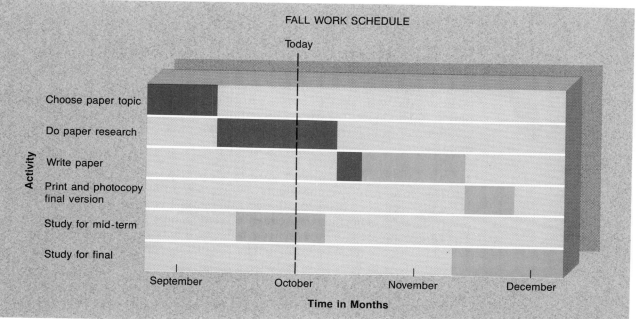

of each activity is then shown by a bar; each bar is shaded to indicate the degree of completion of the activity. As a result, it is possible to determine at a glance the current status of each activity in terms of project deadlines. You could construct a Gantt chart to help you plan and control the major activities necessary for successfully completing a course or even a whole semester or quarter. A status check of the chart in Figure 9-4 for "Today" shows that the individual has chosen a topic for a paper, completed the research, and is ahead of schedule on writing the paper. However, the individual is a bit behind schedule on studying for the midterm and needs to expend special effort to catch up.

Because of the popularity of Gantt charts, they are increasingly available with computer packages designed to help managers plan and control projects.[24] While Gantt charts are extremely useful in a variety of situations, they do have one major weakness. They do not show how various activities are interrelated. For relatively small project situations, interrelationships are fairly obvious. For large, complex projects, more sophisticated means of planning and control frequently are needed.

PERT

Program Evaluation and Review Technique (PERT)
A network planning method for managing large projects

During the 1950s, the U.S. Navy faced the immense task of coordinating the efforts of 11,000 contractors involved in developing the Polaris, the first submarine that could remain submerged while launching a long-range ballistic missile. As a result, the Defense Department, with the help of Lockheed, invented the **Program Evaluation and Review Technique (PERT),** a network planning method for managing large projects. Around the same time, Du Pont, with the help of Remington-Rand, created a similar network planning approach called the Critical Path Method (CPM).[25] Network planning methods involve breaking projects down into activities and determining the required length of time for each, but they go beyond Gantt charts by explicitly considering the interrelationships among activities.

Originally, PERT differed from CPM in that PERT incorporated a method for handling uncertainties about how long various activities would take to complete. On the other hand, CPM had a means for considering how project completion dates would be altered if more or less resources were allocated to various activities. With the increased availability of computer packages, these differences between PERT and CPM have largely disappeared. Most computer packages allow for both handling uncertainties about activity durations and determining trade-offs between resources and project completion times.[26] In addition, the term "PERT" appears to be emerging as the more common designation.[27] Therefore, we use it throughout this discussion.

Setting up PERT to help manage a major project involves the following six main steps:

1. All activities in the project must be clearly specified.
2. The sequencing requirements among activities must be identified (i.e., which activities need to proceed others must be determined).
3. A diagram reflecting the sequence relationships must be developed.
4. Time estimates for each activity must be determined.
5. The network must be evaluated by calculating the critical path. The various activities can then be scheduled.
6. As the project progresses, actual activity times must be recorded so that any necessary schedule revisions and adjustments can be made.[28]

Table 9-3 Major Activities, Predecessor Activities, and Time Estimates for Good Care, Inc.

Activity	Predecessor Activity	TIME ESTIMATES (weeks) t_o	t_m	t_p	Expected time, t_e
A. Build facility	None	20	24	30	24.3
B. Conduct safety inspection	A	2	3	4	3.0
C. Install equipment	A	8	10	20	11.0
D. Decorate interior	B	3	5	9	5.3
E. Recruit staff	None	2	2	3	2.1
F. Train staff	E	4	5	6	5.0
G. Perform pilot	C, D, F	4	5	9	5.5

Source: Adapted from Everett E. Adam, Jr., and Ronald J. Ebert, *Production and Operations Management: Concepts, Models, and Behavior*, 3d ed., Prentice-Hall, Englewood Cliffs, N.J., 1986, p. 535.

In order to understand basically how PERT works, we will walk through a relatively simple example. Suppose an organization that furnishes nursing-home care, Good Care, Inc., decides to expand and upgrade its services to include skilled-level care. Because of federal regulations for skilled care, it is necessary to build a new facility for the skilled-care operation. The administrator of Good Care, Inc., must first develop a list of the major activities that are involved in the project and then determine which activities must precede others (see Table 9-3).

The next step is constructing a **network diagram,** a graphic depiction of the interrelationships among activities. An example of a network diagram for the Good Care project is shown in Figure 9-5. On the diagram, an **activity,** or work component to be accomplished, is represented by an arrow. Activities take a period of time to accomplish. A **node,** or **event,** is an indication of the beginning and/or ending of activities in the network. It represents a single point in time. The nodes are numbered for easy identification, usually using tens (e.g., 10, 20,

Network diagram A graphic depiction of the interrelationships among activities

Activity A work component to be accomplished

Node, or **event** An indication of the beginning and/or ending of activities in the network

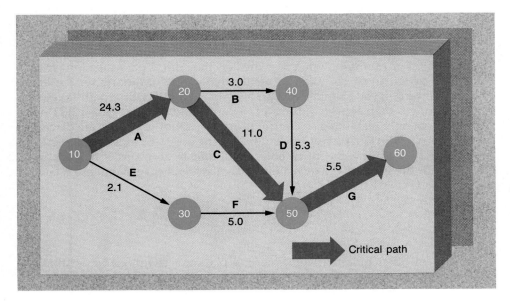

Figure 9-5 Network diagram, critical path, and expected time for each activity in the Good Care, Inc., project. (Adapted from Everett E. Adam, Jr., and Ronald J. Ebert, *Production and Operations Management: Concepts, Models, and Behavior,* 3d ed., Prentice-Hall, Englewood Cliffs, N.J., 1986, p. 537.)

30) so that additions can be made to the network without requiring renumbering. The diagram depicts the interrelationships among the various activities. In Figure 9-5, for example, building the facility must precede the safety inspection, and recruiting staff must precede training staff. However, as the diagram indicates, the building and safety inspection processes can be accomplished at the same time as the staff recruiting and training processes.

Developing the diagram may also include providing initial time estimates for the duration of each activity. Unless the times are well established, an estimate usually is made of the optimistic (t_o), pessimistic (t_p), and most likely (t_m) times necessary to complete each activity (see Table 9-3). The *expected*, or *average*, *time* for each activity is then calculated using the following formula, which gives heavy weight to the most likely time for activity completion:

$$t_e = \frac{(t_o + 4t_m + t_p)}{6}$$

The expected time for each activity is shown next to its respective arrow on the network diagram.

Critical path The path in the network that will take the longest to complete

The next step is identifying the **critical path,** the path in the network that will take the longest to complete. This network has three different paths, 10-20-40-50-60, 10-20-50-60, and 10-30-50-60. By adding up the expected times on each path, we can determine that the path 10-20-50-60 will take the longest (40.8) and, therefore, is the critical path. This means that if there is a delay in any of the activities on this path, project completion will also be delayed. Therefore, the manager needs to pay particular attention to this path. In addition, by allocating further resources to this path, it may be possible to shorten project completion time. For example, if the amount of time required to install equipment could be shortened by 2 weeks, project completion time could be reduced to 38.8. When activity times on the critical path are significantly shortened, another path sometimes becomes critical. This could happen if activity 20-50 was shortened to 8 weeks. Then the path 10-20-40-50-60 would become the critical path. On the noncritical paths, there is some latitude about when various activities can be started without endangering the completion date of the entire project. This latitude is commonly referred to as **slack.**

Slack Latitude about when various activities can be started on the noncritical paths without endangering the completion date of the entire project

Once the critical path is developed, it is important periodically to record the actual times it takes to complete the various activities and then to review the implications. For example, when activities on the critical path take longer than estimated, action must be taken to rectify the situation; otherwise, the entire project will be delayed. Similarly, if an activity on a noncritical path takes substantially longer than expected, the critical path could change. Thus PERT helps managers not only plan but also control projects. (Issues of control are discussed more extensively in Chapters 17 through 20.) The ability of individual managers to use PERT to plan and control both small and large projects has vastly increased with the widespread availability of software packages that are relatively easy to use.[29]

OTHER PLANNING TECHNIQUES

A number of other quantitatively oriented planning techniques exist that can greatly assist managers. Some of the most prominent include the use of linear programming; break-even analysis; queuing, or waiting-line, models; inventory models; routing, or distribution, models; and simulation models.

Linear Programming

Linear programming (LP) is a quantitative tool for planning how to allocate limited or scarce resources so that a single criterion or goal (often profits) is optimized. It is the most widely used quantitative planning tool in business. The technique has been applied to a variety of situations, including minimizing the cost of "hen scratch" (a combination of cereal grains) while maintaining a proper nutritional balance, finding the most profitable product mix in a manufacturing operation, and maximizing capacity usage at modern oil refineries.[30] Linear programming is most likely to be applicable when a single objective (such as maximizing profits) must be achieved, constraints exist that must be satisfied, and variables are linearly related to the objective.[31] A variable is linearly related to an objective when an increase (or decrease) in the variable leads to a proportional increase (or decrease) in the objective. For example, a linear relationship would apply if one chair (variable) produced can be sold for $30 profit (objective), four chairs for $120 profit, six chairs for $180 profit. Likewise, a linear relationship would exist if one sofa produced yields $110 profit, four sofas yield $440 profit, and so on. In each case an increase in the variable leads to a proportional increase in the objective.

> **Linear programming (LP)** A quantitative tool for planning how to allocate limited or scarce resources so that a single criterion or goal (often profits) is optimized

The potential benefits of linear programming can be illustrated by a sample problem.[32] Assume that Concord Chemical wishes to plan how much it should produce of two products, chemical X and chemical Y. Each chemical is manufactured using a two-step process that involves blending and mixing in machine A and packaging on machine B. The processing required by each chemical on each machine and the amount of profits that can be made per unit of each chemical are shown in Table 9-4.

The objective is to maximize profits from the production of the two chemicals, which have a linear relationship to the profit objective in this situation. The relationship between the two chemicals and profit maximization can be stated through an **objective function,** a mathematical representation of the relationship to be optimized in a linear programming problem. The objective function in this problem is the maximization of the sum of the total profit contributions from chemicals X and Y, where Z is the sum, x is the number of units of X, and y is the number of units of Y, or

> **Objective function** A mathematical representation of the relationship to be optimized in a linear programming problem

$$Z = 60x + 50y$$

However, in planning the 2-week production schedule, there are several **constraints,** that is, conditions that must be met in the course of solving a linear programming problem. Information on one constraint, the amount of processing time each chemical needs on each machine, is shown in Table 9-4. Furthermore, for the 2-week production period, machine A has available 80 hours and machine B has available 60 hours of processing time.

On machine A, chemical X requires 2 hours per unit and Y requires 4 hours

> **Constraints** Conditions that must be met in the course of solving a linear programming problem

Table 9-4   Processing Requirements and Profit Contributions for Each Chemical Product

Product	Machine A (hr./unit)	Machine B (hr./unit)	Profit Contribution ($/unit)
X	2	3	60
Y	4	2	50

Source: Adapted from Elwood S. Buffa, *Modern Production/Operations Management*, 7th ed., Wiley, New York, 1983, p. 561.

per unit. Since the total time spent on the two products must be less than or equal to 80 hours, the constraint associated with machine A can be stated as

$$2x + 4y \leq 80$$

Similarly, the constraint for machine B would be

$$3x + 2y \leq 60$$

Forecasts of the market indicate that the maximum amount of each product that Concord can expect to sell is 16 units of chemical X and 18 units of chemical Y. This marketing constraint can be stated as

$$x \leq 16$$

$$y \leq 18$$

Finally, since the minimum production for each product is zero, the minimum production constraints can be stated as

$$x \geq 0$$

$$y \geq 0$$

The next step is to find the values of x and y that provide the highest value for Z and *also* satisfy all the constraint equations. We can gain some insight into the linear programming technique by solving this relatively simple problem graphically. More complex problems cannot be solved graphically. In fact, many business applications of linear programming involve hundreds of variables and constraints and require a computer for solution.

The graphic representation of this problem is shown in Figure 9-6. Since the minimum production constraints require that x and y be no less than zero, the x and y axes on our graph begin at zero. The market constraints are represented by straight lines at $y = 18$ and $x = 16$, indicating that feasible solutions cannot lie beyond those lines on the graph.

The placement of the line indicating the machine A constraint is determined by solving the equation for x when y is zero (thus 40 is marked on the x axis of the graph) and then solving for y when x is zero (thus 20 is marked on the y axis, and the constraint line can be drawn). This line represents all the possible combinations of amounts of chemicals X and Y that can be made with machine A. For example, at one extreme, Concord could make 40 units of chemical X but no units of chemical Y. At the other extreme, it could make 20 units of chemical Y but no units of chemical X. Or Concord could make a number of possible combinations of the two chemicals (as represented by the line for machine A). Similar logic applies to the line for machine B.

The lines representing the various constraints map out the *feasibility space*, the area where feasible solutions can be found (see the area marked by points *abcdef*—the nonshaded part of the graph). Now that we have located the feasibility space, we must find the point within that space that maximizes Z. Suppose, for discussion purposes, that we set Z equal to 900. The dotted line representing possible values of x and y that lead to 900 is shown on the graph. We might see what happens when we set Z equal to 1200 (see this dotted line on the graph).

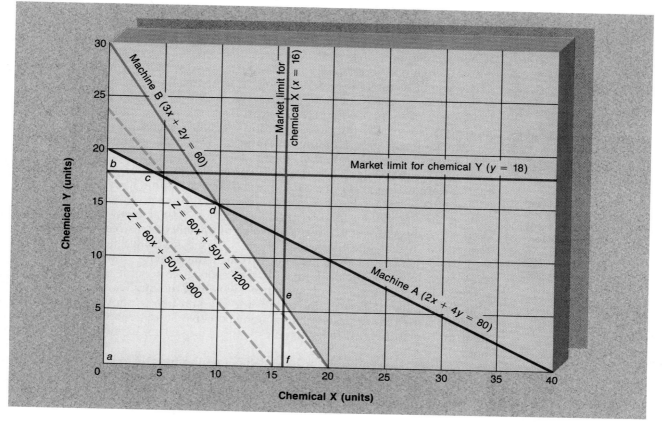

Chemical Y (units)

Machine B $(3x + 2y = 60)$

Market limit for chemical X $(x = 16)$

Market limit for chemical Y $(y = 18)$

$Z = 60x + 50y = 1200$

$Z = 60x + 50y = 900$

Machine A $(2x + 4y = 80)$

Chemical X (units)

Figure 9-6 Graphic representation of linear programming solution for the manufacture of chemicals X and Y. (Reprinted from Elwood S. Buffa, *Modern Production/ Operations Management,* 7th ed., Wiley, New York, p. 563.)

As these dotted lines suggest, various feasible solutions for Z can be represented by a series of lines that parallel those for 900 and 1200. Therefore, the point in the feasible space that represents the highest value of Z will be a parallel dotted line passing through point *d*. Thus we can graphically determine that we could maximize Z at 1350 by making 10 units of chemical X and 15 units of chemical Y. This same solution can be found mathematically by simultaneously solving the equations that we developed.

Linear programming is a valuable aid in helping managers efficiently and effectively allocate resources in a variety of areas. For example, linear programming has recently been used to help plan resource allocations for mental health community support systems; to facilitate controlling production, distribution, and inventory costs at W. R. Grace, one of the largest suppliers of phosphate-based chemical products (such as fertilizer); and to assist in allocating specific types of aircraft to flight schedules at American Airlines.[33]

Queuing, or Waiting-Line, Models

Managers frequently are responsible for providing services under conditions that potentially may require the person or unit needing service to wait in lines, or queues. **Queuing, or waiting-line, models** are mathematical models that describe the operating characteristics of queuing situations. Queuing models were an important part of the Station Manpower Planning System developed by United. Many different queuing models exist because of the need to describe a

Queuing, or waiting-line, models Mathematical models that describe the operating characteristics of queuing situations, in which service is provided to persons or units waiting in line

Devising effective queuing models becomes complicated when there are many servers and many lines, as in this Winn Dixie supermarket in Ocala, Florida.

variety of different queuing situations. For example, *single-server queues,* which involve service provided at a single point, are commonly found at the cashier's desk in a restaurant, a single automated teller at a given location, or a single-window operation at a post office. *Multiple-server queues* occur, for instance, when there are several open windows at the post office but they all draw on a single line of waiting customers. Queuing situations become more complicated when there are many lines and many servers (as in a supermarket) or when the individuals or units needing service must pass through several different service points (as is typically the case in getting a driver's license).

Unlike linear programming, queuing, or waiting-line, models do not provide an optimal solution. Rather, the models allow managers to vary the parameters of the situation and determine the probable effects. For example, suppose that you are the manager of a bank that has four drive-in teller windows.[34] Each of the four windows has a separate line feeding into it, so when drivers approach the lines, they tend to pick the shortest line. However, it frequently occurs that the shortest line turns out to be ultimately the slowest because someone ahead in that line happens to have a very long transaction. The bank is concerned that customers sometimes become irritated when they get stuck in an extremely slow line. In speaking with your colleagues at some other banks, you discover that they have set up systems in which all the cars wait in a single line. This enables the first car in line to move to the first free window. Your study of the situation so far indicates that customers arrive at an average rate of 16 per hour and each drive-in teller handles transactions at an average rate of 8 per hour.

At this point, you could use available queuing models to help you estimate the difference in waiting time between the current system and the alternative of a single line of waiting cars. Suppose your queuing model analysis indicates that customers have to wait an average of 7½ minutes for service under the present system but would wait an average of only .654 minute with a single line of waiting cars.[35] These data would suggest that you might want to make the change in order to achieve this significant improvement in service. Thus, while the queuing models do not specify an optimal decision, they do provide data that is often helpful to managers in planning the best means of delivering effective service to customers and clients. Queuing models for unique and complex situations often are expensive to develop. However, a variety of models exist that can be matched to many situations in which managers may have an interest. The increasing availability of these models in computer software packages is making the use of such models easier and more economically feasible.

Inventory Models

Inventory models
Quantitative approaches to planning the appropriate level for the stock of materials needed by an organization

Inventory models are quantitative approaches to planning the appropriate level for the stock of materials needed by the organization. Goods and stocks in inventory can include raw materials, work-in-process, finished products, and supplies.[36] A major benefit of carrying inventory is that *stockouts,* insufficient inventory to maintain the work flow or fill customer orders, can be avoided. One obvious way to lower the probability of stockouts is to carry large amounts of inventory. Unfortunately, inventory causes organizations to incur *carrying* (or *holding*) *costs,* which include the cost of space where the stock is stored, the cost of handling the stock and maintaining the area where it is kept, and the cost of the money used to finance the inventory. One way to balance stockouts and holding costs is to place orders more frequently for smaller amounts of inventory items. In considering this strategy, however, managers must also consider *order-*

ing costs, the costs associated with placing an order (including such issues as minimum freight charges, paperwork, postage, and time). Thus there are trade-offs among these various options. Inventory models help managers balance these trade-offs in planning inventory levels.[37] According to one estimate, inventories held in the United States exceed $500 billion. Even if half that amount of inventory could be reduced, at 10 percent interest the money saved would amount to $25 billion annually.[38] The Japanese have placed particular emphasis on planning inventory systems that minimize costs, causing American managers to place greater emphasis on this concept as well. Because much of the emphasis in inventory matters focuses on controlling costs, inventory issues are discussed in greater detail in Chapter 18, which deals with control issues.

Routing, or Distribution, Models

For many organizations, it is necessary to distribute a product or service to multiple customers. **Routing, or distribution, models** are quantitative methods that can assist managers in planning the most effective and economical approaches to distribution problems.[39] The development and use of routing and distribution models is sometimes referred to as *network optimization analysis.* For example, Joyce Beverages, a bottler, delivers a variety of soft-drink products to approximately 5000 customers in Maryland, Virginia, and Washington, D.C. Between 500 and 600 customers are visited daily, about 65 percent of them need the deliveries within a specified time frame, and vehicle routes must be changed dramatically from day to day. Adopting a computerized vehicle-routing model helped the company both improve customer service and save money. The company saved money because the routes were more efficient, thus reducing gas utilization, truck wear and tear, and maintenance. Within a year of adapting the quantitative routing approach, sales had increased 30 percent, but the routing model enabled the company to handle the increased deliveries without adding any more vehicles.[40] Routing models have been used in a variety of other industries and environments to solve diverse problems, including increasing the service areas for New York City Police Department patrol cars without adding to response times and helping the New York Department of Sanitation improve the conditions of the streets and, at the same time, save $12 million per year.[41] Routing models frequently draw on a variety of quantitative techniques such as linear programming, queuing theory, and simulation methods.

Routing, or distribution, models Quantitative methods that can assist managers in planning the most effective and economical approaches to distribution problems

Simulation Models

Simulation is a mathematical imitation of reality. The technique is used when the situation of interest is too complex to use more narrow techniques such as linear programming or queuing theory. For example, when queuing situations are very complex, commonly used queuing models may not fit the situation well enough to be used. When this occurs, a simulation may be helpful. Rather than constituting a standardized set of formulas that can be applied to a broad set of problems, simulations usually must be custom-made to fit a situation. In fact, a simulation generally can be divided into a series of smaller mathematical models, in which case the output of some models supplies data for other models in the simulation.[42]

Simulation A mathematical imitation of reality

Simulation has been utilized in production, inventory control, transportation systems, market strategy analysis, industrial and urban growth patterns, environmental control, and a variety of other areas.[43] One advantage of simulation is that it frequently can be less expensive than manipulating a real system.

Indeed, many times it may be totally impractical to conduct tests in a real system to appraise probable effects (e.g., to test the probable effects of alternative zoning regulations on building patterns). Simulation often allows managers to change parameters so that different assumptions and/or approaches can be evaluated. Simulation results depend on the extent to which the mathematical models used are an accurate representation of reality. Simulation accuracy can be difficult to verify because of the complexity of the situation being simulated.[44] In addition, simulations can be very expensive to develop because they typically are custom-designed and require an extensive amount of work by specialists. Nevertheless, their benefits frequently greatly outweigh their costs. One of many examples of the effective use of simulation is provided by the experiences at Canadian National Railway (see the following Case in Point discussion).

CASE IN POINT: Expanding Canadian National Railway's Line Capacity

Canadian National Railway (CN) is one of the oldest and largest of Canada's crown corporations, companies whose only equity holder is the Canadian federal government. Among other things, CN is the operator of Canada's largest railway. The rail system consists of approximately 33,000 miles of track, serving all provinces and most principal cities of Canada and connecting with a number of major U.S. railroads. A multi-billion-dollar company, CN Rail's total traffic volume is approaching 200 billion gross-ton miles (1 gross ton of freight moved 1 mile) per year.

Despite profits in recent years of approximately C$300 million (money amounts are in Canadian dollars), CN needs huge amounts of capital to finance the improvement and expansion of railway services, particularly in western Canada, where forecasts of traffic volumes show rapid increases.

Although during the 1960s traffic on the transcontinental route across Canada was rather light, the volume increased by 50 percent between 1962 and 1972. Most of the growth was concentrated in the mountain region of western Canada, particularly on the 1500-mile section between Winnipeg and Vancouver. To match this traffic growth, the plant improvement program of the 1970s focused on improving the single line of track in this region and changing its operating procedures to achieve maximum capacity. On a single-track line, sidings are typically provided at intervals of 5 to 12 miles so that trains can meet or overtake one another. Specific improvement steps included enhancing the track structure to support heavier trains, lengthening sidings and yard tracks, modernizing the signal system, and operating unit trains of a single commodity (such trains have an engine at each end to eliminate switching at turnaround; because of the single commodity, there is no need for extra track at each end of the line for rearranging the cars to obtain the right configuration for the freight). Individual subdivisions (a section of railroad between two terminals or stations) were already handling 40 to 50 million gross tons in 1980. At that point, traffic forecasts for this region predicted continuing sustained traffic growth throughout the 1980s, with traffic levels reaching 60 to 75 million gross tons by 1990 and peaking much higher in some subdivisions.

Although forecasts pointed to a need for significant stretches of double track by 1990, in the mountain region there were staggering physical impediments to double-track construction. To lay the existing single track, rights of way had been carved across the face of mountains, tunnels had been driven through mountains that could not be circumvented, and bridges had been erected over canyons. Even without considering these geographic difficulties in adding an-

In the 1970s forecasters at Canadian National Railway predicted the need for significant expansion in the Mountain Region of Western Canada, including laying of double track in place of the single track. But how could this be done in stretches of mountainous terrain and through tunnels, such as shown here? The use of simulation models allowed the company's planners to determine where the double track could be laid most advantageously and economically.

other track, double-tracking would be a major financial undertaking, with typical construction costs estimated at C$3 to $5 million per mile in mountainous terrain. Costs would be substantially higher in areas where bridges and tunnels were involved.

On the basis of these forecasts, CN initiated the Plant Expansion program, which called for capital expenditures of C$2.2 billion, including C$1.3 billion for double track on the busiest rail subdivisions. In view of the staggering costs involved, a transportation research group was given the responsibility of determining the most cost-effective method of phasing in the double track.

The transportation group decided to prepare two extensive simulation models of the railroad situation. The simulation models allowed the research team to ask "what if" questions and to evaluate the relative effect of many factors influencing main-line capacity. When used together, the simulation models predicted train delay under various track and signal designs, operating methods, and traffic scenarios. These efforts led to a proposed package of cost-effective improvements for capacity expansion that included closer spacing of intermediate traffic control signals. This crucial change in the control signaling system allowed CN to greatly expand traffic capacity by laying double track only in certain strategic areas identified by the simulation models. These improvements, together with the application of the simulation models to plant design (how, as well as where, track is laid), have enabled CN to save many millions of dollars by deferring capital expenditures of over C$350 million beyond 1990.[45] ■

Simulations also are increasingly being used to evaluate the prospects for new products in the development stages. Kraft used a simulation before deciding to enter three test markets with its Makin' Cajun line of dinner kits and ingredients. The simulation drew on data for another ethnic food, Mexican, in predicting "tens of millions of dollars" in sales for the new product. The test markets subsequently bore out the projections. Simulations often rely on historical data and, hence, have more difficulty making projections for very innovative products like Sony's Walkman.[46] Simulation models developed in the electric utility industry to help balance the costs of holding oil and coal inventories against the risks of running out of fuel have saved more than $125 million.[47]

QUANTITATIVE AIDS FOR DECISION MAKING

Although the aids that we have discussed so far are mainly considered planning tools, they often also assist managers in making the decisions that are part of the planning process. In addition, there are a number of aids that are aimed specifically at helping managers make certain types of decisions. Two particularly well-known quantitative aids for decision making are payoff tables and decision trees. We also include a brief discussion of game theory, a third quantitative approach to decision making that is sometimes useful to managers.

Payoff Tables

Payoff table A two-dimensional matrix that allows a decision maker to compare how different future conditions are likely to affect the respective outcomes of two or more decision alternatives

Decision matrix Another term for payoff table

Payoff The amount of decision-maker value associated with a particular decision alternative and future condition

One helpful method of framing managerial decision situations is the use of the payoff table. A **payoff table** is a two-dimensional matrix that allows a decision maker to compare how different future conditions are likely to affect the respective outcomes of two or more decision alternatives. The payoff table is often also referred to as a **decision matrix.**[48] Typically, in a payoff table, the decision alternatives are shown as row headings in the matrix, and the possible future conditions are shown as column headings. The number at the intersection of a row and a column represents the **payoff,** the amount of decision-maker value associated with a particular decision alternative and future condition. An example will be helpful in clarifying these concepts.[49]

Put yourself in the place of a decision maker at a college where there is a good possibility that enrollments may increase but existing classroom space is being used to capacity. Investigation of the situation reveals that there are three viable alternatives for increasing space: Construct a new building, expand an old building, or rent or lease another building. These alternatives are shown as row headings in Table 9-5. There are also three possible future conditions: Student enrollments may go up, go down, or remain unchanged. These future conditions are shown as column headings in Table 9-5. The potential payoff for each combination of alternative and possible future condition is listed at the appropriate intersection in the table. If it were clear which future condition would occur, then it would be a simple matter to select the alternative that has the highest payoff for that future condition. But, unfortunately, it is not possible to know

Table 9-5 Payoff Table for Classroom Space Problem

Alternatives	POSSIBLE FUTURE CONDITIONS			Expected Value
	Student Enrollments Up [.50]*	Student Enrollments Down [.25]	Student Enrollments Unchanged [.25]	
Construct new building	$500,000	($200,000)†	($100,000)	$175,000
Expand old building	$400,000	$100,000	$100,000	$250,000
Rent or lease another building	$400,000	($100,000)	$200,000	$225,000

*Numbers in brackets are probability estimates for possible future conditions.
†Numbers in parentheses represent losses.
Source: Adapted from E. Frank Harrison, *The Managerial Decision-Making Process,* Houghton Mifflin, Boston, 1980, p. 279.

the exact future condition that will occur. However, on the basis of past experience, current enrollment trends and personal judgment, the decision maker is able to assign probabilities to the possible future conditions. A *probability* is the best estimate of a decision maker regarding the likelihood that a future condition will occur.[50] Such estimates are usually made in the form of a percentage ranging from 0 to 100. For example, as shown in the table, the decision maker estimates that there is a 50 percent probability that student enrollments will go up, while probabilities that enrollments will go down or remain unchanged are each estimated at 25 percent. Which alternative should the decision maker choose?

Decision-making experts recommend choosing the alternative with the highest expected value. The **expected value** for a given alternative is the sum of the payoffs times the respective probabilities for that alternative. For example, the expected value (EV) for expanding an old building is determined as follows:

Expected value The sum of the payoffs times the respective probabilities for a given alternative

$$EV = .50(400,000) + .25(100,000) + .25(100,000) = \$250,000$$

Similarly, the expected value for constructing a new building is

$$EV = .50(500,000) - .25(200,000) - .25(100,000) = \$175,000$$

Similar computations show an expected value of $225,000 for renting or leasing another building. Therefore, the alternative with the highest expected value in this case is expand an old building.

The value of payoff tables is that they help decision makers evaluate situations in which the outcomes to be derived from various alternatives depend on the likelihood of future conditions. As such, payoff tables are most useful when the decision maker is able to determine the major relevant alternatives, the payoffs can be quantified, and reasonably accurate judgments can be made regarding future probabilities.[51] For example, payoff tables have been used to decide which new products to introduce, real estate investments to select, crops to plant, and restaurant staffing levels to implement.[52] Managers at Hallmark, the greeting-card company, use payoff matrices to help determine the production quantities of unique products, such as a special Muppet promotion that includes albums, plaques, gift wrap, stickers, party patterns, and other items.[53]

Decision Trees

A **decision tree** is a graphic model that displays the structure of a sequence of alternative courses of action. A decision tree usually also shows the payoffs associated with various paths and the probabilities associated with potential future conditions.

Decision tree A graphic model that displays the structure of a sequence of alternative courses of action and usually shows the payoffs associated with various paths and the probabilities associated with potential future conditions

An example of a simple decision tree is shown in Figure 9-7. Here, the manager is faced with an initial decision about whether to build a large or a small manufacturing plant given some uncertainty regarding future demand for the product. If a large plant is built and demand is high, the company will make a $12 million profit; however, if demand is low, only a $2 million profit will be made (the profit is low because of the overhead due to the large unused capacity at the plant). This latter amount is less than the profit that will be made with a small plant under conditions of either high or low demand ($8 million and $5 million, respectively). To help make the decision, we compute the expected value for each alternative. The expected value for the large-plant alternative is $8 million [(.60 × $12 million) + (.40 × $2 million)]. The expected value for the

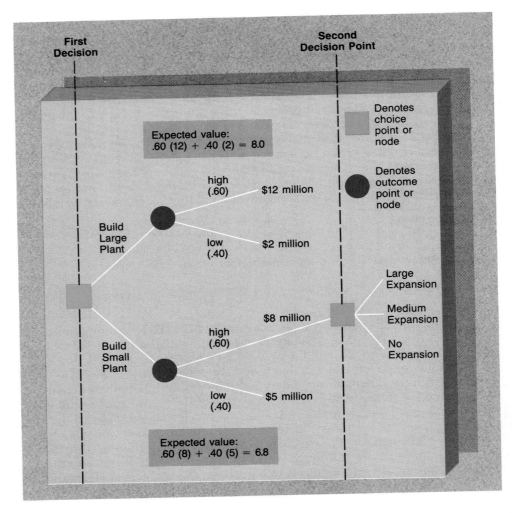

Figure 9-7 Decision tree and expected values for building a large or a small manufacturing plant.

small-plant alternative is $6.8 million [(.60 × $8 million) + (.40 × $5 million)]. This analysis suggests that the manager should seriously consider building the larger plant.

So far, the decision tree operates as a graphic alternative to the payoff table. However, a major advantage of a decision tree is that it allows decision makers to consider the implications of more complex alternatives. For example, a manager may want to consider the implications of initially building a small plant and then possibly expanding it when the nature of the demand becomes more obvious. In our example in Figure 9-7, building a small plant and then facing high demand for the product raises the possibility of a second, later decision point at which time a manager could take further action ranging from a large plant expansion to no expansion. The implication of these later decision possibilities can be considered and their expected values computed by using complex decision trees involving multiple decision points. A decision tree can help managers identify various options, as well as consider the potential impact of various alternative branches of the tree. The device was used recently to assist the U.S. Postal Service in its decision to continue the nine-digit zip code (zip + 4) for first-class business mailers and to purchase additional capital equipment in conjunction with its postal automation efforts.[54]

Break-Even Analysis

Break-even analysis is a graphic model that helps decision makers understand the relationships among sales volume, costs, and revenues in an organization.[55] Although break-even analysis often is conducted graphically, as shown in Figure 9-8, it also can be done mathematically.[56] The technique allows managers to determine the break-even point, which is the level of sales volume at which total revenues equal total costs. The break-even point is so named because it is the point at which the organization neither loses nor makes money—that is, the organization just breaks even. The break-even point is important because only for sales volume beyond that point does the organization begin to make a profit.

Several major elements are included in the break-even analysis shown in Figure 9-8. *Fixed costs* are costs that remain the same regardless of volume of output (e.g., the costs of heating, lighting, administration, mortgage on building, and insurance). Fixed costs in Figure 9-7 are illustrated by the horizontal line at $600,000. *Variable costs* are costs that vary, depending on the level of output (e.g., the costs of raw materials, labor, packaging, and freight). In this particular situation, variable costs are $40 per unit for a unit that sells for $60. These data

Break-even analysis A graphic model that helps decision makers understand the relationships among sales volume, costs, and revenues in an organization

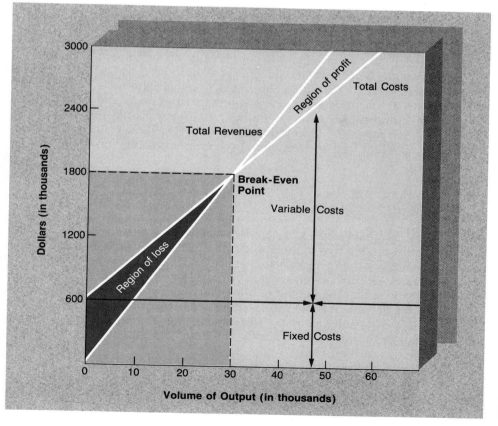

Figure 9-8 Break-even analysis.

can be used to draw the lines on the graph for total costs (fixed costs plus variable costs) and total revenues, respectively. The break-even point, shown graphically, is at 30,000 units. At this point, fixed costs of $600,000 plus variable costs of $1,200,000 [30,000 × $40 (variable cost per unit)] equal $1,800,000. Revenues also equal $1,800,000 [30,000 × $60 (sale price per unit)] at this point. Hence the organization would break even at 30,000 units.

Break-even analysis is useful because it is a rough means of analyzing just how many units of a product or service an organization must sell before that organization begins to make a profit. The analysis also provides a means of assessing the impact of cost cutting on the point at which profits begin. For example, if the organization lowered its fixed and/or variable costs, the total cost line in Figure 9-8 would drop, lowering the break-even point. Along these lines, when Donald E. Petersen was named president of the Ford Motor Company in 1980, he developed a strategy for boosting profitability through the lowering of Ford's break-even point. Petersen cut costs by $5 billion over 6 years, with the result that Ford's break-even point went from 4 million to 2.8 million cars. The new figure, the lowest among Ford, General Motors, and Chrysler, makes it possible for Ford to remain profitable even during downturns in the cyclical automobile market.[57]

This type of analysis also was conducted by John Sculley, head of Apple Computer, in 1986. After concluding that Apple's operations had become too large and expensive, he initiated a cost-cutting program that ultimately reduced Apple's break-even point from $400 million to $325 million per quarter. As a result, profits climbed 23 percent, despite a 23 percent drop in revenues, and cash on hand rose to an unprecedented $441 million at Apple.[58] Break-even analysis also is used to assess the impact of raising prices (and, thereby, total revenues), causing the total revenues line to rise more steeply and the break-even point to be lower.

Break-even analysis makes some simplifying assumptions. For instance, it assumes that a given price will be charged for all units (yet, e.g., some customers may get discounts) and that the fixed costs will remain the same across a wide range of outputs. Such assumptions suggest that the break-even technique is valuable for doing rough analyses, rather than for precisely fine-tuning volumes, costs, and revenues. More complex types of break-even analyses, particularly those involving computers, are becoming available for more precise needs.[59]

Game Theory

Game theory A quantitative technique for facilitating decision making in situations of conflict among two or more decision makers seeking to maximize their own welfares

Game theory is a quantitative technique for facilitating decision making in situations of conflict among two or more decision makers seeking to maximize their own welfares.[60] The theory recognizes explicitly that in situations of competition among adversaries, each adversary must consider the likely actions of competitors. The reason is that the outcomes of one adversary's actions are likely to be affected by the actions of other adversaries. For example, when Hunt-Wesson introduced a new spaghetti sauce, Prima Salsa, the company underestimated the reaction of Ragu, the market leader at that time. Ragu spent a fortune to fight off the challenge, causing Hunt-Wesson to withdraw Prima Salsa within a short period of time. Consequently, when the Campbell Soup Company 1 year later brought out its own challenger, Prego, Ragu assumed that Campbell would not spend the money necessary to market Prego adequately. Ragu was wrong, and the company's relatively mild reaction allowed Campbell's Prego to grab a 26 percent market share.[61] Game theory helps managers analyze such situations. However, game theory has not yet advanced to the stage at which it can handle very complex conflict situations, particularly those involving a number of variables that are difficult to quantify.[62] Nevertheless, even in such situations, game theory can help managers think through major issues involving competitive responses.[63]

The expert in this picture is in the computer, in the form of a compter-based SEC Expert Security Advisor System. A technical manager in the data processing division of Travelers Insurance Company is using the system to get advice on security investments for the company.

DECISION SUPPORT AND EXPERT SYSTEMS

With the proliferation of computers, many organizational computer specialists and software vendors are developing computer software packages that facilitate managerial decision making. Such computer-based aids to decision making fall into two main categories: decision support systems and expert systems. We briefly introduce these two types of computerized decision aids here. (They are covered in greater depth in Chapter 20, on information systems.) These approaches reflect special efforts at innovation and are quickly becoming important elements in gaining and maintaining the competitive edge.

Decision Support Systems

A **decision support system (DSS)** is a computer-based information system that supports the process of managerial decision making in situations that are not well structured. There are many different types of decision support systems, but they typically allow the decision maker to interact with the computer, retrieve data relevant to the decision, and test alternative solutions to the problem under consideration. These systems do not actually provide managers with a decision; rather, they help provide a framework that the manager can use to explore major issues. For example, a DSS might incorporate a payoff-table format in which the manager supplies the input variables, such as alternatives, possible future states, and appropriate probabilities. The system would then compute the expected values and subsequently allow the manager to change the input variables and explore the implications. There are, however, many other types of decision support systems. They are generally most useful with semistructured problems where the judgment of the manager remains an important element in the decision-making process.[64]

Decision support system (DSS) A computer-based information system that supports the process of managerial decision making in situations that are not well structured

Expert Systems

An **expert system (ES)** is a computer-based system that applies the substantial knowledge of an expert to help solve problems in a specific area. Many computer specialists consider expert systems to be special cases of decision support systems. Expert systems typically have an extensive knowledge base and incorporate decision rules that parallel those used by experts. An ES will closely approximate the decision that would be made by an expert facing the same set of circumstances. One of the better known applications of expert systems has been in helping with patient diagnosis in the medical field. The patient's symptoms are entered into the ES, which may then identify the likely possibilities, ask for more information, or suggest a strategy for further tests to more clearly identify the symptom causes. Such systems, in effect, provide the help of experts from many different medical specialties.[65] Expert systems also are being used in such

Expert system (ES) A computer-based system that applies the substantial knowledge of an expert to help solve problems in a specific area

diverse areas as mineral and oil exploration, cement kiln monitoring, equipment fault locating, and the pricing of airline tickets.[66] They also are being developed for use in the insurance industry (see the following Case in Point discussion).

CASE IN POINT: Insurers Race to Develop Expert Systems

At the American International Group of insurance companies, computers are making recommendations to underwriters about how earthquake insurance should be written. At the Hartford Steam Boiler Inspection and Insurance Company, computers are analyzing customers' machinery and suggesting ways that breakdowns can be avoided. At the Aetna Life and Casualty Company, computers soon will be helping new underwriters learn the complex skills and thought processes that experts use in writing workers' compensation coverage.

These programs represent a bold new use of computers in the insurance industry. Computers, long vital in processing vast amounts of data, now are going one step further—they are helping to make judgments and assist insurance professionals in underwriting, claims processing, loss prevention, financial advice, and other tasks.

Called expert systems, these sophisticated software systems for computers have the ability to ask "what if" and "why" questions. The systems emulate human thought through a combination of computer science, electronics, and engineering, which is known in the computer world as *artificial intelligence*. Insurers say that expert systems will increase the consistency, speed, and quality of insurance work, while freeing some human experts from the drudgery of repetitive tasks. Insurance companies believe the systems will enhance their competitiveness and eventually pay for themselves several times over.

Expert systems are not being viewed as replacements for human thinking and expertise, but as powerful tools that can supplement and enhance human knowledge. Companies stress that the systems' recommendations can be modified and their judgments overruled by users.

An example of how an ES works can be seen in the Underwriting Advisor, one of the most sophisticated systems now being used by the American International Group of New York to help write coverage for special risks, including earthquakes. Like a trained underwriter, the system raises a series of questions when analyzing the risk and, after arriving at an assessment, spells out its reasoning. It can also ask for more information or indicate to an underwriter what other information would be useful in reaching a decision.

The battle to develop the best and most far-reaching expert systems is being waged by such companies as the Travelers Corporation, Aetna, the American International Group, Cigna, and the Fireman's Fund Insurance Company. Travelers wants to apply expert systems to property and casualty underwriting, claims, and almost every area of the company, says Ron Bristol, a vice president of computer science. "We're trying to train more and more people in the company. . . . We think these programs give us a competitive edge," Bristol said, noting that Travelers is spending about $500,000 a year on expert systems and that it expects a payoff of three to four times the development cost.[67] ■

Aids like decision support and expert systems help managers make better decisions as part of the planning function. To carry out such decisions, managers also need to give careful consideration to the organizing function, which we consider next in Part Three.

CHAPTER SUMMARY

Largely through advances in management science, there are an increasing number of aids available to help managers gain the competitive edge through innovations in planning and decision making. Many of these aids rely heavily on quantitative methods.

Forecasting, an important tool for planning, falls into three main categories: quantitative; technological, or qualitative; and judgmental. The major types of quantitative forecasting are time-series methods; explanatory, or causal, methods, including regression models, econometric models, and leading indicators; and monitoring methods. Technological, or qualitative, forecasting, a forecasting approach that is particularly useful for promoting innovation, includes the Delphi method, morphological analysis, and La Prospective. The major means used in judgmental forecasting are the jury of executive opinion and sales-force composites. When choosing a forecasting method, managers need to consider such factors as the desired time horizon, type of accuracy needed, ease of understanding, and developmental costs.

Two planning tools are particularly useful to managers who are responsible for significant projects: Gantt charts and PERT. PERT is especially useful for planning and controlling large projects, particularly if there are uncertainties about activity durations and/or trade-offs between resource usage and project completion times.

A number of other quantitatively oriented planning techniques exist that can greatly assist managers. Linear programming is a quantitative tool for planning how to allocate limited or scarce resources so that a single criterion or goal (often profits) is optimized. Queuing, or waiting-line, models help describe the operating charac-teristics of queues and allow managers to vary the parameters of situations and estimate the probable effects. Inventory models assist managers in determining the appropriate level of goods and stocks. Routing, or distribution, models help managers plan the most effective and economical approaches to distribution problems. Simulation is a mathematical modeling approach that allows managers to change parameters and/or assumptions about a situation in order to evaluate the probable effects.

A number of decision aids are available to help managers make certain types of decisions. A payoff table is a two-dimensional matrix that allows a decision maker to compare how different future conditions are likely to affect the outcomes of two or more decision alternatives. A decision tree is a graphic model that displays the structure of a sequence of alternative courses of action and, therefore, can be used to evaluate the implications of a series of decision alternatives. Break-even analysis is a graphic model that helps decision makers understand the relationships among sales volume, costs, and revenues in organizations. Game theory facilitates decision making in situations of conflict among two or more decision makers seeking to maximize their own welfare.

Computerized decision aids in the form of decision support systems and related expert systems provide a growing opportunity for innovation and enhanced competitiveness in organizations. A decision support system is a computer-based information system that supports managerial decision making in situations that are not well structured. An expert system is a computer-based system that applies the substantial knowledge of an expert to help solve problems in a specific area.

MANAGERIAL TERMINOLOGY

activity (307)
break-even analysis (319)
constraints (309)
critical path (308)
decision matrix (316)
decision support system (DSS) (321)
decision tree (317)
Delphi method (301)
econometric models (300)
expected value (317)
expert system (ES) (321)

explanatory, or causal, models (298)
game theory (320)
Gantt chart (305)
inventory models (312)
judgmental forecasting (304)
jury of executive opinion (304)
La Prospective (303)
leading indicators (300)
linear programming (LP) (309)
monitoring methods (300)

morphological analysis (303)
network diagram (307)
node, or event (307)
objective function (309)
payoff (316)
payoff table (316)
Program Evaluation and Review Technique (PERT) (306)
quantitative forecasting (297)
queuing, or waiting-line, models (311)

regression models (299)
routing, or distribution, models (313)
sales-force composite (304)
scenarios (303)
simulation (313)
slack (308)
technological, or qualitative, forecasting (301)
time-series methods (297)

QUESTIONS FOR DISCUSSION AND REVIEW

1. Describe the three major categories of forecasting methods. Under what circumstances would you use each of them?
2. Explain the main forecasting approaches included in the quantitative category. To a large extent, quantitative forecasting methods rely on historical data to predict future events. Under what circumstances might the use of historical data be inappropriate?
3. Enumerate the major approaches included in the technological, or qualitative, forecasting category. Suppose that your college or university is interested in forecasting the need for new academic and support (financial aid, dormitories, etc.) programs for students by the year 2000. How would you use the Delphi method of forecasting to help provide some answers?
4. Explain two major methods of judgmental forecasting. Suppose that you are faced with a sudden situation in which the time requirements make it necessary for you to rely on judgmental forecasting. How can you improve the prospects of getting useful results?
5. Explain the difference between Gantt charts and PERT. Assume that you have just been selected to be the head of a major project involving 75 to 100 interrelated tasks. Evaluate the usefulness of Gantt charts and PERT in helping you effectively plan and control the project.

6. Under what conditions is linear programming likely to be a useful planning aid? Why do you think that linear programming is the most widely used quantitative planning tool in business? What are some of its main limitations?
7. How would you describe each of the following planning techniques to a new boss who has little background in this area: queuing, or waiting-line, models; inventory models; routing, or distribution, models; and simulation models? How might these techniques be used in a hospital?
8. Distinguish among payoff tables, decision trees, and game theory as decision-making tools. Develop a decision tree for the classroom expansion problem discussed in this chapter in the section on payoff tables. How can the decision tree be developed to include the possibility of later expansion decisions after the student enrollment pattern becomes more obvious?
9. Explain the decision-making aid called break-even analysis. Assume that you are advising a friend who is contemplating starting a new business. How could break-even analysis be useful?
10. Explain how decision support and expert systems can enhance managerial decision making. For an organization with which you are familiar, identify areas in which an ES might be helpful. To what extent would the costs of an ES be justified in these situations?

DISCUSSION QUESTIONS FOR CHAPTER OPENING CASE

1. What types of major planning aids were incorporated into United's Station Manpower Planning System?
2. What obstacles confronted the planning group in developing and implementing the new system?

How did the planning group overcome these obstacles?
3. What lessons regarding managerial innovation and change can be gleaned from United's development of the SMPS?

MANAGEMENT EXERCISE: USING PERT[68]

Objectives

■ To learn how to construct a network diagram for use with PERT
■ To gain experience in identifying the critical path

Instructions

Table 9-6 lists the major activities involved in introducing a new product. For each activity, the table gives the length of time that the activity is likely to take and indicates the immediate predecessor activity.

Table 9-6   Activities, Required Sequence, and Time Requirements for the New Product Introduction Project

Activity Code	Description	Immediate Predecessor Activity	Time (weeks)
A	Organize sales office.	—	6
B	Hire salespeople.	A	4
C	Train salespeople.	B	7
D	Select advertising agency.	A	2
E	Plan advertising campaign.	D	4
F	Conduct advertising campaign.	E	10
G	Design package.	—	2
H	Set up packaging facilities.	G	10
I	Package initial stocks.	H, J	6
J	Order stock from manufacturer.	—	13
K	Select distributors.	A	9
L	Sell to distributors.	C, K	3
M	Ship stock to distributors.	I, L	5

Source: Reprinted from Elwood S. Buffa, *Modern Production/Operations Management,* 7th ed., Wiley, New York, p. 423.

1. On the basis of this information, develop a network diagram for the project. (*Hint:* Network diagram developers often start with the final activity and work their way back to the beginning by drawing in the immediate predecessors for each activity.)
2. Identify the critical path.

MANAGEMENT SCIENCE TRANSFORMS CITGO PETROLEUM

In 1983, the Southland Corporation, the 7-Eleven convenience-store giant and retailer of 2 billion gallons of gasoline per year through that chain of stores, took a step to integrate vertically by acquiring the Citgo Petroleum Corporation, the oil-refining and marketing asset of the Occidental Petroleum Corporation. Citgo, with 1985 sales in excess of $4 billion, is one of the nation's largest industrial companies, ranking in the top 150 of the Forbes 500 (on the basis of sales).

Southland was determined, at the time of the acquisition, to establish management priorities and procedures that would make Citgo as successful in the downstream petroleum business (refining and marketing) as Southland is in the convenience-store industry. At the same time, Citgo would supply 7-Eleven stores with quality motor fuels. To achieve these goals, Southland realized that the culture of its acquisition had to change. Citgo had to be transformed from an integrated oil company that produced its own crude oil (while part of Occidental) to an independent refiner and marketer of petroleum products. It was essential that the company turn its financial losses

around and begin making money in its downstream operation. This meant that Citgo had to alter the basis for its decision making, in the process becoming more responsive to the market and less driven by the refining of crude oil.

Toward this end, Southland management made two strategic decisions. First, it established Citgo as a wholly owned subsidiary responsible for its own debts, including those related to its acquisition. This organizational and financial structure was intended to ensure that Citgo would make a profit independent of Southland's vast gasoline retailing business and to provide the most basic motivation (economic survival) for improvements in Citgo's operation. Second, Southland created a task force composed of Southland personnel, Citgo personnel, and external consultants. An external consultant was appointed director of the task force and reported directly to John P. Thompson, chairman of the board of Southland. The task force developed various strategies to help Citgo's management achieve the goals set by Southland. These involved combining mathematical programming, organizational theory, expert systems, decision support systems, and forecasting techniques with the latest information systems technologies.

When the task force began its evaluation of the situation, it

quickly realized that the petroleum industry was in the midst of an information explosion due to several environmental changes. Among the major changes were industry deregulation; a ballooning of the number of new sources of crude oil from which Citgo could make purchases, coupled with volatile prices that could change hourly; increased price competition in selling refined oil at both the wholesale and retail levels; and large increases in the cost of financing working capital that made controlling inventory costs extremely important. Working closely with management, the task force helped make major improvements in the linear programming system, an extremely useful tool for helping management control refinery operating costs. The refinery linear programming system is now used routinely to provide critical decision information in such areas as crude-oil selection and acquisition economics, refinery run levels, and product component production levels.

Another way in which the task force helped management improve Citgo's competitive edge was through the development of a system called TRACS (Tracking, Reporting, and Aggregation of Citgo Segmented Sales) to evaluate the profitability of existing markets. TRACS is a sophisticated expert system that provides an economic comparison between potential sell-

Citgo Petroleum Corporation, whose refinery at Lake Charles, Louisiana, is shown here, became a success story when extensive management science practices, including forecasting techniques and expert systems, were instituted by its parent company, Southland Corporation.

ing options and distribution channels. For example, it can provide comparisons between selling on the "spot" market (the bulk petroleum market delivering within 48 hours) and selling at the wholesale "rack" (terminals in set locations) or between pipeline distribution and barge distribution.

As part of the task force's efforts, price and volume forecasting was centralized and improved. Historically, Citgo forecasted only total volume and those prices necessary for monthly and quarterly budgets. Consequently, each department developed short-term forecasts for its own needs. Now, using management science techniques, including econometric modeling and regression analysis, Citgo's pricing manager has developed models to provide wholesale price forecasts (based on spot-market forecasts, historical time lags, competitive factors, etc.) and wholesale volume forecasts (based on historical price-volume relationships, assumptions about relative positions within the pricing pack, etc.). These forecasts are developed by terminal (for each of the approximately 40 Citgo-owned and -leased terminals and 350 exchange partner terminals), by product, by line of business, and by week for an 11-week planning horizon. The forecasts are reviewed and approved by both pricing and marketing managers before they are entered into an information system that makes the forecasts available to the various Citgo departments that rely on them. Forecasting systems in other areas, such as the gasoline retail sales volume for the 7-Eleven stores, also were developed.

A decision support system was also established to integrate the key economic and physical characteristics of Citgo's supply, distribution, and marketing (SDM) for a short-term (11-week) planning horizon.

This time horizon incorporates both manufacturing and distribution time lags. The SDM system is used by top management to make many operational decisions, such as where to sell products, what price to charge, where to buy or trade products, how much to buy or trade, how much of each product to hold in inventory, and how much to ship by each mode of transportation.

These and other systems created through management science projects were linked to a shared, computerized data base through a system called PASS, a unique aspect of the effort. PASS enables a variety of systems to share the same information base and makes the analyses results available to the various managers who need them.

Over a 2-year period, these efforts have achieved impressive results. Citgo, which had lost money for several years prior to the acquisition, quickly changed from a company that lost $50 million in 1984 to one that achieved a pretax profit of $70 million the following year. Management has been able to reduce working-capital requirements by approximately $150 million. The resulting benefits include an annual decrease in interest expense of approximately $18 million and a substantial reduction in Citgo's vulnerability to falling crude-oil and product prices. Citgo's management also estimates that the effective use of these tools improved marketing profits by $2.5 million and refining profits by $50 million in the first year of implementation. The success of the project was attributed not only to the task force but also to the strong support of top management and the dedicated support of operational managers. During the organizational restructuring of Citgo, new employees were hired and existing employees who supported, and were capable

of implementing, management science tools were promoted. The responsibility of developing and implementing the different systems conceived by the task force was distributed among these employees, who coordinated their efforts with those of the task force.

The total cost of the implemented systems, $20 to $30 million, was the greatest obstacle to the project. However, because of the information explosion in the petroleum industry, top management realized that numerous information systems were essential for gathering, storing, and analyzing data.[69]

Southland sold 50 percent of Citgo to Petroleos de Venezuela, the state-owned Venezuelan oil company, in 1986. By late 1989, Southland was negotiating to sell the other half of Citgo to Petroleos, primarily because Southland itself was struggling under a massive debt incurred through privatization. In 1987, Southland's publicly traded stock had been bought by managers and investors for $4.9 billion, and the company now needed the cash from the sale of Citgo to help meet the interest payments on its debts.[70]

QUESTIONS FOR CHAPTER CONCLUDING CASE

1. What planning and decision aids were used at Citgo in achieving the turnaround?

2. If you were in charge of a task force like the one at Citgo, what aids would you use to plan and manage implementation of the various projects (as opposed to which projects would you implement)?

3. What might the changing information environment and the need for innovation suggest about selection and training for managers at Citgo?

SEARS CHARTS NEW STRATEGIES

Sears, Roebuck and Company is one of the best-recognized names in business. Sears, as it is often called, has more than 800 Sears stores, over 400 separate catalog outlets, and more than 1500 independent catalog merchants in the United States and Canada. Most people are familiar with the organization because they have interfaced with one or more of its major business units: the Sears Merchandise Group, which runs the retail stores and catalog operations; Allstate Insurance; Dean Witter Financial Services; and the Coldwell Banker Real Estate Group. In total, the corporation has annual revenues in the $50 billion range and close to a half million employees.

The company's origins trace back to an 1886 rail shipment of watches that was refused by a jeweler in Redwood Falls, Minnesota. The wayward shipment was accepted instead by 22-year-old Richard Warren Sears, who was working as a freight agent for the Minneapolis and St. Louis Railroad at its station in North Redwood. He began selling the watches (by mail and telegraph) to other agents, who then sold them to railroad customers. Sales were so brisk that he set up the R. W. Sears Watch Company, which he moved to Chicago in 1887.

Since he needed someone to repair the watches that he sold mainly by mail, Sears put a classified ad in the Chicago *Daily News*; it was answered by 23-year-old Alvah Curtis Roebuck. At the time, Roebuck was working in Hammond, Indiana, repairing watches for $3.50 per week plus room and board. Sears hired the cautious

Hoosier and launched an aggressive and very successful newspaper advertising campaign. Still, Sears worried that the watch mail-order business was too vulnerable to economic downturns. By 1893, Richard Sears and Alvah Roebuck had teamed up to form a new company—Sears, Roebuck and Company—which would offer a broader range of goods.

The catalog of the new company included such items as groceries, drugs, tools, bells, furniture, farm implements, boots and shoes, bicycles, pianos, dry goods, stoves, and sporting goods. The timing was ideal for a mail-order business. In the last decades of the nineteenth century, about 65 percent of the people in the United States lived in rural areas, where the few existing stores generally charged high prices. In contrast, because of its high volume, the Sears, Roebuck operation (promoted as the "cheapest supply house on earth") was able to offer more reasonable prices for goods that were delivered by rail and post. Although the official name of the catalog was the *Consumer's Guide*, customers generally referred to it as the "Wish Book," because it included most of the desirable durable consumer goods of the era. The company grew quickly, requiring increased debt levels to pay for inventory and expanded facilities. At the same time, Sears's glowing advertising often generated more demand than the company could meet within a reasonable time. Such developments worried Roebuck, who sold his one-third interest in the company for $25,000 in 1895.

Meanwhile, Chicago manufacturer Julius Rosenwald, who had the planning and organizing skills that the company needed, became an investor and then vice president and treasurer of Sears, Roebuck. By

1906, as annual sales approached a phenomenal $50 million, Sears and Rosenwald offered common and preferred stock to the public for the first time. The company also moved to a $5 million complex that covered 40 acres on Chicago's west side. The mail-order plant in the complex encompassed more than 3 million square feet of floor space, was the largest business building in the world at that time, and operated with an elaborate system of belts and chutes. Henry Ford reportedly visited the famous plant while researching his own plans for an automobile assembly line. A disagreement in 1908 over whether to market aggressively (Sears's preference) or cut costs (Rosenwald's preference) during a sales slump associated with a financial panic in the United States caused Sears to leave the company. Sears sold his stock for $10 million, never again involved himself in the company, and died in 1914 at age 50. Guiding

In the last decade or so, CEOs at Sears, Roebuck and Company have adopted a diversification strategy that has led to the building of the Sears Financial Network. The network's Discover Card—a credit card with no annual fee and a cash-back feature based on the amount of purchases made—has been a very successful part of this new strategy.

CHAPTER TEN

BASIC ELEMENTS OF ORGANIZATION STRUCTURE

CHAPTER OUTLINE

The Nature of Organization Structure
Organization Structure Defined
The Organization Chart
Chain of Command

Job Design
Approaches to Job Design
Alternative Work Schedules

Types of Departmentalization

Methods of Vertical Coordination
The Role of Formalization
Span of Management
Centralization versus Decentralization
Delegation
Line and Staff Positions

Promoting Innovation: Methods of Horizontal Coordination
Slack Resources
Information Systems
Lateral Relations

LEARNING OBJECTIVES

After studying this chapter, you should be able to:

■ Describe the four elements that make up organization structure.

■ Explain the importance of organization charts and the chain-of-command concept.

■ Outline the major approaches to job design, including the main prospects for altering traditional work schedules.

■ Explain five major methods of vertical coordination, including formalization, span of management, centralization versus decentralization, delegation, and line and staff positions.

■ Explain how slack resources and information systems can be used as means of horizontal coordination.

■ Describe the major types of lateral relations and their usefulness in facilitating horizontal coordination.

G A I N I N G   T H E   E D G E

AMERICA'S MOST SUCCESSFUL ENTREPRENEUR

Ken Olsen, president of the Digital Equipment Corporation (DEC), has been tagged by *Fortune* magazine as "America's most successful entrepreneur" with good reason. Over a span of just three decades, he has led DEC from zero to over $12 billion in annual revenues. Adjusting for inflation, that makes DEC bigger than the Ford Motor Company at Henry Ford's death, U.S. Steel when Andrew Carnegie sold it, and Standard Oil during John D. Rockefeller's leadership.

One of Olsen's favorite managerial techniques is issuing his own moral tales, known as "parables" at DEC. He sends them most frequently to senior mangers via the company's electronic mail system. When the parables appear, managers often gather around terminals speculating on the true meaning of the message. Presented below is an edited version of one of his parables, which was ultimately followed by a reorganization:

> I am in the market for a backhoe. The other day I stopped at a Ford place to get literature on tractors. They had colored brochures with beautiful pictures and glowing descriptions, and plain black-on-yellow data sheets filled with numbers.
>
> The four models which I think may cover my needs seem to be made by four different product organizations that compete with each other in who can make the most expensive and beautiful brochure. But no way would the brochures explain why one Ford tractor might have advantages over another. The data sheets vary from two to eight pages, and there is no consistency in the way data is presented. There is no way to compare the four tractors.
>
> If I don't get tired of the whole idea of a backhoe, I'll try seeing the salesman next time. But I am not sure he would understand the differences between the models, and I would feel intimidated by my lack of knowledge. I am always embarrassed when salesmen act surprised that I don't know how deep a ditch I want to dig, how heavy a load I want to lift, or how high I want to lift it.
>
> Sometime I'd like to have you explain whether there is a parallel at Digital in this or not.

In this parable, Olsen was diagnosing organizational difficulties that were plaguing DEC at the time. For 19 years the company had operated with a structure that was somewhat unusual when it was first adopted. Each product line was the responsibility of a product manager who oversaw development, marketing, pricing, inventories, and the profit picture for the product line but who "bought" services from centralized manufacturing, sales, engineering, and field service departments. The services were bought by negotiating a price for needed service and then transferring funds from the product-line budget to the service department providing the support. Over the years the structure had evolved into 18 separate product-line groups, or divisions, each concentrating on developing products for specific industries, such as engineering or education.

Originally, this structure was one of DEC's strong points because it enabled the company to respond quickly to the special demands of each kind of customer. Eventually, however, the product-line groups became fiefdoms that grew more protective of their own interests and lost sight of the company's long-range goals. As a result, DEC found itself behind the prevailing trend toward personal computers and office automation products that could be linked, stymied in efforts to enter new markets that overlapped product groups, and bogged down in increasing product-group conflicts over limited central engineering and manufacturing resources.

Intent upon retaining DEC's innovative character, Olsen turned his attention to a reorganization, staying up nights dictating enough memos to keep four secretaries busy during the day. Finally, Olsen took action to organize the company along more conventional functional lines. To speed up product development and improve coordination among product lines, he combined the engineering and manufacturing operations under one head. Olsen also placed sales and marketing under another senior vice president. Now groups of salespeople would specialize on a given industry, but they would be knowledgeable about all the various DEC products, rather than just selling one small group of products. Combining sales forces also led to a better utilization of salespeople because they could be better aligned to the size of particular markets.

Ken Olsen, the President of Digital Equipment Corporation, took a once innovative organizational structure that was no longer working and revamped it. As a result, DEC was able to develop successful new products and increase its profits.

As part of the changes, the growing headquarters' bureaucracy was pruned and, to help decentralize decision making and encourage innovative ideas, several committees were developed to assist with product strategy, marketing and sales, and management, respectively. The new measures have helped produce successful new products such as the popular VAX computers and related network systems—products based on proprietary DEC technology. Now, DEC faces new challenges as the computer field grows even more fiercely competitive. More organizational changes will likely ensue. Company members say that Olsen's engineering background is reflected in the way that he manages the company: taking things apart that do not work and revamping them until they do.[1]

Put yourself in Ken Olsen's shoes. If you were managing an internationally known and highly successful company, but saw your company start to fall behind competitors in meeting customer needs, you might well do what Ken Olsen did. Olsen engaged in the managerial function of *organizing*, the process of allocating and arranging human and nonhuman resources so that planned goals can be achieved. Organizing is important to managers because it is the means they use to align work with resources so that organizational plans and decisions (discussed in Part Two) can be made and carried out effectively.

As the DEC situation illustrates, even the best intentions and plans can go awry when the way in which the organization is structured and resources are deployed encourages counterproductive actions. Often, means of organizing that work under one set of circumstances become inappropriate as the situation changes. As a result, organizing is an ongoing management function. Managers need to give frequent consideration to organizing issues in order to keep the organization moving on target. As we begin this first chapter of Part Three, we initially probe the nature of organization structure. We also explore major considerations in dividing work in ways that are meaningful to individuals and that are likely to energize their efforts to put forth their best performance. We then review major ways of grouping jobs and units in developing an overall organization structure. We next investigate several important methods of coordinating efforts up and down the hierarchy. Finally, we examine methods of horizontal coordination that not only help various departments and units synchronize their efforts but also encourage innovation.

THE NATURE OF ORGANIZATION STRUCTURE

If you are like most people, you have probably had the experience of running into a problem that made you want to speak to the supervisor or next in command in an organization. Under such conditions, you would probably respond with disbelief if you were told that no one knew who the supervisor was or whose job it was to handle a complaint like yours. We expect such matters to be worked out—at least by organizations that have some hope of long-run survival. In essence, we expect that the organizations with which we deal have developed reasonably effective organization structures.

Organization Structure Defined

Organization structure The formal pattern of interactions and coordination designed by management to link the tasks of individuals and groups in achieving organizational goals

Organization structure is the formal pattern of interactions and coordination designed by management to link the tasks of individuals and groups in achieving organizational goals. The word "formal" in this context refers to the fact that organization structures typically are created by management for specific purposes related to achieving organizational goals and, hence, are official, or formal, outcomes of the organizing function. Organizations also have informal structures, or patterns of interaction, which are not designed by management but which emerge usually because of common interests or friendship. We discuss informal patterns of interaction further when we consider groups in Chapter 16.

Organization design The process of developing an organization structure

The process of developing an organization structure is sometimes referred to as **organization design.** Organization structure consists mainly of four elements:[2]

1. The assignment of tasks and responsibilities that define the jobs of individuals and units
2. The clustering of individual positions into units and of units into departments and larger units to form an organization's hierarchy
3. The various mechanisms required to facilitate vertical coordination, such as the number of individuals reporting to any given managerial position and the degree of delegation of authority
4. The various mechanisms needed to foster horizontal coordination, such as task forces and interdepartmental teams

One aid to visualizing structure is the organization chart. Thus we briefly examine the notion of the organization chart and review the related concept of the chain of command before analyzing the four main elements of organization structure in greater detail.

The Organization Chart

Organization chart A line diagram that depicts the broad outlines of an organization's structure

The **organization chart** is a line diagram that depicts the broad outlines of an organization's structure. Organization charts vary in detail, but they typically show in visual form the various major positions or departments in the organization, the way the various positions are grouped into specific units, reporting relationships from lower to higher levels, and official channels for communicating information.[3] Some charts show titles associated with the positions, as well as the current position holders. An overall organization chart indicating the major managerial positions and departments in the Acacia Mutual Life Insurance Company, based in Washington, D.C., is shown in Figure 10-1.

Because organization charts facilitate understanding the overall structure of organizations, many organizations have found them useful. Such charts are particularly helpful in providing a visual map of the chain of command.

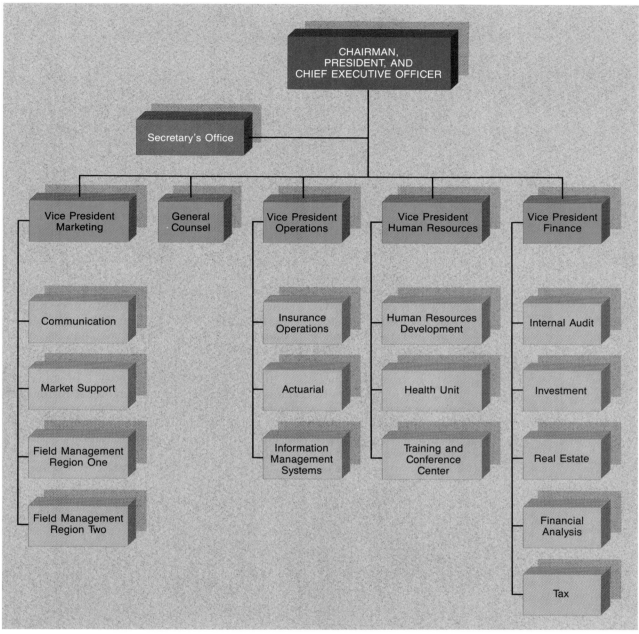

Figure 10-1 Organization chart for the Acacia Mutual Life Insurance Company.

Chain of Command

The **chain of command** is the unbroken line of authority that ultimately links each individual with the top organizational position through a managerial position at each successive layer in between. The concept of chain of command stems from two basic principles developed by contributors to the classical management viewpoint (see Chapter 2): unity of command and the scalar principle. *Unity of command* means that an individual should have only one boss at any

Chain of command The unbroken line of authority that ultimately links each individual with the top organizational position through a managerial position at each successive layer in between

given point in time. The *scalar principle* states that there should be a clear line of authority from the position of ultimate authority at the top to every individual in the organization.[4] Thus the basic idea is that each individual in an organization should be able to identify his or her boss and trace the line of authority through the organization all the way to the very top position.

Today, most organizations that include more than a few individuals are likely to have organization charts showing the chain of command and the basic structure of the organization. Although such charts provide a broad view, they do not include all aspects of the structure picture. For example, organization charts do not normally include detailed information about how work is divided into specific jobs. Yet, as noted earlier in defining organization structure, the design of jobs is an important aspect of structure. Therefore, it is the subject to which we now turn.

JOB DESIGN

Different types of jobs can involve very different activities. A job as a buyer for Macy's, the New York–based department store chain, may involve keeping in contact with various suppliers in a certain specialty area (such as shoes), previewing new offerings, developing sources for in-house brands, and studying trends in consumer tastes. In contrast, the job of a salesperson may include learning about new items in certain departments, keeping merchandise neatly arranged, helping customers, and ringing up sales at the register. The differing activities of the buyer and the salesperson reflect **work specialization,** the degree to which the work necessary to achieve organizational goals is broken down into various jobs. Without some specialization, it would be difficult for most organizations to function, simply because it is usually impossible for every organization member to have the entire range of skills necessary to run an effective organization. Most of us have probably experienced the frustration of attempting to make a purchase only to find that the salesperson filling in for someone else cannot answer our questions about the products we are considering.

Work specialization The degree to which the work necessary to achieve organizational goals is broken down into various jobs

The store manager, buyer, and marketing manager of Scarbrough's Department Store in Austin, Texas, all share the organizational goal of selling merchandise and making a profit, but each specializes in particular tasks to achieve that goal. Their jobs are designed to give them individual challenges but also to aid in the coordination of their efforts.

On the other hand, even jobs with similar titles can differ substantially in the activities performed. For example, a job as an administrative assistant may include typing, filing, and photocopying, or it could involve such activities as coordinating meetings and travel, investigating trouble spots, and making decisions about a certain range of issues. What is included in a given job depends on **job design,** the specification of task activities associated with a particular job.

Job design is important to the organizing function for two major reasons. For one thing, task activities need to be grouped in reasonably logical ways; otherwise, it may be very difficult for organization members to function efficiently. For another, the way that jobs are configured has an important influence on employee motivation to perform well. (We discuss specific concepts of motivation in Chapter 13.) Thus managers need to consider both efficiency and motivational issues in designing jobs that will facilitate effective performance.

Job design The specification of task activities associated with a particular job

Approaches to Job Design

There are four major approaches to job design: job simplification, job rotation, job enlargement, and job enrichment.[5]

Job Simplification. **Job simplification** is the process of configuring, or designing, jobs so that jobholders have only a small number of narrow activities to perform (see Figure 10-2a). Economist Adam Smith was one of the first to highlight the advantages of work specialization and simplification. Using his now-famous example involving pins, Smith pointed out that an individual working alone could make 20 pins per day, while 10 people working on specialized tasks could make 48,000 pins per day.[6] The simplification idea was further popularized by Frederick Taylor through his scientific management viewpoint, which emphasizes reducing jobs to narrow tasks and training workers in the best way to do them (see Chapter 2).

Job simplification The process of configuring jobs so that jobholders have only a small number of narrow activities to perform

Under job simplification, it is possible to gain major production efficiencies by designing optimum ways to perform tasks, having individual workers perform only one or a small number of the tasks, and providing a quality control mechanism (such as quality control inspectors). Because the jobs are simple and repetitive, workers are almost interchangeable, making training new workers relatively easy. Perhaps the most obvious example of job simplification is the assembly-line approach commonly used to make automobiles. Unfortunately, job simplification can be carried too far, creating narrow, repetitive jobs that are not conducive to motivating employees. Instead, such jobs often result in negative side effects, such as worker boredom, low job satisfaction, absenteeism, turnover, and sabotage.[7]

Job Rotation. **Job rotation** is the practice of periodically shifting workers through a set of jobs in a planned sequence (see Figure 10-2b). The approach is often aimed at reducing the boredom associated with job simplification by providing some variety of tasks. Job rotation also has the advantage of *cross-training* workers (training them to do the tasks involved in several jobs) so that there is maximum flexibility in job assignments. Although job rotation can be useful in alleviating monotony and boredom, its advantage with simple jobs may be short-lived. With simple jobs, employees are likely to learn the new jobs quickly and become relatively bored again.

Job rotation The practice of periodically shifting workers through a set of jobs in a planned sequence

Job rotation is generally more successful as an employee development tool, whereby employees are rotated through a series of more challenging jobs in order to increase their capabilities, expand job assignment flexibility, and in-

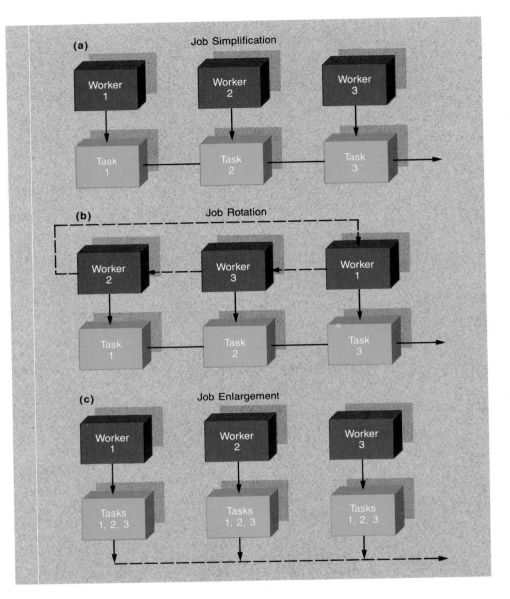

Figure 10-2 Major approaches to job design.

crease their understanding of various aspects of the organization. At Morgan Guaranty, for example, the bank makes a regular practice of rotating managers through various departments. One result is that the managers tend to be more cooperative with one another because they either have been or will be in the other person's job at some point.[8] As part of Digital Equipment Corporation's management training program, new recruits are rotated through three 1-year job assignments.[9] Job rotation across different units or geographic locations may also help stimulate innovation, since it helps promote the exchange of ideas.[10] Potential problems with job rotation are that departments may view the rotating individuals as temporary help (and give them only trivial things to do) and also may question their departmental loyalty.

Job Enlargement. Job enlargement is the allocation of a wider variety of similar tasks to a job in order to make it more challenging (see Figure 10-2c). For exam-

Job enlargement The allocation of a wider variety of similar tasks to a job in order to make it more challenging

This worker at National Steel can fix a hydraulic leak, weld an iron frame, and cut a hose section. By mixing job tasks and broadening responsibilities instead of restricting workers to narrow routine tasks, the company has been able to increase job satisfaction as well as improve the speed and quality of production.

ple, Maytag changed the assembly process for washing machine pumps so that each worker could assemble a complete pump rather than apply only one part on an assembly line.[11] Job enlargement broadens **job scope,** the number of different tasks an employee performs in a particular job. Although it is an improvement over narrow job specialization, job enlargement has generally had somewhat limited success in motivating employees. The primary reason is that a few more similar tasks often do not provide sufficient challenge and stimulation.

Job Enrichment. Job enrichment is the process of upgrading the job-task mix in order to increase significantly the potential for growth, achievement, responsibility, and recognition. The concept of job enrichment was pioneered by Frederick Herzberg, whose work during the late 1960s highlighted the importance of the content of jobs as a significant force in motivation.[12] Job enrichment increases **job depth,** the degree to which individuals can plan and control the work involved in their jobs. For example, U.S. Shoe traded traditional assembly lines for a modular approach at its 11 Ohio and Kentucky factories. Each module has a team of nine workers who switch tasks, decide among themselves about how to meet quality and productivity goals, and receive bonuses for meeting or exceeding them. The company has become the first U.S. shoemaker in a number of years to export women's fashion footwear to European countries.[13]

To guide job enrichment efforts, job design researchers Richard Hackman and Greg Oldham have developed the **job characteristics model.**[14] The model, shown in Figure 10-3, involves three main elements: core job characteristics, critical psychological states, and outcomes. According to the model, motivating through the design of jobs involves providing five *core job characteristics:*

1. **Skill variety** is the extent to which the job entails a number of activities that require different skills.
2. **Task identity** is the degree to which the job allows the completion of a major identifiable piece of work, rather than just a fragment.
3. **Task significance** is the extent to which the worker sees the job output as having an important impact on others.
4. **Autonomy** is the amount of discretion allowed in determining schedules and work methods for achieving the required output.
5. **Feedback** is the degree to which the job provides for clear, timely information about performance results.

The more that these core characteristics are reflected in jobs, the more motivating the jobs are likely to be.

The motivational value of these characteristics stems from workers' experiencing three *critical psychological states:* feeling the work is meaningful, knowing

---

Job scope The number of different tasks an employee performs in a particular job

Job enrichment The process of upgrading the job-task mix in order to increase significantly the potential for growth, achievement, responsibility, and recognition

Job depth The degree to which individuals can plan and control the work involved in their jobs

Job characteristics model A model developed to guide job enrichment efforts that include consideration of core job characteristics, critical psychological states, and outcomes

Skill variety The extent to which the job entails a number of activities that require different skills

Task identity The degree to which the job allows the completion of a major identifiable piece of work, rather than just a fragment

Task significance The extent to which the worker sees the job output as having an important impact on others

Autonomy The amount of discretion allowed in determining schedules and work methods for achieving the required output

Feedback The degree to which the job provides for clear, timely information about performance results

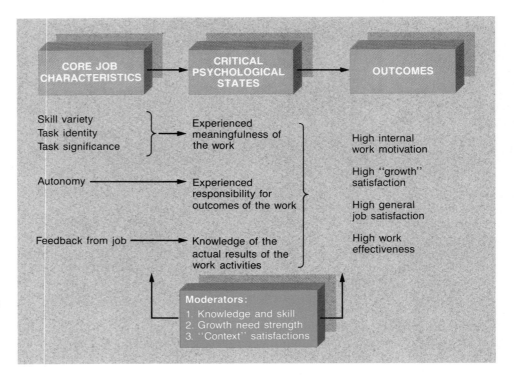

Figure 10-3 Job characteristics model. (Reprinted from J. Richard Hackman and Greg R. Oldham, *Work Redesign*, Addison-Wesley, Reading, Mass., 1980, p. 90.)

that they are responsible for the outcomes, and actually finding out about results. According to the model, these critical states then lead to the major outcomes shown, including higher internal work motivation, greater satisfaction of growth needs, higher general job satisfaction, and increased work effectiveness. The increased work effectiveness usually stems from higher work quality, although greater quantity may sometimes result, depending largely on the improvements made in the flow of work. Research has found that workers may differ in their reactions to increases in the core job characteristics (see the moderators shown in Figure 10-3). Not surprisingly, individuals are more likely to feel motivated by the job changes if they have the knowledge and skills they need to perform well in the redesigned job, if they have high **growth-need strength** (the degree to which an individual needs personal growth and development on the job), and if they feel satisfied with other aspects of the job context (such as supervision, pay, coworkers, and job security). Considerable research support exists for the importance of the job characteristics model, particularly as it relates to the job satisfaction of workers.[15] One organization that has successfully used the job characteristics model to implement job enrichment is First National Bank of Chicago (see the following Case in Point discussion).

Growth-need strength The degree to which an individual needs personal growth and development on the job

CASE IN POINT: Job Enrichment at First National Bank of Chicago

First National Bank of Chicago recently used the job characteristics model to redesign jobs in its unit that prepares letters of credit for businesses. Preparation of the letters, which let businesses know how much credit the bank is willing to extend, was fragmented into a "paperwork assembly line" that involved narrow skills, little sense of the overall product and its impact on client businesses, limited autonomy, and virtually no feedback from clients. For example, one person's whole job was feeding tape into a Telex machine.

Although the unit was notorious for poor service, managers had little success in their attempts to improve the quality and speed of the process. One survey of employees in the line-of-credit department showed that 80 percent of the staff members were dissatisfied with their jobs. The 20 percent who were satisfied were managers and technical professionals. Even the managerial jobs were limited. There was one manager for about every five workers. According to Lawrence F. Buettner, the bank's vice president for documentary products, the tasks of managers "were basically attendance and work-flow monitoring, with a little disciplinary follow-up thrown in." On the basis of the survey, a group of workers were asked to help with the redesign of their jobs. The aim was to involve the entire staff in bringing about change. "We wanted to solicit opinions without threatening people," Buettner says.

The redesign ultimately resulted in eliminating a layer of management and changing the jobs so that each employee would perform customer contact work (resulting in higher task identity, task significance, and feedback) and would perform research, writing, costing, and other letter-preparation tasks (resulting in increased skill variety, autonomy, and task identity) associated with a specific client group. The changes also led to staff reductions (mainly through attrition and transfers) of about 40 percent, extensive training of the staff, and pay increases of $7000 to $8000 per year for those remaining (because they now had higher-skilled jobs). Within a year, profits related to the department rose by $2 million, employee morale rose dramatically, and customer satisfaction increased significantly. The greater customer satisfaction was related to faster turnaround time, greater accuracy, and an increased ability to handle sudden increases in work.[16] ▄▄▄▄

Although the job characteristics model assists managers in redesigning jobs to make them more motivating, related research indicates that the process may be more complex than the model indicates.[17] One complicating factor is suggested by the emerging **social information-processing approach** to job design, which argues that individuals often form impressions of their jobs from socially provided information, such as comments by supervisors and coworkers. Thus individuals' reactions to jobs may reflect not only the reality of job characteristics but also perceptions of them. For example, continual coworker complaints that a job is boring may encourage others to view the work as boring also, despite actual job characteristics to the contrary.[18] The implication of this finding is that managers need to be concerned not only with actual job characteristics but also with other influences on employee job perceptions.[19] Considering the job content is one method of organizing work to meet both organizational and worker needs; another method is devising alternative work schedules.

Social information-processing approach An approach arguing that individuals often form impressions of their jobs from socially provided information, such as comments by supervisors and coworkers

Alternative Work Schedules

A related aspect of designing jobs is creating **alternative work schedules,** schedules based on adjustments in the normal work schedule rather than in the job content or activities. The basic objective of this approach is to increase worker job satisfaction and motivation by arranging work schedules that allow individuals to meet the needs associated with both personal life and work life. Three

Alternative work schedules Schedules based on adjustments in the normal work schedule rather than in the job content or activities

major types of alternative work schedules are flextime, the compressed work-week, and job sharing.

Flextime. **Flextime** is a work schedule that specifies certain core hours when individuals are expected to be on the job and then allows flexibility in starting and quitting times as long as individuals work the total number of required hours per day. For example, a company may have core hours between 10 a.m. and 3 p.m. (with an hour for lunch). Workers may then choose various schedules, such as 7 a.m. to 4 p.m. or 10 a.m. to 7 p.m., that comprise 8 hours of work per day and include the core hours. One recent study showed that the most popular core period is 9 a.m. to 3 p.m., but 9 a.m. to 4 p.m. is also common.

Flextime   A work schedule that specifies certain core hours when individuals are expected to be on the job and then allows flexibility in starting and quitting times as long as individuals work the total number of required hours per day

Major advantages of flextime are improvements in employee morale, accommodation of the needs of working parents, decreased tardiness, and reductions in traffic problems because workers can avoid the peak congestion times. Flextime also often results in lower absenteeism and lower turnover. Major disadvantages include lack of supervision during some hours of work, unavailability of key people during certain periods, understaffing during some periods, and coordination difficulties if the outputs of some employees are inputs for other employees. Also, keeping track of the various schedules may increase administrative work. Overall, however, flextime has been a successful innovation, and its use appears to be growing at a rate of about 1.5 percent per year.[20]

Compressed Workweek. The **compressed workweek** is a work schedule whereby employees work four 10-hour days or some similar combination, rather than the usual five 8-hour days. Some companies close for 3 days each week, which often provides operating economies, such as reduced energy use by cutting down on heating and cooling for the 3 days off. For example, at the Alabama-based Birmingham Steel Corporation, workers put in 12-hour days, working 3 days one week and 4 days the following week. The schedule has had a major positive effect on productivity by cutting the number of shifts and time-consuming changeovers from three to two.[21]

Compressed workweek   A work schedule whereby employees work four 10-hour days or some similar combination, rather than the usual five 8-hour days

Other organizations coordinate employee schedules to remain open for 5 days each week. The basic idea behind the compressed workweek, sometimes called the 4/40 workweek, is to make the job attractive to employees by providing 3 (usually consecutive) days off per week. Potential disadvantages include possible fatigue, loss of productivity, and accidents, as well as difficulties interfacing with other organizations that operate on traditional workweek schedules. More research is needed on the effects of the compressed workweek. According to one study, the compressed workweek had initially led to greater worker job satisfaction and higher performance, but the positive effects disappeared within 2 years.[22]

Job Sharing. **Job sharing** is a work practice in which two or more people share a single full-time job. With job sharing, one person can work in the morning and the other in the afternoon, or they can alternate days or develop some other workable sharing schedule. Individuals who share jobs may be parents who are sharing work and family responsibilities or mothers attempting to juggle both home and work activities. One survey of 348 U.S. and Canadian firms found that 11 percent had job sharing. In 90 percent of the cases in which job sharing existed, each job sharer received half the normal full-time salary for the job.[23]

Job sharing   A work practice in which two or more people share a single full-time job

TYPES OF DEPARTMENTALIZATION

While the way in which individual jobs are arranged is one important dimension of organization structure, a second important aspect is departmentalization. **Departmentalization** is the clustering of individuals into units and of units into departments and larger units in order to facilitate achieving organizational goals.[24] Differing overall patterns of departmentalization often are referred to as *organization designs*.

By determining how individuals will be grouped, departmentalization influences the way an organization operates in several ways.[25] For one thing, the pattern of departmentalization has a direct bearing on the need for supervisors and their linkage into the chain of command. For another, groupings created by departmentalization usually exert a major influence on how resources are shared. For example, members of the same unit often have a common budget, as well as shared facilities (e.g., office space) and equipment (such as photocopy machines). Yet another influence of departmentalization is that individuals often are evaluated to some degree as a unit (e.g., by their overall sales or service record) and, hence, have a structural incentive to coordinate their activities. Finally, members of groups created by departmentalization often must interact frequently and, as a result, may begin to adopt the perspective of their particular group and view others as outsiders. This group perspective often helps members synchronize their productive efforts within their group. Yet this same group perspective may make it more difficult for members to work effectively across units, often necessitating managerial action to encourage coordination. We discuss methods of horizontal coordination later in this chapter.

Four of the most commonly used patterns of departmentalization are functional, divisional, hybrid, and matrix. Briefly, the *functional structure* groups positions into units on the basis of similarity of expertise, skills, and work activities (e.g., marketing, accounting, production or operations, and human resources). In contrast, the *divisional structure* groups positions into units according to the similarity of products or markets (e.g., a separate division for each of several products). The *hybrid structure* combines aspects of both the functional and divisional forms, with some jobs grouped into departments by function and others grouped by products or markets. Finally, the *matrix structure* superimposes, or overlays, a horizontal set of divisional reporting relationships onto a hierarchical functional structure. We discuss these methods of departmentalization, or organization design, in greater detail, including their major advantages and disadvantages, in Chapter 11.[26]

Regardless of the organization design, however, managers typically need to take further steps to achieve the vertical and horizontal coordination that makes a structure effective. In the next section, we discuss methods of vertical coordination.

> **Departmentalization** The clustering of individuals into units and of units into departments and larger units in order to facilitate achieving organizational goals

METHODS OF VERTICAL COORDINATION

Although the functional, divisional, and hybrid types of departmentalization provide basic structures within which individuals carry out organizational work activities, there are a number of additional mechanisms that are important to effective vertical coordination. **Vertical coordination** is the linking of activities at the top of the organization with those at the middle and lower levels in order to achieve organizational goals. Five particularly important means of achieving ef-

> **Vertical coordination** The linking of activities at the top of the organization with those at the middle and lower levels in order to achieve organizational goals

fective vertical coordination are formalization, span of management, centralization versus decentralization, delegation, and line and staff positions.[27]

The Role of Formalization

Formalization The degree to which written policies, rules, procedures, job descriptions, and other documents specify what actions are (or are not) to be taken under a given set of circumstances

One common method of achieving vertical coordination is formalization. **Formalization** is the degree to which written policies, rules, procedures, job descriptions, and other documents specify what actions are (or are not) to be taken under a given set of circumstances.[28] Policies, rules, procedures, and other means of formalization help bring about vertical coordination by specifying expected behaviors in advance.[29] For example, policies provide general guidelines within which organization members are expected to operate; procedures spell out actions to be taken under certain recurring circumstances; and rules specify what should or should not be done in a given situation (see Chapter 5). Job descriptions detail the tasks and activities associated with particular jobs (see Chapter 12). Formal rules and procedures were an important aspect of the ideal bureaucracy outlined by German sociologist Max Weber (see Chapter 2). He saw rules and procedures, along with a well-defined hierarchy, as tools for helping large organizations operate more smoothly.

Indeed, most organizations rely on at least some means of formalization. For example, major student organizations to which you may belong are likely to have written policies about basic qualifications for office, as well as procedures governing how elections should be conducted. Without such means of formalization, it would be necessary to decide these issues each year, a situation that could be time-consuming and might lead to significant inequities. On the other hand, extensive rules and procedures about what activities the organization should sponsor and exactly how everything should be done would likely be stifling. Not surprisingly, research supports the notion that being too highly formalized can lead to cumbersome operations, slowness in reacting to change, and low levels of creativity and innovation.[30] For example, in her study of how and why companies differ in their levels of innovation, management expert Rosabeth Moss Kanter found that narrowly defined job descriptions and high degrees of formalization at the middle management levels depressed the amount of innovation.[31]

Even at lower levels, excessive emphasis on rules and regulations can cause difficulties. When J. Bildner & Sons, Inc., a Boston-based upscale grocery store, began an ill-fated expansion attempt, the company developed formal policies and rules that unwittingly sometimes thwarted the company's intended emphasis on service. In one instance, a customer at a recently opened New York store inquired about the cost of buying a roasted turkey for Christmas. Rather than quoting a price based on the cost of the turkey and a reasonable markup for profit, the manager followed the rules and multiplied the price per slice by the number of slices in a turkey. Naturally, the price was absurd and the customer walked out.[32] As a result of such dysfunctional occurrences, a number of innovative companies, such as Nordstrom's (the Seattle-based apparel, shoe, and soft-goods retailer that is noted for good service), are attempting to allow discretion where possible.

When organizations are small, they usually can run very informally, with few written documents specifying policies and procedures. As they grow, however, organizations tend to require additional degrees of formalization in order to coordinate the efforts of growing numbers of individuals. The challenge is to avoid becoming overly formalized. Consider the experience of Celestial Seasonings as it grew larger, became part of a giant company, and then became an independent company again (see the following Case in Point discussion).

CASE IN POINT: Celestial Seasonings Retains Its Innovative Flair

The origins of Celestial Seasonings, makers of herbal tea, are legendary. In 1970, Mo Siegel and his friend Wyck Hay gathered herbs in the mountains of Colorado, mixed their first blend of herb tea, loaded the mixture in muslin bags sewn by their wives, and began selling the tea to local health stores.

The company took the name "Celestial Seasonings," which was the nickname of an early investor's girlfriend. Tea names, chosen by Mo's friends and company members, were equally whimsical, beginning with Mo's 24 Herb Tea, Red Zinger Herb Tea, and Morning Thunder Tea. The tea was packaged in colorful recyclable boxes that featured such idyllic scenes as charging buffalo and picnicking couples. Up to that time, herb teas had largely been somewhat bitter-tasting brews used for medicinal purposes. The fledgling company changed all that with its flavorful new creations, which soon found themselves on supermarket shelves, and virtually created the herb tea industry.

From the start, the company operated relatively informally, encouraged employee participation in decision making, and had a dedication to all-natural ingredients. In the early days, major decisions were made in all-company meetings lasting as long as 8 hours, volleyball games were played every lunch hour, and toddling children could be found playing in Mo's office. As Celestial grew, the company brought in managers from such major corporations as Pepsi, Coca-Cola, Smuckers, and Lipton to help. Automation became a necessity as the amount of tea blended per day approached 8 tons. Still, the company managed to retain its informality, eschewing such symbols of hierarchical status as time clocks and reserved parking places. Employees were asked to contribute ideas in such areas as new ways to automate, possible new teas, and names for new flavors (often chosen through employee contests).

The success of the innovative herb tea company attracted the attention of Kraft, Inc., which bought Celestial from Mo Siegel in 1984 for approximately $40

Celestial Seasonings' colorful boxes are a familiar sight on supermarket shelves. Beginning as a very informal home-based venture among friends, it quickly grew into a multimillion dollar business entailing various formalized procedures. Nevertheless, Celestial Seasonings has been able to retain a great deal of its original unconventional spirit.

million, with assurances that the company would be left alone to continue its solid growth. By 1989, Kraft decided to get out of the beverage business and attempted to sell Celestial to the tea company's archrival, Thomas J. Lipton, Inc. When an antitrust suit filed by R. C. Bigelow, Inc., a small competitor in the herb tea market, blocked the sale, Kraft agreed to sell Celestial Seasonings to its management and a venture capital firm.

"Although Kraft let us operate as an independent business," says Barnet Feinblum, who was promoted to president when Siegel left, "little by little we were having to comply with Kraft's policies, whether it was employee benefit plans or decisions on purchasing equipment. If we had continued that way, Celestial Seasonings would have gradually and inexorably become just like Kraft." Celestial Seasonings' management came to view its giant parent as hopelessly slow and cautious. Feinblum remembers missing one opportunity because of Kraft's lengthy lead time in purchasing Italian teabagging machines. Caryn Ellison, Celestial Seasonings' vice president of finance, recalls the endless paperwork and says that she produced plans by the ream when she was director of planning. "They wanted our financial results to be completely predictable," says Ellison. "We're used to being much more flexible."

Kraft did double Celestial Seasonings' advertising budget, a move that enabled the company to hire actress Mariette Hartley as a spokesperson for television spots that were extremely successful. By early 1988, sales began to approach $50 million, compared with $27 million in 1983, and Celestial Seasonings had captured 51 percent of the market. Despite the debt stemming from the purchase of the company from Kraft, morale at Celestial Seasonings has soared. Celestial Seasonings is continuing its entrepreneurial spirit with expansion plans and more exotic teas in the development stages.[33] ■

As the Celestial Seasonings situation illustrates, too much formalization can begin to stifle an organization, particularly when it is relatively small. On the other hand, even Celestial Seasonings has had to develop policies, such as using only natural ingredients, and rules, such as procedures for cleaning various spice ingredients imported from all over the world. In addition to formalization, span of management is an important means of vertical coordination.

Span of Management

Span of management, or span of control
The number of subordinates who report directly to a specific manager

Span of management, or **span of control,** is the number of subordinates who report directly to a specific manager. Span of management is important to vertical coordination because it has a direct bearing on the degree to which managers can interact with and supervise subordinates. With too many subordinates, managers can become overloaded, experience difficulty coordinating activities, and lose control of what is occurring in their work units. On the other hand, with too few subordinates, managers are underutilized and tend to engage in excessive supervision of subordinates, leaving subordinates little discretion in doing their work.[34]

Because of the importance of span of control to managers, classical management theorists attempted to identify optimum numbers for such spans. Their estimates ranged from a span of about 5 at upper levels to a span as broad as 25 at lower levels of the organization.[35] Thus classical theorists recognized that the situation has some bearing on the most effective span. More recently, researchers have identified a variety of factors that influence the span of control that will be effective in a given situation.[36]

Factors Influencing Span of Management. In general, research suggests that spans of management can be wider under the following conditions:[37]

■ *Low interaction requirements.* When the work is such that subordinates are able to operate without frequent interaction with each other and/or with their superiors, managers can supervise more individuals.
■ *High competence levels.* High job-related skills and abilities of managers and/or subordinates make it possible for managers to handle more subordinates.
■ *Work similarity.* When employees in a given unit do similar work, it is easier for a manager to maintain adequate supervision than when tasks vary widely.
■ *Low problem frequency and seriousness.* When problems, particularly serious ones, are infrequent, there is less need for managerial attention.
■ *Physical proximity.* When subordinates are located within close physical proximity of one another, managers can coordinate activities more easily.
■ *Few nonsupervisory duties of manager.* Managers can handle more subordinates when they have few nonsupervisory duties to perform, such as doing part of the work themselves.
■ *Considerable available assistance.* Managers can supervise more subordinates when they have considerable additional help, such as assistant and secretarial support.
■ *High motivational possibilities of work.* When the work itself offers a high challenge, subordinates are more likely to increase their performance levels because of opportunities to exercise discretion, making it less necessary for continual managerial involvement.

Levels in the Hierarchy. Although it is not always obvious to the casual observer, spans of management for various managerial positions directly impact the number of hierarchical levels in an organization. A **tall structure** is one that has many hierarchical levels and narrow spans of control. In contrast, a **flat structure** is one that has few hierarchical levels and wide spans of control.

To understand how span of control is related to the number of levels, it is helpful to contrast the two hypothetical organizations depicted in Figure 10-4. In both cases, the organizations have 4096 nonsupervisory employees at the bottom level.[38] However, organization A has seven hierarchical levels, while organization B has only five levels. The reason is tied to differences in spans of control. In organization A, the span of control for each managerial position is 4, requiring 1024 first-line supervisors, 256 at the next level, and so on. In organization B, the span of control for each management position is 8, requiring only 512 first-line supervisors, 64 managers at the next level, and so on. As a result, organization A is 2 levels taller and requires 811 *more* managers.

If one wanted to reduce the number of hierarchical levels in organization A, the only way to do so without reducing the number of employees at the bottom is to increase spans of control. Of course, in a real organization, spans of control would not be uniformly the same throughout the whole organization as they are in Figure 10-4. Still, the principle is the same. When average spans of control in an organization are narrow, the implication is a tall organization. Very tall organizations raise administrative overhead (because there are more managers to be paid, given office space, etc.), slow communication and decision making (because of the many levels), make it more difficult to pinpoint responsibility for various tasks, and encourage the formation of dull, routine jobs.[39]

Because of such problems with tall structures, many companies recently have been downsizing. **Downsizing** is the process of significantly reducing the layers of middle management, expanding the spans of control, and shrinking

Tall structure A structure that has many hierarchical levels and narrow spans of control

Flat structure A structure that has few hierarchical levels and wide spans of control

Downsizing The process of significantly reducing the layers of middle management, expanding spans of control, and shrinking the size of the work force

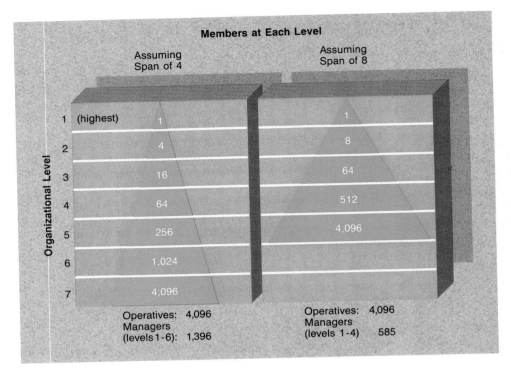

Members at Each Level

Figure 10-4 Contrasting spans of control. (Reprinted from Stephen P. Robbins, *Organization Theory: The Structure and Design of Organizations*, 3d ed., Prentice-Hall, Englewood Cliffs, N.J., 1990, p. 88.)

Restructuring The process of making a major change in organization structure that often involves reducing management levels and also possibly changing components of the organization through divestiture and/or acquisition, as well as shrinking the size of the work force

the size of the work force.[40] The purpose is to increase organizational efficiency and effectiveness. A closely related term that is often used synonymously with "downsizing" is "restructuring." **Restructuring** is the process of making a major change in organization structure that often involves reducing management levels and also possibly changing some major components of the organization through divestiture and/or acquisition.[41] Again, the purpose is to boost efficiency and effectiveness. Restructuring frequently, but not always, involves reducing the size of an organization's work force.

In one example of downsizing, the Ford Motor Company recently reduced its number of management levels after finding that it was laboring under 12 layers of management, compared with 7 layers at Toyota.[42] The additional levels at Ford represented expensive overhead not borne by a significant competitor, causing a competitive disadvantage for Ford. In addition, having many levels made it more difficult for the company to move quickly in its increasingly competitive situation. Soon after Ford made its reductions, Toyota was back cutting management levels of its own (see the following Case in Point discussion).

CASE IN POINT: Toyota Sheds Management Levels

Faced with increasing global competition, management at the Toyota Motor Corporation recently undertook a restructuring aimed at eliminating two management levels. In keeping with the common Japanese tradition of attempting to avoid laying off workers, the company shifted a number of middle managers to "hands-on work," rather than cutting their jobs.

The primary reason that Toyota gave for the restructuring was the desire to streamline decision making by reducing the number of layers through which decisions must travel. The changes affected about 25,000 of the approximately 65,000 Toyota employees, including about 1000 managers. Cost cutting did not seem to be the main reason for the Toyota move because the company has been making admirable profits in recent years. In fact, the company has so much cash that it is often referred to as "the Bank of Toyota."

Instead, the restructuring appeared to stem from the fact that the company often is slower to take competitive action than are its smaller Japanese rivals. For instance, Toyota opened its own U.S. assembly plant only after Honda, Nissan, and Mazda already were manufacturing in the United States. The company also trailed behind Honda in making its entry in the luxury-car market.

At Toyota, there are "so many, many steps to reach top management that it takes time to make a decision," noted a Toyota spokesperson. Furthermore, there were significant numbers of middle managers whose main activities could be summarized as "sit quietly without doing anything," the spokesperson added. Now the displaced managers will need to "become involved in the process of creating and doing hands-on work."

As part of the change, the company is dropping the use of the term *kacho*, meaning "manager." Instead, all employees will use the suffix *-san* in referring to one another—the Japanese equivalent of "Mr.," "Mrs.," or "Ms." In changing the way that employees address one another, Toyota was following the lead of Nissan. Nissan made the change in an effort to reduce employee perceptions of working in a bureaucracy. In an even more radical change, Toyota also said that performance evaluations will weigh performance more heavily than seniority. The company had traditionally considered seniority ahead of performance in evaluating individuals.

At the same time, Toyota announced a plan to spend 100 billion yen (about $730 million) on new housing, recreation facilities, and other comforts for employees. Wall Street analysts interpreted that move, coupled with the restructuring, as an effort to be more competitive in attracting new college graduates, who are in short supply in Japan's labor market. The restructuring allows the new graduates more involvement in decision making because of the reduced number of hierarchical levels.[43] ■

Despite booming profits and production, Toyota underwent a major restructuring in its management, shedding two levels. The aim was to expedite decision making, make the organization less hierarchical, and involve middle level managers in more "hands-on" work. Such changes aid the flow of innovative ideas that improve Toyota's competitive position. For example, at this Takoaka Plant in Japan more than 2000 robots build Corollas by performing some of the heavier and more delicate assembly tasks, thus reducing the number of human workers ultimately needed on the assembly line.

Still, downsizing must be planned and implemented carefully. Done well, it can significantly reduce costs, speed up decision making, energize employees through more challenging jobs, reduce redundancies, and increase innovation. Done poorly, it can lose valuable employees (either because they are laid off or because they decide to leave), demoralize survivors, and result in short-run productivity declines as employees attempt to pick up additional responsibilities.[44] For example, Ireland's Waterford Glass Group PLC, the venerable maker of lead crystal goblets and related items, ran into difficulty in the mid-1980s when it attempted to downsize in part by reducing the size of its highly paid labor force through an early retirement offer. A related step was the purchase of new glass furnaces and diamond-cutting wheels that could speed production. Unfortunately, too many of the most experienced glassblowers chose early retirement. The remaining, less experienced work force could not achieve the same productivity levels, even with the new equipment.[45] While the downsizing trend may reduce the overall number of managerial positions in organizations, it also is likely to provide more challenging and interesting jobs at the middle and lower levels.

Centralization versus Decentralization

Centralization The extent to which power and authority are retained at the top organizational levels

Decentralization The extent to which power and authority are delegated to lower levels

To foster vertical coordination, managers also need to consider the appropriate level of **centralization,** the extent to which power and authority are retained at the top organizational levels. The opposite of centralization is **decentralization,** the extent to which power and authority are delegated to lower levels. Centralization and decentralization form a continuum with many possible degrees of delegation of power and authority in between. The degree of centralization impacts vertical coordination by influencing the amount of decision making that will be done at the upper and lower levels.

One way of judging the degree of centralization in an organization is to study the types of decisions that can be made by managers at lower levels. An organization is relatively centralized if decisions made at lower levels are governed by a *restrictive* set of policies, procedures, and rules, with situations that are not explicitly covered referred to higher levels for resolution. By comparison, an organization is relatively decentralized if decisions made at lower levels are made within a *general* set of policies, procedures, and rules, with situations not covered left to the discretion of lower-level managers.[46] For example, as a result of efforts at the Dana Corporation to decentralize, headquarters gave almost 90 factory managers authority over such decisions as hiring, firing, cost accounting, and purchasing.[47]

Centralization has several positive aspects.[48] If all major decisions are made at the top levels, it can be easier to keep the activities of various units and individuals coordinated. In addition, top managers usually have the most experience and may make better decisions than individuals at lower levels. Also, top-level managers usually have a broader perspective and can better balance the needs of various parts of the organization in making decisions. Another plus is that coordination from the top can help reduce duplication of effort and resources by ensuring that similar activities are not carried on by different organizational units. Finally, centralization promotes strong leadership in an organization because much of the power remains at the top.

Decentralization also has a number of major advantages.[49] Encouraging decision making at lower levels tends to ease the heavy work loads of executives, leaving them more time for major issues. Decentralization also enriches lower-level employees' jobs by offering workers the challenge associated with being able to make significant decisions affecting their work. In addition, it leads to faster decision making at the lower levels, because most decisions do not have to be referred up the hierarchy. Individuals at lower levels may be closer to the problem and, therefore, in a better position to make good decisions. Finally, decentralization often leads to the establishment of relatively independent units, such as divisions, whose output is easier to measure than that of units in a functional design. In assessing this final advantage, though, it is worth noting that a divisional structure is not synonymous with decentralization. It is possible to have a divisional structure in which much of the power and authority is still held at the top and most decisions of significance must be referred to the executive levels.

Given that both approaches have advantages, how does top management decide on the degree of centralization versus decentralization? There are four main factors that begin to tilt the scale from the centralization side of the continuum toward the decentralization side.[50]

Large size tends to require more decentralization simply because it becomes more difficult for top-level managers to have either the time or the knowledge to make all the major decisions. As organizations grow, such decisions become more complex and demanding because there are more factors to consider, such as more products, customers, and markets.

Geographic dispersion of operations makes decentralization more necessary because top executives frequently find it impossible to keep abreast of the details of what is going on at various locations. Moreover, managers on site may be in a better position to assess local situations and make appropriate decisions.

Technological complexity creates pressure for greater decentralization. In situations involving complex technology, it typically is difficult for upper management to keep up technologically. At the same time, there are usually a number of experts who are more capable of making at least the major decisions involving technology. For example, the Digital Equipment Corporation has a reputation for encouraging decision making at the lowest possible levels, partially because of the complex technology involved. Olsen also encourages new ideas and has personally responded to lengthy memos written by newcomers with suggestions.[51]

Environmental uncertainty tends to produce a need for more decentralization. In this case, the fast pace of change interferes with top management's ability to assess situations with the speed necessary to make timely decisions.

The increasing availability of computer networks, which allow information to be shared throughout the organization, has vastly increased the prospects for both centralization and decentralization. Computer networks can facilitate centralization by providing upper-level managers with easy access to information about ongoing operations at the middle and lower levels. With such information, top managers can involve themselves in day-to-day operations. On the other hand, computer networks also can provide upper-level managers with summary information that can enable top managers to obtain timely information regarding how various units are progressing, without having to make so many operating decisions themselves.[52] We discuss the issue of computer-based information systems and management in greater detail in Chapter 20.

Delegation

Another means of vertical coordination that is closely related to the centralization-decentralization issue is delegation. Suppose that you become the manager of a restaurant that is part of a chain. Let's assume that you are one of ten restaurant managers who report to a district manager. When you take over as restaurant manager, you probably expect to be assigned **responsibility,** the obligation to carry out duties and achieve goals related to a position. For example, you might have the responsibility of keeping the restaurant open during certain hours, seeing that food is served, making sure the customers are satisfied, and achieving a certain profit margin. You probably also expect to be given **authority,** the right to make decisions, carry out actions, and direct others in matters related to the duties and goals of a position. For example, as the restaurant manager, you might expect to have the authority to do such things as hire employees, assign work, and order the food and supplies necessary to keep things running smoothly. You would also expect the position to involve **accountability,** the requirement to provide satisfactory reasons for significant deviations from duties or expected results.

Carrying our story a step further, suppose that you soon found that when you attempted to make decisions, such as hiring a new worker, the district manager tended to interfere and even frequently reversed your decisions. Yet,

Responsibility The obligation to carry out duties and achieve goals related to a position

Authority The right to make decisions, carry out actions, and direct others in matters related to the duties and goals of a position

Accountability The requirement to provide satisfactory reasons for significant deviations from duties or expected results

when the end of the month came and you had not achieved your expected profit margin (largely because of interference from the district manager), the district manager still held you accountable for the shortfall in results. Under this set of circumstances, you might correctly conclude that you had been given the responsibility but not the authority needed to do your job.

In this situation, the district manager failed to engage in adequate **delegation,** the assignment of part of a manager's work to others along with both the responsibility and the authority necessary to achieve expected results. Delegation involves moving decision-making authority and responsibility from one level of the organization to the next lower level. With delegation, though, delegating managers are still ultimately responsible for achieving the results and will be held accountable by their own bosses. Delegation is important to vertical integration because it allows the hierarchy to be both more efficient and more effective by enabling work to be done at the lowest level possible.[53] More delegating is done with a decentralized structure than with a centralized one. Even within a centralized structure, top managers must do some delegating. They cannot do everything themselves.

Although even classical theorists placed considerable emphasis on the need to delegate, managers still frequently find delegation difficult. Some of the main reasons why managers are reluctant to delegate are that they may fear blame if subordinates fail, believe they lack the time to train subordinates, wish to hold on to their authority and power, enjoy doing tasks that subordinates could perform, feel threatened that competent subordinates may perform too well and possibly make the manager look poor by comparison, or simply feel that they do not know how to delegate effectively.[54]

At the same time, subordinates may resist delegation by managers, further inhibiting the delegation process. One major reason why resistance sometimes occurs is that subordinates fear that they will fail. Another is that subordinates may believe that the delegation increases the risk of making mistakes but does not provide adequate rewards for taking on the increased responsibility.

The common reluctance of managers to delegate has serious implications for organizing efforts. If managers do not delegate when possible, they can become overloaded. Overloading, in turn, causes vertical coordination to break down because the manager becomes a bottleneck rather than a facilitator. At the same time, subordinates may not be developed to fill future managerial positions, thus weakening prospects for adequate vertical coordination in the future. In addition, recent research shows that subordinates with high job competence perform better in situations in which their bosses engage in high levels of delegation because the subordinates' significant job competence is utilized.[55] Failure to delegate also tends to adversely affect innovation because the ideas of others in the chain of command are underutilized and managers have little time to innovate if they are bogged down in work.[56] Finally, the failure to delegate can hurt managerial careers. A study by the Center for Creative Leadership showed that overmanaging, or the inability to delegate and build a team, was one of the "fatal flaws" that caused executives on the fast track to become derailed for the reasons just described.[57] For some guidelines on how to delegate, see the Practically Speaking discussion, "Guidelines for Effective Delegating."

Line and Staff Positions

Another issue related to vertical coordination is the configuration of line and staff positions. A **line position** is a position that has authority and responsibility for achieving the major goals of the organization. A **staff position** is a position

---

Delegation The assignment of part of a manager's work to others along with both the responsibility and the authority necessary to achieve expected results

Line position A position that has authority and responsibility for achieving the major goals of the organization

Staff position A position whose primary purpose is providing specialized expertise and assistance to line positions

GUIDELINES FOR EFFECTIVE DELEGATING

These guidelines will help you be an effective delegator:

■ The secret of delegating is determining what each member of a work unit can do. Carefully choose the subordinate who should take on the project; usually it is someone immediately below you in the corporate hierarchy. If you want to skip down two ranks, work through that person's supervisor.

■ Next, decide whether you want the subordinate to pinpoint the problem or propose a solution. If the latter, should he or she take action or just present you with alternatives? And do you choose the solution jointly or by yourself?

■ Once you define your goals, consider whether the person you have chosen can handle the responsibility. Will the task be a challenge, but not so difficult that the subordinate gets frustrated? "The art of managing is to figure out what each person is capable of, and create assignments that are within their reach, or slightly above, so they can learn," according to one expert.

■ Do not make the mistake of spelling out in detail how the subordinate should approach the task. Be clear in your objectives, though, because some people fear that they will appear ignorant if they ask questions. Encourage questions. To give a sense of purpose, explain why the task is important. If it is something that seems menial or insignificant, note that it is a prelude to more meaningful assignments later on.

■ Make sure that the subordinate has the time, budget, and data or equipment needed to get the job done—on a deadline. If someone needs training to accomplish the task, be prepared to make the investment. Yes, you could do the job yourself in the time it takes to train someone else, but the hours spent training the individual will be recouped many times over in the future.

■ Unless the project is relatively simple, set up specific checkpoints to review progress so that both you and your subordinate can be sure that work is progressing as planned. That way you can provide additional help, if needed, before the project is in serious trouble. If things are going well, you can let the subordinate know that the good work is appreciated.

■ Be prepared, too, to live with a less than perfect result. Let subordinates know you will support the outcome of their efforts, good or bad. Take responsibility for an occasional blooper, says another expert, and you will have loyal followers for life.[58]

whose primary purpose is providing specialized expertise and assistance to line positions. Sometimes the term "staff" also is used to refer to personal staff, individuals who provide assistance to a particular position as required (e.g., an administrative assistant to a division head).

The positions and related departments that are considered either line or staff vary with the type of organization. For example, in a grocery chain, line departments might be store operations, pharmacy operations, and food operations (directly related to major organizational goals), while staff departments might be human resources and consumer affairs (more indirectly related to major goals). In a manufacturing organization, production and sales are typically considered line departments, while purchasing and accounting are normally staff departments. Among the departments that are often considered staff in many organizations are human resources, legal, research and development, and purchasing. However, each organization must be evaluated in terms of its own major goals in designating line and staff.[59] For instance, in a major law firm, the legal function would be a line department, despite the fact that it often is a staff department in other types of organizations.

The usefulness of the distinction between line and staff departments becomes more clear when one considers the differences between line authority and staff authority. Line departments have **line authority,** which is authority that follows the chain of command established by the formal hierarchy. On the other

Line authority The authority that follows the chain of command established by the formal hierarchy

Functional authority The authority of staff departments over others in the organization in matters related directly to their respective functions

hand, staff departments have **functional authority,** which is authority over others in the organization in matters related directly to their respective functions. For example, in the structure for a bank, shown in Figure 10-5, the line departments receive their authority through the chain of command connected to the president. On the other hand, the staff departments have functional authority in relation to other departments, that is, authority only in their area of staff expertise. Staff departments facilitate vertical coordination by making their considerable expertise available where it is needed, rather than having to follow the strict chain of command.

Still, conflicts frequently arise. For example, staff departments sometimes grow very large and begin to oversee the departments that they are supposed to assist. Before they were cut back, burgeoning staffs at Xerox second-guessed

Figure 10-5 Line and staff departments of a bank.

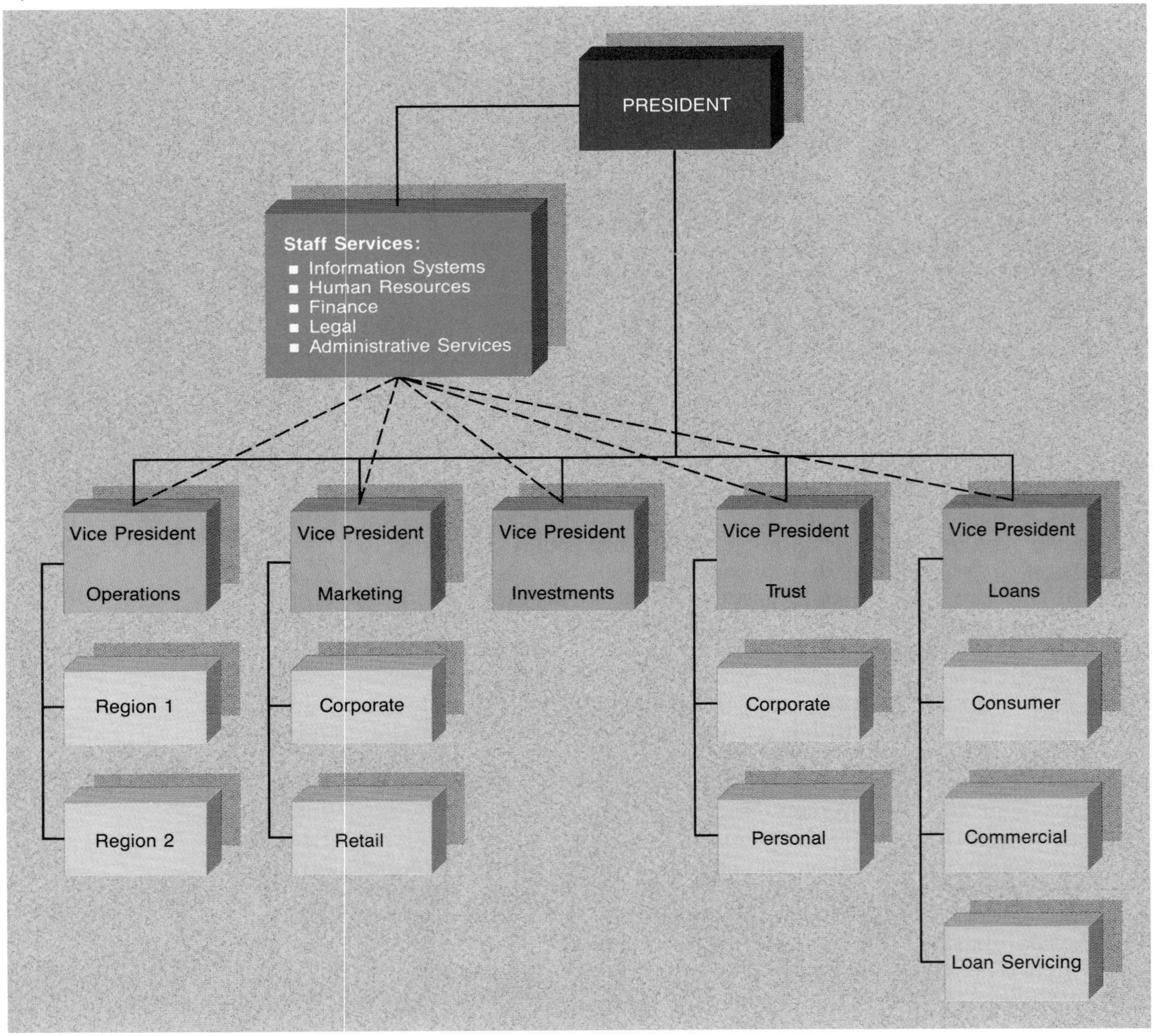

managers to such a point that the ability to adapt existing products to local markets or develop technological breakthroughs was seriously impaired. One former manager explained that moving from the conceptual to the detailed engineering phase of a product, a step that should have taken 2 to 4 weeks, took 2 years because of continual reviews by staff units.[60] On the other hand, line managers sometimes abdicate responsibility in areas in which staff have functional authority. For example, line managers may expect a staff planning department to do all the planning, not just provide support.[61] Nevertheless, such conflicts are not inevitable, particularly if areas of responsibility are clarified and line and staff personnel are encouraged to operate as a team with joint accountability for final results.[62]

Recently, there has been a trend toward reducing the number of corporate-level staff personnel, as companies attempt to cut costs and speed up decision making. For example, Nucor, a North Carolina-based company that runs steel minimills, has annual revenues that exceed $800 million; yet the company operates with a corporate staff of less than 20. Ken Iverson, Nucor's chief executive, has decentralized his 14 divisions, with each operating as an autonomous company in a regional market. The small central office mainly monitors budgets, cash flow, and overall operations.[63] Enhancing vertical coordination is one structural issue in organizations; promoting horizontal coordination is another.

PROMOTING INNOVATION: METHODS OF HORIZONTAL COORDINATION

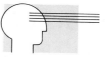

Suppose that you purchased a television set at a large local department store with the understanding that the TV would be delivered within 3 days but the set failed to arrive on time. Imagine that when you called to inquire about the delay, your call was passed up the hierarchy until you were talking with a vice president of the department store. You would probably begin to wonder about an organization in which a vice president is drawn into what should have been a routine transaction between sales and shipping. If all such problems had to be handled vertically, organizations would quickly become paralyzed.

Instead, most organizations take steps to facilitate **horizontal coordination,** the linking of activities across departments at similar levels. One way to think of horizontal coordination is as an additional means of processing information in organizations. Organization structure specialist Jay R. Galbraith argues that the more organizations need to process information in the course of producing their product or service, the more methods of horizontal coordination they will need to use.[64] Organizations typically need to process more information when they face complex and/or changing technology, environmental uncertainty, and growing size. (We discuss these issues further in Chapter 11.) For example, when William H. Wilson founded the Pioneer/Eclipse Corporation, a small company that specializes in a floor-cleaning system, he was able to provide most of the necessary coordination himself within a traditional functional structure. As the company grew larger and more complex, it began to lose money because of insufficient horizontal coordination. In one situation, the sales department launched a promotion only to find that manufacturing and purchasing knew nothing about it and had insufficient materials and stock on hand to fill orders. In another instance, the credit department denied credit to a major account before the sales department could resolve the conflict more amicably. "The left hand," says one observer, "did not know what the right hand was doing."[65]

Because horizontal coordination facilitates processing information across

Horizontal coordination
The linking of activities across departments at similar levels

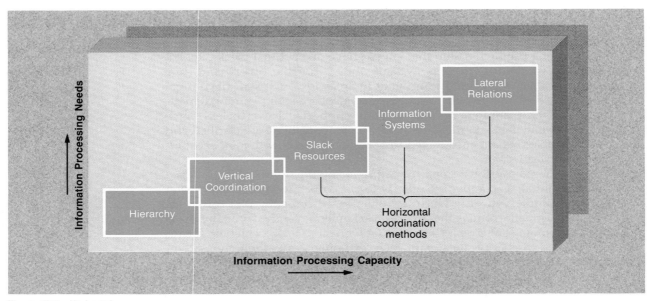

Figure 10-6 Horizontal coordination methods for increasing information-processing capacity as needed.

the organization, it also helps promote innovation.[66] One reason is that new ideas are more likely to emerge when a diversity of views are shared. Another reason is that awareness of problems and opportunities across areas can spark creative ideas. For example, Raytheon's New Products Center, which helps develop and launch new products in conjunction with several of the company's consumer-products divisions, not only keeps in contact with consumers and trade associations but also maintains close ties with units within the various consumer-products divisions. These close internal horizontal linkages have helped the center develop a number of the product ideas that underlie its reputation for successful innovation.[67] Yet another reason why horizontal coordination promotes innovation is that involving others in the development of ideas often positively influences their willingness to help implement the ideas (see Chapter 7).

By facilitating the exchange of information among individuals across units at similar levels, horizontal coordination mechanisms, in essence, supplement the basic hierarchy and related methods of vertical coordination. Three major means that are particularly useful in facilitating horizontal coordination are slack resources, information systems, and lateral relations (see Figure 10-6).[68]

Slack Resources

Slack resources A cushion of resources that facilitates adaptation to internal and external pressures, as well as initiation of changes

One interesting means of supporting horizontal coordination is the use of **slack resources,** a cushion of resources that facilitates adaptation to internal and external pressures, as well as initiation of changes.[69] You have probably benefited from the availability of slack resources in your personal life. For example, in your family, a slack resource might be an extra car, an extra television set, or your own telephone line. Through coordination and tighter programming of mutual schedules, you might be able to get by with less, but doing so would take more effort and you might find it difficult to make quick changes in your plans. Because organizations face similar choices, they, too, often use slack resources, such as extra people, time, equipment, and inventory, to reduce the need for constant coordination among units and to provide some latitude in how resources are used.

A particularly important function of slack resources is that they can help foster creativity and innovation.[70] For example, at 3M, the practice of having researchers spend 15 percent of their time on projects of their own choice that have prospects for long-term payoff (a practice the company calls "bootlegging") is an example of the use of slack resources (time, equipment, and materials) to enhance the prospects for innovation. The latitude in resource use makes it possible for individuals to collaborate on projects in which they have a high interest, thus increasing the likelihood of creative breakthroughs (see Chapter 8).[71]

Information Systems

Another important and growing means of horizontal coordination is the use of information systems, particularly computerized ones, to coordinate various parts of organizations. For example, because of its far-flung international operations and its use of divisional structures, Citicorp found itself with horizontal coordination difficulties. The company frequently was embarrassed when a client of one Citicorp unit would also use the services of other units, perhaps even in other parts of the world, and receive conflicting advice. Even when the advice did not actually conflict, the fragmented guidance offered to clients did not maximize Citicorp's capacity to provide good service. The solution? Citicorp greatly enhanced the ability of various departments to exchange information by instituting a new computerized conferencing system called PARTICIPATE, which allows offices around the world to communicate and coordinate their efforts quickly.[72] (We consider computerized information systems further in Chapter 20.) Such systems also offer means of promoting innovation, not only because they facilitate the exchange of information throughout the organization but also because the new technology itself provides the means of developing innovative methods of operating (like Citicorp's PARTICIPATE system).

Lateral Relations

Another approach to horizontal coordination that is increasingly being used is lateral relations. **Lateral relations** is the coordination of efforts through communicating and problem solving with peers in other departments or units, rather than referring most issues up the hierarchy for consideration. Such collaboration also promotes innovative solutions to difficulties and fosters creative responses to opportunities. Major means of lateral relations are direct contact, liaison roles, task forces, teams, and managerial integrators.[73]

Direct Contact. One means of lateral relations is **direct contact,** communication between two or more persons at similar levels in different work units for purposes of coordinating work and solving problems. The use of direct contact allows many issues to be resolved at middle and lower levels in the hierarchy without having to involve upper-level managers. In fact, problems frequently can be better handled by individuals at middle and lower levels because they may be more familiar with the issues involved.

Liaison Roles. A **liaison role,** another means of lateral relations, is a role to which a specific individual is appointed to facilitate communication and resolu-

Lateral relations The coordination of efforts through communicating and problem solving with peers in other departments or units, rather than referring most issues up the hierarchy for resolution

Direct contact Communication between two or more persons at similar levels in different work units for purposes of coordinating work and solving problems

Liaison role A role to which a specific individual is appointed to facilitate communication and resolution of issues between two or more departments

tion of issues between two or more departments. Liaison roles are typically reserved for situations in which there is a need for almost continuous coordination between two or more different departments in order to function effectively. A common example of a liaison role is an engineer who is appointed to maintain contact between the engineering and manufacturing departments. Under such circumstances, the liaison engineer may even have office space in the manufacturing department. Similarly, the U.S. Department of Defense sometimes uses liaison persons to facilitate communication between the department and major contractors. Liaison persons help solve problems and promote horizontal coordination at lower levels. In this way, they increase the probability that diverse groups can effectively coordinate efforts toward common goals.[74]

Liaison roles also are becoming more common between private businesses and major customers. In this type of situation, the liaison person enhances horizontal coordination by working with various internal departments, as well as the customer, in order to facilitate meeting a customer's needs. The potential advantage of liaison roles in dealing with customers is illustrated by the comments of one steel company executive (who wished to remain anonymous because he was concerned that his comments might create a bad impression of his company). The executive was explaining why he maintains a full-time liaison person on site at Honda's plant in Marysville, Ohio. He noted that if there is a problem with stamping steel to make fenders and other car-body parts and if there were no liaison person, the scenario would go like this: The Honda people affected by the problem would go to their purchasing department. The purchasing department would contact the steel company salesperson. The salesperson would complain to the steel company product office. The product office would pass the issue on to the steel company department that made the steel for Honda. At that point, says the executive, the offending department is likely to deny that the problem is theirs and argue that "it's a Honda stamping problem" (i.e., the problem is not caused by the way in which the steel is made but, rather, by the way in which the steel is being stamped at the Honda plant).[75] A liaison person helps cut through such red tape by dealing directly with the departments in which the problems are occurring. To work effectively, however, the individual in the liaison role must be able to recognize important issues that should have higher-level involvement and must have good interpersonal skills in order to be able to facilitate cooperation across units and companies.

Task Forces and Teams. A *task force* is a temporary interdepartmental group usually formed to make recommendations on a specific issue. Task-force recommendations typically constitute advice. The person or group that appointed the task force can then decide whether or not to implement the recommendations. Task forces promote horizontal coordination by providing a vehicle through which individuals from different organizational units can share their ideas on specific issues and plan viable courses of action.

Teams, on the other hand, are either temporary or ongoing groups that are expected to solve problems and implement solutions related to a particular issue or area. Teams often are composed of individuals from different departments, but they also may be made up of members from the same organizational unit. At its nylon fiber plant in Pensacola, Florida, Monsanto uses an interesting combination of liaison roles and teams in its new Adopt A Customer program, aimed at offering outstanding customer service. Under the program, Monsanto matches top customers with key employees who act as liaison persons. When problems arise, the liaison employees then become "resource team leaders" who help bring about quick resolution of problems. For example, if a customer noti-

A team of Monsanto employees in the Adopt a Customer program consult with the director of quality assurance (second from left) at Shaw Industries, a customer in Georgia. This close attention to customer service generates a great deal of good will. As a Shaw VP notes: "Any time you listen to your customer, you have an edge."

fies the liaison employee that the yarn is breaking during processing, the liaison person then becomes an internal resource team leader who notifies the technical salespeople and quickly puts together a team with the necessary expertise and resources to resolve the difficulty promptly and offer innovative solutions if necessary. "The whole idea of Adopt A Customer is to give top priority to that problem not in three days, but on day one, with the first phone call from our customer," says Monsanto's manager of technical sales for carpet fibers.[76] We discuss teams and task forces further in Chapter 16.

Managerial Integrators. A **managerial integrator,** another means of lateral relations, is a separate manager who is given the task of coordinating related work that involves several functional departments. Such managers typically have titles such as "project manager," "product manager," or "brand manager" and are not members of any of the departments whose activities they help coordinate. *Project managers* usually are responsible for coordinating the work associated with a particular project until its completion. They are used extensively in the aerospace, defense, and construction industries, in which large, technically complex projects must be completed within specified time limits and at contracted costs. *Product managers* orchestrate the launching of new products and services and may then continue coordinating interdepartmental work related to the new products and services. For example, the Buick-Oldsmobile-Cadillac group of General Motors has a functional structure but uses product managers to facilitate horizontal coordination across functional lines.[77] *Brand managers* coordinate organizational efforts involving particular name-brand products, most often within the soap, food, and toiletries industries. Brand managers help devise and implement brand strategies and plans, monitor results, and correct problems as they occur. In essence, managerial integrators act as horizontal coordinating agents. The use of managerial integrators allows fast reaction to environmental change and also efficient use of resources because functional re-

Managerial integrator A separate manager who is given the task of coordinating related work that involves several functional departments

sources can be switched among various projects relatively easily. Managerial integrators also are in a good position to act as sponsors of innovative ideas.

Managerial integrators typically do not have line authority over the individuals and functional departments that they are attempting to coordinate. Rather, they must obtain the cooperation of the functional managers who control the major resources. In doing so, they must compete with others (e.g., managerial integrators for other projects) who also want the help of various functional departments in making their project, product, or brand a success. As a result, managerial integrators must use their knowledge, competence, personality, group management skills, and persuasion abilities in working with functional managers and individuals within the functional departments who are assigned to their project.[78] One recent study suggests that project management using managerial integrators is likely to be more effective when functional managers have influence over technical matters and project managers have influence over organizational issues. The same study also suggests that project performance is likely to be higher when influence over salaries and promotions is perceived by functional specialists working on projects as being balanced between project and functional managers.[79]

Yet, sometimes, forms of lateral relations, such as tasks forces, teams, and managerial integrators, do not provide sufficient horizontal coordination. Under such conditions, matrix departmentalization (discussed further in Chapter 11) may be appropriate.

In this chapter, we have considered several of the major elements of organization structure, including methods of vertical and horizontal coordination. In the next chapter, we explore the link between strategy and organization structure in enhancing organizational effectiveness.

CHAPTER SUMMARY

Organizing is the process of arranging work and resources so that planned goals can be achieved. One important part of the organizing function is determining organization structure. Organization structure consists of four main elements: job design, departmentalization of positions and units methods of vertical coordination, and methods of horizontal coordination. Organization charts provide a graphic depiction of the broad outlines of an organization's structure and help employees trace the chain of command, the line of authority that ultimately connects every position with the top of the organization.

There are four main approaches to job design: job simplification, job rotation, job enlargement, and job enrichment. The job characteristics model helps guide job enrichment efforts by explaining the importance of core job characteristics, critical psychological states, and high growth-need strength to job outcomes. A related aspect of designing jobs involves the possibility of providing alternative work schedules. Major types of alternative work schedules include flextime, the compressed workweek, and job sharing.

Four of the most commonly used forms of departmentalization are functional, divisional, hybrid, and matrix. There are five major means of achieving vertical coordination, which is the linking of activities at the top of the organization with those at the middle and lower levels: formalization, span of management, centralization versus decentralization, delegation, and line and staff positions.

Three major means that are particularly useful in facilitating horizontal coordination are slack resources, information systems, and lateral relations. Slack resources provide a cushion of resources that allows adaptation to change, while information systems enhance information exchange. Lateral relations, which involves coordinating efforts with peers in other departments and units, has several major forms: direct contact, liaison roles, task forces, teams, and managerial integrations. Methods of horizontal coordination are particularly useful in promoting innovation because they facilitate the exchange of ideas across organizational units.

MANAGERIAL TERMINOLOGY

accountability (353)
alternative work
  schedules (343)
authority (353)
autonomy (341)
centralization (352)
chain of command (337)
compressed workweek
  (344)
decentralization (352)
delegation (354)
departmentalization
  (345)
direct contact (359)
downsizing (349)
feedback (341)

flat structure (349)
flextime (344)
formalization (346)
functional authority
  (356)
growth-need strength
  (342)
horizontal coordination
  (357)
job characteristics model
  (341)
job depth (341)
job design (339)
job enlargement (340)
job enrichment (341)
job rotation (339)

job scope (341)
job sharing (344)
job simplification (339)
lateral relations (359)
liaison role (359)
line authority (355)
line position (354)
managerial integrator
  (361)
organization chart (336)
organization design
  (336)
organization structure
  (336)
responsibility (353)
restructuring (350)

skill variety (341)
slack resources (358)
social information-
  processing approach
  (343)
span of management, or
  span of control (348)
staff position (354)
tall structure (349)
task identity (341)
task significance (341)
vertical coordination
  (345)
work specialization (338)

QUESTIONS FOR DISCUSSION AND REVIEW

1. Explain the four elements that make up organization structure. What evidence can you see of these four elements at your college or university?
2. Describe the relationship between an organization chart and an organization's chain of command. If you were new to an organization, how might an organization chart help you get oriented?
3. Contrast the various major approaches to job design. Use the job characteristics model to explain how you might go about enriching a particular job.
4. Distinguish among the three major types of alternative work schedules. What adjustments might be required to accommodate nontraditional work schedules?
5. Explain the role that formalization plays in vertical coordination. Give an example of a policy or rule that is likely to have a dysfunctional impact on organizational effectiveness. In what way should the policy or rule be changed to have a positive influence?
6. Explain the relationship between span of management and the extent to which an organization is flat or tall. Why are a number of major organizations attempting to make their structures more flat? What might be some potential pitfalls associated with the process of making an organization structure flatter?
7. Contrast the advantages of centralization and those of decentralization, and explain when each approach is likely to be most appropriate. Why is delegation important to both?
8. Explain the differences between a line position and a staff position. Which type of position would you prefer to hold? Why?
9. Explain the concepts of slack resources and computer-based information systems as they apply to horizontal coordination. What examples can you cite of the use of slack resources and information systems to facilitate horizontal coordination in organizations?
10. Distinguish among the various types of lateral relations. How could they be used effectively in your college or university?

DISCUSSION QUESTIONS FOR CHAPTER OPENING CASE

1. How would you characterize DEC's organization structure before and after the reorganization by Ken Olsen?
2. What methods of vertical coordination are likely to be useful in making the reorganization successful?
3. What methods of horizontal coordination would you recommend? What other changes might be necessary?

MANAGEMENT EXERCISE:
DESIGNING AN INNOVATING ORGANIZATION

You have just landed a job as the administrative assistant to the CEO of Chameleon Technology, a fast-growing high-technology firm. You took the job because you want to learn more about how to manage high-technology firms. Also, you figure that because the company is growing rapidly, some very good career opportunities will open up quickly.

Chameleon has had tremendous success with its initial product, a small hard-disk drive for personal computers that holds considerably more data and costs less than offerings from competitors. Recently, the company has also introduced a new high-resolution video screen for use with personal computers that also is selling better than anticipated. Because the company is growing so quickly, the CEO is experiencing acute difficulties trying to handle long-range planning as well as the day-to-day developments in what is a rapidly changing competitive environment. For example, in a number of recent instances, sales were made but products were not shipped in a timely manner. In another case, although production was expanded to meet the rising demand, the human resources area was not notified of the need for additional workers. In both situations, the bottleneck

occurred when the CEO's office did not coordinate these activities as well as it had in the past.

In addition, the CEO is concerned with fostering the kind of innovative thinking that will lead not only to improvements in existing products but also to new offerings. The CEO is becoming concerned that Chameleon is too dependent on its two products and that the company may not be moving fast enough in improving the disk drive or developing new products.

Because of your recent management studies, the CEO asks you to develop some ideas about how to achieve better coordination of the company's various activities and also foster innovation. The company is currently organized into a functional structure, with major departments in the following areas: manufacturing, sales, human resources, finance and accounting, and engineering. The company currently has about 600 employees.

Prepare a proposal to present to the CEO outlining the steps that could be taken to achieve better vertical and horizontal coordination, as well as to encourage more innovation.

TEACHING AN ELEPHANT TO DANCE—GM REORGANIZES

When Roger B. Smith became chairman of General Motors in 1981, the automobile giant's share of the U.S. car market was crumbling and the company had just reported its first loss since 1921. One of Smith's first moves was to appoint a task force of 10 select executives to consider a massive reorganization of a structure that had been in existence for decades. At that point, the major skeleton of the company consisted of two huge fiefdoms, Fisher Body and the General Motors Assembly Division (GMAD), as well as the five famous car divisions: Chevrolet, Pontiac, Oldsmobile, Buick, and Cadillac. With centralized design, engineering, and manufacturing, all GM's cars had begun to look remarkably similar, regardless of the nameplate and price tag. The situation had gotten so bad that Ford's Lincoln-Mercury division scored big with ads that poked fun at owners of GM luxury cars trying to pick theirs out from a sea of moderately priced, moderately altered clones. At the same time, GM was criticized because its response to the popular smaller cars manufactured by the Japanese was merely to make shrunken versions of its larger cars, a strategy that was essentially a failure. In addition, the company's structure made responsibility difficult to pinpoint, even though most decisions required multiple organizational units to sign their agreement. Smith wanted a structure that would make it possible for GM to respond more quickly to the market and to measure more easily the performance of major organizational units.

After 15 months of planning,

the world's largest corporation (the first to top $100 billion in sales) began a major structural overhaul in 1984 that was destined to take several years because of the monstrous size of the organization. The main reorganization created two new car groups: Buick, Oldsmobile, Cadillac (BOC) and Chevrolet, Pontiac, GM of Canada (CPC). The BOC group was to concentrate on large cars, while CPC was in charge of smaller cars. The Saturn project, a separate corporation created earlier to design a unique smaller car, would also report to CPC. Each group would have its own design, engineering, and manufacturing resources, while Fisher Body and GMAD were to be dissolved. Spans of control were increased at the top, while a number of management layers in the middle were eliminated.

As might be expected with 800,000 employees, implementation of the logistics of the change has been a horrendous experience for those involved. Even though GM wanted to move as few people as possible, the number still amounted to 10,000. Some managers had to live out of their briefcases and were lucky to have a telephone. Executives in the two new car groups found it difficult to coordinate their scattered forces and found themselves spending large amounts of time on the telephone and traveling among units in their automobiles.

After the reorganization was under way, GM purchased Electronic Data Systems (EDS) from H. Ross Perot in a move to acquire greater expertise in computer software. The software expertise was important to GM's plans to build highly automated factories that would be heavily computerized. As part of the deal, Perot was placed on the GM board of directors,

The pyrotechnics of the robotic welding at this GM plant could symbolize the fireworks that former Chairman Roger B. Smith tried to set off at General Motors. Smith shook up the company with a major reorganization and acquisitions, but he found that change does not come easily in an organization of 800,000 employees. He took rueful note of this: "Everybody says, 'Oh boy, the chairman of GM—what a pot of power.' But you'd better have people going with you instead of trying to drag them along."

where he took the view that "revitalizing GM is like teaching an elephant to tap dance; you find the sensitive spots and start poking." With his "poking," Perot became such a consistent and vocal critic that his substantial number of shares were ultimately purchased for a premium $700 million and he left the board. Meanwhile, the 10,000 GM data-processing employees who had been transferred to EDS became extremely upset with the lower benefits it offered in comparison to GM and with the EDS stringent regulations against such things as beards and tasseled shoes. (Even though EDS was purchased by GM, the software company was to operate as a separate entity with its own policies regarding such matters as compensation, benefits, and dress.) These issues required Smith's intervention to help with the integration of the two groups. Smith then orchestrated the purchase of the Hughes Aircraft Company, thus positioning GM as one of the largest U.S. defense contractors and giving the automaker access to the substantial technical expertise at Hughes. Hughes Aircraft also was to remain a separate entity within the GM structure.

Smith's bold moves were aimed at giving GM "the key to the twenty-first century." Unfortunately, the reorganization took longer than planned, and critics argue that he did not move quickly enough to cut costs. Meanwhile, GM's long-time competitor, the Ford Motor Company, began to outearn GM for the first time in several decades, even though Ford is only about two-thirds the size of GM. GM's share of the U.S. auto market, which was about 45 percent when Smith took over, dropped to around 36 percent. Things began to brighten somewhat when Smith was able to announce record earnings for 1988 that were largely due to cost reduction efforts, truck sales, and brisk auto sales abroad, but, unfortunately, market share continued to slide.

In looking back, Smith says that he would make the same decisions again but wishes that he had done a much better job of communicating his vision of the company to employees. "Then they would have known why I was tearing the place up, taking out whole divisions, changing our whole production structure," says Smith. "If people understand the *why*, they'll work at it." Smith also says that the company operated too autocratically and had to get people to participate more. As a result, he found that he had to spend a great deal of time getting people to support his vision of GM as a twenty-first-century corporation before things began to improve. As Smith retired, his successor, Robert C. Stempel, faced a formidable competitive situation.[80]

QUESTIONS FOR CHAPTER CONCLUDING CASE

1. How would you characterize the changes in organization structure at GM?
2. What could Smith have done to enhance vertical coordination?
3. What could Smith have done to boost horizontal coordination?

CHAPTER ELEVEN

STRATEGIC ORGANIZATION DESIGN

CHAPTER OUTLINE

Designing Organization Structures: An Overview
Which Comes First—Strategy or Structure?
Factors Influencing Organization Design

Assessing Structural Alternatives
Functional Structure
Divisional Structure
Hybrid Structure
Matrix Structure

Weighing Contingency Factors
Technology
Size
Environment
Mintzberg's Five Structural Configurations

Matching Strategy and Structure

Promoting Innovation: Using Structural Means to Enhance Prospects
Vital Roles
Differentiation Paradox
Reservations
Transfer Process

LEARNING OBJECTIVES

After studying this chapter, you should be able to:

■ Summarize current views about the link between strategy and organization structure.

■ Explain the functional, divisional hybrid, and matrix types of departmentalization.

■ Map the major advantages and disadvantages of each type of departmentalization, as well as discuss the basic circumstances under which each is likely to be effective.

■ Explain the major stages of matrix departmentalization and the circumstances under which a matrix design is likely to be appropriate.

■ Assess how major contingency factors, including technology, size, and environment, impact organization structure.

■ Outline Mintzberg's five structural configurations and indicate their relationship to major contingency factors.

■ Delineate how strategy and structure can be matched.

■ Indicate how structure can be used to enhance prospects for innovation.

POST-IT NOTES WIN OUT AT 3M

One company that has earned a solid reputation for innovation is 3M. A look at the development of the famous Post-it note pads illustrates the challenge of the innovation process.

When the four-city marketing tests of Post-it note pads indicated that the product was a dismal failure, it seemed that the matter of the funny little note pads could finally be laid to rest. After all, manufacturing had said all along that they couldn't be mass-produced. And marketing kept asking, "Who would pay a dollar for a scratch pad?"

But two senior executives at 3M decided to give it one last try. Geoffrey Nicholson and Joseph Ramey flew to Richmond, Virginia, one of the test cities. The tests had relied heavily on advertising, but Nicholson and Ramey thought about one factor that had built support at 3M for bringing the product this far. They had given out free pads at 3M, and when people had actually begun to *use* them, they had asked for more. With this experience in mind, the two executives went from door to door in the Richmond business district, giving away packages of the pads. The ploy worked, and sales of the note pads began to take off. Another test blitz in Boise confirmed the popularity of the item, and 3M was in the final stages of launching one of the most successful products in its history.

The path to success had been long and arduous, beginning with the accidental discovery by chemist Spence Silver of an adhesive with odd properties: it was not "aggressively" adhesive. In other words, although it would stick to something, it would not bond tightly; you could pull it off without damaging the item to which it had been attached. Silver was fascinated with the substance, but he couldn't think of a practical application. During the next 5 years, Silver told everyone he could at 3M about his oddball adhesive, but to little avail. Only after a ferocious battle with management was Silver able to get the $10,000 necessary to have the substance patented. Except for Silver's presentations whenever he could find a forum, interest at 3M in the adhesive had long waned. Then, when Silver was transferred to a new research unit in the early 1970s, he met Robert Oliveira, a biochemist, who took an interest in the unique adhesive.

Silver had been to the commercial tape division twice before with his discovery, but it had been rejected both times. When Geoffrey Nicholson took over as head of a new venture team, a group formed to explore innovative product ideas, he was looking for some new products just as Silver and Oliveira were trying once more with the strange adhesive. Recognizing that it was at least different, Nicholson persuaded the new venture team to explore the idea. Still, the substance seemed to be a solution without a problem. Fortunately, one of the people on the team was Arthur Fry, a chemical engineer, who also happened to sing in his church choir. He would use little slips of paper to mark the hymns that were to be sung, but the slips had a habit of falling out of the hymn book, leaving him fumbling furiously in church. He considered putting a little bit of adhesive on the paper, using Silver's adhesive. From that original insight, he envisioned the possibility of creating note pads with many uses and took over the spearheading of the project.

There were further obstacles ahead. Two other members of the new venture team found it necessary to develop a special coating for paper in order to make the product work properly. Then engineering told Fry that there was no reasonable way to manufacture the pads. As a result, Fry constructed a prototype of a machine that is now a closely guarded secret.

Even with its bumpy history, the Post-it note pad story probably would never have occurred without 3M's well-known efforts at fostering innovation. The 3M company has more than 90 product divisions. Each division has its own R&D group that concentrates on projects that can be brought to market in the near future. At 3M, each division is expected to generate at least 25 percent of its revenue each year from products that were not in existence 5 years earlier. In pursuing that aim, there are also multiple places from which one can obtain funding, such as one's own division, other divisions, and new venture teams. In addition, scientists are expected to use up to 15 percent of their time pursuing avenues of discovery of their own choosing. The company makes ample use of teams to explore new product ideas, holds special technical symposia at which researchers present the results of current projects and marketers discuss present strategies and marketplace needs, and is lenient about mistakes on the premise that if individuals are venturing into new areas, mistakes are inevitable. Research and development groups that report to upper-level management concentrate on long-term projects and leading-edge technology.[1]

3M has become famous for its ability to foster innovation and produce a steady stream of successful new products. Because so many of 3M's businesses pursue a differentiation strategy based on unique products, innovation is critical to the company's strategic effectiveness. Thus part of the reason for 3M's success is the ability of its managers to use structural means to support differentiation strategies and encourage innovation.

In the previous chapter, we considered a number of basic organizing elements, such as job design, type of departmentalization, and methods of vertical and horizontal coordination, that can be used to design organization structures. In this chapter, we examine how organizations, like 3M, use various structural tools to design organizations that support critical strategic directions. Accordingly, we begin by presenting a brief overview of the strategy-structure relationship, before outlining the major factors that influence organization design. We next assess the advantages and disadvantages of major structural alternatives. We also examine important contingency factors that are likely to influence the success of different organization structures. We then probe the issue of matching strategy with structure. Finally, we investigate structural devices that help boost the likelihood of significant innovations.

Post-it note pads are one of 3M's most successful products, but they might never have made it to the production line without 3M's strong emphasis on encouraging innovation and supporting research and development. 3M makes strategic use of organization design to promote the development of unique products that give the company an edge on the market.

DESIGNING ORGANIZATION STRUCTURES: AN OVERVIEW

As mentioned in Chapter 10, the process of developing an organization structure is sometimes referred to as organization design. In designing organization structures, what factors do managers need to consider? According to a famous study, one important issue is an organization's strategy.

Which Comes First—Strategy or Structure?

In a landmark book called *Strategy and Structure,* noted business historian Alfred D. Chandler studied the origins of the largest U.S. firms.[2] He was particularly interested in whether strategy development preceded or followed the design of organization structures. On the basis of his studies, Chandler concluded that major companies (such as Du Pont; General Motors; Sears, Roebuck; and Standard Oil) generally follow a similar pattern of strategy development and then structural change, rather than the reverse.

In Chandler's view, organizations often change their strategies in order to better utilize their resources to fuel growth. The changes in strategy then lead to management difficulties because the current structures do not fit the new strategies. Unless organizations subsequently make adjustments in structure, the new strategies cannot realize their potential and serious inefficiencies will result.

Recently, other researchers have questioned the structure-follows-strategy thesis on the basis that it is too simplistic. Instead, the researchers argue that particular structures are also likely to influence the strategies that organizations are apt to adopt.[3] For example, former Eastman Kodak CEO Colby Chandler (no relation to Alfred Chandler) estimates that his company lost about $3.5 billion in sales between 1981 and 1985 to competitors such as Fuji Photo film. Kodak's functional structure did not allow for the kinds of specific strategies needed in Kodak's multiple businesses. Accordingly, Colby Chandler reorganized the $17-billion-per-year company into 34 divisions, ranging from color film to copiers, so that they could operate as strategic business units. Within 2 years, almost every unit had gained market share, and Kodak's exports increased by 23 percent.[4] In the Kodak case, changes in strategy followed changes in structure. Thus it is possible that there are causal linkages each way. Structure may follow strategy at one point; then the new structures may influence the development of new strategies. In any event, Alfred Chandler's work suggests that a mismatch between strategy and structure could lead to organizational difficulties.

Factors Influencing Organization Design

Chandler's research has helped establish the fact that there is an important connection between strategy and the type of organization structure that is needed to reach organizational goals effectively and efficiently.[5] At the same time, the effectiveness of a particular type of organization structure also is influenced by certain major contingency factors, such as the dominant type of technology used or the organization's size. In addition, structural methods for promoting innovation have a bearing on the effectiveness of particular structures in facilitating strategic implementation and the attainment of organizational goals. These components and their relationship to organization structure are shown in Figure 11-1. We explore these various relationships in the remainder of this chapter. We begin by examining in greater detail the major types of organization structure, or departmentalization, that were introduced in Chapter 10, since they represent the principal structural alternatives available to managers.

ASSESSING STRUCTURAL ALTERNATIVES

As discussed briefly in the previous chapter, the four most common types of departmentalization are functional, divisional, hybrid, and matrix. They are often referred to as organization structures or organization designs. Each type has major advantages and disadvantages.[6]

Functional Structure

Functional structure A structure in which positions are grouped according to their main functional (or specialized) area

Functional structure is a type of departmentalization in which positions are grouped according to their main functional (or specialized) area. In other words, positions are combined into units on the basis of similarity of expertise, skills, and work activities.

Common Functions. Several specialties are commonly associated with functional structures in business organizations.[7] For example, the *production*, or *operations*, function combines activities directly related to manufacturing a product or delivering a service. *Marketing* focuses on the promotion and sale of products and services. *Human resources* is responsible for attracting, retaining, and enhancing the effectiveness of organization members. *Finance* is concerned with

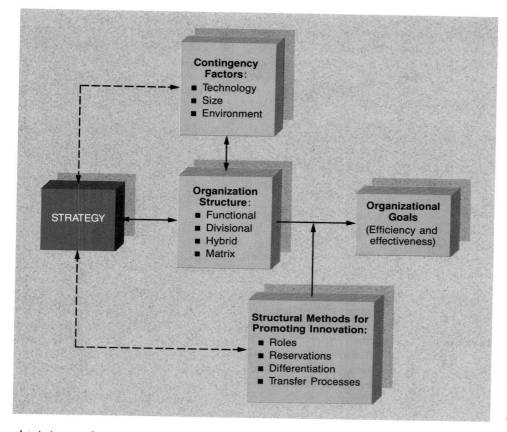

Figure 11-1 Major components influencing the design of effective organization structures.

obtaining and managing financial resources. *Research and development* is responsible for producing unique ideas and methods that will lead to new and/or improved products and services. *Accounting* deals with financial reporting to meet the needs of both internal and external sources. Finally, the *legal* function handles legal matters affecting the organization. Notice that when we are speaking of organization structure, the term "function" (or specialized area of expertise) has a different meaning than it does when we are discussing the major functions of management, that is, planning, organizing, leading, and controlling. The functional organization structure for Celestial Seasonings, the Denver-based herbal tea company, is shown in Figure 11-2. The structure includes many of the common functional areas discussed above.

Figure 11-2 Celestial Seasonings' functional structure.

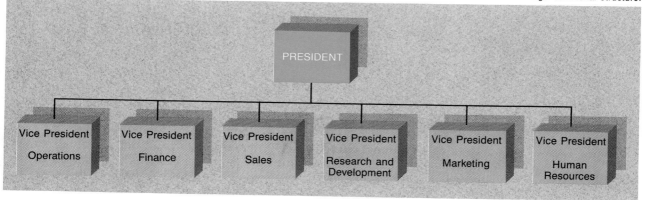

Table 11-1 Major Advantages and Disadvantages of a Functional Structure

Advantages	Disadvantages
In-depth development of expertise	Slow response time on multifunctional problems
Clear career path within function	Backlog of decisions at top of hierarchy
Efficient use of resources	Bottlenecks due to sequential tasks
Possible economies of scale	Restricted view of organization among employees
Ease of coordination within function	Inexact measurement of performance
Potential technical advantage over competitors	Narrow training for potential managers

An organization developing a functional structure must consider the specialized areas that are relevant to its own needs. For example, a functional design for a large utility company might have an energy department that is equivalent to the production, or operations, department often found in other organizations, since it is geared to producing energy. It might also have a distribution department as a major function, because of the importance of energy distribution to a utility. However, a major bank with a functional organization structure might have a functional department for investments and another for loans.

Advantages of Functional Structure. The functional form of organization has several major advantages, which are summarized in Table 11-1. First, it encourages the development of expertise because employees can concentrate on fostering specialties within a single function. For example, if you were the vice president for human resources in a functional structure, you might be able to develop specialists in such areas as recruiting, compensation, and training. Another helpful aspect is that employees have clear career paths within their particular function, giving them further encouragement to develop their expertise. In addition, a functional structure usually facilitates more efficient use of resources because it is fairly easy to shift individuals from one project to another as needed when they work in the same department. Economies of scale also may be possible, either because large amounts of work often can be handled efficiently when individuals specialize or because major equipment can be justified by work volume. An additional advantage is that a functional structure may facilitate ease of coordination within departments, since the activities are all related in one way or another to the same specialized area. Finally, grouping by functions increases the potential for developing specialized technical competencies that can constitute an advantage over competitors.

Disadvantages of Functional Structure. Functional designs also have several disadvantages, as summarized in Table 11-1. For one thing, the coordination across functions that is necessary in handling complex problems may seriously delay responses, because major issues and conflicts must be passed up the chain for resolution. In addition, specialists sometimes become so narrow in orientation that they cannot relate to the needs of the other functions or to the overall goals of the organization. At the same time, performance of the unit may be difficult to measure, because the various functions all have a hand in the organizational results. Finally, a functional structure provides a fairly narrow training ground for managers, because they tend to move up within one function and, hence, have only limited knowledge of the other functions.

Uses of Functional Structure. The functional form of departmentalization is most often used in small and medium-size organizations that are too large to coordinate their activities without some type of formal structure but are not so large as to make coordination across functions difficult. Such organizations frequently have a limited number of related products or services or deal with a relatively homogeneous set of customers or clients. For example, Domino's Pizza, Inc., which deals mainly in pizza and related items, has a functional structure, with operations, distribution, and finance and administration as the major functional departments. A functional design also may be useful in large or more diverse organizations, such as insurance companies, that operate in relatively stable environments in which change occurs at a slow enough rate for the various functions to coordinate their efforts. Another reason why a functional organization structure may be chosen by a large organization is that considerable coordination may be required among products.[8]

Divisional Structure

Divisional structure is a type of departmentalization in which positions are grouped according to similarity of products, services, or markets. Figure 11-3

Divisional structure A structure in which positions are grouped according to similarity of products, services, or markets

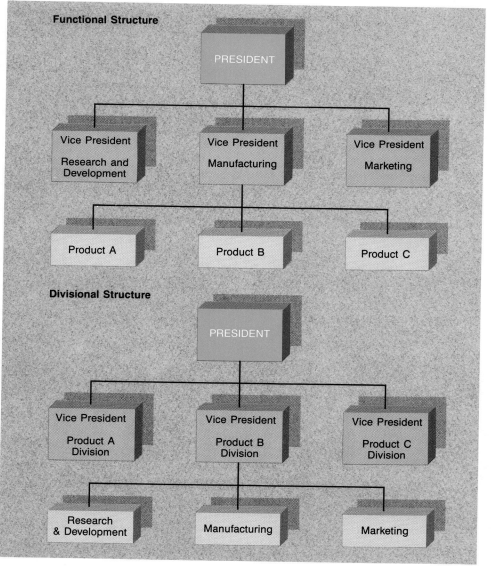

Figure 11-3 Functional versus divisional structure.

shows the difference between a functional and a divisional structure. With a divisional structure, each division contains the major functional resources it needs to pursue its own goals with little or no reliance on other divisions. For example, Figure 11-4 shows a divisional structure for the seven divisions of the Bell Atlantic Corporation that provide local telephone service to customers in different geographic areas. If the seven divisions were organized in a functional structure, then all the telephone operators would be grouped in a central operations department and all the field repair personnel would be grouped in a central repair services department. Instead, with the divisional structure shown, telephone operators and repair personnel are allocated to the various divisions so that each division can operate fairly independently. In this case, the divisions are operated as separate companies. Divisional structures are sometimes referred to as *self-contained structures* because the major functions are generally contained within each division.

Forms of Divisional Structure. There are three major forms of divisional structure, depending on the rationale for forming the divisions. Simplified examples of the three major forms—product, geographic, and customer—are shown in Figure 11-5.

Product divisions Divisions created to concentrate on a single product or service or at least a relatively homogeneous set of products or services

Geographic divisions Divisions designed to serve different geographic areas

Product divisions are divisions created to concentrate on a single product or service or at least a relatively homogeneous set of products or services. When this type of organization structure is chosen, there usually are large differences in the product or service lines that would make coordination within a functional design extremely slow and inefficient. Instead, with a divisional structure, each product department has its own functional specialists, in areas such as marketing, manufacturing, and personnel, who perform work associated with the product of their specific division only.

Geographic divisions are divisions designed to serve different geographic areas. For example, the U.S. Agency for International Development is structured by geography because of the differing needs it serves in various parts of the world. Similarly, The Gap clothing stores in the United States are run by an organization divided into eastern, central, and western zones. Geographic de-

Figure 11-4 Seven divisions of the Bell Atlantic Corporation.

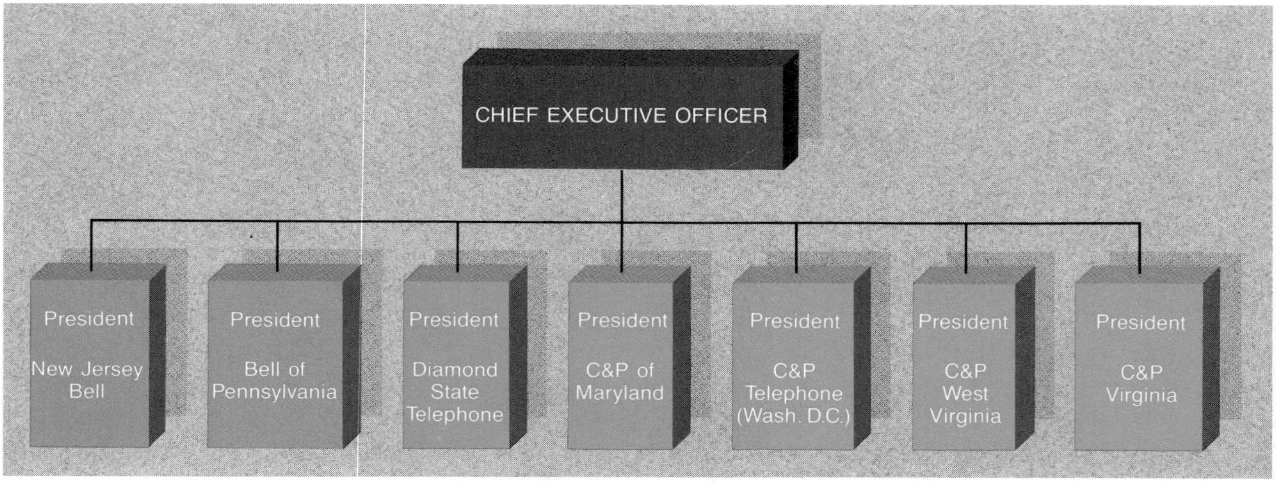

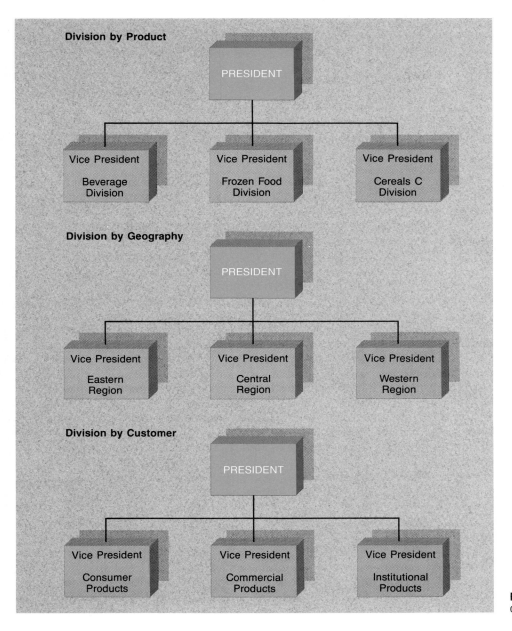

Division by Product

PRESIDENT

Vice President

Beverage
Division

Vice President

Frozen Food
Division

Vice President

Cereals C
Division

Division by Geography

PRESIDENT

Vice President

Eastern
Region

Vice President

Central
Region

Vice President

Western
Region

Division by Customer

PRESIDENT

Vice President

Consumer
Products

Vice President

Commercial
Products

Vice President

Institutional
Products

Figure 11-5 Major forms of divisional structure.

partmentalization often is adopted when it is important to provide products and services that are tailored to the needs of different geographic areas.

Customer divisions are divisions set up to service particular types of clients or customers. This type of organization design is used mainly when there are major differences among types of customers that preclude adequate coordination of the customers' various needs within a standard functional structure. As a result, each department contains individuals who perform the necessary func-

Customer divisions
Divisions set up to service particular types of clients or customers

Table 11-2 Major Advantages and Disadvantages of a Divisional Structure

Advantages	Disadvantages
Fast response to environmental change	Duplication of resources in each division
Simplified coordination across functions	Reduction of in-depth expertise
Strong orientation to customer requirements	Heightened competition among divisions
Simultaneous emphasis on division goals	Limited sharing of expertise across divisions
Accurate measurement of division performance	Restriction of innovation to divisions
Broad training in general management skills	Neglect of overall goals

tions for a specific type of customer. For example, Citicorp Investment Management, Inc., reorganized its institutional-asset management unit from a product structure, the industry's traditional method of organizing, to a customer structure. The new structure included four major divisions: national corporate and public funds group, regional companies group, specialized domestic institutions group, and international institutions group.[9]

Advantages of Divisional Structure. Divisional structure has several major advantages (see Table 11-2). One advantage is that divisions can react quickly when necessary because they normally do not need to coordinate with other divisions before taking actions. Furthermore, necessary coordination across functions is greatly simplified because the various functions are contained within the division itself. The divisional structure also tends to encourage a strong orientation toward serving the customer. This is because the focus is either on a limited number of products or services (product divisions) or on a more limited audience (geographic or customer divisions). In addition, accountability for performance is possible with a divisional structure, since results can be tied to a particular product, service, geographic area, or customer, depending on the form of divisional structure. Finally, the divisional structure provides opportunities for managers to develop more general management skills because, unlike their counterparts in a functional structure, they are likely to deal with multiple functions within their divisions.

Disadvantages of Divisional Structure. Divisional structure also has several disadvantages (see Table 11-2). Organizing by divisions often leads to a duplication of resources. For example, it may be necessary for each division to have its own major computer system (whereas such a system can be shared by the departments in a functional structure), even though in each case it may be somewhat underutilized. Moreover, individuals in a divisional structure will not be able to develop the in-depth areas of specialization to the degree that they could in a functional structure. For example, when an organization changes from a functional to a product design, management may allocate the various specialists in the human resources department to the different product groups. Consequently, an individual who specialized in recruiting may also need to handle compensation and other issues in a product department, since each product department cannot afford to duplicate the entire human resources department that existed under the functional arrangement. Another disadvantage is that divisions may become preoccupied with their own concerns and engage in destructive rivalries for resources.[10] Finally, with a divisional structure, employees sometimes focus on immediate divisional goals to the detriment of longer-term organizational goals.

Uses of Divisional Structure. A divisional structure is likely to be used in fairly large organizations in which there are substantial differences among either the products or services, geographic areas, or customers served. It sometimes is not feasible to organize into self-contained units if the nature of the organization makes it necessary to share common resources, such as expensive manufacturing equipment.

Hybrid Structure

Hybrid structure is a form of departmentalization that adopts parts of both functional and divisional structures at the same level of management.[11] It attempts to incorporate many of the major advantages of functional as well as divisional departmentalization. Many organizations, especially large ones, have some combination of functional and divisional departments. Functional departments are usually created to take advantage of resource utilization efficiencies, economies of scale, or in-depth expertise. At the same time, divisional departments are used when there are potential benefits from a stronger focus on products, services, or markets. IBM's hybrid structure is shown in Figure 11-6. In this case, functional departments handle such areas as law and external relations, science and technology, and personnel—areas in which in-depth expertise is important and resources can be utilized more effectively through a functional arrangement. The rest of the company is divided into four major geographic divisions to better serve differing customer needs throughout the world. The functional departments within a hybrid design are sometimes referred to as corporate departments because they typically have staff authority relative to the divisional departments and their staff authority emanates from the top, or corporate, level of the organization.

Hybrid structure A structure that adopts parts of both functional and divisional structures at the same level of management

Advantages of Hybrid Structure. In general, hybrid structure has several advantages (see Table 11-3). With a hybrid design, an organization can often achieve specialized expertise and economies of scale in major functional areas. At the same time, adaptability and flexibility in handling diverse product or service lines, geographic areas, or customers are possible through a partial divisional structure. Finally, the mix of functional and divisional departmentalization helps align divisional and corporate goals.

Disadvantages of Hybrid Structure. On the other hand, managers need to be alert to the disadvantages of the hybrid structure in order to minimize potential weaknesses (see Table 11-3). For example, hybrid organizations gradually tend to develop excessively large staffs in the corporate-level functional departments. As the corporate departments grow larger, they may also attempt to exercise

Table 11-3 Major Advantages and Disadvantages of a Hybrid Structure

Advantages	Disadvantages
Alignment of corporate and divisional goals	Conflicts between corporate departments and divisions
Functional expertise and/or efficiency	Excessive administrative overhead
Adaptability and flexibility in divisions	Slow response to exceptional situations

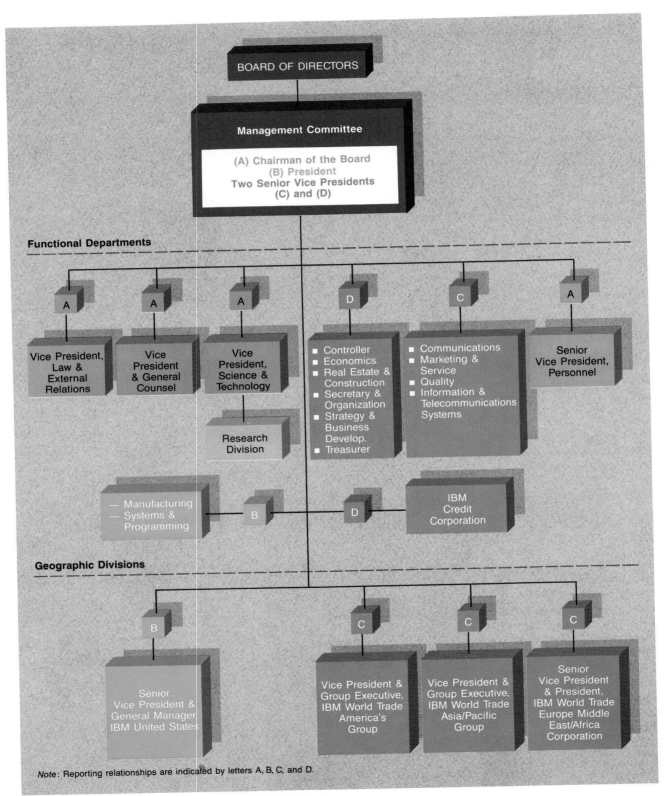

Figure 11-6 IBM's hybrid structure.

increasing amounts of control over the various divisions, causing considerable conflict. Finally, hybrid structures can be slow to respond to exceptional situations that require coordination between a division and a corporate functional department. For example, a personnel matter that requires an exception to policy may take longer to resolve with a hybrid structure than with either functional or divisional departmentalization.

Uses of Hybrid Structure. A hybrid structure tends to be used in organizations that not only face considerable environmental uncertainty that can best be met through a divisional structure but also require functional expertise and/or efficiency. Typically, the hybrid approach is reserved for medium-size or large organizations that have sufficient resources to justify divisions as well as some functional departmentalization.

Matrix Structure

A **matrix structure** is a type of departmentalization that superimposes a horizontal set of divisional reporting relationships onto a hierarchical functional structure. The result is a structure that is both a functional and a divisional organization at the same time. There are two chains of command, one vertical and one horizontal. A basic matrix structure is shown in Figure 11-7. In this case, the vice presidents of operations, marketing, finance, and engineering represent the functional departments that make up the vertical hierarchy. Simultaneously, the managers of businesses A, B, and C represent the divisional units that operate horizontally across the structure. The heads of the major functional and divisional departments that make up the matrix (e.g., the vice presidents and business managers in Figure 11-7) are sometimes referred to as *matrix bosses*.

> **Matrix structure** A structure that superimposes a horizontal set of divisional reporting relationships onto a hierarchical functional structure

One major characteristic of a matrix structure is that employees who work within the matrix report to two matrix bosses. For example, as Figure 11-7 shows, a marketing researcher might report up the vertical chain to the vice president of marketing and across the horizontal chain to the manager of business A. Thus there is a system of dual authority that violates the classical principle of unity of command (an individual should have only one boss at any given point in time), making a matrix structure somewhat complex to operate.

Matrix Stages. Matrix experts Stanley M. Davis and Paul R. Lawrence suggest that organizations ultimately adopting a matrix structure usually go through several identifiable structural stages:[12]

Stage 1 is a *traditional structure,* usually a functional structure, which follows the unity-of-command principle.

Stage 2 is a *temporary overlay,* in which managerial integrator positions are created to take charge of particular projects (e.g., project managers), oversee product launches (e.g., product managers), or handle some other issue of finite duration that involves coordinating across functional departments.

Stage 3 is a *permanent overlay,* in which the managerial integrator positions operate on a permanent basis (e.g., a brand manager coordinates issues related to a brand on an ongoing basis).

Stage 4 is a *mature matrix,* in which matrix bosses have *equal* power.

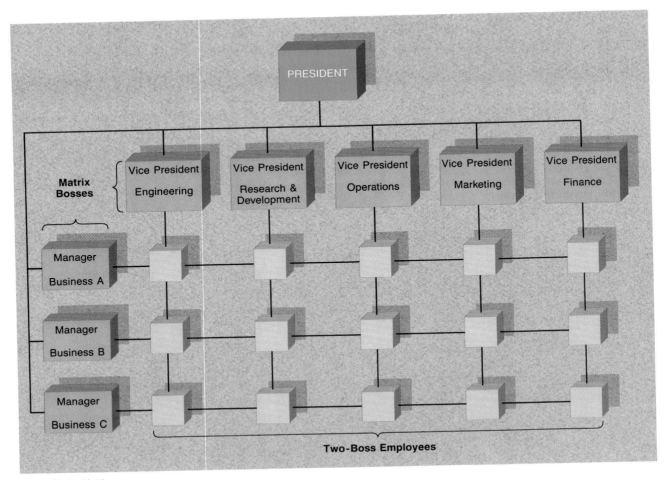

Figure 11-7 Matrix organization structure.

Even though a true matrix incorporates equal power for functional and divisional managers, stages 2 and 3, which involve managerial integrators (see Chapter 10), are often referred to as matrix structures.

Each of the matrix stages offers increasing amounts of horizontal integration, but at the cost of greater administrative complexity.[13] Even with managerial integrators, there is dual authority to some extent because the integrators frequently work directly with various members of functional departments (e.g., engineers or marketing specialists) assigned to help with their project. In their capacity as coordinators, managerial integrators usually informally supervise the work of individuals assigned to their projects, even though they typically do not have direct line authority over these individuals.

With the mature matrix, there is true dual authority.[14] All major decisions must have the approval of both the functional manager and the divisional manager. The mature matrix is used when the functional and divisional dimensions of an organization are both of prime and equal importance. Dow-Corning has experimented with such a design, even adding a third dimension for a simultaneous international focus.[15]

Matrix structures, particularly in the forms of temporary and permanent overlays, operate successfully in a variety of organizations. However, the advantages and disadvantages must be carefully weighed before a matrix design is adopted.[16]

Table 11-4   Major Advantages and Disadvantages of a Matrix Structure

Advantages	Disadvantages
Decentralized decision making	High administrative costs
Strong project or product coordination	Potential confusion over authority and responsibility
Improved environmental monitoring	Heightened prospects for interpersonal conflicts
Fast response to change	Excessive focus on internal relations
Flexible use of human resources	Overemphasis on group decision making
Efficient use of support systems	Possible slow response to change

Advantages of Matrix Structure. The matrix form of organization structure has several major advantages (see Table 11-4). For one thing, decisions can be decentralized so that they are made at the level of the divisional project manager and the functional manager, thereby allowing upper-level management to concentrate on longer-term strategic issues. For another, use of the matrix adds strong horizontal coordination to projects (or products or brands) beyond what is normally possible in the functional design alone, increasing the probability of success. Yet another advantage is that the matrix arrangement facilitates monitoring environmental conditions with respect to both the projects and the various functional areas. The matrix structure can also often react quickly to change because many decisions are made at lower levels. Still another advantage is that functional specialists can be added to or reassigned from projects as needed, allowing effective use of human resources. Finally, support systems, such as computers, special equipment, and software, can be allocated among many projects on an as-needed basis, thereby reducing the costs of such systems.

Disadvantages of Matrix Structure. Matrix designs have several potential disadvantages that must be considered when an organization is thinking about adopting such a structure (see Table 11-4). For example, adding a layer of project managers and their immediate support staff to a functional hierarchy increases administrative costs. In addition, since there are two bosses, individuals working within the matrix may have difficulty determining who has authority and responsibility for various decisions. The increased communication required and the dual-authority arrangements also heighten possibilities of conflicts, particularly between project managers and functional managers. Another potential disadvantage of the matrix structure is that the individuals in the structure can become preoccupied with internal relations at the expense of clients and project goals. Another potential pitfall is that matrix designs can encourage group decision making to the point where even relatively minor decisions are made in groups, causing a serious erosion of productivity. Finally, while the matrix can be particularly adaptable to change, it also can become extremely slow if the interpersonal skills of matrix participants are poor or upper management attempts to retain centralized control. For a time, this latter problem began to cripple the brand management structure at Procter & Gamble (see the following Case in Point discussion).

CASE IN POINT: Brand Management at Procter & Gamble

Since Procter & Gamble (P&G) first used the concept way back in 1927 to manage Camay soap, brand management has been almost synonymous with the Cincinnati-based company. Because of its great success, Procter & Gamble has been viewed almost as a textbook case on how to run a consumer-oriented company—

so much so that major competitors, such as General Mills, began to adopt the brand management approach, often hiring talent from P&G. By the early 1980s, however, P&G's market share in a number of important markets had begun to slip as a result of competition and mature markets, causing P&G to be called a "wounded lion." The company announced its first drop in annual operating earnings in 33 years.

Despite its emphasis on brand management, P&G still had maintained a fairly centralized approach to decision making. In the beginning, the approach worked well; but over the years, excessive centralization began to bog down the company. Gradually, almost every decision was pushed to the top. A former P&G brand manager laughingly relates that the decision about whether the company's new decaffeinated instant Folgers coffee should have a green or a gold cap was elevated all the way to the CEO (he chose gold).

The chief medium in the decision-making process, and the symbol of the growing centralization, became the one-page memo. Managers had to carefully summarize any proposal into a single page, which was rewritten almost endless times as it made its way up the hierarchy.

Brand managers were particularly frustrated by their lack of authority and the fact that they had to answer to layers of management and staff areas such as the legal department. One of many jokes circulating in the company went as follows: "How many brand managers does it take to screw in a light bulb?" The answer: "None. They have to call legal." This lack of authority, together with the tendency of the vertical hierarchy to make most of the significant decisions, effectively canceled the horizontal coordination that the brand managers could provide.

Spurred by the company's difficulties, P&G executives have been taking steps to dismantle the overly bureaucratic practices that have become an anchor on the product management structure. For one thing, the introduction of the "talk sheet" has been welcomed by managers as a significant improvement over strict adherence to the one-page memo. The talk sheet is an informal outline that allows managers on several levels to develop and refine a proposal through discussions, rather than through paper only.

Management also is beginning to decentralize decision making. One method of achieving this objective is the increased use of business teams and task forces that can make decisions in such areas as product development and cost cutting, as well as encourage greater cooperation among functional divisions. In the past, a brand manager might have put together a proposal that would have been passed up the hierarchy for approval by the heads of the various functional units that were affected, as well as by top management. Now, teams are often put together that include representatives from functional areas who help to develop the proposal itself. As a result, brand management is becoming more team-oriented, with greater coordination across functions. The process has speeded product introductions, helping Ivory shampoo get to market in 4 months instead of the usual 18.[17] ▪▬▬▬▪

When to Consider a Matrix Structure. Matrix designs are not necessary for many organizations. For example, Texas Instruments abandoned its much-touted matrix structure after directly blaming it for the company's failure to keep up with the competition.[18] The need for horizontal coordination must be sufficient to justify the additional administrative complexity at the lower levels. Matrix designs usually are appropriate when the following three conditions exist.[19]

1. There is considerable pressure from the environment that necessitates a simultaneous and strong focus on *both* functional and divisional dimensions. For example, the existence of diverse products may call for product orientation, but increasing sophistication in engineering technology may argue for a functional orientation.

2. The demands placed on the organization are changing and unpredictable, making it important to have a large capacity for processing information and coordinating activities quickly. For example, in the microchip industry, foreign competitors frequently make technological improvements and lower prices simultaneously.

3. There is pressure for shared resources. For example, if a company is dominant in its market, it may not feel much pressure to share resources, such as expensive technical specialists, across departments. Instead, the organization could adopt a divisional structure and give each department its own technical specialists. However, in more competitive markets, matrix organizations are one way to attain flexibility in the use of functional resources across projects or products.

There is growing evidence that matrix designs require a corresponding change in an organization's culture to support the increased need for collaborative decision making.[20] In addition, managers may require special training, particularly in interpersonal skills, in order to function effectively within the matrix structure.[21]

While managers need to weigh the advantages and disadvantages of the various structural alternatives in developing an appropriate organization design, they also must consider major contingency factors that can affect structural requirements. We review these factors next.

WEIGHING CONTINGENCY FACTORS

Early in the study of management, classical theorists (see Chapter 2) attempted to develop the ideal organization structure. For example, Henri Fayol offered his ideas about unity of command and the scalar chain. Max Weber, with his notions of the ideal bureaucracy, also provided some concepts (such as formalized rules and regulations) that are useful, particularly in fostering vertical coordination. Still, the one best way to organize proved elusive. A structural configuration that seemed to work for one organization was a deterrent to effectiveness in another. Gradually, contingency theory began to emerge, a management viewpoint arguing that appropriate managerial action depends on the particular parameters of the situation (see Chapter 2). Researchers came to recognize that the best structure for a given organization depends on such major contingency factors as technology, size, and environment.

Technology

One reason why different organizations require different structures can be traced to **technology,** the knowledge, tools, equipment, and work techniques used by an organization in delivering its product or service. Two critical aspects of technology are technological complexity and technological interdependence.[22]

Technology The knowledge, tools, equipment, and work techniques used by an organization in delivering its product or service

Table 11-5 Woodward's Findings on Structural Characteristics and Technology*

Structural Characteristics	TECHNOLOGY		
	Small Batch	Mass Production	Continuous Process
Levels of management	3	4	6
Executive span of control	4	7	10
Supervisory span of control	23	48	15
Industrial workers vs. staff (ratio)	8:1	5.5:1	2:1
Formalization	Low	High	Low
Centralization	Low	High	Low

*Data are medians for the organizations within each technological category.
Source: Joan Woodward, *Industrial Organization: Theory and Practice*, Oxford University Press, London, 1965, pp. 52–62.

Technological Complexity. Famous research that highlighted the importance of technology was conducted during the 1950s by a team led by British sociologist Joan Woodward.[23] Their original intent was to determine the extent to which the principles of management espoused by the classical theorists actually were practiced by a group of 100 British manufacturing firms.

The team was surprised to find that there did not seem to be any connection between the use of the classical management principles in structuring organizations and the success of a firm. In fact, practices varied widely. After careful study, Woodward determined that three different types of technology were reasonably predictive of the structural practices of the firms in the study.

Unit and small-batch production A type of technology in which products are custom-produced to meet customer specifications or they are made in small quantities primarily by craft specialists

Large-batch and mass production A type of technology in which products are manufactured in large quantities, frequently on an assembly line

Continuous-process production A type of technology in which products are liquids, solids, or gases that are made through a continuous process

1. In **unit and small-batch production,** products are custom-produced to meet customer specifications, or they are made in small quantities primarily by craft specialists. Examples are diamond cutting in New York's diamond center and the production of stretch limousines.
2. In **large-batch and mass production,** products are manufactured in large quantities, frequently on an assembly line. Examples are the production of most automobiles and the manufacture of microchips used in computers and related products.
3. In **continuous-process production,** products are liquids, solids, or gases that are made through a continuous process. Examples are petroleum products, such as gasoline, and chemical products.

The research team noted that these types of technologies are increasingly complex to manage, with small-batch and unit production being the least complex and continuous-process production being the most complex. The increasing complexity stems mainly from the use of more elaborate machinery and its greater role in the work process. This technological complexity, in turn, appeared to help explain the differences in the structural practices used by the firms in the study (see Table 11-5).

For example, the researchers found that increasing complexity was associated with more levels of management (a taller structure), more staff personnel per line worker, and larger spans of control at upper management levels. Woodward's results also indicated that formalization and centralization both tended to be high in organizations engaged in large-batch and mass-production technology, in which the efforts of large numbers of workers need to be standardized.

In contrast, formalization and centralization were low in organizations using unit and small-batch, as well as continuous-process, technologies, in which appropriate work decisions must be made at the lower levels.

At the level of the first-line supervisor, the pattern in the span of control was somewhat different than it was at upper levels. For first-line supervisors, the span was greatest with large-batch and mass-production technology because the work involved was fairly routine and one supervisor could handle a relatively large number of workers. The supervisory span of control was somewhat smaller with unit and small-batch technology because of the custom work involved. The span was smallest, though, with continuous-process production because this type of technology is highly automated, requires highly skilled employees at lower levels, and can have very serious implications if there are process difficulties.[24] The chemical leak at the Union Carbide plant in Bhopal, India, in December 1985, which left more than 2000 dead and thousands injured, strongly emphasizes the importance of careful control and supervision in organizations using chemical-process technologies. Recent research suggests that the relatively small spans of control in the continuous-process production category also may be related to the proportionately small number of employees involved and the high interdependence among tasks (requiring smaller work units).[25]

Perhaps the most important outcome of Woodward's research, though, was the finding that the more successful firms had structural characteristics that were close to the median for their particular technology. In contrast, the less successful firms had structural characteristics that deviated more significantly from the median for their main technology. The implication of these results is that appropriate structural characteristics depend, at least to some extent, on the type of technology involved. Research since Woodward's ground-breaking study has largely supported the importance of technological complexity in influencing organization structure.[26]

One recent study suggests that because of advances in technology, Woodward's unit and small-batch category may need to be divided into two categories: traditional batch (equivalent to Woodward's original category) and technical batch, related to new, sophisticated computerized machinery. The use of such

Large batch and mass production, such as is found in the computer chip industry, tends to be highly centralized and formalized. The reason is that the assembly line consists of large numbers of workers using standardized procedures to make intricate chips like this one made at Nixdorf Computer Corporation in Paderborn, Germany.

These people were among thousands injured when toxic chemicals leaked out of the Union Carbide plant in Bhopal, India. In technologically complex industries supervisory spans of control are often kept relatively low so that first-line supervisors can work closely with individuals in their work units and help to prevent accidents like this one.

machinery resembles unit and small-batch production in that the equipment can be set to produce single items or small quantities to meet one customer's specifications and then can be quickly reset to make other custom items; yet the procedure is closely akin to continuous-process production in the degree of technological complexity. The study also suggests that the technical-batch category has structural requirements that closely parallel continuous-process technology, except that decisions tend to be more decentralized with technical batch (because decisions must be made quickly at the bottom levels in order to reset the machine and keep production going).[27]

Technical interdependence The degree to which different parts of the organization must exchange information and materials in order to perform their required activities

Pooled interdependence A relationship in which units operate independently but their individual efforts are important to the success of the organization as a whole

Sequential interdependence A relationship in which one unit must complete its work before the next unit in the sequence can begin work

Reciprocal interdependence A relationship in which one unit's outputs become inputs to the other unit and vice versa

Technological Interdependence. Another way of thinking about how technology affects organizing considerations is to consider **technological interdependence,** the degree to which different parts of the organization must exchange information and materials in order to perform their required activities.[28] There are three major types of technological interdependence: pooled, sequential, and reciprocal.[29]

The type that involves the least interdependence is known as **pooled interdependence,** in which units operate independently but their individual efforts are important to the success of the organization as a whole (hence the term "pooled"). For example, when you go to the local branch of your bank, there is rarely a need for that branch to contact another branch in order to complete your transaction; however, if the branch performs poorly and loses you and other customers, its problems ultimately will have a negative effect on the health of the bank as a whole.

In contrast, with **sequential interdependence,** one unit must complete its work before the next unit in the sequence can begin work. For example, a strike over a local issue at one plant of General Motors frequently causes workers at other plants to be laid off temporarily. The layoffs occur when parts manufactured by the striking plant are needed for the sequentially interdependent assembly process at the nonstriking plants.

Finally, the most complex situation is **reciprocal interdependence,** in which one unit's outputs become inputs to the other unit and vice versa. When an airplane lands, the flight crew turns the plane over to the maintenance crew. After refueling the plane, replenishing supplies, and performing other necessary activities, the maintenance crew releases the plane back to the flight crew so that the plane can continue its journey.[30] Thus the flight crew's output becomes the maintenance crew's input, and then the process is reversed. As you might expect, reciprocal interdependence is likely to require greater efforts at horizontal coordination than do the other two types of technological interdependence. As a result, managers need to give some thought to technological interdependence, as well as complexity, when developing organization structure. In addition, organization size is sometimes a relevant factor.

Size

Woodward's research team also investigated the possibility of a clear relationship between size and various structural characteristics but found nothing definitive. Since that time a number of other studies have attempted to untangle the relationship between size and structure with only modest success. Part of the problem appears to be that there are several other important factors, such as environment and technology, that affect organization structure, leaving size as just one element in the equation. Also, organization size can be measured in various ways, such as gross sales or profits, as well as number of employees (the measure most typically used), sometimes making it difficult to compare studies.

So far, there are four recognizable trends that have been identified by studies of size effects on structure. First, as organizations grow, they are likely to add more departments and levels, making their structures increasingly complex.[31] With functional structures, such growth creates pressure for movement to some type of divisional structure.[32] Second, growing organizations tend to take on an increasing number of staff positions in order to help top management cope with the expanding size. This tendency levels off when a critical mass of staff has been achieved,[33] but it helps lead to the third trend, namely, that additional rules and regulations seem to accompany organizational growth.[34] While rules and regulations can be useful in achieving vertical coordination, the unchecked proliferation of additional rules and regulations may lead to excessive formalization. Fourth, as organizations grow larger, they tend to become more decentralized, probably due in part to the additional rules and regulations that set guidelines for decision making at lower levels.[35]

Because of potential size effects, many successful divisionalized companies try to ensure that various subunits do not become too large by creating new divisions when existing ones become unwieldy. For example, in an effort to reap the advantages of smaller size, Johnson & Johnson operates with more than 150 autonomous divisions. At Worthington Industries, Inc., a steel company with a strong profit record and annual gross sales in the $1 billion range, management operates on the premise that none of its factories (now numbering 27) should have more than 250 workers.[36] Similarly, the president of the W. L. Gore Company, maker of Gore-Tex, a water-repellent fabric that "breathes," likes to limit work units to 150 persons.[37] The actions of these companies are congruent with recent research indicating that larger organizational subunits are often less efficient than their smaller counterparts.[38] While size has a bearing on structural requirements, the impact of environment also is a major factor.

Environment

One of the most famous studies of the effects of environment on organization design was conducted by British scholars Tom Burns and G. M. Stalker.[39] In studying 20 British industrial firms, they discovered that the firms had different characteristics, depending on whether they operated in a stable environment with relatively little change over time or an unstable environment with rapid change and uncertainty.

Mechanistic and Organic Characteristics. The firms that operated in a stable environment tended to have relatively **mechanistic characteristics,** such as high centralization of decision making, many rules and regulations, and mainly hierarchical communication channels. Much of the emphasis was on vertical coordination, but with very limited delegation from one level of management to the next. Still, the researchers found that such firms were able to operate mechanistically and be reasonably successful because changes in the firms' environments usually occurred gradually, making it possible for upper levels of management to stay on top of the changes.

In contrast, the firms that operated in a highly unstable and uncertain environment were far more likely to have relatively **organic characteristics,** such as decentralization of decision making, few rules and regulations, and both hierarchical and lateral communication channels. Much of the emphasis was on horizontal coordination, coupled with considerable delegation from one level to the next. These firms required organic characteristics because their rapidly changing environments made it necessary for individuals at many levels to monitor the environments and help make decisions on how to respond to the chang-

Mechanistic characteristics Characteristics such as high centralization of decision making, many rules and regulations, and mainly hierarchical communication channels

Organic characteristics Characteristics such as decentralization of decision making, few rules and regulations, and both hierarchical and lateral communication channels

Table 11-6 Characteristics of Mechanistic and Organic Organizations

Mechanistic	Organic
Work is divided into narrow, specialized tasks.	Work is defined in terms of general tasks.
Tasks are performed as specified unless changed by managers in the hierarchy.	Tasks are continually adjusted as needed through interaction with others involved in the task.
Structure of control, authority, and communication is hierarchical.	Structure of control, authority, and communication is a network.
Decisions are made by the specified hierarchical level.	Decisions are made by individuals with relevant knowledge and technical expertise.
Communication is mainly vertical, between superior and subordinate.	Communication is vertical and horizontal, among superiors, subordinates, and peers.
Communication content is largely instructions and decisions issued by superiors.	Communication content is largely information and advice.
Emphasis is on loyalty to the organization and obedience to superiors.	Emphasis is on commitment to organizational goals and possession of needed expertise.

Source: Adapted from T. Burns and G. M. Stalker, *The Management of Innovation*, Tavistock, London, 1961, pp. 119–122.

ing conditions. The characteristics of mechanistic and organic organizations are summarized in Table 11-6.

Differentiation and Integration. Two management professors working in the United States, Paul R. Lawrence and Jay W. Lorsch, carried the notion that environment influences organization structure a step further. They reasoned that organizational environments might have different effects on various units within the same organization. To test this possibility, they investigated three departments, manufacturing, sales, and research and development, in three industries with very different environments—plastics, food processing, and containers. Their focus was on **differentiation,** the extent to which organizational units differ from one another in terms of the behaviors and orientations of their members and their formal structures.[40] As expected, Lawrence and Lorsch found significant differentiation among the three types of units studied. The R&D departments tended to concentrate on new developments, operate fairly informally, and be concerned with long-term success. In contrast, the sales departments were mainly oriented toward immediate customer satisfaction, operated more formally, and were interested largely in short-term sales results. Somewhat in between were the manufacturing departments, which primarily concerned themselves with efficiency, operated less formally than the sales departments but more formally than the R&D departments, and were oriented toward an intermediate-term time frame. Interestingly, this differentiation among departments was greatest in the plastics industry, which had the most unstable environment, and was least in the container industry, which operated in the most stable environment.

But differentiation was only half the story. When they considered firm effectiveness, the researchers found that the most effective firms attempted to balance differentiation with efforts toward **integration,** the extent to which there is collaboration among departments that need to coordinate their efforts. The

Differentiation The extent to which organizational units differ from one another in terms of the behaviors and orientations of their members and their formal structures

Integration The extent to which there is collaboration among departments that need to coordinate their efforts

greater the differentiation among departments because of environmental instability, the greater the efforts toward integration in the most successful companies. For example, in the successful container companies, a functional hierarchy and rules and regulations achieved the necessary degree of integration. In the successful plastics companies, however, there was greater use of a variety of vertical and horizontal coordinating mechanisms to achieve effective integration in the face of high differentiation.[41] When the companies were attempting to achieve such integration, methods of horizontal coordination, such as those discussed in Chapter 10 (e.g., teams and managerial integrators) were particularly important.

Mintzberg's Five Structural Configurations

Building on the research about how contingency factors affect structure, management researcher Henry Mintzberg has developed five common structural configurations. He also has outlined the contingency conditions under which the various configurations are likely to be most effective. The five structural configurations are simple structure, machine bureaucracy, professional bureaucracy, divisionalized form, and adhocracy (see Table 11-7).

Table 11-7 Characteristics of Mintzberg's Five Structural Configurations

	STRUCTURAL CONFIGURATIONS				
Characteristics	**Simple Structure**	**Machine Bureaucracy**	**Professional Bureaucracy**	**Divisionalized Form**	**Adhocracy**
BASIC PARAMETERS					
Power concentration	Top executives	CEO and designers of work flow	Professionals	Division executives	Scientists, technocrats, and middle managers
Key coordinating mechanism	Direct supervision	Standardization of work	Standardization of skills	Standardization of outputs	Mutual adjustment
CONTINGENCY FACTORS					
Age and size	Young, small	Old, large	Varies	Old, very large	Young, small to moderate
Technology	Simple, custom	Mass production, large batch	Complex; uses standardized training	Divisible; varies	Sophisticated, automated, or custom
Environmental complexity and dynamism	Simple and dynamic	Simple and stable	Complex and stable	Simple and stable at divisions	Complex and dynamic
STRUCTURAL ELEMENTS					
Departmentalization	Functional	Functional	Functional or hybrid	Divisional or hybrid	Matrix; uses integrators
Formalization	Low	High	Low	High within divisions	Low
Use of horizontal coordination methods	Low	Low	High among professionals	Low between divisions, moderate within divisions	High

Source: Adapted from Henry Mintzberg, *Structure in Fives: Designing Effective Organizations,* Prentice-Hall, Englewood Cliffs, N.J., 1983, pp. 280–281; and Danny Miller, "Configurations of Strategy and Structure: Towards a Synthesis," *Strategic Management Journal,* vol. 7, 1986, p. 242.

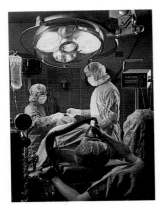

This surgeon, nurse, and anesthesiologist at Winchester Hospital in Winchester, Massachusetts, exemplify a professional bureaucracy. They are skilled professionals who carry on their work with a minimum amount of coordination, a low level of formalization, and a large degree of personal responsibility.

Simple structure A structure characterized by functional departmentalization, a strong concentration of power at the top, low formalization, and emphasis on direct supervision

Machine bureaucracy A structure characterized by functional departmentalization, a strong group of technical specialists, high formalization, and emphasis on standardization of work

Professional bureaucracy A structure characterized by functional or hybrid departmentalization, a strong group of professionals operating at the lower levels, low formalization, and emphasis on standardization of skills

Divisionalized form A structure characterized by divisional departmentalization, a strong management group at the division level, high formalization within divisions, and an emphasis on standardized outputs

Simple Structure. The **simple structure** is a structure characterized by functional departmentalization, a strong concentration of power at the top, low formalization, and emphasis on direct supervision. Because of the structure's simplicity, differentiation among various parts tends to be low, allowing it to function with low usage of horizontal coordination mechanisms. The classic case of the simple structure is the small entrepreneurial firm run by the founder. Simple structures tend to fit best in situations in which the organization is young and small, the technology is relatively simple, and the organization faces a simple, but dynamic, environment. Such structures typically allow rapid innovation, but mainly when the improvements are relatively simple.

Machine Bureaucracy. The **machine bureaucracy** is a structure characterized by functional departmentalization, a strong group of technical specialists (such as engineers, planners, and accountants), high formalization, and emphasis on standardization of work. In contrast to the simple structure, the machine bureaucracy is quite elaborate, largely because of systems of formal planning and work control developed by the technical specialists. A large middle-level management group watches over the operating level and helps resolve the conflicts that grow out of the rigid standardization and the alienation that often accompany routine, narrow jobs. Differentiation among parts is moderate but is handled largely through the work standardization and centralized control. As a result, few forms of horizontal coordination are used.

Machine bureaucracies tend to fit best in situations in which the organization is large, the technology involves large-batch and mass production, and the organization operates in a simple and stable environment. As a result, a machine bureaucracy is likely to be found in large, mature mass-production companies, such as automobile manufacturers, and in large mass-service organizations, such as insurance companies and railroads. Successful machine bureaucracies (e.g., McDonald's) produce goods and services cheaply and efficiently but tend to be relatively slow innovators.

Professional Bureaucracy. The **professional bureaucracy** is a structure characterized by functional or hybrid departmentalization, a strong group of professionals operating at the lower levels, low formalization, and emphasis on standardization of skills. Classic examples of professional bureaucracies are hospitals, universities, and accounting firms, all of which hire large numbers of trained professionals. For the most part, these professionals engage in complex, but fairly standard, activities and are able to operate effectively with a minimum of coordination with others because of their extensive training. Because the success of its operations rely on these trained professionals, the professional bureaucracy decentralizes a considerable amount of decision-making power to them. Differentiation is moderate in a professional bureaucracy, but the extensive use of committees and task forces, particularly at the various managerial levels, helps bring about the necessary horizontal coordination.

Professional bureaucracies operate best in situations in which the technology is complex but standardized and the environment is complex and stable. Because skills are standardized, the professional bureaucracy encourages innovations within narrow skill areas but tends to discourage innovative work that disturbs defined areas and requires interdisciplinary cooperation.

Divisionalized Form. The **divisionalized form** is a structure characterized by divisional departmentalization, a strong management group at the division level, high formalization within divisions, and an emphasis on standardized outputs. The heads of the divisions wield considerable power in the divisionalized form. Since the divisions are created to operate somewhat separately, there is little use of horizontal coordination between divisions, although such mechanisms may be used within divisions. Top management maintains control by visiting the divisions periodically, requiring that they receive top-level approval for some of their most important decisions, and measuring standardized outputs (usually specific, measurable goals). The imposition of this performance control system encourages the divisions themselves to operate as machine bureaucracies in fulfilling the performance requirements.

Divisionalized forms are well suited to situations in which the organization is large and has been in existence for some time, the technology is divisible, and the divisional structure helps make the environments faced by the divisions more simple and stable. Because of the tendency of divisions to become machine bureaucracies, they may have difficulty innovating without specific encouragement and help from top management.

Adhocracy. The **adhocracy** is a structure characterized by various forms of matrix departmentalization, expertise dispersed throughout, low formalization, and emphasis on mutual adjustment. An adhocracy is aimed at innovating in complex ways; as a result, the structure is kept purposely fluid, with power constantly shifting, depending on the particular expertise needed.

The adhocracy has numerous managers, such as functional managers and integrating managers, who help with the extensive horizontal coordination necessary to tap required expertise for particular projects and product areas. In many cases, the ongoing activities of the operating units are kept somewhat independent from much of the rest of the organization so that the need for standardization in producing a product or service does not interfere with the imperative to innovate facing other components. Adhocracies are typically found in situations in which the organization is relative young and small to medium in size, the focus is on sophisticated products involving automation and/or custom work, and the environment is complex and dynamic. Organizations operating in the aerospace, petrochemical, and film-making industries are often adhocracies.

> **Adhocracy** A structure characterized by various forms of matrix departmentalization, expertise dispersed throughout, low formalization, and emphasis on mutual adjustment

Assessing the Configurations. As Mintzberg's configurations illustrate, the success of various organization structures depends on matching them to the appropriate contingency conditions. For example, while a simple structure is well attuned to a simple and dynamic environment, it is not designed to handle more complex situations. At the same time, an adhocracy is too expensive and elaborate for a simple dynamic environment and is too fluid to handle well the mass-production situations that require greater standardization. Mintzberg's five configurations also differ in their appropriateness for implementing given strategies.

MATCHING STRATEGY AND STRUCTURE

Using four of Mintzberg's configurations, strategy specialist Danny Miller recently attempted to match strategies with appropriate structures.[42] In making his assessment, Miller left out the professional bureaucracy because, for the most part, professional bureaucracies are not business organizations.

Miller matched the four remaining structural configurations (simple structure, machine bureaucracy, divisionalized form, and adhocracy) with strategies similar to Porter's competitive strategies (see Chapter 6). The main strategies that Miller considered are:

■ *Niche differentiation*. This strategy is aimed at distinguishing one's products and services from those of competitors for a narrow target market (equivalent to Porter's focus strategy using differentiation).
■ *Cost leadership*. This strategy emphasizes organizational efficiency so that products and services can be offered at prices lower than those of competitors (equivalent to Porter's cost leadership strategy).
■ *Innovative differentiation*. This strategy is aimed at distinguishing one's products and services from those of competitors by leading in complex product or service innovations (similar to Porter's differentiation strategy but more narrowly oriented, specifically to sophisticated innovations).
■ *Market differentiation*. This is a strategy aimed at distinguishing one's products and services from those of competitors through advertising, prestige pricing, and market segmentation (similar to Porter's differentiation strategy but more narrowly oriented, specifically to market approaches). The product and service designs themselves may not necessarily be better than those of competitors, but the firm may offer attractive packaging, good service, convenient locations, and good product or service reliability.

Miller's matches of structure and strategy are shown in Table 11-8. In making these matches, Miller also considered the appropriateness of the environment for the strategy-structure combinations, following much of the logic involved in Mintzberg's typology of structural configurations.

As Table 11-8 indicates, the simple structure is best matched to a niche differentiation, or focus, strategy. Since a simple structure usually is fairly small in size and involves simple technology, cost leadership tends to be impractical. As a result, firms with simple structures are usually more successful pursuing a focus strategy in the form of simple innovations that can be easily implemented and/or marketing efforts that differentiate the product or service for a narrow target market, or niche.

On the other hand, the machine bureaucracy structure is potentially highly compatible with a cost leadership strategy. Because of its large size and high formalization, a machine bureaucracy is particularly well suited to producing

Table 11-8 Major Matches of Structure and Strategy

Mintzberg's Configurations	Type of Departmentalization	Strategy
Simple structure	Functional	Niche differentiation or focus
Machine bureaucracy	Functional	Cost leadership; possibly market differentiation
Divisionalized form	Divisional or hybrid	Market differentiation or cost leadership at division level
Adhocracy	Matrix, integrators	Innovative differentiation

Source: Based on Danny Miller, "Configurations of Strategy and Structure: Towards a Synthesis," *Strategic Management Journal*, vol. 7, 1986, pp. 233–249; and Danny Miller, "Relating Porter's Business Strategies to Environment and Structure: Analysis and Performance Implications," *Academy of Management Journal*, vol. 31, pp. 280–308.

large amounts of standardized goods and to closely controlling costs. Under some circumstances, machine bureaucracies may also benefit from using a market differentiation strategy, as long as they choose a means of differentiation that does not interfere with efficiency and is not easily copied. For example, a machine bureaucracy would likely want to avoid breaking up its product lines into various customized products (which would raise costs and invite imitators). Instead, it may be able to boost quality, improve reliability, or promote its brands through advertising. Machine bureaucracies generally have considerable difficulty pursuing innovation differentiation because of their relative inflexibility.

The divisionalized form of structure is generally well matched with market differentiation or cost leadership strategies at the division levels. Theoretically, divisions can differ greatly in structure from one another, with some being adhocracies and others being more like machine bureaucracies or simple structures. Mintzberg, though, argues that the divisionalized form tends to encourage machine bureaucracies at the division level, largely because of the imposition of controls from above. To the extent that a division approximates a machine bureaucracy, a low-cost strategy or possibly a market differentiation strategy may be appropriate. Divisions that more closely resemble adhocracies, perhaps through specific efforts aimed at encouraging innovation, may be able to pursue successfully an innovative differentiation strategy.

The adhocracy structure generally is compatible with a structure of innovative differentiation. Adhocracies emphasize flexibility and collaboration among specialists, conditions conducive to developing new products. Adhocracies should not orient themselves too broadly, because they may have difficulty innovating across too many markets. On the other hand, they cannot be excessively narrow, since they may find themselves in very small niches or may fail to capitalize on new markets for their innovations.

PROMOTING INNOVATION: USING STRUCTURAL MEANS TO ENHANCE PROSPECTS

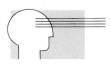

One way of further enhancing the ability of structure to support strategy is by using structural means to encourage innovation. Innovation is particularly critical to differentiation strategies (especially the innovative differentiation strategy), but it also is important in staying ahead of the competition with a focus strategy and pinpointing new ways of shaving costs to implement a cost leadership strategy. Jay R. Galbraith, a specialist on organization structure, offers guidelines for adjusting structures to enhance the prospects for innovation. Although his ideas are particularly compatible with Mintzberg's adhocracy, they are applicable, to some extent, to functional, divisional, and hybrid structures as well.

Generally, Galbraith argues that most existing organizations are aimed at performing similar tasks efficiently on a recurring basis. For example, organizations produce the millionth automobile, process the millionth check, or serve the millionth hamburger. Because their focus is on performing assigned tasks well, most organizations are not particularly well geared to doing new things for the first time. As a result, separate innovating units are needed to increase the likelihood of producing innovations. If units other than the innovating units will be implementing the innovations, attention also needs to be given to transition processes so that innovations can be successfully transferred from the innovating units. In discussing Galbraith's ideas, we consider four major aspects of structuring organizations to facilitate innovation: the vital roles necessary for innovation, the differentiation paradox, the need for innovative units called reservations, and the transfer process.

Vital Roles

Successful innovations are rarely the product of only one person's work. Rather, the innovative process is much more likely to occur in an organization that has individuals who fulfill three different types of vital entrepreneurial roles: idea champion, sponsor, and orchestrator. We discuss these roles in Chapter 1 and review them briefly here.

An *idea champion* is an individual who generates a new idea or believes in the value of a new idea and supports it in the face of numerous potential obstacles. Such individuals often are entrepreneurs, inventors, creative individuals, or risk takers. Since they typically are individuals who are relatively far down in the hierarchy, they often have difficulty getting their innovations accepted without the help of a sponsor. A *sponsor* is a middle manager who recognizes the organizational significance of an idea, helps obtain the necessary funding to continue development of the innovation, and facilitates actual implementation of the new idea. Still, innovations also need the help of an *orchestrator*. An orchestrator is a high-level manager who articulates the need for innovation, provides funding for innovating activities, creates incentives for middle managers to sponsor innovating ideas, and protects idea people. Orchestrators are vital because innovations are usually disruptive in the sense that they disturb the status quo and may, therefore, be resisted by individuals who will need to make adjustments to accommodate the new ideas.

For example, top management at SmithKline Beckman, the Philadelphia drug giant, learned some tough lessons about orchestrating when the company's scientists developed a vaccine for certain types of hepatitis in the early 1980s. Company marketers fought the idea of offering the vaccine because SmithKline did not usually sell vaccines in the United States. Nevertheless, the scientists carried on with clinical trials by siphoning money from other projects. Even after successful trials, the marketers vetoed the project because of concerns about product liability lawsuits. Undaunted, the scientists finally won the backing of the company's international division, which agreed to market the product abroad. After the product found quick acceptance in international markets, SmithKline finally began seeking FDA approval, a process that takes 2 years. "Too bad they didn't listen to us a couple of years ago," says Martin Rosenberg, a SmithKline research vice president. "They would have a $100 million drug by now."[43]

For illustration purposes, a typical organization with a divisional structure is depicted in Figure 11-8*a*. Providing for innovation in this organization means that the three vital roles of idea generator, sponsor, and orchestrator must also appear. Possible innovating roles for the organization structure are indicated in Figure 11-8*b*. The chief executive is shown in an orchestrator role. Certain division managers fulfill the sponsor roles. Idea generation takes place largely in the areas marked "reservations," which are units exclusively devoted to innovation, but a few idea generators are not part of reservations. The reason for the existence of reservations is largely related to the differentiation paradox.

Figure 11-8 Typical divisional structure, vital roles, and reservations for promoting innovation. (Adapted from Jay R. Galbraith, "Designing the Innovating Organization," *Organizational Dynamics*, vol. 10, 1982, pp. 12–13.)

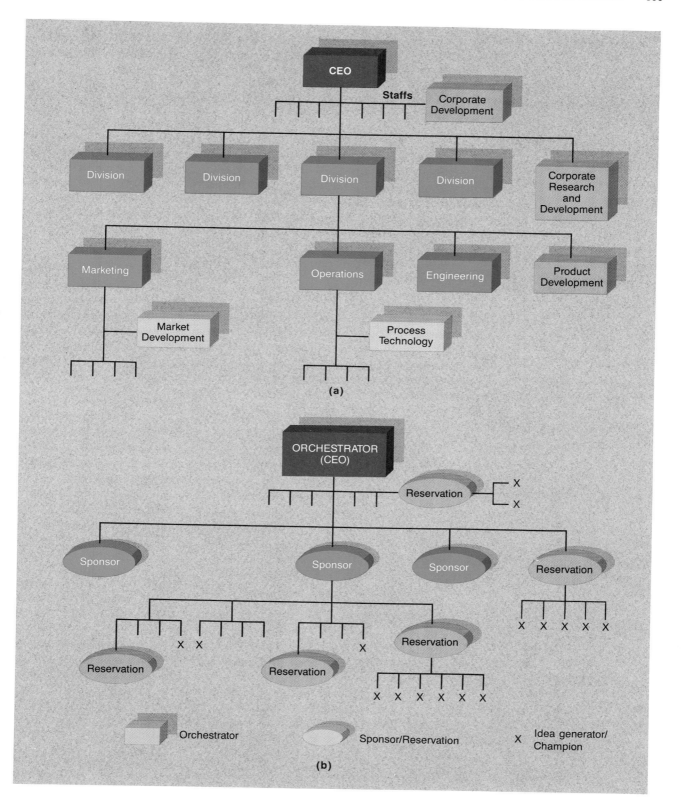

(a)

(b)

Orchestrator

Sponsor/Reservation

X   Idea generator/
Champion

Differentiation Paradox

Considerable research on innovation indicates that major-breakthrough ideas are more likely to occur if the early efforts at development are differentiated, or separated from the operating units of the organization.[44] Differentiation occurs when the innovating activity is separated physically (located in a private work area), financially (given its own budget or funding), and/or organizationally (operated as a separate organizational unit) from ongoing activities. Differentiation also can occur when individuals are allowed to use at least limited amounts of slack resources to test initial ideas without prior hierarchical approval. For example, the Santa Rosa division of Hewlett-Packard has an open-stock policy, whereby engineers are free to use electrical and mechanical components from the lab stock area. They are even encouraged to take components home on the assumption that doing so will foster original thinking and innovation. According to one story, when Bill Hewlett, a company founder, found the lab stock area locked one Saturday, he got a bolt cutter and removed the padlock. He then left a note saying, "Don't ever lock this door again. Thanks, Bill."[45]

There is, however, a paradox associated with differentiation. The **differentiation paradox** poses the idea that although separating efforts to innovate from the rest of the organization increases the likelihood of developing radical ideas, such differentiation also decreases the likelihood that the radical ideas will ever be implemented. This is because the new idea may be perceived as so different that it is threatening or is rejected as nonapplicable. The differentiation paradox is strongest when there is a need for radical innovation that must be implemented by the operating part of the organization. Sometimes, radical innovations generate enough business to justify a whole separate unit or division, and the transfer problem does not occur. Other times, innovations are incremental changes to current business, and the amount of necessary differentiation is less significant. If an organization wants to accelerate the innovation process, the necessary differentiation can be created through reservations.

Differentiation paradox
The idea that although separating efforts to innovate from the rest of the organization increases the likelihood of developing radical ideas, such differentiation also decreases the likelihood that the radical ideas will ever be implemented

Reservations

Reservations are organizational units that devote full time to the generation of innovative ideas for future business. Many research and development units fit this definition. The aim is to create "garagelike" atmospheres in which people can try new approaches. Steven Jobs and Steven Wozniak literally created the first Apple computer in a garage, which became, in effect, a reservation for their work. Reservations can be permanent or temporary. They can take the form of ongoing units, such as research and development units. Sometimes, organizations set up **new venture units** that typically are either separate divisions or specially incorporated companies created for the specific purpose of developing new products or business ideas and initiatives.[46] Reservations can also be temporary task forces or teams made up of individuals who have been relieved of their normal duties in order to develop a new process, product, or program. Such teams are sometimes called **new venture teams.** As a group, the orchestrators, sponsors, and idea generators, working in conjunction with reservations, make up the main innovating part of the organization.

In Figure 11-8a and 11-8b, the following units are viewed as reservations: corporate development, corporate research and development, and product development. In addition, there are smaller reservations under marketing and operations, as well as a few individuals who are viewed as idea generators but who work in units that are not designated as reservations. Three division man-

Reservations
Organizational units that devote full time to the generation of innovative ideas for future business

New venture units Either separate divisions or specially incorporated companies created for the specific purpose of developing new products or business ideas and initiatives

New venture teams
Temporary task forces or teams made up of individuals who have been relieved of their normal duties in order to develop a new process, product, or program

agers have taken on the role of sponsor. Actually, anyone in the organization can be a sponsor or an idea generator, but usually there are certain individuals who show both talent and inclination toward innovating.

Transfer Process

Although the innovation process often can be helped by separating the idea generators from the operating parts of the organization, the differentiation paradox must still be reckoned with. The more that innovators are separated from the rest of the organization, the more difficulty an organization may encounter in ultimately turning innovations into marketable products or services. For example, world-renowned Bell Labs has averaged almost a patent a day since it was founded in 1925 to provide cutting-edge research support to AT&T. Yet AT&T has experienced acute difficulty in translating that research into products and services that will fuel company growth.[47]

It is probably best to think of the transfer, or transition, process as a series of stages. In the first stage, the idea generator, or champion, works on an idea in a reservation. If the initial tests are positive but the idea needs more work, it may be possible to involve people with relevant expertise from other parts of the organization to help hone the idea. Then, if the results are still positive, the next stage may involve testing the idea in one of the operating divisions. In the final stage, the new innovation can be fully implemented. Of course, the process may not always work so smoothly. However, to innovate on a consistent basis, organizations need to foster innovative efforts and provide for the transfer of new ideas from the innovating units to the rest of the organization, if necessary.

Sometimes, organizations set up separate new venture units and then, when they are large enough, transfer them to the main organization as separate divisions, thus lessening the transfer difficulties. One company that has been successful with this method, as well as with other approaches to innovation, is Perstorp, a Swedish specialty chemical maker (see the following Case in Point discussion).

CASE IN POINT: Perstorp Excels at Innovation

Perstorp AB, a large Swedish specialty chemical maker with major businesses in polymers, laminates, and biotechnology, is well known for the variety of methods it uses to encourage innovation. About 25 percent of the products that Perstorp sells did not exist a decade ago. The new products include additives, noise abatement products, carbohydrate-based pharmaceuticals, analysis systems, laminate flooring, and copper foil. Most of the company's other products have been changed radically over the years. In assessing the changes, CEO Karl-Erik Sahlberg notes: "Because we earn most of our profits from relatively mature products that need constant rejuvenation, we have had to develop a commitment to innovation. We think that we have had some success in creating an environment where ideas can thrive and bring us into new business areas."

As part of its drive to increase innovation, Perstorp discontinued its corporate research laboratory in favor of having its divisions conduct more of their own R&D work. The rationale for the reorganization was the desire to place the research efforts closer to the customer base (i.e., in the operating divisions) so that R&D would be oriented toward products for which there is a market. One negative aspect of the change, though, was that it placed the divisions in a

Perstorp AB, a Swedish chemical manufacturer, encourages innovation by funding special cooperative projects undertaken by research centers at universities around the world. The IDEON research center at the University of Lund, shown here, is developing instruments that use fiber optics to control sequences of chemical processes.

situation of conflict between short-run profits and longer-term research for future products.

To encourage a longer-term view, Perstorp has two mechanisms for funding in-house research: the President's Fund and the Research Foundation. The President's Fund supports product development and focuses on long-term projects that divisions would normally not want to undertake because expenditures would affect current profit levels. The Research Foundation provides funding for special projects conducted externally in conjunction with universities and other R&D institutions. Furthermore, Perstorp's general manager of corporate development can offer grants of up to $15,000 without formalities. Higher funding requests are considered frequently by Perstorp's executive management committee. For very large projects, Perstorp gets advice from a council of six university professors with expertise in physics, chemistry, and marketing.

Another major means of encouraging innovation is Perstorp's new business development company, Pernovo AB. Pernovo is a subsidiary that acts like a venture-capital company in that it purchases equity in small, promising high-technology firms in Europe and the United States. The subsidiary invests only in firms that have the potential of involving Perstorp in new technologies with niche products for international markets. Companies that prove to be successful become divisions of Perstorp. Pernovo's president, Stig Eklund, and his two venture managers consider about 1000 new business ideas each year and may invest in 10 or so. One criterion for investing is venture manager support. "No matter how good the idea is, if you can't get a venture manager enthusiastic about it, forget it," says Eklund. "Every idea needs a champion."

Perstorp also maintains a small R&D laboratory at the Ideon research park at the University of Lund in southern Sweden. The company has found that it is easier to recruit engineers and scientists to Ideon because of its campuslike atmosphere.[48]   ■

This chapter has focused on designing structure to support an organization's strategy. In the next chapter, we consider another important aspect of the organizing function, human resources management.

CHAPTER SUMMARY

Alfred Chandler's well-known study of the origins of the largest U.S. firms helped establish the notion that managers should design organization structures to support the organization's strategy. At the same time, structures that are needed to reach organizational goals effectively and efficiently are also likely to be influenced by major contingency factors and structural methods for promoting innovation.

Four of the most commonly used forms of departmentalization are functional, divisional, hybrid, and matrix. Functional structure combines positions into units on the basis of similarity of expertise, skills, and work activities. Divisional structure groups positions according to similarity of products, services, or markets. The three major forms of divisional structure are product divisions, geographic divisions, and customer divisions. Hybrid structure adopts parts of both functional and divisional structures at the same level of management. A mature matrix is a structure that is simultaneously both a functional and a divisional organization, with two chains of command (one vertical and one horizontal). Matrix structures may progress through several stages, beginning with the traditional structure and then moving to a temporary overlay, a permanent overlay, or, perhaps, the mature matrix stage.

Matrix structures are appropriate when pressure from the environment necessitates a strong focus on both functional and divisional dimensions; changing, unpredictable demands call for rapid processing of large amounts of information; and there is pressure for shared resources. Functional, divisional, hybrid, and matrix structures all have advantages and disadvantages. As a result, there are differences in the circumstances under which each is likely to be relatively effective.

Researchers have come to recognize that the best structure for a given organization depends on such major contingency factors as technology, size, and environment. Higher levels of both technological complexity

and technological interdependence require greater efforts at horizontal coordination. Size tends to lead to more departments and levels, a greater number of specialists, more staff positions, and an eventual tendency toward decentralization. Organizations operating in more stable environments tend to have relatively mechanistic characteristics, while those operating in more unstable environments tend to have relatively organic characteristics. Unstable environments also are associated with greater differentiation among internal units, increasing the need for greater efforts at integration, largely through methods of horizontal coordination. Mintzberg offers five structural configurations: simple structure, machine bureaucracy, professional bureaucracy, divisionalized form, and adhocracy. The five configurations differ in the degree to which they are appropriate to particular contingency (technology, size, and environment) conditions.

Some strategies and structures seem to be better matches in terms of likely success: simple structure and niche differentiation; machine bureaucracy and cost leadership or, perhaps, market differentiation; divisionalized form and market differentiation or cost leadership at the division levels; and adhocracy and innovative differentiation.

Enhancement of the prospects for organizational innovation is possible through several mechanisms. The vital roles of idea champion, sponsor, and orchestrator are important ingredients for innovation. The differentiation paradox also must be taken into account. On the one hand, innovation is more likely if the innovating units are separated from the rest of the organization physically, financially, and/or organizationally; therefore, organizations need to designate reservations, units that devote full time to innovation. On the other hand, the separation makes it more difficult to transfer innovations to other parts of the organization.

MANAGERIAL TERMINOLOGY

adhocracy (391)
continuous-process
   production (384)
customer divisions (375)
differentiation (388)
differentiation paradox
   (396)
divisional structure (373)
divisionalized form (390)
functional structure
   (370)

geographic divisions
   (374)
hybrid structure (377)
integration (388)
large-batch and mass
   production (384)
machine bureaucracy
   (390)
matrix structure (379)
mechanistic
   characteristics (387)

new venture teams
   (396)
new venture units (396)
organic characteristics
   (387)
pooled interdependence
   (386)
product divisions (374)
professional bureaucracy
   (390)

reciprocal
   interdependence (386)
reservations (396)
sequential
   interdependence (386)
simple structure (390)
technological
   interdependence (386)
technology (383)
unit and small-batch
   production (384)

QUESTIONS FOR DISCUSSION AND REVIEW

1. Summarize current views about the link between strategy and organization structure. To what extent can these differing views be reconciled?
2. Contrast the functional and divisional types of departmentalization, including their respective advantages and disadvantages. Given your particular career interests, develop a list of pros and cons for working in a company organized by function and another for working in a company organized by product.
3. Describe the hybrid, or mixed, type of departmentalization. How does this type of structure help incorporate some of the advantages of both the functional and divisional types?
4. Outline the advantages and disadvantages of matrix departmentalization. How do they relate to the conditions under which it is appropriate to use matrix structures?
5. Contrast the two critical aspects of technology: technological complexity and technological interdependence. Can you give examples of small-batch, mass-production, and continuous-process technologies? Alternatively, identify examples of three types of technological interdependence.
6. Explain the four recognizable trends in studies of size effects on structure. Can you describe any evidence of these effects in organizations with which you are familiar?
7. Contrast the mechanistic and organic characteristics of organizations. To what extent do you view your college or university as having relatively mechanistic or relatively organic characteristics. Cite examples to support your view. Why might organizations with organic characteristics require greater managerial efforts at integration?
8. Compare and contrast Mintzberg's five structural configurations, including the contingency conditions under which each is likely to be successful. Which type of configuration seems to be the most prevalent?
9. Outline how strategy and structure might be matched to help enhance organizational success. What might be the implications for subsequent changes in strategy or structure?
10. Explain the notion of a reservation as it applies to encouraging organizational innovation. How might the differentiation paradox help explain the difficulties that AT&T has had in utilizing Bell Labs' innovative ideas in marketable products? What might explain Perstorp's success in encouraging innovation?

DISCUSSION QUESTIONS FOR CHAPTER OPENING CASE

1. Classify the type of departmentalization, or structure, used by 3M.
2. Identify the presence of the orchestrator, sponsor, and idea champion roles in the Post-it notes pad situation at 3M. What other evidence indicates that 3M expends considerable effort on encouraging innovation?
3. How does the Post-it note pad situation illustrate the differentiation paradox?

MANAGEMENT EXERCISE: DEVELOPING AN ORGANIZATION STRUCTURE[49]

The Sun Petroleum Products Company, a subsidiary of Sun Company, Inc., is a successful refining company. Its six refineries manufacture three main business products: fuels, petrochemicals, and lubricants. The products are sold to Sunmark Industries (another Sun subsidiary), chemical manufacturers, industrial plants, the auto industry, and a variety of other customers. The $7 billion company has a work force of about 5400.

The company currently has a functional organization structure, with the following major positions reporting directly to the president: chief counsel; vice president, financial services; vice president, technology; director, planning and administration (includes human resources function); and vice president, operations (to whom a vice president of marketing and a vice president of manufacturing and supply distribution report).

Because of changing conditions in the markets for the company's three main products, Sun Petroleum is thinking about changing its organization structure to a hybrid structure. In the process, the president is thinking about adding a senior vice president of resources and strategy to oversee the company's strategic planning.

First, draw an organization chart depicting Sun Petroleum's current organization structure.

Second, draw a proposed chart for changing Sun Petroleum's current structure to a hybrid organization structure.

Third, be prepared to discuss the pros and cons of the proposed new structure and some possible ways of promoting innovation.

THE LOWERING OF THE PIRATES' FLAG AT APPLE

The combination seemed ideal. Steven P. Jobs, charismatic co-founder and chairman of Apple Computer, Inc., woos John Sculley, the young, dynamic president of Pepsi-Cola USA, to be president of Apple. While Jobs oversaw technical innovation, Sculley was to boost Apple's marketing expertise and improve its relationship with retailers and customers. The ultimate goal was to break IBM's stronghold on the business market for personal computers. Under Jobs, the company had had almost a singular focus on products, and Jobs had piqued the imagination of employees with predictions of "insanely great" new computers. One of Sculley's first moves was reorganizing the company's nine product-oriented and highly decentralized divisions into two major divisions, one for the Apple II and one, headed by Jobs himself, for the forthcoming Macintosh. The reorganization allowed resources to be focused on the company's two major product lines and facilitated Sculley's emphasis on marketing them, particularly to the business community.

With Jobs ensconced in the Macintosh division, the reorganization seemed to work at first. Jobs devoted his attention to the further development of the Macintosh, which was not selling quite as well as had been expected. Meanwhile, the Apple II division turned in a record sales performance with the less sophisticated, but highly profitable, Apple IIe. Unfortunately, trouble began to develop. The Mac division employees, touted by Jobs as being superstars, viewed themselves as the Apple elite, since they were developing the new technol-

ogy. Indicative of these feelings, a pirates' flag flew over the building in which the Macintosh division was housed. Morale in the Apple II division was not helped when Jobs addressed the Apple II marketing staff as members of the "dull and boring product division." However, with the largest block of stock (11.3 percent) and the job of chairman, Jobs was an unusually powerful general manager.

Troubles accelerated when sales of personal computers began to slump nationally; the Mac, in particular, continued to sell less well than anticipated. The situation was exacerbated by the fact that the Mac division chronically missed deadlines for the development of crucial parts of the Mac system. Pushed by the board of directors to take greater control, Sculley finally proposed a new organization structure that would, in effect, eliminate the Mac division and with it the general manager position held by Jobs. The proposal (which was ultimately approved by the board) was aimed in part at reducing the duplication of positions, in such areas as marketing, human resources, and manufacturing, that had been necessary under the division by products. It called for a functional structure, which included product operations (comprising R&D, manufacturing, service, and distribution), marketing and sales, finance and management information systems, legal services, and human resources. With the Mac division dissolved, Jobs resigned his position as chairman and left the company.

Within 18 months, sales of the Mac, with its technologically advanced desktop publishing capability and its relative ease of use for computer novices, started to take off. But other companies, including IBM, quickly began to develop products to match the Mac capabili-

ties. Although Sculley professed that Jobs's vision of putting a computer into every person's hands and thus changing the world remained intact, Apple watchers wondered whether Apple could keep innovating under Sculley.

To foster product innovation further, Sculley purchased a supercomputer, doubled the R&D budget, and increased the number of engineers to more than 1000.

Meanwhile, Apple sales had grown from about $580 million in 1984 to more than $5 billion by 1989. The number of employees almost doubled to more than 10,000 worldwide during the same period. This massive growth led Sculley to reorganize once again, this time into major geographic divisions (Apple USA, Apple Pacific, and Apple Europe) with a separate division for Apple products. The Apple products division was responsible for all aspects of product development, ranging from basic research and product definition all the way to manufacturing, introduction, and coordination of marketing. This integrated approach was aimed at competing with Japan on price and quality while incorporating the latest technology and innovation. The major geographic divisions were responsible for selling and servicing the various products in their respective regions.[50]

QUESTIONS FOR CHAPTER CONCLUDING CASE

1. Use your knowledge of organization design to assess the probable effectiveness of Apple's new organization structure.
2. What evidence of the differential paradox related to innovation is manifested in this situation?
3. Trace the various reorganizing efforts by Sculley, and explain his reasons for each reorganization.

CHAPTER TWELVE

HUMAN RESOURCE MANAGEMENT

CHAPTER OUTLINE

Strategic Human Resource Management
The HRM Process: An Overview
The Strategic Importance of HRM

Human Resource Planning
Job Analysis
Demand for Human Resources
Supply of Human Resources
Reconciling Demand and Supply

Staffing
Recruitment
Selection

Development and Evaluation
Training and Development
Performance Appraisal

Compensation
Types of Equity
Designing the Pay Structure
Promoting Innovation: Nontraditional Compensation Approaches
Employee Benefits

Maintaining Effective Work-Force Relationships
Labor-Management Relations
Current Employee Issues

LEARNING OBJECTIVES

After studying this chapter, you should be able to:

■ Outline the human resource management process and trace the development of its strategic importance.

■ Explain how the demand for and supply of human resources are assessed and reconciled within human resource planning.

■ Differentiate between internal and external recruiting.

■ Assess the usefulness of the major selection methods.

■ Explain the main phases in the training process, as well as the major types of training programs.

■ Delineate the major methods for rating performance, common rating errors, and the major roles that supervisors play in the performance appraisal interview.

■ Explain how pay structures are developed and how benefits figure in compensation.

■ Explain the process through which unions are certified and decertified, as well as the growing importance of employee-rights issues.

CHANGES IN HUMAN RESOURCE MANAGEMENT BOOST CARE

CARE, a not-for-profit organization based in New York City, was founded after World War II to provide a means by which Americans could send packages of food and clothing to Europeans who were victims of the war. The program began on a small scale, with packages of mainly food and clothing sent to specified friends and relatives of donors. Gradually, the organization began to expand its efforts through government grants and private donations. CARE started school-lunch and maternal-health programs and engaged in disaster relief. The organization also undertook forestation programs, agribusiness development, and job training as it adjusted its charter to include the underdeveloped countries of Asia, Latin America, and Africa. In the process, the original name that provided the acronym CARE (Cooperative for American Remittances to Europe) was changed to Cooperative for American Relief Everywhere.

By 1980, though, CARE itself was experiencing serious difficulties. Donations in 1979 had fallen about $5 million short of an anticipated $24 million, causing a crisis that necessitated sudden cuts in a number of programs. At about the same time, an executive director who had been appointed head of CARE in 1978 was found to have embezzled $106,000 of the agency's funds. Employee morale plummeted. CARE's board of directors began to conclude that the agency needed to make some drastic changes. With revenues at $200 million in 1980 and projects in 37 countries, CARE's methods of managing had become outmoded. Careful investigation revealed a myriad of problems, including substandard working facilities, an outdated computer system, poor financial management, and inadequate management of human resources. To remedy the situation, the board of directors promoted Philip Johnston from his position as director of CARE Europe to that of executive director of the agency. Johnston immediately hired five experienced managers to help implement the necessary changes.

After a decade of instilling a business orientation, CARE, with approximately $329 million in annual revenues, is now being managed in a manner similar to that of a profit-making organization. Extensive changes have been made in the management of CARE's fund-raising, financial, and computer activities. For one thing, the slow manual procedures used in processing donor contributions have been replaced by a sophisticated computer system and a bank lockbox facility (donations are now sent to a locked mailbox and are picked up directly by the bank for processing). For another, a new financial management team streamlined the financial system, resulting in vastly improved financial management. For example, instead of relying on a bank line of credit to cover cash needs during the slower donor months, CARE now has an operating reserve, which, through aggressive investment management, provides a new income stream for the organization. In another improvement, new computer systems serving various levels of the organization have helped streamline a number of administrative activities.

CARE also purchased its headquarters building, which it had been renting. Along with providing a modern, businesslike work environment for its employees, CARE is able to rent out the additional newly renovated office space at rates that more than cover the costs of purchasing and maintaining the building.

Changes in the management of CARE-funded programs also were warranted. Programs had become larger and more complex but often were not coordinated or evaluated properly. For example, a water system was funded in the Sudan without provisions for its future maintenance. Similarly, a food aid program for mothers and children in Guatemala, Haiti, and the Philippines failed to

403

CARE is now considered one of America's best-run charities, but a decade earlier the organization was struggling. Major changes in the management of human resources contributed significantly to the turnaround. Employees, such as this project manager of small enterprise development in Niger, have been given boosts in salaries, training in job-related skills, and standards for performance.

monitor weight gains. In response to these problems, CARE began planning projects in conjunction with one another, set up mechanisms for receiving improved feedback on how projects were progressing, and developed methods for providing better technical help to go along with funding.

Problems related to human resource management were particularly acute in 1980. Little human resource planning was done. Job descriptions were poorly written, if they existed at all. Many employees did not have appropriate skills for performing their job duties effectively. There were virtually no standards for performance; performance appraisals were rarely conducted; and few formalized training programs were available to help employees improve their job-related skills. The compensation system dispensed inconsistent and inequitable rewards.

As a result, a new team was brought in to revamp human resource management at CARE, and human resource planning is now part of the ongoing planning process. Current job descriptions exist for every job. A new human resource information system allows ready access to various types of information about employees, including an inventory of their skills. A formal orientation program introduces new employees to the organization, and new training programs help employees develop technical and other skills that they need to operate effectively. A new compensation system allocates pay on a more equitable basis, and a new salary structure has helped recruit excellent professional and managerial talent. For example, CARE increased management salaries by 35 to 75 percent in order to attract more experienced people. The salaries still are not generous, but they are more competitive with small companies and other not-for-profit organizations than they were before. As a result of performance standards that are part of a new performance evaluation system based on management by objectives, annual pay raises are awarded on a merit basis. The standards also have induced a portion of the previous management staff to resign over a period of time rather than meet the new expectations for performance.

Although many changes have been made at CARE, the positive results can be attributed in very large degree to the improved management of human resources. In fact, CARE was singled out by *Fortune* magazine in 1987 as one of America's best-run charities—very different, indeed, from the manner in which the organization operated a decade earlier.[1]

While there were multiple causes for the problems that beset CARE by 1980, many of the difficulties can be traced to shortcomings in appropriately acquiring, developing, and utilizing human resources. In the previous two chapters we considered the organizing function as it relates to various means of structuring organizations so that planned goals can be achieved efficiently and effectively. In this chapter, we continue our discussion of the organizing function by examining how organizations, like CARE, can acquire and develop the human resources needed to put the structural elements into effective action. Without organization members who can perform the necessary tasks, organizations have little hope of achieving their goals.

Human resource management (HRM) is the management of various activities designed to enhance the effectiveness of an organization's work force in achieving organizational goals.[2] In exploring various facets of human resource management, we first look at the human resource management process and consider the strategic importance of such management. We next investigate human resource planning and various aspects of staffing the organization with appropriate human resources. We also examine means of developing organization members and evaluating their performance. We then consider major issues relating to adequately compensating organization members, including means of encouraging innovation, particularly through appropriate reward systems for

Human resource management (HRM) The management of various activities designed to enhance the effectiveness of an organization's work force in achieving organizational goals

intrapreneurs. Finally, we examine important issues related to maintaining effective work-force relationships.

STRATEGIC HUMAN RESOURCE MANAGEMENT

At 3M, a company famous for fostering employee innovation, human resource issues are increasingly an integral part of strategic management. Thus 3M is at the forefront of a trend toward recognizing human resources as a crucial element in the strategic success of organizations.[3] In a growing number of organizations, such as 3M and CARE, high-level managers within the human resource management function participate directly in strategy formulation. They also help coordinate human resource aspects of strategy implementation.[4] In this section, we review major aspects of the human resource management process before exploring in greater depth the main reasons for the growing strategic role of human resource management.

The HRM Process: An Overview

As suggested by the HRM process shown in Figure 12-1, human resource management encompasses a number of important activities. One critical aspect of the process, human resource planning, assesses the human resource needs associated with strategic management and helps identify staffing needs. The staffing component of the process includes attracting and selecting individuals for appropriate positions. Once individuals become part of the organization, their ability to contribute effectively is usually enhanced by various development and evaluation efforts, such as training and periodic performance evaluations. Compensating employees for their efforts is another important factor in the HRM process, because adequate rewards are critical not only to attracting but also to motivating and retaining valuable employees. Finally, managers must respond to various issues that influence work-force perceptions of the organization and its treatment of employees.

In order to explore human resource management in an orderly fashion, the various activities that make up the HRM process are discussed sequentially in this chapter. The components, though, are actually highly interrelated. For example, when a group of British financiers took over the British arm of F. W. Woolworth from its American parent in 1982, the chain of 1000 stores had a tarnished image and 30,000 employees with a reputation for poor service. Investigation revealed many interrelated problems, such as poor employment interviewing practices (interviews typically lasted 10 minutes), little training for either sales staff or managers, and a compensation system that did not reward good performance. Thus various components of the HRM process collectively reinforced the service problems.[5]

Human resource professionals operating within human resource depart-

Figure 12-1 The human resource management process.

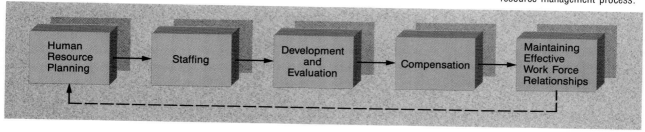

The mutual funds of Fidelity Investments are not always the star performers, but the company maintains a competitive edge in the mutual fund industry by making maximum use of its human resources. Nita Kincaid oversees the company's 1000 telephone representatives, who are rigorously trained in knowledge of the company's products and in telephone courtesy. Kincaid herself monitors the master console of incoming calls to find out how many customers are calling, how many are on hold, and how long they wait. Her goal is to have each call answered within 15 seconds.

ments typically play a major role in designing the various elements in the HRM process and in supporting their use by line managers. Nevertheless, line managers ultimately are responsible for the effective utilization of human resources within their units and, thus, carry out many aspects of the HRM process, particularly as they relate to implementing strategic plans.

The Strategic Importance of HRM

Understanding the strategic potential of human resource management in organizations is a relatively recent phenomenon. In fact, the role of such management in organizations, as it is known today, has evolved through three main stages.[6] From early in this century until the mid-1960s, HRM activities comprised a *file maintenance* stage, in which much of the emphasis was on screening applicants, orienting new employees, recording employee-related data for personnel purposes, and planning company social functions (such as the company picnic).

The second stage, *government accountability*, began with the passage of the Civil Rights Act of 1964 (which forbids employment discrimination based on race, color, religion, sex, or national origin) and continued as additional laws, court rulings, and federal regulatory guidelines increasingly impacted various aspects of employment, such as hiring and promotion decisions, pension plans, and health and safety issues. (We mention several of these laws throughout this chapter.) Of course, some laws, particularly those governing relations with unions, existed before 1964; but the mid-1960s ushered in an era of accelerated governmental regulation of employment issues. As organizations attempted to gain greater control over activities that could result in legal difficulties and large financial settlements, the HRM function gained in importance. Indicative of the expense that can be involved, under a 1973 consent decree (a court-sanctioned agreement in which the accused party does not admit wrongdoing but agrees to discontinue a practice), AT&T agreed to raise the starting pay of women promoted to managerial positions so that their pay levels would be equal to those of similarly promoted men, at a cost of more than $30 million.

The third stage, which began in the late 1970s and early 1980s, can be termed the *competitive advantage* stage. In this stage, human resource management is increasingly viewed as important for both strategy formulation and implementation (see Chapter 6). Thus, under some circumstances, human resources can comprise a source of distinct competence that forms a basis for strategy formulation. For example, 3M's noted scientists enable the company to pursue a differentiation strategy based on innovative products. Under other circumstances, HRM activities may be used to support strategy implementation.[7] For instance, at Honda of America's Marysville, Ohio, plant, an emphasis on differentiation through quality is supported by such HRM activities as training programs, developmental performance appraisal processes, and promises of job security.[8] Human resource management often is an important ingredient in the success of such strategy-related activities as downsizing, mergers, and acquisitions (see Chapters 6 and 10). At the competitive advantage stage, then, human resources are considered explicitly in conjunction with strategic management, particularly through the mechanism of human resource planning.[9]

Human resource planning
The process of determining future human resource needs relative to an organization's strategic plan and devising steps necessary to meet those needs

HUMAN RESOURCE PLANNING

Human resource planning is the process of determining future human resource needs relative to an organization's strategic plan and devising steps necessary to meet those needs.[10] In planning human resource needs, human resource professionals and line managers consider both demand and supply issues, as well as potential steps for addressing any imbalances. Such planning often relies on job analysis as a means of understanding the nature of jobs under consideration.

Job Analysis

Job analysis is the systematic collection and recording of information concerning the purpose of a job, its major duties, the conditions under which it is performed, the contacts with others that performance of the job requires, and the knowledge, skills, and abilities needed for performing the job effectively. Job analysis information can be collected in a variety of ways, including observing individuals doing their jobs, conducting interviews with individuals and their superiors, having individuals keep diaries of job-related activities, and/or distributing questionnaires to be completed by job incumbents and their supervisors.[11]

The results of job analysis often are used to develop job descriptions. A **job description** is a statement of the duties, working conditions, and other significant requirements associated with a particular job. Job descriptions frequently are combined with job specifications (see Table 12-1). A **job specification** is a statement of the skills, abilities, education, and previous work experience that are required to perform a particular job. Formats for job descriptions and job

Job analysis The systematic collection and recording of information concerning the purpose of a job, its major duties, the conditions under which it is performed, the contacts with others that performance of the job requires, and the knowledge, skills, and abilities needed for performing the job effectively

Job description A statement of the duties, working conditions, and other significant requirements associated with a particular job

Job specification A statement of the skills, abilities, education, and previous work experience that are required to perform a particular job

Table 12-1   Sample Job Description and Job Specification

The Port Authority of New York and New Jersey
Data Control Clerk (1127)

Under immediate supervision receives and reviews input and output data for recurring computer reports and records. Receives detailed instructions on assignments which are not routine. Work is checked through standard controls.

DUTIES
Job Description

Operates data processing equipment such as Sorters (IBM 083), Bursters (Std Register and Moore), decollators (Std Register), Communications Terminal (IBM 3775), and interactive operation of IBM 327X family of terminals to process accounting, personnel, and other statistical reports.

Feeds and tends machine according to standard instructions.

Makes minor operating adjustments to equipment.

Submits data with necessary documentation for computer processing.

Reviews output data and corrects problems causing incorrect output.

Revises and maintains lists, control records, and source data necessary to produce reports.

Distributes output reports by predetermined instructions.

Operates magnetic-tape cleaning and testing equipment.

Corrects and/or adjusts files via use of time-sharing terminals.

QUALIFICATIONS
Job Specification

Six months' experience in operating data-processing equipment.

Ability to reconcile differences and errors in computer data.

Source: Reprinted from David J. Rachman, Michael H. Mescon, Courtland L. Bovée, and John V. Thill, *Business Today,* 6th ed., McGraw-Hill, New York, 1990, p. 244.

specifications tend to vary with the organization, but the information typically is used extensively for activities that require a solid understanding of a job and the qualifications necessary for performing it. Such activities include human resource planning, recruitment, selection, and performance appraisal.[12]

Demand for Human Resources

A main aspect of human resource planning is assessing the demand for human resources. Such an assessment involves considering the major forces that affect the demand and using basic forecasting aids to predict it.

Major Forces. One major force affecting the demand for human resources is an organization's *environment*, including factors in both the general environment, or mega-environment, and the task environment (see Chapter 3). For example, an aspect of the general environment, such as the economy, can alter demand for a product or service and, thus, affect the need for certain types of employees. In Chapter 3, we discuss in greater depth the various environmental forces that influence organizations.

In addition to environmental factors, *changing organizational requirements*, such as alterations in the strategic plan, also can influence the demand for human resources. Similarly, internal *work-force changes*, such as retirements, resignations, terminations, deaths, and leaves of absence, frequently cause major shifts in the need for human resources.

Forecasting Demand. Several basic techniques (see Chapter 9) are used to forecast human resource demand in organizations.[13] Judgmental forecasting is mainly based on the views of individuals thought to be knowledgeable, particularly line managers, who often are in a good position to make expert estimates about future needs for various types of workers. For example, at Flour-Daniel, one of the largest construction companies in the United States, organization members with relevant technical skills often help estimate the human resource needs for potential construction projects. Quantitative forecasting, which relies on numerical data and mathematical models, is another approach that is frequently used to forecast human resource needs. Finally, technological, or qualitative, forecasting, which is aimed mainly at predicting long-term trends in technology and other important aspects of the environment (see, e.g., the Delphi method described in Chapter 9), can also help predict future demand.

In one recent study, almost 60 percent of the responding major business organizations reported that they attempt to forecast human resource demand. Of those, more than one-half develop both short-term (covering about 1 year) and long-term (covering about 5 years) forecasts.[14]

Supply of Human Resources

Demand is only one side of the equation governing whether an organization will have sufficient human resources to operate effectively. In assessing the other side, supply, human resource professionals and managers consider both internal and external labor supplies.

Internal Labor Supply. One prime supply source is the pool of current employees who can be transferred or promoted to help meet demands for human re-

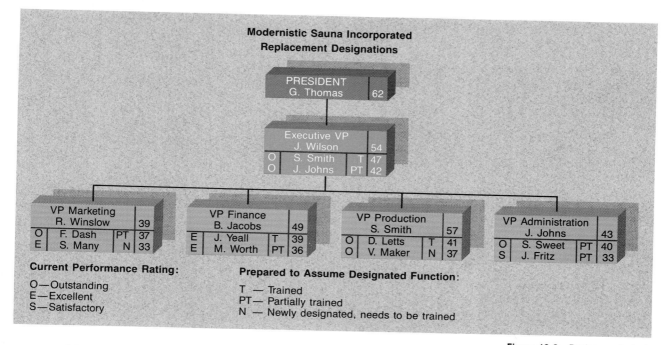

Current Performance Rating:

O—Outstanding
E—Excellent
S—Satisfactory

Prepared to Assume Designated Function:

T — Trained
PT— Partially trained
N — Newly designated, needs to be trained

Figure 12-2 Replacement chart for Modernistic Sauna, Inc.

sources. Major means of assessing the internal labor supply include skills inventories, replacement planning, and succession planning.[15]

A **skills inventory** is a data bank (usually computerized) containing basic information about each employee that can be used to assess the likely availability of individuals for meeting current and future human resource needs. A skills inventory typically contains information regarding each employee's performance, knowledge, skills, experience, interests, and relevant personal characteristics.

Replacement planning is a means of identifying potential candidates to fill specific managerial positions through the use of replacement charts. A **replacement chart** is a partial organization chart showing the major managerial positions in an organization, current incumbents, potential replacements for each position (usually including current performance rating and an assessment of each individual's preparedness to assume the particular position), and the age of each person on the chart (see Figure 12-2). With replacement charts, age is used to track possible retirements, but it is not considered in determining promotions. On the contrary, managers must be careful not to discriminate against older workers in making such choices. The *Age Discrimination in Employment Act* of 1967, as amended in 1978 and 1986, prohibits discrimination against employees and job applicants who are more than 40 years old. The law covers promotion, as well as hiring and termination decisions. Under one provision of the law, with few exceptions, organizations cannot force employees to retire because of age. Exceptions include law enforcement officers and firefighters.[16]

While replacement planning focuses on specific candidates who could fill designated managerial positions, *succession planning* is a means of identifying individuals with high potential and ensuring that they receive appropriate training and job assignments aimed at their long-run growth and development. The purpose of succession planning is to ensure that the organization has a well-qualified pool of individuals from which to draw middle and top managers in the future.

Skills inventory A data bank (usually computerized) containing basic information about each employee that can be used to assess the likely availability of individuals for meeting current and future human resource needs

Replacement chart A partial organization chart showing the major managerial positions in an organization, current incumbents, potential replacements for each position, and the age of each person on the chart

External Labor Supply. Some reliance on the external labor supply usually is necessary because of organizational expansion and/or employee attrition. Periodic estimates of labor supplies in a variety of categories are made by a number of government agencies, including the Bureau of Labor Statistics of the U.S. Department of Labor, the Engineering Manpower Commission, and the Public Health Service of the Department of Health and Human Services. Industry and human resource associations also often can provide helpful information to supplement the knowledge of line managers in specialized areas. In addition, human resource professionals, particularly those heavily engaged in recruitment and selection, often are knowledgeable about supply trends in given areas.[17]

Reconciling Demand and Supply

After estimates are made of the demand and potential supplies of human resources, steps are often necessary to balance the two.[18] If estimates show that the internal supply of employees exceeds the number necessary, then plans must be made to reduce the number of employees. Often, small reductions can be made through employee resignations and retirements. When more major reductions are needed, organizations sometimes offer early retirement to certain categories of employees with a significant number of years of service. In other cases, layoffs may be necessary. On the other hand, if an increase in the number of employees is necessary, then plans must be made for promotions and transfers of current employees, when desirable, as well as for hiring new employees.

Affirmative action Any special activity undertaken by employers to increase equal employment opportunities for groups protected by federal equal employment opportunity laws and related regulations

Affirmative Action Issues. One important aspect of reconciling supply and demand is considering the implications for **affirmative action,** any special activity undertaken by employers to increase equal employment opportunities for groups protected by federal equal employment opportunity laws and related regulations. As mentioned earlier, Title VII of the Civil Rights Act of 1964 (as amended by the Equal Employment Opportunity Act of 1972) forbids employment discrimination on the basis of race, color, religion, sex, or national origin.[19] Groups covered by Title VII and related laws and regulations are often referred to as "protected groups."

Affirmative action plan A written, systematic plan that specifies goals and timetables for hiring, training, promoting, and retaining groups protected by federal equal employment laws and related regulations

Affirmative action is important because organizations often have patterns of employment in which protected groups are underrepresented in certain areas, such as management, relative to the number of group members who have appropriate credentials in the marketplace. As a result, an organization may adopt an **affirmative action plan,** a written, systematic plan that specifies goals and timetables for hiring, training, promoting, and retaining groups protected by federal equal employment laws and related regulations.[20] Such plans are required by federal regulations for organizations with federal contracts greater than $50,000 and with 50 or more employees. The plans, which must be filed with the Office of Federal Contract Compliance Programs (Department of Labor), must include provisions for hiring the disabled (as stipulated by the Rehabilitation Act of 1973). Courts sometimes require that organizations formulate affirmative action plans because of evidence of past discriminatory practices. Many organizations, though, establish affirmative action programs on a voluntary basis.[21]

While courts generally have held that employers may establish such voluntary programs, the programs must balance efforts to assist women and minorities against the rights of others who may be competing for the same jobs. For example, courts generally have been unwilling to approve plans that cause individuals to lose their jobs in order to make room for protected groups, but they

With millions of mothers of preschoolers working outside the home and with dual career families increasing every year, it did not take much genius to forecast the demand for high-quality child care. Many nanny training centers have opened around the country to take advantage of this demand. These nannies are in training at a center in Claremont, California.

have allowed more limited burdens, such as postponements of promotions.[22] Affirmative action programs continue to be challenged in the courts by individuals and groups who do not fit into the protected category and who charge reverse discrimination.

Population Trends. Demographic shifts also are causing organizations to place emphasis on hiring women and minorities. Bureau of Labor Statistics projections indicate that annual work-force growth, which was about 2 percent from 1976 to 1988, has slowed to only 1.2 percent since 1988 and will continue at the lower rate at least until the year 2000. Part of the reason is that most of the baby-boomers wishing to work have already been absorbed into the work force, and there is no similar bulge of workers behind them. One implication, according to the bureau's figures, is that, out of necessity, women will constitute about 47 percent of the work force and minorities and immigrants about 26 percent by the year 2000. In preparation, a number of companies are placing new emphasis on "managing diversity." For example, at a Digital Equipment Corporation factory in Boston that makes computer keyboards, the 350 employees represent 44 countries. Because of the 19 different languages spoken, written plant announcements are printed in English, Chinese, French, Spanish, Portuguese, Vietnamese, and Haitian Creole.[23] Some organizations are filling vacancies with part-time workers, many of whom are senior citizens who have retired from full-time jobs. For example, the Travelers Corporation, an insurance company based in Hartford, Connecticut, runs a job bank for area retirees in order to have workers available for part-time and temporary clerical and administrative jobs.[24] Diversity issues and other considerations that grow out of human resource planning then become the basis for staffing efforts.

STAFFING

Staffing is the set of activities aimed at attracting and selecting individuals for positions in a way that will facilitate the achievement of organizational goals.

Staffing The set of activities aimed at attracting and selecting individuals for positions in a way that will facilitate the achievement of organizational goals

Given the slower growth of the work force, such activities are taking on new meaning as organizations begin to experience greater difficulty in attracting and retaining needed human resources. With relatively fewer workers entering the labor force, recruitment can be more challenging, particularly in regard to entry-level workers.

Recruitment

Recruitment The process of finding and attempting to attract job candidates who are capable of effectively filling job vacancies

Recruitment is the process of finding and attempting to attract job candidates who are capable of effectively filling job vacancies.[25] Job descriptions and job specifications, both mentioned earlier, are important in the recruiting process because they specify the nature of the job and the qualifications required of serious job candidates. Recruiting can be conducted both internally and externally.

Internal Recruitment. Most vacant positions in organizations are filled through internal recruitment, the process of finding potential *internal* candidates and encouraging them to apply for and/or be willing to accept organizational jobs that are open.[26] CARE, Inc., for example, has a policy of filling job vacancies from within and conducts recruiting through external sources only when a job cannot be filled internally.

Job posting A practice whereby information about job vacancies is placed in conspicuous places in an organization, such as on bulletin boards or in organizational newsletters

One major method of recruiting internally is **job posting,** a practice whereby information about job vacancies is placed in conspicuous places in an organization, such as on bulletin boards or in organizational newsletters. The advantages and disadvantages of internal recruitment are summarized in Table 12-2.[27] At CARE, Inc., for instance, all nonunion jobs are posted for at least 15 working days, while union jobs are posted for at least 3 working days, in conformance with union contracts. Skills inventories and replacement charts, mentioned earlier, also are means used to locate potential candidates for internal recruiting.

External Recruitment. For the most part, organizations recruit from the outside only when there are no suitable internal candidates for particular positions.[28] External recruitment is the process of finding potential *external* candidates and encouraging them to apply for and/or be willing to accept organizational jobs that are open. The advantages and disadvantages of external recruitment are listed in Table 12-2.

A wide variety of sources exist for obtaining external job candidates. Advertising is generally the most heavily used recruiting source. Early research indicated that individuals who were recruited informally (such as through referrals by friends, relatives, or employees) were likely to remain with the organization longer, be absent less, and achieve greater productivity than individuals recruited in more formal ways (such as through newspaper advertisements, college recruiting programs, and employment agencies). More recent data suggest that such generalizations may be unwarranted.[29] Rather than focusing on a particular recruitment source per se, organizations may find that it is better to concentrate first on the types of qualifications that are required and then to think of the best way to locate individuals who have those qualifications.[30]

One major issue related to external recruiting is the tendency of recruiters and managers to provide candidates with an overly positive view of the organization in order to attract new employees. Unfortunately, this strategy can backfire, since an individual who accepts a position on such terms may become

Table 12-2   Advantages and Disadvantages of Internal and External Recruitment

Advantages	Disadvantages
INTERNAL RECRUITMENT	
1. Candidates are already oriented to the organization.	1. There may be fewer new ideas.
2. Reliable information is available about candidates.	2. Unsuccessful contenders may become upset.
3. Recruitment costs are lower.	3. Selection is more susceptible to office politics.
4. Internal morale is increased due to upward mobility opportunities.	4. Expensive training may be necessary.
5. Good performance is rewarded.	5. Candidates' current work may be disrupted.
EXTERNAL RECRUITMENT	
1. Candidates are a potential source of new ideas.	1. The probability of mistake is higher because of less reliable information.
2. Candidates may have broader experience.	2. Potential internal candidates may be resentful.
3. Candidates may be familiar with competitors.	3. The new employee may have a slower start because of the need for orientation to the organization.
4. Candidates may have new specialties.	4. The recruitment process may be expensive.

dissatisfied and leave when the position fails to meet his or her inflated expectations. An alternative approach is the **realistic job preview,** a technique used during the recruiting process in which the job candidate is presented with a balanced view of both the positive and the negative aspects of the job and the organization.[31] Studies suggest that even though realistic job previews may somewhat reduce the number of candidates interested in a position, such previews are likely to have a positive effect on the job satisfaction, performance, and length of employment of those ultimately hired.[32] For example, Citizens Bank of Maryland has experienced lower turnover among tellers and customer service representatives partially because of instituting a video preview that frankly describes the job (explaining, e.g., that tellers spend considerable periods of time on their feet).[33] Recruiting, though, is only one part of the staffing process. Decisions must also be made about the candidates to whom job offers will be extended.

Realistic job preview A technique used during the recruiting process in which the job candidate is presented with a balanced view of both the positive and the negative aspects of the job and the organization

Selection

Selection is the process of determining which job candidates best suit organizational needs.[34] During the process of selection, managers must determine the extent to which job candidates have the skills, abilities, and knowledge required to perform effectively in the positions for which they are being considered. To help make such judgments, managers and human resource professionals use various selection methods, such as interviews and tests. Before discussing more specifically the most commonly used selection methods, we examine an important concept underlying their use, validity.

Selection The process of determining which job candidates best suit organizational needs

Validity. In order to make adequate assessments of candidates, selection methods must have validity. **Validity** is the degree to which a measure actually assesses the attribute that it is designed to measure. As applied to selection, validity addresses how well a selection device (such as a test) actually predicts a

Validity The degree to which a measure actually assesses the attribute that it is designed to measure

candidate's future job performance.[35] Although employers obviously want to use selection methods that have high validity, they sometimes use devices that they assume are good predictors without actually investigating them properly. For example, an estimated 2000 to 2500 U.S. organizations use graphology (the analysis of handwriting to infer characteristics about an individual) as part of their selection process, even though considerable data suggest that its ability to predict job candidate performance is dubious.[36]

Organizations often conduct studies to determine the validity of selection methods, particularly if the methods have adverse impact on groups protected by equal employment opportunity laws and regulations. A selection method generally is considered to have **adverse impact** when the job selection rate for a protected group is less than 80 percent of the rate for the majority group. For example, requiring a high school diploma for entry-level positions might have adverse impact because the percentage of minority group members with high school diplomas tends to be smaller than that of majority group members. Under such conditions, an organization can continue to use the selection method if it can demonstrate that the method is a valid predictor of job performance and that there is no other approach that would have similar validity without adverse impact. Still, from a practical point of view, most organizations attempt to use selection devices that not only are valid but also do not have adverse impact. To facilitate identifying such devices, selection experts have conducted considerable research on various methods that can be used in the selection process.[37]

Adverse impact   The effect produced when a job selection rate for a protected group is less than 80 percent of the rate for the majority group

Major Selection Methods. More than one selection method typically is used in assessing job candidates. The most prevalent methods include the use of application blanks, selection interviews, tests, assessment centers, and reference checks.[38]

An **application blank** is a form containing a series of inquiries about such issues as an applicant's educational background, previous job experience, physical health, and other information that may be useful in assessing an individual's ability to perform a job. If you currently hold a job or have ever looked for one, chances are that you have filled out application blanks for employment. An application form serves as a prescreening device to help determine whether an applicant meets the minimum requirements of a position, and it allows preliminary comparisons with the credentials of other candidates.[39] If further consideration of an applicant is warranted, the application form typically also provides a basis for one or more interviews with the individual. Résumés furnished by job applicants also often provide useful background information.

In developing application blanks, organizations need to avoid including questions that are not valid predictors of job performance, especially if such questions tend to have adverse impact. For example, requesting information about whether a job candidate owns a car or a house tends to have an adverse impact on minority group applicants and is usually unrelated to job performance. Similarly, asking where an individual was born may reveal national origin and, again, is usually unrelated to job performance. Essentially, application blanks should require only information that is clearly job-related.[40] The same is true of interviews.

Application blank   A form containing a series of inquiries about such issues as an applicant's educational background, previous job experience, physical health, and other information that may be useful in assessing an individual's ability to perform a job

Another selection method, the **selection interview,** is a relatively formal, in-depth conversation conducted for the purpose of assessing a candidate's knowledge, skills, and abilities, as well as providing information to the candidate about the organization and potential jobs.[41] According to one recent survey of national firms, most outside job candidates who are considered seriously

Selection interview   A relatively formal, in-depth conversation conducted for the purpose of assessing a candidate's knowledge, skills, and abilities, as well as providing information to the candidate about the organization and potential jobs

Is this candidate qualified for a management position at New England Telephone? To obtain relevant information, the interviewer needs to use a semistructured interviewing approach that includes standard questions to be asked of all candidates, but also provides flexibility in probing areas that apply to a particular interviewee.

enough to warrant an interview are interviewed at least twice. Typically, one interview is conducted by a professional recruiter from the human resource department and the other by the supervisor of the unit with the open position.[42]

As one indicator of the perceived importance of the interview, 90 percent of the responding companies in one survey reported that they placed more confidence in the selection interview than in any other selection method.[43] Ironically, despite their popularity, interviews, as they are widely conducted, have relatively low validity as a selection device. A major reason for this is that many interviewers follow a format that constitutes an *unstructured interview*, for which little planning is done regarding the information to be collected and during which the interviewer asks whatever questions happen to come to mind.[44] One result of the lack of structure is that data about candidates are collected in a nonsystematic way that does not yield sufficient information with which to evaluate or compare candidates adequately.

One potential remedy is the *structured interview*, in which the interviewer has a predetermined set of questions that are asked in sequence, with virtually no deviations. The structured interview is sometimes used to advantage if a large number of candidates are to be prescreened or if interviewers are relatively untrained. While a structured interview yields more valid data than an unstructured one, a structured interview has the disadvantage of being almost mechanical and may convey disinterest to the candidate. It also does not allow the interviewer to probe interesting or unusual issues that may arise.

To overcome these disadvantages and still acquire reasonably valid data with which to make a selection decision, interviewers can use a semistructured interview. With a *semistructured interview*, the interviewer has a number of predetermined questions but also asks other questions to probe further into issues that arise that are unique to a particular candidate (such as an unexplained break in work history, unusual work experience, or the individual's particular strengths and weaknesses). A semistructured approach can also make the interview process more comfortable for the candidate and can create a better impression of the organization because the interview can be more conversational. For some hints on how to conduct a semistructured interview, see the Practically Speaking discussion, "How to Conduct an Effective Interview."

HOW TO CONDUCT AN EFFECTIVE INTERVIEW

You have a job vacancy in your unit and you need to interview several job candidates. What should you do? There are a number of steps that you can take before, during, and after the interview to increase the likelihood of obtaining information that will be useful in making your selection decision.

BEFORE THE INTERVIEW
Much of the secret of conducting an effective interview is in the preparation. The following guidelines will enhance your preparatory skills.

Determine the job requirements. Using the job description and job specifications for the job, prepare a list of characteristics that the person will need to possess in order to perform the job. For example, suppose that you are a bank manager and have a job opening for a teller. Important characteristics would include oral communication skills, a willingness to check for errors, the ability to get along with oth-

ers, and a service orientation in handling customers. Once the major characteristics are identified, you can develop an interview guide.

Prepare a written interview guide. A written guide of what you wish to cover during the interview will ensure that major points are addressed with each interviewee. You need to plan questions that assess the degree to which job candidates possess the characteristics that you have identified as necessary to do the job.

Since past performance is often a good predictor of future performance, one useful approach is to frame questions in terms of examples of what a person has done, rather than focusing on generalities or speculations about what the person will do in the future. For example, a relatively *poor* question aimed at assessing how well the individual interacts with customers might be: "How well do you handle problem customers?" For the most part, a candidate is unlikely to answer that he or she has difficulty handling problem customers, even if that is the case.

An *improved* approach is to frame questions in terms of how the individual has dealt with customers in the past. For example, you might ask, "Please describe a time when a customer paid you an especially nice compliment because of something you did; what were the circumstances?" You might follow up by asking, "Tell me about a time when you had to handle a particularly irritating customer; how did you handle the situation?" Answers to these types of specific questions can provide insight into how an individual is likely to treat customers and handle trying situations in the future. (If the individual has no job experience, questions can be adjusted accordingly—for example, " . . . a time when you had to handle a particularly irritating *person*.")

Next, prepare a step-by-step plan of how to present the position to the job candidate. Develop a similar plan for the points you wish to make about the work unit and the organization. Such plans will help you present the information in an organized fashion and will ensure that you cover all the important points you wish to make.

Employment test A means of assessing a job applicant's characteristics through paper-and-pencil responses or simulated exercises

Another selection device that may be used is an **employment test,** a means of assessing a job applicant's characteristics through paper-and-pencil responses or simulated exercises. Three major types of tests used in the selection process are ability, personality, and performance tests.[46]

Ability tests are means of measuring mainly mental (such as intelligence), mechanical, and clerical abilities or sensory capacities (such as vision and hearing). Except for the measures of sensory capacities, the tests are usually the paper-and-pencil type. The use of ability tests declined during the 1970s and early 1980s because they seemed to have adverse impact on the selection of minority candidates. Further study, though, suggests that when ability tests are carefully matched to job requirements developed through job analysis, they can not only be valid predictors of a candidate's future job performance but also have minimal adverse impact. Since ability tests generally are more valid predictors of job performance than most other available means, the use of such tests is again on the rise.[47]

Review the candidate's application and/or résumé. By reviewing the application and/or résumé of the candidate, you will be familiar with the particular experiences and accomplishments that are most relevant to the requirements of the job. Read these background materials before the interview; otherwise, you may appear (correctly so) unprepared for the interview. In addition, it is easy to miss gaps, discrepancies, and relevant experience when the background materials are reviewed quickly in front of the candidate.

DURING THE INTERVIEW

Your carefully prepared questions will help you maintain control of the dialogue during the interview. Here are some additional guidelines for actually conducting the interview.

Establish rapport. Small talk at the beginning of the interview often will help put the candidate at ease. You may be able to comment about some item on the résumé, such as a hobby that you and the candidate have in common or a place where you both have lived. Be careful, though, not to let the interview get too far off track with an extended discussion of, say, your respective golf games.

Avoid conveying the response you seek. Suppose that you are attempting to determine the candidate's ability to work with other tellers, all of whom must work within a relatively small area. You ask, "Do you think that you will be able to work well with the other tellers, especially given our space constraints?" The candidate easily replies, "Of course, no problem." A bright interviewee can quickly realize, from your question, the answer that you are seeking. A better approach would be to say something like this: "We all sometimes have unpleasant experiences with coworkers. Tell me about the most difficult time that you have ever had working with a coworker."

Listen and take notes. Be sure to do a great deal of listening. Some experts recommend that the interviewer talk 20 to 30 percent of the time and allow the interviewee to talk (the interviewer listens) 70 to 80 percent of the time. You want to learn as much as possible about the job candidate in the relatively limited time that you have available. Take a few notes to help you remember important points.

Ask only job-relevant questions. Interviewers sometimes stray into asking questions that have the potential of being discriminatory. One example is asking a female applicant what kind of work her spouse does. Such a question is discriminatory since it is seldom directed at a male candidate and is irrelevant to job requirements or the person's qualifications. The best policy is to ask only questions that are clearly and directly related to job requirements.

AFTER THE INTERVIEW

Write a short report right after the interview, scoring the candidate on the various characteristics that you determined earlier are important to functioning effectively in the job. Briefly indicate your rationale, perhaps using examples or summaries of responses. By documenting your ratings immediately after the interview, you will have good data to help you with your selection decision.[45]

Personality tests are means of measuring characteristics, such as patterns of thoughts, feelings, and behaviors, that are distinctly combined in a particular individual and influence that individual's interactions in various situations. Paper-and-pencil personality tests measure such characteristics as sociability, independence, and need for achievement. The use of personality tests for selection purposes is subject to considerable debate, because of both the difficulty of accurately measuring personality characteristics and the problems associated with matching them appropriately to job requirements. Hence they should be used with caution in selection processes.[48]

The third major type of test, *performance,* or *work sample, tests,* requires that the applicant complete some job activity under structured conditions. For example, a word-processing applicant might be asked to prepare materials on equipment that would be used on the job, while a service representative may be asked to handle a simulated situation involving a complaining customer. In this way, it is possible to make a more direct assessment of an applicant's knowledge, skills, and abilities in regard to performing the required tasks. Although they can be costly if special facilities and equipment are needed, performance tests, when devised to closely reflect important aspects of the job, tend to be valid predictors of future performance. They also tend to be less susceptible to the adverse selection problems that plague many paper-and-pencil tests.

Assessment center A controlled environment used to predict the probable managerial success of individuals mainly on the basis of evaluations of their behaviors in a variety of simulated situations

An **assessment center** is a controlled environment used to predict the probable managerial success of individuals mainly on the basis of evaluations of their behaviors in a variety of simulated situations. The situations (or exercises) are essentially performance tests that reflect the type of work done in managerial positions. For example, a common simulation in an assessment center is an in-basket exercise in which the assessee must decide how to handle a number of items, such as memos, letters, and telephone messages, while under time pressure. Other exercises frequently involve 2 or more of the assessees (usually 12 to 24) in meetings and other simulated work situations. Evaluators, called assessors, are often managers from the organization and/or psychologists who are trained to observe and record behavior for later feedback to the individual assessees. According to one estimate, assessment center programs are in operation in more than 2000 organizations, including AT&T, where the technique was originally pioneered. Research supports the validity of the assessment center method for selecting managers.[49]

Reference checks Attempts to obtain job-related information about job applicants from individuals who are in a position to be knowledgeable about the applicants' qualifications

Reference checks are attempts to obtain job-related information about job applicants from individuals who are in a position to be knowledgeable about the applicants' qualifications. Reference checks can be obtained by mail, by telephone, and in person. Such checks often are aimed at verifying information on application blanks and résumés and may also focus on collecting additional data to facilitate the selection decision. One study of selection practices in a wide range of organizations showed that reference checks were part of the selection procedures in more than 90 percent of the organizations.[50] One reason for widespread reference checks is that, according to one estimate, between 20 and 25 percent of all candidate application blanks and résumés contain at least one major fabrication.[51]

Despite the usefulness of reference checks in selection decisions, an increasing number of employers are adopting policies whereby they will verify only dates of employment of former employees when queried by prospective employers. Others are refusing to divulge any information at all to prospective employers.[52] The reason is fear of defamation suits from former employees who left the organization under less-than-pleasant circumstances and who may warrant less-than-stellar recommendations. Yet, from a legal point of view, employers are generally protected when they provide truthful, nonmalicious information, including honest opinions, about current or former employees to another employer engaging in a legitimate job search.[53] Once an individual meets the selection criteria and is ultimately hired, development and evaluation issues come into play.

DEVELOPMENT AND EVALUATION

Since individuals have tremendous growth potential, both employees and their employing organizations ultimately gain from efforts aimed at enhancing member knowledge, skills, and abilities. Major approaches to increasing the effectiveness of organization members include training and development, as well as performance appraisal.

Training and Development

Training and development is a planned effort to facilitate employee learning of job-related behaviors in order to improve employee performance.[54] Experts sometimes distinguish between the term "training"—denoting efforts to increase employee skills on present jobs—and the term "development"—referring to efforts oriented toward improvements relevant to future jobs.[55] In practice, though, the distinction often is blurred (mainly because upgrading skills in present jobs usually improves performance in future jobs). Accordingly, we adopt the increasingly common practice of using both terms interchangeably.[56] According to one estimate, U.S. businesses spend close to $60 billion annually on internally run training and education, a figure comparable to the yearly operating costs of all the 4-year colleges and universities in the United States.[57]

Phases of the Training Process. Training efforts generally encompass three main phases.[58] The *assessment phase* involves identifying training needs, setting training objectives, and developing criteria against which to evaluate the results of the training program. Within the assessment phase, training requirements are determined by conducting a needs analysis. A **needs analysis** is an assessment of an organization's training needs that is developed by considering overall organizational requirements, tasks (identified through job analysis) associated with jobs for which training is needed, and the degree to which individuals are able to perform those tasks effectively.[59] This phase, as well as the other two phases, typically involves human resource professionals and managers, and outside consultants are sometimes brought in to help with various aspects.

The second phase of training, the *training design and implementation phase*, involves determining training methods, developing training materials, and actually conducting the training. Within this phase there are a number of training methods that can be used, which fall into three main categories.[60] *Information presentation methods* entail teaching facts, skills, attitudes, or concepts without expecting trainees to put what they are learning into practice during the training. Examples are lectures, reading lists, video tapes, and most computerized instruction. *Simulation training methods* involve providing artificial situations that offer trainees a means of practicing their learning during the training. Examples include case analysis, role plays (in which trainees act out the roles of individuals in a situation that is described), and in-basket exercises (described earlier). *On-the-job training (OJT) methods* focus on having the trainee learn while actually performing a job, usually with the help of a knowledgeable trainer. Examples include job rotation (see Chapter 10), vestibule training (in which the trainee learns in a separate area that is set up to approximate as closely as possible the actual job situation), and on-the-job coaching (in which the trainee performs the job under the direct guidance of a trainer).

The third phase of the training process, the *evaluation phase*, entails assessing the results of the training against the criteria developed during the assessment phase. Major ways to evaluate training include measuring participants' reactions to the training to determine how useful they thought it was, assessing actual learning (perhaps through tests before and after the training), determining the extent of behavioral change (possibly by having the supervisor or subordinates of a trainee assess changes in the individual's behavior), and measuring actual results on the job (such as increased output).[61]

Types of Training Programs. From a content point of view, the types of training

---

Training and development A planned effort to facilitate employee learning of job-related behaviors in order to improve employee performance

Needs analysis An assessment of an organization's training needs that is developed by considering overall organizational requirements, tasks associated with jobs for which training is needed, and the degree to which individuals are able to perform those tasks effectively

programs that are most common in organizations are orientation training, technical skill training, and management development training.[62] *Orientation training* usually is a formal program designed to provide new employees with information about the company and their jobs. *Technical skill training* is oriented toward providing specialized knowledge and developing facility in the use of methods, processes, and techniques associated with a particular discipline or trade. Training that helps individuals learn various aspects of their jobs falls into the category of technical skill training. *Management development programs* focus on developing managerial skills for use at the supervisory, managerial, and executive levels (see Chapter 1). Training may be conducted internally, by members of the organization or by outside consultants brought in for that purpose, or externally, by various independent training agencies. Training can have a positive impact on both productivity and employee morale (see the following Case in Point discussion).

CASE IN POINT: Training Makes a Difference at First Service Bank

Service is an important factor in the success of First Service Bank, a small thrift institution headquartered in Leominster, Massachusetts. Yet the bank found its competitive position threatened by its area's low unemployment rate, which made it difficult for the bank to adequately staff its 13 branches located throughout the state's north-central region. With many job alternatives in the area, bank tellers were leaving faster than new applicants could be recruited. In assessing the situation, bank managers and human resource professionals decided that raising pay was not the only answer, although the pay scale was adjusted upward somewhat. Instead, they believed that growth opportunities were also likely to be important to the type of employee that the bank hoped to attract and retain. Thus an extensive training program was devised.

Job analysis revealed that the teller position involved a broader range of skills and abilities than had previously been required. Now employees needed to perform such expanded duties as entering information into the bank data base and retrieving it when necessary for customers; explaining numerous products and services to customers; recognizing opportunities to sell additional products and services; and handling diverse transactions such as commercial checking accounts and credit card payments. Thus, as a first step, the bank changed the title of the teller job to bank service representative (BSR) to reflect more adequately the major changes that had taken place in job duties.

On the basis of needs analysis, a trilevel training and certification program—BSR I, BSR II, and BSR III—was then developed. Most of the training was designed internally and for the most part currently is delivered by in-house staff members. Methods include the use of workbooks, video tapes, and participatory exercises, such as role playing. Seminars average 2 to 4 hours per week and extend over a 3- to 6-month period.

For new hires, the BSR I course begins with a 7-day orientation that includes an overview of various bank policies, as well as training in specific procedures. After subsequent on-the-job training, individuals are encouraged to sign up for other sessions that cover a variety of topics, including government regulations, insurance issues, and effective presentation skills. A series of comprehensive proficiency skills tests must be passed before certification at the BSR I level.

Courses for BSR II certification include skill building related to product knowledge, sales referral, security, and telephone etiquette, as well as a stress reduction session led by a licensed psychologist. Individuals who pass the various proficiency exams and become certified at the BSR II level can then move to BSR III. The third-level course includes more advanced topics, as well as train-the-trainer seminars in which BSRs learn to train new hires.

Although all BSRs must complete the three levels of training, they are eligible for raises and/or promotions at the various levels only if they receive a minimum score of 85 percent on the various exams. Also considered are maintenance of on-the-job standards for quality (such as degree of overages and shortages), absenteeism, and punctuality. Through a sales commission and bonus system, the BSRs receive cash, trips, and tickets to cultural events for meeting certain sales goals. Individuals who aspire to be managers can enroll in additional courses aimed at management development. Within 1 year of the training program's institution, productivity rose by more than 25 percent, turnover declined by 50 percent, and assets of the bank increased by more than 70 percent. Furthermore, openings were attracting a larger pool of better-qualified candidates than before.[63] ▬▬

The BSR training system at First Service Bank also built in a potential career progression, another aspect of development. Because of the particular relevance of career development to most readers of this book, we include an expanded section on the topic in the Appendix. The information it contains may be helpful to you in planning your own career. Another aspect of your work life will undoubtedly include being involved in performance appraisal.

Performance Appraisal

Performance appraisal is the process of defining expectations for employee performance; measuring, evaluating, and recording employee performance relative to those expectations; and providing feedback to the employee.[64] While a major purpose of performance appraisal is to influence, in a positive way, employee performance and development, the process also is used for a variety of other organizational purposes, such as determining merit pay increases, planning future performance goals, determining training and development needs, and assessing the promotional potential of employees.[65] Thus performance appraisal plays several important roles in organizations. In doing so, it poses some special challenges for managers.

Performance appraisal The process of defining expectations for employee performance; measuring, evaluating, and recording employee performance relative to those expectations; and providing feedback to the employee

Major Methods for Rating Performance. Because performance is multidimensional, performance appraisal methods must consider various aspects of a job. Although there are a number of different ways to appraise jobs, the most widely used approaches focus on employee behavior (behavior-oriented) or performance results (results-oriented).[66]

Within the behavior-oriented category, two major assessment means are graphic rating scales and behaviorally anchored rating scales. **Graphic rating scales** list a number of rating factors, including general behaviors and characteristics (such as attendance, appearance, dependability, quality of work, quantity of work, and relationships with people) on which an employee is rated by the supervisor. (See Figure 12-3 for an example of a graphic rating scale.) Supervisors rate individuals on each factor, using a scale that typically has about five gradations (e.g., unsatisfactory, conditional, satisfactory, above satisfactory, and outstanding). Because the rating factors tend to be fairly general, they are relatively flexible and can be used to evaluate individuals in a number of different jobs. On the other hand, the general nature of graphic rating scales makes

Graphic rating scales Scales that list a number of rating factors, including general behaviors and characteristics, on which an employee is rated by the supervisor

Rating Factors	LEVEL OF PERFORMANCE				
	Unsatisfactory	Conditional	Satisfactory	Above Satisfactory	Outstanding
ATTENDANCE					
APPEARANCE					
DEPENDABILITY					
QUALITY OF WORK					
QUANTITY OF WORK					
RELATIONSHIP WITH PEOPLE					
JOB KNOWLEDGE					

Figure 12-3 A portion of a graphic rating scale. (Reprinted from Wayne F. Cascio, *Managing Human Resources*, 2d ed., McGraw-Hill, New York, 1989, p. 326.)

Behaviorally anchored rating scales (BARS) Scales that contain sets of specific behaviors that represent gradations of performance used as common reference points (or anchors) for rating employees on various job dimensions

them somewhat susceptible to inconsistent and inaccurate ratings of employees, mainly because considerable interpretation is needed to apply them to specific jobs (e.g., what does "quality" mean in different jobs?).[67]

In an effort to reduce the subjective interpretation inherent in graphic rating scales, performance appraisal experts have developed behaviorally anchored rating scales. **Behaviorally anchored rating scales (BARS)** contain sets of specific behaviors that represent gradations of performance used as common reference points (or anchors) for rating employees on various job dimensions. An example of one scale, or set of specific behaviors, from a BARS series developed to assess various aspects of police patrol officer performance is shown in Figure 12-4. Here, a police patrol officer being rated can be allocated points ranging from 1 through 9 for job knowledge, depending upon where the supervisor places the individual relative to the anchors. Of course, the officer would be rated on other BARS dimensions as well, such as judgment, use of equipment, relations with the public, oral and written communication, and dependability.[68] Developing BARS, which are based on extensive job analysis and the collection of critical incidents (examples of very good and very bad performance) for a particular job, is expensive and time-consuming. As a result, BARS tend to be used mainly in situations in which relatively large numbers of individuals perform similar jobs. For example, a BARS approach was used successfully to develop a performance appraisal system for reporters, copy editors, and supervising editors at the *Times-Union* and the *Democrat and Chronicle*, two metropolitan newspapers in Rochester, New York, that are owned by the Gannett Company, Inc.[69]

As an alternative, a widely used results-oriented rating method is *management by objectives* (MBO), a process through which specific goals are set collaboratively for the organization as a whole, various subunits, and each individual member (see Chapter 5). With MBO, individuals are evaluated, usually annually (although more frequent discussions of progress often are held), on the basis of how well they have achieved the results specified by the goals. MBO, or goal setting, is particularly applicable to nonroutine jobs, such as those of managers. For example, the various projects undertaken by CARE lend themselves to the MBO approach, which is used extensively by the agency.

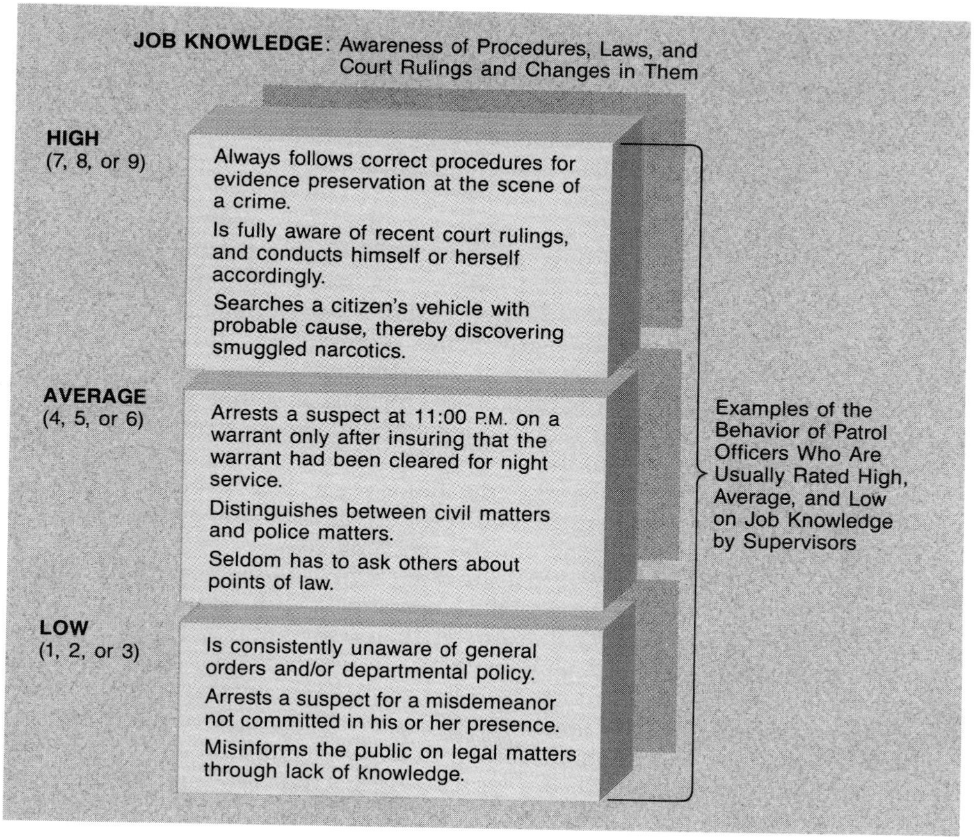

JOB KNOWLEDGE: Awareness of Procedures, Laws, and Court Rulings and Changes in Them

HIGH (7, 8, or 9)

Always follows correct procedures for evidence preservation at the scene of a crime.

Is fully aware of recent court rulings, and conducts himself or herself accordingly.

Searches a citizen's vehicle with probable cause, thereby discovering smuggled narcotics.

AVERAGE (4, 5, or 6)

Arrests a suspect at 11:00 P.M. on a warrant only after insuring that the warrant had been cleared for night service.

Distinguishes between civil matters and police matters.

Seldom has to ask others about points of law.

LOW (1, 2, or 3)

Is consistently unaware of general orders and/or departmental policy.

Arrests a suspect for a misdemeanor not committed in his or her presence.

Misinforms the public on legal matters through lack of knowledge.

Examples of the Behavior of Patrol Officers Who Are Usually Rated High, Average, and Low on Job Knowledge by Supervisors

Figure 12-4 A behaviorally anchored rating scale for assessing the job knowledge of police patrol officers. (Reprinted from Wayne F. Cascio, *Managing Human Resources*, 2d ed., McGraw-Hill, New York, 1989, p. 327.)

Common Rating Errors. The performance appraisal process is complicated by the fact that raters' memories are somewhat fallible and raters are susceptible to biases that produce rating errors.[70] One such bias is the *halo effect*, the tendency to use a general impression based on one or a few characteristics of an individual in order to judge other characteristics of that same individual (see Chapter 15). Another bias is the *contrast error*, the tendency to compare subordinates with one another rather than with a performance standard. Thus, when compared with two unsatisfactory workers, an average worker may end up being rated "outstanding." Still other biases include the *recency error*, in which supervisors assign ratings on the basis of the employee's more recent performance; the *leniency error*, in which raters tend to be unjustifiably easy in evaluating employee performance; and the *severity error*, in which raters tend to be unjustifiably harsh in evaluating employee performance. Finally, another important bias affecting performance appraisal is the *self-serving bias*, the tendency to perceive oneself as responsible for successes and others as responsible for failures (see Chapter 15). The self-serving bias helps set up a scenario in which subordinate and supervisor tend to blame one another for problems and see themselves as responsible for successes. Efforts to use rater training as a means of overcoming such biases have met with mixed success. One review of a number of studies involving rater training suggested that results may be better with simulation training methods that actively involve participants in the training process.[71]

The Performance Appraisal Interview. As might be anticipated given the self-serving bias, numerous studies support the notion that about 80 percent of the individuals who enter a performance appraisal interview believe that they have been performing at an above-average level.[72] While it is indeed possible for all the workers in a particular unit to be above average in performance, the statistical reality, at least across a large organization, is that no more than 50 percent of the individuals can be above-average performers in an organization. Hence the performance appraisal interview is a challenging situation for supervisors to handle.

In order to perform effectively as raters, supervisors must essentially play three different, and somewhat incompatible, roles during the performance appraisal interview: leader, coach, and judge.[73] As leader, the rater must assign work duties; work with the subordinate to establish performance standards, or expectations, about the level of performance required; and furnish resources, such as additional personnel, equipment, time, materials, and space required to do the job. As coach, the rater is responsible for ensuring that the individual is trained adequately to reach the required level of performance and must provide support and encouragement for the subordinate's efforts. Yet, as judge, the rater must evaluate the accomplishments of the employee as objectively as possible, a stance that makes it somewhat difficult to build simultaneously the trust and openness necessary, in particular, for the coaching role.

Given this context, it is not surprising that recent interviews with 60 managers indicate that they are generally more concerned with using the appraisal process to motivate and retain subordinates than with using it to assess performance accurately.[74] Yet the general tendency to inflate ratings not only gives subordinates false feedback but can lead to serious lawsuits should the managers subsequently need to terminate employees who have received performance appraisals indicating that their performance is satisfactory or better.[75] Performance appraisals often have a bearing on pay raises received through the organization's compensation system.

COMPENSATION

Compensation Wages paid directly for time worked, as well as more indirect benefits that employees receive as part of their employment relationship with an organization

Benefits Forms of compensation beyond wages for time worked, including various protection plans, services, pay for time not worked, and income supplements

Compensation consists of wages paid directly for time worked, as well as more indirect benefits that employees receive as part of their employment relationship with an organization.[76] Wages paid for time worked typically are payments made in cashable form that reflect direct work-related remuneration such as base pay, merit increases, or bonuses. **Benefits,** on the other hand, are forms of compensation beyond wages for time worked, including various protection plans (such as health insurance or life insurance), services (such as an organizational cafeteria or drug counseling), pay for time not worked (such as vacations or sick leave) and income supplements (such as stock ownership plans). Benefits are considered a more indirect form of compensation because they generally are not as closely tied to job and performance issues as are other forms of remuneration.

Types of Equity

Most organizations attempt to develop compensation systems that carefully consider issues of equity, or fairness. Equity issues are important because, as equity theory points out (see Chapter 13), individuals tend to compare their own relative inputs and outcomes with those of others in assessing the degree of equitable treatment that they receive. In practice, though, developing fair compensa-

Saturn Corp., a division of GM, has created a partnership of management and labor based on equity. All major decisions must be reached by consensus between management and labor, all employees are salaried, and all eat in the same cafeterias— from the president (shown here in the black sweater) on down.

tion systems is quite challenging, primarily because, with compensation, there are three major types of equity involved.[77] *External equity* is the extent to which pay rates for particular jobs correspond to rates paid for similar jobs in the external job market. *Internal equity* is the degree to which pay rates for various jobs inside the organization reflect the relative worth of those jobs. *Individual equity* is the extent to which pay rates allocated to specific individuals within the organization reflect variations in individual merit. How, then, are these three types of equity incorporated into compensation systems?

Designing the Pay Structure

Because of the complexity involved, many organizations, particularly large ones, have compensation specialists in the human resource department who oversee the compensation system development process. At the foundation of most major compensation systems is a process called job evaluation. **Job evaluation** is a systematic process of establishing the relative worth of jobs within a single organization in order to determine equitable pay differentials among jobs. Job evaluations typically rely on job analysis and resulting job descriptions as the basis for the specific job information used to compare jobs.

Although there are a number of different approaches to job evaluation, the point factor method is the most popular method and the one used by CARE in designing its new compensation system. The **point factor method** is a job evaluation approach in which points are assigned to jobs on the basis of the degree to which the jobs contain selected compensable factors. *Compensable factors* are any characteristics that jobs have in common that can be used for comparing job content.

The first step of job evaluation with the point factor method is selecting the compensable factors that will be used to rate each job. The most commonly used factors include responsibility, skill required, effort required, and working conditions, although others, such as education required and experience required, also are frequently used.

The second step is developing a set of levels, or scale, within each compensable factor and assigning weighted points to each of the levels. For example, Table 12-3 shows a point factor scale for assessing the contribution of education to the relative worth of jobs in an organization. Note that education is divided

Job evaluation A systematic process of establishing the relative worth of jobs within a single organization in order to determine equitable pay differentials among jobs

Point factor method A job evaluation approach in which points are assigned to jobs on the basis of the degree to which the jobs contain selected compensable factors

Table 12-3 Point Factor Scale for Education

Education—300 Points

This factor measures the amount of formal education required to satisfactorily perform the job. Experience or knowledge received through experience is not to be considered in evaluating jobs on this scale.

POINTS		
20	Level 1	Eighth-grade education
90	Level 2	High school diploma or eighth-grade education and four years of formal apprenticeship
160	Level 3	Two-year college degree or high school diploma and three years of formal apprenticeship
230	Level 4	Four-year college degree
300	Level 5	Graduate degree

Source: Reprinted from Marc J. Wallace, Jr., and Charles H. Fay, *Compensation Theory and Practice,* 2d ed., PWS-Kent, Boston, 1988, p. 214.

into five different levels, ranging from eighth-grade education to graduate degree. Each level has been assigned points that constitute the level's weighting within the total of 300 points allocated to the education factor. For example, a job would be rated 20 points for education if the job incumbent normally needs an eighth-grade education and 300 if the incumbent needs a graduate degree to perform at a satisfactory level in the job.

Of course, the job would be rated on other compensable factors as well. For instance, in this case, education can account for a maximum of 300 points; other scales being used in this situation, but not shown in Table 12-3, might be experience, worth a maximum of 300 points; responsibility, worth up to 200 points; and physical demands and working conditions, each worth a possible 100 points. Thus, in this situation, a job could receive a maximum of 1000 points if it rated the highest number of points on each compensable factor. The maximum points for compensable factors differ, depending on how much weight top management (advised by a compensation specialist) wants to give a specific factor in evaluating all jobs.

The third step in the point factor method, then, is measuring each job on each compensable factor to obtain a total score reflecting the worth of each job. These total scores are then used to establish a wage rate for each job. As is probably obvious from the description so far, job evaluation helps establish internal equity by essentially grading the worth of each job relative to the others in the organization. How, then, does external equity figure into the pay scheme?

In order to address the external-equity issue, most organizations utilize information from pay surveys. A **pay survey** (often called a *wage-and-salary survey*) is a survey of the labor market to determine the current rates of pay for benchmark, or key, jobs. *Benchmark,* or *key, jobs* included in the survey represent a cross section of the jobs in an organization, usually reflecting a mix of scores on the compensable factors, various levels in the organization, and a sizable proportion of the organization's work force. At least 25 to 30 percent of an organization's jobs typically are designated as benchmark, or key, jobs.

Most pay surveys are conducted by mailing questionnaires or using the telephone (for relatively short surveys). Organizations may conduct their own surveys and/or use other sources, such as surveys conducted by other organizations (which are often shared with organizations that participate in the survey), by the Bureau of Labor Statistics and other government agencies, by profes-

Pay survey A survey of the labor market to determine the current rates of pay for benchmark, or key, jobs

sional groups (such as industry associations), and by private companies that specialize in compensation issues (such as Sibson and Company).

Pay survey information for benchmark jobs is matched to job evaluation points in order to develop a pay policy line (see Figure 12-5). The pay policy line forms a basis for developing the pay grades and associated minimum and maximum pay rates for each grade that make up the pay structure for the organization. Other jobs are then allocated to the pay grades on the basis of their job evaluation points. Thus organizations typically do not have a wage rate for each job; instead, jobs usually are grouped into grades, or classifications, within some type of pay structure.

For the most part, pay survey information and job evaluation points do not coincide quite as neatly as the pay structure shown in Figure 12-5 might imply. Instead, considerable judgment can be required to design a pay structure that balances the needs of internal equity (represented by job evaluation points) with those of external equity (pay survey information).

Individual equity becomes an issue when specific pay raises are allocated to individuals. Organizations vary in the criteria that they use to award pay raises within the specified pay range for a given grade. The two major determinants of pay increases within the range are seniority and/or performance. Many organizations have recently been attempting to place renewed emphasis on the notion of pay for performance by awarding pay on the basis of merit and/or offering various incentive pay programs tied to performance. Efforts also are being made in a number of organizations to foster innovation through nontraditional forms of compensation.

Promoting Innovation: Nontraditional Compensation Approaches

Organizations have been experimenting with alternatives to traditional approaches to pay that foster flexibility and innovation among employees. One

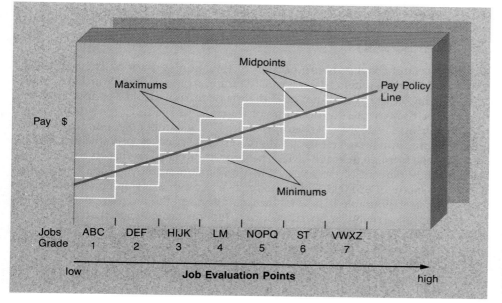

Figure 12-5 Pay structure. (Adapted from George T. Milkovich and Jerry M. Newman, *Compensation*, 3d ed., BPI/Irwin, Homewood, Ill., 1990.)

Skill-based pay A compensation system in which employees' rates of pay are based on the number of predetermined skills the employees have mastered

idea that is growing in popularity is **skill-based pay,** a compensation system in which employees' rates of pay are based on the number of predetermined skills the employees have mastered.[78] For example, at the Santa Clara, California, plant of Northern Telecom, a leading supplier of digital communication switching systems, workers receive a pay increase for each new skill that they master. Workers who once performed narrow tasks now move freely among several different tasks, allowing the company to cut the number of job grades from 25 to 5 and to capitalize on the innovative ideas that result.[79] Another approach that is engendering increased attention is **gainsharing,** in which employees throughout an organization are encouraged to become involved in solving problems and are then given bonuses tied to organizationwide performance improvements.[80] For example, the new Achievement Sharing Plan recently implemented in the fibers division of Du Pont calls for employees to put up to 6 percent of their pay at risk. If profits fall below 80 percent of target, employees forfeit their percentage of pay at risk; otherwise, they receive attractive bonuses, depending on profit levels relative to goals.[81]

Gainsharing A compensation system in which employees throughout an organization are encouraged to become involved in solving problems and are then given bonuses tied to organizationwide performance improvements

Several types of rewards have been recommended for use with intrapreneurs, particularly those who fulfill the entrepreneurial role of idea champion (see Chapters 1 and 7).[82] Since idea champions generate new ideas or support new ideas in the face of numerous potential obstacles, rewards need to recognize the unusual difficulties and uncertainties involved. One reward approach allows intrapreneurs to be promoted and given increased salary without being forced to take on managerial responsibilities. For example, at 3M an intrapreneur can rise to the level of group executive while remaining a specialist rather than becoming a manager. Another type of reward that has been used with idea champions is the cash award. For instance, at International Harvester the scientist who developed key components of a new combine was given an initial award of $10,000, with the potential of receiving more tied to the continuing success of the combine. Finally, another means of compensating idea champions is by awarding an equity interest in new ventures, perhaps by giving stock so that they can share in the profits (or losses).[83]

Much of the discussion of compensation so far has centered on financial remunerations in the form of cashable rewards. Benefits also play a major roll in an employee's total compensation.

Employee Benefits

Benefits account for a growing portion of total compensation. They are sometimes called "fringe" benefits, a term stemming from a federal War Labor Board ruling during World War II that held that pay controls would not apply to benefits because they "were on the fringe of wages."[84] Arguably, benefits no longer fit in the "fringe" category. According to the U.S. Chamber of Commerce, which conducts an annual survey of a national cross section of private-sector firms, benefits rose from an average of 18.7 percent of direct payroll costs in 1951 to an average of 39 percent of payroll by 1987.[85] Thus an employee today who earns an annual salary of $20,000 is likely to receive another $7800 in benefits. The rise in benefits is attributable to several factors.[86] Among the most important are the rise in employer costs for social security, federal tax policies that provide tax advantages to employers and allow employees to receive the benefits on a tax-free or tax-deferred basis, pressure from labor unions for generous benefit packages, employer concern for employee needs, and attempts to encourage productivity improvements through rewards provided by benefits.

Although employers are legally required to make payments so that employees are covered by social security, unemployment compensation, and workers' compensation (in case of injury on the job), most benefits provided by employers are not required by law (even though laws may govern some of the provisions in the event that the benefits are offered). One organization that has a reputation for being particularly generous with benefits is privately owned Hallmark Cards, Inc., where benefits include low-interest $2500-per-year college loans for children of employees, interest-free loans of up to $1000 for emergencies, adoption assistance of up to $3000, paternity or maternity leave of up to 6 months for the parent of a newborn or newly adopted baby, and a physical fitness facility combined with an extensive wellness program.[87]

Perhaps because the amount of a paycheck is more noticeable and easily monitored, employees often fail to recognize the magnitude of their employers' expenditures on benefits. For example, a 1984 Opinion Research Corporation study showed that almost half of the more than 600 respondents estimated that their employers' costs for benefits were less than 10 percent of payroll costs, while 7 percent of the respondents believed that their employers spent *nothing* on benefits.[88] Not surprisingly, employers are seeking ways to communicate the value of benefits to employees through such measures as listing employer expenditures for benefits on employee paycheck stubs or offering "cafeteria" benefit plans, whereby employees have some choice about the benefits that they receive within some dollar limit. At Albany International, a world leader in the manufacture of fabric belts for paper-making machines, a video featuring employees was used successfully to introduce new benefits and explain their value.[89] Such efforts also can help build positive feelings toward the organization.

At Johnson & Johnson, exercising and taking other steps to protect one's health earn special company benefits—"Live-for-Life dollars" that are good for various recreational and health care products. As this employee puts it: "The goodies are psychological incentives that can sometimes motivate me to work out when I might not feel up to it."

MAINTAINING EFFECTIVE WORK-FORCE RELATIONSHIPS

Maintaining positive relations between an organization and its employees is an important aspect of human resource management. Two areas of particular relevance are labor-management relations and employee rights.

Labor-Management Relations

Labor-management relations is the process through which employers and unions negotiate pay, hours of work, and other conditions of employment; sign a contract governing such conditions for a specific period of time; and share responsibilities for administering the resulting contract.[90] **Unions** are employee groups formed for the purpose of negotiating with management about conditions relating to their work. Some employee groups call themselves associations rather than unions (e.g., the American Nurses Association). When recognized by the National Labor Relations Board (NLRB), unions have the legal right to negotiate with employers and help administer the resulting contract. The NLRB is the goverment agency that enforces the unfair labor practice and union election provisions of the Wagner Act of 1935 and the Taft-Hartley Act of 1947, major laws governing labor-management relations.

A number of studies have addressed why employees join unions. A main factor is dissatisfaction with various working conditions, such as wages, job security, benefits, treatment by supervisors, and prospects for promotion. Still, recent studies suggest that even dissatisfied workers will typically not join a union unless they also believe that a union will be effective in remedying the situation.[91]

Labor-management relations
The process through which employers and unions negotiate pay, hours of work, and other conditions of employment; sign a contract governing such conditions for a specific period of time; and share responsibilities for administering the resulting contract

The number of employees who are dues-paying union members has been declining after a peak of 22,618,000 members in 1979. In 1989, 17,002,000 employees were dues-paying union members.[92] Although the causes of the decline are not completely clear, some reasons given are more effective human resource management in organizations, a decrease in union organizing attempts, a decline in the economic well-being of companies (making it more difficult for unions to pressure for better wages and benefits), and increasingly effective management opposition to unions.[93]

Certification Process. Unions are normally established in organizations through an *organizing drive*.[94] The drive begins when employees sign authorization cards designating the union as their exclusive bargaining representative. At least 30 percent of employees within the group to be represented must sign cards before the union can petition the National Labor Relations Board to conduct an election. Once the NLRB verifies that 30 percent of the employees seek union representation, the board notifies management of that fact. At this point, management and the union can attempt to agree on union representation and the group of employees that will be considered the bargaining unit. Usually, though, the two parties do not agree, and the NLRB must determine the unit. Next, an election is held in which the union must receive a majority of the votes cast in order to be certified as the exclusive representative for the bargaining unit. Regardless of the outcome, no further union elections associated with the bargaining unit can take place for 1 year. Recent trends indicate that although unions are experiencing considerable success in obtaining authorization cards from the necessary 30 percent of affected workers, they are subsequently winning certification elections less than half the time (see the following Case in Point discussion).

CASE IN POINT: The UAW versus Nissan

For almost 6 years, the United Auto Workers (UAW), which represents production workers at the "Big Three" automakers (General Motors, Ford, and Chrysler), had been working to unionize a plant owned by the Japan-based Nissan Motor Manufacturing Corporation in Smyrna, Tennessee. The task facing the UAW was formidable.

When the Smyrna plant opened in 1983, it was welcomed by a community that was experiencing double-digit unemployment. More than 120,000 local residents applied for the initial 3200 hourly and salaried jobs at the plant. Those who were hired were reportedly told that they were the "cream of the crop" and that they had become part of a "family" work group. Considering workers as part of an organizational family, attempting to ensure lifetime employment, and involving employees in decisions affecting their work are some of the common characteristics of Japanese management (see Chapter 2; we also discuss international aspects of management in Chapter 21).

Six years later, the $14.80 hourly wage paid to the average worker with 3 years seniority was slightly lower than wages paid at Ford Motor but 37 percent higher than the average manufacturing wage in the nearby Nashville area. In benefits, UAW workers were slightly better off. For example, unlike their Ford counterparts, Nissan employees had to pay part of their health insurance premiums; but, on the plus side, they did not pay a deductible before being able to tap the benefit.

Nissan had built considerable loyalty through such measures as sponsoring an international folk festival, donating funds for civic causes such as the Murfreesboro Symphony, and providing robotics and electronics equipment for high school classes. The $2 million in annual tax payments had allowed local property taxes to be reduced by 25 percent. The company also established a fitness center and offered workers attractive discounts on leasing a new Nissan each year.

For its part, the UAW was able to get the required 30 percent to sign union authorization cards to force an election. Nevertheless, union officials recognized that many workers did not view paying $30 per month in union dues as a good investment, largely because they doubted that the union could improve things appreciably. One potentially important issue was health and safety, which the UAW emphasized in its campaign. At the Nissan plant, workers receive paid breaks totaling 23 minutes per day, compared with the 48 minutes allocated to Ford workers. The UAW charged that the pace at the Smyrna plant resulted in higher injury rates of workers.

Nissan denied the charge about injuries, but refused to allow a group of workers to inspect the injury log, arguing that it wanted to protect doctor-patient confidentiality. Tennessee authorities fined the company $5000 for not following the legal requirement of allowing workers to examine the log. While the company appealed, it continued to make the log unavailable. Meanwhile, the UAW enlisted several injured workers to help with the union drive, brought in 30 professional organizers, distributed leaflets to workers as they entered and left the plant, and had representatives visit more than two-thirds of the employees at their homes.

Company officials used the plant's closed-circuit television system to delivery carefully developed messages, such as one blaming the union for layoffs at GM and pointing out Nissan's no-layoff policy. The company also highlighted the possibility of strikes with the UAW as the bargaining agent. Prounion workers began to wear shirts that said, "Vote Yes for a Safer Workplace," while antiunion workers wore shirts stating, "I Can Spreak for Myself."

Finally, the big day of the election arrived—July 27, 1989. The results were lopsided, with 1622 workers voting against the union and 711 voting in favor.[95] ▬▬▬

Union Decertification. If a union does win an election, it can be decertified in the future, but not earlier than 1 year after the certification election. If there is evidence that at least 30 percent of the employees want to decertify the union, the NLRB can be asked to hold a decertification election. Recent trends indicate that unions have been losing such elections about three-fourths of the time, although about six times more certification than decertification elections are held each year (e.g., 1773 versus 459 in 1988).[96]

Unions Employee groups formed for the purpose of negotiating with management about conditions relating to their work

Current Employee Issues

Maintaining effective work-force relationships requires staying abreast of and making appropriate responses to issues affecting employees. Several areas of current concern include protection from arbitrary dismissal, drug and alcohol abuse, privacy rights, and family issues.[97]

Protection from Arbitrary Dismissal. Issues of job security and protection from arbitrary dismissal are the subject of a growing number of laws and lawsuits.[98] The legal principle that has mainly been followed in the United States during the past century is **employment at will,** which holds that either employee or em-

Employment at will The legal principle that holds that either employee or employer can terminate employment at any time for any reason

ployer can terminate employment at any time for any reason. Recently, the notion of employment at will has been increasingly challenged because of various federal and state laws (such as those forbidding the termination of employees for whistle-blowing or for complaining about safety hazards in the workplace) and certain court rulings (such as one holding that some employment arrangements constitute implied contracts). Although court findings vary considerably, mostly because of differences in state laws, employers are increasingly facing litigation over firings. Adopting a policy of discharging employees only for good cause, following a progressive disciplinary process (e.g., giving oral and written warnings and suspensions before attempting to terminate an individual), and carefully documenting the reasons for dismissal will aid in protecting the rights of both employees and employers.

Drug and Alcohol Abuse. Another important issue affecting employees and their employers is drug and alcohol abuse. Such abuse typically leads to increases in absenteeism, workplace accidents, and use of medical benefits, while causing declines in productivity. According to a 1986 estimate by the Employee Assistance Society of North America, productivity losses related to alcohol problems amount to about $39 billion per year and drug-related losses cost more than $8 billion.[99]

Employee assistance program (EAP) A program through which employers help employees overcome personal problems that are adversely affecting their job performance

As one response to substance abuse problems, more than 10,000 employers have established employee assistance programs.[100] An **employee assistance program (EAP)** is a program through which employers help employees overcome personal problems that are adversely affecting their job performance. Under such programs, supervisors may refer workers to EAP program counselors or outside counselors who help identify problems and arrange for appropriate assistance. Workers usually can also contact EAP counselors themselves. Although drug and alcohol abuse problems are the major aspects covered, such programs increasingly provide assistance for a broader range of issues, including stress, smoking cessation, weight control, financial matters, legal difficulties, and other personal issues that cause difficulties for employees.

Privacy Rights. The employee's right to privacy is another human resource issue of current importance. One privacy concern related to the drug abuse issue just discussed is *drug testing*, the attempt to detect drug usage through analysis of blood, urine, or other body substances. According to one estimate, at least 30 percent of the employers of recent college graduates engage in drug testing of new employees, and the number is growing.[101] Although the legal issues are far from resolved, courts generally have been willing to allow employers to test job applicants, on the premise that applicants choose to submit to the drug tests in order to obtain a job. On the other hand, courts generally are much less tolerant of mandatory testing of employees. In most situations, drug and alcohol testing of employees is more likely to survive legal challenge if the employees have jobs involving public safety (e.g., airline pilots) or dangerous jobs (e.g., electricians), testing is limited to situations in which there is reasonable suspicion of on-the-job impairment, there is a written and publicized substance abuse policy, there are procedural protections (such as careful labeling and secondary tests to confirm positive results), and employers offer voluntary rehabilitation programs rather than firing employees for first offenses.

A related privacy issue is *genetic screening*, attempting to test for genetic factors that may contribute to certain occupational diseases. So far, only a few companies, mainly in the chemical industry, appear to be using genetic screening to attempt to identify those workers who are more likely to contract diseases after exposure to certain chemicals or toxins. While the screening has the potential of protecting workers from hazardous working conditions, it also could possibly be used to deny employment to individuals on the basis of their genetic makeup.[102] As a result, genetic screening appears likely to generate considerable controversy in the future.

Another current privacy-rights issue is the use of *polygraphs* and other mechanical lie detectors by employers. The use of such tests has been severely limited by the Employee Polygraph Protection Act of 1988. The law was passed because of concerns about the accuracy and validity of polygraphs, particularly for routine use. The law largely forbids the use of polygraph tests by private employers for screening job applicants, except in the pharmaceutical industry (because the work involves handling controlled substances) and the security industry. Furthermore, the use of polygraphs to test current employees is substantially limited by the law to situations in which there is a "reasonable suspicion" that the individual was involved in an activity under investigation.

Family Issues. Given the rising proportion of women in the workplace, the growing number of dual-career couples, and the frequency of single parenting, family issues as they affect workers also are increasing in importance. In order to help employees more effectively handle the often conflicting responsibilities of work and family, several major companies, such as Du Pont, now have family issues specialists on their staff. The specialists help develop policies and also assist employees in regard to such issues as leaves from work, child care, and elder care.[103] Such assistance is likely to help maintain positive working relationships with employees and facilitate engaging in the management function of leading. We begin exploring the leading function in the next chapter, which focuses on motivating employees.

CHAPTER SUMMARY

Human resource management is the management of various activities designed to enhance the effectiveness of an organization's work force. Major activities include human resource planning, staffing, development and evaluation, compensation, and maintenance of effective work-force relationships. The strategic importance of HRM has been increasing, particularly since the late 1970s and early 1980s.

Human resource planning considers both demand for and supply of human resources relative to an organization's strategic plan. Such planning relies on job analysis and resulting job descriptions and job specifications. Assessing demand involves considering major forces that can influence demand and using basic forecasting techniques to predict future demand. Assessing supply entails determining internal and external labor supplies. In reconciling future demand and supply, organizations also need to consider affirmative action implications.

Staffing is the set of activities aimed at attracting and selecting individuals for positions in a way that will facilitate the achievement of organizational goals. The attraction aspect of staffing involves recruitment. Most

organizations engage in extensive internal recruitment in order to offer job opportunities to current employees. For the most part, organizations engage in external recruiting only when there are no suitable internal candidates for particular positions. The selection aspect of staffing focuses on determining which job candidates best suit organizational needs. An important issue in selection is validity, which addresses how well a selection device or method actually predicts a candidate's future job performance. The most prevalent selection methods include the use of application blanks, selection interviews, tests, assessment centers, and reference checks, each of which can facilitate the selection process if used properly.

Training and development is a planned effort to facilitate employee learning of job-related behaviors in order to improve employee performance. Training typically includes three main phases: assessment, training design and implementation, and evaluation. Major types of training programs include orientation training, technical skill training, and management development programs. Performance appraisal is the process of defining expectations for employee performance; measuring, evaluating, and recording employee performance relative to those expectations; and providing feedback to the employee. Major methods of performance appraisal include behavior-oriented approaches, such as the use of graphic rating scales and behaviorally anchored rating scales, and results-oriented approaches, such as management by objectives. Because performance raters tend to be susceptible to biases that produce rating errors, they must engage in three somewhat incompatible roles (leader, coach, and judge) in carrying out an effective performance appraisal interview.

Compensation systems need to consider internal, external, and individual equity in developing pay structures and allocating individual pay. The most common approach to devising pay structures depends on the point factor method of job evaluation. Organizations also are attempting to reward intrapreneurs through specialized pay approaches, such as bonus programs, and are encouraging work-force flexibility and innovation through such means as skill-based pay and gainsharing.

Maintaining positive work-force relationships includes engaging in effective labor-management relations and making appropriate responses to current employee issues. Organizations become unionized through a certification process regulated by the National Labor Relations Board. Unions can become decertified through a similar process. Among the major current employee issues are protection from arbitrary dismissal, drug and alcohol abuse, privacy rights, and family matters as they impact work.

MANAGERIAL TERMINOLOGY

adverse impact (414)
affirmative action (410)
affirmative action plan
  (410)
application blank (414)
assessment center (418)
behaviorally anchored
  rating scales (BARS)
  (422)
benefits (424)
compensation (424)
employee assistance
  program (EAP) (432)

employment at will
  (431)
employment test (416)
gainsharing (428)
graphic rating scales
  (421)
human resource
  management (HRM)
  (404)
human resource planning
  (406)
job analysis (407)
job description (407)

job evaluation (425)
job posting (412)
job specification (407)
labor-management
  relations (429)
needs analysis (419)
pay survey (426)
performance appraisal
  (421)
point factor method
  (425)
realistic job preview
  (413)

recruitment (412)
reference checks (418)
replacement chart (409)
selection (413)
selection interview (414)
skill-based pay (428)
skills inventory (409)
staffing (411)
training and development
  (419)
unions (431)
validity (413)

QUESTIONS FOR DISCUSSION AND REVIEW

1. Briefly describe the major elements in the human resource management process and explain why HRM has gradually increased in strategic importance in organizations. To what extent do you believe that effective human resource management is strategically important for your college or university? Explain your reasoning.

2. Explain the role of job analysis in human resource planning. Why might job descriptions (and job specifications) based on job analysis be useful in a variety of human resource activities, such as recruitment, selection, and performance appraisal?

3. Identify the major factors that managers need to consider in attempting to predict future demand for human resources. How can forecasting methods help? What factors do managers need to examine in assessing the future supply of human resources? What options do managers have in reconciling demand and supply imbalances?

4. Distinguish between internal and external recruiting. What might be the major advantages and disadvantages of each?

5. Explain the role of validity in selection. Identify the most widely used selection methods, and assess their potential as valid means of making selection decisions. Assess the probable validity of a selection device used in an organization with which you are familiar.

6. Identify the main phases of training, the major categories of training methods typically used, and the types of training programs that are most common in organizations. Give an example of each type of training method from your own experience as an individual being trained or as a trainer.

7. Explain the major methods for rating performance in organizations, common biases that affect ratings, and major roles that supervisors must play during the performance appraisal interview. Think of a time when your performance was appraised by someone. How well did the individual balance the roles of leader, coach, and judge? Explain your view.

8. Describe how pay structures in organizations are developed using the point factor method. Why might nontraditional compensation systems, such as the ones described in the chapter, be better at encouraging innovation than more traditional approaches?

9. Explain the nature of benefits and the reason why they are growing as a portion of total compensation. Identify several benefits that either you or someone in your family receives as part of job compensation.

10. Describe the process through which unions are certified and decertified. What role might employee-rights issues potentially play in unionization efforts?

DISCUSSION QUESTIONS FOR CHAPTER OPENING CASE

1. Explain the strategic importance of HRM at CARE.
2. Trace evidence of various elements of the HRM process at CARE.

3. Identify and evaluate the recent changes made in human resource management at CARE.

MANAGEMENT EXERCISE: MANAGING HUMAN RESOURCES IN RETAIL HARDWARE

You have just accepted a position as a department head in a large hardware store. The owner, who is the store manager, likes to involve others in decisions. During your interviews for the job, the store manager mentioned that if you became department head, he would be asking you about your views on ways to improve human resource management in the store. He is particularly interested in your input because he is thinking about opening up several other stores in the region. (In fact, you are taking the job partially because you believe that such expansion can only help your career.)

The manager said that he, the assistant manager, and nine other department heads are planning to hold some strategic planning meetings shortly and that they want to consider the impact of human resources in regard to the expansion plans. Also, he anticipates holding subsequent meetings that focus on various aspects of human resource management. He further stated that he wants to maintain a working environment that is stimulating, challenging, and exciting. At the same time, he would prefer to avoid having the store become unionized, since he feels that opening up new stores in the area would be more complicated if a union were involved.

From what you have been able to learn, the 18 percent annual growth of the store and the 15 percent return on investment could definitely be improved. In addition, human resource management seems to be almost nonexistent at this point.

1. What issues will you suggest should be considered as part of human resource planning?
2. What will you be prepared to discuss in regard to recruiting and selecting human resources?
3. What suggestion for training, performance appraisal, and compensation will you have?

NUCOR PROSPERS IN TOUGH STEEL INDUSTRY

Operating its headquarters from a relatively unobtrusive building in a suburb of Charlotte, North Carolina, the Nucor Corporation has gained a reputation for succeeding in an industry where competition is formidable. The company operates so-called minimills, which use a particularly economical method of steelmaking that relies on melting scrap iron to produce basic products such as joists, decking, and steel bars. In contrast, its giant domestic competitors (e.g., USX, LTV, Bethlehem, Inland, Armco, and National Steel) use iron ore that is processed through more expensive, integrated methods. Although the giants can turn out more types of steel, Nucor has carved a lucrative niche for itself, one that has enabled the company to grow at a compound annual rate of more than 20 percent during the past decade.

Nucor, which operates more than 18 minimills in various parts of the United States, recently has taken steps to enter the flat-rolled steel market, a market currently monopolized by the giant steelmakers. The company has built the world's first thin-slab plant in Crawfordsville, Indiana, at a cost of $265 million. The plant is the first to use a patented technology known as thin-slab casting, developed by Schloeman-Siemag A.G. in West Germany. With the technology, 2-inch-thick steel slabs can be immediately rolled into sheets one-tenth of an inch thick. Conventional methods produce slabs that are 8 to 10 inches thick, which then must be reheated before they can be rolled into the thin sheets that major customers, such as auto manufacturers and appliance mak-

ers, need to produce their products. The new Nucor mill eliminates a major step in the process, enabling the mill to produce sheet steel at a lower cost than is possible with conventional methods. With the new technology, Nucor hopes to obtain at least a small part of the $13 billion market for flat-roll steel sheets. The one hitch is that the new mill must operate at 96 percent reliability because if one part of the process has difficulty, the whole mill must be shut down until the problem is rectified.

Nucor has hopes of attaining such high reliability because its 4000 workers are among the best in the industry. Despite Nucor's $1 billion in annual sales, company headquarters operates with a small staff of 16 or so. There are only four management levels. The chairman and CEO, F. Kenneth Iverson, and the company's president, Dave Aycock, serve as one level. The next level consists of vice presidents, who also are general managers of a steel mill, a joist plant, or a division. Next are department heads, who might be a manager of melting and casting, a manager of rolling, a sales manager, or a division controller. The fourth level comprises the first-line supervisors. At the same time, the company tries hard to eliminate distinctions between management and workers. For example, everyone, including Iverson, wears the same color hard hat, eliminating the color distinctions common in many companies. There are no assigned parking spaces, no executive dining rooms, and no hunting lodges, and everyone in the company travels economy class. Management and workers have the same benefits, such as vacation time and insurance.

A particularly unique aspect of Nucor, compared with the rest of both the American and Japanese

In order to be productive, Nucor steel mills must operate at a high level of reliability. Since the mill workers must assume much of the responsibility for this reliability, Nucor manages its human resources in such a way as to attract and retain the best employees. Only three management levels separate the mill worker from the company's CEO, F. Kenneth Iverson (shown here), and all employees and managers share the same benefits. The workers feel free to make suggestions and receive substantial bonus pay under an innovative incentive pay system. The result, as Iverson notes, is that Nucor attracts goal-oriented employees who are willing to work hard.

steel industries, is the company's incentive pay system. Under the system, a significant portion of most organization members' pay depends on worker productivity or on company success. For example, in the steel mills, the company identifies groups of 25 to 35 people doing some complete task and puts them on a bonus program. There typically are nine bonus groups. Each group carries out a particular activity that is involved in the process. In each case, a standard is set for production. The group then receives extra pay based on the amount it produces above the standard. There is no maximum, and the bonuses are paid weekly so that workers can see the fruits of their efforts quickly. Standards about punctuality and attendance also apply. "If you're late even 5 minutes, you lose your bonus for the day," say Iverson. Lateness of more than 30 minutes or absenteeism for any reason results in a bonus loss for the week (there are four "forgiveness days" available to each worker per year). The bonuses received by groups are normally more than 100 percent above base pay, giving the steelworkers an average annual pay of more than $30,000, with some making more than $40,000. Also, the company has a profit-sharing plan, whereby 10 percent of earnings before taxes are distributed to employee accounts within the plan. Money in the plan is invested so that the funds grow over time. Workers can then draw their portions when they retire. There is no retirement program, but some workers have accumulated more than $100,000 in the profit-sharing program.

Although pay is higher at Nucor than at its major competitors, productivity in terms of tons per employee has been running more than double. One reason is that workers are interested in any ideas that improve their productivity and have suggested many innovative ideas. Iverson admits that the Nucor system is not for everyone. When the company starts up a new mill, turnover is usually in the range of 200 percent the first year.

After that, turnover is extremely low. Iverson says that the system appeals best to very goal-oriented individuals who are willing to work hard.

Nucor has a no-layoff policy. Occasionally, there are reduced workweeks to avoid layoffs. When 3½- or 4-day workweeks are necessary, a worker's pay may be cut by as much as 25 percent, but the pay of department heads and officers is cut even more, perhaps as much as 40 percent and 70 percent, respectively. Iverson calls it Nucor's "Share the Pain" program.

New workers receive initial training in the company philosophy and are assigned to group leaders for on-the-job training. Managers receive extensive training, particularly in communication skills. Communication is one reason why Nucor limits the work force at each of its plants to 500 employees. "We don't feel that a general manager can communicate effectively with employees when you have a group larger than that," says Iverson. Company policy requires that the general manager have dinner with every employee in a plant at least once a year, in groups no larger than 50. Most general managers have dinner with employees twice a year. After the first dinner, employees learn that they can speak up. Iverson remembers one incident in particular: "A

fellow got up and said, 'You guys are really rotten. You haven't done anything about the parking lot, and they're stealing us blind out there.' Another one stood up and said, 'They stole so much gas out of my car I couldn't even start it when I came off my shift.' A third had a $400 car stereo stolen. We didn't know about any of this, of course. It took us exactly 3 days to fence the parking lot and put up lights. That's the way we work."

Recently, the company had a few openings at its Darlington, North Carolina, plant and placed a small ad in the local paper stating: "Nucor Steel will take some applications on Saturday morning at 8:30 for new employees." At 8:30 a.m., 1200 people were lined up to fill out applications.[104]

QUESTIONS FOR CHAPTER CONCLUDING CASE

1. Explain the various components of the HRM process that are evident at Nucor.
2. To what extent does human resource management appear to be part of strategic management at Nucor? Cite evidence to support your view.
3. Assess the handling of external, internal, and individual equity in the compensation system at Nucor.

DAIMLER-BENZ DIVERSIFIES

Daimler-Benz AG, West Germany's largest company, is widely known throughout the world as the maker of the Mercedes-Benz luxury-class automobile. Although the firm has recently diversified into a number of other industries, its roots in the auto industry go back many years.

Inventor Gottlieb Daimler's company was producing engines and automobiles around the turn of the century, under the name of Daimler Motors, when Emil Jellinek, a wealthy Austrian diplomat and car-racing enthusiast, purchased a Daimler car and used it to win a number of races. During one of the races, Jellinek witnessed a fatal accident that he believed was caused by the car's design. Accordingly, Jellinek conferred with Daimler's chief engineer about building an automobile with a larger wheelbase, a lower center of gravity, and a more powerful engine. If the company would do so, Jellinek agreed to purchase 36 of the cars for 550,000 gold marks (about $130,000) as long as two additional provisions were met: first, he was to be given sole rights to distribute the car in Austria, Hungary, Belgium, France, and the United States; and, second, the car was to be named "Mercedes" (after his daughter). The new automobile was an instant success. Shortly thereafter, the name "Mercedes" was adopted for all Daimler products.

In 1926, the firm merged with Benz, another German automobile company, to produce the cars and commercial vehicles that are now associated with the name "Mercedes-Benz." The company continued to build its reputation for high-quality engineering and dependability as it gradually forged a global market for its products. By 1985, Daimler-Benz had sales of about $23 billion, placing it fifth among the world's largest industrial companies based outside the United States. At that point, the firm ranked first in the world both in truck and luxury-car sales.

Although automobile production had risen by almost one-third between 1981 and 1985 (from 440,000 to 594,000 cars), the company began to make serious moves toward diversification in 1985. The impetus for diversification was based partially on concerns about the future growth of the luxury-automobile market. With over 95 percent of its 1985 revenues coming from car and truck sales, Daimler-Benz was potentially vulnerable to the effects of a weakened dollar (since the United States is a major market) and to competition from Japanese companies, which are continuing to introduce upscale cars, such as Honda's Acura and Toyota's Lexus. Daimler continues to be a global supplier of trucks and also buses. Another stimulus for diversification was the prospect for applying new technologies in similar or related sectors, such as vehicles, drive systems, aviation, space, electronics, and communication technology. The impending economic unification of Europe and the increasing globalization of its markets provided other incentives to become a broader competitive force.

In pursuing its diversification strategy, Daimler-Benz made its first major acquisition in 1985 when it purchased MTU, an internationally known manufacturer of tur-

The Mercedes-Benz automobile may be Daimler-Benz's most well-known product, but the German company has made major moves toward diversification in recent years. It has acquired a firm that makes aircraft engines and diesel motors, two airplane manufacturers, and an electronics company. The space-plane shown here is part of the "Sanger" project being developed by the new Deutsche Aerospace division of Daimler-Benz. The project is aimed at creating advanced methods of transportation in space.

bines, aircraft engines, and high-speed diesel engines. The unit is well known as the producer of the engine for the Toronado jet fighter plane, a defense project sponsored by Britain, Germany, and Italy. In 1985, Daimler-Benz also purchased Dornier, a major German airplane company that has long traditions in aviation and space, as well as in various sectors of high technology. In an even larger and more controversial move, the next year Daimler acquired AEG, a German electronics company that operates in highly advanced technological fields, such as solar technology, radar systems, communication networks, and automation systems.

Then, in 1989, Daimler-Benz received permission from the then West German government to purchase the German airplane manufacturer Messerschmitt-Boelkow-Blohm (MBB), a step that ultimately transformed Daimler into Germany's largest aerospace and defense conglomerate. The acquisition had been opposed by some critics, and particularly by certain political elements and small businesses who feared that Daimler's growing size would have a stifling effect on competition. At the same time, others argued that the resulting possibilities for economies of scale would significantly strengthen the position of Daimler-Benz in European and world markets. Collectively, the diversification moves have made Daimler-Benz the largest nonoil industrial company in Europe, employing about 350,000.

As implementation of the diversification strategy progressed, top-level managers decided to change the organization structure from one that emphasized functional responsibilities, such as research and development, production, materials, sales, personnel, and finance, to a structure that focused on product markets. The change, implemented in July, 1990, created three major divisions: Mercedes-Benz, for automobiles and trucks; AEG, for electronics; Deutsche Aerospace, for aviation, space, and defense technology, and Daimler-Benz Interservices for various services already existing in various divisions of the company.

The structural revamping included the creation of a new corporate-level R&D center with 1400 employees in the Daimler-Benz research institutes in Stuttgart, Ulm, Frankfurt, and Berlin. Under coordinated management, they work on new concepts in fields such as transport and vehicles, energy, materials, electronics, and communication technology. The center helps divisions to innovate and fosters the exchange of technology across units. Daimler is well known for product innovations. For example, in the area of automobiles, the company reportedly is working on a solar-powered air conditioner embedded in the roof of a car that would keep the interior cool when the car is not being used and is experimenting with a sophisticated information and diagnostic system that will enhance vehicle service. Research and development funding typically receives a high priority in the annual budgeting process. One major aim is to create a high-technology company where new developments and in-depth expertise are utilized in a variety of applications, particularly in the building of integrated systems that incorporate advanced technology from more than one field. For example, the ability to combine transportation expertise with advanced communications technology opens up prospects for unique transportation systems that link various individual elements (such as trains and airplanes) into integrated networks.

In addition to having a strong reputation for research and development innovation, Daimler-Benz also has proven itself able to respond quickly when required. For example, when the accelerator of the 124 model cars purchased by consumers began to stick, despite previous good performance of the model on the test track, the R&D center redesigned the accelerator within 3 months. The company also extended its warranty on the vehicles. Since the response was so rapid, government officials in West Germany and elsewhere did not become involved.

Like most German companies (and quite unlike most U.S. firms), Daimler-Benz has two boards of directors: a supervisory board and a management board. The supervisory board, or senior board of directors, is called the *Aufsichtsrat*. It is composed of equal numbers of stockholders and labor representatives, none of whom is an employee of Daimler. The primary functions of the supervisory board are ensuring that the views of stockholders and labor are appropriately represented in the corporate decision-making process and naming (and removing, if necessary) members of the lower board. The lower board, called the *Vorstand*, is made up of senior managers of Daimler. This board is responsible for the actual management of the company. Several members of the management board represent major functions, such as employment, research and technology, and finance and materials management, while others represent the major product divisions of the company.

The Mercedes-Benz division, traditionally the mainstay of the company, has more than 50 factories and assembly plants located in Germany, Brazil, Argentina, South Africa, Spain, and the United States. In a rather unusual arrangement, each is managed jointly by two individuals, one commercial and one technical. The commercial manager monitors the return on investment, while the technical manager oversees product quality and manufacturing process improvements. Despite the prospects for conflict with such a structure, there is strong pressure to resolve differences. Otherwise, the two managers are forced to contact a member of the Vorstand and admit that they are unable to solve their own mutual issues. Working together, the two managers have

State-of-the-art electronic trains produced by Daimler-Benz's AEG Division serve Las Colinas, a planned, high-density urban center located just north of Dallas, Texas. The trains, which can be operated automatically through a sophisticated computer system, provide convenient transportation for the individuals who live and/or work in the urban center. Gradually the current 3-mile long system, which is known as the Area Personal Transit (APT) system, will be extended to operate on 12 miles of "guideway" or track as the urban center area itself expands.

considerable latitude in making decisions that affect the operations under their jurisdiction.

In assessing the results of various company efforts, until recently only the Vorstand had ultimate profit-making responsibility. Profits were measured on the basis of the performance of the entire corporation because of the heavy functional focus of the organization structure and because many factories deliver parts to and/or receive parts from other units of the organization, making profit measurement below the Vorstand difficult. Of course, the various units did have budget targets and performance goals. For example, the sales division had goals regarding the number of cars to be sold at certain prices. Since the reorganization, major divisions can now also operate as profit centers that are responsible for achieving profit goals.

Traditionally, the company has engaged in considerable planning in conjunction with its car and truck business, and the planning system has been adapted to the requirements of Daimler's recently acquired businesses. The planning cycle includes three major phases: long-term, middle-term, and short-term. The long-term phase addresses strategic planning and is oriented toward periods of 10 years or more into the future. The decision to diversify came from this long-term planning process. The middle-term, or tactical planning process, includes planning for 2 to 10 years and covers the period during which concepts are turned into products. Short-term operational planning is conducted for the current year. Planning for major new products usually is done within this cycle. For example, a new car introduced at Daimler has typically been

in the planning stages for about 10 years and, once introduced, it will probably be manufactured for the next 9 years.

In order to maintain an effective work force, Daimler-Benz has a policy of providing for steady employment for its employees, most of whom are highly skilled. During the occasional periods when sales are slow, workers are transferred from facilities that are adversely affected to others where they are needed. In such instances, the company provides housing for employees because they are working away from home. As a result, Daimler employees have not been subject to the layoffs that have commonly occurred at other large companies. Because the union contracts at Daimler do not include the job restrictions that are common in labor contracts in the United States, there is considerable flexibility in the jobs to which employees can be assigned. At the same time, the company expends considerable effort to provide the necessary training to keep employees at the forefront of changing work requirements.

Besides wages that are generally somewhat higher than those paid by other firms, the company also offers a variety of benefits, such as preventive health care, company pensions, and social advisory services that provide assistance to employees with problems such as alcohol addiction, psychological difficulties, or personal crisis situations.

In addition to a loyal work force, another of Daimler's advantages is the company's large and supportive group of long-term shareholders. Only about one-third of the company's stock is currently held by the general public; the rest is controlled mainly by various banks and institutions. For example, Deutsche Bank holds the largest stake, with 28 percent of the voting stock. Due to the position of Deutsche Bank as Germany's largest banking institution, Daimler-Benz enjoys strong support for its expansion into the eastern sectors of the unified Germany and for capitalizing on new opportunities available with the opening of eastern Europe to ventures by companies from the west. Generally, the nature of the company's shareholders enables Daimler-Benz to make investments aimed at achieving long-term strategic objectives without excessive concern for the impact on short-term profits.

Since the diversification, top management has been pushing for innovations throughout the company, particularly innovations based on microelectronics and new materials. One result is that advanced Mercedes-Benz automobile models with sophisticated electronics are being unveiled to fight the onslaught of Japanese luxury cars. One new offering, the sporty SL roadster, has a backlog of orders extending into the mid-1990's. The company also has been discussing major joint ventures in areas such as aerospace and electronics with United Technologies Corporation of the United States, and with Mitsubishi Corporation of Japan. The formidable challenge ahead is to make the diversified Daimler-Benz as profitable as the more concentrated automobile and truck company was in the past, and to integrate the new acquisitions so that the strengths of each can be used to competitive advantage.*

QUESTIONS FOR DISCUSSION
1. Identify the type of departmentalization currently in use at Daimler-Benz. Assess the likely advantages and disadvantages of this structure.

2. What methods of vertical and horizontal coordination are apparent at Daimler-Benz? What recommendations might you make about additional means of coordination?
3. Which one of Mintzberg's five structural configurations does Daimler-Benz most closely represent? What are the implications for strategy at the division levels?
4. How does Daimler-Benz use structure as a means of enhancing the prospects for innovation? What dangers are posed by the differentiation paradox?
5. What types of compensation are in evidence at Daimler-Benz? To what extent does the company appear to be concerned about external equity? What other means are used at Daimler to maintain effective work-force relationships?

*Sources: See references at back of book.

PART FOUR

LEADING

W hile planning provides direction and organizing arranges the resources, the leading function adds the action ingredient. Leading involves influencing the work behavior of others toward achieving organizational goals. In the process of leading, effective managers can become catalysts in encouraging organizational innovation. Leaders kindle the dynamic spirit that underlies successful organizations.

The energy of an organization comes from the motivation of its workers. As **Chapter 13** notes, managers can utilize several motivational approaches that focus on individual needs, the thought processes involved in deciding whether or not to expend effort, and the reinforcements and rewards available.

Does leadership depend on inherent traits or are there effective leader behaviors that anyone can learn and apply to various situations? **Chapter 14** considers both of these possibilities in exploring the essence of leadership. In order to have influence, leaders must have effective ways of communicating their ideas and visions, as well as workable methods of learning about the thoughts of others. **Chapter 15** discusses the nature of managerial communication, including an exploration of the different types of communication and the various channels involved.

At the same time, many managers have come to realize that groups or teams can be a powerful means of accomplishing organizational goals. As **Chapter 16** explains, understanding group dynamics and being able to encourage the productive power inherent in group activities is an important part of the leading function.

CHAPTER THIRTEEN

MOTIVATION

CHAPTER OUTLINE

The Nature of Motivation
Early Approaches to Motivation
A Simplified Model of Motivation

Need Theories
Hierarchy of Needs Theory
ERG Theory
Two-Factor Theory
Acquired-Needs Theory
Assessing Need Theories

Cognitive Theories
Expectancy Theory
Equity Theory
Goal-Setting Theory
Assessing Cognitive Theories

Reinforcement Theory
Types of Reinforcement
Schedules of Reinforcement
Using Reinforcement Theory

Social Learning Theory
Major Components
Using Social Learning Theory
Promoting Innovation: A Social
  Learning Perspective

LEARNING OBJECTIVES

*After studying this chapter, you
should be able to:*

■ Define motivation, describe
early approaches to the concept, and outline a simplified
model of the motivation
process.

■ Compare and contrast each of
the four major need theories of
motivation.

■ Describe each of the three
major cognitive theories of
motivation and explain how
they facilitate the motivation
process.

■ Explain the reinforcement theory of motivation and how it
can be helpful to managers.

■ Discuss the social learning theory of motivation and its role
in promoting innovation.

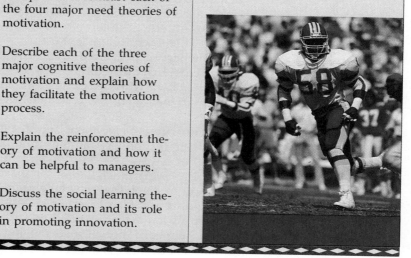

A MOTIVATIONAL BALANCING ACT AT GENENTECH

Imagine a group of scientists chanting "Ahooo! DNA! DNA! DNA!" to recognize a recent breakthrough by a colleague. That's just one approach that helps keep researchers' efforts focused on the cutting edge of science at Genentech, Inc., a San Francisco–based company that is partially owned by Switzerland-based Roche Holding, Ltd., and is widely considered to be a pacesetter in the biotechnology industry. DNA, the basis for the chant, is the genetic code that makes possible the growth and development of living organisms and is also the basis of the scientists' work.

Most often, the leader of the chant is David W. Martin, Jr. (no relative of your author, D.C.M.), vice president of research, who mediates between two competing sets of pressures. Martin's boss, Genentech's CEO, sends a clear message: "More products, more products." The company needs a steady stream of ground-breaking products in order to make a profit. But the 200 top-notch scientists who form Genentech's technical core are dedicated to ideas and scientific discovery. As a result, the scientists do not always have a practical orientation when it comes to pursuing lines of research. To Martin falls the delicate job of keeping his scientists focused on lines of inquiry that are likely to yield new products, without sabotaging their motivation. "You want them to feel they have the freedom to follow their instincts," he says, "but you don't want them to go off on tangents that are unlikely to be productive for the company in the long run."

Martin, formerly a professor of medicine and biochemistry at the University of California in San Francisco, was lured to Genentech by the opportunity to demonstrate that basic research could be profitable. He says that his six-figure salary and generous stock options were not a significant aspect of the job switch because he was already well paid in his previous job. About a third of the 75 to 85 hours that Martin works each week are spent combing the latest medical and scientific journals. "He knows the scientific literature better than anyone else I've ever seen," states one of his scientific directors. "That forces everyone else to keep up."

Beyond his scientific knowledge, Martin uses a potpourri of incentives to help keep motivation levels high. One way he does so is by giving his scientists a stake in the business. All the researchers own Genentech stock, which has risen significantly since the company began to sell stock to the public in 1980, making some of the scientists millionaires.

The best scientists are rewarded with autonomy, the chance to work full-time on research directions of their own choosing with very little interference. In addition, about half the scientists are able to devote 20 percent of their time to projects of their own. The rest are expected to devote all their time to designated projects.

Martin tries to give some latitude when feasible. "If you tell scientists to give 100 percent to a project and they aren't interested, you won't get a product," he says. "But if you say, 'Put 75 percent into this and 25 percent on your own work,' they work much harder." For example, one scientist spends half his time on cancer research that may take years before it leads to a commercial product, but he also assists with other scientific projects, such as recently helping to develop a vaccine for hepatitis and to discover a cost-effective way to produce it.

To help keep the scientists moving in practical directions, Martin uses what he terms "subtle pressure." He enthusiastically supports projects that seem to be moving in useful directions. When a project is successful, he can immediately write a "Genencheck," an instant reward of up to $1000 for small, but significant, breakthroughs. For larger discoveries, he can award stock options.

When a project does not appear to be particularly promising in terms of possible commercial results, he rarely refuses outright to let a scientist work on it. Instead, he sets short-term goals for progress. On one occasion, Martin vetoed a project on leukoregulin, a possible anticancer agent; but then, after the scientist "begged" for more time, he gave the scientist a 6-week progress deadline. When the agreed-upon progress was not made by the deadline, Martin called it quits. By then, the scientist was also ready to abandon the project.

Sometimes scientists keep working on projects after Martin has said no. When suggestions that such scientists spend time on more useful projects do not work, Martin slowly channels away resources, such as technicians and equipment, an extremely effective means of bringing work to a halt.

Most of Genentech's current work involves gene splicing to produce, or clone, human proteins that are used to treat various diseases. Among recent scientific discoveries with commercial applications are a cloned "factor VIII," a blood-clotting agent that helps hemophiliacs, and a tumor necrosis factor that seems to break apart tumor cells. Such discoveries are indications that Martin's approach seems to work. The highest compliment comes from one of Martin's molecular biologists, who notes, "No one good has left since he's been here."[1]

What makes scientists at Genentech spend endless hours pursuing the unknown horizons of biotechnology, come up with new ideas to keep the company at the forefront of the field, and consider the autonomy to pursue directions of interest a reward? When we begin to ask questions like these, we are exploring **motivation,** the force that energizes behavior, gives direction to behavior, and underlies the tendency to persist. This definition of motivation recognizes that in order to achieve goals, individuals must be sufficiently stimulated and energetic, must have a clear focus or end in mind, and must be willing and able to commit their energy for a long enough period of time to realize their aim.[2] Since the leading function of management involves influencing others to work toward organizational goals, motivation is an important aspect of that function.

In this chapter, we explore the basic nature of motivation, including early efforts to learn what motivates people, and we consider a general model of the motivation process. Next, we examine theories of motivation that are based on individual needs, such as the need for achievement. We also look into motivational approaches that emphasize cognitive aspects, focusing on how individuals think about where to direct their efforts and how to evaluate outcomes. We then analyze reinforcement theory, with its emphasis on the power of rewards. Finally, we review a more contemporary extension called social learning theory and consider its implications for promoting innovation.

One source of motivation for scientists at Genentech, a California-based biochemical company, is leeway to spend a certain portion of time on their own projects. A senior scientist at the lab consults here with a postdoctoral fellow (at right) who is developing models for designated diabetes research. Hopefully, the scientists' own research projects will also result in products the company can market.

Motivation The force that energizes behavior, gives direction to behavior, and underlies the tendency to persist

THE NATURE OF MOTIVATION

Because motivation is an internal force, we cannot measure the motivation of others directly. Instead, we typically infer whether or not other individuals are motivated by watching their behavior. For example, we might conclude that our engineering friend who works late every evening, goes to the office on weekends, and incessantly reads the latest engineering journals is highly motivated to do well. Conversely, we might suspect that our engineering friend who is usually the first one out the door at quitting time, rarely puts in extra hours, and

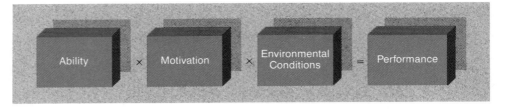

Figure 13-1 The relationship between performance and ability, motivation, and environmental conditions.

generally spends little time reading up on new developments in the field is not very motivated to excel.

In the end, how successful our two engineering friends actually are with their respective projects is likely to depend not only on their motivation, as reflected in effort expended, but also on their ability to handle the engineering subject matter. Environmental conditions, such as numerous interruptions when they are working, extra work assignments, or cramped office space, also may negatively influence respective performance. On the other hand, a quiet place to work, the help of assistants, and ample support resources, such as equipment, may have a positive effect on project performance. Thus actual project performance is likely to be a function of ability, motivation, and environmental conditions, as shown in Figure 13-1.[3] As a result, it is important that managers hire individuals who have the ability to do what is required. Then the management challenge is providing environmental conditions that nurture and support individual motivation to work toward organizational goals.

Early Approaches to Motivation

Perspectives differ on what managers need to do to encourage motivation.[4] One of the first individuals to address worker motivation explicitly was Frederick Taylor, who did so through his writings on scientific management between 1900 and 1915 (see Chapter 2). Because Taylor believed that people are motivated mainly by economic factors, he advocated a wage incentive system to encourage workers to excel at doing the job exactly as specified by management. However, the routine and specialized nature of the work, the tendency of managers to reduce wage incentives as production rose, and worker concerns that higher production would lead to job cutbacks led to worker resistance. Money, especially when it was curbed as production rose, did not seem to have the desired effects.

The apparent limitations of money as the sole motivational tool piqued the curiosity of researchers in the human relations school (see Chapter 2). On the basis of investigations such as the Hawthorne studies, conducted at the Western Electric Company between 1927 and 1932, these researchers argued for devoting greater attention to the social aspects of the job. According to their prescription, managers should make workers feel important, increase vertical communication, allow some decision making on very routine matters related to the job, and pay greater attention to work group dynamics and group incentives. Still, like the scientific management advocates, the human relations school emphasized gaining strict compliance with managerial directives in carrying out extremely routine, specialized jobs. As a result, these efforts met with only limited success in motivating workers' behavior.[5]

By demonstrating the inadequacy of viewing workers as robotlike appendages that can be manipulated into compliance, these early efforts laid the groundwork for more sophisticated approaches and a better understanding of the motivation process.

A Simplified Model of Motivation

Since the early work of the scientific management and human relations theorists, management scholars have developed a number of different theories that help us understand what motivates people at work. Figure 13-2 shows a simplified model of the main elements in the motivation process. As the model indicates, our inner needs (such as needs for food, companionship, and growth) and cognitions (such as knowledge and thoughts about various efforts we might expend and potential rewards we might receive) lead to various behaviors. Assuming that the behaviors are appropriate to the situation, they may result in rewards. The rewards then help reinforce our behaviors, fulfill our needs, and provide input into our cognitions about the linkages between our behaviors and possible future rewards. Conversely, lack of rewards may lead to unfulfilled needs, leave behaviors unreinforced, and influence our thinking about where to expend our efforts in the future. Since motivation is a complex phenomenon, major motivational theories address the various elements in the process (see

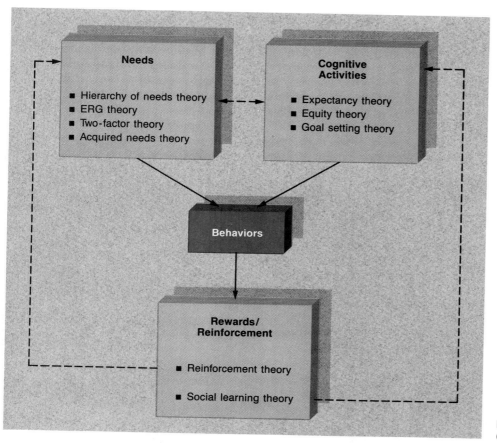

Figure 13-2 A simplified model of the motivation process.

Figure 13-2). In order to understand better the implications of these elements for managers, we explore the respective theories in subsequent sections of this chapter, beginning with need theories.

NEED THEORIES

What makes a person such as Linda Wachner, president of Warnaco, Inc., overcome adolescent spinal surgery that left her in a body cast for over a year, tackle the challenge of successfully turning around the ailing U.S. division of Max Factor & Company, and work 14-hour days to eventually reach her lofty position as head of a Fortune 500 apparel conglomerate?[6] What possessed Kemmons Wilson, founder of the Holiday Inns, to start building another hotel chain at age 75?[7] Need theories argue that we behave the way we do because we have internal needs that we are attempting to fulfill. These theories are sometimes called *content theories* of motivation because they specify *what* motivates individuals (i.e., the content of needs). In this section, we explore four prominent theories that examine what needs individuals are likely to have and how these needs operate as motivators: hierarchy of needs theory, ERG theory, two-factor theory, and acquired-needs theory.

Hierarchy of Needs Theory

Hierarchy of needs theory
A theory (developed by Maslow) that argues that individual needs form a five-level hierarchy

Physiological needs
Survival needs such as food, water, and shelter

One of the most widely known theories of motivation is the **hierarchy of needs theory,** developed by psychologist Abraham Maslow and popularized during the early 1960s, which argues that individual needs form a five-level hierarchy (shown in Figure 13-3). According to this hierarchy, our first need is for survival, so we concentrate on basic **physiological needs,** such as food, water, and shel-

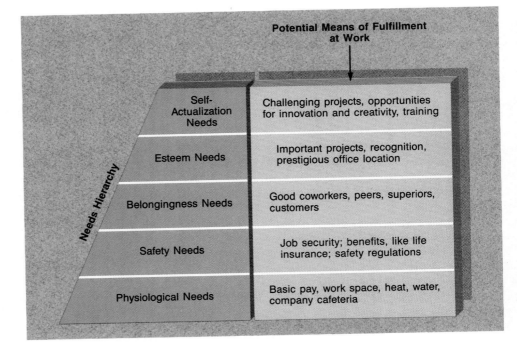

Figure 13-3 Maslow's hierarchy of needs.

ter, until we feel fairly sure that these needs are covered. Next, we concern ourselves with **safety needs,** which pertain to the desire to feel safe, secure, and free from threats to our existence. Once we feel reasonably safe and secure, we turn our attention to relationships with others in order to fulfill our **belongingness needs,** which involve the desire to affiliate with and be accepted by others. With support from loved ones, we focus on **esteem needs,** which are related to the two-pronged desire to have a positive self-image and to have our contributions valued and appreciated by others. Finally, we reach the highest level, **self-actualization needs,** which pertain to the requirement of developing our capabilities and reaching our full potential. Here we concern ourselves with such matters as testing our creativity, seeing our innovative ideas translated into reality, pursuing new knowledge, and developing our talents in uncharted directions. Needs at this highest level are never completely fulfilled, because as we work to develop our capabilities, both our potential and our needs for self-actualization grow stronger. Some possible work-related means of fulfilling the various needs in the hierarchy are shown in Figure 13-3.

Maslow recognized that a need might not have to be completely fulfilled before we start directing our attention to the next level in the hierarchy. At the same time, he argued that once we have essentially fulfilled a need, that need ceases to be a motivator and we begin to feel tension to fulfill needs at the next level.

While Maslow's hierarchy has stimulated thinking about the various needs that individuals have, it has some serious shortcomings. Research suggests that needs may cluster into two or three categories, rather than five. Also, the hierarchy of needs may not be the same for everyone. Entrepreneurs frequently pursue their dreams for years despite the relative deprivation of lower-level needs. Finally, individuals often seem to work on satisfying several needs at once, even though some needs may be more important than others at a given point in time.[8]

ERG Theory

Because of the criticisms of Maslow's hierarchy of needs theory, motivation researcher Clayton Alderfer proposed an alternative known as **ERG theory.**[9] The name stems from combining Maslow's five needs into three need levels: existence, relatedness, and growth. **Existence needs** include the various forms of material and physiological desires, such as food and water, as well as work-related forms such as pay, fringe benefits, and physical working conditions. **Relatedness needs** address our relationships with significant others, such as families, friendship groups, work groups, and professional groups. They deal with our need to be accepted by others, achieve mutual understanding on matters that are important to us, and exercise some influence over those with whom we interact on an ongoing basis. **Growth needs** impel creativity and innovation, along with the desire to have a productive impact on our surroundings.

ERG need levels differ in terms of concreteness, that is, the degree to which their presence or absence can be verified. The existence need level is the most concrete, relating to issues such as our rate of pay and the pleasantness of our work surroundings. The growth need level is the least concrete, involving more nebulous issues such as our level of creativity, the degree to which our capabilities are growing relative to our capacity, and the long-term impact of our efforts on our organization. According to ERG theory, we generally tend to concentrate first on our most concrete requirements. As existence needs are resolved, we have more energy available for concentrating on relatedness needs, which offer a potential source of support that can help us in satisfying growth needs. Then,

Safety needs Needs that pertain to the desire to feel safe, secure, and free from threats to our existence

Belongingness needs Needs that involve the desire to affiliate with and be accepted by others

Esteem needs Needs related to the two-pronged desire to have a positive self-image and to have our contributions valued and appreciated by others

Self-actualization needs Needs that pertain to the requirement of developing our capabilities and reaching our full potential

ERG theory An alternative (proposed by Alderfer) to Maslow's hierarchy of needs theory which argues that there are three levels of individual needs

Existence needs Needs that include the various forms of material and physiological desires, such as food and water, as well as such work-related forms as pay, fringe benefits, and physical working conditions

Relatedness needs Needs that address our relationships with significant others, such as families, friendship groups, work groups, and professional groups

Growth needs Needs that impel creativity and innovation, along with the desire to have a productive impact on our surroundings

Odetics, a high-tech manufacturing company, puts the emphasis on personal values. A sense of family—meeting the needs of relatedness—is nurtured through such perks as a state-of-the-art fitness center, swimming pool, clubs, organized games, and the company's own repertory theatre. Players in ORT (Odetics Repertory Theatre) are shown here in one corner of the manufacturing facility rehearsing for ''Scrooge.''

Satisfaction-progression principle   A principle that states that satisfaction of one level of need encourages concern with the next level

as relatedness needs are somewhat fulfilled, we have the energy and support needed to pursue growth needs. Thus ERG theory incorporates a **satisfaction-progression principle** similar to that of Maslow in that satisfaction of one level of need encourages concern with the next level.

Aside from focusing on three need levels instead of five, ERG theory differs from the hierarchy of needs theory in three significant ways. First, although the general notion of a hierarchy is retained, Alderfer's theory argues that we can be concerned with more than one need category at the same time. Needs at lower levels are not necessarily fairly well satisfied before we concern ourselves with other needs, although satisfaction of lower-level needs can be helpful in allowing us to devote our attention to higher-level needs. For example, even if we have skipped lunch and are extremely hungry, we still may be concerned primarily with solving a challenging customer problem. On the other hand, at some point our hunger may interfere with our problem-solving efforts. Second, ERG theory is more flexible in acknowledging that some individuals' needs may occur in a somewhat different order than that posited by the ERG framework. Inventor Godfrey Hounsfield worked so intensely while developing the CAT scanner at Britain-based EMI, Ltd., that his boss became worried about his health and ordered him to take a vacation (see Chapter 8 for further details).[10]

Frustration-regression principle   A principle that states that if we are *continually* frustrated in our attempts to satisfy a higher-level need, we may cease to be concerned about that need

Third, ERG theory incorporates a **frustration-regression principle.** This principle states that if we are *continually* frustrated in our attempts to satisfy a higher-level need, we may cease to be concerned about that need. Instead, we may regress to exhibiting greater concern for a lower-level need that is more concrete and seemingly more within our grasp. For example, we may become more concerned with establishing strong relationships with coworkers if our continuing efforts to obtain more interesting work are ignored by our boss.

Both Maslow's hierarchy theory and ERG theory are extremely difficult to test because they involve measuring and tracking individuals' changing needs and fulfillment levels over time. So far, the limited research on ERG theory has generally been supportive.[11] If ERG theory is correct in predicting that individuals attempt to fulfill multiple needs at the same time, then motivating individuals is likely to require offering a variety of means for need fulfillment. Because of the frustration-regression aspect of ERG theory, managers need to be particularly concerned with providing opportunities to satisfy growth needs, lest employees cease to be interested in them. At Genentech, the head of research walks a fine line between encouraging the growth needs of scientists and channeling their efforts mainly into endeavors with some hope of company payoff. A different, but also challenging, situation exists at Original Copy Centers, Inc. (see the following Case in Point discussion).

CASE IN POINT: Original Ways of Motivating Behavior

At Original Copy Centers, Inc., a fast-growing corporate and legal copy service in Cleveland, owners Nancy Vetrone and Robert Bieniek use all the originality they can muster to motivate their more than 145 employees, many of whom perform relatively mundane and repetitious tasks, such as operating copy machines or picking up and delivering materials. Noting that the average age of their employees is under 30 and that many are single, Vetrone and Bieniek came up with one unusual, but well-appreciated, employee amenity, a laundry room at work where staff members can wash and dry their clothes. Other provisions include a six-person sauna, locker rooms and showers, a mini-theater, a video library with over 750 titles for employees to rent and view, a game room with a billiards table, an exercise room, company personal computers for employee use, various arcade games, a kitchen, and free coffee. Given the nature of the employees' jobs, Bieniek says, "It makes sense to give employees a pleasant environment. We hope that the Original work environment is as nice or better than their private living conditions, so they'll be in a hurry to get here and they won't be in a hurry to leave."

To afford them greater status, delivery personnel are called "corporate couriers," wear smart, professional-looking uniforms, and seem to view themselves as part of the image of a fast-moving company. Since they are the kingpins in Original's obsessive concern with timely pickups and deliveries, couriers are trained to talk with customers and learn receptionists' names. They have helped develop detailed maps of the inside of every commercial building in Cleveland, a factor that speeds up the almost 300 trips per day made to customer locations. Original employees at all levels (including couriers, receptionists, and production staff) are invited to assist in attracting new customers by staffing the Original booth at trade shows, dispensing the million "I'm an Original" stickers. These stickers promote the individual and require personal interaction with each prospective client. The stickers have shown up at such settings as Cleveland Browns home games, summer river festivals, parades, and marathon races.

These efforts help employees' personal and professional growth. Other means that ensure growth and loyalty within the Original organization are: the use of and training on personal computers, trusting employees to complete their own time cards; flexible schedules and up to 20 overtime hours per week, and encouraging staff members to come up with new ideas that involve the successful company slogan, "I'm an Original." These efforts to motivate employees appear to be working. Counter to industry trends, only three employees at Original have quit in the 15 years that the company has been in operation. Further, members of the staff generally are willing to work extra hours and postpone weekend plans in order to help out in emergencies. As a result, the firm not only has earned a reputation for the fastest copy service turnaround but also is recog-

How do you motivate workers who must perform routine tasks day after day? For one thing, the owners of Original Copy Centers in Cleveland, Ohio, try to make working conditions as pleasant as possible. Their delivery personnel, who are called "couriers" and wear smart-looking uniforms (as shown here), are also made to feel an important part of the commercial photocopy firm. One result of the company's concern with employee morale is that only three workers have quit in fifteen years.

nized as America's largest copy center by *Quick Print* magazine. For four consecutive years, Original has made the INC. 500 fast-growth companies list, a list of the most rapidly growing privately owned small businesses in the United States, compiled each year by *INC.* magazine.[12] ■■■■■■

Two-Factor Theory

In another important quest to learn more about what motivates employees, researcher Frederick Herzberg asked 200 accountants and engineers to describe situations in which they felt particularly satisfied and highly motivated and those in which they felt dissatisfied and unmotivated. When they described motivating situations, the accountants and engineers, from nine companies in the Pittsburgh area, mentioned factors such as the work itself and feelings of achievement (see the right side of Figure 13-4). Herzberg called these factors **satisfiers,** or **motivators,** noting that they relate mainly to the content of the job. On the other hand, when the professionals talked about situations in which they felt unmotivated, they discussed a completely different set of factors, such as working conditions and supervision (see the left side of Figure 13-4). Herzberg called these factors **dissatisfiers,** or **hygiene factors,** pointing out that they are largely associated with the work environment.

On the basis of these interview results, Herzberg developed a **two-factor theory** of motivation, which argues that potential rewards fit into two categories, hygiene factors and motivators, each having distinctly different implications for employee motivation.[13] Hygiene factors are important as a means of keeping workers from being *dissatisfied,* but no amount of hygiene factors will ever lead to work satisfaction and motivation. Instead, to have *satisfied* and *motivated* employees, managers need to ensure that ample motivators are available. They can

Satisfiers, or **motivators** Type of factor that relates mainly to the content of the job (such as the work itself and feelings of achievement)

Dissatisfiers, or **hygiene factors** Type of factor that is largely associated with the work environment (such as working conditions and supervision)

Two-factor theory A theory (developed by Herzberg) which argues that potential rewards fit into two categories, hygiene factors and motivators, each having distinctly different implications for employee motivation

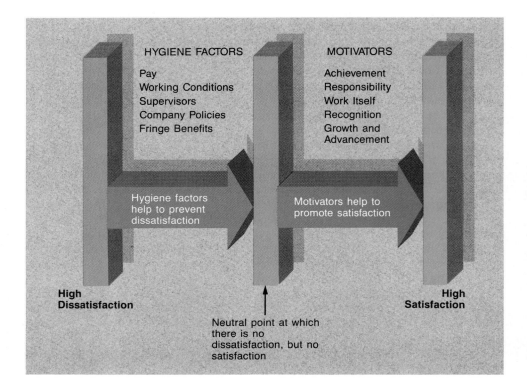

Figure 13-4 Herzberg's two-factor theory.

do this by changing the nature of jobs so that they include opportunities for achievement, challenge, responsibility, growth, and the other motivators. Herzberg called the actual process for change *job enrichment* (see Chapter 10).

Subsequent research has cast doubt on the two-factor idea, since researchers using other methods to study the issue have found that lack of motivators often is associated with dissatisfaction and that hygiene factors frequently are tied to satisfaction.[14] Herzberg may have obtained the results he did because individuals tend to associate positive things (such as accomplishments) with themselves and negative things (such as perceived obstacles) with factors in the environment. Nevertheless, the theory is significant because it focused managers' attention on the importance of motivators, factors that they sometimes underemphasize in attempting to motivate workers.[15] Moreover, the notion of changing the nature of jobs to increase their motivational potential led to a closer look at job design and alternative work schedules, issues that are considered in Chapter 10.[16]

Acquired-Needs Theory

While the hierarchy of needs theory, ERG theory, and the two-factor theory view certain needs as an inherent part of our makeup, psychologist David C. McClelland offers a different perspective, **acquired-needs theory,** which argues that our needs are acquired or learned on the basis of our life experiences. Although such needs tend to be a product of a variety of conditions to which we are exposed, sometimes even a specific event can profoundly influence our desires. For example, Estee Lauder, the billionaire baroness of the beauty supply industry, recounts that while selling her uncle's skin cream in a Manhattan beauty salon during the depression, she (then Josephine Esther Mentzer) admired the blouse of the owner and asked where the owner had purchased it. The owner curtly replied that it was an irrelevant question because a salesgirl would never be able to afford such a blouse. Those words fanned the young saleswoman's desire for achievement. "I wouldn't have become Estee Lauder if it hadn't been for her," she says.[17]

For more than three decades, McClelland has studied mainly three needs: achievement, affiliation, and power. He measures these needs using the Thematic Apperception Test (TAT), which involves having test takers write stories about pictures that are purposely ambiguous. The stories are then scored according to the achievement, affiliation, and power themes that they contain, the assumption being that individuals write about themes that are important to them. For most of us, test results would indicate a blending of the needs for achievement, affiliation, and power, rather than a high level of just one of these needs and none of the others.

McClelland's initial work centered on the **need for achievement (nAch),** the desire to accomplish challenging tasks and achieve a standard of excellence in one's work. Individuals with a high nAch typically seek competitive situations in which they can achieve results through their own efforts and can receive relatively immediate feedback on how they are doing. They like to pursue moderately difficult goals and take calculated risks; but, contrary to what is sometimes believed, high nAchs typically avoid *extremely* difficult goals because of the substantial risk of failure.[18] Since they like problems that require innovative and novel solutions, high-nAch individuals can be a valuable source of creativity and innovative ideas in organizations.[19]

Estimates are that only about 10 percent of the U.S. population has a high nAch. Managers who want to motivate high achievers need to make sure that

These Red Cross workers rescuing a victim of Mexico's earthquake in 1986 likely have a high need for affiliation (nAff). High nAff is associated with the desire to coperate and work with others and is commonly found among health care workers, teachers, and counselors.

Acquired-needs theory   A theory (developed by McClelland) stating that our needs are acquired or learned on the basis of our life experiences

Need for achievement (nAch) The desire to accomplish challenging tasks and achieve a standard of excellence in one's work

Need for affiliation (nAff)
The desire to maintain warm, friendly relationships with others

Need for power (nPow)
The desire to influence others and control one's environment

Personal power A need for power in which individuals want to dominate others for the sake of demonstrating their ability to wield power

Institutional power A need for power in which individuals focus on working with others to solve problems and further organizational goals

such individuals have challenging, but reachable, goals that allow relatively immediate feedback about achievement progress. Although McClelland argues that high-nAch individuals may not be motivated by money per se (because they derive satisfaction mainly from their achievements), they still may place considerable importance on money as a source of feedback on how they are doing.[20]

To a lesser extent, McClelland's work also has addressed the **need for affiliation (nAff),** the desire to maintain warm, friendly relationships with others. High-nAff individuals are particularly likely to gravitate toward professions that involve a large amount of interaction with others, such as health care, teaching, sales, and counseling. To motivate high-nAff individuals, managers need to provide a cooperative, supportive work environment in which individuals can meet both performance expectations and their high affiliation needs by working with others. Individuals with a high nAff can be particular assets in situations that require a high level of cooperation with and support of others, including clients and customers.[21]

As he studied various needs, McClelland gradually came to view the **need for power (nPow),** the desire to influence others and control one's environment, as a particularly important motivator in organizations. Need for power has two forms, personal and institutional. Individuals with a high need for **personal power** want to dominate others for the sake of demonstrating their ability to wield power. They expect followers to be loyal to them personally rather than to the organization, sometimes causing organizational goals to be thwarted. In contrast, individuals with a high need for **institutional power** focus on working with others to solve problems and further organizational goals. Individuals with a high need for institutional power like getting things done in an organized fashion. They also are willing to sacrifice some of their own self-interests for the good of the organization.[22] Motivating individuals with a high need for institutional power involves giving them opportunities to hold positions that entail organizing the efforts of others.

McClelland has analyzed various needs in terms of their relationship to managerial effectiveness. He originally thought that individuals with a high need for achievement would make the best managers. His subsequent work suggests that, to the contrary, high-nAch individuals tend to concentrate on their own individual achievements rather than on the development and achievements of others. As a result, high-nAch individuals often make good entrepreneurs because initial success frequently depends largely on individual achievement. They may not, however, make good managers in situations that require working with a number of others and waiting to learn the results of their efforts. Similarly, individuals with a personal-power orientation run into difficulties as managers because they often attempt to use the efforts of others for their own personal benefit. Critics argue that the demise of E. F. Hutton, the old-line Wall Street brokerage firm that was taken over by the Shearson Lehman brokerage house in the late 1980s, was due largely to the absolute power wielded by CEO Robert Fomon, who headed the firm for 16 years. In addition to hiring and promoting close friends, Fomon apparently personally reviewed the salaries and bonuses of more than 1000 employees, spurned budgets in favor of having employees come to him for resources, spent lavishly on entertainment and perquisites, and made most of the large and small decisions himself.[23] Individuals with a high need for affiliation also may have a managerial weakness, because they tend to concentrate on maintaining good interpersonal relationships rather than achieving goals.[24]

McClelland's work suggests that individuals with a high institutional-power need make the best managers because they are oriented toward coordinating the efforts of others to achieve long-term organizational goals. One study of more than 200 managers at AT&T over a 16-year period before the breakup of the company showed that individuals who were promoted to higher levels tended to have a moderate-to-high need for power and a relatively low need for affiliation. Need for achievement was important only early in the managers' careers, when their success depended more on individual contributions.[25] Other evidence indicates that need for achievement in managers may be more important at higher levels when organizations face highly competitive environments, such as AT&T now confronts.[26] Thus the need profile of successful managers, at least in competitive environments, appears to include (1) a moderate-to-high need for institutional power, (2) a moderate need for achievement to facilitate individual contributions early in one's career and a desire for the organization to maintain a competitive edge as one moves to higher levels, and (3) at least a minimum need for affiliation to provide sufficient sensitivity for influencing others[27]

What happens if an individual wants to be a manager but doesn't have the appropriate need profile? McClelland argues that it is possible to develop certain needs in ourselves and others. Through training, McClelland has successfully increased the need for achievement of individuals who subsequently received faster promotions and made more money than those not trained.[28] This type of training exposes individuals to tasks involving the achievement of goals and gradually makes the situations more challenging as the individuals increase their ability to handle the tasks. Trainees also are exposed to the behavior of appealing entrepreneurial models. Similar approaches apparently can be used to foster the need for institutional powers.[29] Other needs, such as the need for affiliation, may be more difficult to develop through such methods.

Assessing Need Theories

A comparison of the needs identified by the four theories is shown in Figure 13-5. The theories are generally compatible in pointing to the importance of higher-level needs as a source of motivation. The ERG and acquired-needs theories place greater emphasis than the other two theories on the notion that individuals differ in the makeup of their need structures, a stance that has stronger

Figure 13-5 Comparison of needs in four theories. (Adapted from Judith R. Gordon, *A Diagnostic Approach to Organizational Behavior*, 2d ed., Allyn and Bacon, Boston, 1987, p. 92.)

Maslow: Hierarchy of Needs Theory	Alderfer: ERG Theory	Herzberg: Two Factor Theory	McClelland: Acquired Needs Theory
Physiological	Existence		
Safety and security		Hygiene	
Belongingness and love	Relatedness		Need for affiliation
Self-esteem	Growth	Motivators	Need for achievement Need for power
Self-actualization			

research support than the view that the need structures of individuals are basically the same. In fact, McClelland's work demonstrates the possibility of acquiring needs related to managerial success through such mechanisms as training and carefully chosen work assignments.

The frustration-regression aspect of ERG theory, in which workers who are frustrated with attempts at meeting growth needs may revert to being concerned with a more concrete need, could have serious implications for organizations. Given the widespread current requirements for new and innovative ideas, improved quality, and greater capacity to implement needed changes, fostering growth needs is particularly important. Consider, for example, Wal-Mart, the retail chain that is expanding so fast that it has become the largest company job creator in the nation, adding over 150,000 employees to the company since 1982. Although the company typically hires new workers at only 10 percent above the minimum wage, it retains employees (called "associates") by delegating responsibility and offering scholarships of up to $2500 toward college tuition for employees who go to school and work part-time. As a result, approximately 40 percent of Wal-Mart's managers are individuals who began as trainees; this is an unusually high proportion in the turnover-ridden retail business.[30]

COGNITIVE THEORIES

Cognitive theories Theories that attempt to isolate the thinking patterns that we use in deciding whether or not to behave in a certain way

Need theories try to identify the internal desires that influence our behavior, but they do not go very far in explaining the thought processes that are involved. In contrast, **cognitive theories** attempt to isolate the thinking patterns that we use in deciding whether or not to behave in a certain way. Cognitive theories are not necessarily at odds with need theories; rather, they look at motivation from a different perspective. Because they focus on the thought processes associated with motivation, cognitive theories are sometimes called *process theories*. Three major cognitive theories that address work motivation are the expectancy, equity, and goal-setting theories.

Expectancy Theory

Expectancy theory A theory (originally proposed by Vroom) that argues that we consider three main issues before we expend the effort necessary to perform at a given level

Effort-performance expectancy Our assessment of the probability that our efforts will lead to the required performance level

The **expectancy theory** of motivation, originally proposed by Victor H. Vroom, argues that we consider three main issues before we expend the effort necessary to perform at a given level. These three issues are shown in the circles of Figure 13-6, which depicts the basic components of expectancy theory.

Effort-Performance Expectancy. With **effort-performance (E→P) expectancy,** we assess the probability that our efforts will lead to the required performance level. Our assessment may include evaluating our own abilities, as well as considering the adequacy of contextual factors such as the availability of resources. To see how effort-performance expectancy works, imagine that your boss has asked you to consider taking on a major special project. The project involves designing and implementing a new computerized tracking system for customer complaints so that you can vastly improve individual customer service and also learn more quickly about complaint trends. One of the first things that you might think about is the probability of your being able to achieve the high level of performance required, given your abilities and the related environmental factors. If you feel that you don't know very much about developing such systems and/or that the availability of resources is inadequate, you might assess the

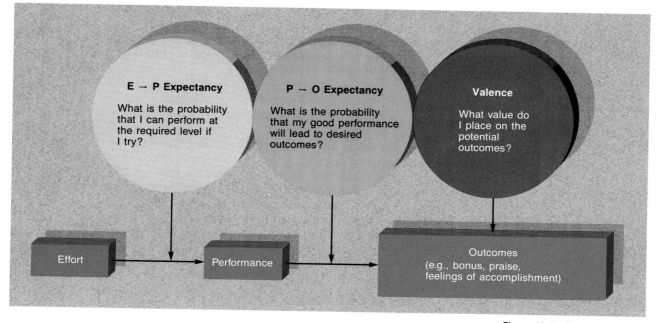

Figure 13-6 Basic components of expectancy theory.

probability of success as low. As a result, your E→P expectancy about this particular assignment might be quite low. On the other hand, if you feel that you are well qualified for the assignment and that the available resources for this particular assignment are adequate, you might assess the probability of your efforts' leading to high performance—the E→P expectancy—as quite high. However, your assessment of the effort-performance expectancy is only part of your evaluation of the situation.

Performance-Outcome Expectancy. With **performance-outcome (P→O) expectancy,** we assess the probability that our successful performance will lead to certain outcomes. The major outcomes that we consider are potential rewards (such as a bonus, a promotion, or a good feeling of accomplishment), although we are also likely to take into account the probability of possible negative outcomes (such as loss of leisure time or family disruption due to putting in extra hours on the job). Among the possible rewards in your special-project situation, perhaps your boss has a history of giving recognition and bonuses to individuals who take on special projects. If so, you might assess the P→O expectancy for taking on the project as very high. On the other hand, if your past experience with special projects and the boss suggests that the boss sometimes arranges for rewards but other times forgets, you might view the P→O expectancy as medium in strength (perhaps a 50–50 probability of being rewarded). In the worst case, if your boss never rewards extra effort, you might assess the P→O expectancy as virtually zero—at least for rewards available from the boss.

In any given situation, there may be many potential outcomes or rewards associated with performance. Rewards, such as bonuses, awards, or promotions, that are provided by others are known as **extrinsic rewards.** Rewards that are related to our own internal experiences with successful performance, such as feelings of achievement, challenge, and growth, are known as **intrinsic rewards.** Considering various possible outcomes or rewards (both positive and negative), we form an assessment of the probability of our performance's leading to de-

Performance-outcome expectancy Our assessment of the probability that our successful performance will lead to certain outcomes

Extrinsic rewards Rewards, such as bonuses, awards, or promotions, that are provided by others

Intrinsic rewards Rewards that are related to our own internal experiences with successful performance, such as feelings of achievement, challenge, and growth

sired outcomes. If our assessment of the P→O expectancy is high, the expectancy will contribute to our motivation; otherwise, our assessment could have a detrimental effect on our willingness to perform at a high level. Still, we have another motivational component to consider—how important the various outcomes are to us.

Valence Our assessment of the anticipated value of various outcomes or rewards

Valence. With the **valence** component, we assess the anticipated value of various outcomes or rewards. If the rewards that are available are ones that interest us, valence will be high. We also consider the value of possible negative outcomes, such as the likely loss of leisure time or the disruption of our family, that may offset the value of rewards in a given situation. The available rewards will have a motivating effect only when we attach a high overall valence to the situation. In the special-project situation, for example, you might view the prospect of a special bonus from the boss in an extremely positive light. On the other hand, if your rich aunt just left you $3 million, the bonus may be much less important. Still, you may attach a high value to the intrinsic rewards that might result if you develop the innovative new project.

Combining the Elements. Expectancy theory argues that in deciding whether or not to put forth effort in a particular direction, we will consider all three elements: E→P expectancy, P→O expectancy, and valence. Originally, expectancy theory indicated that individuals develop complex formulations involving specific probabilities and valence ratings for various outcomes. However, more recent work studying the way in which individuals process information suggests that individuals are more likely to make global judgments about each of the three elements in a given situation and then combine the elements according to the general overall formula posited by expectancy theory: (E→P) × (P→O) × valence = motivation.[31] For example, in the project situation, suppose that you assess all three elements as relatively high. Chances are that you will be fairly highly motivated to pursue the project: high E→P expectancy × high P→O expectancy × high valence = high motivation. On the other hand, consider the implications of assessing one of the elements as extremely low. For the sake of simplicity, let us assume that you assess the P→O expectancy as virtually zero but the other elements as high. The expectancy theory formula would predict that motivation will be zero: high E→P expectancy × zero P→O expectancy × high valence = zero motivation. An assessment of zero for any of the elements leads the whole equation to be equal to zero, regardless of the level of the other two elements. This is because you are unlikely to want to pursue the project if you believe that there is no (or an extremely low) prospect of being able to perform adequately in the situation, assess a zero (or an extremely low) possibility to the chance that successful performance will lead to certain outcomes, or attach a zero (or an extremely low) valence value to potential outcomes. In more mixed situations in which some of the elements are fairly high, you will probably compare the situation with alternatives and choose the one that provides the best prospects of leading to outcomes that you value. In the special-project situation, if you do not rate all three elements highly, you might try to negotiate with your boss either to improve the prospects of good outcomes or to shift assignments so that you receive a task that offers greater motivational potential.

Early research on expectancy theory attempted to use the theory to compare the likely motivation of various individuals in the same situation. These comparisons ran into difficulty primarily because individuals differed in the outcomes that they considered in a given situation. In a sense, they used different yardsticks to measure the same situations. In actuality, the theory was never developed to compare individuals with one another; rather, it was aimed at predicting where a given individual might decide to expend effort, given the choices available.[32] More recent efforts to use the theory as intended have been more successful.[33] For example, the theory has been useful in such situations as predicting whether or not individual naval officers would voluntarily decide to retire, foretelling which job a given undergraduate student would choose after graduation, and determining which M.B.A. program a particular college graduate would ultimately select.[34] The theory can also help explain the success of a revolutionary idea at a Soviet factory (see the following Case in Point discussion).

CASE IN POINT: Soviet Factory Implements Revolutionary Idea

In the early 1980s, the situation was bleak at the Konveyer Industrial Amalgamation, which manufactures automatic loading machines, conveyor belts, and other "transportation systems" outside of Lvov. Valentin Vologzhin, the current plant director, described the state of affairs: "It was bad, really bad. No one wanted to buy our equipment. Our orders were way off. The quality was poor. We couldn't give customers what they needed, so they had to go elsewhere— usually abroad to Italy and France." In addition, the plant was losing large numbers of rubles, necessitating considerable subsidies from Moscow's central financial ministries.

When Vologzhin was brought in as director, he implemented a revolutionary idea, a system known as *aktsiya*, which translates into what westerners think of as corporate ownership. Konveyer is the first Soviet enterprise since Lenin's New Economic Policy in the 1920s to offer workers the opportunity to purchase shares in their organization. Vologzhin was able to sell the Soviet Union's bureaucratic central planners on the *aktsiya* idea for two reasons. First, the shares purchased would provide financing for the plant, so it would not need to tap government resources in Moscow. Second, the shares system would give workers a stake in the success of their organization.

Under the plan, which began in 1988, employees can purchase up to 10,000 rubles' worth of shares, which are valued at 50 rubles each. They can sell them back to the plant at any time for the amount of their original purchase price. Thus the shares themselves do not change value, but they are guaranteed by the central financial ministries in the event that Konveyer loses money or goes bankrupt. The attraction to workers is the safety of the investment and the relatively high dividend, which was 20 percent for the first year because of vast improvements in quality and production at the plant. More than 80 percent of the workers have bought shares in the plan, and the number is growing. Individuals other than workers are not eligible to purchase shares because such an arrangement "amounts to exploitation and the ownership of someone else's labor," says Vologzhin, reflecting the values of the Soviet system. The innovative approach, which has made Vologzhin and the Konveyer plant famous, represents a giant step toward providing incentives for workers to increase productivity.[35]

Thus the Konveyer plant has not only increased available valences but also made major strides in linking performance and outcomes. Of course, the dividend program provides a somewhat weaker connection between worker actions and outcomes than would be the case with an incentive plan based specifically on a worker's own production. Still, for the Soviet system, the notion of purchasing shares in one's own organization is a major innovation and a move toward better utilization of the motivational elements contained in expectancy theory.

Expanding Expectancy Theory. If you ask several people whether they would agree that satisfied workers work harder, they are likely to reply in the affirmative. Although the notion seems to have intuitive appeal, research has not always found a strong link between worker satisfaction and performance. To understand why, Lyman W. Porter and Edward E. Lawler III developed the expanded expectancy theory model shown in Figure 13-7. According to this model, satisfaction does *not* lead to performance. Rather, the *reverse* is true: performance can (but does not always) lead to satisfaction through the reward process.

To follow this model, let us consider three possible scenarios involving Alissa, Bob, and Christen. In the first scenario, Alissa performs well, receives a bonus from the boss (extrinsic reward), feels good about her achievement (intrinsic reward), and ultimately feels satisfied. In this case, we have high performance and high satisfaction. In the second scenario, Bob performs well and feels good about his achievement (intrinsic reward), but the boss does not even say "good job," much less give him a bonus. As a result, even though Bob feels good about his achievement, he is so annoyed with the boss that his satisfaction level is low. So with Bob we have a case of high performance but low satisfaction because he does not feel that he was adequately rewarded. In our third scenario, Christen does very little work but receives a sizable bonus at the end of the year, which pleases her greatly. With Christen, we have a case of low performance but high satisfaction.

How do we get to the ideal of high performance and high satisfaction? As suggested by the extended model, a crucial element is rewarding high performance (as occurred with Alissa but, unfortunately, not with Bob). Rewarding high performance leads to a high P→O expectancy (see the feedback loop in Figure 13-7), an important component of motivation. Equally critical, poor per-

Figure 13-7 An expanded model of expectancy theory. (Adapted from David A. Nadler and Edward E. Lawler III, "Motivation: A Diagnostic Approach," in J. Richard Hackman, Edward E. Lawler III, and Lyman W. Porter (eds.), *Perspectives on Behavior in Organizations*, 2d ed., McGraw-Hill, New York, 1983, p. 75; and Lyman W. Porter and Edward E. Lawler III, *Managerial Attitudes and Performance*, Irwin, Homewood, Ill., 1968, p. 165.)

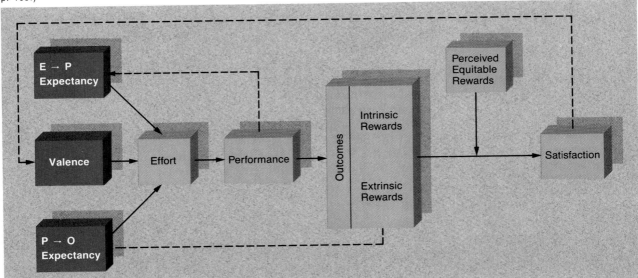

formance should *not* be rewarded (as was done in the case of Christen). Rewarding poor performance leads to a low P→O expectancy and ultimately to low subordinate motivation to perform.

Aside from the issues relating to the P→O expectancy, expectancy theory has some other major implications for managers. For one thing, it is useful for managers to foster a high E→P expectancy in subordinates. This can be done by being very clear about performance expectations, setting performance goals so that they are challenging, but doable, making sure that employees have the training and resources necessary to reach the required performance levels, and providing encouragement. Another major factor in encouraging motivation is offering opportunities for rewards (both extrinsic and intrinsic) with a high valence to employees. As suggested by need theories, valences are likely to differ among employees and are subject to change as some needs are fulfilled and others become paramount.[36]

The logic underlying expectancy theory is the force behind recent trends toward basing pay on performance. Companies are doing more to promote a high P→O expectancy by making sure that various rewards are strongly keyed to performance issues. For example, until recently at the Ford Motor Company, the number of people that a manager supervised was a factor in pay, sometimes causing managers to concentrate on getting more people to report to them rather than on achieving high performance with the smallest possible staff. That has all changed with a new merit pay system that ties raises to increases in productivity.[37] Other examples of the trend toward emphasizing rewards for performance can be found in the John Hancock Mutual Life Insurance Company, whose lower-level managers are eligible for awards of up to 10 percent of their salaries for "extraordinary" work; Hewlett-Packard, whose 200 to 300 special stock options per year are earmarked for employees who deliver extra accomplishments; and Sbarro, Inc., a chain of cafeteria-style restaurants, whose productive managers are given up to 15 percent of a restaurant's net profits.[38] The extended model of expectancy theory also indicates that managers might not get the expected results from their motivational efforts unless employees perceive their outcomes and rewards as equitable, an issue specifically addressed by equity theory.

Equity Theory

On August 20, 1986, Patrick Henry Sherill shot and killed 14 coworkers at the Edmond, Oklahoma, post office before turning the gun on himself. As the story unraveled, it became clear that he felt that he had not been dealt with equitably by a variety of people, including those with whom he worked.[39] Fortunately, such drastic reactions from employees occur infrequently. However, the incident illustrates the fact, as suggested by the extended model of expectancy theory, that feelings of inequitable treatment can have a major impact on employees. To help explain how we identify and react to situations of inequity, J. Stacy Adams developed equity theory while working for the Behavioral Research Service of General Electric.[40]

According to **equity theory,** we prefer situations of balance, or equity, which exists when we perceive the ratio of our inputs and outcomes to be equal to the ratio of inputs and outcomes for a comparison other (or others). The selection of the person or persons with whom we compare ourselves depends on our own view of appropriate comparisons. For example, in considering the equity of a pay raise, we might compare our pay with that of certain coworkers, peers in other units, and/or a friend with similar credentials who works for another company. The inputs we consider in assessing the ratio of our inputs

Equity theory A theory that argues that we prefer situations of balance, or equity, which exists when we perceive the ratio of our inputs and outcomes to be equal to the ratio of inputs and outcomes for a comparison other

Wilber Marshall caused a stir when he left the Chicago Bears to sign a 5-year $6 million contract with the Washington Redskins in 1988. He became the highest paid defensive linebacker in the league as well as the highest paid player on the Redskins team. It is not surprising that Marshall's contract triggered perceptions of inequity among his new teammates, some of whom called for renegotiation of their own contracts.

and outcomes relative to the ratios of others may cover a broad range of variables, including educational background, skills, experience, hours worked, and performance results. Outcomes might include such factors as pay, bonuses, praise, parking places, office space, furniture, and work assignments. The inputs and outcomes that we use to assess the equity of a situation are based strictly on our own perceptions of what is relevant.

According to the theory, situations of inequity exist whenever our inputs-outcomes ratio is either less than or greater than the inputs-outcomes ratio of a comparison other. In making equity judgments, we consider equity in *relative* (compared to another) rather than absolute (compared to a set standard) terms. The implication is that we may feel equitably treated in a situation in which we provide high inputs and receive low outcomes as long as the person with whom we compare ourselves also contributes high inputs and receives low outcomes. Likewise, we are likely to feel equitably treated if other people have higher outcomes than we do as long as we perceive their inputs as sufficiently greater than ours to justify the difference. Although the theory argues that we will feel inequitably treated when we perceive our inputs-outcomes ratio to be greater than that of our comparison other (e.g., we receive a significantly higher pay raise than someone else even though we perceive that our inputs have been the same), research suggests that individuals adjust to such conditions of over-reward rather quickly. Therefore, conditions of underreward (our inputs-outputs ratio is less than that of a comparison other) have much greater impact on motivation than do conditions of overreward.[41]

The motivational aspect of equity theory is based on its two major premises. First, the theory argues that the perception of inequity creates a tension in us. Second, the tension motivates us to eliminate or reduce the inequity. The greater the perceived inequity, the stronger the tension and the greater our motivation to reduce it.

Reducing or Eliminating Inequity. Although the specific actions an individual takes will depend on what appears to be feasible in a given situation, Adams suggests that maintaining one's self-esteem is an important priority. As a result, an individual will probably first attempt to maximize outcomes and to resist personally costly changes in inputs. Changing perceptions about the inputs and outcomes of others or attempting to alter their side of the equation will usually be more palatable than cognitively changing or actually altering one's own side of the equation. Actions to leave the situation will probably be taken only in cases of high inequity when the other alternatives are not feasible. Finally, an individual will be highly resistant to changing the comparison others, especially if the objects of comparison have stabilized over time.

One particularly interesting study demonstrating the potential impact of inequities traced the performance of 23 major-league baseball players who began the 1976 season without contracts. Because of major changes in league contract rules, the researchers speculated that the players would be likely to perceive themselves as underpaid in reference both to others who had signed lucrative contracts and to their own lower compensation as compared to that of the previous year. The prediction that the 23 players would reduce their inputs, one of their few short-term options for reducing the inequity, was confirmed when they logged lower season performance levels for batting average, home runs, and runs batted in.[42]

Although Adams's equity formulation considered one situation at a given point in time, recent work on the theory also considers inequities that extend over a period of time. The addition of the time perspective helps explain why people sometimes blow up over seemingly small inequities. Residues from previous inequities may pile up until the small incident becomes the "straw that broke the camel's back," and we react strongly.[43]

Implications for Managers. Equity theory makes several helpful suggestions to supplement the recommendations of expectancy theory. For one thing, managers need to maintain two-way communication with subordinates so that they have some idea of subordinates' equity perceptions. For another, it is important to let subordinates know the "rules" that will govern the allocation of outcomes relative to inputs. This issue is closely related to the expectancy theory recommendation that the relationship between performance and outcomes (performance-outcome expectancy) be made clear to subordinates. Also, a pattern of inequities over a period of time can build into major difficulties, which is another reason for maintaining good communication with subordinates, superiors, peers, customers, and other individuals associated with the job.

Goal-Setting Theory

The many advantages of establishing goals throughout the organization, as well as methods for doing so, are reviewed in Chapter 5. While goal setting was originally viewed as a technique, it is developing into a motivational theory as researchers attempt to understand better the cognitive factors that influence its success. Goal-setting experts Edwin A. Locke and Gary P. Latham argue that goal setting works by directing attention and action, mobilizing effort, increasing persistence, and encouraging the development of strategies to achieve the goals. Feedback regarding results also is an essential element in motivating through goal setting.[44]

The success of goal setting in motivating performance depends on establishing goals that have the appropriate attributes, or characteristics. In particular, goals should be specific and measurable, challenging, attainable, relevant to the major work of the organization, and time-limited in the sense of having a defined period of time within which the goal must be accomplished. At the Intel Corporation, which makes the microprocessor chips that are the "brains" of personal computers, goals have been successfully used to help cut down on the time it takes to develop and produce new microprocessors. The reduction—from 64 weeks to less than 52 weeks—is an important accomplishment, given the highly competitive environment within which microprocessor producers must operate.[45]

Goal commitment, one's attachment to or determination to reach a goal, is another important element in the goal-setting process. Goal commitment is affected by the major components of expectancy theory: effort-performance expectancy (Can I reach the goal?), performance-outcome expectancy (If I reach it, will I be rewarded?), and valence (Do I value the potential rewards?). Individuals are more likely to be committed to attaining goals when they have high expectations of success in reaching the goals, see strong connections between goal accomplishment and rewards, and value the rewards.[46] Goals themselves help clarify the meanings of performance in E→P expectancy and P→O expectancy, making it easier for individuals to make expectancy assessments. Hence expectancy theory and goal-setting theory are largely compatible.[47]

The usefulness of goal setting in enhancing performance has strong research support.[48] As a result, managers are likely to find it a very helpful motivational tool.

Assessing Cognitive Theories

Each of the cognitive theories of motivation offers a different, though somewhat complementary, perspective. Expectancy theory advises managers to help employees develop positive views of effort-performance expectancy through such means as training and encouragement. It also highlights the importance of a clear link between performance and outcomes, as well as the need to offer rewards that have a positive valence for employees (clues about valence come from need theories). Goal setting is compatible with expectancy theory in that it can help pinpoint the performance levels associated with effort-performance expectancy and performance-outcome expectancy. Finally, equity issues are a component part of the expectancy theory extended model, indicating the importance of maintaining equity in the motivation process.

REINFORCEMENT THEORY

The reinforcement approach to motivation is almost the antithesis of cognitive theories in that it does not concern itself with the thought processes of the individual as an explanation of behavior. The best-known approach to reinforcement theory, sometimes also called *operant conditioning theory* or *behaviorism*, has been pioneered by noted psychologist B. F. Skinner. According to **reinforcement theory**, our behavior can be explained by consequences in the environment and, therefore, it is not necessary to look for cognitive explanations.[49] Instead, the theory relies heavily on a concept called the **law of effect**, which states that behaviors having pleasant or positive consequences are more likely to be repeated and that behaviors having unpleasant or negative consequences are less likely to be repeated.[50]

> **Reinforcement theory** A theory that argues that our behavior can be explained by consequences
> **Law of effect** A concept that states that behaviors having pleasant or positive consequences are more likely to be repeated and that behaviors having unpleasant or negative consequences are less likely to be repeated

The way the reinforcement process works is that a stimulus provides a cue for a response or behavior that is then followed by a consequence. If we find the consequence rewarding, we are more likely to repeat the behavior when the stimulus occurs in the future; otherwise, we are less likely to repeat the behavior. For example, assume that you are the manager of a marketing research unit in a consumer-products company. A product manager from another unit asks you for emergency help with market research data (stimulus). You make the sacrifice of pulling some of your people from other priorities and even stay quite late to produce the needed data (behavior). The product manager makes sure that your unit is recognized for its efforts (a pleasant consequence). As a result, you may be likely to put extra effort into helping the product manager in the future. On the other hand, if the product manager complains about a minor error (an unpleasant consequence) and says nothing about the rest of the data or the extra effort that went into preparing it (a less than pleasant consequence), you will probably be less likely to put the same effort into helping the product manager in the future. The use of techniques associated with reinforcement theory is known as **behavior modification.**

> **Behavior modification** The use of techniques associated with reinforcement theory

Types of Reinforcement

In behavior modification, four types of reinforcement are available to help managers influence behavior: positive reinforcement, negative reinforcement, extinction, and punishment. Positive reinforcement and negative reinforcement are aimed at increasing a behavior, while extinction and punishment focus on decreasing a behavior (see Figure 13-8). Skinner argues that positive reinforce-

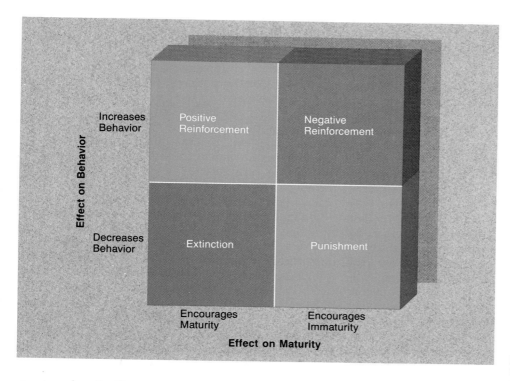

Figure 13-8 Types of reinforcement situations according to Skinner.

ment and extinction encourage individual growth whereas negative reinforcement and punishment are likely to foster immaturity in individuals and eventually contaminate the entire organization.

Positive Reinforcement.   Aimed at *increasing* a desired behavior, **positive reinforcement** involves providing a pleasant, rewarding consequence to encourage that behavior. The rewarding consequence, such as praise, a raise, or time off, is said to be a positive reinforcer if it leads to repetition of the desired behavior. Since individuals differ in regard to what they find pleasant and rewarding, managers need to monitor the effects of a particular reinforcer to determine whether it is effective in encouraging the desired behavior. Because individuals frequently do not execute a new behavior exactly as required when they first try it, managers often find it useful to encourage new behaviors through **shaping,** the successive rewarding of behaviors that closely approximate the desired response until the actual desired response is made. For example, a manager training a new salesperson may compliment the way that the individual greets customers (if this behavior approximates the desired response). The manager also may suggest questions that the salesperson might ask customers to obtain a better idea of their needs. Then the manager can reward the person's efforts to ask better questions and can make a further suggestion. Through this process the individual's behavior is gradually shaped so that the person becomes a competent salesperson.

Negative Reinforcement.   Like positive reinforcement, negative reinforcement focuses on *increasing* a desired behavior, but it operates in a different way. **Negative reinforcement** involves providing a noxious stimuli so that an individual will engage in the desired behavior in order to stop the noxious stimuli. In other words, the desired behavior is reinforced, but in a negative way because the

Positive reinforcement   A technique, aimed at *increasing* a desired behavior, that involves providing a pleasant, rewarding consequence to encourage that behavior

Shaping   The successive rewarding of behaviors that closely approximate the desired response until the actual desired response is made

Negative reinforcement   A technique, aimed at *increasing* a desired behavior, that involves providing a noxious stimuli so that an individual will engage in the desired behavior in order to stop the noxious stimuli

individual must engage in the desired behavior in order to get rid of a negative condition. For example, an engineer may work hard to finish a project on time (desired behavior) in order to stop (consequence) the chief engineer's nagging or yelling (noxious stimuli). With negative reinforcement, either the noxious, or unpleasant, stimuli is actually present or the potential is high for the noxious stimuli to occur unless the individual engages in the desired behavior. For instance, the chief engineer may already be nagging about meeting the project deadline; or the chief engineer may not actually be yelling or nagging yet, but the engineer may know from past experience that late projects trigger such behavior. In either case, the negative reinforcement increases the likelihood that the engineer will complete the project on time.

Although the use of negative reinforcement may encourage the desired behavior, it has the disadvantage of possibly making the individual feel negatively toward the person providing the negative reinforcement. In such cases, individuals may react by doing only what is required, declining to put in extra time when it might be helpful, or even leaving the organization. Negative reinforcement may also foster immature behavior. For example, negative reinforcement may unwittingly encourage the engineer to complete projects on time only when the boss is in the office.

Extinction A technique that involves withholding previously available positive consequences associated with a behavior in order to *decrease* that behavior

Extinction. **Extinction** involves withholding previously available positive consequences associated with a behavior in order to *decrease* that behavior. For example, the first few times that an employee engaged in clowning behavior in a staff meeting the manager laughed. Unfortunately, the laughter tended to reinforce the clowning to such a point that it became disruptive. The employee's clowning behavior gradually was extinguished because the manager proceeded to refrain from (withhold) laughing in response to it.

Punishment A technique that involves providing negative consequences in order to *decrease* or discourage a behavior

Punishment. **Punishment** involves providing negative consequences in order to *decrease* or discourage a behavior. Examples are criticizing the unwanted behavior whenever it occurs, suspending an individual without pay, denying training opportunities, or withholding resources such as new equipment. Punishment differs from negative reinforcement in at least two important ways. First, punishment aims to decrease or discourage an undesirable behavior, whereas negative reinforcement attempts to increase or encourage a desirable behavior. Second, punishment is usually applied after the individual has engaged in an undesirable behavior; conversely, with negative reinforcement, the noxious stimuli stops or is avoided when the desirable behavior occurs. Both punishment and negative reinforcement constitute negative approaches to affecting behavior, approaches that Skinner argues have long-run detrimental effects on individuals and organizations.

Arguments against the use of punishment are that it can have undesirable side effects (e.g., negative feelings toward the punisher) and may eliminate the undesirable behavior only as long as the threat of punishment remains. Also, it does not provide a model of correct behavior. Still, punishment may be necessary under some circumstances, particularly if the undesirable behavior has a serious impact on the organization or endangers others. In such situations, attempts to use extinction to decrease the undesirable behavior might not be practical because immediate action to stop the undesired behavior is necessary. Recent research suggests that if punishment must be used, it is likely to be most effective if there are recognized company policies that govern the situation; the punishment is given as soon as possible after the undesirable behavior; the punishment is moderate, rather than severe; and it is applied consistently.[51]

Schedules of Reinforcement

Reinforcement theory emphasizes using positive reinforcement to encourage desired behaviors. In studying positive reinforcement, researchers have discovered that different patterns of rewarding affect the time required to learn a new behavior and the degree to which the behavior persists. These different patterns, called **schedules of reinforcement,** specify the basis for and timing of positive reinforcement. There are two major types of schedules of reinforcement: continuous and partial. A *continuous* schedule of reinforcement involves rewarding a desired behavior each time it occurs. For example, a manager might praise a worker every time the worker performs a task correctly. This type of reinforcement is very effective during the initial learning process, but it becomes tedious and impractical on an ongoing basis. Further, the desired behavior tends to stop almost immediately (rapid extinction) unless the reinforcement is continued. An alternative, a *partial* schedule of reinforcement, involves rewarding the desired behavior intermittently rather than each time it occurs. With a partial schedule, a desired behavior can be rewarded more often to encourage a behavior during the initial learning process and less so later. There are four major types of partial reinforcement schedules: fixed interval, fixed ratio, variable interval, and variable ratio (see Figure 13-9).

Schedules of reinforcement Patterns of rewarding that specify the basis for and timing of positive reinforcement

Fixed Interval. With a **fixed-interval schedule of reinforcement,** a reinforcer is administered on a fixed time schedule, assuming that the desired behavior has continued at an appropriate level. The pattern exhibited by a plant manager who visits a section of the plant every day at approximately the same time and praises efforts being made to increase production quality would be an example of a

Fixed-interval schedule of reinforcement A pattern in which a reinforcer is administered on a fixed time schedule, assuming that the desired behavior has continued at an appropriate level

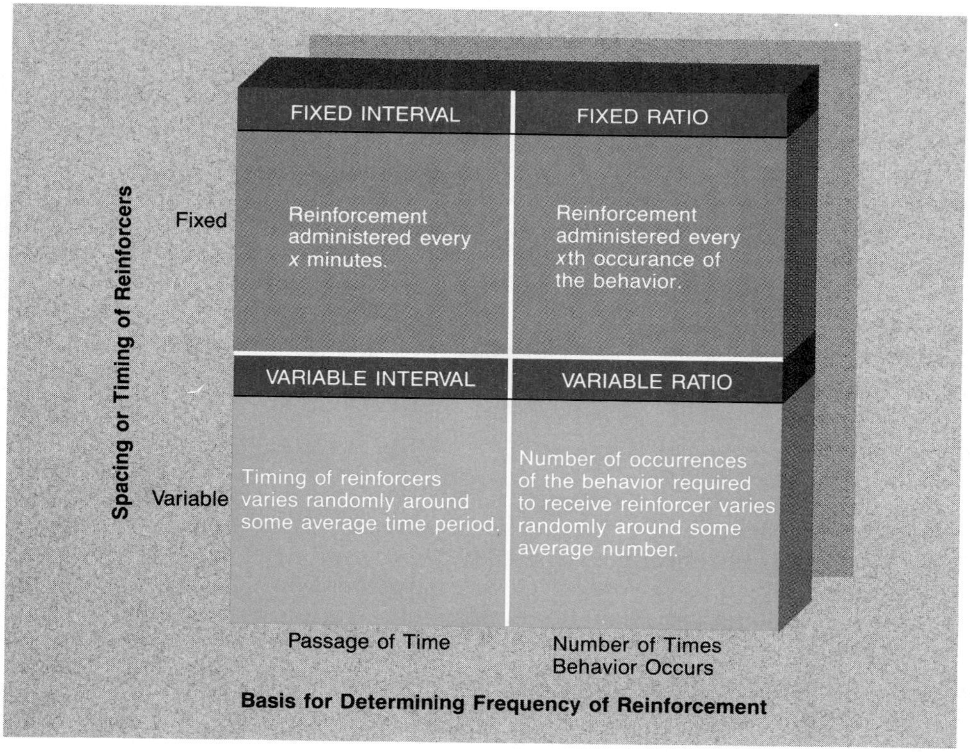

Figure 13-9 Types of partial reinforcement schedules. (Adapted from Hugh J. Arnold and Daniel C. Feldman, *Organizational Behavior,* McGraw-Hill, New York, 1986, p. 70.)

fixed-interval reinforcement schedule. This schedule tends to produce an uneven response pattern, with the desired behavior peaking just before the expected reinforcement and then declining somewhat until the next anticipated reinforcement. With a fixed-interval schedule, extinction is rapid if the reinforcement is delayed or stopped.

Fixed-ratio schedule of reinforcement   A pattern in which a reinforcer is provided after a fixed number of occurrences of the desired behavior

Fixed Ratio. With a **fixed-ratio schedule of reinforcement,** a reinforcer is provided after a fixed number of occurrences of the desired behavior, rather than according to a fixed time schedule. For example, special awards for innovative ideas might be given to individuals after they have contributed five implemented ideas. Piecework incentive pay systems, in which workers earn an incentive for producing a specified number of units, are also an example of fixed-ratio reinforcement. A fixed-ratio schedule tends to elicit a high response rate, but rapid extinction occurs if the reinforcer is discontinued even temporarily.

Variable-interval schedule of reinforcement   A pattern in which a reinforcer is administered on a varying, or random, time schedule that *averages* out to a predetermined time frequency

Variable Interval. With a **variable-interval schedule of reinforcement,** a reinforcer is administered on a varying, or random, time schedule that *averages* out to a predetermined time frequency. For example, a plant manager might visit a section of the plant to praise good quality an average of five times per week, but at varying times. This type of reinforcement schedule tends to promote a high, steady response rate with slow extinction.

Variable-ratio schedule of reinforcement   A pattern in which a reinforcer is provided after a varying, or random, number of occurrences of the desired behavior in such a way that the reinforcement pattern *averages* out to a predetermined ratio of occurrences per reinforcement

Variable Ratio. With a **variable-ratio schedule of reinforcement,** a reinforcer is provided after a varying, or random, number of occurrences of the desired behavior (rather than on a varying time schedule) in such a way that the reinforcement pattern *averages* out to a predetermined ratio of occurrences per reinforcement. For example, special awards for innovative ideas might be given to individuals on a ratio average of one award per five innovative ideas (i.e., an award after three ideas one time, after seven ideas another time, etc.). Slot-machine payoff patterns, which provide rewards after a varying number of pulls on the lever, are one of the best examples of a variable-ratio schedule. This type of schedule is likely to produce a very high response rate and is the partial reinforcement method with the slowest extinction rate. One recent example of variable-ratio reinforcement is the McDonald's Monopoly promotion, in which customers were given game pieces that contained stamps corresponding to the properties on a Monopoly game board. Although the odds for the top prize of $2 million were very long (1 in 724,214,000 in the 1988 version), more immediate reinforcement was provided because customers could win instant McDonald's food prizes at much better odds (1 in 12), as well as collect stamps for possible bigger prizes. The promotion was so successful that it was repeated 2 years in a row.

Using Reinforcement Theory

Researchers have proposed several guidelines to help managers effectively use the reinforcement approach. They advise that managers should emphasize positive reinforcement to encourage desired behaviors and to let subordinates know what behaviors will be rewarded. Once desired behaviors have been learned, variable-interval and variable-ratio reinforcement patterns seem to be the most effective approaches to maintaining the behaviors. Finally, if it is necessary to punish, punishment of moderate severity administered quickly and consistently seems to yield the best results.[52] The Union National Bank in Little Rock, Arkansas, has used positive reinforcement principles to increase output in the proof department, where employees encode machine-readable numbers onto the bottom of checks so that the checks can be credited to the appropriate accounts. As a result of putting up a graph that shows daily production and praising high performers, production increased from 1065 items per hour to 2100 items per hour. With the addition of individual bonuses based on daily output, production rose to 3500 items per hour.[53]

SOCIAL LEARNING THEORY

On the basis of his extensive work on reinforcement theory, noted psychologist Albert Bandura became convinced that the apparent success of the approach could not be explained without taking into account the cognitive, or thinking, capacity of individuals. Accordingly, he and others developed **social learning theory,** which argues that learning occurs through the continuous reciprocal interaction of our behaviors, various personal factors, and environmental forces. Individuals influence their environment, which in turn impacts the way in which they think and behave. In other words, we learn much of our behavior by observing, imitating, and interacting in a reciprocal manner with our social environment. Although social learning theory combines elements of both the cognitive and the reinforcement approaches, it is discussed at this point because it builds on reinforcement theory.

> **Social learning theory** A theory that argues that learning occurs through the continuous reciprocal interaction of our behaviors, various personal factors, and environmental forces

Major Components

Social learning theory argues that three cognitively related processes are particularly important in explaining our behavior: symbolic processes, vicarious learning, and self-control.[54] Figure 13-10 illustrates the interactions among these components.

Symbolic Processes. According to social learning theory, we rely heavily on **symbolic processes,** the various ways that we use verbal and imagined symbols to process and store experiences in representational forms (words and images) that can serve as guides to future behavior. For example, through the use of symbols, we can attempt to solve problems without actually trying all the alternative courses of action. We also may be able to visualize an intriguing vacation spot in the South Pacific even if we have never actually been there. Images of desirable futures allow us to set distant goals and fashion actions that will lead to the accomplishment of those goals. Our symbolic processes also incorporate a cognitive element called **self-efficacy,** the belief in one's capabilities to perform a specific task. Although somewhat similar to the effort-performance expectancy component of expectancy theory, self-efficacy is more oriented toward our convictions about our own capacities; it may be useful in explaining the levels of goals that we set, as well as task effort and persistence. For example, one study found that faculty members who feel competent at research and writing tend to produce more articles and books, which, in turn, increases their self-confidence and the likelihood of future productivity. Similar findings have emerged from studies of sales performance among life insurance agents.[55]

> **Symbolic processes** The various ways that we use verbal and imagined symbols to process and store experiences in representational forms that can serve as guides to future behavior

> **Self-efficacy** The belief in one's capabilities to perform a specific task

Vicarious Learning. **Vicarious learning,** or observational learning, refers to our ability to learn new behaviors and/or assess their probable consequences by observing others. This concept is important because, contrary to the arguments

> **Vicarious learning** Our ability to learn new behaviors and/or assess their probable consequences by observing others

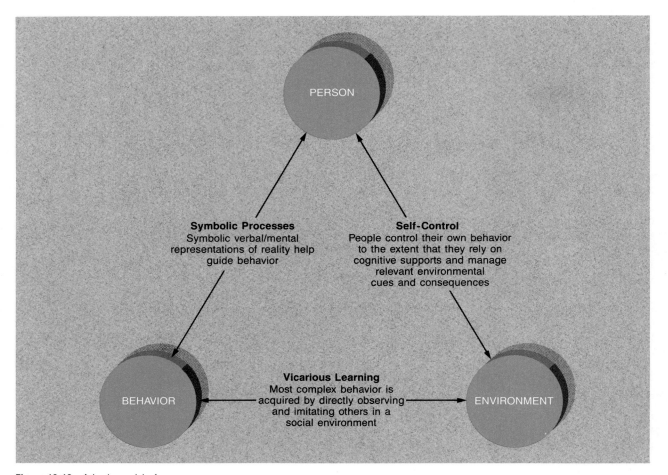

In the center of the triangle, labels connect the three circles:

PERSON (top circle)

BEHAVIOR (bottom left circle)

ENVIRONMENT (bottom right circle)

Symbolic Processes
Symbolic verbal/mental representations of reality help guide behavior

Self-Control
People control their own behavior to the extent that they rely on cognitive supports and manage relevant environmental cues and consequences

Vicarious Learning
Most complex behavior is acquired by directly observing and imitating others in a social environment

Figure 13-10 A basic model of social learning theory. (Reprinted from Robert Kreitner and Fred Luthans, ''A Social Learning Approach to Behavioral Management: Radical Behaviorists 'Mellowing Out,''' *Organizational Dynamics*, Autumn 1984, p. 55.)

Modeling Actually observing and attempting to imitate the behaviors of others

associated with reinforcement theory, we do not actually have to perform a behavior ourselves to learn about the consequences. The process of observing and attempting to imitate the behaviors of others is called **modeling.** If you have learned to swim or play tennis by imitating the behaviors of others (perhaps a proficient friend or an instructor), then you have engaged in modeling. Modeling usually takes place in four stages. In the *attention* stage, we select a model for observation, usually because we perceive the model to be skilled and successful, and we pay attention to the relevant aspects of behavior. In the *retention* stage, we retain information about the behavior through mental images and words. In the *reproduction* stage, we attempt to reproduce the behavior, perhaps being only partially successful and requiring further adjustment through feedback. In the *motivation* stage, we are motivated to adopt the model behavior. For this stage to lead to our actual adoption of the behavior, reinforcement must be present, usually from one of three sources. First, our behavior can be reinforced by the consequences in the environment in a manner similar to that noted by reinforcement theory. Second, reinforcement can occur vicariously through our observations of the consequences that have accrued to others engaging in the particular behavior. Third, we can engage in self-reinforcement through the process of self-control.

Self-Control. Self-control, or self-regulation, is our ability to exercise control over our own behavior by setting standards and providing consequences (both rewards and punishments) for our own actions. Self-control increases performance when we make our self-rewards conditional on reaching a challenging preset level of performance.[56] For example, we may promise ourselves a 15-minute break if we finish an assignment by a certain time, treat ourselves to something new when we get an A on an exam, or internally congratulate ourselves on a job well done. Since we are able to reinforce ourselves according to social learning theory, this approach gives us more credit for control over our own behavior than is the case with reinforcement theory.

Self-control Our ability to exercise control over our own behavior by setting standards and providing consequences for our own actions

Using Social Learning Theory

The social learning theory approach has considerable research support, although investigators have only recently begun to explore fully its implications for organizations.[57] The theory has two major managerial implications beyond those offered by other motivational theories. First, providing positive models appears to accelerate greatly the learning of appropriate behaviors, particularly if there are opportunities to try the new behaviors in a supportive setting and obtain feedback. Modeling can be particularly useful for training new workers. Second, the notion of vicarious learning indicates that employees are likely to draw conclusions about prospects for rewards and punishments, not only from their own experiences but also from those of others. One company whose operations reflect social learning theory principles, including modeling and various types of reinforcement, is Domino's Pizza, Inc. (see the following Case in Point discussion).

CASE IN POINT: Learning the Domino Theory

Begun as one small shop in 1960, Domino's Pizza almost went bankrupt before emerging in the late 1980s as the world's largest pizza delivery empire. A large part of Domino's success is attributable to the company's founder, Tom Monaghan, whose innovative ideas include the guarantee that Domino's will deliver an ordered pizza within 30 minutes or reduce the price and the use of the "hot box," which ensures that the delivered pizza will taste as if it just came out of the oven. With rapid growth, gross annual sales topping more than $1.5 billion, and over 4000 outlets, the need to train new workers and managers is almost insatiable.

To help meet this challenge, the company has developed a variety of video tapes, most of them aimed at the five basic worker positions in an outlet—phone answerer, pizza maker, oven tender, router, and driver. The videos cover such topics as orientation, image, dough management, pizza making, oven tending and maintenance, delivery, and safe driving. They combine detailed instructions with generous sprinklings of humor to hold the attention of new recruits. To incorporate humor, for example, one award-winning video on dough management shows a funeral scene featuring uncooked pizza dough that has "died" before its time; another, on safe driving, shows a hapless driver gradually turning into a werewolf, consumed by the pressure to deliver pizzas within the 30-minute limit. Managers are trained to show the videos; have individuals perform the various tasks in the desired manner, as clearly illustrated on the videos; and give workers appropriate feedback and reinforcement. The videos are sup-

Every Monday, the owner of the Domino's Pizza franchise in Washington takes his store managers for a six-mile jog. The run is in keeping with Domino founder Tom Monaghan's philosophy that, "our whole business is built on speed." Monaghan himself religiously runs 6½ miles a day. By providing good models and by reinforcing employee efforts through store contests and other incentives, the Domino organization motivates its workers.

plemented with a plethora of well-designed posters that provide further models of desired behaviors. For example, just above the counters where the pizzas are actually made, detailed glossy posters show exactly how a pizza should look at various stages in the process.

To make the grade at Domino's, employees must also meet challenging time performance standards. Order takers must answer the telephone within three rings and take an order within 45 seconds; pizza makers are expected to have the ordered pizza made and in the oven within 1 minute; and oven tenders are given 5 seconds to load one pizza while unloading another. Management trainees also must be able to meet these same standards, as well as others spelled out in detailed behavioral terms in the performance evaluation system.

Reinforcement comes from pay incentives and a heavy dose of competition based on employee contests within stores for the fastest service and delivery times and the highest sales figures. The contests frequently escalate to regional and national competitions, with results printed as "box scores" in the company newspaper, *The Pepperoni Press*. A powerful and unusual incentive is the prospect that high performers can become store managers within a year and franchisees within 2 years under very generous terms (30 percent of the outlets are company-owned; the rest are franchises). In fact, company policy holds that franchises are available only to individuals who have been store managers, and store managers themselves are normally promoted from within. As the number of desirable locations for franchises becomes more limited in the United States, additional motivational strategies may be needed. Other incentives for successful managers currently include company-paid luxury vacations, weekends on the corporate yacht, and the possibility of being awarded a $12,000 Patek Philippe gold watch for beating the company record for weekly store sales.[58] ▬

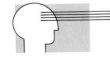

Promoting Innovation: A Social Learning Perspective

Bandura explicitly uses social learning theory to explore two major facets of innovation: the creation of innovative ideas and their acquisition and adoption through the diffusion of innovation.

Creating Innovative Ideas. Bandura argues that one way to encourage individuals to develop new, innovative ideas is to provide diverse models as stimulators of our creative thinking. When we are exposed to diverse models, we are more likely to be innovative in our thinking. With diversity, we rarely copy any one model exactly; rather, we improvise somewhat, taking those ideas we perceive to be the best and building upon them. In business, the existence of patents, copyrights, and other barriers to entry often precludes direct copying of models. Still, exposure to new ways of doing things can get us thinking about unforeseen prospects.[59] In areas in which innovation is desired, managers may need to think in terms of providing a diversity of models to encourage creative thinking.

At the same time, self-reinforcement may help explain what makes individuals persist on innovative projects and ideas. Bandura argues that without self-generated reinforcement, innovative efforts are difficult to sustain because the unconventional is usually resisted.[60] Domino's founder Monaghan keeps a "Dream File," filled with ideas about things he would like to own, places he would like to go, and individuals he would like to meet. His reputation for letting people try new ideas is based on his philosophy: "If you're not making mistakes, you're not working."[61] Innovative organizations, such as 3M, work hard to provide external reinforcement that complements, rather than conflicts with, self-reinforcement of innovation, thus increasing the possibilities that innovators will be motivated to persist. For example, successful innovators are often given their own laboratories or business organizations to run. As the situation at Genentech illustrates, managers walk a thin line between providing insufficient support of innovation and supporting efforts in directions that are unlikely to yield usable results.

Diffusion of Innovation. According to social learning theory, modeling assists the diffusion of the innovation process by helping individuals learn appropriate new behaviors. Early adopters usually come from the group of individuals that has had the greatest exposure to the new ideas. As the early adopters model the new ideas, the adoptive behavior tends to spread along existing networks of communication. Observers are initially reluctant to adopt the new innovation until they see the advantages gained by the early adopters. According to social learning theory, adoptive behavior is highly susceptible to reinforcement influences. Individuals are more likely to be motivated to adopt new ideas that produce tangible results. Because the benefits of innovations cannot be experienced until the ideas are actually tried, promotions of innovations usually rely heavily on anticipated and vicarious reinforcement. Thus, according to social learning theory, motivating individuals in organizations to adopt innovations may depend on providing appropriate models so that the necessary behavior can be learned easily. It also is necessary to ensure that the potential gains are not only articulated but demonstrated by the appropriate models so that vicarious learning can take place. When 3M developed the now-famous Post-it note pads, the project team found that it was difficult to motivate people to adopt the pads unless they actually used them or saw them being used. In one of the strategic moves to get the new product into organizations, the secretary of 3M's CEO sent free packages of Post-it pads to the secretaries of the CEOs of all the Fortune 500 companies and included a letter about their many uses. As the pads began to be used at the top of many of these organizations, others in the companies followed suit and sales mushroomed.[62] Thus a knowledge of motivation can be an important asset in attempting to influence innovation and other behaviors in organizations, and it is a critical factor in effective leadership, a subject to which we turn in the next chapter.

CHAPTER SUMMARY

Motivation is the force that energizes behavior, gives direction to behavior, and underlies the tendency to persist. Early efforts by Frederick Taylor to use money and by the human relations school of management to use attention to workers and group dynamics as motivators on extremely routine, specialized jobs met with only limited success. Since then, more sophisticated approaches have centered on several major elements in the motivation process: needs, cognitive activities, and reward and reinforcement issues.

Need theories argue that we behave the way we do because we have internal needs that we are attempting to fulfill. These theories are sometimes called content theories because they focus on what motivates others. Maslow's widely known hierarchy of needs theory argues that our needs form a five-level hierarchy, ranging from physiological to self-actualization needs. ERG theory updates Maslow's approach by proposing three need levels and including a frustration-regression principle in addition to the satisfaction-progression explanation of movement among need levels. Herzberg offers a two-factor theory that has helped emphasize the importance of factors included in the motivator categories. However, research has cast doubt on the wisdom of viewing his hygiene factors as useful only in keeping employees from being dissatisfied. While the hierarchy of needs, two-factor, and ERG theories view certain needs as inherent, McClelland's acquired-needs theory argues that needs are acquired or learned on the basis of our life experiences. His work has focused particularly on needs for achievement, affiliation, and power, as well as on how these needs affect managerial success.

Cognitive theories, sometimes called process theories, attempt to isolate the thinking patterns that we use in deciding whether or not to behave in a certain way. Expectancy theory posits that in deciding how much ef-

fort to expend in a given direction, we consider effort-performance expectancy (the probability that our efforts will lead to the required performance level), performance-outcome expectancy (the probability that our successful performance will lead to certain outcomes), and valence (the anticipated value of the various outcomes or rewards). As the expanded model of expectancy theory suggests, managers need to consider all three elements in achieving both high performance and high job satisfaction among employees. Equity theory indicates that we prefer situations of balance, or equity, which occurs when we perceive the ratio of our inputs and outcomes to be equal to the ratio of inputs and outcomes of a comparison other (or others). Goal-setting theory highlights the importance of goal commitment, specific and challenging goals, and feedback. Goal setting works by directing attention and action, mobilizing effort, increasing persistence, and encouraging the development of strategies to achieve the goals.

Reinforcement theory argues that our behavior can be explained by consequences in the environment. The four major types of reinforcement are positive reinforcement, negative reinforcement, extinction, and punishment. Schedules of reinforcement specify the basis for and timing of positive rewards and include fixed-interval, fixed-ratio, variable-interval, and variable-ratio schedules. Social learning theory argues that learning occurs through the continuous reciprocal interaction of our behaviors, various personal factors, and environmental forces. Three cognitively related processes are particularly important: symbolic processes, vicarious learning, and self-control. Social learning theory is useful in explaining both the creation of innovative ideas and their acquisition and adoption through the diffusion of innovation.

MANAGERIAL TERMINOLOGY

acquired-needs theory (453)
behavior modification (464)
belongingness needs (449)
cognitive theories (456)
dissatisfiers, or hygiene factors (452)
effort-performance expectancy (456)
equity theory (461)
ERG theory (449)

esteem needs (449)
existence needs (449)
expectancy theory (456)
extinction (466)
extrinsic rewards (457)
fixed-interval schedule of reinforcement (467)
fixed-ratio schedule of reinforcement (468)
frustration-regression principle (450)
growth needs (449)

hierarchy of needs theory (448)
institutional power (454)
intrinsic rewards (457)
law of effect (464)
modeling (470)
motivation (445)
need for achievement (nAch) (453)
need for affiliation (nAff) (454)
need for power (nPow) (454)

negative reinforcement (465)
performance-outcome expectancy (457)
personal power (454)
physiological needs (448)
positive reinforcement (465)
punishment (466)
reinforcement theory (464)
relatedness needs (449)

safety needs   (449)
satisfaction-progression
   principle   (450)
satisfiers, or motivators
   (452)

schedules of
   reinforcement   (467)
self-actualization needs
   (449)
self-control   (471)
self-efficacy   (469)

shaping   (465)
social learning theory
   (469)
symbolic processes   (469)
two-factor theory   (452)
valence   (458)

variable-interval schedule
   of reinforcement   (468)
variable-ratio schedule of
   reinforcement   (468)
vicarious learning   (469)

QUESTIONS FOR DISCUSSION AND REVIEW

1. Briefly describe the concept of motivation, early approaches to the concept, and a simplified model of motivation. Describe a situation that illustrates the idea that performance is a function of ability and environmental conditions, as well as motivation.

2. Explain the hierarchy of needs theory and ERG theory. Assume that you are the manager of a large fast-food outlet. How might these theories help you motivate the various individuals who work for you?

3. Describe the acquired-needs theory of motivation. Based on McClelland's work on the need for achievement, what might be some difficulties in attempting to motivate high-nAch individuals in organizations? How could you encourage the need for achievement in others? How might you encourage the need for institutional power?

4. Outline the expectancy theory of motivation. Suppose that you are in charge of a group of engineers who are responsible for the completion of various projects. How would you use expectancy theory to motivate them to perform at a high level? How might the expanded expectancy theory help you keep them motivated?

5. Explain equity theory. In part, equity theory argues that our judgments of equity (or inequity) are based on our own perceptions of situations. What poten-

tial difficulties does the perceptual aspect of equity judgments present for managers?

6. Assess the role of goal setting in motivation. Analyze a student group or other organization to which you belong in terms of its goals or lack thereof. To what extent are goals set that are specific and challenging? To what extent is there commitment to the goals? What is the impact of these goals on organizational effectiveness?

7. Explain the four main types of reinforcement. For each one, identify a situation in which you have seen that type used and assess the outcome.

8. Contrast the four major types of partial reinforcement schedules. Provide an example of each of these types from your own experience.

9. Explain the social learning theory of motivation. Describe an instance in which you obtained important information through vicarious learning. Also describe a situation in which you learned through modeling. To what extent can you identify the steps in the modeling process in your own situation?

10. Use social learning theory to explain how diffusion of an innovation can occur. Describe a situation with which you are familiar that illustrates how social learning theory can be used to facilitate the diffusion of innovation.

DISCUSSION QUESTIONS FOR CHAPTER OPENING CASE

1. How can need theories help provide clues about what is likely to motivate scientists at Genentech?

2. What aspects of expectancy theory appear to be particularly important in the Genentech situation?

Where are goal-setting theory and equity theory applicable?

3. What evidence exists for the use of various types of reinforcement, vicarious learning, and self-control?

MANAGEMENT EXERCISE: MARKETEER OR ENTREPRENEUR

Lee Brown has been a market planning specialist for the Sweet Tooth Candy Company for the past 2 years. This is her first job following graduation from college, and

she is quite pleased with her progress in the organization. She has received three merit raises and expects to be promoted to the position of senior market planning specialist soon. She enjoys her work, and her immediate boss is one of the finest market planners she could ever hope to work with. Her boss gives her autonomy, support, and resources when she needs them. Similarly, he seems to know when she needs help and gives it to her in a way that seems to bring out the best in her. Lee frequently wonders how anyone could be happier than she is with her job and company.

Last week she met Jamie Wilson, one of her former schoolmates, at the local shopping center. Lee recalled that Jamie, an excellent student who majored in human resources management, had accepted a position as a compensation analyst with a local health-care corporation. While catching up on the events of their lives during the previous 2 years, Jamie indicated that she had a business proposition that she had been considering for some time but did not believe she could pursue alone. She needed a partner and suggested that Lee be that person.

Her proposition was that child-care centers were desperately needed in their area. The city of approximately 35,000 people had only one small child-care facility, which had a very long waiting list and very high rates. Jamie's research had revealed that three different churches in the area would gladly support additional child-care centers by furnishing their facilities, at little or no cost, provided the centers were managed as separate businesses. Jamie had also located a building that could be developed into an excellent child-care center in the future. Jamie reasoned that she and Lee could start the business in one or more of the churches and expand into the building she had found. Financially, the return from operating one child-care center would not quite equal Lee's current total compensation; however, two or more centers would yield a very nice income for both partners. Jamie had determined that appropriate licenses could be obtained in a few weeks and that the financing required to start the business was available at very favorable rates. Other materials and supplies were readily available as well.

Lee was intrigued with this proposition and told Jamie that she wanted a week to think it over. She intends to discuss her interest in this proposition with Jamie tomorrow.

Requirement

Using expectancy theory, indicate the factors that would have an impact on Lee's decision and the strength of her motivation to participate in the proposed child-care business.

MAKING VISIBLE CHANGES

In an industry characterized by fragmentation, poor management, and mediocre profits, a Houston-based beauty salon chain, called Visible Changes, is breaking all the records. Average sales at the chain's 16 salons are triple the industry figure; sales per customer are almost twice the industry average; sales of retail products as a percentage of revenues typically beat the industry average by almost a factor of four; and turnover is one-third the industry rate.

When they launched their first salon in 1976, John and Maryanne McCormack envisioned a chain of elegant salons located in shopping malls, providing excellent service to both men and women, requiring no appointments, attracting high-volume business, and making large profits. To make their vision a reality, they would need to motivate the hairdressers to provide better service—no small challenge, since hairdressers tended to be recent graduates of hairdressing schools who, with salaries of less than $10,000, were trying to find a better way to make a living.

As a solution, the McCormacks came up with an elaborate incentive plan geared to encouraging their hairdressers to provide excellent service. Hairdressers at Visible Changes receive a 35 percent commission on the payments from customers who request them by name, as opposed to 25 percent on payments from regular walk-in customers who make no requests. Further, when they are requested more than 75 percent of the time, they can charge a premium price (about $10 more than the basic fee); for a request rate of 65 percent, there also is an add-on to the basic price (about $6 + 50 percent = $3 more).

Thus hairdressers who please customers are more likely to be requested and are rewarded for their efforts. Hairdressers can also receive health insurance (an industry rarity) by selling $160 worth of hair-care products per week; for sales beyond that figure hairdressers receive 15 percent commission. There also are annual bonuses. Once each quarter, each hairdresser is rated on a scale of 1 to 10, with points related to attitude, customer service, and the extent to which individual and salon goals have been met. Individuals who receive all 10 points each quarter receive an additional bonus amounting to 10 percent of their annual commissions. There are "superbonuses" for the most requested hairdressers and the best achievers in product sales. In addition, there is profit sharing, which recently was 15 percent of gross pay for everyone in the company. For one top hairdresser, these incentives added up to more than $60,000, not counting the trips that employees can win under special promotions. On average, Visible Changes hairdressers earn about $33,000 per year, while the national average is about $12,000.

Advanced training sessions in the latest haircutting techniques must be earned by meeting one's goals. Maryanne also makes video tapes showing the latest cutting techniques so that the hairdressers use standardized terminology and follow the same methods. High performers, who are by definition also the high earners, are asked to act as role models and share their techniques for success. In addition, the hairdressers compete to be chosen for the "artistic team" that travels throughout the United States and abroad developing and demonstrating new haircuts. The McCormacks work hard to make sure that employees understand

Maryanne McCormack has made visible changes in the hairdressing industry. She and her husband John have built a highly successful chain of salons (called Visible Changes) in Houston shopping malls. Their enterprise is quickly becoming a model for the industry. The secret behind their spectacular results is employee motivation: those haircutters who give good service to their customers and who reach their goals for sales of the salon's hair products receive special pay incentives and bonuses. On average, the company's hairdressers earn close to $33,000 a year, compared with an industry average of $12,000.

the incentive system and the rationale behind each element. In addition, the hairdressers often contribute ideas for refining the system. John keeps track of these indicators, as well as data about customer traffic and trends, through a computer system that gives him access to data within seconds.[63]

QUESTIONS FOR CHAPTER CONCLUDING CASE

1. Assess the extent to which it appears possible for hairdressers to meet various needs at Visible Changes.
2. Using the cognitive theories of motivation, evaluate the incentive system at Visible Changes.
3. Explain how reinforcement and vicarious learning are used at Visible Changes.

CHAPTER FOURTEEN

LEADERSHIP

CHAPTER OUTLINE

How Leaders Influence Others
Sources of Leader Power
Effective Use of Leader Power

Searching for Leadership Traits

Identifying Leader Behaviors
Iowa Studies
Michigan Studies
Ohio State Studies
The Managerial Grid
Female versus Male Leader Behaviors

Developing Situational Theories
Fiedler's Leadership Theories
Situational Leadership Theory
Revised Normative Leadership Model
Path-Goal Theory

Promoting Innovation:
  Transformational Leadership

Are Leaders Necessary?
The Romance of Leadership
Substitutes for Leadership
Leadership and the Organizational
  Life Cycle

LEARNING OBJECTIVES

*After studying this chapter, you
should be able to:*

■ Outline the major sources of
leader power and explain how
leaders can use power to encourage subordinate commitment.

■ Describe the current state of
efforts to identify leadership
traits.

■ Explain the different strategies
used by the Iowa, Michigan,
and Ohio State researchers in
studying leader behaviors and
discuss the implications of their
findings.

■ Describe the Managerial Grid
approach to leadership and assess the extent to which females and males behave differently as leaders.

■ Delineate Fiedler's situational
model of leadership and the
related cognitive resource approach.

■ Compare and contrast the following situational approaches
to leadership: situational leadership theory, normative leadership model, and path-goal theory.

■ Describe transformational leadership and explain its link to
innovation.

■ Evaluate the extent to which
leaders are necessary in organizations.

LEADERSHIP HELPS APPLE SHINE

When John Sculley, president of the Pepsi-Cola division of PepsiCo, accepted the CEO post at Apple Computer, Inc., in 1983, he was expected to apply his marketing expertise to improve Apple's relationship with retailers and customers. Stephen P. Jobs, Apple's legendary cofounder and Chairman, in whose now-famous garage the first Apple computer was made, was to oversee technical innovation.

Within 2 years, the scheme ran into trouble as sales of personal computers began to slump nationally; the Macintosh computer was not selling as well as anticipated, and some outsiders began to wonder whether the company would survive. The situation was exacerbated by the fact that the Macintosh division, headed by Jobs, chronically missed deadlines for developing crucial additional parts for the Macintosh system. Furthermore, there were no other new major products under way. After a clash over who would run the company, the board of directors and most of the top executives sided with Sculley, causing Jobs to leave Apple.

Once firmly in charge, Sculley moved quickly to reorient the company. He laid off 20 percent of the work force, closed three plants, slashed overhead, and imposed new controls to raise Apple's gross profit margins to the highest in years. Recognizing that businesses provided a better market than did homes for the Macintosh, Sculley channeled greater efforts toward Fortune 500 customers. He also reemphasized the importance of meeting goals and deadlines, resolving to discontinue Apple's habit of making public promises and then taking them lightly. Asked later about the difficulties of potentially being perceived as a bad guy, Sculley says, "I wasn't really focused on popularity. What I had to do was convince people that we were in a crisis, and that we weren't going to get out of it unless we pulled together."

Some critics argued that Sculley's changes would sap the innovative, entrepreneurial spirit of the company. In order to try to keep the creative juices flowing, Sculley spent a great deal of time meeting with groups of managers to talk about mistakes, as well as successes, and to try to determine which future directions were really important. Sculley wanted new products to "percolate freely from within" rather than be "dictated" from above. He also placed all the product development efforts into a single group, doubled the R&D budget, hired more engineers, and brought the marketing and manufacturing people into the developmental process earlier. At the same time, he promoted a number of talented managers into slots with greater responsibilities.

One such manager was Deborah A. Coleman, who had left Hewlett-Packard to join Apple as a financial specialist. After becoming controller of the Macintosh division under Jobs, she expressed interest in running the Macintosh factory and was given the position. The factory had been continually falling short of its goals in areas such as production, costs, inventory turns, and quality.

She began by having the assembly area painted, a cafeteria built, and the bathrooms remodeled. "The changes had nothing to do with morale," she says. "They had to do with my sense of order. I just didn't see how you could do clean thinking in an unclean environment."

Next, she learned about everything that was going on in the factory, spending several hours each day on the factory floor and often coming in for parts of all three shifts. "I knew every operation, every piece of equipment, and almost every operator by name," she says. "She wanted to meet everybody," states one former assembler. "And that was three or four hundred people at least. And she

When conditions began to decline at Apple Computer in the mid-1980s, CEO John Sculley launched a major reorganization that promoted several talented managers. One of these managers was Deborah Coleman, who turned around the faltering Macintosh factory. Coleman's effective leadership earned her several other major positions including Vice President of Worldwide Manufacturing, Chief Financial Officer, and Vice President of Finance. Coleman describes her approach this way: "I like to optimize. I like to take something that is and make it even better."

Leadership The process of influencing others toward the achievement of organizational goals

didn't want to hide anything from the employees that would affect us out here." She also reduced inventory 37 percent, developed new delivery schedules, and cut the number of suppliers by more than one-third. Once her innovative moves turned the factory around, she prepared a report for Sculley that included ideas on "the strategic role that operations could and should have at Apple." When Sculley reorganized after Jobs left, Coleman got the job of vice president for worldwide manufacturing and was later promoted to the position of chief financial officer of Apple before taking a 5-month leave of absence and returning as vice president of finance.

Coleman describes her own management style as "very participative—and very directive." Ralph R. Russo, who succeeded Coleman as vice president of worldwide operations, concurs: "She is directive in the sense that she paints a big picture of the direction in which the organization is heading. Then she looks for credibility in people—credibility meaning doing what you say you're going to do. And then she gives quite a bit of autonomy." Russo says that some of the things that he has been able to accomplish were a direct result of "her management style: her constant challenge to do better, to bring the best out. We don't settle for the norm or even a little bit above average. It's what we call Class 4, or the best in the world—not *one* of the best in the world."

The efforts of Sculley, Coleman, and others at Apple have generally paid off handsomely with strong growth, relatively high profits, and a pipeline full of new Macintosh-related products. The future holds even greater innovative challenges for the company and its leaders, as competitors begin to match the easy-to-use commands and powerful graphics that have made the Macintosh so popular with customers.[1]

Faced with watching Apple start to decline after some initial successes, what would you have done in Sculley's place? Sculley decided to take firm hold of the reins and provide the leadership that Apple needed. Other talented managers such as Debi Coleman also were crucial to the successful turnaround through their leadership in important segments of Apple. Such leaders also will play a critical role in Apple's future. But what is leadership? **Leadership** is the process of influencing others toward the achievement of organizational goals. This definition recognizes that leadership is typically an ongoing activity, is oriented toward having an impact on the behaviors of others, and is ultimately focused on realizing the specific aims of the organization. Since it involves influencing others, leadership is considered the foundation of the management function known as leading.

In this chapter, we explore the means that leaders have for influencing others. We consider the possibility that leaders have common traits, and we review the quest to identify universal leader behaviors that leaders can use in any situations. We then probe recent efforts to develop situational approaches that help leaders decide when certain types of behaviors are applicable. Next, we examine transformational leadership and its linkage to innovation. Finally, we consider the question of whether and under what circumstances leaders are necessary.

HOW LEADERS INFLUENCE OTHERS

Why do people accept the influence of a leader? One major reason is that leaders have power, although Katharine Graham, chairman of the influential Washington Post Company, notes, "Nobody ever has as much power as you think they do."[2] In this section, we examine the major sources of power and the ways that leaders can effectively use the power they potentially have available.

Sources of Leader Power

Power is the capacity to affect the behavior of others.[3] Leaders in organizations typically rely on some or all of six major types of power: legitimate, reward, coercive, expert, information, and referent.[4]

Power The capacity to affect the behavior of others

Legitimate Power. **Legitimate power** stems from a position's placement in the managerial hierarchy and the authority vested in the position. When we accept a job with an organization, we usually are aware that we will be receiving directions related to our work from our immediate boss and others in the hierarchy. Normally, we accept such directions as legitimate because these persons hold positions of authority. Hence legitimate power relates to the position, rather than to the person per se.

Legitimate power Power that stems from a position's placement in the managerial hierarchy and the authority vested in the position

Reward Power. **Reward power** is based on the capacity to control and provide valued rewards to others. Most organizations offer an array of rewards, including pay raises, bonuses, interesting projects, promotion recommendations, a better office, support for training programs, assignments with high visibility in the organization, recognition, positive feedback, and time off. The greater a manager's control over valued rewards, the greater that manager's reward power.

Reward power Power that is based on the capacity to control and provide valued rewards to others

Coercive Power. **Coercive power** depends on the ability to punish others when they do not engage in desired behaviors. Forms of coercion or punishment include criticisms, terminations, reprimands, suspensions, warning letters that go into an individual's personnel file, negative performance appraisals, demotions, and withheld pay raises. The greater the freedom to punish others, the greater a manager's coercive power.

Coercive power Power that depends on the ability to punish others when they do not engage in desired behaviors

Expert Power. **Expert power** is based on the possession of expertise that is valued by others. Managers often have considerable knowledge, technical skills, and experience that can be critical to subordinates' success. To the extent that a leader possesses expertise and information that is needed or desired by others, the leader has expert power.

Expert power Power that is based on the possession of expertise that is valued by others

Information Power. **Information power** results from access to and control over the distribution of important information about organizational operations and future plans.[5] Managers usually have better access to such information than do subordinates and have some discretion over how much is disseminated to work-unit members. The greater the control over important information, the greater the information power.

Information power Power that results from access to and control over the distribution of important information about organizational operations and future plans

Referent Power. **Referent power** results from being admired, personally identified with, or liked by others. When we admire people, want to be like them, or feel friendship toward them, we more willingly follow their directions and exhibit loyalty toward them. Some observers argue that Lee Iacocca's initial success in turning around the Chrysler Corporation was based partially on the fact that he possessed referent power in relation to the work force. The more that a leader is able to cultivate the liking, identification, and admiration of others, the greater the referent power.

Referent power Power that results from being admired, personally identified with, or liked by others

Effective Use of Leader Power

Although all six types of power are potential means of influencing others, in actual usage they may engender somewhat different levels of subordinate motivation. Subordinates can react to a leader's direction with commitment, compliance, or resistance. With commitment, employees respond enthusiastically and exert a high level of effort toward organizational goals. With compliance, employees exert at least minimal efforts to complete directives but are likely to deliver average, rather than stellar, performance. With resistance, employees may appear to comply but actually do the absolute minimum, possibly even attempting to sabotage the attainment of organizational goals. For example, when Chicago scrap-metal czar Cyrus Tang bought the ailing McLouth Steel Products Corporation, he relied on legitimate and coercive power to gain worker cooperation. Workers reacted with production slowdowns and a wildcat strike that eventually led to the further deterioration of the company and its sale to employees.[6]

The relationship between a leader's use of the different sources of power and likely subordinate reactions is summarized in Table 14-1. As the table illus-

Table 14-1   Major Sources of Leader Power and Likely Subordinate Reactions

Source of Leader Influence	Basis for Power	TYPE OF OUTCOME		
		Commitment	**Compliance**	**Resistance**
Referent power	Admiration and liking by others	LIKELY* If request is believed to be important to leader	POSSIBLE If request is perceived to be unimportant to leader	POSSIBLE If request is for something that will bring harm to leader
Expert power	Possession of valued expertise	LIKELY* If request is persuasive and subordinates share leader's task goals	POSSIBLE If request is persuasive but subordinates are apathetic about task goals	POSSIBLE If leader is arrogant and insulting or subordinates oppose task goals
Legitimate power	Hierarchical position and authority	POSSIBLE If request is polite and very appropriate	LIKELY* If request or order is seen as legitimate	POSSIBLE If arrogant demands are made or request does not appear proper
Information power	Access to important information	POSSIBLE If request is substantiated by data	LIKELY* If request is reasonable	POSSIBLE If leader is arrogant, secretive, or manipulative
Reward power	Capacity to provide valued rewards	POSSIBLE If used in a subtle, very personal way	LIKELY* If used in a mechanical, impersonal way	POSSIBLE If used in a manipulative, arrogant way
Coercive power	Ability to punish	VERY UNLIKELY	POSSIBLE If used in a helpful, nonpunitive way	LIKELY* If used in a hostile or manipulative way

*Indicates most common outcome.

Source: Adapted from Gary A. Yukl, *Leadership in Organizations,* 2d ed., Prentice-Hall, Englewood Cliffs, N.J., 1989, p. 44.

trates, expert power and referent power are most likely to lead to subordinate commitment, while legitimate power, information power, and reward power tend to result in compliance. The use of coercive power has a strong tendency to provoke resistance in subordinates; hence effective leaders tend to minimize its use as much as possible. Alluding to the wisdom of avoiding heavy-handed use of power, particularly the overuse of coercive power, Allen Jacobson, chief executive of 3M, observes, "I guess if you're doing it right, you don't feel like you're wielding power."[7]

Managers usually rely on several different types of power in order to be effective. When Jim Lynn was chosen to be chairman of the Aetna Life & Casualty Company, the firm had just been through the painful process of a competitive price-cutting program, had suffered write-offs from several ill-fated acquisitions in noninsurance areas, and was facing the lowest earnings in 9 years. At that point, Lynn, a 6-year veteran on Aetna's board of directors, a previous partner in two prestigious law firms, and a former Nixon administration cabinet member, had a reputation for being effective with both handling people and solving problems. In establishing himself at Aetna, he clearly had the legitimate power of his new chairman's position. However, he relied heavily on building referent power. According to one former Aetna senior vice president, Lynn went out of his way to "portray a peer relationship with everybody." He also used reward power to boost the morale of the heads of Aetna's three principal businesses, each with revenues of more than $3 billion, by awarding them the title of president in recognition of their major roles in the company. Since he was not an insurance professional himself, Lynn was careful to respect the insurance expertise (and related power) of others, while using his own expert power in managerial and legal issues. He also shared information about company activities with organization members when it would be helpful to them. Thus he supplemented his legitimate power mainly with referent, reward, expert, and information power to help gain employee commitment to needed changes.[8] While power helps explain the inducements behind leader influence, we need to look to other concepts to explore the nature of the influence attempts themselves.

Part of John Reed's power at Citicorp stems from his position as Chairman of the Board and Chief Executive Officer of the largest banking company in the United States. Power that is related to a position is called legitimate power. Reed will likely be using other forms of power, such as expert, referent, and reward power, as he works toward his goal of making Citicorp the world's first global consumer bank. If Reed has his way Citicorp branch banking, credit cards, and mortgages and other consumer services will be offered all over the world.

SEARCHING FOR LEADERSHIP TRAITS

Although individuals have speculated for centuries on the nature of effective leadership, Army psychologists seeking methods to select officers during World War I set the stage for earnest postwar scientific research on the subject.[9] To early researchers, it seemed logical to try to identify significant traits that distinguish effective leaders from nonleaders.[10] **Traits** are distinctive internal qualities or characteristics of an individual, such as physical characteristics (e.g., height, weight, appearance, energy), personality characteristics (e.g., dominance, extroversion, originality), skills and abilities (e.g., intelligence, knowledge, technical competence), and social factors (e.g., interpersonal skills, sociability, and socioeconomic position).[11]

For the most part, early researchers initially measured various traits of individuals and then typically had the individuals work in leaderless groups (without appointed leaders). The idea was to see whether certain traits would predict the individuals who would emerge (be identified by members of the group) as leaders. A turning point away from the trait approach, however, came when two researchers, Ralph M. Stogdill in 1948 and Richard D. Mann in 1959, re-

Traits Distinctive internal qualities or characteristics of an individual, such as physical characteristics, personality characteristics, skills and abilities, and social factors

viewed earlier studies and suggested that there were no traits that consistently distinguished leaders from nonleaders.[12]

The efforts to identify universal leadership traits ran into difficulties for two main reasons. For one thing, although a number of traits were associated with leadership, the relationships were often weak. For another, the traits that were important, as well as their strengths, seemed to vary depending on the situation, making the specification of a universal set of leadership traits difficult. Still, in conducting an updated review in 1974, Stogdill noted that researchers may have interpreted his earlier review too pessimistically, and he argued that some general qualities may be associated with leadership.[13]

Recent efforts support the notion that the trait approach may have been abandoned prematurely. Using sophisticated statistical techniques that allow researchers to better assess results across studies, one group of researchers reexamined the early studies of personality traits, as well as subsequent related research.[14] Their results showed that several of the traits originally studied by Mann were associated with being identified as leaders by others—namely, intelligence, dominance, and aggressiveness and decisiveness.[15] Thus traits may be more closely associated with leadership emergence than earlier reviews have led us to believe.

Meanwhile, other researchers have suggested that it may be possible to isolate leadership traits that apply to specific types of situations.[16] For example, one famous study conducted at AT&T found that traits such as oral communication skills, human relations skills, need or motive for advancement, resistance to stress, tolerance of uncertainty, energy, and creativity were predictive of managerial advancement.[17]

Thus it is possible that future research may isolate traits that cause people to identify individuals as leaders, at least in some situations. However, it is still an open question whether those same traits, if they could be found, would predict actual performance in leadership positions. Many researchers believe that performance is more closely related to the things leaders actually do than to the traits they possess. As a result, most recent leadership research has focused on leader behaviors.

IDENTIFYING LEADER BEHAVIORS

Why was Chairman Raymond L. Hixon able to build the Bonneville Pacific Corporation into a thriving independent power company, while John Kuhns, the Catalyst Energy chief, ran into difficulties leading a similar company?[18] A number of researchers have focused on the intriguing prospect that it may be specific *behaviors* that make some leaders more effective than others. Whereas many inherent traits may be difficult to change, it might be possible—if universally effective behaviors could be identified—for most of us to learn those behaviors and become successful leaders. In this section, we review major efforts at identifying important leader behaviors. This research largely grew out of work at the University of Iowa, the University of Michigan, and Ohio State University. We also consider a popularized outgrowth of some of the research on leader behaviors, the Managerial Grid, and explore the question of whether females and males exhibit different behaviors in leadership positions.

Iowa Studies

University of Iowa researcher Kurt Lewin and his colleagues conducted some of the earliest attempts at scientifically identifying the leader behaviors that are most effective.[19] They concentrated on three leader behaviors, or styles: autocratic, democratic, and laissez-faire. **Autocratic** leaders tend to make unilateral decisions, dictate work methods, limit worker knowledge about goals to just the next step to be performed, and sometimes give feedback that is punitive. In contrast, **democratic** leaders tend to involve the group in decision making, let the group determine work methods, make overall goals known, and use feedback as an opportunity for helpful coaching. **Laissez-faire** leaders generally give the group complete freedom, provide necessary materials, participate only to answer questions, and avoid giving feedback—in other words, they do almost nothing.

To determine which leadership style is most effective, the Lewin researchers trained different adults to exhibit each of the styles and then placed them in charge of various groups in preadolescent boys' clubs. They quickly found that groups with laissez-faire leaders underperformed both the autocratic and democratic groups on every criteria in the study. On the other hand, while quantity of work was equal in the groups with autocratic and democratic leaders, work quality and group satisfaction were higher in the democratic groups. Thus it appeared that democratic leadership could lead to both good quantity and quality of work, as well as satisfied workers. Perhaps the key to effective leadership had been found.

Unfortunately, later work by other researchers produced more mixed results. Sometimes democratic leadership produced higher performance than did autocratic leadership, but other times performance was lower than or merely equal to that under the autocratic style. Results related to subordinate satisfaction were more consistent; satisfaction levels were generally higher with a democratic leadership style than they were with an autocratic one.[20]

These research results, though, created a dilemma for managers. While a democratic leadership style seemed to make subordinates more satisfied, it did not always lead to higher, or even equal, performance. Furthermore, many managers were not used to operating in a democratic mode. To help managers sort out this dilemma, particularly with regard to making decisions, researchers Robert Tannenbaum and Warren H. Schmidt developed the continuum of leader behaviors shown in Figure 14-1.[21] The continuum represents various gradations of leadership behavior, ranging from the autocratic (or boss-centered) approach at the extreme left to the democratic (or subordinate-centered) approach on the extreme right. A move away from the autocratic end of the continuum represents a move toward the democratic end and vice versa. In developing the continuum, the researchers softened the meaning of "autocratic" somewhat, so that it did not necessarily include tendencies to be punitive or keep the ultimate goal of task activities hidden from subordinates. At the autocratic end of the continuum, it did mean that the boss makes the decision and lets others know what they are supposed to do, rather than involving them in the decision.

In deciding which leader behavior pattern to adopt, according to Tannenbaum and Schmidt, managers need to consider forces within themselves (such as comfort level with the various alternatives), within subordinates (such as readiness to assume responsibility), and within the situation (such as time pressures). Tannenbaum and Schmidt argued that in the short run managers need to exercise some flexibility in their leader behavior depending on the situation. The researchers advised that in the long run managers should attempt to move toward the employee-centered end of the continuum, on the premise that such leader behavior has a higher potential for increasing employee motivation, decision quality, teamwork, morale, and employee development.

Autocratic Behavioral style of leaders who tend to make unilateral decisions, dictate work methods, limit worker knowledge about goals to just the next step to be performed, and sometimes give feedback that is punitive

Democratic Behavioral style of leaders who tend to involve the group in decision making, let the group determine work methods, make overall goals known, and use feedback as an opportunity for helpful coaching

Laissez-faire Behavioral style of leaders who generally give the group complete freedom, provide necessary materials, participate only to answer questions, and avoid giving feedback

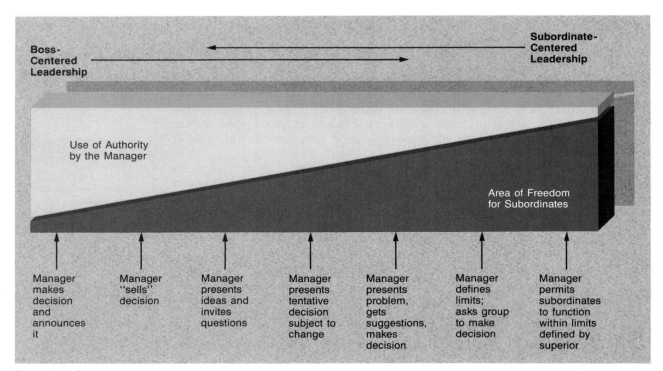

Boss-
Centered
Leadership

Subordinate-
Centered
Leadership

Use of Authority
by the Manager

Area of Freedom
for Subordinates

| Manager makes decision and announces it | Manager "sells" decision | Manager presents ideas and invites questions | Manager presents tentative decision subject to change | Manager presents problem, gets suggestions, makes decision | Manager defines limits; asks group to make decision | Manager permits subordinates to function within limits defined by superior |

Figure 14-1 Continuum of boss-centered and subordinate-centered leader behaviors. (Robert Tannenbaum and Warren H. Schmidt, "How to Choose a Leadership Pattern," *Harvard Business Review*, vol. 51, May–June 1973, p. 164.)

Michigan Studies

Building on the democratic leadership findings of the Lewin group, researchers at the University of Michigan conducted a number of studies using a somewhat different strategy. Instead of training leaders and then assessing their impact on groups, as the Lewin group did, the Michigan group pinpointed effective and ineffective work groups in a variety of business, government, military, educational, and not-for-profit settings.[22] They then studied the leaders of the effective and ineffective groups to determine what the leaders in the two types of groups did differently from each other.

On the basis of interviews and questionnaires, they identified two major types of leader behaviors that form a continuum, with employee-centered behavior at one end and job-centered behavior at the other. With the **employee-centered** approach, managers channel their main attention to the human aspects of subordinates' problems and to the development of an effective work group dedicated to high performance goals. With the **job-centered** approach (sometimes called the *production-centered* approach), leaders divide work into routine tasks, determine work methods, and closely supervise workers to ensure that the methods are followed and productivity standards are met. Results of the early studies generally showed that in the high-producing work units (compared with low-producing work units), supervisors were likely to be employee-centered, use general (rather than close) supervision, and react to problems in a nonpunitive, helpful manner. However, there were some low-producing units with employee-centered supervisors and some high-producing units with job-centered supervisors, suggesting that other factors also were at work.[23] Unfortunately, many adopters of the employee-centered approach tended to interpret it as meaning "Be nice to subordinates," erroneously ignoring the emphasis on setting high performance goals that was central to the research findings.[24]

Employee-centered A leadership approach in which managers channel their main attention to the human aspects of subordinates' problems and to the development of an effective work group dedicated to high performance goals

Job-centered A leadership approach in which leaders divide work into routine tasks, determine work methods, and closely supervise workers to ensure that the methods are followed and productivity standards are met

Ohio State Studies

Meanwhile, a group of researchers at Ohio State University developed a third strategy for studying leadership. They attempted to identify important leader behaviors and develop a questionnaire to measure them. With a leadership questionnaire, they would be able to measure the behaviors of different leaders and track factors such as group performance and satisfaction to see which leader behaviors were most effective. Although the researchers isolated a number of different leader behaviors, or styles, two stood out as particularly important: initiating structure and consideration.

Initiating structure is the degree to which a leader defines his or her own role and the roles of subordinates in terms of achieving unit goals. It includes many basic managerial functions, such as planning, organizing, and directing, and focuses primarily on task issues. Initiating structure is similar to the job-centered leader behavior of the Michigan studies, but it includes a broader range of functions for managers. It involves emphasis on task-related issues.

Consideration is the degree to which a leader builds mutual trust with subordinates, respects their ideas, and shows concern for their feelings. A consideration-oriented leader is more likely to be friendly toward subordinates, maintain good two-way communication, and encourage participation in decision making. Consideration is similar to the employee-centered leader behavior of the Michigan studies. It involves emphasis on people-related issues.

These two styles are illustrated by managers Lynn Shostack and Gertrude Crain, respectively (see the following Case in Point discussion).

Initiating structure The degree to which a leader defines his or her own role and the roles of subordinates in terms of achieving unit goals

Consideration The degree to which a leader builds mutual trust with subordinates, respects their ideas, and shows concern for their feelings

Two successful managers with two different leadership styles: *(top)* Gertrude Crain, chairman of Crain Communications, and *(bottom)* Lynn Shostack, CEO of Joyce International, an office-furniture company. Both women combine aspects of initiating structure and consideration in exercising leadership, but Crain puts the emphasis on consideration in the way she treats her employees like extended family while Shostack is known for her strategic approach to task-related issues.

CASE IN POINT: Successful Leaders at Joyce and Crain

Lynn Shostack, who left a job as head of the Bankers Trust consumer division to take over as CEO of ailing Joyce International, has a reputation for being "tough, but fair," and for letting employees know what is expected of them. Joyce is an office-furniture company with $350 million in annual sales and 4043 employees. Considered to be a brilliant strategist, Shostack excels at developing plans and organizing others to achieve the necessary goals. She sets high standards and rewards employees who meet them. During her first 21 months at Joyce, Shostack worked hard on innovative cost-cutting measures to stem serious losses. Her efforts produced immediate results: a $5 million pretax profit in her first year.[25] Shostack is a manager who has been successful with a leadership style that emphasizes initiating structure.

On the other hand, Gertrude Crain, chairman of Crain Communications, Inc., is known for treating employees as if they were part of an extended family. Crain is a major midwest publisher of trade and consumer-oriented publications, including *Advertising Age, Automotive News, Crain's New York Business, Detroit Monthly, Autoweek,* and others. After inheriting the company from her husband, Gertrude Crain enlarged the company from 5 publications to 26, while gross revenues climbed from $10 million to more than $120 million and the number of employees rose to more than 1000. "She gives this company a really soft, comfortable feeling," says the editor of one Crain publication. "She makes it a wonderful place to work, and I've been here 14 years. It makes people feel very good about the company, that she takes the time to say hi to the editors and to meet new people on staff." She is known for sending notes and flowers to people when they are ill, mailing a check when a new baby arrives, and attending weddings of employees. She also fosters an entrepreneurial spirit and nurtures creativity and innovation in others, including her two sons, who help run the company.[26] Crain is a successful manager who relies heavily on a consideration leadership style. ▬▬▬

In a major departure from the Iowa and Michigan studies, both of which considered their leadership dimensions to be opposite ends of the same continuum, the Ohio State researchers proposed that initiating structure and consideration were two independent behaviors.[27] This meant that they operated on separate continuums. A leader could be high on both, low on both, or high on one and low on the other or could display various gradations in between. The Ohio State two-dimensional approach is depicted in Figure 14-2. This configuration made sense, since many leaders seemed to have characteristics of both initiating structure and consideration. For example, Lynn Shostack of Joyce International is known for encouraging and supporting good employees, while Gertrude Crain still personally signs all major Crain checks so that she can keep a watchful eye on expenditures and the bottom line.[28]

The two-dimensional approach led to the interesting possibility that a leader might be able to place high emphasis on task issues and still engender high levels of subordinate satisfaction by simultaneously exhibiting consideration behavior. While initial studies supported the idea that a leader exhibiting both high initiating structure and high consideration would produce the best results, the notion of the great high-high leader was later pronounced a myth.[29] Why did the high-high approach fall from favor? The main reason was that, like the Iowa and Michigan studies, it was too simplistic. As studies began to accumulate, it became clear that situational factors, such as the nature of the task and subordinate expectations, also affect the success of leadership behaviors.[30]

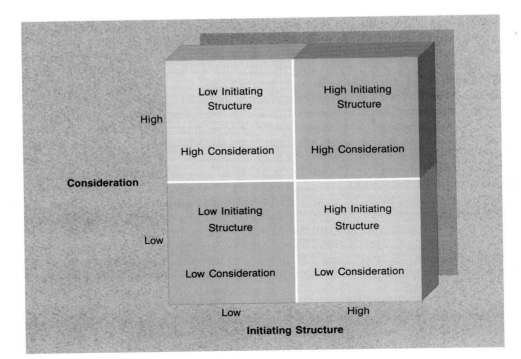

Figure 14-2   Ohio State two-dimensional model of leader behaviors.

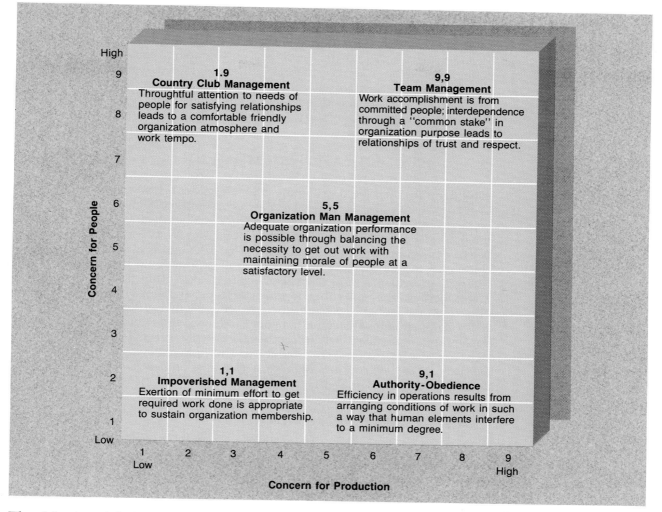

High

9
1,9
Country Club Management
Throughtful attention to needs of
people for satisfying relationships
leads to a comfortable friendly
organization atmosphere and
work tempo.

9,9
Team Management
Work accomplishment is from
committed people; interdependence
through a "common stake" in
organization purpose leads to
relationships of trust and respect.

8

7

6
5,5
Organization Man Management
Adequate organization performance
is possible through balancing the
necessity to get out work with
maintaining morale of people at a
satisfactory level.

5

4

3

2
1,1
Impoverished Management
Exertion of minimum effort to get
required work done is appropriate
to sustain organization membership.

9,1
Authority-Obedience
Efficiency in operations results from
arranging conditions of work in such
a way that human elements interfere
to a minimum degree.

1

Low

Concern for People (vertical axis)

1   2   3   4   5   6   7   8   9
Low   High

Concern for Production

Figure 14-3 The Managerial
Grid. (Reprinted from Robert A.
Blake and Jane S. Mouton, *The
Managerial Grid® III*, Gulf
Publishing, Houston, 1985,
p. 12.)

The Managerial Grid

One popularized outgrowth of the emphasis on leader behaviors aimed at both
task and people issues is the Managerial Grid® developed by Robert Blake and
Jane Srygley Mouton.[31] Rather than focusing directly on the leader behaviors
addressed by the Ohio State studies, the grid approach uses parallel leader attitudes—concern for people and concern for production. A recent version of the
grid, which has been used as a training device in a large number of organizations, is shown in Figure 14-3. Depending on the degree of concern for people
and production, a manager can fall anywhere on the grid. However, Blake and
Mouton argue that the most desirable leadership approach is the 9,9 orientation,
involving a high concern for both people and production. Of course, the Ohio
State studies suggest that a 9,9 orientation might not always be the best. Blake
and Mouton do allow for some flexibility in actual leader behaviors, depending
on a leader's diagnosis of the people and production issues in a given situation.

Female versus Male Leader Behaviors

In the course of studying various leader behaviors, some researchers began to
wonder whether female managers exhibit different leader behaviors than do

male managers. Early survey data indicated that a number of people viewed females as being highly oriented toward interpersonal issues and, therefore, possibly ill-suited for leadership positions. Males were seen as more oriented toward task issues and better candidates for leadership slots.[32] As its turns out, neither stereotype is correct. Studies indicate that female and male leaders are similar in the amounts of interpersonal and task behaviors that they exhibit. Furthermore, they are equally effective in terms of eliciting subordinate job satisfaction and performance.[33]

DEVELOPING SITUATIONAL THEORIES

Situational theories
Theories of leadership that take into consideration important situational factors

Although they attempted to identify effective leader behaviors that would work in every situation, the various researchers pursuing the behavioral view of leadership eventually found that leader behaviors that worked well in one situation often were not as effective in another situation. As a result, the researchers began developing theories of leadership that take into consideration important situational factors. Such approaches are called **situational theories** because of their situational emphasis. They also are often called *contingency theories* of leadership because they hold that appropriate leader traits or behaviors are *contingent*, or dependent, on relevant situational characteristics. Since there are potentially many situational factors that could influence the effectiveness of leaders, several different situational approaches have evolved. Among the most prominent are Fiedler's contingency theory and his recent revision called cognitive resource theory, Hersey and Blanchard's situational theory, the revised normative leadership model, and path-goal theory.

Fiedler's Leadership Theories

Fiedler's contingency model
A situational approach originally developed by Fred Fiedler and his associates

Arguably the most well known of the situational approaches is **Fiedler's contingency model,** originally developed by leadership researcher Fred Fiedler and his associates. We first explore various aspects of his contingency model and then consider a recent revision and extension called cognitive resource theory.[34]

Contingency Theory

LPC orientation A personality trait measured by the least preferred coworker (LPC) scale

The LPC Scale. A cornerstone of the contingency model is a leader's **LPC orientation,** a personality trait measured by the least preferred coworker (LPC) scale. The LPC scale consists of 18 (originally 16) sets of bipolar adjectives. A leader is asked to describe the "person with whom [he or she] can work least well" by rating the person on a range of 1 to 8 points for each set. An example of one of the sets is

Pleasant _____ : _____ : _____ : _____ : _____ : _____ : _____ : _____ Unpleasant
                    8   7   6   5   4   3   2   1

Although the scale and its precise meaning have been controversial and have undergone changes, the most recent interpretation by Fiedler and his colleagues is that the LPC score measures a motivational hierarchy indicating the extent to which an individual places a higher priority, or value, on task accomplishment rather than on personal relationships. According to this interpretation, if a leader describes a least preferred coworker in relatively negative terms on the LPC scale, the leader is likely to be task-motivated and inclined to put "business before pleasure." Conversely, if the leader describes the least preferred coworker in relatively positive terms, the leader is likely to be people-motivated and to believe that a close relationship with coworkers is an important variable for team success. According to Fiedler, a leader's LPC personality factor (a trait) is relatively stable and difficult to change. The basic idea behind the contingency model, then, is that the leader's personality (as measured by the LPC scale) should be carefully matched to situational factors that favor that type of leader's prospects for success.

Assessing the Situation. The contingency model cites three situational factors that affect the degree of favorability (or, as Fiedler has more recently called it, the degree of situational control) for a leader:

> *Leader-member relations* refers to the extent to which a leader has the support of group members. It is the most important situational variable and is related to the degree to which group members trust and like the leader and are willing to accept guidance and direction. To assess this factor, a leader considers the issue "Will the group members do what I tell them, are they reliable, and do they support me?"
>
> *Task structure* is the extent to which a task is clearly specified with regard to goals, methods, and standards of performance. When task assignments are vague, it is difficult to know what to do and assess how one is doing. Therefore, low task structure reduces the favorableness, or situational control, of the leader, while high task structure raises it. To analyze this factor, a leader evaluates the question "Do I know what I am supposed to do and how the job is to be done?"
>
> *Position power* is the amount of power that the organization gives the leader to accomplish necessary tasks. It is strongly related to the ability to reward and punish. To evaluate this factor, a leader considers the issue "Do I have the support and backing of the 'big boss' and the organization in dealing with subordinates?"

On the basis of recent research findings, Fiedler estimates that in assessing degree of favorability, or situational control, the weighting of these factors should normally be 4:2:1, with leader-member relations receiving four times as much weight and task structure receiving twice as much as position power.[35]

Matching Leadership Style and Situation. The contingency model combines different levels of these three situational factors into the eight situations, or octants, shown in Figure 14-4, representing different degrees of favorability, or situational control (e.g., good leader-member relations, high task structure, and strong position power—octant 1—represents the most favorable situation). The boxes below the octants indicate the type of leader (low LPC or high LPC) that matches the situation and thus is likely to be the most effective. According to the contingency model, in situations of either high favorability (octants 1, 2, and 3, on the left) or extremely low favorability (octant 8, on the extreme right), a low-LPC leader does best; in situations of moderate favorability (octants 3 through 7), a high-LPC leader excels.

The logic behind the contingency model is that when the situation is very unfavorable, the leader will need to provide strong task orientation and direction in order to get the group moving toward its goal. On the other hand, when the situation is very favorable, a task-oriented leader can easily provide what-

Elements of Situation	Leader-Member Relations	Good				Poor			
	Task Structure	High		Low		High		Low	
	Position Power	Strong	Weak	Strong	Weak	Strong	Weak	Strong	Weak
Octant		1	2	3	4	5	6	7	8
Characteristics of Leader	Relationship-Oriented (High LPC)	Mismatch	Mismatch	Mismatch	Match	Match	Match	Match	Mismatch
	Task-Oriented (Low LPC)	Match	Match	Match	Mismatch	Mismatch	Mismatch	Mismatch	Match

Decreasing Situational Favorability/Control →

Note: Leaders perform best when there exists a match between characteristics of leader and elements of situation.

Figure 14-4 Fiedler's contingency model of leadership. (Adapted from Arthur G. Jago, ''Leadership: Perspectives in Theory and Research,'' *Management Science*, vol. 28, 1982, p. 324.)

ever task direction is necessary for the cooperative group to complete the task, because workers willingly follow. When the situation is only moderately favorable, either because of poor leader-member relations or an unstructured task, a supportive, relationship-oriented leader can help smooth over relations with group members or provide support as the group seeks to cope with an unstructured task.[36]

The contingency model helps us understand why a leader who is doing well can run into trouble. For example, when Thomas F. Faught, Jr., became president and CEO of the Dravo Corporation, an international engineering and construction company, he helped reverse 3 years of losses, sell off unprofitable businesses, and get the company moving in a better direction. Chosen for his ability to shrink the company, he made tough decisions and gave orders, but subordinates sometimes complained that the orders were contradictory. In the process, he alienated a number of employees—and was finally fired by the board of directors. Although Faught may have been a bit heavy-handed with his task approach, he was successful in getting results in an unfavorable situation. As the situation started to improve somewhat, the board felt that a more relationship-oriented approach was needed.[37]

Fiedler believes that managers cannot easily change their LPC orientation or management style. As a result, he argues that when a leader's LPC orientation and a situation do not constitute a good match in terms of likely effectiveness, the situation should be changed or possibly the individual should move to a situation in which there is a good match. He calls this approach ''engineering the job to fit the manager.'' Following this line of argument, perhaps Faught should specialize in turnarounds and plan to move on as each situation improves.

The contingency model has been severely criticized because of the changing interpretation of the LPC scale and the lack of clarity about exactly how LPC orientation translates into behaviors that are successful in the various octants. Critics have also pointed to confusion about how managers should actually assess the degree of favorability, or situational control, and cited studies that have questioned findings for various octants of the model.[38] Despite these criticisms, recent sophisticated analyses of the various studies have found considerable support for the model. However, these analyses suggest that there are other factors also at work that are not accounted for in the contingency model.[39]

Cognitive Resource Theory. To address these deficiencies, Fiedler and his colleague, Joseph E. Garcia, developed the **cognitive resource theory.** The theory, a major revision and extension of the contingency model, considers the additional factor of a leader's cognitive resource use in predicting performance.[40]

In searching for other major variables that could influence leader effectiveness, Fiedler and Garcia identified **cognitive resources,** the intellectual abilities, technical competence, and job-relevant knowledge (acquired through either formal training or job experience) that leaders bring to their jobs. Research evidence related to traits, as we saw earlier, supports the potential importance of intelligence in leadership. Not surprisingly, there also is considerable research support for the importance of technical competence and job-related knowledge in leaders, at least in certain situations.[41] Still, as the research on traits suggests, simply having certain traits and competencies does not necessarily lead to effective leadership. More seems to be involved.

Fiedler and Garcia believe that leader cognitive resources translate into group performance through directive behavior on the part of a leader. Cognitive resources enable leaders to develop better plans, decisions, and action strategies, which are then conveyed to subordinates through directive behavior. Directive leaders let employees know in fairly specific terms what is expected of them, provide instructions, and make clear the standards by which employees' work will be evaluated. These steps potentially can maximize the impact of a leader's cognitive resources. In contrast, nondirective leaders consult their subordinates, ask for their opinions, and involve them in planning and making decisions.[42] This approach reduces the likely impact of the leader's own cognitive resources but makes it possible to take advantage of those of others.

To predict when a given leader will be directive, Fiedler and Garcia use the major elements from the contingency model—the leader LPC score and the degree of situational control (as determined by leader-member relations, task structure, and position power). Essentially, they build on the latest interpretation of the LPC scale as measuring a motivation hierarchy related to the extent to which an individual places a higher value on either task accomplishment or personal relationships. When situational control is high, high-LPC leaders tend to feel satisfied that their relationship concerns (their primary orientation) are met, and they engage in directive behavior (their secondary orientation) in pursuit of task accomplishment. In the same situation, low-LPC leaders feel assured that task concerns (their primary orientation) are being addressed, and they engage in nondirective behavior aimed at personal relationships (their secondary concern). The opposite occurs when situational control is low. A high-LPC leader faced with low control focuses on relationships and becomes nondirective; conversely, a low LPC leader worries about task accomplishment and becomes directive. In other words, both types of LPC leaders follow their primary concern when situational control is low and their secondary concern when situational control is high. Determining when a leader will be directive is important because cognitive resource theory argues that a leader's cognitive resources contribute highly to group performance only when the leader is directive.

Besides the directiveness of the leader, there are a few other supporting conditions that also help determine whether a leader's cognitive resources will contribute highly to performance. Assuming that the task requires cognitive abilities in the first place, the situation must be relatively stress-free (this de-

Cognitive resource theory A theory, which is a major revision and extension of Fiedler's contingency model, that considers the additional factor of a leader's cognitive resource use in predicting performance

Cognitive resources The intellectual abilities, technical competence, and job-relevant knowledge that leaders bring to their jobs

pends on how much stress a particular person can withstand before it begins to interfere with good thinking; then experience becomes a major factor). In addition, the group must support the leader and/or the organizational goals to be achieved (otherwise the group may consider only some or perhaps none of the leader's directives and ideas). On the other hand, when the leader is nondirective and the group supports the leader and/or the organizational goals, the cognitive abilities of members become important. These conditions are illustrated in the schematic representation of cognitive resource theory shown in Figure 14-5.

While cognitive resource theory is very new and will require testing beyond the extensive supporting data already offered by Fiedler and Garcia, it has a number of interesting implications for managers. For one thing, if intelligent leaders with high technical competence and job-related skills are to make a difference in group performance levels, the leaders need to be in situations in which they are likely to be directive and in which they have a relatively stress-free relationship with a supportive group. For another, when members of a group have high cognitive abilities, a nondirective leader who lets the group participate may get the best results. Therefore, whether directive or nondirective leaders get the best results depends on the situation. Consequently, Fiedler suggests that if you want to be directive, you should know what you are doing; otherwise, get subordinates involved.[43] Chung Ju-Yung illustrates a directive leadership style that has been successful at Korea's Hyundai group (see the following Case in Point discussion).

Figure 14-5 Schematic representation of cognitive resource theory. (Adapted from Fred E. Fiedler and Joseph E. Garcia, *New Approaches to Effective Leadership: Cognitive Resources and Organizational Performance*, Wiley, New York, 1987, p. 9.)

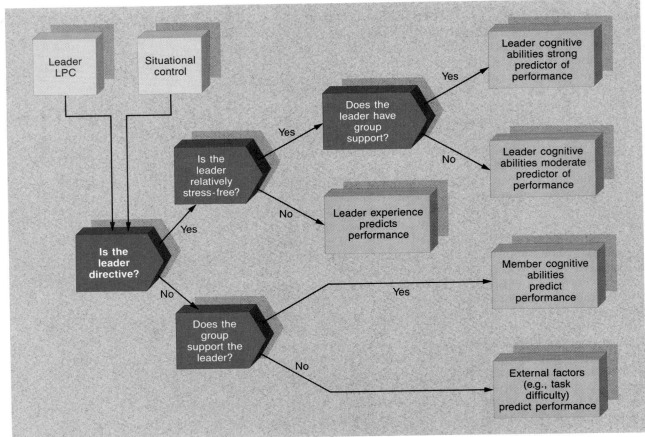

CASE IN POINT: Company Founder Chung Ju-Yung Builds Hyundai

One manager with a reputation for being at the far end of highly directive leadership is Chung Ju-Yung, founder and long-time chairman of one of Korea's foremost conglomerates, or *chaebol* (the name often given to large Korean companies operating in many diverse industries). Chung's organization, the Hyundai group, ranks among the largest organizations in the world.

Chung, who comes from a peasant background and has only a grade-school education, started Hyundai in 1947 as a general contracting firm that built barracks and repaired trucks for the U.S. Army. When the Korean war ended in 1953, Chung turned his company to construction, winning major contracts from the South Korean government to build roads, bridges, office buildings, and other structures. The company has also moved into a variety of other businesses, including shipbuilding, automobiles, and electronics. The Hyundai name became famous in the United States after the company launched its low-priced Excel in 1986, a car that broke automotive import records for first-year sales. Chung has spent millions of advertising dollars to make the Hyundai name familiar to Americans by pointing out that it rhymes with "Sunday."

Chung's name has been synonymous with major moves made by the Hyundai group because of his notoriously directive leadership style. Described as having a "tremendous analytical mind," he has dominated those who work for him, including two brothers and six sons. For years, every morning, he held a meeting of executives that often included lower-level managers; but, according to one former executive, no one had the "guts" to ever tell him when he was wrong. At the company's Ulsan complex, where 60,000 of Hyundai's more than 150,000 workers produce ships and automobiles, discipline has been described as almost military in nature. Reputed to be a billionaire, Chung continues to live in a modest home with sparse furnishings and to eschew foreign luxuries such as coffee. Now in his seventies and honorary chairman, he still plays a prominent role.[44] ■

Chung Ju-Yung, honorary chairman of Korea's Hyundai group, can claim only a grade school education, but he is widely credited with a keen analytical mind. Chung's considerable skills allowed him to take on a highly directive role at the company he founded. As he built the Hyundai group, he dominated his subordinates and maintained strict discipline within the firm.

With his directive behavior, Chung has helped Hyundai become a major international success. His leadership behavior contrasts strongly with that of Kim Woo-Choong, chairman of Daewoo, another of Korea's major conglomerates. Kim, who started Daewoo in the mid-1960s, is a graduate of the prestigious Yonsei University and depends on professional managers and task forces. He involves himself only in major strategic decisions and encourages the managers below him to be innovative and take risks. "The bottom of Daewoo's management is becoming more visible as the group relies less on Kim's dynamism, expertise, and leadership," says one financial analyst who tracks the company.[45]

Since Fiedler believes that people cannot change their LPC orientation (and related behaviors) very easily, he argues that managers need to make sure they are in situations that match their leadership style. For example, if managers tried to use Chung's approach in situations for which they did not have the appropriate cognitive skills, they would probably fail. Similarly, Kim's leadership approach without competent employees would also likely lead to disaster. Of course, not everyone concurs with Fiedler on the notion that leaders have difficulty adjusting their behaviors to the situation. Most situation theories, including the situational leadership theory that we examine next, are premised on the ability of leaders to adjust their behaviors to differing conditions.

Situational Leadership Theory

Situational leadership theory
A theory (developed by Hersey and Blanchard) based on the premise that leaders need to alter their behaviors depending on the readiness of followers

Another widely known contingency theory is the **situational leadership theory,** developed by Paul Hersey and Ken Blanchard. Originally called the life-cycle theory of leadership, this theory is based on the premise that leaders need to alter their behaviors depending on the readiness of followers.[46]

The theory focuses on two leader behaviors that are similar to the initiating structure and consideration behaviors pioneered by the Ohio State researchers:

Task behavior refers to the extent to which the leader engages in spelling out the duties and responsibilities of an individual or group. These behaviors include telling people what to do, how to do it, when to do it, where to do it, and who is to do it.

Relationship behavior refers to the extent to which the leader engages in two-way or multiway communication. It includes listening, facilitating, and supportive behaviors.[47]

Since these behaviors, like the Ohio State leader behaviors, are considered to be two independent dimensions, it is possible for a leader to be high on both, low on both, or high on one and low on the other. See the four quadrants in Figure 14-6.

To determine which combination of leader behaviors to use in a given situation, according to situational leadership theory, a leader needs to take into consideration the readiness levels of followers.[48] Follower readiness is the ability and willingness of followers to accomplish a particular task. Assessing readiness involves considering two factors, ability and willingness. *Ability* (job readiness) includes the ability, skill, knowledge, and experience that are needed to do a specific task. *Willingness* (psychological readiness) comprises the confidence, commitment, and motivation that are needed to complete a specific task. As can be seen at the bottom of Figure 14-6, the readiness continuum is divided into four levels: low (R1), low to moderate (R2), moderate to high (R3), and high (R4).

The bell-shaped curve running through the four leadership quadrants prescribes the appropriate leadership style for a given level of readiness:

Telling is used in situations of low readiness, when followers are unable and also unwilling or too insecure to take responsibility for a given task. Here, the telling style (S1) involves giving individuals specific directions on what to do and how to do it. It consists of high task and low consideration behaviors. Consideration is de-emphasized because too much supportive behavior may give low-readiness individuals the impression that the leader will be permissive and reward low performance.

Selling is used for low to moderate readiness, when followers are unable to take responsibility but are willing or feel confident to do so. The selling style (S2) is aimed at giving specific directions, but it also is supportive of the individual's willingness and enthusiasm. Explaining, persuading, and clarifying are particularly important here to provide directions and still maintain the individual's willingness to take responsibility when he or she is ready. This style utilizes high task and high relationship behaviors.

Participating is used with moderate to high readiness, when followers are able to take responsibility but are unwilling or too insecure to do so. Usually their unwillingness is related to lack of confidence, but it may also be related

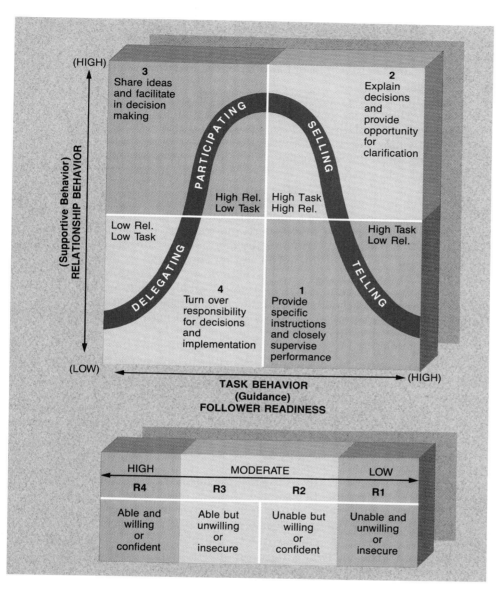

Figure 14-6 Situational leadership theory. (Adapted from Paul Hersey and Kenneth H. Blanchard, *Management of Organizational Behavior: Utilizing Human Resources*, 5th ed., Prentice-Hall, Englewood Cliffs, N.J., 1988, p. 188.)

to low motivation. Since they are able to perform, a supportive, participating style (S3), in which the leader emphasizes two-way communication and collaboration, is most likely to be effective. This style involves high relationship and low task behaviors.

Delegating is used for high readiness, when followers are able and willing or confident enough to take appropriate responsibility. At this point, they need relatively little support or direction; hence the delegating style has the best prospect of success. This style involves low task and low relationship behaviors.

To use the situational theory of leadership, leaders need to determine what task areas they would like to influence, assess the readiness level of the individual, and select the leadership style that corresponds to the individual's readiness level. Underlying the situational theory is the notion that leaders should help increase the task-related readiness of followers as quickly as feasible by appropriately adjusting their own leadership styles to move through the cycle from S1 to S4.

Although the theory has intuitive appeal, it has been the subject of only limited research to verify its validity as a guideline to managers. The theory has been criticized particularly for its ambiguity about assessing follower readiness (e.g., an unwilling but able follower is considered to be more mature than a willing but unable follower), changing definitions of relationship behavior (e.g., in S3, treating relationship behavior as equivalent to follower participation), and the failure to include other important situational factors (such as the nature of the task).[49] Its positive contributions are its focus on the situational nature of leadership, its emphasis on the importance of subordinates as determinants of appropriate leadership style, and its fairly innovative notion that a leader may be able to change the leadership situation by increasing subordinate skills and confidence.[50] Results of one of the most comprehensive tests of the theory to date indicate that its best application may be with newly hired employees or employees in new jobs, who seem to benefit from the highly structured, telling leadership behavior associated with S1. The study also suggests that subordinates may need more task leader behaviors in S3 and more of both task and relationship leader behaviors in S4 than the theory recommends.[51]

Andrew S. Grove, president of Intel, a high-technology company well known for its semiconductor technology, makes extensive use of the situational leadership approach. He assesses a subordinate's task-relevant readiness to help him decide what type of leadership style to use. Grove points out that it is very possible for an individual to have high task-relevant readiness in one job but not in another. He uses as an example a very productive sales manager who was moved from the field to a plant and placed in charge of a factory unit. Although the size and scope of the two jobs were similar, the manager's performance began to deteriorate and he appeared to be overwhelmed by the assignment. Grove explains that while the individual was extremely capable in his former position, his readiness for the new job was "extremely low, since its environment, content, and task were all new to him." Over time, he gained more experience with the job and his task-relevant readiness began to increase. Simultaneously, his performance began to rise to the outstanding level that the top managers had expected when they promoted him. "What happened here should have been totally predictable," notes Grove, "yet we were surprised."[52]

Revised Normative Leadership Model

Normative leadership model
A model (designed by Vroom and Yetton) that helps leaders assess important situational factors that affect the extent to which they should involve subordinates in particular decisions

Another situational leadership theory, called the **normative leadership model,** was designed for a fairly narrow, but important, purpose. It helps leaders assess important situational factors that affect the extent to which they should involve subordinates in particular decisions. The original model, sometimes called the *Vroom-Yetton model,* was developed in 1973 by researchers Victor Vroom and Philip Yetton and became well known as a helpful leadership decision tool for managers. However, research on its usefulness highlighted a number of shortcomings, including its omission of some important situational considerations.[53]

As a result, Vroom and Arthur Jago recently developed a revised and expanded normative leadership model that has an enhanced capacity to more adequately reflect the decision-making environment of managers.[54] Like the original model, the revised model includes five types of management decision

Table 14-2 Normative Leadership Model Decision Styles

Symbol	Definition
AI	You solve the problem or make the decision yourself using the information available to you at the present time.
AII	You obtain any necessary information from subordinates, then decide on a solution to the problem yourself. You may or may not tell subordinates the purpose of your questions or give information about the problem or decision on which you are working. The input provided by them is clearly in response to your request for specific information. They do not play a role in the definition of the problem or in generating or evaluating alternative solutions.
CI	You share the problem with the relevant subordinates individually, getting their ideas and suggestions without bringing them together as a group. Then *you* make the decision. This decision may or may not reflect your subordinates' influence.
CII	You share the problem with your subordinates in a group meeting. In this meeting you obtain their ideas and suggestions. Then *you* make the decision, which may or may not reflect your subordinates' influence.
GII	You share the problem with your subordinates as a group. Together you generate and evaluate alternatives and attempt to reach agreement (consensus) on a solution. Your role is much like that of chairperson, coordinating the discussion, keeping it focused on the problem, and making sure that the critical issues are discussed. You can provide the group with information or ideas that you have, but you do not try to "press" them to adopt "your" solution, and you are willing to accept and implement any solution that has the support of the entire group.

Source: Reprinted from Victor H. Vroom and Philip W. Yetton, *Leadership and Decision Making,* University of Pittsburgh Press, 1973.

methods for group problems (problems in which the decision can affect more than one subordinate in the work unit). The five methods are shown in Table 14-2. Each method is designated by a letter and a number. "A," "C," and "G" stand for "autocratic," "consultative," and "group," respectively. The autocratic and consultative approaches each have two variations, designated I and II. The decision methods become progressively more participative as one moves from AI (decide yourself) to GII (let the group decide).

To help managers determine which method to use in a given situation, the revised normative leadership model includes 12 questions about attributes of the decision problem:

1. *How important is the technical quality of this decision?* For most managerial decisions, technical quality is important in the sense that some solutions are more likely than others to facilitate the reaching of external objectives (e.g., better quality, lower cost, more long lasting).
2. *How important is subordinate commitment to the decision?* For some decisions, subordinate commitment in the form of enthusiastic support is vital for decision success. In other cases, compliance may do.
3. *Do you have sufficient information to make a high-quality decision?* If your subordinates have additional information and expertise that would be important in making a high-quality decision, then you may need to obtain their input in some way.

4. *Is the problem well structured?* With structured problems, it is clear where you are, where you want to go, and what you need to get there (e.g., deciding when to schedule the manufacturing of extra batches of an existing product). Unstructured problems are more "fuzzy" in terms of understanding the current situations, formulating goals, and determining how to achieve the goals (e.g., deciding which new products to develop). Unstructured problems often require creative input and expertise from others.

5. *If you were to make the decision by yourself, is it reasonably certain that your subordinates would be committed to the decision?* Here, you consider the likelihood of whether subordinates would enthusiastically support your decision if you made it autocratically.

6. *Do subordinates share the organizational goals to be attained in solving this problem?* It is easier to involve them heavily in the process if they are likely to think about organizational goals, rather than mainly about their own self-interest.

7. *Is conflict among subordinates over preferred solutions likely?* Here, you consider the extent to which subordinates are likely to have widely varying views about what should be done.

8. *Do subordinates have sufficient information to make a high-quality decision?* If subordinates *collectively* have enough information and expertise to make the decision themselves, then heavy involvement becomes more feasible.

9. *Does a critically severe time constraint limit your ability to involve subordinates?* A time constraint exists if *both* these conditions apply: (1) Any reasonably decent decision would be better than a decision that comes too late, and (2) involving subordinates would probably cause the decision to be made too late.

10. *Are the costs involved in bringing together geographically dispersed subordinates prohibitive?* You need to make a judgment weighing expense, if any, against the importance of the decision.

11. *How important is it to you to minimize the time it takes to make the decision?* If other work is pressing, time may be extremely important.

12. *How important is it to you to maximize the opportunities for subordinate development?* This question addresses how much importance you attach to enhancing the decision-making and related technical skills of subordinates. The importance of developing subordinates and that of saving time (question 11) often are in conflict in decision-making situations.

With the revised model, a software package is available for use on personal computers so that a manager can answer these questions and then have the software determine the best decision-making method (AI through GII) to use in the particular circumstance. In most situations, though, managers can gain adequate guidance from two decision trees that contain the first eight questions and can be used without computers. Questions 9 to 12 pertain to when the decision trees can be used and which one to use. The decision trees (instead of the computer software) can be used when the answers to questions 9 (severe time constraint?) and 10 (cost of group meeting prohibitive?) are both no. The development-driven decision tree (see Figure 14-7) is used when developing subordinates is more important than conserving time (question 12). A separate time-driven decision tree (not shown) is available for use when minimizing time is more important than developing subordinates (question 11).

To see how a decision tree works, let us consider what happened when the Springfield Remanufacturing Corporation of Springfield, Missouri, ran into a

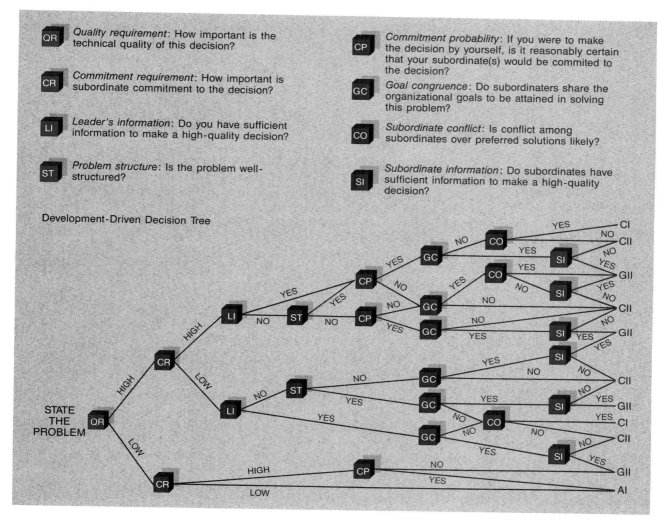

QR **Quality requirement**: How important is the technical quality of this decision?

CR **Commitment requirement**: How important is subordinate commitment to the decision?

LI **Leader's information**: Do you have sufficient information to make a high-quality decision?

ST **Problem structure**: Is the problem well-structured?

CP **Commitment probability**: If you were to make the decision by yourself, is it reasonably certain that your subordinate(s) would be commited to the decision?

GC **Goal congruence**: Do subordinaters share the organizational goals to be attained in solving this problem?

CO **Subordinate conflict**: Is conflict among subordinates over preferred solutions likely?

SI **Subordinate information**: Do subordinates have sufficient information to make a high-quality decision?

Development-Driven Decision Tree

Figure 14-7 Decision trees for normative leadership model. (Reprinted from Victor H. Vroom and Arthur G. Jago, *The New Leadership: Managing Participation in Organizations*, Prentice-Hall, Englewood Cliffs, N.J., 1988, pp. 184, 185.)

crisis. The company had signed a 10-year, $75 million agreement with General Motors to remanufacture automotive diesel engines. The contract helped revive the company, which had previously spent a number of years as a dying division of International Harvester. After spending a couple of hectic years getting production lined up and meeting schedules, Springfield received a sudden call from GM's material scheduling division, which wanted to cut 5000 engines from the annual schedule. Jack Stack, Springfield's CEO, won a 90-day delay in the cuts; during that time he pondered what to do. Analysis showed that the cuts would force him to lay off 100 people, an action Stack had somehow managed to avoid for 19 years. As the end of the 90 days drew closer, Stack agonized over what to do. He had narrowed down the prospects. If he kept everyone, the workers would need to go out and generate 50,000 person-hours' worth of business. But if they weren't successful, there would be no time to recoup. Instead of having to lay off 100, Stack would have to lay off 200. How should he make this decision?

Using the development-driven decision tree (Figure 14-7), the analysis would go like this:

Quality requirement: Low, because both alternatives would allow the company to stay in business.

Commitment requirement: High, because commitment is needed to make it work.

Commitment probability: No, because there might be resentment over the layoffs.

Model's suggested approach: Let the group decide.

Stack called a meeting of all 350 employees, presented the alternatives, and asked them what they wanted to do. Almost unanimously they replied: "Go for it. Let's keep the people." For the next year, they all worked extremely hard, taking any jobs they could get, selling in any kind of market they could get into, and starting product lines with which they had no previous experience. It was brutal, but they did it. The company made $2 million more than in the previous year and even had to add people. "If we had done that layoff," Stack says, "I don't think we ever would have recovered. We'd have lost momentum. As tired as everybody is, they really feel great that they did it."[55]

Notice that for this situation it was not necessary to answer all eight decision-tree questions. The decision tree skips over questions that are irrelevant to certain paths. (In this case, use of the development-driven decision tree would yield the same result; however, most often the results for the two alternative decision trees differ.) Our example considered the normative leadership model as it applies to possible involvement of a group, but there is also a version of the model that can be used for individual decision problems—those involving just one other person. Because the revision of the normative leadership model is so recent, there has not been sufficient time for independent researchers to conduct and publish research verifying the effectiveness of the improvements. However, the revision was guided by research on the original model's shortcomings and appears to have at least attempted to address major known flaws.

Path-Goal Theory

Path-goal theory A theory that attempts to explain how leader behavior impacts the motivation and job satisfaction of subordinates

The last major situational leadership theory that we consider, the **path-goal theory** of leadership, attempts to explain how leader behavior impacts the motivation and job satisfaction of subordinates.[56] Although other individuals had a hand in its early development, path-goal theory is mainly associated with leadership researcher Robert J. House and his colleagues.[57] The theory grew partially out of attempts to explain the various discrepant findings of the Ohio State leadership studies, particularly the finding that initiating structure was often, but not always, associated with higher performance. It is called path-goal theory because it focuses on how leaders influence the way that subordinates perceive work goals and possible paths to reaching both work goals (performance) and personal goals (intrinsic and extrinsic rewards).

Path-goal theory relies heavily on the expectancy theory of motivation. As discussed more thoroughly in Chapter 13, expectancy theory involves three main elements: effort-performance expectancy (the probability that our efforts will lead to the required performance level), performance-outcome expectancy (the probability that our successful performance will lead to certain outcomes or rewards), and valence (the anticipated value of the outcomes or rewards). Path-goal theory uses expectancy theory for guidance in determining ways that a leader might make the achievement of work goals easier or more attractive.

How do you make a raft out of 50-gallon drums, two-by-fours, and rope? That's the task that top executives at General Foods are asked to do as part of their leadership training. This group found out that reaching the goal of a workable raft requires a combination of directive, supportive, participative, and achievement-oriented behaviors.

Leader Behaviors. In order to affect subordinate perceptions of paths and goals, path-goal theory identifies four major leader behaviors that can be used:

Directive leader behavior involves letting subordinates know what is expected of them, providing guidance about work methods, developing work schedules, identifying work evaluation standards, and indicating the basis for outcomes or rewards. It is similar to task orientation or initiating structure.

Supportive leader behavior entails showing concern for the status, well-being, and needs of subordinates; doing small things to make the work more pleasant; and being friendly and approachable. It is similar to relationship-oriented or consideration behavior.

Participative leader behavior is characterized by consulting with subordinates, encouraging their suggestions, and carefully considering their ideas when making decisions.

Achievement-oriented leader behavior involves setting challenging goals, expecting subordinates to perform at their highest level, and conveying a high degree of confidence in subordinates.

Situational Factors. Although the four leader behaviors potentially can be used to enhance the path-goal motivation and job satisfaction of subordinates, path-goal theory argues that leaders also need to consider two types of situational factors: subordinate characteristics and environmental characteristics. *Subordinate characteristics* include personality traits, skills, abilities, and needs. For example, an individual with low skills in a particular area is likely to be motivated by directive leadership, while a highly skilled individual is apt to appreciate a participative leader.

Environmental characteristics fall into three main categories: the task itself, the work group, and the organization's formal authority system (such as levels in the hierarchy, degree of decision centralization, nature of formal reward system). For example, supportive leadership may foster motivation on a boring

Directive Leader behavior that involves letting subordinates know what is expected of them, providing guidance about work methods, developing work schedules, identifying work evaluation standards, and indicating the basis for outcomes or rewards

Supportive Leader behavior that entails showing concern for the status, well-being, and needs of subordinates; doing small things to make the work more pleasant; and being friendly and approachable

Participative Leader behavior that is characterized by consulting with subordinates, encouraging their suggestions, and carefully considering their ideas when making decisions

Achievement-oriented Leader behavior that involves setting challenging goals, expecting subordinates to perform at their highest level, and conveying a high degree of confidence in subordinates

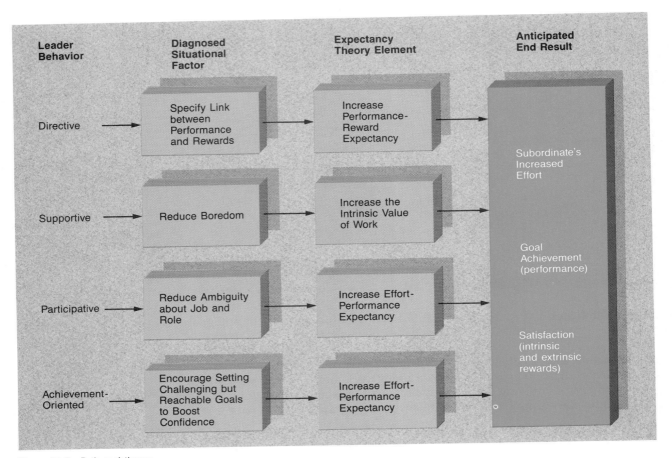

Leader Behavior	Diagnosed Situational Factor	Expectancy Theory Element	Anticipated End Result
Directive	Specify Link between Performance and Rewards	Increase Performance-Reward Expectancy	Subordinate's Increased Effort
Supportive	Reduce Boredom	Increase the Intrinsic Value of Work	Goal Achievement (performance)
Participative	Reduce Ambiguity about Job and Role	Increase Effort-Performance Expectancy	Satisfaction (intrinsic and extrinsic rewards)
Achievement-Oriented	Encourage Setting Challenging but Reachable Goals to Boost Confidence	Increase Effort-Performance Expectancy	

Figure 14-8 Path-goal theory examples. (Adapted from Gary A. Yukl, *Leadership in Organizations*, Prentice-Hall, Englewood Cliffs, N.J., 1981, pp. 148, 150.)

task, while achievement orientation may increase motivation on an interesting task.

Choosing Leader Behaviors. In using path-goal theory to choose appropriate leader behaviors, leaders need to diagnose various situational factors in terms of their effects on the three expectancy theory elements (the path) and ultimately on the desired end results (the goals). A practical way to do this is first to think in terms of the expectancy theory elements, then diagnose situational factors that could be changed to positively affect the expectancy theory elements (operate to increase motivation), and finally initiate appropriate leader behaviors to change the situational factors. Several examples of how path-goal theory works are shown in Figure 14-8.

For instance, a leader may recognize that subordinates' performance-reward expectancies are low because the formal reward system (a formal authority system situational factor) does a poor job of communicating the connection between performance and rewards to employees. As a result, a leader may engage in directive behavior to specify clearly the link between performance and rewards. Similarly, a leader may engage in supportive behavior to reduce the boredom of a routine job (a task situational factor) and increase the intrinsic value of the work. A leader may use participative leadership to reduce the ambiguity of an unstructured task (a task situational factor) and increase a subordinate's effort-performance expectancy. Finally, achievement-oriented leadership may help encourage a subordinate who has low self-confidence (an individual characteristic situational factor) to set challenging, but reachable, goals that increase effort-performance expectancy.

Since it is a situational leadership theory, path-goal theory argues that leadership behavior that is effective in one situation will not necessarily be effective in another. For example, the use of directive leadership to clarify task demands when they are already clear will, at best, have little effect because the behavior is redundant; it might, at worst, frustrate employees and reduce the intrinsic valence of work. Notice, however, that unlike Fiedler's contingency and cognitive resource approaches, path-goal theory assumes that leaders can be flexible in their behaviors and can potentially learn to engage in any of the four major leader behaviors as the situation requires. One manager who has been successful by making sure that employees clearly understand paths to organizational and personal goals is Hervey Feldman, president of Embassy Suites Hotels (see the following Case in Point discussion).

CASE IN POINT: Leading Embassy Suites to an Enviable Reputation

President Hervey Feldman has built a high-quality service reputation for Embassy Suites, a subsidiary of the Holiday Corporation, which specializes in hotels that offer only suites. Part of his approach is helping his employees set high goals for themselves. "Historically hotel managers have believed that minimum-wage workers aren't smart or ambitious," says Feldman. "That's just not true. With training and experience, they all have the curiosity and intelligence to go beyond making beds." To ensure that his views permeate the organization, he makes a special effort to hire managers with good interpersonal skills who tend to view others as basically competent.

Feldman helps encourage employees to reach for higher personal goals through a pay system based on skills. A housekeeper who wants to work the front desk, for example, could sign up for a company-sponsored training course

The service workers at Embassy Suites Hotels are encouraged to develop their skills, meet personal and company goals, and move into higher positions. The credit for this highly successful leadership approach goes to Hervey Feldman, President of the organization. Feldman utilizes all four leadership behaviors associated with path-goal theory in encouraging workers to uphold Embassy Suite's standards for high quality service.

in that skill. Although successfully completing the course does not necessarily lead to a promotion right away, it does mean an immediate raise, in the range of 25 cents per hour, and opportunities to work the front desk during peak periods. About one-fourth of the 4500 employees are enrolled in various training courses. As proof that Feldman does provide opportunities, more than two dozen managers and assistant managers have come out of the training program to date.

To make sure that employees understand the goals and the potential pay-offs, Feldman has hotel managers post a daily report in the employee lounge. The report gives the hotel's occupancy rate, average room rate, and estimated profits, as well as comments from five or more customers interviewed randomly the previous day. When the hotel is meeting its goals, even employees who are at the bottom of the pay scale are eligible for a monthly bonus of more than $100.[58] ▄▄▄▄

Feldman uses achievement-oriented behavior in encouraging employees toward high, but reachable, personal and organizational goals. He also is directive in making sure that employees have the skills they need to do their jobs and that they understand the link between performance and reward. He is participative in involving employees in their own development. In addition, he makes efforts to be supportive, particularly in attempting to ensure that employees are treated as competent members of the organization.

Because path-goal theory can encompass multiple leader behaviors and a potentially large number of situational variables that operate simultaneously, only limited testing of the theory has been conducted thus far. Although some studies have produced mixed results, a recent evaluation of research to date indicates general support for the theory.[59] Its flexibility will allow further refinements and extensions as additional related research accumulates.[60] In the meantime, it does provide managers with a useful framework for thinking about the likely impacts of their leader behaviors on subordinate motivation, goal attainment, and job satisfaction. For example, Apple's Debi Coleman uses a directive style to outline broad directions but also tends to be participative by involving others in bringing about changes.[61]

PROMOTING INNOVATION: TRANSFORMATIONAL LEADERSHIP

Transactional leaders
Leaders who motivate subordinates to perform at expected levels by helping them recognize task responsibilities, identify goals, acquire confidence about meeting desired performance levels, and understand how their needs and the rewards that they desire are linked to goal achievement

One interesting issue involving leadership is the prospect that managers and leaders are not necessarily one and the same.[62] According to one argument, managers do the same things over and over (do things right), but it takes leaders to innovate (do the right things), bring about major change, and inspire followers to pursue extraordinary levels of effort.[63] In studying the issue, leadership expert Bernard M. Bass and his colleagues have made a distinction between transactional and transformational leaders.[64]

Transactional leaders motivate subordinates to perform at expected levels by helping them recognize task responsibilities, identify goals, acquire confidence about meeting desired performance levels, and understand how their needs and the rewards that they desire are linked to goal achievement. As you have probably recognized, transactional leadership is closely allied to the path-goal theory of leadership. The other situational leadership theories discussed in this chapter also can be characterized as transactional leadership approaches.

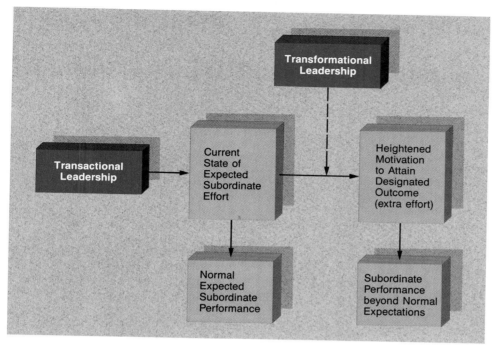

Figure 14-9 Add-on effect of transformational leadership. (Adapted from Bernard M. Bass, *Leadership and Performance Beyond Expectations*, Free Press, New York, 1985, p. 23.)

In contrast, **transformational leaders** motivate individuals to perform beyond normal expectations by inspiring subordinates to focus on broader missions that transcend their own immediate self-interests, to concentrate on intrinsic higher-level goals (such as achievement and self-actualization) rather than extrinsic lower-level goals (such as safety and security), and to have confidence in their abilities to achieve the extraordinary missions articulated by the leader.

Transformational leadership is not a substitute for transactional leadership. It is a supplemental form of leadership with add-on effects: performance beyond expectations (see Figure 14-9). The logic is that even the most successful transformational leaders need transactional skills as well to manage effectively the day-to-day events that form the basis of the broader mission.

According to Bass, three leader factors are particularly important to transformational leadership: charisma, individualized consideration, and intellectual stimulation. Of these, charisma is the most important. **Charisma** is the leader's ability to inspire pride, faith, and respect; to recognize what is really important; and to articulate effectively a sense of mission, or vision, that inspires followers. Various individuals in history, such as Martin Luther King, Mahatma Gandhi, John F. Kennedy, and Franklin D. Roosevelt, have been said to have had charisma.[65]

Although a number of researchers in political science and sociology have studied the concept for decades, serious interest by management researchers is relatively recent. Early researchers visualized charisma as an inborn personality trait. However, whether or not a leader is charismatic seems to depend on the eye of the follower. As a result, more recent efforts have aimed at understanding the leader behaviors that prompt followers to identify a leader as having charisma. Some results from one recent effort to identify behavioral components associated with charismatic leaders suggest that such leaders strive to change the status quo, project future goals that are idealized visions very different from current conditions, behave in ways that are somewhat unconventional and

Transformational leaders Leaders who motivate individuals to perform beyond normal expectations by inspiring subordinates to focus on broader missions that transcend their own immediate self-interests, to concentrate on intrinsic higher-level goals rather than extrinsic lower-level goals, and to have confidence in their abilities to achieve the extraordinary missions articulated by the leader

Charisma A leadership factor that comprises the leader's ability to inspire pride, faith, and respect; to recognize what is really important; and to articulate effectively a sense of mission or vision that inspires followers

counter to existing norms, rely heavily on referent and expert power, and attempt to get others to share a radical vision of changes. In contrast, noncharismatic leaders are more likely to attempt to maintain the status quo, project future goals closely related to current conditions, behave generally in conventional ways that conform to existing norms, utilize several power bases (mainly legitimate, referent, reward, and expert), and nudge or order others to share their views.[66]

The second leadership factor associated with transformational leadership, **individualized consideration,** involves delegating projects to help develop each follower's capabilities, paying personal attention to each follower's needs, and treating each follower as an individual worthy of respect. The third leadership factor, **intellectual stimulation,** involves offering new ideas to stimulate followers to rethink old ways of doing things, encouraging followers to look at problems from multiple vantage points, and fostering creative breakthroughs in obstacles that had seemed insurmountable.

Not everyone agrees that transformational leaders must have charisma, although one recent study showed that a charismatic style is highly effective in enhancing subordinate performance and job satisfaction.[67] There does seem to be agreement that transformational leaders need to provide a vision of a desired future state, mobilize commitment, and bring about changes that enable reaching the vision.[68] When she ran Apple's Macintosh factory, Debi Coleman encouraged workers to make the facility Class 4, or the best in the world. Similarly, in speaking about John Sculley, Apple's chairman and CEO, Coleman says, "He and I can talk ideas for hours. When I walk into his office, it's like I become mesmerized by the future." Noting that she feels as if she were stepping 5 years into the future and beyond, Coleman says, "It's a little like being in *Star Wars*. Like you're on the mother ship, guiding the federation."[69] Hence both Coleman and Sculley demonstrate transformational leadership. Others sometimes mentioned as transformational leaders include Lee Iaccoca, who inspired major changes at Chrysler that were instrumental in its survival; the late An Wang, who built Wang Laboratories into a major electronics and software corporation (its recent troubles notwithstanding—see the concluding case in Chapter 7); and Sam Walton, who is in the process of establishing Wal-Mart as one of the largest retailers in the United States (see the concluding case in Chapter 5).[70]

ARE LEADERS NECESSARY?

Some critics argue that the importance of leadership is greatly overrated and that in many contexts leaders make little or no difference.[71] In this section, we explore the notion of the romance of leadership, as well as the related prospect that there may be substitutes for leadership, and we consider the organizational life-cycle approach to understanding when different leadership styles may be most applicable.

The Romance of Leadership

Noting the extensive research that is still trying to pinpoint just what leadership really is, several groups of researchers have argued that leaders may not be as important as we sometimes think.[72] Rather, we may use the concept of leadership to try to make sense out of the world around us. The tendency to do so appears to be greatest when things are going well. In one intriguing study, researchers spent 11 years tracking the headlines of *Wall Street Journal* articles

---

Individualized consideration A leadership factor that involves delegating projects to help develop each follower's capabilities, paying personal attention to each follower's needs, and treating each follower as an individual worthy of respect

Intellectual stimulation A leadership factor that involves offering new ideas to stimulate followers to rethink old ways of doing things, encouraging followers to look at problems from multiple vantage points, and fostering creative breakthroughs in obstacles that had seemed insurmountable

about 34 major U.S. companies. They then coded the headlines according to whether or not corporate leadership was mentioned in some form (e.g., "top management," "senior executive," "top brass," and names of specific managers) and tied the results to company performance data. Results showed that leadership is much more likely to be highlighted in a headline when a company is performing well. A related study showed that articles about leadership are more likely to appear in general business periodicals when the economy is doing well, causing the researchers to label the phenomenon "the **romance of leadership.**"[73]

Other studies also support the idea that leadership may sometimes get more than its due credit for positive results, even though there is ample evidence that leaders can and do affect outcomes.[74] Another reason why leadership may not be as important as it seems is that substitutes for leadership may be present.

Substitutes for Leadership

An interesting aspect of path-goal theory is the notion that situational factors may sometimes render certain leader behaviors unnecessary and/or ineffective. For example, directive behavior related to the task may not be necessary when the task is clear. However, path-goal theory stops short of attempting to specify explicitly the conditions under which leader behavior may be unnecessary because of situational factors.

The **substitutes for leadership** approach attempts to specify some of the main situational factors likely to make leader behaviors unnecessary or to negate their effectiveness.[75] According to this approach, **neutralizers** are situational factors that make it *impossible* for a given leader behavior to have an impact on subordinate performance and/or satisfaction. In other words, they cancel out, or negate, the effects of a leader's behavior. Examples of neutralizers that can negate the impact of both relationship-oriented and task-oriented leader behaviors are high need for subordinate independence, low subordinate valence for available rewards (see Chapter 13), and physical distance between leader and subordinates. On the other hand, **substitutes** are situational factors that make leadership impact not only *impossible* but also *unnecessary*. Substitutes for relationship-oriented leader behavior include intrinsically satisfying work and subordinates who have a professional work orientation. Substitutes for task-oriented behavior include able and experienced subordinates and work that is routine, has clearly specified methods, and/or provides clear feedback.

Neutralizers can create leadership vacuums that result in dysfunctional outcomes. Hence managers need to assess the presence of neutralizers and attempt to alter the situation, if possible, so that appropriate leader behaviors can have the intended effect. (For instance, a manager may develop new reward possibilities, such as training opportunities, if subordinates have a low valence for currently available rewards.) On the other hand, situational factors that are substitutes for leadership can enable a leader to concentrate on other areas in need of leader attention, since the substitutes are likely to have the desired positive impact on subordinate performance and satisfaction. For example, Sally Minard, a partner in Lotas Minard Patton McIver, Inc., a New York advertising agency, has a reputation for giving experienced subordinates latitude. "Sally was one of the best management supervisors I have ever had," says one former subordinate. "She didn't watch over our shoulders. She was aware of what was happening, but she would give us responsibility.[76]

The small amount of research that has directly addressed the substitutes for leadership approach has generally been supportive. Sometimes, though, situa-

Romance of leadership The phenomenon of leadership's possibly being given more that its due credit for positive results

Substitutes for leadership An approach that attempts to specify some of the main situational factors likely to make leader behaviors unnecessary or to negate their effectiveness

Neutralizers Situational factors that make it *impossible* for a given leader behavior to have an impact on subordinate performance and/or satisfaction

Substitutes Situational factors that make leadership impact not only *impossible* but also *unnecessary*

Table 14-3 Leadership and the Organizational Life Cycle

Organizational Life-Cycle Stage	Most Important Leadership Emphasis
Entrepreneurial	Transformational
Collectivity	Transactional
Formalization and control	Transactional
Elaboration of structure	Transformational

tional factors substitute only partially for leadership behaviors, making some leadership still necessary.[77] For instance, a task that provides feedback on how a subordinate is doing may provide some guidance, but some direction from a leader may still be necessary until the subordinate is completely proficient or when unusual circumstances arise. Aside from being concerned about the leadership needs of specific subordinates and work groups, managers also need to consider the broader perspective of the organizational life cycle.

Leadership and the Organizational Life Cycle

The view of organizations as having life cycles, or predictable stages of development (see Chapter 7), provides some guidance about when either transactional or transformational leadership is likely to be most appropriate (see Table 14-3).[78] When an organization is at its entrepreneurial, or beginning, stage, transformational leadership is particularly instrumental in creating a vision that allows the organization to be born and take a few first steps. At the collectivity stage, additional workers begin to join the initial core group, and transactional leadership becomes an important aid in handling the accelerating growth. By the formalization and control stage, organizational growth requires even greater emphasis on transactional leadership to maintain direction and control. By the elaboration of structure stage, excessive formalization and control often reduce innovation to a low level, and heavy emphasis on transformational leadership is again needed. Although both transactional and transformational styles of leadership are likely to be utilized at every stage in effective organizations, the amount of emphasis is different in each case. Thus managers need to understand both approaches to leadership in order to function effectively. Inherent in putting these leadership approaches into practice is the need to be well versed in organizational communication processes, a subject to which we turn in the next chapter.

CHAPTER SUMMARY

Leadership is the process of influencing others toward the achievement of organizational goals. Leaders use six major types of power to help affect the behavior of others: legitimate, reward, coercive, expert, informational, and referent. Leaders need to use their power carefully in ways that encourage commitment and build power rather than diminish it.

Researchers have had only limited success in attempting to identify common traits that distinguish leaders from nonleaders. Recent efforts suggest that

there may be some general distinguishing traits, such as intelligence and dominance, and that some traits may apply only to specific types of situations.

Studying leader behaviors has provided a more promising research direction. The Iowa, Michigan, and Ohio State studies represent prominent initial efforts to identify effective leadership behaviors, or styles. The Ohio State studies identified two important leadership styles, initiating structure and consideration, that they viewed as independent dimensions rather than opposite ends of a continuum. Unfortunately, leaders exhibiting both high initiating structure and high consideration did not necessarily get the best results. The Managerial Grid popularized a related approach, which emphasized concern for people and concern for productions. Studies indicate that female and male managers are similar in the amounts of interpersonal and task behaviors that they exhibit.

Situational leadership theories grew out of the recognition that leader behaviors that work well in one situation often are not as effective in another situation. Fiedler's contingency model holds that a leader's LPC orientation measures the extent to which a leader is likely to be task- or people-motivated. The effectiveness of a leader depends on whether the leader's LPC orientation matches the situation as determined by leader-member relations, task structure, and position power. Cognitive resource theory argues that a leader's cognitive resources will have a major effect on group performance only when the leader is directive, the situation is relatively stress-free for the leader, and the group supports the leader and/or the organizational goals to be achieved. When the leader is nondirective in the same situation, member cognitive abilities become important.

The situational leadership theory argues that leaders need to alter their combination of task and relationship behaviors depending on the task readiness of their followers. The revised normative leadership model helps leaders determine the extent to which they should involve subordinates in particular decisions. The path-goal theory of leadership relies heavily on the expectancy theory of motivation and attempts to explain how leader behavior impacts the motivation and job satisfaction of subordinates.

Transformational leadership can be an important factor in innovation because it motivates individuals to perform beyond normal expectations in pursuit of new visions. It is an add-on to transactional leadership, since both are needed.

There is some evidence that leadership may sometimes get more than its due credit for positive results, particularly when things are going well. Researchers call this phenomenon the romance of leadership. One reason why leadership may not be as important as it seems is that there are a number of substitutes for leadership. The organizational life cycle also may affect the emphasis that needs to be placed on transactional and transformational leadership.

MANAGERIAL TERMINOLOGY

achievement-oriented (503)
autocratic (485)
charisma (507)
coercive power (481)
cognitive resource theory (493)
cognitive resources (493)
consideration (487)
democratic (485)
directive (503)
employee-centered (486)

expert power (481)
Fiedler's contingency model (490)
individualized consideration (508)
information power (481)
initiating structure (487)
intellectual stimulation (508)
job-centered (486)
laissez-faire (485)
leadership (480)

legitimate power (481)
LPC orientation (490)
neutralizers (509)
normative leadership model (498)
participative (503)
path-goal theory (502)
power (481)
referent power (481)
reward power (481)
romance of leadership (509)

situational leadership theory (496)
situational theories (490)
substitutes (509)
substitutes for leadership (509)
supportive (503)
traits (483)
transactional leaders (506)
transformational leaders (506)

QUESTIONS FOR DISCUSSION AND REVIEW

1. Outline the major types of power available to managers. Think of a situation in which you were a leader. What types of power were available to you? Which ones did you use most? What were the results in terms of follower commitment, compliance, and resistance?

2. Explain the current status of research efforts to identify leader traits. What traits can you identify in an individual whom you consider to be a good

leader? Do other leaders with whom you are familiar have any of these same traits?

3. Describe the continuum of boss-centered (authoritarian) and subordinate-centered (democratic) behaviors. Identify situations in which ou have seen a democratic leader in action and situations in which you have seen an authoritarian one. How did the followers react? Did situational factors make a difference in the followers' reactions?

4. Explain the different strategies used by the Iowa, Michigan, and Ohio State researchers in investigating leadership. What did each group find? Use these findings to evaluate the degree to which the Managerial Grid is likely to help managers lead more effectively.

5. Outline the basic ideas in Fiedler's contingency model of leadership. Analyze a student association or other leadership situation in terms of leader-member relations, task structure, and position power. On the basis of Fiedler's contingency model, what type of leader behavior would the situation require?

6. Explain the cognitive resource theory of leadership. Identify a situation in which a leader's directive behavior made a significant difference in group performance and one in which it did not. To what extent can cognitive resource theory help explain these outcomes?

7. Describe the revised normative theory of leadership. Consider a leadership situation that you experienced in which a decision had to be made. Use the appropriate decision tree to determine the extent to which the group should have been involved. How closely does the recommendation of the decision tree match what was done? What were the results?

8. Explain the basic ideas comprising the path-goal theory of leadership. Use the theory to determine how a leader might improve motivation in a group with which you are familiar.

9. Contrast transactional and transformational leadership. Identify a transactional leader and a transformational leader. To what extent is each one's leadership emphasis appropriate given the state in the life cycle of the organization in which each manages?

10. Differentiate between neutralizers and substitutes for leadership. Identify two neutralizers and two substitutes for leadership in an organization with which you are familiar.

DISCUSSION QUESTIONS FOR CHAPTER OPENING CASE

1. What sources of power usage by Sculley and Coleman are evident?

2. Use one of the situational theories to analyze the leadership styles of Sculley and Coleman. What situational factors may have influenced their success?

3. Would you characterize either Sculley or Coleman as a transformational leader? Why, or why not?

MANAGEMENT EXERCISE: THE QUESTION OF SUBORDINATE INVOLVEMENT

Read the following situation.[79] Then get together with a group designated by your instructor, and use the normative leadership model to determine the degree to which you should involve subordinates in the decision.

Case: Purchasing Decision Problem

You have recently been appointed vice president in charge of purchasing for a large manufacturing company. The company has twenty plants, all located in the midwest. Historically, the company has operated in a highly decentralized fashion with each of the plant managers encouraged to operate with only minimal control and direction from the corporate office. In the area of purchasing, each of the purchasing executives who report to the plant manager does the purchasing for his/her plant. There seems to be little or no coordination among them, and the relationships that do exist are largely ones of competition.

Your position was created when it began to appear to the president that the company was likely to face increasing difficulty in securing certain essential raw materials. In order to protect the company against this possibility, the present haphazard decentralized arrangement must be abandoned or at least modified to meet the current problems.

You were chosen for the position because of your extensive background in corporate purchasing with another firm that operated in a much more centralized fashion. Your appointment was announced in the last issue of the company house organ. You are anxious to get started, particularly since the peak buying season is now only three weeks away. A procedure must be established that will minimize the likelihood of serious shortages and secondarily achieve the economies associated with the added power of centralized purchasing.

GE'S CONTROVERSIAL LEADER

Back in the late 1970s, Reginald Jones, General Electric's CEO and chairman at the time, began to make plans for a successor who would be able to steer the company through the stiff foreign competition on the horizon. To facilitate the selection process, he placed a possible successor in charge of each one of the six major sectors of the company. By 1979, John W. Welch, Jr., and two other finalists were made vice-chairmen. In 1981, Welch succeeded Jones, ushering in an era of disdain for the elaborate planning and centralized control that had been Jones's hallmark. "Jones felt the others would be caretakers," says one former GE vice president. "Welch was the one who would take the company in radical directions if necessary."

Indeed, Welch has proved to be anything but a caretaker. He quickly articulated a plan to change GE from a manufacturing company that derives more than half its revenues from heavy industry to one that reaps a larger share of its earnings from technology and services. To illustrate his plan, he sketched three circles labeled "core," "services," and "technology." He also said that GE would sell those of its businesses that weren't either first or second in their markets. Welch argued, "The managements and companies in the '80s that don't do this, that hang on to losers for whatever reason—tradition, sentiment, their own management weakness—won't be around in 1990."

Since becoming CEO, Welch has sold more than 200 businesses and used more than $16 billion to purchase 300 new ones, including the RCA Corporation, the Employ-ers Reinsurance Company, 80 percent of Kidder, Peabody & Company, the medical-equipment business of Thomson S.A., the appliance-making Roper Corporation, and the chemical business of the Borg-Warner Corporation. In the process, he has eliminated more than 120,000 jobs through forced retirements, layoffs, resignations, and outright divestitures.

His moves have doubled revenues and caused earnings to rise by nearly 20 percent. He is using the cash flow from earnings and the sale of businesses to buy still other businesses in a move to make GE's market valuation more closely approach that of giant IBM. "Welch is the best CEO in the world today," says former GE executive Richard W. Miller. "There is no corporation in the world with stronger management." Miller's view is shared by a number of other past and present GE executives, as well as a number of academics. Admirers say that Welch has vision and is transforming GE from a stodgy bureaucracy to a nimble company much more fit for the challenges ahead.

A notorious disliker of bureaucracy and red tape, Welch has cut layers of management, eliminating the group and sector levels that once fell between the heads of the various businesses and the CEO. Having fewer hierarchical levels fits in with his basic philosophy that managers should have the freedom to run their businesses as they see fit and to react to the fast-changing environment. He also wants to deliberately spread managers thin so that they are forced to focus on the major decisions and cannot get involved in bureaucratic nit-picking. "We like to think of trying to become a big company and a small company simultaneously. That literally is the message that we're trying to get across."

Some observers consider John F. Welch, Jr., chairman of General Electric, to be a transformational leader who has succeeded in orienting a conservative company towards major new directions. But critics fault Welch's leadership style in dealing with employees. He has eliminated more than 120,000 jobs and sold a number of divisions, leading many employees to feel that loyalty to the company doesn't count. One GE executive has described Welch's philosophy as: "Those who do, get, and those who don't go."

Welch first tried to get his message across to the more than 300,000 GE employees by talking about the idea of employees having "ownership"—by which he meant that lower-level managers should have enough responsibility and freedom to make them feel as if they had "ownership" of the business, much like the situation with entrepreneurs. But the notion of "ownership" puzzled employees, so Welch has recently changed his approach and now talks more about freedom, challenge, and excitement in the job, as well as taking charge of one's own actions. To facilitate the process of change, Welch is making extensive use of the company's manager-training school overlooking the Hudson at Crotonville, New York, where the emphasis is on action and risk taking.

Welch's approach has its critics. Harvard strategy expert Michael Porter says that investing only in businesses that are first or second in their industry is a 15-year-old idea that places emphasis on size instead of competitive advantage. *In Search of Excellence* coauthor Tom Peters says the approach stifles creativity.

The employee cuts have earned Welch the nickname "Neutron Jack," after the bomb that destroys people but leaves buildings intact. For example, at one point he announced that he wanted to attempt a turnaround in consumer electronics. Some employees, lured by the opportunity, moved over from GE's major appliance business only to be shocked when Welch suddenly sold the electronics business to Paris-based Thomson. Welch explains that it was the only way to get Thomson's medical-equipment business, which had better prospects for profits. He claims that the employees will do better because the consumer electronics business will be more successful under Thomson. Still, the incident reportedly added fuel to employee feelings that loyalty to the company doesn't count. Welch, however, feels that loyalty is an outmoded concept. He argues that if a worker and manager are communicating, they will make good decisions for the company. This will lead to "happier, more self-confident, more energized" individuals. Other complaints by managers and workers center on the feeling that the cuts have left them overburdened and forced them to work long, hectic hours just to keep things afloat.

Welch is known for his abrasiveness and calls his managers "turkeys" and "grunts." One former head of GE's lighting business, who was "retired" without warning in 1986, says, "You can't even say hello to Jack without it being confrontational. If you don't want to step up to Jack toe-to-toe, belly-to-belly and argue your point, he doesn't have any use for you. He's very smart, so he has an opinion about everything." Edward E. Hood, Jr., GE's vice chairman, admits that Welch can be "excitable to excess."

Some observers say that the ranks of executives increasingly reflect Welch's own ambition and temperament. Notes John M. Trani, handpicked to run GE's medical systems business, "The Welch theory is those who do, get, and those who don't, go." Compensation systems at GE are being changed to give substantial bonuses to high producers and low or no bonuses to mediocre performers.[80]

QUESTIONS FOR CHAPTER CONCLUDING CASE

1. What sources of power does Welch use as a leader? What appear to be the effects?
2. Use path-goal theory to analyze Welch's leadership approach.
3. Do you consider Welch to be a transformational leader? Why, or why not?

CHAPTER FIFTEEN

MANAGERIAL COMMUNICATION

CHAPTER OUTLINE

The Nature of Managerial Communication
Types of Communication
Managerial Communication Preferences
Basic Components of the Communication Process

Factors That Impede or Enhance Individual Communication
Perceptual Processes
Semantics
Verbal and Nonverbal Consistency
Communication Skills

Group Communication Networks

Organizational Communication Channels
Vertical Communication
Horizontal Communication
Informal Communication: The Grapevine
Promoting Innovation: Multiple Communication Channels
The Growing Potential of Electronics

LEARNING OBJECTIVES

After studying this chapter, you should be able to:

■ Explain the major types of managerial communication and discuss managerial communication preferences.

■ Outline the basic components of the communication process.

■ Describe how perceptual processes influence individual communication.

■ Explain the role of semantics, verbal and nonverbal consistency, and communication skills in communication by individuals.

■ Assess the usefulness of centralized and decentralized group communication networks.

■ Distinguish among major organizational communication channels and explain how multiple communication channels can be used to promote innovation.

■ Discuss the growing potential of electronics in regard to organizational communication channels.

GAINING THE EDGE

STEW LEONARD'S BRAND OF COMMUNICATING

The tone is set when you drive up to Stew Leonard's in Norwalk, Connecticut, billed as the world's largest dairy store. Two cows and a number of goats, hens, and geese grace "The Little Farm," right alongside the 550-car parking lot. A life-size plastic cow stands at the door. The store's motto is chiseled into the 3-ton granite rock standing by the front door: "Rule 1: The customer is always right! Rule 2: If the customer is ever wrong, reread Rule 1."

Inside, a dairy plant is enclosed in glass so that you can actually see the milk being processed. A cow's head juts out of the wall of the dairy and obligingly moos at the press of a button. More mooing is heard at the cash registers whenever a tab goes over $100. An employee in a black-and-white cow costume picks up little children and dances with more mature shoppers. In the produce section, an employee in a bright yellow chicken suit twirls little shoppers around. Over the frozen-food locker an 8-foot mechanical dog dressed in a Confederate gray uniform entertains the crowd with singing and banjo playing, belting out such favorites as "Dixie" and "I'm a Yankee Doodle Dandy." "Everybody likes to have fun," says company president Stew Leonard, Jr. (Stewie), 36, who is the son of the founder.

Unique and astoundingly successful, the store began in 1969 when the state of Connecticut decided to build a highway through the family dairy plant. At that point, Stew Leonard, Sr., was a milk delivery person serving homes. His customers advised him to open a dairy store and offer low prices. As a result, he and his wife risked everything they owned to open a small dairy store that stocked eight items. Since then, the store has expanded 26 times and now offers 750 carefully chosen items (the average supermarket carries 10,000 to 15,000 items), many bearing a Stew Leonard label. "We have to sell at least 1000 units of an item a week to include it in inventory," says Leonard, Jr. As a result, the store carries only four types of cereal, two brands of yogurt, one peanut butter label, and one brand of chicken. For staples such as flour and sugar or for cleaning items, customers must go elsewhere.

The store sells immense quantities of what it does stock. For example, in a given week, customers carry out 5 tons of cookies, 40,000 croissants, 100,000 pounds of chicken, and 25 tons of salad-bar items. Every year the store's more than 3 million customers generate over $100 million in sales and purchase 10 million quarts of milk, 100 tons of cottage cheese, and 1 million ice-cream cones. On weekends, families come from as far away as Massachusetts, Pennsylvania, Rhode Island, and New York to take advantage of low prices (the Leonards say that they try to make sure that prices are 10 percent lower than those in stores within a 5-mile radius) and enjoy the carnival-like atmosphere. "This is the funniest place I ever shopped," notes James Ballantoni, a Norwalk resident who says that he also makes sure to partake of the free samples of lemonade, horseradish cheese, gazpacho, cupcakes, nuts, and chocolate cookies. "You come in here just for milk and you walk out with a shopping cart full of food."

Attention to detail shows in every aspect of the store, from the fresh flowers in the restrooms and the English muffins stacked next to the bacon and eggs to the paper towels for wiping rain off of shopping carts. And there's no waiting at the 25 cash registers. "Cleanliness, quality and fun," qualities espoused by Walt Disney (Leonard, Sr.'s hero), and a dedication to treating customers the way you would like to be treated form the underpinnings of this extremely popular place to shop.

Leonard's philosophy about running the store grew out of an incident involving a customer:

About a week after opening day, I was standing at the entrance when a customer came up to me and angrily said, "This eggnog is sour." It tasted all right to me, so I said, "You're wrong, it's perfect." Then, to prove the customer *really* was wrong, I said, "We sold over 300 half-gallons of eggnog this week, and you're the only one who's complained." The customer was boiling mad and demanded her money back. I reached into my pocket and gave it to her. She grabbed the money, and as she was heading out the door, the last thing I heard her say was, "I'm never coming back to this store again."

That night, at home, I couldn't get the incident out of my head. As I carefully analyzed it, I realized that I was in the wrong. First, I didn't listen. Second, I contradicted the customer and told her she was wrong. Third, I humiliated her and practically called her a liar by saying 300 other customers had not complained.

Leonard, Sr.'s efforts to communicate better with customers now extend to a suggestion box; it is opened religiously each morning, and its contents are given meticulous attention. Leonard, Jr. periodically meets with small groups of customers who volunteer their time to communicate what they like and don't like about what is arguably their favorite place to shop. The Leonards also spend a great deal of time walking around the store, greeting and talking with customers.

Communicating with members of the "team," as the 650 employees are called, also receives a high level of attention from management. Members of the team help keep each other informed through a monthly newsletter called *Stew's News.* Originally suggested by a team member, the newsletter sports more photos than text and usually is between 30 and 50 pages long. It's a conglomeration of critical, useful, and/or interesting information, compiled by anyone who wants to help. Leonard, Jr. is the publisher; other family members often lend a hand; and anyone in the company can write for it or make suggestions to improve it. In a typical issue, there are as many as 40 names on the masthead, a list

The owners and the employees at Stew Leonard's, a huge grocery and dairy store in Norwalk, Connecticut, all chip in to produce the monthly newsletter, *Stew's News.* Called "the last word in newsletters," the publication profiles employees, gives tips on store management, and serves as a company-wide bulletin board. The newsletter was the suggestion of a store employee, who "thought it would be a good way to tie everything together."

that changes frequently to reflect the various contributors. Except for the full-time editor, all contributors are volunteers and range from the Leonards to cashiers, baker's assistants, and salad-bar managers.

The walls of the store are covered with various plaques and framed pictures that highlight the star employees of the month and year. Other employees' pictures also abound, and certificates for completed training programs are on prominent display. As signals that team members are encouraged to offer new ideas, one can find framed pictures of such individuals as Henry Gordon, who "eliminated $2300 in motor repairs," and Tony Serrano, who "saved over $6200 by eliminating one dumpster pickup per week."

To further let members of the team know that their efforts to follow S.T.E.W. (Satisfy the customer, Teamwork, Excellence, Wow) are appreciated, management presents them with awards such as gift certificates and $100 dinners. Managers participate in a profit-sharing plan.[1]

The Stew Leonard approach has transformed what could have been a small, ordinary dairy store into what is virtually a regional institution. When we trace this innovative and successful business back to its roots, we find that Stew Leonard, Sr. learned a very valuable lesson early. His unsuccessful interaction with the woman complaining about the eggnog taught him the importance of good communication.

As a result, the Leonards expend considerable effort to solicit the thoughts and ideas of both customers and employees. They also work to convey their notion of the importance of cleanliness, quality, fun, and satisfied customers. As the running of *Stew's News* suggests, good communication in an organization requires the efforts of many individuals. Such efforts are likely to pay off in terms of organizational effectiveness.[2] Although effective communication is critical to all four major management functions, communication is particularly vital to the leading function because it provides a necessary conduit through which efforts to influence others take place. In this chapter, we closely examine the nature of managerial communication, including the different types of communication that managers use, managerial communication preferences, and the basic components of the communication process. We consider several major factors that can impede or enhance the way that individuals communicate, and we take a brief look at communication networks involving groups. Finally, we consider various communication channels in organizations, investigate how the use of multiple communication channels can help promote innovation, and explore the growing potential of electronics.

THE NATURE OF MANAGERIAL COMMUNICATION

Communication The exchange of messages between people for the purpose of achieving common meanings

Communication is the exchange of messages between people for the purpose of achieving common meanings.[3] Unless common meanings are shared, managers find it extremely difficult to influence others. For example, in looking back on his efforts to revitalize General Motors, former CEO Roger Smith says that he would make the same decisions again regarding the implementation of major changes to rebuild the company for global leadership in the twenty-first century. But, says Smith:

> I sure wish I'd done a better job of communicating with GM people. I'd do that differently a second time around and make sure they understood and shared my vision for the company. Then they would have known why I was tearing the place up, taking out whole divisions, changing our whole production structure. If people understand the

why, they'll work at it. Like I say, I never got all this across. There we were, charging up the hill right on schedule, and I looked behind me and saw that many people were still at the bottom, trying to decide whether to come along. I'm talking about hourly workers, middle management, and even some top management. It seemed like a lot of them had gotten off the train.[4]

As Smith's predicament illustrates, communication is a critical part of every manager's job. Without effective communication, even the most brilliant strategies and best-laid plans may not be successful. As a result, it is not surprising that high-level executives, as well as managers at other levels, often mention effective communication skills, both oral and written, as crucial elements for managerial success.[5]

Types of Communication

In their work, managers use two major types of communication: verbal and nonverbal. Each type plays an important part in the effective transmission of messages within organizations.

Verbal Communication. **Verbal communication** is the written or oral use of words to communicate. Both written and oral communications are pervasive in organizations.

> **Verbal communication** The written or oral use of words to communicate

Written communication occurs through a variety of means, such as business letters, office memorandums, reports, résumés, written telephone messages, newsletters, and policy manuals. In many cases, considerable time and effort are expended in preparing written communications. According to several estimates, the cost of producing a single letter or memo has risen to more than $7, with one recent estimate placing the figure as high as $25 for the average memo.[6] Yet one study of 800 randomly selected letters from a variety of industries indicates that written business correspondence suffers from significant deficiencies in such areas as proper word usage, clear sentence construction, and precision.[7] A related study shows that more than 80 percent of managers judge the quality of the written communications they receive as either fair or poor. They also did not give themselves very high grades, with 55 percent describing their own writing skills as fair or poor.[8]

Despite some possible shortcomings in writing skills, written communication generally has several advantages over oral communication. Written communication provides a record of the message, can be disseminated widely with a minimum of effort, and allows the sender to think through the intended message carefully. Written communication also has several disadvantages, including the expense of preparation, the relatively impersonal nature of written communications, possible misunderstanding by the receiver, and the delay of feedback regarding the effectiveness of the message.[9]

In contrast to written communication, oral communication, or the spoken word, takes place largely through face-to-face conversations with another individual, meetings with several individuals, and telephone conversations. Oral communication has the advantage of being fast, is generally more personal than written communication, and provides immediate feedback from others involved in the conversation. Disadvantages include the fact that oral communication can be time-consuming, can be more difficult to terminate, and requires that additional effort be expended to document what is said if a record is necessary.[10]

Given the advantages and disadvantages of written and oral communication, it is not surprising that both types of verbal communication are used by managers. Later in this chapter we give further consideration to managerial preferences for written and oral communication. First, though, we consider another type of communication that is important to managers.

Nonverbal communication
Communication by means of elements and behaviors that are not coded into words

Nonverbal Communication. Nonverbal communication is communication by means of elements and behaviors that are not coded into words. Studies estimate that nonverbal aspects account for between 65 and 93 percent of what gets communicated.[11] Interestingly, it is quite difficult to engage in verbal communication without some accompanying form of nonverbal communication. Important categories of nonverbal communication include kinesic behavior, proxemics, paralanguage, and object language.

Kinesic behavior Body movements, such as gestures, facial expressions, eye movements, and posture

Kinesic behavior refers to body movements, such as gestures, facial expressions, eye movements, and posture. We often draw conclusions regarding people's feelings about an issue, not only from their words but also from their nonverbal behavior, such as their facial expressions.

Proxemics The influence of proximity and space on communication

Proxemics refers to the influence of proximity and space on communication. For example, some managers arrange their offices so that they have an informal area where people can sit without experiencing the spatial distance and formality created by a big desk. Another example of proxemics, which you have probably experienced, is that you are more likely to get to know students whom you happen to sit near in class than students who are sitting in other parts of the room.

Paralanguage Vocal aspects of communication that relate to how something is said rather than to what is said

Paralanguage refers to vocal aspects of communication that relate to how something is said rather than to what is said. Voice quality, tone of voice, laughing, and yawning fit in this category.

Object language The communicative use of material things, including clothing, cosmetics, furniture, and architecture

Object language refers to the communicative use of material things, including clothing, cosmetics, furniture, and architecture.[12] If you have prepared a job résumé lately, you probably gave some thought to the layout and to the type of paper on which you wanted your résumé printed—nonverbal aspects of your communication about yourself and your credentials. Nonverbal elements form an important part of the messages that managers communicate.

Managerial Communication Preferences

Research on managerial job activities indicates that managers spend most of their time communicating in one form or another. Most studies have focused on

Proxemics at work: Two employees of Bell Laboratories are shown conferring in the aisle at the company's New Jersey office. An open floor plan with work modules allows employees to circulate freely and facilitates communication among them.

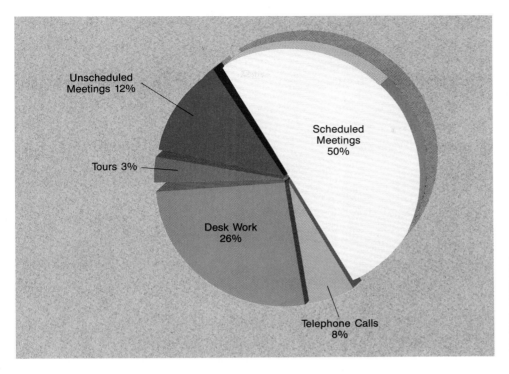

Figure 15-1 Proportion of time top managers spent on various activities. (Based on Lance B. Kurke and Howard Aldrich, ''Mintzberg Was Right!: A Replication and Extension of *The Nature of Managerial Work*,'' *Management Science*, vol. 29, 1983, p. 979.)

verbal rather than nonverbal communication. Such studies show that managers tend to prefer oral over written communication, largely because oral communication is usually more informal and timely.[13] One detailed study showed that four top managers in four different types of organizations spent almost 74 percent of their working hours communicating orally with others, through informal and formal meetings, telephone calls, and tours of the organization (see Figure 15-1). These results are similar to those of an earlier well-known study by Henry Mintzberg, which showed that five chief executives spent an average of about 78 percent of their work time engaging in oral communication.[14] The top executives in both studies spent about 50 percent of their oral communication time with subordinates. The board of directors, peers, trade organizations, clients, and suppliers accounted for most of the remaining contact time. Although these studies focused on top-level managers, there is evidence that managers at other levels also lean toward the spoken rather than the written word.[15]

Managers serve as communication centers through the use of several managerial roles that were discussed in Chapter 1 (such as monitor, disseminator, and spokesperson). Managers acting in these roles form the basis for the organization's communication network. If managers and those with whom they interact do not communicate effectively, the repercussions can be serious, not only for a particular manager's work unit but for the rest of the organization. Miscommunications have the potential to slow down and even short-circuit communications throughout the organization.

On the other hand, concerted efforts to promote effective communication can be a key ingredient in an organization's success. Recent events at the Scandinavian Airlines System (SAS) help illustrate the potential importance of both verbal and nonverbal managerial communication (see the following Case in Point discussion).

SAS has built a strong reputation for good service to business travelers by concentrating on "moments of truth." That is the term that the airline's CEO, Jan Carlzon, uses for the average of 15 seconds of communication between agent and customer. Carlzon wants this contact to convey SAS's commitment to service and customer satisfaction. Carlzon is no slouch himself at communication; he distributed to all his employees a book that spells out the company's vision, and he spends half of his working time talking with employees.

CASE IN POINT: Communication Helps SAS Stage Turnaround

When Jan Carlzon became the president and chief executive officer of SAS in 1981, the airline was suffering its second consecutive year of serious losses. Within a year, SAS, whose ownership is shared among private interests and the governments of Denmark, Norway, and Sweden, was posting a profit. The turnaround was based on a clear strategy directed at becoming known as "the best airline in the world for the frequent business traveler." In implementing the strategy, SAS spent heavily to upgrade its facilities so that it could better serve business customers. Yet Carlzon recognized that if the airline was really to be the best at serving the business traveler, he had to get the employees behind the shift in strategy. In particular, he needed the help of what he calls SAS's "front line," the ticket agents, flight attendants, baggage handlers, and all others who directly interact with customers.

To help articulate the change in strategy, all 20,000 employees received a little red book entitled *Let's Get in There and Fight*. The book spelled out in concise terms the company's vision and prime goal. Once they understood the vision, the employees began to support the strategy. Carlzon says, "The new energy at SAS was the result of 20,000 employees all striving towards a single goal every day." During that first year, Carlzon also spent half his working hours talking with employees and demonstrating his own enthusiasm and involvement in the strategy. Carlzon wanted the staff to understand his notion of "moments of truth," by which he meant the average time of 15 seconds during which the customer has contact with an SAS employee. Arguing that those brief moments form the basis of customers' impressions of SAS, Carlzon emphasized that the front line needs to take actions that communicate to business customers the fact that SAS is serious about service. One of Carlzon's favorite stories is about an SAS ticket agent at the Stockholm airport who sent a limousine to retrieve an American businessman's ticket. The businessman had left the ticket on the bureau in his hotel room, checked out, and traveled to the airport; he would have missed his plane had it not been for the quick-thinking agent.

Carlzon, who is known for his capacity to communicate complicated messages in simple, but meaningful, ways, also understands the importance of non-verbal communication. "Leaders should be aware of how far nonverbal communication can go in illustrating the style that others in the organization should follow," he says. He notes, as an example, that SAS passes out magazines and newspapers for customers to read during their flight, but often there are not enough to go around. As a result, when he flies on SAS, the staff sometimes tries to accommodate him first. "Out of the question," he tells the attendants. "I cannot take any myself until I know that all the passengers have gotten what they want!" Thus, by taking the magazine or newspaper only after all customers have been served, Carlzon reinforces both verbally and nonverbally (by example) that he really means what it says in the red book. In other words, the strategy is excellent service, and customers do come first.

Furthermore, top management is willing to support the front line. To celebrate the initial turnaround, Carlzon sent every one of the 20,000 employees a gold wristwatch. Since then, his major efforts to communicate with employees have helped SAS earn an international reputation for good service and higher profits as well.[16] ▪▪▪▪

Basic Components of the Communication Process

A look at the basic components of the communication process helps one appreciate the challenge of effective communication in organizations.[17] The basic elements of the process are shown in Figure 15-2.

Sender. The **sender** is the initiator of the message. Messages are usually initiated in response to an outside stimulus, such as a question, a meeting, an interview, a problem, or a report. The stimulus triggers a need or desire for the sender to communicate, or attempt to achieve a common meaning, with an individual or group.

Encoding. Before the message exchange can take place, however, the sender must engage in **encoding,** the process of translating the intended meaning into

Sender   The initiator of the message

Encoding   The process of translating the intended meaning into symbols

Figure 15-2 Basic components of the communication process. (Adapted from Phillip V. Lewis, *Organizational Communication: The Essence of Effective Management,* 2d ed., Prentice-Hall, Inc., Englewood Cliffs, N.J., 1980, p. 55.)

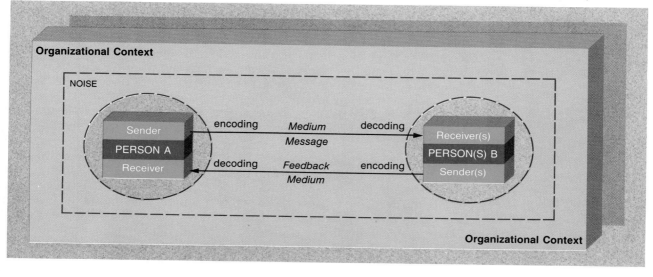

symbols. Translation must occur because we cannot transmit our intended meanings directly to another individual without the use of symbols, such as words and gestures. The sender's choice of symbols will depend upon such factors as sender encoding skills, assessments of the ability of the intended receiver to understand various symbols, judgments regarding the appropriateness of the use of certain symbols, past experience in similar situations, job status, education, and emotional state at the time of the communication attempt.

For example, since Americans often do not speak foreign languages, they frequently fail to recognize the problems that the idioms and regional sayings in English conversation cause individuals for whom English is a second language. Hence they do not consider such factors in the encoding process. Jarold Kieffer, chairman of Senior Employment Resources, a not-for-profit organization in Annandale, Virginia, that helps individuals find employment, noticed the puzzled looks that sometimes appear on the faces of foreign-born clients. Still, he did not recognize the magnitude of the communication problem until he asked one of his counselors who is Vietnamese to help him move a table. "Give me a hand, will ya?" said Kieffer. The bewildered counselor looked at his hands and exclaimed, "But I need them both." Since then, Kieffer has prepared a pocket-size book of common phrases, such as "foot the bill," "dyed-in-the-wool," and "go fly a kite," to help foreign-born job seekers.[18] Of course, similar problems often occur in international business communications, in which one or more participants may be conversing in other than his or her native language. Interpreters may even be involved, raising the prospects for encoding problems because additional individuals must engage in encoding as part of the communication process.

Message The encoding-process outcome, which consists of verbal and nonverbal symbols that have been developed to convey meaning to the receiver

Medium The method used to convey the message to the intended receiver

Message. The outcome of the encoding process is a **message** consisting of the verbal (oral or written) and nonverbal symbols that have been developed to convey meaning to the receiver. The **medium** is the method used to convey the message to the intended receiver. Examples include written words in a memo, spoken words over the telephone, graphics on a slide, and gestures in face-to-face situations. The sender of a message must consider the appropriateness of the medium. For example, a telephone call may be an effective means of resolving a conflict over a minor item, but a face-to-face meeting may be more appropriate for negotiating a major change in a project. Advantages and disadvantages of common communication methods in organizations are shown in Table 15-1.

Receiver The person with whom the message is exchanged

Receiver. The **receiver** is the person with whom the message is exchanged. If no exchange takes place (i.e., the receiver does not receive the message), then there has been no communication. There may be one receiver of the message, as in a conversation between two individuals, or many receivers, as in the case of a report sent to various members of the organization. Unintended receivers also can emerge if they overhear our private conversation or read our mail.

Decoding The process of translating the symbols into the interpreted message

Decoding. When the message is received, the receiver engages in **decoding,** the process of translating the symbols into the interpreted message. When the communication is effective, the sender and the receiver achieve a common meaning. However, the decoding process may result in misunderstandings of the message if the receiver does not decode the message as the sender intended. For example, because the Vietnamese counselor at Senior Employment Resources attempted to translate Kieffer's request ("Give me a hand") literally, there was no shared meaning. In the decoding process the receiver may also consider both the

Table 15-1 Advantages and Disadvantages of Common Communication Methods

Method	Advantages	Disadvantages
Telephone	Verbally fast Permits questions and answers Convenient Two-way flow Immediate feedback	Less personal. No record of conversation. Message might be misunderstood. Timing may be inconvenient. May be impossible to terminate.
Face-to-face	Visual Personal contact Can "show" and "explain" Two-way flow Immediate feedback	Timing may be inconvenient. Requires spontaneous thinking. May not be easy to terminate. Power or status of one person may cause pressure.
Meeting	Can use visuals Involves several minds at once Two-way flow	Time-consuming. Timing may be inconvenient. One person may dominate the group.
Memorandum	Brief Provides a record Can prethink the message Can disseminate widely	No control over receiver. Less personal. One-way flow. Delayed feedback.
Formal report	Complete, comprehensive Can organize material at writer's leisure Can disseminate widely	Less personal. May require considerable time in reading. Language may not be understandable. Expensive. One-way flow. Delayed feedback.

Source: Reprinted from Phillip V. Lewis, *Organizational Communication: The Essence of Effective Management,* 2d ed., Prentice-Hall, Inc., Englewood Cliffs, N.J., 1980, p. 11.

medium and various aspects of the context in which the communication takes place. For example, we are likely to attribute a different meaning to a message relayed from the boss by telephone to our home at 2 a.m. than to the same message uttered casually in the cafeteria line.

Noise. Noise is any factor in the communication process that interferes with exchanging messages and achieving common meaning. Noise can range from interruptions while the sender is encoding to static on telephone lines as a message is being transmitted and to fatigue on the part of the receiver while decoding takes place. Thus noise can occur during any stage of the communication process, and it has the effect of reducing the probability of achieving common meaning between senders and receivers.

Noise Any factor in the communication process that interferes with exchanging messages and achieving common meaning

Feedback. Feedback is the basic response of the receiver to the interpreted message. This feedback response involves a reversal of the communication process so that the receiver now becomes the sender and the sender becomes the receiver. Feedback provides preliminary information to the sender about the success of the communication process. It often takes further loops through the communication process to establish that the sender and receiver have been successful in communicating effectively—achieving common meaning. Without

Feedback The basic response of the receiver to the interpreted message

feedback, managers have difficulty assessing the effectiveness of their communication attempts.

When the communication process does not allow for feedback, it is called **one-way communication.** Memos, newsletters, and announcements often are examples of one-way communication—at least when they do not explicitly provide for feedback from those to whom the message is directed. When managers do not build means for immediate feedback into the communication process, they run the risk that the intended message will not be understood by the receiver. With one-way communication, they might not find out about miscommunications until it is too late to correct them.

Conversely, when the communication process explicitly includes feedback, as illustrated in Figure 15-2, it is called **two-way communication.** Two-way communication has a better chance of resulting in a reasonably accurate exchange of common meaning. Still, effective two-way communication requires that careful attention be paid to the communication process, particularly if several layers of the organization are involved in the message transmission. One reason for this is that each additional link adds to the possibility that the encoding and decoding processes and/or noise will distort the information. Another is that subordinates are often reluctant to provide negative information to upper layers of the hierarchy because they fear that they will be criticized.[19] As a result, managers need to expend considerable effort to obtain accurate information even with two-way communication, as top management at Ashland Oil learned when a serious difficulty turned into a crisis (see the following Case in Point discussion).

One-way communication
The communication that results when the communication process does not allow for feedback

Two-way communication
The communication that results when the communication process explicitly includes feedback

CASE IN POINT: Ashland Oil Faces a Major Crisis

The CEO of Ashland Oil, Inc., John R. Hall, learned firsthand about the perils of information transmission when 1 million gallons of diesel fuel spilled from a company storage tank into the Monongahela River near Pittsburgh on a quiet Sunday in January 1988. After he and the company's president spent much of the day in his office (at headquarters in Ashland, Kentucky) in front of a speakerphone talking with colleagues at the accident site and elsewhere, Hall believed the situation was under control. He decided against going to the accident scene himself, convinced that his emergency-management team could handle the logistical arrangements. It was still unclear what had caused the leakage.

In fact, the next morning he decided against devoting his regular 3-hour weekly meeting with top executives exclusively to the spill. By midmorning, however, it was clear that Hall had not obtained sufficient and accurate information about the situation, which was quickly evolving into a major crisis. Reporters had been told by the company spokesperson that the storage tank was new and that a permit had been obtained to build it. Now new information "from several sources" was indicating that the storage tank involved had been recently reconstructed from steel that was 40 years old, that the construction was done without a permit, and that less testing than usual had been done on the tank. As he considered these emerging facts, Hall became unusually quiet. "It was obvious that he was frustrated, upset, and eager to get the right information," an Ashland vice president said.

The degenerating situation turned into a major crisis when the arrangements that had been made to contain the spill proved to be inadequate because of unusually strong river currents. There was no contingency plan in place. As a result, the spill formed a 100-mile oil slick and interrupted water supplies for 750,000 Pennsylvania residents, as well as those of many communities in Ohio and West Virginia. Schools closed in several localities. By the following morning, Hall was jetting to Pittsburgh to investigate the situation himself and help subordinates deal with the crisis. In retrospect, Hall "would have wanted more accurate information faster," said his vice president and media chief. Says Hall, "I suppose you always should be prepared for the unexpected—and are never as prepared as you'd like to be."[20] ▬▬▬▬

In addition to the unusual communication difficulties, such as encoding, decoding, noise, and the reluctance of subordinates to provide negative information, the stress of the situation likely exacerbated the communication breakdown at Ashland Oil. Factors that influence the way in which particular individuals communicate in organizations also probably played a part.

FACTORS THAT IMPEDE OR ENHANCE INDIVIDUAL COMMUNICATION

You may have experienced the frustration of arriving for a meeting only to find that some of the anticipated participants did not seem to know about it. How is it that some individuals receive a particular communication and others do not? While some of the reasons may relate to misdirected mail and lost messages, miscommunications often can be traced to individual factors, such as perceptual issues, semantics, verbal and nonverbal consistency, and communication skills, that can impede or enhance the communication process in organizations.

Perceptual Processes

Perception is the process that individuals use to acquire information from the environment. The process is quite complex and involves three main stages. The first stage is *selecting*, the filtering of stimuli that we encounter so that only certain information receives our attention. For example, suppose that a manager taking over a new unit has heard a rumor that a particular individual in the unit has a short temper. If the manager is not careful, this piece of information may cause the manager to pay particular attention to situations in which the person *is* impatient or angry. Individuals select certain elements in the environment for attention and ignore others, often without consciously realizing that they are doing so.

The second stage of the perceptual process is *organizing*, the patterning of information from the selection stage. Slowly pronounce each of the following four words:[21]

M-A-C-T-A-V-I-S-H

M-A-C-D-O-N-A-L-D

M-A-C-B-E-T-H

M-A-C-H-I-N-E-R-Y

Like many people, you may have pronounced the last word as "MacHinery." This happens because the previous pattern leads us to expect another word with the same type of pronunciation. This exercise illustrates an interesting characteristic of perception: the tendency to organize information into the

Perception The process that individuals use to acquire information from the environment

patterns that we expect to perceive. In the example of the individual rumored to have a short temper, the manager may begin to organize the selectively perceived behavior into a pattern of incidents in which the individual was angry.

The third stage is *interpreting,* attaching meaning to the information that we have selected and organized. In our example, the manager may, over time, begin to interpret (perhaps unfairly) the organized information as indicating that the person does, indeed, have a short temper.

The perceptions of individuals are affected by a variety of factors such as experiences, needs, personality, and education. As a result, it is very likely that there will be differences among individuals in their perceptions of the very same situations and messages. Several common tendencies to distort perceptions are particularly applicable to managerial communication situations. These tendencies are stereotyping, the halo effect, projection, perceptual defense, and self-serving bias.[22] Awareness of these common perceptual tendencies can help managers avoid the misunderstandings that such distortions often create.

Stereotyping The tendency to attribute characteristics to an individual on the basis of an assessment of the group to which the individual belongs

Stereotyping. Stereotyping is the tendency to attribute characteristics to an individual on the basis of an assessment of the group to which the individual belongs. When a manager engages in stereotyping, two steps occur. First, the manager categorizes the individual as belonging to a group whose members are perceived to share certain common characteristics. Second, the manager uses those perceived common characteristics to draw conclusions about the characteristics of the individual, rather than acquiring information about those characteristics more directly.

In some cases, stereotyping can help us navigate our world. For example, we might be fairly close to the mark in speculating that an individual wearing a dark-colored uniform and sitting at a desk just inside a building entrance is a member of the building security force. On the basis of our general perceptions of security guards, we might further speculate that the individual will help us locate the office that we are seeking. Fortunately, our speculations can be easily verified in this instance.

Stereotyping leads to problems when the generalizations do not apply or do not apply equally to all members of the group or when people try to generalize about less specifically related characteristics. In such situations, managers may communicate expectations that are inappropriate. For example, at American Medical International, Inc., a publically owned hospital company based in Beverly Hills, California, the president and chief operating officer, Gene Burleson, ran into communication difficulties because of stereotyping. Burleson was explaining some new changes in the company to several hundred employees when one asked why the company did not have any women directors or top executives. Although the exact words were not recorded, observers reported that Burleson said something implying that women cannot deal with the stress of the executive suite, a reply that offended many members of the audience and caused the incident to be reported in *The Wall Street Journal.* A company spokesperson noted that about 80 percent of the organization's employees are females (nurses and other health-care professionals) and reported that Burleson later "admitted he gave a lame and a stupid answer" to the question.[23]

Halo effect The tendency to use a general impression based on one or a few characteristics of an individual to judge other characteristics of that same individual

Halo Effect. The **halo effect** refers to the tendency to use a general impression based on one or a few characteristics of an individual to judge other characteristics of that same individual. The halo effect often occurs in interviewing situations, in which an interviewer may form an impression (positive or negative) of the individual on the basis of dress or a few initial statements and then use this early impression to evaluate other characteristics, such as competence in specific job-related areas.[24] A similar situation can occur when a manager uses a general impression formed on the basis of one thing a worker does, such as compiling a well-done or poorly prepared report, to judge other areas of work, such as handling customers. To avoid the halo effect, interviewers and managers need to make special efforts to collect enough data to make reasonable judgments in all the specific areas that they are trying to evaluate.

Projection. **Projection** is the tendency of an individual to assume that others share his or her thoughts, feelings, and characteristics. Unfortunately, projection can encourage managers to engage in one-way communication because they assume that they know how their employees feel on various issues. For example, on the basis of personal feelings, a manager may make assumptions about the kind of work that an employee might consider to be challenging and interesting. Hence the manager may think of certain work assignments as rewards. Yet the employee may have very different feelings, become frustrated with continual assignments in certain areas, and even feel punished. Remembering to engage in two-way communication to learn how other individuals feel about various issues helps managers avoid the potential ill effects of projection.

Projection The tendency of an individual to assume that others share his or her thoughts, feelings, and characteristics

Perceptual Defense. **Perceptual defense** is the tendency to block out or distort information that one finds threatening or that challenges one's beliefs.[25] As a result, managers or workers may not be very receptive to certain types of information. One common outcome is sometimes referred to as the "shoot the bearer of bad news" syndrome, a tendency of some managers to "behead" the bearer of bad news, even though the bearer was not the cause of the problem. Thus some managers get angry at employees who provide information about serious problems that cannot be ignored, even though the manager needs to know about them.

Perceptual defense The tendency to block out or distort information that one finds threatening or that challenges one's beliefs

Self-Serving Bias. **Self-serving bias** is the tendency to perceive oneself as responsible for successes and others as responsible for failures.[26] This tendency sets the stage for serious communication problems between managers and their subordinates. When a subordinate is successful with a project, the manager may attribute the positive outcomes to the manager's own effective leadership. However, when a subordinate fails with a project, the manager is likely to conclude that the failure is due to the subordinate's shortcomings. Subordinates, on the other hand, tend to see successes as the result of their own hard work and ability and to view failures as stemming from bad luck or factors in the work environment, including areas controlled by their supervisor. By recognizing this bias, managers can attempt to avoid making self-serving assumptions when communicating with subordinates and can be prepared for possible self-serving tendencies on the part of subordinates and others.[27]

Self-serving bias The tendency to perceive oneself as responsible for successes and others as responsible for failures

Semantics

Words are symbols; therefore, they do not necessarily have the same meaning for everyone. The study of the meanings and choice of words is called semantics. A **semantic net** is the network of words and word meanings that a given individual has available for recall.[28] Individuals have their own semantic nets that overlap, but do not correspond exactly, with those of others. **Semantic**

Semantic net The network of words and word meanings that a given individual has available for recall
Semantic blocks The blockages or difficulties in communication that arise from word choices

Table 15-2 Examples of Semantic Blocks in Communications between Manager and Subordinate

What the Manager Said	What the Manager Meant	What the Subordinate Heard
I'll look into hiring another person for your department as soon as I complete my budget review.	We'll start interviewing for that job in about 3 weeks.	I'm tied up with more important things. Let's forget about hiring for the indefinite future.
Your performance was below par last quarter. I really expected more out of you.	You're going to have to try harder, but I know you can do it.	If you screw up one more time, you're out.
I'd like that report as soon as you can get to it.	I need that report within the week.	Drop that rush order you're working on and fill out that report today.

Source: Reprinted from Richard M. Hodgetts and Steven Altman, *Organizational Behavior*, Saunders, Philadelphia, 1979, p. 305.

blocks are the blockages or difficulties in communication that arise from word choices.[29] Such blocks are commonplace because of the different meanings and shades of meanings that can be attached to words by individuals using their own semantic nets. Receivers decode words and phrases in conformity with their own semantic networks, which may be very different from those of the senders. Of course, the skill of the sender in choosing appropriate words also is important to the communication process. Yet it is the receiver, not the sender, who ultimately attaches the meaning to the message.[30] Examples of the high potential for semantic blocks in communications between manager and subordinate are illustrated in Table 15-2.

Within organizations, different units can have terminology that has evolved through tradition or is related specifically to the type of work being done. A common cause of semantic blocks is the use of *professional jargon,* language related to a specific profession but unfamiliar to others outside the profession. For example, the use of professional jargon by individuals from the data-processing department when speaking with others in the rest of the organization can quickly lead to communication breakdowns. In addition, organizations often have a number of terms that are unique to the particular organization. Such language must be used with care because it can be somewhat bewildering to newcomers, customers, or visitors. On the other hand, organization-specific language can help build cohesion among employees, reinforce the corporate culture, and, in the case of the Walt Disney Company, support a competitive edge (see the following Case in Point discussion).[31]

CASE IN POINT: At Many Firms, Employees Speak a Language
of Their Own

A hipo, a Wallenda, and an imagineer order drinks at a bar. They do a little work—edit a violin, non-concur with a wild duck, take care of some bad Mickey—and then ask for the bill. "This is on the mouse," says one of the three.

Who picks up the tab?

Organizations often evolve a language of their own that becomes part of the daily communication of employees. In fact, outsiders may need help translating messages.

For example, a veteran employee at IBM says that a "hipo" (short for "high potential") is an insider designation for an employee who appears to be on the fast track to success. Another IBMer claims that, conversely, an employee perceived as having low potential is known as an "alpo." IBM employees do not disagree with their bosses; instead they "non-concur." An individual who non-concurs fairly frequently, but does so constructively, is known as a "wild duck." The "wild duck" designation was a favorite of the company's former chairman, Thomas Watson, Jr., who borrowed it from Kierkegaard.

Corporate slang can be particularly prevalent in publishing operations, whose employees frequently have a way with words. At *Newsweek,* top editors are often called "Wallendas," after the famous family of aerialists. The designation is an overt recognition of the editors' job vulnerability. Editors' offices are sometimes referred to as "Wallendatoriums." Writers at *Newsweek* speak of the weekly's top national story as the "violin." According to a company spokesperson, this is because the top story is chosen to "reflect the tone" of the news. She adds that the second national story was at one time known as the "cello" and the top business story as the "kazoo," terms that are now rarely used.

In an unusual move, the Walt Disney Company has consciously developed its own corporate jargon to directly support its efforts to have employees think of the Disney theme parks as stages. At orientation and training sessions, employees are taught to say that they are "onstage" when working in the theme park itself and "backstage" when they are in the lower environs, where they cannot be seen by the public. They also learn to refer to coworkers as "cast members." The division that does theme-park planning is called "Walt Disney Imagineering."

Jack Herrman, formerly a Disney World publicist, remembers that his coworkers would label anything positive a "good Mickey" and anything negative (like a cigarette butt on the pavement) a "bad Mickey." When employees take someone to lunch on the Disney World expense account, they say that the meal is "on the mouse." "You're immersed in the jargon they impose upon you as a way of life," Herrman says. Through the use of such language, Disney continually reminds organization members of their roles in the production being performed at the theme parks and, in this way, uses language to support the company's competitive edge.[32] ▆▆▆▆▆

The issue of organization-specific language becomes even more complicated in companies such as the Economy Color Card Company, where as many as 30 percent of the 900 employees do not speak English. On one assembly line at the textile company, which is based in Elizabeth, New Jersey, the 14 workers are legal immigrants from Colombia, Honduras, Peru, Argentina, Ecuador, the Dominican Republic, India, Haiti, Cuba, El Salvador, and Portugal. Supervisors use dictionaries and say they "muddle through with pointing and sign language." The situation emphasizes the need for verbal and nonverbal consistency.[33]

Verbal and Nonverbal Consistency

A friend who is about to give a speech may tell you, "I'm not nervous," as she continuously twists her note cards and shifts from one foot to the other. When

When Disneyland employees are at work, they are said to be "on stage." The Walt Disney organization deliberately encourages the use of theater jargon in its theme parks to convey to employees the idea that they are putting on a production and performing for their customers.

we receive a message, we consider both the verbal and nonverbal communication elements. There are six major ways that these elements can interrelate. In the first four ways, the nonverbal communication reinforces the verbal message:

1. *Repeating* the verbal message (e.g., explaining the location of a certain department to a visitor and pointing in the appropriate direction)
2. *Complementing,* or adding to, the verbal message (e.g., having a look of embarrassment when talking to a supervisor about a poor performance issue)
3. *Accenting,* or emphasizing, a verbal message (e.g., pounding the table while stating that quality must be improved)
4. *Regulating* the verbal exchange (e.g., making a head nod, an eye movement, or a shift in position that signals another person to continue speaking or stop speaking)

In the fifth way that verbal and nonverbal communication elements are related, the nonverbal message replaces the verbal one:

5. *Substituting* for the verbal message (e.g., using facial expressions or body movements to communicate a message without speaking a word)

The sixth type of interrelationship shows that verbal and nonverbal communication elements can also combine to send an inconsistent message:

6. *Contradicting* the verbal message (e.g., yelling "I am *not* angry!" or shaking and perspiring heavily before giving a speech while insisting "I'm not nervous").[34]

Evidence suggests that when the verbal and nonverbal messages contradict each other, the receiver is most likely to interpret the nonverbal message as the true message.[35] This means that managers must give some attention to the nonverbal as well as the verbal part of the messages that they send. In addition, managers may be able to gain better insight into the thoughts and feelings of others by scrutinizing the nonverbal as well as the verbal parts of their messages. Furthermore, they may be able to use nonverbal aspects to reinforce verbal messages as Carlzon does at SAS.

The importance of both the verbal and the nonverbal aspects of communication often is highlighted in dealings in the international realm. For example, a recent article giving advice to American businesspeople visiting Asia not only includes guidance about what to say and not say but also provides the following tips aimed at showing respect nonverbally: Be punctual; use both hands to present and receive business cards, and be sure to read them carefully; and use a handshake and a simple nod when greeting people, but be sure to avoid additional physical contact, such as backslapping.[36]

To be effective communicators in the various settings in which they must function, managers need effective communication skills. Such skills usually can take considerable time and concerted practice to develop.

Communication Skills

Two communication skills of prime importance to managerial effectiveness are listening skills and feedback skills. These two skills are particularly critical because such a large proportion of a manager's time is spent in communicating orally.

PRACTICALLY SPEAKING

HOW TO LISTEN ACTIVELY

The following guidelines will help you be an active listener.

1. Listen patiently to what the other person has to say, even though you may believe it is wrong or irrelevant. Indicate simple acceptance (not necessarily agreement) by nodding or injecting an occasional "um-hm" or "I see."
2. Try to understand the feeling the person is expressing, as well as the intellectual content. Most of us have difficulty talking clearly about our feelings, so careful attention is required.
3. Restate the person's feeling, briefly but accurately. At this stage, simply serve as a mirror and encourage the other person to continue talking. Occasionally make summary responses, such as "You think you're in a dead-end job" or "You feel the manager is play-ing favorites"; but in doing so, keep your tone neutral and try not to lead the person to your pet conclusions.
4. Allow time for the discussion to continue without interruption, and try to separate the conversation from more official communication of company plans. That is, do not make the conversation any more "authoritative" than it already is by virtue of your position in the organization.
5. Avoid direct questions and arguments about facts; refrain from saying "That's just not so," "Hold on a minute, let's look at the facts," or "Prove it." You may want to review evidence later, but a review is irrelevant to how a person feels now.
6. When the other person does touch on a point you do want to know more about, simply repeat his or her statement as a question. For instance, if the person remarks, "Nobody can break even on his expense account," you can probe by replying, "You say no one breaks even on expenses?" With this encouragement, he or she will probably expand on the previous statement.
7. Listen for what isn't said—evasions of pertinent points or perhaps too-ready agreement with common clichés. Such omissions may be clues to a bothersome fact the person wishes were not true.
8. If the other person appears genuinely to want your viewpoint, be honest in your reply. But in the listening stage, try to limit the expression of your views, since these may condition or suppress what the other person says.
9. Focus on the content of the message; try not to think about your next statement until the person is finished talking.
10. Don't make judgments until all information has been conveyed.[37]

Listening Skills. As the earlier discussion of the communication process suggests, receivers need to expend considerable effort to be sure that they have decoded and interpreted the message that the sender intended. Since managers rely heavily on the information inputs that they receive from oral communication, their listening skills are particularly crucial.[38] Experts on listening often differentiate between listening that is relatively passive, in the sense of following the general gist of the words being spoken, and listening that is active. **Active listening** is the process in which a listener actively participates in attempting to grasp the facts and the feelings being expressed by the speaker. Actively listening for both the content and the feelings is important in understanding the total meaning of the message.[39] Managers leave themselves at a disadvantage when they are not good listeners. For example, they may have difficulty in negotiations because they cannot assess what the other person truly wants or might accept. If managers tend not to listen, they also may discourage subordinates from bringing problems to their attention. Finally, without good listening skills, managers may have difficulty in a crisis, when it is important to size up situations quickly.[40] For some guidelines on enhancing your listening skills, see the Practically Speaking discussion, "How to Listen Actively."

Active listening The process in which a listener actively participates in attempting to grasp the facts and the feelings being expressed by the speaker

This "Video Point" at London's Gatwick Airport records the comments of British Airways passengers. Customer service managers review the videos and respond to the complaints. Feedback from customers is important, because those who feel their complaints are listened to are more likely to continue to do business with the company.

Feedback. Other interpersonal communication skills that are particularly important for managers center around the issue of feedback, both giving and receiving. Giving feedback is a continuous part of managing. Although managers may give feedback to a variety of individuals with whom they interact (such as individuals in other work units or suppliers), much of the feedback that managers give involves subordinates. Managers need to let subordinates know when they are performing well in relation to unit goals and when they are performing poorly. Telling an individual subordinate that performance in some area is not up to required standards is sometimes difficult for managers. Effective feedback, in such circumstances, has several main characteristics. For one thing, it focuses on the relevant behaviors or outcomes, rather than on the individual as a person. For another, it deals with specific, observable behavior, rather than dwelling on generalities. Yet another characteristic of effective feedback is that perceptions, reactions, and opinions are labeled as such, rather than presented as facts. Finally, it spells out what individuals can do to improve themselves.[41] Being skilled in giving feedback makes the task of handling subordinates with substandard performance considerably easier and increases the prospects for success.

In addition to giving feedback, being able to receive feedback also is important. Typically, individuals have no difficulty receiving positive feedback; receiving feedback that is negative is generally more difficult. Yet the way in which managers and others react to feedback is often a factor influencing how much feedback they receive from others.[42] When you are receiving negative feedback, it often is helpful to paraphrase what is being said (so that you can check your perceptions), ask for clarification and examples regarding any points that are unclear or with which you disagree, and avoid reacting defensively.[43]

Organizations also are learning that it pays to get feedback from customers, particularly dissatisfied ones. For example, Roger Nunley, manager of industry and consumer affairs at Coca-Cola USA, says studies indicate that only 1 dissatisfied consumer in 50 complains; the rest switch brands. Yet, when a complaint is redressed, the individual is highly likely to remain a customer. As a result, a number of companies, such as Coca-Cola, American Express, and Procter &

Gamble, maintain 800 numbers in an attempt to encourage customers to voice their complaints. According to an estimate by the American Management Association, more than half of all companies exceeding $10 million in annual sales maintain such numbers for purposes of complaints, inquiries, and orders. British Airways has a video booth in London's Heathrow Airport where unhappy passengers can tape their complaints.[44]

GROUP COMMUNICATION NETWORKS

When tasks require input from several individuals, managers need to give some thought to the **communication network,** or pattern of information flow among task group members. Considerable research has assessed the impact of different networks on communication and task outcomes. Five of these major network structures are shown in Figure 15-3.

> **Communication network**
> The pattern of information flow among task group members

Three of the networks are fairly centralized in that most messages must flow through a pivotal person in the network. In the *wheel network,* the most centralized, all messages must flow through the individual at the center of the wheel. In the *chain network,* some members can communicate with more than one member of the network, but the individual in the center of the chain still tends to emerge as the controller of the messages. In the *Y network,* the member at the fork of the "Y" usually becomes the central person in the network. The last two networks shown in Figure 15-3 are more decentralized in that there is freer communication among the various members. In the *circle network,* each member can communicate with the individual on either side. Finally, with the *star network,* the most decentralized of the networks, each member can communicate with any other member.

Research on the effects of these networks on various aspects of communication has produced some interesting results. For relatively simple, routine tasks, the centralized networks are usually faster and more accurate. The reason is that

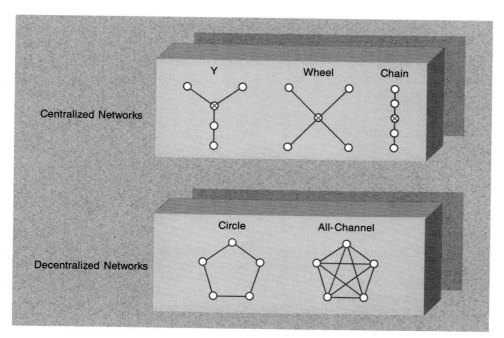

Figure 15-3 Group communication networks. (Adapted from Otis W. Baskin and Craig E. Aronoff, *Interpersonal Communication in Organizations,* Scott, Foresman and Company, Glenview, Ill., 1980, p. 77.)

Centralized Networks
Y   Wheel   Chain

Decentralized Networks
Circle   All-Channel

in each of the centralized networks, the individual in the central position (marked with an "x" in Figure 15-3) tends to become the coordinator, which facilitates the completion of routine tasks. In contrast, when the tasks are more complex, the decentralized networks most often prove to be faster and more accurate, with the star network showing the best performance. With complex tasks, the free exchange of information provided by the circle and the star facilitate the process, whereas the central position in a centralized network has difficulty adequately coordinating all the activities and tends to stifle creativity.

An intriguing aspect of the research findings is that group morale in the networks studied was higher in the decentralized ones, regardless of the type of task. These results pose somewhat of a dilemma for managers. Centralized networks appear to be the best for achieving accurate performance on simple tasks, particularly when time is an important factor. However, morale may suffer. For more complex tasks, the decentralized networks achieve both high performance and high morale. From a practical point of view, many organizational tasks are likely to fit into the complex category.[45] If tasks are relatively simple and call for more centralized communication networks, one potential solution to the morale dilemma may be for managers to provide subordinates with some opportunities for working on more complex tasks that allow interactions with others in a more decentralized network.

ORGANIZATIONAL COMMUNICATION CHANNELS

Communication channels Various patterns of organizational communication flow that represent potential established conduits through which managers and other organization members can send and receive information

An important consideration in assessing communication in organizations is the movement of information throughout various organizational parts. When information does not reach the individuals and groups that need it for their work, serious organizational effectiveness and efficiency problems can result. Various patterns of organizational communication flow are sometimes referred to as **communication channels** because they represent potential established conduits through which managers and other organization members can send and receive information. In this section, we consider the two major directions of communication flow in organizations: vertical and horizontal. We also examine an informal means of communication flow, the organizational "grapevine." Finally, we consider the implications of communication channel usage for organizational innovation, as well as the growing potential of electronics in facilitating communication in organizations.

Vertical Communication

Vertical communication Communication that involves a message exchange between two or more levels of the organizational hierarchy

Vertical communication is communication that involves a message exchange between two or more levels of the organizational hierarchy (see Figure 15-4). Vertical communication can involve a manager and a subordinate or can involve several layers of the hierarchy. It can flow in a downward or an upward direction. Studies generally find that managers spend about two-thirds of their communication time engaging in vertical communication.[46]

Downward communication Vertical communication that flows from a higher level to one or more lower levels in the organization

Downward Communication. When vertical communication flows from a higher level to one or more lower levels in the organization, it is known as **downward communication.** Downward communication can take many forms, such as staff meetings, company policy statements, company newsletters, informational memos, and face-to-face contact. Most downward communication involves information in one of five categories: (1) job instructions related to specific tasks,

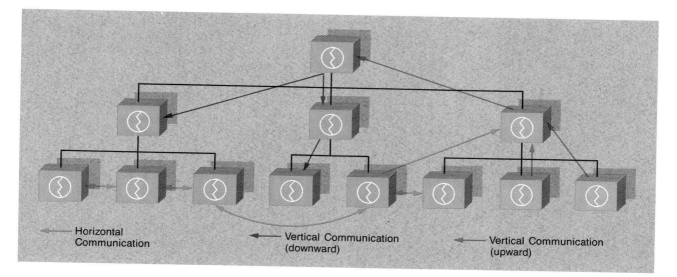

Horizontal Communication

Vertical Communication (downward)

Vertical Communication (upward)

Figure 15-4 Vertical and horizontal organizational communication. (Adapted from R. Wayne Pace, *Organizational Communication*, Prentice-Hall, Englewood Cliffs, N.J., 1983, p. 40.)

(2) job rationales explaining the relationship between a task and other organizational tasks, (3) procedures and practices of the organization, (4) feedback on individual performance on assigned tasks, and (5) efforts to encourage a sense of mission and dedication to the goals of the organization.[47]

Downward communication across several levels is prone to considerable distortion. As illustrated by Figure 15-5, as much as 80 percent of top management's message may be lost by the time the message reaches five levels below. There are three main reasons for the distortion. One reason is that faulty message transmission may occur because of sender carelessness, poor communication skills, and the difficulty of encoding a message that will be clearly understood by individuals at multiple levels. Another is that managers tend to overuse one-way communication methods, such as memos, manuals, and newsletters, leaving little possibility for immediate feedback regarding receiver understand-

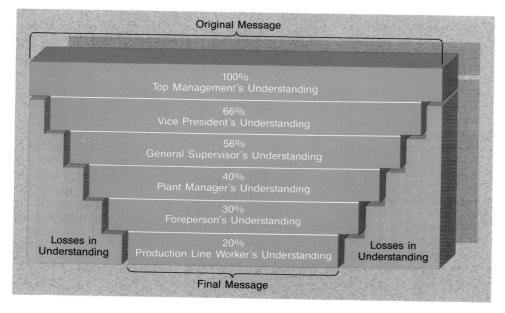

Original Message

100% Top Management's Understanding

66% Vice President's Understanding

56% General Supervisor's Understanding

40% Plant Manager's Understanding

30% Foreperson's Understanding

20% Production Line Worker's Understanding

Losses in Understanding

Losses in Understanding

Final Message

Figure 15-5 Levels of understanding as information is transmitted down the organization. (Reprinted from Phillip V. Lewis, *Organizational Communication: The Essence of Effective Management*, 2d ed., Prentice-Hall, Inc., Englewood Cliffs, N.J., p. 131; and Edward E. Scannell, *Communication for Leadership*, McGraw-Hill, New York, 1970.)

ing. Finally, some managers may intentionally or unintentionally filter communications by withholding, screening, or manipulating information. Intentional filtering typically occurs when a manager seeks to enhance personal power over subordinates by tightly controlling organizational information.[48]

One means of increasing the effectiveness of downward communication systems is the use of multiple channels and repetition. For example, James D. Robinson III, chairman of American Express, is credited with communicating the importance of service as a competitive edge by repeating the message—incessantly—to employees. He uses multiple vehicles, including over 100 programs to recognize and reward individuals who take unusually good care of customers. The service message, after years of repetition, has become part of the way employees view their jobs and has given American Express an important edge in the highly competitive credit card business.[49] Another means of increasing the effectiveness of downward communication systems is through encouraging feedback in the form of upward communication.

Upward Communication. When the vertical flow of communication is from a lower level to one or more higher levels in the organization, it is known as **upward communication.** Forms of upward communication include one-to-one meetings with one's immediate superior, staff meetings with superiors, memos and reports, suggestion systems, grievance procedures, and employee attitude surveys. At Stew Leonard's, the many individuals involved in *Stew's News* make it an upward, as well as a downward, means of communication. The information disseminated through upward communication typically pertains to (1) progress of current work projects, (2) serious unsolved problems and situations in which subordinates need help from superiors, (3) new developments arising within or affecting the work unit or organization, (4) suggestions for improvements and innovations, and (5) employee attitudes, morale, and efficiency.[50]

The distortion that characterizes downward communication also plagues upward communication for two main reasons. First, as mentioned previously, individuals are likely to be extremely selective about the information that they transmit upward. Information favorable to the sender is very likely to be sent upward. In contrast, information that is unfavorable to the sender will probably be blocked, even when it is important to the organization. Subordinates are more likely to filter information when they do not trust their superiors, perceive that their superiors have considerable influence over their careers, and have a strong desire to move up.[51] Second, managers do not expend sufficient effort in encouraging upward communication. In one study, 43 percent of training specialists across a variety of organizations reported that management does "little" or "very little" to encourage upward communication.[52] In fact, managers often behave in manners that exacerbate the situation, usually through punishing the bearer of bad news or allowing themselves to be isolated from subordinates at lower levels.[53] In a creative effort to overcome these problems, Robert Darvin, head of Scandinavian Design, Inc., distributes special stationery to every employee at his 21-year-old retail furniture company, including warehouse workers, corporate executives in Natick, Massachusetts, and salespeople in the 70 stores located in the northeastern United States and Hawaii. The stationery is used exclusively for communicating with Darvin, and employees are encouraged to use it to send up bad, as well as good, news.[54]

One technique that has helped managers keep from becoming isolated is **management by wandering around (MBWA),** a practice whereby managers frequently tour areas for which they are responsible, talk to various employees,

Upward communication
The vertical flow of communication from a lower level to one or more higher levels in the organization

Management by wandering around (MBWA) A practice whereby managers frequently tour areas for which they are responsible, talk to various employees, and encourage upward communication

and encourage upward communication.[55] For instance, Gerry Mitchell, chairman of the Dana Corporation, a major maker of auto parts that is based in Toledo, Ohio, makes 50 scheduled and 100 unscheduled visits to Dana's plants each year.[56] Of course, if the "wandering around" is done for the purpose of finding problems so that people can be punished, the wandering will probably build mistrust and increase managerial isolation.

Horizontal Communication

Horizontal communication is lateral or diagonal message exchange either within work-unit boundaries, involving peers who report to the same supervisor, or across work-unit boundaries, involving individuals who report to different supervisors (see Figure 15-4). Horizontal communication can take many forms, including meetings, reports, memos, telephone conversations, and face-to-face discussions between individuals. Studies show that managers spend about one-third of their communication time in horizontal communication.[57] Considerable horizontal communication in organizations stems from staff specialists, in areas such as engineering, accounting, and human resources management, who provide advice to managers in various departments. Horizontal communication usually relates to one or more of the following areas: (1) task coordination, (2) problem solving, (3) information sharing, (4) conflict resolution, and (5) peer support.[58]

Three major factors tend to impede necessary, work-related horizontal communication. First, rivalry among individuals or work units can influence individuals to hide information that is potentially damaging to themselves or that may aid others. Second, specialization may cause individuals to be concerned mainly about the work of their own unit and to have little appreciation for the work and communication needs of others. For example, scientists in an R&D unit that is focused on long-term projects may find it difficult to interrupt their work to help with current customer problems identified by the sales department. Third, motivation may be lacking when subordinate horizontal communication is not encouraged or rewarded. Committees, task forces, and matrix structures are common means that managers use to help encourage horizontal communication, particularly across work-unit boundaries (see Chapters 10 and 11). The effective use of horizontal communication in organizations requires that peers doing the communicating across work units keep their respective bosses informed of significant developments. Otherwise, the vertical chain of command begins to break down, and the managers in the hierarchy soon do not know what is going on.[59]

> **Horizontal communication** Lateral or diagonal message exchange either within work-unit boundaries, involving peers who report to the same supervisor, or across work-unit boundaries, involving individuals who report to different supervisors

Informal Communication: The Grapevine

The vertical and horizontal communication patterns that we have just discussed are sometimes referred to as **formal communication** patterns, or channels, because the communication follows paths specified by the official hierarchical organization structure and related task requirements. You might think of formal communication as communication relating to one's *position* in the organization. In contrast, **informal communication,** better known as the **grapevine,** is communication that takes place without regard to hierarchical or task requirements. Informal communication can be thought of as relating to *personal* rather than positional issues.[60] For example, personal relationships unrelated to organizational positions might exist because of such factors as riding to work in the same

> **Formal communication** Vertical and horizontal communication that follows paths specified by the official hierarchical organization structure and related task requirements
>
> **Informal communication** Communication that takes place without regard to hierarchical or task requirements
>
> **Grapevine** Another term for informal communication

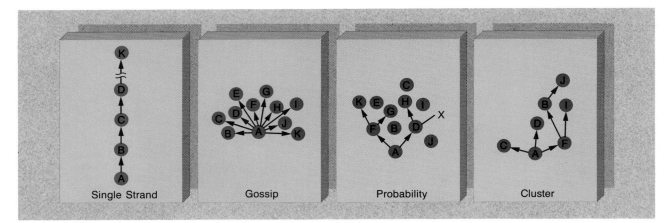

Figure 15-6 Types of grapevine chains. (Reprinted from Keith Davis, ''Management Communication and the Grapevine,'' in Stewart Ferguson and Sherry Devereaux Ferguson (eds.), *Intercom: Readings in Organizational Communication*, Hayden Book Company, Rochelle Park, N.J., 1980, p. 59.)

carpool, attending the same church, or having children in the same school as others in the organization. Grapevine communications stem largely from such personal relationships, which may overlap, but frequently do not coincide with, communication requirements associated with the hierarchy and the task.

The term ''grapevine'' can be traced back to the Civil War, when telegraph lines that were strung from tree to tree in grapevinelike patterns often provided intelligence messages that were garbled.[61] Grapevines exist in virtually all organizations, and grapevine communication patterns are likely to include both vertical and horizontal elements. One classic study investigated four possible configurations for grapevine chains (see Figure 15-6). In the *single-strand chain*, communication moves serially from person A to B to C and so on. With the *gossip chain*, person A seeks out and tells others. When following the *probability chain*, person A spreads the message randomly, as do individuals F and D. In the *cluster chain*, person A tells three selected individuals, and then one of these tells three others. The study found that the cluster chain was the most predominant form, which suggests that individuals who are part of grapevines are likely to be selective about the persons to whom they relay information and that only some of those persons will in turn pass the information further.[62]

Overall, grapevines tend to be fast, carry large amounts of information, and produce data that ranges in accuracy from 50 to 90 percent.[63] Although grapevine communications are often perceived by organization members as being fairly inaccurate, the problems seem to stem largely from misinterpretation when details are incomplete.[64] For example, Jack Shields, a senior vice president at the Digital Equipment Corporation who is often mentioned as a possible successor to President Kenneth Olson, did not attend a recent ''state of the company'' meeting for top managers. When asked where Shields was, Olson responded somewhat vaguely. Then a new organization chart of U.S. field operations did not include Shields. As a result, rumors that Shields had been fired started to move through the sales force and to sources outside the company. Soon the gossip reached Wall Street, raising questions about succession at Digital and causing the company's stock to fall more than a point. Shields, however, had not been at the meeting because he was attending the annual meeting of a company on whose board of directors he serves. His name did not appear on the U.S. field operations chart because the chart did not extend up to the level of the executive committee of which he is a member.[65]

Despite the fact that grapevines sometimes create difficulties when they carry gossip and false rumors, they are a fact of life in organizations, and it is unrealistic of managers to think that they can eliminate grapevines. In fact, researchers have recently suggested that grapevine gossip, by dwelling on transgressions, may be a valuable aid in communicating organizational rules, values, and morals. The grapevine also helps disseminate information about organizational traditions and history.[66] Managers may be able to enlist the help of the grapevine to reinforce important messages sent through formal communication channels, to test certain proposals before they become official, and to obtain feedback about employee feelings and ideas.[67] The grapevine may also help foster innovation by facilitating communication among various parts of the organization.

Promoting Innovation: Multiple Communication Channels

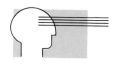

Rosabeth Moss Kanter, a researcher on innovation, argues that the use of multiple communication channels is especially critical for innovation.[68] In order to nurture innovative behavior, managers need to emphasize the use of both vertical and horizontal communication channels.

Vertical Communication. Managers can use vertical communication to encourage innovation in four key ways:

■ *Signaling organizational expectations for innovation* both through words and through specific actions, such as providing special funds for innovation and giving public recognition for successful innovations, aids the innovation process.
■ *Fostering the upward communication of innovative ideas* helps organizations promote innovation. Some innovative companies have "open-door" policies that, theoretically, mean all levels can have access to anyone in order to ask questions, present ideas, or even criticize. For example, on one occasion Rubbermaid's CEO, Stanley Gault, came in at 5 a.m. to meet with a worker whose shift ends at that time.[69]
■ *Encouraging managers in the chain of command to act as sponsors* in funding, protecting, and testing potential innovations in their developmental stages is another way to use vertical communication to encourage innovation.
■ *Facilitating extensive use of horizontal communication channels* in the organization also can be a useful method of promoting innovation.

Horizontal Communication. Considerable research support is accumulating for the particular importance of horizontal communication in the process of innovation.[70] Horizontal communication is critical to the innovation process in four ways:

■ *Connecting potential recognizers of opportunities for innovation* can set the stage for possible breakthroughs. When individuals in various parts of the organization are closely connected through various communication channels, they are more likely to be aware of opportunities and problems, which are the grist for innovation.
■ *Linking different areas of expertise* through horizontal communication channels can vastly increase the prospects of spawning a unique idea. The importance of a variety of views is related to Kanter's notion of "kaleidoscopic thinking."

The formation of teams can lead to quicker and more innovative solutions to problems by aiding horizontal communication both within and across functions. At Honeywell's Air Transport Systems Division, a 30-person engineering team (part of which is shown here) won recognition for contributing to the success of a collision avoidance system.

The kaleidoscope has multiple elements that form a pattern, but they are not locked in place. Shaking, twisting, or changing the angle provides a new pattern. Similarly, fresh approaches to existing patterns form the basis for new innovations.

■ *Building coalitions of individuals* who can help develop innovations and/or support their implementation is easier when both vertical and horizontal communication channels are active. Innovative companies often use teams with representatives from various functional areas to help with developments that are likely to lead to critical changes. For example, 3M and Honeywell utilize internal conferences and "idea fairs" to connect ideas with those who can use them or develop them into usable innovations. Other means of encouraging horizontal communication include setting up special units to study and write about innovations and appointing product managers to help bridge development and implementation efforts across functional areas. When Linda Bos took over as sales vice president of McKesson Office Products, she instituted monthly sales meetings of district managers to encourage the sharing and generating of innovative ideas.[71]

■ *Emphasizing boundary spanning*, the creating of roles within the organization that interface with important elements outside the organization, can help keep organization members linked to important sources of information in the environment. For example, encouraging scientists to maintain close ties with their respective fields through association memberships, conferences, and the like is a means of boundary spanning. Another is maintaining close ties with customers. One study of 500 important industrial innovations found that over three-fourths originated with user suggestions, while only one-fifth developed from technical ideas seeking applications.[72] For example, at Ballard Medical Products, Inc., in Midvale, Utah, sales representatives train customers to use new products and, in the process, often call headquarters with suggestions for improvements that come out of the training sessions. The continual effort to gain suggestions from customers has helped relatively small Ballard (annual sales of about $10 million) produce innovative products in the hospital supply industry, which is dominated mainly by very large companies such as American Hospital Supply and Johnson & Johnson.[73] Similarly, at Stew Leonard's many new ideas come from customers through such vehicles as suggestion boxes and focus groups.

Thus, efforts at enhancing both vertical and horizontal communication are an important element in encouraging innovation in an organization. Both forms of communication receive special attention from Arthur E. Morrissette, president and founder of Interstate Van Lines, Inc., a $30-million-a-year moving and storage company in Springfield, Virginia. Although Morrissette publishes a newsletter, called *Under the Top Hat*, his main communication media are the training session and the sing-along.

The training sessions, attended by more than 200 employees, are scheduled daily for 7:30 to 8:30 a.m. During this time managers provide information to movers and packers about various business-related issues. Every couple of weeks, there is a sing-along. The sing-along format, which calls for all the employees to meet in the convention hall and mingle, has been designed to discourage employees from thinking of themselves as belonging to separate groups or camps. The occasions also serve as a forum for Morrissette to emphasize a team spirit and to provide recognition for good work and new ideas by distributing individual achievement awards, cash prizes, and points toward performance evaluations. In addition, participants sing patriotic songs, as well as the company anthem:

> Work that you do is more than just a job.
> It's important to keep a smile on your face.
> You are the one the shipper comes to trust.
> You are the image of Interstate.

Evidently, the sing-alongs work: Interstate Van Lines has one of the highest profit ratios in its industry.[74]

The Growing Potential of Electronics

Electronic advances are providing managers with new methods and channels of communication. Two of the most prominent advances are electronic mail systems and video teleconferencing.

An **electronic mail system** is a mail system that allows high-speed exchange of written messages through the use of computerized text-processing and communication networks. Anyone who has access to a computer terminal can develop and send a written message to anyone else who has a computer mailbox on the network. Electronic mail systems typically have three general characteristics.[75] First, they are *asynchronous*; that is, message sending and receiving take place serially, rather than simultaneously. As with ordinary mail, a message is sent at one point in time and an answer is received at a later point in time. In contrast, the telephone is an example of a synchronous system, because senders and receivers are concerned with the same message at the same time. Second, electronic mail systems are fast. Messages can be transmitted in seconds to another office in the same building or to an office thousands of miles away, as long as the locations are served by the network. Third, they are text-based. The message can be conveyed only through written text or graphics. According to one estimate, the number of messages sent on private corporate electronic mail systems could exceed 10 billion per year by 1992.[76]

Managers at the Digital Equipment Corporation indicate that they save about 7 hours per week because their electronic mail system has increased the speed of decision making.[77] Managers at Manufacturers Hanover Trust estimate that their electronic mail system saves them about 3 hours per week, mainly by eliminating unreturned phone calls and reducing other internal correspondence.[78] One recent study of messages in units of two divisions of a Fortune 500 office equipment firm showed that the managers sent a daily average of 2.4 messages and received 20.6 messages.[79]

There also is evidence that electronic mail systems lead to exchanges of information among managers who previously did not communicate either by mail or telephone and that they receive new types of information through the system.[80] Electronic mail systems not only enhance vertical communication but also can facilitate horizontal communication.[81]

One disadvantage of electronic mail is that it eliminates the nonverbal cues (e.g., facial expressions, body movements, tone of voice) that serve as aids in face-to-face communication. (Of course, regular mail also has far fewer nonverbal cues than does face-to-face message exchange.) Another is that the ease of sending mail electronically can cause individuals to receive excessive amounts of mail that does not interest them. As Mitchell Kapor, former chairman of the Lotus Development Corporation, notes, "It's a well-known phenomenon in large corporations that when you come back from a long weekend you'll find 50

Electronic mail system A mail system that allows high-speed exchange of written messages through the use of computerized text-processing and communication networks

Video teleconferencing The holding of meetings with individuals in two or more locations by means of closed-circuit television

pieces of electronic mail in your mailbox, spend hours going through it, and end up with most of it being stuff you don't want to see."[82]

Another form of electronic communication, **video teleconferencing,** is the holding of meetings with individuals in two or more locations by means of closed-circuit television. Teleconferencing usually has three general characteristics. First, it is *synchronous*, meaning that senders and receivers can engage in simultaneous communication of the type associated with face-to-face conversation. Second, like electronic mail, it is fast. Third, it usually allows oral and written, as well as nonverbal, message exchange through the use of cameras and supplementary equipment such as facsimile devices and electronic blackboards. Although the teleconferencing facilities themselves can be expensive, teleconferencing has the potential advantage of eliminating the travel time and costs associated with bringing people from multiple locations to one spot for a meeting. However, the cost, reduced nonverbal information, and lessened spontaneity associated with teleconferencing, as compared with traditional meetings, have made adoption of teleconferencing rather slow.[83] A recent study indicates that teleconferencing use is still in the embryonic stages, at least in Fortune 500 companies.[84] James Treybig, head of Tandem Computers, uses a form of teleconferencing in monthly television broadcasts over the company's in-house TV station. Employees throughout the world can watch the broadcast and call in with questions and comments.[85] Other companies with their own private television networks include IBM, J. C. Penney, Federal Express, Ford, Merrill Lynch, Xerox, and A. L. Williams Insurance.[86]

Since communication involves interacting with others, managers usually find it helpful to have a working knowledge of group dynamics and conflict management. We explore these topics in the next chapter.

CHAPTER SUMMARY

Effective communication is important in gaining and maintaining the competitive edge in organizations. Communication is the exchange of messages between people for the purpose of achieving common meanings. In their work, managers use two types of communication: verbal (including written and oral) and nonverbal. Studies indicate that managers tend to prefer oral over written communication, spending approximately 75 percent of their working hours communicating orally with others.

The process of communication has several basic components: sender, encoding, message, receiver, decoding, noise, and feedback. When the communication process provides for relatively immediate feedback, it is called two-way communication. Without a feedback provision, it is known as one-way communication.

A number of factors affect individual communication. Perception is susceptible to five major types of distortion: stereotyping, the halo effect, projection, perceptual defense, and self-serving bias. Semantic blocks sometimes occur because of different meanings and shades of meanings that can be attached to words by individuals using their own semantic nets. The consist-

ency of verbal and nonverbal communication elements can reinforce a message in various ways. When the elements contradict each other, the receiver is most likely to interpret the nonverbal message as the true message. Individual communication is facilitated by the development of communication skills in such areas as listening, giving feedback, and receiving feedback.

When tasks require input from several individuals, managers need to give some thought to the communication network among task group members. Centralized networks are represented by the wheel, chain, and Y; decentralized networks consist of the circle and the star. For relatively simple, routine tasks, the centralized networks tend to be faster and more accurate. When tasks are more complex, decentralized networks are likely to be faster and more accurate.

Managers also need to be concerned with the flow of information among the various parts of the organization. Formal communication in organizations follows channels specified by the official hierarchical organization structure and related task requirements, and it flows in two main directions, vertical and horizontal. When vertical communication flows from a higher level to one or more lower levels, it is known as downward communication. When it moves from a lower level to one or more higher levels, it is known as upward communication. On the other hand, horizontal communication is lateral message exchange. Informal communication, better known as the grapevine, takes place without regard to hierarchical or task requirements or organiza-tional position. In order to nurture innovative behavior in an organization, managers need to emphasize the use of both vertical (upward and downward) and horizontal communication channels. Electronic mail systems and teleconferencing are examples of new communication methods being made available to managers through advances in electronics.

MANAGERIAL TERMINOLOGY

active listening (533)
communication (518)
communication channels
    (536)
communication network
    (535)
decoding (524)
downward
    communication (536)
electronic mail system
    (543)
encoding (523)
feedback (525)

formal communication
    (539)
grapevine (539)
halo effect (528)
horizontal communication
    (539)
informal communication
    (539)
kinesic behavior (520)
management by
    wandering around
    (MBWA) (538)
medium (524)
message (524)

noise (525)
nonverbal communication
    (520)
object language (520)
one-way communication
    (526)
paralanguage (520)
perception (527)
perceptual defense (529)
projection (529)
proxemics (520)
receiver (524)
self-serving bias (529)
semantic blocks (529)

semantic net (529)
sender (523)
stereotyping (528)
two-way communication
    (526)
upward communication
    (538)
verbal communication
    (519)
vertical communication
    (536)
video teleconferencing
    (544)

QUESTIONS FOR DISCUSSION AND REVIEW

1. Explain the major types of communication that managers use and discuss managerial communica-tion preferences. For an organization with which you are familiar, identify examples of each type. Classify the nonverbal communication examples in terms of kinesic behavior, proxemics, paralan-guage, and object language.
2. Outline the basic components of the communica-tion process. Trace these components for a conver-sation that you witness.
3. Delineate several common tendencies to distort perceptions. Give an example of how each could adversely affect communication.
4. Explain the notion of semantic blocks. Identify some words that are used at your university that might cause semantic blocks to outsiders who are unfamiliar with the terminology.
5. Explain how nonverbal communication can rein-force or substitute for a verbal message and how it can contradict a verbal message. Give an example that illustrates each situation.
6. Outline the major types of centralized and decen-tralized group communication networks. Explain the conditions under which centralized and decen-

tralized networks are likely to result in the best per-formance. Evaluate how well suited they appear to be for the situations involved.
7. Differentiate between vertical and horizontal com-munication. Identify the major methods used in your college or university for downward communi-cation from chief administrators to students and for upward communication from students to chief administrators. What mechanisms exist for hori-zontal communication among students?
8. Assess the organizational implications of the grapevine. What evidence points to the existence of a student grapevine in your department at your college or university?
9. Explain how vertical and horizontal communica-tion channels might be used to foster innovation in an organization. How could communication be used to promote innovation in a campus organiza-tion to which you belong?
10. How can managers use electronic mail systems and video teleconferencing to advantage in communi-cating? What potential problems exist with these methods?

DISCUSSION QUESTIONS FOR CHAPTER OPENING CASE

1. Identify the vertical communication methods, both downward and upward, used at Stew Leonard's.
2. What methods are used to provide horizontal communication?
3. Would you characterize the management at Stew Leonard's as attempting to foster innovation? What evidence exists for your view?

MANAGEMENT EXERCISE: A QUESTION OF INFERENCES

Read the story presented below, and indicate whether you believe the statements that follow the story are true (T), false (F), or unknown (?). Then get together with a group designated by your instructor, and determine as a group whether each of the statements is true, false, or unknown.

Haney Test of Uncritical Inferences (1979)[87]

The Story*

A businessman had just turned off the lights in the store when a man appeared and demanded money. The owner opened a cash register. The contents of the cash register were scooped up, and the man sped away. A member of the police force was notified promptly.

Statements about the Story

1.	A man appeared after the owner had turned off his store lights.	T	F	?
2.	The robber was a *man*.	T	F	?
3.	The man who appeared did not demand money.	T	F	?
4.	The man who opened the cash register was the owner.	T	F	?
5.	The store owner scooped up the contents of the cash register and ran away.	T	F	?
6.	Someone opened a cash register.	T	F	?
7.	After the man who demanded the money scooped up the contents of the cash register, he ran away.	T	F	?
8.	While the cash register contained money, the story does *not* state *how much*.	T	F	?

9.	The robber demanded money of the owner.	T	F	?
10.	A businessman had just turned off the lights when a man appeared in the store.	T	F	?
11.	It was broad daylight when the man appeared.	T	F	?
12.	The man who appeared opened the cash register.	T	F	?
13.	No one demanded money.	T	F	?
14.	The story concerns a series of events in which only three persons are referred to: the owner of the store, a man who demanded money, and a member of the police force.	T	F	?
15.	The following events occurred: someone demanded money; a cash register was opened; its contents were scooped up; and a man dashed out of the store.	T	F	?

*The story and statements are a portion of the Uncritical Inference Test, copyrighted 1955, 1964, 1979 by William V. Haney. The full-length test is available for educational purposes from The International Society for General Semantics, P.O. Box 2469, San Francisco, California 94126.

CHAIRMAN'S COST-CUTTING HUMOR AT BEAR, STEARNS

Even before cost cutting replaced scandal dodging as the latest game on Wall Street, one firm kept a sharp eye on its bottom line—thanks mainly to advice from the revered Haimchinkel Malintz Anaynikal, a reclusive philosopher of budgetary restraint.

The fictional Anaynikal resides in the fertile imagination of Alan C. (Ace) Greenberg, the chairman and chief executive of Bear, Stearns & Company, a noted Wall Street investment firm. "I have no further comment about him," Greenberg said when asked to supply details of Anaynikal's biography. "If other firms found out about him, there might be big trouble."

It's easy to see why. For years, Greenberg and Anaynikal have been tough on costs, but now the rest of Wall Street seems to be catching up. After the stock market difficulties of October 1987, Salomon, Inc., another Wall Street investment firm, announced it would eliminate 800 jobs as part of a plan to save $150 million a year; other investment firms that grew rapidly during the bull market also took a fresh look at possible staff reductions.

In contrast, through a series of internal memos distributed to employees at Bear, Stearns &

Company, Ace Greenberg and Anaynikal have worked overtime to slash costs at the firm. One typical memo begins:

It may come as a surprise to some of you, but Federal Express is not a wholly owned subsidiary of Bear, Stearns & Co. I mention this because we have been spending $50,000 a month with them and there is no explanation to justify this expenditure unless it was an intercompany transfer.

The company's memos typically contain nuggets of Haimchinkel Malintz Anaynikal's instructive—and diverting—wisdom. What follows, in chronological order, are excerpts from a few of these memos.

FR: Alan C. Greenberg

June 19, 1985

The month of May is history, but it looks like we did get 10 runs in the first inning. I frankly cannot remember any time in the past where we ever broke even in the month of May, much less made money.

Haimchinkel Malintz dropped down, saw the figures and made some suggestions. . . . . He pointed out to me that the tendency is to cut expenses when things are tough and how stupid that line of reasoning is. When

things are good you should be even more careful of expenses. . . .

The partners of this firm must continue to work together and learn to overlook petty differences. We are all expendable and I hope that your Executive Committee does not have to prove that to any of us.

August 9, 1985

I was just shown the results for our first quarter. They were excellent. When mortals go through a prosperous period, it seems to be human nature for expenses to balloon. We are going to be the exception. I have just informed the purchasing department that they should no longer purchase paper clips. All of us receive documents every day with paper clips on them. If we save these paper clips, we will not only have enough for our own use, but we will also in a short time be awash in the little critters. Periodically, we will collect excess paper clips and sell them. . . .

In addition to the paper clip caper, we also are going to cut down on ordering the blue envelopes used for interoffice mail. These envelopes can be used over and over again. . . .

You have probably guessed by now that these thoughts are not

Figure 15-7 Penny-wise tips for the busy executive of today by H. M. Anaynikal. (Drawn by Richard Thompson, *The Washington Post*, Oct. 18, 1987, p. H1.)

original. They came from one of Haimchinkel Molonitz [sic] Anaynikal's earlier works. His thoughts have not exactly steered us wrong so far. Let's stick with his theories till he lets us down.

August 15, 1985

Thank you, thank you, thank you! The response to the memo on paper clips and envelopes has been overwhelming. It seems that we already have an excess of paper clips. . . . If we can save paper clips from incoming mail, we can save rubber bands, and my hope is that we can become awash in those little stretchies also. Obviously, if we can handle the rubber band challenge, I have something even bigger in mind.

September 10, 1985

We have been supplying everyone with memo pads. These pads have, at the top, our logo and also a person's name and telephone number. This is conceptually wrong. We are in a person-to-person business. It would be much warmer if the sender of a note signed it with his name and telephone number along with some sweet words, such as "I love you" or "I need more business to feed my family."

. . . Haimchinkel Malintz Anaynikal just informed me that this superior way of communicating will save us $45,000 a year.

February 25, 1986

The [profits] for our first three months of [public ownership] are certainly something to be proud of. Before we fall into one of the traps that Haimchinkel Malintz Anaynikal so often warned us about, please keep in mind that we were aided and abetted by a great stock and bond market. . . .

We must continue to be alert for scams and con artists. We must watch for unusual behavior by the people we work with. What is unusual behavior? Something subtle like somebody who drives a Rolls-Royce on a salary that can barely support roller skates.

. . . Are all phone calls returned? I couldn't care less what a person does in his own home, but I am a nut about returning phone calls that are made to personnel during the work day. I do not care if the caller is selling malaria. Calls must be returned!

. . . Do you and your associates leave word where you are at all times so that finding you is not like hunting for the *Andrea Doria*? . . .

August 29, 1986

Because we are rolling along, it is essential that we review the fundamentals of Haimchinkel Malintz Anaynikal. . . . Do not get conceited or cocky. . . . Check on the people that answer telephones. Are they courteous? . . . Return all calls as soon as possible. . . . Watch expenses—like a hawk. Now is the time to cut out fat! The rest of the world cuts expenses when business turns sour. With your help, we will be different, smarter and richer.

December 9, 1986

This is going to be hard for you to believe, but it is actually a fact. I called the head of one of our major areas yesterday, and although the man was in, his secretary did not know where to find him! I know this tests my creditability [sic] with you, but it is true. You are well aware that this violates one of Haimchinkel

Malintz Anaynikal's cardinal rules. . . .

It also hurts me to report that I saw somebody throw away a used envelope before it made 22 trips around the office. I can't stand to see people burn money. . . . Rubber bands can be used even when they break. Take the two ends and tie a square knot.

August 21, 1987

I would like to announce at this time a freeze on expenses and carelessness. We probably throw away millions every year with stupidities and slop. In fact, I have seen more slop in the last three weeks than in the previous six months. Stop it now.

Haimchinkel Malintz Anaynikal is really something. . . . He hates slop even more than I do. In fact, he pointed out to me where our stock could be if we ran a neat, tight shop. I am tired of cleaning up poo-poos. The next associate of mine that does something "un-neat" is going to have a little meeting with me and I will not be the usual charming, sweet, understanding, pleasant, entertaining, affable, yokel from Oklahoma.[88]

QUESTIONS FOR CHAPTER CONCLUDING CASE

1. Compare the Anaynikal memos sent by Ace Greenberg with other possible communication options. Do you feel that the memos are effective in sending the message regarding the cost-cutting competitive edge?

2. Evaluate the Anaynikal memos in terms of the basic components of the communication process.

3. To what extent do the memos encourage vertical (upward and downward) and horizontal communication? Give evidence to support your answer.

CHAPTER SIXTEEN

MANAGING GROUPS

CHAPTER OUTLINE

Foundations of Work Groups
What Is a Group?
Types of Work Groups
How Informal Groups Develop
How Work Groups Operate

Work Group Inputs
Work Group Composition
Member Roles
Group Size

Work Group Processes
Group Norms
Group Cohesiveness
Group Development

Promoting Innovation: Special Work Group Applications
Task Forces
Teams

Normative Model of Group Effectiveness
Components of the Model
Using the Model

Managing Conflict
Causes of Conflict
Reducing and Resolving Conflict
Stimulating Conflict

LEARNING OBJECTIVES

After studying this chapter, you should be able to:

■ Differentiate among different types of groups in the workplace and explain how informal groups develop.

■ Use a systems approach to describe the major factors that influence the way that groups operate.

■ Describe the major work group inputs, including group composition, member roles, and group size, and how they affect group functioning.

■ Explain the significance of major group processes, such as group norms, group cohesiveness, and group development.

■ Discuss how special group applications, such as task forces and teams, can be used to promote innovation.

■ Outline the normative model of group effectiveness.

■ Explain the causes of conflict and how to reduce, resolve, and stimulate conflict.

COMPAQ SUCCEEDS WITH TEAMS

According to Compaq Computer Corporation lore, in 1982, Rod Canion and two other Texas Instruments (TI) employees sat in the Houston House of Pies and sketched on a place mat an idea for a portable personal computer. Ten months later the product hit the market. Thus began the computer company whose annual sales would pass the $1 billion mark by 1988, giving it one of the fastest sales growths for a start-up company in U.S. business history.

Although the product idea was a good one, there was another essential ingredient involved—an emphasis on the use of teams and a spirit of teamwork throughout the company. "When we left Texas Instruments, we were determined to start a company with people who could work in a Fortune 500 company," explains Canion. "We wanted to combine the discipline of a big company with an environment where people felt they could participate in a success. We wanted the best of both worlds. And we wanted to do it right." From the start, Compaq was dedicated to teamwork.

As a result, the three cofounders hired a number of seasoned industry veterans whom they felt could work well together. The outcome was what one Compaq vice president has called the "United Nations of high tech," referring to the fact that experts were brought in from such luminary companies as TI, IBM, Apple, Digital Equipment, and GTE. In the early months of the company, the cofounders and the other new managers set up shop in an executive suite. The suite consisted of modest private offices located near a large and comfortable conference area where all the major company decisions were made by a special top management team consisting of experts in the various relevant areas. The idea was to make decisions by consensus; the group would try to reach an agreement on the key directions that the company would take. The team members would then work together to implement their ideas.

The team approach was put to the test early in 1983 when Canion became enthralled with the idea of producing a lap-top computer. Although the special top management team basically supported the idea, it asked market researcher Mary Dudley to survey the market. She concluded that the product would not sell at that point in time. After Dudley presented, reanalyzed, and reiterated her negative assessment, Canion backed away from the idea—fortunately. Lap-top computers soon introduced by the Gavilan Computer Corporation and the Data General Corporation proved to be colossal market failures. (More recently, Compaq has introduced not only a successful lap-top computer but also a computer the size of a notebook.)

As Compaq has grown, the team concept has spread to other parts of the company and is widely credited for Compaq's phenomenal success in introducing new products in record time. For example, in late 1984, Compaq faced a crisis when IBM began producing a more powerful line of PCs. Kevin Ellington, a 21-year veteran of TI, was given the job of developing a response. Ellington created a special development team by drawing individuals from every department in the company to work in tandem specifically on the project. While the engineers designed a new product line, manufacturing specialists established a new factory to produce it, a marketing executive prepared a promotion campaign, and an assistant treasurer lined up funding. Compaq was shipping its new, quickly successful Deskpro 286 line within 6 months, much faster than the average development time in the industry. As luck would have it, the Deskpro 286 line came out just in time to fill a void created by IBM production and quality

Compaq Computer Corp. started as a team effort, and now the spirit of teamwork pervades the company. Shown here is the "Salespaq" team going over the company's products and software programs. Compaq makes a point of hiring employees who have a cooperative attitude and enjoy working in groups.

control problems. In commenting on the success, Ellington says, "The first, second, and third reason for that was teamwork. . . . That's what has kept Compaq free from the perils of this world."

Canion strives to encourage the use of teams throughout the company. "We're not only looking for experts, we're looking for experts who can work on a team. If they lack a positive and cooperative attitude, then we're willing to forgo the benefits of their expertise because they would more than offset it by undermining the team approach." In support of a general spirit of teamwork, Canion lets employees know company goals at quarterly meetings and stresses the importance of everyone's job to company success. At Compaq, everyone's ID badge has name and department only; parking spots are on a first-come, first-served basis; soft drinks are free; sick leave is unlimited; and all permanent employees are eligible for stock options. As a result, Compaq employees tend to be extremely loyal.

Much of Compaq's success has hinged on producing high-quality personal computers and related equipment that are compatible with IBM personal computers. Typically, Compaq has introduced machines that can do everything that IBM personal computers do but also have attractive additional features for a similar price. Sometimes, Compaq has plunged ahead on new technology, as in 1986, when the company was the first to introduce a personal computer using a powerful new 80386 microprocessor chip from the Intel Corporation. More recently, Compaq has assumed more of a leadership position in introducing computers that depart from IBM standards.

Operating in a fiercely competitive environment, Canion says: "I am really the pilot of a ship looking out ahead for the obstacles on the course and for the opportunities. My top priority is seeing that the company stays in navigable waters and realizes its potential." With his emphasis on teams and group involvement, so far his efforts have paid off.[1]

Canion is a manager who recognizes that individuals working effectively in groups can often be a powerful competitive force. However, in order to take advantage of the power of groups, managers need to have a solid understanding of group behavior—often referred to as group dynamics because of the ongoing interchanges that characterize groups. Managers also need to be aware of their own potential to influence groups as part of the leading function.

In this chapter, we examine some basic characteristics of groups, including types of work groups, the development of informal groups, and the operation of groups. We investigate some of the major inputs and processes that affect group outcomes. We explore some special work group applications that are particularly appropriate for fostering innovation. We also review a normative model of effectiveness that helps managers design effective work teams. Finally, we analyze how conflict within and between groups can be managed, addressing possibilities for both reducing and stimulating conflict.

FOUNDATIONS OF WORK GROUPS

What Is a Group?

Group   Two or more interdependent individuals who interact and influence each other in collective pursuit of a common goal

A **group** is two or more interdependent individuals who interact and influence each other in collective pursuit of a common goal.[2] This definition recognizes that a group can involve as few as two people, that group success depends on the interdependent and collective efforts of various group members, and that group members are likely to have significant impacts on one another as they work together. This definition also helps differentiate a group from a mere aggregate of individuals, perhaps several strangers who happen to leave by the same door at the theater or who can be found studying in the reference section of a library. In neither case are those individuals interdependent, nor do they interact and influence one another in collectively attempting to achieve a shared goal. Groups also differ from organizations in that the latter involve systematic efforts (such as using the four major management functions and having a formal structure), as well as the production of goods or services. Groups typically do not engage in systematic efforts to the same extent as organizations and may or may not produce goods or services.

Although groups have always been a central part of organizations as we know them, they are gaining increasing attention as potentially important organizational assets. Organizations that are making more extensive use of groups range from mammoth General Motors to much smaller Castite, a Cleveland firm that employs 17 people and is just approaching its first $1 million in annual sales. At Castite, for example, when an order for a new part comes in, President Joan Lamson has a salesperson, a quality assurance person, and a production worker meet together. They determine exactly what the customer wants, how to get the job done in the best possible way, and how to maximize quality. Castite, which uses an epoxylike resin to fill the tiny holes that are left by gas bubbles in molten metal as it is cast, has customers that include the "Big Three" automakers.[3]

Types of Work Groups

A number of different types of groups exist in the workplace. One useful way of classifying them is to think of them as falling into two main categories: formal and informal. These categories and several subcategories that we discuss below are shown in Figure 16-1.

Formal group   A group officially created by an organization for a specific purpose

Formal Groups.   A **formal group** is a group officially created by an organization for a specific purpose. There are two major types of formal groups: command and task.

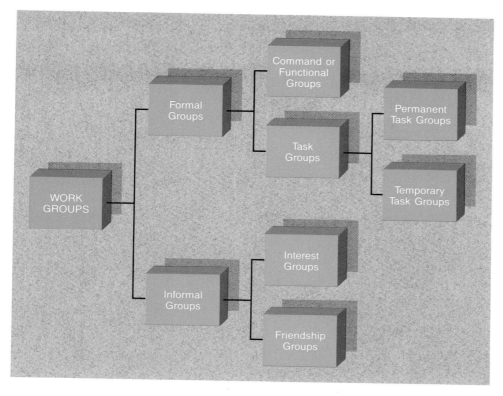

Figure 16-1 Types of work groups.

A **command,** or **functional, group** is a formal group consisting of a manager and all the subordinates who report to that manager. In other words, each identifiable work unit (manager and subordinates) in an organization is considered to be a command group. For example, if you stay in a large Marriott hotel, your room will be cleaned by one of several housekeepers who report to an area housekeeping supervisor, making up one command group. If you attend a luncheon, the individuals who wait on the tables report to a catering supervisor, forming part of another command group. Each supervisor reports to a respective higher-level manager and belongs to that higher-level command group. In this way, each supervisor forms a linking pin between a lower-level and a higher-level group. A **linking pin** is an individual who provides a means of coordination between command groups at two different levels by fulfilling a supervisory role in the lower-level group and a subordinate role in the higher-level group (see Figure 16-2). Thus, from one vantage point, organizations are made up of command, or functional, groups arranged in pyramidal fashion, with linking pins tying them together.

A **task group** is a formal group that is created for a specific purpose that supplements or replaces work normally done by command groups. Task groups can be either relatively permanent or temporary. A *permanent* task group, often called a **standing committee** or *team,* is charged with handling recurring matters in a narrowly defined subject area over an indefinite, but generally lengthy, period of time. An example is the Quality Improvement Team of Hazleton Laboratories America, Inc., a high-level permanent task group charged with facilitating quality improvement efforts across various units of the biotechnology firm. A *temporary* task group is created to deal with a specific issue within a specific time frame. For example, as part of its Profitability Improvement program and accompanying strategy to be a low-cost producer, Heinz USA frequently orga-

Command, or **functional, group** A formal group consisting of a manager and all the subordinates who report to that manager

Linking pin An individual who provides a means of coordination between command groups at two different levels by fulfilling a supervisory role in the lower-level group and a subordinate role in the higher-level group

Task group A formal group that is created for a specific purpose that supplements or replaces work normally done by command groups

Standing committee A permanent task group of individuals charged with handling recurring matters in a narrowly defined subject area over an indefinite, but generally lengthy, period of time

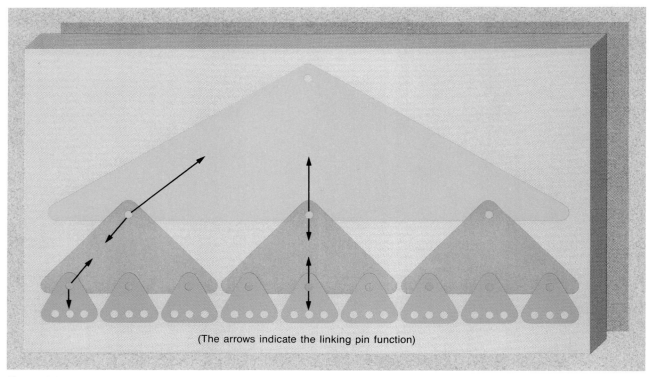

(The arrows indicate the linking pin function)

Figure 16-2 The linking-pin concept. (Reprinted from Rensis Likert, *New Patterns of Management*, McGraw-Hill, New York, 1961, p. 113.)

nizes temporary teams of managers from different departments to seek out and prioritize projects that can lead to major cost savings.[4] Temporary task groups often are called *ad hoc committees, task forces,* and *project groups* or *teams.*[5] Names vary somewhat across organizations, so it may be necessary to ask about time frames to establish whether a particular task group is relatively permanent or temporary. We discuss task forces and teams in greater detail later in this chapter.

Informal Groups. An **informal group** is a group that is established by employees, rather than by the organization, in order to serve group members' interests or social needs. Such groups may or may not also further the goals of the organization. Sometimes, informal groups have the same members as does a formal group, as when members of a work group begin to have lunch together. Other times, informal groups are made up of only some members of a formal group and/or cut across two or more formal groups (see Figure 16-3). There are two major types of informal groups: interest and friendship.

An **interest group** is an informal group created to facilitate employee pursuits of common concern. The types of interests that spawn informal groups can be wide-ranging and may include a radical new technology that may not be practical for the company to pursue at a given time (but which a group of engineers investigate informally), a sport such as volleyball, a hobby such as amateur radio, a desire to get the company to alter some policy, or a concern about getting something done as effectively as possible within the company. Interest groups can benefit the organization, but they can also create difficulties. R. R. Donnelly & Sons, one of the four companies that print over 1 million copies of *Business Week* each week, found it necessary to fire several employees who alleg-

Informal group A group that is established by employees, rather than by the organization, in order to serve group members' interests or social needs

Interest group An informal group created to facilitate employee pursuits of common concern

edly conspired to sell early copies of the magazine to stock brokers. The brokers were interested in gaining early access to stocks mentioned in the magazine's weekly "Inside Wall Street" column so that they could buy the stocks before demand for them pushed prices up.[6]

A **friendship group** is an informal group that evolves primarily to meet employee social needs. Such groups typically stem from mutual attraction, often based on characteristics in common, such as similar work, backgrounds, and/or values. Members of a friendship group may eat lunch together frequently, attend plays, go golfing, or engage in other friendship-related social activities. Friendship groups can benefit an organization by enhancing the flow of information and reinforcing the willingness of employees to work cooperatively together. They can also be detrimental when employees place social concerns above important work goals or when friends have a serious falling out. Four

Friendship group An informal group that evolves primarily to meet employee social needs

Figure 16-3 Formal and informal groups in an organization.

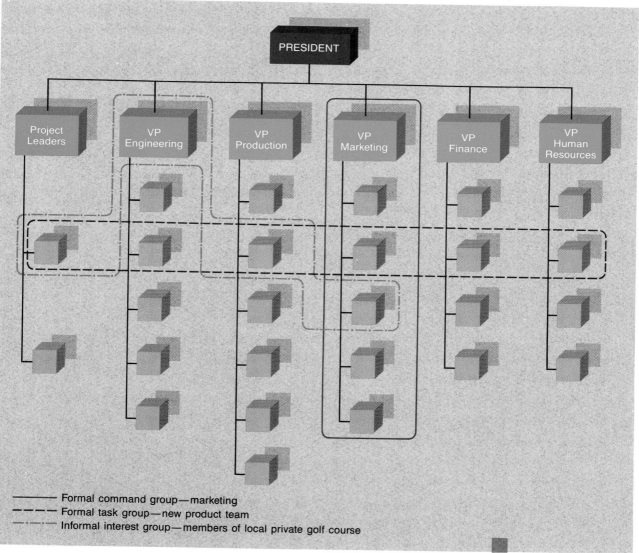

———— Formal command group—marketing
– – – – Formal task group—new product team
–·–·–· Informal interest group—members of local private golf course

months after opening the doors of Ranieri Wilson & Co., the friendly partners of that popular New York investment banking firm found themselves enmeshed in internal strife that led to the firing of one partner and the resignations of at least two others.[7] Thus managers need to understand informal groups because of their potential for influencing organizational effectiveness.

How Informal Groups Develop

Work by sociologist George Homans on required versus emergent behaviors and sentiments helps explain how informal groups often arise from the dynamics of formal groups.[8] When a formal group is established, certain behaviors and sentiments are required (see Figure 16-4) of its members: *Required activities* are the behaviors necessary to perform job tasks; *required interactions* are the dealings with others that are specified as part of the job; *required sentiments* are the views and feelings that are necessary to do the job. Also involved are *given sentiments*, the nonrequired feelings and values that individuals inevitably bring to their jobs.

For example, when Federal Express was a fledgling company in the early 1970s, there were some basic, but limited, requirements that its employees were expected to meet. Couriers were expected to pick up packages on time, somehow get them to the airport, look clean and professional, and keep their trucks washed (required activities). They were also expected to interact with customers when they picked up and dropped off packages, as well as to cooperate with Federal Express pilots, plane loaders, and other company employees at airports (required interactions). Finally, they were supposed to be courteous and polite to customers (required sentiments). No doubt, the couriers also held feelings about a variety of issues, such as the way the organization was run, other employees, sports, and politics (given sentiments and values).[9]

During this period, the company was operating on the edge of financial disaster, was involved in a major lawsuit, and was engaged in strenuous efforts to get federal laws on freight weights changed so that it could use bigger planes. Skeptics were certain the endeavor would fail. As the couriers in their formal groups performed their required behaviors, other behaviors, interactions, and

Employees of the Meredith Corporation lunch together in the company cafeteria. Such friendship groups can result in beneficial exchanges of information and establish a sense of cooperation. But when friends who work together have a falling out, the strained relations can have a detrimental effect on the quality and productivity of their work.

It's clear what brought together the members of this particular group at Northwestern Mutual Life Insurance: a mutual interest in music. The band, which helps promote United Way, is shown here rehearsing at company headquarters.

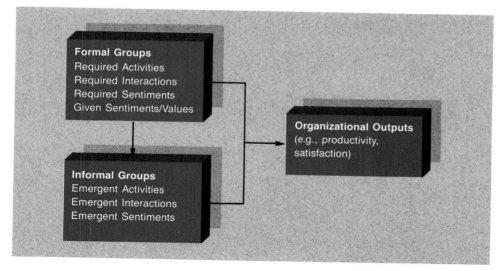

Figure 16-4 The informal-group emergence process.

sentiments began to emerge. According to Homans, *emergent behaviors* are actions that either supplant or supplement required behaviors. Similarly, *emergent interactions* and *emergent sentiments* are actions that either supplant or supplement required interactions and sentiments. These emergent behaviors, interactions, and sentiments are associated with informal groups.

In the Federal Express case, the couriers began to form a strong, informal camaraderie with the pilots, plane loaders, and others involved with their packages. For example, stories abound about couriers who were so dedicated to getting their packages picked up and delivered that they did things like pawning watches to buy gasoline (emergent behaviors). They bent over backward to make sure that they built not only good but outstanding relationships with customers (emergent interactions), prompting customers to make notations on Federal Express customer surveys such as "Say hello to Ginny in Wichita for me." One observer likened the informal team spirit that arose to that of bomber crews in movies about World War II (emergent sentiments). For Federal Express, the emergence of informal groups led to emergent behaviors, interactions, and sentiments that supplemented those required and were a major factor in the survival of the company.[10] In the Federal Express situation, fortunately, the informal groups were largely supportive of company goals. Depending on their nature, informal groups may have positive, minimal, or negative effects on the achievement of organizational goals.

Not surprisingly, most organizations have many formal and informal groups. While formal groups generally spawn informal ones, sometimes the process works in reverse. Informal groups can lead to formal ones, as occurred when Rod Canion, Bill Murton, and Jim Harris, all of whom were working at Texas Instruments at the time, teamed up to form Compaq.[11]

How Work Groups Operate

A number of major factors affect the way that groups operate and their ultimate effectiveness. One useful approach to analyzing these various factors is to think of groups as systems that use inputs, engage in various processes or transformations, and produce outcomes (see Chapter 2 for a further explanation of the systems approach to analyzing organizations). Figure 16-5 shows a number of

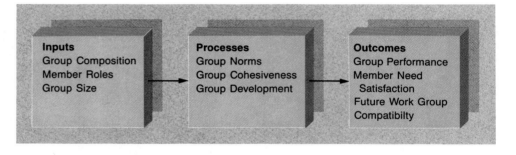

Figure 16-5 A general model of work group behavior.

general factors that are important in understanding the interactions and outcomes of groups. These factors are organized under the input, process, and outcome categories.

Before we investigate the work group inputs and processes that ultimately lead to work group outcomes, we need to consider the importance of potential outcomes. What outcomes should we look for when assessing the extent to which a work group is effective? Several criteria are likely to be involved.[12]

For one thing, performance is likely to be important. Good performance entails meeting the quality, quantity, and timeliness expectations of those who receive, review, or use a group's output. In some situations, evaluations of the quality and quantity of performance may include assessments of innovations made by the group, particularly if innovation is part of the group's explicit mission. Another criterion might be the satisfaction of group members' needs, including growth and development. Satisfying the various needs of individuals can be a powerful motivating force (see Chapter 13, on motivation).

Still another criterion is the degree to which the experience will enable group members to work together productively in the future. Sometimes, group members develop mutual antagonisms that make it difficult for them to function as a group, thus potentially limiting future group operations. On the other hand, interaction can enhance the capabilities of groups to operate as high-performing units, thus increasing their value to the organization.

In the next two sections, we consider the input and process categories that ultimately affect major group outcomes. We concentrate on factors within the groups themselves, recognizing that there are many factors in the context within which groups operate that also influence them, such as organizational culture, human resources policies, and outside competition.

WORK GROUP INPUTS

In order for groups to operate, they must have certain basic inputs. Some of the major inputs that affect groups are the composition of the group, the roles that members play, and the size of the group. In this section, we explore each of these major inputs.

Work Group Composition

The composition of a work group has a major bearing on a group's ultimate success. Two compositional factors that are particularly important are the characteristics of members and the reasons that members are attracted to a particular group.

Member Characteristics. Group expert J. Richard Hackman argues that managers need to consider three major issues when selecting members for work groups.[13] For one thing, individual group members need to have task-relevant expertise.[14] While this may seem fairly straightforward, it sometimes happens that for convenience or political reasons individuals other than those with the necessary expertise are placed in a work group. Another compositional consideration is that group members need to have appropriate interpersonal skills. The greater the need for coordination among members, the more important such skills become. Finally, for tasks that involve at least some challenge, a moderate degree of diversity in the makeup of a group is useful. If a group is too homogeneous, members may get along well but lack enough differing perspectives to generate new ideas. On the other hand, if a group is too heterogeneous, the advantages of the breadth of talent may be lost because the group may have difficulty coordinating the diverse efforts.[15] At W. L. Gore & Associates, managers pay little attention to the location of people on the organization chart when they put together task forces; instead, it is the contribution particular skills can make that counts. The company is best known for Gore-Tex, a breathable but waterproof fabric used in sportswear, and for Gore-Tex artificial blood vessels, which have been implanted inside more than half a million people.[16]

Attraction to the Group. Another issue to consider in composing a group is potential members' attraction to the group. While employees are not always able to choose the groups in which they work, there often is some discretion, particularly for certain types of task groups, such as task forces and committees.

Why do individuals join or agree to participate in groups?[17] Some may be attracted to or like other members of a group. Others may enjoy the activities of a group—perhaps a committee is exploring new ideas in a technical area of interest. Still others may value the goals or purposes of a group. For example, Michael J. Daly left a $45,000 accounting job with Manufacturers Hanover Bank to join the Peace Corps in the Dominican Republic for $200 per month plus room and board. Daly took on the job of teaching peasant-owned financial cooperatives how to operate at a profit and compete with local banks.[18] Yet another reason that people join groups is that groups help meet individual needs for affiliation. McClelland's acquired needs theory of motivation, for example, posits that such needs may be higher in some individuals than others but that we are all likely to have at least some need for affiliation (see Chapter 13). Finally, individuals may join a group because the group can be instrumental in achieving a goal outside the group (e.g., joining a fraternity to facilitate meeting members of sororities or vice versa). Individuals may join groups for any or all of these reasons.

Given the many potential reasons for joining groups, managers often may be able to enhance the attractiveness of particular work groups. For example, they may be able to place individuals who like working together on the same project, make assignments interesting and challenging so that group activities are appealing, clarify group goals while choosing individuals who are likely to support them, and let group members know about ways that group membership may be instrumental to other desirable outcomes.

Member Roles

Why are we likely to expect that the designated chair of a committee will call the meeting to order, a group member from the finance department will provide relevant financial expertise, and the designated secretary will take notes? One

Role   A set of behaviors expected of an individual who occupies a particular position in a group

reason is that each of these individuals is fulfilling a **role,** a set of behaviors expected of an individual who occupies a particular position in a group. When operating in a work group, individuals typically fulfill several roles. For example, a person may be operating in the role of an expert in a given area, a representative of a particular command group, and a member of the work force interested in the implications of the matter under discussion.

In addition, the fact that an individual is a member of a group brings with it other potential roles. Some expectations are set initially, particularly if supervisors are in charge or leaders have been named. Others develop as the group operates and members take on various roles that differentiate them from others in the group. Common member roles in groups fit into three categories: group task roles focus on getting the task done, group maintenance roles address maintaining good relationships among group members, and individual roles serve individual needs rather than those of the group.[19]

Group task roles   Roles that help a group develop and accomplish its goals

Group task roles help a group develop and accomplish its goals and include the following:

■ *Initiator-contributor:* Proposes goals, suggests ways of approaching tasks, and recommends procedures for approaching a problem or task
■ *Information seeker:* Asks for information, viewpoints, and suggestions about the problem or task
■ *Information giver:* Offers information, viewpoints, and suggestions about the problem or task
■ *Coordinator:* Clarifies and synthesizes various ideas in an effort to tie together the work of the members
■ *Orienter:* Summarizes, points to departures from goals, and raises questions about discussion direction
■ *Energizer:* Stimulates the group to higher levels of work and better quality

Group maintenance roles   Roles that do not directly address a task itself but, instead, help foster group unity, positive interpersonal relations among group members, and development of the ability of members to work effectively together

Group maintenance roles do not directly address a task itself but, instead, help foster group unity, positive interpersonal relations among group members, and development of the ability of members to work effectively together. Group maintenance roles include the following:

■ *Encourager:* Expresses warmth and friendliness toward group members, encourages them, and acknowledges their contributions
■ *Harmonizer:* Mediates disagreements between other members and attempts to help reconcile differences
■ *Gatekeeper:* Tries to keep lines of communication open and promotes the participation of all group members
■ *Standard setter:* Suggests standards for the way in which the group will operate and checks whether members are satisfied with the functioning of the group
■ *Group observer:* Watches the internal operations of the group and provides feedback about how participants are doing and how they might be able to function better
■ *Follower:* Goes along with the group and is friendly, but relatively passive

Self-oriented roles   Roles that are related to the personal needs of group members and often negatively influence the effectiveness of a group

Self-oriented roles are related to the personal needs of group members and often negatively influence the effectiveness of a group. These roles include:

■ *Aggressor:* Deflates the contributions of others by attacking their ideas, ridiculing their feelings, and displaying excessive competitiveness

- *Blocker:* Tends to be negative, stubborn, and resistive of new ideas, sometimes in order to force the group to readdress a viewpoint that they have already dealt with
- *Recognition seeker:* Seeks attention, boasts about accomplishments and capabilities, and works to prevent being placed in an inferior position in the group
- *Dominator:* Tries to assert control and manipulates the group or certain group members through such methods as flattery, giving orders, or interrupting others

To accomplish their goals and also develop the capacity to work effectively, groups need to have members who take on the various group task roles and group maintenance roles. Otherwise, groups will have difficulty functioning. If it should happen that members of a group tend mainly toward task roles, the group may have trouble reaching goals because relationships among group members are likely to deteriorate. Conversely, if group members lean mainly toward maintenance roles, members may get along very well but may become stymied in terms of completing tasks. The more that members tend toward self-oriented roles, the more that task and maintenance roles are needed to counteract the negative impact of the self-orientation.[20]

Group leaders often assume many of the task roles. In leaderless groups (those with no appointed leader), the individuals who are most likely to emerge as leaders (be perceived by others as leaders) are active participants who adopt task roles.[21] When groups have formal appointed leaders, such leaders also often take on many of the task roles. In addition, group leaders may use some maintenance roles to facilitate group progress. Often, however, it is difficult for a leader to engage in all the necessary task and maintenance behaviors without some help from others in the group.

Even when a group has a formally designated leader, one or more informal leaders may develop. An **informal leader** is an individual, other than the formal leader, who emerges from a group, has major influence, and is perceived by group members as a leader. Although some individuals in a group may attempt to exercise informal leadership regardless of the behavior of the formal leader, the emergence of informal leaders in groups with formal leaders is most likely to occur when the formal leaders have difficulty facilitating group progress.[22] In addition to roles, another important group input factor is group size.

Informal leader An individual, other than the formal leader, who emerges from a group, has major influence, and is perceived by group members as a leader

Group Size

Research on small groups provides some interesting insights into the effects of group size. One thrust has considered how different numbers of members affect interactions, while another has investigated how group size affects performance.[23]

Size and Group Interactions. The number of individuals in a group influences how the members interact. With two-person groups, or dyads, there are no other members to help resolve differences. Yet, if one leaves the group, the task may not be able to be completed. As a result, dyads often follow one of two patterns. Either the pair is extremely polite and attempts to avoid disagreements or the two disagree frequently, causing relations to be somewhat strained. Adding a third person often does not resolve the interaction difficulties because there is a tendency for the group to split into a "two against one" situation. Groups with four or six members are susceptible to deadlocks because the groups can easily split into factions of equal size.

On the other hand, midsize groups of five—or possibly seven—members have a number of advantages, at least in situations that involve making decisions or completing tasks that require a number of interactions. One advantage is that deadlocks cannot occur, because of the odd number of members. The groups are also large enough to generate a number of different ideas but small enough to allow various members to participate fully in the group.

As groups grow beyond seven—and even more so beyond eleven or twelve—it becomes more difficult for all members to participate actively. As a result, the interaction tends to become more centralized, with a few individuals taking more active roles relative to the rest; disagreements may occur more easily; and group satisfaction may decline unless group members put a good deal of effort into group maintenance roles. Sometimes, because of the way in which the work must be done or the number of viewpoints that must be included, large-size groups are necessary. However, interactions in large groups are fairly lengthy when complex issues are involved.[24] In an effort to be responsive to competitive pressures, Procter & Gamble recently revamped its highest-ranking group, the administrative committee. Traditionally, the 40-member committee met every Tuesday at 10 a.m. to approve all significant promotions and spending plans. In its place, a 20-member executive committee will meet weekly to review only extremely important issues, pushing other decisions down to lower levels in the organization for handling. The change was made because the difficulty of engaging in meaningful dialogue in such a large group bogged down the whole decision-making process.[25]

Size and Performance. What impact does size have on group performance? This is not an easy question to answer because the effects of size depend to some degree on the nature of the task. For example, the effects might be different in a group whose members work somewhat independently (such as waiters in a restaurant) than one in which they must coordinate their efforts closely (such as a rescue team). Generally, though, the impact of size on group performance is shaped like an inverted "U" (see Figure 16-6).[26] Thus, as managers initially add workers to a group, performance goes up; but after a certain point, the added impact of more workers begins to level off and may even go down.

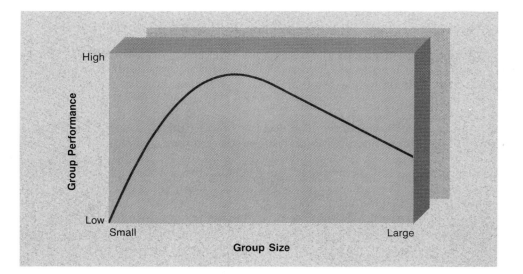

Figure 16-6   Effects of group size on performance.

Why does performance stop rising and even possibly decline as group size increases? One reason is **social loafing,** the tendency of individuals to expend less effort when working in groups than when working alone.[27] The notion of social loafing is illustrated by a simple, but interesting, experiment that involved having different numbers of individuals pull on a rope attached to a device that measures the amount of pulling force. While one person tended to exert 63 kilograms of force and two persons exerted 118 kilograms of force, eight persons exerted only 248 kilograms of force (31 kilograms per person). Thus at least some of the individuals exerted less effort as the group grew larger.[28] The effects can snowball if others detect the social loafing and consequently reduce their own efforts.[29] The reasons behind social loafing are still under investigation, but individual "selfish" interests appear to play a part, as some individuals recognize that they may be able to expend less effort and still reap the group benefits. Another factor may be the difficulty of assessing the adequacy of one's own performance in group situations that lack feedback.[30] Individuals who engage in social loafing in a group often are called **free riders** because they benefit from the work of the group without bearing their proportional share of the costs involved.[31] As a result, social loafing is sometimes called *free riding.*

Managers can take several steps to reduce the likelihood of social loafing. Assigning just enough people to do the work is one prime step. Others are having each group member do different tasks, making each individual's work visible in some way, providing for individual feedback, and making rewards contingent on individual, as well as group, performance. Finally, since social loafing is less likely to occur when the group is committed to the task, it may be possible to design interesting, challenging tasks or select group members who are likely to be committed to particular tasks.[32]

Besides social loafing, another factor that affects productivity as group size grows is the increase in the amount of coordination required.[33] The coordination issue is closely related to the matter of group process, the topic that we take up next.

WORK GROUP PROCESSES

Why do some groups seem to accomplish very little, while others with similar inputs achieve a great deal? Part of the reason stems from *group processes,* the dynamic, inner workings of groups as they operate over a period of time. As members of a group go about their work, some of their energy must be allocated to developing and operating the group itself. This energy is, in essence, diverted from the task and, therefore, is sometimes called process loss because it represents a loss of energy that could have been devoted to the task.[34] Some process loss is inevitable, given the interdependence that is characteristic of groups.

On the other hand, there are possibilities of tremendous gains from the combined force, or synergy, of group members.[35] **Positive synergy** occurs when the combined gains from group interaction (as opposed to individuals operating alone) are greater than group process losses. When there is positive synergy, the whole (the total effect of the group) is greater than the sum of its parts (what the members could accomplish individually). For instance, Procter & Gamble's premium diaper, Luvs Deluxe, made it to market in half the usual 18 months because of a multidisciplinary team that cut through departmental barriers.[36] **Negative synergy** occurs when group process losses are greater than any gains achieved from combining the forces of group members. If you have ever enlisted the help of a group that proved to be so ineffective that you felt you could have

Social loafing The tendency of individuals to expend less effort when working in groups than when working alone

Free riders Individuals who engage in social loafing, thus benefiting from the work of the group without bearing their proportional share of the costs involved

Positive synergy The force that results when the combined gains from group interaction are greater than group process losses

Negative synergy The force that results when group process losses are greater than any gains achieved from combining the forces of group members

done the job faster yourself, then you have witnessed negative synergy. Scientific Computer Systems, founded to develop a machine that could run the software for high-speed Cray computers more slowly, but also more cheaply, experienced the difficulties of negative synergy. Development of the new machine ran into severe problems when the company had its software specialists work out of Wilsonville, Oregon, and its hardware experts operate in San Diego. The coordination difficulties, aggravated by the geographic separation, slowed completion by many months and greatly increased costs.[37] We next discuss three of the major group process factors that affect group synergy and effectiveness: norms, cohesiveness, and group development.

Group Norms

Norms Expected behaviors sanctioned by a group that regulate and foster uniformity in member behaviors

Norms are expected behaviors sanctioned by a group that regulate and foster uniformity in member behaviors.[38] Therefore, for a behavior to fit into the norm category, there must be some recognition among group members that the behavior is generally expected for membership in the group.

Work groups do not attempt to regulate all behavior through norms. Instead, they attempt to develop and enforce norms that are related mainly to certain central issues.[39] One such issue involves production processes. For example, groups typically develop norms regarding standards of quality and quantity, as well as how to get the job done. Informal social arrangements form another common central issue about which norms are apt to arise. That is, groups often establish norms regarding when and where to have lunch; what type of social function, if any, to have when someone leaves; and how much socializing to do both at and outside of work. Finally, work groups frequently have norms about the allocation of resources, including materials, equipment, the assigned work area (e.g., near a window), and pay.

Recent research indicates that norms typically develop through one of the following four mechanisms: explicit statements, critical events, primacy, and carryover behaviors.[40]

Explicit Statements. *Explicit statements* made by supervisors and coworkers can provide important information about the expectations of various group members. Such statements provide a particularly good opportunity for the supervisor to influence the norms of the group. Supervisory statements may be especially important when a new group is formed or when a new person is added to a group. Recognizing the potential power of explicit statements, Thomas Tyrrell, CEO of 5-year-old American Steel & Wire in Cuyahoga Heights, Ohio, has every new employee come to his office for a get-acquainted chat. He also visits each of the company's three plants for 1 day every month to let workers know how business is going and what they can do to cut costs.[41]

Critical Events. In any group, there can be *critical events* in the group's history that set precedents for the future. Tyrrell's efforts at American Steel & Wire are aided by the fact that the company's three plants were acquired from USX, including the Cuyahoga works that had been shut down for 2 years because of a labor dispute. The difficult competitive position of the plants and the past labor disputes have encouraged cooperation among employees within the plant.

Primacy. *Primacy* as a source of norms stems from the tendency for the first behavior pattern that emerges in a group to establish group expectations from

Tom Tyrrell, CEO of American Steel & Wire, uses explicit statements to make it clear what he expects of his workers. He holds private get-acquainted meetings with each new employee, and he pays monthly visits to his plants where he meets with the workers in small groups to discuss company goals and progress. His intention is to build "a new culture" that keeps the employees motivated and involved in the company.

that point on. In order to get new workers to take responsibility for their actions, Tyrrell insists that all new hires invest at least $100 cash in company stock on their first day of work, despite the fact that many are steelworkers who have been unemployed for a significant period of time. He wants the new workers to develop a norm of concern for the welfare of the company right from the start. The plants shut down for the annual stockholders' meeting, and the company also has a profit-sharing plan.

Carryover Behaviors. Many norms are *carryover behaviors* from other groups and perhaps other organizations. When group members have shared similar experiences in the past (such as working on similar committees in the company), the establishment of norms progresses quickly. Otherwise, norms may evolve more slowly.[42] Tyrrell wants to encourage more worker involvement in figuring out ways to cut costs and improve operations, but he finds that it is difficult to break down the old norms and taboos that discourage workers from speaking out when they feel that something should be changed.

Group Cohesiveness

Another factor related to group process is **group cohesiveness,** the degree to which members are attracted to a group, are motivated to remain in the group, and are mutually influenced by one another. We take a look at some of the consequences of group cohesiveness before exploring more specifically its determinants.[43]

Group cohesiveness The degree to which members are attracted to a group, are motivated to remain in the group, and are mutually influenced by one another

Consequences of Group Cohesiveness. The degree of cohesiveness in a group can have important positive consequences for communication and job satisfaction. For example, members in groups that are relatively cohesive tend to communicate more frequently and be more sensitive to one another, and they are generally better able to gauge the feelings of other members of the group. Members of highly cohesive groups are apt to feel more satisfied with their jobs than are members of groups that are not very cohesive.[44] For example, Cleveland Track Materials, a maker of rail joints used by railroads to lay and repair track, has achieved success by training workers in several skills so that work groups can react quickly to the varying product specifications of customers. Welding supervisor Willie Smith says, "This is the best job I've ever had. All the guys—black, white—we're like a family. Everyone is important."[45] Although there are some negative possibilities (such as excessive amounts of communication among group members), the communication and job satisfaction consequences of group cohesiveness are generally positive from an organizational point of view.

Group cohesiveness also tends to impact the degree of hostility and aggression that one group exhibits toward another. Whether the impact is an organizational asset or liability depends largely on where the group's energy is directed. For example, cohesiveness may be helpful when it leads to friendly competition among groups that do the same type of work but do not depend upon each other to get the work done. Aggressiveness as a by-product of group cohesiveness can also energize a group to fight outside competition. On the other hand, among groups that depend on one another to reach organizational goals, hostility or aggression usually leads to a lack of cooperation and related dysfunctional consequences, such as missing deadlines, raising costs, and frustrating customers.

Another area in which group cohesiveness has an impact is performance, since performance levels of group members tend to be more *similar* in highly

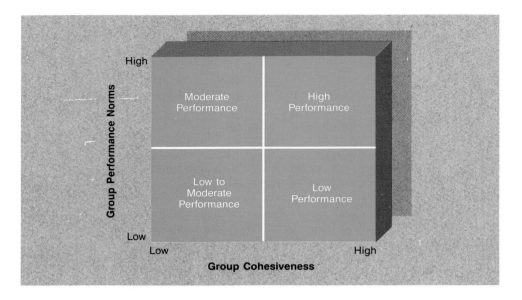

Figure 16-7 Effects of cohesiveness and performance norms on group performance.

cohesive groups. This is because members of highly cohesive groups tend to avoid either letting the group down by underperforming or showing up other group members by performing at a significantly higher level.

The impact of cohesiveness on the actual *level* of performance in a group, however, depends not only on the degree of cohesiveness in a group but also on existing performance norms. This relationship is shown in Figure 16-7. When group cohesiveness is high, group performance tends to be either high or low, depending on performance norms. Groups perform at their *highest* level when group cohesion and performance norms are both high, thus encouraging all group members to perform at the same high level. In contrast, when group cohesion is high but performance norms are low, group performance tends to be at its *lowest* level.[46] Here, the high group cohesion bolsters adherence to the low performance norms. For example, former M.B.A. student Glen Huston tells of his summer-job experience in a highly cohesive lawn-care crew with low performance norms. As he was diligently raking grass clippings on his first day of work, members of the crew, and even the crew leader, told him to slow down because they would all get tired if they worked at that pace. Then the crew leader explained how to use a handkerchief to mop one's brow while leaning on one's rake so that it would appear that one had been working strenuously and had just stopped to wipe off the resulting perspiration. The handkerchief routine was for use if one got caught standing around when the supervisor drove up on periodic checks of the various work crews.

On the other hand, when group cohesiveness itself is low, performance levels tend to be more mixed regardless of performance norms. The reason is that there tends to be more variability in performance levels when group cohesiveness is low. Therefore, even when performance norms are high, it is likely that not everyone will adhere closely to the high norms and, thus, that moderate group performance will result. Similarly, mixed adherence to low performance norms results in low to moderate group performance.

Group cohesiveness can also affect a group's willingness to innovate and change. Changes will be more difficult to implement when they are opposed by a highly cohesive group, but they can be greatly facilitated when they have the strong backing of such a group.

Overall, group cohesiveness can be an extremely positive organizational force when it helps unite a group behind organizational goals. On the other hand, it can sometimes be a negative factor when it impedes productivity and causes opposition to needed changes.

Determinants of Group Cohesiveness. A number of factors have a positive effect on group cohesiveness. For example, similar attitudes and values make it easier for individuals to communicate, find common ground, and develop mutual understandings. External threats, such as fierce outside competition or challenges to survival, can provide a compelling reason for a group to pull together into a cohesive unit. Similarly, outstanding successes often create strong positive feelings about group membership and establish linkages among group members. The difficulty encountered in joining a group can build a common bond based on such factors as high standards (college), sacrifice (the Peace Corps), or difficult training (the Green Berets). Finally, group size can be a factor because cohesiveness is much easier to attain when groups are relatively small and becomes much more difficult to achieve and maintain as groups grow larger. At Patagonia, Inc., a mail-order company well known for its expensive, high-performance outdoor clothing, positive norms about quality and innovation, as well as high cohesiveness among employees, have been important factors in the company's success. While the founder spends about half the year traveling the world, employees maintain his vision of producing high-quality, very durable clothing that can be worn during such activities as scaling Kilimanjaro or sailing the Atlantic in a one-person boat. Group cohesion is aided by the fact that employees are encouraged to engage in outdoor activities on company time, as long as their work is done.[47]

Group Development

New groups are constantly being formed in organizations. They may result from the formation of various formal groups, such as new work units, committees, and task forces, or arise as informal interest or friendship groups. Even existing groups often are in a state of flux as current members leave and new members are added. Such comings and goings also affect the inner workings of groups.

A number of researchers argue that groups go through developmental stages that are relatively predictable. Understanding these stages can help managers both participate more effectively in groups and assist groups for which they have managerial responsibility. One of the best-known approaches to analyzing group development, proposed by group researcher Bruce W. Tuckman, holds that there are five major stages: forming, storming, norming, performing, and adjourning (see Figure 16-8).[48] New groups may progress through these phases, but if there are changes in group membership, the development of the group may regress to an earlier stage—at least temporarily.

Stage 1: Forming. In the **forming** stage of group development, group members attempt to assess the ground rules that will apply to a task and to group interaction. At this point, members seek basic information about the task, make a preliminary evaluation of how the group might interact to accomplish it, and begin to test the extent to which their input will be valued. Some members may begin to try out the acceptability of various interpersonal behaviors, such as engaging in small talk, making jokes, being sarcastic, or leaving the meeting to make telephone calls. Often, because of the uncertainty associated with form-

Forming A stage in which group members attempt to assess the ground rules that will apply to a task and to group interaction

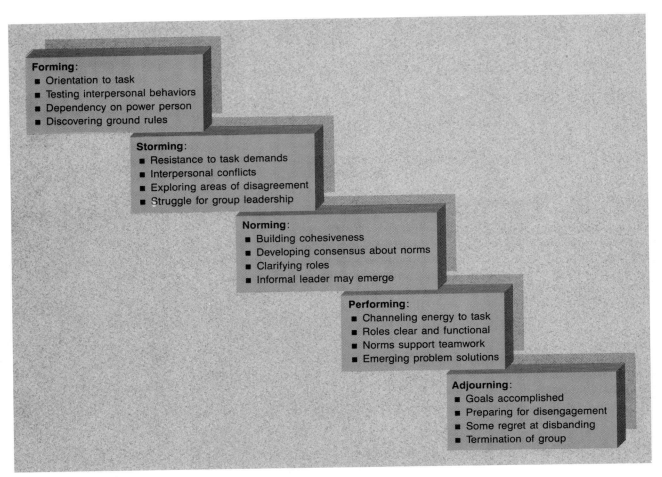

Forming:
- Orientation to task
- Testing interpersonal behaviors
- Dependency on power person
- Discovering ground rules

Storming:
- Resistance to task demands
- Interpersonal conflicts
- Exploring areas of disagreement
- Struggle for group leadership

Norming:
- Building cohesiveness
- Developing consensus about norms
- Clarifying roles
- Informal leader may emerge

Performing:
- Channeling energy to task
- Roles clear and functional
- Norms support teamwork
- Emerging problem solutions

Adjourning:
- Goals accomplished
- Preparing for disengagement
- Some regret at disbanding
- Termination of group

Figure 16-8   Stages of group development.

ing, members may initially accept dependence on a powerful person, if one is present, or on existing norms, if they are commonly known. Because of the need to make some sense of the ground rules, groups at the forming stage often require some time to get acquainted with the task and with each other before attempting to proceed in earnest with task responsibilities.

Storming A stage in which group members frequently experience conflict with one another as they locate and attempt to resolve differences of opinion regarding key issues

Stage 2: Storming. During the **storming** stage, group members frequently experience conflict with one another as they locate and attempt to resolve differences of opinion regarding key issues. The issues in contention might revolve around task requirements and possible resistance to them. Another common area of conflict centers on interpersonal relations—how various group members relate to one another. Often, at this stage, there is a struggle among members for leadership of the group if a leader has not been appointed. Listening to one another and attempting to find mutually acceptable resolutions of major issues are important approaches during this period. Otherwise, the group is not likely to operate effectively; it may not progress beyond this stage, and it may even disband.

Norming A stage in which group members begin to build group cohesion, as well as develop a consensus about norms for performing a task and relating to one another

Stage 3: Norming. With the **norming** stage, group members begin to build group cohesion, as well as develop a consensus about norms for performing a task and relating to one another. The idiosyncrasies of individual members are generally accepted, and members start to identify with the group. Member roles in the group also become clearer, while the group shows a greater willingness to engage in mutual problem solving. If there is no appointed leader or the appointed leader is weak, an informal leader may emerge. At this stage, clarifying norms and roles, building cohesiveness, and attempting to use the resources of the group to solve problems are particularly important.

Stage 4: Performing. Providing that a group reaches this stage of development, the **performing** stage is the period in which energy is channeled toward a task and in which norms support teamwork. Solutions from the problem solving of the previous stage begin to emerge. The roles of various group members become clearer and more functional as the group works to achieve positive synergy and group goals. Groups that reach this stage are likely to be effective as long as they devote their energies to the task and work to maintain good group relationships.

Performing A stage in which energy is channeled toward a task and in which norms support teamwork

Stage 5: Adjourning. During the **adjourning** stage, group members prepare for disengagement as the group nears successful completion of its goals. While members may be pleased with completing their tasks, they also may feel some regret at the imminent disbanding of the group. The adjourning stage applies more frequently to temporary task groups, such as committees, task forces, or teams of limited duration. With ongoing or permanent formal groups, adjournments apply less frequently, although reorganizations and related phenomena such as takeovers and mergers can also bring about the adjourning stage of groups.

Adjourning A stage in which group members prepare for disengagement as the group nears successful completion of its goals

Do All Groups Have These Stages? Recent research suggests that the five stages of group development apply mainly to newly formed, relatively unstructured groups. They are less likely to appear in groups with members who work frequently together or in those with fairly well established operating methods or ground rules.[49]

One major forum for group development is meetings. According to a recent survey, senior executives spend an average of 23 hours per week in meetings, while middle managers attend meetings about 11 hours per week.[50] Many other members of organizations are likely to spend several hours per week in meetings. Meetings are frequently maligned because they often are not run well or do not achieve useful purposes.[51] One way of facilitating group development in meetings is by giving careful attention to how the meetings are conducted. Meetings are more productive when they are well organized and operate with appropriate ground rules. To learn more about running effective meetings, see the Practically Speaking discussion, "How to Lead a Meeting."

PROMOTING INNOVATION: SPECIAL WORK GROUP APPLICATIONS

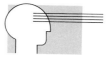

Groups are used in many contexts in which organizations can benefit from the experience and ideas of two or more individuals. Increasingly, they are being tapped when creativity and innovation are important to organizational success. Some of the major mechanisms that organizations use to benefit from groups as resources are task forces and teams. In this section, we explore the nature of task forces, as well as investigate some current special uses of teams.

HOW TO LEAD A MEETING

There are three major phases in leading a meeting: preparation, meeting in progress, and follow-up.[52]

PREPARATION

The preparation stage is a key element in conducting an effective meeting. The following five major steps are involved.

Make sure the meeting is necessary. According to one estimate, it costs about $100 per hour, including overhead, to have a manager attend a meeting. Therefore, a 2-hour meeting attended by 10 managers can quickly add up to $2000. Colleagues will appreciate not being asked to attend meetings for routine matters that could be handled just as well with a memo.

Define the meeting's objectives. An objective might be to involve others in a decision, coordinate important activities, or provide important information that will require a discussion. It is helpful to orient attendees by briefly describing each objective either in the memo announcing the meeting or on the agenda. Be specific when stating objectives. For example, "Decide between using sales reps or an in-house sales force" is much more helpful than "Discuss sales."

Identify participants. Try to limit participation to those who are the decision makers, have needed expertise, and/or are affected by the outcome. As noted earlier, a group of five to seven is an ideal number for group interaction, but sometimes meetings must be larger to involve all the necessary participants. Be careful, though; if the group gets too large, the meeting will be more difficult to handle.

Prepare an agenda. When there is time, circulate the agenda early and obtain feedback to get participants involved. The agenda should be a short list of the main topics to be discussed. It helps key participants focus on what preparations they need to make for the meeting and also assists in ensuring that the important topics are covered. Send the final agenda out 2 or 3 days in advance.

Distribute needed background information. Consider what information participants will need to review in advance, and send it out with the final agenda. Avoid sending out huge reports that participants are unlikely to read. A better strategy is to send a summary and note that the full report is available if needed.

MEETING IN PROGRESS

Good preparation helps the meeting progress more smoothly. Actually running the meeting involves the five main steps discussed below.

Review the agenda. Start on time, and review the agenda and major objectives. The review will help focus participants on why they are there and what outcomes are needed. It often helps to print the agenda on a blackboard or flip chart so that you can refer to it easily to keep the meeting on track.

Get reports from individuals with preassigned tasks. This should be done as early as feasible, although it may be necessary to wait for a particular agenda item to ask for a report or presentation. Getting reports as early as possible will ensure that presenters have adequate time and will provide recognition for their premeeting work. It will also provide some of the necessary background information for various other parts of the agenda.

Encourage participant input. Group effectiveness and member satisfaction are likely to be greater when all the various members are able to provide input in their areas of expertise. A meeting leader should ensure that the meeting is not dominated by one faction or a few members. If someone speaks excessively, the leader might say something like "Well, Joan, let me see if I understand what you are saying." Then, after summarizing, the leader might follow with "Perhaps others have views on this issue." If an individual has said little, the leader might say, "Jim, we haven't heard from you yet. What are your views on this issue?"

Keep the meeting on track. Sticking to the agenda helps keep the meeting on track. If the discussion wanders, refer to a point someone made just before the digression to get the discussion back on track. If an issue is raised that cannot be resolved because of insufficient information, ask someone to check into it and report back.

Summarize and review assignments. Summarize what has been agreed upon or accomplished in the meeting. Also, review what each person has agreed to do and make sure that deadlines are set. In addition, review plans for the next meeting if that is appropriate. End the meeting on time.

FOLLOW-UP

It is important for the meeting leader to follow up on the meeting. The following two major steps are involved.

Send out a memo summarizing the meeting. The memo should summarize the main things that were accomplished, and it should specify the actions that each person agreed to take and the deadlines that were set.

Follow up on assignments where appropriate. This involves checking with the various individuals about their progress, usually in preparation for a subsequent meeting.

Meeting leadership takes some practice. Therefore, it is usually a good idea for individuals to volunteer to chair small, lower-level meetings early in their careers in order to gain some practice.

Task Forces

A **task force** is a temporary task group usually formed to make recommendations on a specific issue (see also Chapter 10).[53] A task force is sometimes called an **ad hoc committee** or a *temporary committee*.[54] Because the issues with which they deal typically involve several parts of the organization, task forces often are composed of individuals from the main command groups affected by a given issue. Individuals from these various groups usually are needed to provide the necessary expertise, to furnish information about the needs of their command groups, and to help develop innovative ideas for solving problems or taking advantage of opportunities. Because they provide a vehicle for interaction among individuals from diverse departments, task forces are particularly well suited to fostering creativity and innovation.

Task force A temporary task group usually formed to make recommendations on a specific issue

Ad hoc committee Another term for a task force

Teams

A **team** is a temporary or ongoing task group whose members are charged with working together to identify problems, form a consensus about what should be done, and implement necessary actions in relation to a particular task or organizational area (see also Chapter 10). Two major characteristics distinguish a team from a task force: Team members typically identify problems in a given area (rather than deal with them after they have been identified by others), and they not only reach a consensus about what should be done but actually implement the decisions as a team (rather than make recommendations that are then implemented by others). Of course, team members (unless they are top-level managers) usually keep their superiors informed, as necessary, and are likely to need their superiors' concurrence on decisions that have major implications for others and the organization.

Team A temporary or ongoing task group whose members are charged with working together to identify problems, form a consensus about what should be done, and implement necessary actions in relation to a particular task or organizational area

Teams are often, but not always, task groups made up of individuals who cross command groups. Temporary teams handle a specific project to completion, whereas permanent teams have ongoing responsibilities in a given area. Teams sometimes have a fluid membership consisting of individuals who join when their expertise is needed and leave when their work is done. Because of the very visible success of teams in such organizations as Compaq, General Motors, and many Japanese companies, teams are gaining increasing attention, particularly as means of fostering innovation, increasing quality, and facilitating successful implementation of changes.[55] Teams are created for a number of different purposes. Two types of teams that are of particular current importance are entrepreneurial teams and self-managing teams.

Entrepreneurial Teams. An **entrepreneurial team** is a group of individuals with diverse expertise and backgrounds who are brought together to develop and implement innovative ideas aimed at creating new products or services or significantly improving existing ones.[56] Entrepreneurial teams focus on new business either by pioneering completely different types of endeavors or by devising novel products and services that are congruent with existing lines of business. Such teams are usually temporary, since they are typically configured to confront a particular entrepreneurial challenge. For example, an entrepreneurial team at the Ford Motor Company was responsible for the introduction of the very successful Taurus and its companion car, the Mercury Sable (see the following Case in Point discussion).

Entrepreneurial team A group of individuals with diverse expertise and backgrounds who are brought together to develop and implement innovative ideas aimed at creating new products or services or significantly improving existing ones

CASE IN POINT: Team Taurus Scores Big

During the dark recession days of 1980, Ford Motor Company executives found themselves facing not only a slowed economy but also the toughest foreign-car competition that they had ever encountered. "It was painfully obvious that we weren't competitive with the rest of the world in quality," says John A. Manoogian, who was Ford's chief of quality during that period. Company members decided to fight back. Their basic strategy involved using some of their competitors' methods, such as thoroughly studying the competition, making quality a top priority, and changing the organization of the firm's developmental efforts.

One major step was departing from the traditional approach to new car development. Normally, the company followed a sequential 5-year process to launch a new automobile. Product planners would start with a basic concept. Then a design team would develop the look. Their work would then go to engineering for specifications before going on to manufacturing and suppliers for process design. Each step in the sequence would be done with little ongoing communication with the other parties.

This time, the company put an unprecedented $3 billion behind a new group, dubbed Team Taurus. With the team approach, representatives from all the affected units—planning, design, engineering, and manufacturing—worked together. The team had the overall final responsibility of developing the vehicle. With appropriate representatives on the team, issues could be resolved early. For example, manufacturing suggested changes in the design that made it easier to build in quality during manufacturing.

In its developmental effort, the team engaged in "reverse engineering," a practice often used by Japanese companies to study their competitors and learn how parts were assembled as well as designed. For this purpose, the team bought a Honda Accord and a Toyota Corolla; then, says Lewis C. Veraldi, head of Team Taurus, "[we] tore them down layer by layer, looking for things we could copy or make better." Before they were finished, team members had intensely investigated over 50 midsize cars in their search for the best features. They discovered, for example, that the Toyota Supra had the best fuel-gauge accuracy, while honors for the best tire and jack storage belonged to the BMW 528e. Ford says that the Taurus and Sable meet or exceed 80 percent of the 400 identified "best-in-class" features.

Some of the investigative work was done by special subteams. For example, a five-member group had the job of developing comfortable, easy-to-use seats. In the course of their work, the group members took seats from 12 different cars, put them in Crown Victorias, and conducted 100,000 miles of driving tests using a variety of different drivers who indicated what they liked and didn't like.

In a major departure from traditional modes of operation, the team asked assembly-line workers for advice during the design phase and was flooded with helpful ideas. Worker suggestions led to changes such as reducing the parts in a door panel from eight to two for easier handling and ensuring that all the bolts had the same-size head to eliminate the need for different wrenches. "In the past we hired people for their arms and their legs," says Manoogian. "But we weren't smart enough to make use of their brains." In another unusual move, supplier ideas also were tapped during the design stage, and long-term contracts were signed with suppliers so that they had a strong stake in the new car development. "We never had the supplier input we had on this car," says Veraldi. "Now we'll never do it any other way."

The success of the Taurus and Sable has sold Ford on the team idea for new car development. Teams also have been a significant factor in the strong sales of the new Lincoln Continental and Thunderbird automobiles. Still, there is more work to be done. There have been some recalls of the Taurus and Sable, as well as some problems with repair records that have not been as good as originally hoped. While the team approach has been a strong success, there is more work ahead for Ford teams in achieving their goals for high quality.[57] ▬

Self-Managing Teams. A **self-managing team** is a work group given responsibility for a task area without day-to-day supervision and with authority to influence and control both group membership and behavior.[58] Another name for a self-managing team is an **autonomous work group.** One of the most famous examples of an autonomous work group is A. B. Volvo's automobile plant in Kamar, Sweden, where autonomous work teams of about 20 workers are responsible for putting together entire units of cars, such as the electric system or the engine. The cars move about the plant on a separate computer-controlled carrier. Each worker typically performs a series of tasks over several minutes, rather than the single task taking a few seconds that is typical of U.S. automobile assembly lines. In addition, workers on a team are taught several jobs to build in variety and to allow them to cover for sick or vacationing team members. After some initial efforts to fine-tune the system, during the last decade or so, the autonomous work group approach has helped Volvo reduce the labor hours that go into making a car by 40 percent, increase inventory turnover from 9 times per year to 22, and cut the number of defects by 40 percent. The company has recently built a new plant at Uddevalla, where work teams will complete an even greater variety of tasks.[59]

A number of companies in the United States are experimenting with self-managing teams.[60] One of the most prominent examples is the NUMMI project, a joint venture of General Motors and the Toyota Motor Corporation, which builds automobiles in Fremont, California, using a self-managing team approach. At GM's new Saturn plant, work units are teams of 6 to 15 workers, each led by an elected United Auto Workers "counselor" who is a member of the team. Groups of three to six work units are then led by a company "work-unit

Self-managing team A work group given responsibility for a task area without day-to-day supervision and with authority to influence and control both group membership and behavior

Autonomous work group Another name for self-managing team

Workers at the Volvo plant in Kalmar, Sweden, are organized into self-managed teams responsible for assembling entire units of cars. Not only does this approach alleviate the boredom of assembly line production, it also allows each worker to learn a variety of tasks, enabling the team to fill in for absent members. The company benefits, too, because of reduced labor hours per car, increased turnover of inventory, and fewer defects.

adviser.'' Since external leaders of self-managing teams do not exercise day-to-day supervision, their role becomes more oriented toward facilitating the team's self-management through liaison work with company experts in areas such as engineering, marketing, and personnel.[61] Compared with its traditional plants, Digital Equipment Corporation's Enfield, Connecticut, facility with self-managing teams builds products 40 percent faster, uses fewer workers, maintains lower inventories, has double to triple the quality, and generates lower turnover.[62]

NORMATIVE MODEL OF GROUP EFFECTIVENESS

Figure 16-9 Overview of normative model of effectiveness. (Reprinted from J. Richard Hackman, ''The Design of Work Teams,'' in Jay W. Lorsch (ed.), *Handbook of Organizational Behavior*, Prentice-Hall, Englewood Cliffs, N.J., 1987, p. 331.)

Building on the work of a number of researchers who have attempted to describe how groups actually operate, group expert J. Richard Hackman has developed a normative model of work group effectiveness (see Figure 16-9).[63] The normative model differs from descriptive approaches in that it specifies how groups *should* operate. Although it applies to any type of work group, the model is particularly applicable to designing effective work teams. Hackman's model focuses specifi-

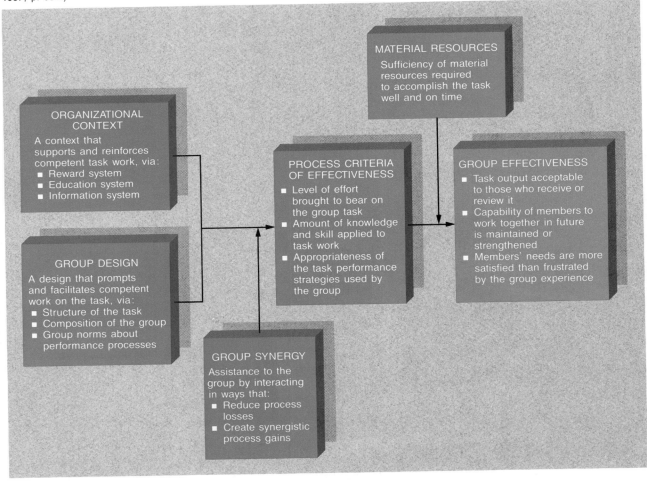

cally on those aspects of work groups that a manager has the best chance to influence in encouraging group effectiveness. The model also is aimed at helping managers diagnose the strengths and weaknesses of groups as performing work units.

Components of the Model

The various main elements in Hackman's model are organizational context, group design, group synergy, process criteria of effectiveness, and material resources. Because the model is normative, we discuss the various elements in terms of the way Hackman's model says that they should be handled.

Organizational Context. For purposes of the model, the organizational context includes factors in the organization that are outside of the group but influence its work. According to the model, three such factors that are especially likely to affect the success of groups are the reward system, the education system, and the information system. To promote group effectiveness, then, organizations should build their reward systems on challenging and specific performance objectives, positive consequences that are tied to performance, and rewards and objectives that focus on group, rather than individual, behavior. The education system, through training and outside consultation for the group, as necessary, can ensure that group members have the appropriate task expertise to do the job. The information system should be used to clarify the parameters of the work situation (such as task requirements and constraints that may affect how the group approaches the task, material resources available, and the standards that will be used by those who will receive, review, or use the group output). The information system should also provide enough data so that the group can assess the likely consequences of alternative strategies. For example, information about inventory costs may be relevant to a group attempting to decide whether it is better to build a backlog of components and then go to final assembly or to divide the work simultaneously between component makers and final assemblers.

Group Design. Group design in the model refers to input factors that managers often have some control over and that influence the effectiveness of the group. Important factors in this category are the structure of the task, the composition of the group, and group norms about performance processes. According to the model, the group task should be one that engages and motivates group members (see Chapter 10 for related material on work design). The composition of the group, discussed earlier in this chapter, should consist of the right number and mix of members who have the skills necessary for group effectiveness. The group norms factor, also discussed earlier in the chapter, suggests that it may be possible for managers to help the group build positive performance norms. Hackman argues that managers should encourage two particular norms. First, groups need to develop norms of self-regulation, whereby the group takes responsibility for the performance of its members. Second, groups need norms that support the idea of analyzing the performance situation and planning the best ways to execute tasks.

Group Synergy. We have already discussed the concepts of positive and negative group synergies in conjunction with group processes. Hackman's model places strong emphasis on efforts to reduce process losses and create synergistic gains. Some of his suggestions include cultivating member skills at working with one another, building a shared commitment through group-building activities (such as encouraging work-team members to develop team names, decorate their work areas, or participate in an athletic activity as a team), and fostering group learning through such approaches as information sharing and cross-training so that members can do a number of different tasks and be somewhat interchangeable. Another important means of attaining positive group synergy is encouraging interactions that foster creativity and innovative approaches to work (see Chapter 8 for ways of enhancing group creativity). For example, managers can encourage groups to develop innovative ways to surmount obstacles, use materials, or perform tasks.

Process Criteria of Effectiveness. In Hackman's model, the process criteria of effectiveness are parameters that help a manager monitor the extent to which the group's task processes are likely to lead to group effectiveness. Three main questions are important: First, is the group expending the effort necessary to achieve high performance in a timely manner? Second, do members have the appropriate expertise, and are they able to apply their knowledge and skills to task performance? Third, has the group developed an appropriate work strategy, and have members been able to implement it in performing tasks? If the answers to these questions are negative, then corrective action is necessary. Hackman argues, though, that managers will not succeed by trying to affect the process criteria directly—for instance, by urging members to put forth more effort or instructing them in performance strategies—since such actions do not address the root causes of the problem (they are essentially only symptoms). Instead, managers need to address the root elements—organizational context, group design, or group synergy—that influence group effectiveness.

Material Resources. Another important contextual element that is included separately is material resources—tools, equipment, space, raw materials, money, or human resources. Its placement in the model reflects the fact that even if the process criteria of effectiveness are positive, performance will suffer if the group does not have adequate materials with which to work.

Using the Model

Managers can use the model to help determine major ingredients necessary for an effective work group. It provides guidelines about the appropriate organizational context and group design for success. The model also highlights the need for a group process that leads to positive synergy. A particularly valuable aspect of the model is its inclusion of the process criteria of effectiveness, which managers can use to make ongoing assessments of the likelihood of group effectiveness. By using the process criteria, managers may be able to take corrective action before there is an outcome problem, such as unacceptable task output, that may be difficult to reverse. Finally, the model points out the importance of monitoring material resources levels, since inadequate materials can ultimately block what otherwise might be very effective group outcomes. The use of groups at Semco S/A, Brazil's largest marine and food-processing machinery manufacturer, shows how the group effectiveness model can work (see the following Case in Point discussion).

CASE IN POINT: Groups Make a Difference at Brazil's Semco

In 1980, when Richard Semler joined the company that his father had founded 27 years before, Semco had about 100 employees, manufactured hydraulic pumps for ships, produced about $4 million in revenues, and tottered on the edge of bankruptcy. For the next 2 years, top managers constantly sought bank loans, fought off continual rumors that the company was about to sink, and traveled four continents seeking the seven license agreements that enabled the company to reduce its cyclical marine business to 60 percent of total sales.

Today, Semco has five factories, which produce a range of sophisticated products, including marine pumps, digital scanners, commercial dishwashers, truck filters, and mixing equipment for a variety of substances that run the gamit from bubble gum to rocket fuel. Customers include Alcoa, Saab, and General Motors. Semco is frequently cited in the press as one of the best companies in Brazil for which to work.

One principal reason for the company's survival and ultimate success was that Semco made a major change in its management approach, shifting toward an emphasis on three fundamental values—democracy, information, and profit sharing. These values ultimately led to reliance on work groups as a primary mechanism for managing the company.

After some experimentation, Semco found that the optimal number for an effective production unit is about 150 people per factory. In one case the company divided a factory of 300 people into two separate groups of 150, which were further subdivided into smaller work teams of about 10 employees each. In the spirit of democracy and worker involvement, work teams were given major responsibility for outcomes associated with their areas. Initially, costs rose because of duplicated effort and lost economies of scale. Within a year, though, sales doubled, inventory dropped from 126 to 46 days, eight new products appeared that had been tied up in R&D for 2 years, and the product rejection rate at inspection dropped from 33 to 1 percent. Increased productivity enabled the company to reduce the work force by 32 percent through attrition and offers of early retirement.

At Semco, once the members of a group agree on a monthly production schedule, they meet it. In one situation, a group determined that it could make 220 meat slicers. As the end of the month approached, everything was completed except for motors that had not yet arrived, despite repeated phone calls to the supplier. Finally, two employees went to the supplier's plant, talked to the supplier, and got delivery on the last day of the month. Then everyone stayed until 4:45 the next morning in order to finish production of the meat slicers on time.

Part of the reason that the system works is that everyone in the company has access to information about all major aspects. Each employee gets a balance sheet, a profit-and-loss analysis, and a cash-flow statement for his or her division each month. All workers voluntarily attend monthly classes so that they can learn to read and understand the numbers. Although top-level managers are strict about meeting the financial targets, workers have wide latitude in deciding the necessary actions and carrying them out. (In one plant, workers hired one of Brazil's best-known artists to paint the inside and outside walls of the facility and the machinery as well.) Another reason for the success is that the workers share in profits. Twice a year, employees receive 23 percent of the after-tax profits for their division. Employees vote on how to disburse the funds; usually,

At Semco S/A, a manufacturer of machinery in Brazil, employees are divided into work groups of about 10 members each. These teams decide on their production goals and cooperate in meeting them. In this system "managing" from above is kept to a minimum. The approach is working: Semco's sales have doubled and productivity has increased since it was implemented.

they are distributed equally. Semco doesn't bother to advertise job openings because word of mouth brings up to 300 applications for every open position.[64] ▬▬▬

MANAGING CONFLICT

Conflict A perceived difference between two or more parties that results in mutual opposition

Of course, the positive results at Semco do not occur without some conflict. In organizations, conflicts within and between groups are common. By **conflict** we mean a perceived difference between two or more parties that results in mutual opposition.[65]

While conflict often is considered to be a negative factor, it potentially can have constructive, as well as destructive, consequences. Some of the destructive prospects are well known. For example, conflict can cause individuals or groups to become hostile, withhold information and resources, and interfere with each other's efforts. It can delay projects, drive up costs, and cause valued employees to leave. On the other hand, conflict can yield a number of constructive consequences. For one thing, conflict highlights problems and the need for solutions. For another, it promotes change as parties work to resolve problems. Conflict also can enhance morale and cohesion, as group members deal with areas of concern and frustration. Finally, conflict can stimulate interest, creativity, and innovation by encouraging new ideas.[66]

As a result, some conflict in an organization is important, but too much can have a detrimental effect on organizational performance (see Figure 16-10). Conflict levels that are very low may indicate that problems are being hidden and new ideas stifled. For instance, a major factor in the famous failed Edsel project of the Ford Motor Company was the fact that subordinates withheld information because conflict was discouraged and because they felt that managers were already committed to the project.[67] In contrast, too much conflict may indicate that excessive amounts of energy are aimed at dissension and opposition. Accordingly, managers need to understand the causes of conflict, know how to reduce or resolve conflict, and also be able to stimulate it in a positive way when appropriate.

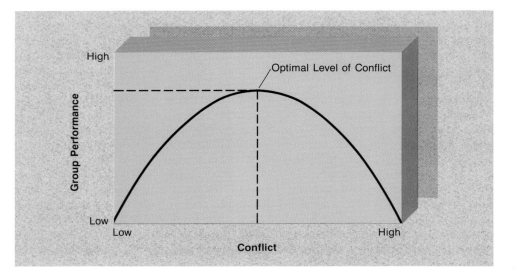

Figure 16-10 Effects of conflict on group performance.

Causes of Conflict

A number of factors contribute to conflict.[68] Several of the most important causes are discussed below.

Task Interdependence. Two types of task interdependence are particularly prone to conflict. One is sequential interdependence, in which one individual or work unit is heavily dependent on another. For example, waiters generally are more reliant on cooks than the reverse because waiters must depend on cooks to furnish good meals in a timely manner. Line and staff conflicts often arise because staff members frequently are dependent upon the line to implement their ideas. The second form of task interdependence is reciprocal interdependence, in which individuals or work units are mutually interdependent. For instance, purchasing agents want engineers to provide detailed generic specifications so that they can negotiate lower costs from suppliers. At the same time, engineers need to obtain materials of the proper quality on a timely basis, so they may find it more convenient to specify a brand name.[69]

Scarce Resources. Possibilities for conflict expand when there are limited resources, such as office space, equipment, training, human resources, operating funds, and pay allocations.[70]

Goal Incompatibility. Out of necessity, organization members frequently pursue goals that are somewhat different from one another, setting the stage for potential conflicts. For example, sales personnel may find it easier to battle the competition by promising very quick deliveries, while people in manufacturing may find that small production runs on short notice interfere with their cost-cutting efforts.

Communication Failures. Breakdowns in communication due to distortions or lack of communication often lead to conflicts. See Chapter 15 for a more thorough discussion of communication in organizations.

Individual Differences. Differences in personality, experience, and values make frequent conflicts likely. For example, conflicts with Robert A. Schoellhorn, chairman of Abbott Laboratories, led three potential successors to leave the company and caused concern among board members about who would succeed to the chairman's position. Critics say Schoellhorn is intolerant of dissent and undermines executives who build power of their own.[71]

Poorly Designed Reward Systems. Reward systems can unwittingly lead to destructive conflict when they reward competition in situations that require cooperation for success.[72] For instance, Solar Press, Inc., based in Napier, Illinois, found that a bonus system that rewarded team production undermined cooperation in a situation that entailed sequential dependence among teams. So far, a bonus system tied to company results seems to be an improvement.[73]

Reducing and Resolving Conflict

Managers can use a number of different approaches to reduce or resolve conflict.[74] Such efforts are typically aimed at minimizing the destructive impact of conflict.

Changing Situational Factors. One obvious way to reduce conflict is to change the factors in the situation that are causing the conflict. For example, a manager might increase the resources available, reorganize to reduce interdependence, redesign reward systems (as Solar Press did), or take steps to improve communication systems. Unfortunately, these solutions may not always be feasible or may be extremely expensive.

Appeal to Superordinate Goals. If the situations causing excessive conflict are difficult to change, managers sometimes are able to refocus the individuals or groups on **superordinate goals,** major common goals that require the support and effort of all parties. Examples are ensuring the survival of the organization and beating highly visible competition. The success of appeals to superordinate goals depends heavily on identifying goals that are sufficiently important to both parties. For instance, word of a serious defect in factory floor sweepers shipped to Japan and Toyota's announcement of a competing product in 1979 coalesced the various elements of the Tennant Company in a lifesaving push for quality. Today, the Minneapolis-based company has approximately 60 percent of the North American market and 40 percent of the world market for floor maintenance equipment, such as sweepers and scrubbers.[75]

Use an Interpersonal Conflict-Handling Mode. Aside from attempting to reduce conflict by changing the situation or encouraging the parties to pursue superordinate goals despite the situation, managers have five major interpersonal modes that they can use to attempt to resolve conflicts in which they are involved.[76]

■ **Avoidance** involves ignoring or suppressing a conflict in the hope that it will either go away or not become too disruptive.
■ **Accommodation** focuses on solving conflicts by allowing the desires of the other party to prevail. Essentially, the manager voluntarily lets the other party have his or her way rather than continue the conflict.
■ **Competition** involves attempting to win a conflict at the other party's expense. In other words, one party wins and the other loses.
■ **Compromise** aims to solve conflict issues by having each party give up some desired outcomes in order to get other desired outcomes. Compromise often involves bargaining by the conflicting parties and generally requires a situation that offers both parties the chance to be in a better position or at least in no worse position after the conflict is resolved. With compromise each person wins some major issues and loses others.
■ **Collaboration** strives to resolve conflicts by devising solutions that allow both parties to achieve their desired outcomes. In other words, the solution is such that both parties win at least their major issues. Collaboration frequently involves considerable creativity in developing solutions that suit the needs of both parties in the conflict.

Although collaboration is often an advantageous way to handle conflict because both sides are likely to be satisfied, there frequently are reasons to use the other approaches as well. Table 16-1 summarizes situations in which each of the conflict-handling modes might apply, as reported by 28 chief executives.

Stimulating Conflict

Since too little conflict can lead to apathy, lethargy, and low performance, at times managers also need to be able to stimulate conflict. Obviously, conflict

---

Superordinate goals Major common goals that require the support and effort of all parties

Avoidance A conflict-handling mode that involves ignoring or suppressing a conflict in the hope that it will either go away or not become too disruptive

Accommodation A conflict-handling mode that focuses on solving conflicts by allowing the desires of the other party to prevail

Competition A conflict-handling mode that involves attempting to win a conflict at the other party's expense

Compromise A conflict-handling mode that aims to solve conflict issues by having each party give up some desired outcomes in order to get other desired outcomes

Collaboration A conflict-handling mode that strives to resolve conflicts by devising solutions that allow both parties to achieve their desired outcomes

Table 16-1   Situations in Which to Use the Five Conflict-Handling Modes, as Reported by Chief Executives

Conflict Mode / Situation	Conflict Mode / Situation
COMPETING 1. When quick, decisive action is vital—e.g., emergencies 2. On important issues where unpopular actions need implementing—e.g., cost cutting, enforcing unpopular rules, discipline 3. On issues vital to company welfare when you know you're right 4. Against people who take advantage of noncompetitive behavior **COLLABORATING** 1. To find an integrative solution when both sets of concerns are too important to be compromised 2. When your objective is to learn 3. To merge insights from people with different perspectives 4. To gain commitment by incorporating concerns into a consensus 5. To work through feelings which have interfered with a relationship **COMPROMISING** 1. When goals are important, but not worth the effort or potential disruption of more assertive modes 2. When opponents with equal power are committed to mutually exclusive goals 3. To achieve temporary settlements to complex issues 4. To arrive at expedient solutions under time pressure 5. As a backup when collaboration or competition is unsuccessful	**AVOIDING** 1. When an issue is trivial, or more important issues are pressing 2. When you perceive no chance of satisfying your concerns 3. When potential disruption outweighs the benefits of resolution 4. To let people cool down and regain perspective 5. When gathering information supersedes immediate decision 6. When others can resolve the conflict more effectively 7. When issues seem tangential or symptomatic of other issues **ACCOMMODATING** 1. When you find you are wrong—to allow a better position to be heard, to learn, and to show your reasonableness 2. When issues are more important to others than yourself—to satisfy others and maintain cooperation 3. To build social credits for later issues 4. To minimize loss when you are outmatched and losing 5. When harmony and stability are especially important 6. To allow subordinates to develop by learning from mistakes

Source: Reprinted from Kenneth W. Thomas, "Toward Multi-Dimensional Values in Teaching: The Example of Conflict Behaviors," *Academy of Management Review,* vol. 2, 1977, p. 487.

stimulation needs to be initiated in as positive a way as possible—and with caution, to prevent the amount of conflict from reaching a destructive stage that outweighs its advantages. There are several prime means of increasing constructive conflict.[77] Adding individuals with more diverse backgrounds to a group is one means. Another is communicating information that will cause organization members to engage in constructive dialogue about the potential need for change. For example, at Textronix, once a major competitor in high technology, managers grew comfortable and complacent about their success; as a result, the company began to decline seriously. A new chief executive has replaced a number of managers and now is attempting to work with various organization members to reenter the computer workstation market, in which the company has fallen behind.[78] Still another means is encouraging internal competition.[79] Of course, in stimulating conflict, managers must have mechanisms in place to monitor the situation and maintain control, a subject we consider in the next four chapters, which examine the controlling function.

CHAPTER SUMMARY

Work groups are becoming an increasingly important competitive factor in organizations. There are two major types of work groups, formal and informal. Formal groups include command, or functional, groups and task groups. Informal groups include interest and friendship groups. Required aspects of formal groups lead to the emergent behaviors, interactions, and sentiments associated with informal groups.

A useful way to analyze groups is to view them as systems that use inputs, engage in various processes or transformations, and produce outcomes. Important group inputs are group composition, particularly member characteristics and reasons for attraction to the group; member roles, including group task roles, group maintenance roles, and individual roles; and group size.

Hopefully, work group processes result in positive synergy. Important factors influencing group processes are group norms, group cohesiveness, and group development. Group norms stem from explicit statements by supervisors and coworkers, critical events in a group's history, primacy, and carryover behaviors. A number of factors contribute to group cohesiveness, which in turn has important consequences for group communication, satisfaction, performance, hostility and aggression toward other groups, and a group's willingness to innovate and change. New groups typically go through five stages of development: forming, storming, norming, performing, and adjourning. Because of the widespread presence of groups, managers spend a considerable amount of their time in meetings. Therefore, it is important for managers to know how to lead a meeting effectively. Important outcomes to consider in evaluating the effectiveness of groups are group performance, member need satisfaction, and future work group compatibility.

Some of the major mechanisms that organizations use to tap the creativity and innovative capacity of groups include task forces, or ad hoc committees, and teams, particularly entrepreneurial and self-managing teams.

The normative model of group effectiveness focuses specifically on those aspects of work groups that a manager has the best chance of influencing. It is particularly useful for designing work teams. Major elements of the model include organizational context, group design, group synergy, process criteria of effectiveness, and material resources leading to group effectiveness.

Managing conflict is also an important managerial skill related to groups. Causes of conflict include task interdependence, scarce resources, goal incompatibility, communication failures, individual differences, and poorly designed reward systems. Methods of reducing or resolving conflict include changing situational factors, appealing to superordinate goals, and using interpersonal conflict-handling modes. In addition, managers may need to simulate conflict in order to encourage creativity and innovation.

MANAGERIAL TERMINOLOGY

accommodation (580)
ad hoc committee   (571)
adjourning   (569)
autonomous work group
   (573)
avoidance   (580)
collaboration   (580)
command, or functional,
   group   (553)
competition   (580)
compromise   (580)
conflict   (578)

entrepreneurial team
   (571)
formal group   (552)
forming   (567)
free riders   (563)
friendship group   (555)
group   (552)
group cohesiveness
   (565)
group maintenance roles
   (560)
group task roles   (560)

informal group   (554)
informal leader   (561)
interest group   (554)
linking pin   (553)
negative synergy   (563)
norming   (568)
norms   (564)
performing   (569)
positive synergy   (563)
role   (560)
self-managing team
   (573)

self-oriented roles   (560)
social loafing   (563)
standing committee
   (553)
storming   (568)
superordinate goals
   (581)
task force   (571)
task group   (553)
team   (571)

QUESTIONS FOR DISCUSSION AND REVIEW

1. Outline the major types of work groups. Identify several work groups at your college or university. Classify them according to work group type.
2. Explain how informal groups develop in organiza-

tions. Choose an organization with which you are familiar and identify two informal groups. Trace how the informal groups came about.
3. Using a systems perspective, identify the main fac-

tors that influence the way that groups in organizations operate. Evaluate the effectiveness of a work group with which you are familiar.

4. Explain the basic inputs that groups require to operate. Analyze the basic inputs of a work group that you think runs effectively. What are the member characteristics that help it operate successfully? What attracts the various members to the group? What roles do members play? How does the number of members affect the group interaction?

5. Explain the significance of group norms and group cohesiveness in group functioning. Think of a group to which you belong. What are four important norms in the group. How did they develop? Assess the level of group cohesiveness and its consequences.

6. Explain how groups develop. Trace the group development of a group in which you have participated.

7. Differentiate among task forces and teams. Explain how each can be used to promote innovation. Identify examples of task forces and teams in the business section of your local paper, *The Wall Street Journal,* and/or business magazines, such as *Business Week* and *Fortune.*

8. Explain the components of the normative model of group effectiveness. Use the model to analyze the effectiveness of a group to which you belong. Pay particular attention to the process criteria of effectiveness. What changes might you suggest in organizational context, group design, or group synergy to make the group more effective?

9. Explain the causes of conflict in organizations. Identify an organizational conflict situation of which you are aware and trace the causes.

10. Describe several ways to reduce or resolve conflict and to stimulate conflict. Think of a conflict situation that you have witnessed in a group. What are some ways that you might reduce or resolve the conflict?

DISCUSSION QUESTIONS FOR CHAPTER OPENING CASE

1. What types of groups are evident in the Compaq situation?

2. What group composition factors helped Compaq use teams successfully?

3. If Rod Canion wanted to check on the effectiveness of a team developing a new product line, how would you suggest that he proceed?

MANAGEMENT EXERCISE: LOST AT SEA[80]

The Situation

You are adrift on a private yacht in the South Pacific. As a consequence of a fire of unknown origin, much of the yacht and its contents have been destroyed. Your location is unclear because critical navigation equipment was destroyed and because you and the crew were distracted trying to bring the fire under control. Your best estimate is that you are approximately 1000 miles south-southwest of the nearest land.

The Problem

On the following page is a list of 15 items that are intact and undamaged after the fire. You have, in addition, a serviceable rubber life raft with oars that is large enough to carry yourself, the crew, and all the items listed. The total contents of all the survivors' pockets are a package of cigarettes, several books of matches, and five $1 bills.

Your task is to rank these items in terms of their importance to your survival. Place "1" by the most important item, "2" by the second most important item, and so on, ending with "15" by the least important. Enter the numbers in the column labeled "Individual Ranking."

Your instructor will tell you the number of individuals in the crew. When you have completed the ranking, your instructor will give you further instructions.

	Scoring Sheet					
Items	**Individual Ranking**	**Group Ranking**	**Expert's Ranking**	**Influence**	**Individual Accuracy**	**Group Accuracy**
Sextant						
Shaving mirror						
5-gallon can of water						
Mosquito netting						
One case of U.S. Army C-rations						
Maps of Pacific Ocean						
Seat cushion (flotation device approved by Coast Guard)						
2-gallon can of oil-gas mixture						
Small transistor radio						
Shark repellent						
20 square feet of opaque plastic						
1 quart of 160-proof Puerto Rican rum						
15 feet of nylon rope						
Two boxes of chocolate bars						
Fishing kit						
	Your accuracy score:			Group accuracy score:		

BEN & JERRY'S THRIVES ON COMPANY SPIRIT

Known for its rich ice cream generously laced with tasty tidbits and the black-and-white cow logo, Ben & Jerry's Homemade, Inc., began simply enough as an ice cream parlor in a renovated gas station. When it opened in 1978 in Burlington, Vermont, it was a social experiment. Cofounders Ben Cohen and Jerry Greenfield wanted to demonstrate that their business could operate differently than many—that it could be weird and unconventional, share its prosperity with employees, interact responsibly with the community, and still do well from a business point of view. In fact, they intended to sell the business as soon as it was established and they had proved their point.

But things didn't turn out quite as they planned. Happily, the ice cream was an instant success. Yet there always seemed to be some new factor that forced the company to grow beyond the cofounders' original expectations, such as the need to increase sales just enough to cover the chronic repair bills on the company's ancient ice cream truck. Ben and Jerry soon found that their company was growing rapidly and—to their chagrin—becoming more businesslike. By 1982, they even hired an M.B.A., nicknamed "Chico," as a chief operating officer. With Chico's help, the company reduced costs, increased production, and began making some real money. Chico was eventually promoted to company president.

The magnitude of the business success caused philosophical problems for Ben and Jerry. Jerry even left the company for 3 years. Ben put the company up for sale until another entrepreneur persuaded him to use the profits for social change. At that point, Ben began to consider the company as being held in trust for the community, and, therefore, growth became important. Growth, however, would necessitate building a new factory, so Ben took the company public. The first shares were offered only to residents of Vermont to make the company really part of the community, and the minimum buy price was set relatively low. Now that there were shareholders to be concerned about, further growth was clearly a must. The more the company grew, the greater the attention it began to receive from competitors, particularly from Richard Smith of Steve's Homemade, who threatened to go national with a similar ice cream. To preclude being preempted, Ben & Jerry's suddenly had to enter eight new major markets over a 9-month period. Company sales edged close to $50 million.

As the company grew, though, Ben and Jerry worked hard to foster fun, charity, and goodwill toward coworkers. The company founded The Ben & Jerry's Foundation, Inc., which receives 7.5 percent of the company's pretax income and spends it on various social causes. Ben & Jerry's has a 5-to-1 salary ratio, whereby the highest salaries paid cannot equal more than five times the lowest. Even Ben and Jerry have salaries that abide by the ratio. This provision has meant that some upper-level managers from other companies had to take pay cuts when they came to work for Ben & Jerry's. It has also sometimes

Ben Cohen (right) and Jerry Greenfield started their ice cream company, Ben & Jerry's, with a dream—a caring, sharing, socially responsible company—only to find that as the company grew it had to become more "businesslike." Yet the company has managed to keep its socially conscious orientation through such means as giving Tuskegee Institute part of the revenues from Tuskegee Chunk, a peanut butter chocolate chunk ice cream honoring the institution. Despite its growing size the company is also attempting to keep employees heavily involved, partially through holding monthly group meetings.

made it difficult to recruit managers.

In the process of making ice cream, the company tries to be a model employer through such programs as hiring the handicapped; providing for free therapy sessions, including drug and alcohol counseling for any worker; and taking employees on all-company trips to see baseball and hockey games. Dedication to the company runs high among the workers.

The group spirit that characterizes the company is reflected in the monthly staff meetings, which all the approximately 325 employees are invited to attend. The meetings, held in the receiving bay of the Waterbury plant, usually begin at 8 a.m. on a Friday with fresh coffee and donuts for all. Looking in on one such occasion, an observer would see more than 150 managers and workers sitting in folding chairs. Most are wearing Levis. Ben is absent, but Jerry is there. First, Jerry handles some routine reports. He talks of Ben's effort to open an ice cream parlor in Moscow, with profits earmarked for east-west exchange programs. He gives the latest on another of Ben's ideas, the plan to refurbish and maintain a New York City subway station for a year, a project that has run into considerable bureaucracy, as well as transit authority debate.

Jerry, who since his return to the company has been attempting to serve as keeper of Ben & Jerry's spiritual soul and whose title is "Minister of Joy," talks about joy and proposes a joy committee charged with putting more joy into the workday. No one laughs. He asks if anyone is interested. The group applauds as hands go up. Chico announces the birthday of an employee, and the group joins in to sing "Happy Birthday." The tenor of the meeting is upbeat. The group seems to like being there. Members appear to like and appreciate one another.

Despite the good times that employees experience, the pattern of somewhat unplanned growth tends to leave the company in a state of continual crisis. Instead of planning, Ben & Jerry's has depended upon an energetic, dedicated staff that would pitch in whenever the alarm was sounded.

Milly Badger, company controller, tells new recruits to work in running shoes and be prepared to move quickly from one task to another as needs arise.

One major crisis occurred in Spring 1987, when the company wanted to be the first ice cream maker to offer tamper-resistant seals on containers. A machine was ordered that supposedly could do the job. At the same time, the company also bought another machine to fill pints automatically. Unfortunately, neither machine seemed to work properly—leading to less ice cream production just as seasonal demand began to rise. One Friday, Chico checked the loading dock to see how things were going and discovered that the company would be short in the coming week by more than 300 pallets of ice cream. He quickly called for everyone to work the production line, and just about everyone did—including Chico, Ben, and Jerry. Jerry even hired a masseuse to give workers massages during their breaks. Some workers made dinner for the rest of the staff; pizzas were ordered. As always, the group spirit came through. One positive aspect of the struggle was that it helped build cohesion in the group. On the negative side, as Chico pointed out, once again the company was struggling to put out fires.

When the company was small, everyone knew everyone else and everything that was going on. As the company has grown and the crises keep coming, it has become more difficult to preserve the family feeling. For example, employees learned about the new Springfield, Vermont, plant from the newspaper. Milly Badger complains that she found out only at the last minute about a plan to open 50 new stores, a move that required heavy support from her department.

In the old days, Ben kept himself informed through the monthly staff meetings. Employees would break into small groups and provide input on solutions to problems. Lately, the meetings are characterized by one-way communication from Ben and other managers. Recently, Ben attempted to institute the old format by posing the question: "What are the most pressing problems confronting us?" One manager who spent a night helping Ben categorize the responses said, "It was like having this 8-ton dump truck back up and dump its load over you." The message to Ben was that the employees were beginning to feel left out. They wanted to know where the company was heading and what the company wanted to be. Meanwhile, Chico announced that he planned to resign so that he could try "working for a while at a more relaxed pace."[81]

QUESTIONS FOR CHAPTER CONCLUDING CASE
1. What group norms are evident at Ben & Jerry's?
2. What factors have contributed to the development of high cohesiveness among Ben & Jerry's employees? What is your prognosis for the future?
3. What might Ben and Jerry be able to do to preserve some of the positive aspects of group dynamics at Ben & Jerry's?

HERMAN MILLER: WHERE INNOVATION AND PARTICIPATION ARE GOSPEL

Herman Miller, Inc., the prominent publicly owned office furniture maker located in Zeeland, Michigan, is noted both for its innovative products and its participatory management methods. The furniture firm was purchased by D. J. DePree in 1923 and renamed Herman Miller in honor of DePree's father-in-law, who loaned him the money for the acquisition. DePree and later his two sons, Hugh and Max (who currently is chairman of the board), helped build the company into the second-largest office furniture manufacturer in the United States, with 5400 employees and annual revenues of about $800 million.

The company began to establish its reputation for innovation in the 1930s after industrial designer Gilbert Rohde suggested that DePree shift from the heavy classical furniture it was making for Sears, Roebuck to smaller, simpler, "more honest" furniture that was better suited to the size of most homes. DePree liked the idea of greater integrity of design and 2 years later presented the first offerings based on Rohde's designs at the 1933 World's Fair in Chicago. Although the furniture was ridiculed at first, within 4 years it had set a trend toward lighter, less expensive, and more functional pieces. It had also cemented Herman Miller's dedication to innovative design, as the company began to concentrate exclusively on producing furniture for the burgeoning office market.

Since then, Herman Miller has produced a steady stream of intriguing office furniture. For example, three chairs designed by Charles Eames for Herman Miller rank among the top-100 greatest product designs of all times according to a survey of designers conducted by the Illinois Institute of Technology. A chair produced by Herman Miller is included in the permanent collection of the Museum of Modern Art in New York City. The Walker Art Center in Minneapolis devoted a special exhibit to a recently developed Herman Miller chair, the Equa. The company also received a medal from the American Institute of Architects for its dedication to design and technical innovations.

With its extremely successful "Action Office" components, introduced in 1968, the company is generally credited with pioneering the move toward the open-space concept in office arrangement. The Action Office components (desk consoles, flexible panels, cabinets, etc.) can be moved around easily to create open space, yet they still afford workers some privacy at their individual workstations. By furnishing offices in this way, organizations can avoid the heavy costs associated with putting up and taking down walls as space needs change.

More recently, the company has introduced "Ethospace," a concept whereby rectangular tiles and windows can be snapped into a structural frame to make many different movable wall configurations that furnish varying amounts of privacy. Unlike the Action Office line, in which panels, desks, and cabinets are hooked together, Ethospace allows some furniture (such as desks) to be freestanding; the system provides considerable latitude in arranging an office, yet it retains much of the flexibility of the open-space concept. Due to manu-

The factory workers at Herman Miller, Inc., a major office furniture manufacturer, are part of an unusually egalitarian culture that is a major factor in the company's success. Work teams are routinely evaluated by managers, but the workers themselves also regularly evaluate their bosses. Each employee is covered by a silver parachute in the event the company is the victim of a hostile takeover. The CEO's salary cannot be more than 20 times the salary of the average factory worker. Such practices have earned Herman Miller a rating among the top ten corporations in management excellence. In fact, one management professor maintains that "if every company in America were managed like Herman Miller, we would not be concerned about the Japanese right now."

facturing problems and delays, the new line got off to a rocky start in the market when it was first introduced in the mid-1980s, but it is now generating acceptance despite prices that are about 20 percent higher than those for Action Office components (still the company's best-selling line).

As is typical of a major new entry from Herman Miller, Ethospace spent a number of years in the design stages. Such extensive efforts reflect the philosophy of

D. J. DePree, who wanted his company to be "dedicated to manufacturing modern furniture for moral reasons." The company is committed to producing only products that reflect good design, a stance in keeping with its strong sense of the value of individuals that permeates the manner in which the company is run.

A legendary story helps explain the philosophy underlying management at Herman Miller. About a decade after he purchased the company, D. J. DePree visited the widow of a millwright who had died. The widow read a number of passages of poetry from a bound book. Impressed with the beauty of the poems, DePree asked who the author was. The widow replied that her husband had written the poetry. DePree left wondering, "Did we have a poet who did millwright's work, or did we have a millwright who wrote poetry?" On the basis of the episode, DePree decided that the company should treat workers as if they were the former, a philosophy that continues today. DePree's son Max notes, "In addition to all their ratios and goals and parameters and bottom lines, it is fundamental that corporations have a concept of persons. In our company this begins with an understanding of the diversity of people's gifts."

As part of the effort to encourage participation at Herman Miller, employees are organized into work teams with team leaders. The team leaders evaluate team members every 6 months, and each team member in turn evaluates his or her team leader. In many departments, the various teams elect representatives to caucuses that meet periodically with supervisors to discuss company progress, grievances, and potential improvements. If caucus members are not happy with the

results of their discussions, they can ask to meet with managers at upper levels. Each month, top-level managers hold a panel discussion to discuss strategic goals, performance toward planned goals, special achievements of the past month, and goals and areas needing particular focus during the next month. The discussion is videotaped, and the tape is then shown at monthly work-team meetings so that everyone at Herman Miller is kept informed about matters affecting the company.

The team meetings and various other approaches to communication mesh well with the Scanlon Plan in operation at Herman Miller. The Scanlon Plan is a type of gainsharing and participative management system whereby workers receive quarterly bonuses based mainly on goals achieved, net savings from suggestions, results of customer satisfaction surveys, and the company's return on assets. In addition to the quarterly bonus system, recognition for ideas from workers or groups of workers also is provided through the Idea Club. The criterion for membership is having 10 suggestions accepted during the year and/or having suggestions implemented that save more than $100,000 during the year. Members of the club are honored at a special dinner.

In keeping with corporate values about the worth of all organization members, Herman Miller has established a "silver parachute" plan, which provides that all employees are eligible for payments under certain conditions in the event of a hostile takeover of the company. The payments (up to 2½ years' salary) would be triggered if the employee's job was eliminated or the job situation was adversely affected (e.g., by salary or benefits reductions). The silver parachute at

Herman Miller (believed to be the first of its kind when it was instituted in 1986) is an extension of the so-called golden parachutes, common at many companies, which provide that only top-level managers are protected with payments in the event of negative impacts from hostile takeovers.

As another symbol of Herman Miller's high regard for employee contributions, the chief executive's salary is limited to a figure that is no more than 20 times higher than the average wage of Herman Miller's factory workers. According to the current CEO, Richard Ruch, "One of the real keys to leadership in making sure you don't find yourself defending the wrong things, such as your own inflated salary."

Max DePree calls the view that employees have the right to be meaningfully involved in the company and to receive adequate rewards for their efforts the "convenant model of leadership." "The majority of people who work can be classified as volunteers," he says. "They could probably find jobs in any number of organizations, so they choose to work somewhere for reasons less tangible than salary or position. Volunteers do not need contracts, they need covenants." In the case of Herman Miller, everyone in the company, including production workers, shares the firm's dedication to good design and to employee participation. Herman Miller may be the only company in the United States in which the head of the human resources function has the title "Vice President for People."

Interestingly, Herman Miller designers are not employees of the company. "We have all our designing done on contract by outside consultants because they are ideally students of life, and we do not want them to be encumbered by a bureaucracy," says Robert Harvey, vice president in charge of design. The company does provide designers with studios at its Zeeland headquarters, called the "design yard," which is styled to resemble a midwestern farm. Nonetheless, Herman Miller encourages the designers to seek stimulation elsewhere and even pursue related activities, such as architecture, if it helps foster innovative ideas. To allay designer concerns about money, Herman Miller often puts designers on generous yearly retainers for a lengthy period, such as 10 years. In addition, a number of designers have become wealthy because of royalties associated with their designs for Herman Miller.

Despite all its efforts, things have not always gone smoothly for the innovative company. For example, during the mid-1980s, just as Herman Miller was launching Ethospace, the electronics industry—on which the company relied for almost 30 percent of its sales—experienced a slump that caused electronics firms to severely curtail office furniture purchases. The ensuing serious decline in earnings at Herman Miller led the company to reevaluate its position in the marketplace. As a result, Herman Miller began concerted efforts to attract new customers and also to change its relationship with its distributors (which had been free to sell the office furniture of other makers) by offering them financial and marketing help if they would handle only or mostly Herman Miller products. In contrast, privately owned Steelcase, the largest office furniture manufacturer in the United States and Herman Miller's archrival, has long relied on a system of dealers that handle Steelcase products exclusively. Herman Miller management also decided that the company was too internally oriented and began focusing more employee attention on business and competitive factors, which is one reason why bonuses now also depend on customer satisfaction and return on assets. In addition, Herman Miller currently is diversifying somewhat by designing furniture systems for the aged and health-care markets, lines that are slated for introduction in the 1990s.

Meanwhile, the company faces increased competition from small furniture makers attracted by the vast market for office furnishings, as well as from foreign competitors. For instance, BIF Korea is attempting to invade the office furniture market in the United States with its low-cost offerings. Fortunately, the dedicated and creative work force of Herman Miller has a history of constituting formidable competition.*

QUESTIONS FOR DISCUSSION
1. To what extent are need theories of motivation reflected in the management approach at Herman Miller?
2. Evaluate the management of Herman Miller from the standpoint of cognitive and reinforcement theories of motivation. As part of your analysis, use the social learning perspective to help explain innovation at Herman Miller.
3. Assess the leadership at Herman Miller, using both the transactional and the transformational leadership approaches.
4. Trace evidence of the use of vertical and horizontal communication channels at Herman Miller.
5. Identify several group norms that exist at Herman Miller and evaluate the extent of group cohesiveness. To what extent do these factors help and/or hinder organizational effectiveness at Herman Miller?

* *Sources:* See references at back of book.

PART FIVE

CONTROLLING

As we learned in the previous parts, the planning function provides the direction, the organizing function arranges the resources, and the leading function adds the action ingredient. Still, how does a manager ensure that an organization performs up to standards and actually achieves its intended goals? The controlling function adds that vital regulatory element, allowing managers to make use of a variety of methods for monitoring performance and taking corrective action when necessary. Controls must be used flexibly, though, because too much control can stifle innovation.

In exploring the controlling function, **Chapter 17** takes a close look at the overall control process, including the steps in the process, the major types of controls, various managerial approaches to implementing the controls that are available, and the problems associated with attempting to control innovation.

As part of the control process, managers use certain major control systems to increase the probability of meeting organizational goals. **Chapter 18** focuses on four of these systems: financial control, budgetary control, quality control, and inventory control.

Another major control system is operations management, which involves overseeing the processes entailed in actually producing a product or service. As **Chapter 19** points out, a key aspect of operations management is productivity. Managers must devise operations strategies, develop operating systems, utilize facilities, and promote innovative technology with productivity in mind.

Finally, as **Chapter 20** shows, information systems are an important means of control. Computer-based systems provide managers with information to help them make whatever decisions are necessary to adjust performance to meet goals. But information systems do not simply aid in improving an organization's operating efficiency; they also can be used in innovative ways to give an organization a distinctive competitive edge.

CHAPTER SEVENTEEN

CONTROLLING THE ORGANIZATION

CHAPTER OUTLINE

Control as a Management Process
Significance of the Control Process
Role of Controls
Levels of Control

The Control Process
Steps in the Control Process
Deciding What to Control: A Closer
 Look

Types of Controls
Major Control Types by Timing
Multiple Controls
Cybernetic and Noncybernetic Control

**Managerial Approaches to
 Implementing Controls**
Market Control
Bureaucratic Control
Clan Control
Blending the Approaches
Choosing a Managerial Control Style
Promoting Innovation: Control and
 the Innovation Process

Assessing Control Systems
Potential Dysfunctional Aspects of
 Control Systems
Overcontrol versus Undercontrol
Characteristics of an Effective Control
 System

LEARNING OBJECTIVES

*After studying this chapter, you
should be able to:*

■ Explain the major roles of controls in organizations.

■ Describe how control responsibilities change with the level of
management.

■ Outline the general process
that can be applied to most
control situations.

■ Delineate the major conditions
that managers need to consider
in deciding what to control.

■ Explain the major control types
by timing and the use of multiple controls.

■ Differentiate between cybernetic
and noncybernetic control.

■ Describe the major managerial
approaches to implementing
controls, including means of
appropriately controlling the
innovation process.

■ Outline the potential dysfunctional aspects of control systems and explain the implications of overcontrol and
undercontrol.

■ Delineate the major characteristics of effective control systems.

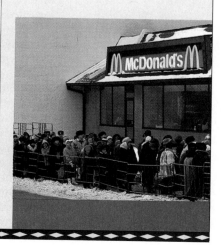

CONTROLLING SUCCESS AT McDONALD'S

The original McDonald's drive-in restaurant in San Bernadino, California, was doing a brisk business in 1955 when the franchising rights (legal rights to allow other people to use the name and methods of a business for a fee) were sold to a milk-shake-mixer salesperson named Ray Kroc. Although Kroc, at the time, did not know the restaurant business and was not wealthy, he was going into competition against well-established fast-food chains, such as Kentucky Fried Chicken, InstaBurger King (later shortened to Burger King), Dairy Queen, and Big Boy.

Nevertheless, while selling milk-shake mixers, Kroc had witnessed many franchised outlets go out of business because of poor management, uneven quality, and financial draining by parent companies. On the basis of his observations, Kroc believed that an organization could run a tremendously successful franchising operation if it could control the quality of both the food and the service offered at the franchised outlets. Offering franchisees good financial incentives for adhering to a fair, but closely controlled, system would be another essential element for success.

To develop the kind of controls needed, Kroc designed training programs that were unusual at the time and remain the best in the fast-food industry. He also put together a training manual that has grown to about 600 pages. The manual detailed operating procedures and standards for virtually every aspect of outlet management. Instructions ranged from the cooking time for french fries to expected standards of cleanliness for rest rooms. To help ensure that employees followed the provisions outlined in the manual, Kroc had field inspectors visit outlets and grade their operations against the standards set forth.

Kroc also demanded that suppliers conform to high standards. For example, potato distributors were shocked to learn that McDonald's technicians measured the moisture levels in potatoes by using devices called hydrometers and rejected batches in which the solids content did not meet requirements. Because cheating on hamburger quality was a common practice in the meat industry at that time, McDonald's inspectors were known to use tactics such as showing up at a meat-packing plant at 3 a.m., ready to cancel contracts if they found anything amiss. McDonald's still keeps close tabs on suppliers, right down to conducting laboratory tests on the thickness of pickle slices.

Another unique aspect of the McDonald's operation was Kroc's approach to granting franchises. While the usual practice of other chains, such as Dairy Queen and Burger King, was to license whole territories in return for sizable front-end payments, Kroc sold franchises one outlet at a time. Only if an operator demonstrated a willingness and ability to live up to McDonald's standards would that operator be considered for additional outlets. Kroc also made sure that the franchisees would get to keep a good chunk of the fruits of their labors, giving them ample incentive to work hard. Franchises originally cost $950 and a 1.9 percent slice of gross revenues. Today an average-size McDonald's costs a franchisee more than $375,000 and 12 percent of gross sales for the duration of the franchise, which is normally 20 years.

When Kroc began his franchising operations, most organizations that franchised fast-food outlets had staffs of about 10 people whose primary job was selling more franchises and properly managing the income resulting from the sales. In contrast, McDonald's central staff was several times larger because of its broader mission, which included training franchisees and their managerial staffs and monitoring the way in which the stores were operated. This approach, coupled with the strategy of low franchise fees and low sales percentages from franchises, was costly at first. Although McDonald's outlets grossed $75 million during the first 6 years of operations, headquarters made net profits of only $159,000. Still, because he had the foresight to concentrate on the long run, Kroc began to achieve a vision that would ultimately prove difficult for the competition to duplicate: nationwide standardization. Gradually, customers started to notice that regardless of where they were, the local McDonald's restaurant could be counted on to offer reliable food, quick service, and clean rest rooms. Yet there often have been innovations, such as the recent testing of new menu items (e.g., the McRib sandwich, low-fat milk, and sherbert) and the recent decision to gradually begin offering the new 14-inch McDonald's pizza at all U.S. outlets. The durable reputation of McDonald's was recently confirmed in a survey in which Americans indicated that McDonald's was fifth among America's most powerful brands.

A Big Mac in Moscow should taste exactly the same as one in Minneapolis. Ray Kroc, founder of McDonalds, instituted strict controls to ensure consistency in products and service at every franchise. He implemented these controls through such measures as training programs, a comprehensive training manual, field inspectors, exacting standards for suppliers, and the rigorous screening of potential franchisees.

Today, there are more than 10,875 McDonald's outlets located in the United States and in more than 42 other countries. For example, there are approximately 675 outlets in Japan, 600 in Canada, and 300 in West Germany. Overseas franchisees often modify the menu and/or prices to be locally competitive. The company's gross sales of more than $13 billion are increasing at a rate of more than 10 percent annually. A new McDonald's outlet opens every 15 hours someplace in the world. About 75 percent of the outlets in the United States are franchised operations. McDonald's typically owns or leases the property on which outlets are located, but the franchisee purchases the equipment and furnishings used. Overseas outlets are most often joint ventures in which both the company and local owners have 50 percent shares. Increasingly, the company is expanding internationally, an approach which presents even greater challenges to controlling food and service.

Although Kroc placed heavy emphasis on controlling the food and service offered, he still left room for considerable innovation among franchisees in addition to the innovating initiated by headquarters. For example, franchisees originated the ideas for the Big Mac, the Egg McMuffin, the McDLT, and now-famous Ronald McDonald. They also have considerable influence over outlet decor, which is one reason why decor varies from one outlet to another. One of the busiest McDonald's in America, located north of Chicago's Loop, draws an estimated 320,000 visitors per month. The visitors step back into the 1950s and 1960s among such memorabilia as a telephone booth from the 1950s television series *Superman*, a Wurlitzer jukebox, and old movies shown on elevated screens. Lunchtime customers at a McDonald's in Los Angeles enjoy violin serenades. McDonald's outlets also are popping up in some unique locations, such as on a reproduction of a riverboat on the Mississippi River in St. Louis, at St. Joseph's hospital in Phoenix, on several university campuses, and at the U.S. naval base in Cuba.[1]

What explains McDonald's spectacular success? One major factor is the extent to which the company maintains strong controls over most aspects of its operations. These controls have helped McDonald's develop a competitive edge in the form of high product and service consistency. A Big Mac is likely to taste pretty much the same whether we are eating it in Boston or Bangkok. As noted economist Robert J. Samuelson reported recently in praising McDonald's, his Big Mac ordered at an outlet in Tokyo did not "merely taste like an American Big

Mac"; it tasted "exactly the same."[2] Still, the company has allowed room for innovation, as described earlier. How are successful companies such as McDonald's able to design and implement effective controls?

To explore this issue, we devote the next four chapters to various aspects of controlling, the fourth major function of management. In this chapter, we consider the significance of control as a management process and examine the control process itself, including a discussion of how managers decide what to control. We also review the major types of controls and the appropriate times for instituting these controls. We then describe some differences in the way in which managers can approach the process of implementing controls, including considerations of how to institute controls without unduly hampering innovation. Finally, we analyze how managers can effectively assess the control systems that they use.

CONTROL AS A MANAGEMENT PROCESS

Controlling The process of regulating organizational activities so that actual performance conforms to expected organizational standards and goals

Like their McDonald's counterparts, managers in other organizations also face important issues related to the function of controlling. **Controlling** is the process of regulating organizational activities so that actual performance conforms to expected organizational standards and goals.[3] As the definition suggests, controlling means that managers develop appropriate standards, compare ongoing performance against those standards, and take steps to ensure that corrective actions are taken when necessary. Since most aspects of organizations ultimately depend on human behavior, controlling is largely geared toward ensuring that organization members behave in ways that facilitate the reaching of organizational goals. Thus controls both highlight needed behaviors and discourage unwanted behaviors.[4] For instance, during their 2-year training program, management trainees preparing to become McDonald's franchisees work their way through a thick guide that spells out various aspects of what to do and not do in properly running a McDonald's outlet.[5]

Significance of the Control Process

As you might expect, the controlling function is closely allied to the other three major functions of management: planning, organizing, and leading. It builds most directly on the planning function by providing the means for monitoring and making adjustments in performance so that plans can be realized. Still, controlling also supports the organizing and leading functions by helping ensure that resources are channeled toward organizational objectives (see Figure 17-1). For example, feedback from the control process might signal the need to reorganize, provide more training to workers, clarify communications, increase leadership influence, or take other actions associated with the respective organizing and leading functions. For instance, after detecting a shortage of workers who could assume some supervisory responsibilities, six McDonald's restaurants in Fairfax, Virginia, have been experimenting with a training program to teach English to workers who have management potential but speak little English.[6]

Control system A set of mechanisms that are designed to increase the probability of meeting organizational standards and goals

As part of the control process, managers set up control systems. A **control system** is a set of mechanisms that are designed to increase the probability of meeting organizational standards and goals.[7] Control systems can be developed to regulate any area that a manager considers important, such as quantity produced, resources expended, profit margins, quality of products or services, cli-

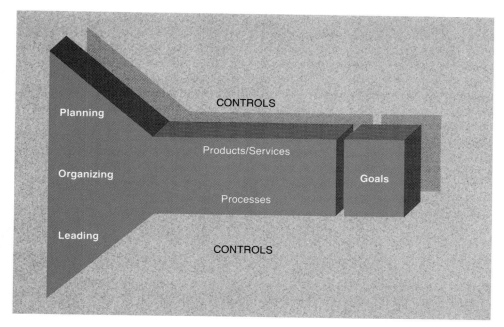

Figure 17-1 Relationship of controls to the other functions of management.

ent satisfaction, timeliness of deliveries, or specific activities that are performed in producing a product or service.

For example, McDonald's has a 19-step procedure that workers must rigidly follow when they are cooking and bagging french fries. Local managers are expected to ensure that employees prepare and bag french fries in accordance with these steps to that the french fries will conform to McDonald's standards. This procedure also is one of the operations that corporate evaluation teams check during their unannounced inspections of outlets.[8] Thus the local managers, the corporate evaluation teams, and the standards embodied in the procedure form part of a control system aimed at achieving consistently good french fries at all McDonald's outlets.

Role of Controls

In evaluating the role of controls, it is useful to consider what can happen when controls are inadequate. Worlds of Wonder, Inc., a producer of exotic toys for children, went from being a Wall Street sensation to seeking Chapter 11 bankruptcy protection within 2 years, mainly because of poor controls. You may have heard of some of its more famous toys, such as the popular $80 talking Teddy Ruxpin or the $100 intelligent Julie doll that reads. For all the wizardry incorporated in its toys, the company (often known as "WOW") lacked the control systems needed to ensure that its products would reach retailers when required. Either the company could not produce enough of a popular product or deliveries were too late to generate substantial sales. In one case, the company spent heavily on promoting Lazer Tag (a game in which players tag each other using infrared light beams), generated enormous demand for the toy, but then could not produce it in sufficient quantities. In another situation, a line of school products reached retailers too late to produce significant back-to-school sales. The toys also sometimes had serious quality shortcomings. For example, the talking Teddy Ruxpin bears exhibited mechanical problems that resulted in the return of almost 20 percent of them by dissatisfied customers.[9]

The hot toy in 1989 was Tyco Toys' Oopsie Daisy doll, which can crawl, fall down, cry, and pick herself up again. Demand for the doll outran supply, a situation that can fuel retailer and consumer resentment and hurt a company that relies on one popular item. But Tyco's strategy is to control the roller coaster effects of faddish toys by diversifying its product line and not depending on one successful product.

Controls can help managers, like those at WOW, avoid such problems. More specifically, controls play important roles in assisting managers with five particular challenges: coping with uncertainty, detecting irregularities, identifying opportunities, handling complex situations, and decentralizing authority.

Coping with Uncertainty. Uncertainty arises because organizational goals are set for future events on the basis of the best knowledge at the time, yet things do not always go according to plan. A variety of factors in the environment typically operate to bring about changes in such areas as customer demand, technology, and the availability of raw materials. By developing control systems, managers are better able to monitor specific activities and react quickly to significant changes in the environment. For example, contrast WOW's situation with that of Levi Strauss. By pioneering efforts to put a universal product code (the scannable black lines on many grocery store products) on its jeans, Levi Strauss has been able to obtain computerized information from retailers on purchasing trends and regional preferences.[10] The information helps the company react quickly to changing customer demands.

Detecting Irregularities. Controls also help managers detect undesirable irregularities, such as product defects, cost overruns, or rising personnel turnover. Early detection of such irregularities often can save a great deal of time and money by preventing minor problems from mushrooming into major ones. Finding aberrations early also sometimes avoids problems that can be difficult to rectify, such as missing important deadlines or selling faulty merchandise to customers. For example, Worlds of Wonder might have been able to avoid the ill will that it generated among retailers and customers with its often-defective Teddy Ruxpin bear if it had instituted better controls over design and related manufacturing processes.

Identifying Opportunities. Controls also help highlight situations in which things are going better than expected, which alerts management to possible future opportunities.[11] At St. Louis–based May Department Stores, division managers prepare special monthly reports that specify the items that are selling well and the amount of money the items are generating. The chain then uses these data to develop successful merchandising strategies for all its stores, including what to buy, which vendors to buy from, and how to display the merchandise.[12]

Handling Complex Situations. As organizations grow larger or engage in more complex operations and projects, controls enhance coordination.[13] Controls help managers keep track of various major elements to be sure that they are well synchronized. Operating on an international basis often increases complexity and calls for further consideration of necessary controls. Consider what has happened to British retailer Marks & Spencer as the company has struggled to become a significant force in North American retailing (see the following Case in Point discussion).

CASE IN POINT: Marks & Spencer Struggles in North America

Marks & Spencer, PLC, is a household name in Britain, where its many conveniently located stores carry well-made, low-priced clothing and feature food counters with fresh, prepared meals bearing the St. Michael label. With more than $8 billion in annual revenues, "Marks & Sparks," as it is often called by British customers, is Great Britain's most successful retailer. Its admirable net profit margins of about 7 percent are approximately double those of comparable U.S. firms.

Because Marks & Spencer began to saturate its home market, the company purchased three Canadian chains in 1973: D'Allaird's, which features clothing for older women; People's, which carries budget-priced general merchandise; and Walker's, which, at the time, was a general clothing store. While retaining the basic thrust of D'Allaird's and People's, Marks & Spencer changed the name of Walker's to Marks & Spencer Canada and remodeled the stores to resemble smaller versions of their famous British counterparts. Unfortunately, the Marks & Spencer Canada stores, with their sturdy British clothing, relatively plain decor, and imported biscuits and teas, did not fare well compared with the more attractive stores and merchandise of Canadian shopping-mall competitors. Yet Marks & Spencer was very slow to sense the problem and take corrective action. Only very gradually did Marks & Spencer Canada begin to carry Canadian-made merchandise and to improve the look of its stores. The chain also expanded its food offerings to include such fare as frozen entrées, tinned Brazilian beef products, and, more recently, fresh foods. Still, after more than 16 years, the three Canadian chains of Marks & Spencer recently registered combined annual losses of about $19 million (Canadian).

Seeking improved company growth, Marks & Spencer decided to enter the U.S. market in 1987. Determined not to repeat the same mistakes that the company had made in Canada, a team of executives studying the situation concluded that the company would not attempt to export its successful British formula for Marks & Spencer stores to the United States. Rather, it would establish a base by purchasing existing chains with good performance records and expanding them. Accordingly, in 1988, Marks & Spencer bought the famous Brooks Brothers chain, then owned by the Canada-based Campeau Corporation. The purchase price of $750 million—two and a half times the chain's annual revenue—was relatively high for the purveyor of conservative, but rather expensive, clothes. Brooks Brothers, with its $600 suits, $475 casual jackets, and shoes that begin around $260, handles a vastly different type of merchandise than the low-priced clothing that is Marks & Spencer's hallmark in Britain. In order to broaden the appeal of Brooks Brothers merchandise to younger and less-affluent men and women, Marks & Spencer is offering new styles, particularly in sportswear. Brooks Brothers' best suits are being cut more trimly, trousers now often have pleats, and many suits and shirts reflect a British look. At the same time, the company is taking some shortcuts that are uncharacteristic of Brooks Brothers, such as offering the $475 casual jackets in small, medium, large, and extra-large sizes, rather than the usual, more specifically calibrated sizes. Instead of its subdued week-long clearance sales, Brooks Brothers now runs 6-week sales that mirror the practices of its more ordinary competitors.

Marks & Spencer also purchased Kings Super Markets, a 16-store New Jersey grocery chain, in 1988 to provide a means of entry into the U.S. food market. Yet the 2000 items (including soup, entrées, and desserts) marketed in Britain under the St. Michael label are mainly made in central kitchens, delivered overnight, and marketed as fresh and ready to eat (or requiring only a brief heating in an oven). ■

In attempting to broaden the appeal of Brooks Brothers' merchandise, Marks & Spencer will need to monitor the situation closely so that the chain does not lose its prestigious reputation in the process. At the same time, it remains to be seen whether Marks & Spencer can successfully adapt its carefully controlled British food operations to the vastly different U.S. grocery industry, with its orientation toward mass-produced foods and national name brands. So far, Marks & Spencer has not demonstrated the ability to adequately control company activities overseas.[14]

Decentralizing Authority. Another major role of controls is in affording managers more latitude to decentralize authority. With controls, managers can foster decision making at lower levels in the organization but still maintain a handle on progress. Alfred Sloan, the noted former chairman of General Motors, once wrote that he implemented control by setting the standard for the level of return on investment that he expected various units of General Motors to achieve. This approach let him exercise control over major units by monitoring return on investments, yet it allowed him to maintain a philosophy of decentralization.[15] Sloan, of course, was operating at the very top of an organization. As you might expect, control issues tend to vary according to managerial level in the hierarchy.

Levels of Control

Just as planning responsibilities differ by managerial level (see Chapter 5), there are parallel control responsibilities at each level (see Figure 17-2). Strategic, tactical, and operational levels of control increase the probabilities of realizing plans at respective levels.[16]

Strategic control involves monitoring critical environmental factors that could affect the viability of strategic plans, assessing the effects of organizational strategic actions, and ensuring that strategic plans are implemented as intended. Control at the strategic level is mainly the domain of top-level managers, who generally take an organizationwide perspective. For strategic control, managers often concentrate on relatively long time frames, such as quarterly, semiannual, and annual reporting cycles. If environments are somewhat unstable and/or competition is especially keen, managers may use shorter reporting cycles for strategic control. Even though they are primarily concerned with strategic issues, top-level managers also may make use of tactical and operational control to ensure that tactical and operational plans are being implemented as intended at the middle and lower management levels.

Tactical control focuses on assessing the implementation of tactical plans at department levels, monitoring associated periodic results, and taking corrective action as necessary. Control at the tactical level involves mainly middle managers, who are concerned with department-level objectives, programs, and budgets and who concentrate on periodic or middle-term time frames and often use weekly and monthly reporting cycles. They also test how the environment reacts to the tactical initiatives of their departments. Although their prime concern is tactical control, middle managers are likely to engage in some strategic control in the sense of providing information to upper-level managers on strategic issues. They also are involved in operational control, at least to the extent of checking on some of the more critical aspects of operating plan implementation.

Operational control involves overseeing the implementation of operating plans, monitoring day-to-day results, and taking corrective action when required. Control at the operating level is largely the responsibility of lower-level managers, who are concerned with schedules, budgets, rules, and specific outputs normally associated with particular individuals. Operating control provides

Strategic control A control type that involves monitoring critical environmental factors that could affect the viability of strategic plans, assessing the effects of organizational strategic actions, and ensuring that strategic plans are implemented as intended

Tactical control A control type that focuses on assessing the implementation of tactical plans at department levels, monitoring associated periodic results, and taking corrective action as necessary

Operational control A control type that involves overseeing the implementation of operating plans, monitoring day-to-day results, and taking corrective action when required

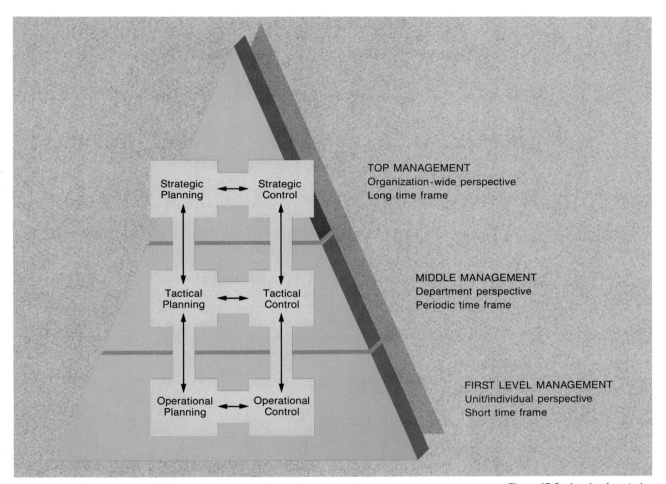

TOP MANAGEMENT
Organization-wide perspective
Long time frame

MIDDLE MANAGEMENT
Department perspective
Periodic time frame

FIRST LEVEL MANAGEMENT
Unit/individual perspective
Short time frame

Figure 17-2 Levels of control. (Adapted in part from Peter Lorange, Michael F. Scott Morton, and Sumantra Ghoshal, *Strategic Control Systems*, West, St. Paul, Minn., 1986, p. 12.)

feedback about what is happening in the very near term to achieve both the short-term and long-term goals of the organization.

The levels of control—strategic, tactical, and operational—are strongly interrelated in much the same way that planning systems at the different levels are integrated. For example, if an organization decides that quality will be an important part of its strategy, then quality becomes an important element for control not only at the strategic control level but also at the tactical and operational levels. Thus, for controls at the various levels to be effective, it is important that they operate in concert.

For example, at fast-growing Waldenbooks, top managers keep track of the overall effects of such strategies as publishing the company's own books under the Longmeadow Press label and attempting to turn relatively unknown mystery writer Bernard Cornwell (author of *Wildtrack*) into a best-selling author whose new works can stimulate sales. Middle-level managers monitor the implementation of these strategies throughout the various parts of the bookstore chain and keep tabs on important indicators, such as sales figures in various areas. At the operating level, individual store managers are responsible for ensuring that prominent display areas, such as the front of the store and the main traffic artery (called the "poweraisle"), are used to display specific materials that support major strategic directions.[17]

THE CONTROL PROCESS

Although control systems must be tailored to specific situations, such systems generally follow the same basic process. In this section, we first consider the steps in the control process and then examine more closely the issues related to deciding what to control.

Steps in the Control Process

The basic process used in controlling is shown in Figure 17-3. The process has several major steps.

Determine Areas to Control. The first major step in the control process is determining the major areas to control. Managers must make choices because it is expensive and virtually impossible to control every aspect of an organization's activities. In addition, employees often resent having their every move controlled. Managers usually base their major controls on the organizational goals and objectives developed during the planning process. For example, Briggs & Stratton, the maker of small, four-cycle, air-cooled engines used on lawn mowers, has been focusing heavily on market share since the company began to face serious Japanese competitors. The company has been raising advertising budgets, increasing research and engineering funding, and lowering production costs in an effort to regain and maintain its former market share of more than 50 percent.[18] The company, of course, is monitoring other indicators as well. (We further discuss the issue of what to control later in this section.)

Figure 17-3 Steps in the control process.

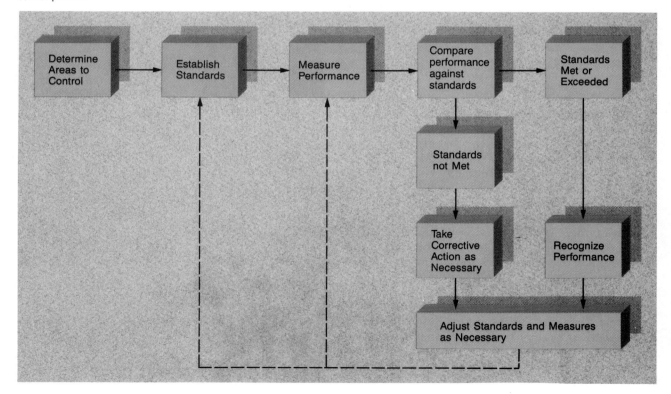

The first step in the control process is determining what areas are in particular need of control. Sea Containers Ltd. of London found that it needed to control debt, especially after sustaining too large a fleet in the 1980s caused it to lose millions of dollars. This Sea Container ship is loading irrigation piping in Houston to be transported to Saudi Arabia.

Establish Standards. The second step in the control process is establishing standards. Standards spell out specific criteria for evaluating performance and related employee behaviors. For example, standards might indicate how well a product is to be made or how effectively a service is to be delivered. Standards may also reflect specific activities or behaviors that are necessary to achieve organizational goals, such as coming to work on time, observing safety rules, and following ethical guidelines in conducting organizational business. Often such standards are incorporated into the goals as they are set in the planning process. When Chicago-based Marshall Field & Company began its recent service-improvement program, it discovered that salespeople took an average of 10 minutes to approach a customer. With the help of training programs, special incentives for salespeople, and a computerized scheduling program that assigns salespeople to areas where they are most likely to be needed, Field has been able to set a standard of 2 minutes for salespeople to approach customers.[19]

Generally, standards serve three major purposes related to employee behavior.[20] For one thing, standards help employees understand what is expected and how their work will be evaluated. Knowing what is expected helps employees do an effective job. For another, standards provide a basis for detecting job difficulties that are related to personal limitations of organization members. Such limitations can be based on a lack of ability, training, or experience or on any other job-related deficiency that prevents an individual from performing properly on the job. Timely identification of deficiencies makes it possible to take corrective action before the difficulties become serious and possibly irresolvable. Finally, standards help reduce the potential negative effects of goal incongruence. **Goal incongruence** is a condition in which there are major incompatibilities between the goals of an organization member and those of the organization. Such incompatibilities can occur for a variety of reasons, such as lack of support for organizational objectives (e.g., viewing a job as temporary and attempting to

Goal incongruence A condition in which there are major incompatibilities between the goals of an organization member and those of the organization

do the minimum), and often result in behaviors that are incompatible with reaching organizational goals.

One common manifestation of goal incongruence is employee theft, which includes wasting an organization's resources, as well as taking equipment, materials, and money.[21] Related problems almost led to the demise of Intermedics, Inc., a small pacemaker company located near Houston. A new manager, who subsequently saved the company from impending bankruptcy, recalls: "Intermedics was a country club. Most employees were arriving to work late, expense account abuse was rampant, and nobody ever thought we owed the stockholders anything. Values around here were really warped."[22] According to one study, about 15 percent of employees are highly likely to steal from their organization, while another 20 percent are highly unlikely to do so. The other 65 percent will steal if they observe others engaging in theft without being apprehended or suffering negative consequences—in other words, when controls are inadequate.[23]

Measure Performance. Once standards are determined, the next step is measuring performance. For a given standard, a manager must decide both how to measure actual performance and how often to do so. One of the more popular techniques used to help set standards and coordinate the measurement of performance is management by objectives (see Chapter 5).

The means of measuring performance will depend on the standards that have been set, but they can include such data as units produced, dollar amount of service rendered, amount of materials used, number of defects found, scrap rate, steps or processes followed, profits, return on investment, quality of output, or stores opened. At American Express, where good service is an important organizational goal, the 12 departments responsible for card operations were asked by top management to develop their own performance standards and measure their own achievements. The departments all seemed to be doing well under this arrangement, but overall service did not seem to be improving. Consequently, the company developed a system for measuring the impact of all the departments' activities on customers. The system, called the service tracking report, measures success in processing new applications for cards within 15 days, replacing lost or stolen cards in 1 day, sending out errorless bills, and performing more than 100 other tasks.[24]

In some cases performance must be measured continuously. This is certainly true of nuclear power plants, where the potential for disaster is constant. Control at the Three Mile Island nuclear power plant (shown here) has been especially strict since a near disaster in 1979.

Although quantitative measures often are used whenever possible, many important aspects of performance can be difficult to measure quantitatively. For example, although it may be relatively easy to measure the number of minutes between taking an order and filling it in a McDonald's drive-through line, it will probably take some managerial judgment to determine the extent to which the objective of being polite to customers is being fulfilled. Similarly, areas such as research and development can be difficult to measure quantitatively in the short run because it may take years to determine the final outcomes of research programs. As a result, qualitative judgments by peers are often utilized.[25] Hence most organizations use combinations of both quantitative and qualitative performance measures in carrying out the control function.

Once they have selected the means of measurement, managers must decide how often they will measure performance for control purposes. In some cases, managers need control data on a daily, hourly, or even more frequent basis (as in the case of supervisors of air traffic controllers). In other cases, weekly, monthly, quarterly, semiannual, or even annual data may be sufficient. Lower-level managers at American Express need to keep close tabs on the day-to-day activities that ultimately make up the service tracking report; middle-level managers are more likely to track weekly progress; and top management reviews the report on a monthly basis to check on customer service at operations in various parts of the world. Each year, employees receive an annual summary of how the company is doing on service.[26] Some industries, such as manufacturers of outdoor furniture and fireplace equipment, are particularly concerned with seasonal results. Basically, the period of measurement generally depends upon the importance of the goal to the organization, how quickly the situation is likely to change, and the difficulty and expense of rectifying a problem if one were to occur. Nuclear power plants, for example, have elaborate systems of controls that continuously provide data on all major aspects of the process. The elaborate controls are important given the potentially serious consequences of a power-plant accident.

Compare Performance against Standards. This step consists of comparing the performance measured in step 3 with the standards established in step 2. Managers often base their comparisons on information provided in reports that summarize planned versus actual results. Such reports may be presented verbally, forwarded in written form, or generated automatically in conjunction with computerized processes. The proliferation of computers tied into networks has made it possible for managers to obtain up-to-the-minute status reports on a variety of quantitative performance measures.

Such computer systems lend themselves particularly well to applications of **management by exception,** a control principle which suggests that managers should be informed of a situation only if control data show a significant deviation from standards.[27] Use of the management by exception principle, with or without computers, helps save managers time by bringing to their attention only those conditions that appear to need managerial action. While the management by exception principle can often be used effectively, managers need to be careful that they do not become so preoccupied with problems that they ignore positive accomplishments of subordinates.

Managers often make comparisons of performance and standards by walking around work areas and observing conditions, a practice sometimes referred to as management by wandering around (see Chapter 15). For example, Sam M. Walton, chief of the phenomenally successful Wal-Mart discount chain, is a habitual visitor to company stores, where he constantly checks merchandise displays and talks with customers.[28]

Management by exception A control principle which suggests that managers should be informed of a situation only if control data show a significant deviation from standards

If Standards Are Met or Exceeded, Recognize Performance. When performance meets or exceeds the standards set, usually no corrective action is necessary. However, managers do need to consider recognizing the positive performance. The type of recognition given can vary from a verbal "well done" for a routine achievement to more substantial rewards, such as bonuses, training opportunities, or pay raises, for major achievements or consistently good work. These approaches are consistent with motivation theories, such as expectancy theory and reinforcement theory, which emphasize the importance of rewarding good performance in order to sustain it and encourage further improvements (see Chapter 13). For instance, in an effort to reinforce Marshall Field's standard of 2 minutes or less for approaching a customer, managers give a silver coin called a "Frangloon" to any salesperson who is observed being extra helpful to a customer. Ten coins earn a box of Field's Frango mint chocolates, while 100 coins can be exchanged for an extra day of paid vacation.[29]

If Standards Are Not Met, Take Corrective Action as Necessary. When standards are not met, managers must carefully assess the reasons why and take corrective action. As part of their evaluation, managers often personally check the standards and the related performance measures to be sure that they are still realistic. Sometimes, managers may conclude that corrective action to meet standards is not desirable because the standards are, in fact, inappropriate—usually because of changing conditions. More often, though, corrective actions are needed to reach standards.

Adjust Standards and Measures as Necessary. Control is a dynamic process. As a result, managers need to check standards periodically to ensure that the standards and the associated performance measures are still relevant for the future. For one thing, standards and measures can be inappropriate, either because they were not set appropriately to begin with or because circumstances have changed. For another, exceeding a standard may signal unforeseen opportunities, the potential to raise standards, and/or the need for possible major adjustments in organizational plans. Finally, even if standards have been met, changing conditions, such as improvements in the skill levels of employees, may make it possible to raise standards for future efforts. Conversely, a manager may feel that achieving a particular standard consumes too many resources and may decide to lower that standard. Thus managers use the control process to keep track of various activities, but they must also be prepared to review the process itself as necessary to be sure that it meets current needs.

Deciding What to Control: A Closer Look

Well-formulated objectives, strategic plans, and supporting goals provide guidance about what is important to the organization. As a result, they suggest areas for control. While it is important for managers to collect data regarding the extent to which desired ends are being achieved, they may also need to control various elements that lead to those ends.

Resource dependence An approach to controls which argues that managers need to consider controls mainly in areas in which they depend on others for resources necessary to reach organizational goals

Strategic control points Performance areas chosen for control because they are particularly important in meeting organizational goals

One recent approach that helps managers decide what to control takes a resource dependence point of view.[30] The **resource dependence** approach to controls argues that managers need to consider controls mainly in areas in which they depend on others for resources necessary to reach organizational goals. Resources in this context can be parts, information, service, funding, or any other type of resource that a manager might need in pursuing objectives. Still, just because a manager is dependent upon others does not necessarily mean that an area should be controlled. There are four conditions that need to be met in making a final determination. Areas that meet all four conditions constitute **strategic control points,** performance areas chosen for control because they are particularly important in meeting organizational goals. The conditions and a related decision tree are shown in Figure 17-4.

Four Conditions for Control. The first two conditions relate to whether or not controls are needed. The second two assess whether controls are feasible and practical.

The first and most basic condition is relatively *high dependence* on the resource. The more important the dependence and the less the resource is available from other sources, the higher the dependence on the resource. High dependence increases the likelihood that a manager will need to develop controls to monitor the area. If you were running a McDonald's outlet, for example, you would probably find yourself highly dependent on resources such as food, food

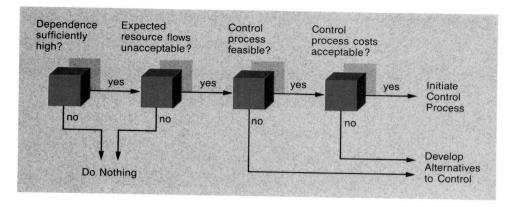

Figure 17-4 Resource dependence decision tree. (Adapted from Stephen G. Green and M. Ann Welsh, "Cybernetics and Dependence: Reframing the Control Concept," *Academy of Management Review*, vol. 13, pp. 287–301.)

containers, water, napkins and related items, and equipment that is in good working order. These resources are crucial to operations. On the other hand, if the resource is not very important or a substitute can be obtained easily (e.g., a replacement for a trampled shrub), then the resource is probably not worth elaborate controls.

The second condition for control is a strong likelihood that the *expected resource flow will be unacceptable.* In other words, the manager anticipates that there may be some problems with the resource or at least feels uncertain about it. The anticipated problems can be related to any relevant aspect, but usually they are tied to the quantity of the resource, certain characteristics (such as specifications and quality), and timeliness. The more that the manager feels that the resource will be a source of problems, the greater the need for controls. For instance, as a manager of a McDonald's outlet, you might find it difficult to stockpile many food products (such as lettuce, hamburger buns, and milk) that can spoil. Yet shifting customer patterns can affect usage, making control of food inventory very important. On the other hand, even though water is also an important resource, water supplies (at least in most parts of the United States) are quite reliable and a formal control system generally is not needed.

The third condition that influences whether to institute controls is *control process feasibility.* Sometimes the basic control process—establishing standards of performance, measuring performance, comparing performance to standards, feeding back information about discrepancies, and allowing for corrective action—is not feasible. Typically, feasibility is an issue when it is difficult to specify standards of performance or when there are problems either with measuring performance or with measuring it in a timely manner. For example, it is difficult for McDonald's to establish rigid standards in the area of price competition overseas. In Japan, McDonald's recently instituted the "Thank You Seeto" (combination deal), which offered a burger, a small drink, and a small order of fries for a relatively low 390 yen (about $3). If purchased individually, these items would cost about $4.15. The promotion was billed as a thank-you to customers for making McDonald's the largest burger operation in Japan in terms of annual sales ($1.1 billion) and profitability. The combination deal was initiated at a point when market growth was slowing and competitors were beginning to attract more business. Even though other Japanese fast-food outlets followed suit with their own specials, McDonald's sales increased approximately 12 percent, and some Japanese business analysts predicted that the weaker local fast-food outlets would cease to exist. In this case, price issues were controlled locally, because it was infeasible for McDonald's to make adequate and timely assessments of pricing issues governing its Japanese operations from its central headquarters in Oak Brook, Illinois.[31]

Finally, an important condition influencing whether to institute a control process is *cost acceptability*. Managers need to weigh the costs of control against the benefits. It is possible for a control system to cost more than an organization gains from the controls. For example, McDonald's central headquarters could maintain even better control than it does over outlets through a video teleconferencing network, which includes a two-way video-audio connection tied into every store (see Chapter 15); but at this point, the cost would be prohibitive given the potential gains. On the other hand, if costs are acceptable and the other conditions are met, then it is reasonable to institute a control process in the given situation.

Alternatives to Control. What happens if the first two conditions (questions 1 and 2 in Figure 17-4) indicate that controls are needed, but a control process is either infeasible or too costly? Then managers need to develop alternatives to control.

One way to develop an alternative to control is to change the dependence relationship so that control is no longer necessary. For example, a manager might line up several suppliers so that controls are much less important. Alternatively, a manager can work with the source of dependence to make it more reliable, thus reducing the need for extensive controls. This approach was used when McDonald's experts helped local farmers in Thailand learn how to cultivate Idaho russet potatoes, a key element in meeting McDonald's standards for french fries at Thai outlets.[32]

Another alternative approach to control is to change the nature of the dependence to one that is more feasible and/or cost-effective to control. For instance, redesigning complex jobs so that they involve narrower, simpler tasks reduces dependence on experienced workers. Although there are a number of disadvantages to job simplification (see Chapter 10), the approach may make a situation easier to control in a tight labor market. Another example of an alternative to control is the use of vertical integration, producing inputs previously provided by suppliers or replacing a customer role by disposing of one's own outputs (see Chapter 6). McDonald's used this approach when the company ran into continuous problems with suppliers of hamburger buns in Britain and finally put up money, with two partners, to build its own plant.[33]

Still another alternative approach to control is to change organizational goals and objectives so that the organization is no longer dependent on the particular source of resources. Changing goals is a fairly drastic approach and is not likely to be adopted until other approaches are ruled out. Still, it may be the best alternative in some situations.

TYPES OF CONTROLS

While managers determine the areas that they want to control, they also need to consider the types of controls that they wish to use. In this section, we discuss the major types of controls based on timing, consider the use of multiple controls, and contrast cybernetic and noncybernetic types of controls.

Major Control Types by Timing

Using a systems perspective, one can think of the productive cycle of an organization as encompassing inputs, transformation processes, and outputs that occur at different points in time (see Chapter 2). Accordingly, one major way of classifying controls is based on their timing, or stage in the productive cycle—in other words, on whether they focus on inputs, transformation processes, or outputs (see Figure 17-5). Managers often have options regarding the stage in the transformation cycle at which they institute controls. The three respective types of controls based on timing are feedforward, concurrent, and feedback.

Feedforward Control. **Feedforward control** focuses on the regulation of inputs to ensure that they meet the standards necessary for the transformation process (see Figure 17-5). Inputs that can be subject to feedforward control include materials, people, finances, time, and other resources used by an organization. Feedforward control attempts to evaluate potential inputs and reject or correct those that do not meet standards. The emphasis of feedforward control is on prevention in order to preclude later serious difficulties in the productive process. Feedforward control also is sometimes called *preliminary control, precontrol, preventative control,* or *steering control.*

At its $550 million factory in Flat Rock, Michigan, the Mazda Motor Manufacturing Corporation uses feedforward control by carefully selecting and training workers. Generally, Mazda's efforts at feedforward control have been successful in that the company has hired relatively competent workers. Still, its efforts have run into some difficulty because first-year absenteeism rates have been 8 percent, compared with the expected 5 percent, and turnover has been 2 percent above the expected 5 percent level. One result is that the company has been forced to reduce training for new workers from 3 weeks to 1 in the struggle to meet annual production quotas.[34] Thus, even though feedforward controls often make a significant contribution to organizational effectiveness, they frequently cannot cover every possible contingency. Instead, other types of controls may also be needed.

Concurrent Control. **Concurrent control** involves the regulation of ongoing activities that are part of the transformation process to ensure that they conform to

Feedforward control The regulation of inputs to ensure that they meet the standards necessary for the transformation process

Concurrent control The regulation of ongoing activities that are part of the transformation process to ensure that they conform to organizational standards

Figure 17-5 Major control types by timing.

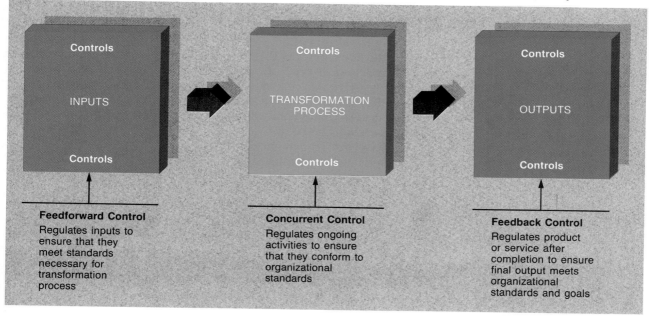

Feedforward Control
Regulates inputs to ensure that they meet standards necessary for transformation process

Concurrent Control
Regulates ongoing activities to ensure that they conform to organizational standards

Feedback Control
Regulates product or service after completion to ensure final output meets organizational standards and goals

organizational standards. With concurrent control, the emphasis is on identifying difficulties in the productive process that could result in faulty output (see Figure 17-5). Concurrent control sometimes is called *screening* or *yes-no control*, because it often involves checkpoints at which determinations are made about whether to continue progress, take corrective action, or stop work altogether on a product or service. Since concurrent control involves regulating ongoing tasks, it requires a thorough understanding of the specific tasks involved and their relationship to the desired end product.[35] In other words, it must be possible to clearly specify standards for how various activities are to be conducted. At Mazda, standards cover every aspect of the automobile production line, including how long it takes to move a car through the body shop, the paint shop, and final assembly (about 27 hours compared with about 32.5 hours at one of GM's most modern plants in Wilmington, Delaware).[36]

As you may have surmised, it can be difficult to use this type of control for endeavors that require creativity and innovation, such as creating advertising or conducting research and development. The reason is that, in such areas, it typically is not possible to specify exactly what should be done to achieve the desired results. Thus, when creativity and innovation are important, the emphasis is most often placed on feedforward control (e.g., competent people, necessary equipment), as well as feedback control.

Feedback control
Regulation exercised after a product or service has been completed in order to ensure that the final output meets organizational standards and goals

Feedback Control. **Feedback control** is regulation exercised after a product or service has been completed in order to ensure that the final output meets organizational standards and goals (see Figure 17-5). Feedback control, sometimes called *postaction control* or *output control*, fulfills a number of important functions.

For one thing, it often is used when feedforward and concurrent controls are not feasible or are too costly. For example, suppose that you are the sales manager for a company that manufactures machine tools. Even if it were possible for you to clearly specify the exact activities that lead to good sales (an unlikely prospect), it still would be difficult for you to use concurrent control beyond a minimum level (e.g., information about scheduled contacts) to check on the specific ongoing task activities of each salesperson in the field. Therefore, you would likely emphasize feedforward control by carefully selecting new hires and then use feedback control by periodically comparing sales quotas (standards) with actual sales.

Feedback control also is often used when the exact processes involved in producing a product or service (e.g., performing complex surgery) are difficult to specify in advance. This type of control can also serve as a final means of checking for deviations that were not detected earlier. Recently, many major companies have been expending great efforts to improve quality so that either feedback control is unnecessary or there are few deviations to detect and, hence, very little scrap or rework to be done (see Chapter 18). During early operations at the new Mazda plant, 70 percent of the finished cars were parked outside, waiting for repairs of defects identified in final inspections. Still, refusing to ship cars that do not adhere to its high standards, the company is working instead to reduce the proportion of cars with defects found by feedback control to 15 percent.[37]

Another function of feedback control is providing information that will facilitate the planning process. Such information, which may include number of units made or sold, cost of various aspects of production, quality measures, return on investment, or clients served, can be used in revising existing plans and formulating new ones. Finally, feedback control provides output information that is particularly useful in the process of rewarding employee performance.

Multiple Controls

Organizations typically set up **multiple control systems,** systems that use two or more of the feedforward, concurrent, and feedback control processes and involve several strategic control points. As mentioned earlier, strategic control points are performance areas chosen for control because they are particularly important in meeting organizational goals. Multiple control systems develop because of the need to control various aspects of a productive cycle, including inputs, transformations, and outputs. For example, the GM assembly plant in Fisherville, Missouri, uses a multiple control system that focuses on the assembly cycle. Plant personnel inspect components prior to using them in cars (a strategic control point); the assembly process has several inspection points (strategic control points); and each car undergoes a final inspection prior to shipping (a strategic control point). The plant goes a step further with feedback control by sending car buyers a postcard with a checklist for indicating comments concerning the condition and operation of the car (another strategic control point). Thus a multiple control system with strategic control points helps General Motors maintain standards and learn about weaknesses in the assembly process that need correcting.

When organizations do not have multiple control systems that focus on strategic control points, they often can experience difficulties that cause managers to reevaluate their control processes. For example, the Lotus Development Corporation increased all three types of timing controls as part of its renewed effort to meet organizational goals related to the revision of its popular Lotus 1-2-3 software package (see the following Case in Point discussion).

> **Multiple control systems** Systems that use two or more of the feedforward, concurrent, and feedback control processes and involve several strategic control points

CASE IN POINT: Developing Better Controls at Lotus

The name "Lotus" is well known in the field of business because of the company's highly successful Lotus 1-2-3 computerized spreadsheet program. At the same time, the field of software development is highly competitive, requiring a steady stream of innovations to stay ahead of challengers. Knowing this, Lotus has developed updated versions of the spreadsheet, as well as produced new versions of its Freelance Plus graphics package that also has sold well. Unfortunately, sales of other new products have lagged, leaving the company precariously dependent on the 1-2-3 spreadsheet for more than 70 percent of its revenues. Lotus's problems were partly related to a disturbing pattern. The company had developed a penchant for announcing new products prior to their completion and then too often found itself unable to deliver them on schedule—to such a point that its announcements began to be ridiculed by industry analysts as "vaporware."

Its most serious problem stemmed from the chronic delays in an announced new version (Release 3.0) of Lotus 1-2-3, a delay that frustrated and angered customers. Many of the customers were forced to shelve plans that depended on the availability of the new version of 1-2-3 as scheduled. Others switched to rival products. One reason for the difficulties in completing the new version was the sheer size of the massive program.

As the revision situation grew more critical, Lotus hired W. Frank King III as senior vice president in charge of the company's Software Products Group. King, a 17-year veteran of IBM with much greater knowledge of software development processes than his Lotus predecessor, quickly began instituting controls. He banned vaporware, a move that required everyone at Lotus to stop talking to outsiders about the new version of 1-2-3 and other major products

> From "vaporware" to software: Lotus' penchant for promising more than it could deliver earned it the reputation of producing "vaporware" until a take-charge manager instituted multiple controls that tracked the production of its most important software product, Lotus 1-2-3. Such controls helped the company to release the new version (Release 3) of the 1-2-3 within a year. (Since then Lotus has produced another version—Release 3.1.)

under development. He also appointed 19 technology "czars" to help make sure that all new Lotus software would share the same standard systems and features. To further enhance coordination and control, he established daily meetings for code writers and program testers to discuss exactly what each was doing and to solve the problems they jointly faced. Schedules detailed exactly what each programmer was to do daily. The entire Software Products Group began meeting monthly. A group of quality assurance testers concentrated on locating errors in the 1-2-3 revision and other products under development. Because of the seriousness of the situation, King even had the quality assurance testers send him daily reports, electronically, of every error found so that he could personally keep close tabs on progress and ensure that corrective action was taken.

Although King was changing the culture by bringing more discipline to the informal way of operating, the controls generally were well received by both management and the work force. The feeling seemed to be that King was instituting the kind of controls that Lotus needed to keep it competitive. His control efforts ultimately led to the release of the new version of 1-2-3 within a year. Release 3.0 received good reviews from computer users because of such features as improved graphs and charts and a three-dimensional spreadsheet. The new release enabled Lotus to retain its dominance in computer-based spreadsheets, with more than 60 percent of the market.[38] ▬

Thus King used feedforward control by attempting to make sure that certain inputs, in this case agreements about standard systems and features to be used across programs, were clear to all participants. He also exercised concurrent control by requiring meetings that were crucial to the ongoing software development activities. Finally, he made use of feedback control by instituting a strong group of quality assurance experts to ensure that the output was free of errors. King's controls required considerable human discretion. The degree of human discretion required forms another means of distinguishing types of control systems.

Cybernetic and Noncybernetic Control

Cybernetic control system
A self-regulating control system that, once it is put into operation, can automatically monitor the situation and take corrective action when necessary

A basic control process can be either cybernetic or noncybernetic, depending on the degree to which human discretion is part of the system. A **cybernetic control system** is a self-regulating control system that, once it is put into operation, can automatically monitor the situation and take corrective action when necessary. A heating system controlled by a thermostat is often used as an example of a cybernetic control system; once the thermostat is set, the self-regulating system keeps the temperature at the designated level without requiring human discretion and intervention. Computerized inventory systems sometimes use cybernetic control by automatically placing an order when inventories of certain items reach a designated level. The ordering is done without requiring human discretion, such as managerial approval before an order is placed.

Noncybernetic control system
A control system that relies on human discretion as a basic part of its process

Although the growing use of computers is increasing the possibilities for cybernetic control, most control systems used by organizations are the noncybernetic type. A **noncybernetic control system** is a control system that relies on human discretion as a basic part of its process. By their very nature, areas that require control in organizations typically go awry in ways that are difficult to predict in advance. Further, they are apt to be complex enough to require human discretion in determining what corrective action is needed. Strictly speaking, even systems that require relatively little human discretion, such as a computerized inventory system with automatic ordering capacity, generate reports for human perusal. They also typically have built-in monitoring systems designed to alert appropriate organization members if things are not progressing as intended. Thus it is difficult to identify significant organizational control systems that do not rely to at least some degree on human discretion, although some may depend more on ongoing human involvement than others.

MANAGERIAL APPROACHES TO IMPLEMENTING CONTROLS

In addition to considering the types of controls they will employ, managers also have options regarding the mechanisms they will use to implement controls. There are three basic managerial approaches to control: market, bureaucratic, and clan. It sometimes is useful to think of these managerial approaches in terms of how the control is exercised—whether through the market, bureaucratic rules, or the clan. Although market control has a somewhat more limited use in organizations than bureaucratic or clan control, all are likely to be used to some extent.

Market Control

Market control relies on market mechanisms to regulate prices for certain clearly specified goods and services needed by an organization, thus relieving managers of the need to establish more elaborate controls over costs. In order to use market control, there must be a reasonable level of competition in the goods or service area and it must also be possible to specify requirements clearly. For example, purchasing departments frequently develop detailed standards or specifications for goods needed by the organization and then initiate a competitive bidding process. Without the specifications and bidding process (or at least alternative sources for the goods or services that can be compared), purchasing agents might have to expend considerable time and effort attempting to control costs by determining whether particular price quotes are reasonable on the basis of the productive processes involved.

While market control often is used to obtain outside goods and services, it also is sometimes used to regulate internal operations as well. In some circumstances, organizations set up profit centers, such as photocopying operations or computer services, which charge other parts of the organization for services rendered.

Since market control works well only when there is a clearly specified product or service involved and considerable competition, its usage as a control mechanism in organizations is somewhat limited. In many situations involving control of internal operations, it may be difficult to specify exact requirements because of uncertainty or changing circumstances (e.g., shifting demand) and there may be little or no competition on which to base pricing (e.g., R&D projects).

Interestingly, General Motors has been making somewhat greater use of market control in pressuring internal divisions to either become more efficient in making parts or face losing the work to outside sources. The automaker currently produces about 70 percent of the parts used in its cars. In making its

Market control A managerial approach that relies on market mechanisms to regulate prices for certain clearly specified goods and services needed by an organization

decisions about who will manufacture certain parts, GM has been comparing the price and quality available through outside suppliers with its own internal costs and quality. Internally, divisions are being told to become more competitive, and many have been making major improvements. For instance, in 1986, workers at GM's inland division plant in Livonia, Michigan, required 48 hours, 6 minutes to complete the interior section of the door for a Chevy Cavalier sedan. Within 3 years, they had cut the time to 12 hours, 7 minutes.[39]

At the same time, in a countertrend to market control, U.S. automakers have also been moving toward establishing long-term contracts with suppliers in order to forge closer relationships, develop better products, and foster improved service (as the Japanese have done). Since the long-run nature of the contracts makes it more difficult for a company to rely on market control, such contracts may lend themselves to the rules and policies that are characteristic of another commonly used managerial approach to control, bureaucratic control.

Bureaucratic Control

Bureaucratic control A managerial approach that relies on regulation through rules, policies, supervision, budgets, schedules, reward systems, and other administrative mechanisms aimed at ensuring that employees exhibit appropriate behaviors and meet performance standards

Bureaucratic control relies on regulation through rules, policies, supervision, budgets, schedules, reward systems, and other administrative mechanisms aimed at ensuring that employees exhibit appropriate behaviors and meet performance standards. Several major characteristics likely to be associated with heavy emphasis on bureaucratic control are shown in Table 17-1. As indicated, with bureaucratic control, the sources of control are mainly external to the individual, the emphasis tends to be on a fixed set of duties that are often narrowly defined, and the focus is on top-down hierarchical control.

Table 17-1 Characteristics Associated with Bureaucratic and Clan Control

Characteristics	Bureaucratic Control	Clan Control
Means of control	Rules, policies, and hierarchy	Shared goals, values, and tradition
Source of control	Mainly external mechanisms	Mainly internal motivation
Job design	Narrow subtasks; doing, rather than thinking	Whole task; doing and thinking
Definition of duties	Fixed	Flexible; contingent on changing conditions
Accountability	Usually individual	Often team
Structure	Tall; top-down controls	Flat; mutual influence
Power usage	Emphasis on legitimate authority	Emphasis on relevant information and expertise
Responsibility	Performing individual job	Upgrading performance of work unit and organization
Reward emphasis	Extrinsic	Intrinsic
Innovation	Less likely	More likely
Likely employee reactions	Compliance	Commitment

Source: Adapted from Richard E. Walton, ''From Control to Commitment in the Workplace,'' *Harvard Business Review,* March–April 1985, p. 81.

One advantage of bureaucratic control is that, unlike the case with market control, it is not necessary to specify all requirements in advance or to rely on competition for control. With bureaucratic control, rules and policies are developed over time to handle a variety of recurring conditions. When unforeseen circumstances or infrequent exceptions occur, supervisors then can decide what corrective action, if any, is necessary. Supervisors also are charged with checking to be sure that individuals follow various rules and other administration mechanisms.

While bureaucratic control is useful for keeping recurring, relatively predictable activities running smoothly, a heavy dosage of this type of control does have some disadvantages. Bureaucratic control is not particularly conducive to innovation, may inhibit needed changes in situations in which the environment shifts rapidly, and tends to engender compliance, rather than commitment, in employees (because of the emphasis on following regulations developed by others; see also Chapter 14 on leadership). For these reasons, a number of organizations are attempting to place greater emphasis on clan control.

Clan Control

Clan control relies on values, beliefs, traditions, corporate culture, shared norms, and informal relationships to regulate employee behaviors and facilitate the reaching of organizational goals. Several major characteristics likely to be related to heavy use of clan control are listed in Table 17-1. In contrast to bureaucratic control, clan control places greater emphasis on internal motivation, flexible duties and broad tasks, and influence based on relevant information and expertise rather than on position in the hierarchy.

With clan control, as the name implies, there is greater emphasis on groups, and teams are often the focus of responsibility. Clan control is often used in situations involving professionals, in which professional training and norms, as well as group identification, help substitute for the strong emphasis on rules and regulations characteristic of bureaucratic control.

Partially because of the greater prospects for commitment to organizational objectives and the increased willingness to help bring about improvements in the workplace, a number of organizations with relatively routine types of jobs are also attempting to incorporate greater emphasis on clan control. One such organization is Cummins Engine, a manufacturer of heavy-duty truck engines, which has been making a concerted effort to inform employees about the business, encourage participation and ideas from everyone, and develop jobs with greater flexibility and responsibility.[40] Teams are being used in a variety of industries, including the insurance, automobile, aerospace, electronics, food-processing, paper, steel, and financial services industries (see also Chapter 16).[41]

Generally, clan control is more conducive to innovation than is bureaucratic control, although it is possible that a group with strong norms toward conformity and the status quo could tend to inhibit innovation. In order to counter such possibilities, organizations with strong reputations for innovation generally work hard to build norms and values that support efforts toward innovation and change.

Clan control A managerial approach that relies on values, beliefs, traditions, corporate culture, shared norms, and informal relationships to regulate employee behaviors and facilitate the reaching of organizational goals

Blending the Approaches

Most organizations do not rely totally on either bureaucratic or clan control. Rather, the managerial approach to control depends on placing greater emphasis on one and lesser emphasis on the other, as well as using some market control. In the situation with Lotus, for example, the company relied heavily on clan control, but King interjected some bureaucratic control to supplement the clan control. One organization that has been successful in blending strong clan control with advantageous use of bureaucratic control is United Parcel Service (see the following Case in Point discussion).

CASE IN POINT: UPS Runs a Tight Ship

A recent company slogan, "We run the tightest ship in the shipping business," sets the theme. Today, United Parcel Service (UPS) is the most profitable transportation company in the United States, with more than 116,000 vehicles and over 100 aircraft delivering packages around the clock to 180 countries and territories. Founded in 1907 in Seattle, Washington, as a messenger service that would be owned by its managers and managed by its owners, the company has kept most of its stock in the hands of its 20,000 managers through a generous annual bonus plan. Some managers who began as clerks or drivers retire as millionaires. When managers leave or retire, they must sell their stock back to the company, thus keeping company ownership in the hands of current managers. This closely held ownership allows the company to make long-term strategic decisions without being concerned about reactions of outside investors.

With few exceptions, employees move up only by starting at the bottom and learning firsthand about the company. Because UPS employs about 82,000 college students as part-time package sorters, it has a vast army of workers from which to select full-time employees. For those chosen, the next step is van, or package-car, driver—a job that pays relatively well and is held in high esteem. According to one observer, "The drivers are the real heroes of the company— living, breathing Norman Rockwell portraits. They are 365-day-a-year Santa Clauses bringing the goodies." On average, a middle manager with 10 years of service makes a modest $54,000 in salary but also usually receives about $14,000 in stock and a $7500 dividend check.

Part of the uniqueness of UPS is its corporate culture, described by one former member of the board of directors as half Marine Corps and half Quaker meeting. Teamwork is emphasized over individual glory, and there is a strong norm of egalitarianism. The Greenwich, Connecticut, headquarters and the regional centers are extremely spartan; there are no designated parking places for executives; first names are used for everyone; and no one has a private secretary—not even the chairman of the board. One board member notes, "When we have our meetings in Greenwich, we directors troop downstairs to the cafeteria, stand in line, and pay our $2.17 for a tuna sandwich." One result is that company employees exhibit an enviable commitment to hard work and an unusually strong dedication to the company. It is not uncommon for some 80 percent of the work force to attend voluntary workshops on the company's competitive position that are held after working hours. Thus clan control is strong at UPS.

On the other hand, UPS establishes policies and procedures over every aspect of its operations. Tasks are carefully analyzed to determine appropriate productivity standards. For example, sorters at the massive company hub in Addison (near Chicago), Illinois, are expected to load delivery vans at the rate of

UPS Chairman John W. Rogers determined that by the end of 1989 UPS vehicles and their uniformed drivers would be "seen throughout much of the world." Whether the driver is in Hong Kong (as shown here) or Rome or San Francisco, UPS' close control over policies and procedures ensures that the vehicles are clean and that the uniforms look sharp. But UPS also relies on clan control: almost all UPS shares are owned by employees, and they take great pride in the efficiency and egalitarianism of their company.

500 to 650 packages each hour and unload them almost twice as fast. Pickup and delivery routes are also meticulously timed for each regular stop on the routes. Supervisors regularly recheck these times to ensure that conditions have not changed. When drivers leave in the morning, their supervisors usually can estimate to within 6 minutes just how long their pickups and deliveries will take. All vehicles are washed every day and are rigorously maintained in accordance with computerized schedules. As a result, the vans or package cars used to deliver packages to customers remain in service an astounding average of 22 years, and long-haul trucks often run 2 million miles or more.

Competitors such as Federal Express, which uses high technology to track exactly where a package is at any given time, are forcing UPS to move more boldly into the high-tech era. UPS is currently adding airplanes to its fleet and implementing such devices as electronic scanners in its sorting centers and computers on its delivery vans. It is also experimenting with innovations like computerized clipboards that will reproduce signatures for delivered goods and show exact times of all transactions. These devices will provide even more control over operations. At the same time, these changes are forcing the company to hire experts, such as pilots, airplane mechanics, and computer programmers, from the outside—posing a potential threat to the cohesive corporate culture.[42]

Choosing a Managerial Control Style

Since most organizations use a combination of approaches in implementing controls, individual managers need to give some consideration to the control approach, or style, that is most appropriate for the operations for which they are directly responsible.[43] In deciding on a particular managerial control style, it is helpful to consider the four questions shown in Table 17-2, which deal with managerial leadership style, organizational, structural issues, accuracy and reliability of measures, and subordinate orientations toward participation.

Table 17-2   Questions Managers Should Ask Themselves When Choosing a Control Style

1. In general, what kind of managerial style do I have?

PARTICIPATIVE	DIRECTIVE
I frequently consult my subordinates on decisions, encourage them to disagree with my opinion, share information with them, and let them make decisions whenever possible.	I usually take most of the responsibility for and make most of the major decisions, pass on only the most relevant job information, and provide detailed and close direction for my subordinates.

2. In general, what kind of climate, structure, and reward system does my organization have?

PARTICIPATIVE	NONPARTICIPATIVE
Employees at all levels of the organization are urged to participate in decisions and influence the course of events. Managers are clearly rewarded for developing employee skills and decision-making capacities.	Most important decisions are made by a few people at the top of the organization. Managers are not rewarded for developing employee competence or for encouraging employees to participate in decision making.

3. How accurate and reliable are the measures of key areas of subordinate performance?

ACCURATE	INACCURATE
All major aspects of performance can be adequately measured; changes in measures accurately reflect changes in performance; and measures cannot be easily sabotaged or faked by subordinates.	Not all critical aspects of performance can be measured; measures often do not pick up on important changes in performance; good performance cannot be adequately defined in measurement terms, and measures can be easily sabotaged.

4. Do my subordinates desire to participate and respond well to opportunities to take responsibility for decision making and performance?

HIGH DESIRE TO PARTICIPATE	LOW DESIRE TO PARTICIPATE
Employees are eager to participate in decisions, are involved in the work itself, can make a contribution to decision making, and want to take more responsibility.	Employees do not want to be involved in many decisions, do not want additional responsibility, have little to contribute to decisions being made, and are not very involved in the work itself.

Source: Reprinted from Cortlandt Cammann and David Nadler, "Fit Control Systems to Your Management Style," *Harvard Business Review,* January–February 1976, p. 70.

The four questions relate to the decision tree shown in Figure 17-6 and provide guidance regarding the overall control approach that is likely to be most appropriate. For example, a clan approach with emphasis on internal motivation is most appropriate when a manager's leadership style tends to be participative, the organization's climate and structure are oriented toward participation, and subordinates want and are able to participate. Conversely, a bureaucratic approach with emphasis on external control will likely be more effective when a manager's leadership style is directive, the organization's climate and structure lean toward nonparticipation, performance is relatively easy to measure, and subordinates have little desire to participate. Other branches of the decision tree, representing more mixed conditions, point toward modified general approaches, using elements of both clan and bureaucratic control.

The decision tree can assist a manager in deciding on a general approach to control style. However, even a manager who chooses a clan approach is likely to use at least some bureaucratic control. For example, the head of a research laboratory who depends heavily on clan control is still apt to implement some bureaucratic controls, such as rules regarding levels of expenditures that do not

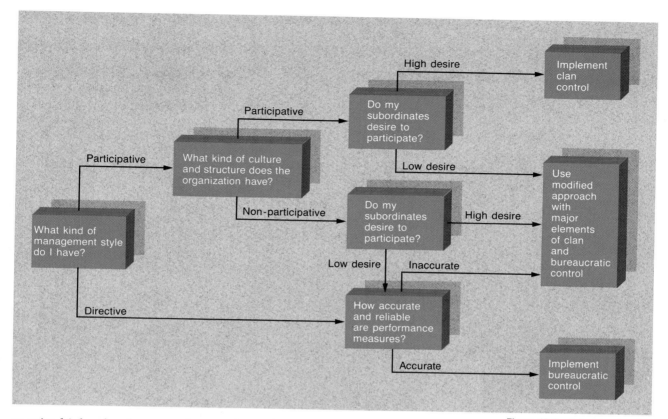

Figure 17-6 A decision tree for choosing a managerial control style. (Adapted from Cortlandt Cammann and David A. Nadler, "Fit Control Systems to Your Managerial Style," *Harvard Business Review*, January–February 1976, pp. 69, 71.)

require higher-level approval, procedures for ordering equipment, and policies regarding visitors. Similarly, managers supervising routine operations with strong bureaucratic controls may attempt to build at least some group norms that support organizational goals (see also Chapter 16 on managing groups).

Promoting Innovation: Control and the Innovation Process

When it comes to controlling major innovative efforts, such as R&D projects, innovation expert James Brian Quinn argues that it helps to view the ideal innovation process as "controlled chaos." On the one hand, the process of innovation is fairly unpredictable and, hence, somewhat chaotic. On the other hand, the process can be controlled to some degree by combining heavy reliance on clan control with the use of some carefully considered bureaucratic controls. Unfortunately, many companies unwittingly establish bureaucratic controls that constitute substantial barriers to major innovations. In this section, we consider some of the ways that bureaucratic controls create barriers to innovations, as well as explore an incrementalist approach to providing some control over the process without stifling innovations.[44]

Bureaucratic Barriers. There are a number of common ways that controls create bureaucratic barriers to innovation. For one thing, controls often are geared to relatively short time horizons, largely because of pressures on companies to report a steady stream of quarterly profits. These pressures can lead to an emphasis on quick marketing pushes, cost cutting, and acquisitions. Such short-term tactics operate to the detriment of process and product innovations, which typically entail 7 to 15 years in the discovery-to-development phase but have greater long-run potential. Another barrier to innovation is the use of accounting controls that assess direct, indirect, overhead, overtime, and service costs against projects in their embryonic stages. Early cost emphasis may make a project appear to be impractical before the real potential of the project can be reasonably assessed. To counter this problem, innovative companies, such as 3M, encourage scientists to "bootleg," that is, to allocate a certain portion of their work time to new research directions without the necessity of receiving hierarchical approval. (For further details about innovation at 3M, see the opening case in Chapter 11.) Another common bureaucratic barrier to innovation is excessive rationalism, the expectation that the innovative process will proceed according to an orderly, predetermined timetable with specified control points. Unfortunately, major innovations rarely follow such a predictable timetable, and such unrealistic expectations discourage innovative efforts. Still another barrier is the presence of excessive rules and regulations requiring that approvals be received for virtually every move, thus interfering with timely feedback to the innovation process and raising costs. Finally, controls and the related reward systems often are geared to minimizing surprises by ensuring that individuals behave in conformity with current expectations. While such predictability may be functional in many instances (e.g., in producing service consistency), it also is the antithesis of major innovations, which by definition include an inherent element of surprise.

Incrementalist Approach. One solution to the problem of controlling major innovation efforts is the use of the incrementalist approach.[45] The **incrementalist approach** to controlling an innovation project relies heavily on clan control but also involves a phased set of plans and accompanying bureaucratic controls that begin at a very general level and grow more specific as the project progresses. In early stages of the incrementalist approach, managers set general goals, select key individuals for the project, set a few critical limits (such as spending limits), and establish a few major decision points for checking progress.

At the middle stages of the project, when more is known about its technical aspects and/or when market needs become more evident, managers set a few more critical performance goals, limitations, and checkpoints. Still, managers allow the members of the technical groups to decide how they will pursue the goals, within the limits and checkpoints, since there are likely to be many questions remaining.

At later stages of the innovation process, when many of the key variables are understood and perhaps demonstrated in laboratory experiments, more concrete controls may be possible to accompany more specific planning. Even at this stage, many factors may be unknown and several technical options may still be pursued. However, at the specified review points, options that cannot meet performance targets will be eliminated. The decision to kill a project is a difficult one and will likely involve a judgment call due to the fact that there are still unknowns. Because of the uncertainty, managers often continue some of the options that appear less promising, but at a lower resource level. It is not uncommon for the smaller-scale options to produce significant breakthroughs, while the planned option fails. Sony's famous Walkman, a miniature stereo cassette player with lightweight earphones, grew out of a failed attempt to produce a miniature tape recorder with stereo sound. The idea to combine a miniature player, which was the creation of one engineering group, with the earphones being made by another group came from Honorary Chairman Masaru Ibuka, founder of Sony. Still, the company originally put a minimum amount of money and personnel into the product launch, thinking of it primarily as a toy for young people.[46]

Incrementalist approach
An approach to controlling an innovation project that relies heavily on clan control but also involves a phased set of plans and accompanying bureaucratic controls that begin at a very general level and grow more specific as the project progresses

The incrementalist approach requires that managers strike an appropriate balance among the control approaches in order to encourage innovation. Otherwise, control systems can themselves stifle innovation and inhibit long-term organizational effectiveness.

ASSESSING CONTROL SYSTEMS

Whether controls are developed for facilitating innovation or for other purposes, managers need to assess control systems continually to be sure that the systems are achieving the results intended. In this section, we consider potential dysfunctional aspects of control systems. The presence of any of these aspects indicates that a control system needs adjusting. We also examine the issue of overcontrol versus undercontrol, and we conclude by reviewing the characteristics of an effective control system.

Potential Dysfunctional Aspects of Control Systems

As you might imagine, not all effects of control systems are positive. When controls are designed poorly and/or are excessive, they may result in one or more of four major dysfunctional side-effects: behavioral displacement, game playing, operating delays, or negative attitudes.[47]

Behavioral Displacement. **Behavioral displacement** is a condition in which individuals engage in behaviors that are encouraged by controls and related reward systems even though the behaviors actually are inconsistent with organizational goals. In one case, a research laboratory decided to use the number of patents filed as an indicator of effectiveness. Unfortunately, there was a major increase in the number of patents filed but a decrease in the number of successful research projects.[48] Displacement usually can be traced to three basic causes: inadequate analysis of the relationship between the controls and the desired outcomes, overemphasis on quantification of control measures when qualitative aspects also are important, and overemphasis on activities, rather than on necessary end results.

Behavioral displacement
A condition in which individuals engage in behaviors that are encouraged by controls and related reward systems even though the behaviors actually are inconsistent with organizational goals

Game Playing. Game playing with controls occurs when managers attempt to improve their standing on performance measures by manipulating resource usage and/or data rather than by achieving bona fide performance improvements. Manipulating resource usage usually involves negotiating for more resources than necessary to do a job so that objectives can be easily met or exceeded. Some slack in resource levels may be functional in that it provides a buffer against unforeseen contingencies; carried too far, it can undermine the competitive position of the organization through inflated costs. Manipulating data involves either actually falsifying performance data or influencing performance results during the time period for which the data are reported.

Operating Delays. Operating delays often develop as the result of actions required by feedforward and concurrent controls. To the extent that they are excessive, such controls can seriously cripple, rather than facilitate, efforts to reach organizational goals. They may also engender actions that undermine the effects of the controls. For example, one study in a diversified corporation showed that 74 percent of the general managers reported obtaining required expenditure approvals *after* the money had in fact been spent.[49]

Negative Attitudes. Controls often lead to negative attitudes, particularly when they seem excessive or are poorly designed.[50] Professionals, in particular, are likely to resist controls, especially bureaucratic controls that seem to hinder, rather than help, the attainment of organizational goals.

Overcontrol versus Undercontrol

Overcontrol The limiting of individual job autonomy to such a point that it seriously inhibits effective job performance

Undercontrol The granting of autonomy to an employee to such a point that the organization loses its ability to direct the individual's efforts toward achieving organizational goals

Since excessive amounts of control can make the occurrence of dysfunctional aspects of control systems more likely, managers need to avoid overcontrol. **Overcontrol** is the limiting of individual job autonomy to such a point that it seriously inhibits effective job performance. At the same time, managers need to avoid going too far in the other direction, which results in a situation of undercontrol. **Undercontrol** is the granting of autonomy to an employee to such a point that the organization loses its ability to direct the individual's efforts toward achieving organizational goals. In fact, undercontrol is the reason frequently given to explain why organizations do not achieve their goals.

For instance, undercontrol at JWT Group, Inc. (formerly the seventh-largest advertising agency in the United States) was a major factor in its being purchased by the London-based WPP Group, PLC, in the late 1980s. At the time, JWT was suffering from management upheavals and runaway costs. The culture of the organization was one that encouraged big spending, overstaffing, and laxness in collecting receivables that typically became long overdue. Little attention was given to serious financial management. (We discuss financial controls in Chapter 18.) The year before the company was purchased by the WPP Group, JWT revenues rose 11 percent but pretax profits dropped 40 percent. After purchasing the company, WPP instituted cost-cutting measures, tight financial controls, and a goal of a 10 percent profit margin by the early 1990s. Now six regional finance directors receive daily cash balances, weekly receivables, monthly profit statements, and 2-year rolling budgets from their subordinates. The traditional practice of giving generous raises to managers has been replaced by a bonus system tied to the agency's profits. The response to these controls has been fairly good, with the agency beginning to make a profit, yet further work on effective controls still is required.[51]

Determining the appropriate amount of control that should exist in an organization is a significant managerial decision. With the appropriate amount of control, a manager can be reasonably certain that no major unpleasant surprises will occur and that employees will achieve organizational goals.[52]

Characteristics of an Effective Control System

Effective control systems have certain characteristics.[53] They form a checklist for assessing control systems that are being designed or are in operation.

Future-Oriented. To be effective, control systems need to help regulate future events, rather than fix blame for past events. A well-designed control system focuses on letting managers know how work is progressing toward unit objectives, pinpointing areas in which future corrective action is needed, and uncovering unforeseen opportunities that might be developed—all aids to future action.

Multidimensional. In most cases, control systems need to be multidimensional in order to capture the major relevant performance factors. For example, the GM assembly plant in Fisherville, Missouri, mentioned earlier, would quickly run into difficulty if it focused only on quantity without concern for other issues, such as quality, scrap rate, and overhead.

Cost-Effective. The cost of controls is an important consideration. One major control factor at McDonald's is clean rest rooms. The company manual specifies how often the rest rooms must be cleaned, and there are provisions for both the outlet manager and the company inspection teams to check this factor.[54] Still, McDonald's could control rest-room cleanliness even further by dedicating one person at each outlet to do nothing but ensure cleanliness. The costs of doing so, however, may well be greater than the benefits to be derived from the additional controls, since McDonald's already has one of the best reputations in the industry for cleanliness. Essentially, the benefits should outweigh the costs.

Accurate. Since controls provide the basis for future actions, accuracy is vital. Control data that are seriously inaccurate may be worse than no controls at all, since managers may make poor decisions on the basis of faulty data that they believe to be accurate.

Realistic. Control systems should incorporate realistic expectations about what can be accomplished. Otherwise, employees are likely to view the control system as unreasonable and may ignore or even sabotage it.

Timely. Control systems are designed to provide data on the state of a given production cycle or process as of a specific time, for example, a monthly sales report, a weekly update on a project, a daily production report, or quality inspections on a production line. In order for managers and employees to respond promptly to irregularities, control systems must provide relevant information soon enough to allow corrective action before there are serious repercussions.

Monitorable. Another desirable characteristic of control systems is that they can be monitored to ensure that they are performing as expected. One way of checking a control system is to deliberately insert an imperfection, such as a defective part, and then observe how long it takes the system to detect and report it to the correct individual. Obviously, it is important to keep close tabs on the test to be sure that the imperfection does not cause significant difficulties if the control system fails (as in, e.g., a test of maintenance quality for airplanes). Other methods of monitoring control systems are by conducting audits of various kinds. (We discuss financial audits in Chapter 18.)

Acceptable to Organization Members. Control systems operate best when they are accepted by the organization members who are affected by them. Otherwise, members may take actions to override and undermine the controls. Control systems are apt to be accepted when they focus on important issues that are compatible with organizational goals, when they provide useful data to various levels, when the data collected give a fair and accurate picture of employee performance, and when the emphasis is on using the data for making improvements (as opposed to setting blame).

Flexible. Just as organizations must be flexible to respond rapidly to changing environments, control systems need to be flexible enough to meet new or revised requirements. Accordingly, they should be designed so that they can be changed quickly to measure and report new information and track new endeavors.

While this chapter has focused on basic concepts underlying control systems in organizations, the next chapter examines more closely several specific managerial control methods, such as financial control and quality control.

CHAPTER SUMMARY

Controlling is the process of regulating organizational activities so that actual performance conforms to expected organizational goals and standards. Controls play important roles in helping managers handle five particular challenges: coping with uncertainty, detecting irregularities, identifying opportunities, handling complex situations, and decentralizing authority. Just as planning responsibilities differ by level, there are parallel control responsibilities at the strategic, tactical, and operational levels.

The basic process used in control has several major steps: Determine areas to control; establish standards; measure performance; compare performance against standards; if standards are met or exceeded, recognize performance; if standards are not met, take corrective action as necessary; and adjust standards and measures as necessary. The resource dependence approach to controls argues that managers need to consider controls mainly in areas in which they depend on others for resources necessary to reach organizational goals. Four conditions that help delineate when controls should be used are a high dependence on the resource, an expectation that resource flows may be unacceptable without controls, the feasibility of instituting a control process, and acceptable control process costs.

There are several different types of controls. Major types of controls by timing are feedforward control, concurrent control, and feedback control. In addition, managers often need to use multiple control systems, systems that use two or more of the feedforward, concurrent, and feedback control processes and involve several strategic control points. Finally, control systems can be cybernetic or noncybernetic, depending on the degree to which human discretion is part of the system.

Managers also have options regarding the approaches that they will use to implement controls. The three basic approaches are market, bureaucratic, and clan. Although market control has a somewhat more limited application in organizations than bureaucratic or clan control, all are likely to be used to some extent. In choosing the managerial control approach, or style, that is most appropriate, managers need to consider their leadership style, organizational structural issues, the accuracy and reliability of measures, and subordinate orientation toward participation.

Managers often find it helpful to view the innovation process as "controlled chaos." Bureaucratic controls often create barriers to innovation. One solution to the problem of controlling major innovation efforts is to use the incrementalist approach, which relies heavily on clan control but also involves a phased set of plans and accompanying bureaucratic controls that begin at a very general level and grow more specific as the project progresses.

Potential dysfunctional aspects of control systems are behavioral displacement, game playing, operating delays, and negative attitudes. As a result, managers need to avoid engaging in either overcontrol or undercontrol. Effective control systems should be future-oriented, multidimensional, cost-effective, accurate, realistic, timely, monitorable, acceptable to organization members, and flexible.

MANAGERIAL TERMINOLOGY

behavioral displacement (619)
bureaucratic control (612)
clan control (613)
concurrent control (607)
control system (594)
controlling (594)

cybernetic control system (610)
feedback control (608)
feedforward control (607)
goal incongruence (601)
incrementalist approach (618)

management by exception (603)
market control (611)
multiple control systems (609)
noncybernetic control system (610)
operational control (598)

overcontrol (620)
resource dependence (604)
strategic control (598)
strategic control points (604)
tactical control (598)
undercontrol (620)

QUESTIONS FOR DISCUSSION AND REVIEW

1. Explain the five major roles of controls. Give three examples from your college or university of controls that fulfill at least one of these roles.

2. Describe the three major levels of controls in organizations. For an organization with which you are familiar, identify a control at each level.

3. Outline the general process that can be applied to most control situations. Using the control process, explain how you would develop a system to control the home delivery staff for a local pizzeria.

4. Explain the major factors, or conditions, that managers need to consider in deciding what to control. Use these conditions to assess a control that exists at your college or university.

5. Describe each of the major types of controls by timing. Suppose that you are managing a small factory that makes specialized microchips for a well-known computer manufacturer. Explain how you might use each of the major types of controls to help maintain adequate control over the manufacturing process. What strategic control points might you use? For each type of control that you explain, indicate whether you consider it to be cybernetic or noncybernetic.

6. Explain the three basic approaches to implementing controls. For each approach, give an example based on an organization with which you are familiar.

7. Outline the major factors that should be considered in choosing a managerial control style. Suppose that you are a manager supervising experienced professionals who have a high desire to participate in decision making and whose work is somewhat difficult to measure accurately. Which type of managerial control style would you probably adopt? Why? Describe a situation in which you believe that the opposite type of style might be more appropriate.

8. Explain the incrementalist approach to controlling innovation. How does the development of Sony's famous Walkman illustrate the incrementalist approach?

9. Identify the major potential dysfunctional aspects of control systems in organizations. How might overcontrol or undercontrol contribute to these dysfunctional aspects?

10. Delineate the major characteristics of effective control systems. Use these characteristics to evaluate controls at United Parcel Service.

DISCUSSION QUESTIONS FOR CHAPTER OPENING CASE

1. Assess the extent to which the major roles of controls are evidenced at McDonald's.

2. Explain how McDonald's managers use major control types by timing to increase the prospects for reaching organizational goals.

3. Use the characteristics of effective control systems to assess the effectiveness of controls at McDonald's.

MANAGEMENT EXERCISE: OPPORTUNITY KNOCKS

You and a friend have what you believe to be the opportunity of a lifetime. You are both graduating from college this year, and your friend's father has asked the two of you whether you would like to buy the air conditioning and heating business he founded and has operated for the last 30 years. It has been a very lucrative business for him; today he is a millionaire many times over. You are aware that his firm is the leader in its field in your area, and you see the possibility of expanding because many new homes are being built in the local three-county region.

Your friend's father will finance the buyout through a loan, which would be paid off over the next 10 years. Both you and your friend have some degree of expertise in the heating and air-conditioning field as you have both worked for his father the past four summers and sometimes during the Christmas break from college. His father has agreed to be a consultant to the two of you for a year or two if you need his advice.

The firm has almost 60 well-qualified employees, a large inventory, 40 service trucks that are in excellent condition, and a well-established list of clients. At the same time, the return on investment has been lower than average for the past 3 years, labor costs are very high, and the company has attracted only a few new clients during the past 2 years. In addition, you have some indication that the firm is not carrying the most up-to-date heating or air-conditioning equipment, and the four large structures used to house the showrooms and service centers need refurbishing very badly.

You and your friend are discussing the possibility of buying the firm. In considering the situation, you are reviewing the forms of control and the control process you will implement to ensure effective control in the firm.

Exercise Requirement

Discuss the types of control you and your friend would use and the control process the two of you would implement as the new owners of the firm.

LOOSE CONTROLS LEAD TO THE DEMISE OF E. F. HUTTON

In December 1987, the deal was completed. Shearson Lehman Brothers, the nation's biggest investment firm, had purchased E. F. Hutton, the tenth-largest investment firm, for about $1 billion. Actually, the demise of the 84-year-old Hutton organization had started several years before.

There were many indicators that the firm was not operating as it should. As one former Hutton officer put it, between 1983 and 1985, Robert Fomon, the chairman and chief executive officer, "lost control of the firm and no one ever regained it."

In 1985, the firm's plea of guilty to 2000 counts of mail and wire fraud conducted between 1980 and 1982 brought extensive criticism from the press and Congress. The firm had intentionally overdrawn enormous sums from many of its bank accounts for a day or two to gain interest-free cash. As part of the guilty plea, Hutton agreed to pay a $2 million fine and $750,000 in legal costs to the government and to reimburse $8 million to the banks that had been victimized.

Another indicator of lack of control was the way the firm was managed by Robert Fomon, who wielded almost absolute power over the organization for 16 years. Fomon apparently hired and promoted whomever he wanted, including close friends. He personally reviewed the salaries and bonuses of over 1000 employees, disdained organizational budgets and planning, had affairs with a number of Hutton employees, and put his girlfriends on the payroll. His liking for young women was brought to the public's attention on several occasions, but most notable and embarrassing to the firm was a profile presented in *M*, a men's fashion magazine. One picture in this article showed him at a party with his arms around two attractive young women. Fomon told the interviewer that he was old enough to be the grandfather of some of the women he dated and that they were decorative, nice to look at, and had keen senses of humor. The board of directors found this kind of publicity entirely inappropriate. To make matters worse, Hutton was hiring women from various escort services to be present at parties he attended and then was charging the expenses under the category of temporary clerical and secretarial help.

Money was also being squandered in various other areas. One officer charged $900,000 in travel and entertainment expenses in 1986, a year during which the firm was losing money. During the same general period, Hutton spent $30 million sending its best-paid brokers and their wives on all-expenses-paid trips. In some cases, commissions were prepaid; in others, loans were given interest-free to certain employees. Perhaps the most flagrant unnecessary expenditure of funds was the huge cost of moving the firm's headquarters from downtown to expensive midtown facilities when the firm was not doing well financially.

There were some bright spots in the otherwise steady decline of the firm. Robert Rittereiser, hired as the chief operating officer in 1985, was able to set up some legal and financial controls. Unfortunately, the controls were too little, too late to turn the firm around. Although in the second quarter of 1987 Hutton reported a profit, its first for some time, the profit came from the sale of E. F. Hutton Insurance Group, Inc.

Hutton was a prime target for a takeover prior to the October 19, 1987, stock market crash. With the crash, its stock fell from $35 to $15 a share within a 2-week period. The decline made Hutton an even more attractive target for Shearson Lehman Brothers, a rival investment firm largely owned by American Express. Shearson Lehman, which had been doing very well and had a stable management structure, acquired Hutton for $960 million, absorbed the Hutton assets, changed its name to Shearson Lehman Hutton Holdings, Inc., and set about trying to rein in the out-of-control organization. Unfortunately, successfully combining the two firms into one investment firm was more difficult than anticipated. Part of the reason was that although the stock market strongly rebounded from its 1987 low, individual investors continued to shun the market, leaving Shearson Lehman Hutton with too many stockbrokers and insufficient customers. By 1990, American Express was forced to invest roughly $1.35 billion in the investment firm and finally purchase the remaining 30 percent of the shares owned by the public in order to protect Shearson Lehman Hutton's credit rating and quell rumors of the investment firm's possible collapse.[55]

QUESTIONS FOR CHAPTER CONCLUDING CASE

1. Discuss the controls employed by Hutton from 1982 to 1987.
2. Evaluate Fomon's actions in terms of goal incongruence and the effects on organizational control.
3. Assume that you accepted the position of controller at Hutton prior to its demise. In an agreement with the firm, you were assured that your recommendations would be implemented. What would you have done to establish a control system?

CHAPTER EIGHTEEN

MANAGERIAL CONTROL METHODS

CHAPTER OUTLINE

Major Control Systems
Managerial Level
Timing Emphasis

Financial Control
Financial Statements
Ratio Analysis
Comparative Financial Analysis
Financial Audits
Avoiding Financial Control Pitfalls

Budgetary Control
Responsibility Centers
Types of Budgets
The Budgetary Process
Zero-Base Budgeting
Impacts of the Budgeting Process

Quality Control
Strategic Implications of Quality
Total Quality Control
Promoting Innovation: Quality Circles
   and Beyond
Statistical Aids to Quality Control

Inventory Control
Significance of Inventory
Costs of Inventory
Economic Order Quantity
Just-in-Time Inventory Control

LEARNING OBJECTIVES

After studying this chapter, you should be able to:

■ Explain how major control systems differ according to managerial level and timing.

■ Describe the financial statements, ratio analyses, comparative analyses, and financial audits used in financial control.

■ Distinguish among the different types of responsibility centers and budgets.

■ Contrast top-down, bottom-up, mixed, and zero-base budgeting.

■ Describe the eight dimensions of quality and their implications for competing on quality.

■ Explain total quality control, quality circles, employee involvement teams, and statistical quality control aids.

■ Discuss the significance of inventory and the related costs.

■ Explain the economic order quantity and just-in-time approaches to inventory control.

CONTROLS MAKE FOOD LION A ROARING SUCCESS

When Ralph Ketner went to his friend Paul Ritchie, a postal clerk at the time, and asked him to buy some stock in a grocery store that he was going to open in their hometown of Salisbury, North Carolina, Ritchie did not hesitate. "Knowing how smart Ralph is, I thought, 'Somewhere along the line that's bound to be a good stock.'" The 10 shares that Ritchie bought for $100 in 1957 have grown to 129,000 shares worth more than $1.4 million today. Eighty-six other people from the Salisbury and local Rowan County area are now million-aires—including Ralph Ketner, currently chairman of the board—because of their small early investments.

The original food store has grown into a chain, called Food Lion, that will number 1000 stores by 1992. The stores, located in eight southeastern states stretching from Delaware to Florida, collectively take in $3 billion per year, an amount that is expected to reach $5 billion in the 1990s. Food Lion's numbers are impressive. For the past 20 years, annual sales have increased an average of 37 percent and annual profits an average of 55 percent, giving shareholders annual returns on equity averaging 24 percent. During the 1970s, Delhaize, a Belgian supermarket company, acquired a 50.4 percent stake in Food Lion for $16 million, but it has strictly kept its hands off operations as the worth of its holdings has increased tenfold.

Food Lion's strategy is quite simple—low cost. The chain implements the strategy by handling only fast-moving products, selling them in large volumes at low prices, and being tenacious about controlling expenses. For example, the average Food Lion store carries only about 15,000 products, compared to the 20,000 carried by the competition. Limited shelf space is allocated according to how well products and brands sell, with allocations reviewed every 6 months. Food Lion's aggressive low-pricing policy is based on its approach of selling certain basic items at cost, including baby food, coffee, shortening, cat food, dog food, rice, and detergents. Most other goods, such as produce and frozen foods, are priced slightly lower than or at a comparable level with the prices of competitors.

Food Lion uses a nontraditional form of inventory control to its advantage. Many companies have limited warehouse space and strive to turn their inventory over as many times as possible annually in order to achieve low storage or holding costs per item and to avoid tying up funds for lengthy periods (since suppliers must be paid while items are sitting in the warehouse waiting to be used or sold). In contrast, Food Lion invests in large warehouses to support its strategy of buying very large quantities of products when they are at their lowest prices. The costs associated with having the larger warehouses and paying for products that are stored for relatively long periods of time are more than offset by the lower purchase prices of the products. Company buyers try to take advantage of the special promotion deals that manufacturers offer periodically. For example, if Ocean Spray is offering a discount on CranApple juice, Food Lion will buy enough to last until the next promotion. "They use inventory as a weapon," says Bob Goodale, president of a competing chain.

Although Food Lion offers low prices, its profit margins are enviable by industry standards. During the past decade, the company has averaged an annual 2.7 percent return on sales, compared with the 1.5 percent typical for the industry. Recently, its selling and administrative costs have been running about

12.3 percent of sales, significantly below the 20 percent that is common for major competitors.

Innovative expense cutting also is a key element in the company's low-cost strategy. At Food Lion, employees save everything possible for reuse, such as boxes, tires, and envelopes. Former banana crates are used as bins for cosmetics. Heat that is generated by refrigeration units is recycled. Grinding up fat and bones cut from meat and selling them as fertilizer nets the company $1 million per year. No one is allowed to fly first class. By producing their own television spots, often starring CEO Tom Smith, the company keeps advertising costs to less than 0.5 percent of sales, or one-fourth the industry average. Food Lion's spartan stores are slightly smaller than those of the competition, but consequently cost just $650,000 to build, compared with the normal $1 million. The company also saves money by locating stores within 200 miles of its warehouses. Food Lion usually builds stores in clusters and then expands to new markets from warehouses on the periphery.

To make sure that expenses stay low and sales high, headquarters keeps close control over a number of major factors. For example, lights, heating, and refrigeration for all stores are controlled by computer from headquarters. Major decisions about buying, pricing, merchandising, and displaying are made by a central group of specialists. Regional staffs do make some adjustments to fit local markets, but for the most part, a bottle of ketchup will be located in the same place in a store in Ocean City, Maryland, as in one in Richmond, Virginia, and is likely to cost the same. "Keep it simple" is one maxim of the company. The favorite motto, though, is "We may not do anything 1000 percent better, but we do 1000 things 1 percent better."[1]

When Ketner first started out, he was not so successful. In fact, within the first decade, he had opened 16 stores, but closed 9. His success came when he initiated the low-cost strategy, coupled with effective controls. How do managers like Ketner decide what kinds of control systems they need to be successful? In the previous chapter, we examined the basic concepts associated with controls, such as the need for controls, the control process itself, and types of controls available to managers. In this chapter, we build on those ideas by focusing on specific methods that managers use to maintain control in organizations. Although many control systems must be custom-designed, most organizations share a common need for certain major control systems. Accordingly, we first describe the general nature of six major control systems that organizations are apt to require to some degree. Throughout the remainder of the chapter, we explore four of these major control systems in greater depth. In conjunction with considering one of these systems, quality control, we examine the prospects of promoting innovation through the use of quality circles and related techniques. Two other major control systems are covered in greater detail in subsequent chapters.

These are some of the 87 millionaires in Rowan County, North Carolina, who bought stock in a friend's grocery store in 1957. That grocery store is now the fastest growing supermarket chain in America (Food Lion), and a share of stock that cost $10 in 1957 is worth $140,000 today. The secret of Food Lion's success lies in its innovative cost control and inventory control measures. To help maintain its effective controls, a headquarters group makes all buying, pricing, and merchandising decisions, and centralized warehouses distribute goods efficiently.

MAJOR CONTROL SYSTEMS

If you decided to investigate major control systems in prominent business organizations such as IBM, RJR Nabisco, or American Express, you would likely find the systems shown in Figure 18-1.[2] Since the purpose of control systems is to increase the probability of meeting organizational goals and standards, managers use these major control systems to boost their prospects for success. For example, a financial control system helps managers keep track of important

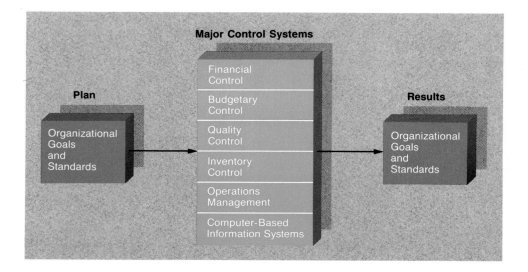

Figure 18-1 Major organizational control systems.

overall money matters, such as whether the organization is making a profit or taking on too much debt. Budgetary control systems assist managers of various units by giving them quantitative tools to monitor how closely the revenues and costs associated with various organizational activities match what has been planned. Quality control systems provide a means of assessing the quality of products and services, an increasingly important competitive issue. Inventory control systems offer a way to ensure that the necessary inputs are available when needed, while keeping the costs involved at a minimum. Operations management involves controlling the processes associated with actually producing a product or service. Finally, computer-based information systems are increasingly being used to develop sophisticated systems geared to maintaining better control over information and related functions. We discuss operations management and computer-based information systems in Chapters 19 and 20, respectively. (Management by objectives, which also can be used as a control system, is described in Chapter 5.)

For the remainder of this chapter, we concentrate on financial, budgetary, quality, and inventory control systems. Before considering each of these major control systems individually, we first explore some ways that they differ in terms of the level of management to which they are mainly oriented and their timing emphasis.

Managerial Level

Control systems tend to differ somewhat in the degree to which they are used by different managerial levels (see Figure 18-2). For example, financial control systems are a primary control mechanism used by top-level management because such systems relate mainly to the overall financial health of the organization, although middle managers also have an interest in monitoring the financial matters as they impact their particular specialized area. On the other hand, middle and lower-level managers make the main use of budgetary controls, since it is typically their job to run organizational activities so that various budgets are met. Still, top management may monitor overall budget performance, as well as major deviations from what is expected. When it comes to quality, related control is mainly the purview of lower-level managers in the sense that they are the ones who primarily work at the operational level, where product and service quality is directly affected. Middle and top managers may also be interested in trends in quality, but they are less involved in the hands-on issues. Finally, inventory control rests largely with lower-level and middle managers, although upper management may use some indexes to evaluate costs.

Timing Emphasis

Major control systems also lean toward different emphases on timing in regard to the degree to which controls take place before (feedforward), during (concurrent), or after (feedback) the transformation process that produces a product or service (see Chapter 17). Financial control systems tend to constitute feedback control because the data usually are evaluated at the end of particular reporting periods. Although it is too late at that point to make changes that will affect the particular data, the data are useful in planning changes that can affect organizational performance and results for future periods. In contrast, budgetary control often has more of a concurrent focus, since it can be used to regulate ongoing activities so that planned budget levels are met. For example, budgets may be checked during expenditure decisions. To the degree that budgets are considered only at the end of particular periods, budgetary control moves closer to a form of feedback control. At the same time, quality control increasingly is used as concurrent control in the sense that checks are made during the actual production or service process to be sure that quality standards are being met. When checks are not made until after production, when materials must be scrapped or rejected if they are faulty, the timing of quality control fits into the feedback category. Finally, inventory control is mainly oriented toward feedforward control, because it is geared to ensuring that materials and products will be available when needed. In the remaining sections of this chapter, we consider these major control systems in greater detail.

FINANCIAL CONTROL

Suppose that you are a top manager at a giant organization such as RJR Nabisco. What types of financial controls might you use? In this section, we review some

Figure 18-2 Major control systems by managerial level and timing.

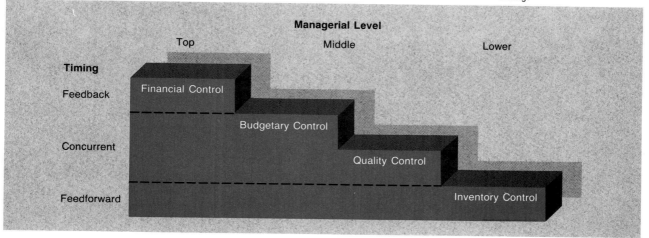

of the more common financial control techniques, including the use of financial statements, ratio analysis, comparative financial analysis, and financial audits. We also consider how managers can avoid some of the major pitfalls associated with financial controls.

Financial Statements

Financial statement   A summary of a major aspect of an organization's financial status

A **financial statement** is a summary of a major aspect of an organization's financial status. The information contained in various financial statements is essential in maintaining financial control over organizations. Two basic types of financial statements that are typically used by business organizations are the balance sheet and the income statement.[3] Financial statements typically are prepared at the end of reporting periods, such as quarterly and annually, although the widespread availability of computers is facilitating more frequent preparation.

Balance sheet   A financial statement that depicts an organization's assets and claims against those assets at a given point in time

Balance Sheet. A **balance sheet** is a financial statement that depicts an organization's assets and claims against those assets at a given point in time.[4] A balance sheet for the Eagle Manufacturing Company, a maker of industrial parts, is shown in Table 18-1. You may find it helpful to think of a balance sheet as a financial "snapshot" that is made up of two main sections. The top half shows current assets, and the bottom half documents existing claims against assets.[5]

Assets, the resources that an organization controls, fall into two main categories: current and fixed. *Current assets* are cash and other assets that usually are converted to cash or are used within 1 year (e.g., marketable securities, such as U.S. Treasury bills or money market mutual funds that can be converted to cash within a relatively short period; accounts receivable, which are sales on credit for which payment has not yet been received; and inventory). *Fixed assets* are assets that have a useful life that exceeds 1 year (such as property, buildings, and equipment). In the case of Eagle Manufacturing, the balance sheet indicates that the company has $40 million in current assets and $42 million in fixed assets (after depreciation) for total assets of $82 million.

The bottom half of the balance sheet, devoted to claims, includes both liabilities and shareholders' equity. *Liabilities* are claims by nonowners against company assets (in other words, debts owed to nonowners, such as banks). Liabilities also fall into two main categories: current and long-term. *Current liabilities* are accounts that typically are paid within 1 year (such as accounts payable—current bills the company must pay—and short-term loans). *Long-term liabilities* are debts usually paid over a period that exceeds 1 year (such as bonds). Eagle Manufacturing has $18 million in current liabilities and $27 million in long-term liabilities, for a total of $45 million in liabilities.

Shareholders' equity represents claims by owners against the assets. As you might expect, shareholders' equity is equal to the company's assets minus liabilities. Shareholders' equity is, in essence, the organization's net worth; it is represented on the balance sheet by stock and retained earnings (funds accumulated from the profits of the organization). In the case of Eagle Manufacturing, shareholders' equity is equal to $37 million. Since shareholders' equity equals assets minus liabilities, by placing the assets on the top ($82 million) and the liabilities and shareholders' equity ($45 million plus $37 million, for a total of $82 million) on the bottom, the balance sheet "balances." By using a comparative balance sheet, which shows figures from one year to the next (as in Table 18-1), it is possible to track trends in the growth of assets, the state of liabilities, and current net worth.

Table 18-1

Eagle Manufacturing Company		
Comparative Balance Sheet December 31, 1989 and 1990 (in thousands of dollars)		
	1990	**1989**
ASSETS		
Current assets		
Cash	$ 2,500	$ 3,000
Marketable securities.......	1,000	1,300
Accounts receivable	16,000	12,000
Inventories.......	20,500	18,700
Total current assets	$40,000	$35,000
Fixed assets		
Land and buildings.........	$28,700	$24,200
Machinery and equipment.........	31,600	29,000
Total fixed assets	$60,300	$53,200
Less: Accumulated depreciation.........	18,300	17,200
Net fixed assets	$42,000	$36,000
Total assets	$82,000	$71,000
LIABILITIES AND SHAREHOLDERS' EQUITY		
Current liabilities		
Accounts payable	$ 7,200	$ 6,000
Notes payable (10% bank)	5,500	7,000
Accrued liabilities.........	900	700
Current maturity of long-term debt	3,000	3,000
Other liabilities.........	1,400	1,200
Total current liabilities.........	$18,000	$17,900
Long-term liabilities		
Long-term debt (12% mortgage bonds)	27,000	30,000
Total liabilities	$45,000	$47,900
Shareholders' equity		
Common stock ($5 par, 2,000,000 shares authorized; 1,300,000 shares outstanding in 1990 and 1,000,000 shares outstanding in 1989).........	$ 6,500	$ 5,000
Capital in excess of par	14,000	5,350
Retained earnings	16,500	12,750
Total shareholders' equity	$37,000	$23,100
Total liabilities and shareholders' equity	$82,000	$71,000

Source: Adapted from H. Kent Baker, *Financial Management,* Harcourt Brace Jovanovich, San Diego, 1987, p. 90.

Income Statement. Whereas the balance sheet focuses on the overall financial worth of the organization at a specific point in time, an **income statement** is a financial statement that summarizes the financial results of company operations over a specified time period, such as a quarter or a year. An income statement shows revenues and expenses. *Revenues* are the assets derived from selling goods and services. *Expenses* are the costs incurred in producing the revenue (such as cost of goods sold, operating expenses, interest expense, and taxes).

Income statement A financial statement that summarizes the financial results of company operations over a specified time period, such as a quarter or a year

The difference between revenues and expenses represents the profits or losses over a given period of time and is often referred to as the *bottom line*.

Like the balance sheet, income statements for different periods of time are frequently compared. A comparative income statement for Eagle Manufacturing Company is shown in Table 18-2. The statement indicates that net income (revenues minus expenses) is about $6.7 million, up from about $5 million the previous year.

Ratio Analysis

Ratio analysis The process of determining and evaluating financial ratios

In assessing the significance of various financial data, managers often engage in **ratio analysis,** the process of determining and evaluating financial ratios.[6] A *ratio* is an index that measures one variable relative to another and is usually expressed in the form of percentages or times. The notion of a ratio will become clearer as we consider specific examples below. Ratios are meaningful only when compared with other information. Since ratios often are compared to industry data, they help managers understand their company's performance compared with that of competitors and are often used to track performance over time. There are four types of financial ratios that are particularly important to managerial control: liquidity, asset management, debt management, and profitability. Formulas and end-of-the-year data for Eagle Manufacturing for the four types of ratios are shown in Table 18-3.

Liquidity ratios Financial ratios that measure the degree to which an organization's current assets are adequate to pay current liabilities (current debt obligations)

Liquidity Ratios. **Liquidity ratios** are financial ratios that measure the degree to which an organization's current assets are adequate to pay current liabilities (current debt obligations). A major type of liquidity ratio is the *current ratio,*

Table 18-2

Eagle Manufacturing Company		
Income Statement For the Years Ended December 31, 1989 and 1990 (in thousands of dollars)		
	1990	**1989**
Net sales...	$120,000	$110,000
Cost of goods sold...	90,000	83,000
Gross profit...	$ 30,000	$ 27,000
Operating expenses		
Selling..	5,000	4,800
General and administrative................................	8,000	7,600
Depreciation..	1,100	800
Lease payments..	1,650	1,600
Earnings before interest and taxes (EBIT).............	$ 14,250	$ 12,200
Interest expense		
Interest on bank notes....................................	550	700
Interest on other debt.....................................	3,600	3,960
Earnings before taxes.......................................	$ 10,100	$ 7,540
Taxes (34%)...	3,434	2,564
Net income...	$ 6,666	$ 4,976

Source: Adapted from H. Kent Baker, *Financial Management,* Harcourt Brace Jovanovich, San Diego, 1987, p. 91.

Table 18-3   Ratio Analyses for Eagle Manufacturing Company

					EVALUATION		
Ratio	Formula	Calculation	Current Year	Previous Year	Industry Averages*	Trend	Current Status*
LIQUIDITY RATIOS							
Current ratio	$\dfrac{\text{Current assets}}{\text{Current liabilities}} =$	$\dfrac{\$40,000}{\$18,000} =$	2.22x	1.96x	2.00x	↑	Good
ASSET MANAGEMENT RATIOS							
Average collection period	$\dfrac{\text{Accounts receivable}}{\text{Sales per day}} =$	$\dfrac{\$16,000}{\$328.8} =$	48.67 days	39.82 days	35.00 days	↓	Poor
Inventory turnover	$\dfrac{\text{Cost of goods sold}}{\text{Inventory}} =$	$\dfrac{\$90,000}{\$20,500} =$	4.39x	4.44x	6.00x	↓	Poor
DEBT MANAGEMENT RATIOS							
Debt ratio	$\dfrac{\text{Total liabilities}}{\text{Total assets}} =$	$\dfrac{\$45,000}{\$82,000} =$	54.88%	67.47%	45.00%	↑	Poor
PROFITABILITY RATIOS							
Net profit margin	$\dfrac{\text{Net income}}{\text{Net sales}} =$	$\dfrac{\$6,666}{\$120,000} =$	5.56%	4.52%	6.00%	↑	Fair
Return on investment	$\dfrac{\text{Net income}}{\text{Total assets}} =$	$\dfrac{\$6,666}{\$82,000} =$	8.13%	7.01%	12.00%	↑	Poor
Return on equity	$\dfrac{\text{Net income}}{\text{Shareholders' equity}} =$	$\dfrac{\$6,666}{\$37,000} =$	18.02%	21.54%	21.82%	↓	Poor

*Industry averages are assumed to remain constant for 1989 and 1990.
Source: Adapted from H. Kent Baker, *Financial Management*, Harcourt Brace Jovanovich, San Diego, 1987, p. 108.

which measures a company's ability to meet the claims of short-term creditors by using only current assets. The current ratio shown in Table 18-3 indicates that Eagle Manufacturing has $2.22 in current assets for every dollar in current liabilities. Eagle's ratio is just a bit better than the industry average of $2.00, suggesting that the company is in reasonable shape on liquidity (unless the industry itself is experiencing liquidity troubles).

Asset Management Ratios. Asset management ratios (sometimes called *activity ratios*) measure how effectively an organization manages its assets. Two of the most used asset management ratios are inventory turnover and average collection period.

Inventory turnover helps measure how well an organization manages its inventory. Low inventory turnover may point to either excess or obsolete inventory. High inventory turnover generally signals effective handling of inventory relative to selling patterns, because less money is tied up in inventory that is waiting to be sold. It is, of course, possible to have an inventory turnover ratio that is too high, if it means that significant sales are lost because items ordered by potential customers are out of stock. With an industry average of 6.00, Eagle's inventory turnover of 4.39 (shown in Table 18-3) does not stack up well and needs investigating. Higher inventory levels relative to goods sold are generally not desirable because money tied up in inventory waiting to be sold cannot be used for other purposes. In addition, companies often must borrow funds to cover the costs of large inventories, a factor that ultimately raises costs relative to those of competitors. Of course, Food Lion has been successful with a nontraditional type of inventory strategy. Instead of attempting to keep inventory small and turn it over frequently, Food Lion builds large inventories of items ordered

Asset management ratios
Financial ratios that measure how effectively an organization manages its assets

in quantity and stores them in its giant warehouses. The low prices outweigh the holding costs, making the strategy effective for Food Lion.

The *average collection period* ratio measures how many days it takes for a company to receive payment from sales. If the average collection period extends considerably beyond a company's credit terms (how long customers are given to pay for purchases), it may signal either poor performance in collecting accounts receivable or a tendency to extend credit to poor risks (customers with weak credit records). If the average collection period is too short, it may mean that the company is too restrictive on credit (extends credit only to customers with extremely strong credit ratings) or is too aggressive with collections (requires that customers pay bills within a relatively short time, perhaps making it more attractive for customers to conduct their business elsewhere). In the case of Eagle Manufacturing, the average collection period (shown in Table 18-3) is 48.67 days.[7] Since the company grants 30-day credit terms, this average suggests a problem in either the way that money is collected or the way that credit is extended.

Debt management ratios
Financial ratios that assess the extent to which an organization uses debt to finance investments, as well as the degree to which it is able to meet its long-term obligations

Debt Management Ratios. The third category of financial ratios is **debt management ratios** (often called *leverage ratios*), which assess the extent to which an organization uses debt to finance investments, as well as the degree to which it is able to meet its long-term obligations. The more that an organization uses debt to finance its needs, the more it must commit funds to pay interest and repay principal. As debts increase, so does the risk that the organization may not be able to pay its debts and may end up in bankruptcy. Thus one of the most important ratios is the *debt ratio*, which measures the percentage of total assets financed by debt (including current liabilities). The higher the percentage, the more the organization's assets are furnished by creditors rather than owners. Eagle Manufacturing's debt ratio of 54.88 percent (shown in Table 18-3) indicates that creditors have supplied about 55 cents of every dollar in assets, a figure that is higher than the industry average of 45 percent. This higher-than-average debt ratio may be problematic if the organization needs to take on additional debt. Future creditors may require a higher rate of return on their money because of the additional risk associated with the high debt ratio.

Profitability ratios
Financial ratios that help measure management's ability to control expenses and earn profits through the use of organizational resources

Profitability Ratios. Profitability ratios, the fourth category of financial ratios, help measure management's ability to control expenses and earn profits through the use of organizational resources.[8] Three commonly used profitability ratios are net profit margin, return on investment, and return on equity.

The *net profit margin* indicates the percentage of each sales dollar that is left after deducting all expenses. In the case of Eagle Manufacturing, the net profit margin (shown in Table 18-3) is 5.56 percent. According to this figure, Eagle earns about 5½ cents on every dollar of sales, a bit less than the industry average of 6 percent. Comparatively speaking, Eagle's sales may be too low or its expenses too high, or both.

The *return on investment* (ROI; also called *return on assets*) measures the overall effectiveness of management in generating profits from its total investment in assets. The ROI for Eagle (shown in Table 18-3) is 8.13 percent. Given the industry average of 12 percent, Eagle's ROI is considerably lower. The company may want to consider either increasing sales relative to costs or reducing costs relative to sales.

The *return on equity* (ROE) measures management's effectiveness in terms of earning a rate of return on the investment of shareholders. The ROE is based on shareholders' equity only, whereas the ROI is based on total assets. A high return on equity is considered indicative of good management, as long as the organization does not have an excessive amount of debt. A low return on equity is generally considered a sign of ineffective management, but it may also indicate conservative financing and low debt. Eagle's ROE of 18.02 percent is somewhat below the industry average of 21.82 percent, indicating that the company needs to consider increasing sales, reducing costs, and/or reviewing debt and financing strategies.

Top managers in most major companies, including RJR Nabisco, make strong use of financial controls (see the following Case in Point discussion).

CASE IN POINT: Giant RJR Nabisco Goes by the Numbers

Many of the brand names of RJR Nabisco, such as Oreo, Ritz, Premium, Planters, Life Savers, Camel, Winston, and Salem, are familiar to consumers in the United States and various other parts of the world. The company became RJR Nabisco in 1985, when R. J. Reynolds bought Nabisco Brands for $4.9 million. At the time, R. J. Reynolds was noted for its southern genteel, methodical, take-care-of-the-people style of operating, while Nabisco Brands was regarded as a risk-taking, freewheeling, decentralized organization. The outgrowth of the purchase has been a blend of both styles at RJR Nabisco, although the company tends more toward the Nabisco Brands approach by requiring few approvals to get jobs done, having few policies to which one must conform, and rewarding managers well for good performance. To maintain control over the organization, yet allow managers considerable latitude in running their particular specialized areas, top management relies heavily on financial controls.

In fact, since the two companies were joined, RJR Nabisco has been literally run by the book when it comes to financial controls. Each of the 173 unit managers prepares a report that is forwarded up the chain. The reports are then assembled into books for senior executives at various levels. Each division president gets a green book that depicts information concerning that division; the members of the board of directors get a blue book that includes a corporate summary; and the chief executive officer gets a red book that outlines the problem areas in each reporting unit. The reports track such financial statement items as receivables, inventories, and working capital—all of which are considered critical indicators of the state of the business. Reportedly, newcomers have not looked forward to the reports, particularly the one to the CEO because "it says nothing nice about no one."

With the takeover of the company by the leveraged-buyout firm Kohlberg Kravis Roberts in 1989, top management has more reason than ever to keep a close eye on the financial picture. Chairman and CEO Louis V. Gerstner, Jr., a former president of American Express who was brought in to run the company, must find ways to pay off the $25 billion debt associated with the takeover. The company is doing very well in a number of areas. For example, it has been able to claim half the market share in cookies and crackers, with at least twice the profitability of its nearest competitor, and company profits have been running ahead of projections. On the other hand, it faces difficulties in the tobacco business, its traditional cash cow, because of the growing public concern about the health hazards of tobacco. The company recently canceled the debut of Premier, its much-talked-about smokeless cigarette, after market research indicated that it tasted like "a smoldering Hefty Bag."[9] ■

RJR Nabisco is known as a low-cost cookie producer. Instead of striving for that "just-baked" look, which results in greater variation in quality and less efficiency in production, the Oreo division uses a computerized process to guarantee consistency in the product. The researcher shown here is using an image analyzer to measure roundness, width, and the coefficient of friction on the Oreo. Financial figures are analyzed just as meticulously at RJR Nabisco to ensure consistency in profits.

Comparative Financial Analysis

Financial statements and ratios are more meaningful when managers can compare the data against some standard. Managers are expected to explain significant variances (positive and negative) from standards, in order to help top-level managers better understand why the variances are occurring and their implications. The three major standards that managers most often use to compare data are management goals, historical standards, and industry standards.

Management financial goals frequently are set during the planning process and then become standards against which actual achievements are compared during the control process. In the case of Eagle Manufacturing, top management had set a goal of reaching the industry averages on the major ratios shown in Table 18-3 by the end of the reporting period, but the company has fallen short in a number of areas.

In contrast to management goals, which project future standards, *historical financial standards* are financial data from past years' statements or ratios that are used as a basis for comparing the current year's financial performance. The balance sheet and income statement for Eagle Manufacturing, as well as the chart of the company's financial ratios, include data from the previous year for comparison, illustrating uses of historical standards.

Another method of comparison is the use of *industry financial standards*, financial data based on averages for the industry. Financial ratios for a variety of industries are published by several sources, including Robert Morris Associates and Dun & Bradstreet.[10] Our discussion of Eagle Manufacturing's financial ratios and the data in Table 18-3 reflect the use of industry standards.

In making comparisons, managers can use one of two main approaches: cross-sectional analysis or time-series analysis. With *cross-sectional analysis,* managers typically compare the financial data for their organization at a given point in time with industry averages for the same period. For example, the analysis of ratios in Table 18-3 is cross-sectional because it compares ratios for the end of a fiscal year with industry averages for the same fiscal year. With *time-series analysis,* managers compare financial data over a period of time, usually to identify trends. For example, a time-series analysis of the current ratio for Eagle Manufacturing over the past 5 years, as compared with the industry average over the past 5 years, shows that Eagle's liquidity position declined faster than that of the industry but has now increased relative to the industry average (see Figure 18-3).

Financial data provide managers with major indicators about the overall direction of the organization. For example, Rupert Murdoch, who runs his Australia-based News Corporation, Ltd., from New York, makes heavy use of financial data to maintain control over his media holdings on four continents. Among the data he receives are weekly reports with itemized profit and loss figures for every single business, "whether it be from Perth, in western Australia, or in London or in San Antonio. Those figures," he says, "are what keeps us up to date." Modern communication systems and computers enable Murdoch to receive timely information from all over the world.[11] Still, while financial information helps identify problem areas, managers must investigate beyond the surface of the numbers to determine the root causes of the data's results before taking action.

Financial Audits

Given the importance of financial data for control at the top management levels, it is crucial that the data be accurate and follow accepted standards of account-

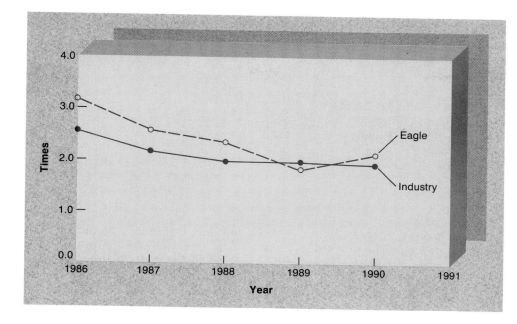

Figure 18-3 Time-series analysis of Eagle Manufacturing Company's current ratio versus the industry average. (Reprinted from H. Kent Baker, *Financial Management*, Harcourt Brace Jovanovich, San Diego, 1987, p. 109.)

ing. As a result, another means of managerial control is the financial audit. An *audit* is a review conducted by an outside agency or office to determine whether or not specified rules and procedures are being followed. There are two types of financially related audits that are used extensively: external and internal.

An **external audit** is a review and verification of the fairness of an organization's financial statements that is conducted by an independent auditor. Such audits are usually performed by certified public accounting firms, such as Ernst and Young or Arthur Anderson. External auditors are interested in ensuring that an organization follows generally accepted accounting principles and practices in reporting its financial data.[12]

An **internal audit** is a review of both financial statements and internal operating efficiency that is conducted by members of the organization. Internal auditors inspect financial statements and the related accounting system in much the same way as do external auditors. As a result, the use of internal auditors often can lower the high fees that must be paid to external auditing teams by improving account controls and gathering some of the information that is used in external audits.

Unlike external auditors, internal auditors also give attention to potential cost savings and to the effectiveness with which various units meet organizational goals.[13] Many large organizations have internal-audit staffs. For example, Teresa M. LeGrand, head of the internal-audit department for General Electric, dispatches 120 auditors to factories and offices around the world, where they delve into all of the company's businesses.[14]

External audit A review and verification of the fairness of an organization's financial statements that is conducted by an independent auditor

Internal audit A review of both financial statements and internal operating efficiency that is conducted by members of the organization

Avoiding Financial Control Pitfalls

While financial controls can be extremely helpful to top management, there are six primary pitfalls that can short-circuit their usefulness (see Table 18-4).[15] For one thing, the controls need to be tailored, to some extent, to the needs of the organization. Concentrating too much on the financial numbers helped blind Xerox's management to the coming intense competition from Japanese copy

Table 18-4   Six Potential Financial Control Pitfalls

1. Failing to tailor financial controls to the specific requirements of the organization
2. Neglecting to link financial controls to the strategic planning process
3. Instituting controls that send mixed messages about desired behaviors
4. Allowing financial controls to stifle innovation and creativity
5. Forcing the same financial controls on various subunits that have different control requirements
6. Implementing financial controls that are too sophisticated for organizational needs

machine makers. A second pitfall is failing to link the controls to the strategic planning process. The purpose of controls is to help increase the prospects of realizing goals rather than to constitute ends in themselves. A third potential problem is instituting controls that send mixed messages to managers. For example, it is sometimes difficult to maximize both return on investment and sales growth at the same time, because sales growth may involve spending extra money in the present to reap more sales in the future (thus lowering ROI in the short run). At Corning Glass Works, both the long-term and short-term implications are considered in setting financial goals for its various businesses. A fourth problem is allowing financial controls to stifle innovation and creativity by making it extremely difficult to get financial backing for new ideas. During the mid-1970s, product development at Xerox, from inception to implementation, required more than 100 sign-offs before a proposal reached top management. A fifth pitfall is failing to meet subunit needs by forcing the same financial controls on various subunits and businesses that may be very different. Finally, systems that are too sophisticated may cause trouble when just providing information to the system begins to use up excessive managerial time. Reginald Jones, the previous chief at General Electric, used his financial background to change the company from being chronically short of cash to having tremendous financial strength. Unfortunately, the financial reporting got out of hand. The present chief financial officer, Dennis Dammerman, reports that he had to stop computers in one GE business from producing seven daily reports, one of which was 12 feet high and contained sales data on hundreds of thousands of items, accurate to the penny.[16]

BUDGETARY CONTROL

While financial controls are a major tool of top management, budgetary control is a mainstay for middle managers. Lower-level managers also use budgets to help track progress in their own units. **Budgeting** is the process of stating in quantitative terms, usually dollars, planned organizational activities for a given period of time. Budgets, the quantitative statements prepared through the budgeting process, may include such figures as projected income, expenditures, and profits. Budgets are useful because they provide a means of translating diverse activities and outcomes into a common measure, such as dollars.

Budgets typically are prepared for the organization as a whole, as well as for various subunits (such as divisions and departments). For budgetary purposes, organizations define various subunits as responsibility centers.

Budgeting The process of stating in quantitative terms, usually dollars, planned organizational activities for a given period of time

Responsibility Centers

A **responsibility center** is a subunit headed by a manager who is responsible for achieving one or more goals.[17] In fact, organizations can be thought of as forming a hierarchy of responsibility centers, ranging from small subunits at the bottom to large ones at the top. For example, the local AT&T phone store and the marketing division of AT&T are responsibility centers at different levels of the organization. There are five major types of responsibility centers: standard cost centers, discretionary expense centers, revenue centers, profit centers, and investment centers. The particular designation that a unit receives for budgetary purposes depends on the degree to which a unit has control over the major elements, such as revenues and expenses, that contribute to profits and return on investment.

Responsibility center A subunit headed by a manager who is responsible for achieving one or more goals

Standard Cost Centers. A **standard cost center** is a responsibility center whose budgetary performance depends on achieving its goals by operating within standard cost constraints. Because standard costs often are determined by using engineering methods, this type of center is also called an *engineered expense center*. With a standard cost center, managers face the challenge of controlling input costs (e.g., labor, raw materials) so that the costs do not exceed predetermined standards. For example, at RJR Nabisco, the bakery operations have standard costs for cracker production that are based on such factors as ingredients, expected breakage rates of between 5 and 7 percent, and an 8 percent "giveaway" rate (the overweight amount in an average package of Nabisco crackers).[18] Therefore, one measure of the efficiency of baking operations is the unit's ability to turn out the required number of boxes of crackers at a given level of quality within specified cost constraints. A standard cost center is appropriate only if standards for costs involved in producing a product or service can be estimated with reasonable accuracy and if the unit cannot be held directly responsible for profit levels because it does not have significant control over other expenses and/or revenues.

Standard cost center A responsibility center whose budgetary performance depends on achieving its goals by operating within standard cost constraints

Discretionary Expense Centers. A **discretionary expense center** is a responsibility center whose budgetary performance is based on achieving its goals by operating within predetermined expense constraints set through managerial judgment or discretion. Discretionary expense centers are commonly used with departments such as research and development, public relations, human resources, and legal units, in which it is difficult to determine standard costs or to measure the direct profit impact of the unit's efforts.

Discretionary expense center A responsibility center whose budgetary performance is based on achieving its goals by operating within predetermined expense constraints set through managerial judgment or discretion

Revenue Centers. A **revenue center** is a responsibility center whose budgetary performance is measured primarily by its ability to generate a specified level of revenue. Prime examples of revenue centers are sales and marketing divisions, which are typically evaluated on the sales (and thus revenues) that they generate in relation to the level of resources that they are allocated. For example, Nabisco's cookies are delivered directly to supermarkets and other outlets by combination driver-salespersons, who are part of revenue centers. They can influence revenues but have little control over the costs of the products they handle.[19] Revenue centers are used when the unit in question is responsible for revenues but does not have control over all the costs associated with a product or service, which makes it difficult to hold the unit responsible for profit levels. Individual Food Lion stores operate as revenue centers that are expected to generate a specific amount of revenues with the resources that they are given.

Revenue center A responsibility center whose budgetary performance is measured primarily by its ability to generate a specified level of revenue

GE's lighting division is on the move again. By treating the once-faltering division as an investment center, a new management team has boosted productivity and held competition at bay.

Profit center   A responsibility center whose budgetary performance is measured by the difference between revenues and costs—in other words, profits

Profit Centers. A **profit center** is a responsibility center whose budgetary performance is measured by the difference between revenues and costs—in other words, profits. Profit centers are appropriate only when the organizational unit in question has significant control over both costs and revenues, since these are the elements that ultimately affect profit levels. At RJR Nabisco, large divisions, such as Reynolds Tobacco USA, are considered profit centers because they have major control over both costs and revenues.[20] Organizations as a whole also are considered to be profit centers.

Investment center   A responsibility center whose budgetary performance is based on return on investment

Investment Centers. An **investment center** is a responsibility center whose budgetary performance is based on return on investment. The ROI ratio, discussed earlier in this chapter, involves not only revenues and costs but also the assets involved in producing a profit. Thus investment centers provide an incentive for managers to concern themselves with making good decisions about investments in facilities and other assets. Of course, this type of center works best if the unit has at least some control over decisions to invest in facilities, as well as over both revenues and expenses. For example, at General Electric, major businesses such as its aircraft engine, broadcasting (NBC), and major appliance divisions are operated as investment centers.[21]

Uses of Responsibility Centers. The uses of responsibility centers depend to a great extent on the type of organization structure involved (see Chapter 11).[22] Standard cost centers, discretionary expense centers, and revenue centers are more often used with functional organization designs and with the function units in a matrix design. Thus manufacturing or production units are likely to be treated as standard cost centers, while accounting, finance, and human resources usually are designated as discretionary expense centers. Sales or marketing units are normally considered to be revenue centers.

In contrast, with a divisional organization design, it is possible to use profit centers because the large divisions in such a structure usually have control over both the expenses and the revenues associated with profits. Of course, within divisions, various departments may operate as other forms of responsibility centers. Major companies that operate their divisions as separate and autonomous businesses often use investment centers for budgetary purposes. At Hanson PLC, a British-based conglomerate, businesses are run as investment centers, although managers of operating units must obtain permission from superiors for all significant capital investments (see the following Case in Point discussion).

CASE IN POINT: Budgets Are Sacred at Hanson PLC

At budget time, Hanson managers from all over the world go to Iselin, New Jersey, or London to present their cost and revenue projections for the forthcoming year to the senior management of Hanson PLC. This sprawling transatlantic conglomerate has products ranging from jacuzzi whirlpool baths and Smith Corona typewriters to bricks and cement. Hanson has grown to be Britain's seventh-largest business empire by following a simple formula: Buy undervalued companies with poor management in mature industries, and then improve the management practices. In the process, Hanson typically sells off some businesses of the acquired companies and keeps others, particularly low-technology businesses that do not require continual major capital expenditures. For more than 20 years, Hanson has posted record profits, and its earnings per share have frequently been as high as 38 percent annually.

Hanson has a reputation for granting a great deal of autonomy to local managers, yet the company maintains control through budgets. At Hanson, budgets are considered sacred. For each business, "it's a promise from the operating CEO to us," says one senior vice president. In the United States alone, some 150 Hanson investment centers file monthly and quarterly reports to their Iselin headquarters. The reports, a little more than a yard high when stacked up, are generally considered to be the company bible. Several group vice presidents and their controllers review the reports, which show how pretax profits and

Hanson Trust specializes in buying low-technology businesses that don't require huge infusions of capital, such as London Brick, which owns enough clay to make bricks well into the next century. By paying close attention to budgets and avoiding the risks inherent in high technology, the British conglomerate has achieved impressive results.

other financial data compare with budget projections. One expectation is that Hanson managers will produce a pretax payback on investment in 3 years. For meeting their return on investment targets, the managers are rewarded well with bonuses that can be as much as 60 percent of base pay.

At Hanson, capital expenditures are very closely controlled. Every capital investment of $1000 or more must be approved by headquarters. Such requests engender close perusal by company accountants. If a manager argues that an investment in more efficient machinery will reduce labor costs, the manager must furnish the names of employees who will be cut from the payroll as a result. Critics argue that such tight control discourages managers from requesting capital investments that may be important for future earnings. Still, the Hanson brand of budgetary control has produced a number of successes. For example, Smith Corona was operating in the red under SCM but flourished with Hanson, allowing Hanson to sell some of SCM's assets at premium prices.[23] ■■■■■■

Types of Budgets

In order to maintain budgetary control, organizations usually have a master budget that includes a number of other budgets that together summarize the planned activities of the organization. The format of the master budget depends on the nature and size of the organization involved, but it typically includes three major types of budgets: operating budgets, capital expenditures budgets, and financial budgets (see Figure 18-4).[24]

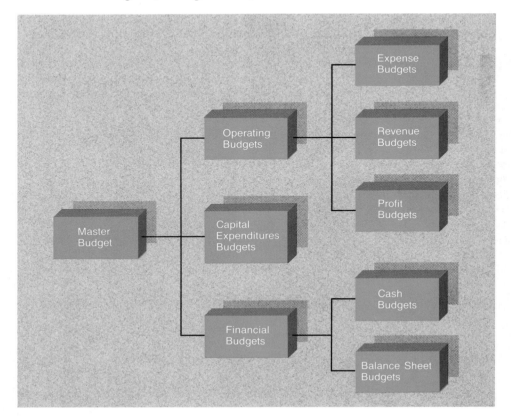

Figure 18-4 Major types of budgets.

Operating Budgets. An **operating budget** is a statement that presents the financial plan for each responsibility center during the budget period and reflects operating activities involving revenues and expenses.[25] Three types of operating budgets are most common and are closely related to the responsibility centers discussed in the previous section: expense, revenue, and profit budgets.[26]

An **expense budget** is an operating budget that documents expected expenses during the budget period. It reflects fixed, variable, and discretionary expenses, or costs. *Fixed costs* are costs that remain the same regardless of changes in the volume of output. Items such as mortgages, certain taxes, insurance, payments for capital expenditures, and leases are fixed costs. *Variable costs* are costs that change in direct proportion to output volume.[27] Raw materials, labor, energy, packaging, freight, and sales commissions are examples of variable costs. *Discretionary costs* are costs that depend on managerial judgment because they cannot be determined with certainty. Legal fees, accounting fees, R&D expenses, and supplies are examples of discretionary costs that must be estimated by managers. Discretionary costs figure heavily in the preparation of budgets for discretionary expense centers, whereas variable costs that can be reliably calculated for different levels of output are an important ingredient in the budgets of standard cost centers.

A **revenue,** or **sales, budget** is an operating budget that indicates anticipated revenues. In the case of business organizations, the anticipated revenue is based on the estimated dollar volume of the organization's products and services. In contrast, government agencies may estimate revenues on the basis of current tax rates, while associations are likely to use membership figures to make revenue estimates.

A **profit budget** is an operating budget that focuses on the profit to be derived from the difference between anticipated revenues and expenses. As such, it includes both revenue and expense figures, but the emphasis is on the profits. Profit centers have profit budgets, and there usually is a profit budget for the organization as a whole. The controller develops the overall profit budget on the basis of inputs from the expense and revenue budgets of various units so that the top managers can check the resultant overall profit levels. If profits are too small, managers need to plan actions that will raise revenues (such as conducting marketing promotions that will increase sales) and/or reduce expenses (such as cutting proposed expenditures for travel or delaying the purchase of nonessential equipment). Profit budgets are used to make final resource allocations, check on the adequacy of expense budgets relative to anticipated revenues, control activities across units, and assign responsibility to managers for their shares of the organization's financial performance.[28]

Capital Expenditures Budgets. A **capital expenditures budget** is a plan for the acquisition or divestiture of major fixed assets, such as land, buildings, or equipment. Acquisitions of major fixed assets are often referred to as *capital investments*. Since capital investments must be paid for over a long period of time and companies often borrow to cover the investments, they represent important organizational decisions. As a result, top-level managers are usually heavily involved, and the decision process often includes the board of directors. During the 1970s, many companies in energy-related businesses made heavy capital investments on the premise that oil prices would continue to rise in the 1980s. When prices plunged instead, many of these companies experienced acute difficulties because they did not have sufficient revenue to pay the long-term obligations associated with their capital investments.[29]

Marginal glossary:

Operating budget A statement that presents the financial plan for each responsibility center during the budget period and reflects operating activities involving revenues and expenses

Expense budget An operating budget that documents expected expenses during the budget period

Revenue, or sales, budget An operating budget that indicates anticipated revenues

Profit budget An operating budget that focuses on the profit to be derived from the difference between anticipated revenues and expenses

Capital expenditures budget A plan for the acquisition or divestiture of major fixed assets, such as land, buildings, or equipment

Financial budgets Budgets that outline how an organization is going to acquire its cash and how it intends to use the cash

Cash budget A financial budget that projects future cash flows arising from cash receipts and disbursements by the organization during a specified period

Balance sheet budget A financial budget that forecasts the assets, liabilities, and shareholders' equity at the end of the budget period

Financial Budgets. Financial budgets outline how an organization is going to acquire its cash and how it intends to use the cash. Two major types of financial budgets are the cash budget and the balance sheet budget.[30]

A **cash budget** projects future cash flows arising from cash receipts and disbursements by the organization during a specified period. The cash budget shows the likely availability of cash in terms of both magnitude (how much cash) and timing (when and for how long).[31] The cash budget helps managers determine whether they will have adequate amounts of cash to handle required disbursements when necessary, when there will be excess cash that needs to be invested, and when cash flows deviate from budgeted amounts.[32]

A **balance sheet budget** forecasts the assets, liabilities, and shareholders' equity at the end of the budget period. A balance sheet budget is also known as a *pro forma (projected) balance sheet*. It is like the balance sheet financial statement that we discussed earlier, except that it is based on future projections rather than past performance. Financial ratios may be computed on the basis of a balance sheet budget. Such ratios and the raw figures can help managers analyze changes in internal operations or an organization's environment that may significantly affect organizational success. Often, pro forma income statements also are prepared.[33]

The Budgetary Process

The information contained in the various budgets makes it fairly obvious that considerable coordination is involved in the budgetary process, the putting together of organizational budgets. How does the budgetary process work? There are a number of different ways that an organization can proceed.[34] Some organizations use **top-down budgeting,** a process of developing budgets in which top management outlines the overall figures and middle and lower-level managers plan accordingly. Other organizations use **bottom-up budgeting,** a process of developing budgets in which lower-level and middle managers specify their budgetary needs and top management attempts to accommodate them to the extent possible. Both approaches have advantages (see Figure 18-5).

Top-down budgeting A process of developing budgets in which top management outlines the overall figures and middle and lower-level managers plan accordingly

Bottom-up budgeting A process of developing budgets in which lower-level and middle managers specify their budgetary needs and top management attempts to accommodate them to the extent possible

The top-down approach allows top managers to incorporate their comprehensive knowledge of the organization and its environment, including their familiarity with the company's goals, strategic plans, and overall resource availability. The top-down approach works particularly well when there is an economic crisis, when unit managers have a limited knowledge of the current situation, and when business needs necessitate close coordination among various units.

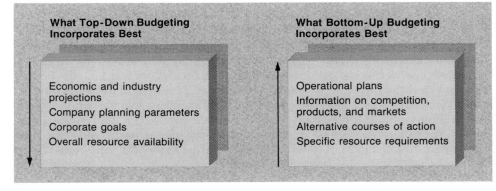

Figure 18-5 Top-down and bottom-up budgeting. (Reprinted from Neil C. Churchill, ''Budget Choice: Planning vs. Control,'' *Harvard Business Review*, July–August 1984, pp. 150–164.)

In contrast, the bottom-up approach builds on the specialized knowledge of operating managers about the environment and marketplace, which they have gleaned from day-to-day operations. When innovation is important, budget input from lower-level managers is particularly vital, because it is these managers who are more likely to understand the opportunities, the alternative courses of action, and the resource needs. Furthermore, managers of the operating units at various levels are more likely to be committed to the budget when they have had some hand in developing it. Bottom-up budgets work especially well when competitive pressures require quick responses. Yet, when there is a considerable degree of interdependence among units, the bottom-up approach may not provide sufficient coordination.

In reality, the budgetary process usually involves a mixture of both styles that addresses the question of how much emphasis should be placed on each approach. Blending the two approaches can capture many of the advantages of each. One way to blend the two approaches involves the following six steps:

Step 1: Top management sets forth in broad terms, and sends to the various unit managers, an overview of the environment, the corporate goals for the year, and the resource constraints.

Step 2: Each unit manager formulates in broad terms the unit's operating plans, performance targets, and resource requirements.

Step 3: Top management collects, combines, and evaluates information for all the various units.

Step 4: Top management assesses and revises target and resource availabilities and assigns preliminary estimates to each unit.

Step 5: Unit managers plan their activities in detail, determine their resource needs, and prepare their final budgets, which are sent to top management.

Step 6: Top management combines these unit budgets, fine-tunes them if necessary, approves them, and sends them back to the unit managers for implementation.[35]

The budgetary process usually produces the best results if it is conducted as close to the beginning of the budget period as possible. For large companies, the process might start 6 to 9 months in advance, while for small companies, 1 or 2 months may be sufficient.

Zero-Base Budgeting

The conventional budgeting process that we have just described does have one major disadvantage. Managers tend to prepare new budget requests by adding an incremental amount to their previous year's budget requests, rather than reevaluating the need for things already included. One potential solution, **zero-base budgeting (ZBB),** is a budget approach in which responsibility centers start with zero in preparing their budget requests and must justify the contributions of each of their activities to organizational goals, rather than focus on increments to the previous year's budget.[36]

The zero-base budgeting process was pioneered by Texas Instruments in the late 1960s and has been adopted at various times by a large number of organizations. For instance, Xerox and Ford Motor have credited the approach with

Zero-base budgeting (ZBB)
A budget approach in which responsibility centers start with zero in preparing their budget requests and must justify the contributions of each of their activities to organizational goals

saving millions through the elimination of outdated and marginally useful activities.[37] Jimmy Carter used ZBB when he was the governor of Georgia, and in the late 1970s he brought the system with him to Washington, where it was incorporated into the federal budgetary process during his presidential administration.[38] The system also is used by a number of state and local governments, although some researchers have questioned its use in governmental processes, in which political considerations also come into play.[39]

While ZBB forces managers to justify their activities in terms of future goals rather than past practices, the process can be costly and time-consuming to administer since every ongoing activity must be evaluated. The process also tends to overload upper-level management with information and may unnerve employees because of the yearly prospect of having one's activities eliminated. As a result, zero-based budgeting is not widely used in business organizations. Nevertheless, the concept is of interest because it serves to remind managers of the requirement of carefully evaluating the continuing need for various activities, rather than automatically adding incremental amounts to the previous year's budget. One recent study suggests that ZBB might work more effectively in organizations that have a longer time frame for the budgeting process, a larger budgeting staff, better standard operating procedures for the process, and increased training in ZBB.[40]

Impacts of the Budgeting Process

Depending on how they are used, budgets can have both positive and negative effects on managerial behavior in organizations. Among the positive effects, budgets can help keep managers informed about organizational activities, enhance coordination across various units, provide standards against which managers' efforts will be evaluated, and offer a means of making adjustments when corrective action is needed. At the same time, budgets also can have negative effects, particularly if they are used in a rigid manner and managers have concerns about fair treatment. Negative managerial behaviors that sometimes grow out of poorly run budgetary processes are politicking to increase budget allocations, overstating needs so that allocations will be increased, and abandoning potential innovations because the fight for resources is too formidable.[41]

QUALITY CONTROL

While budgetary control and financial control typically receive considerable emphasis in most organizations, the issue of quality control is currently receiving greater attention than in the past. A major reason is that a number of companies based in Japan and elsewhere are making serious inroads into U.S. and global markets by offering products and services of superior quality. As a result, in one recent Gallup poll, top executives of major U.S. companies rated improvements in service quality and product quality as the most critical challenge currently facing their companies.[42]

Quality The totality of features and characteristics of a product or service that bear on its ability to satisfy stated or implied needs

Although quality has been defined in many ways, the American Society for Quality Control offers this standard definition: **Quality** is "the totality of features and characteristics of a product or service that bear on its ability to satisfy stated or implied needs."[43] This definition recognizes that quality can involve every aspect of a product or service, that quality affects the ability of a product or service to satisfy needs, and that customer needs for quality may not always be explicitly stated. In examining the issue of quality and the need for quality control, we explore the strategic implications of quality, the concept of total quality control, quality circles and related recent developments, and statistical aids to quality control.

Strategic Implications of Quality

Quality expert David A. Garvin argues that quality can be used in a strategic way to compete effectively.[44] Choosing an appropriate quality strategy, though, depends on a thorough understanding of the important dimensions of quality. As a result, we first explore these dimensions before considering the issue of how to compete through quality.

Eight Dimensions. There are eight dimensions of quality that are important from a strategic point of view.

Performance involves a product's primary operating characteristics. For an automobile, performance would include acceleration, braking, handling, and fuel usage. In service industries, such as fast-food restaurants, airlines, or hotels, performance is apt to mean prompt service.[45]

Features are supplements to the basic functioning characteristics of the product or service. Examples include complimentary newspapers for hotel guests, extra options on autofocus cameras, or stereo tape decks in automobiles.

Reliability addresses the probability of a product's not working properly or breaking down altogether within a specific period. Since a significant period of usage is typically involved in assessing reliability, this quality dimension does not apply as readily to products and services that are used immediately. Reliability is becoming increasingly important, particularly for major items such as home appliances. For example, when General Electric introduced its new SpaceCenter 27 refrigerator with crushed-ice and cold-water dispensers on the door, it had a revolutionary new rotary compressor that provided the cooling. Unfortunately, some of the new compressors failed, particularly in warm-weather states such as Florida. While working to resolve the bugs in the new compressor, GE took the expensive steps of switching back to the usual reciprocating compressor used by the competition and replacing compressors in refrigerators already sold. The company did not want to ruin its carefully cultivated reputation for quality.[46]

Conformance refers to the degree to which a product's design or operating characteristics conform to preestablished standards. Typically, products and services are developed with some standards or specifications in mind. For instance, when the Michigan-based Van Dresser Corporation showed Toyota engineers a new prototype part designed for use in Toyota's Kentucky automobile plant, one Toyota engineer got "down on his hands and knees measuring the gap" between the automobile's steel door frame and the interior panel by Dresser. The engineer said, "Look, the gap is a millimeter too wide." Van Dresser retooled the mold that produced the panel.[47]

Durability is a measure of how much use a person gets from a product before it deteriorates or breaks down to such a point that replacement makes more sense than continual repair. For instance, one study conducted in the early 1980s indicated that durability for major home appliances varied widely, ranging from 5.8 to 18 years for washing machines and from 6 to 17 years for vacuum cleaners.[48]

Serviceability refers to the promptness, courtesy, proficiency, and ease of repair. In a Florida Power & Light Company push for quality, the utility has developed a number of unique computer programs, one of which geographically groups customer complaints about blackouts. After comparing the location of

the customers against service routes, the computer system automatically figures out whether the problem is a downed line, disabled transformer, or blown household fuse. The system has helped FP&L cut the average duration of blackouts from 70 minutes to 48.[49]

Aesthetics refers to how a product looks, feels, sounds, tastes, or smells—all subjective issues highly dependent on personal judgment and preference. For example, Herman Miller, Inc., an office furniture maker, places a great deal of emphasis on ensuring that its products are artistically attractive and functional.[50]

Perceived quality refers to individuals' subjective assessments of product or service quality. Such assessments may be based on incomplete information, but often it is perceptions that count with customers. Ironically, Honda, which produces cars in Marysville, Ohio, and Sony, which makes television sets in San Diego, have been reticent about noting that their products are "made in America" because of fears that the products will be perceived as lower in quality than counterparts made in Japan.[51]

Competing on Quality. While some dimensions of quality reinforce one another, others do not. For example, adding more features often will reduce reliability, while aesthetics sometimes interferes with durability. As a result, organizations do not usually attempt to compete through exceptionally high quality on all dimensions simultaneously. In fact, competing on all eight dimensions is usually not possible without charging very high prices. For example, a few products that probably do rank high on all eight dimensions, such as Cross pens, Rolex watches, and Rolls Royce automobiles, cost premium prices.

Instead, companies often must make trade-offs. For example, Cray Research, a manufacturer of high-speed supercomputers, found that it was not possible to build its computers for maximum speed without accepting the fact that the machines would likely fail every month or so (a sacrifice of reliability). Similarly, Japanese automobile manufacturers marketing in the United States often highlight the reliability (low repair rates) and conformance (good fits of parts and smooth finishes) of their cars, while de-emphasizing the limited options in the features category.

In pursuing quality as a competitive advantage, then, most companies choose a quality niche rather than attempt to emphasize all eight dimensions simultaneously. Not surprisingly, choosing a quality niche that customers consider important is critical. After deregulation, AT&T assumed that customers equated expensive features with quality in telephones, but actually durability and reliability proved to be more important.[52] Of course, another crucial issue is actually delivering the intended level of quality, once it has been decided upon.

Total Quality Control

Total quality control (TQC)
A quality control approach that emphasizes organizationwide commitment, integration of quality improvement efforts with organizational goals, and inclusion of quality as a factor in performance appraisals

To improve quality, a number of organizations, such as Xerox and Corning, are adopting a quality stance known as total quality control. **Total quality control (TQC)** is a quality control approach that emphasizes organizationwide commitment, integration of quality improvement efforts with organizational goals, and inclusion of quality as a factor in performance appraisals.[53] In essence, it highlights collective responsibility for the quality of products and services. It also encourages individuals in different, but related, departments (such as product design and manufacturing) to work together to improve quality.

Total quality control represents a change in the way quality is perceived. The traditional approach thinks of quality in terms of the degree of deviation

P R A C T I C A L L Y   S P E A K I N G

DEMING'S 14 POINTS ON HOW TO IMPROVE QUALITY

In the course of his work, Deming developed 14 management points that summarize what he believes managers, especially at the upper levels, must do to produce high-quality products:

1. Make a long-term commitment to improve products and services, with the aim of becoming competitive, staying in business, and providing jobs.
2. Adopt the new philosophy of concern for quality. We are in a new economic age. Western management must awaken to the challenge, learn its responsibilities, and take on leadership for change.
3. Cease dependence on mass inspection to achieve quality; build quality into the product in the first place.

4. End the practice of awarding business on the basis of price tag. Instead, minimize total cost. Move toward a single supplier for any one item, and build a long-term relationship of loyalty and trust.
5. Constantly improve the system of production and service so that quality and productivity also constantly improve and costs decrease.
6. Institute training on the job.
7. Institute leadership. The aim of supervision should be to help people and machines and gadgets do a better job.
8. Drive out fear so that everyone may work effectively for the company.
9. Break down barriers between departments so that people work as a team.
10. Eliminate slogans, exhortations, and targets that ask the work force for zero defects and new levels of productivity.

Such exhortations only create adversarial relationships because most of the causes of low quality and low productivity can be traced to the system of production and thus lie beyond the power of the work force.
11. Eliminate work standards (quotas) and the use of numerical goals on the factory floor. Substitute leadership instead.
12. Remove barriers that rob workers of the right to take pride in their work. Change the emphasis from sheer numbers to quality.
13. Institute a vigorous program of education and self-improvement.
14. Put everybody in the organization to work on accomplishing the transformation. The transformation is everybody's job.[54]

from standards that is deemed allowable for products and services. Speaking of U.S. suppliers, Osamu Nobuto, president of Mazda Motor Manufacturing, the U.S. unit of the Mazda Motor Corporation, complains, "It often seems that if something is 90 percent right, there is a tendency to believe that further improvement is either unnecessary or not worth the extra effort."[55] In contrast, the total quality control approach is aimed at achieving **zero defects,** a quality mentality in which the work force strives to make a product or service conform exactly to desired standards.[56]

Although Japanese companies are generally credited with pioneering total quality control, the roots of the concept actually originated in the United States. American quality control expert W. Edwards Deming took his ideas on statistical methods for improving quality to Japan in the late 1940s after they were ignored in the United States. He also promoted the concept of involving employees and various units throughout the organization in the quality effort, and he developed 14 management points that portray his overall philosophy. His ideas were embraced by Japanese companies, eager to rebuild after World War II. In fact, his contributions were so well appreciated that the Japanese established the Deming prize, a coveted annual award for excellence in quality control. In the 1950s, another American quality expert, J. M. Juran, also helped Japanese companies develop their total quality control efforts.[57] For some ideas about how to im-

Zero defects A quality mentality in which the work force strives to make a product or service conform exactly to desired standards

prove quality in organizations, see the Practically Speaking discussion, "Deming's 14 Points on How to Improve Quality."

An important aspect of TQC is its emphasis on the cost of quality, the cost of not doing things right the first time.[58] According to one estimate, the typical U.S. factory spends between 20 and 25 percent of its operating budget on finding and fixing mistakes.[59] Quality experts argue that if just some of these funds were spent on prevention, the number of mistakes requiring fixing (and the associated costs) could be substantially lowered. Dow Chemical USA credits its 5-year quality improvement effort with saving $100 million in operating costs.[60] Other examples of benefits from total quality efforts include a 60 percent reduction in scrap and rework at Harley-Davidson, a 69 percent cutback in customer returns at Westinghouse's semiconductor division, and savings of more than $52 million in 60 days at AT&T by eliminating errors in service documents.[61] A total quality effort also has paid off handsomely for Spectrum Control, Inc. (see the following Case in Point discussion).

CASE IN POINT: Upgrading Quality at Spectrum Control, Inc.

When Thomas L. Venable, president and chairman of Spectrum Control, Inc., announced with fanfare a new companywide commitment to quality, Ed Leofsky, a process engineer at Spectrum's Fairview, Pennsylvania, electromagnetic division, knew it was time to act. Each week, Leofsky's division solders terminals to about 75,000 tubular ceramic capacitors that are manufactured at Spectrum's material science division in nearby Saegertown. The capacitors are then used in one of the company's primary products, electronic filters.

Unfortunately, for the previous 12 years Leofsky had faced a chronic problem—for unknown reasons, the solder often would not stick. When that happened all sorts of unusual steps had to be taken, such as inspecting each soldering point with a microscope. Leofsky's efforts to get a vice president at Saegertown interested in solving the problem got nowhere. This time, just as the quality program was being announced, the soldering problem grew worse. The reject rate jumped from 3 to 32 percent. Leofsky wrote a letter to the vice president at Saegertown, with copies to everyone he could think of who could help.

The letter got people's attention, including concern from Venable himself. Venable and others in top management had begun to be seriously concerned about quality when a Japanese company purchased a major competitor and when Spectrum's principal customers, such as Hewlett-Packard and IBM, announced that they were adopting a zero-defects approach. Spectrum's sales and marketing personnel also were complaining that the company was not very good at meeting delivery dates. Recognizing that these problems were related to the overall lack of a quality orientation, senior management began reviewing quality programs, attending training programs, and adapting materials to fit the Spectrum situation. Next, all employees were trained in how to work toward error-free performance.

Leofsky's letter was the first major test of the quality commitment. Laboratory tests showed that surface contaminants were the problem, but finding the sources was tough. Just as one was identified and eliminated, another would appear. Solving the problem took capital, people, and time resources that would have been unthinkable in the past. "We would never have gotten beyond justifying the return on investment," says Leofsky. Soon other victories also began to occur. The rejection rate on shielded windows, which are the artfully crafted

This employee involvement team at a Monsanto plant in Springfield, Massachusetts, corrected a defect in one of its products, Saflex, a material used in laminating windshields. Employee teams such as this one have proved effective at resolving problems related to quality and productivity.

panels of dark, curved glass fastened to the front of computer screens, went from 15 percent to .08 percent, allowing Spectrum to reduce prices on the product line. Overall sales returns and related allowances on Spectrum products plummeted 75 percent, saving more than $767,000 annually. The company profit sharing plan, which had been dispensing $150,000 per year, recently has been budgeted for more than $1 million.[62] ■■■■■■

Savings such as those attained by Spectrum Control add significantly to profit levels. Quality efforts typically make use of two important tools that we consider in the next two sections: quality circles or related team approaches and statistical aids to quality control.

Promoting Innovation: Quality Circles and Beyond

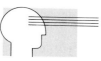

A **quality circle (QC)** is a small group of employees who meet periodically to solve quality problems related to their jobs. Typically, circles consist of eight to twelve employees, the members do similar work, supervisors are included, and the leader may be an employee rather than the supervisor. Participation is usually voluntary, although there may be considerable organizational and peer pressure to become involved. Often, members are trained in problem solving, data gathering, and statistical methods that help them with their innovative quality improvement efforts.[63]

Quality circle (QC) A small group of employees who meet periodically to solve quality problems related to their jobs

Although quality circles began in Japan in 1962, they did not spread to the United States until 1974, when the Lockheed Corporation began quality circles after sending six employees to Japan to investigate the approach. Still, quality circles did not catch on until a recession in the late 1970s caused organizations to seek ways to increase productivity and cut sales losses related to the higher quality of Japanese products. A national survey conducted by the New York Stock Exchange shows that by 1982, 44 percent of all companies with more than 500 employees had quality circles. In 3 out of 4 cases, the circles had been started within the previous 2 years.[64]

Some QC programs have reported impressive results. For example, Blue Cross of Washington and Alaska reported that more efficient employee procedures saved $430,000 over 3 years. Similarly, Hertz Rent a Car in Oklahoma City boosted car availability information by 27 seconds by moving from microfiche to computers. Nevertheless, the QC approach began to lose momentum by the mid-1980s. While many companies have continued their quality circles, others have disbanded or modified them.[65]

Why did interest in quality circles wane? For one thing, some organizations felt that the results did not justify the costs involved. For another, managers may have had unrealistic expectations about what could be accomplished, especially in the short run. In some cases, the quality circles were implemented with minimum or no training on quality issues, making it difficult for employees to make the necessary contributions. In addition, quality circle efforts sometimes were misdirected. For example, early quality circles at Honeywell made suggestions such as painting walls, putting salads in the cafeteria, and adding granola bars to vending machines.[66] Finally, quality circles were sometimes instituted by upper-level managers without the involvement and support of middle managers, who then resisted them.[67]

Recent research on quality circles suggests that, on average, quality circles have resulted in positive results in such areas as productivity and quality, as well as job satisfaction and morale. Still, positive results are by no means ensured; negative outcomes also have been reported.[68] One major study indicates that employee job satisfaction, organizational commitment, performance, and intentions to remain with rather than leave the organization improved initially but then dropped back to previous levels. The same was true of management's perceptions of the effectiveness of the QC program.[69] In one case, the Lake Financial Corporation, a major metropolitan banking institution, successfully reintroduced quality circles by providing proper training, but a great deal of senior management support was involved.[70]

One result of the mixed success is that a number of companies are moving toward a second generation of quality circles, often called employee involvement teams, which use a more structured approach to quality innovations. **Employee involvement teams** are small groups of employees who work on solving specific problems related to quality and productivity, often with stated targets for improvement. Typically, membership in employee involvement teams is mandatory, problems may be offered by management as well as workers, and the groups often set specific improvement goals and compete with one another.[71] In keeping with the new approach, Monsanto formed a quality improvement team when Ford Motor reported trouble with Saflex, a Monsanto material used to make laminated windshields. The material was changing dimensions by the time it was delivered to Ford. The quality improvement team traced the trouble to packaging, designed a new prototype, tested it, and implemented a new packaging process that eliminated Ford's complaints within 2 months.[72]

Statistical Aids to Quality Control

A mainstay of quality control is the use of statistical techniques that facilitate the tracing of quality difficulties. Two statistical approaches are most common: acceptance sampling and statistical process control.[73]

Acceptance sampling is a statistical technique that involves evaluating random samples from a group, or "lot," of produced materials to determine whether the lot meets acceptable quality levels. An **acceptable quality level (AQL)** is a predetermined standard against which the random samples are compared. If a certain number of the samples fall below the AQL, the entire lot will be rejected. Since this type of procedure is typically done after production is completed, it normally represents feedback control. On the other hand, acceptance sampling can be used as a method of feedforward control if it is aimed at determining whether incoming components from suppliers meet standards for inputs to a production process.

Statistical process control is a statistical technique that uses periodic random samples taken during actual production to determine whether acceptable quality levels are being met or production should be stopped for remedial action. In contrast to acceptance sampling, statistical process control assesses quality during production so that problems can be resolved before materials are completed. Since the emphasis is on prevention of poor-quality output during the actual process, this approach represents concurrent control. Because most production processes produce some variations, statistical process control works by using statistical tests to determine when variations fall outside a narrow range around the acceptable quality level and signal systematic fluctuations attributable to some malfunction in the production process.

Employee involvement teams Small groups of employees who work on solving specific problems related to quality and productivity, often with stated targets for improvement

Acceptance sampling A statistical technique that involves evaluating random samples from a group, or "lot," of produced materials to determine whether the lot meets acceptable quality levels

Acceptable quality level (AQL) A predetermined standard against which random samples of produced materials are compared in acceptance sampling

Statistical process control A statistical technique that uses periodic random samples taken during actual production to determine whether acceptable quality levels are being met or production should be stopped for remedial action

INVENTORY CONTROL

Another major type of control system found in most organizations is inventory control. **Inventory** is a stock of materials that are used to facilitate production or to satisfy customer demand. There are three major types of inventory: raw materials, work in process, and finished goods.[74]

Raw materials inventory is the stock of parts, ingredients, and other basic inputs to a production or service process. For example, McDonald's uses raw materials inventory such as hamburgers, cheese slices, buns, potatoes, and soft-drink syrup, while a bicycle factory uses such items as chains, sprockets, handlebars, and seats.

Work-in-process inventory is the stock of items currently being transformed into a final product or service. For McDonald's, work-in-process inventory includes the hamburgers being assembled, the salads being made, and the syrup and water being mixed to make a soft drink, while a bicycle frame with only the handlebars and seat attached would be work-in-process at a bicycle factory.

Finished-goods inventory is the stock of items that have been produced and are awaiting sale or transit to a customer. At McDonald's, finished-goods inventory includes the hamburgers waiting on the warmer and the salads in the refrigerated case, while bicycles constitute the finished-goods inventory at a bicycle factory. Organizations that provide services, rather than products, such as hospitals, beauty salons, or accounting firms, do not have finished-goods inventory, since they are not able to stockpile finished goods (e.g., kidney operations, haircuts, and audits).

Inventory A stock of materials that are used to facilitate production or to satisfy customer demand

Raw materials inventory The stock of parts, ingredients, and other basic inputs to a production or service process

Work-in-process inventory The stock of items that are currently being transformed into a final product or service

Finished-goods inventory The stock of items that have been produced and are awaiting sale or transit to a customer

Significance of Inventory

Inventory serves several major purposes in organizations.[75] For one thing, inventory helps deal with uncertainties in supply and demand. For example, having extra raw materials inventory may preclude shortages that hold up a production process. Having extra finished-goods inventory also makes it possible to serve customers better. Worlds of Wonder, the California-based toy maker, ended up going into Chapter 11 bankruptcy partly because it used advertising to generate enormous demands for items such as Laser Tag and then could not fill orders because of insufficient inventory.[76] Another purpose of inventory is to facilitate more economic purchases, since it sometimes is more economical to purchase large amounts of materials at one time. As pointed out earlier, Food Lion buys huge amounts of products during supplier promotions. Finally, inventory may be a useful means of dealing with anticipated changes in demand or supply, such as seasonal fluctuations or an expected shortage. Caution must be exercised in predicting changes. During the summer of 1988, Apple Computer, Inc., got burned badly when it paid high prices to stockpile memory chips worth hundreds of millions of dollars in anticipation of a continued shortage. Instead, the shortage eased and prices of the chips fell. When the company tried to raise computer prices to cover the costs of its high-priced chips, sales fell and quarterly profits plunged almost 43 percent.[77]

Costs of Inventory

Inventory is important to organizations because it represents considerable costs. For one thing, there is **item cost,** the price of an inventory item itself (the cost of

Item cost The price of an inventory item itself

Ordering cost The expenses involved in placing an order (such as paperwork, postage, and time)

Carrying, or holding, cost The expenses associated with keeping an item on hand (such as storage, insurance, pilferage, breakage)

Stockout cost The economic consequences of running out of stock (such as loss of customer goodwill and possibly sales)

Economic order quantity (EOQ) An inventory control method developed to minimize ordering plus holding costs, while avoiding stockout costs

the handlebars or seats). Then there is the **ordering cost,** the expenses involved in placing an order (such as paperwork, postage, and time). There also is the **carrying,** or **holding, cost,** the expenses associated with keeping an item on hand (such as storage, insurance, pilferage, breakage). Finally, there is **stockout cost,** the economic consequences of running out of stock. Stockout costs include the loss of customer goodwill and possibly sales because an item requested by customers is not available. Inventory control aims to minimize the costs of inventory (including considerations of stockout costs). One approach to minimizing such costs is the use of an inventory method called the economic order quantity.

Economic Order Quantity

The **economic order quantity (EOQ)** is an inventory control method developed to minimize ordering plus holding costs, while avoiding stockout costs. The method uses an equation that includes annual demand (D), ordering costs (O), and holding costs (H). Assume that a bicycle manufacturer estimates a total annual demand of 1470 bicycle frames for use in the manufacturing process, ordering costs of $10 per order, and holding costs of $6 per unit per year. Substituting these estimates into the equation indicates that the economic order quantity is 70 bicycle frames:

$$\text{EOQ} = \frac{2DO}{H} \text{ (square root)} = \frac{2(1470)(10)}{6} = 70$$

Reorder point (ROP) The inventory level at which a new order should be placed

The EOQ equation helps managers decide how much to order, but they also need to determine the **reorder point (ROP),** the inventory level at which a new order should be placed. To determine the reorder point, managers estimate *lead time* (L), the time between placing an order and receiving it. In the case of the bicycle manufacturer, the lead time for obtaining frames from a nearby producer is 7 days. In the formula for ROP, lead time is multiplied by average daily demand (annual demand ÷ 365 days). Conceptually, the bicycle frames should be ordered when there are just enough frames to keep making bicycles until the new frames come in. Substituting the data for the bicycle manufacturer into the ROP formula indicates that an order should be placed when the stock of bicycle frames reaches 29:

$$\text{ROP} = (L)\frac{D}{365} = (7)\frac{1470}{365} = 28.19, \text{ or } 29 \text{ (rounded)}$$

The EOQ inventory control system, which requires continuous monitoring of inventories, is depicted in Figure 18-6. Although the approach assumes that demand and unit costs are constant, in many cases demand may vary substantially and suppliers may offer quantity discounts and special promotions. Still, the EOQ often gives a useful approximation. (We consider more sophisticated approaches to inventory issues in Chapter 19.) In using the EOQ, an organization often will add some slack to the system in the form of *fluctuation*, or *safety*, *stock*, extra inventory kept on hand in case of unforeseen contingencies such as quality problems or reorder delays.[78] On the other hand, a number of U.S. companies are taking a completely different approach to inventory control by emulating the "just-in-time" method pioneered in Japan.

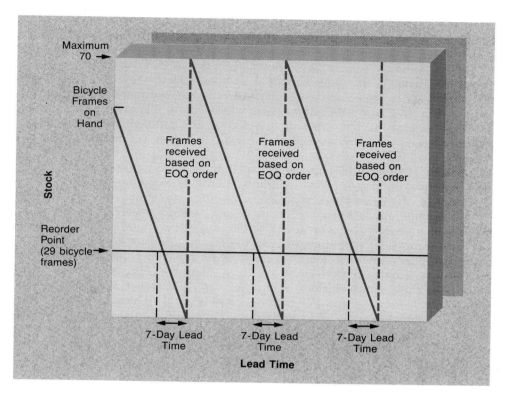

Figure 18-6 EOQ inventory control system.

Just-in-Time Inventory Control

Just-in-time (JIT) inventory control is an approach to inventory control that emphasizes having materials arrive just as they are needed in the production process.[79] The JIT approach to inventory is actually part of a broader JIT philosophy of manufacturing that attempts to eliminate all sources of waste, including any activities that do not add value, by focusing on having the right part at the right place at exactly the right time. By having materials arrive only as required, rather than holding backup parts in inventory for a period of time, the JIT approach as applied to inventory allows an organization to minimize holding costs. The JIT approach also saves space that is usually taken up by inventory waiting in the production area.

The JIT philosophy was popularized by the Toyota Motor Company in Japan during the mid-1970s and was transferred to the United States at Kawasaki's Lincoln, Nebraska, plant around 1980. One report indicates that a Japanese plant designed to produce 1000 cars per day requires 1 million square feet and a just-in-time inventory of $150 per car. In contrast, a U.S. car manufacturer producing the same number of cars per day without using a just-in-time system requires 2 million square feet and a conventional inventory of $775 per car.[80] With such potential savings, it is not surprising that the JIT inventory approach has been adopted to some degree by most of the Fortune 1000 largest industrial companies.[81] In its focus on eliminating waste, the JIT philosophy also calls for utilizing the full capabilities of workers, giving them greater responsibilities for the production process, and involving them in continual efforts at improving the production process.

Just-in-time (JIT) inventory control An approach to inventory control that emphasizes having materials arrive just as they are needed in the production process

Kanban A simple parts-movement system that depends on cards and containers to pull parts from one work center to another

For handling inventory, the JIT approach uses a subsystem called **Kanban** (Japanese for "card" or "signal"), a simple parts-movement system that depends on cards and containers to pull parts from one work center to another. With the Kanban system, workstations along the production process produce only enough to fill the containers that they are given; they begin producing again only when they receive a card and an empty container from the next workstation, indicating that more parts will be needed shortly. If the process stops because of machine breakdowns and quality problems, all the workstations involved in the process will produce only until their containers are full and then they will stop.

With a JIT system, high quality is a vital necessity. Since materials are either delivered by suppliers or made in various internal work centers just before they will be used, the items must be perfect. Otherwise, not only is there waste, but the production process itself must be halted because there is no significant amount of inventory to cover mistakes. Because of the high need for coordination and control, JIT inventory systems often help forge close relationships between suppliers and customers. In the case of Polycom Hunstman, Inc., and GM's Harrison radiator division in Lockport, New York, the relationship is exceptionally close—just 1500 feet, to be exact. After GM invited suppliers to move closer to its Harrison plant, Polycom built a new plant right next door so that a pneumatic conveying system could connect the two plants, eliminating even shipping costs. Now, when the GM plant begins to run low on the plastic compounds that Polycom supplies, a computer-based control system automatically begins sending materials from Polycom's facility to the Harrison plant.[82] Of course, it takes time to install a JIT system, and the system is dependent on near-perfect coordination. We discuss other inventory and production-related concepts in conjunction with operations management, the subject of the next chapter.

CHAPTER SUMMARY

Among the major control systems used in organizations are financial control, budgetary control, quality control, and inventory control. These systems vary in the degree to which they are used at different managerial levels, ranging from financial controls, which are used more at the top, to inventory controls, which are used more at the lower levels. Timing also varies, with financial control representing mainly feedback control, budgetary and quality control being more concurrent, and inventory control often matching feedforward timing.

Financial controls consist mainly of financial statements, ratio analysis, and comparative financial analysis, and financial audits. The primary financial statements are the balance sheet and the income statement. The major types of ratios used in financial control are liquidity, asset management, debt management, and profitability ratios. Financial statements and ratios can be assessed through the use of comparative financial analysis based on management financial goals, historical financial standards, or industry financial standards. The comparisons can be made using either the cross-sectional or the time-series approach. To help ensure the

integrity of the data used for financial controls, organizations usually have the data audited through external audits and, often, through internal audits as well. Managers need to guard against major pitfalls associated with financial controls.

Budgetary control requires that various organizational units be designated as responsibility centers, such as standard cost centers, discretionary expense centers, revenue centers, profit centers, and investment centers. The specific designation depends mainly on the type of organization structure involved. Organizations have three major types of budgets: operating budgets, capital expenditures budgets, and financial budgets. In developing these budgets, organizations can follow a top-down or bottom-up approach, each of which has advantages, or they can use a mixed style that encompasses many of the advantages of both approaches. Another alternative is the use of the zero-base budgeting process. Depending on how they are used, budgets can have both positive and negative effects on managerial behavior in organizations.

Quality control has strategic implications that are

related to the eight dimensions of quality: performance, features, reliability, conformance, durability, serviceability, aesthetics, and perceived quality. Organizations usually find it difficult to compete on all dimensions simultaneously and must make trade-offs. To improve quality, a number of organizations are adopting a quality stance known as total quality control. The approach is aimed at achieving zero defects, a quality mentality in which the work force strives to make a product or service conform exactly to desired standards. Quality efforts typically make use of quality circles or the more recent employee involvement teams, as well as statistical aids to quality control.

Inventory control serves a number of important purposes in organizations and involves a number of significant costs. Two major inventory control methods are the economic order quantity and just-in-time inventory control.

MANAGERIAL TERMINOLOGY

acceptable quality level (AQL) (652)
acceptance sampling (652)
asset management ratios (633)
balance sheet (630)
balance sheet budget (644)
bottom-up budgeting (644)
budgeting (638)
capital expenditures budget (643)
carrying, or holding, cost (654)
cash budget (644)
debt management ratios (634)

discretionary expense center (639)
economic order quantity (EOQ) (654)
employee involvement teams (652)
expense budget (643)
external audit (637)
financial budgets (644)
financial statement (630)
finished-goods inventory (653)
income statement (631)
internal audit (637)
inventory (653)
investment center (640)
item cost (653)

just-in-time (JIT) inventory control (655)
Kanban (656)
liquidity ratios (632)
operating budget (643)
ordering cost (654)
profit budget (643)
profit center (640)
profitability ratios (634)
quality (646)
quality circle (QC) (651)
ratio analysis (632)
raw materials inventory (653)
reorder point (ROP) (654)
responsibility center (639)

revenue center (639)
revenue, or sales, budget (643)
standard cost center (639)
statistical process control (652)
stockout cost (654)
top-down budgeting (644)
total quality control (TQC) (648)
work-in-process inventory (653)
zero-base budgeting (ZBB) (645)
zero defects (649)

QUESTIONS FOR DISCUSSION AND REVIEW

1. How do major control systems differ in their emphasis on timing control? In what ways might the timing of these control systems be altered?

2. Identify and briefly explain the main types of financial statements and financial ratios used by organizations. Suppose that your friend calls upon you to help rescue a motorcycle factory that is losing money. How might you use the various financial analyses to help assess the situation?

3. There are a number of potential pitfalls associated with financial controls. Could any of these pitfalls occur at Hanson PLC (see the Case in Point)?

4. Explain each type of responsibility center, and show the connection with organization structure. How do the different types of budgets relate to the responsibility centers?

5. Contrast top-down and bottom-up budgeting. Why do many organizations use a mixed approach? How might the positive and negative impacts of the budgetary process on managers differ depending on which approach is used?

6. Explain the main steps in the zero-base budgeting

process. If you were a lower-level or middle manager, would you advocate the use of zero-base budgeting? Explain your position.

7. Describe the eight dimensions of quality. Choose an item that you recently purchased, and rate your purchase on each of the dimensions of quality. What dimension was most important in your decision to purchase the item you did instead of one produced by a competitor?

8. Explain the total quality control approach. Why might employee involvement teams work better than quality circles?

9. Contrast acceptance sampling and statistical process control. From the point of view of a consumer, how would you like to see these quality control aids used by the companies whose products you buy?

10. Compare and contrast the economic order quantity and just-in-time approaches to inventory control. Why do you think that so many companies are attempting to make greater use of the just-in-time approach?

DISCUSSION QUESTIONS FOR CHAPTER OPENING CASE

1. How can Food Lion use financial and budgetary control techniques to help lower costs?
2. In what ways does Food Lion use the dimensions of quality to compete? Can you suggest other ways that the chain might be able to use quality control techniques?
3. What are the inventory considerations associated with buying massive amounts of products such as CranApple juice? Under what circumstances might the Food Lion approach not work as well?

MANAGEMENT EXERCISE: MEETING WATER BED DEMAND

A recent announcement from your state health department has proclaimed that water beds are very good for people with minor back pains. This has resulted in an extremely high demand for the water beds your firm produces. This is very good news; however, as the operating manager of the firm, you are concerned that your ability to produce may be impeded by several considerations. You review these:

Market share: The firm currently has about 12 percent of the local market. You recognize that you will need to increase productivity 5 percent just to maintain the current market position. However, to reach your goal of a 5 percent increase in market share, you must further increase productivity.

Capacity: You believe that you have the plant capacity to expand productivity to 6500 water beds annually. The firm now produces and sells 5000 water beds annually. The increase in market share, for both maintaining the current position and achieving your stated goal, will require 5500 water beds per year.

Inventory: You have storage capacity for raw materials for 450 water beds per month, and your work-in-process inventory is normally 470 beds per month. The finished-goods inventory is normally 8 percent of monthly production.

Quality: Inspections conducted after the water beds are made typically result in about 10 percent of them being rejected because of quality problems. Only about 50 percent of these can be repaired; the others must be scrapped.

Human resources: You have the skilled employees required to support increased production but will need additional unskilled workers. There are many potential employees in the local labor market.

Tomorrow you must tell the president of the firm whether or not you can meet the projected production schedule. If you need to make some modifications in your procedures in order to meet the projected schedule, these modifications should be included in your discussion with the president. What are you going to tell the president tomorrow morning?

C O N C L U D I N G   C A S E

POOR QUALITY LEADS TO FINANCIAL PROBLEMS FOR REGINA

The Regina Company, one of America's largest makers of vacuum cleaners, recently had severe problems with the quality of its products. The market response to this lack of quality caused financial problems for the company.

In late 1988 the company began having return rates as high as 30 to 50 percent on some of its Housekeeper and Housekeeper Plus models. These lines were sold primarily through discount stores for $59 to $79 and $100 to $150, respectively. Further, Regina's Stutz vacuum cleaner, an upgraded version sold in specialty stores, was introduced in 1988 with many quality problems. The specific problems identified for the Housekeeper and Housekeeper Plus lines were associated with faulty belts and weak suction. The Stutz had the following problems: The agitator was melting and making a loud noise, the foot pedals were breaking, and the steel-encased motor (which had been advertised as the power source for the vacuum cleaner) had been replaced with a less desirable, less reliable motor.

As a result of these problems, the Dayton Hudson Corporation dropped one line. Target Stores discontinued Regina's Housekeeper Plus 500 line after reporting that "at least half of those sold were returned." At K Mart, which accounts for about a quarter of the Housekeeper 1000 sales, 1 out of every 5 machines sold was returned, and to help service customer complaints Regina set up an 800 telephone number for customers to contact the firm directly.

It should be recognized that the Hoover Company and the Eureka Corporation, both leaders in the vacuum cleaner industry, have reported return rates for their machines of less than 1 percent. They further indicated that they would have cause for alarm if the return rate reached 3 percent.

The many returns caused Regina's shareholders to question the 1988 fiscal earnings report. Furthermore, both inventories and accounts receivable doubled during the 1988 fiscal year. In 1987 inventories were $19.6 million, but they climbed to $39.1 million by the end of 1988. About $17 million was finished goods in 1988, up from $10 million in 1987. Accounts receivable rose to $51 million in 1988, from $27.8 million in 1987. However, at the end of the 1988 fiscal year, Regina's chairman and 40 percent stockholder resigned. His resignation was closely followed by a company announcement stating that the financial results reported for the 1988 fiscal year were materially incorrect and had been withdrawn. This announcement brought a suit from shareholders who had bought Regina stock after the 1988 results had been announced. It also prompted an audit of the 1988 results and a request to another accounting organization to work on Regina's business and accounting controls. In addition, both the Securities and Exchange Commission and the National Association of Securities Dealers began investigating the company's affairs. The company filed for bankruptcy protection under Chapter 11 of the Federal Bankruptcy Code in 1989; a few months later, it agreed to be acquired by a unit of Electrolux, a vacuum cleaner and water-purification company based in Marietta, Georgia.[83]

QUESTIONS FOR CHAPTER CONCLUDING CASE

1. What type of controls would you have established to preclude the major returns experienced by Regina?
2. How would you have controlled the finished-goods inventory to preclude its growing to twice the size that it was in the previous year?
3. What actions would you have taken to reduce Regina's accounts receivable?

CHAPTER NINETEEN

OPERATIONS MANAGEMENT

CHAPTER OUTLINE

Defining Operations Management
The Productivity–Operations
  Management Linkage
Manufacturing versus Service
  Organizations
The Operations Management Process

Formulating Operations Strategy
Strategic Role Stages
Types of Operations Strategies

**Developing and Implementing
  Operating Systems**
Forecasting
Capacity Planning
Aggregate Production Planning
Scheduling
Materials Requirements Planning
Purchasing

Designing and Utilizing Facilities
Expansion and Contraction Decisions
Facilities Location
Facilities Layout

**Promoting Innovation: Process
  Technology**
Computer-Integrated Manufacturing
Implementing CIM Systems
Services Applications

Improving Productivity

LEARNING OBJECTIVES

*After studying this chapter, you
should be able to:*

■ Explain the concept of productivity and its linkage to the
operations management process.

■ Contrast manufacturing and
service organizations.

■ Identify four strategic role
stages that govern the role of
operations management in
strategy development and describe the two most common
operations strategies.

■ Explain each of the major systems used in operations management and discuss their interrelationships.

■ Outline the steps involved in
making expansion and contraction decisions regarding facilities and pinpoint the major
policy options.

■ Identify the four major types of
facility location problems and
the three main types of facility
layouts.

■ Explain the role of process
technology in promoting innovation through computer-integrated manufacturing and related means.

■ Discuss the major steps involved in improving productivity.

FANUC LEADS THE WORLD IN ELECTRONIC FACTORY HELP

If you had an opportunity to visit some of the most highly automated factories in the world, chances are that you would quickly run into the name "Fanuc." Japanese-based Fanuc (pronounced fa-NUKE) is the world's top supplier of devices that control the machines in automated factories. The company also is the foremost producer of industrial robots. The name "Fanuc" is an acronym for Fuji Automatic Numerical Control.

Fanuc's products are usually easy to recognize because they typically are painted bright yellow—or at least have bright-yellow nameplates. In fact, yellow is obtrusively evident at Fanuc headquarters. The company helicopter, the buildings, the jackets or smocks that employees wear—just about everything connected with Fanuc—all are bright yellow. The color yellow was chosen by Fanuc's chief executive Dr. Seiuemon Inaba because he perceives it to be an "emperor's color," befitting a premier company.

Fanuc constantly beats the competition by being the lowest-cost producer of high-quality automation components. In fact, the components are considered to be the highest quality available anywhere in the world. Fanuc's efforts to drive down costs are relentless, and Fanuc plants are among the most automated to be found anywhere. The 400 robots at the Mount Fuji complex slightly outnumber the production workers. The other 1700 workers are research engineers, administrators, and salespersons. In one plant, which cost about one-tenth of a conventional facility, 70 workers and 130 robots turn out 18,000 electric motors per month. To make a factory of this type possible, Fanuc had to redesign the motors, greatly reducing the number of parts needed for each motor.

Such efforts have helped Fanuc counteract the effects of the recently rising yen on the prices that Fanuc would otherwise have needed to charge its international customers. For example, in one instance, engineers drastically reduced the number of parts in a motor controller, a device that regulates the speed of a motor. The controller now has 573 parts compared with an earlier 1070; in addition, all cables and metal-stamping processes have been eliminated.

A large part of Fanuc's success can be attributed to Dr. Inaba, a directive leader, who is uncompromising in his emphasis on product quality and reliability. Subordinates generally do not speak in meetings unless he addresses them. Yet Inaba has been able to provide a vision for the company that has inspired employees to put forth their best efforts.

An additional factor is that Inaba rewards employees exceptionally well. The earnings of managers at Fanuc are generally about 50 percent more than the usual salaries at other Japanese companies, and engineers earn about 30 percent more than their counterparts in other organizations. The company also takes care of employees in other significant ways. For example, within the factory grounds there is family housing, as well as yellow dorms for single men, single women, and married people living away from their families. Workers may stay in these living facilities even past retirement—until death if they wish. Employees and their families can pursue leisure interests by studying such subjects as flower arranging or the tea ceremony in the Fanuc cultural center. They can exercise in the Fanuc gym or vacation in Fanuc-owned lodges in Japan, Spain, and the United States (Wisconsin). One outcome is that the workers are extremely loyal and hardworking, even by Japanese standards. For example, employees frequently sleep in beds provided on the premises so that they can work longer hours than they would otherwise to help the company maintain its preeminent position. Inaba located the company's headquarters at the base of Mount Fuji because he feels that people work best when there is a chill in the air.

Fanuc, nestled at the foot of Japan's Mount Fuji, produces high-quality automation products. In order to lower costs and compete effectively in the world market, Fanuc makes extensive use of robotic automation at its own plants. Fanuc's production methods are among the best in the world.

Another reason is that foreign dignitaries can have their picture taken with one of Japan's most famous landmarks as a background.

In urging his workers toward success, Inaba once told his engineers, "No matter how excellent a product may be produced, we will not be able to win a war if we should fail to market it at the proper time." Accordingly, he gave the product development lab a legendary wall clock that turns at 10 times the normal speed. "That saved me making a speech," he says. Inaba also expects at least $400,000 in sales per employee and an operating income that is 35 percent of sales.

General Motors formed a joint venture with Fanuc in 1982, after the automaker was unable to expand its own robot production enough to meet its own demand and also sell to others. Since then, the joint enterprise, called the GMFanuc Robotics Corporation, has become the world's largest supplier of robots.

More recently, another giant, General Electric, gave up its attempts to become the number-one company in factory automation after losing at least $200 million. Instead, GE formed a joint venture with Fanuc, its most formidable competitor. The new venture, the GE Fanuc Automation Corporation, specializes in devices that control automated machines, particularly computerized numerical controls. The controls are the electronic boxes that form the brains and nervous systems of automated versions of such tools as lathes and milling machines. When GE's plant in Charlottesville, Virginia, began making Fanuc models in 1988, the Fanuc versions incorporated refinements that one GE executive termed "awesome."[1]

Few leaders are as directive as Dr. Inaba. Yet, within the broad parameters and major directions that he outlines, workers have considerable latitude in pursuing the innovations that have made Fanuc a world-class supplier of factory automation devices. Although the company has been at the forefront in supplying others with automation devices, much of its success can be attributed to the internal emphasis on innovation within its own factory operations. The company's tireless efforts have made Fanuc the lowest-cost producer of automation equipment, yet its quality is unsurpassed. Thus Fanuc has been able to achieve high-quality outputs, yet, compared with the competition, it uses relatively fewer inputs. How has Fanuc been able to achieve such enviable productivity? A major part of the company's success can be attributed to its excellence in operations management, the functional area responsible for producing the goods and services that Fanuc has to offer.

In this chapter, we examine how companies like Fanuc can achieve high productivity by emphasizing effective operations management. The topic of operations management is considered in this part of the text, on the controlling function, because operations management constitutes a major control system used to increase the probability of meeting organizational goals and standards (see also Chapter 18). In considering operations management, we first explore its basic nature, as well as examine its linkage to productivity issues. We next investigate how operations management can be tied to an organization's overall strategy. We then explore several other major aspects of operations management, including operating systems, facilities, and the potential usefulness of process technology in promoting innovation. Finally, we take a closer look at the major steps involved in improving productivity within operations management.

DEFINING OPERATIONS MANAGEMENT

Operations management is the management of the productive processes that convert inputs into goods and services.[2] Because of its close association with manufacturing, operations management is sometimes called *production-operations management.* Recently, though, the term "production" is increasingly being dropped in favor of simply "operations management," a term that has less of a manufacturing connotation. The operations management function is that part of the organization directly involved in producing the primary goods and services.

In the case of a manufacturing organization such as Fanuc, the operations management function would include plant managers and all the other managers who work in the factories (e.g., production managers, inventory control managers, quality assurance managers, and line supervisors). When an organization's structure has a corporate level, operations would also encompass any manufacturing or operations vice presidents that exist at the corporate level, as well as related corporate operations staff (such as those primarily concerned with production, inventory, quality, facilities, and equipment).

In a service industry such as the hotel business, the operations management function would include hotel managers and the various managers who work in the hotels (e.g., housekeeping managers, food and beverage managers, and convention managers). Again, if there is a corporate level, operations would also comprise managers and staff at the corporate level who are directly involved in actually running the hotels (as opposed to managers who are involved in other related functions, such as marketing and finance). Regardless of whether an organization produces a service, a product, or both, operations managers need to be acutely concerned about productivity.

> **Operations management** The management of the productive processes that convert inputs into goods and services

The Productivity–Operations Management Linkage

Productivity is an efficiency concept that gauges the ratio of outputs relative to inputs into a productive process.[3] In Chapter 1, we discuss the concepts of organizational *effectiveness* and *efficiency* in performance. Effectiveness relates to the extent to which performance reaches organizational goals. In contrast, efficiency addresses the resource usage (inputs) involved in achieving outcomes (outputs). Productivity is aimed at assessing the efficiency aspect of organizational performance—the ratio of outputs relative to inputs. As such, productivity can be a useful tool for managers because it helps them track progress toward the more efficient use of resources in producing goods and services.

Organizational productivity is often measured by using this equation:

$$\text{Productivity} = \frac{\text{goods and services produced (outputs)}}{\text{labor + capital + energy + technology + materials (inputs)}}$$

An approach, like this one, that considers all the inputs involved in producing outputs is sometimes referred to as **total-factor productivity.** Managers also use **partial-factor productivity,** a productivity approach that considers the total output relative to a specific input, such as labor. For example:

$$\text{Productivity} = \frac{\text{goods and services produced (outputs)}}{\text{labor hours (labor input)}}$$

> **Productivity** An efficiency concept that gauges the ratio of outputs relative to inputs into a productive process

> **Total-factor productivity** A productivity approach that considers all the inputs involved in producing outputs

> **Partial-factor productivity** A productivity approach that considers the total output relative to a specific input, such as labor

In addition, managers often develop specific ratios that gauge productivity for particular outputs and inputs. Examples include sales per square foot of floor space, profit per sales dollar, return on investment, claims processed per employee, and lab tests completed per dollar of labor cost. For example, at Fanuc, Dr. Inaba uses the annual rate of return per employee as one of his productivity gauges; his goal: an annual return of $400,000 per employee. Managers typically devise several ratios that help them track important aspects of their work units. Top management, of course, is particularly interested in productivity measures that relate to the organization as a whole.

To illustrate the implications of productivity differences in organizations, we might consider a recent comparison of a Honda plant and a Jeep plant in Ohio. At the Honda plant 2432 workers turned out 875 four-wheel vehicles per day (about 2.8 workers per vehicle), while at the Jeep plant it took almost 5000 workers to produce 750 vehicles (about 6.7 workers per vehicle).[4] While workers per vehicle is only one gauge of productivity, the figures point to the reason why managers must concern themselves with productivity issues. If competitors can produce a given level of output with fewer inputs, they will be more profitable and have greater resources to expend on strengthening their competitive position.[5]

Productivity trends in the United States are troublesome, despite the fact that the United States is still the most productive country in the world. The nation had fairly high productivity growth in the private business sector from the period after World War II to the early 1970s. During the last half of the 1970s, however, U.S. productivity lagged, particularly in relation to that of other major countries.[6] For example, during the period from 1977 to 1987, manufacturing productivity in terms of output per labor hour climbed 32.4 percent in the United States, compared with 70.5 percent in Japan. Productivity growth in several other countries (e.g., France, Italy, Sweden, and the United Kingdom) also exceeded U.S. gains during the same period. A 1989 report by the Massachusetts Institute of Technology Commission on Industrial Productivity summed up the situation by observing, "American industry is not producing as well as it ought to produce, or as well as it used to produce, or as well as the industries of some other nations have learned to produce."[7]

During the 1980s, output per labor hour in manufacturing has again begun to climb. Unfortunately, in service and nonmanufacturing sectors, which employ almost four-fifths of all workers in the United States, output per worker is growing less than 0.6 percent per year (see Figure 19-1).[8] Differences in the nature of manufacturing and service organizations help explain some of these discrepancies.

Manufacturing versus Service Organizations

Manufacturing and service organizations differ in several important respects.[9] *Manufacturing organizations* are organizations that transform inputs into identifiable, tangible goods, such as soft drinks, cars, or videocassette recorders. Typically, the tangible goods they produce can be stored (at least to some degree), and the ultimate customer does not usually need to be present while the transformation process is taking place. As a result, manufacturing can often be done in centralized places, and the products can be shipped to customers. In addition, a manufacturing concern can often avoid wasting capacity during slack periods by using available capacity to produce inventory in anticipation of future sales.

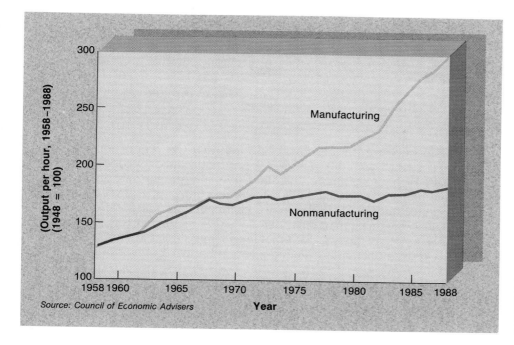

Figure 19-1 Lagging productivity in the service sector. (Reprinted from *The Wall Street Journal*, June 1, 1989, p. A1.)

Thus manufacturing organizations typically have considerable control over when and how their manufacturing operations will run, and they can attempt to organize their activities to maximize productivity.

In contrast, *service organizations* are organizations that transform inputs into intangible outcomes, such as education, health care, transportation services, and personal services. Such outcomes are produced and consumed more or less simultaneously, cannot be stored, and involve customer participation. For example, you are involved with a service organization when you take a class, see a doctor, visit a bank, catch an airplane flight, or get a haircut—all are activities in which you must participate in order to receive the service, and all are activities that cannot be stored. Unlike their manufacturing counterparts, service organizations cannot use idle capacity to produce stored inventory, and they often must operate in geographically dispersed locations where the customers are, rather than being able to store services and ship them. Compared with manufacturing organizations, service operations often have somewhat less control over when and exactly how their operations take place, since their activities may depend on customer volume and customer needs that are difficult to determine fully in advance.

In reality, many organizations provide both goods and services. As illustrated in the continuum shown in Figure 19-2, some organizations (such as factories, farms, and mines) produce mainly goods. Others (such as consulting firms, hospitals, and government agencies) produce mainly services. Still others produce a combination of goods and services. For example, in addition to the cars that they sell, Ford and General Motors provide many services, such as financing, insurance, and repairs. Similarly, when you visit your local Burger King outlet, you are receiving services in the form of order taking, order filling, and availability of tables for eating, yet you also receive a product in the form of, perhaps, a newly produced cheeseburger.

One way to classify organizations according to the degree of service they

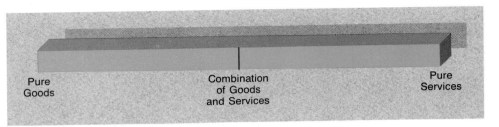

Figure 19-2 Continuum of goods and services.

provide is to measure the percentage of time that the production process involves direct contact with the customer.[10] A pure producer of goods would have zero contact with the ultimate customer, while a pure producer of services would have 100 percent contact. High customer contact often reduces organizational efficiency and productivity, since customers' arrival patterns may vary and customers may make particular demands that require customized service.[11] For example, you may have noticed that lines move slower at Burger King when individuals order nonstandard items, like a Whopper burger without pickles.

The Operations Management Process

In the process of transforming inputs into goods and services, operations management involves several major elements (see Figure 19-3).[12] For one thing, there is *operations strategy*, the role played by operations management in both formulating and implementing strategies to achieve organizational goals (see Chapter 6). For another, operations management includes various *operating systems*, major methods used to achieve efficiency and effectiveness in manufacturing and service operations. Yet another major element is *facilities*, the land, buildings, equipment, and other major physical assets that directly affect an organization's capacity to deliver goods and services. Finally, *process technology*, the technology used in transforming inputs into goods and services, also is an important ingredient in operations management. We consider each of these major elements in the next several sections of this chapter.

FORMULATING OPERATIONS STRATEGY

When IBM decided to enter the business of making printers for personal computers in 1983, it turned to manufacturing as a means of gaining the competitive

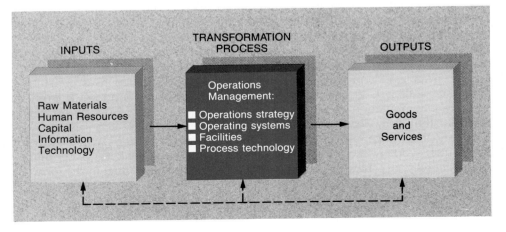

Figure 19-3 Operations management process.

edge over other makes, particularly those from Japan. The result was the very successful IBM Proprinter, manufactured in an award-winning plant in Charlotte, North Carolina. IBM took a relatively unique approach at the time: the printer was actually designed with the manufacturing process in mind. In fact, according to one IBM executive, "The manufacturing people literally shared the same coffee machine as the design people" as they worked together to consider simultaneously both the product design and the manufacturing process in developing the product.[13] The result was an advanced popular printer that could be manufactured in a very cost-effective manner, thus achieving high productivity in the Charlotte plant and enabling IBM to offer the printer at an attractive price. Such strategic use of operations management is becoming more commonplace in the face of increasing world competition.

Strategic Role Stages

Operations experts Steven C. Wheelwright and Robert H. Hayes argue that operations management plays different roles in determining strategy, depending on an organization's strategic role stage.[14] The four stages are shown in Figure 19-4.

Stage 1: Minimize Negative Potential. At stage 1, top managers attempt to neutralize any negative impact that internal operations may have on the organization. They take this stance because they regard operations management as essentially neutral in the sense of being incapable of positively affecting the organization's competitive success. In this mode, top managers typically use detailed measures and controls to be sure that the operations function does not veer too far off track before corrective action is taken. Generally, top managers minimize their involvement with operations areas, except for concerning themselves with major investment decisions (such as new facilities or major equipment purchases) through the vehicle of the capital budgeting process. Many consumer-products and service companies fit in this category.

Stage 2: Achieve Parity with Competition. At stage 2, top managers seek to have operations management maintain parity, or stay even, with the competition. Organizations at this stage typically attempt to maintain equality with the competition by adopting industry practices related to work-force matters (such as labor negotiations), equipment purchases, and upgrades of capacity. They

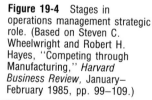

Figure 19-4 Stages in operations management strategic role. (Based on Steven C. Wheelwright and Robert H. Hayes, "Competing through Manufacturing," *Harvard Business Review*, January–February 1985, pp. 99–109.)

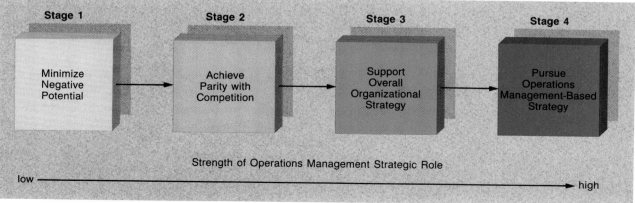

Stage 1	Stage 2	Stage 3	Stage 4
Minimize Negative Potential	Achieve Parity with Competition	Support Overall Organizational Strategy	Pursue Operations Management-Based Strategy

Strength of Operations Management Strategic Role

low ⟶ high

also are likely to avoid introducing major changes that will disrupt the status quo, to view capital investments in new equipment and facilities as the best means of gaining a temporary jump on the competition, and to consider economies of scale (producing in large amounts) as the best source of efficiency. Traditional manufacturing-intensive industries, such as steel, autos, and heavy equipment, are among the organizations often found in this stage.

Stage 3: Support Overall Organizational Strategy. At stage 3, top managers expect the operations management function to actively support and strengthen the organization's overall strategy. The role of operations managers, then, is to gain a thorough understanding of the organizational strategy as formulated by top management and to consider innovations that will help implement that strategy effectively. In this mode, top management wants operations managers to be creative and take a longer-term view of the operations management function. In contrast to those at stage 2, organizations at stage 3 see technological progress as a viable option that can enhance an organization's competitive position. Nonetheless, at this stage, operations managers are involved in implementing and supporting strategy but not in formulating it. The beer industry includes many stage-3 organizations. After building a number of new, large-scale facilities in the 1970s and rationalizing their existing operations, they began to drift back into a "business as usual" attitude toward the manufacturing function.

Stage 4: Pursue Operations Management-Based Strategy. At stage 4, top managers include operations managers in the strategy development process and formulate a strategy that depends to a significant degree on operations capabilities. Top managers view operations management as a strong strategic resource that can be used as a basis for strategy development. At stage 4, managers try to anticipate potential technological advances that could affect operations and to gain the necessary internal expertise well before the implications are obvious. At this stage, organizations attempt to use innovation as a means of making incremental strategic jumps ahead of the competition. Stage 4 is characteristic of all companies that have reached the status of world-class manufacturers. Such companies typically place a great deal of emphasis on ongoing innovations developed within the organization. In operations, these innovations are aimed at improving the processes used to produce goods and services. Because such organizations are at the forefront of new operations processes, they often develop their own innovative production equipment. Such efforts help them keep up with the various operations technologies that can affect their competitive position. (We discuss process technology further in a later section of this chapter). For example, Motorola has reached stage 4 through its "Operation Bandit" robotic production line (see the following Case in Point discussion).

CASE IN POINT: Motorola's Bandit Line Makes 29 Million Variations

A dominant force in the U.S. market for pocket pagers, Motorola watched as Japanese producers forced out half a dozen other domestic pager makers. Determined to stay competitive, Motorola's paging division developed a $9 million state-of-the-art manufacturing assembly line that debuted in 1988, operating along one wall of Motorola's Boynton Beach plant in southern Florida. The production line is called "Operation Bandit" because it borrows heavily from the best legally available manufacturing methods, including those used by Seiko and Honda.

On the Bandit line, robots dominate. The robots receive production orders by computer and then perform all the assembling, adjusting, and checking. They perform all these functions within one-hundredth of the time and with half the defect rate of conventional manufacturing methods. The Bandit robots are aided by about a dozen human employees who monitor the system and load it with sufficient parts to operate for an 8-hour stretch.

The Bandit line is geared to producing one type of pager, the "Bravo," which is marketed under several different brand names. Because the pagers work by a unique combination of access codes and radio frequencies, the Bandit line is able to produce pagers in an astronomical 29 million variations.

It took Motorola 18 months to design and install the Bandit system. In the process, the design team also redesigned the insides of the Bravo pager to make it easier to assemble by robot. About half of all Motorola's pagers will be built at this facility in the early 1990s. The entire Motorola Corporation has a goal of reducing defects and errors in every aspect of its business to three mistakes per million operations within that same time frame. Programs such as Operation Bandit have been crucial to that effort.[15] ■■■■■■

In order to survive in the highly competitive market for pocket pagers, Motorola has adopted the best manufacturing innovations available. The result is an automated assembly line that produces a sophisticated pager in 2 hours (rather than the 4 weeks required by conventional manufacturing means). Motorola's pager is now a top seller in the world market, including Japan.

Moving from One Stage to Another. Normally, organizations have difficulty moving from one stage to higher stages without passing through the stages in between. For example, an organization would find it almost impossible to jump from stage 2 to stage 4 without going through stage 3. One reason is that operations management personnel need to acquire new skills to function at each progressive stage. Another reason is that higher stages also require changes in the way that the rest of the organization views operations management and interacts with it. In dealing with the growing competition from Japan, Motorola went through an evolution in which managers first ignored the competition and then attempted to fight it through legal means (by trying to stop the selling of pagers in the U.S. market at below cost and to open up the Japanese market to U.S. manufacturers). Finally, they began learning from Japan and others to the point at which Motorola has finally moved to stage 4, developing a world-class manufacturing operation to produce pagers. In fact, Motorola pagers rank among the top sellers in Japan.[16] While existing organizations find it difficult to skip stages, a new organization may be able to start at any stage, provided that the necessary skills and strategy orientation are in place.

Of course, the role stages apply to service types of organizations as well as to manufacturing enterprises. For example, American Express has gained a reputation for outstanding service by continually refining its service processes to achieve high standards, such as a 7-second standard for operators to answer the telephone at its service centers and a 48-hour standard for customers reporting a lost card to receive a replacement in the mail. The head of one report service that monitors the credit card industry describes service at American Express as "incomparable."[17]

Types of Operations Strategies

In strategic role stages 3 and 4, the two operations strategies that are most commonly used are low-cost producer and innovative producer. The low-cost producer approach to operations strategy fits well with an overall organizational strategy of low cost, while the innovative producer approach meshes with an overall strategy of differentiation (see Chapter 6). In the low-cost situation, operations management emphasizes low costs for a given level of quality and typically focuses on superior production processes, high volume, bureaucratic control, cost-reducing innovations, and mainly low-skilled workers (because they perform the same duties on a high volume of output). ServiceMaster exemplifies the use of this strategy (see the following Case in Point discussion).

CASE IN POINT: ServiceMaster Cleans, Repairs, and Maintains

ServiceMaster provides a wide range of services for its clients. The services performed by this almost $2 billion (annual revenues) organization include pest control, plumbing, lawn care, maid service, and appliance maintenance.

ServiceMaster was founded in 1958 by Marion Wade, a devout Christian who established four commandments for the organization. The first, "To honor God in all we do," is the basis for the firm's name ("ServiceMaster" is short for "Service to the Master"). The second commandment is "To help people develop"; the third is "To pursue excellence"; and the last is "To grow profitably."

The company, headquartered in Downers Grove, near Chicago, earned its stellar reputation by furnishing cleaning services for hospitals and factories. Today it has almost 3500 franchisees located throughout the United States. The franchisees are allowed to provide ServiceMaster services in various areas; in return, they pay ServiceMaster various fees and/or royalties, as well as agree to follow the company's standard operating procedures.

In order to facilitate efficient and effective service, the company has produced a 3-inch-thick manual which provides detailed instructions for franchisees and their workers. For example, the task of polishing floors is broken into a series of specific 5-minute steps. Other services are similarly addressed, with very precise instructions for their completion. In addition to standardizing tasks in its manual, ServiceMaster makes its own chemicals and designs its own equipment. For example, when polishing a floor, ServiceMaster workers use a specially made floor-finish product with a prescribed drying time. Similarly, the ServiceMaster vacuum cleaner is battery-operated so that the operator does not have to waste time moving an electric cord.

After years of unprecedented growth, ServiceMaster's sales began to level off in 1987. The company responded by adding additional services and a maintenance contract, for both commercial and residential properties, which includes a wide range of services such as unclogging toilets, repairing stove burners, fixing leaky faucets, checking and spraying for unwanted insects, and taking care of the lawn. So far, market tests of the maintenance contract concept indicate that it has high potential for success.[18] ■

In contrast to the low-cost strategy, the innovative producer approach concentrates on innovations that distinguish a company's products or services from those of the competition. In an innovative producer situation, operations management spotlights production flexibility, superior products or services, low volume, clan control, flexibility innovations, and skilled workers who can deal with constant product and service changes. The Motorola strategy for pagers fits in the innovative producer category since it is aimed at producing 29 million variations of a high-quality pager much more quickly than could be done by conventional means.

DEVELOPING AND IMPLEMENTING OPERATING SYSTEMS

Successfully carrying out an operations strategy requires the design and implementation of well-conceived operating systems, the major methods used to achieve efficiency and effectiveness in manufacturing and service operations. The primary operating systems used in operations management are forecasting, capacity planning, aggregate production planning, scheduling, materials requirements planning, and purchasing (see Figure 19-5). Quality control, another

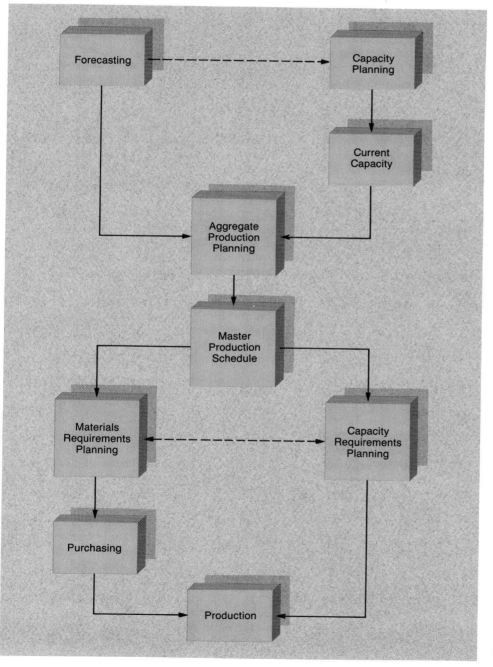

Figure 19-5 Major systems used in operations management.

major system that is important in operations management, is discussed extensively in Chapter 18.

Forecasting

Forecasting is a process aimed at predicting changing conditions and future events that may significantly affect the business of an organization. Major forecasting methods are explained in Chapter 9.

For operations management purposes, forecasting efforts are mainly aimed at predicting goods or services *demand*. Forecasts of demand can range from short to long term and typically depend on quantitative and judgmental forecasting methods. Forecasting short-term demand (up to 1 year, but often ranging from less than a month to 3 months) is important because demand predictions affect relatively short-run conditions, such as scheduling production and having sufficient materials on hand to meet the production schedule. For example, in Rubbermaid's home products division, quantitative methods are used each month to make 30-day, 60-day, 90-day, and annual forecasts of demand for 600 item packs (because products are often marketed in several different packaging schemes). The various product managers then add their judgment to the statistical data to achieve the final forecasts.[19]

Forecasting intermediate-term (1 to 5 years) or long-term (5 years or more) demand has a major impact on expansion decisions, such as acquiring additional major equipment and new facilities. Organizations often enlist outside help in making such forecasts. For example, most of the major automobile manufacturers use the services of J. D. Power & Associates of Los Angeles, one of the foremost forecasters of automobile sales. One recent 5-year report on specific models predicted that Japanese automakers will increase their share of the luxury-car market from 3 to 20 percent in the early 1990s.[20]

After preparing demand forecasts, managers then use the information in two major ways. As indicated in Figure 19-5, forecasts of demand influence capacity planning, as well as aggregate production planning. We consider the capacity-planning issue first.

Capacity Planning

Capacity planning The process of determining the people, machines, and major physical resources, such as buildings, that will be necessary to meet the production objectives of the organization

Capacity planning is the process of determining the people, machines, and major physical resources, such as buildings, that will be necessary to meet the production objectives of the organization.[21] *Capacity* is the maximum output capability of a productive unit within a given period of time. For example, a car wash can handle only so many cars within an hour because of the physical constraints of the facility. Similarly, a beauty salon can handle only so many customers per day without serious declines in service. Some common measures of capacity according to the type of organization are shown in Table 19-1.

Time Horizons. Capacity planning involves three different time horizons: long, medium, and short range. Each time horizon involves somewhat different capacity-related issues.[22]

Long-range capacity planning focuses on the human, physical, and financial resources necessary to meet long-term organizational goals. Because adding significantly to long-term capacity usually requires major capital expenditures for facilities and has major implications for employment, such decisions typically are made by top management. We discuss long-range capacity changes in the next section, which deals with facilities.

Table 19-1 Measures of Capacity According to Type of Organization

Type of Organization	Capacity Measure
Auto plant	Number of autos
Steel plant	Tons of steel
Beer plant	Cases of beer
Nuclear power plant	Megawatts of electricity
Airline	Available seat-miles (ASMs)
Hospital	Available bed-days
Movie theater	Available seat-performances
Restaurant	Available seat-turns
Jobbing machine shop	Available labor hours
School of business administration	Available semester or quarter sections

Source: Adapted from Elwood S. Buffa, *Modern Production/Operations Management,* Wiley, New York, 1983, p. 128.

Medium-range capacity planning provides information on the capacities of current major facilities, as well as on possible means of making limited adjustments in capacity during the intermediate and short run (such as hiring and laying off employees, using overtime, and building up inventory). We discuss these limited means of adjusting capacity in further detail under "Aggregate Production Planning."

Short-range capacity planning is aimed at ensuring that the capacities of current major facilities are being utilized effectively within the context of the master production schedule. Planning within this time horizon may make use of **capacity requirements planning,** a technique for determining what personnel and equipment are needed to meet short-term production objectives (see Figure 19-5). Unanticipated or late changes, such as a shortage of materials or an emergency order from an important customer, may necessitate temporary reshufflings of scheduled work to utilize productive capacity effectively.

Capacity requirements planning A technique for determining what personnel and equipment are needed to meet short-term production objectives

Aggregate Production Planning

Short-term forecasts of demand, as well as intermediate- and short-range capacity planning, are particularly important in aggregate production planning.[23] **Aggregate production planning** is the process of planning how to match supply with product or service demand over a time horizon of about 1 year (see Figure 19-5). Although the planning process typically covers 1 year, the plan is updated periodically (often monthly). In some organizations the aggregate plan may cover as little as 3 months or as much as 18 months, depending on the manufacturing or service lead time. The basic idea of an aggregate plan is to achieve a rough balance between market demand and the capacity of the organization. The term "aggregate" is used because production plans at this point are stated in global units of output, such as number of automobiles, tons of steel, or seat-miles, rather than individual car models, specific steel products, or particular airline flights.

Aggregate production planning The process of planning how to match supply with product or service demand over a time horizon of about 1 year

Aggregate planning relies on two major assumptions. One is that the maximum capacity of major facilities, such as plants, retail outlets, or extensive equipment, cannot be altered within the time frame. The second assumption is that short- and intermediate-term demand is subject to fluctuations due to uncertainties, seasonal influences, or other market-related factors. As a result, operations managers need to plan how to meet the fluctuating demand within the fixed major facilities.

Table 19-2   Major Approaches and Potential Costs of Adjusting to Fluctuating Demand

	COSTS OF ADJUSTING TO:	
Major Approach	**Increased Demand**	**Decreased Demand**
Hiring and laying off workers	Hiring and training Use of less experienced workers	Unemployment insurance Loss of skilled workers Decreased employee morale Adverse community (and union) effects
Overtime and idle time	Overtime pay Potential decreased product quality Skill shortages	Fixed costs of underutilized workers
Building up inventory	Carrying costs Increased purchasing Reduced service level if safety stock used up	Carrying costs Obsolescence Increased stock levels may take up working space
Back orders	Stockout costs of lost or dissatisfied customers	Negligible
Subcontracting	Cost premium Decreased quality control	Negligible

Source: Adapted from Joseph G. Monks, *Operations Management*, 3d ed., McGraw-Hill, New York, 1987, p. 314.

Operations managers can use several approaches to meet short-term and intermediate-term fluctuating demand. These approaches, along with the costs of adjusting to increasing or decreasing demand (if forecasts turn out to be wrong), are summarized in Table 19-2.

Hiring and Laying Off Employees. One way to adjust to short-term demand fluctuations is to hire employees as needed and lay them off when they are not needed. Although this strategy is often used, many companies attempt to avoid this approach. One reason is that hiring and training costs are usually substantial. Another reason is that the most skilled workers may tend to gravitate toward companies with more stable employment patterns. In addition, unemployment insurance and related costs can be quite high for companies with chronic layoff patterns. Finally, chronic layoffs might lead to a major cost in terms of damage to employee morale and community relations. Nevertheless, GMFanuc Robotics was forced to lay off 200 members of its work force in 1986, after General Motors suddenly canceled or delayed orders totaling about $88 million because of a slump in auto sales.[24]

Using Overtime and Idle Time. Another approach to handling demand fluctuations is to hire the average number of employees needed, knowing that at some times overtime will be required and that at other times the employees will not be fully utilized even though they are at work. Since overtime pay costs range between 150 and 200 percent of regular pay, depending on when the overtime is scheduled, heavy of overtime has a high impact on production costs. Also, quality may suffer under conditions of extensive overtime.

Building Up Inventory. For organizations that produce goods, inventory is one means of attempting to meet fluctuating demands. Operations managers can use slack periods to produce goods that can be held as finished-goods inventory.

Such goods are often referred to as *anticipation*, or *seasonal*, *inventories* because the products are produced to meet expected rather than current demand. Of course, this strategy involves carrying costs, the expenses associated with keeping the items on hand. If the demand is much greater than expected, stockouts still may occur. On the other hand, if the anticipated demand does not materialize, it is possible that the products may become obsolete. This strategy is not feasible for pure services, since they cannot build up inventory.

Taking Back Orders. One potential solution to fluctuating demand is to take **back orders,** orders for goods which cannot be filled immediately but which will be honored as more goods or service slots become available. The danger with the back-order approach is that the customer might go elsewhere or might feel dissatisfied with having to wait for goods or a service. The advantage, of course, is that if the expected demand does not occur, the costs of adjusting to the decreased demand are negligible.

Back orders Orders for goods which cannot be filled immediately but which will be honored as more goods or service slots become available

Subcontracting. Subcontracting involves using other organizations to supply all or part of the goods and services needed to fulfill demand. Subcontracting may add to product or service costs, particularly if it is difficult to line up the necessary expertise on relatively short notice. Also, control over quality is usually lessened, since the subcontracting often is done at another location. On the other hand, subcontractors are usually hired only as needed, making it easier to react to downturns in demand. For example, Liz Claiborne, Inc., the apparel company, has relied largely on subcontracting the production of its clothing to avoid tying up funds required for buying factories and to provide additional flexibility in adjusting to demand changes.[25]

Combining Approaches. While any of these approaches can be used alone, in most complex situations several are used in combination to meet fluctuating customer demand. A number of researchers have been experimenting with a variety of mathematical models, simulations, and other analytical efforts to make it easier for operations managers to conduct effective aggregate planning and decide how best to react to demand fluctuations. To date, few of these analytical approaches have been successfully used in real organizations, partially because many of these approaches make simplifying assumptions that limit their usefulness in solving actual production problems.[26] Continual work in this area, coupled with the widespread use of computers, is likely to yield more sophisticated help for managers conducting aggregate production planning.

Scheduling

Aggregate planning lays the rough groundwork for the next step, creating the master production schedule (see Figure 19-5). The **master production schedule (MPS)** translates the aggregate plan into a formalized production plan encompassing specific products to be produced or services to be offered and specific capacity requirements over a designated time period. Thus the master production schedule includes greater detail than the aggregate plan about the actual products and models to be produced or services to be offered, making it possible to more closely assess capacity requirements. Master scheduling involves some trial-and-error work and typically begins with a tentative schedule that is refined through several iterations.

Master production schedule (MPS) A schedule that translates the aggregate plan into a formalized production plan encompassing specific products to be produced or services to be offered and specific capacity requirements over a designated time period

Time Horizon. The time horizon covered by a master schedule may be a few weeks or may range to a year or more, depending on product or service characteristics and the lead times necessary for obtaining materials. Within the master schedule, the various activities are often broken down on a weekly basis. Some organizations use weekly intervals for 13 weeks (one quarter) and monthly intervals beyond the quarter.

MPS Advantages. Using a master production schedule has several advantages. For one thing, master scheduling helps managers evaluate alternative schedules. Many computerized production and inventory control systems enable managers to simulate the effects of a proposed production schedule. By means of the simulation, planners can determine what lead times for materials and what delivery dates to customers would result from alternative schedules. If these lead times or delivery dates are not acceptable, then schedule revisions must be made. Another advantage of the master scheduling process is that it helps determine the materials required. It does so by providing specific information about what is to be produced for the materials requirements system (discussed below; see also Figure 19-5) so that materials are purchased and delivered in time to meet scheduled production. Still another advantage of developing an MPS is that it provides specific information about immediate capacity requirements (such as labor and equipment resources) for use in capacity requirements planning (see Figure 19-5). If the requirements exceed the available capacity, schedule adjustments, such as delaying the production of some items or services, may be required. On the other hand, underutilization of capacity may call for producing some items ahead of schedule, if feasible, or possibly generating greater demand (perhaps through a special promotion). Finally, the master schedule facilitates sharing relevant information about marketing (such as customer deliveries), inventory, and personnel matters (such as personnel needs).

Materials Requirements Planning

Materials requirements planning (MRP) A computer-based inventory system that develops materials requirements for the goods and services specified in the master schedule and initiates the procurement actions necessary to acquire the materials when needed

Dependent demand inventory A type of inventory consisting of raw materials, components, and subassemblies that are used in the production of an end product or service

Independent demand inventory A type of inventory consisting of end products, parts used for repairs, and other items whose demand is tied more directly than that for dependent demand inventory items to market issues

While developing a master schedule is important, scheduled production cannot occur unless the appropriate materials are in place at the right time to do the job. One effective means of handling materials issues is the use of materials requirements planning, which must be closely coordinated with the master production schedule (see Figure 19-5). **Materials requirements planning (MRP)** is a computer-based inventory system that develops materials requirements for the goods and services specified in the master schedule and initiates the procurement actions necessary to acquire the materials when needed.

MRP systems can handle various types of inventory, but they are particularly adept at dealing with **dependent demand inventory,** the raw materials, components, and subassemblies that are used in the production of an end product or service. For example, if a company makes wheelbarrows, components such as tires, wheels, and axles are considered to be dependent demand inventory items because they are used to create end products (wheelbarrows), rather than being end products in themselves. In other words, the inventory *demand* for these items is *dependent* on the need for the end products. In contrast, **independent demand inventory** consists of end products, parts used for repairs, and other items whose demand is tied more directly to market issues. An MRP system was first available from IBM in the 1960s, when computers became more widely used as a tool to facilitate operations management. Since that time, many manufacturing companies either have installed an MRP system or are planning to do so.[27] The MRP concept is only beginning to be applied to service organizations, but there are tremendous possibilities for improvements in productivity stemming from MRP systems in service operations such as restaurants, hotels, legal offices, and health care.[28]

Inputs to MRP Systems. In manufacturing, MRP systems use three major inputs: the master production schedule, bill-of-materials information, and inventory status information. The MRP system obtains specific information about products to be produced from the master production schedule.

The MRP system then consults the bill of materials for each product and model in order to determine the exact materials required. A **bill of materials (BOM)** is a listing of all components, including partially assembled pieces and basic parts, that make up an end product. The bill of materials usually includes the part numbers and quantities required per unit of end product. The information is often organized in a hierarchy of component levels so that it is possible to determine the most basic ingredients as well as the subassemblies that make up the various parts. For example, Figure 19-6 shows a product structure tree indicating the BOM levels for a wheelbarrow. As the figure indicates, the bars and grips at level 2 are assembled to make up the handle assembly in level 1. Similarly, the tire from level 3 (the most basic level) and the axle, bearings, and wheel from level 2 make up the wheel assembly in level 1. The top level (0) shows the end product. Bill-of-materials information is kept in computer files for ready access by the MRP system so that exact materials requirements for a proposed master schedule can be determined rapidly. The larger the number of levels in the BOM, the more likely that an MRP system is needed to help manage materials in the production process.[29]

The MRP system also makes extensive use of computerized inventory status

Bill of materials (BOM) A listing of all components, including partially assembled pieces and basic parts, that make up an end product

Figure 19-6 Bill-of-materials levels for a wheelbarrow. (Reprinted from Joseph G. Monks, *Operations Management*, McGraw-Hill, New York, 1987, p. 444.)

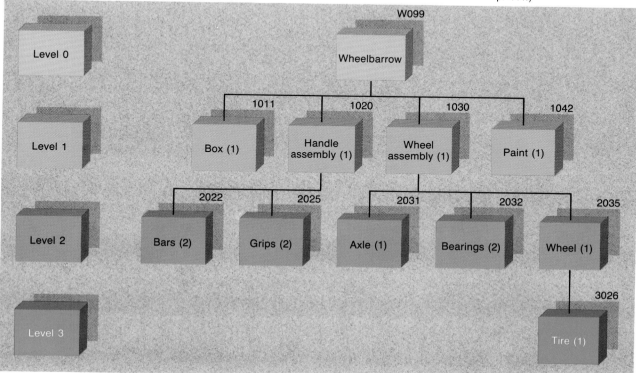

information. The system accesses inventory data to determine quantities of needed materials on hand, scheduled receipts of already ordered materials, and orders about to be released. The inventory status file also includes related information such as lead times for obtaining materials and desirable safety stock levels.

For service applications, the bill of materials might be replaced by a bill of activities. Combined with the master production schedule and inventory status information, the bill of activities might be used as a basis for determining all the activities and personnel required to produce a particular combination of services. If materials are an important part of the service to be delivered, a bill of materials may also be needed. In one application of the MRP system at a utility, new customer requests for electric service are entered into a computer system which prepares a detailed estimate of the labor, materials, and work activities required. Estimates for various service requests are then combined to determine whether sufficient capacity is available. Ultimately, utility work crews are given work orders from the system; the crews report back to the system as work is completed.[30]

Benefits from MRP Systems. Four major types of outputs come from MRP systems. First, the system triggers orders for materials that go to purchasing for handling or to internal departments that will supply the necessary components. Second, the system supplies information to master production schedulers, indicating any materials procurement difficulties that will interfere with the proposed master schedule. Third, the MRP system gives information to individuals in charge of capacity planning, who can make short-run changes such as shifting equipment and adding people (through capacity requirements planning) or can consider longer-run changes based on trends. Fourth, the system can provide management with valuable information in such areas as costs, quality, and supplier activities.

MRP is a much more sophisticated approach to inventory control than the traditional economic order quantity (EOQ) method discussed in Chapter 18. The EOQ approach is aimed at keeping inventories from falling below certain minimum levels, whereas MRP is tailored to the specific needs of the current master schedule. MRP systems can be difficult to implement, and they depend heavily on the accuracy of data fed into the system, particularly data on current inventory and bills of materials (or activities).[31] According to one study, the major problems associated with implementing MRP are failure to educate adequately those who are going to use the system, lack of top management support, and insufficient time and personnel for properly setting up the system.[32] MRP systems can also be costly to install. One study put the average cost at more than $600,000. That same study indicates that MRP systems improve inventory turnover, reduce product delivery lead time, increase the percentage of product delivery promises met, and reduce the number of expediters needed to iron out inventory-related production problems.[33]

MRP systems also operate very differently from the just-in-time (JIT) inventory approach described in Chapter 18.[34] Like the JIT approach, MRP is aimed at reducing inventory costs and keeping the production line supplied with the materials necessary to keep it running smoothly. However, MRP systems do so by planning extensively and using lead times to order exactly what is needed on the basis of the master production schedule (plus perhaps a small amount of safety stock to allow for some schedule changes). MRP systems also can handle master schedules that vary considerably from day to day and involve producing many different products and services. In contrast, the JIT approach relies on a stable master schedule that varies little from day to day, has relatively high volume requirements, and emphasizes close relationships with suppliers, who deliver the needed materials just before they are required. Typically, the JIT approach includes a production control system known as Kanban, which is based on reusable cards that specify materials needs within the production process. In essence, the JIT approach is better suited to relatively stable situations in which very close relationships can be developed with suppliers. MRP has the edge in more complex and dynamic situations that require sophisticated planning.

Manufacturing Resource Planning. On the basis of the success of MRP systems, a number of organizations have taken a further step in instituting manufacturing resource planning. **Manufacturing resource planning (MRP II)** is a computer-based information system that integrates the production planning and control activities of basic MRP systems with related financial, accounting, personnel, engineering, and marketing information. MRP II systems tie operations management information into a common system with other organizational functions.[35] For example, when an organization with an MRP II system produces an item, the system analyzes the labor and materials costs, captures the cash-flow implications, and notifies marketing that the product is in stock. These and other activities make it possible for the operations management function to coordinate its efforts with the rest of the organization.[36]

> **Manufacturing resource planning (MRP II)** A computer-based information system that integrates the production planning and control activities of basic MRP systems with related financial, accounting, personnel, engineering, and marketing information

Although MRP II systems can be expensive and time-consuming to implement successfully, results have been impressive. For example, at Tektronix, a manufacturer of oscilloscopes, computer workstations, and related products, an MRP II system led to a 61 percent cut in inventory (from $180 to $70 million) and a 47 percent reduction in needed warehouse space.[37] According to one estimate, there are more than 45,000 MRP II–packaged computer systems in operation in the United States, with pharmaceutical firms, aerospace and defense contractors, and automotive and parts manufacturers being the biggest users.[38] Again, such systems are potentially applicable to service organizations, but they are only just beginning to be implemented in the service sector.

Purchasing

In order to conduct their business, most organizations need materials and services that they obtain through **purchasing,** the process of acquiring necessary goods or services in exchange for funds or other remuneration.[39] Purchasing needs are identified through materials requirements planning (see Figure 19-5). The purchasing process then provides major contributions such as investigating vendors to determine whether they are qualified to provide supplies, seeking alternative sources of supplies, and negotiating low, favorable purchasing prices. Traditionally, though, the purchasing function has been viewed as almost a clerical function aimed at buying commodities that meet specifications, rather than as a technical or managerial task.

> **Purchasing** The process of acquiring necessary goods or services in exchange for funds or other remuneration

More recently the traditional view of purchasing has been changing because of environmental and competitive developments.[40] One reason for the change is that materials and supplies can amount to significant expenditures, and small savings on purchases can make a significant difference to a company's bottom line.

Another reason for the growing importance of purchasing is that advancing technology has made products for purchase more complex and difficult to evaluate. As a result, greater technical expertise is necessary to make good purchasing decisions; companies such as Eli Lilly and Motorola have begun to hire M.B.A.s with technical backgrounds to take charge of purchasing in crucial technical areas. Yet another reason for highlighting purchasing is the rising importance of obtaining high-quality materials and services from suppliers. Without high-quality inputs, organizations have a much greater difficulty producing the high-quality outputs that are necessary to compete effectively in the marketplace.

Finally, the increasing rate of technological change has led to more new product and service introductions with shorter lead times. One implication is that organizations are finding that they can shorten development time and expense by obtaining more materials from outside vendors and involving the vendors in the actual product or service design phase. This approach, of course, requires identifying specialized vendors and establishing ongoing relationships with them. For example, General Electric's jet engine division has used 16 design teams to work on various aspects of its new commercial engine. Each of the teams included members from the purchasing staff who could help to involve vendors in the design process. GE expects that the involvement of purchasing and vendors will ultimately reduce product development costs by as much as 20 percent.

DESIGNING AND UTILIZING FACILITIES

Facilities The land, buildings, equipment, and other major physical inputs that substantially determine productive capacity, require time to alter, and involve significant capital investments

An area closely related to capacity planning is the question of facilities. **Facilities** are the land, buildings, equipment, and other major physical inputs that substantially determine productive capacity, require time to alter, and involve significant capital investments. Facilities issues confronting managers focus mainly on expansion and contraction decisions, facilities location, and facilities layout.

Expansion and Contraction Decisions

Making decisions about expanding or contracting available facilities is directly related to long-range capacity planning. Typically, the facilities decision process involves four steps.[41]

Decision Steps. First, managers use forecasts to determine the probable future demand for products or services. Since facilities often take 2 or more years to arrange and put into operation, relevant forecasts must extend over several years, adding to the uncertainty involved.

Second, managers compare current capacity with projected future demand. *Current capacity* is the maximum output rate possible from current operations. By comparing current capacity with future demand, managers can determine whether current capacity is insufficient, about right, or excessive. For example, in 1988, Robert Stempel, who is currently chairman of General Motors and who was president at the time, announced a 5-year plan to reduce plant capacity to bring it more in line with projected demand. He recognized that he may have to close four factories and eliminate more than 100,000 jobs in North America to achieve full-capacity utilization in the early 1990s.[42]

Third, when there is either insufficient or excess capacity, managers need to generate and then evaluate alternatives. In many cases, the number of alternatives available for making changes in facilities is large. In others, it may be difficult to develop even one feasible alternative. Alternatives typically involve location considerations, an issue we discuss below.

Finally, managers carefully consider the risks and decide on a plan that includes the timing of capacity expansion or contraction, if any. Facilities decisions usually involve considerable risk because additional facilities raise fixed costs that must be paid even if the expected demand does not materialize. On the other hand, insufficient capacity may provide competitors with opportunities to attract customers that otherwise would have been yours.

Options for Expanding Capacity. In expanding capacity, top managers generally have three major policy options—at least when demand is expected to grow somewhat steadily.[43]

First, with a *capacity-leads-demand* policy, an organization tries not to run short. Following this policy produces a capacity cushion so that there is a relatively small likelihood of not being able to fill orders from customers. Although the capacity cushion will add fixed costs, an organization might choose such a cushion in order to take care of demand surges, provide better service to customers, or put itself in a good position to attract customers from competitors that do not have a cushion. For example, Echlin, based in Branford, Connecticut, makes and stocks nearly 150,000 automobile parts, including parts for the Model T and the Rolls-Royce. The company prospers by offering speedy and reliable service in delivering parts to a variety of garages, automakers, and mass merchandisers. To retain its unchallenged eminence in parts, Echlin maintains a capacity that stays ahead of demand.[44]

Second, with a policy of *capacity in approximate equilibrium with demand,* an organization attempts to match capacity as closely as possible to anticipated demand. Since demand usually does not grow at a strictly even pace, this policy will sometimes lead to overcapacity and other times to undercapacity. This approach is often used when both the costs of some overcapacity and some inability to meet demand because of undercapacity can be tolerated, at least for a short period of time.

Third, with a *capacity-lags-demand* policy, an organization tries to maximize capacity utilization. In a sense, this policy implies a *negative* cushion, since there is a high likelihood of running short. This approach requires less capital investment than is needed for a positive cushion and, therefore, provides a higher return on manufacturing investment than is possible with a lower utilization of capacity rate. The danger, of course, is that the organization will lose sales and seriously erode its market share. Ford Motor's top executives have faced difficult decisions because they foresee a worldwide capacity glut in the automobile industry during the 1990s and have been reluctant to add to capacity by building new plants. Yet Ford automobiles have been selling so well that the company has been unable to meet the demand, even with extensive overtime that is straining both its employees and machines.[45]

Facilities Location

The location of plants, warehouses, and service facilities is an important aspect of facilities decisions. In fact, for the most part, decisions about additional facilities are closely connected to location considerations. Most facilities location problems fall into one of four categories: single facility, multiple factories and warehouses, competitive retail outlets, and emergency services. Each of these categories involves somewhat different criteria in deciding facilities locations.

Benetton, the retail clothing chain based in Italy, experienced a leveling off of sales in the United States during the late 1980s. Part of the reason was an oversaturation of stores in some markets and poor store locations in others. One result is that the general manager of Benetton USA has been directing greater attention to determining optimal locations and sizes for the more than 600 independently owned outlets licensed by Benetton in the United States.

A *single-facility* location involves a facility that does not need to interact with any other facilities that the organization might have. A single factory or warehouse or a single retail store would fit into this category. Location decisions for a single facility typically revolve around multiple criteria, such as labor costs, labor supply, raw materials, transportation availability, community services, taxes, and other relevant issues.

Locations for *multiple factories and warehouses* usually involve strong consideration of distribution costs and effects on total production costs owing to the various interfaces. For complex problems involving multiple facilities, operations research methods may be used to help determine locations that will minimize distribution costs.[46] A large part of the phenomenal success of Wal-Mart comes from carefully locating warehouses and then opening multiple stores within a 400-mile radius in order to pool distribution and advertising overhead.[47] Recently, efforts to adapt just-in-time inventory methods are causing manufacturing organizations to consider facility sites closer to major customers.

Locations for *competitive retail outlets* must be oriented toward consideration of the revenue that can be obtained from various locations. For example, the location of a bank, shopping center, or movie theater relative to both customers and competitors usually has a strong bearing on how much revenue the facility generates. There are a number of commercially available computer programs that use census and other data to help major retailers, like Woolworth, choose new locations for retail outlets.[48]

The location of *emergency services* often is connected to response time. For example, police and fire departments must be located where they can provide an acceptable level of service, which often includes a speedy response in emergencies.

Facilities Layout

Another important aspect of facilities is the layout, the configuration of processing components (departments, workstations, and equipment) that make up the production sequence. There are three main types of layouts for facilities: process, product, and fixed position.[49]

Process Layout. A **process layout** is a production configuration in which the processing components are grouped according to the type of function that they perform. The product being made or the client receiving service moves from function to function depending on the particular needs for that product or client. As a result, the demand for any particular function is somewhat intermittent, stemming from the fact that there may be some products or clients not requiring the use of a given function. Intermittent demand may cause a function to be idle at times and backed up with waiting work at other times. See Figure 19-7a for examples of process layouts for a product (machine shop) and a service (medical clinic), respectively. A process layout makes sense when a variety of products

Process layout A production configuration in which the processing components are grouped according to the type of function that they perform

Figure 19-7 (a) Two examples of a process layout. (Reprinted from Elwood S. Buffa, *Modern Production/Operations Management*, Wiley, New York, 1983, pp. 32–33.)

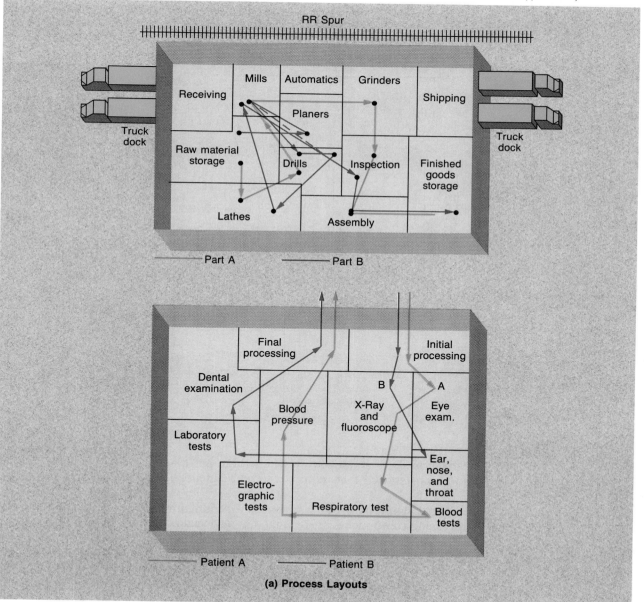

(a) Process Layouts

(Continued)

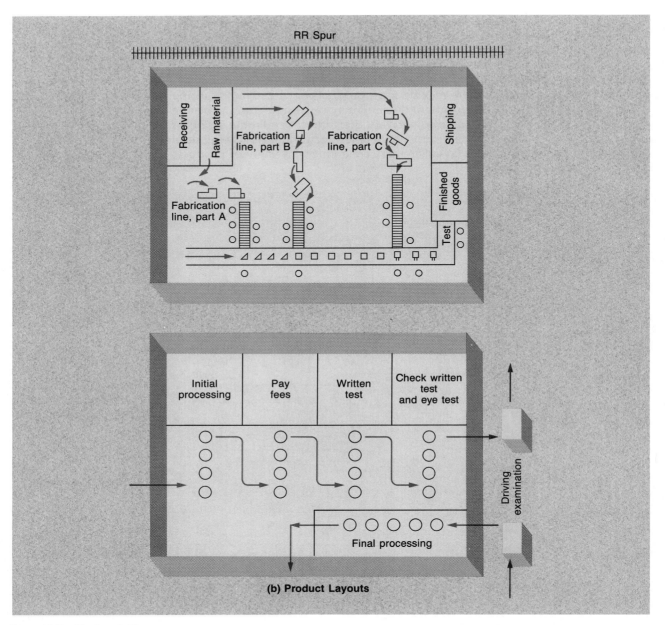

(b) Product Layouts

Figure 19-7 *(Continued)* (*b*) Two examples of a product layout.

Product layout A production configuration in which the processing components are arranged in a specialized line along which the product or client passes during the production process

and services are produced or when there are many variations of a particular product or service that require different functions for production.

Product Layout. A **product layout** is a production configuration in which the processing components are arranged in a specialized line along which the product or client passes during the production process. With this arrangement, a product or service is produced through a somewhat standardized production sequence geared specifically to the particular characteristics of a product or service. Examples of a product layout for a product (a separate, specialized assembly line for each of three products) and a service (a driver's license processing center set up to render one type of specialized service) appear in Figure 19-7*b*. Other common examples of product layouts include automatic car washes, cafeteria lines, and mass medical examinations for military recruits.

Product layouts are used mainly when one standardized product or service is produced, usually in large volume. Each item or service being produced requires essentially the same or a similar production process. Although there may be some variations in products or services, such variations are typically limited in number or scope. The problems at Winnebago Industries, Inc., illustrate the difficulties that can ensue when too many product variations are attempted with a product layout (see the following Case in Point discussion).

CASE IN POINT: Winnebago's Production Lines Go Awry

When Gerald Gilbert, a former vice president of the Control Data Corporation, took the job of chief executive officer of Winnebago Industries, Inc., in 1986, it was a major change from the city life he was used to in Minneapolis. Forest City, Iowa, where Winnebago is the major employer, is a quiet town whose 4300 residents can enjoy the tranquil country life. Gilbert was the sixth CEO to run Winnebago in 14 years, while founder John K. Hanson continued as chairman of the board.

Gilbert assessed conditions in the factory as "still in the Dark Ages." He found excess inventory, outdated design methods, and few standardized parts. "There were something like 800 different cabinet doors, some an eighth of an inch apart" in measurement, according to Gilbert. To solve these problems, he quickly hired Richard Berreth, his friend and a manufacturing expert, as executive vice president. Berreth had been a vice president at Control Data and had managed factories making key components and employing between 2000 and 7200 people.

Berreth tackled inventory costs by having workers unload heavily used components from trucks and take them directly to the assembly line. He created employee teams that were responsible for the quality of particular parts of the assembly process. His various efforts soon cut in half the time it took to make a motor home.

Unfortunately, the stock market crashed in October 1987, and sales of the motor-home recreation vehicles slowed to a crawl. Berreth took the opportunity created by the slower sales to institute an even bigger change on the assembly lines: merging three assembly lines into two. The move would make room for a new approach to assembly, one in which appliances and cabinets would be attached to the walls before they were hoisted onto the vehicle on the assembly line. Previously, workers assembled walls on the vehicle and then loaded the appliances and cabinets through windows or the side door, a process that often led to dents and scratches.

The merged lines progressed well until April. Sales began to pick up significantly just as another big change was being implemented. The latest move involved changing from batch production, in which 50 to 100 vehicles of the same model would be made at one time, to mixed production, in which any of 58 models could come down the line. With the batch system, the workers quickly adjusted to a change in the model and soon picked up their production rhythm again. With the new system, every vehicle was a different model from the previous one, and the workers began to get confused and frustrated.

Going to two lines also meant that the workers were crowded together. As production accelerated in response to the growing number of orders, the assembly lines began to get jammed. Soon overtime, including Saturdays, became mandatory. Meanwhile, new models were also being rushed into production. A sign over one of the production lines read, "Quality is chief on this reservation." In actuality, the lines were producing anything but quality. Holes in parts wouldn't line up; fasteners couldn't be inserted; parts weren't available when they were needed. The parking lot began to fill up with motor homes needing further work before they could be shipped.

As if conditions were not bleak enough, a summer heat wave arrived that sent temperatures in the factory, which had no air-conditioning, soaring to almost 100 degrees. Tempers flared out of control. Workers punched holes in carpeting and scrawled epithets on plant walls. Some quit. The chaos caused Winnebago to lose an estimated 1000 motor-home sales because orders could not be filled. In late September, after checking with the board of directors, John K. Hanson fired both Gilbert and Berreth. Soon after, Winnebago switched back to three production lines, instead of two, and once again began filling its orders as it struggled to regain market share.[50] ▬▬▬

Fixed-position layout A production configuration in which the product or client remains in one location and the tools, equipment, and expertise are brought to it, as necessary, to complete the productive process

Fixed-Position Layout. A **fixed-position layout** is a production configuration in which the product or client remains in one location and the tools, equipment, and expertise are brought to it, as necessary, to complete the productive process. Fixed-position layouts are typically used when it is not feasible to move the product—because of size, shape, or any other characteristic—or when it makes more sense to take the service to the client. For example, the fixed-position layout often is used in building ships, locomotives, and aircraft. This type of layout also can be used for services, such as furnace repair (in which the equipment, supplies, and repairing expertise are brought to the home or building) or a mobile CAT scanner (in which the mobile three-dimensional X-ray units are brought to various hospitals because it is more economical to share a scanner). Having appropriate facilities in which to work, of course, is critical to another major aspect of operations management, process technology.

Corporate jets have become a lucrative business for Cessna, a subsidiary of General Dynamics. Here on Cessna's Wichita, Kansas, assembly line, the jets are made using a fixed-position layout, in which workers bring tools, parts, and expertise to the aircraft under production.

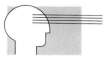

PROMOTING INNOVATION: PROCESS TECHNOLOGY

Process technology is the technology used in transforming inputs into goods and services. It includes the tools, methods, procedures, equipment, and various steps involved in the production process.[51] Increasingly, process technology is an important factor in competitive success. One reason is that prospects for using sophisticated technology in producing goods and services have mushroomed with advances in computer software, computer-controlled machines, and robots such as those made by Fanuc. In this section, we explore recent innovations in computer-integrated manufacturing, examine some of the challenges in successfully implementing a computer-integrated manufacturing system, and consider the application of advanced technology to service organizations.

Computer-Integrated Manufacturing

Computer-integrated manufacturing (CIM) is the computerized integration of all major functions associated with the production of a product. Such functions typically include designing and engineering products, instructing machines, handling materials, controlling inventories, and directing the production process. Operations that use CIM are sometimes referred to as "factories of the future" because they use the latest in technology to produce world-class production facilities. CIM systems typically make extensive use of sophisticated materials requirements planning (MRP) systems and rely on several other types of computerized systems, such as computer-aided design, computer-aided manufacturing, and flexible manufacturing systems.

Computer-Aided Design. **Computer-aided design (CAD)** is a system that uses computers to geometrically prepare, review, and evaluate product designs. Engineers and designers can alter and evaluate initial designs easily, saving considerable time and expense over more conventional means such as making physical mock-ups of various designs. Because the design is in a computer data base, it can be accessed later for further work and additional tests. CAD systems also allow designers to test such factors as stress tolerance and reliability by computer.

Computer-Aided Manufacturing. **Computer-aided manufacturing (CAM)** is a system that uses computers to design and control production processes. CAM systems access the computer-stored information on product designs developed through CAD in order to put the products into production. CAM usually includes the ability to change machine setups automatically by computer, as well as the capacity to move materials and work in progress from one machine to the other automatically. For example, at GM's Saginaw Vanguard plant, which essentially is an experimental factory of the future, computer linkages to sophisticated machinery allow the factory to switch production from one product line to another in just 10 minutes (compared with the 10 hours to 10 days more typical of conventional automobile factories).[52] Another example of computer-aided manufacturing is the Cassino automobile factory in central Italy. The factory opened in 1988 to build Fiat's Tipo, a medium-size car that has been an immediate success in Europe. The factory features computer-aided machinery, such as 403 robots and 24 lasers that are used for mounting subassemblies and components, gluing moldings, and welding. The Cassino factory has raised annual production from 48 cars per worker to over 60 cars per worker.[53]

Computer-integrated manufacturing (CIM) The computerized integration of all major functions associated with the production of a product

Computer-aided design (CAD) A system that uses computers to geometrically prepare, review, and evaluate product designs

Computer-aided manufacturing (CAM) A system that uses computers to design and control production processes

Flexible manufacturing system (FMS) A manufacturing system that uses computers to control machines and the production process automatically so that different types of parts or product configurations can be handled on the same production line

Group technology The classification of parts into families (groups of parts or products that have some similarities in the way they are manufactured) so that members of the same family can be manufactured on the same production line

Flexible Manufacturing Systems. Computer-integrated manufacturing often incorporates another computer-related manufacturing concept, flexible manufacturing systems. A **flexible manufacturing system (FMS)** is a manufacturing system that uses computers to control machines and the production process automatically so that different types of parts or product configurations can be handled on the same production line. Flexible manufacturing typically makes use of **group technology,** the classification of parts into families (groups of parts or products that have some similarities in the way they are manufactured) so that members of the same family can be manufactured on the same production line. By grouping similar products together for manufacture, a flexible manufacturing system can be programmed for rapidly setting up machines to handle both very small and very large quantities of particular parts through the same production process. This flexibility can make it cost-effective to manufacture products in lots as small as one and enables manufacturers to be more responsive to customers.[54] For example, Allen-Bradley, a subsidiary of Rockwell International, took 3 years to install computer-integrated manufacturing in its contactor (a device that turns motors on and off) plant in Milwaukee, Wisconsin. The plant produces 600 units per hour in more than 777 varieties in lot sizes as small as one or two.[55]

Implementing CIM Systems

Although there have been a number of spectacular successes, such as Fiat's Cassino plant, attempts to implement computer-integrated manufacturing systems often encounter formidable barriers. One study of more than 200 managers and operating employees found that the barriers fall into three main categories: structural, human, and technical.[56]

Structural Barriers. Structural barriers are situational factors that deter the adoption and successful use of technology. For example, one major structural barrier is a reward system that emphasizes quick and dramatic results, making implementation of CIM systems extremely high-risk undertakings for managers. Another major structural barrier stems from unrealistically high hopes about ease of implementation, coupled with ignorance of hidden costs. Often, productivity is reduced in the short run as employees struggle to learn the new ways of doing things. At the same time, hidden costs frequently arise because of needing additional computer experts and extensive training of employees.

Major structural barriers to automation constitute one reason why some experts warn that it often is better to seek other means of improving production before turning to automation. For example, Corning examined the manufacturing process in two factories that make pollution control devices and found it could eliminate 115 of 235 processing steps. The changes cut production time from 4 weeks to 3 days without requiring Corning to turn to automation.[57]

Human Barriers. The human barriers to implementation of CIM systems center around change issues. One barrier, uncertainty avoidance, can be traced back to fear of change and the uncertainty that comes with the new, complex CIM systems. The second major barrier, resistance, often is associated with potential losses of power and status due to new relationships and expertise associated with the new technology. Companies that have been successful in overcoming the resistance barrier often make extensive use of a strong and persuasive innovation champion (see Chapter 7) who is able to help the various players work effectively toward CIM system implementation.

Technical Barriers. Technical barriers to CIM system implementation are related largely to problems arising from the purchase of incompatible systems, such as a CAD system that cannot communicate with a CAM system or machines from different vendors. Some solutions are buying only systems that can be integrated with one another easily, developing software internally (a major task), or developing "neutral," or shared, files of information that use a third language that both the CAD and CAM systems can understand. General Motors has developed a manufacturing automation protocol, known as MAP, that establishes a means of connecting computer-based factory-floor equipment from a variety of companies.[58] Interestingly, despite the technical problems associated with CIM systems, most study respondents saw the structural and human barriers as the most formidable.[59]

Services Applications

Prospects for using advanced technology such as computers in service industries are also providing possibilities for innovation, although the vast potential is only beginning to be tapped.[60] For example, automated teller machines (ATMs) enabled the Wells Fargo Bank to eliminate 700 employees from its work force and close 30 bank branches within 2 years of installing the ATMs. The machines also allowed the East Lansing State Bank to target a low-cost service for Michigan State University students by offering them no-minimum-balance, all-ATM checking accounts. The students are able to write five checks per month for a $1 service charge; but bank window transactions cost 50 cents, encouraging the students to use the ATMs rather than tying up tellers.[61]

Super Valu, a grocery wholesaler that serves mainly independently owned supermarkets, offers a SLASH (Site Location Analysis Strategy Heuristic) program that helps its independent retailer customers select advantageous store locations. Part of the program incorporates a computer-aided design system that helps architects to assess more than 100 store plans on a computer screen. Similarly, Fidelity Investments, the largest mutual fund company in the world, emphasizes good customer service with such measures as a telephone system that can handle 672 calls simultaneously through automated, toll-free lines. A master computer console at headquarters in Boston routes calls to available operators in telephone centers throughout the United States. Meanwhile, Nita Kincaid, who supervises the firm's 1000 telephone representatives, can monitor the situation on a computer screen that provides her with constant information about the status of calls, such as how long customers have been kept on hold.[62] In an effort to extend the use of robotics to service industries, robotics manufacturers are experimenting with service possibilities. For instance, an experimental robot designed to be a nurse's aide that carries dinner trays is being tested in a Connecticut hospital.[63]

Still, some efforts to apply information technology to service organizations have been disappointing.[64] Effective use of technology requires careful identification of the areas in which technology can make a major difference in services offered and productivity. Otherwise, technology applied to service organizations may not achieve the desired results. For example, expenditures for personal computers and spreadsheet programs at GTEL, the retail subsidiary of the General Telephone Company of California, provided disappointing outcomes, partially because the time saved with the technology was not necessarily channeled in productive directions through reduced staff or new assignments.[65] Expenditures for technology to be applied to the service industry are likely to be more effective with careful consideration of productivity issues.

IMPROVING PRODUCTIVITY

As the clock struck noon in Appleton, Wisconsin, the entire 500-member insurance staff of the Aid Association for Lutherans (AAL), a fraternal society that operates as a large insurance business, piled their personal belongings on chairs and rolled the chairs to other parts of headquarters. Corridors were jammed as "organized chaos" brought a reorganization of insurance operations into reality. Within 2 hours, the move transformed the functionally organized bureaucracy into self-managing teams (see Chapter 16) that would eventually operate without several layers of supervisors. Under the new arrangement, all the policies related to a particular customer would be handled by a single team, rather than being routed to separate departments. Within a year of the move, productivity rose 20 percent—a significant amount, particularly for a service organization.[66]

The results at AAL constitute only one example of what can be accomplished when productivity improvements in operations are given high priority. Within organizations, attempts to improve productivity—that is, to generate more outputs from the same or fewer inputs—depend on the five-step process described below.

The first step in improving productivity is for managers to *establish a base point* against which to assess future improvements. Examples of measures that could be used to establish a base point include the number of claims processed daily, dollar income per square foot of selling space, amount produced per day, percentage of output passing inspection, percentage of repaired items that had to be returned for further repairs, or customers served per hour. The important thing is to choose measures that focus on important aspects of productivity for the particular organization or work unit.

The second step involves setting goals in order to *establish the desired productivity level.* A number of studies in a wide variety of jobs and industries support the usefulness of goal setting as a means of raising productivity levels.

The third step is to *review methods for increasing productivity.* Extensive reviews of productivity studies indicate that useful methods for increasing productivity include improving employee selection techniques, placing people in jobs that are well matched to their qualifications, training workers in job-related skills, redesigning jobs to give workers more control over their own productivity, providing financial incentives that are carefully tied to productivity issues, and using feedback and performance appraisals to let workers know how they are doing.[67]

Still other approaches aimed at improving productivity include many of the operations management techniques considered in this chapter, such as aggregate planning, master production scheduling, MRP and related systems, well-thought-out purchasing programs, appropriate facilities and layouts, and new process technologies.

Productivity expert Wickham Skinner argues that managers sometimes overemphasize cost cutting as the principal means of increasing productivity and fail to adopt major new process technologies that would make significant breakthroughs in productivity and competitiveness.[68] Often, rethinking the work process itself also leads to breakthroughs. The new Sleep Inn hotel chain introduced by Manor Care has been developed with labor productivity in mind. For example, the hotels have a sophisticated washer and dryer installed behind the desk so that the night-shift desk operator can also do the laundry by pushing a few buttons. Concrete and shrubs eliminate grass cutting. Shower stalls are round so that they are easier to keep clean. These and other labor-saving changes will allow a typical 100-bed Sleep Inn to employ only 12 full-time employees, 13 percent fewer than the average for a no-frills hotel.

The fourth step is *select a method and implement*. This step involves choosing a method that appears to have the best chance of success in the particular situation. Implementation is likely to involve some considerations about the best way to bring about change (see Chapter 7).

Finally, the last step in improving productivity is to *measure results and modify as necessary*. Further modifications are necessary only if productivity is not improving as planned. Met goals, of course, lead to new goals, since increasing productivity is a continual challenge for successful organizations. One means of meeting the challenge is through judicious use of information technology, the subject of the next chapter.

CHAPTER SUMMARY

Operations management is the management of the productive processes that convert inputs into goods and services. The concept applies to both manufacturing and service industries, even though their characteristics differ to some degree. Major aspects of operations management include operations strategy, operating systems, facilities, and process technology.

Productivity is an efficiency concept that gauges the ratio of outputs relative to inputs into a productive process. Although the United States continues to be the most productive country in the world, productivity increases lagged during the late seventies. Productivity increases in the manufacturing sector have been picking up in the 1980s, but productivity growth in the service sector continues to lag.

Operations management plays different roles in determining strategy, depending on the strategic role stage into which an organization falls: stage 1, minimize negative potential; stage 2, achieve parity with competition; stage 3, support overall organizational strategy; and stage 4, pursue operations management–based strategy. Within stages 3 and 4, two of the most commonly used operations strategies are low-cost producer and innovative producer.

A number of systems are particularly important for effective operations management. Forecasting helps predict the demand for goods and services. Capacity planning is the process of determining the people, machines, and major physical resources, such as buildings, that will be necessary to meet the production objectives of the organization. Capacity planning involves three different time horizons: long, medium, and short. Aggregate production planning helps match supply with product or service demand over a time horizon of about 1 year. The master production schedule translates the aggregate plan into a formalized production plan en-

compassing specific products to be produced and specific capacity requirements over a designated period. Materials requirements planning is a computer-based inventory system that develops materials requirements for the goods and services specified in the master schedule and initiates the procurement actions necessary to acquire the materials when needed. Manufacturing resource planning expands MRP systems to include related financial, accounting, personnel, engineering, and marketing information. Purchasing is the process of acquiring necessary goods and services in exchange for funds or other remuneration.

Facilities issues focus mainly on expansion and contraction decisions, facilities location, and facilities layout. In expanding facilities, top managers usually have three major policy options: capacity leads demand, capacity is in approximate equilibrium with demand, or capacity lags demand. Most facilities location problems fall into one of four categories: single facility, multiple factories and warehouses, competitive retail outlets, and emergency services. There are three major types of facilities layouts: process, product, and fixed position.

Recent innovations in process technology center on computer-integrated manufacturing. Major aspects of CIM include computer-aided design, computer-aided manufacturing, and flexible manufacturing systems. Because of their complexity, CIM systems often face formidable implementation barriers that fall into three main categories: structural, human, and technical. Process technology advances also are increasingly applicable to organizations in service industries.

Improving productivity involves five major steps: determine a base, establish a desired productivity level, review methods for increasing productivity, select a method and implement, and measure results and modify as necessary.

MANAGERIAL TERMINOLOGY

aggregate production
  planning   (673)
back orders   (675)
bill of materials (BOM)
  (677)
capacity planning   (672)
capacity requirements
  planning   (673)
computer-aided design
  (CAD)   (687)
computer-aided

manufacturing (CAM)
  (687)
computer-integrated
  manufacturing (CIM)
  (687)
dependent demand
  inventory   (676)
facilities   (680)
fixed-position layout
  (686)
flexible manufacturing
  system (FMS)   (688)

group technology   (688)
independent demand
  inventory   (676)
manufacturing resource
  planning (MRP II)
  (679)
master production
  schedule (MPS)   (675)
materials requirements
  planning (MRP)   (676)
operations management
  (663)

partial-factor productivity
  (663)
process layout   (683)
product layout   (684)
productivity   (663)
purchasing   (679)
total-factor productivity
  (663)

QUESTIONS FOR DISCUSSION AND REVIEW

1. Explain the concept of productivity, including its linkage to operations management. Why is the operations management process a focal point for productivity improvements in organizations?

2. Describe the major ways in which producing manufactured goods differs from producing a service. Use two services that you have received recently to illustrate the characteristics of a service.

3. Describe each of the four strategic role stages that influence the role operations management plays in an organization's strategy development. What information would you need to determine the strategic role stage of a particular organization? Why is moving from one stage to another so difficult?

4. Explain how each of the following systems is used in operations management and how they relate to one another: forecasting, capacity planning, aggregate planning, scheduling, materials requirements planning, and purchasing.

5. Suppose that you are in charge of aggregate planning for an organization and need to consider how to cope with short- and intermediate-term fluctuations in demand. What are several approaches that you could use? Which do you feel would be most

advantageous if there is a strong possibility that the forecasted demand is much too optimistic?

6. Explain the major steps involved in making expansion and contraction decisions about facilities. What major policy options do top managers have when demand is expected to grow somewhat steadily? Can you identify an organization that seems to have chosen each option?

7. Contrast the criteria used in locating facilities for each of the following types of organizations: single facility, multiple factories and warehouses, competitive retail outlets, and emergency services. Think of a retail outlet that you have seen go out of business. To what extent do you think location affected its demise?

8. Identify an example of each of the three main types of facilities layouts.

9. Explain several of the computerized systems that typically are used in computer-integrated manufacturing. How might managers overcome the major barriers to implementing CIM systems?

10. Explain the main steps involved in productivity improvement. For a job with which you are familiar, identify five ways that productivity could be increased.

DISCUSSION QUESTIONS FOR CHAPTER OPENING CASE

1. In relation to operations management, in which strategic role stage would you place Fanuc? What is your evidence?

2. What process technologies are in evidence at Fanuc? How does Dr. Inaba attempt to overcome potential

barriers to computer-integrated manufacturing and related technologies?

3. What evidence of attempts to increase productivity exist at Fanuc? How are these efforts tied to Fanuc's operations strategy?

MANAGEMENT EXERCISE: OPERATION LANDSCAPING

You have a landscaping company that has been very successful, growing in sales at the rate of about 20 percent annually. In addition to designing landscapes and selling, planting, pruning, and caring for plants, shrubs, and trees, your organization also provides complete lawn-care service. Your organization has a reputation for high-quality work, a reputation of which you are quite proud.

A local developer has just asked you to do the landscaping and lawn-care work for the general-use areas of a very large local community he is going to develop. This job is quite massive, and a quick estimate of its size and duration indicates that you may have to double the size of your work force, buy additional equipment, and construct a building (the developer will give you the land) in the area for your operations.

You recognize that there are many issues to be considered prior to making the decision to accept this job, which will last at least 5 years. Among them are several related to operations management, including forecasting, capacity planning, aggregate production planning, scheduling, MRP, facilities layout, and type of process technology that could be used.

Explain the major issues to be addressed in each category of operations management.

CATERPILLAR USES OPERATIONS MANAGEMENT TO BECOME COMPETITIVE AGAIN

Caterpillar is a name known for quality. Since the 1920s, it has been the world pacesetter in earth-moving equipment. More than half its business is conducted overseas. The company had experienced 50 straight years of profits until 1982, when it lost $180 million. During the next 2 years, Caterpillar lost approximately $770 million more. The almost $1 billion in losses stemmed from a number of causes, including construction markets that collapsed around the globe; oil and other commodity prices that plummeted, killing the demand for mining, logging, and pipe-laying equipment; competition from other companies, particularly Japan-based Komatsu; the rising dollar, which made its products more expensive for international customers; a slowdown in major highway projects; and a 7-month strike by Caterpillar workers. "Almost overnight the whole world changed for us," recalls George Schaefer, Cat's chairman and chief executive officer. The company knew that it had to change. By 1985, Caterpillar had turned around, and it has been making a profit ever since.

Caterpillar's return to profitability came about as a result of very deliberate actions. The company began to concentrate on driving costs down and improving its enviable reputation for quality. Cat slashed its work force by one-third, or 30,000 jobs. It also closed seven factories and canceled construction of its partially completed 1.8-million-square-foot parts distribution center in its headquarters town of Peoria, Illinois.

An important part of its new direction is the decision to completely redesign and outfit its remaining 30 factories, a sweeping $1.2 billion modernization program. The program, called Plant with a Future (PWAF), is aimed at overhauling all 36 million square feet of Caterpillar's factory space. If things go as expected, the program, which began in 1985, will have more than paid for itself by the early 1990s. Because of a new computerized inventory system alone, the company expects to save a cumulative $850 million. PWAF is bringing about a complete change in Cat's tooling and manufacturing methods. "We are not going to compete with the Japanese by doing what they did 5 years ago," says Pierre Gueridon, the executive vice president in charge of PWAF.

As part of the change, Cat is reworking its traditional manufacturing process, whereby components or products are worked on in specialized areas, such as grinding or heat treating. Instead, activities will be grouped by "cells," a form of flexible manufacturing whereby machines and workers operate in groups that together can perform a variety of operations on products. For example, it previously took 11 workers to machine, burr, balance, and wash planet carriers, a basic part of a transmission. Now two workers do it, running a manufacturing cell consisting of six flexible computerized machines. With the new machines in the cells, setup time for working on new tasks takes seconds (compared with 4 hours to 2 days with older machines). Furthermore, there is little need for adjustments because the computer monitors the machine settings, so there is little scrap. Ultimately, the various cells will be linked by computer and will also be tied into the materials supply sys-

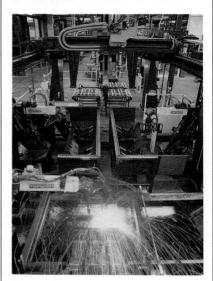

Staggering losses in the 1980s forced Caterpillar's management to make drastic changes in the manufacturing of its earth-moving equipment. This photo shows the new setup at the tractor-tread plant in East Peoria, Illinois. This manufacturing "cell" accomplishes the cutting, drilling, and heat treating of steel beams that formerly required three separate assembly lines. Computers instantly adjust the machine tools to meet specifications of new orders, a changeover process that previously took a full day.

tem. The revamped factories will use computerized machine tools, laser-read bar codes, and automated carrier systems for materials, but they will stop short of computerized integration of everything from engineering to finance.

The changes have not been implemented without some difficulties. For example, the changes in the manufacturing process have required radical changes in attitudes about how products are made. Workers now need to work in teams, be trained to handle multiple tasks, and take responsibility for the quality of their work. First-line and middle managers worry about the prospect of their authority eroding as the system becomes less hierarchical and everyone becomes more dependent on the latest technology. "When you go through changes, there's just a fear of the unknown," notes Gerald Flaherty, vice president for employee relations. "You're asking some people to go into a classroom who haven't been in one for 25 years." During the last several years, the union has made some grudging concessions, such as allowing the number of job classifications to be reduced from 418 to 150. Such concessions came only after Caterpillar agreed to stringent job security provisions.

In an attempt to stimulate more worker involvement in the operations and improvement efforts, machinists take part in certifying suppliers. Since 1982, the company has certified 800 of its major suppliers, a designation that means the suppliers get preferential treatment as long as they agree to furnish parts that are close to perfect. The reject rate from certified suppliers runs 0.6 percent versus 2.8 percent for noncertified suppliers.

The company also has begun vigorously developing new products, particularly smaller machines that lend themselves to the shift in the market toward smaller construction projects. Since 1984, it has more than doubled its original product line of 150 models. As fewer superhighways are being built, the emphasis has shifted to smaller pieces of equipment. A new sprocket design has been put on all its tractors, an innovation that makes tractors last longer. In addition, Caterpillar now makes light construction equipment with Mitsubishi Heavy Industries, Ltd., a company with which Cat has had several joint ventures over the past 25 years. The joint venture manufactures products for sale both in the United States and in Pacific Rim countries.[69]

QUESTIONS FOR CHAPTER CONCLUDING CASE

1. What strategy role stage would you place Caterpillar in during the early 1980s? Where would you place the company now? Why?

2. What approach did Caterpillar take to adjust to the suddenly shifting demand for its products that took place in the early 1980s? What approaches could the company use now?

3. What operations management systems and new process technologies are in evidence as Caterpillar changes its manufacturing methods?

CHAPTER TWENTY

INFORMATION SYSTEMS FOR MANAGEMENT

CHAPTER OUTLINE

Computer-Based Information Systems: An Overview
The Nature of Information Systems
Computer Components of Information Systems
Characteristics of Useful Information
Information Needs by Managerial Level
Information Needs by Specialized Area

Types of Information Systems
Transaction-Processing Systems
Office Automation Systems
Management Information Systems
Decision Support Systems
Executive Support Systems

Promoting Innovation: Strategic Implications of Information Systems
Strategic Targets
Strategic Thrusts

Developing Computer-Based Information Systems
The Systems Development Life Cycle
Alternative Means of Systems Development
Selecting a Development Approach

Managing Information System Resources
Factors Favoring Centralization
Factors Favoring Decentralization
Trends in Centralization and Decentralization
Managing End-User Computing

Impacts of Information Technology on Organizations
Organization Structure
Individual Jobs
Organizational Risk

LEARNING OBJECTIVES

After studying this chapter, you should be able to:

■ Distinguish between data and information, as well as describe how the systems view helps managers understand information processing.

■ Explain the computer components of information systems and describe the characteristics of useful information.

■ Indicate how information needs differ by managerial level and specialized area.

■ Compare and contrast the major types of information systems.

■ Outline how considering strategic targets and strategic thrusts can help managers use information systems to competitive advantage.

■ Delineate the systems development life cycle and identify the major alternative means of systems development.

■ Contrast the factors favoring centralization and decentralization of information system resources.

■ Evaluate the impact of information technology on organizations in the areas of organization structure, individual jobs, and organizational risk.

MRS. FIELDS'S SECRET INGREDIENT

Although the tantalizing aroma, just-baked warmth, and wonderful taste have made Mrs. Fields Cookies famous, the success of the chain of cookie stores based in Park City, Utah, also depends on a secret ingredient that is not in the cookies. The company makes extensive use of a computer-based information system to help manage its more than 650 company-owned stores in the United States, the United Kingdom, Japan, Hong Kong, Australia, and Canada.

In an unusual move, Debbi Fields and her husband, Randy, have kept all the stores under direct company ownership, rather than following the usual pattern of franchising (allowing others to open Mrs. Fields outlets in return for payment of various fees or royalties and agreement to follow certain standard operating procedures; see Chapter 22). Companies with multiple retail outlets typically franchise because they experience difficulty maintaining day-to-day control over operations as the number of outlets grows.

The communication patterns at Mrs. Fields make it possible for a manager such as Wee-kiat, who runs a number of Mrs. Fields stores in San Francisco, to maintain contact with Debbi through advanced technology and a personal computer in the back of each store. The computers are equipped with a specially designed software package, called Retail Operations Intelligence (ROI), which has a number of modules, or components, that help managers like Wee-kiat perform various aspects of their jobs.

On a typical morning in one of his shops, Wee-kiat brings up the Daily Production Planner program on his personal computer, inserts the day's sales projection (based on the previous year's sales, adjusted for growth), and answers questions that the program displays on the screen, such as whether it is a normal day, sale day, school day, holiday, etc.

Suppose, for example, that the day is Tuesday and a school day. The computer uses that particular store's hour-by-hour, product-by-product performance on the last three Tuesdays that were school days to produce hour-by-hour, product-by-product projections for this particular Tuesday. On the basis of the projections, the computer lets the manager know how many customers will be needed each hour and how much will need to be sold to meet store goals. The computer also provides information on how many cookie batches to make and when they should be made in order to minimize leftovers.

When sales are made, cash registers feed sales information to the computer, which then revises the hourly projections and even makes suggestions. If the number of customers is about right, but the amount of the average sale is low, the message on the computer screen might inquire whether team members are doing enough to encourage additional purchases. On the other hand, if the customer count is down, the computer might suggest that the manager take some action to lure more customers into the store—such as offering samples. If these steps do not work, the computer, which is programmed to recognize fluctuations in sales upward or downward, adjusts baking requirements accordingly.

A Labor Scheduler module helps the manager schedule workers ("the team") by using the store's daily sales projections for 2 weeks hence to provide the best estimate of how many people with the proper skills will be needed for each shift. The scheduling, which previously took almost an hour to do manually, can be done in minutes on the computer.

In addition, the manager can use the Interview module to help interview job applicants by having them answer a series of questions at the computer. On the basis of an applicant's responses, the computer lets the manager know whether

Debbi Fields, president of Mrs. Fields Cookies, keeps up to date with the operations of her more than 650 company-owned retail outlets via computer. Each store manager uses a computer and specially designed software to help project sales, track inventory, hire and schedule workers, and communicate with headquarters. A company division, the Fields Software Group, even markets the computer system to other multi-unit companies.

the applicant fits the profile of a successful Mrs. Fields employee. When an individual is hired, the manager can key information into the computer, which then produces a personnel folder and a payroll entry in Park City. Several other modules in the ROI system, such as the Inventory module, the Repair and Maintenance module, and the Sales Reporting and Analysis module, also help make Wee-kiat's job easier, freeing him to concentrate on other aspects of his job, such as working with team members and talking with customers.

If Wee-kiat wants to send a message to Debbi, he calls up the FormMail module on the computer and types his message; the next morning it is in her hands. Debbi responds to every message by FormMail and frequently initiates messages herself. FormMail, then, is used as a vehicle for exchanging ideas, providing suggestions, sharing anecdotes, and enhancing motivation.

Randy Fields, chairman of the board, wants the system to keep Debbi in close contact with the stores even as the company grows larger. He also wants to keep the managers managing, not immersed in paperwork. The system is set up so that the individual stores provide data and receive it back in the form of useful information and assistance with routine jobs.

To help maintain control over the growing number of stores, computer-based information systems at Mrs. Fields can compare expected against anticipated results and pinpoint major discrepancies in "flash reports." The reports can be easily brought up on computer screens by the area vice presidents, regional directors, and district sales managers who work with Debbi in managing the network of stores.

When Mrs. Fields acquired a bakery group called La Petite Boulangerie from PepsiCo in March 1987, the chain had habitually been a money loser. With the ROI system installed (within 30 days), the bakeries were profitable during their first year under Mrs. Fields ownership. Building on the La Petite Boulangerie concept, there are now 14 new Mrs. Fields Bakeries, which offer Mrs. Fields cookies, a variety of other baked goods, and sandwiches made with freshly baked bread that can be eaten on the premises at café tables. Through the Fields Software Group, the company now markets the system to other multiunit establishments. As part of the arrangement, the Fields Group helps tailor the system to the particular needs of the businesses who adopt the ROI approach.[1]

Although Debbi Fields makes extensive use of the computer in a number of ways, perhaps its greatest role is in helping her maintain control over her large and growing network of stores. One could argue that without computers and the ability to communicate by computer with various stores, Mrs. Fields would not be able to operate the stores as a wholly owned chain. The information system at Mrs. Fields is just one example of how technological change has opened up vast possibilities for using computers to enhance the process of management. Such systems, though, take considerable creativity and effort to develop. In the Mrs. Fields case, for example, Randy Fields's vision was invaluable in developing and implementing the company's ROI system.

Although computer-based information systems can be helpful in carrying out all four major functions of management, we discuss these systems in this part of the text because they are particularly germane to the controlling function. Information systems can greatly facilitate the process of regulating organizational activities so that actual performance conforms to expected organizational standards and goals.

In exploring the usefulness of computer-based information systems to management, we first investigate the basic nature of such systems, including various information needs of managers. We next analyze five major types of information systems found in organizations and examine the growing importance of using these systems innovatively to enhance organizational strategies. We then explore major ways to develop effective information systems and consider potential ways to manage an organization's information system resources. Finally, we look at major impacts of information technology on organizations.

COMPUTER-BASED INFORMATION SYSTEMS: AN OVERVIEW

Most experts seem to agree that information technology is causing vast changes in the way in which information is handled and used in organizations. For one thing, the number of personal computers in offices is expected to quadruple to about 46 million by the year 2000.[2] Increasingly, there is the potential for managers to have more and better information at their fingertips. One implication of the proliferation of personal computers is that managers need to have a solid understanding of computer-based information systems and their various characteristics.

The Nature of Information Systems

Despite the sophisticated technology, the basic concepts involved in information systems are fairly straightforward and somewhat familiar. In order to understand such systems, it helps to differentiate between data and information, as well as to use a systems view to examine the nature of information processing.

Data versus Information. Although we might frequently use the terms "data" and "information" interchangeably, professionals in the computer field make important distinctions between the two terms. **Data** are unanalyzed facts and figures. For example, when you go to a major supermarket to buy a quart of milk, the cash register hooked to a central computer records that a quart of milk

Data Unanalyzed facts and figures

has been sold. However, this piece of data has little direct relevance to management.

Information Data that have been analyzed or processed into a form that is meaningful for decision makers

To be useful in managing the supermarket, the data need to be transformed into **information,** data that has been analyzed or processed into a form that is meaningful for decision makers. For instance, the data on the sold quart of milk may be processed with other related data to produce current inventory figures for milk in the store. This information may be useful to individuals in charge of purchasing, delivery, and stocking. The milk data may also be processed to develop figures on store sales—perhaps broken down by shift for the store manager, by the day for the district manager, and by the week for upper management. Thus the milk-purchase data may become an analyzed element in these and many other informational reports. **Electronic data processing (EDP)** is the transformation of data into meaningful information through electronic means. Sometimes the major computer-related function in an organization is referred to as the EDP department, although more recently the function is likely to be called management information systems, information services, or information systems.[3]

Electronic data processing (EDP) The transformation of data into meaningful information through electronic means

The difference between data and information is important for managers, as well as for computer professionals. For example, faced with stiff foreign competition and the need to operate with a smaller work force, Bethlehem Steel began to explore information technology to help keep the company competitive. A special internal management team worked with 14 handpicked experts from IBM to carefully study the information needs of the $4.3 billion steelmaker. After interviews with 239 workers from all levels of the organization, one issue stood out. "There was too much data and too little information," says George T. Fugere, vice president of information services at Bethlehem Steel. As a result, the company is attempting to build better systems that transform data into the information that organization members need to be more productive.[4]

Information Processing: A Systems View. In order to obtain the information needed for various purposes, organizations develop information systems. The notion of an information system is closely akin to the systems approach to understanding organizations (see Chapter 2), in that an information system can be thought of as involving inputs, transformations, and outputs. The basic elements of an information-processing system are shown in Figure 20-1.

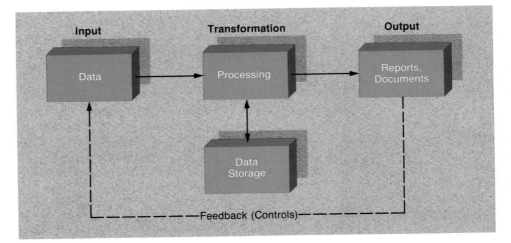

Figure 20-1 Basic components of an information system.

With an information system, data are the *inputs*. The data then undergo transformation, or processing. *Processing* involves the various forms of data manipulation and analyses (such as classifying, sorting, calculating, and summarizing) that transform data into information. Information-processing systems also typically make use of *data storage*, a system of storing data for use at a later point—such as predetermined desired inventory levels and data on item usage to date. The *outputs* are the reports, documents, and other system outcomes that supply needed information to decision makers. *Controls*, represented in the figure by the feedback loop, are safeguards to ensure that the outputs are appropriate and serve their intended purposes. Such safeguards can take the form of checks within the system to verify the accuracy (to the extent possible) of the data and processing, as well as steps to determine the usefulness of the outputs to users.

Given its nature, then, an **information system** can be defined as a set of procedures designed to collect (or retrieve), process, store, and disseminate information to support planning, decision making, coordination, and control.[5] Information systems are not necessarily computerized. For example, a manager of a Mrs. Fields store could probably figure out, without using a computer, how many cookie batches to make on a given day to minimize leftovers (although doing so would be more difficult without the computer). Our focus here, however, is on **computer-based information systems (CBISs).** Therefore, when we speak of information systems during the remainder of this chapter, we will mean information systems that involve the use of computer technology.

Information system A set of procedures designed to collect (or retrieve), process, store, and disseminate information to support planning, decision making, coordination, and control

Computer-based information systems (CBISs) Information systems that involve the use of computer technology

Computer Components of Information Systems

As shown in Figure 20-2, the components of a computer-based information system fall into two categories: hardware and software. We examine each of these two categories before considering the major types of computers.

Hardware. The **hardware** is the physical equipment, including the computer and related devices. For example, there are input devices, such as keyboards, optical bar-code scanners (e.g., those used in major grocery stores), optical scanning machines (e.g., those that sense the pencil marks on examination answer sheets), and voice recognition devices. These input devices allow data to be entered in machine-readable form into the main memory and processing section of a computer, called the **central processing unit (CPU).**

There also are secondary storage devices. Some of these devices, such as magnetic-disk storage units, allow large amounts of data to be available for almost immediate access. When data can be accessed and processed immediately, the arrangement is called **on-line processing.** For example, when you call an airline to make a reservation, the airline representative at the other end of the telephone line usually can tell you right away what flights are available on a given day and can process your reservation immediately. The representative can do this by using some type of input device that is communicating with a computer and a secondary storage device that allows immediate access to large amounts of information. On the other hand, when immediate transactions are not necessary, it is sometimes more efficient to use **batch processing,** whereby data are accumulated and then processed as a group. Such an arrangement typically makes use of magnetic-disk storage units or possibly other secondary storage devices (such as magnetic tape and magnetic-tape drives). Chances are that your college or university uses batch processing to prepare grade reports at

Hardware Physical computer equipment, including the computer itself and related devices

Central processing unit (CPU) The main memory and processing section of a computer

On-line processing An arrangement whereby data can be accessed and processed immediately

Batch processing An arrangement whereby data are accumulated and then processed as a group

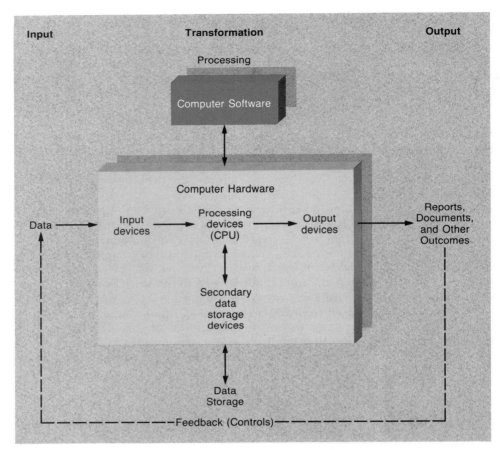

Figure 20-2 Basic components of a computer-based information system.

the end of the semester, waiting until grading sheets have been received from a number of professors before updating the computer records for the whole batch of grades.

Output devices allow the computer to produce information in a form that is useful to managers and others. Output devices include printers, visual displays on computer display monitors or terminals, and graphics plotters.

Software The set of programs, documents, procedures, and routines associated with the operation of a computer system that makes the hardware capable of its various activities

Data base A set of data organized efficiently in a central location so that it can serve a number of information system applications

Data-base management system The software that allows an organization to build, manage, and provide access to its stored data

Software. Most computers are general-purpose machines that can be made to perform a variety of tasks, such as computing the appropriate amount of pay for an individual, keeping track of a customer's charges, or assessing current inventory levels. What makes the hardware capable of these various activities is the **software,** the set of programs, documents, procedures, and routines associated with the operation of a computer system.[6] The software provides the instructions that enable the computer to perform various tasks.

There are many software packages that can be purchased. Among the most well known are packages for word processing (e.g., *WordPerfect* and *WordStar*) and spreadsheets (e.g., *Lotus 1-2-3*). Almost as familiar are packages for data-base management (e.g., the *dBASE* series). A **data base** is a set of data organized efficiently in a central location so that it can serve a number of information system applications. A **data-base management system** is the software that allows an organization to build, manage, and provide access to its stored data.[7]

For example, major catalog companies, such as Lands End, depend heavily on a data base of customer-related information (names, addresses, ordering history, status of current orders, etc.). The data-base management system that facilitates building the data base also allows access to the data for such activities as producing mailing labels for catalogs, processing orders that come in by telephone and mail, printing shipping labels and invoices, and providing various reports to management.

In addition to the software packages already available for use, software is often developed by an organization's own computer specialists for unique applications. Such custom-designed software can be expensive to create, but it can be developed to suit a particular organization's needs and may be more difficult for competitors to duplicate.

At Mrs. Fields Cookies, for example, the company has developed a special centralized data base containing information on many of the important aspects of the company (e.g., cookie sales, payroll records, suppliers' invoices, inventory reports, and utility charges). Then various software programs, such as the Daily Production Planner module used by store managers, work off the data base located in a large computer in Park City. Managers gain access to the data through their personal computers, which are located at their stores and tied into the Park City central computer.

Many organizations, particularly large and diverse ones, may have a number of different data bases oriented to different types of needs (such as accounting and human resources). Increasingly, efforts are being made to create systems that are able to share information from a variety of data bases. The software development issue will be discussed more thoroughly in a later section.

Types of Computers. To understand contemporary issues related to computers, it is helpful to have a working knowledge of the major types of computers. For a brief description of each type, see the Practically Speaking discussion, "A Guide to Major Types of Computers."

Until the last decade, most information processing in organizations was done on *mainframe computers* operated by a central data-processing department. The emergence of *personal computers* (sometimes called *microcomputers*) during the 1980s, as well as the decreasing cost and increasing capacity of *minicomputers*, super-minicomputers, and mini-supercomputers, has greatly expanded organizational information-processing options. *Supercomputers*, with their great processing speed, have made it possible to tackle problems that involve highly complex and time-consuming calculations. For example, United Airlines recently purchased a supercomputer for a new application—crew- and aircraft-schedule modeling and optimization problems. United found that solving the linear programming equations (see Chapter 9) associated with the complex, highly numerical applications took much too long (15 hours of CPU time) on a mainframe computer. Involved is the scheduling of 200,000 to 250,000 flights per day, as well as the planning of various fare classes and allocating of seat assignments.[8] Overall, the trend toward greater computer hardware power for less cost is gradually reducing the differences among types of computers.

Characteristics of Useful Information

Because computers can produce information very quickly, it is easy for managers to become overloaded. For instance, one recent survey of 1000 large British firms indicated that top executives are being deluged with reports but that the

P R A C T I C A L L Y   S P E A K I N G

A GUIDE TO MAJOR TYPES OF COMPUTERS

Several different types of computers are available for use in organizations. The major types are described and illustrated below.

PERSONAL COMPUTERS

General-purpose desktop computers that use 16- or 32-bit microprocessors (the more bits, the faster a computer works). Price: less than $1000 to $5000.

WORKSTATIONS

High-performance 32-bit computers used by engineers, scientists, and technical professionals who need superior graphics. Workstations, commonly used in computer-aided design, offer the performance of minicomputers but serve one person. The station often sits on or beside a desk and connects to other workstations in a network. Price: $5000 to $100,000.

MINI/SUPER-MINICOMPUTERS

Minicomputers have largely been supplanted by more powerful super-minicomputers. Machines in this category can handle the general needs of more than 100 people, who typically work on terminals wired to the computer. Super-minicomputers are about as big as a two- or four-drawer filing cabinet; several often connect to form a companywide network. Increasingly, such networks are replacing mainframes. Less powerful minicomputers: $20,000 to $100,000; super-minicomputers: $100,000 to $1 million.

MINI-SUPERCOMPUTERS

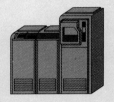

Computers that handle complex math computations for engineers, scientists, and researchers. Because of basic differences in design, mini-supercomputers outperform conventional computers in vector processing—simultaneously performing calculations on different lists of numbers. About the size of a refrigerator, mini-supercomputers deliver a quarter to half the performance of a supercomputer at only one-tenth the cost. Price: $100,000 to $1.5 million.

MAINFRAME COMPUTERS

Large, general-purpose computers that serve hundreds or thousands of users, all tied to a corporate data-processing center. A typical mainframe is slightly smaller than a Volkswagen Beetle and requires an atmospherically controlled room. Mainframes generally handle the major data-processing needs of large corporations, such as the weekly payroll. Despite encroachments by networks of super-minicomputers, mainframes remain the staple of large data-processing centers. Price: as much as $5 million.

SUPERCOMPUTERS

The world's fastest computers, used in science, engineering, and research for the most difficult processing challenges, such as weather forecasting. An average supercomputer is no larger than a mainframe, but packs faster processors that are more closely connected, to provide greater computing speed. Several organizations often share time on one supercomputer to offset the high cost of these machines. Price: $2.5 million to $25 million.[9]

---

reports need further refinement to be useful. The executives said that they want more emphasis put on information quality, rather than quantity.[10] Five characteristics are important in making information useful to managers.[11]

Relevant. First of all, it helps if the information is *relevant*—that is, directly related to the decision at hand. Of course, the more unstructured the situation, the more difficult it may be to determine exactly what information is relevant.

Accurate. Information needs to be *accurate* or correct enough to form the basis for effective decision making. Just how precisely correct information needs to be will depend on the situation. For example, if you are running an off-site training program, it may be important to keep precise information on how many students have enrolled so that room reservations, meals, and other support arrangements can be made. On the other hand, to help your boss decide whether to authorize further sessions of the training program, information such as "about 30 have signed up" may be sufficient.

Timely. For information to be useful, it needs to be *timely*—that is, available when needed.

Complete. Information also needs to be *complete* in the sense that it comes from the appropriate sources and covers all the areas that are required by the decision maker.

Concise. Finally, information should be *concise*, providing the level of summarization that is appropriate to the particular decision. For example, a sales manager interested in how closely the sales staff's travel expenses conform to budget would hardly want a listing of every individual expense item turned in by each individual. Instead, a summary of expenses for each person and overall as compared to target would probably be most useful.

Information Needs by Managerial Level

Since managerial responsibilities in such areas as planning and control differ according to level, it is not surprising to find that managerial needs for information also differ by level.[12] Some of these major differences are summarized in Table 20-1.

Top Management. At the top levels of management, organizational executives are mainly concerned about strategic issues, such as strategic planning and strategic control. Although they need some information about internal matters, top-

Table 20-1   Information Needs According to Management Level

	Main Issues	Informational Sources	Time Horizon	Decision Type	Level of Aggregation	Information Currency
Top management	Strategic	Mainly external	Long	Unstructured	Summarized	Less current
	↑	↑	↑	↑	↑	↑
Middle management	Tactical	External/ internal	Medium	Semistructured	Intermediate detail	Somewhat current
	|	|	|	|	|	|
First-line management	Operational	Mainly internal	Short	Structured	Detailed	Very current

Source: Adapted from Lee L. Gremillion and Philip J. Pyburn, *Computers and Information Systems in Business: An Introduction*, McGraw-Hill, New York, 1988, p. 182.

level managers are likely to require considerable information from external sources to help them monitor environmental factors. Generally, executives require information that is summarized and relevant to long-term issues and unstructured decision making. Because of its summarized nature, the information tends to be less current than that used by managers at lower levels in an organization. For instance, Debbi Fields needs information on sales and profit trends, particularly by region and overall. She also needs to keep an eye on such environmental factors as major competitors (e.g., David's Cookies, Blue Chip Cookies, The Original Great Chocolate Chip Cookies, and a number of other local and regional competitors), growth trends that affect the location of stores, and the general economic picture as it impacts likely profits.

Middle Management. At the middle levels, managers need to deal with tactical issues, such as tactical planning and tactical control. As a result, they require more of a balance between internal and external information. This balance enables them to handle internal matters that affect the implementation of tactical plans and to keep abreast of external changes that can potentially affect tactical plans. The information needs to be relevant to the medium-range time horizons and semistructured decisions that are the main concern of middle managers. These managers generally use information that is more detailed and more current than that required by their top management counterparts. For example, a regional director for Mrs. Fields Cookies may pay particular attention to weekly and monthly sales trends in the region, as well as monitor tactical moves by competitors operating in the area.

First-Line Management. At the first-line level, managers handle operational issues that are largely of a day-to-day nature. Not surprisingly then, first-level managers require information that comes mainly from internal sources, focuses on short-term issues, and is oriented toward fairly structured decisions. Because of their operational responsibilities, first-line managers typically need information that is considerably more detailed and more current than that required by managers at higher levels. The information needs of a manager of a Mrs. Fields Cookies store include hour-by-hour advice on how many batches of different types of cookies to make.

Information Needs by Specialized Area

In most companies, particularly medium- and large-size ones, information needs also vary by specialized area—such as manufacturing, finance, and human resources. When computers began to be used extensively in organizations during the late 1960s and early 1970s, computer specialists often envisioned a future in which the information needs of all the specialized areas would be met through one single, giant information system. More recently, computer specialists are increasingly recognizing that it is difficult to simultaneously meet the information needs of an entire major organization, particularly a very large one like American Express or Sears. In addition, the information requirements of various organizational parts are dynamic and can change rapidly, making one major system all the more difficult to design and implement.

   A more contemporary view is that information system efforts are likely to be more productive if they are aimed at developing specialized systems to meet the needs of specific areas (see Figure 20-3). The data used and the information produced, of course, may also be shared by other systems for various purposes.

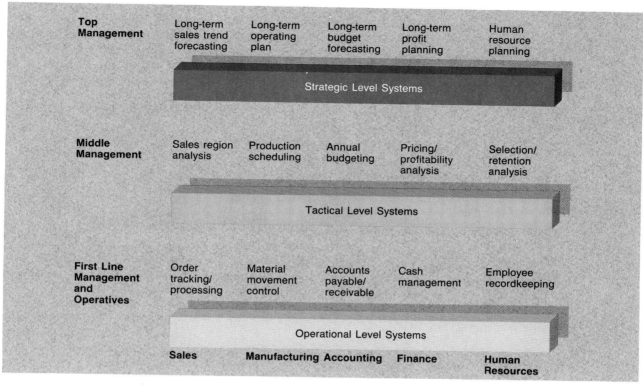

Top Management	Long-term sales trend forecasting	Long-term operating plan	Long-term budget forecasting	Long-term profit planning	Human resource planning

Strategic Level Systems

Middle Management	Sales region analysis	Production scheduling	Annual budgeting	Pricing/ profitability analysis	Selection/ retention analysis

Tactical Level Systems

First Line Management and Operatives	Order tracking/ processing	Material movement control	Accounts payable/ receivable	Cash management	Employee recordkeeping

Operational Level Systems

Sales	Manufacturing	Accounting	Finance	Human Resources

Figure 20-3 Examples of information systems for various functional areas by management level. (Adapted from Kenneth C. Laudon and Jane Price Laudon, *Management Information Systems: A Contemporary Perspective*, Macmillan, New York, 1988, p. 7.)

TYPES OF INFORMATION SYSTEMS

To serve the needs of different organizational levels, there are five major types of information systems: transaction processing, office automation, management information, decision support, and executive support.[13] These types of systems, the organizational level to which each is primarily geared, and the organization members mainly served by each are shown in Figure 20-4.

Transaction-Processing Systems

A **transaction-processing system (TPS)** is a computer-based information system that executes and records the day-to-day routine transactions required to conduct an organization's business. For example, each time we charge gas at a major service station, register to take a college or university class, renew a driver's license, or make a withdrawal from a bank account, a computerized transaction-processing system is at work. Transaction systems are used in highly structured and repetitive situations in which the tasks to be done and the criteria involved are clear. The structured nature of the situation makes it possible to write detailed and unequivocal instructions that allow the computer to handle and record the transactions properly. A TPS provides direct assistance to the operational level of an organization.

Two aspects of transaction-processing systems are particularly important. First, a TPS can be a vital aid to organizational boundary spanning or interfacing with important elements in the environment (see Chapter 3), because the system is often a major part of interactions with individuals outside the organization,

Transaction-processing system (TPS) A computer-based information system that executes and records the day-to-day routine transactions required to conduct an organization's business

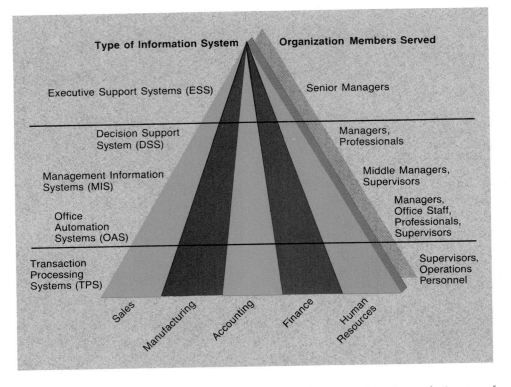

Type of Information System

Organization Members Served

Executive Support Systems (ESS) — Senior Managers

Decision Support System (DSS) — Managers, Professionals

Management Information Systems (MIS) — Middle Managers, Supervisors

Office Automation Systems (OAS) — Managers, Office Staff, Professionals, Supervisors

Transaction Processing Systems (TPS) — Supervisors, Operations Personnel

Sales Manufacturing Accounting Finance Human Resources

Figure 20-4 Types of information systems by level and organization members served. (Adapted from Kenneth C. Laudon and Jane Price Laudon, *Management Information Systems: A Contemporary Perspective*, Macmillan, New York, 1988, p. 37.)

particularly customers and suppliers. For example, Roger Milliken, chairman of Milliken & Company, a major textile firm, recently headed an effort by 220 top retail and clothing executives to establish technical standards for electronic data interchange (EDI), which allows specially formatted documents, such as purchase orders and shipping documents, to be sent directly from the computer of one company to the computer of another. Likewise, by increasing the speed of ordering and reducing prospects for human error, an EDI transaction-processing system enabled the Seminole Manufacturing Company to reduce by 50 percent the delivery time required to resupply its major customer, Wal-Mart Stores, with Seminole's men's slacks.[14] Second, a TPS is a main source of data used by other types of computer-based information systems within an organization.

Office Automation Systems

Office automation system (OAS) A computer-based information system aimed at facilitating communication and increasing the productivity of managers and office workers through document and message processing

An **office automation system (OAS)** is a computer-based information system aimed at facilitating communication and increasing the productivity of managers and office workers through document and message processing. The earliest, most widely used, and best-known application of OASs is the use of *word-processing* systems, which allow text to be created, edited, and printed quickly and easily. A more recent and growing aspect of OASs is the use of *electronic mail* systems, which allow the high-speed exchange of written messages by means of computer text processing and communications networks (see Chapter 15). An OAS may also include such applications as voice mail (a means of recording a message by telephone that is stored in a special form in a computer's secondary storage for retrieval by an intended receiver), electronic calendaring (a method of maintaining an appointments schedule electronically), teleconferencing (a means of communicating between two or more geographically separated locations by using electronic and/or image-producing facilities), document retrieval (the use of one or more electronic devices to store documents on microfilm or some other medium and facilitate the later location and copying of stored images), facsimile transmission (a means of sending documents over telephone lines to be printed at the receiving location), and graphics.[15]

There are generally two different views of office automation systems. Initially, such systems were viewed as a means of increasing the productivity of clerical and secretarial staffs. As part of this orientation, experts during the 1970s quoted figures indicating that capital investments to support an office worker generally fell into a range of $2000 to $4000 compared with expenditures of about $25,000 per worker in manufacturing. More recently, a second view has emerged that sees OASs as a means of aiding not only clerical and secretarial workers but managers and professionals as well.[16]

Management Information Systems

A **management information system (MIS)** is a computer-based information system that produces routine reports and often allows on-line access to current and historical information needed by managers mainly at the middle and first-line levels. MISs are oriented principally to tactical and operational issues and are particularly important in planning, decision making, and controlling. Typically, they summarize information from transaction-processing systems to produce routine and exception reports for use by managers and supervisors. For example, materials requirements planning systems used in operations management (see Chapter 19) supply information to master schedulers concerning any potential difficulties with materials procurement that will affect the schedule, provide information to capacity planners about necessary short- or long-run needs for capacity changes, and produce reports for first- and middle-level managers in such areas as costs, quality, and supplier activities.

Some computer specialists use the term "management information system" in a broad sense to describe all computer-related systems relevant to management, including the five major types of systems under discussion here. The term is also often used to designate the field of management that focuses on designing and implementing computer-based information systems for use by management. On the basis of work by researchers Kenneth C. Laudon and Jane Price Laudon, in this chapter we use "computer-based information systems" as the overall term denoting all computer-based systems related to the various levels of management. In turn, we reserve the term "management information systems" for the more narrow meaning just described above.

Management information system (MIS) A computer-based information system that produces routine reports and often allows online access to current and historical information needed by managers mainly at the middle and first-line levels

Decision Support Systems

A *decision support system (DSS)* is a computer-based information system that supports the process of managerial decision making in situations that are not well structured (see Chapter 9). Such systems generally do not actually provide "answers" or point to optimal decisions for managers. Rather, they attempt to improve the decision-making *process* by providing tools that help managers and professionals analyze situations more clearly.

Texas Air recently developed a DSS called Gatekeeper to aid gate control managers at Houston and Miami airports. The sophisticated computer aid became necessary as the airline changed from scheduling connecting flights at many different airports to utilizing hub operations, whereby many of the air-

The AT&T System 85 is an example of a state-of-the-art office automation system that enables managers and office workers to leave messages, exchange information, send, receive, and store memos, and schedule meetings and appointments.

line's flights stop at the central locations of Houston and Miami. With so many Texas Air flights coming into and leaving the same airport, managers had much greater difficulty allocating gates for incoming planes, particularly when incoming flights arrived late or outgoing flights were delayed. Gatekeeper helps managers reallocate gate designations quickly by suggesting configurations that maximize efficient use of the airline's gates.[17]

There are several differences between a DSS and an MIS. For one thing, compared to an MIS, a typical DSS provides more advanced analysis and greater access to various models that managers can use to examine a situation more thoroughly. For another, a DSS often relies on information from external sources, as well as draws from the internal sources that are largely the domain of the TPS and MIS. Finally, a DSS tends to be more highly interactive than an MIS, allowing managers to communicate directly (often back and forth) with computer programs that control the system and to obtain the results of various analyses almost immediately (see the following Case in Point discussion).

CASE IN POINT: Decision Support at Hidroeléctrica Española

Hidroeléctrica Española is one of the largest electric utilities in Spain, with about 19 percent of the market. The company owns a major interest in three large nuclear generating facilities, runs numerous thermal plants that use coal and oil for fuel, and controls about 19 percent of the hydroelectric generating capability in Spain. Managing the generation of hydroelectric energy effectively is particularly important to the company because the greater the amount of hydro-generated energy, the less the company is required to use more expensive fuels, such as coal and oil, to meet the energy demands of its customers. Yet maximizing the use of hydro-generated energy is a challenging task.

Within Hidroeléctrica, the Departamento de Operacion del Sistemas (DOS) makes the decisions about hydro releases, the discharge of water from various reservoirs within its purview. The DOS concerns itself particularly with generating hydro power on the lower Tajo river system, which runs from about 100 kilometers (about 62 miles) southwest of Madrid to the Portuguese border. There are three main interconnected rivers and ten reservoirs in the system. Rainfall in the area varies drastically from one year to the next, with most of the rain falling between November and May. When precipitation does occur, it tends to fall within a relatively short time period. As a result, the water levels in the reservoirs may become very high, making it necessary to release water without generating energy. Decisions to release water without energy generation have high importance because doing so precludes using that water to generate energy at a future date; furthermore, such releases can be dangerous since they may be adding water to the river system at a time of considerable precipitation. Yet failure to release water may cause spilling (reservoir overflow), a situation that can result in considerable damage. On the other hand, keeping the reservoirs too low can prevent the company from generating hydro power when necessary if expected additional rainfall does not materialize. Decisions made on a given day about the generation of hydroelectric power and water release depend on such factors as electricity demand, expected rainfall, current and anticipated reservoir levels, and availability of the hydro turbines that generate electricity at the various reservoirs. In dealing with the situation in the past, managers tended to focus on the immediate situation, using general and sometimes inconsistent notions about the implications of their decisions for future time periods of up to a year or so.

In order to help managers make better assessments of the yearlong implications of their actions, Hidroeléctrica hired a management science consultant to help develop a decision support system. The resulting system is based on mathematical models and incorporates forecasts for both energy demand and likely precipitation that are based on historical data, current indicators, and estimates by managers. Managers can vary their estimates of future conditions and then evaluate the computer-generated implications before making their final decisions about water release and hydrogeneration of energy. At first, DOS managers had difficulty accepting the decision support system because it made suggestions about water release that ran counter to their intuition. Since then, managers have made many suggestions that have helped refine the support system, which is now used extensively to help guide water release and hydrogeneration decisions. Use of the model has led to estimated annual savings ranging from $1 million to $3 million (depending on rainfall levels) and decreased the risk of reservoir overflows.[18] ■

One specialized type of DSS that is coming into increased use is the expert system.[19] *Expert systems* are computer-based systems that apply the substantial knowledge of an expert to help solve specialized problems (see Chapter 9). These systems are sometimes called *knowledge-intensive systems* because they attempt to incorporate much of the relevant knowledge that experts draw upon to solve problems in their area of expertise. In fact, in developing such systems,

Sometimes managerial decision making is aided by analyses that a computer is uniquely able to provide—at least in a timely manner. In the situation shown here, managers at New York State Electric and Gas (NYSEG) are checking on coal inventories at power plants. By using a computer, managers can convert aerial photos of coal piles into three-dimensional diagrams and then calculate the volume of coal in the piles.

designers typically work with experts to determine the information and heuristics, or decision rules, that the experts use when confronted with particular types of problems. One well-known example is XCON (for "eXpert CON-figurer"), developed by the Digital Equipment Corporation. The system uses more than 3000 decision rules and 5000 product descriptions to analyze sales orders and design layouts to be sure that the equipment will work when it reaches DEC's customers. XCON catches most configuration errors and eliminates the need for completely assembling a computer system to check it and then breaking it down again for shipment to the customer.[20]

Artificial intelligence A field of information technology aimed at developing computers that have humanlike capabilities, such as seeing, hearing, and thinking

Expert systems represent one outgrowth of **artificial intelligence,** a field of information technology aimed at developing computers that have humanlike capabilities, such as seeing, hearing, and thinking.[21] Artificial intelligence is an area of scientific inquiry, rather than an end product such as an expert system. In pursuing the prospect of getting computers to think, researchers during the 1960s attempted to develop machines that could play chess. They made tremendous strides in developing elaborate decision trees mapping out possible moves, but the resulting programs encompassed so many potential alternatives that even today's large supercomputers cannot assess them within a reasonable amount of time. Since then, the number of alternatives to consider has been reduced through the use of heuristics, or decision rules; today, chess programs operating on a mainframe computer can play at the level of a chess master. Still, the computers are not intelligent; they are simply processing enormous amounts of data on alternative moves. In essence, computers today are far from intelligent in the sense of being able to conceptualize or reason.[22] Nevertheless, efforts in the area of artificial intelligence have laid the groundwork related to significant developments, such as expert systems.

Some researchers argue that the "flamboyant quality" of the terms "artificial intelligence" and "expert systems" has created unrealistic expectations about what such systems can do.[23] Indeed, expert systems are extremely difficult and costly to develop. A moderate-size expert system, comprising about 300 decision rules, generally costs about $250,000 to $500,000 to design. The Digital Equipment Corporation spends $2 million per year just to update its XCON system.[24]

Executive Support Systems

Executive support system (ESS) A computer-based information system that supports decision making and effective functioning at the top levels of an organization

An **executive support system (ESS)** is a computer-based information system that supports decision making and effective functioning at the top levels of an organization. Such systems, which are a relatively recent development, are sometimes called *executive information systems* (EIS).

Unlike a DSS, which tends to be more narrowly focused, an ESS involves more general computing capabilities, telecommunications, and display options (such as graphs and charts) that are applicable to many different problems. An ESS tends to make less use of analytical models than does a DSS, delivers information from a variety of sources on demand, and allows more general queries in a highly interactive way. For instance, at the Phillips 66 Company, a division of the Phillips Petroleum Company, top-level managers have an ESS that helps them watch important indicators, such as oil-pricing trends, refinery operating results, and chemical-plant product statistics. President Robert G. Wallace, who reports that he uses the system all day and even now has a computer at home, says the system saves him an hour per day because he no longer needs to work with pages of paper reports. He also figures that the system could help increase profits by as much as $100 million annually because top executives get better,

Table 20-2   Characteristics of Information-Processing Systems

Type of CBIS	Data Inputs	Processing	Information Outputs
ESS	Aggregate data; external, internal	Graphics; simulations; interactive	Projections; responses to queries
DSS	Low-volume data; analytic models	Interactive; simulations; analysis	Special reports; decision analyses; responses to queries
MIS	Summary transaction data; high-volume data; simple models	Routine reports; simple models; low-level analysis	Summary and exception reports
OAS	Office documents; schedules	Word processing, storage, retrieval	Documents; schedules; graphics; mail
TPS	Transactions; events	Sorting, listing, merging, updating	Detailed reports; lists; summaries

Source: Reprinted from Kenneth C. Laudon and Jane Price Laudon, *Management Information Systems: A Contemporary Perspective,* Macmillan, New York, 1988, p. 34.

more timely information that helps particularly with buying and selling oil futures.[25]

In essence, ESSs are information systems that are tailor-made to fit the needs of executives working in particular situations and are often geared to the individual work habits of those managers. The general characteristics of executive support systems, as well as of the other major types of systems, are summarized in Table 20-2.

PROMOTING INNOVATION: STRATEGIC IMPLICATIONS OF INFORMATION SYSTEMS

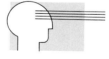

During the 1980s, a number of strategic planning experts began to highlight the innovative possibilities and strategic implications of the emerging information technology.[26] Before then, top-level managers had generally viewed computers as a means of streamlining internal processes in order to operate more efficiently. Even so, some companies were ahead of their time in using computers in innovative ways as essential elements in their competitive strategies.

One of the most famous examples of the innovative use of information technology to gain a competitive advantage is the American Airlines SABRE system, a computerized reservation system that basically falls into the category of a sophisticated transaction-processing system. The system was developed in the 1970s, partially to preclude travel agencies from joining together to develop their own system; it cost more than $300 million. SABRE serves more than 11,000 travel agencies. The travel agents rent the terminals from American, and other airlines pay a service fee whenever the terminals are used to make reservations on one of their flights. American has expanded the system to cover reservations for hotels, cars, and other services. Almost 400 programmers work full-time to keep the system functioning and to develop new services associated with it. Robert Crandall, American's chairman and CEO, indicates that he expects the company to spend in the neighborhood of $1 billion on the system over the next few years to cover expansion, upgrading of services, and telecommunications. United Airlines has the only major competing system, called Apollo.[27]

One aid in helping managers think about how to use information technol-

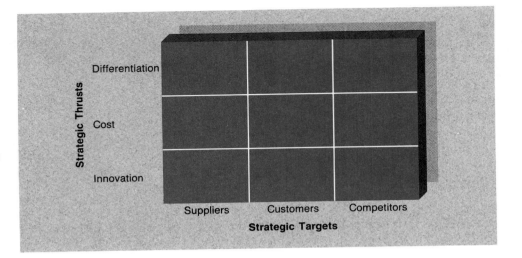

Figure 20-5 Matrix of strategic options related to information technology. (Adapted from Charles Wiseman and Ian C. MacMillan, "Creating Competitive Weapons from Information Systems," *The Journal of Business Strategy*, Fall 1984, p. 45.)

ogy to competitive advantage is a matrix of major strategic options for information technology, developed by strategy experts Charles Wiseman and Ian C. MacMillan. Related to Michael Porter's work on competitive strategy (see Chapter 6), the matrix considers two main dimensions: strategic targets and strategic thrusts (see Figure 20-5).[28]

Strategic Targets

According to the matrix, organizations have three major strategic targets on which they can focus in attempting to use information systems to gain competitive advantage. The targets are suppliers, customers, and competitors (see Figure 20-5).

Suppliers as Target. Suppliers include providers of raw materials, capital, labor, or services. In one system aimed at suppliers, Equitable Life Assurance, one of the nation's largest insurance companies, installed a telecommunications network that links its field offices with regional offices, four warehouses, and its New York headquarters. The company also installed a new inventory and purchasing system. Before its installation, warehouse purchasing agents had experienced difficulty assessing vendor prices and choosing the best deals. With the new system, corporate headquarters makes major purchases of needed items from a New York distributor and offers them to the warehouses at somewhat higher prices. The warehouses can buy supplies from headquarters or shop elsewhere if they can get better prices. The system enables them to compare prices and check the terms of recent contracts for similar purchases made by the company. Thus the system puts the purchasing agents and the company in a better bargaining position relative to suppliers.[29]

Customers as Target. Customers include organizations that retail, wholesale, warehouse, distribute, or use a company's products or services. In one strategic use of information technology aimed at customers, Metpath, a large clinical laboratory, installed computer terminals in doctors' offices and connected the terminals to laboratory computers. By means of the terminals, Metpath is able to provide the doctors with quick access to test results for a small monthly fee. Metpath also keeps records of patient tests in a computer data base and offers doctors financial processing services linking billing and accounts payable systems. These steps represent a Metpath strategy to differentiate its services from those offered by competitors and to raise barriers to entry for new and existing competitors.[30]

Competitor as Target. Competitors include current industry members, potential entrants, organizations in other industries that have substitute products, and other organizations that require the same scarce resources. The Hewlett-Packard Company, the Palo Alto electronics manufacturer, has been aggressively designing systems to give itself an edge in direct competition for customers. In connection with one new system, Hewlett-Packard is providing its 3000-person U.S. sales force with lap-top computers. The computers tie into new company data bases that give promising sales leads, as well as helpful historical information about customers and their purchases over a considerable period of time.[31]

Strategic Thrusts

The matrix (see Figure 20-5) also suggests three major strategic thrusts, or approaches, that combine well with information technology. The thrusts are differentiation, cost, and innovation.

Differentiation. The goal of the differentiation approach is either to increase the differentiation advantages of an organization in relation to those of others (suppliers, customers, or competitors) or to decrease the differentiation advantages of others relative to those of the organization. One company that has been successful in the fiercely competitive shipping industry is American President Companies (APC), whose subsidiary, American President Lines, ships containerized freight for customers throughout North America and Asia. Faced with heavy competition from foreign carriers, APC felt that it could charge premium prices for better service on urgently needed or high-value items, such as materials for just-in-time production systems or parts for computers. The company's strategy involved making huge investments in information technology to offer such services as coordinated shipping over both land and water, computerized aid for cargo clearance by U.S. Customs, and customer access to computerized information that lets clients track their shipments 24 hours per day.[32]

Cost. A cost approach is oriented toward reducing an organization's costs in relation to the costs of others (suppliers, customers, or competitors), helping suppliers or customers reduce their costs so that they want to do business with the organization, or increasing competitors' costs. General Motors and the Ford Motor Company, for example, have indicated that they will make purchases only from suppliers that have telecommunications equipment for sending and receiving messages electronically. The automobile companies want to use telecommunications to reduce inventory costs by moving toward just-in-time inventory methods (in which parts arrive just shortly before they are needed). Already, Ford sends daily electronic messages on parts needs to 700 suppliers of its Wixom, Michigan, assembly plant instead of the weekly communications it relied on in the past. The two automakers also want to use the system to reduce the cost of paying supplier bills. For instance, GM ultimately hopes to eliminate the 300,000 paper checks that it sends out each month to almost 6000 suppliers.[33]

Innovation. The innovation approach is focused on finding major new ways to conduct business by using information technology. In a sense, the differentiation and cost approaches also involve some innovation. However, the innovation thrust is included in the matrix to highlight prospects for major changes in directions, such as making drastic changes in current practices, moving into new businesses or industries, redefining existing businesses, or developing businesses that did not exist previously. Innovative applications of information technology are preemptive strikes that are difficult for others to match because of the advantages that accrue to organizations that take the initial actions. An example of a major innovative use of information technology to gain competitive advantage is the information system called Economost, developed by the McKesson Corporation, a drug wholesaler based in San Francisco (see the following Case in Point discussion).

CASE IN POINT: McKesson Forges Strong Computer Links with Customers

Consider the mundane business of restocking shelves at the corner drugstore. Philip Cavavetta buys merchandise for his Boston-area drugstores from two wholesalers. One of them, McKesson, is getting more of his business these days. Why? "Their computer system is so good," he says.

Not long ago, sales representatives from McKesson, as well as those from other wholesalers, would drop by Cavavetta's Econo Drug Marts to take orders for cough syrup, aspirin, penicillin, and similar items. When the store ran short between sales representatives' visits, clerks would read new orders over the phone to tape recorders at McKesson's warehouse.

Today, a clerk in Cavavetta's store walks the aisles once a week with a McKesson-supplied computer in his palm. If the store is low on, say, bottles of cough syrup, the clerk waves a scanner over a McKesson-provided label stuck to the shelf. The computer takes note and, when the clerk is finished, transmits the order to McKesson.

At first glance, it appears that McKesson has simply automated a costly, labor-intensive chore. But far more has happened: McKesson's computers not only dispatch the orders to a warehouse but also print price stickers that add in the precise profit margin that Cavavetta has selected. In addition, the computers generate monthly reports on the profitability of each of his departments.

If Cavavetta buys from his alternative supplier, a regional wholesaler, he gets none of these services. And if he wants to switch to a McKesson competitor with a similar computer service, he will have to relabel his shelves and learn another computer system.

Other McKesson computer services keep tabs on prescription-drug use by drugstore customers, check to be sure no one is taking medicines that should not be taken simultaneously, and bill insurers for subscribers' medicines.[34] ■

McKesson offers similar services for supermarkets and hospitals. In the late 1970s, McKesson actually considered giving up its drug distribution business because it was doing so poorly. Now the business is its biggest, with more than 25,000 customers, 50 distribution centers throughout the country, and sales exceeding $6.6 billion annually.[35]

DEVELOPING COMPUTER-BASED INFORMATION SYSTEMS

Developing computer-based information systems can be difficult and expensive, particularly when the applications are large and complex. In fact, time and cost overruns are common. In one recent survey of 600 large clients by Peat Marwick Mitchell & Company, about 35 percent of the clients reported that they currently had information system projects with major cost and/or time overruns.[36] For example, in 1982, the Allstate Insurance Company, a subsidiary of Sears, Roebuck & Company, began developing a sophisticated information system that would automate office operations. It was also slated to cut the time needed to introduce new policies from 3 years to 1 month, a move calculated to gain competitive advantage over competitors. An outside contractor was hired to help develop the system; the target date was set for December 1987; and the expected cost was projected at $8 million. During the first year things ran fairly smoothly, but then the programming and hardware testing started to fall behind schedule. Things got worse when conflicts arose among Allstate technical personnel over their roles and over the parameters of the project. By 1988, after spending $15 million, the company found it necessary to hire a new outside contractor, revise the projected target date to 1993, and boost the cost estimate to $100 million.[37]

Furthermore, the resulting systems sometimes spew out errors that cause serious business problems. In 1987, when the Bank of America attempted a conversion to MasterNet, a new information system developed to better manage $34 billion in institutional trust accounts and to attract new business, the system failed. The bank could not provide customers with adequate statements about their accounts for months, and large pension funds withdrew at least $1.5 billion. Finally, in early 1988, the bank scrapped MasterNet, wrote off its $20 million investment in the system, set up a $60 million fund to correct the problems with customer accounts, and contracted the work out to other banks.[38] The disastrous dimensions of such problems, as well as the potential strategic value of information technology, have made it important for managers to have at least a general knowledge of what is involved in information systems development.

The Systems Development Life Cycle

Traditionally, the development of new information systems has followed a process known as the systems development life cycle. The **systems development life cycle** is a series of stages that are used in the development of most medium- and large-size information systems. The approach was first devised in the 1950s as a means of creating large transaction-processing systems, and it still is the basic approach used in major systems development today. The life cycle also is often used more informally in developing small-scale systems. Typically, systems development is carried out by a project team consisting of managers, users, systems analysts, programmers, and other technical personnel needed for successful development of the project.

Systems development life cycle A series of stages that are used in the development of most medium- and large-size information systems

Although there are several different versions of the life cycle and the terminology used may differ, the basic elements are fairly similar across versions. The systems life cycle has three distinct stages: definition, physical design, and implementation and operation (see Figure 20-6).[39] We first explore these stages and then assess the life-cycle approach to systems development.

Definition Stage. The *definition stage* is aimed at evaluating the proposed idea and defining system parameters. This stage is extremely important because,

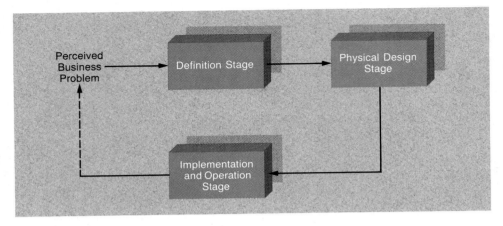

Figure 20-6 The systems development life cycle. (Adapted from Lee L. Gremillion and Philip J. Pyburn, *Computers and Information Systems in Business: An Introduction,* McGraw-Hill, New York, 1988, p. 259.)

according to one estimate, mistakes and omissions that are not detected until later can cost from 10 to 100 times more to fix than oversights detected during the definition stage.[40] Furthermore, results of one recent study suggest that projects on which considerable effort is expended in the definition stage are likely to be more successful on a variety of dimensions.[41] Yet for complex situations, particularly if the initial project idea is fairly vague, it can be difficult to reliably assess feasibility and to identify all the important functions and outputs of the proposed system at this early stage.

Physical Design Stage. The *physical design stage* carries the project from concept to reality. This stage includes developing a detailed systems design, carrying out the necessary programming and debugging, and planning the implementation. At the end of the physical design stage, the system exists physically—that is, the hardware and software are ready—and it awaits implementation.

Implementation and Operation Stage. The *implementation and operation stage* includes implementing the system, evaluating its effectiveness, and maintaining effective operation of the system. A typical medium-size development project requires about 2 years to reach the conversion phase of the implementation stage and is likely to have an expected life span of 5 to 8 years from that point, during which ongoing maintenance will need to be conducted and operating costs will be incurred.[42] According to one estimate, the average new information system will require about 50 cents for operation and maintenance each year for every dollar spent on development and initial implementation.[43]

Assessing the Life-Cycle Approach. The life-cycle approach has several advantages. For one thing, it provides a series of stages and phases as guidelines for major systems development efforts. For another, it focuses considerable effort on early definition of both the necessary functions and the outputs of the system. Finally, the approach allows for the involvement of potential users, particularly at the definition stage.

Unfortunately, the life-cycle approach also has some disadvantages. One disadvantage is that the cycle is very costly, particularly because it involves spending considerable time on investigating various aspects of the system. Backlogs of 2 or 3 years before new applications of computer technology can be developed are common, partially because of the chronic shortage of experienced computer specialists. Another disadvantage is that the intended users often have difficulty specifying all the functions and outputs of the system early in the life cycle, as required. One reason is that users often are not familiar enough with the technical aspects of computers to understand what is intended or even possible. Finally, another disadvantage of the life-cycle approach is that it tends to discourage changes in the system definition once the definition stage is over. Even within the life-cycle approach, though, it is possible to loop back through the definition stage periodically. Unfortunately, such loops add still more to the time and cost of the project.

Overall, the life-cycle approach appears to be the best alternative available when projects are very large and/or complex and when the applications are fairly well structured so that parameters can be reasonably well defined early in the project. Evidence suggests that systems development efforts that run into difficulty usually have not adequately followed the steps involved in the life cycle.[44]

Alternative Means of Systems Development

Given the potential problems associated with custom-designed information systems developed through the traditional life cycle, other alternatives are emerging.[45] Among the most prominent are applications software packages, prototyping, and end-user development.[46]

Applications Software Packages. **Applications software packages** are software programs available for sale or lease from commercial sources. The packages typically are geared to handle specialized areas that are required by a large number of organizations. Payroll, inventory control, work scheduling, accounts receivable, and graphics are examples of applications for which there are a number of software packages available from various vendors. Commercial vendors take on the considerable expense of developing such packages because they are able to make a profit by selling the same packages at reasonable prices to a large number of organizations. One result is that organizations can often obtain such packages at considerably less cost than in-house, custom-developed software. Using an off-the-shelf applications software package also may make it possible to implement a new system much sooner, since much of the development work has been done by the commercial vendor.

There are, however, disadvantages to using commercial packages. The most major one stems from the fact that the packages are somewhat generic in orientation; although they usually offer some options, they often cannot accommodate extraordinary circumstances or uncommon procedures. On the other hand, if the savings are substantial, it may sometimes be feasible to change the organization's operations in order to make them compatible with the parameters of the software package. A second major disadvantage of applications software packages is that their use in attempts to exploit information technology ahead of competitors may make it easy for competitors to follow suit quickly. A third disadvantage is that such packages can have major errors that cause serious malfunctions, a situation that occurred when dBASE IV, a revision of the popular dBASE III data-base software package developed by the Ashton-Tate Corporation, was found to contain serious errors.[47]

Prototyping. **Prototyping** is the process of building a rough, working model of all or parts of a proposed information system for purposes of preliminary evaluation and further refinement. Unlike the traditional approach that involves attempting to specify clearly all user needs in the early development stages, the

Applications software packages Software programs available for sale or lease from commercial sources

Prototyping The process of building a rough, working model of all or parts of a proposed information system for purposes of preliminary evaluation and further refinement

prototype approach is based on the idea of providing a quick response to loosely defined user specifications. The prototype system may then go through a number of modifications and enhancements before the system finally meets evolving user requirements. Companies that are using prototyping report that the approach can cost 25 percent less than the traditional development approach, usable results are usually produced faster, and the systems typically earn better acceptance from users because they meet user needs.[48]

User An individual, other than an information system professional, who is engaged in the development and/or management of computer-based information systems

End user The same as a user

End-user computing The development and/or management of information systems by users

User-Developed Systems. In the world of information systems, a **user** is an individual, other than an information system professional, who is engaged in the development and/or management of computer-based information systems. (A user is often called an **end user**.) **End-user computing,** the development and/or management of information systems by users, is a growing trend in organizations. For example, during the early 1980s over 40 percent of the computer resources at Xerox were devoted to supporting end-user computing, a figure that rose to about 75 percent by 1990.[49]

User-developed systems, then, are created with little or no help from information system professionals. The trend toward increasing end-user computing stems from several sources. First, the rise of microcomputers, or personal computers, has enabled users to gain basic experience with computers. Second, falling prices for computer hardware have made it practical in many cases for departments and divisions to have their own computers. Third, the availability of applications software packages and other user-friendly tools makes it more feasible for individuals who are not computer professionals to tackle information system development. Fourth, the long queue of projects waiting to be developed by information system departments has caused users to take matters into their own hands.

End-user computing has a number of advantages. The possibility of increasing individual performance through the use of computers is one advantage. Another, of course, is that users learn about the capabilities and limitations of computers. This learning can then lead to the third advantage, the increased possibility that users will recognize innovative ideas for information systems that can lead to a competitive advantage.[50] Finally, end-user development often results in speedier implementation of systems.

Still, end-user development may not be best in all circumstances. Some types of systems may be too complex for nonprofessionals to tackle. There also is the danger of poorly designed systems which make errors that are not detected until considerable damage has been done. In addition, the systems may not tie in well to other systems in the organization. Finally, such systems may be developed by individuals who keep poor notes or documentation about how the systems work, possibly crippling the ability of others to work with a system should the key person leave.

Selecting a Development Approach

Three project criteria are useful in helping to determine the appropriate development approach.[51] The first is *commonality*, the degree to which there is likely to be a common need for the type of system in other organizations. When commonality is high, commercial software packages probably exist that are at least worth investigating as a possible alternative to custom development. The second criteria is *impact*. The more widespread the impact and the more important the system is to ongoing operations and strategic directions, the more information system professionals should be involved in the development effort. The third criteria is *structure*, the degree to which the problem and its probable solution are understood. When structure is low, prototyping begins to look more attractive, particularly if the system is likely to have broad impact.

MANAGING INFORMATION SYSTEM RESOURCES

The computer revolution has brought with it the necessity of managing the information system resources themselves. A major issue in managing information system resources is the extent to which the information specialists (such as the systems analysts and programmers who help design and develop information systems) and other computer-related resources (such as hardware and software) will be centralized in an information system department that has overall control of the organization's information systems. The opposite alternative is to decentralize information system resources and control into the divisions, departments, or groups that use the systems. In between the two extremes, there are a number of variations, such as having a corporate information system department responsible for overall planning and control issues, with systems development and operations managed by divisions.[52]

Factors Favoring Centralization

A number of factors favor centralization. Enhanced staff professionalism is one. When computer specialists are centralized in one department, it is easier to create the kind of challenging atmosphere and the career paths that allow specialists to progress to higher-level jobs in their profession. Another factor, of course, is staff specialization, whereby individuals can develop in-depth specialties because they can be given narrower job duties. Another advantage is the potential for economies of scale, because specialists can be shifted among projects that need their assistance. Still another advantage of centralization is that it is easier to maintain control of corporate data bases, including data integrity (accuracy and completeness) and security. Finally, centralization allows greater control over standards and procedures for information system development, computer purchases, and computer operations.

Factors Favoring Decentralization

On the other hand, a number of factors favor decentralization of computing resources. For one thing, in some circumstances, using several smaller computers (such as minicomputers) may be more cost-effective than using one large mainframe. For another, the current relatively low cost of acquiring computers and the increasing availability of user-friendly software make it feasible for decentralized locations to computerize without help from a centralized group of specialists. Yet another argument for decentralization is the fact that there is usually a heavy backlog of projects awaiting development by central information system groups. Finally, users often want control over computer operations when they feel that the information systems are critical to their own performance.[53]

Trends in Centralization and Decentralization

During the relatively short history of computer usage by organizations, the pendulum has swung back and forth between centralization and decentralization, largely because of technological developments and the accompanying cost factors (see Table 20-3).[54] When computers first began to be used extensively for commercial applications in the early 1950s, the machines were so expensive that computer resources were generally located only at headquarters. Field offices both forwarded data for input and received output by mail.

As lower-priced units became available in the late 1950s, field operations began to have their own computers. By the mid-1960s, the first software for telecommunications made it feasible and less costly to have large mainframe computers at headquarters with terminals at field offices.

When minicomputers, and then microcomputers, became popular in the mid-1970s, the low cost of these new machines made it attractive—especially for large, geographically dispersed companies—to decentralize computing to some extent. In addition, further developments in telecommunications made it possible to interconnect the computers distributed to various locations.

Distributed processing
An arrangement in which computers are distributed to various organizational locations where they serve the organization's local and/or regional needs and are interconnected for electronic communication

The distribution of computers to various organizational locations where they serve the organization's local and/or regional needs and are interconnected for electronic communication is known as **distributed processing.** Frequently, the computers are connected to a host computer (often a large mainframe) at headquarters that handles data exchange. For example, Sears has small computers at each store that are connected in a distributed network to mainframe computers in Chicago. The store computers handle the local transaction processing and supply data to the headquarters mainframe computers, which are used for centralized purchasing, inventory management, and a variety of other management information system applications.[55]

Managing End-User Computing

The prevalence of the microcomputer (or personal computer) in the early 1980s has accelerated the trend toward distributed processing and end-user computing, as well as tying computers together in networks.[56] Yet many companies are finding that with complete decentralization, various parts of the organization are purchasing many different types of equipment and software, a development that inhibits creating the networks that are becoming increasingly useful.[57] For example, a number of organizations are installing **local area networks (LANs),** interconnections (usually by cable) that allow communications among computers within a single building or in close proximity.

Local area networks (LANs)
Interconnections (usually by cable) that allow communications among computers within a single building or in close proximity

Table 20-3 Trends in Centralization and Decentralization of Computer Resources

	1951–1958	1958–1965	1965–1975	1975–Present
Headquarters	Large systems	Large systems	Large systems	Large systems
Outlying offices	No computing equipment	Small systems not connected to headquarters	Terminals connected to headquarters	Mini- and microcomputers often connected to headquarters
Overall emphasis	*Centralized*	*Decentralized*	*Centralized*	*Distributed*

Source: Reprinted from Raymond McLeod, Jr., *Management Information Systems,* Science Research Associates, Inc., Chicago, 1986, p. 293.

Multiple-vendor equipment also makes it more difficult for organizations to establish **wide area networks,** networks that provide communications among computers over long distances, usually through the facilities and services of public communications companies (in most countries) or private companies (in the United States), such as AT&T, MCI, and Sprint. For example, Mrs. Fields Cookies operates a wide area network that connects the personal computers in all its stores with the main computer in Park City, Utah.

One recent attempt to allow users some latitude but also to maintain some control is the information center.[58] An **information center** is a centrally located group of hardware, software, and information system professionals dedicated to assisting users with information system development. These centers often help establish policies on issues such as the number of types of equipment that can be purchased. They also frequently set standards regarding the use of certain types of software packages for basic applications, such as word processing, so that individuals do not need to learn a whole new system when they change departments. Information centers also frequently arrange for educational programs to help users, as well as provide technical advice. Such steps still can leave ample room for user innovation. At Rayovac, within 2 years of the company's developing an information center, over 100 clients from within the company were using the center to run more than 300 information systems. Most of the systems were developed by user departments.[59]

Wide area networks
Networks that provide communications among computers over long distances, usually through the facilities and services of public or private communications companies

Information center A centrally located group of hardware, software, and information system professionals dedicated to assisting users with information system development

IMPACTS OF INFORMATION TECHNOLOGY ON ORGANIZATIONS

As computers grow more pervasive, information technology is having a considerable impact on many aspects of organizations. Major areas of influence include organization structure, individual jobs, and organizational risk.[60]

Organization Structure

Aside from the issue of how to organize the information system function itself, CBISs are gradually impacting the overall structures of organizations. Early researchers anticipated that computers would eventually reduce the need for middle managers, cause top management to assume more of the responsibility for innovating and planning, and lead large organizations to recentralize decision making.[61] Indeed, there does appear to be a recent trend toward eliminating some layers of middle management in organizations, a move made possible to some extent by the increased ability of top-level managers to obtain needed information through computers. At the same time, early researchers did not foresee the onslaught of microcomputers, a technological breakthrough that allows information to be shared and decision making to be decentralized. The overall impact of computers on organization structure appears to be that they increase the structural options available to managers by potentially facilitating decentralized decision making while still allowing higher-level managers to retain control by enabling them to keep informed through integrated computer networks.[62]

The Westin St. Francis Hotel in San Francisco installed a network that allows four personal computers to trade programs and information. As a result, word processing output increased by one-third. When computer equipment and software have been purchased from different vendors, such networks can be particularly difficult and expensive to implement.

Individual Jobs

Computers can impact individual jobs in a number of ways. Three of the most significant effects are alterations in the design of jobs, the job-related stress and health consequences of computers, and increasing options regarding the location of work.

Nature of Jobs. The relatively recent invasion of personal computers in the workplace has made it difficult to gauge accurately the total impact of computers on work.[63] For clerical jobs, the trends so far suggest that computers can lead either to jobs that are extremely simple and require little skill or to jobs that involve considerable creativity and skill.[64] At the professional level, computers seem to be reducing the number of routine tasks while increasing the ability of professionals to communicate with others and use some of the same decision-making tools being developed for managers. At the managerial level, computers offer managers new aids to help with decision making, communication, and control.

Stress and Health Consequences. Stress and health issues related to computers largely center on the impact on lower-level white-collar jobs. One continuing controversy is over the effects of **electronic monitoring,** the practice of using computers to continually assess employee performance. For example, computers are used by a number of airlines to monitor both telephone and computer use. At Pacific Southwest Airlines, spokesman William Hastings says, "Our customer complaints have gone down since we've instituted monitoring. Our productivity numbers have improved markedly." Still, critics argue that monitoring reduces customer service and increases stress.[65] One recent study concluded that monitoring has the effect of degrading the quality of customer service and of the work environment itself. Nevertheless, the study found that some workers were able to internalize the standards of the system, used the data for feedback on how they were doing, and were not bothered by the monitoring. Thus using the system to give employees direct, regular feedback, but providing feedback to supervisors less frequently, may be a more effective approach to monitoring.[66]

A related issue stems from the possible health hazards associated with sitting in front of a video display terminal (VDT) for extended periods of time. Hypothesized health hazards include possible eye, back, and wrist injuries. Also, there is some evidence that women who spend more than 20 hours per week in front of VDTs early in their pregnancy may be more likely to have miscarriages than women who do not use terminals. It is not clear whether the problem stems from the VDTs themselves or other factors such as ergonomic (the degree to which the work environment is suited to the worker) influences and stress. Some companies, such as Con Edison, the Brooklyn-based utility, are attempting to reduce the possibility of hazards by offering eye examinations, making changes in the work environment (e.g., providing ergonomically designed furniture, i.e., furniture designed to support the human body and reduce strain), and providing training in how to position arms and hands to avoid muscle strain. Similar measures at Norwegian STK's telephone plant at Knosvinger, near Oslo, reduced turnover by 22 percent.[67]

Location of Work. Advances in information technology are increasing the options related to the location of work. One outgrowth is **telecommuting,** a form of working at home that is made possible by using computer technology to remain in touch with the office. Studies indicate that telecommuting may not be satisfactory for many individuals because of their need for social interaction with co-workers and the difficulties inherent in separating work and home roles.[68] One

Electronic monitoring The practice of using computers to continually assess employee performance

Telecommuting A form of working at home that is made possible by using computer technology to remain in touch with the office

study found that if given a choice between telecommuting or working at the office, 56 percent of respondents would prefer to work at the office, 36 percent would like to split their time between home and office, and just 7 percent would want to work only at home.[69]

Another possibility that derives from advanced technology is the **logical office,** the concept that portable microcomputers allow an individual's office to be anywhere the individual is, rather than being restricted to one specific location. Portable microcomputers, which run on batteries and usually plug into modular phone jacks for transmission, often are referred to as *lap-top computers*. Ruth L. Otte, president of the Discovery Channel, has found it possible to operate with 40 percent fewer people than a major competitor by using lap-tops. Based in Landover, Maryland, the Discovery Channel acquires, promotes, and transmits some 200 television programs per month to more than 30 million U.S. homes. Otte uses a sophisticated communications system to keep in touch with her 105-member staff and receives an average of 100 memos per day wherever she is. "I feel like I'm never out of the office," she says.[70] Nonetheless, managers who use lap-tops as they travel often have to cope with such inconveniences as extra scrutiny by airport security, batteries that lose power, and inadequate phone-jack facilities in hotel rooms.[71]

Logical office The concept that portable microcomputers allow an individual's office to be anywhere the individual is, rather than being restricted to one specific location

Organizational Risk

Despite all the potential benefits, information technology does pose some considerable risks to organizations. Among the most significant are possible errors, physical calamities, theft, sabotage and security breaches, and resistance to and underutilization of major systems.

Errors. With complex software, it is almost impossible to test for every possible error and contingency. As a result, errors and problems do occur. For instance, in 1990, a software problem caused the AT&T long-distance phone network to malfunction, shutting off service to tens of millions of customers throughout the United States for several hours and disrupting many businesses that depend heavily on telephone communication, such as airline reservation systems.[72]

Physical Calamities. Physical damage caused by fires, floods, power failures, earthquakes, and similar factors can severely disrupt an organization's information flows. For example, in 1988, a fire at an Illinois Bell switching station outside Chicago shut down communication over telephone lines in several Illinois towns for weeks. Among those affected were the headquarters of McDonald's Corporation and the Motorola Corporation. Large corporations were forced to use emergency microwave radio systems in order to reestablish communications.[73]

Recognizing the seriousness of having its computers damaged, American Airlines has spent $34 million to create an underground facility in Tulsa, Oklahoma, where its SABRE system operates. The facility has foot-thick concrete walls, a 42-inch steel-reinforced concrete ceiling covered with 7½ feet of earth, and a barbed-wire fence. It is made to withstand earthquakes, floods, and winds of up to 350 miles per hour.[74]

Theft. According to one estimate by consultants at the accounting firm of Ernst & Whinney, theft committed by using computers amounts to $3 to $5 billion per year in the United States alone. Computer theft is often internal in origin. In one incident, a group of employees wired $54 million from the London office of the

Union Bank of Switzerland to another Swiss bank by using all the proper authorization codes. They were caught only because the second bank's computer malfunctioned, bringing the attention of the auditors to the transaction. While the average bank robber usually steals about $5000, electronic thefts average about $500,000 per incident.[75]

Sabotage and Security Breaches. Both sabotage and security breaches are growing into major problems plaguing information technology. Computer sabotage is the deliberate disruption of computer-related activities and/or the destruction of computer equipment, software, or data. Computer security breaches include gaining unauthorized entry to computers or computer-related networks, as well as gaining access to stored data.

Sometimes the sabotage comes from disgruntled parties. For example, the USPA & IRA Company, a Fort Worth securities trading firm, alleged that a former programmer erased 168,000 computer records. The company said that the programmer, who was fired after numerous arguments over pay, entered company headquarters 2 days later, erased the records, and then planted a program designed to wipe out records of sales commissions each month. Company officials admitted that they procrastinated about changing passwords, which would have thwarted the programmer's dirty work. The programmer was subsequently convicted, sentenced to 7½ years on probation, and ordered to pay his former employer $11,800.[76]

In other cases, the sabotage may be pranks perpetrated by employees or by hackers. **Hackers** are individuals who are knowledgeable about computers and who gain unauthorized entry to, and sometimes tamper with, computer networks and files of organizations with which they have no affiliation. In one famous incident, a West German law student, by using an academic research network, gained access to IBM's 145-country electronic mail network in December 1987 and planted a seemingly innocuous picture of a Christmas tree and a holiday message. To get rid of the greeting, individuals were instructed to type "Christmas." However, when they did so, they unwittingly triggered a program that caused the greeting to be reproduced and sent to others in chain-letter fashion. Before long, the entire system was forced to shut down.[77] The tool of the prank was a **computer virus,** a small program, usually hidden inside another program, that replicates itself and surfaces at a predetermined time to cause disruption and possibly destruction.

Data security is also subject to threats. Privacy issues surround such data as personnel and credit records. Crucial corporate data bases and proprietary software also can be compromised. Recently, a group of West German hackers gained access to NASA computers and several U.S. military networks before being detected.[78]

As a result of these sabotage and security issues, many companies are tightening their computer security through such means as increasingly sophisticated password systems, dial-back systems that check to be sure that an incoming call is from an authorized phone number, and encryption hardware that disguises data by converting it to a code that is difficult for outsiders to decipher.

Resistance and Underutilization. Another risk is that significant resources might be allocated to developing systems that managers and their subordinates will resist using. For example, one group of division heads at AT&T was reluctant to provide data to a system that could be used by top-level executives in assessing the progress of various operations at any point in time. The division heads apparently feared that top-level managers would be able both to check on

Hackers Individuals who are knowledgeable about computers and who gain unauthorized entry to, and sometimes tamper with, computer networks and files of organizations with which they have no affiliation

Computer virus A small program, usually hidden inside another program, that replicates itself and surfaces at a predetermined time to cause disruption and possibly destruction

and to interfere with their activities more directly with the new system. On the other hand, top-level executives often are particularly adverse to operating computers, mostly because they tend to associate using a keyboard with lower-level work. Nevertheless, these views are gradually changing as various organization members begin to appreciate more fully the usefulness of computers for obtaining needed information quickly.[79] For example, companies such as Eastman Kodak are building worldwide computer linkages to facilitate international management, a subject to which we turn in the next chapter.

CHAPTER SUMMARY

An information system is a set of procedures designed to collect (or retrieve), process, store, and disseminate information to support planning, decision making, coordination, and control. A useful way to visualize information systems is to think of them as involving inputs, transformations, and outputs. Such systems transform data into information that has meaning for decision makers. Information systems that make use of computers are often referred to as computer-based information systems. The computer components of a CBIS fall into two categories: hardware and software. Effective CBISs produce information that is useful in that it is relevant, accurate, timely, complete, and concise, given the particular managerial need. Managerial needs for information tend to differ for top, middle, and first-line management levels and also to vary by specialized area.

To serve the needs of different organizational levels, there are five major types of information systems: transaction processing, office automation, management information, decision support, and executive support. Decision support systems and related expert systems represent outgrowths of a specialized information technology field called artificial intelligence.

One aid in helping managers think about how to use information technology to achieve competitive advantage is a matrix of major strategic options for information technology. The matrix consists of two main dimensions: strategic targets (suppliers, customers, and competitors) and strategic thrusts (differentiation, cost, and innovation).

Traditionally, the development of new information systems has followed a process known as the systems development life cycle, which includes three stages: definition, physical design, and implementation and operation. Among the most prominent alternative means of systems development are software packages, prototyping, and end-user development.

Managing information system resources raises the issue of how much centralization versus decentralization should be fostered. Each approach has its advantages. Trends have varied since the early 1950s, when computers were first used for commercial applications. The trend is currently leaning toward distributed processing, whereby computers are allocated to various organizational locations to serve local and/or regional needs and are interconnected for electronic communication.

As computers grow more pervasive, information technology is having a considerable impact on many aspects of organizations. Major areas of influence include organization structure, individual jobs, and organizational risk.

MANAGERIAL TERMINOLOGY

applications software
    packages   (719)
artificial intelligence
    (712)
batch processing   (701)
central processing unit
    (CPU)   (701)
computer-based
    information systems
    (CBISs)   (701)
computer virus   (726)
data   (699)

data base   (702)
data-base management
    system   (702)
distributed processing
    (722)
electronic data processing
    (EDP)   (700)
electronic monitoring
    (724)
end user   (720)
end-user computing
    (720)

executive support system
    (ESS)   (712)
hackers   (726)
hardware   (701)
information   (700)
informaton center   (723)
information system   (701)
local area networks
    (LANs)   (722)
logical office   (725)
management information
    system (MIS)   (709)

office automation system
    (OAS)   (708)
on-line processing   (701)
prototyping   (719)
software   (702)
systems development life
    cycle   (717)
telecommuting   (724)
transaction-processing
    system (TPS)   (707)
user   (720)
wide area networks (723)

QUESTIONS FOR DISCUSSION AND REVIEW

1. Differentiate between data and information, and use the systems view to explain the general process by which information is created. Give an example from your own experience of data versus information.

2. Identify the major components of computer-based information systems. Describe the types of computers that you have used or seen used. For what major purposes were they being used?

3. Discuss the characteristics of useful information, and explain how information needs differ by managerial level. How are information needs likely to vary among levels of administration at your college or university?

4. Distinguish among the five major types of information systems. List five activities in which you engage that involve interacting with a transaction-processing system in some way.

5. Describe how considering strategic targets and strategic thrusts can facilitate the development of information systems that provide a competitive advantage. Identify an information system that you believe provides a competitive advantage in some way. Where would it fit on the matrix of major strategic options for information technology?

6. Describe the systems development life cycle. Research suggests that systems development efforts that run into difficulty often have deviated from the systems development life cycle. Why are such deviations likely to create problems?

7. Identify three alternative means of systems development, and explain the advantages of each. Which means would likely to be appropriate for developing an information system to record routine employee information and produce basic reports? Which means would you probably consider for developing a unique new application involving better servicing of client needs, some of which are unclear and evolving? Give your reasoning.

8. Explain the advantages of centralized and decentralized management of information system resources. Which means might be used to help resolve the centralization versus decentralization issue and best utilize information system resources?

9. Describe the major impacts of CBISs on organization structure and individual jobs. Give an example from your own experience and observations that illustrates how computers and information technology have influenced jobs.

10. Explain the major risks associated with information technology in organizations. To what extent do you expect such risks to increase or decrease in the future? Explain the reasons for your view.

DISCUSSION QUESTIONS FOR CHAPTER OPENING CASE

1. Evaluate, in terms of their usefulness, the different types of information that are available at Mrs. Fields Cookies.

2. How has Mrs. Fields Cookies used information technology to achieve a competitive advantage? What other steps could be taken?

3. What has been the likely impact of information technology on Mrs. Fields Cookies in such areas as organization structure, individual jobs, and organizational risk?

MANAGEMENT EXERCISE: SOXSPORT, INC.

You have just landed a job with a relatively new and growing company by the name of Soxsport. The company makes socks that are designed for particular sports, such as running, tennis, golf, and skiing. The socks are designed to give the best foot comfort (through padding, materials, weave, etc.) when the wearer is engaged in the particular sport for which the socks were made. Recently, the company has begun to move into sports clothing designed to coordinate with the fashionable colors of the socks and to meet the needs of individuals seriously engaged in sports. The company's prod-

ucts have proved to be extremely popular, particularly with sporting-goods stores, and sales have been rising steadily.

One major difficulty confronting management is that it takes about 16 people to process an order from the initial customer contact to shipping. One person takes the order; another checks the customer's credit rating; another checks inventory to be sure the items are in stock; another prepares the invoice; another pulls the items from inventory; another boxes the items; etc. Furthermore, it takes almost a week to fill a customer's order. So far, the delay is not much of a problem with individual orders that come through the company's small catalog operation, but it is somewhat of an annoyance to the growing list of sporting-goods stores and specialty shops that are the main source of business.

A related problem is that on telephone orders, it isn't possible to check whether the items are in inventory while the customer is on the telephone. As a result, if the items are not available, a member of the staff needs to call the customer back and ask if a partial shipment is acceptable. It is difficult to talk about substituting other items, since that takes a further trip to check inventory. Some of the customers have been grumbling lately that they get better service from other vendors, and Soxsport's president, Jerry Clark, is beginning to get concerned.

Clark also is having some difficulty determining which items are most profitable. The company deals mainly in stacks of invoices and related materials. Clark has someone plow through these materials periodically to try to get a handle on what is selling and what is not.

Unfortunately, the information is somewhat dated by the time it is available for Clark, the designers, and the production group. In addition, some of the company's merchandise is made abroad, and it is difficult to make adjustments in orders unless they are made on a very timely basis.

When Clark is away from the office, which is often due to sales promotions, the work of the president's office falls way behind. Clark would like to find some ways of keeping things moving even when frequent trips are necessary.

With your background in business courses, Clark is hoping that you will be able to make some useful suggestions about what types of information systems Soxsport might need to operate more efficiently internally. Since company products appear to be ahead of the competition, it would also be useful to think in terms of how the company might use information technology to ensure competitive advantage over potential competitors.

DU PONT'S EDGE IN MANAGING INFORMATION TECHNOLOGY

Du Pont, the chemical and energy giant, has earned a reputation for being at the forefront of managing information technology. The company spends about $500 million per year on computers, software, and related salaries. The large budget reflects the belief that information systems are essential to Du Pont's competitive position. Raymond E. Cairns, Du Pont's vice president for information systems, has told managers that they should look at computers not only as a means of cutting costs but also as a potential tool for increasing revenues and market share.

Du Pont managers have been following Cairns's guidance in a variety of ways. For example, one major Du Pont business that has a strategy of growth through acquisition found itself with a number of different manufacturing approaches because of the various types of manufacturing equipment and processes used by the acquired companies. In order to take a comprehensive view of the problem, a team consisting of both manufacturing and information technology specialists was formed. Having the information technology specialists involved during the problem definition stage enabled the team to develop an innovative approach using information technology. The resulting computer-based system united manufacturing operations and helped them operate at significantly less cost—a change that has enhanced the competitive position of the business.

In another instance, a Du Pont business faced a very competitive environment in which a fairly long distribution chain (e.g., wholesalers, distributors, retailers) existed between the point of manufacturing the product and the point of the product reaching the ultimate consumer. Because of the multiple links in the chain, Du Pont had difficulty obtaining sound market knowledge about the consumers; yet such information was critical to an effective marketing effort. In assessing the problem, marketing managers recognized that using computer-based information systems could help to change the situation. Accordingly, a team of marketing and information specialists was formed; they conceived of an information system that could be used to alter the role of a major part of the distribution chain and, in the process, provide access to previously unavailable market information. Within 1 year of implementation, the new system had helped Du Pont significantly increase its market share.

Du Pont also makes use of expert systems and other types of decision support systems, says Ed G. Mahler, manager of decision support and artificial intelligence. For example, one type of expert system helps manufacturers design items such as squeezable ketchup bottles or microwave containers, a very complex engineering design problem. Du Pont sells the system to manufacturers as a means of expanding the market for one of its products—resin—a substance used by manufacturers in making the various bottles and containers that can be designed with the expert system.

In attempting to utilize its information resources effectively and efficiently, Du Pont has centralized some aspects and decentralized others, says Thomas F. Holmes, division manager of architecture and planning within the computer and systems function. For example, Du Pont has centralized such areas as the basic operations of large computers, implementing and maintaining communiciation networks, setting common data standards, and developing applications that are basically similar across businesses (e.g., computer-based cost systems). Most other resources, though, are allocated to various businesses so that the businesses can use the technology to develop competitive advantages in their various marketplaces. These efforts are linked to some degree with centralized efforts through a goal-setting process. The basic philosophy, Holmes notes, is that information technology resources should be located as close to the individuals running the various Du Pont businesses as possible.

To facilitate the process of decentralizing resources, individuals within the computer and systems function often are given training in a particular business. The training helps them be more effective in identifying how business can use information technology to differentiate itself from competitors.[80]

QUESTIONS FOR CHAPTER CONCLUDING CASE

1. Place two of the information systems developed by Du Pont on the matrix of major strategic options for information technology. Give reasons for your placement decisions.
2. Explain how Du Pont uses the definition stage of the systems development life cycle to enhance the prospects for success.
3. Discuss the advantages and disadvantages of Du Pont's approaches to managing information systems resources—that is, the company's efforts at centralization and decentralization.

MILLIKEN & COMPANY SETS THE PACE FOR QUALITY

Little did Seth Milliken and his partner, William Deering, realize when they started Milliken & Company in 1865 that 124 years later the company would be recognized throughout the world as a leader in quality. In 1989, the company won the coveted Malcolm Baldridge award, sharing the honors with Xerox. The award is presented annually by the U.S. Department of Commerce to honor companies (up to six per year) that have achieved world-class excellence in quality. In presenting the prestigious award to Roger Milliken, chairman and CEO of Milliken, President George Bush said, "The company's management style is sheer twenty-first century."

A major textile manufacturer based in Spartanburg, South Carolina, Milliken produces products that are all around us. Often, though, they are unlabeled because they constitute materials contained in other labeled products. For example, Milliken has about 30 percent of the $1.2 billion U.S. market for the stretchable fabrics used in swimsuits and sportswear. It produces the cloth used in uniforms worn by employees at McDonald's and many other fast-food restaurants. Milliken controls about 40 percent of the $300 million or more market for acetate and acetate blends that are used in coats and women's outerwear. Overall, Milliken manufactures more than 48,000 textile and chemical products, including 60 percent of the upholstery in GM cars, the yellow fabric on Wilson tennis balls, and the washable materials in Crayola markers. Annual sales of the pri-

vately owned company are estimated as easily surpassing $1 billion.

Although the company has long had an established reputation for high-quality products and advanced technology, about a decade ago company executives began to question why some Japanese textile companies were able to produce higher-quality products with less waste, achieve greater productivity, and receive fewer customer complaints while using less sophisticated technology than that employed by Milliken. On the basis of their investigations, Milliken managers found that, in addition to technology, management practices were a key factor in improving quality and efficiency. Accordingly, in 1981 top-level managers launched Milliken's Pursuit of Excellence (POE) program, denoting a commitment to quality and customer satisfaction. Roger Milliken himself and Thomas J. Malone, chief operating officer, have allocated more than half their work time to furthering the POE process.

In one step, the company reduced the number of levels in its hierarchy, reassigning more than 700 managers as specialists to improve the manufacturing process or other aspects of company operations, such as billing and customer service. This reorganization has helped achieve a 60 percent reduction in the cost of nonconformances, such as discounts for products that do not meet quality standards or payments for freight costs for items that customers return. One way that Milliken avoids customer returns is by having no defects. The zero-defects program has been so successful that many customers do not even inspect Milliken shipments. Such high quality has helped increase profits and has attracted additional business. For

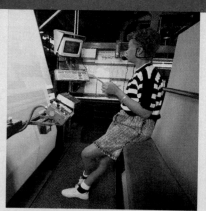

Effective controls are a key to Milliken & Co.'s international reputation for excellence in quality. For example, computers at the giant textile manufacturer monitor productivity and defects by keeping track of every horizontal thread in the looms. Automation also helps control labor costs; 400 looms can be run by only 3 or 4 workers per shift. At the same time, teams of employees, known as "associates," focus on improvements in specific areas, such as supplier and customer relations. The result is that Milliken is one of the most successful companies in the textile industry. Its products are so defect-free that most customers don't even bother to inspect shipments, and its percentage of on-time deliveries is 99 percent.

example, the company is the only U.S. firm to earn approval to ship braided polyester tire cord to Michelin.

In another part of the POE process, Milliken delegated greater authority to its employees, who are referred to as "associates." For example, associates can stop the production process in the event of a quality or safety problem. Many associates are organized into self-managing teams, which have jurisdiction over such activities as scheduling work and setting goals for individual performance. In its improvement efforts, Milliken spends considerable amounts of money on associate training ($1300 per associate in one recent year). In addition, the company recently formed 1600 corrective action teams that focus on making improvements in specific areas inside Milliken. Another 200 supplier action teams concentrate on upgrading relationships with suppliers. Still another 500 customer action teams consider methods of improving service to customers; their efforts so far have led to the development of new products and have helped generate additional sales.

At the end of each assembly line at Milliken plants, there is a bulletin board that is usually heavily covered with notes containing ideas for improvement offered by various associates. The action person, normally the supervisor, must acknowledge receipt of an idea within 24 hours and respond within 72 hours. Frequently, another associate provides additional ideas or offers a solution to a problem. On the average, associates submit about 19 suggestions per year and close to 87 percent of the ideas for improvement are ultimately implemented. When all the members of a team have submitted at least 20 ideas, the team throws a party.

Part of the improvement process involves obtaining customer feedback and engaging in extensive self-evaluation of company performance. Through such efforts, Milliken was able to improve its percentage of on-time deliveries from 75 percent in 1984 to 99 percent by 1988, giving it the best rate in the industry.

Roger Milliken's grandfather, Seth Milliken, originally built up the company mainly by purchasing mills that had fallen into economic difficulty. Gerrish Milliken, Seth's son, continued the expansion before turning the leadership over to his son Roger, who has headed the firm for more than four decades. There are about 200 stockholders of the company, mostly family members. Roger Milliken is generally credited with turning the company into a powerful leader in the textile industry, one that excels in research, technology, quality, and customer service. Describing his management style as "management by wandering around," Milliken spends a considerable amount of his time visiting his 57 plants, several of which are abroad (e.g., in Britain, France, and Belgium). Although he is in his midseventies, Milliken continues to work 90 to 100 hours per week. "The world makes it [hard work] necessary," he says. "Competition gets tougher and things move faster."

One of the ways that Milliken keeps his company ahead of the competition is by investing heavily in new technology. He habitually has his managers purchase the fastest looms, the highest-quality knitting machines, and the most efficient yarn spinners. When a new spinning or knitting machine is introduced, Milliken has been known to buy all the available machines, giving his company an edge over the competition. Recently, he bought 500 additional Belgian looms that can stop automatically to locate defects and then start themselves again.

Because of the heavy volume of business, Milliken is sometimes able to negotiate 6- or 12-month exclusive rights to new fibers from companies such as Du Pont and Hoechst Celanese. The rights enable him to offer new products ahead of the competition.

The company also has more than 1200 patents, reflecting its heavy research in a variety of areas ranging from color-enhancing chemicals to computerized carpet dyers. The company's most famous proprietary development is Visa, an easy-care fabric finish that is used in a wide variety of products, such as clothing, napkins, and tablecloths. As is typical of virtually all aspects of the company, Milliken steadfastly continues to improve Visa, which has undergone major transformations since it was first introduced in the 1960s.

Automation is used to help control labor costs at Milliken. Company plants with as many as 400 high-speed looms can be run with only three or four weavers per shift. As a result, Milliken employs only about 14,800 associates, compared with about 25,000 employees at Springs Industries, a competitor with 30 percent lower sales. Milliken generally does not hire managers from other textile companies; instead, the company chooses promising college graduates and starts them on the factory floor. If they prove themselves, they are given opportunities to move up. Salaries are good, with plant managers usually earning about 30 percent more than counterparts at other firms. Managers typically work about 60 hours per week.

Milliken is a pioneer in the use of profit centers. The company has about 50 strategic business units, which make products ranging from Lycra fabric for bathing suits to upholstery for automobiles. Each unit reports profit and loss results every 4 weeks.

In a departure from its usual practice of developing standard costs as a basis for controls throughout the company, Milliken recently has been placing greater emphasis on the actual costs of processes. The reason is to encourage managers to concentrate on reducing actual costs rather than meeting some standard. Standard costs are still used to evaluate performance at the plant level, but they are updated quarterly (rather than annually, as in the past) to reflect the improvements continually being made in various areas. In addition, the company has placed increased emphasis on nonfinancial measures of process and cost control, emphasizing in particular the following factors: reductions in lead, or throughput, time; reductions in change, or set-up, time; reductions in downtime; reductions in turnaround time for customer samples; increases in on-time deliveries; audits of machinery maintenance; and audits of quality assurance.

The company also pays close attention to its accounts receivables. For example, in the unfinished gray-goods division, customers are expected to pay their bills within 30 days, compared with the 60 days allowed by most competitors. Customers who do not pay on time may find further shipments delayed and may also be charged for storage.

To support the company's production and control systems, computers are used extensively at Milliken. The company has a large mainframe computer at its corporate offices in Spartanburg that maintains the company's major business systems. The mainframe is linked to various plants through minicomputers, which are tied by way of additional communications systems to various personal computers and workstations. Such systems have been essential in Milliken's major move toward computer-aided manufacturing, but they are also used extensively in computer-based information systems that support various controls. Milliken no longer thinks of its information systems as providing only managerial information. In fact, the company has changed the name of its management information center to "Milliken Information Center" to reflect the utilization of the information by all associates.

In one information system application, computers are used to monitor productivity at weaving plants by measuring picks, rather than output of yards of fabric. A pick is a horizontal insertion of thread into a vertical set of threads. Computers monitor each pick and automatically record the data, as well as keep track of machine downtime and the causes. Associates can then use desktop and personal computers to retrieve statistics on individual machines and overall performance, including the printing of graphs that can be displayed on plant bulletin boards. The information, of course, also can be consolidated into reports for upper management on overall productivity. Another recent application is Quick Response, a computerized order service linked to major customers, through which Milliken provides just-in-time service. These systems are just one more manifestation of Milliken's dedication to high quality and innovation.*

QUESTIONS FOR DISCUSSION

1. Identify an example of Milliken's use of each of the following types of control by timing: feedforward, concurrent, and feedback. To what extent does Milliken appear to rely on market, bureaucratic, and/or clan control? Give evidence to support your answer.

2. Explain how Milliken makes use of budgetary controls. Evaluate the likely impact of the increasing emphasis on nonfinancial controls at Milliken.

3. Assess the use of quality control as a competitive advantage at Milliken. Which dimensions of quality appear to receive the most emphasis at Milliken?

4. Identify the strategic role stage that is characteristic of operations management at Milliken. Which of the two major strategic alternatives for operations management has Milliken adopted?

5. Describe two types of computer-based information systems in use at Milliken. Explain how the matrix of major strategic options for information technology applies to the use of information systems at Milliken.

*Sources: See references at back of book.

PART SIX

ACROSS ALL FUNCTIONS

Previous parts of this book introduce management and examine its four major functions: planning, organizing, leading, and controlling. Now in Part Six, we see how these various functions apply in two particularly significant management situations: conducting business in the international arena, and engaging in entrepreneurship and small business management. Fostering innovation is particularly important within these realms because global businesses must keep pace with rapidly changing world conditions, new technology, and increasing competition, while new ventures and small businesses often must maintain a competitive edge just to stay alive.

Since managers in many organizations increasingly must take a worldwide perspective, **Chapter 21** pinpoints the strategic issues and the structural al-lternatives associated with conducting business across national boundaries. One necessary part of being an international manager is learning how to adapt to cultural differences and how to deal with the special social and ethical concerns that can arise in the international domain.

At the same time, most businesses in the United States are relatively small, and even large businesses typically start small. The implication is that it is important to understand the phenomenon of entrepreneurship, which involves the creation of new businesses or ventures, and as well as the particular issues related to managing a small business. **Chapter 22** examines the role of the entrepreneur and explores major considerations that managers of small businesses must address.

CHAPTER TWENTY-ONE

INTERNATIONAL MANAGEMENT

CHAPTER OUTLINE

The Nature of International Management
Changing Character of International Business
Organizations Engaging in International Management
Orientations toward International Management

Assessing the International Environment
Environmental Elements
Promoting Innovation: The Competitive Advantage of Nations

Gauging International Strategic Issues
Methods of International Entry
Multinational Corporation Strategies

Organizing International Business
Worldwide Functional Divisions
Worldwide Product Divisions
International Division
Geographic Regions
Global Matrix

Adapting to Cultural Differences
Managing International Human Resources
Adjusting Leadership Styles

Handling Social Responsibility and Ethical Issues
International Social Responsibility
International Value Conflicts
Questionable-Payments Issue

LEARNING OBJECTIVES

After studying this chapter, you should be able to:

■ Explain the concept of a multinational corporation and explain three major orientations toward international management.

■ Delineate several major elements that are important in assessing the international environment.

■ Explain the concept of the competitive advantage of nations and its linkage to innovation.

■ Outline the major methods of entry into the international business arena.

■ Contrast three major strategies for multinational corporations.

■ Enumerate the major structural alternatives for conducting international business.

■ Explain the major issues related to assignment policies and the recruitment, selection, and training of managerial personnel.

■ Describe the adjustments in leadership style that may be necessary because of cultural differences.

■ Delineate the major social responsibility and ethics issues related to international management.

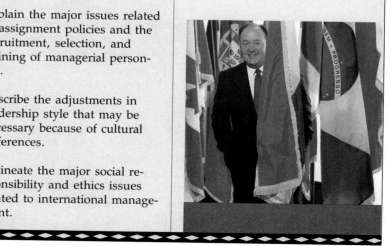

UNILEVER: ONE OF THE WORLD'S LARGEST MULTINATIONAL CORPORATIONS

It is said that the sun never sets on Unilever. The company's more than 300,000 employees operate 500 businesses in 70 countries. Although its corporate name, Unilever, may not be readily recognized, its products are household names and include such famous labels in the United States as Lipton, Dove, Caress, Wisk, Impulse, Aim, Dawn, Snuggle, Surf, Pepsodent, Ragu spaghetti sauces, Pond's face creams, Elizabeth Taylor's Passion perfume, and Calvin Klein cosmetics, to name only a few. With more than $34 billion in annual revenues, Unilever is one of the world's largest consumer goods companies. The company is the foremost producer of margarines throughout the world, and it is the premier seller of detergents outside the United States.

A unique aspect of Unilever is its dual structure—it is actually two companies with two sets of shareholders and two headquarters. Unilever PLC (for Public Limited Company) is based in London, while Unilever NV (for Naamloze Vennootschap, meaning "limited-liability company") is based in Rotterdam. The dual structure can be traced back to a merger of two companies (British Lever Brothers, Ltd., and Dutch Margarine Unie) in 1930. While the two companies remain legally distinct, they are linked by a series of agreements. One major aspect ensures that shareholders of each company participate in the prosperity of the entire Unilever organization by receiving dividends that are equalized across the two companies.

Despite the legal duality, Unilever is run as if it were one company, often referred to by employees as the "Concern." Although each company must have its own board of directors for legal reasons, both boards consist of the same 18 directors (mostly Dutch and British) of the company. At the top executive level, Unilever is run by a triumvirate modestly called the "Special Committee." The Special Committee is made up of the chairman of PLC, the chairman of NV, and a third senior director. All top-level decisions are made by this group. There are 15 directors who report directly to the Special Committee. Beneath them are the subsidiary companies. Various product coordinators help develop and implement product strategies worldwide.

One of the reasons why the seemingly awkward Special Committee structure works is that the committee believes strongly in decentralized decision making. The company follows a policy called "-ization," or nationalization of management, whereby efforts are made to develop local managers in the various countries; the policy is based on the belief that such managers will understand local needs better than managers who were raised elsewhere. At any given point in time, the Special Committee carefully tracks as many as 200 managers, who are moved through various developmental assignments all over the world. In this group, 25 may be considered potential stars, individuals who are slated for eventual assignments at the highest levels of the company.

Unilever recently changed its long-range planning horizon from 5 years to 2 or 3 in recognition of the fast pace of change in the international arena. For example, a business coordinator may submit a 3-year plan for margarine that includes anticipated sales, the number of people required, expected cash flows, and actions that will be taken to increase profit. The plan is then approved or modified by the Special Committee. Within this framework, various business and product coordinators also submit annual plans that are approved by the Special Committee mainly to identify substantial deviations from expectations.

Wherever possible, Unilever likes to sell the same product throughout the world. Lux toilet soap is perhaps the classic example. It's in every country, and it's largely the same in every country. Other products, such as a shampoo called Sunsilk and a body spray called Impulse, also appear in many countries, although the formulation may change somewhat. Food, however, is unlikely to be the same everywhere. As a result, Unilever's strategy is to standardize wherever possible. The company also works to provide customers with new and improved products. Among its innovations introduced in Europe are hamburgers in high-tech foil packages that keep fresh without refrigeration and ketchup bottles made to stand upside down.

Unilever, the world's largest packaged goods company, pitches its worldwide products (such as soap and detergents) to local tastes and makes extensive use of local managers for its more than 500 businesses in 78 countries. Decentralization of decision making and standardization of products are part of the firm's international management strategy.

The major U.S. subsidiary until recently has been Lever Brothers, which handled most of the products mentioned above. Following its decentralized policy, Unilever generally allowed Lever Brothers to operate relatively independently. Unfortunately, the subsidiary, which competes head-on with Procter & Gamble in many areas, performed rather poorly during the 1970s and early 1980s, causing Unilever to send in a new director to take charge. The company wanted to improve its operations because the United States would constitute 40 percent of the potential world market for Unilever goods. Furthermore, Procter & Gamble and other U.S. packaged-goods companies were increasingly penetrating the world markets that Unilever had previously dominated. Analysis of the problems at the U.S. subsidiary revealed that low profitability had caused managers to cut back on expenditures in areas such as advertising. This approach then led to market share problems, lower sales volumes, and higher costs that, in turn, exacerbated the profitability problems.

The new management acted fast, first closing outmoded plants and acquiring more modern production facilities. Next, Lever Brothers took a more aggressive stance in the U.S. detergent business. First came Sunlight dishwasher detergent, then Snuggle fabric softener, and then Surf laundry powder to complement Wisk, its successful heavy-duty laundry detergent. This burst of new products made Lever Brothers a more formidable opponent of Procter & Gamble.

Unilever also enhanced its influence in the United States when it purchased Chesebrough-Pond's, Inc., in December 1986, a move that brought Ragu spaghetti sauces, Ragu pasta meals, Prince Matchabelli fragrances, and Pond's face creams under its control. In 1989 Unilever significantly strengthened its position in the U.S. and worldwide cosmetics field by buying Fabergé and the Elizabeth Arden line of cosmetics, as well as Minnetonka, Inc. (which includes Calvin Klein cosmetics). In 1989, the Lever Brothers Company was reorganized into five separate divisions: Lever Brothers (soap and laundry products), Unilever Personal Products Group, USA (personal-care items and cosmetics), Thomas J. Lipton (teas, dried soups, and other foods), Van den Bergh Foods (margarine and edible fats), and Ragu Foods (spaghetti sauce). On an operational basis, the U.S. companies now report to the appropriate product coordinators.[1]

Unilever is just one of many international companies that touch our lives. We can easily name others that are even more visible, such as Fiat, Honda, Volvo, Michelin, Nestlé, Sony, NEC, Toyota, and Volkswagen. Many observers argue that organizations increasingly need to adopt a global view in planning and carrying out their various activities. Such a perspective enables managers to view their operating area as encompassing the entire world, thus allowing them to tap vast worldwide markets and conduct business activities wherever conditions appear to be most conducive to meeting organizational goals. In fact, one expert argues that a worldwide outlook is already a necessity for competing effectively in a number of industries, such as automobiles, banking, consumer electronics, entertainment, pharmaceuticals, publishing, travel services, and washing machines.[2]

Not only are managers increasingly likely to be engaging in international business themselves, but they are also highly likely to face competition from international organizations or to deal with them in other capacities (e.g., as suppliers or customers). Such developments make it imperative that managers have a solid understanding of international management issues. Accordingly, in this chapter, we explore the basic nature of international management, building further on the coverage of international management issues provided throughout this text. We also probe various environmental factors that are likely to affect managerial success in the international arena, and we consider the notion of the competitive advantage of nations and its relationship to innovation. We then examine a number of strategic issues associated with international management and consider structural alternatives that aid in conducting international business. We next investigate several means of adapting to cultural differences. Finally, we turn to ethical questions that may arise when organizations are conducting business throughout the world.

THE NATURE OF INTERNATIONAL MANAGEMENT

If you took an inventory of the items that are in your living quarters, you would probably find many that reflect the increasing volume of business conducted on an international basis. For example, you might have shoes from Italy or Brazil, a television and VCR from Japan, and a shirt made in Korea. Even items that bear the brand names of a U.S.-based company may have been produced in a far-off land in the course of international business. **International business** refers to profit-related activities conducted across national boundaries.[3] Such activities encompass importing supplies from other countries, selling products or services to customers abroad, or providing for the transfer of funds to subsidiaries in other countries. **International management** is the process of planning, organizing, leading, and controlling in organizations engaged in international business.

International business
Profit-related activities conducted across national boundaries

International management
The process of planning, organizing, leading, and controlling in organizations engaged in international business

Changing Character of International Business

As was pointed out in earlier chapters, there is strong evidence that the United States is losing its competitive edge in international trade and is facing increasing competition in world markets.[4] According to some accounts, the United States enjoyed an abnormal advantage for several decades after World War II because the productive facilities of other large industrial powers had been severely damaged by wartime activities.[5] Now countries such as Japan and Germany have become formidable competitors, and developing nations such as Brazil, India, and South Korea also are emerging as potential major players. Despite the increased competition, though, international markets are growing rapidly, providing expanded opportunities for many U.S.-based businesses. For example, the creation of a unified 12-nation European market (by "harmonizing" various national rules, such as adopting common standards for electric plugs) beginning in December, 1992, has caused many companies to take actions to become major players. For instance, Motorola, which is already an important force in cellular telephones in Europe, is constructing a new $160 million manufacturing plant in Scotland. Similarly, Emerson Electric paid $460 million for Leroy-Somer, a French maker of electric drives and motors in order to establish improved access to the massive new Western European market.[6] Another part of the lure behind such efforts is the prospect of additionally gaining entry to the emerging new markets in Eastern Europe as communism ebbs in the former East bloc. Business potential in the Soviet Union also is improving as a result of *perestroika*, the economic restructuring that is moving the country toward a more market-oriented economy. As one sign of the changes, major Western oil companies, such as France's Societe Nationale Elf Aquitaine, are being allowed to drill for oil on Soviet territory for the first time.[7] India, too, is showing increasing willingness to open up its vast market to foreign business endeavors.[8]

Meanwhile, the recent free-trade agreement between the United States and Canada and similar talks with Mexico raise the possibility of a huge integrated North American market. In anticipation, General Electric Co.'s consumer appliance division is building a gas-range factory in San Luis Potosi in central Mexico that will be able to supply consumers not only in the United States, but also in Canada and Mexico.[9]

While these and other related developments throughout the world present opportunities, conducting business in other countries poses some hazards. A shortage of foreign currency in early 1990 caused the Soviet Union to delay payments for goods obtained from dozens of Western companies. Such problems led Dow Chemical Co. to temporarily stop deliveries of more than $25 million in basic chemicals.[10] As a result of the massacre of pro-democracy protesters in China's Tiananmen Square in 1989, major companies, such as Xerox and Johnson & Johnson, cancelled expansion plans in the country.[11] In Brazil, a recent economic reform plan implemented by President Fernado Collor de Mello to halt the country's serious inflation and other economic problems decreed a temporary freeze on much of the country's money, created foreign exchange losses for many companies, and sparked a recession. As a result, companies like Caterpillar, Whirlpool, and Aluminum Co. of America experienced sudden and serious profit declines.[12] Thus, organizations operating in the international realm typically face considerable challenges as well as opportunities.

Organizations Engaging in International Management

Organizations that engage in international management vary considerably in size and in the extent to which their business activities cross national boundaries. One special type of organization involved in international management is the multinational corporation. Although definitions differ somewhat, the term **multinational corporation (MNC)** is typically reserved for an organization that engages in production or service activities through its own affiliates in several countries, maintains control over the policies of those affiliates, and manages from a global perspective.[13]

Multinational corporations are not always easy to identify, since it may be difficult to determine from the outside how much control management maintains over the policies of affiliates or whether management actually uses a global perspective. As a result, for purposes of gathering statistics, an arbitrary percentage (such as 25 percent of sales from foreign sources) is sometimes used to distinguish multinational corporations from other types of international businesses. However, there is no single universally accepted percentage of foreign sales that clearly separates multinational corporations from others.[14] A listing of the 25 largest industrial multinational corporations in the world is shown in Table 21-1.

Multinational corporation (MNC) An organization that engages in production or service activities through its own affiliates in several countries, maintains control over the policies of those affiliates, and manages from a global perspective

Table 21-1   The World's 25 Largest Industrial Multinational Corporations

RANK 1988*/1987		Company	Headquarters	Industry
1	1	General Motors	Detroit	Motor vehicles
2	4	Ford Motor	Dearborn, Mich.	Motor vehicles
3	3	Exxon	New York	Petroleum refining
4	2	Royal Dutch/Shell Group	London/The Hague	Petroleum refining
5	5	International Business Machines	Armonk, N.Y.	Computers
6	8	Toyota Motor	Toyota City (Japan)	Motor vehicles
7	10	General Electric	Fairfield, Conn.	Electronics
8	6	Mobil	New York	Petroleum refining
9	7	British Petroleum	London	Petroleum refining
10	9	IRI	Rome	Metals
11	11	Daimler-Benz	Stuttgart	Motor vehicles
12	16	Hitachi	Tokyo	Electronics
13	21	Chrysler	Highland Park, Mich.	Motor vehicles
14	18	Siemens	Munich	Electronics
15	17	Fiat	Turin	Motor vehicles
16	19	Matsushita Electric Industrial	Osaka	Electronics
17	15	Volkswagen	Wolfsburg (W. Ger.)	Motor vehicles
18	12	Texaco	White Plains, N.Y.	Petroleum refining
19	14	E.I. Du Pont de Nemours	Wilmington, Del.	Chemicals
20	20	Unilever	London/Rotterdam	Food
21	24	Nissan Motor	Tokyo	Motor vehicles
22	22	Philips' Gloeilampenfabrieken	Endhoven (Netherlands)	Electronics
23	27	Nestle	Vevey (Switzerland)	Food
24	32	Samsung	Seoul	Electronics
25	25	Renault	Paris	Motor vehicles

*▮ U.S.   ▮ EUROPE   ▮ ASIA

Source: Reprinted from *Fortune,* July 31, 1989, p. 282.

Although multinational companies tend to be rather large and to engage in a substantial amount of business transactions across borders, international business also is conducted by a number of midsize companies. For example, members of the American Business Conference (ABC), a coalition of 100 high-growth, midsize companies (average sales of $360 million), constitute one particularly successful group in foreign markets. According to a McKinsey and Company study, group members have expanded their world trade primarily by emphasizing innovation, providing good value rather than necessarily the lowest price, and maintaining good communication with customers. Members of the group include the Millipore Corporation, a worldwide manufacturer of advanced products for fluid analysis and purification; Hasbro, Inc., the toy maker; and Dunkin' Donuts, the donut chain found throughout most of the United States.[15]

Even fairly small companies may engage in international business if they offer a unique product and/or good value. Thorneburg Hosiery, a $10 million company based in Statesville, North Carolina, found that its line of athletic socks, designed and padded for specific sports such as tennis and jogging, quickly appealed to the Japanese attendees at a trade show, leading to a $300,000 initial order.[16]

Regardless of their size, companies may decide to expand internationally for a number of different reasons. Some organizations may become involved through unsolicited orders from foreign customers. Others may initiate international efforts in order to open new markets or to preclude foreign companies from entering specific foreign markets and eventually becoming domestic competitors. Still others may be motivated by the need to develop sources of supplies, possibilities of acquiring needed technology, or prospects for reducing costs by operating in foreign countries.[17] Whatever the reason, managers need to think through their basic orientation toward international management.

Orientations toward International Management

Top-level managers in companies that are expanding internationally (particularly those in multinational corporations) tend to subscribe to one of three basic orientations, or philosophies, regarding the degree to which methods of operating are influenced by headquarters or by company members in other parts of the world. The three orientations are ethnocentric (home-country oriented), polycentric (host-country oriented), and geocentric (world oriented).[18] A *home country* is the country in which an organization's headquarters is located, whereas a *host country* is a foreign country in which an organization is conducting business.

An **ethnocentric** (or home-country) **orientation** is an approach to international management whereby executives assume that practices which work in the headquarters or home country must necessarily work elsewhere. For example, during the period 1973 to 1986, Procter & Gamble lost an estimated quarter of a billion dollars of business in Japan partially because of an ethnocentric orientation. As one former Japanese employee stated, "They did not listen to anybody." One of the most serious blunders was a commercial for Camay soap that was used in the late 1970s. The commercial showed a Japanese man meeting a Japanese woman for the first time and immediately comparing her skin to that of a fine procelain doll. Although this commercial had worked well in the Philippines, South America, and Europe, it was a disaster in Japan. A Japanese advertising specialist who worked on the commercial had warned Procter & Gamble that only an unsophisticated or rude man would say something like that to a Japanese woman, but company representatives would not listen. As the vice-chairman of Procter & Gamble later noted, "We learned a lesson here [in Japan] about tailoring your products and marketing to the market." Today Procter & Gamble is doing somewhat better in Japan.[19] Although an ethnocentric orientation often is a phase that organizations go through when they enter the international arena, it can prove extremely difficult to eradicate.

A **polycentric** (or host-country) **orientation** is an approach to international management whereby executives view host-country cultures and foreigners as difficult to fathom and, therefore, believe that the parts of the organization located in a given host country should be staffed by local individuals to the fullest extent possible. Locals—or nationals, as they are sometimes called—are thought to know their own culture, mores, work ethics, and markets best. As a result,

Ethnocentric orientation An approach to international management whereby executives assume that practices that work in the headquarters or home country must necessarily work elsewhere

Polycentric orientation An approach to international management whereby executives view host-country cultures and foreigners as difficult to fathom and, therefore, believe that the parts of the organization located in a given host country should be staffed by local individuals to the fullest extent possible

subsidiaries in various countries operate almost independently under the direction of local individuals and are tied to the parent company mainly through financial controls. The parent company may maintain a very low public profile relative to the subsidiary, as was the case until recently with Unilever and its U.S. subsidiary, Lever Brothers. It is very possible that you only discovered that Lever Brothers was owned by a foreign company when you read the introductory case to this chapter. Although with a polycentric orientation local individuals run operations in the host countries, they have little prospect of holding senior executive positions at headquarters, largely because they are perceived as having only a local perspective and expertise. Still, a polycentric approach may be successful when decision making is largely decentralized to host-country personnel.

Geocentric orientation An approach to international management whereby executives believe that a global view is needed in both the headquarters of the parent company and its various subsidiaries and that the best individuals, regardless of home- or host-country origin, should be utilized to solve company problems anywhere in the world

The **geocentric** (or world) **orientation** is an approach to international management whereby executives believe that a global view is needed in both the headquarters of the parent company and its various subsidiaries and that the best individuals, regardless of home- or host-country origin, should be utilized to solve company problems anywhere in the world. Major issues are viewed from a global perspective at both headquarters and subsidiaries, which consider questions such as "Where in the world shall we raise money, build our plant, conduct R&D, develop and launch new ideas to serve our present and future customers?"[20] The geocentric approach is the most difficult to achieve because it requires that managers acquire both local and global knowledge.

A geocentric approach helped Boeing save its 737 airplane. Introduced more than 20 years ago to compete with McDonnell Douglas's DC-9, the 737 received a number of initial orders before sales began to slow in the early 1970s. Because the competitor's DC-9 had a somewhat faster speed and a few other superior features, Boeing was ready to scrap its 737 program. When a group of Boeing engineers was given the task of making one final effort to salvage the plane, the engineers began to recognize that they had not given enough attention to a major potential market, the developing regions of the world—mainly the Middle East, Africa, and South America. While developing countries wouldn't buy a large number of planes at once, over a period of time their purchases could be substantial. The engineers decided not to follow the common procedure of developing specifications according to their own ideas of what was needed, using U.S. requirements as the standard; instead, they visited the various countries and got firsthand information. They found that runways in developing countries generally were too short for the 737 and were mainly asphalt, a softer material than concrete. So they redesigned the wings to allow shorter landings on soft pavement and changed the engine so that takeoffs would be quicker. When they went to Africa, they found that the pilots tended to bounce planes when landing, which meant the brakes couldn't work properly and the arriving planes would run out of runway. So they redesigned the landing gear and installed low-pressure tires. Boeing soon began to get small orders for the 737 from a number of developing countries, which later bought larger Boeing planes because of their satisfaction with the 737. Recently, the 737 has become the best-selling commercial jet in aviation history.[21] The Boeing situation helps illustrate the importance of understanding the international environment within which one is attempting to conduct business.

ASSESSING THE INTERNATIONAL ENVIRONMENT

While international management opens up vast opportunities, it also presents the challenge of attempting to understand a much broader set of environmental factors than those typically encountered in managing a strictly domestic business. In this section, we explore the effects of various elements of the international environment and also consider a relatively new concept, the competitive advantage of nations.

Environmental Elements

The notion of the general environment, or mega-environment, can be helpful in exploring the nature of international management. The general environment is the segment of the external environment that reflects broad conditions and trends in the societies within which an organization operates (see Chapter 3). Major elements of the general environment, such as economic, legal-political, sociocultural, and technological, can be used to explore the international realm more thoroughly.

The Economic Element. Different types of economic systems of countries are discussed in Chapter 3. Additional important economic factors that influence the ability of organizations to conduct international business successfully are the levels of economic development in various countries, the presence of adequate infrastructures, a country's balance of payments, and monetary exchange rates.

Countries, other than the communist ones, fall into two major classifications based on the economic or industrial level of development. The first group, known as **developed countries,** is characterized by a high level of economic or industrial development and includes the United States, western Europe, Canada, Australia, New Zealand, and Japan. The other noncommunist countries fit into the second group, known as **less developed countries (LDCs)** or *developing countries*. The LDC category, often called the "third world," consists primarily of relatively poor nations characterized by low per capita income, little industry, and high birthrates. Within the LDCs, countries that are emerging as major exporters of manufactured goods are often referred to as **newly industrialized countries (NICs),** a designation that covers such countries as Hong Kong, Taiwan and South Korea.

While we often may think of multinational corporations as operating extensively in developing countries, actually about 95 percent of such companies are based in developed countries and about 75 percent of foreign investment has been channeled to developed countries. Nevertheless, the rising prosperity of many less developed countries (particularly those in the NIC group) provides the potential for tremendous expansion of current world markets.[22] Such prospects, however, must be carefully assessed on a country-by-country basis to ensure that the level of economic development supports adequate markets for particular products.

The decision to conduct business in a given area also will depend heavily on the availability of an adequate infrastructure. **Infrastructure** is a broad term that refers to the highways, railways, airports, sewage facilities, housing, educational institutions, recreation facilities, and other economic and social amenities that signal the extent of economic development in an area. For example, transportation facilities are important for moving various supplies and products, while educational facilities may be a factor in the availability of an adequately educated work force. Similarly, recreational and cultural facilities influence a company's ability to attract managerial and professional employees to a given area. For example, in an effort to develop Manaus, an inland city on the Amazon River that is surrounded by jungle for about 1000 miles in every direction, the Brazilian government built a modern airport, improved communications facilities, and encouraged the establishment of a renowned opera, a world-class

Developed countries A group of countries that is characterized by a high level of economic or industrial development and that includes the United States, western Europe, Canada, Australia, New Zealand, and Japan

Less developed countries (LDCs) A group of noncommunist countries, often called the "third world," that consists primarily of relatively poor nations characterized by low per capita income, little industry, and high birthrates

Newly industrialized countries (NICs) Countries within the LDCs that are emerging as major exporters of manufactured goods, including such nations as Hong Kong, Taiwan, and South Korea

Infrastructure The highways, railways, airports, sewage facilities, housing, educational institutions, recreation facilities, and other economic and social amenities that signal the extent of economic development in an area

With generous tax incentives and transportation improvements, Brazil has lured some 400 international and local companies to locate in Manaus, an inland city on the Amazon River. The government has been so successful in developing the city that some environmentalists fear that the continual expansion will have a detrimental effect on the surrounding jungle.

Balance of payments An account of goods and services, capital loans, gold, and other items entering and leaving a country

Balance of trade The difference between a country's exports and imports

hotel, and other amenities to attract outside workers. More than 300 multinational corporations and about 100 local companies now have factories in the city, since operating in Manaus is a key to doing business in Brazil.[23]

Another significant economic variable is a country's **balance of payments,** an account of goods and services, capital loans, gold, and other items entering and leaving a country. The **balance of trade,** the difference between a country's exports and imports, is generally the most critical determinant of a country's balance of payments. Constant trade deficits result in the exportation of a country's wealth, whereas surpluses enhance a country's ability to expand and conduct even more international trade. Recently, the United States has been suffering from an imbalance in trade due to more imports than exports.[24] A country's balance of payments may affect its willingness to allow profits and certain types of currencies to leave the country. For example, the Soviet Union generally does not allow foreign businesses operating there to take profits out of the country unless they are earned in foreign currencies or taken out in the form of Soviet-made goods, such as Russian dolls or Ukrainian carvings.[25] Because of such limitations in some countries, Unilever sometimes makes further investments in particular countries with the profits earned in those places; for example, it has invested in cultivating sunflowers in Kenya and establishing palm plantations in Nigeria and the Ivory Coast.[26]

Exchange rate The rate at which one country's currency can be exchanged for another country's currency

A related issue is the **exchange rate,** the rate at which one country's currency can be exchanged for another country's currency. Exchange rates fluctuate depending on a variety of international economic factors, including shifts in world demand for a particular country's exports. Changes in exchange rates can have a profound impact on the ability of a firm to engage in international business because exchange rates affect the relative prices of goods from various countries. For example, the declining value of the dollar in the late 1980s made automobiles imported from Japan more expensive in the United States because Japanese companies needed to charge more dollars to earn the same amount of profit in their own currency. Conversely, the declining dollar made U.S. goods cheaper on world markets, helping companies such as Caterpillar, a U.S. maker of tractors and other earth-moving machinery, which has been locked in ferocious competition with foreign companies, particularly Komatsu, Ltd., of Japan.[27]

The Legal-Political Element. Both legal and political conditions affect the ability of organizations to conduct business in a given country. Major considerations include the level of political risk associated with doing business in a particular country, the degree to which trade barriers are erected by various governments, and the business incentives offered by governments.

Corporations must closely assess the political risk involved in establishing themselves in a given country.[28] **Political risk** is the probability of the occurrence of political actions that will result in loss of either enterprise ownership or significant benefits from conducting business.[29] The seizure of a foreign company's assets by a host-country government is called **expropriation.** In the past such countries as Cuba, Zambia, and Iran have expropriated assets of foreign-owned corporations located within their borders. Iran seized the assets of many American companies, including the Iranian operations of Xerox, R. J. Reynolds, and United Technologies, which were valued at an estimated $5 billion when the Ayatollah Khomeini took over the Iranian government in 1979. Since 1960 more than 1535 companies have been expropriated by 76 nations.[30] Other political risks are less severe but may make it more difficult or expensive to conduct business in a host country. Managers at Exxon have developed a policy for dealing with political risk after the company has established itself in a host country. If there appears to be a major escalation of risk, the managers may add 1 to 5 percent to the required return on investment for further expansion of operations in that country.[31]

Another aspect of the legal-political environment is trade control, the creation of barriers or limitations on goods entering or leaving a country.[32] Such barriers often are erected so that domestically produced goods will have a competitive price advantage over the goods of foreign competitors. Other major reasons include raising governmental revenue or discouraging domestic purchases of foreign-made goods. The most common type of barrier is the **tariff,** a customs duty, or tax, levied mainly on imports. The impact of tariffs can be seen in the relative prices of an American-built Chrysler Reliant K car that during the late 1980s could be purchased in the United States for $10,000 but cost $48,000 in Korea.[33] Another type of barrier is an **import quota,** a limit on the amount of a product that may be imported over a given period of time. Import quotas can protect a domestic market by restricting the availability of foreign competitors' products. The United States implemented an import quota on Japanese-made cars during the 1980s, when the large number of imports was severely damaging the domestic automobile industry.[34] The quotas were a factor in causing a number of Japanese companies to begin manufacturing automobiles in the United States.

Because tariffs and quotas tend to engender direct reprisals from countries whose products are affected, a country may use the more subtle approach of **administrative protections,** various rules and regulations that make it more difficult for foreign firms to conduct business in a particular country. Examples include veterinary regulations, such as quarantines for imported animals; buy-national policies, which give preference to domestic products or require that imports contain a certain percentage of domestic parts; and complex customs regulations, which can cause delays and add to costs. In one well-known situation, Japanese video recorders were required to pass through French customs at a small facility at Poitiers, where they were inspected one by one, creating tremendous delays. Because actual importation of the recorders slowed to a dribble, the Japanese manufacturers eventually agreed to a "voluntary export quota," limiting the number of recorders that they shipped to France.[35]

While countries often institute various barriers to international trade for a host of reasons, they also frequently take action to encourage foreign companies

Political risk The probability of the occurrence of political actions that will result in loss of either enterprise ownership or significant benefits from conducting business

Expropriation The seizure of a foreign company's assets by a host-country government

Tariff A type of trade barrier in the form of a customs duty, or tax, levied mainly on imports

Import quota A type of trade barrier in the form of a limit on the amount of a product that may be imported over a given period of time

Administrative protections A type of trade barrier in the form of various rules and regulations that make it more difficult for foreign firms to conduct business in a particular country

to operate within their borders in order to boost economic development. In the United States, attempts to attract foreign industry are largely made through inducements (such as tax breaks, road building, and subsidies for worker training) offered by state and local governments. Through massive recruiting efforts and special incentives, Tennessee has managed to attract about 12 percent of the total Japanese manufacturing investment in the United States, creating at least 7000 jobs.[36] Many other countries (such as Mexico, South Korea, Taiwan, and Brazil) also offer a variety of tax breaks, cash grants, and other financial incentives to foreign companies that locate operations within their borders.[37]

The Sociocultural Element. The sociocultural element of the environment includes the attitudes, values, norms, beliefs, behaviors, and associated demographic trends that are characteristic of a given geographic area. When comparing individuals in different nations, it is common to speak in terms of cultural differences.

Dutch social scientist Geert Hofstede has developed a framework for studying the effects of societal culture on individuals.[38] In developing his framework, he researched the values and beliefs of more than 100,000 IBM employees working in 40 countries throughout the world. Although the study has been criticized for focusing on only one organization, the framework is proving to be useful for studying other organizations and countries. Hofstede's approach involves four cultural dimensions that can be used to analyze societies: power distance, uncertainty avoidance, individualism-collectivism, and masculinity-femininity. Each dimension represents a continuum from high to low.

Power distance is the degree to which individuals in a society accept differences in the distribution of power as reasonable and normal. In low-power-distance societies, such as those of Sweden, Denmark, and Israel, people from different backgrounds interact more frequently with one another, and members of lower status can move more easily to higher-status positions. In contrast, in societies with high power distance, such as those of Mexico, the Philippines, and India, individuals of high status have very limited interaction with lower-status individuals, and it is very difficult to raise one's status. Such differences affect the degree of collaboration between subordinates and their bosses. With high power distance, managers are more likely to tell subordinates what to do rather than consult with them. On the other hand, greater collaboration between managers and subordinates is likely in a low-power-distance society.

The second dimension in Hofstede's framework, **uncertainty avoidance,** is the extent to which members of a society feel uncomfortable with and try to avoid situations that they perceive as unstructured, unclear, or unpredictable. For example, in low-uncertainty-avoidance countries, such as Sweden, Great Britain, and the United States, organizations tend to have fewer written rules and regulations in order to facilitate the development of generalists (who know about many different areas) as opposed to specialists (who know a great deal about a narrow area) and to encourage risk taking among managers. Organizations operate in opposite ways in countries with high uncertainty avoidance, such as Japan, Peru, and France.

Individualism-collectivism, the third dimension, refers to the degree to which individuals concern themselves with their own interests and those of their immediate family as opposed to the interests of a larger group. In cultures that place a high value on individualism, managers are more likely to switch companies when opportunities arise, feel less responsible for the general welfare of employees, and rely more on individual than on group decision making.

Power distance A cultural dimension that involves the degree to which individuals in a society accept differences in the distribution of power as reasonable and normal

Uncertainty avoidance A cultural dimension that involves the extent to which members of a society feel uncomfortable with and try to avoid situations that they perceive as unstructured, unclear, or unpredictable

Individualism-collectivism A cultural dimension that involves the degree to which individuals concern themselves with their own interests and those of their immediate family as opposed to the interests of a larger group

High-individualism countries include the United States, Great Britain, and Canada. In contrast, in cultures that value collectivism, managers tend to focus on team achievements rather than individual ones, emphasize employee welfare, and view the organization as if it were a family. Countries that are high on collectivism include Venezuela, Taiwan, and Mexico.

The fourth dimension, **masculinity-femininity,** involves the extent to which a society emphasizes traditional male values such as assertiveness, competitiveness, and material success rather than traditional female values such as passivity, cooperation, and feelings. In relatively masculine societies, such as those of Japan, Italy, and Mexico, employees tend to believe that jobs should provide vehicles for recognition, growth, and challenge. In more feminine societies, such as those of Sweden, Finland, and Yugoslavia, there is greater emphasis on good working conditions, security, feelings, and intuition in decision making. Masculine societies tend to define very different roles for men and women; as a result, opportunities for women in organizations tend to be limited to some degree. Of course, Hofstede's labels reflect common stereotypes about male and female values, which may not apply to particular individuals.

In the course of his work, Hofstede developed clusters, or groups, of countries that have similarities on the four value dimensions. The United States falls in a cluster that is characterized by lower-than-average power-distance and uncertainty-avoidance values, higher-than-average masculinity values, and high individualism. Hofstede's study showed that Americans placed a higher value on individualism than did people in any other country in the study. Other researchers argue that the United States reflects this individualism through such heroes as Lee Iacocca of Chrysler; H. Ross Perot, formerly of EDS; and Sam Walton of Wal-Mart Stores.[39]

Still, there are many differences among countries and within countries that must be taken into account. Even within the United States, we recognize significant regional differences. For example, PepsiCo divides its U.S. operations into four regions to take into consideration the variations in regional markets. McDonald's works with 74 different advertising agencies serving various parts of its U.S. market.[40]

The Technological Element. The technological environment is also a particularly significant aspect because the level of technology in various countries affects the nature of markets and the ability of companies to conduct business. In fact, considerable technological transfer typically takes place in the course of engaging in international business. **Technological transfer** is the transmission of technology from those who possess it to those who do not. The technology can be in the form of tangible goods or processes, such as component parts or machinery, or in the form of intangible know-how, such as advanced knowledge of road-building techniques. International technological transfers occur through a variety of means such as joint ventures, licensing agreements for the use of technology within certain parameters, in-house transfers of technology to foreign subsidiaries, attendance at educational institutions in other countries, and the purchase of products or services (by means of which competitors can obtain information about a given technology). After General Electric Co. purchased the Tungsram Co., a state-owned light bulb maker based in Budapest, Hungary, in order to boost its position in lighting in Europe, Tungsram's factories and computer systems required major technological overhauls.[41]

Technological innovation is important both for competing in global markets and for protecting domestic markets from foreign competition. While the United States is the source of considerable technological transfers to other countries,

Masculinity-femininity A cultural dimension that involves the extent to which a society emphasizes traditional male values such as assertiveness, competitiveness, and material success rather than traditional female values such as passivity, cooperation, and feelings

Technological transfer The transmission of technology from those who possess it to those who do not

several researchers argue that U.S. companies need to take greater advantage of possible technological advances in other countries. For example, between 1966 and 1981, Japanese companies paid U.S. firms about $3.8 billion in royalties and fees for licensed technology, while U.S. firms paid Japanese companies only approximately $165 million.[42] These figures indicate that Japanese companies have licensed considerable technology from U.S. companies, while the reverse is not true. In addition, approximately 800 U.S. citizens are studying at Japanese universities, compared with about 13,000 Japanese citizens studying at U.S. universities.[43] Thus there is evidence that U.S. companies need to expend greater efforts in obtaining technology from others, rather than engaging in one-way technological transfer.

Promoting Innovation: The Competitive Advantage of Nations

Competitive advantage of nations The concept that environmental elements within a nation can foster innovation in certain industries, thereby increasing the prospects for the success of home-based companies operating internationally within those industries

In considering the impact of environmental factors on organizations, strategy expert Michael E. Porter has developed the notion of the competitive advantage of nations.[44] The **competitive advantage of nations** is a concept which holds that environmental elements within a nation can foster innovation in certain industries, thereby increasing the prospects for the success of home-based companies operating internationally within those industries. The competitive success of such companies, of course, has positive implications for national prosperity as well.

Porter's views are based on the argument that companies achieve competitive advantage through innovations. Such innovations may be radical breakthroughs or small incremental improvements (see Chapter 7), as long as organizations continually upgrade their innovative efforts to stay ahead of the competition. The likelihood of innovation among companies in given industries, though, is influenced by the characteristics of the nations within which the companies are based.

The Diamond of National Advantage. In explaining why certain companies are able to innovate on a consistent basis, Porter identifies four national attributes that individually and as a system establish the diamond of national advantage (see Figure 21-1). The national attributes depicted in the diamond determine the conditions within which a nation's industry players must operate.

Factor conditions are components of production, such as skilled labor or infrastructure, that are needed to compete effectively in a particular industry. Factors have the most impact on competitive success when they are highly specialized, require continual heavy investment, and are directly related to a particular industry's needs. Examples are a scientific institute that specializes in optics and major sources of capital that will fund new software companies—factors that can foster innovation in home-based companies. For example, Holland, with leading research institutes in the cultivating and shipping of flowers, is the world's principal flower exporter.

Demand conditions are the characteristics of the domestic demand for the products and services of an industry. While home demand for products and services may appear to be of lesser importance to organizations operating internationally, domestic demand conditions can be a critical factor in establishing a competitive advantage. The reason is that the makeup of the home market often has a major impact on how companies envision and respond to customer needs. When home buyers are sophisticated and exacting, companies are pressured to innovate and meet high standards. Demand conditions can further aid a nation's companies in gaining a competitive advantage when domestic consumers tend

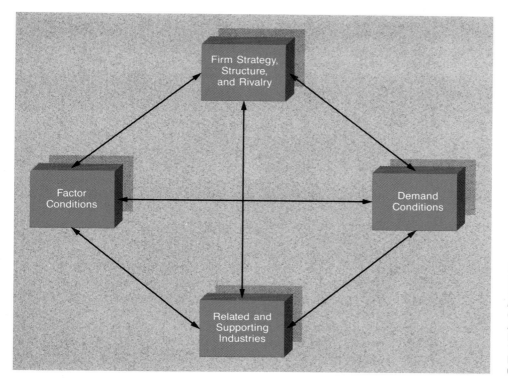

Figure 21-1 Determinants of national competitive advantage. (Reprinted by permission of *Harvard Businessd Review*. An exhibit from ''The Competitive Advantage of Nations,'' by Michael E. Porter, March/April 1990. Copyright © 1990 by the President and Fellows of Harvard College; all rights reserved.)

to anticipate and even influence the needs of consumers in other nations. For example, strong environmental concerns in Denmark have prodded companies in that country to develop world-class expertise in water-pollution control equipment and windmills.

The attribute of *related and supporting industries* refers to the availability within the nation of supplier and other related industries that compete effectively on an international basis. Such industries can help create competitive advantages in several ways. For one thing, they can provide cost-effective inputs and the latest developments rather quickly to home-based companies. In addition, the lines of communication frequently are shorter, allowing for the relatively free flow of information and the constant exchange of information that increase the likelihood of innovations (see Chapter 15). Moreover, companies can become testing sites for potential supplier breakthroughs, thus hastening the tempo of innovation.

Firm strategy, structure, and rivalry comprise the major conditions in a nation that affect the way in which organizations are created, organized, and managed, as well as the character of domestic rivalry. For example, successful international firms in Italy tend to be small- or medium-size companies that are privately owned and that function almost as extended families. This profile is well suited to the industries in which Italian firms tend to excel, such as lighting, furniture, footwear, and woolen fabrics—all of which require strategies that include customized products, fast change, and ample flexibility. On the other hand, companies in Germany are likely to be fairly hierarchical in orientation and to have top managers with strong technical backgrounds. The German approach has been particularly successful in industries that rely on strong technical and engineering expertise, such as optics, chemicals, and complicated machinery. These industries also typically involve complex and precise design and manufacturing processes that are compatible with the German management approach. In addition, the prestige that a nation accords to various industries affects the flow of capital and human resources to those industries and influences their prospects for competitive advantage. Finally, one of the most important factors in the diamond is the presence of strong domestic rivalry, which stimulates innovation and the development of competitive advantage. Porter argues that domestic rivalry is a vital factor precisely because it pressures all the local members of an industry to innovate and upgrade their efforts. For example, the rivalry among the major Swiss drug firms (Hoffman-La Roache, Ciba-Geigy, and Sandoz) serves to enhance their leading global positions. A similar point could be made about the computer industry in the United States, and about the machine tool, semiconductor, audio equipment, and camera industries in Japan.

Implications for Organizations and Their Managers. In the final analysis, though, companies themselves must develop competitive advantages. Porter argues that they must take action on the basis of the factors contained in the diamond of national advantage and particularly must recognize the "central role" played by innovation in achieving a competitive advantage. Among the most important steps that a company's management should take is fostering pressures for innovation through such means as seeking sophisticated and demanding buyers, working with advanced suppliers, establishing high performance standards, and working to develop and retain valuable human resources. Another important step is establishing early warning systems by continually assessing critical aspects of the environment. Another is helping to improve the national diamond by working closely with home-based buyers, suppliers, and other channels in encouraging them to innovate and improve. Still another is welcoming domestic rivalry. Another useful step for companies is expanding international business dealings on a selective basis that allows the tapping of advantages in other nations, such as sophisticated buyers or important research (in other words, expanding to enhance a competitive advantage rather than for expansion alone). For example, the Electro Rent Corporation, which rents and leases electronic equipment, entered the Japanese market in order to facilitate staying abreast of technological developments in both the United States and Japan.[45] Another step is using alliances with foreign companies only selectively, mainly because such alliances tend to preclude developing an independent competitive advantage. Finally, an additional step is locating company headquarters (or the headquarters of substantial businesses) in nations that will support a competitive advantage for the business. Although Porter's ideas are based on considerable research, they are quite new; further investigations will be necessary for a complete assessment of their applicability. Nevertheless, the issues raised by Porter help to further highlight the importance of long-range planning and strategic management in the realm of international business.

GAUGING INTERNATIONAL STRATEGIC ISSUES

Many companies involved in international business, particularly multinational corporations, engage in long-range planning. The planning period normally incorporates a 3-, 5-, or 7-year horizon. Studies of U.S., German, and Japanese multinationals indicate that much of the planning is done at the headquarters level, with some involvement by subsidiaries.[46]

Although most companies conducting international business appear to en-

The Biggest Roach in Japan contest won this Okinawa woman a weekend in Tokyo but it also helped earn a quarter share of the insecticide market in Japan for American Cyanamid's cockroach killer, Combat. The product itself is exported to Japan where packaging is then done to meet local language and regulatory requirements. Since this promotion, the Combat brand has been acquired by Clorox Company.

gage in long-range planning, their initial efforts to do business in the international arena are likely to focus on more narrow goals than becoming a full-fledged multinational corporation. Accordingly, we first consider the major methods of international entry before examining several strategic approaches for multinational corporations.

Methods of International Entry

Companies contemplating entering or expanding international business typically have several alternative methods of entry. There are four main entry methods that organizations can use to expand into different countries: exporting, licensing, establishing joint ventures, and operating wholly owned subsidiaries.[47]

Exporting. **Exporting,** the process of making a product in the home country and sending it overseas, is a common means of entering international markets for organizations that manufacture products. A major advantage of exporting is that it requires very little in the way of additional capital if the product does not need modifications for sale abroad. There also is relatively low risk involved, especially if the company ships products only after payment has been guaranteed.

    Exporting does have some serious potential disadvantages. For one thing, various tariffs and taxes, as well as transportation costs, are typically involved. In addition, the exporter may have difficulty promoting products adequately in other countries. If the product is successful, local competition may emerge. As one means of minimizing the disadvantages of exporting, many companies engage *foreign sales representatives*, local individuals who have a good understanding of product and market needs and whose activities may also help to deter the emergence of competition.

Exporting The process of making a product in the home country and sending it overseas

Licensing. **Licensing** is an agreement in which one organization gives limited rights to another to use certain of its assets, such as expertise, patents, copyrights, or equipment, for an agreed-upon fee or royalty. Typically, a license allows the licensee to use the assets within a certain territory and for a specified length of time. A main advantage of licensing is that an organization can make profits without the large outlays required to conduct business directly. Also, since the licensee is usually from the particular country involved, the licensee is familiar with the culture and the methods of doing business there.

    Licensing has several major potential disadvantages, however. Perhaps the most important is that it usually precludes the licenser from conducting business involving the licensed product or service in a given territory for 5, 10, or even 20 years. If the product or service is very successful, the licenser will have given up the much greater profits associated with doing business directly. Another major disadvantage is that the licenser may be establishing a potential competitor, since licensees often have the right to produce an equivalent product or service after the license has expired. Also, the licensee may not perform at a desired level, affecting licensing revenues and long-term business potential. Coca-Cola recently engaged in a legal battle to buy back the license that it granted to Pernod Ricard, a major French beverage maker. A principal reason was Pernod's tendency to push its own brands at the expense of Coke.[48] Still, licenses may be the only feasible means a given organization has of doing business abroad, owing to lack of resources for international expansion or limitations on imports imposed by certain countries.

Licensing An agreement in which one organization gives limited rights to another to use certain of its assets, such as expertise, patents, copyrights, or equipment, for an agreed-upon fee or royalty

Joint Ventures. A *joint venture* is an agreement involving two or more organizations that arrange to produce a product or service jointly (see Chapter 3). Examples of international joint ventures include the fiber-optics venture between Siemens A.G. and Corning, the robotics venture between Fujitsu and General Electric, and the factory automation venture between Westinghouse Electric and Siemens A.G.[49] Joint ventures typically represent a **direct investment,** the establishment of operating facilities in a foreign country, although with a joint venture the direct investment is limited to the degree of ownership that a company has in the venture. According to one estimate, approximately 20 percent of direct investments are in joint ventures.[50] Many companies seek to have a majority interest in joint ventures so that they can maintain control over operations. However, in a number of countries, foreign companies are limited to a minority interest or have been required to reduce their proportion of interest over a specified period of time. For example, in the People's Republic of China, joint ventures with companies from capitalist countries have been permitted only since 1980, and such companies may not hold majority interest in the ventures.

> **Direct investment** The establishment of operating facilities in a foreign country

One advantage of joint ventures is that they can provide a means of gaining access to countries where full equity is not permitted. Other advantages include possibilities for lowering the risk of introducing new products, for staying abreast of new technology, and for combining the technical expertise and capital of one partner company with the local knowledge held by the host-country partner. Major disadvantages include possible losses if the venture is not successful, possibilities of expropriation, and potential disagreements among partners that may be difficult and time-consuming to resolve. For example, a joint agreement between the American Motors Corporation (now owned by the Chrysler Corporation) and the Chinese government to produce jeeps in Beijing resulted in an endless series of exasperating incidents and few profits for American Motors.[51]

Wholly Owned Subsidiaries. A **wholly owned subsidiary** is an operation on foreign soil that is totally owned and controlled by a company with headquarters outside the host country. Like joint ventures, wholly owned subsidiaries represent direct investments; however, in this case, the productive facilities are totally owned by one company. Wholly owned subsidiaries can be established either through acquisitions (buying an existing company in a foreign country) or through start-ups (developing a company from scratch).

> **Wholly owned subsidiary** An operation on foreign soil that is totally owned and controlled by a company with headquarters outside the host country

Wholly owned subsidiaries offer several major advantages. The parent company has sole management authority to operate the subsidiary within the existing laws of the foreign country where it is located; profits do not need to be shared with partners; technology and expertise remain under the control of the parent company; and the subsidiary may enhance the ability of the parent company to service worldwide customers. The most important disadvantage, aside from the substantial costs involved, is that the facilities and considerable expertise—representing a substantial investment and completely located within foreign borders—may be subject to expropriation if there is a major shift in the political environment. IBM, which generally establishes wholly owned subsidiaries, declined to make direct investments in India because of limits to total ownership of subsidiaries and other onerous conditions. The Coca-Cola Company also closed its operations in India rather than give up majority control and risk revealing its secret formula for Coke.[52] Italy's Benetton Group is a good example of a company that has used licensing, and wholly owned subsidiaries, to expand worldwide (see the following Case in Point discussion).

CASE IN POINT: Benetton Makes Unique Ideas
Work Worldwide

Sometimes called "the McDonald's of fashion," Italy's Benetton Group now has about 5000 sportswear shops, featuring brightly colored knit clothing, in over 75 countries. The development of Benetton constitutes a rags-to-riches story about four siblings, one sister and three brothers, who built a billion-dollar empire beginning in the early sixties after Giulianna (the sister) began designing attractive knitwear. The knitwear sold well, spawning what was to become a major multinational corporation and the largest wool consumer in the world.

The basic idea behind the company's success is to make clothing that not only is fashionable but also can be produced on a major scale so that prices are affordable. To boost affordability, the Benettons have eliminated the wholesaler and all the intermediaries. They rely mainly on independent licensees who sell Benetton merchandise directly to customers in specially designed stores with the now-famous Kelly-green fronts. Benetton's licensees pay no fees or royalties. Instead, they commit to selling only Benetton-made goods. Although it can cost more than $100,000 for a licensee to set up a Benetton store in the United States, profits can be sizable if the sales volume is high. The profits come from the markup on the clothing purchased from the Benetton Group.

Benetton goods are manufactured mainly in Italy, where the company has seven factories. The company also has wholly owned manufacturing facilities in other countries, such as France, Spain, the United Kingdom, and the United States. The U.S. facility in Rocky Mount, North Carolina, opened in 1986 to help meet domestic demand for cotton and denim goods and to shorten ordering time. Manufacturing in the United States also has helped shelter Benetton's U.S. licensees against the impact of the falling dollar, which had been pushing up the prices of Italian-made Benetton goods.

Part of the company's prosperity is attributable to a special technique for making sweaters in undyed wool and dyeing them a short time before shipping. This approach allows the company to react rapidly to fashion trends and fill orders from licensees quickly. To make the system work, the company has invested in a computerized inventory system and a huge $20 million computer-controlled warehouse that is bigger than a domed sports arena. The warehouse has 16 robots and a complex conveyor system to help handle 12,000 boxes per day.

Benetton works at keeping a steady stream of new merchandise in its stores. Besides the traditional outlets aimed at its core market of women between the ages of 15 and 30, the company is developing Benetton 012 stores for children, Sisley higher-priced boutiques, and Benetton Uomo shops for men. It is also expanding product lines by adding such items as Bulova watches, Polaroid sunglasses, Giulianna Benetton shoes, and Colors de Benetton fragrances.

As the number of stores in the United States moves toward the 650 range, some U.S. licensees have complained that Benetton is licensing too many stores in close proximity and that the company has violated a number of oral agreements with store owners. Licensees are chosen by one of Benetton's nine U.S. agents. These company representatives also show new collections to licensees every 6 months, earning a 5.5 percent commission on orders they receive. To help increase company service to licensees and respond to their complaints, Benetton recently has named an individual to head U.S. operations and has organized Benetton USA, an autonomous New York–based company.[53]

Multinational Corporation Strategies

As companies such as Benetton expand their international business dealings, they need to develop appropriate international strategies. Multinational corporations, and to a lesser extent other organizations conducting business in the international arena, must weigh two important factors: the need to make optimum economic decisions on a global basis and the requirement to be responsive to significant host-country differences. Accordingly, multinationals have three major strategy options: worldwide integration, national responsiveness, and multifocal emphasis.

Worldwide Integration. A **worldwide integration strategy,** sometimes called **globalization** (or globalism), is aimed at developing relatively standardized products with global appeal, as well as rationalizing operations throughout the world. Rationalizing operations, or **rationalization,** involves assigning activities to those parts of the organization, regardless of their location, that are best suited to produce the desired results and then selling the finished products where they are likely to yield the best profits. Thus a multinational might consider such factors as costs, expertise, raw materials, and availability of capacity in deciding where particular work is to be done. Rationalization facilitates taking advantage of economies of scale and making the best use of worldwide organizational resources.

Automobile production represents a classic case of globalization. The Japanese, in particular, have been extremely successful in designing automobiles that can be manufactured on a massive scale to meet global markets, thus achieving major economies of scale. Recently, several Japanese auto manufacturers, such as Mazda, Honda, and Nissan, have established automobile plants in the United States as well as in other countries. In addition, more than 150 Japanese parts companies now have facilities in the United States, a number that is expected to double in the 1990s.[54]

Globalization is based on the notion that there are a number of products that can be used around the globe with little alteration of specifications. Coca-Cola, which is sold in 155 countries, is a classic example of a global product requiring only limited alterations of formula. Not all products and situations lend themselves to globalization. Thus, under some circumstances, multinational organizations may need to consider alternative strategies that are more responsive to local needs.

National Responsiveness. A **national responsiveness strategy** allows subsidiaries to have substantial latitude in adapting products and services to suit the particular needs and political realities of the countries in which they operate. As such, a national responsiveness strategy sacrifices many of the potential advantages of worldwide integration. Subsidiaries operate almost as if they were national companies, although they retain many of the substantial benefits of being affiliated with a multinational company, such as shared financial risks and access to global R&D resources. However, it may be a successful approach in situations in which globalization is not feasible because of the need to cater to national differences.

For example, Parker Pen, Ltd., was doing well with a national responsiveness strategy that involved about 500 styles of pens produced in 18 plants. Local offices in about 150 countries created their own packaging and advertising geared to local tastes. Then, in 1983, company officials read a *Harvard Business Review* article highlighting the advantages of globalization, arguing that technol-

Whirlpool Corp., under CEO David Whitwam, is pursuing a global strategy. The giant appliance manufacturer is developing a "world washer" program that includes spending $110 million on a marketing campaign in Europe, moving some of its production to Mexico to take advantage of lower labor costs, and designing a smaller-than-average washer with 30 percent fewer parts for consumers in developing nations.

Worldwide integration strategy, or **globalization** A strategy aimed at developing relatively standardized products with global appeal, as well as rationalizing operations throughout the world

Rationalization The strategy of assigning activities to those parts of the organization, regardless of their location, that are best suited to produce the desired results and then selling the finished products where they are likely to yield the best profits

National responsiveness strategy A strategy of allowing subsidiaries to have substantial latitude in adapting products and services to suit the particular needs and political realities of the countries in which they operate

ogy has created immense global markets for standardized consumer products, and contending that "different cultural preferences, national tastes and standards, and business institutions are vestiges of the past."[55]

Taking the globalization argument to heart, Parker Pen officials consolidated pen styles down to about 100 choices manufactured in 8 plants, and they developed one international advertising campaign that was then translated into a number of local languages. Profits plunged when local managers resisted the singular advertising approach, which ultimately failed, leading to a $12 million loss for fiscal 1985 and the sale of the company to a group of its British managers the following year. Profits rebounded when the company switched back to a national responsiveness strategy.[56] Thus, in developing an international strategy, managers need to evaluate their situations extremely carefully, testing for a global market before making massive moves in that direction.

National responsiveness often is needed in such industries as nuclear engineering and electric power, since political factors often necessitate considerable product customizing in these fields. Other products that typically must be tailored to respond to national tastes are food and personal-care items, such as cosmetics. On the other hand, the significantly larger costs normally associated with a national responsiveness strategy must be justified by the existence of a clear need for that type of responsiveness.

Multifocal Emphasis. A **multifocal strategy** is aimed at achieving the advantages of worldwide integration whenever possible, while still attempting to be responsive to important national needs. For example, Citicorp is attempting to create the largest investment bank in the world. The expansion involves constructing a multi-million-dollar global communications network to service worldwide client investment needs, but it also is aimed at providing in-depth investment coverage in a growing number of countries where Citicorp has offices.[57] Thus the strategy involves both worldwide integration and national responsiveness. Organizations with multifocal strategies are typically more difficult to manage because they need to be concerned with two dimensions simultaneously. The integration aspect requires careful coordination from headquarters, yet the national responsiveness aspect requires considerable feedback from subsidiary personnel and strong efforts to integrate local information into the global perspective. Another organization that is attempting to implement a multifocal strategy is Texas Instruments, a long-time leader in microchips (see the following Case in Point discussion).

> **Multifocal strategy** A strategy aimed at achieving the advantages of worldwide integration whenever possible, while still attempting to be responsive to important national needs

CASE IN POINT: Texas Instruments Strives for a Multifocal Perspective

Although Texas Instruments (TI) operated throughout the world, including Asia, for more than two decades, the company was deriving only some of the potential benefits of a multinational corporation. For the most part, the subsidiaries in various countries operated as separate fiefdoms, with little regard for the overall needs of the company or other subsidiaries. One implication of this approach was that the various subsidiaries operating independently contributed to a huge buildup of excess capacity. This excess caused the company serious problems when the international semiconductor market took a severe downturn in 1985. Jerry R. Junkins, who took over as CEO of TI at that point, has since been working to take better advantage of the company's global position.

Junkins wants managers to consider the capabilities and needs of the company as a whole, as well as the requirements of their own particular subsidiaries

A Japanese engineer works with an American and an Indian at Texas Instruments in Dallas. TI's international subsidiaries used to operate as separate fiefdoms, but now the company is switching to a multifocal strategy—combining some of the advantages of worldwide integration with the need to be responsive to national needs. For instance, TI's top executive in Japan is also responsible for the company's worldwide strategy for memory chips.

when making decisions. He is taking decisive steps to bring about the desired multifocal perspective. For example, he has given Akira Ishikawa, the executive in charge of TI operations in Japan, responsibility for TI's global memory-chip business. Because Japan is such a heavy user of memory chips, it is tempting for Ishikawa to add local production capacity. But because he is responsible for the global business as well, Ishikawa must weigh carefully any further investments in Japanese plants when chip capacity is available in other parts of TI. As a result, he placed a large order with a TI plant in Lubbock, Texas, for chips slated for export to Japan. As part of the deal, he exacted a commitment from the Lubbock plant that the order would receive first priority even if chip demand increased in the United States.

Another aspect of Junkins's campaign for a multifocal view is the company's requirement that managers with global responsibilities meet once each quarter to set worldwide strategy. The executives work in small groups to resolve the various conflicts that arise from attempts to coordinate their individual investment and product development plans. They ultimately produce a detailed agreement that spells out how much money will be spent on each program and where. In order to signal commitment to the plan, each manager must individually stand up and write his or her name on a blackboard, while the group leader makes a permanent record of the event with a Polaroid picture. TI managers and their staffs keep in touch through the company's worldwide private communications network, involving 40,000 terminals in 50 countries.

Junkins is trying to create an organization that can learn to effectively utilize global economies of scale to make a profit in the viciously competitive memory-chip business. At the same time, he wants the company to gain and maintain the competitive edge that comes from producing customized chips. With customized chips, customers design their own products around state-of-the-art chips produced by companies such as TI. The worldwide strategy meetings help managers pinpoint various customers' needs so that investments can be geared to satisfying the largest number of buyers regardless of their global location. Helped by a worldwide increase in the demand for chips, TI's new multifocal approach appears to be working.[58] ■

ORGANIZING INTERNATIONAL BUSINESS

In addition to considering strategic issues, managers involved in international business need to choose the most appropriate organization structure, given the nature of their organization's global pursuits. Most of the research on appropriate organizational designs has centered on multinational corporations. Such corporations tend to adopt one of five types of organization structures: worldwide functional divisions, worldwide product divisions, international division, geographic regions, and global matrix.[59]

Worldwide Functional Divisions

With worldwide functional divisions, top-level functional executives at the parent company have worldwide responsibility for the separate functions, such as manufacturing, marketing, and finance (see Figure 21-2). Thus the various functional units within a foreign subsidiary report directly to the respective functional units of the parent company. The strength of this structure is that it provides strong functional expertise to foreign subsidiaries in areas such as manufacturing and engineering. However, because actions must be coordinated

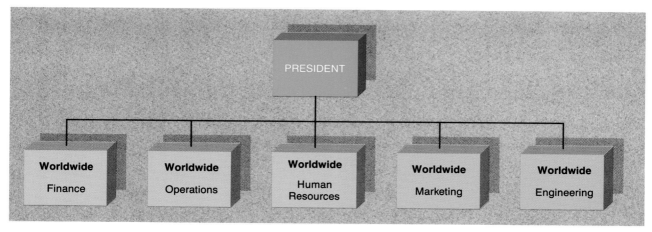

Figure 21-2   Worldwide functional divisions structure.

across various functional units, the structure can hamper quick reactions to changing circumstances in various countries and to competition if there are a number of diverse products. Generally, this structure works best when a few related products are sold in a relatively uniform market worldwide and there are few foreign subsidiaries.

Worldwide Product Divisions

With worldwide product divisions, top-level executives are responsible for particular product areas worldwide (see Figure 21-3). With this type of structure, there is a tendency for the parent company to put particular emphasis on coordination of product-related decisions but to allow the foreign subsidiaries to run other aspects of their organizations. Because of its product focus, this structure

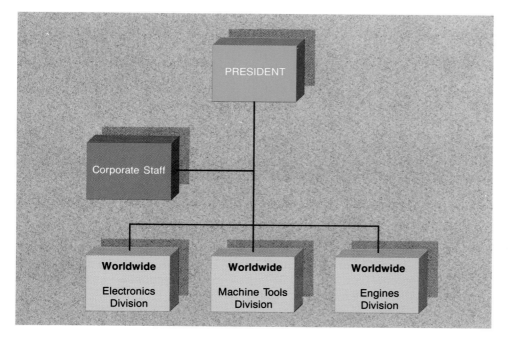

Figure 21-3   Worldwide product divisions structure.

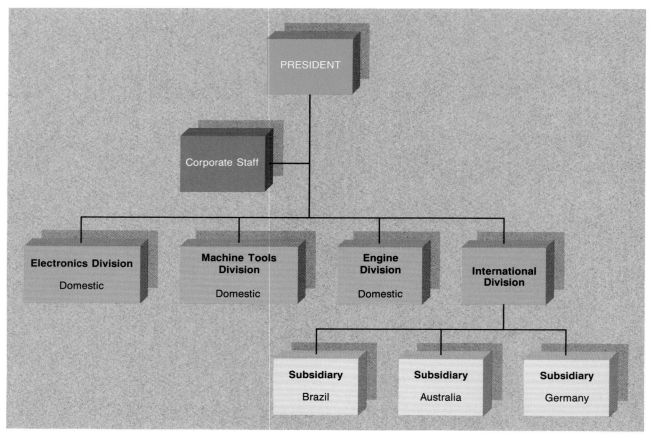

Figure 21-4 International division structure.

is likely to be most effective in organizations whose products are technologically complex, highly diverse, or subject to rapid change. It is highly compatible with a worldwide integration strategy when there are a number of diverse products to consider.

International Division

With an international division structure, a separate division is created to which all foreign subsidiaries report. Figure 21-4 shows a multinational company with domestic product divisions and an international division (an international division could also be added to a functional structure, but the form is less prevalent).[60] The addition of the international division creates representation for geographic issues at the same level as that of the product interests, but makes it more difficult to coordinate information between domestic product divisions and the international division. The international division structure is an asset when foreign sales are proportionally large enough to justify centralizing international expertise at a single point in the organization, while subsidiaries are still able to take advantage of the technological- and product-related strengths offered by the parent. One study of 37 large U.S. multinationals showed that the international division was the most prevalent form.[61]

Geographic Regions

Under this organizational design, the world is divided into regional divisions, with subsidiaries reporting to the appropriate one according to location (see Figure 21-5). This type of structure facilitates the flow of information within regions but inhibits information exchange across regions. As a result, it is particularly well suited to catering to national differences and provides strong support for a national responsiveness strategy. This approach is generally impractical unless foreign sales are a relatively large proportion of total sales and important regional differences justify duplication of functional or product staffs for each region. The geographic regions structure is used much more widely by European than by U.S. multinational firms because U.S. firms tend to have relatively large domestic markets, making one of the other structural alternatives somewhat more suitable.[62]

Global Matrix

The global matrix structure is one in which equal authority and responsibility are assigned along at least two dimensions, with one dimension being region and the second usually being either product or function. A global matrix, with region and product as the two dimensions, is shown in Figure 21-6. Under this matrix structure, middle-level executives report to two bosses who share authority over decisions affecting a particular region and particular product area of business. Dow-Corning, a multinational company, has experimented with a global matrix design involving three dimensions so that middle managers reported to three bosses (one each for region, function, and product). Some authors have argued that a global matrix structure, usually with two dimensions (region and prod-

Figure 21-5 Geographic regions structure.

- PRESIDENT
- Corporate Staff
- North American Division
- Latin American Division
- European Division
- Middle Eastern/African Division
- Far Eastern Division

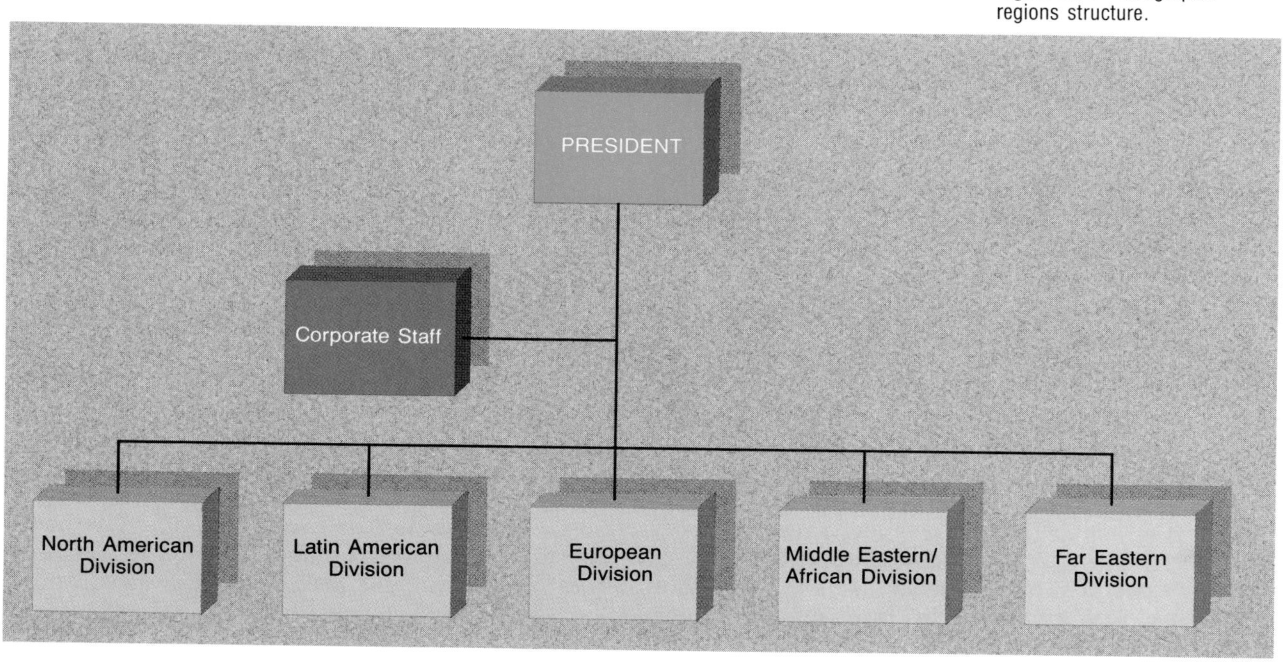

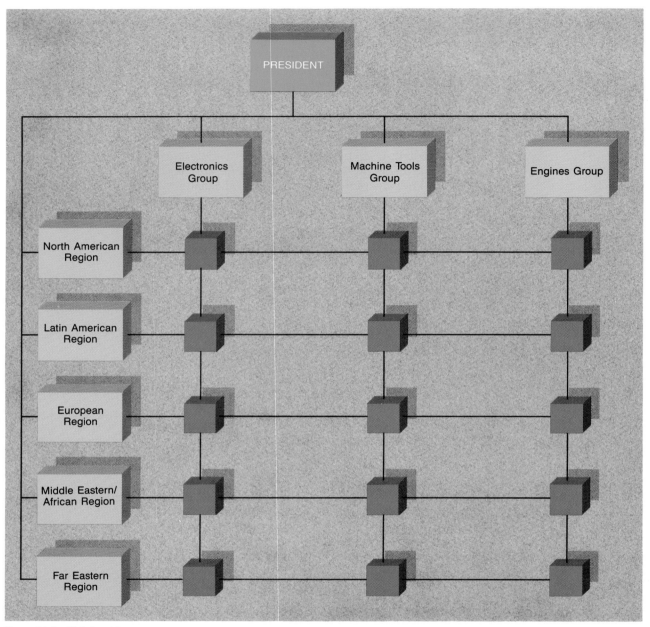

Figure 21-6 Global matrix structure.

uct), is necessary when an organization is pursuing a multifocal strategy.[63] However, a recent survey of 93 U.S. multinationals found that only one had a global matrix structure. Several executives reported that they prefer to use other mechanisms to address multifocal issues, such as task forces and liaison positions (see Chapter 10).[64]

ADAPTING TO CULTURAL DIFFERENCES

While structural considerations are important, another major aspect of effective international management is adapting to cultural differences. Critical issues include managing international human resources and adjusting leadership styles.

Managing International Human Resources

One prominent researcher on international management, Rosalie Tung, argues that U.S. companies operating overseas need to place greater emphasis on the strategic management of human resources in order to gain a competitive edge in international markets. Multinationals, in particular, require a carefully developed cadre of managerial talent in order to function effectively. Areas of particular concern are assignment policies, recruitment approaches, and the selection and training of managerial personnel.

Assignment Policies. An international organization has basically four major policy options regarding staffing sources for key managerial slots in overseas operations: local nationals, parent company personnel, international personnel, or mixed sources. With a *local option,* key positions for each subsidiary are filled with nationals from the country where the subsidiary is located. This approach has the advantage of filling important positions with individuals who are familiar with the local context; it is likely to result in lower salary levels, and it eliminates the need for cross-cultural adjustments. However, local managers may not be as knowledgeable about the management techniques, products, and technology of the parent company as managers from the home office would be.

With the *parent company option,* the parent has a representative in each subsidiary who is well versed in the policies and procedures of the overall multinational company, may be more knowledgeable than local employees about the latest technological developments of the parent, and likely has good lines of communication back to parent headquarters. This option often is used in the early stages of internationalization, when there usually is a major need to transplant various aspects of the parent company, particularly technological expertise, to the subsidiary. Its major disadvantages are resistance from host governments that want foreign subsidiaries to be staffed by local nationals, the blocking of promotion possibilities for local managers, the possibility that too much parent direction may inhibit necessary responsiveness to the particular national situation, and the expense of keeping parent company personnel at various subsidiaries. In addition to normal salaries and benefits, expenses may include allowances for such items as a car, education for children, housing, cost-of-living adjustments, international medical coverage, and moving costs. For example, typical first-year expenses for sending a U.S. executive to Great Britain are likely to be in the $300,000 range. Costs related to particularly expensive areas such as Stockholm or Tokyo will be substantially higher. In some locations, it may be necessary to provide other special arrangements to accommodate personnel from outside the host country. For example, Lockheed Aircraft developed a color television broadcasting station in Saudi Arabia for its 4000 employees assigned there.[65]

With the *international option,* multinationals attempt to assign the best person to do the job, regardless of the person's nationality or the location of the job. Such a policy aids a multinational in fostering a geocentric approach to global management and developing truly multinational managers. Thus this approach has considerable appeal. It also has the advantage of providing considerable upward mobility for managers throughout the organization. From a practical point of view, the international option often runs into difficulty due to the major expenses involved in training and relocating a large number of executives and their families. Another substantial stumbling block is the tendency of host countries to want foreign subsidiaries to be staffed by local nationals, which is also somewhat of an impediment to the parent company option. Currently, most multinationals follow a mixed option, generally assigning mostly local nationals to foreign subsidiaries, home-country nationals to headquarters, and a mixture of the two to regional offices, if regions exist.[66]

Recruitment. Regardless of the assignment policy followed, ample evidence suggests that companies engaged in international business need to expend greater effort in recruiting competent individuals for key overseas positions. For example, U.S.-educated foreign students provide a potential, but underutilized, source of national management talent for foreign subsidiaries.[67]

Expatriates Individuals who are not citizens of the countries in which they are assigned to work

Women constitute another virtually untapped source of managerial talent. A 1983 study by international management researcher Nancy J. Adler indicated that women constituted only 3 percent of expatriate managers in a sample of 686 U.S. and Canadian companies engaged in international business. **Expatriates** are individuals who are not citizens of the countries in which they are assigned to work. In a follow-up study with international personnel managers from 60 of the American and Canadian multinational firms, Adler found that the personnel managers perceived major barriers facing women in overseas assignments compared to domestic ones.[68] For example, 72.7 percent of the personnel managers cited foreigners' prejudice, while 53.8 percent noted the reluctance of company managers to select women for foreign assignments.

To gain information about the actual experiences of female expatriate managers, Adler interviewed 52 such managers either while they were on assignment in Asia or after they returned to North America. Because some had had more than one overseas assignment, they represented working experiences in 61 countries. The women came from many different types of industries, including financial, manufacturing, and service sectors. More than 90 percent of the managers were the first females in their positions, and almost 25 percent were the first females their companies had sent overseas. However, 97 percent of the women reported success in their jobs, with most firms sending another female manager expatriate after witnessing the performance of the first female manager. Interestingly, almost half the women (42 percent) reported that being a female was advantageous in their assignments, largely because of being highly visible. Only 20 percent saw their gender as being mainly a negative factor in their work abroad.[69]

Selection and Training. Most organizations engaging in international business to a substantial degree are likely to have at least some managers working overseas within all the assignment options. Unfortunately, the failure rate of expatriates assigned to various countries is substantial, ranging between 25 and 40 percent. Such failures are expensive in terms of the direct costs of bringing an expatriate home early and providing a replacement. Indirect costs, such as loss of self-esteem of the executives and resultant business difficulties in the subsidiary, add to the total.[70] At least part of the high failure rate for expatriates stems from serious shortcomings in expatriate selection and training.

In the selection area, most multinational corporations tend to use technical skills as the major criterion for selecting individuals for overseas assignments. While technical skills are extremely important for expatriate success, considerable evidence also points to the need to consider *relational skills,* the ability of the expatriate to relate effectively with host nationals. For one thing, expatriates need to be able to develop long-lasting friendships with host nationals so that they can really learn about the country where they are assigned. For another, they must be able to communicate effectively with host nationals. The necessary communication skills typically involve a willingness to use the host nationals' language; confidence in carrying on communication with others; the ability to engage in local small talk, such as anecdotes, jokes, and comments on movies and sports events; and the desire to understand and relate well with host nationals.[71] Indicative of the flexibility required, Ben Lochtenberg, an Australian who is currently chairman of the American subsidiary of Great Britain's Imperial Chemical Industries (ICI), has found the need to adjust his communication style even in countries with a common language. For example, when he worked in England, he found that his direct Australian manner created difficulties, so he learned the more indirect British approach (e.g., saying "Perhaps you ought to think about this a little more" to convey "You must be mad—forget it"). In the United States, though, Lochtenberg found that when he used the same sentence ("Perhaps you ought to think about this a little more"), the subordinate interpreted it literally and forged ahead with the project.[72]

Unfortunately, sufficient training of expatriates for assignments is often lacking. One study of 80 U.S. multinationals found that only 32 percent of the respondent firms had formalized training programs aimed at preparing individuals for overseas assignments.[73] Some of the main reasons for the lack of training appear to be feelings among human resources administrators that such training is ineffective, dissatisfaction of expatriate trainees with the training, insufficient time for adequate training before departure, or views that such assignments are too short to warrant expensive training.[74] Yet evidence suggests that rigorous training programs geared to preparing expatriates for extensive contact with host nationals are important for expatriate success.[75] For example, one American manager recently assigned to France rented a luxurious apartment and invited all the personnel in his office to a large party. Unfortunately, he did not realize that it is unusual for French employees to be invited to their superior's home. Furthermore, the party involved people from all levels of the organization, as well as employees' spouses, individuals who normally did not mix socially. This extremely awkward situation got things off to a bad start, from which the manager was never able to recover.[76]

Adjusting Leadership Styles

Although some scholars argue that behavior in organizations is becoming more similar across nations, managers may still find the need to adjust their leadership styles because of cultural factors.[77] In studying leadership issues, management scholars have found it difficult to isolate the effects of culture from other variables such as differences in economic development and resources in various countries. As a result, there is still a great deal to be learned about effective leadership in different nations and cultures.

On the basis of his major study of a large American multinational (discussed earlier in this chapter), Hofstede argues that managers need to consider particularly the power-distance index in determining appropriate leadership styles in different countries. In high-power-distance countries (such as Mexico, the Philippines, and India), in which individuals tend to accept large differences in the distribution of power in institutions and organizations, subordinates are likely to expect superiors to act fairly autocratically, be somewhat paternalistic, be subject to different rules than are subordinates, and enjoy privileges not available to subordinates. In medium-power-distance countries (such as the United States, Japan, and Italy), subordinates are likely to expect to be consulted but will accept some autocratic behavior. They also expect laws and rules to apply to all, but they accept some level of privileges and status symbols for superiors that are not available to subordinates. In low-power-distance countries (such as Sweden, Denmark, and Israel), subordinates expect to be consulted on most issues, prefer a participative democratic style of leadership, and may rebel or strike if superiors appear to be stepping outside their authority. Typically, laws and rules are seen as applying to all employees, and privileges and status symbols for superiors are not viewed as acceptable. Thus there is some evidence that managers operating in different cultures need to adjust their leadership behaviors according to the different power-distance expectations of subordinates.[78] Recent work using Hofstede's four cultural dimensions—power distance, uncertainty avoidance, individualism-collectivism, and masculinity-femininity—indicates that these dimensions may also be useful in predicting the behavior of CEOs in different cultures.[79] Research such as Hofstede's provides a basic framework for thinking about leadership issues in different cultures. Organizational social responsibility and managerial ethics are other important areas that require special managerial consideration when organizations are operating in the international realm.

HANDLING SOCIAL RESPONSIBILITY AND ETHICAL ISSUES

Issues of organizational social responsibility and managerial ethics are addressed extensively in Chapter 4. In this section, we examine several major concerns that are related particularly to international management.

International Social Responsibility

Many of the issues relating to social responsibility are compounded when an organization engages in a substantial amount of international business. A major reason is the large increase in the number of social stakeholders involved (customers in various countries, communities in various countries, etc.; see Chapter 4), particularly when business is conducted through subsidiaries in multiple countries. During the early 1970s, large multinational corporations came under severe criticism for their potentially harmful effects in developing nations in regard to such issues as exhausting natural resources, diverting wealth to developed nations, and attempting to manipulate LDC governments. Currently, the severity of the criticisms has dissipated, largely because of stronger LDC governments, the rise of multinationals based in developed countries besides the United States, the emergence of LDC multinationals, the growing number of smaller multinationals, and greater adaptability of multinationals to local conditions.[80] Still, the debate continues to some degree regarding the benefits of versus the harm wrought by large, powerful multinational corporations, particularly in LDCs.[81]

International Value Conflicts

The public in the home country often monitors aspects of multinational corporate behavior abroad and may institute pressure if it finds some policy or mode of operation unacceptable. For example, on the basis of views in the United States and throughout most of the world, many major companies, including General Motors, IBM, Eastman Kodak, and Coca-Cola, either sold or discontinued their operations in South Africa during the 1980s because of that country's apartheid policies. Other issues are less clear-cut. For example, General Foods, a company with a good reputation in the area of social responsibility, came under pressure for its policy of buying coffee from El Salvador and Guatemala. A group of shareholders prepared a petition citing concern over human-rights violations in the two countries, but company officials expressed concern about having a business corporation take independent action to affect political change in a country.[82] Such situations illustrate the complex ethical issues that companies are likely to encounter when doing business in the international arena.

Questionable-Payments Issue

One of the most pervasive international ethical issues involves **questionable payments,** business payments that raise significant ethical questions of right or wrong either in the host nation or in other nations.[83] Difficulties with questionable payments arise because of differences in the customs, ethics, and laws of various countries regarding different types of payments. The most common forms of questionable payments are political payments (usually funds to support a political party or candidate), bribes (money or valuables given to a powerful person to influence decisions in favor of the giver), extortion (payments made to protect a business against some threatened action like cancellation of a franchise), sales commissions (payments of a percentage of a sale, which become questionable if paid to a government official or political figure or if unusually large), and expediting payments (normally, money given to lower-level government officials to ensure cooperation and prompt handling of routine transactions). Many of these types of payments are considered to be legal and acceptable in many parts of the world, but they are generally viewed as unethical and/or illegal in the United States.

The U.S. Foreign Corrupt Practices Act, passed in 1977 and recently amended, prohibits most of the questionable payments just described when they are made by U.S. companies doing business in other nations. Making expediting payments to low-level government officials is generally permitted. Supporters argue that the law will ensure ethical conduct, encourage other nations to discontinue questionable payments, help discourage corruption in the governments of other nations, and increase accurate reporting to shareholders. Detractors contend that the law represents an ethnocentric attempt to impose U.S. ethical standards on the rest of the world regardless of other nations' laws and customs. They also say that the law places U.S. companies at a disadvantage when they are competing with businesses from other countries where such payments are allowed. In a *Business Week* survey of 1200 senior U.S. executives, 78

Questionable payments
Business payments that raise significant ethical questions of right or wrong either in the host nation or in other nations

percent agreed that the law makes it difficult to do business in countries where bribery is an accepted way of life and felt that the law hurts U.S. exports. About 20 percent said that they had actually lost business because of the act.[84]

With its complex issues and intriguing prospects, the international realm also offers a rich source of opportunities for new ventures and small businesses, subjects that we explore further in the next chapter.

CHAPTER SUMMARY

International management is the process of planning, organizing, leading, and controlling in organizations engaged in international business. A considerable amount of international business is conducted by multinational corporations. Multinational corporations are organizations that engage in production or service activities through their own affiliates in several countries, maintain control over the policies of those affiliates, and manage from a global perspective. Multinationals and other organizations engaged in international business typically subscribe to one of three basic orientations or philosophies in engaging in international management: ethnocentric, polycentric, and geocentric.

Various elements of the international environment affect the ability of organizations to engage in business beyond national borders. The economic element includes the level of economic development in various countries, the presence of adequate infrastructures, a country's balance of payments, and monetary exchange rates. Major issues related to the legal-political element are the degree of political risk associated with a particular country, the degree to which trade barriers are erected by governments, and various business incentives offered to encourage foreign business investments. Within the sociocultural element, Hofstede has identified four major dimensions related to cultural values: power distance, uncertainty avoidance, individualism-collectivism, and masculinity-femininity. The technological element includes various methods of technological transfer, an important aspect of international business. The concept of the competitive advantage of nations refers to elements within a nation that can foster innovation in certain industries, thereby increasing the pros-

pects for the success of home-based companies operating internationally within those industries. The elements make up the diamond of national advantage and include factor conditions, demand conditions, related and supporting industries, and firm strategy, structure, and rivalry.

Most companies involved in international business engage in both short- and long-range planning. Organizations have four main entry methods that they can use to expand into different countries: exporting, licensing, establishing joint ventures, and operating wholly owned subsidiaries. Major strategies used by multinational corporations include worldwide integration, national responsiveness, and multifocal emphasis. Major organization structures for multinational corporations are worldwide functional divisions, worldwide product divisions, international division, geographic regions, and global matrix.

Adapting to cultural differences requires careful consideration of managing international human resources, including assignment policies, recruitment approaches, and the selection and training of managerial personnel. Although some scholars argue that leadership issues are becoming more similar across nations, there still appear to be differences in the leadership styles that are likely to be effective in various cultures.

Conducting international business raises complex issues regarding social responsibility, international value conflicts, and questionable payments. The U.S. Foreign Corrupt Practices Act prohibits most questionable payments when they are made by U.S. companies doing business in other nations.

MANAGERIAL TERMINOLOGY

administrative protections (745)
balance of payments (744)
balance of trade (744)
competitive advantage of nations (748)

developed countries (743)
direct investment (752)
ethnocentric orientation (741)
exchange rate (744)
expatriates (762)

exporting (751)
expropriation (745)
geocentric orientation (742)
globalization (754)
import quota (745)

individualism-collectivism (746)
infrastructure (743)
international business (738)
international management (738)

less developed countries (LDCs) (743)
licensing (751)
masculinity-femininity (747)
multifocal strategy (755)
multinational corporation (MNC) (739)

national responsiveness strategy (754)
newly industrialized countries (NICs) (743)
political risk (745)
polycentric orientation (741)

power distance (746)
questionable payments (765)
rationalization (754)
tariff (745)
technological transfer (747)

uncertainty avoidance (746)
wholly owned subsidiary (752)
worldwide integration strategy, or globalization (754)

QUESTIONS FOR DISCUSSION AND REVIEW

1. Explain the concept of a multinational corporation. Identify several major companies that probably are multinational corporations. Give reasons for your selections.
2. Describe three major orientations toward international management. Find a newspaper or magazine article that discusses a company engaged in international business. Which orientation appears to best depict the company's approach to international management?
3. Outline several major elements that are useful in assessing the international environment. How could you use these elements to help provide advice to a foreign company interested in doing business in the United States?
4. Explain the concept of the competitive advantage of nations. Use the concept to assess the ability of conditions in the United States to foster innovation among home-based companies in an industry of your choice. What suggestions might you have to improve conditions?
5. Enumerate the major methods of entry into international business. Explain the advantages and disadvantages of each method. Which would you be likely to use if you were running a small company with few resources but had a product with potentially broad international appeal? Would you use a different approach if you were running a large company that had considerable funds available? Give your reasoning.
6. Explain the three major strategic alternatives for conducting international business. For each strategic alternative, recommend a type of business that would likely be successful if it adopted that strategy.
7. Describe the five major organization structures used by international businesses. Identify a type of business that you would like to manage on an international basis, and explain the organization structure that you believe would be most appropriate. Explain your reasoning.
8. Describe the major issues related to assignment policies and the recruitment, selection, and training of managerial personnel for international assignments. What recommendations would you make to companies that are just beginning their international expansions?
9. Assess the types of adjustments in leadership style that managers may need to make because of cultural differences. What advice might you give to members of a local company who are going to set up a wholly owned subsidiary in the Philippines? How might your advice differ if the subsidiary was to be in Denmark?
10. Explain the social responsibility and ethical issues that international managers are likely to confront. What steps might you, as a manager, take to prevent questionable payments from being made by subordinates engaging in international business in behalf of your company?

DISCUSSION QUESTIONS FOR CHAPTER OPENING CASE

1. Unilever prefers to have local managers for its subsidiaries, yet it has mainly British and Dutch employees on its board of directors and "Special Committee." Is this approach viable or not? Would you insist that other nationalities be represented on the board of directors and the Special Committee? Why, or why not?
2. What general strategy does Unilever follow in conducting international business? Is its approach appropriate given the current international environment?
3. Assess Unilever's use of organization structure to support its international management orientation. What are the implications of the recent shift in structure relating to its operations in the United States?

MANAGEMENT EXERCISE: GOING INTERNATIONAL

You have worked many years on a revolutionary combination automatic washer and dryer, which went into production for the first time last year. It has been an astounding success in the United States, and you are now considering going international with your new product. You have had numerous inquiries and offers from businesses around the world but believe that you will concentrate on business in Canada, Great Britain and western Europe, Australia, and New Zealand for the near future. You are going to meet with your director of marketing tomorrow to discuss expanding your business into Canada. You recognize that there are several options available to you, including exporting, licensing, joint ventures, and wholly owned subsidiaries. In addition, you must consider your philosophy of international management, select a strategy, decide on a structure, determine how you will select and train your managers, and determine the appropriate leadership style to use.

Consider the issues indicated above; then, with two other classmates, discuss how you would proceed with the possibility of conducting business in Canada. You want to expand into the international marketplace and believe this is the place to start. Explain your rationale for the decisions you make, pointing out the advantages and disadvantages of each of your choices.

LOCTITE CREATES INTERNATIONAL COHESION

The Loctite Corporation is hardly a household word, but one of its products, Super-Glue, is widely known. Headquartered in Newington, Connecticut, Loctite is a multinational corporation, with about 60 percent of its more than $300 million in annual sales coming from business conducted in 80 countries. Most of that business is in anaerobic adhesives, which form a tight bond when air is removed. The adhesives work well with bolts and other types of airtight applications.

Loctite began pursuing international business when it was very small, with only $1 million in annual sales. Because its adhesives are useful for joining the components of the flat motors that run videocassette recorders and compact disc players, it has developed considerable business in Japan. Nevertheless, building its business in Japan involved a series of small steps. At first, Loctite had a licensing arrangement and then a joint venture before it was able to develop a wholly owned subsidiary.

A key to its success is its large team of Japanese engineers, who work with designers of videocassette recorders and compact disc players to show them how Loctite adhesives can be used. As a result, Loctite dominates the industrial market in Japan and is able to sell its adhesives at higher prices than most domestic competitors. The process also has helped Loctite improve its products, since Japanese customers demand high quality. Loctite received an additional bonus from its work in Japan: when Nissan and Honda built plants in

Mexico and California, they incorporated Loctite products into the manufacturing process. Loctite may also benefit from further movements of Japanese companies to the United States.

Loctite's Australian-born chairman and CEO, Kenneth W. Butterworth, is particularly proud of the company's multinational work force. "Out of 3000 people in the company worldwide, probably 55 to 60 percent are not Americans," he says. The company has only two or three Americans working outside the United States, and five of its six top executives have lived and worked in three or more other countries. Being able to operate effectively abroad is important for Loctite personnel, because they must work so closely with customers to develop applications of its adhesive. For example, the head of Loctite's international division took a special team to a government-run factory in China to help with a serious leakage problem. The team spent 2000 hours in testing and field trials to find a way to assemble engines through the use of adhesives that form gaskets and hold bolts in place. Five years of further negotiations finally allowed Loctite to form a 50-50 joint venture with the Chinese to build a Loctite plant in Shandong Province. Loctite is already training Baosheng Xu, a Chinese native who earned an M.B.A. in Boston, to manage the plant. Baosheng exemplifies the Loctite approach to managing in foreign markets: recruit a local national. "I have the language, and—most important—I know where to get things done," says Baosheng.

Loctite is continually attempting to innovate and make its products more valuable to customers. Recently, the company has had success in developing new ultraviolet-cured silicones, which have a

Loctite prefers employing local nationals in its foreign subsidiaries and joint ventures. Chinese native Baosheng Xu, shown here, is being trained by Loctite to manage a plant in China's Shandong Province.

variety of applications in electronics, such as sealing switches in automobiles. The newer products set in seconds rather than hours and can help expedite assembly processes for manufacturers.

Loctite officials argue that American companies pursuing foreign business are too impatient and unwilling to expend enough effort to ensure success. As one manager has said, "Americans cannot go to China, Japan, or Korea one time and walk away with an agreement. It takes a tremendous amount of work." The company also has factories in Ireland and Brazil and is expanding into the Far East and Latin America. It also operates in Europe.[85]

QUESTIONS FOR CHAPTER CONCLUDING CASE

1. What strengths have made Loctite a successful multinational?
2. Characterize Loctite's basic philosophy of international management and its strategy. How appropriate are its approaches for a company in this type of business?
3. Considering Loctite's success overseas, how should its current expansion into the Far East and Latin America proceed?

CHAPTER TWENTY-TWO

ENTREPRENEURSHIP AND SMALL BUSINESS

CHAPTER OUTLINE

The Nature of Entrepreneurship
Defining Entrepreneurship
Promoting Innovation: Assessing
  Entrepreneurial Opportunities
Economic and Social Contributions of
  Entrepreneurship

Factors Influencing Entrepreneurship
Personal Characteristics
Life-Path Circumstances
Favorable Environmental Conditions
Perceptions of Desirability and
  Feasibility

**Deciding What Type of Business to
  Pursue**
Starting a New Firm
Buying an Existing Business
Purchasing a Franchise

**Preparing to Operate a Small
  Business**
Developing a Business Plan
Obtaining Resources
Selecting an Appropriate Site

Managing a Small Business
Stages of Small-Business Growth
Entrepreneurship versus
  Intrapreneurship
Major Issues and Problems

LEARNING OBJECTIVES

*After studying this chapter, you
should be able to:*

■ Define entrepreneurship and
explain the role that innovation
plays in creating entrepreneurial opportunities.

■ Outline the major economic
and social contributions made
by entrepreneurship and the
small businesses that it
spawns.

■ Explain the major factors that
influence the decision to engage in entrepreneurship.

■ Explain the main types of small
businesses that one might consider pursuing.

■ Enumerate the major purposes
of developing a business plan.

■ Describe what is involved in
obtaining resources and selecting an appropriate business
site.

■ Trace the major stages in new
venture growth.

■ Explain several special issues
and problems associated with
entrepreneurship and small-
business ownership.

PHIL ROMANO KEEPS SCORING ENTREPRENEURIAL SUCCESSES

Phil Romano is perhaps best known for one of his most intriguing creations, Fuddruckers, the upscale hamburger chain that he founded in 1979. When developing a new venture, Romano typically starts with a "concept," a basic idea about what he wants to do. He then thinks about it, talks with others, and puts the concept on paper. Next, he is likely to get help from experts, such as architects and market researchers. If conditions look favorable, he usually puts together a business plan that includes a detailed description of the concept and related business issues. The business plan is particularly helpful during the process of lining up financing for the new venture.

In creating Fuddruckers, for example, Romano built his concept around freshness and quality. At Fuddruckers, butchers trim, cut, and grind meat in full view of customers. Bakers in white uniforms mix and bake rolls. Customers can watch the 8-ounce burgers being grilled and then can add their trimmings at a condiment bar that looks like a produce stand, with lettuce, tomatoes, onions, jalapeño peppers, and other good-tasting fixings. The decor is distinctly functional, with the aisles defined by stacks of supplies, such as bags of flour, beer cases, sacks of potatoes and onions, and boxes of catsup, salt, and sauerkraut. The restaurants also feature chili, hot dogs, wurst, and taco salads. The total effect is an informal, warm, inviting atmosphere in which customers feel involved in the whole process. To ensure that each restaurant in the chain is operated in a manner that supports the basic concept, Romano developed Fuddruckers University and an 8-week course for store managers. By the time Fuddruckers had gone public and developed into a $25 million company with restaurants in 19 states and Canada, Romano had already trained his successor as CEO. After selling a large part of his interest in Fuddruckers, Romano left the business in January 1985 to create more new ventures.

Actually, Fuddruckers was the twelfth new venture that Romano had started. During college, Romano's father took out a second mortgage on the family house so that Phil could start a restaurant. The budding entrepreneur made $60,000 that he added to a $150,000 loan from the U.S. Small Business Administration to start a succession of other businesses that culminated in the extremely successful Fuddruckers chain. Among his previous restaurants was Shuckers A Real Seafood Place, which was heavily oriented toward fresh seafood. Another was the First National Bar and Grill, located in an office building with a potentially large lunch crowd. To encourage customers to eat and then go, Romano charged by the minute (so much for the first 30 minutes and then an additional charge for each 10 minutes thereafter) rather than by the food they ate. Another successful restaurant was Enoch's, where customers paid $100 for a key and recommended the names of 10 friends who then would be given the opportunity to buy a key. Romano creates businesses using a heavy dose of creativity and innovation. Then he sells them. Romano thrives on the joy of business creation and initial start-up—the phase that most entrepreneurs say is the most difficult.

Within a year of leaving Fuddruckers, Romano started two new businesses, a restaurant named Stix and a fashionable men's clothing store named Baroni. Both were opened in 1986 in his hometown of San Antonio, Texas. Romano called Stix an eating spa because it was oriented toward serving healthy food. The menu included such items as spinach salad, cold pasta, broiled scallops or chicken, and a chocolate-covered strawberry for dessert. Unfortunately, it did

Phil Romano is the quintessential entrepreneur. This dynamic Texan has started up dozens of ventures—including hamburger chains, a company specializing in automated retrieval systems, and a restaurant featuring soft tacos—and succeeded in most of them. Romano likes the challenge of creating solutions to problems and finding a niche in an industry.

not do well financially, and Romano closed it after a little more than a year of operation. Market research showed that while there was 100 percent acceptance of the product, the average customer was from a family with an annual income of $75,000 or more. There just were not enough of these families in the geographic area to support such a restaurant. This was the first restaurant that Romano had financed himself, and he lost a little more than a million dollars.

Baroni, featuring men's clothing imported primarily from Italy and catering to an affluent clientele, suffered a similar fate after the shop was in business about a year. Romano lost about half a million dollars of his money prior to selling out.

Undaunted by these relatively rare setbacks, the following year Romano and others provided research and development funding to a biotechnical organization researching a device for keeping coronary arteries open. The device, known as the PALMAZ stent, is a small, expandable tube of wire mesh that is designed to be put into arteries that are obstructed by cholesterol and plaque. The mesh holds the arteries open so that the proper amount of blood can pass through. The device was later purchased by Johnson & Johnson, netting Romano several million dollars and part ownership of the patent from which he collects royalties. At about the same time, he started DocuCon, an organization that specializes in setting up systems that convert paper files to automated retrieval systems. DocuCon is growing into a multi-million-dollar business.

In 1988, Romano's Macaroni Grill opened and won the Silver Spoon award as the best restaurant in San Antonio. Featuring some Romano family recipes, the restaurant specialized in fresh vegetables, grilled meats, gourmet pizzas, and other northern Italian fare. At that time, the Macaroni Grill was a family operation that included Rose Romano (Phil's mother); his wife, Libby; sister Rosalie; and several nieces and nephews. The concept for the restaurant emphasized openness and the flavor of an Italian kitchen, reminiscent of Romano's own childhood. Counters along a wall of the entryway are refrigerated shelves that show off the meat and fish to customers. Counters facing the large dining area display the dishes. The cooking areas, food, and wine are visible from the eating area, and waiters work from counters located in the center of the room. The counters are loaded with appetizers, condiments, and desserts. The tables have white tablecloths, and the trimming is in green and red, making it a very attractive setting. To show gratitude to customers, Romano's had one free night, a Monday or a Tuesday, per month (not announced beforehand) when customers were not given bills. In December 1989, Phil Romano sold the popular restaurant and concept to Dallas-based Chili's, Inc., for a reported $4.5 million. Chili's intends to build several more Macaroni Grills and has retained Phil Romano as a consultant to assist in ensuring that the new chain is successful. Chili's has indicated that the free night each month will continue.

Recently, Romano also started Texas Tortilla Bakery Incorporated, with an initial site in New York City's Greenwich Village. The Tex-Mex restaurant serves soft tacos made with a new machine developed by Romano. This venture, started with his high school friend Arthur C. (Christy) Howard, features an open-style kitchen. Tacos are produced right in front of the customer and sold by the bucket; they come with a choice of fillings and can be eaten at tables or stands outside the bakery.

Romano's advice to potential entrepreneurs is straightforward. Find an industry you really like, search out the problems in the industry, and create solutions.[1]

If there are heroes and heroines in American business in recent years, they are the entrepreneurs like Phil Romano. Entrepreneurs create new organizations, provide innovative services and products, pique our imagination, and stimulate the economy. The insights into Phil Romano's world help us better understand entrepreneurs and the phenomenon called entrepreneurship. An understanding of entrepreneurship is particularly important for aspiring managers because 99 percent of the businesses in the United States are small businesses, most of which have been created by entrepreneurs. Many of you who read this book will likely become entrepreneurs or operate one of the small businesses that result from entrepreneurial activities. Of course, some businesses created by entrepreneurs quickly become relatively large businesses, as was the case with the Compaq Computer Corporation (see Chapter 16). Most, though, spend a significant period of time as relatively small businesses, assuming that they survive beyond the initial start-up period. In this chapter, we explore the nature of entrepreneurship, including the role of innovation in entrepreneurial endeavors. We investigate the major factors that influence the entrepreneurship phenomenon. We also analyze the types of businesses that entrepreneurs and small-business owners can pursue and review the major preparations necessary to operate a small business. Finally, we consider some of the major issues involved in the ongoing management of small businesses.

THE NATURE OF ENTREPRENEURSHIP

What is entrepreneurship? In this section, we explore the meaning of the term, consider the importance of innovation in assessments of entrepreneurial opportunities, and examine some of the major economic and social contributions of entrepreneurship.

Defining Entrepreneurship

In order to understand entrepreneurship, it is useful to trace the meaning of the closely related term "entrepreneur." "Entrepreneur" is actually a French word that, translated literally, means "go-between" or "between-taker."[2] As applied to activities related to business, the term has had a long and meandering evolution. For instance, in the Middle Ages, the term was used to refer to both an actor and an individual overseeing large projects. At that point, the project manager–entrepreneur was not expected to take any risks, but just to use the materials provided. By the seventeenth century, the term "entrepreneur" carried the notion of risk and was applied to individuals who entered into contractual arrangements to furnish goods or services to the government at a fixed price. Because the contract price was fixed, the entrepreneur could reap the benefits of any economies of production but would also need to absorb any losses—hence the basis for the risk. In the eighteenth century, the term came to connote individuals in need of capital to carry out their activities, as opposed to providers of capital. By the present century, the noted economist Joseph Schumpeter added the notion of innovation to the growing list of meanings for "entrepreneur," viewing the entrepreneur as one who tries new combinations and unexplored technologies.

Although the varying meanings of entrepreneur have been used as a basis for attempting to define entrepreneurship, the exact meaning of entrepreneurship remains controversial today.[3] Recently though, scholars have begun to emphasize the creation of organizations as the essence of entrepreneurship.[4] Along these lines, a definition that also captures some of the flavor of risk and innovation has recently been proposed by entrepreneurship scholars Murray

Entrepreneurship The "creation of new enterprise"

Low and Ian MacMillan. We adopt their definition of **entrepreneurship** as the "creation of new enterprise."[5] Although one could conceivably engage in entrepreneurship geared toward establishing a new not-for-profit organization (such as an association or a cultural center), most entrepreneurship activities involve profit-oriented businesses. Accordingly, this chapter focuses on entrepreneurship aimed at profit making.

Entrepreneur An individual who creates a new enterprise

On the basis of our definition of entrepreneurship, an **entrepreneur,** then, is an individual who creates a new enterprise. Many of today's familiar product names were born in enterprises created by entrepreneurs. Some examples include Brooks Brothers apparel (Henry Sands Brooks), Gerber baby food (Dan Gerber), Gucci loafers (Guccio Gucci), Barbie dolls (Barbara Handler), Wurlitzer instruments (Rudolph Wurlitzer), Calvin Klein jeans (Calvin Klein), Hummel figurines (Berta Hummel), Post cereals (Charles W. Post), and Heinz ketchup (Henry J. Heinz).[6] When an enterprise is in the process of being created by an entrepreneur, it often is referred to as a **new venture.**

New venture An enterprise that is in the process of being created by an entrepreneur

New ventures typically fall into the category of "small businesses," a classification that is itself somewhat difficult to define. The U.S. Chamber of Commerce suggests that businesses employing fewer than 500 persons are small; others sometimes use a figure of fewer than 100 persons. With either figure, small businesses would still constitute 99 percent of all U.S. businesses, as mentioned earlier.[7] Another criterion that often is used to identify a small business is that it is independently owned—in other words, it is not a subsidiary of a larger organization. Accordingly, we consider a *small business* to be an independently owned business that employs fewer than 500 persons. Using this definition, most new ventures would be small businesses, but not all small businesses would be considered new ventures (since they are not all in the creation stage). We make this differentiation because we will be exploring some aspects of management that are unique to entrepreneurs and the creation of new enterprises, while other aspects will be applicable to small businesses in general. For the most part, we will use the terms "entrepreneurship" and "entrepreneur" in conjunction with creating new ventures. Otherwise, we will use "small business" or "small-business owner" when the discussion applies more generally. In some cases we may refer to both small businesses and new ventures (or owners and entrepreneurs) to make clear that the discussion applies to both. So far, researchers have experienced difficulty determining precisely when the creation phase attributable to entrepreneurship ends.

Promoting Innovation: Assessing Entrepreneurial Opportunities

In his book *Innovation and Entrepreneurship,* noted management consultant and writer Peter Drucker observes, "Innovation is the specific tool of entrepreneurs, the means by which they exploit change as an opportunity for a different business or a different service."[8] Essentially, it is difficult to be an entrepreneur without engaging in at least some innovation, since merely duplicating what already is being done will not usually attract sufficient customers.[9] The innovation dilemma related to entrepreneurship is illustrated in Table 22-1.

As shown in the table, three criteria that we can use to consider the probable opportunity conditions associated with different degrees of innovation are risk, evaluation, and profit potential. *Risk* is the probability of the venture's failing. *Evaluation* is the ease of estimating the significance and feasibility of a new venture idea. *Profit potential* is the likely level of return or compensation to the entrepreneur for taking on the risk of developing an idea into an actual business venture. As the table indicates, if a new venture is very much like the competi-

Table 22-1 Opportunity Conditions Associated with New Venture Innovation

Opportunity Conditions	LEVELS OF INNOVATION				
	New Invention	Highly Innovative	Moderately Innovative	Slightly Innovative	Copycat
Risks	Very high	High	Moderate	Moderate to low	Very high
Evaluation	Very difficult	Difficult	Somewhat difficult	Easy	Easy
Profit potential	Very high	High	High to moderate	Moderate to low	Low to nil

Source: Reprinted from John G. Burch, *Entrepreneurship*, Wiley, New York, 1986, p. 72.

tion (a copycat), it is easy to evaluate its significance and feasibility (since others are already doing it). Unfortunately, such a venture involves high risk because there is little to attract customers, making the profit potential low. As new venture ideas become somewhat more innovative, the risk goes down because there is something new to offer the customer. As ideas become more innovative, though, the significance and feasibility become more difficult to evaluate and the risk increases. As innovation and risk both increase, so does profit potential because of the possibility of being able to offer a unique product or service that is highly desirable. At the invention end of the spectrum, the entrepreneur often is not the actual inventor of a product or service. Rather, the entrepreneur is the one who recognizes the commercial applications. In any event, innovation is an important part of the entrepreneurial process, because without innovation the prospects of success are extremely low.

Economic and Social Contributions of Entrepreneurship

A major reason why entrepreneurship has been receiving increasing attention from both scholars and the popular press is the growing recognition of the substantial economic and social contributions of entrepreneurship and the small businesses it spawns. In this section, we consider major contributions associated with entrepreneurship in the areas of economic growth, innovation, employment opportunities, and career alternatives for women and minorities.

Economic Growth. Entrepreneurship leads to the creation of many new businesses that help fuel economic growth. Since there is no central source of data collection on new company formations, completely accurate numbers are impossible to obtain. According to one report, more than 1,115,500 new companies were formed during the period 1981 to 1987 alone.[10] Of course, many of these new ventures fail. While statistics vary, as many as 50 to 70 percent of new ventures fail or merge with other organizations within their first 5 years.[11] Nevertheless, there is little doubt that new ventures make a significant contribution to economic expansion.[12]

Innovation. As might be anticipated given the innovation requirements for successful entrepreneurship that were just discussed, entrepreneurs have introduced many new products and services that have changed the way we live. Henry Ford's automobile, Joyce Hall's Hallmark greeting cards, Isaac Singer's sewing machine, and King Gillette's razors are just a few examples of new products developed by entrepreneurs.[13] Evidence suggests that new ventures produce a disproportionately large share of product and process innovations, compared with larger, more established firms.[14]

Employment Opportunities. New ventures and small businesses provide the majority of new job opportunities in the United States. This source of job creation has received a great deal of attention since researcher David L. Birch conducted a study in 1979 which demonstrated that small businesses with fewer than 20 employees are a significant generator of new jobs in the U.S. economy.[15] According to one estimate, between 1980 and 1986, 31.8 million new jobs were created by small businesses.[16] Recent research suggests that the most significant job growth can be attributed to a small number of fast-growing new ventures and that the economic impact of small-business job growth is likely to be the greatest during times of economic slowdown, when larger companies are cutting back.[17] During such reductions, many individuals whose jobs are eliminated find employment with small businesses. Because of the difficulty of tracking new ventures and because of disputes over which businesses should be included in the figures, the exact contributions of entrepreneurial endeavors and ongoing small businesses to employment opportunities are likely to be controversial for some time to come.

Opportunities for Women and Minorities. Entrepreneurship offers an alternative avenue into business for women and minorities. One major attraction is the possibility of avoiding patterns of discrimination common in established organizations, whereby women and minorities may be channeled to relatively lower-level and poorly paid positions. Another attraction is the prospect of material independence and the ability to control the outcomes of one's own efforts.[18] Finally, some government agencies, at the federal, state, and local levels, have attempted to encourage diversity of entrepreneurship through programs which favor businesses owned by minorities and women in the awarding of some government contracts.

During the period 1980 to 1986, the number of women-owned sole proprietorships (a legal form of business with one owner) increased from 2,535,240 to 4,120,000.[19] Although the percentage of businesses started and operated by women is relatively small (estimates range from 4.6 to 5.7 percent), women are making significant inroads.[20] Minorities also are starting more new businesses. For instance, even though blacks presently own less than 2 percent of U.S. businesses, the number of black-owned businesses is rising rapidly.[21] One example of these new entrepreneurs is Lillian Lincoln, the daughter of a Virginia subsistence farmer. She attended segregated schools before managing to earn a Harvard M.B.A. Since then, she has founded Centennial One, a successful company based in Crofton, Maryland, that provides cleaning and pest-control services to major corporations, such as IBM and Westinghouse. As she notes, "Where I have to go can't be as rough climbing as where I've been."[22]

FACTORS INFLUENCING ENTREPRENEURSHIP

What makes someone like Lillian Lincoln create a successful new business? To find the answer, researchers have explored several different avenues. For one thing, they have focused on characteristics of the entrepreneur, theorizing that there may be some special traits involved. For another, researchers have begun to examine more closely the life-path circumstances of individuals that might

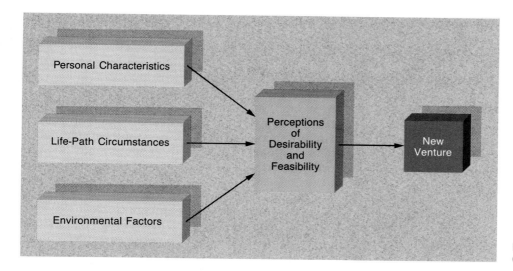

Figure 22-1 Factors influencing entrepreneurship.

influence them to become entrepreneurs. Researchers have also considered the possibility that certain environmental factors might encourage entrepreneurship. Finally, perceptions of the desirability and feasibility of becoming an entrepreneur also appear to affect the decision to engage in entrepreneurship.[23] These factors are shown in Figure 22-1 and examined further below.

Personal Characteristics

One fascinating question surrounding entrepreneurship is whether entrepreneurs have personality traits and background experiences that set them apart from others. If so, an awareness of such characteristics might make it easier to determine which individuals would have the best chance of successfully launching new ventures. A number of studies have addressed just this issue, focusing mainly on personality, background, and other personal characteristics that could explain why some people become entrepreneurs and others do not.[24]

Personality Characteristics. Given the wide variety of businesses that entrepreneurs have created, identifying characteristics that entrepreneurs have in common is a formidable task. So far, the search for personality characteristics has yielded only a few results that may be helpful in separating potential entrepreneurs from the general population, but these same traits also are often indicative of managers.

Psychologist David C. McClelland, who is the chief architect of acquired-needs theory (see Chapter 13), has argued that entrepreneurs tend to have a *high need for achievement* (nAch). Individuals who have a high nAch gravitate toward situations in which they can achieve results through their own efforts, pursue moderately difficult goals, and receive relatively immediate feedback on how they are doing.[25]

Evidence suggests that entrepreneurs do have a relatively high need for achievement but that high nAch, by itself, does not single out entrepreneurs because high nAch can also be found among salespeople, professionals, and managers. Moreover, researchers have also not been able to establish a direct link between high nAch and the propensity to actually start a new business. It is likely that high nAch is an important ingredient in entrepreneurial success, just

Michael Dell began his computer company selling computer parts by mail when he was a freshman in college. Now 24, he runs the fastest growing personal computer company in the country. Dell has a strong internal locus of control: "I wanted to control my own destiny and basically always felt I would be successful. I had a pretty strong inclination to create a business" (*Fortune*, February 12, 1990, p. 120).

as it is a useful trait in other occupations that involve taking personal responsibility in order to reach significant achievements.

Another characteristic that has been found in entrepreneurs is an *internal locus of control*. Individuals with an internal locus of control tend to feel that they control their fate largely through their own efforts (their opposites, individuals with an external locus of control, view their fate as mainly determined by outside forces and luck). Again, though, an internal locus of control also is often characteristic of managers. One researcher suggests that the internal locus of control may be useful in separating successful from unsuccessful entrepreneurs. The reason is that entrepreneurs with an internal locus of control may be more likely to engage in active efforts to affect the success of the endeavor, particularly in the face of adversity.[26]

One characteristic that does seem to separate entrepreneurs from managers is a *high tolerance for ambiguity*. A high tolerance for ambiguity means that an individual is able to continue to function effectively and persist even when situations are highly uncertain. Since entrepreneurship involves starting new organizations, there frequently is a great deal of uncertainty involved. Hence, high levels of tolerance for ambiguity may be one factor that explains why an individual becomes an entrepreneur rather than a manager. Managers often also have fairly high levels of tolerance for ambiguity, but not as high as those of entrepreneurs.[27]

Background and Other Personal Characteristics. A variety of studies have also attempted to isolate important background and other personal characteristics of entrepreneurs. Much of the focus has been on the areas of childhood family environment, education, age, and work history.[28]

Inquiries into the *childhood family environment* of entrepreneurs have considered issues such as birth order and occupations of parents. One recurring question is the degree to which entrepreneurs tend to be the firstborn or only children in the family. The basic idea is that such children are likely to gain a greater share of their parents' time, leading to an increased self-confidence that may fuel entrepreneurship. Although some studies have found a firstborn or only-child effect, others have not, leaving the theory in doubt.[29]

On the other hand, there is considerable evidence that entrepreneurs tend to have self-employed fathers. They also often have self-employed mothers or parents who jointly own (or owned) a business.[30] Apparently, having one or both parents as business owners provides a salient role model for potential entrepreneurs.

Another focus of inquiry has been the level of *education* of entrepreneurs. Although popularized books on entrepreneurship often state that entrepreneurs are less educated than the general population, recent studies suggest that the opposite is likely to be true. Generally, studies have found that entrepreneurs tend to be better-educated than the general population, although they may be less well educated than individuals who pursue managerial careers, particularly in large organizations. Within the entrepreneurial ranks there is wide variation in educational attainment, with some entrepreneurs lacking high school diplomas and others having graduate degrees.[31] Female entrepreneurs are particularly likely to have college degrees.[32]

Age has been another variable of interest in explaining entrepreneurial activity. Although the ages between 25 and 40 are frequently mentioned as periods when individuals are most likely to become entrepreneurs, actually the span appears to be wider—more like 22 to 55. Individuals can become entrepreneurs before age 22, but such endeavors are less likely because these individuals do not have the education, experience, and financial resources to take on creating new ventures. After about 55 years of age, reduced energy and physical problems can impede some, though certainly not all, would-be entrepreneurs. For example, the late Ray Kroc founded McDonald's when he was over 50.[33] There also appear to be "milestone years" that occur in approximate 5-year increments (20, 25, 30, 35, 40, 45, 50), when individuals are more likely to assess their current status and decide to take the plunge into entrepreneurship.

Not surprisingly, there is evidence that *work history* and related experience is an important factor in initiating a new enterprise. Several studies indicate that in new ventures at least one of the company founders had previously worked in the same industry as the new business. Moreover, creating new ventures seems to become easier after the first one, giving rise to the corridor principle. The **corridor principle** states that the process of beginning a new venture helps entrepreneurs visualize other opportunities that they could not envision or take advantage of until they started the initial venture.[34] For example, Phil Romano developed ideas for several other businesses after he created Fuddruckers. One implication of the corridor principle is that individuals who begin their entrepreneurial careers at the lower end of the age scale may be able to exploit the corridor principle better because of their potentially longer entrepreneurial career.

All in all, there do appear to be a few characteristics that separate entrepreneurs from the general population and even, in some cases, from managers. Yet personal characteristics are relatively weak predictors of entrepreneurship. Only some of the individuals who seem to have the characteristics and background of entrepreneurs actually start enterprises. What distinguishes those who make the decision to become entrepreneurs from those who do not? Some further clues come from recent efforts to study the life-path circumstances of entrepreneurs.

Corridor principle A principle which states that the process of beginning a new venture helps entrepreneurs visualize other opportunities that they could not envision or take advantage of until they started the initial venture

Life-Path Circumstances

Several types of life-path, or individual, circumstances seem to increase the probability that an individual will become an entrepreneur. The four major types of circumstances are unsatisfactory work environment, negative displacement, career transition points, and the presence of positive-pull influencers.[35]

Unsatisfactory Work Environment. An unsatisfactory work environment refers to circumstances in an individual's job situation that impel that person to think about leaving and starting a new venture. One common factor is strong dissatisfaction with either the work itself or some other aspect of the work environment such as supervision. A second frequent factor is refusal of an employer to recognize the value of an innovative idea.[36] For example, H. Ross Perot tried to get IBM to adopt his idea of selling customers computer software services along with their hardware. When IBM refused to support his idea, he quit and started Electronic Data Services. The company netted him close to a billion dollars when he sold his final holdings in 1984, 22 years after founding the company.[37]

Negative Displacement. Negative displacement, or disruption, refers to circumstances in a person's life situation that make it necessary to make major changes in lifestyle. Major factors in this category include being fired, getting a divorce, becoming widowed, reaching middle age, or emigrating from another country. For instance, when brother and sister Marty and Helen Shih came to Los Angeles from Taiwan in 1979, they had $500 between them to start a new business.

Marjory Williams used adversity as a springboard for action, resulting in the ownership of Laura Caspari, Ltd.–SHE, Inc., a successful string of boutiques that cater to working women. In the early 1970's, Williams, then recently divorced and the mother of a baby, decided that a career in business was the way to independence and success. She graduated from Harvard Business School and landed a job as a buyer at Dayton-Hudson, the department store chain. Two years later, she developed her idea of catering to career women. When Dayton-Hudson showed no interest, she started up her own company; it was profitable in its first month.

The pair started a flower shop because they felt that their English language skills were not sufficient to land good corporate jobs, despite their good educational backgrounds. Today, they operate as Shih's Flowers, Inc.; they own nine shops (the downtown store alone grosses $1 million per year), and the business is still growing.[38]

Career Transitions. Career transition points are circumstances in which an individual is moving between one type of career-related activity and another, such as completing studies or a degree, being discharged from military service, finishing a major project, or having children leave home. For example, when Nancy Barocci returned to Wilmette, Illinois, with her husband and children after several years in Europe, she wanted to put her studies of Italian food and wines to good use. So, in 1980, she opened an Italian restaurant that was an immediate hit. She has since moved the original Convito Italiano to a larger location and opened a second—even larger and equally successful—Convito in Chicago.[39]

Positive-Pull Influencers. Positive-pull influencers are individuals, such as mentors, investors, customers, or potential partners, who urge an individual to start a business. For instance, Scott McNealy, who is cofounder and chief executive of Sun Microsystems, Inc., got involved in starting the company when his former Stanford roommate, Vinod Khosia, approached him with the idea. The pair teamed up with two other Stanford M.B.A.s in 1982 and have built the company into a billion-dollar player in the field of engineering workstations.[40] The pull notion is in contrast to the other life-path changes discussed above, which fit more into the category of pushing individuals toward the entrepreneurial life. The reason for the push is that individuals are in situations that require them to take action or suffer negative consequences. While life-path circumstances can be an impetus for entrepreneurship, environmental conditions also are an ingredient.

Favorable Environmental Conditions

A review of a number of relevant studies indicates that there are a number of environmental conditions that appear to stimulate entrepreneurship. Many of these conditions deal with the basic prerequisites of running a business, such as adequate financing, a technically skilled labor force, accessibility of suppliers, accessibility of customers or new markets, availability of land or facilities, accessibility of transportation, and availability of supporting services. Other, more indirect conditions provide support, such as the presence of experienced entrepreneurs and incubator organizations, government influences, proximity of universities, attitude of the area's population, and living conditions.

One factor mentioned above that requires further explanation is the notion of an incubator. An **incubator** is an organization whose purpose is to nurture new ventures in their very early stages by providing space (usually at a site housing other new ventures as well), stimulation, support, and a variety of basic services, often at reduced fees. (The term "incubator" also is sometimes used to refer to the organization that an entrepreneur previously worked for while "hatching" the idea for a related new venture. In this case, the organization usually unwittingly serves as an incubator.) The idea is to help the new ventures during their first 2 or 3 years or so, until they have grown enough to "hatch" and join the normal business world.[41] Although there were only about 50 incubators in the United States in 1984, there were more than 330 by 1989, according to figures from the National Business Incubation Association.[42]

Incubator An organization whose purpose is to nurture new ventures in their very early stages by providing space (usually at a site housing other new ventures as well), stimulation, support, and a variety of basic services, often at reduced fees

Perceptions of Desirability and Feasibility

Even if there are personal characteristics, life-path circumstances, and environmental conditions that tend to either push or pull individuals toward entrepreneurship, individuals still are unlikely to take action unless they perceive entrepreneurship as both desirable and feasible.[43]

Some factors that influence desirability are related to the personal characteristics mentioned earlier, such as family members who have owned their own businesses and/or who encourage independence. Others are related mainly to life-path circumstances, such as the presence of positive-pull influencers—peers who have created new ventures, teachers (especially in courses on entrepreneurship) who point out the potential for success, and supportive colleagues in the organization that the individual worked for before initiating the new venture.

Even with perceived desirability, would-be entrepreneurs must also make an assessment of the feasibility of creating a new enterprise. While personal characteristics and life-path circumstances play a part, environmental conditions are an important aspect of feasibility assessments. Thus perceptions of feasibility are influenced by seeing oneself as having the necessary background, the presence of successful role models, the availability of advice from knowledgeable others, and the availability of financial support. For example, after graduating from college and moving to Hong Kong, Katha Diddel began to perceive that she, too, could start her own business (see the following Case in Point discussion).

CASE IN POINT:　Katha Diddel Launches Her Home Collection

When Katha Diddel graduated from college in 1979, she went directly to mainland China seeking a job in which she could use her 6 years of intensive language training in Mandarin Chinese. After a few short-term jobs as an interpreter, she landed a position in the China trade division of the Associated Merchandising Corporation (AMC) in Hong Kong. She worked as a merchandiser and market guide for American retailers who wanted to meet Chinese suppliers on the mainland. This position allowed her to build a network of business contacts at a time when China was beginning to show interest in exporting products to U.S. markets. In the process, she began to slowly put together a business plan to fulfill her dream of having a business of her own—a company that would market exquisite Chinese embroidery in the United States.

Her dream took a step closer to reality when Diddel met a stationery and paper-goods exporter at a cocktail party in Shanghai. She offered the importer some ideas about how he could change his products to make them more marketable in the United States. Six weeks later, he invited her to Shanghai to show her the beautiful samples that he had developed on the basis of her ideas. Seeing the samples gave her confidence that her own ideas for a business were feasible.

Diddel traveled around the country visiting dozens of tiny villages and remote islands before finally finding what she was looking for in an old factory in a mountain community. There she located workers doing lovely embroidery in patterns that earlier generations had learned from European missionaries. Unfortunately, the workers were using "garish" colors and cheap polyester fabric. After her proposal to have workers embroider fine linens was accepted by the plant managers, she stayed to supervise the learning process, including picking out the thread colors and showing the artisans where to put the designs on the fabric.

Having developed the products, Diddel now needed to find interested importers in the United States. In New York, she made numerous calls to importers listed in the telephone book, went to trade shows and collected names of potential customers, advertised in trade journals, and sent out over 1000 letters to prospects. "The process took a very long time," she says. "It was not the most pleasant period of my life." Nevertheless, she was ultimately successful. To finance her operation, she obtained a $5000 loan from a Hong Kong bank. She also worked out an arrangement with her importers that guaranteed immediate payment for products received.

With the pieces in place, Diddel launched Twin Panda, Inc., in 1981, just when the U.S. home-furnishings market was expanding rapidly. From 1981 to 1986, sales boomed. Then, suddenly, she began to notice signs of trouble. Diddel says that competitors, taking note of her success, went to her sources and set up rival contracts for imitations using cheaper materials that allowed them to undercut her prices. Since copyright laws in China are weak, Diddel decided to fight the low-cost approach of her competitors by choosing a differentiation strategy in the form of top-of-the-line, hand-worked products and a greater variety of designs. As part of the implementation process, Diddel went to China and renegotiated contracts for higher volumes in return for guaranteed protection of her designs. She also has renamed her company the Katha Diddel Home Collection, to denote that the products are created by a designer. The change has been accompanied by new catalogs, new promotional strategies, and new advertising. Her expanding product line recently included baby-bed linens that were an instant hit. Her instinct for discovering new ideas is keeping her company on a successful track.[44]   ■■■■■■

Because of the major current interest in entrepreneurs like Katha Diddel, our emphasis here has been on factors that influence individuals to create new ventures. Of course, creating a new organization is not the only way to engage in small-business ownership; there are alternative types of business opportunities available.

DECIDING WHAT TYPE OF BUSINESS TO PURSUE

One major aspect of both entrepreneurship and small-business ownership is determining the type of business to pursue.[45] There are three general approaches: starting a new firm, buying an existing business, or purchasing a franchise.

Starting a New Firm

Start-up A type of new firm or venture started from scratch by an entrepreneur

A new firm started from scratch by an entrepreneur is often referred to as a **start-up.** Some clues about the types of new firms, or start-ups, that one might create can be gleaned from a recent study of 106 entrepreneurs by researchers William B. Gartner, Terence R. Mitchell, and Karl H. Vesper.[46] On the basis of interviews with a sample of entrepreneurs that was reasonably representative of the general population of U.S. entrepreneurs, the researchers identified eight types of new business ventures that the entrepreneurs actually tended to undertake. In developing the types, the researchers considered such factors as the kinds of individuals involved, the competitive strategies used, the sort of competitive environment that the business operates in, and the kinds of activities required by the entrepreneurs. Seven of the types are classified under the general approach of starting a new firm.

Who hasn't played UNO? Today's best selling card game was being sold out of a trunk of a car in in Louisville, Kentucky, when Joe Cusimano (shown here) and his brother-in-law bought the rights to the game in 1973. UNO is easy to play and inexpensive to produce—the perfect example of a unique idea making it big.

Escaping to Something New. In starting a new firm, the entrepreneur in this category is attempting to escape from his or her previous type of job, which the individual feels did not offer prospects for sufficient rewards in terms of salary, challenging work, promotion opportunities, or other factors. As a result, the new venture is typically in a different industry and involves a different type of work than did the individual's previous job. This company enters a highly competitive market with a product or service that is fairly similar to those of its competitors.

Putting the Deal Together. The individual in this category aims to bundle the different aspects of the business (such as suppliers, wholesale and retail channels, and customers) into a "deal," from which each participant will gain. Contacts are a vital ingredient.

Rolling Over Skills and Contacts. Before establishing the new firm in this category, the individual worked in a position that involved technical skills and expertise closely related to those needed in the new enterprise. As an entrepreneur, he or she devotes little time to selling, marketing, or advertising because customer contacts exist from the previous position. The venture offers goods and services that rely on the owner's professional expertise and are most often generic services (e.g., auditing or advertising). The enterprise competes by providing better service than that offered by competitors.

Leveraging Expertise. The individual is one of the top people in his or her technical field. The entrepreneur brings in partners to help start the firm. The venture enters an established market and competes through flexibility in adapting to customer needs, which is based on the entrepreneur's keen awareness of environmental changes. A substantial amount of time is devoted to sales. The environment involves a high degree of technical change and complexity.

Forming an Aggressive Service. The entrepreneur creates a very aggressive service-oriented firm, usually a consulting firm in a very specialized area. The competitive situation is such that the entrepreneur must have very specific professional or technical expertise of some type. Knowing the right people is extremely important in making sales or gaining access to those who influence sales decisions.

Pursuing the Unique Idea. The venture develops because of an idea for a product or service that is not being offered. The product or service is not technically sophisticated or difficult to produce. Since this enterprise is the first into the market with the product or service, some uncertainty exists about the existence and size of the potential market.

Organizing Methodically. The entrepreneur in this category uses extensive planning both to acquire the skills and to perform the tasks required in the new venture. The products or services are similar to those of competitors, but the firm provides a new twist, usually either a slightly different way to produce the product or service or a slightly different customer to whom to sell.

One entrepreneur who has parlayed a knack for new twists into a British company that now has annual revenues of more than $1 billion is Alan Michael Sugar (see the following Case in Point discussion).

CASE IN POINT: Europe's Most Successful New Entrepreneur

Alan Michael Sugar was born in 1947 and grew up in London's working-class East End, where his achievement orientation exhibitied itself early. By taking various odd jobs, such as photographing neighbors on Sunday outings and rising at the crack of dawn to stock grocery shelves, Sugar was earning more than his father by the time Sugar left school at 16. Soon after, he started his own business by renting a van and using it as a base from which to sell car-radio antennas. In 1968, he started Amstrad (for "Alan Michael Sugar Trading"), a wholesale distributor of cassette players, speakers, and other electronic gear for cars.

The seeds of Amstrad's subsequent success were sewn during the mid-1970s when Sugar began visiting Japan and Hong Kong in the search for suppliers. Sugar credits the Japanese for teaching him the value of fastidious attention to detail, the importance of reaching for volume when attempting a market assault, and the advantages of a strong corporate culture. By 1978, Sugar had his first major success, a stackable stereo unit priced for the ordinary consumer. Sales were impressive enough that he was able to get Amstrad listed on the London stock exchange 2 years later and immediately acquired a net worth of $8 million.

Sugar's basic strategy is offering established technology at prices so low that specialty markets are immediately transformed into mass markets—a phenomenon that stock market analysts have dubbed "the Amstrad effect." For example, when Amstrad introduced its first word-processing computer in 1985, British industry experts figured that it would sell about 50,000 units per year. Sugar set the price of the unit about equal to the price of a good electronic typewriter and soon was selling 50,000 per month. A year later, Amstrad became the first European company to offer a low-priced IBM personal computer clone. The price was set at below $600, or less than half the price of equivalent machines from other sources. As a result, Amstrad more than doubled the British PC market before pushing into France and Spain. Now Amstrad tops everyone but IBM in European sales of personal computers.

Amstrad is able to offer such low prices by subcontracting most of its production to Asian factories. That way, the company can get in and out of markets quickly. For example, at one point Sugar stopped selling VCRs, a major money-maker, because profit margins had plummeted. The company was back within 18 months with a new product, a combination TV and VCR in a single unit, that was developed by Amstrad's small design unit. Recently, Amstrad worked out an agreement with IBM to gain worldwide access to IBM patents, and the company will likely be offering more high-powered personal computers in the future. In another recent move, Amstrad has been preparing to provide satellite disks in conjunction with a new European satellite TV network announced by communications magnate Rupert Murdoch. Under the plan, Amstrad will supply retailers with 100,000 24-inch dishes a month priced at about $340, compared with the usual $650 for similar dishes based on a different technology. Once again, the Amstrad effect is in action. Such moves have transformed Sugar's original wholesale distributor into an electronics giant in less than two decades. In keeping with his low-cost emphasis, Sugar continues to work from Amstrad's spartan headquarters overlooking the railroad tracks in a drab commuter town by the name of Brentwood.[47] ■■■■■■

For many types of new ventures, entrepreneurs need technical expertise and experience in the industry. According to one estimate, as many as 95 percent of new firms have founders who have worked in basically the same marketplace, technology, and industry as the new firm. The more sophisticated the technology and marketplace, the more important this type of experience is likely to be. On the other hand, many entrepreneurs have been successful at launching businesses in new areas, particularly in nontechnological and service-type businesses.[48] In any case, it may take some searching to find the right idea. (See the section on creativity in Chapter 7 for ways to generate novel ideas).

Buying an Existing Business

The last type of new venture discussed by Gartner et al. constitutes the second major approach to developing a new venture, purchasing an existing business. This category can also apply to acquiring and managing a small business. Entrepreneurs typically acquire an existing business when they believe that they can quickly change its direction in a fairly substantial way so that it will grow in major new directions. Often the organization may be faltering. For example, in 1988, a group of entrepreneurs purchased Cuisinarts, Inc., the company that pioneered the food processor after it failed to capitalize on its name in developing new products. Unfortunately, the entrepreneurs were not experienced in the small-kitchen-appliance business and 1 year later were forced to file for bankruptcy protection themselves.[49] In contrast, prospective small-business owners tend to purchase an existing business with the idea of retaining the business in basically the same form, although it possibly may need to be managed more effectively (especially if it was doing poorly). In the long run, of course, small-business owners may make substantial changes.

Several of the major considerations that go into purchasing an existing business are shown in Figure 22-2. A product or service area that fits one's expertise and interests, of course, is important. Other critical issues include the current financial condition of the firm, prospects for turnaround (if the financial condition is poor), potential for substantial growth, and possibilities of purchasing the firm for a reasonable price. It usually is imperative to obtain professional help, particularly from a lawyer (to review such things as current contracts with suppliers and to set up an acquisition agreement) and an accountant (to audit the financial records and help determine a purchase price).[50]

Purchasing a Franchise

The third major approach to developing a small business is purchasing a franchise (Gartner et al. did not include franchises in their study). A **franchise** is a continuing arrangement between a franchiser and a franchisee in which the franchiser's knowledge, image, manufacturing or service expertise, and marketing techniques are made available to the franchisee in return for the payment of various fees or royalties and conformity to standard operating procedures.[51] A **franchiser** is usually a manufacturer or sole distributor of a trademarked product

Franchise A continuing arrangement between a franchiser and a franchisee in which the franchiser's knowledge, image, manufacturing or service expertise, and marketing techniques are made available to the franchisee in return for the payment of various fees or royalties and conformity to standard operating procedures

Franchiser A manufacturer or sole distributor of a trademarked product or service who typically has considerable experience in the line of business being franchised

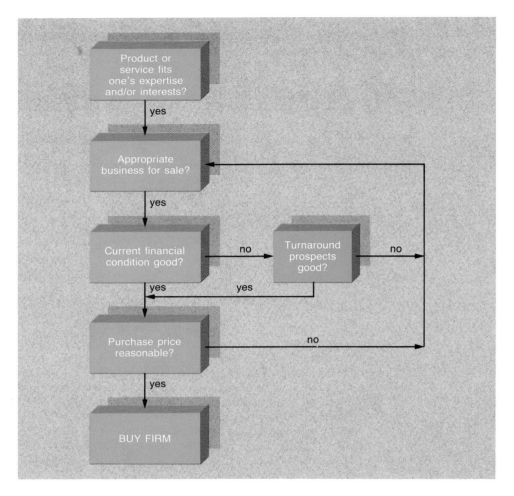

Figure 22-2 Considerations in purchasing an existing business. (Adapted from Nicholas C. Siropolis, *Small Business Management.* Houghton Mifflin, Boston, 1990, p. 103.)

Franchisee An individual who purchases a franchise and, in the process, is given an opportunity to enter a new business hopefully with an enhanced chance of success

or service who typically has considerable experience in the line of business being franchised. A **franchisee** is an individual who purchases a franchise and, in the process, is given an opportunity to enter a new business hopefully with an enhanced chance of success.[52] When one mentions franchises, fast-food operations, such as McDonald's and Kentucky Fried Chicken, often come to mind. Actually, though, auto dealers and gas stations represent greater franchise sales volumes (see Figure 22-3 for the biggest franchised industries).

Franchises are normally considered to be small businesses but not new ventures, since the creation process is largely controlled by the franchiser, rather than the franchisee. In fact, some writers do not include most franchise arrangements in the small-business category; instead, they view franchises as appendages of larger organizations.[53]

The primary advantage of a franchise is that the franchisee gains access to the proven business methods, established reputation, training, and assistance of the franchiser, so the new venture risk is minimized. On the other hand, there are a number of disadvantages, including a lack of independence in regard to making major modifications, the considerable difficulty involved in canceling franchise contracts, the likelihood of continual monitoring by the franchiser, and the substantial expense that may be involved in establishing a franchise with a well-known company (see Table 22-2 for some recent examples of the most and least expensive franchises).[54] Nevertheless, for individuals who lack expertise in a viable business specialty, a franchise may be the answer.

PREPARING TO OPERATE A SMALL BUSINESS

Regardless of which type of business an individual decides to enter, there are major preparations involved. Major preparatory steps include developing a business plan, obtaining the necessary resources, and selecting an appropriate site for the business.

Developing a Business Plan

Most small-business and entrepreneurship experts strongly recommend the development of a business plan. A **business plan** is a document written by the prospective owner or entrepreneur that details the nature of the business, the product or service, the customers, the competition, the production and marketing methods, the management, the financing, and other significant aspects of the proposed business venture.[55]

A well-prepared business plan can take 200 to 400 hours or even more to complete, depending on the complexity of the business contemplated, the

Business plan A document written by the prospective owner or entrepreneur that details the nature of the business, the product or service, the customers, the competition, the production and marketing methods, the management, the financing, and other significant aspects of the proposed business venture

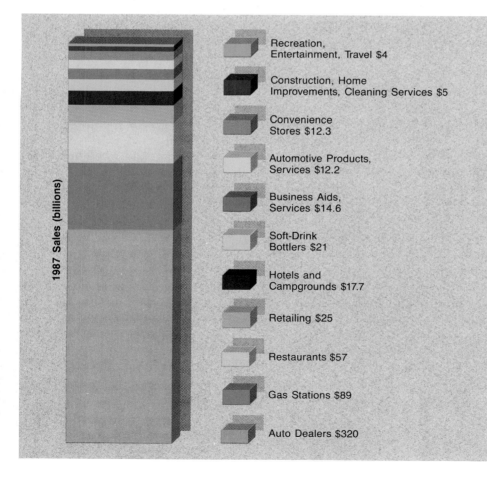

Recreation, Entertainment, Travel $4

Construction, Home Improvements, Cleaning Services $5

Convenience Stores $12.3

Automotive Products, Services $12.2

Business Aids, Services $14.6

Soft-Drink Bottlers $21

Hotels and Campgrounds $17.7

Retailing $25

Restaurants $57

Gas Stations $89

Auto Dealers $320

1987 Sales (billions)

Figure 22-3 Biggest franchised industries. (Reprinted from *USA Today*, Feb. 11, 1988, p. 8D.)

Table 22-2   Ten Most and Ten Least Expensive Franchises

Company	Start-Up Cost and Franchise Fee ($)
10 MOST EXPENSIVE FRANCHISES	
1. Hampton Inn	2,300,000
2. Quality Inns Intl.	1,900,000
3. Econo Lodge	1,800,000
4. Hardee's	433,000
5. Roy Rogers	396,000
6. McDonald's	363,000
7. Ponderosa Steakhouses	342,000
8. Jack in the Box	331,000
9. Round Table Pizza	322,000
10. Super 8 Motels	320,000
10 LEAST EXPENSIVE FRANCHISES	
1. Packy the Shipper	995
2. Novus Windshield Repair	2,000
3. Sunshine Polishing System	2,675
4. Coverall	4,200
5. Stork News	5,000
6. Chem-Dry	9,000
7. Coustic-Glo	11,250
8. Jani-King	13,500
9. Duraclean	16,800
10. Video Data Services	16,950

Source: Reprinted from *USA Today*, Feb. 11, 1988, p. 8B.

strength of the competition, the number of different parties involved, and the number of other factors that must be considered.[56] For an outline of the major steps involved in developing a business plan, see the Practically Speaking discussion, "Steps in Developing a Business Plan."

A business plan serves several important purposes.[57] For one thing, it helps prospective owners and entrepreneurs carefully think through every aspect of their proposed endeavor. Since the business plan requires writing down information about such aspects as the risks involved, financing requirements, and intended markets, prospective owners and entrepreneurs are forced to think concretely about such matters.

Another important purpose of a business plan is to help prospective owners and entrepreneurs obtain financing. For example, the U.S. Small Business Administration (SBA) requires that a business plan accompany applications for the agency's small-business loan program. Most private investors will not even consider financing a venture without seeing a well-thought-out business plan. For example, Phil Romano uses business plans to help obtain outside funding for his various ventures. Obtaining significant funding from banks also will involve submitting a business plan. Even short-run loans may be easier to negotiate when an entrepreneur can demonstrate that a new business venture is progressing according to plan.

Still another important purpose of a business plan is to provide a basis for measuring plan progress. Some experts argue that planning is particularly important for new ventures because of the inherent instability involved. A business plan can help establish milestones for periodic reviews, during which assumptions and accomplishments can be compared. Careful monitoring

P R A C T I C A L L Y   S P E A K I N G

STEPS IN DEVELOPING A BUSINESS PLAN

The steps below will give you a good idea of what is involved in putting together a business plan. The timetable for developing the plan will depend on the complexity of the situation and your own time schedule.[58]

1. Make commitment to go into business for yourself.
2. Analyze your strengths and weaknesses, paying special attention to your business experience, business education, and desires. Then answer this question:

   Why should I be in business for myself?
3. Choose the product or service that best fits your strengths and desires. Then answer these questions:

   What need will my product or service fill?

   What is unique about my product or service? How do I know it is unique?

   What will my product or service do for customers? What will it not do?

   What should it do later that it does not now do?
4. Research the market for your product or service to find answers to such questions as these:

   Who are my customers? Where are they? What is their average income? How do they buy? At what price? In what quantities? When do they buy? When will they use my product or service? Where will they use it? Why will they buy it?

   Who are my competitors? Where are they? How strong are they?

   What is the total market potential? Is it growing?
5. Forecast your share of market, if possible. Then forecast your sales revenues over a 3-year period, broken down as follows:

   First year—monthly

   Second year—quarterly

   Third year—yearly

   Next, answer this question:

   Why do I believe my sales revenue forecast is realistic?
6. Choose a site for your business; then answer this question:

   Why do I prefer this site to other possible sites?
7. *This step applies only to entrepreneurs who plan to go into manufacturing.* Develop your production plan, answering these questions:

   How big should my plant be?

   How should my production process be laid out?

   What equipment will I need? In what size?

   How will I control the waste, quality, and inventory of my product?
8. Develop your marketing plan, answering such questions as these:

   How am I going to create customers? At what price? By what kinds of advertising and sales promotion? Through personal selling? How?
9. Develop your organizational plan, answering this question:

   What kinds of skills and talents will I need to make my business grow?

   Draw up an organization chart that spells out who does what, who has what authority, and who reports to whom.
10. Develop your legal plan, focusing on whether to form a sole proprietorship, a partnership, or a corporation, and then explain your choice.
11. Develop your accounting plan, explaining the kinds of records and reports you need and how you will use them.
12. Develop your insurance plan, answering this question:

    What kinds of insurance will I need to protect my venture against possible loss from unforeseen events?
13. Develop a computer plan, spelling out the ways that computer services may help you plan and control your business.
14. Develop your financial plan by preparing these statements:

    A 3-year cash budget. Show how much cash you will need before opening for business, and how much cash you expect will flow in and out of your business, broken down as follows:

    First year—monthly

    Second year—quarterly

    Third year—yearly

    An income statement for the first year only.

    Balance sheets for the beginning and end of the first year.

    A profit graph (breakeven chart), showing when you will begin to make a profit.

    Then determine how you will finance your business and where you expect to raise money.
15. Write a cover letter summarizing your business plan, stressing its purpose and its promise.

Sue Ling Gin became a millionaire by speculating in Chicago real estate. Now she is in a position to help finance new ventures, including an airline food company.

increases the likelihood of identifying significant deviations from the plan and making modifications before the frail new venture is forced out of business.[59]

Finally, business plans often help prospective owners and entrepreneurs establish credibility with others, which is required for the organization's success. For example, potential employees may need to be convinced that they are joining an organization with a strong chance of success. Suppliers may be more willing to extend a line of credit when the business plan appears sound. Major customers may be more inclined to place orders when there are convincing arguments that the new venture or small business will be able to deliver the necessary products or services.

Obtaining Resources

Two of the most important resources typically needed in starting a new firm or acquiring an existing small business are financing and human resources. Each plays a crucial role.

Financing. New ventures, even small ones, require funds to operate. Moreover, most of their revenues in the early years must be plowed back into the business in order to fuel growth. Of course, purchasing and operating a small business also requires considerable funding. There are many sources of financing for entrepreneurs and prospective small-business owners. The most common are personal savings and loans from family and friends. For example, Mark Turner, who with a friend founded the Columbus-based Great Steak Escape restaurant chain, borrowed $20,000 from his parents to fund his part of the start-up costs. Katha Diddel started her business with a $5000 loan from a Hong Kong bank. Phil Romano has initiated several businesses with loans from banks, money borrowed from friends, loans from the U.S. Small Business Administration, and funds from stock sold to private investors, as well as with his own funds. Potential sources of funding for entrepreneurs and prospective small-business owners are shown in Table 22-3. For the most part, venture capitalists tend to be mainly interested in new ventures and small businesses with promising high-growth prospects and may not be a good source of funding for purchases of existing small businesses whose growth possibilities appear more moderate.

One of the major issues associated wit securing funding is the amount of equity (or ownership of the firm) and potential control an entrepreneur or prospective small-business owner must relinquish in order to obtain the necessary financing. There are two major types of funding available.[60] The first is debt capital. **Debt capital** is financing that involves a loan to be repaid, usually with interest. Typically, part of the loan arrangement involves putting up some asset (such as a car, a house, or machinery) as collateral in case the firm is not able to repay the debt. Banks are the major source of debt capital to new ventures and small businesses, although some debt capital is available through other sources, such as the Small Business Administration.

The second major type of funding available to entrepreneurs is equity capital. **Equity capital** is financing which usually requires that the investor be given some form of ownership in the venture. The investor shares in the profits and in any proceeds from the sale of assets in proportion to the equity held. For example, Phil Romano gave up 48 percent of his equity in Fuddruckers to obtain the $150,000 that he needed to start the business. When he later sold the company, the investors were entitled to 48 percent of the proceeds. Because of the success of the venture, a $15,000 investment in Fuddruckers was worth about $3.5 million 3 years later. One recent study of entrepreneurs showed that the overall

Debt capital A type of financing that involves a loan to be repaid, usually with interest

Equity capital A type of financing which usually requires that the investor be given some form of ownership in the venture

Table 22-3   Potential Sources of Funding a New Ventures and Small Businesses

Wealthy individuals: Go to these individuals either directly or through a third party. These people normally prefer common stock and secured loans, expect a substantial ownership stake in the company, and like to keep tabs on their investment.

Venture capitalists: These institutional risk takers are normally located through CPAs, attorneys, and bankers. They usually have formulas for evaluating a business, tend to specialize in certain types of businesses, and prefer strong minority positions. They often structure deals with both equity and debt characteristics.

Small Business Administration: The SBA has a variety of loan programs for small businesses that cannot borrow from conventional vendors on reasonable terms. There are normally limits on the amount of money available, but the interest rates are slightly lower than those on regular commercial loans.

Commercial banks: Banks generally require security and guarantees before making start-up loans and sometimes impose other restrictions on the borrower. A borrower can expect to pay the prime rate plus 1 to 4 points.

Business development corporations: BDCs are privately owned corporations charted by about half the states to make loans to small businesses. They can develop creative financing packages, and their loans are generally guaranteed by the SBA.

State venture capital funds: About half the states have programs which provide venture-capital funds. Most make loans, and some provide equity capital. Information about these sources of funding can normally be obtained from the local state economic or industrial development office.

Shares sold by the entrepreneur or small-business owner: To attract outside investors, some entrepreneurs and small-business owners sell shares at private or public offerings. Such offerings are very technical and require expert legal help to conform to the federal securities laws and appropriate state laws.

Source: Adapted from *Changing Times*, September 1985, pp. 38–43. [Also reprinted in "How to Bank-roll Your Future," in Clifford M. Baumback and Joseph Mancuso (eds.), *Entrepreneurship and Venture Management*, Prentice-Hall, Englewood Cliffs, N.J., 1987, pp. 188–189.]

equity relinquished by their firms in order to obtain capital during the early stages averages 45.1 percent.[61]

New venture capital recently has been playing a major role in the creation of start-up companies in eastern Europe. In one such case, Jan Bednarek, the general manager of Wistom, a state-owned synthetic fiber company in Poland, has used some of the profits from the company to furnish seed money for 18 start-up companies. His goal is to create enough jobs and pump enough profits into the local economy of Tomaszow Mazowiecki (a town of 70,000 people, located 60 miles southwest of Warsaw) to enable his antiquated synthetic fibers plant to be closed. Wistom invests in new ventures for an agreed-upon amount of stock. In one case, a new venture began by designing and producing improved lighting fixtures for the Wistom factory. Another start-up, which specializes in factory automation and industrial processing equipment, is housed in the Wistom facility. It is currently making $20,000 per month in profits, and Bednarek is looking forward to its employees' buying out Wistom's stake in the company.[62]

In the United States, new ventures typically use a combination of debt and equity capital. Debt capital tends to be used for short-time financing (funds needed for a year or less) to pay for such things as monthly expenses, advertising, special sales from suppliers, and unforeseen emergencies. For the longer range, both long-term debt capital (funds for 1 to 5 years or more) and equity capital are often used to finance basic start-up costs, the purchase or replacement of equipment, expansions, and other major expenditures. Small businesses that are aiming for relatively moderate growth frequently used mainly debt capital, with the owners retaining most or all of the equity.

Human Resources. Although many new ventures are initiated by entrepreneurs, others have multiple founders who are often referred to as a venture team. A **venture team** is a group of two or more individuals who band together for the purpose of creating a new venture. Several studies indicate that venture teams are particularly likely to be involved in the start-up of high-technology companies.[63] Ideally, venture-team members complement one another's skills, thus strengthening the prospects of the new venture. Mutual trust and strong commitment to the start-up are also essential ingredients. Potential venture-team members need to explore their mutual expectations carefully, since a breakup of the team early in the venture can have a serious detrimental effect on the success of the endeavor.[64]

Venture team   A group of two or more individuals who band together for the purpose of creating a new venture

Of course, new ventures and small businesses typically require the help of others besides entrepreneurs or owners. In fact, a recent poll shows that small-business owners believe their most difficult problem is finding competent workers and then motivating them to perform.[65] Since each employee in a small business represents a large percentage of the work force, a given individual's contribution can be particularly significant to the success of the organization. Thus entrepreneurs and small-business owners need to use good selection processes in order to find individuals who will be strong assets as the organization grows. (Selection issues are discussed in Chapter 12.) For example, Leo Imperiali, the founder of the Tile World chain of tile stores, hired many workers who were inexperienced but showed a willingness to learn and an enthusiasm for the venture. As the venture grew, Imperiali generally followed a policy of good training and hiring from within. As a result, he had the human resources to support his expansion plans.[66]

Selecting an Appropriate Site

Choosing a location for a business is typically an important decision, although the criticality varies according to the type of business involved. for instance, location can be crucial to the success of a business like a fast-food restaurant, which depends heavily on potential customers passing by. On the other hand, a business like a general contracting operation that relies heavily on advertising to reach customers will not be as directly affected by its location. In selecting an appropriate business site, entrepreneurs and small-business owners usually take into consideration major factors such as the community, the trade area, lease or buy trade-offs, zoning or licensing requirements, and cost per square foot.[67]

Community. The community in which an entrepreneur or small-business owner chooses to operate is often a matter of personal choice. Some may prefer a specific geographic location, such as the northwest; others may wish to operate in a small town; while still others will opt for a large metropolitan area. Some local governments offer benefits and incentives to businesses willing to locate in their areas.

Trade Area. Usually, location decisions also involve identifying a *trade area*, the geographic area that contains the firm's prospective customers. Determining a trade area includes deciding who the customers will be and learning about their buying habits. For example, a study of food-store purchases in a major city found that close to 70 percent of the customers shopped at stores within one to five blocks of their homes. For suburban locations, the majority of customers lived within 3 miles of the stores, although some traveled as far as 5 miles. In rural locations, most of the customers lived a 10-minute drive away, with the trade area extending as far as a 20-minute drive.

Lease or Buy. New businesses typically lease facilities, sometimes with an option to buy. One reason is that financing sources are normally reluctant to provide funds for the purchase of physical facilities when a firm has no established track record. New ventures and small businesses are also usually discouraged from making major renovations while leasing, because the changes may increase the value of the property that the firm may ultimately wish to buy. As the business develops, small-business owners tend to purchase facilities. Of course, when owners purchase an existing small business, buying the facilities may be part of the contract agreement.

Zoning and Licensing. Zoning laws could have some bearing on the location of new ventures and small businesses. For example, many types of businesses, such as light manufacturing or automobile sales, are usually not permitted in residential areas. Moreover, licenses are frequently required in many jurisdictions in order to operate certain types of businesses, such as restaurants, dry cleaners, gas stations, liquor stores, and bars. For these reasons, a thorough investigation into zoning and licensing requirements is usually conducted early in the site selection process.

Cost per Square Foot. Rental or lease costs will vary and can be very substantial for a new venture or other small business. Commercial property is usually rented or leased on a cost-per-square-foot basis. These costs are normally determined by location, condition of property, services furnished, and availability of parking for both employees and customers. sometimes starting a business in an incubator can greatly reduce such costs, although the location of the incubator may not be suitable in many cases. Regardless of the choice, with a business plan developed, resources acquired, and a site determined, issues of managing the ongoing business grow in importance.

MANAGING A SMALL BUSINESS

As new ventures begin to take shape and other small businesses engage in commerce, they must be managed. In this section we consider the growth stages of small businesses as they emerge and develop, the transition from entrepreneurship to intrapreneurship, and some special issues and problems associated with entrepreneurship and small-business management.

Stages of Small-Business Growth

Although a number of researchers have examined the growth stages of organizations (see Chapter 7), recently some efforts have been made to develop a

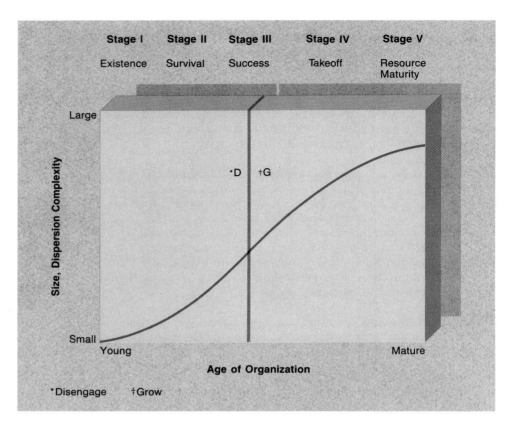

model of the stages of small-business growth in order to understand better the very early life of business organizations.[68] The results of one such effort are shown in Figure 22-4. According to the model, there are five major stages.

Stage I: Existence. In the existence stage, the small business is just getting started. The main problems it faces are attracting customers and delivering the products and services required. Critical questions center around whether or not sufficient customers can be lined up, whether the production process can actually fulfill the needs of customers, and whether there are sufficient funds to cover the emerging start-up costs. At this point, the organization is simple, usually involving an entrepreneur or owner who performs many of the required tasks and perhaps a few employees. Companies at this stage are struggling for their existence. Many times, customers or adequate production capabilities do not materialize before funds run out. If that happens, the new venture collapses or perhaps is sold for asset value.

Stage II: Survival. In the survival stage, the problem changes from concern for mere existence to concern for revenues relative to expenses. One critical question focuses on whether the company can break even and make enough profit to repair and replace assets as required. Another addresses the need to generate enough funds to finance the growth necessary for eventually earning a good return on assets and labor. At this point, the organization is still relatively simple, with a limited number of employees who may be supervised by a manager other than the owner. The main concern at this stage is survival, and the owner still makes most of the important decisions concerning the organization. Some organizations may remain at this level for some time, barely making ends meet, until the owner gives up or retires. Others may grow in size and begin to earn a reasonable profit, moving them to the next stage.

Stage III: Success. At the success stage, owners face the decision of whether to stabilize at a profitable level that can be used to support the owner's other interests (success-disengagement substage) or build on the accomplishments so far and go for further growth (success-growth substage).

In *substage III-D* (for disengagement), the company has good economic health and earns average or above-average profits. The company may be able to stay at this stage for some time as long as it is adaptive enough to ensure that an environmental change does not destroy its market niche or inept management does not create internal difficulties. The organization is usually large enough to warrant several functional managers who take over some of the duties previously performed by the owner, who often becomes involved in at least some activities elsewhere. If it does not adapt to environmental changes, the organization may go under or revert back to the survival stage.

In *substage III-G* (for growth), the owner pulls together the cash and borrowing power of the company to invest in significant further growth. Important tasks are managing the business so that it continues to be profitable and developing managers to handle the expansion. Often, additional managers are brought on board to help with the future growth. Strategic planning becomes critical, and the owner is involved in all phases of the company. If successful, the company moves to the next stage. If not, it may be able to shift to III-D; otherwise, it may slide back to the survival stage or be sold.

Stage IV: Takeoff. In the takeoff stage, the key problems are how rapidly to grow and how to finance the growth. One critical question centers around whether the owner is willing to delegate responsibilities to others in order to handle the growing enterprise. Another is whether the cash flow will be sufficient. Often, inadequate controls over expenses and poor investments by an impatient owner erode cash flow. At the same time, failure to develop other managers and unwillingness to delegate sufficiently may undermine the management structure. Both operational planning and strategic planning are extremely important. Entrepreneurs, and some small-business owners, often do not have the breadth of managerial skills and experience that is needed to handle a company at this stage. In some cases entrepreneurs recognize their shortcomings and move aside so that professional managers can steer the company at this stage.

J. Bruce Llewellyn is an entrepreneur who not only can get businesses to take off but also knows how to manage them. He started out by developing a small supermarket chain in New York City. He then went on to manage a bank, buy a majority interest in and manage a Coca-Cola bottling company, and buy and manage a network-affiliated TV station.

One example of a company in which entrepreneurs successfully turned the operation of an organization over to professional managers is BDM International, headquartered in McLean, Virginia. The high-technology consulting firm was founded in 1959 by three physicists. The first major contract was awarded to the company by the U.S. Army in 1960. The current president, Earle Williams, who was hired as a senior engineer in 1962, gradually was given greater management responsibilities and finally was made president in 1972. The founders remained major shareholders and advisers to the organization. Whereas the company had $8.1 million in contract awards and 434 employees in 1972, by 1988—when the company was acquired by the Ford Motor Company—its annual contract awards totaled $487 million and the company employed 3500 people.[69]

If efforts at this stage are unsuccessful, a company may fold or revert back to one of its former stages. One company that ran into difficulty attempting to move from substage III-G (success-growth) to stage IV (takeoff) is J. Bildner & Sons (see the following Case in Point discussion).

CASE IN POINT: James Bildner's Spectacular Rise and Fall

When James Bildner opened his first upscale grocery store in 1984, it was greeted with rave reviews. Bildner and his company, J. Bildner & Sons, Inc., were even featured in a *Newsweek* cover story on yuppies. Within 3 years, the company had 21 stores, more than 2000 employees, and sales approaching $50 million. Yet 1 year later, the company was in proceedings under Chapter 11 of the Federal Bankruptcy Code, with debts exceeding assets by about $30 million. The number of stores had shrunk to six, and the work force had been cut to 250 members. How could a business that started up so well turn so sour?

When Bildner, who was then 30 years old, opened his first store in Boston in late 1984, he envisioned a grocery store that offered more service and convenience than a normal supermarket, as well as lower prices and higher-quality food than a convenience store. Bildner had experience with both types of stores. He had worked at Kings, a regional New Jersey grocery chain that his father now manages. He also did a stint as vice president of operations for a chain of convenience stores called The Store 24, Inc.

The first J. Bildner & Sons was located in an ornate Boston building dating back to 1865. It stayed open long hours, took phone orders, allowed credit cards, and offered free delivery. In fact, delivery people would even pick up a customer's dry cleaning on the way and shop at other stores for items that Bildner's didn't have. Bildner's itself was well stocked with an enticing array of selections, including such delights as hot red-pepper fettucine and salmon-spinach, prepared in Bildner's own kitchens.

The store was extremely popular from the day it opened. Since the store's success relied on a concept, rather than a patentable product, Bildner was concerned that competitors would attempt to establish similar stores. Also, he figured that he could do more advertising if he could spread the cost across a number of stores. Accordingly, he opened five more stores in the Boston area in 1985. The following year, he opened eight more, including locations in Atlanta and in Birmingham, Alabama.

In September 1986, the company sold stock to the public at $13 per share in order to raise $15 million for further expansion. Shortly thereafter, Bildner's had a store in New York City, as well as leases for seven additional stores in New York. Leases also were signed for nine other stores in such cities as Philadelphia; Chicago; and Fairfax, Virginia. The expansion had reached a feverish pace.

By the following summer, though, trouble signs were appearing. That's when the company closed its Birmingham store and its first two New York stores. By July 1988, the company had to file for bankruptcy protection.

In sorting out what went wrong, some observers say that company executives didn't do enough planning before expanding. For example, in New York, the company expected costs to be about 10 percent higher than in Boston, but they were actually 40 percent more. Construction delays and an attempt to unionize the New York stores also delayed openings and drove up costs. In addition, company executives underestimated the competition in New York, where the company's offerings were not as unique as those in Boston. Furthermore, the expansion into some other cities involved locating outlets in department stores, a concept far different from the original Bildner's site.

The company's management also found it difficult to make the transition from a small number of stores with a local orientation to a larger company in multiple cities. Top managers became so absorbed in the expansion that soon they began to lose touch with what was going on in individual stores. Financial controls were fairly loose, so the company's good cash position faded quickly. Now Bildner is working hard with the remaining stores to being them back into line with his original concept while he tries to work his way out of bankruptcy.[70] ■

Unfortunately, James Bildner was not able to effectively navigate his company from success-growth to takeoff. Had he been successful, J. Bildner & Sons would have been ready to move on to the next stage, resource maturity.

Stage V: Resource Maturity. At this stage, the company needs to consolidate and control the financial gains resulting from rapid growth, but it also must attempt to retain the spirit that brought it this far. However, at this stage, growing size may cause **ossification,** a condition characterized by lack of innovation and avoidance of risk (which may be in marked contrast to the company's orientation in its early days). Eventually, depending on how quickly the environment changes, ossification can lead to eventual decline, perhaps even back to the survival stage or to the end of the business. At this stage, the company must begin aggressive steps to encourage innovation. Here the emphasis shifts from entrepreneurship to intrapreneurship.

Ossification A condition that is characterized by lack of innovation and avoidance of risk

Entrepreneurship versus Intrapreneurship

We have discussed many means of promoting innovation in the various Promoting Innovation sections throughout this book. By the time a company reaches the resource maturity stage, the emphasis has switched from building on the initial momentum of entrepreneurship to having a strong need for intrapreneurship. *Intrapreneurship* is the practice of innovating by developing new products, processes, or services while one is part of an organization (see Chapters 1 and 7). Entrepreneurship, as we have seen, also involves innovating, but the innovations are carried out by creating a new organization.

Major Issues and Problems

New ventures and small businesses offer the potential for considerable satisfaction in terms of both accomplishments and financial remuneration. On the other hand, such endeavors involve several relatively unique issues and problems.

Bankruptcy and Failure Prospects. For one thing, as we saw with J. Bildner & Sons, things do not always progress smoothly. In fact, the odds of failure are quite high. When things do go wrong and a company fails, what are the major reasons? The results of one study of 570 businesses that went bankrupt (see Table 22-4) show that the opinions of business owners are not always the same as those of their creditors. Actually, these results are not too surprising given what we know from psychology about the self-serving perceptual bias—the tendency to perceive oneself as responsible for successes and to blame outside factors for failures (see Chapter 15). Still, the data do cast some doubt on the explanations frequently given by small-business owners and managers to the effect that the blame lies mainly with outside factors.

Table 22-4   Perceived Causes of Business Bankruptcies

Cause of Bankruptcy	PERCENTAGE CITING PARTICULAR CAUSE	
	Owner's Opinion	Creditors' Opinion
Business depression	68	29
Inefficient management	28	59
Insufficient capital	48	33
Bad-debt losses	30	18
Competition	40	9
Decline in value of assets	32	6
Poor business location	15	3
Excessive interest charaged on borrowed money	11	2
Unfavorable changes in trading area	11	2

Source: Adapted from Clifford M. Baumback, *How to Organize and Operate a Small Business,* 8th ed., Prentice-Hall, Englewood Cliffs, N.J., 1988, p. 17.

Dark Side of Entrepreneurship. One researcher writes of the "dark side of entrepreneurship," alluding to the creative energy of the entrepreneur that can, at the same time, be a destructive force in building a company. For example, their bias toward action sometimes causes entrepreneurs to act without thinking. Moreover they often experience great difficulty taking directions from others and have high needs for control that make it difficult for them to delegate responsibility.[71]

Family-Life Stresses. Both small-business owners and entrepreneurs often work grueling hours, frequently neglecting their families in the process. One recent survey conducted by the National Federation of Independent Businesses found that entrepreneurs commonly work 60 to 70 hours per week and sometimes more during the early years of establishing their businesses. Although some managers, particularly top-level executives of large corporations, also work similar long hours, the high odds of failure add to the pressure when young small businesses are involved. In one case, business pressures led entrepreneur Carl R. Zwerner and his wife of 19 years to get a divorce. Zwerner, who runs Glass, Inc., a glass-importing firm in Miami, recently donated $500,000 to Georgia State University for a professorship in family-run businesses, with strong emphasis on the conflict between family and business.[72]

Need for Outside Assistance. Entrepreneurs and small-business owners often do not recognize the need to seek outside assistance from local agencies, such as a state-sponsored small-business development center, or from other advisers. Yet recent studies indicate that small firms that receive such outside assistance tend to perform better than those which do not. Assistance on administrative matters and operations management often is helpful. However, the results tend to be best when the assistance also addresses strategic management issues, an area likely to be somewhat neglected by small businesses.[73]

Ethical Issues. Some experts believe that small businesses are particularly vulnerable to unethical practices. One reason for this assessment is the weak financial condition of many small firms, which may make the owners more vulnerable to demands for bribes. Likewise, problems competing with larger companies may induce owners to offer bribes in order to obtain business. Still another reason for possible vulnerability is that there usually are fewer checks and balances in place in small firms (compared with their larger counterparts), a situation that may make it fairly easy for owners to engage in unethical behaviors (such as pocketing cash from a sale or charging personal items to the company account). On the other hand, other experts argue that small businesses have an advantage in being able to maintain ethical standards because their small size enables the owner to detect unethical practices within the firm.[74]

CHAPTER SUMMARY

Entrepreneurship is the "creation of new enterprise," and it involves innovation. Three criteria that can be used to evaluate the entrepreneurial opportunity condition associated with different degrees of innovation are risk, evaluation, and profit potential. The topic of entrepreneurship has been the subject of increasing research and public interest because of important contributions made by new ventures and related small businesses in the areas of economic growth, innovation, employment opportunities, and alternatives for women and minorities.

Research studies indicate that a number of factors influence the decision of whether to engage in entrepreneurship. Entrepreneurs tend to have a few similarities in personality, background, and other characteristics, but these same characteristics are often also indicative of managers and individuals in other occupations. Certain life-path circumstances seem to increase the probability that an individual will become an entrepreneur: unsatisfactory work environment, negative displacement, career transition points, and the presence of positive-pull influencers. Favorable environmental conditions and positive perceptions of desirability and feasibility also are factors that influence individuals to become entrepreneurs.

In considering what type of business to pursue, entrepreneurs and prospective small-business owners have three main choices. Entrepreneurs most often start a new firm, although sometimes they may acquire an existing firm and quickly make major changes in its direction. Other small-business owners may acquire existing businesses and retain their basic direction. Alternatively, they may purchase a franchise.

Most experts on small business and entrepreneurship strongly recommend that individuals preparing to start a business develop a business plan. Two of the most important resources needed in starting a new firm are adequate financing and human resources. There are a number of major factors that need to be considered when selecting an appropriate site for a business, including the community, the trade area, lease or buy trade-offs, zoning or licensing requirements, and cost per square foot.

The process of managing and developing new ventures and small businesses comprises five major stages of growth: existence, survival, success (including disengagement or growth substages), takeoff, and resource maturity. As businesses reach the resource maturity stage, the emphasis needs to shift from entrepreneurship to intrapreneurship. Entrepreneurs and owners face several particularly important issues and problems in managing their small businesses, including high bankruptcy and failure prospects, behaviors of entrepreneurs that can undermine a growing organization, family-life stresses, the need for outside help, and ethical issues.

MANAGERIAL TERMINOLOGY

business plan 787	entrepreneurship 774	franchiser 785	ossification 797
corridor principle 779	equity capital 790	incubator 780	start-up 782
debt capital 790	franchise 785	new venture 774	venture team 792
entrepreneur 774	franchisee 786		

QUESTIONS FOR DISCUSSION AND REVIEW

1. Define entrepreneurship. What difficulties might you have in attempting to use this definition to separate entrepreneurship from managing a small business?

2. Outline three criteria that can be used to assess the probable opportunity conditions associated with different degrees of new venture innovation. Use the criteria to evaluate the probable opportunity conditions inherent in two recent new ventures in your geographic area.

3. Explain the major economic and social contributions of new ventures and other small businesses. Identify specific situations in your geographic area in which entrepreneurship and small-business ownership has made such contributions.

4. What personality traits and other personal characteristics might you use to identify potential entrepreneurs? What advantages and disadvantages might exist in using this approach to determine who should receive a loan for a new venture?

5. Explain other major factors that might influence an individual to become an entrepreneur. To what extent might it be possible to use this information to encourage entrepreneurship among one's friends and associates?

6. What major options exist in deciding on the type of business for a new venture? If you were considering a new venture, which would you prefer and why? What might be some major advantages and disadvantages of purchasing an existing small business or a franchise?

7. Explain the major purposes of a business plan. Why is a well-constructed business plan an important factor in obtaining outside financing and other resources for a new venture?

8. Enumerate several major considerations involved in selecting an appropriate site for a new business. Use these considerations to evaluate the sites of two small businesses in your geographic area.

9. Outline the major stages in new venture growth. Explain how the J. Bildner & Sons new venture (see the Case in Point) got off track.

10. Identify three major pitfalls associated with entrepreneurship. What might be done to minimize these pitfalls?

DISCUSSION QUESTIONS FOR CHAPTER OPENING CASE

1. What factors probably influence Phil Romano to continually start new ventures?

2. Considering the discussion of new firms, how would you classify Phil Romano's various enterprises?

3. What entrepreneurial process does Phil Romano follow? What role do you think this process plays in his various successes? How do you account for his failures?

MANAGEMENT EXERCISE: AN ENTREPRENEURAL OPPORTUNITY

You have been working as an appliance salesperson at a local store for 3 years. This is your first job after graduating from college, and you took the job for several reasons: you wanted to see how a small business is organized and operates; you wanted some practical, "hands-on" small-business experience; you were looking for a niche in which you could eventually set up your own business; and, finally, the business is located in an area where you thought you might want to set up a business in the future. You believe your experience in this job has been very valuable.

Yesterday, while you were talking to the owner, he confided in you that he had long dreamed of setting up a kitchen design and appliance shop in an affluent area on the other side of town. The population of the area is expanding and is expected to continue to do so for the next two decades. The shop would be oriented toward dual-career couples who share some cooking chores, and it would focus on kitchen atmosphere, as well as utility. The owner said that he would be willing to finance such a start-up but could not actually take charge of setting it up himself because of family obligations. He wondered if you knew anyone who would be interested in developing such a project for a large chunk of equity.

You are surprised to learn of his interest in the kitchen design and appliance shop and are definitely interested in the opportunity yourself. The next day, you indicate your interest to the owner, who tells you how much financing he could make available and what equity he would expect in return. His proposal seems fair to you, and you talk it over with several people whom you trust. You are convinced that you could be successful in this type of business, but must study it further.

You recognize that you will need much more information prior to deciding whether or not to take on this entrepreneurial endeavor. Describe the information you will need and the decisions you should make prior to involving yourself in this start-up.

BARBARA GROGAN BEATS OUT BIG-NAME COMPETITION

At 35, Barbara Grogan found herself out of work and ending a 12-year marriage. For the first time in her life, she was confronted with the problem of how to make mortgage payments and put food on the table for her two children. In figuring out what to do, Grogan chose a relatively unusual niche in the construction industry—millwrighting. Her company, Denver-based Western Industrial Contractors, Inc. (WIC), moves and installs mammoth industrial equipment. Millwrighting involves projects such as hanging a four-story theater screen, putting in place a freestanding stack of storage cubicles eight stories high where the maximum vertical variance cannot exceed an eighth of an inch, and guiding a 100-ton cooling system into a plant with a crane that comes within one-sixteenth of an inch of the building's main support.

Grogan had heard of millwrighting during a 9-month period when she served as general manager of her husband's crane-and truck-rental company, but she didn't know very much about the business. Millwrighting requires huge equipment, such as cranes up to 20 stories high, trucks that are as big as railroad cars, and lots of other intricate equipment that must be synchronized perfectly in getting the job done.

In order to compete with the other 4600 millwrighting contractors nationwide, Grogan works hard to get her customers and then tries to keep them through outstanding service. "Once I get the clients, I service their socks off," Says Grogan. "The client has to win for us to win." For example, Gro-

gan recently received a call at 6 a.m. from a client at a cement factory where a kiln had been knocked out of service by an explosion. Thousands of dollars were being lost for every hour the kiln was out of commission. Grogan had a staff of 12 there by 9 a.m. and had shifts work around the clock for 4 days to repair the kiln. Nevertheless, Grogan charged only her usual fees. She says that she does not like to take advantage of clients when they have troubles. She's more interested in building long-term relationships, and this is one reason why she has been able to build her company to the point at which recent annual sales exceeded $5 million.

When she began, Grogan had $50,000 in capital and a limited knowledge of cranes. She managed to find a man with 15 years' experience as a millwright to be her partner. When she started in 1982, the Denver economy was experiencing the beginnings of an economic decline linked to problems in the energy industry. One result was that many construction companies were abandoning union contracting. In a contrary move, Grogan allied herself with the millwright's union. "My business is so specialized," she says. "When you are installing a Mylar press and it can have a vertical variance of only one ten-thousandth of an inch every 80 feet, you need people who know what they are doing." By being a union contractor, Grogan can get the skilled help she needs.

Start-up, though, was difficult. Her initial business plan was sketchy and people were skeptical. Finally, when she began interviewing people in insurance companies to determine her insurance needs, she found two people who were receptive to her plans and who helped her make connections with

When Barbara Grogan started up Western Industrial Contractors, Inc., a company that moves and installs huge industrial equipment, she was establishing a relatively unusual business—millwrighting. Grogan picked an experienced partner, actively pursued customers, and provided top service. As a result, her company is now one of the most successful in the business.

bankers and CPA. At this point, she was finally ready for customers and began making calls. One of the places that she tried was Anheuser-Busch in St. Louis, where she grew up. Most of her contact attempts were rebuffed, but she managed to talk with an engineer who, it turned, out, had once worked on her grandfather's farm. The engineer then introduced her to others, and she finally got a contract to install equipment in a bakery.

Her major breakthrough, though, came after she was in business for 8 months and was running out of money. She bid on a contract from the Manville Corporation to disassemble a pipe-manufacturing plant in Florida, ship it to Malaysia, and reassemble it. Although her own experience was meager, she highlighted the credentials of her employees and won the bid for the 5-month job. Successful completion of this project gave her the credibility that she needed to win other big jobs.

When Grogan and her partner broke up amicably in 1985, Grogan was free to move the company toward the really big contracts that she wanted. One of her efforts led to a small contract with United Airlines to modify an odd-size conveyor belt at Denver's airport. United was impressed with WIC's service orientation. A series of other contracts with United finally led to a major contract to install an underground baggage-sorting system at Chicago's O'Hare International Airport. The project involved 3 miles of conveyor belts and took 1 year to complete. WIC also does millwrighting for other major firms, including AT&T, Ralston Purina, Nabisco Brands, IBM, and ITT and the company's good reputation is leading to more work every year.

"Bidding is an act of faith," says Grogan, because each job is different. Fortunately, she has a chief estimator who has been in the business 26 years and has a real gift for judging how long a project will take and how much it will cost. In addition, Grogan has been able to finance growth from sales, leaving the company in a sound financial position with very little debt. She has kept her basic staff to a minimum. She now has a secretary, a controller, an estimator, three project managers, and twelve superintendents who supervise field operations. She hires millwrights to work on specific projects as needed, allowing her to avoid the overhead of carrying employees between projects.[75]

QUESTIONS FOR CHAPTER
CONCLUDING CASE
1. What factors entered into Barbara Grogan's decision to become an entrepreneur?
2. Assess the process that Grogan followed in setting up her business.
3. At what stage of the small-business growth cycle would you place Grogan's company? What factors have led to Barbara Grogan's success, and how did she manage to enhance her company's success? What dilemmas does she now face in terms of the small-business growth cycle?

SOHO NATURAL SODA: FROM THE KITCHEN TO THE WORLD

When Connie Best and Sophia Collier began experimenting with different flavors of natural soda in their Brooklyn kitchen in 1977, Best was 24 years old and Collier was 21. Convinced that there was a market for a healthful soft drink, the two childhood friends pooled $10,000 each to start the American Natural Beverage Corporation. By 1988, the company's product, Soho Natural Soda, was sold in 37 states and overseas; annual sales had reached almost $30 million.

Even before starting their company, both Collier and Best had shown an entrepreneurial bent. Collier graduated from high school in New York at age 16 and then lived on an Indian reservation in Arizona for a period of time before starting a small construction company and a grocery store in Maine. She subsequently returned to New York at age 20 to write her autobiography, *Soul Rush,* which earned her the $10,000 that became her share of the start-up funding for American Natural. Best was a free-lance writer who knew nothing about business, but she had a history of setting difficult goals for herself and striving very hard to achieve them. Best borrowed her $10,000 stake from a friend who believed in her abilities and in the idea of making a soft drink solely from natural ingredients.

To develop their natural soft-drink product, Best and Collier obtained information about the latest soda-making techniques, as well as more traditional methods, from the New York Public Library. On the basis of their research, the friends produced two formulas, which they then "tested" on their neighbors. The tests produced a stalemate, with one neighbor preferring one formula and the other neighbor preferring the other formula. To resolve the issue, Best and Collier took the two alternatives to a local health food store, where they held a tasting contest at the checkout counter. The winner, which became the first natural soda to be sold by the company, was "Fruit Punch." Best christened the product "Soho Natural Soda," a name chosen to reflect the avant-garde image of New York's famous artist neighborhood.

Best and Collier also conducted library research on the soft-drink industry. They knew that, at the time, Coca-Cola's share of the market was about 24 percent and Pepsi's was about 19 percent. In their view, that left more than half the market to other firms. With their innovative soft drink, they believed that they could get at least one-tenth of 1 percent of the $26 billion soft-drink market, or $26 million of the business available. The fact that the soft-drink business was dominated by a handful of huge consumer-product companies, was considered "mature," and had not seen many new product introductions in recent years did not deter them. They believed that a targeted "niche," or focus, approach to such a market might make the difference for a small brand. Best decided that the way to take on the mass-market soft drinks was to position Soho as a "class" alternative, an idea borrowed from the gourmet food industry but never before applied to soft drinks. As a result, the design and marketing of Soho expanded the concept of "natural" beyond the good-for-you approach to one that emphasized full, rich flavors and a sophisticated, artistic image.

When in their early 20s, Connie Best (top) borrowed $10,000 from a friend and Sophia Collier (bottom) used the proceeds of an autobiography to create a company that would produce natural flavor sodas. This fledgling business grew in 11 years into a flourishing corporation (American Natural Beverage Corporation) with annual sales of $30 million. Credit and penny-pinching saw them through the early lean years until they were able to get bank loans. Then, creative marketing and close distributor relationships helped promote the product and get it on store shelves. Because expanding the market further would require large-scale investments and debt financing, Best and Collier decided to sell their company to Seagram Beverage Co. in 1989, a transaction that left the two entrepreneurs multimillionaires in search of further ventures.

Having a prototype product was just the beginning. Next, they needed a bottler. They looked in the Yellow Pages and found 28 bottling plants in the northeastern United States. Next, Best or Collier visited each plant, a process that proved to be an ordeal because neither of the two owned a car and the bottling plants generally were not located near bus lines. When they finally reached each of the bottlers, they typically found little enthusiasm for their product. Some bottlers even indicated that a natural soda was a contradiction in terms. Nevertheless, by persisting, they eventually found a local bottler who had three things in common with them. For one thing, he, too, was an entrepreneur who had started with very little money. For another, he had previously bottled sodas that included "true fruit" (natural) flavors. Finally, and perhaps most importantly, he believed in the idea of a soda made with natural ingredients and thought that the two entrepreneurs could be successful. To assist them in getting started, he agreed to bottle the first 50 cases of soda on credit. The credit was significant because the income of the two entrepreneurs had dwindled to fees that Best generated by running a typing service.

Best and Collier had planned their business fairly well, writing a business plan after studying library books and materials they had received from the U.S. Small Business Administration. Nevertheless, they had little success in convincing banks to finance the endeavor. They discussed the company with several venture capitalists as well, all of whom were certain that a small consumer-product company in an industry of giants would not last long. Trade credit, such as that received from their bottler, and minimal overhead saw them through their first couple of years until Chemical Bank provided them with a $20,000 loan through a women's business task force. Until the company succeeded in growing significantly, Best and Collier continued to rely mainly on credit from suppliers and working capital from friends.

In following their high-end niche, or focus, strategy, Best and Collier targeted their product to young, affluent, urban dwellers who would be willing to pay a premium price for a soda made with real fruit extracts, natural spices, and vanilla beans and free from caffeine, sodium, artificial flavorings, colorings, and preservatives. Reaching that group with their product, however, proved to be a challenge. Best and Collier soon found that beverage distributors would not handle their product because the distributors believed that there was no market for it. Undaunted, Best and Collier personally delivered the cases of Soho Natural Soda to the few delicatessens in Soho and lower Manhattan that would give them a small amount of shelf space. Their first year in business, 1979, was not encouraging. Gross sales totaled $729, yielding a net profit of $1.

The two entrepreneurs recognized that they had to solve their distribution problem. Natural foods, with which their soft drink could be identified, are basically low-volume, high-margin products. On the other hand, most soft drinks constitute a high-volume, low-margin product. In contrast, Soho Natural Soda was intended to be a medium-volume, high-margin product. Hence, distributors of natural foods were ill-equipped to handle Soho Natural Soda, and regular beverage distributors continued to be uninterested. As a result, Best and Collier decided to set up their own distribution system. With additional credit from their bottler and a $60,000 loan from the Small Business Administration, the two organized a Manhattan distributorship. Under the new system,

Soho Natural Soda's distinctive label, designed by an award-winning illustrator, emphasises the product's rich natural flavors and reinforces its sophisticated, artistic image.

route salespeople visited delicatessens, explained the benefits and potential possibilities of the new product to the owners, and then delivered the cases of Soho Natural Soda.

At the same time, Best and Collier took another step that would help boost their product to new sales levels. The entrepreneurs wanted to improve the packaging of their product by providing a very distinctive label that would identify Soho Natural Soda as an upscale drink. To provide this unique packaging, they hired an award-winning illustrator and theater designer who had never created a label before. Since Best and Collier could not afford his fee, they agreed to give him a royalty on every can of Soho Natural Soda sold using his design. As a result, the designer ultimately made much more than would have been the case if Best and Collier could have afforded to pay him immediately in cash for the design. The new design, introduced in 1982, helped boost sales, and by 1983 Best and Collier had sold over $400,000 worth of Soho Natural Soda.

In 1984, the beer business in the United States began to slip as beer consumption leveled off and consumers became more interested in nonalcoholic beverages. As a result, distributors began looking for new products. This market change provided an important opportunity for Soho to gain access to a network of large professional distributors. Soho Natural Soda was a hit at the 1984 Interbev Trade Show. It gave the distributors, who sell on a wholesale basis, just what they needed. Soho was a natural drink, free of the preservatives, sodium, and other ingredients that the public was trying to avoid. At the same time, the distributors could make a high profit on a product that complemented, but did not compete with, their main lines. This fortunate turn of events, however, also caused a problem. The partners began to recognize that additional funding would be required to expand the business fast enough to take advantage of the growing opportunities.

During the period 1981 to 1985, Best and Collier were able to expand slowly through the prudent management of their funds and the help of supportive suppliers. Because soda is a seasonal product in the northeastern part of the United States, American Natural made the bulk of its revenues in the summer, with profits generated in late summer and fall. Yet the company needed to expend considerable funds to get its product and promotions in place in new territories and with new distributor accounts before the late spring and summer. By working very closely with distributors, Best and Collier managed to conserve funds. Still, they found that they needed additional capital to support the expansion necessary to meet the increasing demand for their product. Accordingly, in 1984

they began making sales presentations to potential investors. These presentations resulted in the sale of 28 percent of the company's stock in 1985 for a reported $3 million. This funding allowed the firm to expand further.

During 1987, rumors surfaced that Anheuser-Busch, the largest American brewer of beer, with revenues of $7.6 billion, was planning to enter the natural-soda market. The rumors were confirmed when Collier made a visit to American Natural's main bottler in Havre de Grace, Maryland, and discovered that a test run of a new soda was in progress on behalf of Anheuser-Busch. If Best and Collier ever had doubts about the viability of the natural-soda market, the discovery of a major competitor on the scene convinced them that the natural-soda category was now being taken seriously.

Soon, they both obtained information indicating that Anheuser-Busch planned to purchase the Havre de Grace plant. Best and Collier quickly located another bottler, but not before Anheuser-Busch had purchased the Havre de Grace facility, giving the brewer access to Soho's formulas and customer information. Interestingly, at this time American Natural relied on Anheuser-Busch distributors for a significant part of its business. Fortunately, these wholesalers were not pressured to abandon Soho.

At about the same time, Best received a promotional photo of the new Anheuser-Busch soft drink, called Zeltzer Seltzer, and was shocked by the strong resemblance of the label to Soho's own award-winning logo. Collier quickly sent a letter directly to August Busch, informing him of the confusing similarity in logo design and asking him to immediately change the Zeltzer

Seltzer label. The Anheuser-Busch lawyers replied that American Natural's assertions were without merit, so Best and Collier chose to defend their brand identity by seeking an injunction against the sale of Zeltzer Seltzer. After some media attention unfavorable to Anheuser-Busch, Best and Collier were countersued by the brewer for defamation. The night before the hearing on the injunction, Anheuser-Busch agreed to stop using the Zeltzer Seltzer design and dropped its countersuit. The entrepreneurs had taken on the giant and won.

By this time, Soho Natural Soda faced two or more competitors in most markets across the country. The "alternative," or "new age," beverage category, as it became known in the trade publications, was growing at double-digit rates, far outstripping the sales growth of mainstream soft drinks. Despite the new competition, American Natural continued to expand.

The marketing success of Soho was a result of a strategy of local and regional grass-roots distribution and promotion programs developed by Best. Building on the strength of the product itself, American Natural committed its modest promotional budget to dramatic, colorful, and nontraditional point-of-sale materials. Also working at the point of sale, the company arranged for thousands of in-store samplings, based on the conviction that most people would buy Soho if they had a chance to taste the product. Most summer sale seasons centered on a display promotion, supported by an array of local tastings, event sponsorships, special pricing, and limited advertising. Again, breaking from the conventions of soft-drink marketing, Soho Natural Soda sought out amateur athletic events, as well as artistic and cultural sponsorships. In an industry in which a new product is usually dependent on a multi-million-dollar advertising campaign featuring television, Soho built its franchise market by market, seeking to identify itself with its consumers through highly visible, but targeted, local media promotions.

Best and Collier also created a small, but very active, sales force that worked side by side with Soho distributors in every market, teaching beer distributors how to sell upscale soda. The closeness of these distributor relationships allowed American Natural to achieve a greater "share of mind" in the trade than the actual sales volume of Soho warranted.

Collier, as chairperson, and Best, as vice chairperson, managed their organization mainly by delegating responsibility and authority to appropriate members of their staff. Both recognized that as the organization grew, it would need to operate through others. Their management style could best be described as outlining the requirements of people's jobs and allowing individuals considerable latitude in fulfilling them.

As with many rapidly growing, entrepreneurial companies, creating middle management was a challenge. Collier and Best sought experienced managers from outside, as well as selected individuals to be promoted from within. Their vision of making an excellent product, and marketing it independently and creatively, attracted a core of bright, enthusiastic, generally young employees who were noted in the trade for their hard-working commitment to the brand. Moreover, by 1986 both founders had reached the point of recognizing the necessity of taking 4 weeks' vacation each year to relax.

Both Collier and Best had come to believe that American Natural Beverage had the potential of becoming a company with annual sales of $100 million. They also realized that additional advertising, expanded distribution, and overseas marketing agreements would likely be required for that goal to be reached. Licensing and joint ventures were also possibilities for expanding overseas. These steps, however, would require additional investments, which in turn would mean either selling more equity or incurring additional debt. For these reasons, Best and Collier decided that a prudent step would be to sell American Natural Beverage in order to ensure a well-financed future for Soho Natural Soda. Accordingly, they sold the company to the Seagram Beverage Company in March 1989 for a reputed $15 million. At the time of its sale, American Natural Beverage had 125 distributors, 12 flavors of sodas, and three major bottlers. Soho Natural Soda was offered in more than 39,000 outlets in the United States, and it was sold overseas in Japan, England, France, Germany, Guam, Okinawa, and Singapore through importers or distributors.

Entrepreneurs Best and Collier, who started with a solid idea and $20,000, are now multimillionaires considering their next venture.*

QUESTIONS FOR DISCUSSION

1. Identify the favorable environmental conditions that influenced the creation of the American Natural Beverage Corporation. What factors likely contributed to Best and Collier's perceptions that starting the corporation was both desirable and feasible?

2. Which of the seven types of new firms or ventures does American Natural Beverage represent? Give reasons for your answer.

3. How did Best and Collier develop a business plan for their new venture? What role did it play in helping them launch their new business?

4. Assess the prospects for further expansion into overseas markets. What environmental factors might be important? What strategic issues would you consider?

5. Use the stages of small-business growth to trace the development of the American Natural Beverage Corporation. Evaluate Best and Collier's decision to sell their company to the Seagram Beverage Company.

*Sources: See references at back of book.

MANAGING YOUR CAREER

Few women hold the post of chief financial officer in U.S. corporations. How did Judy Lewent rise to her position as CFO of Merck & Co., the pharmaceutical firm? First, she earned a master's degree in finance, and then held finance-related positions at Banker's Trust and Pfizer before working her way further up the corporate ladder at Merck. By her own admission "intense and aggressive," Lewent has not seen gender as an issue. As she says, "I have never experienced overt bias. I've never been impeded in anything I wanted to do."

When Judy C. Lewent was promoted to corporate vice president for finance and chief financial officer (CFO) of Merck & Company, the drug giant, in 1990, her appointment gained national attention. She had become one of the few women to hold a top financial post in a major U.S. corporation. Studying her career path is instructive for individuals pursuing careers of their own.

Lewent became interested in finance at an early age, first reading the stock pages at age 7 on her grandfather's knee. She grew up in Manhattan, where her mother was an accountant and her father was an import-export executive who treated her as an "intellectual peer." After receiving a bachelor's degree in economics from Goucher College in Towson, Maryland, in 1970, Lewent earned a master's degree in finance from the Sloan School of Management at the Massachusetts Institute of Technology in 1972. She decided to pursue the graduate degree because a series of summer jobs during college convinced her that she would need such a degree to be viewed seriously in the corporate world.

After receiving her graduate degree, she became an associate in the corporate finance office of E. F. Hutton. In 1974, she accepted a position at Bankers Trust as an assistant vice president, before moving to the Roering division of Pfizer as controller. By 1980, she was invited to join the laboratory division at Merck, Sharp, and Dohme (the predecessor of Merck & Company), where she initially held a position as the director of acquisition and analysis. She later served as assistant controller of the laboratory division (1983); corporate executive director of financial evaluation and analysis (1985); and, finally, corporate vice president and treasurer (1987), the position she held until her most recent promotion. While working in the laboratory division, she became acquainted with and later worked for the division's director, P. Roy Vagelos, who subsequently became chairman and chief executive officer at Merck (see the opening case in Chapter 7). Lewent refers to Vagelos as her mentor and says that she would not be in her present position without his help. Vagelos says simply that Lewent was the best candidate for the job.

"I am an intense, aggressive, and definitely hard-charging person," says Lewent in describing herself. For example, her idea of an ideal vacation with her husband, Mark L. Shapiro, includes 2 hours of vigorous tennis per day, followed by swimming 50 or 60 laps in the pool, and then walking on the beach. As CFO, Lewent oversees all financial matters at Merck, including the handling of $1 billion in cash and short-term investments and $1 billion in pension funds.[1]

THE NATURE OF CAREER MANAGEMENT

Career A sequence of work-related activities and experiences that span the course of a person's life

As Lewent's path to date illustrates, a **career** is a sequence of work-related activities and experiences that span the course of a person's life.[2] This definition recognizes that a career develops over time, encompasses objective conditions (such as specific job duties and levels of responsibility), and also includes subjective reactions (such as enthusiasm or boredom). The subjective assessment of career aspects is particularly important, since it is the individual who ultimately must judge the success of a career. While success sometimes is framed in terms of advancement (as in our depiction of Judy Lewent), career specialists increasingly emphasize that individuals must establish their own criteria for success and that such criteria can be far-ranging (e.g., pay, adventure, working in new areas, or helping others). For example, Philip Seiden, an IBM physicist, voluntarily resigned from a senior management position 15 years ago to channel his efforts into research on such issues as galactic structures. "Have you made it in your own eyes? That's what really matters," Seiden says.[3]

Regardless of the criteria, one noted career expert argues that the crucial element in one's career is experiencing *psychological success*, which basically is feeling a sense of personal accomplishment and fulfillment.[4] Psychological success energizes our efforts and impels us to undertake the new challenges that foster our development over time. In order to establish a career that encompasses the enhancement of skills and the growth likely to be associated with psychological success, though, individuals need to engage in career management. **Career management** is the continuing process of setting career goals, formulating and implementing strategies for reaching the goals, and monitoring the results.[5] Without engaging in career management, individuals leave the development of their careers virtually to chance—a risky proposition. In this Appendix, then, we examine several career management issues that are relevant to developing careers as managers but also can be applied to pursuing other types of careers as well.

Career management The continuing process of setting career goals, formulating and implementing strategies for reaching the goals, and monitoring the results

ENGAGING IN CAREER MANAGEMENT

Career management can be undertaken by an individual alone or in conjunction with the career development program of an organization. In either case, there are important factors to consider, including the main steps in the career management process, major stages in career development, and potential means of effectively utilizing the career development programs offered by organizations.[6]

Steps in the Career Management Process

Four major steps make up the career management process. These steps can be used on a recurring basis to periodically reassess career directions and rechannel efforts when necessary.

1. *Explore career options.* The career exploration step involves collecting and analyzing information that is relevant to one's career-related decisions. To carry out this step effectively, individuals need to gather information about their own values, interests, and talents, as well as about opportunities and obstacles in the environment that are likely to affect career options. Means of self-assessment include writing one's personal life story (e.g., educational experiences, hobbies, work experiences, significant changes and turning points, key decisions, and visualizations about the future), taking vocational interest tests at a college or university career center, and developing a description of an ideal job. Evaluating opportunities means analyzing various occupations, organizations, and types of jobs to help prepare for making informed career decisions. One useful source of information on opportunities is the *Occupational Outlook Handbook,* published by the U.S. Department of Labor, which provides data on such issues as job duties, earnings, educational and other requirements, and demand outlooks for over 200 occupations. Other possibilities include career-related materials available at a local library and personal interviews with individuals in occupations in which one has an interest. In Chapter 1, we discuss several skills,

educational credentials, and experience factors that are associated with individuals who have become top-level managers.

2. *Set career goals.* The next major step in the career management process is setting specific career goals. Generally, individuals are likely to be more successful in their careers when they set specific goals that they wish to achieve. Some goals may be long-run targets, such as becoming vice president for human resources at a major company. Others may focus on shorter-term outcomes, such as obtaining a position as a recruiter or achieving a promotion to director of human resources for a plant. Of course, such goals must be realistic and should reflect the information analyzed in the previous step.

3. *Develop and implement career strategy.* Once individuals determine career goals, they also need to develop and implement a *career strategy,* a set of activities formulated to help an individual achieve career goals. A number of possible major career strategies are shown in Table 1. These strategies can be used alone or in combination. For example, an individual might strive to perform very competently in a current job and also attempt to make extra contributions. Judy Lewent, for instance, typically works 70 hours per week and has a history of making innovative contributions. One of her innovations is a computer program called the Drug Research Uncertainty Game (DRUG), a simulation that is designed to instruct new Merck managers about the risks involved in drug development (e.g., invest too little and the hypothetical company, "Drugs R Us," goes out of business).[7] Of course, various strategies should be carefully matched to the characteristics of the situation, including the type of job, nature of the industry, and character of the corporate culture.

Table 1 Major Career Strategies

Career Strategy	Description of Strategy
Competence in current job	Attempting to perform effectively in one's current job
Extended work involvement	Deciding to devote considerable amounts of time, energy, and emotion to one's work role
Skill development	Attempting to acquire or enhance work-related skills and abilities through training and/or job experience
Opportunity development	Performing actions designed to make one's interests and aspirations known to others and to make oneself aware of opportunities that are consistent with those aspirations
Development of mentor relationships	Performing actions designed to seek, establish, and utilize relationships with a significant other in order to receive or provide information, guidance, support, and opportunities
Image building	Attempting to communicate the appearance of acceptability, success, and/or potential for success
Organizational politics	Attempting to use flattery, conformity, coalitions, and trading of favors and influence as a means of attaining desired outcomes

Jeffrey H. Greenhaus, *Career Management,* Table 2.1. Copyright © 1987 by the Dryden Press, a division of Holt, Rinehart and Winston, Inc. Adapted by permission of the publisher.

4. *Appraise career progress.* After implementing a career strategy, individuals must continually appraise their progress toward their career goals by acquiring and using career-related feedback. Constructive feedback allows individuals to assess the extent to which their goals are realistic and their strategies are effective. Major sources of feedback include work performance, recognition from one's boss, performance appraisal and coaching sessions with one's boss, input from peers, data from other significant persons at work, and reactions from nonwork segments (e.g., working long hours on weekends may engender praise from the boss but complaints from family members). The appraisal process may lead individuals to reassess their career options, revise career goals, and/or reevaluate strategies. Thus the career management process is essentially a loop through which individuals continually reassess their situation throughout the course of their careers.

Such reassessments may sometimes lead to major changes in direction. For example, Richard Faulkner sold his Illinois dairy farm in 1958 to acquire funding to open a McDonald's franchise in Colorado Springs, Colorado. He added nine more McDonald's outlets before selling them in 1986, after he began to have eye problems brought on by diabetes. Unhappy with retirement, though, Faulkner purchased 80 percent of the floundering Business Radio Network, which offers radio stations 24 hours of business news per day. Today, the company is on its way to becoming an industry leader.[8] As most experts on career management note, the career management process must be somewhat flexible to take advantage of unanticipated opportunities that may arise, such as Faulkner's discovery of the troubled radio network.

Stages in Career Development

One reason why continual career reappraisal is necessary is that careers tend to evolve through several stages. Knowledge of these stages is helpful in anticipating major tasks to be accomplished in managing one's career. Although a number of researchers have attempted to define these stages, career expert Jeffrey H. Greenhaus argues that it is helpful to visualize a career as consisting of the five main stages discussed below.

Stage 1: Preparation for Work. This first stage involves forming a self-image about the types of occupations that one might pursue, reviewing alternative occupations, making at least an initial choice of occupation, and obtaining the necessary educational credentials to pursue that choice. This stage, which usually takes place during the period from birth to about age 25, entails significant exploration of one's talents, interests, values, and desired lifestyle, as well as assessment of the various requirements, opportunities, and rewards that are characteristic of different occupations. Thus this stage involves a considerable degree of concentration on the career exploration step of career management discussed earlier, at least if one is to be adequately prepared for the next stage.

Stage 2: Organizational Entry. In the organizational entry stage, the individual has the task of selecting a first job and an organization in which to begin pursuing one's chosen occupation. The job search associated with this stage may take a number of months to complete and may lead to a job choice that is compatible with one's talents and career values. Unfortunately, individuals often make poor job selections, either because of insufficient preparation in the previous stage and/or an inadequate job search. For example, one recent survey found that only

41 percent of the respondents were on a career or job path that they had planned (most of the others either got started on their careers through chance circumstances, took the only jobs they found available, or were heavily influenced by friends and relatives).[9] Organizational entry typically takes place sometime between the ages of 18 and 25, depending for the most part on the years of education that one elects to pursue. Some individuals, of course, may choose to start a business (at this point or possibly looping back from a later stage).

Stage 3: Early Career. With occupational and initial job choices made, the early career stage brings two major phases: establishing oneself in one's career and organization and striving to achieve success at chosen career goals. In the first phase, the individual is usually concerned mainly with learning about the job and organization, as well as being accepted as an able contributor. In the second phase, the individual is typically heavily oriented toward building a record of significant accomplishments that relates to success as the individual has defined it. This stage typically extends from age 25 to about 40.

Stage 4: Midcareer. The midcareer stage encompasses the midlife transition from early to middle adulthood. During this stage, an individual is likely to engage in a major reappraisal of career accomplishments and reaffirm or modify earlier career goals. This process can be repeated several times during a period that typically extends from about age 40 to 55. For some, the midcareer stage can be a difficult period as they attempt to cope perhaps with unfulfilled dreams, feelings of lost youth, or prospects of mortality. For others, the midcareer stage is a time of adjusting to middle adulthood and attempting to find ways of continuing growth (rather than stagnating or allowing one's skills to become obsolete).

Stage 5: Late Career. The late career stage usually involves two main tasks: remaining a productive contributor with a strong sense of self-worth while also anticipating and planning for eventual retirement. This stage begins somewhere around age 55 and extends until a person actually retires. With the declining number of young workers entering the work force between now and the year 2000, some observers argue that measures will be necessary to encourage individuals to retire later in order to make up for the impending shortfall. This situation may open up new work-related growth prospects during this stage.[10]

Assessing the Stages. Of course, these career stages constitute general guidelines regarding the major career phases that one is likely to encounter. Ages at which individuals go through these stages are particularly likely to vary. Rather than comprising a rigid progression, the stages simply serve to provide some basic notions about the ways in which careers are likely to unfold and the means by which individuals address career issues at different stages in their lives. As the above-mentioned situation with Richard Faulkner illustrates, individuals may make major changes in directions during the course of their careers and revert to earlier stages as they pursue alternative dreams, accept new jobs, and/or join other organizations.

Linkages into Organizational Career Development Programs

As noted previously, individuals can engage in career planning on their own or in conjunction with career development programs sponsored by their organizations. Unfortunately, though, career development programs in most organiza-

Pitney Bowes takes an active part in managing the career paths of those who are considered to have potential for top positions. Shown here are seven managers on the rise at the company. Sometimes managers are encouraged to take lateral moves to broaden their experience or position themselves for promotion in another area.

tions tend to be fairly informal and somewhat fragmented. According to one survey of 225 companies conducted for the American Management Association, the most common type of career development is informal counseling by human resources staff members.[11] Still, such counseling may be a useful addition to one's own efforts. Also, supervisors sometimes are trained to provide career counseling, often as part of the performance appraisal process.

Career-planning workshops are used by some organizations, such as the Continental Insurance Company, the Gulf Oil Company, the Ford Motor Company, and Xerox, to help employees engage in career planning.[12] Career-planning workbooks, often developed specifically for a particular company, can be another aid in career management. (One popular commercially available workbook, not tied to a particular company, is Richard Bolle's *What Color Is Your Parachute?*; it is updated frequently and provides a variety of information and exercises geared to helping individuals engage in career planning.)[13] Other means that may be available, particularly to managerial and professional employees, are personality and other occupationally related testing programs, as well as assessment centers (see Chapter 12). Some organizations have specific programs aimed at the particular requirements of certain groups, such as women and minority employees, who often are underrepresented at higher levels in organizations (see Chapter 12); individuals in the late career stage, who are preparing for retirement; and management trainees, particularly those perceived to have strong future potential.[14]

SPECIAL CAREER ISSUES

Within the context of career management, several contemporary career issues warrant special attention because of the particular challenges they present. These issues focus on dealing with the particular difficulties facing dual-career couples, obtaining help from mentors, and handling career plateaus and lateral moves.

Dual-Career Couples

Largely due to the influx of women into the work force since World War II, the number of dual-career couples has been rising rapidly.[15] By one estimate, almost 90 percent of all married couples will be dual-career couples in the 1990s.[16] Aside from the obvious problems of running a household while perhaps spending extra hours at work, such couples (particularly when both parties pursue professional careers) often experience difficulties in finding acceptable employment for both parties in the same geographic location. Sometimes, couples solve dual-career problems by working in separate locations during the week and spending only weekends together. According to one estimate, about 700,000 couples in the United States have so-called commuter marriages.[17]

Raising children often adds to the pressure as the couples attempt to expend further effort juggling their work and family responsibilities.[18] In such cases, one parent may leave the work force for a period of time in order to provide child care, particularly when the children are very young. A recent study, though, indicates that the negative impact of such employment gaps may be more severe for men than for women in terms of future income and career satisfaction, unfortunately suggesting that males are particularly likely to suffer discrimination when they do not follow a traditional career path.[19]

Gradually, a number of organizations are attempting to provide help for dual-career couples. For example, Martin Marrietta, the aerospace and defense contractor, has found that it can attract top people by being willing to hire both members of a dual-career couple.[20] Other steps include providing flextime (see Chapter 10), special career counseling, greater leave flexibility for child-care purposes, and help in locating jobs for spouses in transfer situations.[21]

Mentors and Mentoring

A **mentor** is an individual who contributes significantly to the career development of a junior colleague or a peer. Mentoring usually takes place either by providing specific career advancement assistance (e.g., coaching, opportunities for visibility, challenging assignments) and/or by offering interpersonal support (e.g., counseling, friendship, and encouragement). While mentors often are managers at senior levels who draw upon their experience, organizational rank, and influence to enhance the careers of junior colleagues, mentoring expert Kathy E. Kram notes that peers also are a valuable source of mentoring assistance. Some of the ways in which peers can help are by sharing information, aiding with career strategies, offering job-related feedback, and providing emotional support.[22] In fact, Kram suggests that individuals may function best if they seek to build several developmental alliances—with bosses, senior colleagues, and peers—rather than just one, particularly at the early career stages. The reason is that various relationships are likely to be limited in the range of help that is offered and in the duration of such assistance. Thus, while it is sometimes possible to locate a senior colleague who provides major enduring guidance, the search for such a mentor in many cases may be futile. Friends outside of work and family members can also provide valuable counseling, coaching, and support.

Mentor An individual who contributes significantly to the career development of a junior colleague or a peer

Career Plateaus and Lateral Moves

Common trends in many organizations are restructuring and downsizing, measures that typically make significant reductions in the layers of middle management (see Chapter 10). One implication is that individuals in organizations are likely to find themselves plateaued, at least periodically, since there are not as many levels for potential promotion. A *career plateau* is a point in an individual's career at which the likelihood of future promotion to a higher-level position is very low. When an individual who is otherwise qualified for a higher position cannot move up because higher-level openings are lacking, the person is sometimes said to be *organizationally plateaued*. (Others may be plateaued by personal choice or because their performance and/or qualifications do not warrant their promotion.)[23]

Because restructuring and downsizing are creating greater numbers of organizationally plateaued individuals, lateral position changes are becoming a more common means of stimulating individual growth and enhancing expertise. For example, after being promoted roughly every year as he worked in manufacturing operations, David Hogberg of Quaker Oats remained manager of manufacturing for Kibbles 'n Bits dog food for 3 years. He then made a lateral move into product development before accepting a position in marketing as assistant brand manager for Cap'n Crunch cereal 3 years later. These lateral moves helped him ultimately gain a promotion to manager of marketing for all "semimoist" pet foods, such as Gaines Burger. In sizing up his career progress, Hogberg says, "My lateral moves have been deliberate, and they worked."[24]

acceptable quality level (AQL) A predetermined standard against which random samples of produced materials are compared in acceptance sampling. (652)

acceptance sampling A statistical technique used in quality control that involves evaluating random samples from a group, or "lot," of produced materials to determine whether the lot meets acceptable quality levels. (652)

acceptance theory of authority A theory connected with the administrative management approach which argues that authority does not depend as much on "persons of authority" who *give* orders as on the willingness of those who *receive* the orders to comply. (53)

accommodation A conflict-handling mode that involves solving conflicts by allowing the desires of the other party to prevail. (580)

accountability The requirement to provide satisfactory reasons for significant deviations from duties or expected results. (353)

achievement-oriented A leader behavior identified in path-goal theory that involves setting challenging goals, expecting subordinates to perform at their highest level, and conveying a high degree of confidence in subordinates. (503)

acquired-needs theory A content theory of motivation (developed by David C. McClelland) which argues that our needs are acquired or learned on the basis of our life experience. (453)

acquisition The purchase of all or part of one organization by another, and a means of implementing growth strategies. (204)

action research A method used in the diagnosis phase of organiza-

tional development that places heavy emphasis on data gathering and collaborative diagnosis before action is taken. (251)

active listening The process in which a listener actively participates in attempting to grasp the facts and the feelings being expressed by the speaker. (533)

activity A work component to be accomplished, represented by an arrow on a PERT network diagram. (307)

Ad hoc committee Another term for a task force. (569)

adaptive mode An approach to strategy formulation that emphasizes taking small incremental steps, reacting to problems rather than seeking opportunities, and attempting to satisfy a number of organizational power groups. (194)

adhocracy The structural configuration in Mintzberg's typology characterized by various forms of matrix departmentalization, expertise dispersed throughout, low formalization, and emphasis on mutual adjustment. (391)

adjourning A stage of group development in which group members prepare for disengagement as the group nears successful completion of its goals. (569)

administrative management An approach within classical management theory that focuses on principles that can be used by managers to coordinate the internal activities of organizations. (51)

administrative protections A type of trade barrier in the form of various rules and regulations that make it more difficult for foreign firms to conduct business in a particular country. (745)

adverse impact The effect produced when a job selection rate for a protected group is less than 80 percent of the rate for the majority group. (414)

advertising An approach to influencing the environment involving the use of communications media to gain favorable publicity for particular products and services. (99)

affirmative action Any special activity undertaken by employers to increase equal employment opportunities for groups protected by federal equal employment opportunity laws and related regulations. (410)

affirmative action plan A written, systematic plan that specifies goals and timetables for hiring, training, promoting, and retraining groups protected by federal equal employment laws and related regulations. (410)

aggregate production planning A primary operating system used in operations management that is concerned with planning how to match supply with product or service demand over a time horizon of about 1 year. (673)

alternative work schedules Schedules based on adjustments in the normal work schedule rather than in the job content or activities. (343)

amoral management An approach to managerial ethics that is neither immoral nor moral but, rather, ignores or is oblivious to ethical considerations. (136)

anchoring and adjustment A decision-making bias that involves the tendency to be influenced by an ini-

Note: The glossary contains definitions for the terms in text that appear in boldface type.

tial figure, even when the information is largely irrelevant. (276)

antifreeloader argument   An argument that indicates that since businesses benefit from a better society, they should bear part of the costs by actively working to bring about solutions to social problems. (123)

application blank   A form used widely as a selection method that contains a series of inquiries about such issues as an applicant's educational background, previous job experience, physical health, and other information that may be useful in assessing an individual's ability to perform a job. (414)

applications software packages   Software programs available for sale or lease from commercial sources. (719)

artificial intelligence   A field of information technology aimed at developing computers that have humanlike capabilities, such as seeing, hearing, and thinking. (712)

assessment center   A controlled environment used to predict the probable managerial success of individuals mainly on the basis of evaluations of their behaviors in a variety of simulated situations, thereby facilitating selection. (418)

asset management ratios   Financial ratios that measure how effectively an organization manages its assets. (633)

authority   The right to make decisions, carry out actions, and direct others in matters related to the duties and goals of a position. (353)

autocratic   The behavioral style of leaders who tend to make unilateral decisions, dictate work methods, limit worker knowledge about goals to just the next step to be performed, and sometimes give feedback that is punitive. (485)

autonomous work group   Another name for a self-managing team. (573)

autonomy   A core job characteristic involving the amount of discretion allowed in determining schedules and work methods for achieving the required output. (341)

availability   A decision-making bias that involves the tendency to judge the likelihood of an occurrence on the basis of the extent to which other like instances or occurrences can easily be recalled. (276)

avoidance   A conflict-handling mode that involves ignoring or suppressing a conflict in the hope that it will either go away or not become too disruptive. (580)

back orders   Orders for goods which cannot be filled immediately but which will be honored as more goods or service slots become available. (675)

balance of payments   An international economic element that is an account of goods and services, capital loans, gold, and other items entering and leaving a country, and a factor influencing the ability of an organization to conduct international business in that country successfully. (744)

balance of trade   The difference between a country's exports and imports and, generally, the most critical determinant of a country's balance of payments. (744)

balance sheet   A financial statement that depicts an organization's assets and claims against those assets at a given point in time. (630)

balance sheet budget   A financial budget that forecasts the assets, liabilities, and shareholders' equity at the end of the budget period. (644)

bankruptcy   A defensive strategy in which an organization that is unable to pay its debts can seek court protection from creditors and from certain contract obligations while it attempts to regain financial stability. (205)

batch processing   An arrangement whereby data are accumulated and then processed as a group. (701)

BCG growth-share matrix   A portfolio approach involving a four-cell matrix (developed by the Boston Consulting Group) that compares various businesses in an organization's portfolio on the basis of relative market share and market growth rate. (206)

behavior modification   The use of

techniques associated with reinforcement theory. (464)

behavioral displacement   A condition which is a side effect of poorly designed and/or excessive controls in which individuals engage in behaviors that are encouraged by controls and related reward systems even though the behaviors actually are inconsistent with organizational goals. (619)

behavioral science   An approach that emphasizes *scientific research* as the basis for developing theories about human behavior in organizations that can be used to develop practical guidelines for managers. (61)

behavioral viewpoint   A perspective on management that emphasizes the importance of attempting to understand the various factors that affect human behavior in organizations. (53)

behaviorally anchored rating scales (BARS)   Performance appraisal scales containing sets of specific behaviors that represent gradations of performance used as common reference points (or anchors) for rating employees on various job dimensions. (422)

belongingness needs   The needs in Maslow's hierarchy that involve the desire to affiliate with and be accepted by others. (449)

benefits   Forms of compensation beyond wages for time worked, including various protection plans, services, pay for time not worked, and income supplements. (424)

bill of materials (BOM)   An input to MRP systems that consists of a listing of all components, including partially assembled pieces and basic parts, that make up an end product. (677)

bottom-up budgeting   A process of developing budgets in which lower-level and middle managers specify their budgetary needs and top management attempts to accommodate them to the extent possible. (644)

boundary spanning   An approach to influencing the environment that involves creating roles within the organization that interface with important elements in the environment. (99)

bounded rationality A concept that suggests that the ability of managers to be perfectly rational in making decisions is limited by such factors as cognitive capacity and time constraints. (265)

brainstorming A technique for enhancing group creativity that encourages group members to generate as many novel ideas as possible on a given topic without evaluating them. (287)

break-even analysis A quantitative technique based on a graphic model that helps decision makers understand the relationships among sales volume, costs, and revenues in an organization. (319)

budgeting The process of stating in quantitative terms, usually dollars, planned organizational activities for a given period of time. (638)

buffering A method of adapting to environmental fluctuations that involves stockpiling either inputs into or outputs from a production or service process in order to cope with environmental fluctuations. (97)

bureaucratic control A managerial approach that relies on regulation through rules, policies, supervision, budgets, schedules, reward systems, and other administrative mechanisms aimed at ensuring that employees exhibit appropriate behaviors and meet performance standards. (612)

bureaucratic management An approach within classical management theory that emphasizes the need for organizations to operate in a rational manner rather than relying on the arbitrary whims of owners and managers. (49)

business-level strategy A type of strategy that concentrates on the best means of competing within a particular business while also supporting the corporate-level strategy. (193)

business plan A document written by the prospective owner or entrepreneur that details the nature of the business, the product or service, the customers, the competi-

tion, the production and marketing methods, the management, the financing, and other significant aspects of the proposed business venture. (787)

capacity argument An argument which states that the private sector, because of its considerable economic and human resources, must make up for recent government cutbacks in social programs. (123)

capacity planning A primary operating system used in operations management that is concerned with determining the people, machines, and major physical resources, such as buildings, that will be necessary to meet the production objectives of the organization. (672)

capacity requirements planning A technique for determining what personnel and equipment are needed to meet short-term production objectives. (673)

capital expenditures budget A type of budget that involves a plan for the acquisition or divestiture of major fixed assets, such as land, buildings, or equipment. (643)

capitalist economy An economy in which economic activity is governed by market forces and the means of production are privately owned by individuals. (82)

career A sequence of work-related activities and experiences that span the course of a person's life. (807)

career management The continuing process of setting career goals, formulating and implementing strategies for reaching the goals, and monitoring the results. (808)

carrying, or **holding, cost** An inventory cost comprised of the expenses associated with keeping an item on hand (such as storage, insurance, pilferage, breakage). (654)

cash budget A financial budget that projects future cash flows arising from cash receipts and disbursements by the organization during a specified period. (644)

central processing unit (CPU) The main memory and processing section of a computer. (701)

centralization A vertical coordina-

tion method that addresses the extent to which power and authority are retained at the top organizational levels. (352)

ceremonial A system of rites performed in conjunction with a single occasion or event. (104)

chain of command The unbroken line of authority that ultimately links each individual with the top organizational position through a managerial position at each successive layer in between. (337)

change Any alteration of the status quo. (226)

change agent An individual with a fresh perspective and a knowledge of the behavioral sciences who acts as a catalyst in helping the organization approach old problems in new or innovative ways and thus plays a key role in OD interventions. (250)

charisma A leadership factor that comprises the leader's ability to inspire pride, faith, and respect; to recognize what is really important; and to articulate effectively a sense of mission or vision that inspires followers. (507)

clan control A managerial approach that relies on values, beliefs, traditions, corporate culture, shared norms, and informal relationships to regulate employee behavior and facilitate the reaching of organizational goals. (613)

classical viewpoint A perspective on management that emphasizes finding ways to manage work and organizations more effectively. (45)

clients The element of the task environment that includes those individuals and organizations that purchase an organization's products and/or services. (87)

closed system A system that does little or no interacting with its environment and receives little feedback. (64)

coercive power Power that depends on the ability to punish others when they do not engage in desired behaviors. (481)

cognitive resource theory A theory, which is a major revision and extension of Fiedler's contingency model, that considers the additional factor of a leader's cognitive resource use in predicting performance. (493)

cognitive resources Factors identified in cognitive resource theory that involve the intellectual abilities, technical competence, and job-relevant knowledge that leaders bring to their jobs. (493)

cognitive theories Theories that attempt to isolate the thinking patterns that we use in deciding whether or not to behave in a certain way. (456)

collaboration A conflict-handling mode that strives to resolve conflict by devising solutions that allow both parties to achieve their desired outcomes. (580)

command group A formal group consisting of a manager and all the subordinates who report to that manager. (553)

communication The exchange of messages between people for the purpose of achieving common meanings. (518)

communication channels Various patterns of organizational communication flow that represent potential established conduits through which managers and other organization members can send and receive information. (536)

communication network The pattern of information flow among task group members. (535)

compensation Wages paid directly for time worked, as well as more indirect benefits that employees receive as part of their employment relationship with an organization. (424)

competition A conflict-handling mode that involves attempting to win a conflict at the other party's expense. (580)

competitive advantage A significant edge over the competition in dealing with competitive forces. (191)

competitive advantage of nations The concept that environmental elements within a nation can foster innovation in certain industries, thereby increasing the prospects of success of home-based companies operating internationally within those industries. (748)

competitors The element of the task environment that includes other organizations that either offer or have a high potential of offering rival products or services. (88)

complacency A condition preventing effective decision making in which individuals either do not see the signs of danger or opportunity or ignore them. (272)

compressed workweek An alternative work schedule whereby employees work four 10-hour days or some similar combination, rather than the usual five 8-hour days. (344)

compromise A conflict-handling mode that aims to solve conflict issues by having each party give up some desired outcomes in order to get other desired outcomes. (580)

computer-aided design (CAD) A system on which CIM systems rely that uses computers to geometrically prepare, review, and evaluate product designs. (687)

computer-aided manufacturing (CAM) A system on which CIM systems rely that uses computers to design and control production processes. (687)

computer-based information systems (CBISs) Information systems that involve the use of computer technology. (701)

computer-integrated manufacturing (CIM) The computerized integration of all major functions associated with the production of a product. (687)

computer virus A small program, usually hidden inside another program, that replicates itself and surfaces at a predetermined time to cause disruption and possibly destruction. (726)

concentration A growth strategy that focuses on effecting the growth of a single product or service or a small number of closely related products or services. (201)

conceptual skills Key management skills related to the ability to visualize the organization as a whole, discern interrelationships among organizational parts, and understand how the organization fits into the wider context of the industry, community, and world. (18)

concurrent control A control type based on timing involving the regulation of ongoing activities that are part of the transformation process to ensure that they conform to organizational standards. (607)

conflict A perceived difference between two or more parties that results in mutual opposition. (578)

consideration The degree to which a leader builds mutual trust with subordinates, respects their ideas, and shows concern for their feelings. (487)

constraints Conditions that must be met in the course of solving a linear programming problem. (309)

contingency planning The development of alternative plans for use in the event that environmental conditions evolve differently than anticipated, rendering original plans unwise or unfeasible. (179)

contingency theory A viewpoint that argues that appropriate managerial action depends on the particular parameters of the situation. (67)

continuous-process production A type of technology in which products are liquids, solids, or gases that are made through a continuous process. (384)

control system A set of mechanisms, established as part of the control process, that are designed to increase the probability of meeting organizational standards and goals. (594)

controlling The management function that is aimed at regulating organizational activities so that actual performance conforms to expected organizational standards and goals. (8, 594)

convergent thinking A way of thinking related to creativity in which an individual attempts to solve problems by beginning with a problem and attempting to move logically to a solution. (282)

co-opting An approach to influencing the environment that involves absorbing key members of important environmental elements into the leadership or policy-making structure of an organization. (100)

corporate culture A term sometimes used for organizational culture. (103)

corporate-level strategy A type of strategy that addresses what businesses the organization will operate, how the strategies of those businesses will be coordinated to strengthen the organization's competitive position, and how resources will be allocated among the businesses. (192)

corporate philanthropy Corporate contributions for charitable and social responsibility purposes. (124)

corporate social responsibility A term often used to refer to the concept of organizational social responsibility as applied to business organizations. (115)

corporate social responsiveness A term used to refer to the concept of organizational social responsiveness as applied to business organizations. (126)

corridor principle A principle which states that the process of beginning a new venture helps entrepreneurs visualize other opportunities that they could not envision or take advantage of until they started the initial venture. (779)

cost leadership strategy A generic business-level strategy outlined by Michael E. Porter that involves emphasizing organizational efficiency so that the overall costs of providing products and services are lower than those of competitors. (211)

creativity The cognitive process of developing an idea, concept, commodity, or discovery that is viewed as novel by its creator or a target audience. (281)

crisis problem A type of problem in managerial decision making involving a serious difficulty that requires immediate action. (262)

critical path The path in a PERT network that will take the longest to complete. (308)

customer divisions A form of divisional structure involving divisions set up to service particular types of clients or customers. (375)

customers The element of the task environment that includes those individuals and organizations that purchase an organization's products and/or services. (87)

cybernetic control system A self-regulating control system that, once it is put into operation, can automatically monitor the situation and take corrective action when necessary. (610)

data Unanalyzed facts and figures. (699)

data base A set of data organized efficiently in a central location so that it can serve a number of information system applications. (702)

data-base management system The software that allows an organization to build, manage, and provide access to its stored data. (702)

debt capital A type of financing available to entrepreneurs that involves a loan to be repaid, usually with interest. (790)

debt management ratios Financial ratios that assess the extent to which an organization uses debt to finance investments, as well as the degree to which it is able to meet its long-term obligations. (634)

decentralization A vertical coordination method that addresses the extent to which power and authority are delegated to lower levels. (352)

deciding to decide A response in which decision makers accept the challenge of deciding what to do about a problem and follow an effective decision-making process. (273)

decision making The process through which managers identify organizational problems and attempt to resolve them. (261)

decision matrix Another term for payoff table. (316)

decision support system (DSS) A computer-based information system that supports the process of managerial decision making in situations that are not well structured. (321)

decision tree A quantitative decision-making aid based on a graphic model that displays the structure of a sequence of alternative courses of action and usually shows the pay-offs associated with various paths and the probabilities associated with potential future conditions. (317)

decoding The process, in communication, of translating the symbols into the interpreted message. (523)

defensive avoidance A condition preventing effective decision making in which individuals either deny the importance of a danger or an opportunity or deny any responsibility for taking action. (273)

defensive strategies Grand strategies (sometimes called *retrenchment strategies*) that focus on the desire or need to reduce organizational operations usually through cost and/or asset reductions. (204)

delegation A means of vertical coordination that involves the assignment of part of a manager's work to others along with both the responsibility and the authority necessary to achieve expected results. (354)

Delphi method A method of technological or qualitative forecasting that uses a structured approach to gain the judgments of a number of experts on a specific issue relating to the future. (301)

democratic The behavioral style of leaders who tend to involve the group in decision making, let the group determine work methods, make overall goals known, and use feedback as an opportunity for helpful coaching. (485)

departmentalization An aspect of organization structure involving the clustering of individuals into units and of units into departments and larger units in order to facilitate achieving organizational goals. (345)

dependent demand inventory A type of inventory consisting of raw materials, components, and subassemblies that are used in the production of an end product or service. (676)

descriptive decision-making models Models that attempt to document how managers actually *do* make decisions. (268)

developed countries A group of countries that is characterized by a high level of economic or industrial development and that includes the United States, western Europe, Canada, Australia, New Zealand, and Japan. (743)

devil's advocates Individuals who are assigned the role of making sure that the negative aspects of any attractive decision alternatives are considered and whose involvement in a group helps avoid groupthink. (281)

dialectical inquiry A technique used to help avoid groupthink that involves approaching a decision situation from two opposite points of view. (281)

differentiation The extent to which organizational units differ from one another in terms of the behaviors and orientations of their members and their formal structures; also used to refer to the tendency for open systems to become more complex. (66, 388)

differentiation paradox The idea that although separating efforts to innovate from the rest of the organization increases the likelihood of developing radical ideas, such differentiation also decreases the likelihood that the radical ideas will ever be implemented. (396)

differentiation strategy A generic business-level strategy outlined by Michael E. Porter that involves attempting to develop products and services that are viewed as unique in the industry. (213)

direct contact A means of facilitating lateral relations that involves communication between two or more persons at similar levels in different work units for purposes of coordinating work and solving problems. (359)

direct interlock A situation in which two companies have a director in common. (100)

direct investment A means of entering international markets involving the establishment of operating facilities in a foreign country. (752)

directive A leader behavior identified in path-goal theory that involves letting subordinates know what is expected of them, providing guidance about work methods, developing work schedules, identifying work evaluation standards, and indicating the basis for outcomes or rewards. (503)

discretionary expense center A responsibility center whose budgetary performance is based on achieving its goals by operating within predetermined expense constraints set through managerial judgment or discretion. (639)

dissatisfiers A type of factor which figures in the two-factor theory of motivation that is largely associated with the work environment (such as working conditions and supervision) and that can influence the degree of worker dissatisfaction. (452)

distinctive competence An organizational strength that is unique and not easily matched or imitated by competitors. (200)

distributed processing An approach to controlling information system resources in which computers are distributed to various organizational locations where they serve the organization's local and/or regional needs and are interconnected for electronic communication. (722)

divergent thinking A way of thinking related to creativity in which an individual attempts to solve problems by generating new ways of viewing the problem and seeking novel alternatives. (282)

diversification A growth strategy that entails effecting growth through the development of new areas that are clearly distinct from current businesses. (203)

divestiture A defensive strategy that involves an organization's selling or divesting of a business or part of a business. (205)

divisional structure A type of

departmentalization in which positions are grouped according to similarity of products, services, or markets. (373)

divisionalized form The structural configuration in Mintzberg's typology characterized by divisional departmentalization, a strong management group at the division level, high formalization within divisions, and an emphasis on standardized outputs. (390)

domain shifts Changes in the mix of products and services offered so that an organization will interface with more favorable environmental elements. (101)

downsizing A method of increasing organizational efficiency and effectiveness that involves significantly reducing the layers of middle management, expanding spans of control, and shrinking the size of the work force. (349)

downward communication Vertical communication that flows from a higher level to one or more lower levels in the organization. (536)

driving forces Forces studied in force-field analysis that involve factors that pressure *for* a particular change. (243)

econometric models Explanatory models based on systems of simultaneous multiple regression equations involving several predictor variables that are used to identify and measure relationships or interrelationships that exist in the economy. (300)

economic element The part of the mega-environment that encompasses the systems of producing, distributing, and consuming wealth. (82)

economic order quantity (EOQ) An inventory control method developed to minimize ordering plus holding costs, while avoiding stockout costs. (654)

effectiveness A dimension of organizational performance involving the ability to choose and achieve appropriate goals. (20)

efficiency A dimension of organizational performance involving the ability to make the best use of available resources in the process of achieving goals. (20)

effort-performance expectancy A component of expectancy theory that concerns our assessment of the probability that our efforts will lead to the required performance level. (456)

electronic data processing (EDP) The transformation of data into meaningful information through electronic means. (700)

electronic mail system The mail system that allows high-speed exchange of written messages through the use of computerized text-processing and communications networks. (543)

electronic monitoring An issue in job-related stress and health that involves the use of computers to continually assess employee performance. (724)

employee assistance program (EAP) A program through which employers help employees overcome personal problems that are adversely affecting their job performance. (432)

employee-centered A leadership approach in which managers channel their main attention to the human aspects of subordinates' problems and to the development of an effective work group dedicated to high performance goals. (486)

employee involvement teams Small groups of employees who work on solving specific problems related to quality and productivity, often with stated targets for improvement. (652)

employment at will The legal principle that holds that either employee or employer can terminate employment at any time for any reason. (431)

employment test A selection method involving the assessment of a job applicant's characteristics through paper-and-pencil responses or simulated exercises. (416)

encoding The process, in communication, of translating the intended meaning into symbols. (523)

end user The same as a user. (720)

end-user computing The development and/or management of information systems by users. (720)

enlightened self-interest argument An argument that holds that businesses exist at society's pleasure and that, for their own legitimacy and survival, businesses should meet the expectations of the public regarding social responsibility. (123)

entrepreneur An individual who creates a new enterprise. (774)

entrepreneurial mode An approach to strategic management in which strategy is formulated mainly by a strong visionary chief executive who actively searches for new opportunities, is heavily oriented toward growth, and is willing to make bold decisions or to shift strategies rapidly. (194)

entrepreneurial team A special type of project team comprising a group of individuals with diverse expertise and backgrounds who are brought together to develop and implement innovative ideas aimed at creating new products or services or significantly improving existing ones. (571)

entrepreneurship The "creation of new enterprise." (774)

environmental complexity A factor affecting the level of environmental uncertainty that involves the number of elements in an organization's environment and their degree of similarity. (94)

environmental dynamism A factor affecting the level of environmental uncertainty that involves the rate and predictability of change in the elements of an organization's environment. (94)

environmental munificence The extent to which the environment can support sustained growth and stability. (95)

environmental uncertainty A condition of the environment in which future conditions affecting an organization cannot be accurately assessed and predicted. (94)

equity capital A type of financing available to entrepreneurs that usu-

ally requires that the investor be given some form of ownership in the venture. (790)

equity theory A cognitive theory of work motivation which argues that we prefer situations of balance, or equity, which exist when we perceive the ratio of our inputs and outcomes to be equal to the ratio of inputs and outcomes for a comparison other. (461)

ERG theory An alternative (proposed by Clayton Alderfer) to Maslow's hierarchy of needs theory which argues that there are three levels of individual needs. (449)

escalation situations Situations that signal the strong possibility of escalating commitment and accelerating losses. (277)

esteem needs The needs in Maslow's hierarchy related to a two-pronged desire to have a positive self-image and to have our contributions valued and appreciated by others. (449)

ethnocentric orientation An approach to international management (also known as home-country orientation) in which executives assume that practices that work in the headquarters or home country must necessarily work elsewhere. (741)

event An indication of the beginning and/or ending of activities in a PERT network. (307)

exchange rate An international economic element that is the rate at which one country's currency can be exchanged for another country's currency. (744)

executive support system (ESS) A computer-based information system that supports decision making and effective functioning at the top levels of an organization. (712)

existence needs The needs in ERG theory that include the various forms of material and physiological desires, such as food and water, as well as such work-related forms as pay, fringe benefits, and physical working conditions. (449)

expatriates Individuals who are not citizens of the countries in which they are assigned to work. (762)

expectancy theory A cognitive theory of work motivation (originally proposed by Victor H. Vroom) which argues that we consider three main issues before we expend the effort necessary to perform at a given level. (456)

expected value The sum of the payoffs times the respective probabilities for a given alternative. (317)

expense budget An operating budget that documents expected expenses during the budget period. (643)

expert power Power that is based on the possession of expertise that is valued by others. (481)

expert system (ES) A computer-based system that applies the substantial knowledge of an expert to help solve problems in a specific area. (321)

explanatory, or causal, models Methods of quantitative forecasting that attempt to identify the major variables that are related to or have caused particular past conditions and then use current measures of those variables (predictors) to predict future conditions. (298)

exporting A means of entering international markets that involves an organization's making a product in the home country and sending it overseas. (751)

expropriation The seizure of a foreign company's assets by a host-country government. (745)

external audit A financial audit involving the review and verification of the fairness of an organization's financial statements that is conducted by an independent auditor. (637)

external environment The major forces outside the organization that have the potential of significantly impacting on the likely success of products or services. (77)

extinction A type of reinforcement in behavior modification that involves withholding previously available positive consequences associated with a behavior in order to *decrease* that behavior. (466)

extrinsic rewards Rewards, such as bonuses, awards, or promotions, that are provided by others. (457)

facilities The land, buildings, equipment, and other major physical inputs that substantially determine productive capacity, require time to alter, and involve significant capital investment. (680)

feedback A term that generally denotes information about the results of actions; used in conjunction with systems theory to signify information about results and organizational status relative to the environment; as applied to the job characteristics model of job design, specifies core job characteristic associated with the degree to which the job provides for clear, timely information about performance results; also used to indicate an element in the communication process that refers to the basic response of the receiver to the interpreted message in the communciation process. (64, 341, 525)

feedback control A control type based on timing that involves regulation exercised after a product or service has been completed in order to ensure that the final output meets organizational standards and goals. (608)

feedforward control A control type based on timing that focuses on the regulation of inputs to ensure that they meet the standards necessary for the transformation process. (607)

Fiedler's contingency model A situational leadership approach originally developed by Fred Fiedler and his associates. (490)

financial budgets Budgets that outline how an organization is going to acquire its cash and how it intends to use the cash. (644)

financial statement A summary of a major aspect of an organization's financial status which is used as a financial control technique. (630)

finished-goods inventory The stock of items that have been produced and are awaiting sale or transit to a customer. (653)

first-line managers Managers at the lowest level of the hierarchy who are directly responsible for the work of operating (nonmanagerial) employees. (22)

first-line supervisors The same as first-line managers. (22)

five competitive forces model A model developed by Michael E. Porter and used in the examination of an organization's task environment that offers an approach to analyzing the nature and intensity of competition in a given industry in terms of five major forces. (196)

fixed-interval schedule of reinforcement A type of partial reinforcement schedule based on a pattern in which a reinforcer is administered on a fixed time schedule, assuming that the desired behavior has continued at an appropriate level. (467)

fixed-position layout A type of facilities layout having a production configuration in which the product or client remains in one location and the tools, equipment, and expertise are brought to it, as necessary, to complete the productive process. (686)

fixed-ratio schedule of reinforcement A type of partial reinforcement schedule based on a pattern in which a reinforcer is provided after a fixed number of occurrences of the desired behavior. (468)

flat structure A structure that has few hierarchical levels and wide spans of control. (349)

flexible manufacturing system (FMS) A manufacturing system on which CIM systems rely that uses computers to control machines and the production process automatically so that different types of parts or product configurations can be handled on the same production line. (688)

flextime An alternative work schedule that specifies certain core hours when individuals are expected to be on the job and then allows flexibility in starting and quitting times as long as individuals work the total number of required hours per day. (344)

focus strategy A generic, business-level strategy outlined by Michael E. Porter that entails specializing by establishing a position of overall cost leadership, differentiation, or both, but only within a particular portion or segment of an entire market. (213)

force-field analysis A method that involves analyzing the two types of forces that influence any proposed change: driving forces and restraining forces. (243)

formal communication Vertical and horizontal communication that follows paths specified by the official hierarchical organization structure and related task requirements. (539)

formal group A group officially created by an organization for a specific purpose. (552)

formalization A method of vertical coordination that addresses the degree to which written policies, rules, procedures, job descriptions, and other documents specify what actions are (or are not) to be taken under a given set of circumstances. (346)

forming A stage of group development in which group members attempt to assess the ground rules that will apply to a task and to group interaction. (567)

framing A decision-making bias that involves the tendency to make different decisions depending on how a problem is presented. (275)

franchise A continuing arrangement between a franchiser and a franchisee in which the franchiser's knowledge, image, manufacturing or service expertise, and marketing techniques are made available to the franchisee in return for the payment of various fees or royalties and conformity to standard operating procedures. (785)

franchisee An individual who purchases a franchise and, in the process, is given an opportunity to enter a new business hopefully with an enhanced chance of success. (786)

franchiser A manufacturer or sole distributor of a trademarked product or service who typically has considerable experience in the line of business being franchised. (785)

free riders Individuals who engage in social loafing, thus benefiting from the work of the group

without bearing their proportional share of the costs involved. (563)

friendship group An informal group that evolves primarily to meet employee social needs. (555)

frustration-regression principle A principle incorporated into ERG theory which states that if we are *continually* frustrated in our attempts to satisfy a higher-level need, we may cease to be concerned about that need. (450)

functional audit A technique for evaluating internal strengths and weaknesses that involves an exhaustive appraisal of an organization and/or its individual businesses conducted by assessing the important positive and negative attributes of each major functional area. (200)

functional authority The authority of staff departments over others in the organization in matters related directly to their respective functions. (356)

functional group A formal group consisting of a manager and all the subordinates that report to that manager. (553)

functional-level strategy A type of strategy that focuses on action plans for managing a particular functional area within a business in a way that supports the business-level strategy. (193)

functional managers Managers who have responsibility for a specific, specialized area of the organization and supervise mainly individuals with expertise and training in that specialized area. (29)

functional structure A type of departmentalization in which positions are grouped according to their main functional (or specialized) area. (370)

futurists Individuals useful in social forecasting who track significant social and other trends in the environment and attempt to predict their impact on the organization. (126)

gainsharing A compensation system in which employees throughout an organization are encouraged

to become involved in solving problems and are then given bonuses tied to organizationwide performance improvements. (428)

game theory A quantitative technique for facilitating decision making in situations of conflict among two or more decision makers seeking to maximize their own welfares. (320)

Gantt chart A type of planning and control model developed by Henry L. Gantt that relies on a specialized bar chart showing the current progress on each major project activity relative to necessary completion dates. (305)

garbage-can model A nonrational model of managerial decision making stating that managers behave in virtually a random pattern in making nonprogrammed decisions. (267)

GE business screen A portfolio approach involving a nine-cell matrix (developed by General Electric with McKinsey & Company) that is based on long-term industry attractiveness and on business strength. (208)

general managers Managers who have responsibility for a whole organization or a substantial subunit that includes most of the common specialized areas within it. (29)

geocentric orientation An approach to international management (also known as *world orientation*) whereby executives believe that a global view is needed in both the headquarters of the parent company and its various subsidiaries and that the best individuals, regardless of home- or host-country origin, should be utilized to solve company problems anywhere in the world. (742)

geographic divisions A form of divisional structure involving divisions designed to serve different geographic areas. (374)

globalization A strategy aimed at developing relatively standardized products with global appeal, as well as at rationalizing operations throughout the world. (754)

goal A major planning component that is a future target or end result that an organization wishes to achieve. (156)

goal commitment   A critical goal-setting element that involves one's attachment to, or determination to reach, a goal. (166)

goal incongruence   A condition in which there are major incompatibilities between the goals of an organization member and those of the organization, the effects of which can be reduced by the establishment of standards. (601)

government agencies   The element of the task environment that includes agencies that provide services and monitor compliance with laws and regulations at local, state or regional, and national levels. (91)

grand strategy   A master strategy that provides the basic strategic direction at the corporate level. (201)

grapevine   Another term for informal communication. (539)

graphic rating scales   Performance appraisal scales that list a number of rating factors, including general behaviors and characteristics, on which an employee is rated by the supervisor. (421)

group   Two or more interdependent individuals who interact and influence each other in collective pursuit of a common goal. (552)

group cohesiveness   A major group process factor that concerns the degree to which members are attracted to a group, are motivated to remain in the group, and are mutually influenced by one another. (565)

group maintenance roles   Roles that do not directly address a task itself but, instead, help foster group unity, positive interpersonal relations among group members, and development of the ability of members to work effectively together. (560)

group task roles   Roles that help a group develop and accomplish its goals. (560)

group technology   The classification of parts into families (groups of parts or products that have some similarities in the way they are manufactured) so that members of

the same family can be manufactured on the same production line. (688)

groupthink   A phenomenon of group decision making in which cohesive groups tend to seek agreement about an issue at the expense of realistically appraising the situation. (280)

growth-need strength   The degree to which an individual needs personal growth and development on the job. (342)

growth needs   The needs in ERG theory that impel creativity and innovation, along with the desire to have a productive impact on our surroundings. (449)

growth strategies   Grand strategies that involve organizational expansion along some major dimension. (201)

hackers   Individuals who are knowledgeable about computers and who gain unauthorized entry to, and sometimes tamper with, computer networks and files of organizations with which they have no affiliation. (726)

halo effect   The tendency to use a general impression (based on a few characteristics) of an individual to judge other characteristics of that same individual. (528)

hand of government   A view of corporate social responsibility which argues that the interests of society are best served by having the regulatory hands of the law and the political process, rather than the invisible hand, guide the results of corporations' endeavors. (116)

hand of management   A view of corporate social responsibility which states that corporations and their managers are expected to act in ways that protect and improve the welfare of society as a whole, as well as advance corporate economic interests. (116)

hardware   Physical computer equipment, including the computer itself and related devices. (701)

harvest   A defensive strategy that entails minimizing investments while attempting to maximize short-run profits and cash flow,

with the long-run intention of exiting the market. (205)

Hawthorne effect   The possibility that individuals singled out for a study may improve their performance simply because of the added attention they receive from the researchers, rather than because of any specific factors being tested. (57)

Hawthorne studies   A group of studies conducted at the Hawthorne plant of the Western Electric Company during the late 1920s and early 1930s whose results ultimately led to the human relations view of management. (55)

hierarchy of needs theory   A content theory of motivation (developed by Abraham Maslow) which argues that individual needs form a five-level hierarchy. (448)

horizontal communication   Lateral or diagonal message exchange either within work-unit boundaries, involving peers who report to the same supervisor, or across work-unit boundaries, involving individuals who report to different supervisors. (539)

horizontal coordination   An aspect of organization structure involving the linking of activities across departments at similar levels. (357)

human resource management (HRM)   The management of various activities designed to enhance the effectiveness of an organization's work force in achieving organizational goals. (404)

human resource planning   The process of determining future human resources needs relative to an organization's strategic plan and devising the steps necessary to meet those needs. (406)

human skills   Key management skills associated with a manager's ability to work well with others both as a member of a group and as a leader who gets things done through others. (18)

hybrid structure   A type of departmentalization that adopts parts of both functional and divisional structures at the same level of management. (377)

hygiene factors A type of factor which figures in the two-factor theory of motivation that is largely associated with the work environment (such as working conditions and supervision) and that can influence the degree of worker dissatisfaction. (452)

idea champion An individual who generates a new idea or believes in the value of a new idea and supports it in the face of numerous potential obstacles. (26)

immoral management An approach to managerial ethics that not only lacks ethical principles but is actively opposed to ethical behavior. (134)

import quota A type of trade barrier in the form of a limit on the amount of a product that may be imported over a given period of time. (745)

income statement A financial statement that summarizes the financial results of company operations over a specified time period, such as a quarter or a year. (631)

incremental model A nonrational model of managerial decision making stating that managers make the smallest response possible that will reduce the problem to at least a tolerable level. (266)

incrementalist approach An approach to controlling an innovation project that relies heavily on clan control but also involves a phased set of plans and accompanying bureaucratic controls that begin at a very general level and grow more specific as the project progresses. (618)

incubator An organization whose purpose is to nurture new ventures in their very early stages by providing space (usually at a site housing other new ventures as well), stimulation, support, and a variety of basic services, often at reduced fees. (780)

independent demand inventory A type of inventory consisting of end products, parts used for repairs, and other items whose demand is tied more directly than that for dependent demand inventory items to market issues. (676)

indirect interlock A situation having environmental influence in which two companies each have a director on the board of a third company. (100)

individualism-collectivism A cultural dimension in Geert Hofstede's framework for analyzing societies that involves the degree to which individuals concern themselves with their own interests and those of their immediate family as opposed to the interests of a larger group. (746)

individualized consideration A leadership factor that involves delegating projects to help develop each follower's capabilities, paying personal attention to each follower's needs, and treating each follower as an individual worthy of respect. (508)

informal communication Communication that takes place without regard to hierarchical or task requirements. (539)

informal group A group established by employees, rather than by the organization, in order to serve group members' interests or social needs. (554)

informal leader An individual, other than the formal leader, who emerges from the group as a major influence and is perceived by group members as a leader. (560)

information Data that has been analyzed or processed into a form that is meaningful for decision makers. (700)

information center A centrally located group of hardware, software, and information system professionals which is dedicated to assisting users with information system development and which can be used to manage end-use computing. (723)

information power Power that results from access to and control over the distribution of important information about organizational operations and future plans. (481)

information system A set of procedures designed to collect (or retrieve), process, store, and disseminate information to support planning, decision making, coordination, and control. (701)

infrastructure The highways, railways, airports, sewage facilities, housing, educational institutions, recreation facilities, and other economic and social amenities that signal the extent of economic development in an area and constitute an economic factor that influences the ability of organizations to conduct business in that area successfully. (743)

initiating structure The degree to which a leader defines his or her own role and the roles of subordinates in terms of achieving unit goals. (487)

innovation A new idea applied to initiating or improving a process, product, or service. (26, 226)

inputs The components of an organizational system that include the various human, material, financial, equipment, and informational resources required to produce goods and services. (63)

institutional power A need for power in which individuals focus on working with others to solve problems and further organizational goals. (454)

integration The extent to which there is collaboration among departments that need to coordinate their efforts. (388)

intellectual stimulation A leadership factor that involves offering new ideas to stimulate followers to rethink old ways of doing things, encouraging followers to look at problems from multiple vantage points, and fostering creative breakthroughs in obstacles that had seemed insurmountable. (508)

interest group An informal group created to facilitate employee pursuits of common concern. (554)

interlocking directorates A situation in which organizations have board members in common either directly or indirectly. (100)

internal audit A financial audit involving a review of both financial statements and internal operating efficiency that is conducted by members of the organization. (637)

internal environment The general conditions that exist within an organization. (77)

international business Profit-related activities conducted across national boundaries. (738)

international element The element of the mega-environment that includes the developments in countries outside an organization's home country that have the potential of impacting on the organization. (84)

international management The process of organizing, leading, and controlling in organizations engaged in international business. (738)

interventions OD change strategies developed and initiated with the help of a change agent. (250)

intrapreneurs Individuals who engage in entrepreneurial roles inside organizations. (26)

intrapreneurship The process of innovating within an existing organization. (26)

intrinsic rewards Rewards that are related to our own internal experiences with successful performance, such as feelings of achievement, challenge, and growth. (457)

inventory A stock of materials that are used to facilitate production or to satisfy customer demand. (653)

inventory models Quantitative approaches to planning the appropriate level for the stocks of materials needed by an organization. (312)

investment center A responsibility center whose budgetary performance is based on return on investment. (640)

invisible hand A classical view of corporate social responsibility which holds that the entire social responsibility of a corporation can be summed up as "make profits and obey the law." (116)

iron law of responsibility A law connected with the enlightened self-interest argument which states that "in the long run, those who do not use power in a manner that society considers responsible will tend to lose it." (123)

issues management The process of identifying a relatively small number of emerging social issues of particular relevance to the organization, analyzing their potential impact, and preparing an effective response. (127)

item cost An inventory cost that is the price of an inventory item itself. (653)

Japanese management An approach that focuses on aspects of management in Japan that may be appropriate for adoption in the United States. (68)

job analysis A key activity in human resources planning that involves the systematic collection and recording of information concerning the purpose of a job, its major duties, the conditions under which it is performed, the contacts with others that performance of the job requires, and the knowledge, skills, and abilities needed for performing the job effectively. (407)

job-centered A leadership approach in which leaders divide work into routine tasks, determine work methods, and closely supervise workers to ensure that the methods are followed and productivity standards are met. (486)

job characteristics model A model developed to guide job enrichment efforts that include consideration of core job characteristics, critical psychological states, and outcomes. (341)

job depth An aspect of job design that addresses the degree to which individuals can plan and control the work involved in their jobs. (341)

job description A statement of the duties, working conditions, and other significant requirements associated with a particular job. (407)

job design An aspect of organization structure that involves the specification of task activities associated with a particular job. (339)

job enlargement A job design approach that involves the allocation of a wider variety of similar tasks to a job in order to make it more challenging. (340)

job enrichment A job design approach that upgrades the job-task mix in order to increase significantly the potential for growth, achievement, responsibility, and recognition. (341)

job evaluation A systematic process of establishing the relative worth of jobs within a single organization in order to help establish pay differentials among jobs; it is the foundation of most major compensation systems. (425)

job posting An internal recruiting practice whereby information about job vacancies is placed in conspicuous places in an organization, such as on bulletin boards or in organizational newsletters. (412)

job rotation A job design approach that involves periodically shifting workers through a set of jobs in a planned sequence. (339)

job scope An aspect of job design that addresses the number of different tasks an employee performs in a particular job. (341)

job sharing An alternative work schedule in which two or more people share a single full-time job. (344)

job simplification A job design approach whereby jobs are configured so that jobholders have only a small number of narrow activities to perform. (339)

job specification A statement of the skills, abilities, education, and previous work experience that are required to perform a particular job. (407)

joint venture An agreement involving two or more organizations that arrange to produce a product or service jointly. (100)

judgmental forecasting A type of forecasting that relies mainly on individual judgments or committee agreements regarding future conditions. (304)

jury of executive opinion A method of judgmental forecasting in which organization executives hold a meeting and estimate, as a group, a forecast for a particular item. (304)

just-in-time (JIT) inventory control An approach to inventory control that emphasizes having materials arrive just as they are needed in the production process. (655)

Kanban A subsystem of the JIT approach involving a simple parts-movement system that depends on cards and containers to pull parts from one work center to another. (656)

kinesic behavior A category of nonverbal communication that includes body movements, such as gestures, facial expressions, eye movements, and posture. (520)

La Prospective A method of technological or qualitative forecasting that addresses a variety of possible futures by evaluating major environmental variables, assessing the likely strategies of other significant actors, devising possible counter-strategies, developing ranked hypotheses about the variables, and formulating alternative scenarios that do not greatly inhibit freedom of choice. (303)

labor-management relations The process through which employers and unions negotiate pay, hours of work, and other conditions of employment; sign a contract governing such conditions for a specific period of time; and share responsibilities for administering the resulting contract. (429)

labor supply The element of the task environment that consists of those individuals who are potentially employable by an organization. (90)

laissez-faire Behavioral style of leaders who generally give the group complete freedom, provide necessary materials, participate only to answer questions, and avoid giving feedback. (485)

large-batch and mass production A type of technology in which products are manufactured in large quantities, frequently on an assembly line. (384)

lateral relations An approach to horizontal coordination that involves coordinating efforts through communicating and problem solving with peers in other departments or units, rather than referring most issues up the hierarchy for resolution. (359)

law of effect A concept on which reinforcement theory relies heavily which states that behaviors having pleasant or positive consequences are more likely to be repeated and that behaviors having unpleasant or negative consequences are less likely to be repeated. (464)

leadership The process of influencing others toward the achievement of organizational goals. (480)

leading The management function that involves influencing others to engage in the work behaviors necessary to reach organizational goals. (8)

leading indicators Explanatory models based on variables that tend to be correlated with the phenomenon of major interest but also tend to occur in advance of that phenomenon. (300)

legal-political element The part of the mega-environment that includes the legal and governmental systems within which an organization must function. (83)

legitimate power Power that stems from a position's placement in the managerial hierarchy and the authority vested in the position. (481)

less developed countries (LDCs) A group of noncommunist countries, often called the "third world," that consists primarily of relatively poor nations characterized by low per capita income, little industry, and high birthrates. (743)

liaison role A role to which a specific individual is appointed to facilitate communication and resolution of issues between two or more departments, thereby facilitating lateral relations. (359)

licensing A method of international entry that involves an agreement in which one organization gives limited rights to another to use certain of its assets, such as expertise, patents, copyrights, or equipment, for an agreed-upon fee or royalty. (751)

life cycles Predictable stages of development. (228)

line authority The authority that follows the chain of command established by the formal hierarchy. (355)

line position A position that has authority and responsibility for achieving the major goals of the organization. (354)

linear programming (LP) A quantitative tool for planning how to allocate limited or scarce resources so that a single criterion or goal (often profits) is optimized. (309)

linking pin An individual who provides a means of coordination between command groups at two different levels by fulfilling a supervisory role in the lower-level command group and a subordinate role in the higher-level command group. (553)

liquidation A defensive strategy that entails selling or dissolving an entire organization. (205)

liquidity ratios Financial ratios that measure the degree to which an organization's current assets are adequate to pay current liabilities (current debt obligations). (632)

local area networks (LANs) Interconnections (usually by cable) through which end-user computing can be managed that allow communications among computers in a single building or within close proximity. (722)

logical office The concept that portable microcomputers allow an individual's office to be anywhere the individual is, rather than being restricted to one specific location. (725)

LPC orientation A personality trait in Fiedler's contingency model that is measured by the least preferred coworker (LPC) scale. (490)

machine bureaucracy The structural configuration in Mintzberg's typology characterized by functional departmentalization, a strong group of technical specialists, high formalization, and emphasis on standardization of work. (390)

management The process of achieving organizational goals through engaging in the four major functions of planning, organizing, leading, and controlling. (6)

management by exception A control principle associated with comparing performance against standards which suggests that managers should be informed of a situation only if control data show a significant deviation from standards. (603)

management by objectives (MBO) A process through which specific goals are set collaboratively for the organization as a whole and every unit and individual within it; the goals are then used as a basis for planning, managing organizational activities, and assessing and rewarding contributions. (179)

management by wandering around (MBWA) A practice whereby managers frequently tour areas for which they are responsible, talk to various employees, and encourage upward communication. (538)

management information system (MIS) A computer-based information system that produces routine reports and often allows on-line access to current and historical information needed by managers mainly at the middle and first-line levels; the name also given to the field of management that focuses on designing and implementing computer-based information systems for use by management. (62, 709)

management science An approach within the quantitative management viewpoint that is aimed at increasing decision effectiveness through the use of sophisticated mathematical models and statistical methods. (62)

managerial ethics Standards of conduct and moral judgment used by managers of organizations in carrying out their business. (115)

managerial integrator A separate manager who is given the task of coordinating related work that involves several functional departments and who facilitates lateral relations. (361)

manufacturing resource planning (MRP II) A computer-based information system that integrates the production planning and control activities of basic MRP systems with related financial, accounting, personnel, engineering, and marketing information. (679)

market control A managerial approach that relies on market mechanisms to regulate prices for certain clearly specified goods and services needed by an organization. (611)

masculinity-femininity A cultural dimension in Geert Hofstede's framework for analyzing societies that involves the extent to which a society emphasizes traditional male values such as assertiveness, competitiveness, and material success rather than traditional female values such as passivity, cooperation, and feelings. (747)

master production schedule (MPS) A schedule that translates the aggregate plan into a formalized production plan encompassing specific products to be produced or services to be offered and specific capacity requirements over a designated time period. (675)

materials requirements planning (MRP) A primary operating system used in operations management which consists of a computer-based inventory system that develops materials requirements for the goods and services specified in the master schedule and initiates the procurement actions necessary to acquire the materials when needed. (676)

matrix structure A type of departmentalization that superimposes a horizontal set of divisional reporting relationships onto a hierarchical functional structure. (379)

mechanistic characteristics The likely characteristics of firms operating in a stable environment, such as high centralization of decision making, many rules and regulations, and mainly vertical communication channels. (387)

medium The method used in the communication process to convey the message to the intended receiver. (524)

mega-environment The segment of the external environment that reflects the broad conditions and trends in the societies within which an organization operates. (78)

mentor An individual who contributes significantly to the career development of a junior colleague or a peer. (813)

merger The combining of two or more companies into one organization and thus a means of implementing growth strategies. (204)

message The encoding-process outcome, which consists of verbal and nonverbal symbols that have been developed to convey meaning to the receiver. (524)

middle managers Managers beneath the top levels of the hierarchy who are directly responsible for the work of other managers below them. (22)

mission The organization's purpose or fundamental reason for existence. (157)

mission statement A broad declaration of the basic, unique purpose and scope of operations that distinguishes the organization from others of its type. (157)

modeling A component of social learning theory that involves observing and attempting to imitate the behaviors of others. (470)

monitoring methods Methods of quantitative forecasting that provide early warning signals of significant changes in established patterns and relationships so that managers can assess the likely impact and plan responses if necessary. (300)

moral management An approach to managerial ethics that strives to follow ethical principles and precepts. (136)

morphological analysis A method of technological or qualitative forecasting that focuses on predicting potential technological breakthroughs by breaking the possibilities into component attributes and evaluating various attribute combinations. (303)

motivation The force that energizes behavior, gives direction to behavior, and underlies the tendency to persist. (445)

motivators A type of factor that figures in the two-factor theory of motivation that relates mainly to the content of the job (such as the work itself and feelings of achievement) and that can influence the degree of worker satisfaction. (452)

multifocal strategy A strategy aimed at achieving the advantages of worldwide integration whenever possible, while still attempting to be responsive to important national needs. (755)

multinational corporation (MNC) An organization that engages in production or service activities through its own affiliates in several countries, maintains control over the policies of those affiliates, and manages from a global perspective. (739)

multiple control systems Systems that use two or more of the feedforward, concurrent, and feedback control processes and involve several strategic control points. (609)

national responsiveness strategy A strategy of allowing subsidiaries to have substantial latitude in adapting products and services to suit the particular needs and political realities of the countries in which they operate. (759)

natural selection model A term sometimes used for the population ecology model. (91)

need for achievement (nAch) The desire to accomplish challenging tasks and achieve a standard of excellence in one's work. (453)

need for affiliation (nAff) The desire to maintain warm, friendly relationships with others. (454)

need for power (nPow) The desire to influence others and control one's environment. (454)

needs analysis An assessment of an organization's training needs that is developed by considering overall organizational requirements, tasks associated with jobs for which training is needed, and the degree to which individuals are

able to perform those tasks effectively. (419)

negative entropy The ability of open systems to bring in new energy in the form of inputs and feedback from the environment in order to delay or arrest entropy. (66)

negative reinforcement A type of reinforcement in behavior modification, aimed at *increasing* a desired behavior, that involves providing a noxious stimuli so that an individual will engage in the desired behavior in order to stop the noxious stimuli. (465)

negative synergy The result that occurs when group process losses are greater than any gains achieved from combining the forces of group members. (563)

negotiating contracts An approach to influencing the environment that involves seeking favorable agreements on matters of importance to the organization. (100)

network A management process element consisting of a set of cooperative relationships with individuals whose help is needed in order for a manager to function effectively. (11)

network diagram A diagram constructed as a step in setting up PERT that constitutes a graphic depiction of the interrelationships among the activities in a project. (307)

neutralizers Situational factors that make it *impossible* for a given leader behavior to have an impact on subordinate performance and/or satisfaction. (509)

new venture An enterprise that is in the process of being created by an entrepreneur. (774)

new venture teams Temporary task forces or teams made up of individuals who have been relieved of their normal duties in order to develop a new process, product, or program. (396)

new venture units Either separate divisions or specially incorporated companies created for the specific purpose of developing new products or business ideas and initiatives. (396)

newly industrialized countries (NICs) Countries within the LDCs that are emerging as major exporters of manufactured goods, including such nations as Hong Kong, Taiwan, and South Korea. (743)

node An indication of the beginning and/or ending of activities in a PERT network. (307)

noise Any factor in the communication process that interferes with exchanging messages and achieving common meaning. (525)

nominal group technique (NGT) A technique for enhancing group creativity that integrates both individual work and group interaction within certain ground rules. (287)

noncrisis problem A type of problem in managerial decision making involving an issue that requires resolution but does not simultaneously have the importance and immediacy characteristics of a crisis. (262)

noncybernetic control system A control system that relies on human discretion as a basic part of its process. (610)

nonprogrammed decisions Managerial decisions for which predetermined decision rules are impractical because the situations are novel and/or ill-structured. (263)

nonrational escalation The tendency to increase commitment to a previously selected course of action beyond the level that would be expected if the manager followed an effective decision-making process; also called *escalation phenomenon*. (278)

nonrational models Models of managerial decision making which suggest that information-gathering and -processing limitations make it difficult for managers to make optimal decisions. (265)

nonverbal communication Communication by means of elements and behaviors that are not coded into words. (520)

normative decision-making models Models of decision making that attempt to prescribe how managers *should* make decisions. (268)

normative leadership model A situational leadership theory model (designed by Vroom and Yetton) that helps leaders assess important situation factors that affect the extent to which they should involve subordinates in particular decisions. (498)

norming A stage of group development in which group members begin to build group cohesion, as well as develop consensus about norms for performing a task and relating to one another. (568)

norms A major group process factor involving expected behaviors sanctioned by the group that regulate and foster uniformity in member behaviors. (564)

not-for-profit organization An organization whose main purposes center on issues other than making profits. (9)

object language A category of nonverbal communication that involves the communicative use of material things, including clothing, cosmetics, furniture, and architecture. (520)

objective function A mathematical representation of the relationship to be optimized in a linear programming problem. (309)

office automation system (OAS) A computer-based information system aimed at facilitating communication and increasing the productivity of managers and office workers through document and message processing. (708)

ombudsperson Usually an executive operating outside the normal chain of command whose job is to handle issues involving hot-line-communicated employee grievances and warnings about serious ethical problems. (144)

on-line processing An arrangement whereby data can be accessed and processed immediately. (701)

one-way communication The communication that results when the communication process does not allow for feedback. (526)

open system A system that operates in continual interaction with its environment. (64)

operating budget A type of bud-

get involving a statement that presents the financial plan for each responsibility center during the budget period and reflects operating activities involving revenues and expenses. (643)

operational control A control type concerning mainly lower-level managers that involves overseeing the implementation of operating plans, monitoring day-to-day results, and taking corrective action when required. (598)

operational goals Targets or future end results set by lower management that address specific measurable outcomes required from the lower levels. (162)

operational plans The means devised to support implementation of tactical plans and achievement of operational goals; such plans are usually developed by lower management in conjunction with middle management. (173)

operations management The management of the productive processes that convert inputs into goods and services; the name also given to the function or field of expertise that is primarily responsible for managing the production and delivery of an organization's products and services. (62, 663)

operations research Another name commonly used for management science. (62)

opportunity problem A type of problem in managerial decision making involving a situation that offers a strong potential for significant organizational gain if appropriate actions are taken. (262)

orchestrator A high-level manager who articulates the need for innovation, provides funding for innovating activities, creates incentives for middle managers to sponsor new ideas, and protects idea people. (27)

ordering cost An inventory cost that is comprised of the expenses involved in placing an order (such as paperwork, postage, and time). (654)

organic characteristics The likely characteristics of firms operating in a highly unstable environment,

such as decentralization of decision making, few rules and regulations, and both hierarchical and lateral communication channels. (387)

organization Two or more persons engaged in a systematic effort to produce goods or services. (6)

organization chart A line diagram that depicts the broad outlines of an organization's structure. (336)

organization design The process of developing an organization structure. (336)

organization structure The formal pattern of interactions and coordination designed by management to link the tasks of individuals and groups in achieving organizational goals. (336)

organizational cultural change An intervention involving the development of a corporate culture that is in synchronization with organizational strategies and other factors, such as structure. (252)

organizational culture A system of shared values, assumptions, beliefs, and norms that unite the members of an organization. (78)

organizational development (OD) A change effort that is planned, focused on an entire organization or a large subsystem, managed from the top, aimed at enhancing organizational health and effectiveness, and based on planned interventions. (250)

organizational problems Discrepancies between a current state or condition and what is desired. (268)

organizational social responsibility The obligation of an organization to seek actions that protect and improve the welfare of society along with its own interests. (115)

organizational social responsiveness A term that refers to the development of organizational decision processes whereby managers anticipate, respond to, and manage areas of social responsibility. (126)

organizational termination The process of ceasing to exist as an identifiable organization. (228)

organizing The management function that focuses on allocating and arranging human and non-human resources so that plans can be carried out successfully. (7)

ossification A condition that may occur in stage V (resource maturity) of small-business growth that is characterized by lack of innovation and avoidance of risk. (797)

outputs The components of an organizational system that include the products, services, and other outcomes produced by the organization. (64)

overconfidence The tendency to be more certain of judgments regarding the likelihood of a future event than one's actual predictive accuracy warrants. (276)

overcontrol The limiting of individual job autonomy to such a point that it seriously inhibits effective job performance. (620)

panic A reaction preventing effective decision making in which individuals become so upset that they frantically seek a way to solve a problem. (273)

paralanguage A category of nonverbal communication that involves vocal aspects of communication that relate to how something is said rather than to what is said. (520)

partial-factor productivity A productivity approach that measures organizational productivity by considering the total output relative to a specific input, such as labor. (663)

participative A leader behavior identified in path-goal theory that is characterized by consulting with subordinates, encouraging their suggestions, and carefully considering their ideas when making decisions. (503)

path-goal theory A situational leadership theory that attempts to explain how leader behavior impacts the motivation and job satisfaction of subordinates. (502)

pay survey A survey of the labor market to determine the current rates of pay for benchmark, or key, jobs which is used to address the issue of external equity (of compensation). (426)

payoff The amount of decision-maker value associated with a particular decision alternative and future condition in a payoff table. (316)

payoff table A quantitative decision-making aid consisting of a two-dimensional matrix that allows a decision maker to compare how different future conditions are likely to affect the respective outcomes of two or more decision alternatives. (316)

perception The process that individuals use to acquire information from the environment. (527)

perceptual defense The tendency to block out or distort information that one finds threatening or that challenges one's beliefs. (529)

performance appraisal The process of defining expectations for employee performance; measuring, evaluating, and recording employee performance relative to those expectations; and providing feedback to the employee. (421)

performance-outcome expectancy A component of expectancy theory that is our assessment of the probability that our successful performance will lead to certain outcomes. (457)

performing A stage of group development in which energy is channeled toward a task and in which norms support teamwork. (569)

personal power A form of need for power in which individuals want to dominate others for the sake of demonstrating their ability to wield power. (454)

physiological needs The needs in Maslow's hierarchy that are required for survival, such as food, water, and shelter. (448)

plan A major planning component that is the means devised for attempting to reach a goal. (157)

planned change Change that involves actions based on a carefully thought-out process for change that anticipates future difficulties, threats, and opportunities. (235)

planning The management function that involves setting goals and deciding how best to achieve them. (7)

planning mode An approach to strategy formulation that involves systematic, comprehensive analysis, along with integration of various decisions and strategies. (195)

planning staff A small group of individuals who assist top-level managers in developing the various components of the planning process. (178)

plant closings A generic term that refers to shutting down operations at a factory or nonfactory site either permanently or for an extended period of time (an issue connected with a corporation's responsibility to employees). (119)

point factor method A job evaluation approach in which points are assigned to jobs on the basis of the degree to which the jobs contain selected compensable factors. (425)

policy A standing plan that provides a general guide specifying the broad parameters within which organization members are expected to operate in pursuit of organizational goals. (174)

political risk The probability of the occurrence of political actions that will result in loss of either enterprise ownership or significant benefits from conducting business. (745)

polycentric orientation An approach to international management (also known as *host-country orientation*) whereby executives view host-country cultures and foreigners as difficult to fathom and, therefore, believe that the parts of the organization located in a given host country should be staffed by local individuals to the fullest extent possible. (741)

pooled interdependence A type of technological interdependence in which units operate independently but their individual efforts are important to the success of the organization as a whole. (386)

population ecology model A view of the organization-environment interface that focuses on populations or groups of organizations and argues that environmental factors cause organizations with appropriate characteristics to survive and others to fail. (91)

portfolio strategy approach A corporate-level strategy approach that involves analyzing an organization's mix of businesses in terms of both individual and collective contributions to strategic goals. (205)

positive reinforcement A type of reinforcement in behavior modification, aimed at *increasing* a desired behavior, that involves providing a pleasant, rewarding consequence to encourage that behavior. (465)

positive synergy The force that results when the combined gains from group interaction are greater than group process losses. (563)

power The capacity to affect the behavior of others. (481)

power distance A cultural dimension in Geert Hofstede's framework for analyzing societies that involves the degree to which individuals in a society accept differences in the distribution of power as reasonable and normal. (746)

procedure A standing plan that involves a prescribed series of related steps to be taken under certain recurring circumstances. (174)

process consultation An intervention concerned with the interpersonal relations and dynamics operating in work groups. (252)

process layout A type of facilities layout having a production configuration in which the processing components are grouped according to the type of function that they perform. (683)

product divisions A form of divisional structure involving divisions created to concentrate on a single product or service or at least a relatively homogeneous set of products or services. (374)

product layout A type of facilities layout having a production configuration in which the processing components are arranged in a specialized line along which the product or client passes during the production process. (684)

product/market evolution matrix A portfolio approach involving a 15-cell matrix (developed by Charles W. Hofer) in which businesses are plotted according to the business unit's business strength, or competitive position, and the industry's stage in the evolutionary product/market life cycle. (210)

productivity An efficiency concept that gauges the ratio of outputs relative to inputs into a productive process. (663)

professional bureaucracy The structural configuration in Mintzberg's typology characterized by functional or hybrid departmentalization, a strong group of professionals operating at the lower levels, low formalization, and emphasis on standardization of skills. (390)

profit budget An operating budget that focuses on the profit to be derived from the difference between anticipated revenues and expenses. (643)

profit center A responsibility center whose budgetary performance is measured by the difference between revenues and costs, in other words, profits. (640)

profitability ratios Financial ratios that help measure management's ability to control expenses and earn profits through the use of organizational resources. (634)

program A comprehensive single-use plan that coordinates a complex set of activities related to a major nonrecurring goal. (174)

Program Evaluation and Review Technique (PERT) A network planning method for managing large projects. (306)

programmed decisions Managerial decisions made in routine, repetitive, well-structured situations through the use of predetermined decision rules. (263)

project A single-use plan that coordinates a set of limited-scope activities that do not need to be divided into several major projects in order to reach a major nonrecurring goal. (174)

project managers Managers who have responsibility for coordinating efforts involving individuals in several different organizational units who are all working on a particular project. (29)

projection The tendency of an individual to assume that others share his or her thoughts, feelings, and characteristics. (529)

prospect theory A theory explaining certain decision-making biases which posits that decision makers find the prospect of incurring an actual loss more painful than giving up the possibility of a gain. (275)

prototyping A means of developing an information system that involves building a rough, working model of all or parts of a proposed system for purposes of preliminary evaluation and further refinement. (719)

proxemics A category of nonverbal communication that involves the influence of proximity and space on communication. (520)

public affairs department A permanent department, used as a mechanism for facilitating an organization's internal social response, that coordinates various ongoing social responsibilities and identifies and recommends policies for new social issues. (130)

public relations An approach to influencing the environment involving the use of communications media and related activities to create a favorable overall impression of the organization among the public. (99)

punishment A type of reinforcement in behavior modification that involves providing negative consequences in order to *decrease* or discourage a behavior. (466)

purchasing A primary operating system used in operations management that is involved with acquiring necessary goods or services in exchange for funds or other remuneration. (679)

qualitative forecasting A type of forecasting aimed primarily at predicting long-term trends in technology and other important aspects of the environment. (301)

quality The totality of features and characteristics of a product or service that bear on its ability to satisfy stated or implied needs. (646)

quality circle (QC) A small group of employees who meet periodically to solve quality problems related to their jobs. (651)

quantitative forecasting A type of forecasting that relies on numerical data and mathematical models to predict future conditions. (297)

questionable payments An international social responsibility issue concerning business payments that raise significant ethical questions of right or wrong either in the host nation or in other nations. (765)

queuing models A quantitative planning technique based on mathematical models that describe the operating characteristics of queuing situations in which service is provided to persons or units waiting in line. (311)

ratio analysis A financial control technique that involves determining and evaluating financial ratios. (632)

rational model A model of managerial decision making which suggests that managers engage in completely rational decision processes, ultimately make optimal decisions, and possess and understand all information relevant to their decisions at the time they make them. (265)

rationalization The strategy of assigning activities to those parts of the organization, regardless of their location, that are best suited to produce the desired results and then selling the finished products where they are likely to yield the best profits. (754)

rationing A method of adapting to environmental fluctuations that involves limiting access to a product or service that is in high demand. (98)

raw materials inventory The stock of parts, ingredients, and other basic inputs to a production or service process. (653)

reactive change Change that occurs when one takes action in response to perceived problems, threats, or opportunities. (234)

realistic job preview A technique used during the recruiting process in which the job candidate is presented with a balanced view of both the positive and the negative aspects of the job and the organization. (413)

receiver The person with whom the message is exchanged in the communication process. (524)

reciprocal interdependence A type of technological interdependence in which one unit's outputs become inputs to the other unit and vice versa. (386)

recruitment An activity in the staffing process that involves finding and attempting to attract job candidates who are capable of effectively filling job vacancies. (412)

reference checks A selection method involving attempts to obtain job-related information about job applicants from individuals who are in a position to be knowledgeable about the applicants' qualifications. (418)

referent power Power that results from being admired, personally identified with, or liked by others. (481)

regression models Explanatory models based on equations that express the fluctuations in the variable being forecasted in terms of fluctuations among one or more other variables. (299)

reinforcement theory A theory of motivation that argues that our behavior can be explained by consequences in the environment and, therefore, that it is not necessary to look for cognitive explanations. (464)

relatedness needs The needs in ERG theory that address our relationships with significant others, such as families, friendship groups, work groups, and professional groups. (449)

reorder point (ROP) The inventory level at which a new order should be placed. (654)

replacement chart A partial organization chart showing the major managerial positions in an organization, current incumbents, potential replacements for each position, and the age of each person listed on the chart. (409)

representativeness A decision-making bias that involves the tendency to be overly influenced by stereotypes in making judgments about the likelihood of occurrences. (276)

reservations Organizational units that devote full time to the generation of innovative ideas for future business. (396)

resource dependence An approach to controls that argues that managers need to consider controls mainly in areas in which they depend on others for resources necessary to reach organizational goals. (604)

resource dependence model A view of the organization-environment interface that highlights organizational dependence on the environment for resources and argues that organizations attempt to manipulate the environment to reduce that dependence. (92)

responsibility The obligation to carry out duties and achieve goals related to a position. (353)

responsibility center A subunit headed by a manager who is responsible for achieving one or more goals. (639)

restraining forces Forces studied in force-field analysis that involve factors that pressure *against* a change. (243)

restructuring A method of increasing organizational efficiency and effectiveness that involves making a major change in organization structure and often includes reducing management levels and also changing components of the organization through divestiture and/or acquisition, as well as shrinking the size of the work force. (350)

revenue budget An operating budget that indicates anticipated revenues. (643)

revenue center A responsibility center whose budgetary performance is measured primarily by its ability to generate a specified level of revenue. (639)

revitalization The renewal of the innovative vigor of organizations sought in the elaboration-of-structure stage of the organizational life cycle. (231)

reward power Power that is based on the capacity to control and provide valued rewards to others. (481)

risk The possibility, characteristic of decisions made under uncertainty, that a chosen action could lead to losses rather than the intended results. (264)

rite A relatively elaborate, dramatic, planned set of activities intended to convey cultural values to participants and, usually, an audience. (104)

role A major work group input that involves a set of behaviors expected of an individual who occupies a particular position in a group; also used to denote a management process element consisting of an organized set of behaviors associated with a particular office or position. (11, 560)

romance of leadership The phenomenon of leadership's possibly being given more than its due credit for positive results. (509)

routing, or distribution, models Quantitative methods that can assist managers in planning the most effective and economical approaches to distribution problems. (313)

rule A standing plan that is a statement spelling out specific actions to be taken or not taken in a given situation. (175)

safety needs The needs in Maslow's hierarchy that pertain to the desire to feel safe, secure, and free from threats to our existence. (449)

sales budget An operating budget that indicates anticipated revenues. (643)

sales-force composite A method of judgmental forecasting that is used mainly to predict future sales and typically involves obtaining the views of various salespeople, sales managers, and/or distributors regarding the sales outlook. (304)

satisfaction-progression principle A principle incorporated into ERG theory which states that satisfaction of one level of need encourages concern with the next level. (450)

satisficing model A nonrational model of managerial decision making stating that managers seek alternatives only until they find one that looks *satisfactory*, rather than seeking the optimal decision. (266)

satisfiers Motivating factors which figure in the two-factor theory of motivation that relate mainly to the content of the job (such as the work itself and feelings of achievement). (452)

scenarios Outlines of possible future conditions, including possible paths the organization could take that would likely lead to these conditions. (303)

schedules of reinforcement Patterns of rewarding that specify the basis for and timing of positive reinforcement. (467)

scientific management An approach within classical management theory that emphasizes the scientific study of work methods in order to improve worker efficiency. (45)

selection An activity in the staffing process that involves determining which job candidates best suit organizational needs. (413)

selection interview A relatively formal, in-depth conversation conducted for the purpose of assessing a candidate's knowledge, skills, and abilities, as well as providing information to the candidate about the organization and potential jobs. (414)

self-actualization needs The needs in Maslow's hierarchy that pertain to the requirement of developing our capabilities and reaching our full potential. (449)

self-control A component of social learning theory involving our ability to exercise control over our own behavior by setting standards and providing consequences for our own actions. (471)

self-efficacy The belief in one's capabilities to perform a specific task. (469)

self-managing team A work group given responsibility for a task area without day-to-day supervision and with authority to influence and control both group membership and behavior. (573)

self-oriented roles Roles that are related to the personal needs of group members and often negatively influence the effectiveness of a group. (560)

self-serving bias The tendency to perceive oneself as responsible for successes and others as responsible for failures. (529)

semantic blocks The blockages or difficulties in communication that arise from word choices. (529)

semantic net The network of words and word meanings that a given individual has available for recall. (529)

sender The initiator of the message in the communication process. (523)

sequential interdependence A type of technological interdependence in which one unit must complete its work before the next unit in the sequence can begin work. (386)

shaping A technique associated with positive reinforcement that involves the successive rewarding of behaviors that closely approximate the desired response until the actual desired response is made. (465)

simple structure The structural configuration in Mintzberg's typology characterized by functional departmentalization, a strong concentration of power at the top, low formalization, and emphasis on direct supervision. (390)

simulation A quantitative planning technique that uses mathematical models to imitate reality. (313)

single-use plans Plans aimed at achieving a specific goal that, once reached, will most likely not recur in the future. (174)

situational leadership theory A contingency theory (developed by Paul Hersey and Ken Blanchard) based on the premise that leaders need to alter their behaviors depending on the readiness of followers. (496)

situational theories Theories of leadership that take into consideration important situational factors. (490)

skill-based pay A compensation system in which employees' rates of pay are based on the number of predetermined skills that the employees have mastered. (428)

skill variety A core job characteristic involving the extent to which the job entails a number of activities that require different skills. (341)

skills inventory A data bank (usually computerized) containing basic information about each employee that can be used to assess the likely availability of individuals for meeting current and future human resources needs. (409)

slack Latitude about when various activities can be started on the noncritical paths in a PERT network without endangering the completion date of the entire project. (308)

slack resources A means of facilitating horizontal coordination that involves a cushion of resources that aids adaptation to internal and external pressures, as well as initiation of changes. (358)

smoothing A method of adapting to environmental fluctuations that involves taking actions aimed at reducing the impact of fluctuations, given the market. (97)

social audit A systematic study and evaluation of the social, rather than the economic, performance of an organization. (127)

social forecasting The process of identifying social trends, evaluating the organizational importance of those trends, and integrating these assessments into the organization's forecasting program. (126)

social information-processing approach A job design approach arguing that individuals often form impressions of their jobs from socially provided information, such as comments by supervisors and coworkers. (343)

social learning theory A theory of motivation having aspects of both cognitive and reinforcement theories which argues that learning occurs through the continuous recip-

rocal interaction of our behaviors, various personal factors, and environmental forces. (469)

social loafing The tendency of individuals to expend less effort when working in groups than when working alone. (563)

social scanning The general surveillance of various elements in the task environment to detect evidence of impending changes that will affect the organization's social responsibilities. (128)

socialist economy An economy in which the means of production are owned by the state and economic activity is coordinated by plan. (82)

sociocultural element The element of the mega-environment that includes the attitudes, values, norms, beliefs, behaviors, and associated demographic trends that are characteristic of a given geographic area. (84)

software The set of programs, documents, procedures, and routines associated with the operation of a computer system that makes the hardware capable of its various activities. (702)

soldiering A work practice whereby workers deliberately work at less-than-full capacity, the resolution of which led Taylor to develop his scientific management approach. (45)

span of management, or **span of control** A means of vertical coordination involving the number of subordinates who report directly to a specific manager. (348)

sponsor A middle manager who recognizes the organizational significance of an idea, helps obtain the necessary funding for development of the innovation, and facilitates its actual implementation. (27)

stability strategy A grand strategy that involves maintaining the status quo or growing in a methodical, but slow, manner. (204)

staff position A position whose primary purpose is providing specialized expertise and assistance to line positions. (354)

staffing The set of activities aimed

at attracting and selecting individuals for positions in a way that will facilitate the achievement of organizational goals. (411)

standard cost center A responsibility center whose budgetary performance depends on achieving its goals by operating within standard cost constraints. (639)

standing committee A permanent task group of individuals charged with handling recurring matters in a narrowly defined subject area over an indefinite, but generally lengthy, period of time. (553)

standing plans Plans that provide ongoing guidance for performing recurring activities. (174)

start-up A new firm or venture started from scratch by an entrepreneur. (782)

statistical process control A statistical technique employed in quality control that uses periodic random samples taken during actual production to determine whether acceptable quality levels are being met or production should be stopped for remedial action. (652)

stereotyping The tendency to attribute characteristics to an individual on the basis of an assessment of the group to which the individual belongs. (528)

stockout cost An inventory cost that involves the economic consequences of running out of stock (such as loss of customer goodwill and possibly sales). (654)

storming A stage of group development in which group members frequently experience conflict with one another as they locate and attempt to resolve differences of opinion regarding key issues. (568)

story A narrative based on true events, which sometimes may be embellished to highlight the intended value. (104)

strategic business unit (SBU) A distinct business, with its own set of competitors, that can be managed reasonably independently of other businesses within the organization. (193)

strategic control A control type concerning mainly top managers that involves monitoring critical environmental factors that could affect the viability of strategic plans, assessing the effects of organizational strategic actions, and ensuring that strategic plans are implemented as intended. (598)

strategic control points Performance areas chosen for control because they are particularly important in meeting organizational goals. (604)

strategic goals Broadly defined targets or future end results set by top management. (161)

strategic management A process through which managers formulate and implement strategies geared to optimizing strategic goal achievement, given available environmental and internal conditions. (190)

strategic plans Detailed action steps mapped out to reach strategic goals; such plans are developed by top management in consultation with the board of directors and middle management. (172)

strategies Large-scale action plans for interacting with the environment in order to achieve long-term goals. (190)

strategy formulation The part of the strategic management process that involves identifying the mission and strategic goals, conducting competitive analysis, and developing specific strategies. (190)

strategy implementation The part of the strategic management process that focuses on carrying out strategic plans and maintaining control over how those plans are carried out. (190)

substitutes Situational factors that make leadership impact not only *impossible* but also unnecessary. (509)

substitutes for leadership An approach that attempts to specify some of the main situational factors likely to make leader behaviors unnecessary or to negate their effectiveness. (509)

sunk costs Costs that, once incurred, are not recoverable and should not enter into considerations of future courses of action. (278)

superordinate goals Major common goals that require the support and effort of all parties and on which the manager is sometimes able to refocus individuals or groups in conflict, thus reducing or resolving the conflict. (580)

suppliers The element of the task environment that includes those organizations and individuals that supply the resources an organization needs to conduct its operations. (90)

supportive A leader behavior identified in path-goal theory that entails showing concern for the status, well-being, and needs of subordinates; doing small things to make the work more pleasant; and being friendly and approachable. (503)

SWOT analysis A method of analyzing an organization's competitive situation that involves assessing organizational strengths (S) and weaknesses (W), as well as environmental opportunities (O) and threats (T). (196)

symbol An object, act, event, or quality that serves as a vehicle for conveying meaning. (104)

symbolic processes Components of social learning theory involving the various ways that we use verbal and imagined symbols to process and store experiences in representational forms that can serve as guides to future behavior. (469)

synectics A technique for enhancing creativity that relies on analogies to help group members look at problems from new perspectives. (288)

synergy A major characteristic of open systems that is the ability of the whole to equal more than the sum of its parts. (66)

system A set of interrelated parts that operate as a whole in pursuit of common goals. (63)

systems development life cycle A series of stages that are used in the development of most medium- and large-size information systems. (717)

systems theory A view of management based on the notion that

organizations can be visualized as systems. (63)

tactical control A control type concerning mainly middle managers that focuses on assessing the implementation of tactical plans at department levels, monitoring associated periodic results, and taking corrective action as necessary. (598)

tactical goals Targets or future end results usually set by middle management for specific departments or units. (162)

tactical plans The means charted to support implementation of the strategic plan and achievement of tactical goals; such plans are developed by middle management potentially in consultation with lower management. (173)

takeover A form of acquisition involving the purchase of a controlling share of voting stock in a publicly traded company and thus a potential reason for organizational termination. (234)

tall structure A structure that has many hierarchical levels and narrow spans of control. (349)

tariff A type of trade barrier in the form of a customs duty, or tax, levied mainly on imports. (745)

task environment The segment of the external environment made up of the specific outside elements with which an organization interfaces in the course of conducting its business. (87)

task force A temporary task group usually formed to make recommendations on a specific issue. (571)

task group A formal group that is created for a specific purpose that supplements or replaces work normally done by command groups. (553)

task identity A core job characteristic involving the degree to which the job allows the completion of a major identifiable piece of work, rather than just a fragment. (341)

task significance A core job characteristic involving the extent to which the worker sees the job output as having an important impact on others. (341)

team A temporary or ongoing task group whose members are charged with working together to identify problems, form a consensus about what should be done, and implement necessary actions in relation to a particular task or organizational area. (571)

team building An intervention aimed at helping work groups become effective at task accomplishment. (252)

technical skills Key management skills that reflect both an understanding of and a proficiency in a specialized field. (18)

technological element The part of the mega-environment that reflects the current state of knowledge regarding the production of products and services. (79)

technological forecasting A type of forecasting aimed primarily at predicting long-term trends in technology and other important aspects of the environment. (301)

technological interdependence The degree to which different parts of the organization must exchange information and materials in order to perform their required activities. (386)

technological transfer The transmission of technology from those who possess it to those who do not. (747)

technology The knowledge, tools, equipment, and work techniques used by an organization in delivering its product or service. (383)

technostructural activities An intervention involving activities intended to improve work technology and/or organization structure. (252)

telecommuting A form of working at home that is made possible by using computer technology to remain in touch with the office. (724)

Theory Z A concept that combines positive aspects of American and Japanese management into a modified approach aimed at increasing U.S. managerial effectiveness while remaining compatible with the norms and values of American society and culture. (68)

third-party intervention A technique concerned with helping individuals, groups, or departments resolve serious conflicts that may relate to specific work issues or may be caused by suboptimal interpersonal relations. (252)

time-series methods Methods of quantitative forecasting that use historical data to develop forecasts of the future. (297)

top-down budgeting A process of developing budgets in which top management outlines the overall figures and middle and lower-level managers plan accordingly. (644)

top managers Managers at the very top levels of the hierarchy who are ultimately responsible for the entire organization. (23)

total-factor productivity A productivity approach which measures organizational productivity by considering all the inputs involved in producing outputs. (663)

total quality control (TQC) A quality control approach that emphasizes organizationwide commitment, integration of quality improvement efforts with organizational goals, and inclusion of quality as a factor in performance appraisals. (648)

trade associations Organizations that are composed of individuals or firms with common business concerns and which have environmental influence. (100)

training and development A planned effort to facilitate employee learning of job-related behaviors in order to improve employee performance. (419)

traits Distinctive internal qualities or characteristics of an individual, such as physical characteristics, personality characteristics, skills and abilities, and social factors. (483)

transaction-processing system (TPS) A computer-based information system that executes and records the day-to-day routine transactions required to conduct an organization's business. (703)

transactional leaders Leaders who motivate subordinates to perform at expected levels by helping them recognize task responsibilities, identify goals, acquire confidence about meeting desired performance levels, and understand how their needs and the rewards that they desire are linked to goal achievement. (506)

transformation processes The components of an organizational system comprising the organization's managerial and technological abilities that are applied to convert inputs into outputs. (64)

transformational leaders Leaders who motivate individuals to perform beyond normal expectations by inspiring subordinates to focus on broader missions that transcend their own immediate self-interests, to concentrate on intrinsic higher-level goals rather than extrinsic lower-level goals, and to have confidence in their abilities to achieve the extraordinary missions articulated by the leader. (507)

turnaround A defensive strategy designed to reverse a negative trend and restore the organization to appropriate levels of profitability. (205)

two-factor theory A content theory of motivation (developed by Frederick Herzberg) which argues that potential rewards fit into two categories, hygiene factors and motivators, each having distinctly different implications for employee motivation. (452)

two-way communication The communication that results when the communication process explicitly includes feedback. (526)

uncertainty An aspect of nonprogrammed decisions that is a condition in which the decision maker must choose a course of action without complete knowledge of the consequences that will follow implementation. (264)

uncertainty avoidance A cultural dimension in Geert Hofstede's framework for analyzing societies that involves the extent to which members of a society feel uncomfortable with and try to avoid situations that they perceive as unstructured, unclear, or unpredictable. (746)

undercontrol The granting of autonomy to an employee to such a point that the organization loses its ability to direct the individual's efforts toward achieving organizational goals. (620)

unions Employee groups formed for the purpose of negotiating with management about conditions relating to their work. (431)

unit and small-batch production A type of technology in which products are custom-produced to meet customer specifications or they are made in small quantities primarily by craft specialists. (384)

upward communication The vertical flow of communication from a lower level to one or more higher levels in the organization. (538)

user An individual, other than an information system professional, who is engaged in the development and/or management of computer-based information systems. (720)

valence A factor in expectancy theory that is our assessment of the anticipated value of various outcomes or rewards. (458)

validity A concept underlying the use of various selection methods that concerns the degree to which a measure actually assesses an attribute that it is designed to measure. (413)

variable-interval schedule of reinforcement A type of partial reinforcement schedule based on a pattern in which a reinforcer is administered on a varying, or random, time schedule that *averages* out to a predetermined time frequency. (468)

variable-ratio schedule of reinforcement A type of partial reinforcement schedule based on a pattern in which a reinforcer is provided after a varying, or random, number of occurrences of the desired behavior in such a way that the reinforcement pattern *averages* out to a predetermined ratio of occurrences per reinforcement. (468)

venture team A group of two or more individuals who band together for the purpose of creating a new venture. (792)

verbal communication The written or oral use of words to communicate. (519)

vertical communication Communication that involves a message exchange between two or more levels of the organizational hierarchy. (536)

vertical coordination An aspect of organization structure involving the linking of activities at the top of the organization with those at the middle and lower levels in order to achieve organizational goals. (345)

vertical integration A growth strategy that involves effecting growth through the production of inputs previously provided by suppliers or through the replacement of a customer role by disposing of one's own outputs. (201)

vicarious learning A component of social learning theory involving our ability to learn new behaviors and/or assess their probable consequences by observing others. (469)

video teleconferencing The holding of meetings with individuals in two or more locations by means of closed-circuit television. (544)

waiting-in-line models A quantitative planning technique based on mathematical models that describe the operating characteristics of queuing situations in which service is provided to persons or units waiting in line. (311)

whistle-blower An employee who reports a real or perceived wrongdoing under the control of his or her employer to those who may be able to take appropriate action. (144)

wholly owned subsidiary An operation on foreign soil, by means of which organizations can conduct business internationally, that is totally owned and controlled by a company with headquarters outside the host country. (752)

wide area networks Networks through which end-user computing can be managed that provide communications among computers over long distances, usually through the facilities and services of public or private communications companies. (723)

work agenda A management process element composed of a loosely connected set of tentative goals and tasks that a manager is attempting to accomplish. (15)

work-in-process inventory The stock of items that are currently being transformed into a final product or service. (653)

work specialization The degree to which the work necessary to achieve organizational goals is broken down into various jobs. (338)

worldwide integration strategy A strategy aimed at developing relatively standardized products with global appeal, as well as rationalizing operations throughout the world. (754)

zero-base budgeting (ZBB) A budget approach in which responsibility centers start with zero in preparing their budget requests and must justify the contributions of each of their activities to organizational goals. (645)

zero defects A quality mentality that the total quality control approach attempts to achieve in which the work force strives to make a product or service conform exactly to desired standards. (649)

CHAPTER 1

1. Mary Jane Madigan, *Steuben Glass, An American Tradition in Crystal*, Abrams, New York, 1981; "Corning and Innovation: Old Friends, New Partners," *The Gaffer*, June–July 1986, pp. 8–9; James R. Houghton, "The Old Way of Doing Things Is Gone," *Quality Progress*, September 1986; Jagannath Dubashi, "Through a Glass Lightly," *Financial World*, May 19, 1987, pp. 20–29; Gerald J. Barry, "Stay Tuned," *The Quality Review*, Spring 1988, pp. 34–39; Philip H. Dougherty, "Steuben Has New Form of Expression," *The New York Times*, Apr. 20, 1988; Betty Sargent, "Steuben Breaks the Mold," *Connoisseur*, June 1988; "At Corning, A Vision of Quality," *Fortune*, Oct. 24, 1988, p. 64; Judith D. Schwartz, "Adding Sparkle and Style to the Glassware at Steuben," *Adweek's Marketing Week*, July 17, 1989, pp. 66–67; John Holusha, "The Search for Flexibility on the Line," *The New York Times*, July 16, 1989, sec. 3, pp. 1, 8; *About Steuben*, Steuben Glass, Corning, N.Y., n.d.; conversations between Susan B. King, Dick Jack, and Linda Moonschein of Steuben Glass and Kathryn M. Bartol, July 1989.
2. Todd Mason, "The Downfall of a CEO," *Business Week*, Feb. 16, 1987, pp. 76–84.
3. See Stephen J. Carroll and Dennis J. Gillen, "Are the Classical Management Functions Useful in Describing Managerial Work?" *Academy of Management Review*, vol. 12, 1987, pp. 38–51, for a recent review of the continuing importance of the functions of management as a framework for studying management.
4. Alex Taylor III, "Why the Bounce at Rubbermaid?" *Fortune*, Apr. 13, 1987, pp. 77–78; Maria Mallory, "Profits on Everything but the Kitchen Sink," *Business Week*, Innovation 1989 issue, June 16, 1989, p. 122.
5. Todd Mason, "The Downfall of a CEO," *Business Week*, Feb. 16, 1987, pp. 76–84.
6. Alex Taylor III, "Why the Bounce at Rubbermaid?" *Fortune*, Apr. 13, 1987, pp. 77–78; Maria Mallory, "Profits on Everything but the Kitchen Sink," *Business Week*, Innovation 1989 issue, p. 122.
7. Todd Mason, "The Downfall of a CEO," *Business Week*, Feb. 16, 1987, pp. 76–84.
8. Kenneth Labich, "The Seven Keys to Business Leadership," *Fortune*, Oct. 24, 1988, pp. 58–66.
9. Alex Taylor III, "Why the Bounce at Rubbermaid?" *Fortune*, Apr. 13, 1987, pp. 77–78; Maria Mallory, "Profits on Everything but the Kitchen Sink," *Business Week*, Innovation 1989 issue, June 16, 1989, p. 122.
10. Todd Mason, "The Downfall of a CEO," *Business Week*, Feb. 16, 1987, pp. 76–84.
11. William H. Newman, *Constructive Control*, Prentice-Hall, Englewood Cliffs, N.J., 1975.
12. Alex Taylor III, "Why the Bounce at Rubbermaid?" *Fortune*, Apr. 13, 1987, pp. 77–78; Maria Mallory, "Profits on Everything but the Kitchen Sink," *Business Week*, Innovation 1989 issue, June 16, 1989, p. 122.
13. Todd Mason, "The Downfall of a CEO," *Business Week*, Feb. 16, 1987, pp. 76–84.
14. Steven J. Carroll and Dennis J. Gillen, "Are the Classical Management Functions Useful in Describing Managerial Work?" *Academy of Management Review*, vol. 12, 1987, pp. 38–51.

15. Ran Lachman, "Public and Private Sector Differences: CEOs' Perceptions of Their Role Environments," *Academy of Management Journal*, September 1985, pp. 671–680.
16. Gary A. Yukl, *Leadership in Organizations*, 2d ed., Prentice-Hall, Englewood Cliffs, N.J., 1989.
17. Henry Mintzberg, *The Nature of Managerial Work*, Prentice-Hall, Englewood Cliffs, N.J., 1980.
18. Ford S. Worthy, "How CEOs Manage Their Time," *Fortune*, Jan. 18, 1988, pp. 88–97.
19. Ibid.
20. J. H. Horne and Tom Lupton, "The Work Activities of Middle Managers: An Exploratory Study," *Journal of Management Studies*, vol. 2, 1965, pp. 14–33; Colin P. Hales, "What Do Managers Do? A Critical Review of the Evidence," *Journal of Management Studies*, vol. 23, 1986, pp. 88–115; Henry Mintzberg, *The Nature of Managerial Work*, Prentice-Hall, Englewood Cliffs, N.J., 1980; Lance B. Kurke and Howard E. Aldrich, "Mintzberg Was Right!: A Replication and Extension of *The Nature of Managerial Work*," *Management Science*, vol. 29, 1983, pp. 975–984.
21. Robert H. Guest, "Of Time and the Foreman," *Personnel*, vol. 32, 1955–1956, pp. 478–486.
22. Henry Mintzberg, *The Nature of Managerial Work*, Prentice-Hall, Englewood Cliffs, N.J., 1980.
23. Based on Allan R. Cohen and David L. Bradford, "Influence without Authority: The Use of Alliances, Reciprocity, and Exchange to Accomplish Work," *Organizational Dynamics*, Winter 1989, pp. 5–17.
24. Ronni Sandroff, "The Manager Who Never Says Never," *Working Woman*, December 1989, pp. 90–94, 124.
25. Ibid.
26. M. W. McCall and C. A. Segrist, *In Pursuit of the Manager's Job: Building on Mintzberg*, Center for Creative Leadership, Greensboro, N.C., 1980; A. W. Lau, A. R. Newman, and L. A. Broedling, "The Nature of Managerial Work in the Public Sector," *Public Management Forum*, vol. 19, 1980, pp. 513–521; H. H. Snyder and T. L. Wheelen, "Managerial Roles: Mintzberg and the Management Process Theorists," in *Proceedings of the Academy of Management*, 1981, pp. 249–253.
27. Stephen J. Carroll and Dennis J. Gillen, "Are the Classical Management Functions Useful in Describing Managerial Work?" *Academy of Management Review*, vol. 12, 1987, pp. 38–51.
28. John P. Kotter, *The General Managers*, Free Press, New York, 1982.
29. Adapted (with minor changes) from John P. Kotter, "What Effective General Managers Really Do," *Harvard Business Review*, November–December 1982, pp. 156–167.
30. Rosemary Stewart, "A Model for Understanding Managerial Jobs and Behavior," *Academy of Management Review*, vol. 7, 1982, pp. 7–13.
31. John P. Kotter, *The General Managers*, Free Press, New York, 1982.
32. Richard E. Boyatzis, *The Competent Manager: A Model for Effective Performance*. Wiley, New York, 1982.
33. Lucy Kraus, "Tough, with a Velvet Glove," *American Way*, Fall 1988, pp. 48–51.
34. Peter F. Drucker, *The Effective Executive*,

Harper & Row, New York, 1967.
35. Joan O'C. Hamilton, "Why Rivals Are Quaking as Nordstrom Heads East," *Business Week*, June 15, 1987, pp. 99–100.
36. Ibid.
37. Steven Kerr, Kenneth D. Hill, and Laurie Broedling, "The First-Line Supervisor: Phasing Out or Here to Stay?" *Academy of Management Review*, vol. 11, 1986, pp. 103–117.
38. Ibid.
39. Peter F. Drucker, "Tomorrow's Restless Managers," *Industry Week*, Apr. 18, 1988, pp. 25–27; Ron Zemke, "Putting the SQUEEZE on Middle Managers," *Training*, December 1988, pp. 41–46.
40. Kenneth Labich, "Making Over Middle Managers," *Fortune*, May 8, 1989, pp. 58–64.
41. Ron Zemke, "Putting the SQUEEZE on Middle Managers," *Training*, December 1988, pp. 41–46.
42. Kenneth Labich, "Making Over Middle Managers," *Fortune*, May 8, 1989, pp. 58–64.
43. Rosabeth Moss Kanter, "The New Managerial Work," *Harvard Business Review*, November–December 1989, pp. 85–92.
44. Approximations of importance are based on Thomas A. Mahoney, Thomas H. Jerdee, and Stephen J. Carroll, "The Job(s) of Management," *Industrial Relations*, February 1965, pp. 97–110, and Luis R. Gomez-Mejia, Joseph E. McCann, and Ronald C. Page, "The Structure of Managerial Behaviors and Rewards," *Industrial Relations*, vol. 24, Winter 1985, pp. 147–154.
45. Robert L. Katz, "Skills of an Effective Administrator," *Harvard Business Review*, September–October 1974, pp. 90–102.
46. Derek Torrington and Jane Weightman, "Middle Management Work," *Journal of General Management*, vol. 13, 1987, pp. 74–89.
47. Kenneth Labich, "The Seven Keys to Business Leadership," *Fortune*, Oct. 24, 1988, p. 62.
48. Cynthia M. Pavett and Alan W. Lau, "Managerial Work: The Influence of Hierarchical Level and Functional Specialty," *Academy of Management Journal*, vol. 26, 1983, pp. 170–177.
49. Morgan W. McCall, Jr., and Michael M. Lombardo, "What Makes a Top Executive?" *Psychology Today*, February 1983, pp. 26–31.
50. Henry Mintzberg, *The Nature of Managerial Work*, Prentice-Hall, Englewood Cliffs, N.J., 1980.
51. Cynthia M. Pavett and Alan W. Lau, "Managerial Work: The Influence of Hierarchical Level and Functional Specialty," *Academy of Management Journal*, vol. 26, 1983, pp. 170–177.
52. Ibid.
53. Rosabeth Moss Kanter, "The Middle Manager as Innovator," *Harvard Business Review*, July–August 1982, pp. 95–105; Andrall E. Pearson, "Tough-Minded Ways to Get Innovative," *Harvard Business Review*, May–June 1988, pp. 99–106.
54. For a similar definition, see Rosabeth Moss Kanter, *The Change Masters*, Simon and Schuster, New York, 1983, p. 20.
55. Jay R. Galbraith, "Designing the Innovating Organization," *Organizational Dynamics*, Winter 1982, pp. 5–25; Andrall E. Pearson, "Tough-Minded Ways to Get Innovative," *Harvard Business Review*, May–June 1988, pp. 99–106.
56. Based on "JVC and VCR Miracle: 'You

Should Be Very Polite and Gentle,'" in P. Ranganath Nayak and John M. Ketteringham, *Break-Throughs*, Rawson Associates, New York, 1986, pp. 23–49.
57. John P. Kotter, *The General Managers*, Free Press, New York, 1982; see also Andrall E. Pearson, ''Six Basics for General Managers,'' *Harvard Business Review*, July–August 1989, pp. 94–101.
58. Stanley M. Davis and Paul R. Lawrence, *Matrix*, Addison-Wesley, Reading, Mass., 1977.
59. Luis R. Gomez-Mejia, Joseph E. McCann, and Ronald C. Page, ''The Structure of Managerial Behaviors and Rewards,'' *Industrial Relations*, vol. 24, 1985, pp. 147–154.
60. Cynthia M. Pavett and Alan W. Lau, ''Managerial Work: The Influence of Hierarchical Level and Functional Specialty,'' *Academy of Management Review*, vol. 26, 1983, pp. 170–177.
61. Louis E. Boone, David L. Kurtz, and C. Patrick Fleenor, ''CEOs: Early Signs of a Business Career,'' *Business Horizons*, September–October 1988, pp. 20–24.
62. Harold Stieglitz, *Chief Executives View Their Jobs: Today and Tomorrow*, Conference Board, New York, 1985.
63. Lise M. Saari, Terry R. Johnson, Steven D. McLaughlin, and Senise M. Zimmerle, ''A Survey of Management Training and Education Practices in U.S. Companies,'' *Personnel Psychology*, vol. 41, 1988, pp. 731–743.
64. Quoted in Louis E. Boone, David L. Kurtz, and C. Patrick Fleenor, ''CEOs: Early Signs of a Business Career,'' *Business Horizons*, September–October 1988, pp. 20–24.
65. Louis E. Boone and David L. Kurtz, ''CEOs: A Group Profile,'' *Business Horizons*, July–August 1988, pp. 38–42; see also Joel E. Ross and Darab Unwalla, ''Making It to the Top: A 30-Year Perspective,'' *Personnel*, April 1988, pp. 70–78.
66. Scott Tiver, ''The Boss at RJR Likes to Keep 'Em Guessing,'' *Business Week*, May 23, 1988, pp. 175–182; John Helyar and Bryan Burrough, ''How Underdog KKR Won RJR Nabisco without Highest Bid,'' *The Wall Street Journal*, Dec. 2, 1988, pp. A1, A11; Judith H. Dobrzynski, ''Running the Biggest LBO,'' *Business Week*, Oct. 2, 1989, pp. 72–79.
67. Amanda Bennett, ''Early to Bed . . . ,'' *The Wall Street Journal*, Mar. 20, 1987, p. 22D; see also Louis E. Boone and David L. Kurtz, ''CEOs: A Group Profile,'' *Business Horizons*, July–August 1988, pp. 38–42.
68. Harold Stieglitz, *Chief Executives View Their Jobs: Today and Tomorrow*, Conference Board, New York, 1985.
69. Fred Luthans, ''Successful vs. Effective Real Managers,'' *Academy of Management Executive*, vol. 2, no. 2, 1988, pp. 127–132.
70. Brian Dumaine, ''What the Leaders of Tomorrow See,'' *Fortune*, July 3, 1989, pp. 48–62.
71. Constance Mitchell, ''Partnerships Have Become a Way of Life for Corning,'' *The Wall Street Journal*, July 12, 1988, p. 6.
72. Amanda Bennett, ''The Chief Executives in Year 2000 Will Be Experienced Abroad,'' *The Wall Street Journal*, Feb. 27, 1989, pp. A1, A9.
73. Lester B. Korn, ''How the Next CEO Will Be Different,'' *Fortune*, May 22, 1989, pp. 157–158.
74. Based on David Garfinkel, ''What I Do on the Job: Bank Manager,'' *Business Week Careers*, February 1987, pp. 50–56.

CHAPTER 2

1. Based on Peter F. Drucker, *Management*, Harper & Row, New York, 1973, p. 53; Robert Lacey, *Ford—The Men and the Machine*, Little, Brown, Boston, 1986; and Peter Collier and David Horowitz, *The Fords*, Summit, New York, 1987.
2. Claude S. George, Jr., *The History of Management Thought*, Prentice-Hall, Englewood Cliffs, N.J., 1972; Richard L. A. Sterba, ''The Organization and Management of the Temple Corporations in Ancient Mesopotamia,'' *Academy of Management Review*, vol. 1, 1976, pp. 16–26; Daniel A. Wren, *The Evolution of Management Thought*, 2d ed., Wiley, New York, 1979.
3. Cited in W. Jack Duncan, *Great Ideas in Management*, Jossey-Bass, San Francisco, 1989.
4. Ibid.
5. Daniel A. Wren, *The Evolution of Management Thought*, 2d ed., Wiley, New York, 1979; W. Jack Duncan, *Great Ideas in Management*, Jossey-Bass, San Francisco, 1989.
6. W. Jack Duncan, *Great Ideas in Management*, Jossey-Bass, San Francisco, 1989.
7. Charles Babbage, *On the Economy of Machinery and Manufactures*, Charles Knight, London, 1832; reprinted by Agustus Kelly, New York, 1963.
8. W. Jack Duncan, *Great Ideas in Management*, Jossey-Bass, San Francisco, 1989.
9. Daniel A. Wren, *The Evolution of Management Thought*, 2d ed., Wiley, New York, 1979.
10. Henry R. Towne, ''The Engineer as an Economist,'' *Transactions of the American Society of Mechanical Engineers*, vol. 7, 1886, pp. 428–432; David F. Noble, *America by Design: Science, Technology and the Rise of Corporate Capitalism*, Knopf, New York, 1977; Daniel A. Wren, ''Years of Good Beginnings: 1886 and 1936,'' in Daniel A. Wren and John A. Pearce II (eds.), *Papers Dedicated to the Development of Modern Management*, Academy of Management, 1986, pp. 1–4; W. Jack Duncan, *Great Ideas in Management*, Jossey-Bass, San Francisco, 1989.
11. Hannah Sampson, ''The Army's Clausewitz of the Meeting Room,'' *Army*, vol. 38, no. 1, January 1988, pp. 49–50.
12. For a fascinating series of reviews of the works of major contributors to the classical viewpoint, see Allen C. Bluedorn (ed.), ''Special Book Review Section on the Classics of Management,'' *Academy of Management Review*, vol. 11, 1986, pp. 442–464.
13. W. Jack Duncan, *Great Ideas in Management*, Jossey-Bass, San Francisco, 1989.
14. Frederick Winslow Taylor, *The Principles of Scientific Management*, Hive, Easton, Pa., 1985.
15. See review of Frederick Winslow Taylor, *Scientific Management*, by Allen C. Bluedorn, *Academy of Management Review*, vol. 11, 1986, pp. 443–447.
16. Frederick Winslow Taylor, *The Principles of Scientific Management*, Hive, Easton, Pa., 1985.
17. Edwin A. Locke, ''The Ideas of Frederick W. Taylor: An Evaluation,'' *Academy of Management Review*, vol. 7, 1982, pp. 14–24.
18. Frederick Winslow Taylor, *The Principles of Scientific Management*, Hive, Easton, Pa., 1985.
19. Ibid.
20. W. Jack Duncan, *Great Ideas in Management*, Jossey-Bass, San Francisco, 1989.
21. Daniel A. Wren, *The Evolution of Management Thought*, 2d ed., Wiley, New York, 1979.
22. John Breeze, ''Paul Devinat's Scientific Management in Europe—A Historical Perspective,'' in Daniel A. Wren and John A. Pearce II (eds.), *Papers Dedicated to the Development of Modern Management*, Academy of Management, 1986, pp. 58–63.
23. See, for example, John H. Hoagland, ''Management before Taylor,'' in Paul M. Dauten (ed.), *Emerging Concepts in Management*, Houghton Mifflin, Boston, 1957; Charles D. Wrege and Amedeo G. Perroni, ''Taylor's Pig-Tale: A Historical Analysis of Frederick W. Taylor's Pig Iron Experiment,'' *Academy of Management Journal*, vol. 17, 1974, pp. 6–27; and Charles D. Wrege and Anne Marie Stotka, ''Cooke Creates a Classic: The Story behind F. W. Taylor's Principles of Sci-
24. Louis W. Fry, ''The Maligned F. W. Taylor: A Reply to His Many Critics,'' *Academy of Management Review*, vol. 1, 1976, pp. 124–129; Edwin A. Locke, ''The Ideas of Frederick W. Taylor: An Evaluation,'' *Academy of Management Review*, vol. 7, 1982, pp. 14–24.
25. Peter F. Drucker, ''The Coming Rediscovery of Scientific Management,'' *Conference Board Review*, June 1976, pp. 23–27; W. Jack Duncan, *Great Ideas in Management*, Jossey-Bass, San Francisco, 1989.
26. Daniel A. Wren, *The Evolution of Management Thought*, 2d ed., Wiley, New York, 1979.
27. Milton J. Nadworny, ''Frederick Taylor and Frank Gilbreth—Competition in Scientific Management,'' *Business History Review*, vol. 31, 1957, pp. 23–34.
28. Daniel A. Wren, *The Evolution of Management Thought*, 2d ed., Wiley, New York, 1979.
29. L. M. Gilbreth, *The Psychology of Management*, Sturgis and Walton, 1914; reissued by Macmillan, New York, 1921.
30. W. Jack Duncan, *Great Ideas in Management*, Jossey-Bass, San Francisco, 1989.
31. Daniel A. Wren, *The Evolution of Management Thought*, 2d ed., Wiley, New York, 1979.
32. Frank B. Gilbreth, Jr., and Ernestine Gilbreth Carey, *Cheaper by the Dozen*, Crowell, New York, 1948.
33. Daniel A. Wren, *The Evolution of Management Thought*, 2d ed., Wiley, New York, 1979.
34. Ibid.
35. This section is based on ibid., and W. Jack Duncan, *Great Ideas in Management*, Jossey-Bass, San Francisco, 1989.
36. This section is based mainly on ibid.; see also Arnold Eisen, ''The Meanings and Confusions of Weberian 'Rationality,''' *British Journal of Sociology*, March 1978, pp. 57–70.
37. Richard M. Weiss, ''Weber on Bureaucracy: Management Consultant or Political Theorist?'' *Academy of Management Review*, vol. 8, 1983, pp. 242–248.
38. Jeffrey M. Laderman, ''The Family That Hauls Together Brawls Together,'' *Business Week*, Aug. 29, 1988, pp. 64–68.
39. This section is based mainly on Daniel A. Wren, *The Evolution of Management Thought*, 2d ed., Wiley, New York, 1979, and W. Jack Duncan, *Great Ideas in Management*, Jossey-Bass, San Francisco, 1989.
40. The work was originally published in French in book form in 1925; it was translated by A. Coubrough as *Industrial and General Administration* (International Management Institute, Geneva) in 1930 and by Constance Storrs (Pitman & Sons, London) in 1949.
41. This section is mainly based on W. Jack Duncan, *Great Ideas in Management*, Jossey-Bass, San Francisco, 1989.
42. Kenneth R. Andrews, in the introduction to the thirtieth-anniversary edition of Chester I. Barnard, *The Function of the Executive*, Harvard, Cambridge, Mass., 1968.
43. Daniel A. Wren, *The Evolution of Management Thought*, 2d ed., Wiley, New York, 1979.
44. Kenneth R. Andrews, in the introduction to the thirtieth-anniversary edition of Chester I. Barnard, *The Function of the Executive*, Harvard, Cambridge, Mass., 1968; W. Jack Duncan, *Great Ideas in Management*, Jossey-Bass, San Francisco, 1989.
45. John A. Pearce II, ''The Company Mission as a Strategic Tool,'' *Sloan Management Review*, Spring 1982, pp. 15–24.
46. Arthur M. Louis, ''The Controversial Boss of Beatrice,'' *Fortune*, July 22, 1985, pp. 110–116, and ''A Big Raider Gets the Last Laugh,'' *Fortune*, July 4, 1988, pp. 62–69.
47. Correspondence to Daniel A. Wren from William B. Wolf, cited in Daniel A. Wren, *The Evolution of Management Thought*, 2d ed., Wiley, New York, 1979, p. 250.
48. Thirtieth-anniversary edition of Chester I. Barnard, *The Functions of the Executive*, Harvard, Cambridge, Mass., 1968.

49. Claude S. George, Jr., *The History of Management Thought*, Prentice-Hall, Englewood Cliffs, N.J., 1972.
50. L. D. Parker, "Control in Organizational Life: The Contribution of Mary Parker Follett," *Academy of Management Review*, vol. 9, 1984, pp. 736–745; W. Jack Duncan, *Great Ideas in Management*, Jossey-Bass, San Francisco, 1989.
51. "How Power Will Be Balanced on Saturn's Shop Floor," *Business Week*, Aug. 4, 1985, pp. 65–66.
52. Kenneth R. Andrews, in the introduction to the thirtieth-anniversary edition of Chester I. Barnard, *The Function of the Executive*, Harvard, Cambridge, Mass., 1968; W. Jack Duncan, *Great Ideas in Management*, Jossey-Bass, San Francisco, 1989.
53. Henry C. Metcalf and Lyndall Urwick (eds.), *Dynamic Administration: The Collected Papers of Mary Parker Follett*, Harper & Row, New York, 1940, pp. 32–33.
54. Daniel A. Wren, *The Evolution of Management Thought*, 2d ed., Wiley, New York, 1979; L. D. Parker, "Control in Organizational Life: The Contribution of Mary Parker Follett," *Academy of Management Review*, vol. 9, 1984, pp. 736–745.
55. L. D. Parker, "Control in Organizational Life: The Contribution of Mary Parker Follett," *Academy of Management Review*, vol. 9, 1984, pp. 736–745.
56. Ronald G. Greenwood and Charles D. Wrege, "The Hawthorne Studies," in Daniel A. Wren and John A. Pearce II (eds.), *Papers Dedicated to the Development of Modern Management*, Academy of Management, 1986, pp. 24–35.
57. Ibid.
58. John G. Adair, "The Hawthorne Effect: A Reconsideration of the Methodological Artifact," *Journal of Applied Psychology*, vol. 69, 1984, pp. 334–345.
59. Ronald G. Greenwood and Charles D. Wrege, "The Hawthorne Studies," in Daniel A. Wren and John A. Pearce II (eds.), *Papers Dedicated to the Development of Modern Management*, Academy of Management, 1986, pp. 24–35.
60. Berkeley Rice, "The Hawthorne Defect: Persistence of a Flawed Theory," *Psychology Today*, February 1982, pp. 70–74.
61. John G. Adair, "The Hawthorne Effect: A Reconsideration of the Methodological Artifact," *Journal of Applied Psychology*, vol. 69, 1984, pp. 334–345.
62. Daniel A. Wren, *The Evolution of Management Thought*, 2d ed., Wiley, New York, 1979; Dana Bramel and Ronald Friend, "Hawthorne, the Myth of the Docile Worker, and Class Bias in Psychology," *American Psychologist*, August 1981, pp. 867–878.
63. For criticisms and clarifications, see, for example, Alex Carey, "The Hawthorne Studies: A Radical Criticism," *American Sociological Review*, June 1967, pp. 403–416; John M. Shepard, "On Alex Carey's Radical Criticisms of the Hawthorne Studies," *Academy of Management Journal*, March 1971, pp. 23–32; Dana Bramel and Ronald Friend, "Hawthorne, the Myth of the Docile Worker, and Class Bias in Psychology," *American Psychologist*, August 1981, pp. 867–878; Ronald G. Greenwood, Alfred A. Bolton, and Regina A. Greenwood, "Hawthorne a Half Century Later: Relay Assembly Participants Remember," *Journal of Management*, vol. 9, 1983, pp. 217–231; and Jeffrey A. Sonnenfeld, "Shedding Light on the Hawthorne Studies," *Journal of Occupational Behavior*, vol. 6, 1985, pp. 111–130.
64. John G. Adair, "The Hawthorne Effect: A Reconsideration of the Methodological Artifact," *Journal of Applied Psychology*, vol. 69, 1984, p. 334.
65. Ronald G. Greenwood and Charles D. Wrege, "The Hawthorne Studies," in Daniel A. Wren and John A. Pearce II (eds.), *Papers Dedicated to the Development of Modern Management*, Academy of Management, 1986, pp. 24–35; see also Elton Mayo, *The Human Problems of an Industrial Civilization*, Harvard Graduate School of Business Administration, Boston, 1933; Elton Mayo, *The Social Problems of an Industrial Civilization*, Harvard, Cambridge, Mass., 1945; F. J. Roethlisberger, and W. J. Dickson, *Management and the Worker*, Wiley, New York, 1939.
66. W. Jack Duncan, *Great Ideas in Management*, Jossey-Bass, San Francisco, 1989.
67. A. H. Maslow, "A Theory of Human Motivation," *Psychological Review*, vol. 50, 1943, pp. 370–396, and *Motivation and Personality*, Harper & Row, New York, 1954.
68. Douglas McGregor, *The Human Side of Enterprise*, McGraw-Hill, New York, 1960.
69. Edwin A. Locke, Karyll N. Shaw, Lise M. Saari, and Gary P. Latham, "Goal Setting and Task Performance: 1969–1980," *Psychological Bulletin*, vol. 90, 1982, pp. 125–152; Robert D. Pritchard, Steven D. Jones, Philip L. Roth, Karla K. Stuebing, and Steven E. Ekeberg, "Effects of Group Feedback, Goal Setting, and Incentives on Organizational Productivity," *Journal of Applied Psychology*, vol. 73, 1988, pp. 337–358.
70. Norman Gaither, "Historical Development of Operations Research" in Daniel A. Wren and John A. Pearce II (eds.), *Papers Dedicated to the Development of Modern Management*, Academy of Management, 1986, pp. 71–77.
71. James R. Miller and Howard Feldman, "Management Science—Theory, Relevance, and Practice in the 1980s," *Interfaces*, October 1983, pp. 56–60.
72. Hicks Waldon, "Putting a New Face on Avon," *Planning Review*, July 1985, pp. 18–25; John Thackray, "Planning an Avon Turnaround," *Planning Review*, January 1985, pp. 6–11.
73. William J. Sawaya, Jr., and William C. Giauque, *Production and Operations Management*, Harcourt Brace Jovanovich, San Diego, 1986.
74. Edward O. Welles, "The Company Money Almost Killed," *INC.*, November 1988, pp. 46–60.
75. Fremont E. Kast and James E. Rosenzweig, "General Systems Theory: Applications for Organization and Management," *Academy of Management Journal*, vol. 15, pp. 447–465.
76. Ludwig von Bertalanffy, "General Systems Theory: A New Approach to the Unity of Science," *Human Biology*, vol. 23, December 1951, pp. 302–361, and "General Systems Theory—A Critical Review," *General Systems*, vol. 7, 1962, pp. 1–20; Daniel Katz and Robert L. Kahn, *The Social Psychology of Organizations*, Wiley, New York, 1978; see also Kenneth E. Boulding, "General Systems Theory—The Skeleton of Science," *Management Science*, vol. 2, 1956, pp. 197–208.
77. Arkalgud Ramaprasad, "On the Definition of Feedback," *Behavioral Science*, January 1983, pp. 4–13.
78. Donde P. Ashmos and George P. Huber, "The Systems Paradigm in Organization Theory: Correcting the Record and Suggesting the Future," *Academy of Management Review*, vol. 12, 1987, pp. 607–621.
79. J. Miller, *Living Systems*, McGraw-Hill, New York, 1978.
80. Fremont E. Kast and James E. Rosenzweig, *Organization and Management: A Systems Approach*, 2d ed., McGraw-Hill, 1974.
81. Fremont E. Kast and James E. Rosenzweig, "General Systems Theory: Applications for Organization and Management," *Academy of Management Journal*, vol. 15, 1972, pp. 447–465; Daniel Katz and Robert L. Kahn, *The Social Psychology of Organizations*, Wiley, New York, 1978.
82. Fred Luthans, "The Contingency Theory of Management," *Business Horizons*, June 1973, pp. 67–72; Fred Luthans and Todd I. Stewart, "A General Contingency Theory of Management," *Academy of Management Journal*, vol. 20, 1977, pp. 181–195; Sang M. Lee, Fred Luthans, and David L. Olson, "A Management Science Approach to Contingency Models of Organizational Structure," *Academy of Management Journal*, vol. 25, 1982, pp. 553–566.
83. Joan Woodward, *Industrial Organization: Theory and Practice*, Oxford University, London, 1965.
84. Jay W. Lorsch, "Making Behavioral Science More Useful," *Harvard Business Review*, March–April 1979, pp. 171–180; Henry L. Tosi, Jr., and John W. Slocum, Jr., "Contingency Theory: Some Suggested Directions," *Journal of Management*, vol. 10, 1984, pp. 9–26.
85. Based on Anne B. Fisher, "Ford Is Back on the Track," *Fortune*, Dec. 23, 1985, pp. 18–22; Steve Kichen and Jerry Flint, "Supercharged," *Forbes*, Sept. 5, 1988, pp. 74–78; Paul Ingrassia and Bradley A. Stertz, "Ford's Strong Sales Raise Agonizing Issue of Additional Plants," *The Wall Street Journal*, Oct. 26, 1988, p. 1; Kate Ballen, "The No. 1 Leader Is Petersen of Ford," *Fortune*, Oct. 24, 1988, pp. 69–70; Jerry Flint, "It's a New World," *Forbes*, Nov. 14, 1988, p. 172; Alex Taylor III, "Why Fords Sell Like Big Macs," *Fortune*, Nov. 21, 1988, pp. 122–125; Paul Ingrassia and Gregory A. Patterson, "Restyled Fords Take on GM's Coupes," *The Wall Street Journal*, Dec. 7, 1988, p. B1; 1988 Annual Report, Ford Motor Company, Detroit; Joann S. Lublinard and Craig Forman, "Ford Snares Jaguar, but $2.5 Billion Is High Price for Prestige," *The Wall Street Journal*, Nov. 3, 1989, p. A1; "How to Go Global—And Why," *Fortune*, Aug. 28, 1989, pp. 73–74; Podr Davis, "Ford Australia Made Long Climb to Top Sales Spot," *Automotive News*, Feb. 22, 1988, p. 31; Joyce Heard, Jonathon Kapstein, and Frank J. Comes, "How Business Is Creating Europe Inc.," *Business Week*, Sept. 7, 1987, pp. 40–41; John Marcom, Jr., "Detroit's Euro-Boom," *Forbes*, Mar. 20, 1989, p. 39; and Warren Brown, "Ford Chairman Announces He'll Retire 18 Months Early," *The Washington Post*, Nov. 11, 1989, p. D 12.

CHAPTER 3

1. Based on Rayna Skolnik, "Retail Merchandising Programs That Both Make Sales and Track Them Turn Liz Claiborne, Inc., into the Hot Player in Women's Apparel," *Sales and Marketing Management*, Sept. 9, 1985, pp. 50–51; Lisa Belkin, "Redesigning Liz Claiborne's Empire," *The New York Times*, May 4, 1986, p. F29; Patricia Sellers, "Liz Claiborne: The Rag Trade's Reluctant Revolutionary," Jan. 5, 1987, pp. 36–38; Kathleen Deveny, "Can Ms. Fashion Bounce Back?" *Business Week*, Jan. 16, 1989, pp. 64–70; Michele Morris, "The Wizard of the Working Woman's Wardrobe," *Working Woman*, June 1988, pp. 74–80; and James Hirsch, "Claiborne Founders to Retire," *The New York Times*, Feb. 27, 1989, pp. D1, D5.
2. Linda Smircich, "Concepts of Culture and Organizational Analysis," *Administrative Science Quarterly*, vol. 28, 1983, pp. 339–358; Ralph H. Kilmann, Mary J. Saxton, and Roy Serpa, "Issues in Understanding and Changing Culture," *California Management Review*, vol. 28, 1986, pp. 87–94.
3. Eric Morgenthaler, "A 19th-Century Firm Shifts, Reinvents Itself and Survives 100 Years," *The Wall Street Journal*, May 9, 1989, pp. A1, A16.
4. Fred R. David, *Concepts of Strategic Management*, Merrill, Columbus, Ohio, 1987, pp. 104–121; Richard H. Hall, *Organizations: Structures, Processes, and Outcomes*, 4th ed., Prentice-Hall, Englewood Cliffs, N.J., 1987, pp. 219–225.
5. Michael L. Tushman and Philip Anderson,

"Technological Discontinuities and Organization Environments," *Administrative Science Quarterly*, vol. 31, 1986, pp. 439–465.

6. William M. Bulkeley, "Frontiers of Science," *The Wall Street Journal*, Nov. 10, 1986, p. 1D.

7. "R&D Spending by Country as a Percent of Gross National Product," *The Wall Street Journal*, Nov. 10, 1986, p. 5D.

8. Jonathan P. Hicks, "Steelmakers' Inferiority Syndrome," *The New York Times*, Aug. 7, 1989, pp. D1, D7.

9. Gary Lee, "Reform Key to Growth by Soviets," *The Washington Post*, Jan. 11, 1987, p. G6.

10. Edwin A. Finn, Jr., "Megatort Mania," *Forbes*, June 1, 1987, pp. 114–120.

11. Michele Galen, "A Seat on the Board Is Getting Hotter," *Business Week*, July 3, 1989, pp. 72–73.

12. Cindy Skrzycki, "Just Who's in Charge Here, Anyway?" *The Washington Post*, Jan. 29, 1989, pp. H1, H8.

13. For a comparison of the United States and Japan, see William Ouchi, *Theory Z—How American Business Can Meet the Japanese Challenge*, Addison-Wesley, Reading, Mass., 1981; John Child compares Great Britain and Germany in "Culture, Contingency and Capitalism in the Cross-National Study of Organizations," in L. L. Cummings and Barry M. Staw (eds.), *Research in Organizational Behavior*, vol. 3, JAI, Greenwich, Conn., 1981, pp. 303–356.

14. Kathleen Deveny, "McWorld?" *Business Week*, Oct. 13, 1986, pp. 80–81.

15. Sandra Kresch, "The Impact of Consumer Trends on Corporate Strategy," *Journal of Business Strategy*, Winter 1983, p. 59; Daniel Bell, "The World and the United States in 2013," *Daedalus*, Summer 1987, pp. 1–31.

16. Stratford P. Sherman, "America's New Abstinence," *Fortune*, Mar. 18, 1985, pp. 20–23.

17. Damon Darlin, "Most U.S. Firms Seek Extra Profits in Japan, at the Expense of Sales," *The Wall Street Journal*, May 15, 1987, pp. 1, 6.

18. Otis Port, "Back to Basics," *Business Week*, Innovation 1989 issue, June 16, 1989, pp. 14–18.

19. Based on Jennifer Lin, "IKEA's U.S. Translation," *Stores*, April 1986, pp. 60–63; Eugene Carlson, "How a Major Swedish Retailer Chose a Beachhead in the U.S.," *The Wall Street Journal*, Apr. 7, 1987, p. 37; Peter Fuhrman, "The Workers' Friend," *Forbes*, Mar. 21, 1988, pp. 124–128; and Janet Bamford, "Why Competitors Shop for Ideas at IKEA," *Business Week*, Oct. 9, 1989, p. 88.

20. Fred R. David, *Concepts of Strategic Management*, Merrill, Columbus, Ohio, 1987, p. 105.

21. Jerry Flint with William Heurslein, "An Urge to Service," *Forbes*, Sept. 18, 1989, pp. 172–176.

22. Kathleen Deveny, "The Health Industry Finally Asks: What Do Women Want?" *Business Week*, Aug. 25, 1986, p. 81.

23. Susan Caminiti, "Seeking Big Money in Paper and Pens," *Fortune*, July 31, 1989, pp. 173–174.

24. Based on Leonard M. Fuld, "How to Get the Scoop on Your Competition," *Working Woman*, January 1989, pp. 39–42, and Leonard M. Fuld, *Monitoring the Competition*, Wiley, New York, 1988.

25. Maggie McComas, "Cutting Costs without Killing the Business," *Fortune*, Oct. 13, 1986, p. 71.

26. John A. Byrne, "Culture Shock at Xerox," *Business Week*, June 22, 1987, pp. 106–110.

27. Luther Jackson, "In Tune with Out-Sourcing," *Detroit Free Press*, Mar. 2, 1987, p. C1.

28. Eugene Carlson, "For the New England Story, Turn to the Help-Wanted Ads," *The Wall Street Journal*, June 2, 1987, p. 33; Selwyn Feinstein, "Labor Letter," *The Wall Street Journal*, June 9, 1987, p. 1.

29. Rudolph A. Pyatt, Jr., "AAA's Lesson for Fairfax," *The Washington Post*, Oct. 3, 1986, pp. F1–F2.

30. Sylvia Nasar, "Jobs Go Begging at the Bottom," *Fortune*, Mar. 17, 1986, pp. 33–34.

31. This section relies heavily on Richard H. Hall, *Organizations*, 4th ed., Prentice-Hall, Englewood Cliffs, N.J., 1987, and David Ulrich and Jay B. Barney, "Perspectives in Organizations: Resource Dependence, Efficiency, and Population," *Academy of Management Review*, vol. 9, 1984, pp. 471–481.

32. Michael T. Hannan and John Freeman, "The Population Ecology of Organizations," *American Journal of Sociology*, vol. 82, 1977, pp. 929–964; W. Graham Astley and Andrew H. Van de Ven, "Central Perspectives and Debates in Organization Theory," *Administrative Science Quarterly*, vol. 28, 1983, pp. 245–273; John Betton and Gregory G. Dess, "The Application of Population Ecology Models to the Study of Organizations," *Academy of Management Review*, vol. 10, 1985, pp. 750–757.

33. "It's Tough Up There," *Forbes*, July 13, 1987, pp. 145–160.

34. Jeffrey Pfeffer and Gerald Salancik, *The External Control of Organizations*, Harper & Row, New York, 1978; David Ulrich and Jay B. Barney, "Perspectives in Organizations: Resource Dependence, Efficiency, and Population," *Academy of Management Review*, vol. 9, 1984, pp. 471–481.

35. G. Pascal Zachary, "Software Makers Get a Chill from Microsoft's Windows," *The Wall Street Journal*, Oct. 10, 1989, pp. B1, B8.

36. Brenton R. Schlender, "How Steve Jobs Linked Up with IBM," *Fortune*, Oct. 9, 1989, pp. 48–61.

37. Jeffrey Pfeffer and Gerald Salancik, *The External Control of Organizations*, Harper & Row, New York, 1978.

38. Lawrence G. Hrebiniak and William F. Joyce, "Organizational Adaptation: Strategic Choice and Environmental Determinism," *Administrative Science Quarterly*, vol. 30, 1985, pp. 336–349.

39. Masoud Yasai-Arkekani, "Structural Adaptations to Environments," *Academy of Management Review*, vol. 11, 1986, pp. 9–21.

40. Jeffrey Pfeffer and Gerald Salancik, *The External Control of Organizations*, Harper & Row, 1978, p. 67.

41. Frances J. Milliken, "Three Types of Perceived Uncertainty about the Environment: State, Effect, and Response Uncertainty," *Academy of Management Review*, vol. 12, 1987, pp. 133–143.

42. Gregory G. Dess and Donald W. Beard, "Dimensions of Organizational Task Environments," *Administrative Science Quarterly*, vol. 29, 1984, pp. 52–73; Gregory G. Dess and Nancy K. Origer, "Environment, Structure, and Consensus in Strategy Formulation: A Conceptual Integration," *Academy of Management Review*, vol. 12, 1987, pp. 313–330.

43. Gregory G. Dess and Donald W. Beard, "Dimensions of Organizational Task Environments," *Administrative Science Quarterly*, vol. 29, 1984, pp. 52–73.

44. Ibid.

45. Frances J. Milliken, "Three Types of Perceived Uncertainty about the Environment: State, Effect, and Response Uncertainty," *Academy of Management Review*, vol. 12, 1987, pp. 133–143.

46. Howard E. Aldrich, *Organizations and Environments*, Prentice-Hall, Englewood Cliffs, N.J., 1979, pp. 63–66; Gregory G. Dess and Donald W. Beard, "Dimensions of Organizational Task Environments," *Administrative Science Quarterly*, vol. 29, 1984, pp. 52–73.

47. Based on Barry Stavro, "Loser and Still Champion," *Forbes*, Nov. 17, 1986, p. 176; Stephen Phillips, "Champion Is Starting to Show a Little Spark," *Business Week*, Mar. 21, 1988, p. 87; and Jacob M. Schlesinger, "Champion Spark to Be Acquired for $800 Million," *The Wall Street Journal*, Feb. 22, 1989, p. A4.

48. James D. Thompson, *Organizations in Action*, McGraw-Hill, New York, 1967, pp. 20–37; John P. Kotter, "Managing External Dependence," *Academy of Management Review*, vol. 4, 1979, pp. 87–92.

49. James D. Thompson, *Organizations in Action*, McGraw-Hill, New York, 1967, pp. 20–23.

50. Beth McGoldrick, "The Corporate Guru of Global Economics," *Working Woman*, November 1988, pp. 118–124.

51. Peter Fuhrman, "The Workers' Friend," *Forbes*, Mar. 21, 1988, pp. 124–128.

52. John P. Kotter, "Managing External Dependence," *Academy of Management Review*, vol. 4, 1979, pp. 87–92.

53. Howard Aldrich and Diane Herker, "Boundary Spanning Roles and Organization Structure," *Academy of Management Review*, vol. 2, 1977, pp. 217–230; Michael L. Tushman and Thomas J. Scanlan, "Boundary Spanning Individuals: Their Role in Information Transfer and Their Antecedents," *Academy of Management Journal*, vol. 24, 1981, pp. 289–305.

54. "Sharing of Director Seen as Posing Threat for Antitrust," *The Wall Street Journal*, Apr. 24, 1978, p. 5.

55. F. David Schoorman, Max H. Bazerman, and Robert S. Atkin, "Interlocking Directorates: A Strategy for Reducing Environmental Uncertainty," *Academy of Management Review*, vol. 6, 1981, pp. 243–251.

56. Mark S. Mizruchi, "Who Controls Whom? An Examination of the Relation between Management and Boards of Directors in Large American Corporations," *Academy of Management Review*, vol. 8, 1983, pp. 426–435.

57. David Remnick, "H. Ross Perot to GM: I'll Drive," *The Washington Post Magazine*, Apr. 19, 1987, p. 24.

58. Mark Potts, "Toys 'R' Us and McDonald's Take on Japanese Toy Market," *The Washington Post*, Sept. 27, 1989, p. B1.

59. Jonathan B. Levine and John A. Byrne, "Corporate Odd Couples," *Business Week*, July 21, 1986, pp. 100–105.

60. "Washington, D.C.: Home of the Association Business," *The Washington Times*, Jan. 29, 1986, p. 3E.

61. Caroline E. Mayer, "Minn. Passes Bill to Aid Dayton Hudson," *The Washington Post*, June 26, 1987, p. F1.

62. Burr Leonard, "Life after Death," *Forbes*, May 4, 1987, pp. 132–133.

63. Michael Oneal, "Harley-Davidson: Ready to Hit the Road Again," *Business Week*, July 21, 1986, p. 70; Shirley Cayer, "Harley's New Manager-Owners Put Purchasing Out Front," *Purchasing*, Oct. 13, 1988, pp. 50–54; Peter C. Reid, "How Harley Beat Back the Japanese," *Fortune*, Sept. 25, 1989, pp. 155–164.

64. Peter C. Reid, "How Harley Beat Back the Japanese," *Fortune*, Sept. 25, 1989, pp. 155–164.

65. Linda Smircich, "Concepts of Culture and Organizational Analysis," *Administrative Science Quarterly*, vol. 28, 1983, pp. 339–358; Ralph H. Kilmann, Mary J. Saxton, and Roy Serpa, "Issues in Understanding and Changing Culture," *California Management Review*, vol. 28, 1986, pp. 87–94.

66. Ralph H. Kilmann, Mary J. Saxton, and Roy Serpa, "Issues in Understanding and Changing Culture," *California Management Review*, vol. 28, 1986, pp. 87–94.

67. Daniel R. Denison, "Bringing Corporate Culture to the Bottom Line," *Organizational Dynamics*, 1984, pp. 5–22; Guy S. Saffold III, "Culture Traits, Strength, and Organizational Performance: Moving Beyond 'Strong' Culture," *Academy of Management Review*, vol. 13, 1988, pp. 546–558.

68. Ralph H. Kilmann, "Five Steps for Closing Culture-Gaps," in Ralph H. Kilmann, Mary J. Saxton, Roy Serpa, and Associates, *Gaining Control of the Corporate Culture*, Jossey-Bass, San Francisco, 1985, pp. 351–369.

69. Penny Moser, "The McDonald's Mystique," *Fortune*, July 4, 1988, pp. 112–116.
70. This section relies heavily on Ralph H. Kilmann, Mary J. Saxton, and Roy Serpa, "Issues in Understanding and Changing Culture," *California Management Review*, vol. 28, 1986, pp. 87–94.
71. Howard Schwartz and Stanley M. Davis, "Matching Corporate Culture and Business Strategy," *Organizational Dynamics*, Summer 1981, pp. 30–48; Jay B. Barney, "Organizational Culture: Can It Be a Source of Sustained Competitive Advantage?" *Academy of Management Review*, vol. 11, 1986, pp. 656–665.
72. Kenneth Labich, "The Innovators," *Fortune*, June 6, 1988, pp. 51–61.
73. Linda Smircich, "Concepts of Culture and Organizational Analysis," *Administrative Science Quarterly*, vol. 28, 1983, pp. 339–358.
74. Harrison M. Trice and Janice M. Beyer, "Studying Organizational Cultures through Rites and Ceremonials," *Academy of Management Review*, vol. 9, 1984, pp. 653–669.
75. Jagannath Dubashi, "Through a Glass Lightly," *Financial World*, May 19, 1987, pp. 20–29.
76. Jacob M. Schlesinger and Paul Ingrassia, "GM Woos Employees by Listening to Them, Talking of Its 'Team,'" *The Wall Street Journal*, Jan. 12, 1989, p. 1.
77. Harrison M. Trice and Janice M. Beyer, "Studying Organizational Cultures through Rites and Ceremonials," *Academy of Management Review*, vol. 9, 1984, pp. 653–669.
78. Terrence E. Deal and Allan A. Kennedy, *Corporate Cultures: The Rites and Rituals of Corporate Life*, Addison-Wesley, Reading, Mass., 1982.
79. Ibid.
80. This section is based on Howard H. Stevenson and David E. Gumpert, "The Heart of Entrepreneurship," *Harvard Business Review*, March–April 1985, pp. 85–94.
81. Jay W. Lorsch, "Managing Culture: The Invisible Barrier to Strategic Change," *California Management Review*, Winter 1986, pp. 95–109; Christian Scholz, "Corporate Culture and Strategy—The Problem of Strategic Fit," *Long Range Planning*, vol. 20, 1987, pp. 78–87; Thomas H. Fitzgerald, "Can Change in Organizational Culture Really Be Managed?" *Organizational Dynamics*, Autumn 1988, pp. 5–15.
82. Ralph H. Kilmann, "Five Steps for Closing Culture-Gaps," in Ralph H. Kilmann, Mary J. Saxton, Roy Serpa, and Associates, *Gaining Control of the Corporate Culture*, Jossey-Bass, San Francisco, 1985, pp. 351–369.
83. "Yea Team!" *Industry Week*, Nov. 10, 1986, pp. 20–21; Gary Jacobson and John Hillrirk, *Xerox, American Samurai*, Macmillan, New York, 1986; Howard Rudnitsky, "World's Largest Up & Comer," *Forbes*, May 18, 1987, pp. 78–80; John A. Byrne, "Culture Shock at Xerox," *Business Week*, June 22, 1987, pp. 106–110; James R. Norman, "Xerox Rethinks Itself—And This Could Be the Last Time," *Business Week*, Feb. 13, 1989, pp. 90–93; Barbara Hetzer, "How Xerox Zapped the Japanese," *Business Month*, June 1989, pp. 81–82; John Holusha, "Stress on Quality Lifts Xerox's Market Share," *The New York Times*, Nov. 9, 1989, pp. D1–D11.

CHAPTER 4

1. Frederick G. Harmon and Garry Jacobs, "Company Personality: The Heart of the Matter," *Management Review*, October 1985, pp. 36–37; Thaddeus F. Tuleja, *Beyond the Bottom Line: How Business Leaders Are Turning Principles into Profits*, Facts on File, New York, 1985, pp. 78–80; Sana Siwolop and Christopher Eklund, "The Capsule Controversy: How Far Should the FDA Go?" *Business Week*, Mar. 3, 1986, p. 37.
2. Edward C. Baig, "America's Most Admired Corporations," *Fortune*, Jan. 19, 1987, pp. 18–23.
3. James O'Toole, *Vanguard Management: Redesigning the Corporate Future*, Doubleday, Garden City, N.Y., 1985, pp. 235–236.
4. Robert Johnson, John Koten, and Charles F. McCoy, "Anheuser-Busch Co. Is Shaken by Its Probe of Improper Payments," *The Wall Street Journal*, Mar. 31, 1987, pp. 1, 31.
5. James B. Stewart and Janet Buyon, "How GE and Kidder Managed to Ward Off an Impending Disaster," *The Wall Street Journal*, June 8, 1987, p. 1.
6. Elizabeth Tucker, "Former CEO of Intelsat Pleads Guilty," *The Washington Post*, July 15, 1987, p. D1.
7. Milton R. Moskowitz, "Company Performance Roundup," *Business and Society Review*, Summer 1989, pp. 66–72.
8. Amy Dockser Marcus, "Donations Land Charities in Trouble," *The Wall Street Journal*, Oct. 27, 1989, p. B1.
9. Stephen H. Wildstrom, "A Risky Tack for Democrats," *Business Week*, July 20, 1987, p. 71.
10. William C. Frederick, Keith Davis, and James E. Post, *Business and Society*, 6th ed., McGraw-Hill, New York, 1988.
11. Lee E. Preston, *Social Issues and Public Policy in Business and Management: Retrospect and Prospect*, Center for Business and Public Policy, University of Maryland, 1986; Archie Carroll, *Business and Society: Ethics and Stakeholder Management*, South-Western, Cincinnati, 1989.
12. The framework is based on Kenneth E. Goodpaster and John B. Matthews, Jr., "Can a Corporation Have a Conscience?" *Harvard Business Review*, January–February 1982, pp. 134–141.
13. Milton Friedman, *Capitalism and Freedom*, University of Chicago, Chicago, 1962, pp. 133–136.
14. One proponent of this view is John Kenneth Galbraith, *The New Industrial State*, University of Chicago, Chicago, 1962, and *The Age of Uncertainty*, Houghton Mifflin, Boston, 1975.
15. William G. Frederick, Keith Davis, and James E. Post, *Business and Society*, 6th ed., McGraw-Hill, New York, 1988.
16. Gladwin Hill, "The Shifting Sands of Public Consent," *New Management*, Spring 1987, pp. 47–50.
17. Archie B. Carroll, "A Three-Dimensional Conceptual Model of Corporate Performance," *Academy of Management Review*, vol. 4, 1979, pp. 499–500.
18. William C. Frederick, Keith Davis, and James E. Post, *Business and Society*, 6th ed., McGraw-Hill, New York, 1988.
19. "Public Service," *Business Week*, Jan. 11, 1988, p. 156.
20. Janice E. Simpson, "Here's the Newest Top 10: Companies with a Conscience," *The Wall Street Journal*, Mar. 3, 1987, p. 18.
21. Michael Kinsley, "Companies as Citizens: Should They Have a Conscience?" *The Wall Street Journal*, Feb. 19, 1987, p. 29.
22. Dalton E. McFarland, *Management and Society: An Institutional Framework*, Prentice-Hall, Englewood Cliffs, N.J., 1982.
23. Thaddeus F. Tuleja, *Beyond the Bottom Line: How Business Leaders Are Turning Principles into Profits*, Facts on File, New York, 1985, pp. 41–131.
24. This section relies heavily on William C. Frederick, Keith Davis and James E. Post, *Business and Society*, 6th ed., McGraw-Hill, New York, 1988.
25. Barry Z. Posner and Warren H. Schmidt, "Values and the American Manager: An Update," *California Management Review*, vol. 26, 1984, pp. 202–216.
26. William C. Frederick, Keith Davis, and James E. Post, *Business and Society*, 6th ed., McGraw-Hill, New York, 1988.

27. Stuart Auerbach, "Ex-Wall Street Workers Test Plant-Closing Law," *The Washington Post*, Apr. 25, 1989. p. E1.
28. Cathy Trost, "Bhopal Disaster Spurs Debate over Usefulness of Criminal Sanctions in Industrial Accidents, *The Wall Street Journal*, Jan. 7, 1985, p. 18.
29. Robert Levering, Milton Moskowitz, and Michael Katz, *The 100 Best Companies to Work for in America*, Signet, New York, 1987.
30. James O'Toole, *Vanguard Management: Redesigning the Corporate Future*, Doubleday, Garden City, N.Y., 1985, p. 101.
31. This section relies heavily on Thaddeus F. Tuleja, *Beyond the Bottom Line: How Business Leaders Are Turning Principles into Profits*, Facts on File, New York, 1985, pp. 57–74.
32. Mark Potts, "Bic Stock Dives after Report about Lighters," *The Washington Post*, Apr. 11, 1987, p. D10.
33. Robert Johnson, "Fast-Food Chains Draw Criticism for Marketing Fare as Nutritional," *The Wall Street Journal*, Apr. 6, 1987, p. 31.
34. Thaddeus F. Tuleja, *Beyond the Bottom Line: How Business Leaders Are Turning Principles into Profits*, Facts on File, New York, 1985, pp. 75–85.
35. William C. Frederick, Keith Davis, and James E. Post, *Business and Society*, 6th ed., McGraw-Hill, New York, 1988.
36. Milton R. Moskowitz, "Company Performance Roundup," *Business and Society Review*, Winter 1989, pp. 72–78.
37. Myron Magnet, "What Merger Mania Did to Syracuse," *Fortune*, Feb. 3, 1986, pp. 94–98.
38. Lisa Atkinson and Joseph Galaskiewicz, "Stock Ownership and Company Contributions to Charity," *Administrative Science Quarterly*, vol. 33, 1988, pp. 82–100.
39. This section is based largely on Thaddeus F. Tuleja, *Beyond the Bottom Line: How Business Leaders Are Turning Principles into Profits*, Facts on File, New York, 1985, pp. 115–118.
40. William C. Frederick, Keith Davis, and James E. Post, *Business and Society*, 6th ed., McGraw-Hill, New York, 1988.
41. Cited in Thaddeus F. Tuleja, *Beyond the Bottom Line: How Business Leaders Are Turning Principles into Profits*, Facts on File, New York, 1985, p. 118.
42. Peter Arlow and Martin J. Gannon, "Social Responsiveness, Corporate Structure, and Economic Performance," *Academy of Management Review*, vol. 7, 1982, pp. 235–241; Arieh A. Ullmann, "Data in Search of a Theory: A Critical Examination of the Relationships among Social Performance, Social Disclosure, and Economic Performance of U.S. Firms," *Academy of Management Review*, vol. 10, 1985, pp. 540–557; Kenneth E. Aupperle, Archie B. Carroll, and John D. Hatfield, "An Empirical Examination of the Relationship between Corporate Social Responsibility and Profitability," *Academy of Management Journal*, vol. 28, 1985, pp. 446–463.
43. Jean B. McGuire, Alison Sundgren, and Thomas Schneeweis, "Corporate Social Responsibility and Firm Financial Performance," *Academy of Management Journal*, vol. 31, 1988, pp. 854–872.
44. Wallace N. Davison III and Dan I. Worrell, "The Impact of Announcements of Corporate Illegalities on Shareholder Returns," *Academy of Management Journal*, vol. 31, 1988, pp. 195–200.
45. Richard E. Wokutch and Barbara A. Spencer, "Corporate Saints and Sinners: The Effects of Philanthropic and Illegal Activity on Organizational Performance," *California Management Review*, vol. 29, 1987, pp. 62–77.
46. Thaddeus F. Tuleja, *Beyond the Bottom Line: How Business Leaders Are Turning Principles into Profits*, Facts on File, New York, 1985.
47. Adapted (with minor changes) from Bill Paul, "Utility Aids Customer's Welfare Needs," *The Wall Street Journal*, July 8, 1987, p. 6.

48. Timothy S. Mescon and Donn J. Tilson, "Corporate Philanthropy: A Strategic Approach to the Bottom-Line," *California Management Review,* vol. 29, 1987, pp. 49–61.

49. James O'Toole, *Vanguard Management: Redesigning the Corporate Future,* Doubleday, Garden City, N.Y., 1985; see also Mark Pastin, *The Hard Problems of Management: Gaining the Ethics Edge,* Jossey-Bass, San Francisco, 1986.

50. James O'Toole, *Vanguard Management: Redesigning the Corporate Future,* Doubleday, Garden City, N.Y., 1985, p. 350.

51. William C. Frederick, Keith Davis, and James E. Post, *Business and Society,* 6th ed., McGraw-Hill, New York, 1988.

52. Milton R. Moskowitz, "Company Performance Roundup," *Business and Society Review,* Summer 1989, pp. 67–72.

53. John E. Fleming, "Public Issues Scanning," in Lee Preston (ed.), *Research in Corporate Social Performance and Policy,* vol. 3, JAI, Greenwich, Conn., 1981, pp. 154–174; Steven L. Wartick and Philip L. Cochran, "The Evolution of the Corporate Social Performance Model," *Academy of Management Review,* vol. 10, 1985, pp. 758–769.

54. Stephen E. Littlejohn, "Competition and Cooperation: New Trends in Corporate Public Issues Identification and Resolution," *California Management Review,* vol. 29, Fall 1986, pp. 109–123.

55. Richard L. Daft, Juhani Sormunen, and Don Parks, "Chief Executive Scanning, Environmental Characteristics, and Company Performance: An Empirical Study," *Strategic Management Journal,* vol. 9, 1988, pp. 123–139.

56. Sadahei Kusumoto, "We're Not in Honshu Anymore," *Across the Board,* June 1989, pp. 49–50.

57. Rich Strand, "A Systems Paradigm of Organizational Adaptations to the Social Environment," *Academy of Management Review,* vol. 8, 1987, pp. 93–94.

58. This section is based mainly on Sandra L. Holmes, "Adapting Corporate Structure for Social Responsiveness," *Business Horizons,* Fall 1978, pp. 47–54.

59. Michael L. Lovdal, Raymond A. Bauer, and Nancy H. Treverton, "Public Responsibility Committees on the Board," *Harvard Business Review,* May–June 1977, pp. 41–64.

60. James E. Post, Edwin A. Murray, Jr., Robert B. Dickie, and John F. Mahon, "Managing Public Affairs: The Public Affairs Function," *California Management Review,* Fall 1983, pp. 135–136.

61. Arvind Bhambri and Jeffrey Sonnenfeld, "Organization Structure and Corporate Social Performance: A Field Study in Two Contrasting Industries," *Academy of Management Journal,* vol. 31, 1988, pp. 642–662.

62. Adapted (with minor changes) from Rod Willis, "The Levi Strauss Credo: Fashion and Philanthropy," *Management Review,* July 1986, pp. 51–54.

63. Walter Shapiro, "What's Wrong," *Time,* May 25, 1987, pp. 14–17.

64. Susan Gervasi, "Moral Dilemmas, All in the Game," *The Washington Post,* Apr. 20, 1987, p. B5.

65. "How You Play the Game Says Whether You Win," *The Wall Street Journal,* Apr. 18, 1989, p. B1.

66. Stephen Koepp, "Having It All, Then Throwing It All Away," *Time,* May 25, 1987, pp. 22–23.

67. For related definitions, see Henry C. Finney and Henry R. Lesieur, "A Contingency Theory of Organizational Crime," *Research in the Sociology of Organizations,* vol. 1, 1982, pp. 255–299.

68. Stephen Koepp, "Having It All, Then Throwing It All Away," *Time,* May 25, 1987, pp. 22–23; Ezra Bowen, "Looking to Its Roots," *Time,* May 25, 1987, pp. 26–29.

69. Bryan Burrough, "Broken Barrier: More Women Join Ranks of White-Collar Criminals," *The Wall Street Journal,* May 29, 1987, p. 29.

70. *Business Ethics Program: Local Office Reference Guide,* Arthur Andersen & Co., St. Charles, Ill., 1989.

71. William C. Frederick, Keith Davis, and James E. Post, *Business and Society,* 6th ed., McGraw-Hill, New York, 1988.

72. This section, including the examples, is based on Archie B. Carroll, "In Search of the Moral Manager," *Business Horizons,* March–April 1987, pp. 7–15.

73. Thaddeus F. Tuleja, *Beyond the Bottom Line: How Business Leaders Are Turning Principles into Profits,* Facts on File, New York, 1985.

74. These guidelines are offered by James O'Toole, *Vanguard Management: Redesigning the Corporate Future,* Doubleday, Garden City, N.Y., 1985, p. 349; see also Thaddeus F. Tuleja, *Beyond the Bottom Line: How Business Leaders Are Turning Principles into Profits,* Facts on File, New York, 1985, and Mark Pastin, *The Hard Problems of Management: Gaining the Ethics Edge,* Jossey-Bass, San Francisco, 1986.

75. Lee Berton, "Wedtech Used Gimmickry, False Invoices to Thrive," *The Wall Street Journal,* Feb. 23, 1987, p. 6.

76. Milton R. Moskowitz, "Company Performance Roundup," *Business and Society Review,* Winter 1987, pp. 69–70.

77. Paul B. Carroll, "IBM Launches Retirement Plan to Cut Outlays," *The Wall Street Journal,* Oct. 2, 1989, p. A7.

78. Thaddeus F. Tuleja, *Beyond the Bottom Line: How Business Leaders Are Turning Principles into Profits,* Facts on File, New York, 1985, p. 25.

79. Milton R. Moskowitz, "Company Performance Roundup," *Business and Society Review,* Winter 1987, p. 69.

80. Ibid., pp. 70–71.

81. Reprinted from Laura L. Nash, "Ethics without the Sermon," *Harvard Business Review,* November–December 1981, p. 81.

82. This section is based on Arvind Bhambri and Jeffrey Sonnenfeld, "The Man Who Stands Alone," *New Management,* Spring 1987, pp. 29–33.

83. Abridged from Martha Brannigan, "Auditor's Downfall Shows a Man Caught in Trap of His Own Making," *The Wall Street Journal,* Mar. 4, 1987, p. 32.

84. "Aftermath of Huge Fraud Prompts Claims of Regret," *The Wall Street Journal,* Mar. 4, 1987, p. 32.

85. This section relies heavily on Henry C. Finney and Henry R. Lesieur, "A Contingency Theory of Organizational Crime," in *Research in the Sociology of Organizations,* vol. 1, 1982, pp. 255–299; see also Linda Klebe Trevino, "Ethical Decision Making in Organizations: A Person-Situation Interactionist Model," *Academy of Management Review,* vol. 11, 1986, pp. 601–617.

86. Chris Welles, "What Led Beech-Nut Down the Road to Disgrace," *Business Week,* Feb. 22, 1988, pp. 124–128; Joe Queenan, "Juice Men," *Barrons,* June 20, 1988, pp. 37–38.

87. Bruce Ingersoll, "Generic-Drug Scandal at the FDA Is Linked to Deregulation Drive," *The Wall Street Journal,* Sept. 13, 1989, pp. A1, A14.

88. Jeffry A. Trachtenberg, "American Express Makes Apology to Safra," *The Wall Street Journal,* July 31, 1989; Steven Mufson, "Safra Donation Doubled," *The Wall Street Journal,* Aug. 2, 1989, p. F3.

89. Barry Z. Posner and Warren H. Schmidt, "Values and the American Manager: An Update," *California Management Review,* vol. 26, 1984, pp. 202–216.

90. Alan L. Otten, "Ethics on the Job: Companies Alert Employees to Potential Dilemmas," *The Wall Street Journal,* July 14, 1986, p. 21.

91. Janelle Brinker Dozier and Marcia P. Miceli, "Potential Predictors of Whistle-Blowing: A Prosocial Behavior Perspective," *Academy of Management Review,* vol. 10, 1985, pp. 823–836; Michael Brody, "Listen to Your Whistleblower," *Fortune,* Nov. 24, 1986, pp. 77–78.

92. Adapted (with minor changes) from "A Question of Ethics," *National Business Employment Weekly,* Special Edition, Managing Your Career, Spring 1987, p. 4.

93. Abridged (with minor changes) from Arvind Bhambri and Jeffrey Sonnenfeld, "The Man Who Stands Alone," *New Management,* Spring 1987, pp. 30–31.

Sources for Part Ending Case for Part 1: Mary Lu Carnevale, "Marriott to Build 150 Retirement Sites at Cost of $1 Billion in Next 5 Years," *The Wall Street Journal,* July 21, 1989, p. B3; Pat Guy, "Marriott's Courtyards Head to City," *USA TODAY,* Sept. 19, 1989, p. B1; Paul Farhi, "Three Deals Announced by Marriott," *The Wall Street Journal,* Sept. 12, 1989, p. D1; Carol Kennedy, "How Marriott Corporation Grew Fivefold in Ten Years," *Long Range Planning,* vol. 21, 1988, pp. 10–14; "Chief Executive of the Year," *Chief Executive,* July–August 1988, pp. 2–6; E. C. B., "The 25 Most Fascinating Business People of 1988," *Fortune,* Jan. 2, 1989, p. 62; "How Master Lodger Bill Marriott Prophesied Profit and Prospered," *Fortune,* June 5, 1989; 1988 Annual Report, Marriott Corporation, Washington, D.C.; Paul Farhi, "Marriott Executive Resigns to Join Northwest Airlines," *The Wall Street Journal,* Nov. 21, 1989, p. C1; Janet Novack, "Tea, Sympathy, and Direct Mail," *Forbes,* Sept. 18, 1989, pp. 210–211; Judith H. Dobrzynski, "The CEO on the Move," *Business Week,* Oct. 21, 1989; Robert O'Brien, *Marriott—The J. Willard Marriott Story,* Deseret, Salt Lake City, Utah, 1987; Mary Lu Carnevale, "Marriott Corporation Realigns Its Operations into Two Segments, Shifts Some Officials," *The Wall Street Journal,* Apr. 26, 1988, p. 46; Doug Carroll, "Heart Attack Forces Exec to Downshift," *USA Today,* Dec. 11, 1989, p. B1; Paul Farhi, "Marriott to Sell 800 Restaurants," *The Washington Post,* Dec. 19, 1989, pp. A1, A14; "Marriott Announces Major Restructuring Moves, Completes Transfer of Airline Catering Division," *Marriott News,* Dec. 18, 1989; Paul Farhi, "Can Marriott Fatten Up without Fast Food?" *The Washington Post,* Dec. 25, 1989, pp. 1, 19; Paul Farhi, "Marriott to Sell Its Roy Rogers Chain to Hardee's," *The Washington Post,* Jan. 31, 1990, pp. A1, A5.

CHAPTER 5

1. Steve Kaufman, "Turbo MBOs Spell Success for Chip Maker," *San Jose Mercury News,* June 1, 1987, p. 2D; Allan E. Alter, "Compact Competitors," *CIO,* July 1989, pp. 40–44; Steven B. Kaufman, "The Goal System That Drives Cypress," *Business Month,* July 1987, pp. 30–32.; interview with Dr. T. J. Rodgers, Aug. 21, 1989; "Corporate Critics Confidential-Technology/Semiconductors," *The Wall Street Transcript,* Mar. 13, 1989, p. 95; Stan Baker, "Rodgers' Revolution," *Electronic Engineering Times,* July 17, 1989, pp. 1, 67–68; 1988 Annual Report, Cypress Semiconductor.

2. "Thriving on Order," *INC.,* December 1989, pp. 47–62.

3. Leslie W. Rue and Phyllis G. Holland, *Strategic Management: Concepts and Experiences,* 2d ed., McGraw-Hill, New York, 1989.

4. John A. Pearce II and Richard B. Robinson, Jr., *Strategic Management,* Irwin, Homewood, Ill., 1988.

5. Laura Nash, "Mission Statements—Mirrors and Windows," *Harvard Business Review,* March–April 1988, pp. 155–156.

6. Peter F. Drucker, *Management: Tasks, Responsibilities, and Practices,* Harper & Row, New York, 1973.

7. Jerome H. Want, "Corporate Mission: The Intangible Contributor to Performance," *Management Review,* August 1986, pp. 46–50;

George L. Morrisey, "Who Needs a Mission Statement? You Do," *Training and Development Journal*, March 1988, pp. 50–52.

8. John A. Pearce II and Fred David, "Corporate Mission Statements: The Bottom Line," *Academy of Management Executive*, vol. 1, 1987, pp. 109–116.

9. Fred R. David, "How Companies Define Their Mission," *Long Range Planning*, vol. 22, 1989, pp. 90–97.

10. Laura Nash, "Mission Statements—Mirrors and Windows," *Harvard Business Review*, March–April 1988, pp. 155–156.

11. Fred R. David, "How Companies Define Their Mission," *Long Range Planning*, vol. 22, 1989, pp. 90–97.

12. John A. Pearce II and Fred David, "Corporate Mission Statements: The Bottom Line," *Academy of Management Executive*, vol. 1, 1987, pp. 109–118.

13. Thomas W. Lee, Edwin A. Locke, and Gary P. Latham, "Goal Setting Theory and Job Performance," in Lawrence A. Pervin (ed.), *Goal Concepts in Personality and Social Psychology*, Lawrence Erlbaum, Hillsdale, N.J., 1989, pp. 291–326.

14. Edwin A. Locke and Gary P. Latham, *Goal Setting: A Motivational Technique That Works!* Prentice-Hall, Englewood Cliffs, N.J., 1984; Max D. Richards, *Setting Strategic Goals and Objectives*, 2d ed., West, St. Paul, Minn., 1986; Robert D. Pritchard, Philip L. Roth, Steven D. Jones, Patricia J. Galgay, and Margaret D. Watson, "Designing a Goal-Setting System to Enhance Performance: A Practical Guide," *Organizational Dynamics*, Summer 1988, pp. 69–78.

15. Robert D. Pritchard, Philip L. Roth, Steven D. Jones, Patricia J. Galgay, and Margaret D. Watson, "Designing a Goal-Setting System to Enhance Performance: A Practical Guide," *Organizational Dynamics*, Summer 1988, pp. 69–78.

16. Charles Siler, "The Goal is 0%," *Forbes*, Oct. 30, 1989, pp. 95–98; information from a company official, March 1990.

17. Gary P. Latham, and Edwin A. Locke, "Goal Setting—A Motivational Technique That Works," *Organizational Dynamics*, Autumn 1979, pp. 68–80.

18. Thomas W. Lee, Edwin A. Locke, and Gary P. Latham, "Goal Setting Theory and Job Performance," in Lawrence A. Pervin (ed.), *Goal Concepts in Personality and Social Psychology*, Lawrence Erlbaum, Hillsdale, N.J., 1989.

19. Charles Perrow, "The Analysis of Goals in Complex Organizations," *American Sociological Review*, vol. 26, 1961, pp. 854–866; Max S. Richards, *Setting Strategic Goals and Objectives*, 2d ed., West, St. Paul, Minn., 1986.

20. 1988 Annual Report, Cypress Semiconductor.

21. Ibid.

22. Correspondence from John W. Hamburger, marketing communications manager, Cypress Semiconductor, Aug. 24, 1989.

23. Thomas W. Lee, Edwin A. Locke, and Gary P. Latham, "Goal Setting Theory and Job Performance," in Lawrence A. Pervin (ed.), *Goal Concepts in Personality and Social Psychology*, Lawrence Erlbaum, Hillsdale, N.J., 1989, pp. 291–326; Edwin A. Locke and Gary P. Latham, *A Theory of Goal Setting & Task Performance*, Prentice-Hall, Englewood Cliffs, N.J., 1990.

24. Laura Jereski, "I'm a Bad Manager," *Forbes*, Feb. 8, 1988, pp. 134–135.

25. Edwin A. Locke and Gary P. Latham, *Goal Setting: A Motivational Technique That Works!* Prentice-Hall, Englewood Cliffs, N.J., 1984.

26. Joseph Pereira, "L. L. Bean Scales Back Expansion Goals to Ensure Pride in Its Service Is Valid," *The Wall Street Journal*, July 31, 1989, p. B3.

27. Maria Mallory, "Profits on Everything but the Kitchen Sink," *Business Week*, Innovation 1989 issue, June 16, 1989, p. 122.

28. Gary P. Latham and Kenneth N. Wexley, *Increasing Productivity through Performance Appraisal*, Addison-Wesley, Reading, Mass., 1981.

29. "Being the Boss," *INC.*, October 1989.

30. Edwin A. Locke, Gary P. Latham, and Miriam Erez, "The Determinants of Goal Commitment," *Academy of Management Review*, vol. 13, 1988, pp. 23–39.

31. Edwin A. Locke and Gary P. Latham, *Goal Setting: A Motivational Technique That Works!* Prentice-Hall, Englewood Cliffs, N.J., 1984.

32. Francine Schwadel, "Nordstrom's Push East Will Test Its Renown for the Best in Service," *The Wall Street Journal*, Aug. 1, 1989, pp. A1, A4.

33. Ibid.

34. Edwin A. Locke, Gary P. Latham, and Miriam Erez, "The Determinants of Goal Commitment," *Academy of Management Review*, vol. 14, 1988, pp. 23–39.

35. Robert E. Wood, A. J. Mento, and Edwin A. Locke, "Task Complexity as a Moderator of Goal Effects: A Meta Analysis," *Journal of Applied Psychology*, vol. 72, 1987, pp. 416–425.

36. Edwin A. Locke, Karyl N. Shaw, Lisa M. Saari, and Gary P. Latham, "Goal Setting and Task Performance," *Psychological Bulletin*, vol. 90, 1981, pp. 125–152.

37. Based on excerpts from a talk by Denis A. Ossola reported in *Manufacturing Productivity Frontiers*, May 1981, pp. 1–8, and James L. Riggs and Glenn H. Felix, *Productivity by Objectives*, Prentice-Hall, Englewood Cliffs, N.J., 1983, pp. 130–131.

38. Edwin A. Locke and Gary P. Latham, *Goal Setting: A Motivational Technique That Works!* Prentice-Hall, Englewood Cliffs, N.J., 1984, and *A Theory of Goal Setting & Task Performance*, Prentice-Hall, Englewood Cliffs, N.J., 1990.

39. Edwin A. Locke and Gary P. Latham, *Goal Setting: A Motivational Technique That Works!* Prentice-Hall, Englewood Cliffs, N.J., 1984.

40. Arthur A. Thompson, Jr., and A. J. Strickland III, *Strategic Management: Concepts and Cases*, Business Publications, Plano, Tex., 1987.

41. William H. Newman and James P. Logan, *Strategy, Policy, and Central Management*, 8th ed., South-Western, Cincinnati, 1981.

42. Robert T. Grieves, "Hold the Phone," *Forbes*, June 13, 1988, p. 52; William C. Symonds, "People Aren't Laughing at U.S. Sprint Anymore," *Business Week*, July 31, 1989, pp. 82–86.

43. William C. Symonds, "People Aren't Laughing at U.S. Sprint Anymore," *Business Week*, July 31, 1989, pp. 82–86.

44. This section relies heavily on Leslie W. Rue and Phyllis G. Holland, *Strategic Management, Concepts and Experiences*, 2d ed., McGraw-Hill, New York, 1989.

45. Patricia Sellers, "How to Handle Customers' Gripes," *Fortune*, Oct. 24, 1988, pp. 88–100.

46. This section is based mainly on Teresa M. Amabile, "A Model of Creativity and Innovation in Organizations," *Research in Organizational Behavior*, vol. 10, 1988, pp. 123–167.

47. 1988 Annual Report, Cypress Semiconductor.

48. Based on Russell Mitchell, "Mining the Work Force for Ideas," *Business Week*, Innovation 1989 issue, June 16, 1989, p. 121.

49. "Thriving on Order," *INC.*, December 1989, pp. 47–62.

50. Henry Mintzberg, *The Nature of Managerial Work*, Prentice-Hall, Englewood Cliffs, N.J., 1980.

51. Daniel H. Gray, "Uses and Misuses of Strategic Planning," *Harvard Business Review*, January–February 1986, pp. 89–97.

52. Thomas L. Wheelen and J. David Hunger, *Strategic Management and Business Policy*, 3d ed., Addison-Wesley, Reading, Mass., 1989.

53. Leslie W. Rue and Phyllis G. Holland, *Strategic Management: Concepts and Experiences*, 2d ed., McGraw-Hill, New York, 1989.

54. "The New Breed of Strategic Planner," *Business Week*, Sept. 17, 1984, pp. 62–68.

55. Paul Miesing and Joseph Wolfe, "The Art and Science of Planning at the Business Unit Level," *Management Science*, vol. 31, 1985, pp. 773–781.

56. George S. Odiorne, *M.B.O. II*, Fearon Pitman, Belmont, Calif., 1979.

57. Peter F. Drucker, *The Practice of Management*, Harper, New York, 1954; Roland G. Greenwood, "Management by Objectives: As Developed by Peter Drucker, Assisted by Harold Smiddy," *Academy of Management Review*, vol. 6, 1981, pp. 225–230.

58. Eugene J. Seyna, "MBO: The Fad That Changed Management," *Long Range Planning*, vol. 19, 1986, pp. 116–123.

59. Anthony P. Raia, *Managing by Objectives*, Scott, Foresman, Glenview, Ill., 1974; Max D. Richards, *Setting Strategic Goals and Objectives*, 2d ed., West, St. Paul, Minn., 1986.

60. Mark L. McConkie, "A Clarification of the Goal Setting and Appraisal Processes in MBO," *Academy of Management Review*, January 1979, pp. 29–40.

61. Anthony P. Raia, *Managing by Objectives*, Scott, Foresman, Glenview, Ill., 1974; Max D. Richards, *Setting Strategic Goals and Objectives*, 2d ed., West, St. Paul, Minn., 1986.

62. Steven J. Carroll and Henry L. Tosi, *Management by Objectives: Applications and Research*, Macmillan, New York, 1973; Anthony P. Raia, *Managing by Objectives*, Scott, Foresman, Glenview, Ill., 1974; Joseph W. Leonard, "Why MBO Fails So Often," *Training and Development Journal*, June 1986; Max D. Richards, *Setting Strategic Goals and Objectives*, 2d ed., West, St. Paul, Minn., 1986.

63. F. L. May, "How We Got Our Association Out of a Slump," *Association Management*, September 1979, pp. 83–87.

64. Andy Zipser, "How Pressure to Raise Sales Led MiniScribe to Falsify Number," *The Wall Street Journal*, Sept. 11, 1989, pp. A1, A8.

65. Susan C. Faludi, "At Nordstrom Stores, Service Comes First—But at a Big Price," *The Wall Street Journal*, Feb. 20, 1990, pp. A1, A16.

66. Jack N. Kondrasuk, "Studies in MBO Effectiveness," *Academy of Management Review*, vol. 6, 1981, pp. 419–430.

67. Jan P. Muczyk, "Dynamics and Hazards of MBO Application," *Personnel Administrator*, May 1979, pp. 51–61.

68. John Huet, "WAL-MART Will It Take Over the World?" *Fortune*, Jan. 30, 1989, pp. 52–59; "The Five Best," *Business Month*, December 1988, pp. 30–44; Fact Sheet about Wal-Mart Stores Inc., Wal-Mart Stores, Inc., Corporate Public Relations Office, Bentonville, Ark., n.d.; Arthur A. Thompson, Jr., and A. J. Strickland III, *Strategic Management, Concepts and Cases*, 4th ed., Business Publications, Plano, Texas, 1987, pp. 936–954; Steve Weiner, "Gold Balls, Motor Oil and Tomatoes," *Forbes*, Oct. 30, 1989, pp. 130–134; discussion between Brenda Lockhart, corporate coordinator of public relations, and David C. Martin, November 1989.

CHAPTER 6

1. Based on Stephen J. Sansweet, "Disney's 'Imagineers' Build Space Attraction Using High-Tech Gear," *The Wall Street Journal*, Jan. 6, 1987, pp. 1, 24; Ronald Grover, "Disney's Magic," *Business Week*, Mar. 9, 1987, pp. 62–69; Walter Roessing, "Michael D. Eisner, Frank G. Wells, the Walt Disney Company," *Sky*, September 1987, pp. 50–56; Stephen Koepp, "Do You Believe in Magic?" *Time*, Apr. 25, 1988, pp. 66–73; Howard Rudnitsky, "Mickey Is Eating My Lunch!" *Forbes*,

Sept. 18, 1989, pp. 86–92; Christopher Knowlton, "How Disney Keeps the Magic Going," *Fortune*, Dec. 4, 1989, pp. 111–132; Richard Turner, "Disney's Ship May Come In at Long Beach," *The Wall Street Journal*, Feb. 6, 1990, p. B1; and "Disney Plans Massive Mall, Residential Project in Florida," *The Washington Post*, Mar. 13, 1990, p. C4.

2. Lawrence R. Jauch and William F. Glueck, *Business Policy and Strategic Management*, 5th ed., McGraw-Hill, New York, 1988; John A. Pearce II and Richard B. Robinson, Jr., *Strategic Management: Strategy Formulation and Implementation*, 3d ed., Irwin, Homewood, Ill., 1988.

3. Arthur A. Thompson, Jr., and A. J. Strickland III, *Strategic Management: Concepts and Cases*, 5th ed., BPI/Irwin, Homewood, Ill., 1990.

4. Arthur A. Thompson, Jr., and A. J. Strickland III, *Strategic Management: Concepts and Cases*, 4th ed., Business Publications, Plano, Tex., 1987; Leslie W. Rue and Phyllis G. Holland, *Strategic Management: Concepts and Experiences*, 2d ed., McGraw-Hill, New York, 1989.

5. Arthur A. Thompson, Jr., and A. J. Strickland III, *Strategic Management: Concepts and Cases*, 5th ed., BPI/Irwin, Homewood, Ill., 1990.

6. Ibid.

7. Michael E. Porter, *Competitive Advantage: Creating and Sustaining Superior Performance*, Free Press, New York, 1985.

8. Steve Weiner, "Electrifying," *Forbes*, Nov. 30, 1987, pp. 196–198.

9. Warren Keith Schilit, "An Examination of the Influence of Middle-Level Managers in Formulating and Implementing Strategic Decisions," *Journal of Management Studies*, May 1987, pp. 271–293.

10. Ibid.

11. D. Robley Wood, Jr., and R. Lawrence LaForge, "The Impact of Comprehensive Planning on Financial Performance," *Academy of Management Journal*, vol. 22, 1979, pp. 516–526; Lawrence C. Rhyne, "The Relationship of Strategic Planning to Financial Performance," *Strategic Management Journal*, vol. 7, 1986, pp. 423–436.

12. Arthur A. Thompson, Jr., and A. J. Strickland III, *Strategic Management: Concepts and Cases*, 5th ed., BPI/Irwin, Homewood, Ill., 1990. Thompson and Strickland also include an operating strategy level that addresses strategy for managers within functional areas.

13. Ibid.

14. Robert Mueller, "Criteria for the Appraisal of Directors," *Harvard Business Review*, vol. 57, 1979, p. 48–56.

15. Leslie W. Rue and Phyllis G. Holland, *Strategic Management: Concepts and Experiences*, 2d ed., McGraw-Hill, New York, 1989.

16. John A. Pearce II and Richard B. Robinson, Jr., *Strategic Management: Strategy Formulation and Implementation*, 3d ed., Irwin, Homewood, Ill., 1988.

17. Arthur A. Thompson, Jr., and A. J. Strickland III, *Strategic Management: Concepts and Cases*, 5th ed., BPI/Irwin, Homewood, Ill., 1990.

18. Leslie W. Rue and Phyllis G. Holland, *Strategic Management: Concepts and Experiences*, 2d ed., McGraw-Hill, New York, 1989.

19. Henry Mintzberg, "Strategy-Making in Three Modes," in James Brian Quinn, Henry Mintzberg, and Robert M. James (eds.), *The Strategy Process: Concepts, Contexts, and Cases*, Prentice-Hall, Englewood Cliffs, N.J., 1988, pp. 82–89.

20. Danny Miller and Peter H. Friesen, *Organizations: A Quantum View*, Prentice-Hall, Englewood Cliffs, N.J., 1984.

21. Henry Mintzberg, "Strategy-Making in Three Modes," in James Brian Quinn, Henry Mintzberg, and Robert M. James (eds.), *The Strategy Process: Concepts, Contexts, and Cases*, Prentice-Hall, Englewood Cliffs, N.J., 1988, pp. 82–89.

22. Danny Miller and Peter H. Friesen, *Organizations: A Quantum View*, Prentice-Hall, Englewood Cliffs, N.J., 1984.

23. Walecia Konrad, "Shoney's Needs a Recipe for Succession," *Business Week*, Dec. 25, 1989, p. 52.

24. Henry Mintzberg, "Strategy-Making in Three Modes," in James Brian Quinn, Henry Mintzberg, and Robert M. James (eds.), *The Strategy Process: Concepts, Contexts, and Cases*, Prentice-Hall, Englewood Cliffs, N.J., 1988, pp. 82–89.

25. Mark Maremont, "Trying to Get Burger King Out of the Flames," *Business Week*, Jan. 30, 1989, pp. 29–30; Richard Gibson and Barbara Marsh, "Burger King Reviews Hard Sell for Service," *The Wall Street Journal*, Sept. 28, 1989, pp. B1, B6.

26. Danny Miller and Peter H. Friesen, *Organizations: A Quantum View*, Prentice-Hall, Englewood Cliffs, N.J., 1984. Miller and Friesen's conclusions about innovation apply to Mintzberg's adhocracy, but they also draw parallels to the adaptive mode.

27. Howard Rudnitsky, "Mickey Is Eating My Lunch!" *Forbes*, Sept. 18, 1989, pp. 86–92.

28. Henry Mintzberg, "Strategy-Making in Three Modes," in James Brian Quinn, Henry Mintzberg, and Robert M. James (eds.), *The Strategy Process: Concepts, Contexts, and Cases*, Prentice-Hall, Englewood Cliffs, N.J., 1988, pp. 82–89.

29. Ibid.; John A. Pearce II and Richard B. Robinson, Jr., *Strategic Management*, 3d ed., Irwin, Homewood, Ill., 1988.

30. Arthur A. Thompson, Jr., and A. J. Strickland III, *Strategic Management: Concepts and Cases*, 5th ed., BPI/Irwin, Homewood, Ill., 1990.

31. Patrick M. Reilly, "As Magazine Industry Faces a Shakeout, Some Publishers Start to Close the Books," *The Wall Street Journal*, Jan. 31, 1990, pp. B1, B4.

32. Norm Alster, "Unlevel Playing Field," *Forbes*, June 26, 1989, pp. 53–57.

33. Stewart Toy, "Waiter, a Magnum of Your Best Portland Champagne," *Business Week*, Dec. 11, 1989, pp. 92–94.

34. Julia Flynn Siler, "A Warning Shot from the King of Beers," *Business Week*, Dec. 18, 1989, p. 124.

35. Betsy Morris, "Coke Unveils Compact Dispenser, Hoping to Sell More Soft Drinks in Small Offices," *The Wall Street Journal*, Nov. 17, 1988, p. B1.

36. Charles W. L. Hill and Gareth R. Jones, *Strategic Management: An Integrated Approach*, Houghton Mifflin, Boston, 1989.

37. Ibid.

38. Leslie W. Rue and Phyllis G. Holland, *Strategic Management: Concepts and Experiences*, 2d ed., McGraw-Hill, New York, 1989.

39. *Hewlett-Packard in Brief*, Hewlett-Packard, Palo Alto, Calif., 1989.

40. Toni Mack, "Playing with the Majors," *Forbes*, Nov. 13, 1989, pp. 92–94.

41. Leslie W. Rue and Phyllis G. Holland, *Strategic Management: Concepts and Experiences*, 2d ed., McGraw-Hill, New York, 1989.

42. Ibid.

43. Arthur A. Thompson, Jr., and A. J. Strickland III, *Strategic Management: Concepts and Cases*, 5th ed., BPI/Irwin, Homewood, Ill., 1990.

44. John A. Pearce II and Richard B. Robinson, Jr., *Strategic Management: Strategy Formulation and Implementatin*, 3d ed., Irwin, Homewood, Ill., 1988.

45. This section is based heavily on Leslie W. Rue and Phyllis G. Holland, *Strategic Management: Concepts and Experiences*, 2d ed., McGraw-Hill, New York, 1989.

46. E. S. Browning, "Long-Term Thinking and Paternalistic Ways Carry Michelin to Top," *The Wall Street Journal*, Jan. 5, 1990, pp. A1, A8.

47. Ted Kumpecb and Piet T. Bolwijn, "Manufacturing: The New Case for Vertical Integra-

tion," *Harvard Business Review*, March–April 1988, pp. 75–81.

48. Richard Behar, "Spreading the Wealth," *Forbes*, Aug. 10, 1987, pp. 74–81.

49. Kathryn Rudie Harrigan, "Vertical Integration and Corporate Strategy," *Academy of Management Journal*, vol. 28, 1985, pp. 397–425.

50. Raphael Amit and Joshua Livnat, "A Concept of Conglomerate Diversification," *Journal of Management*, vol. 14, 1988, pp. 593–604.

51. Howard Banks, "Being a Conglomerate Is Not All Bad," *Forbes*, Dec. 11, 1989, pp. 40–41.

52. Stephen P. Robbins, *Organization Theory: The Structure and Design of Organizations*, Prentice-Hall, Englewood Cliffs, N.J., 1983.

53. Based on Brian O'Reilly, "Leslie Wexner Knows What Women Want," *Fortune*, Aug. 19, 1985, pp. 154–160; Steven B. Weiner, "The Unlimited?" *Forbes*, Apr. 6, 1987, pp. 76–80; Carol Hymowitz, "Limited Inc. Struggles to Lure Back Customers," *The Wall Street Journal*, Oct. 13, 1988, p. B6; "The Limited's Approach," *Chain Store Age Executive*, December 1988, pp. 28–36; and Carol Hymowitz, "Upscale Look for Limited Puts Retailer Back on Track," *The Wall Street Journal*, pp. B1, B5.

54. David J. Jefferson, "Dream to Nightmare: When Growth Gets Out of Hand," *The Wall Street Journal*, Jan. 23, 1990, p. B2.

55. John A. Pearce II and Richard B. Robinson, Jr., *Strategic Management: Strategy Formulation and Implementation*, 3d ed., Irwin, Homewood, Ill., 1988.

56. Arthur A. Thompson, Jr., and A. J. Strickland III, *Strategic Management: Concepts and Cases*, 5th ed., BPI/Irwin, Homewood, Ill., 1990.

57. Jack Willoughby, "The Last Iceman," *Forbes*, July 13, 1987, pp. 183–204.

58. Cynthia A. Montgomery, Ann R. Thomas, and Rajan Kamath, "Divestiture, Market Valuation, and Strategy," *Academy of Management Journal*, vol. 27, 1984, pp. 830–840.

59. "Bankruptcy Petition Brings Fresh Risks for Allied, Federated," *The Wall Street Journal*, Jan. 16, 1990, pp. A1, A10; Todd Mason, "It'll Be a Hard Sell," *Business Week*, Jan. 29, 1990, pp. 30–31.

60. Sometimes other criteria, such as a 10 percent growth rate, are used to gauge high and low market growth; see Leslie W. Rue and Phyllis G. Holland, *Strategic Management: Concepts and Experiences*, 2d ed., McGraw-Hill, New York, 1989.

61. Janet Guyon, "GE to Acquire Borg-Warner's Chemical Lines," *The Wall Street Journal*, June 17, 1988, p. 3.

62. Richard Phalon, "Roto-Rooter's New Drill," *Forbes*, Dec. 11, 1989, pp. 176–178.

63. Ibid.

64. Laura Landro and Douglas R. Sease, "General Electric to Sell Consumer Electronics Lines to Thomason SA for Its Medical Gear Business, Cash," *The Wall Street Journal*, July 23, 1987, p. 3; Janet Guyon, "GE Chairman Welch, Though Much Praised, Starts to Draw Critics," *The Wall Street Journal*, Aug. 4, 1988, pp. 1, 8.

65. Donald C. Hambrick, Ian C. MacMillan, and Diana L. Day, "Strategic Attributes and Performance in the BCG Matrix—A PIMS-Based Analysis of Industrial Product Businesses," *Academy of Management Journal*, vol. 25, 1982, pp. 510–531.

66. Arthur A. Thompson, Jr., and A. J. Strickland III, *Strategic Management: Concepts and Cases*, 5th ed., BPI/Irwin, Homewood, Ill., 1990.

67. Ibid.

68. Graham Turner, "Inside Europe's Giant Companies: Daimler-Benz Goes Top of the League," *Long Range Planning*, vol. 19, 1986, pp. 12–17.

69. Bill Saporito, "The Tough Cookie at RJR Nabisco," *Fortune*, July 18, 1988, pp. 32–46; Peter Waldman, "New RJR Chief Faces a

Daunting Challenge at Debt-Heavy Firm," *The Wall Street Journal,* Mar. 14, 1989, pp. A1, A19.

70. Anil K. Gupta and V. Govindarajan, "Build, Hold, Harvest: Converting Strategic Intentions into Reality," *Journal of Business Strategy,* March 1984, pp. 34–47.

71. Donald C. Hambrick, Ian C. MacMillan, and Diana L. Day, "Strategic Attributes and Performance in the BCG Matrix—A PIMS-Based Analysis of Industrial Product Businesses," *Academy of Management Journal,* vol. 25, 1982, pp. 510–531.

72. This section is based mainly on Charles W. L. Hill and Gareth R. Jones, *Strategic Management: An Integrated Approach,* Houghton Mifflin, Boston, 1989, and Arthur A. Thompson, Jr., and A. J. Strickland III, *Strategic Management: Concepts and Cases,* 5th ed., BPI/Irwin, Homewood, Ill., 1990.

73. John A. Pearce II and Richard B. Robinson, Jr., *Strategic Management: Strategy Formulation and Implementation,* 3d ed., Irwin, Homewood, Ill., 1988.

74. Charles W. Hofer and Dan Schendel, *Strategy Formulation: Analytical Concepts,* West, St. Paul, Minn., 1978.

75. Arthur A. Thompson, Jr., and A. J. Strickland III, *Strategic Management: Concepts and Cases,* 5th ed., BPI/Irwin, Homewood, Ill., 1990.

76. Charles W. L. Hill and Gareth R. Jones, *Strategic Management: An Integrated Approach,* Houghton Mifflin, Boston, 1989.

77. Malcolm Schofield and David Arnold, "Strategies for Mature Businesses," *Long Range Planning,* vol. 21, 1988, pp. 69–76.

78. Gregory Stricharchuk, "Westinghouse Relies on Ruthless Pruning," *The Wall Street Journal,* Jan. 24, 1990, p. A4.

79. This section is based mainly on Michael E. Porter, *Competitive Strategy: Techniques for Analyzing Industries and Competitors,* Free Press, New York, 1980.

80. James Cook, "We're the Low-Cost Producer," *Forbes,* Dec. 25, 1989, pp. 65–66.

81. Gregory L. Miles, "Heinz Ain't Broke, but It's Doing a Lot of Fixing," *Business Week,* Dec. 11, 1989, pp. 84–88.

82. Based on Richard C. Morais, "Cock-a-Leekie," *Forbes,* Sept. 7, 1987, pp. 68–69.

83. Kerry Hannon, "Shifting Gears," *Forbes,* Dec. 11, 1989, pp. 124–130.

84. W. K. Hall, "Survival in a Hostile Environment," *Harvard Business Review,* vol. 58, 1980, pp. 75–85; Gregory G. Dess and Peter S. Davis, "Porter's (1980) Generic Strategies as Determinants of Strategic Group Membership and Organizational Performance," *Academy of Management Journal,* vol. 27, 1984, pp. 467–488; R. E. White, "Generic Business Strategies, Organizational Context, and Performance: An Empirical Investigation," *Strategic Management Journal,* vol. 7, 1986, pp. 217–231.

85. W. K. Hall, "Survival in a Hostile Environment," *Harvard Business Review,* vol. 58, 1980, pp. 75–85; R. E. White, "Generic Business Strategies, Organizational Context, and Performance: An Empirical Investigation," *Strategic Management Journal,* vol. 7, 1986, pp. 217–231.

86. See, for example, Charles W. L. Hill, "Differentiation versus Low Cost or Differentiation and Low Cost: A Contingency Framework," *Academy of Management Review,* vol. 13, 1988, pp. 401–412; see also Alan I. Murray, "A Contingency View of Porter's 'Generic Strategies,'" *Academy of Management Review,* vol. 13, 1988, pp. 390–400.

87. Jay R. Galbraith and Robert K. Kazanjian, *Strategy Implementation: Structure, Systems and Process,* 2d ed., West, St. Paul, Minn., 1986.

88. Charles W. L. Hill and Gareth R. Jones, *Strategic Management: An Integrated Approach,* Houghton Mifflin, Boston, 1989.

89. Theodore T. Herbert and Helen Deresky, "Should General Managers Match Their Business Strategies?" *Organizational Dynamics,* Winter, 1987, pp. 40–51.

90. Marc Beauchamp, "Food for Thought," *Forbes,* Apr. 17, 1989, p. 73.

91. Helen Deresky and Theodore Herbert, "Senior Management Implications of Strategic Human Resource Management Programs," in *Proceedings, Human Resources Management Organizational Behavior Conference,* The Association of Management, November 1986.

92. Based on Tom Alexander, "Cray's Way of Staying Super-Duper," *Fortune,* Mar. 18, 1985, pp. 56–76; John W. Verity, "Street Smarts: The Supercomputer Becomes a Stock Strategist," *Business Week,* June 1, 1987, pp. 84–85; Richard Gibson, "Cray Research Cancels a Supercomputer Plan and Loses a Superstar," *The Wall Street Journal,* Sept. 3, 1987, pp. 1, 10; George Melloan, "Staying Ahead of the Pack at Cray Research," *The Wall Street Journal,* Feb. 23, 1988, p. 31; John Burgess and Evelyn Richards, "Can U.S. Protect Lead in Supercomputers?" *The Washington Post,* May 7, 1989, pp. H1, H7; Richard Gibson, "Cray Plans to Spin Off Founder's Efforts on New Computer; Cites Research Costs," *The Wall Street Journal,* May 16, 1989, p. A3; William M. Bulkeley, "Long a U.S. Province, Supercomputer Market Feels a Japanese Threat," *The Wall Street Journal,* May 24, 1989, pp. A1, A9; Russell Mitchell, "Now Cray Faces Life without Cray," *Business Week,* May 29, 1989, p. 31; Carla Lazzareschi, "Cray Left His Company to Prevent Internal Conflict," *Los Angeles Times,* June 4, 1989, part IV, p. 4; Willy Schatz, "Cray to Offer New Low-End Supercomputer," *The Washington Post,* Nov. 15, 1989, p. F3; Jim Bartimo, "Can Convex Throw the Big Boys a Curve?" *Business Week,* Dec. 18, 1989, p. 104D; and Russell Mitchell, "The Genius," *Business Week,* Apr. 30, 1990, pp. 81–88.

CHAPTER 7

1. Based on Stuart Gannes, "Merck Has Made Biotech Work," *Fortune,* Jan. 19, 1987, pp. 58–64; John A. Byrne, "The Miracle Company," *Business Week,* Oct. 19, 1987, pp. 84–90; and Michael Waldholz, "Merck Says Near-Term Profit Will Slow from Recent History of 25 Percent Growth," *The Wall Street Journal,* Nov. 14, 1989, p. A8.

2. Peter F. Drucker, "A Prescription for Entrepreneurial Management," *Industry Week,* Apr. 29, 1985, pp. 33–38.

3. "The New Breed of Strategic Planner," *Business Week,* Sept. 17, 1984.

4. Boyce Rensberger, "Lessons of the VCR Revolution: How U.S. Industry Failed to Make American Ingenuity Pay Off," *The Washington Post,* Apr. 13, 1987, pp. 1, 10.

5. For a similar definition, see Rosabeth Moss Kanter, *The Change Masters,* Simon and Schuster, New York, 1983, p. 20.

6. Brian Bremmer, "Asbestos Makers Run Out of Breathing Room," *Business Week,* Nov. 20, 1989, pp. 36–38.

7. Luther Jackson, "Industrial Evolution," *Detroit Free Press,* Sept. 12, 1988, pp. B1–B8.

8. Gerald Zaltman, Robert Duncan, and Jonney Holbek, *Innovations and Organizations,* Wiley, New York, 1973; Andrew H. Van de Ven, "Central Problems in the Management of Innovation," *Management Science,* vol. 32, 1986, pp. 590–607.

9. Otis Port, "Innovation in America," *Business Week,* Innovation 1989 issue, pp. 14–18.

10. Neil Gross, "A Wave of Ideas, Drop by Drop," *Business Week* Innovation 1989 issue, June 16, 1989, pp. 22–30.

11. Richard Phalon, "Couch Potatoes Don't Dine Out," *Forbes,* Oct. 30, 1989, pp. 209–216.

12. Ibid.

13. Christopher Tucher, "How Ames Is Digesting Its 'Whale,'" *Business Week,* Sept. 11, 1989, p. 62; Joseph Pereira and Jeffrey A. Trachtenberg, "Ames Seeks Protection under Chapter 11 after Retailers' Talks with Lenders Stall," *The Wall Street Journal,* Apr. 27, 1990, p. A3.

14. This section on organizational life cycles is based primarily on Robert E. Quinn and Kim Cameron, "Organizational Life Cycles and Shifting Criteria of Effectiveness: Some Preliminary Evidence," *Management Science,* vol. 29, 1983, pp. 33–51, and Larry Greiner, "Evolution and Revolution as Organizations Grow," *Harvard Business Review,* July–August, 1972, pp. 37–46; see also Ken G. Smith, Terrence R. Mitchell, and Charles E. Summer, "Top Level Management Priorities in Different Stages of the Organizational Life Cycle," *Academy of Management Journal,* vol. 28, 1985, pp. 799–820.

15. James Brian Quinn, "Technological Innovation, Entrepreneurship, and Strategy," *Sloan Management Review,* Spring 1979, p. 20.

16. Dyan Machan, "DEC's Democracy," *Forbes,* Mar. 23, 1987.

17. Bro Uttal, "Behind the Fall of Steve Jobs," *Fortune,* Aug. 5, 1985, p. 20.

18. "The Shrinking of Middle Management," *Business Week,* Apr. 25, 1983, p. 56.

19. Jay R. Galbraith, "Designing the Innovating Organization," *Organizational Dynamics,* Winter 1982, p. 5.

20. Maggie McComas, "Cutting Costs without Killing the Business," *Fortune,* Oct. 13, 1986, pp. 70–71.

21. Barbara Gray and Sonny S. Ariss, "Politics and Strategic Change across Organizational Life Cycles," *Academy of Management Review,* vol. 10, 1985, pp. 707–723.

22. Kim S. Cameron, David A. Whetten, and Myung U. Kim, "Organizational Dysfunctions of Decline," *Academy of Management Journal,* vol. 30, 1987, pp. 126–138.

23. Alex Beam and Gordon Bock, "Wang Labs Wrestles with the Question: What Happens after An Wang?" *Business Week,* June 30, 1986, pp. 78–82; Arthur M. Louis, "Doctor Wang's Toughest Case," *Fortune,* Feb. 3, 1986, pp. 106–109; Gary McWilliams, "Pulling It All Together: A Troubled Wang Labs Tries to Put Itself Back on Track," *Datamation,* Mar. 1, 1987, pp. 24–30; John R. Wilke, "Wang Founder Apparently Forces His Son to Step Down as President," *The Wall Street Journal,* Aug. 9, 1989, pp. A3, A4; William M. Bulkeley, "Wang, Bogged Down by Debt, Could Face Loss of Independence," *The Wall Street Journal,* July 14, 1989, "Wang Labs Names Computer Novice President and Chief Operating Officer," *The Wall Street Journal,* Aug. 24, 1989, p. B6, and "Wang Laboratories Founder Dies at 70; Family Will Retain Control of Concern," *The Wall Street Journal,* Mar. 26, 1990, p. B4.

24. Donald P. Baker, "Robins Files Reorganization Plan," *The Washington Post,* Apr. 17, 1987, p. G1; Malcolm Gladwell, "Robins Reorganization Plan Upheld by Appeals Court," *The Washington Post,* June 17, 1989, p. C11.

25. Leslie W. Rue and Phyllis G. Holland, *Strategic Management: Concepts and Experiences,* 2d ed., McGraw-Hill, New York, 1989.

26. Caroline E. Mayer, "A Downtown Tradition Calls It Quits," *The Washington Post,* Mar. 2, 1987, Washington Business section, pp. 1, 34–35.

27. Mark Potts, "Burroughs Changes Its Name," *The Washington Post,* Nov. 11, 1986, pp. E1, E5.

28. Milo Geyelin, "Robins Acquisition Opens Way to Settle Claims by Women," *The Wall Street Journal,* Dec. 15, 1989, p. B8.

29. "After Its Recovery, New Headaches for Tylenol," *Business Week,* May 14, 1984, p. 137.

30. Sana Siwolop and Christopher Eklund, "The Capsule Controversy: How Far Should the FDA Go?" *Business Week,* Mar. 3, 1986, p. 37.

31. For discussions of the innovative process,

see Gerald Zaltman, Robert Duncan, and Jonny Holbek, *Innovations and Organizations*, Wiley, New York, 1973, and Modesto A. Maidique, ''Entrepreneurs, Champions, and Technological Innovation,'' *Sloan Management Review*, Winter 1980, pp. 59–76.

32. Peter F. Drucker, ''A Prescription for Entrepreneurial Management,'' *Industry Week*, Apr. 29, 1985, pp. 33–34.

33. Stratford P. Sherman, ''Eight Big Masters of Innovation,'' *Fortune*, Oct. 15, 1984, p. 76; Joseph Weber, ''M'm! M'm! Bad! Trouble at Campbell Soup,'' *Business Week*, Sept. 25, 1989, pp. 68–70.

34. Thomas J. Peters and Robert H. Waterman, Jr., *In Search of Excellence*, Harper & Row, New York, 1982, pp. 200–234.

35. John A. Byrne, ''Giving Free Rein to Merck's Best and Brightest,'' *Business Week*, Oct. 19, 1987, p. 90.

36. Alison Leigh Cowan, ''Getting Rich on Other People's Pay Checks,'' *Business Week*, Nov. 17, 1986, pp. 148–149; Fleming Meeks, ''Tom Golisano and the Red Tape Factory,'' *Forbes*, May 15, 1989, pp. 80–82.

37. Russell Mitchell, ''The Health Craze Has Kellogg Feeling G-r-r-reat,'' *Business Week*, Mar. 30, 1987, p. 53.

38. Ibid.

39. Bill Saporito, ''A Smart Cookie at Pepperidge,'' *Fortune*, Dec. 22, 1986, pp. 67–74; Dyan Machan, ''Pepperidge Farm's Doughboy,'' *Forbes*, Mar. 20, 1989, pp. 198–199.

40. John P. Kotter and Leonard A. Schlesinger, ''Choosing Strategies for Change,'' *Harvard Business Review*, March–April 1979, pp. 106–114.

41. ''Citicorp Loses Top Investment Talent Abroad,'' *Dun's Business Month*, November 1986, p. 21.

42. Bill Saporito, ''The Revolt against 'Working' Smarter,'' *Fortune*, July 21, 1986, pp. 58–65.

43. Kurt Lewin, ''Frontiers in Group Dynamics: Concept, Method, and Reality in Social Science,'' *Human Relations*, vol. 1, 1947, pp. 5–41; Edgar F. Huse and Thomas G. Cummings, *Organization Development and Change*, 3d ed., West, St. Paul, Minn., 1985.

44. John P. Kotter and Leonard A. Schlesinger, ''Choosing Strategies for Change,'' *Harvard Business Review*, March–April 1979, pp. 106–114.

45. Paul C. Nutt, ''Tactics of Implementation,'' *Academy of Management Journal*, vol. 29, 1986, pp. 230–261.

46. Ibid.

47. Maggie McComas, ''Cutting Costs without Killing the Business,'' *Fortune*, Oct. 13, 1986, pp. 70–78.

48. Paul C. Nutt, ''Tactics of Implementation,'' *Academy of Management Journal*, vol. 29, 1986, pp. 230–261.

49. Jacob M. Schlesinger, ''Plant-Level Talks Rise Quickly in Importance; Big Issue: Work Rules,'' *The Wall Street Journal*, Mar. 16, 1987, p. 16.

50. David Kirkpatrick, ''What Givebacks Can Get You,'' *Fortune*, Nov. 26, 1986, p. 61.

51. Paul C. Nutt, ''Tactics of Implementation,'' *Academy of Management Journal*, 1986, vol. 29, pp. 230–261.

52. Kurt Lewin, *Field Theory in Social Science: Selected Theoretical Papers*, Harper, New York, 1951.

53. David Kirkpatrick, ''What Givebacks Can Get You,'' *Fortune*, Nov. 24, 1986, pp. 60–72.

54. Gifford Pinchot III, *Intrapreneuring*, Harper & Row, New York, 1985.

55. Ibid.

56. Ibid.

57. Ibid. (adapted from pp. 124–125).

58. Harold J. Leavitt, ''Applied Organization Change in Industry: Structural, Technical, and Human Approaches,'' in W. W. Cooper, H. J. Leavitt, and M. W. Shelly II (eds.), *New Perspectives in Organization Research*, Wiley, New York, 1964, pp. 55–71; Edgar F. Huse

and Thomas G. Cummings, *Organization Development and Change*, 3d ed., West, St. Paul, Minn., 1985.

59. John Child, *Organization: A Guide to Problems and Practice*, Harper & Row, New York, 1977.

60. George Russell, ''Rebuilding to Survive,'' *Time*, Feb. 16, 1987, p. 44.

61. Danny Miller and Peter H. Friesen, ''Structural Change and Performance: Quantum versus Piecemeal-Incremental Approaches,'' *Academy of Management Journal*, vol. 25, 1982, pp. 867–892.

62. Andrew Tanzer, ''Create or Die,'' *Forbes*, Apr. 6, 1987, p. 57.

63. Marilyn Chase, ''Robot Apprentices,'' *The Wall Street Journal*, Nov. 16, 1986, p. 16D.

64. Aaron Bernstein, Scott Ticer, and Jonathan B. Levine, ''IBM's Fancy Footwork to Sidestep Layoffs,'' *Business Week*, July 7, 1986, pp. 54–55; Frank Swoboda, ''IBM Begins New Round of Early Retirement,'' *The Washington Post*, Oct. 3, 1989, p. 1C.

65. V. Sathe, ''Implications of Corporate Culture: A Manager's Guide to Acting,'' *Organizational Dynamics*, Autumn 1983, pp. 5–23; Linda Smircich, ''Concepts of Culture and Organizational Analysis,'' *Administrative Science Quarterly*, vol. 28, 1983, pp. 339–358; Ralph H. Kilmann, Mary J. Saxton, and Roy Serpa, ''Issues in Understanding and Changing Culture,'' *California Management Review*, vol. 28, 1986, pp. 87–94.

66. Edgar F. Huse and Thomas G. Cummings, *Organization Development and Change*, 3d ed., West, St. Paul, Minn., 1985, p. 350.

67. Noel M. Tichy, *Managing Strategic Change: Technical, Political, and Cultural Dynamics*, Wiley, New York, 1983, p. 254; W. Brooke Tunstall, ''The Breakup of the Bell System: A Case Study in Cultural Transformation,'' *California Management Review*, Winter 1986, pp. 110–124; Zane E. Barnes, ''Change in the Bell System,'' February 1987, pp. 43–46.

68. Based on Graham Turner, ''Inside Europe's Giant Companies: Cultural Revolution at Philips,'' *Long Range Planning*, vol. 19, 1986, pp. 12–17; Jonathan Kapstein, ''Enough with the Theory—Where's the Thingamajig?'' *Business Week*, Mar. 21, 1988, pp. 155–158; and Jonathan Kapstein and Thane Peterson, ''Look Out, World, Philips Is on a War Footing,'' *Business Week*, Jan. 15, 1990, pp. 44–45.

69. Richard Beckhard, *Organizational Development: Strategies and Models*, Addison-Wesley, Reading, Mass., 1969; Michael Beer, *Organization Change and Development: A Systems View*, Goodyear, Santa Monica, Calif., 1980.

70. Michael Beer, *Organization Change and Development: A Systems View*, Goodyear, Santa Monica, Calif., 1980, p. 10; see also Noel M. Tichy, *Managing Strategic Change*, Wiley, New York, 1983.

71. Michael Beer, *Organization Change and Development: A Systems View*, Goodyear, Santa Monica, Calif., 1980, p. 10.

72. Wendell L. French and Cecil H. Bell, Jr., *Organization Development: Behavioral Interventions for Organizational Improvement*, Prentice-Hall, Englewood Cliffs, N.J., 1978; Edgar F. Huse and Thomas G. Cummings, *Organization Development and Change*, 3d ed., West, St. Paul, Minn., 1985.

73. Larry Reibstein, ''A Finger on the Pulse: Companies Expand Use of Employee Surveys,'' *The Wall Street Journal*, Oct. 27, 1986, p. 31.

74. Wendell L. French and Cecil H. Bell, Jr., *Organizational Development: Behavior Science Interventions for Organizational Improvement*, 2d ed., Prentice-Hall, Englewood Cliffs, N.J., 1978; Noel M. Tichy, *Managing Strategic Change: Technical, Political, and Cultural Dynbamics*, Wiley, New York, 1983; Edgar F. Huse and Thomas G. Cummings, *Organization Development and Change*, 3d ed., West, St. Paul, Minn., 1985.

75. W. Warner Burke, Lawrence P. Clark, and Cheryl Koopman, ''Improve Your OD Project's Chances for Success,'' *Training and Development Journal*, September 1984, pp. 62–68; Edgar F. Huse and Thomas G. Cummings, *Organization Development and Change*, 3d ed., West, St. Paul, Minn., 1985; Marshall Sashkin and W. Warner Burke, ''Organization Development in the 1980's,'' *Journal of Management*, vol. 13, 1987, pp. 393–417; Michael Beer and Anna Elise Walton, ''Organization Change and Development,'' *Annual Review of Psychology*, vol. 38, 1987, pp. 339–367.

76. John M. Nicholas, ''The Comparative Impact of Organizational Development Interventions on Hard Criteria Measures,'' *Academy of Management Review*, vol. 7, 1982, pp. 531–542.

77. Based on Kurt Lewin, *Field Theory in Social Science: Selected Theoretical Papers*, Harper, New York, 1951.

78. Based on James L. Rowe, Jr., ''Armacost to Resign as BankAmerica Chief,'' *The Washington Post*, Oct. 11, 1986, pp. C1–2; Gary Hector, ''A Dubious Act II at BankAmerica,'' *Fortune*, Nov. 10, 1986, pp. 69–72, and ''The Most Beleaguered Banker,'' *Fortune*, Jan. 5, 1987, p. 86; Robert N. Beck, ''Visions, Values, and Strategies: Changing Attitudes and Culture,'' *Academy of Management Executive*, February 1987, pp. 33–39; Charles McCoy, ''A Slashing Pursuit of Retail Trade Brings BankAmerica Back,'' *The Wall Street Journal*, Oct. 2, 1989, pp. A1, A8; Charles McCoy, ''BankAmerica's Rosenberg to Succeed A. W. Clausen,'' *The Wall Street Journal*, Jan. 25, 1990, p. B1; and Carrie Dolan, ''BankAmerica's Rosenberg Will Succeed Clausen as Chief; Dividend Lifted 66%,'' *The Wall Street Journal*, Feb. 6, 1990, p. B8.

CHAPTER 8

1. Based on Thomas Moore, ''He Put the Kick Back into Coke,'' *Fortune*, Oct. 26, 1987; also Jaclyn Fierman, ''How Coke Decided a New Taste Was It,'' *Fortune*, May 27, 1985, p. 80; Scott Scredon and Marc Frons, ''Coke's Man on the Spot,'' *Business Week*, July 29, 1985, pp. 56–61; Betsy Morris, ''Shaking Things Up at Coca-Cola Foods,'' *The Wall Street Journal*, Apr. 3, 1987, p. 36; ''Some Things Don't Go Better with Coke,'' *Forbes*, Mar. 21, 1988, pp. 34–35; ''New Coke,'' *Chief Executive*, May–June 1988, pp. 36–40; Scott Ticer, ''The Cola Superpowers' Outrageous New Arsenals,'' *Business Week*, Mar. 20, 1989, pp. 162–166; Walecia Konrad, ''Bottling Is Hardly a Classic for Coke,'' *Business Week*, Dec. 11, 1989, pp. 130–135; Michael J. McCarthy, ''As a Global Marketer, Coke Excels by Being Tough and Consistent,'' *The Wall Street Journal*, Dec. 19, 1989, pp. A1, A6; and Anthony Ramirez, ''It's Only Soft Drinks at Coca-Cola,'' *The New York Times*, May 21, 1990, pp. D1, D3.

2. Lois Therrien, ''The Rival Japan Respects,'' *Business Week*, Nov. 13, 1989, pp. 108–118.

3. See Alvin Elbing, *Behavioral Decisions in Organizations*, Scott, Foresman, Glenview, Ill., 1978.

4. George P. Huber, *Managerial Decision Making*, Scott, Foresman, Glenview, Ill., 1980, pp. 8–9.

5. Henry Mintzberg, Duru Raisignhani, and Andre Theoret, ''The Structure of 'Unstructured' Decision Processes,'' *Administrative Science Quarterly*, vol. 21, 1976, pp. 246–275; Paul C. Nutt, ''Types of Organizational Decision Processes,'' *Administrative Science Quarterly*, vol. 29, 1984, pp. 414–450.

6. Betsy Morris, ''Shaking Things Up at Coca-Cola Foods,'' *The Wall Street Journal*, Apr. 3, 1987, p. 36.

7. Paul C. Nutt, ''Types of Organizational Decision Processes,'' *Administrative Science Quarterly*, vol. 29, 1984, pp. 414–450.

8. Arthur M. Louis, "America's New Economy: How to Manage in It," *Fortune*, June 23, 1986, pp. 21–25.

9. David Henry, "No Customers, No Profits," *Forbes*, Feb. 23, 1987, pp. 52–56.

10. Bernard M. Bass, *Organizational Decision Making*, Irwin, Homewood, Ill., 1983, p. 13.

11. Marc Beauchamp, "Smooth Flying," *Forbes*, Sept. 18, 1989, pp. 94–96.

12. See, for example, Max H. Bazerman, *Judgment in Managerial Decision Making*, Wiley, New York, 1986.

13. Ronald N. Taylor, *Behavioral Decision Making*, Scott, Foresman, Glenview, Ill., 1984, pp. 121–122.

14. Katherine Weisman, "Safe Harbor," *Forbes*, Sept. 4, 1989, pp. 58–62.

15. Bernard M. Bass, *Organizational Decision Making*, Irwin, Homewood, Ill., 1983, pp. 27–28.

16. See, for example, Herbert A. Simon, "A Behavioral Model of Rational Choice," *Quarterly Journal of Economics*, vol. 69, 1955, pp. 99–118, and "Rational Choice and the Structure of the Environment," *Psychological Review*, vol. 63, 1956, pp. 129–138.

17. Max H. Bazerman, *Judgment in Managerial Decision Making*, Wiley, New York, 1986, p. 5.

18. George P. Huber, *Managerial Decision Making*, Scott, Foresman, Glenview, Ill., 1980.

19. Pranay Gupte, "Merge in Haste, Repent in Leisure," *Forbes*, Aug. 22, 1988, p. 85.

20. Charles E. Lindblom, *The Intelligence of Democracy*, Free Press, New York, 1965; Bernard M. Bass, *Organizational Decision Making*, Irwin, Homewood, Ill., 1983, pp. 34–35.

21. George P. Huber, *Managerial Decision Making*, Scott, Foresman, Glenview, Ill., 1980, p. 27.

22. Michael D. Cohen, James G. March, and Johan P. Olsen, "A Garbage Can Model of Organizational Choice," *Administrative Science Quarterly*, vol. 17, 1972, pp. 1–25; Anna Grandori, "A Prescriptive Contingency View of Organizational Decision Making," *Administrative Science Quarterly*, vol. 29, 1984, pp. 192–209.

23. Myron Magnet, "How Top Managers Make a Company's Toughest Decisions," *Fortune*, Mar. 18, 1985, pp. 52–57.

24. Steve Weiner, "Taking the Pledge," *Forbes*, June 29, 1987, pp. 41–42; Stephen Kindel, "The 10 Worst Managed Companies in America," *Financial World*, July 26, 1988, pp. 28–39; Michael Oneal, "Gould Is So Thin You Can Hardly See It," *Business Week*, Aug. 29, 1988, p. 74; "Japan Makes a Bid for the Merger Business," *The Economist*, Sept. 17, 1988, pp. 85–86.

25. Daniel D. Wheeler and Irving L. Janis, *A Practical Guide for Making Decisions*, Free Press, New York, 1980.

26. This section is based on David A. Cowan, "Developing a Process Model of Problem Recognition," *Academy of Management Review*, vol. 11, 1986, pp. 763–776.

27. The information about the American Can Company is based on Myron Magnet, "How Top Managers Make a Company's Toughest Decision," *Fortune*, Mar. 18, 1985, pp. 52–57, and Colin Leinster, "Jerry Tsai Listens to His Mother," *Fortune*, Aug. 17, 1987, pp. 82–86.

28. Ronald N. Taylor, *Behavioral Decision Making*, Scott, Foresman, Glenview, Ill., 1984, pp. 36–59.

29. A. F. Osborn, *Applied Imagination*, Scribner, New York, 1963.

30. Norman R. F. Maier, *Problem-Solving Discussions and Conferences: Leadership Methods and Skills*, McGraw-Hill, New York, 1963.

31. Harvey Gittler, "Decisions Are Only as Good as Those Who Can Change Them," *The Wall Street Journal*, October 7, 1985, p. 22.

32. Ibid.

33. Robert L. Desatnick, "Service: A CEO's Perspective," *Management Review*, October 1987, pp. 41–45.

34. Daniel D. Wheeler and Irving L. Janis, *A Practical Guide for Making Decisions*, Free Press, New York, 1980, pp. 17–36.

35. Giora Keinan, "Decision Making under Stress: Scanning of Alternatives under Controllable and Uncontrollable Threats," *Journal of Personality and Social Psychology*, vol. 52, 1987, pp. 639–644.

36. Paul C. Nutt, "Types of Organizational Decision Processes," *Administrative Science Quarterly*, vol. 29, 1984, pp. 414–450.

37. This section, including the problems, is based on Kevin McKean, "Decisions," *Discover*, June 1985, pp. 22–31.

38. For recent research on prospect theory and the framing effect, see David V. Budescu and Wendy Weiss, "Reflection of Transitive and Intransitive Preferences: A Test of Prospect Theory," *Organizational Behavior and Human Decision Processes*, vol. 39, 1987, pp. 184–202; N. S. Fagley and Paul M. Miller, "The Effects of Decision Framing on Choice of Risky vs. Certain Options," *Organizational Behavior and Human Decision Processes*, vol. 39, 1987, pp. 264–277; Margaret A. Neale, Vandra L. Huber, and Gregory B. Northcraft, "The Framing of Negotiations: Contextual versus Task Frames," *Organizational Behavior and Human Decision Processes*, vol. 39, 1987, pp. 228–241; and Howard Rachlin, *Judgment, Decisions, and Choice*, Freeman, New York, 1989.

39. S. Lichtenstein, P. Slovic, B. Fischhoff, M. Layman, and B. Combs, "Judged Frequency of Lethal Events," *Journal of Experimental Psychology: Human Learning and Memory*, vol. 4, 1978, pp. 551–578.

40. Adapted from Max H. Bazerman, *Judgment in Managerial Decision Making*, Wiley, New York, 1986, p. 28.

41. Ronald N. Taylor, *Behavioral Decision Making*, Scott, Foresman, Glenview, Ill., 1984, p. 141.

42. Max H. Bazerman, *Judgment in Managerial Decision Making*, Wiley, New York, 1986, p. 36.

43. Reprinted from John Merwin, "A Billion in Blunders," *Forbes*, Dec. 1, 1986, p. 111.

44. A. Koriat, S. Lichtenstein, and B. Fischhoff, "Reasons for Confidence," *Journal of Experimental Psychology: Human Learning and Memory*, vol. 6, 1980, pp. 107–118.

45. This example and section rely heavily on work by Max H. Bazerman, *Judgment in Managerial Decision Making*, Wiley, New York, 1986, pp. 67–69.

46. Barry M. Staw and Jerry Ross, "Behavior in Escalation Situations: Antecedents, Prototypes, and Solutions," in L. L. Cummings and Barry M. Staw (eds.), *Research in Organizational Behavior*, JAI, Greenwich, Conn., vol. 9, 1987, pp. 39–78.

47. Max H. Bazerman, *Judgment in Managerial Decision Making*, Wiley, New York, 1986, p. 69. For an alternative view of the reasons for the phenomenon, see Michael G. Bowen, "The Escalation Phenomenon Reconsidered: Decision Dilemmas or Decision Errors?" *Academy of Management Review*, vol. 12, 1987, pp. 52–66.

48. J. Z. Rubin, "Experimental Research on Third Party Intervention in Conflict: Toward Some Generalizations," *Psychological Bulletin*, vol. 87, 1980, pp. 379–391.

49. Adapted from Barry M. Staw and Jerry Ross, "Behavior in Escalation Situations: Antecedents, Prototypes, and Solutions," in L. L. Cummings and Barry M. Staw (eds.), *Research in Organizational Behavior*, JAI, Greenwich, Conn., vol. 9, 1987, pp. 67–68; see also Barry M. Staw and Jerry Ross, "Good Money after Bad," *Psychology Today*, February 1988, pp. 30–33. For an extended treatment, see Jerry Ross and Barry M. Staw, "Expo 86: An Escalation Prototype," *Administrative Science Quarterly*, vol. 31, 1986, pp. 274–297.

50. Elizabeth M. Fowler, "Management Participation by Workers," *The New York Times*, Dec. 27, 1988, p. D6.

51. This section is based largely on George P. Huber, *Managerial Decision Making*, Scott, Foresman, Glenview, Ill., 1980, and Norman R. F. Maier, "Assets and Liabilities in Group Problem Solving: The Need for an Integrative Function," in Michael T. Matteson and John M. Ivancevich (eds.), *Management and Organizational Behavior Classics*, 4th ed., BPI/Irwin, Homewood, Ill., 1989.

52. Larry K. Michaelsen, Warren E. Watson and Robert H. Black, "A Realistic Test of Individual versus Group Consensus Decision Making," *Journal of Applied Psychology*, vol. 74, 1989, pp. 834–839.

53. Irving L. Janis, *Groupthink*, 2d ed., Houghton Mifflin, Boston, 1982.

54. Arie W. Kruglanski, "Freeze-think and the Challenger," *Psychology Today*, August 1986, pp. 48–49.

55. Carrie R. Leana, "A Partial Test of Janis' Groupthink Model: Effects of Group Cohesiveness and Leader Behavior on Defective Decision Making," *Journal of Management*, vol. 11, 1985, pp. 5–17. For alternative explanations of groupthink, see Glen Whyte, "Groupthink Reconsidered," *Academy of Management Review*, vol. 14, 1989, pp. 40–56.

56. Daniel D. Wheeler and Irving L. Janis, *A Practical Guide for Making Decisions*, Free Press, New York, 1980.

57. Charles R. Schwenk and Richard A. Cosier, "Effect of the Expert, Devil's Advocate, and Dialectic Inquiry Methods on Prediction Performance," *Organizational Behavior and Human Performance*, vol. 26, 1980, pp. 409–424; David M. Schweiger and Phyllis A. Finger, "The Comparative Effectiveness of Dialectical Inquiry and Devil's Advocate: The Impact of Task Biases on Previous Research Findings," *Strategic Management Journal*, vol. 5, 1984, pp. 335–350.

58. Max H. Bazerman, *Judgment in Managerial Decision Making*, Wiley, New York, 1986, p. 81.

59. Teresa M. Amabile, *The Social Psychology of Creativity*, Springer-Verlag, New York, 1983, p. 31.

60. Quoted in Alfie Kohn, "Art for Art's Sake," *Psychology Today*, September 1987, p. 54.

61. Gene Bylinsky, "Trying to Transcend Copycat Science," *Fortune*, Mar. 30, 1987, pp. 42–46.

62. This analogy is based on Edward de Bono, *New Think*, Basic Books, New York, 1968; see also Edward de Bono, *Lateral Thinking for Management*, American Management Association, New York, 1971.

63. Reprinted from Diane E. Papalia and Sally Wendkos Olds, *Psychology*, 2d ed., McGraw-Hill, New York, 1988, p. 293.

64. Teresa M. Amabile, *The Social Psychology of Creativity*, Springer-Verlag, New York, 1983, pp. 67–77.

65. J. W. Haefele, *Creativity and Innovation*, Reinhold, New York, 1962; Max H. Bazerman, *Judgment in Managerial Decision Making*, Wiley, New York, 1986, pp. 89–91.

66. Based on "Problems! We've Got to Have Problems!" in P. Ranganath Nayak and John M. Ketteringham, *Breakthroughs*, Rawson Associates, New York, 1986, pp. 151–178.

67. Niles Howard, "Business Probes the Creative Spark," *Dun's Review*, January 1980, pp. 33–34.

68. Emily T. Smith, "Are You Creative?" *Business Week*, Sept. 30, 1985, pp. 80–84.

69. Rick Wartzman, "Aluminum Maker's Big Coup: The Resealable Beverage Can," *The Wall Street Journal*, Oct. 30, 1987, p. 25.

70. Andre L. Delbecq, Andrew H. Van de Ven, and D. H. Gustafson, *Group Techniques for Program Planning*, Scott, Foresman, Glenview, Ill., 1975, pp. 66–69; see also George P. Huber, *Managerial Decision Making*, Scott, Foresman, Glenview, Ill., 1980, pp. 200–205.

71. See W. R. Street, "Brainstorming by Indi-

viduals, Coacting and Interacting Groups,'' *Journal of Applied Psychology*, vol. 59, 1974, pp. 433–436; A. H. Van de Ven and A. L. Delbecq, ''The Effectiveness of Nominal, Delphi, and Interacting Group Processes,'' *Academy of Management Journal*, vol. 17, 1974, pp. 605–621; and T. B. Green, ''An Empirical Analysis of Nominal and Interacting Groups,'' *Academy of Management Journal*, vol. 18, 1975, pp. 63–73.

72. Niles Howard, ''Business Probes the Creative Spark,'' *Dun's Review*, January 1980, pp. 32–36; Ronald N. Taylor, *Behavioral Decision Making*, Scott, Foresman, Glenview, Ill., 1984, pp. 47–48.

73. Niles Howard, ''Business Probes the Creative Spark,'' *Dun's Review*, January 1980, pp. 32–36.

74. Emily T. Smith, ''Are You Creative?'' *Business Week*, Sept. 30, 1985, pp. 80–84.

75. Adapted from Laurie Hays, ''Book Maps USA Today's Costly Road,'' *The Wall Street Journal*, July 14, 1987, p. 6.

76. Paul Farhi, ''USA Today: Looking Ahead to Tomorrow,'' *The Washington Post*, August 29, 1988, Washington Business section, pp. 1, 22.

CHAPTER 9

1. Based on Thomas J. Holloran and Judson E. Byrn, ''United Airlines Station Manpower Planning System,'' *Interfaces*, January–February 1986, pp. 39–50; and Kenneth Labich, ''Winners in the Air Wars,'' *Fortune*, May 11, 1987, pp. 68–79.

2. Hans Levenbach and James P. Cleary, *The Modern Forecaster: The Forecasting Process through Data Analysis*, Lifetime Learning, Belmont, Calif., 1984, p. 3.

3. J. T. Mentzer and J. E. Cox, ''Familiarity, Application and Performance of Sales Forecasting Techniques,'' *Journal of Forecasting*, vol. 3, 1984, pp. 27–36.

4. This section relies heavily on Steven C. Wheelwright and Spyros Makridakis, *Forecasting Methods for Management*, Wiley, New York, 1985.

5. Jeffrey Trachtenberg, ''Firms Seek to Ring in New Customers,'' *The Wall Street Journal*, Mar. 23, 1989, p. B1.

6. Cynthia Green and Ellen Farley, ''Coke's Man on the Spot,'' *Business Week*, July 29, 1985, pp. 56–61; Betsy Morris, ''Coke and Pepsi Step Up Bitter Price War,'' *The Wall Street Journal*, Oct. 10, 1988, p. B1.

7. Charles A. Gallagher and Hugh J. Watson, *Quantitative Methods for Business Decisions*, McGraw-Hill, New York, 1980, p. 116.

8. John Merwin, ''A Billion in Blunders,'' *Forbes*, Dec. 1, 1986, p. 104.

9. This example is based on Charles A. Gallagher and Hugh J. Watson, *Quantitative Methods for Business Decisions*, McGraw-Hill, New York, pp. 131–135.

10. Peter Finch and Marc Frons, ''Gurus Who Called the Crash—Or Fell on Their Faces,'' *Business Week*, Nov. 30, 1985, pp. 124–125.

11. Dexter Hutchins, ''And Now, the Home-Brewed Forecast,'' *Fortune*, Jan. 20, 1986, pp. 53–54.

12. Susan Caminiti, ''A Quiet Superstar Rises in Retailing,'' *Fortune*, Oct. 23, 1989, pp. 167–174.

13. George P. Huger, *Managerial Decision Making*, Scott, Foresman, Glenview, Ill., 1980, p. 206.

14. John F. Preble, ''The Selection of Delphi Panels for Strategic Planning Purposes,'' *Strategic Management Journal*, vol. 5, 1984, pp. 157–170.

15. Ibid.

16. Ted G. Eschenbach and George A. Geistauts, ''A Delphi Forecast for Alaska,'' *Interfaces*, November–December 1985, pp. 100–109.

17. Other examples can be found in George P. Huber, *Managerial Decision Making*, Scott, Foresman, Glenview, Ill., 1980, pp. 206–209; and Steven C. Wheelwright and Spyros Makridakis, *Forecasting Methods for Management*, Wiley, New York, 1985, pp. 289–290.

18. V. D. Garde and R. R. Patel, ''Technological Forecasting for Power Generation—A Study Using the Delphi Technique,'' *Long Range Planning*, August 1985, pp. 73–79.

19. This example is taken from William C. Miller, *The Creative Edge: Fostering Innovation Where You Work*, Addison-Wesley, Reading, Mass., 1987, pp. 68–69.

20. Steven C. Wheelwright and Spyros Makridakis, *Forecasting Methods for Management*, Wiley, New York, 1985, p. 286.

21. M. Godet, ''From Forecasting to 'La Prospective': A New Way of Looking at Futures,'' *Journal of Forecasting*, vol. 1, 1982, pp. 293–301.

22. Steven C. Wheelwright and Spyros Makridakis, *Forecasting Methods for Management*, Wiley, New York, 1985, pp. 311–366.

23. For a recent review of forecasting literature, as well as commentary by several forecasting experts, see J. Scott Armstrong, ''The Ombudsman: Research on Forecasting: A Quarter-Century Review, 1960–1984,'' *Interfaces*, January–February 1986, pp. 89–109.

24. See, for example, Mike Hack, ''Harvard Project Manager Serves Pros, Casual Users,'' *InfoWorld*, Jan. 30, 1989, pp. 54–55.

25. John O. McClain and L. Joseph Thomas, *Operations Management: Production of Goods and Services*, Prentice-Hall, Englewood Cliffs, N.J., 1985, pp. 50–51.

26. Edward A. Wasil and Arjang A. Assad, ''Project Management on the PC: Software, Applications, and Trends,'' *Interfaces*, March–April 1988, pp. 75–84.

27. K. Roscoe Davis and Patrick G. McKeown, *Quantitative Models for Management*, 2d ed., Kent, Boston, 1984, pp. 242–243.

28. These steps and the following material on PERT are based heavily on Everett E. Adam, Jr., and Ronald J. Ebert, *Production and Operations Management*, 3d ed., Prentice-Hall, Englewood Cliffs, N.J., 1986, pp. 533–538.

29. For a recent review of software packages that include Gantt charts and PERT, see Edward A. Wasil and Arjang A. Assad, ''Project Management on the PC: Software, Applications, and Trends,'' *Interfaces*, March–April 1988, pp. 75–84.

30. William E. Pinney and Donald B. McWilliams, *Management Science: An Introduction to Quantitative Analysis for Management*, Harper & Row, New York, 1982, p. 95.

31. K. Roscoe Davis and Patrick G. McKeown, *Quantitative Models for Management*, 2d ed., Kent, Boston, 1984, pp. 24–25.

32. This problem is based on Elwood S. Buffa, *Modern Production/Operations Management*, 7th ed., Wiley, New York, 1983, pp. 560–564.

33. H. Stephen Leff, Maqbool Dada, and Stephen C. Graves, ''An LP Planning Model for a Mental Health Community Support System,'' *Management Science*, vol. 32, 1986, pp. 139–155; Darwin Klingman, John Mote, and Nancy V. Phillips, ''A Logistics Planning System at W. R. Grace,'' *Operations Research*, vol. 36, 1988, pp. 811–822; Jeph Abara, ''Applying Integer Linear Programming to the Fleet Assignment Problem,'' *Interfaces*, July–August 1989, pp. 20–28.

34. This example is based on K. Roscoe Davis and Patrick G. McKeown, *Quantitative Models for Management*, 2d ed., Kent, Boston, 1984, pp. 592–610.

35. For further information regarding the specific queuing models used to develop these data, see ibid., pp. 607–610.

36. Everett E. Adam, Jr., and Ronald J. Ebert, *Production and Operations Management: Concepts, Models, and Behavior*, 3d ed., Prentice-Hall, Englewood Cliffs, N.J., 1986.

37. William E. Pinney and Donald B. McWil-

38. John O. McClain and L. Joseph Thomas, *Operations Management: Production of Goods and Services*, 2d ed., Prentice-Hall, Englewood Cliffs, N.J., 1985.

39. For recent advances in this area, see Bruce L. Golden and Arjang Assad (eds.), *Vehicle Routing: Methods and Studies*, North-Holland, Amsterdam, 1988.

40. Bruce L. Golden and Edward A. Wasil, ''Computerized Vehicle Routing in the Soft Drink Industry,'' *Operations Research*, vol. 35, 1987, pp. 6–17.

41. Richard C. Larson and Thomas F. Rich, ''Travel-Time Analysis of New York City Police Patrol Cars,'' *Interfaces*, March–April 1987, pp. 15–20; Lucius J. Riccio, Joseph Miller, and Ann Litko, ''Polishing the Big Apple: How Management Science Has Helped Make New York Streets Cleaner,'' *Interfaces*, January–February 1986, pp. 83–88.

42. William E. Pinney and Donald B. McWilliams, *Management Science: An Introduction to Quantitative Analysis for Management*, Harper & Row, New York, 1982, pp. 460–461.

43. K. Roscoe Davis and Patrick G. McKeown, *Quantitative Models for Management*, 2d ed., Kent, Boston, 1984, p. 625.

44. William E. Pinney and Donald B. McWilliams, *Management Science: An Introduction to Quantitative Analysis for Management*, Harper & Row, New York, 1982, pp. 460–461.

45. Adapted from Norma Welch and James Gussow, ''Expansion of Canadian National Railway's Line Capacity,'' *Interfaces*, January–February 1986, pp. 51–64; see also John F. Burns, ''Trains to Be Cut in Canada,'' *The New York Times*, Oct. 5, 1989, pp. D1, D2.

46. Toni Mack, ''Let the Computer Do It,'' *Forbes*, Aug. 10, 1987, p. 84.

47. Hung-Po Chao, Stephen W. Chapel, Charles E. Clark, Jr., Peter A. Morris, M. James Sandling, and Richard C. Grimes, ''EPRI Reduces Fuel Inventory Costs in the Electric Utility Industry,'' *Interfaces*, January–February 1989, pp. 48–67.

48. George P. Huber, *Managerial Decision Making*, Scott, Foresman, Glenview, Ill., 1980, p. 91.

49. The example is based on E. Frank Harrison, *The Managerial Decision-Making Process*, 2d ed., Houghton Mifflin, Boston, 1981, p. 279.

50. For several different definitions of probability, see William E. Pinney and Donald B. McWilliams, *Management Science: An Introduction to Quantitative Analysis for Management*, Harper & Row, New York, 1982, pp. 48–49.

51. E. Frank Harrison, *The Managerial Decision-Making Process*, 2d ed., Houghton Mifflin, Boston, 1981, p. 280.

52. George P. Huber, *Managerial Decision Making*, Scott, Foresman, Glenview, Ill., 1980, p. 90; Dennis H. Ferguson and Thomas I. Selling, ''Probability Analysis: A System for Making Better Decisions,'' *The Cornell H.R.A. Quarterly*, August 1985, pp. 35–42.

53. F. Hutton Barron, ''Payoff Matrices Pay Off at Hallmark,'' *Interfaces*, July–August 1985, pp. 20–25.

54. Jacob W. Ulvila, ''Postal Automation (ZIP + 4) Technology: A Decision Analysis,'' *Interfaces*, March–April 1987, pp. 1–12.

55. Everett E. Adam, Jr., and Ronald J. Ebert, *Production and Operations Management*, 3d ed., Prentice-Hall, Englewood Cliffs, N.J., 1986.

56. See Jerry A. Viscione and Gordon S. Roberts, *Contemporary Financial Management*, Merrill, Columbus, Ohio, 1987, for a mathematical treatment of break-even analysis.

57. Lynn Adkins, ''Such a Grand Design,'' *Business Month*, December 1987, p. 31.

58. Deborah C. Wise and Geoff Lewis, ''Apple, Part 2: The No-Nonsense Era of John Sculley,'' *Business Week*, Jan. 27, 1986, pp. 96–98.

59. See, for example, Thomas L. Powers, "Breakeven Analysis with Semifixed Costs," *Industrial Marketing Management*, vol. 16, 1987, pp. 35–41.
60. See E. Frank Harrison, *The Managerial Decision-Making Process*, 2d ed., Houghton Mifflin, Boston, 1980, p. 286.
61. "Futurist Laural Cutler," *INC.*, November 1987, pp. 48–49.
62. Charles A. Gallagher and Hugh J. Watson, *Quantitative Methods for Business Decisions*, McGraw-Hill, New York, 1980, pp. 101–102.
63. For a recent application of game theory, see M. Edward Goretsky, "When to Bid for Government Contracts," *Industrial Marketing Management*, vol. 16, 1987, pp. 25–33.
64. Peter G. W. Keen, "'Interactive' Computer Systems for Managers: A Modest Proposal," *Sloan Management Review*, Fall 1976, pp. 1–18; Gordon B. Davis and Margrethe H. Olson, *Management Information Systems: Conceptual Foundations, Structure, and Development*, 2d ed., McGraw-Hill, New York, 1985, p. 368.
65. Gordon B. Davis and Margrethe H. Olson, *Management Information Systems: Conceptual Foundations, Structure, and Development*, 2d ed., McGraw-Hill, New York, 1985, p. 375.
66. "Expert Systems: Taking the Plunge," *Electronic Business*, Feb. 1, 1986, p. 78; Kenneth Fordyce, Peter Norden, and Gerald Sullivan, "Review of Expert Systems for the Management Science Practitioner," *Interfaces*, March–April 1987, p. 74.
67. Peter H. Stone, "Insurers Making Computers a Matter of Policy," *The Washington Post*, Dec. 6, 1987, p. H8.
68. This exercise is adapted from Elwood S. Buffa, *Modern Prouction/Operations Management*, 7th ed., Wiley, New York, pp. 423–429.
69. Adapted from Darwin Klingman, Nancy Phillips, David Steiger, and Warren Young, "The Successful Deployment of Management Science throughout Citgo Petroleum Corporation," *Interfaces*, January–February 1987, pp. 4–25.
70. Karen Blumenthal, "Southland Mulls Sale of Citgo to Venezuela," *The Wall Street Journal*, Nov. 7, 1989, p. A4; Steven Mufson, "Southland Struggling under Debt," *The Washington Post*, Nov. 15, 1989, p. F1.

Sources for Part Ending Case for Part 2: Based on Peter F. Drucker, *Management: Tasks, Responsibilities, Practices*, Harper & Row, New York, 1974; Michael Barrier, "Changing Gears at Sears," *Nation's Business*, August 1985, pp. 31–35; Edward R. Telling, "How Sears Restructured for Growth in Financial Services," *Management Review*, May 1986, pp. 31–40; Brian McGinty, "Mr. Sears & Mr. Roebuck," *American History Illustrated*, vol. 21, 1986, pp. 34–49; *Sears Yesterday & Today*, Sears, Roebuck and Co., Chicago, 1986; Steven Weiner, "They Buy Their Stocks Where They Buy Their Socks," *Forbes*, Mar. 7, 1988, pp. 60–67; Rick Gallagher, "Sears Strategy: Pursue Specialty Formats," *Chain Store Age Executive*, April 1988, pp. 17–20; David Snyder, "Last Chapter for Big Catalog?" *Advertising Age*, July 18, 1988, p. 26; Jay L. Johnson, "Sears Succumbs to National Brands," *Discount Merchandiser*, November 1988, pp. 44–46; Andrea Stone, "Retailer Goes Back to Basics," *USA Today*, Nov. 1, 1988, pp. B1, B2; Francine Schwadel, "Its Expansion Lagging, Sears Now Struggles to Stay Independent," *The Wall Street Journal*, Nov. 2, 1988, pp. A1, A8; "Shielding Sears from Would-Be Raiders," *The New York Times*, Nov. 6, 1988, p. 11; Kate Fitzgerald, "Financial Network a Bad Fit at the Big Store," *Advertising Age*, Nov. 14, 1988, pp. S1–S6; Steve Weiner, "Don't Write Sears Off," *Forbes*, Nov. 28, 1988, p. 27; Michael Oneal, "Sears Faces a Tall Task," *Business Week*, Nov. 14, 1988, pp. 54–55; Patricia Sellers, "Why Bigger Is Badder at Sears," *Fortune*, Dec. 5, 1988, pp. 79–84; B. H. Lawrence, "Sears' Discounting Gamble," *The Washington Post*, Mar. 26, 1989, pp. H1, H6; "Now Sears Has Everyday Low Profits, Too," *Business Week*, Aug. 21, 1989, p. 28; Martha T. Moore, "Slow Start for Pricing Strategy," *USA Today*, Sept. 7, 1989, pp. 1B, 2B; Francine Schwadel, "Sears Expects Only Modest Sales Gains," *The Wall Street Journal*, Nov. 3, 1989, p. 4B; Neil Barsky, "Sears Roebuck to Mortgage Headquarters," *The Wall Street Journal*, Nov. 16, 1989, p. A4; John Waggoner, "Sears Crows Over Card's Success," *USA Today*, Jan. 29, 1990, pp. 1B, 2B; 1989 Annual Report, Sears, Roebuck and Co., Chicago, pp. 4–7; and Steve Weiner, "It's Not Over until It's Over," *Forbes*, May 28, 1990, pp. 58–64.

CHAPTER 10

1. "A New Strategy for No. 2 in Computers," *Business Week*, May 2, 1983, pp. 66–75; Peter Petre, "America's Most Successful Entrepreneur," *Fortune*, Oct. 27, 1986, pp. 24–32; William M. Bulkeley, "A 'Tekkie' on the Inside Track at Digital," *The Wall Street Journal*, Sept. 1, 1987, p. 36; John R. Wilke, "At Digital Equipment, Slowdown Reflects Industry's Big Changes," *The Wall Street Journal*, Sept. 15, 1989, pp. A1, A5; conversation with Jeff Gibson of Digital Equipment Corporation.
2. John Child, *Organization: A Guide to Problems and Practice*, Harper & Row, New York, 1977, p. 10.
3. Alfred D. Chandler, Jr., "Origins of the Organization Chart," *Harvard Business Review*, March–April 1988, pp. 156–157.
4. W. Jack Duncan, *Great Ideas in Management*, Jossey-Bass, San Francisco, 1989.
5. George T. Milkovich and William F. Glueck, *Personnel/Human Resource Management: A Diagnostic Approach*, 4th ed., Business Publications, Plano, Tex., 1985.
6. Adam Smith, *The Wealth of Nations*, Dent, London, 1910.
7. J. Richard Hackman and Greg R. Oldham, *Work Redesign*, Addison-Wesley, Reading, Mass., 1980.
8. Robert H. Waterman, Jr., "The Power of Teamwork," *Best of Business Quarterly*, Spring, 1988, pp. 17–25.
9. Dyan Machan, "DEC's Democracy," *Forbes*, Mar. 23, 1987, pp. 154–156.
10. Beverly L. Kaye, *Up Is Not the Only Way: A Guide for Career Development Practitioners*, Prentice Hall, Englewood Cliffs, N.J., 1982.
11. M. D. Kilbridge, "Reduced Costs through Job Enrichment: A Case," *Journal of Business*, vol. 33, 1960, pp. 357–362.
12. Frederick Herzberg, *Work and the Nature of Man*, World Publishing, Cleveland, 1966, and "One More Time: How Do You Motivate Employees?" *Harvard Business Review*, January–February 1968, pp. 53–62.
13. James M. Odato, "U.S. Shoe Revamps," *USA Today*, Mar. 24, 1988, p. 8B.
14. J. Richard Hackman and Greg R. Oldham, *Work Redesign*, Addison-Wesley, Reading, Mass., 1980.
15. See, for example, Brian T. Lohner, Raymond A. Noe, Nancy L. Moeller, and Michael P. Fitzgerald, "A Meta-Analysis of the Relation of Job Characteristics to Job Satisfaction," *Journal of Applied Psychology*, vol. 70, 1985, pp. 280–289.
16. F. K. Plous, Jr., "Focus on Innovation: Chicago Bank Eliminates Paperwork Assembly Line," *World of Work Report*, November 1986, pp. 1–2.
17. For a recent, more complex model, see Ricky W. Griffin, "Toward an Integrated Theory of Task Design," *Research in Organizational Behavior*, vol. 9, 1986, pp. 79–120.
18. G. Salancik and J. Pfeffer, "A Social Information Processing Approach to Job Attitudes and Task Design," *Administrative Science Quarterly*, vol. 22, 1977, pp. 427–456.
19. Ricky W. Griffin, "Toward an Integrated Theory of Task Design," *Research in Organizational Behavior*, vol. 9, 1987, pp. 79–120.
20. R. T. Golembiewski and C. W. Proehl, "A Survey of the Empirical Literature on Flexible Workhours: Character and Consequences of a Major Innovation," *Academy of Management Review*, vol. 3, 1978, pp. 837–853; Simcha Ronen and Sophia B. Primps, "The Compressed Work Week as Organizational Change: Behavioral and Attitudinal Outcomes," *Academy of Management Review*, vol. 6, 1981, pp. 61–74; Simcha Ronen, *Flexible Working Hours: An Innovation in the Quality of Work Life*, McGraw-Hill, New York, 1981; Edward G. Thomas, "Workers Who Set Their Own Time Clocks," *Business & Society Review*, Spring 1987, pp. 49–51.
21. "Why a Big Steelmaker Is Mimicking the Minimills," *Business Week*, Mar. 27, 1989, p. 92.
22. J. M. Ivancevich and H. L. Lyon, "The Shortened Workweek: A Field Experiment," *Journal of Applied Psychology*, vol. 62, 1977, pp. 34–37.
23. Edward G. Thomas, "Flextime Doubles in a Decade," *Management World*, April–May 1987, pp. 18–19.
24. John Child, *Organization: A Guide to Problems and Practice*, Harper & Row, London, 1984.
25. Henry Mintzberg, *The Structuring of Organizations*, Prentice-Hall, Englewood Cliffs, N.J., 1979.
26. This section is based largely on Robert Duncan, "What Is the Right Organization Structure? Decision Tree Analysis Provides the Answer," *Organizational Dynamics*, Winter 1979, pp. 59–80; and Daniel Robey, *Designing Organizations*, Irwin, Homewood, Ill., 1986, pp. 210–213.
27. Richard L. Daft, *Organization Theory and Design*, 3d ed., West, St. Paul, Minn., 1989; John Child, *Organization: A Guide to Problems and Practice*, Harper & Row, London, 1984.
28. Richard H. Hall, *Structures, Processes, and Outcomes*, Prentice-Hall, Englewood Cliffs, N.J., 1987; John Child, *Organization: A Guide to Problems and Practice*, Harper & Row, London, 1984.
29. Jay Galbraith, *Organization Design*, Addison-Wesley, Reading, Mass., 1977, p. 43.
30. James W. Frederickson, "The Strategic Decision Process and Organizational Structure," *Academy of Management Review*, vol. 11, 1986, pp. 280–297; Alfred A. Marcus, "Responses to Externally Induced Innovation: Their Effects on Organizational Performance," *Strategic Management Journal*, vol. 9, 1988, pp. 387–402.
31. Rosabeth Moss Kanter, "When a Thousand Flowers Bloom: Structural, Collective, and Social Conditions for Innovation in Organizations," *Research in Organizational Behavior*, vol. 10, 1988, pp. 169–211.
32. Buck Brown, "James Bildner's Spectacular Rise and Fall," *The Wall Street Journal*, Oct. 24, 1988, p. B1.
33. Eric Morgenthaler, "Herb Tea's Pioneer: From Hippie Origins to $16 Million a Year," *The Wall Street Journal*, May 6, 1981, p. 1; Nora Gallagher, "'We're More Aggressive Than Our Tea,'" *Across the Board*, July–August, 1983, pp. 45–50; Janet Neiman and Jennifer Pendleton, "Celestial Fits Kraft to a Tea," *Advertising Age*, Mar. 26, 1984, p. 73; Sandra D. Atchinson, "An Herbal Tea Party Gets a Bitter Response," *Business Week*, June 20, 1988, p. 52, and "Kraft Is Celestial Seasonings' Cup of Tea," *Business Week*, July 28, 1986; John Birmingham, "Strange Brew," *Adweeks' Marketing Week*, Nov. 21, 1988, pp. 18–22; Robert Ebisch, "Celestial after the LBO," *Business Plus/Daily Camera* (Denver, Colo.), July 4, 1989, pp. 1, 8–9.
34. John Child, *Organization: A Guide to Problems and Practice*, Harper & Row, London, 1984.

35. David D. Van Fleet and Arthur G. Bedeian, "The History of the Span of Management," *Academy of Management Review*, vol. 2, 1977, pp. 356–372.

36. Dan R. Dalton, William D. Todor, Michael J. Spendolini, Gordon J. Fielding, and Lyman W. Porter, "Organization Structure and Performance: A Critical Review," *Academy of Management Review*, vol. 5, 1980, pp. 49–64; Robert D. Dewar and Donald P. Simet, "A Level Specific Prediction of Spans of Control Examining the Effects of Size, Technology, and Specialization," *Academy of Management Journal*, vol. 24, 1981, pp. 5–24; David D. Van Fleet, "Span of Management Research and Issues," *Academy of Management Journal*, vol. 26, 1983, pp. 546–552.

37. C. W. Barkdull, "Span of Control: A Method of Evaluation," *Michigan Business Review*, vol. 15, 1963, pp. 25–32; John Child, *Organization: A Guide to Problems and Practice*, Harper & Row, London, 1984, pp. 58–59; David D. Van Fleet, "Span of Management Research and Issues," *Academy of Management Journal*, vol. 26, 1983, pp. 546–552.

38. This example is based on Stephen P. Robbins, *Organization Theory: Structure, Design, and Applications*, 3d ed., Prentice-Hall, Englewood Cliffs, N.J., 1990.

39. John Child, *Organization: A Guide to Problems and Practice*, Harper & Row, London, 1984, p. 53.

40. W. Norman Smallwood and Eliot Jacobsen, "Is There Life after Downsizing?" *Personnel*, December 1987, pp. 42–46; George Bailey and Julia Szerdy, "Is There Life after Downsizing?" *The Journal of Business Strategy*, January–February 1988, pp. 8–11.

41. Norman R. Horton, "Restructurings and Dismemberments," *Management Review*, March 1988, pp. 5–6; George Bailey and David Sherman, "Downsizing: The Alternatives May Be Cheaper," *Management Review*, April 1988, pp. 54–55.

42. Phil Nienstedt and Richard Wintermantel, "Motorola Restructures to Improve Productivity," *Management Review*, January 1987, p. 47 (reprinted from *Personnel*, August 1985).

43. Joseph B. White, "Toyota Wants More Managers Out on the Line," *The Wall Street Journal*, Aug. 2, 1989, p. A10; Yumiko Ono and Marcus W. Brauchli, "Japan Cuts the Middle-Management Fat," *The Wall Street Journal*, Aug. 8, 1989, p. B1.

44. George Bailey and David Sherman, "Downsizing: The Alternatives May Be Cheaper," *Management Review*, April 1988, pp. 54–55; Robert M. Tomasko, "Planned Downsizing: A Sustainable Alternative," *Management Review*, April 1988, pp. 55–58; Philip R. Nienstedt, "Effectively Downsizing Management Structures," *Human Resource Planning*, vol. 12, 1989, pp. 155–156.

45. Mark Maremont, "Waterford Is Showing a Few Cracks," *Business Week*, Feb. 20, 1989, pp. 60–61.

46. Richard H. Hall, *Organizations: Structures, Processes, and Outcomes*, 4th ed., Prentice-Hall, Englewood Cliffs, N.J., 1987, p. 88.

47. Thomas J. Peters and Robert H. Waterman, Jr., *In Search of Excellence: Lessons from America's Best-Run Companies*, Harper & Row, New York, 1982, pp. 112, 212.

48. Howard M. Carlisle, "A Contingency Approach to Decentralization," *Advanced Management Journal*, July 1974, pp. 9–18.

49. Ibid.

50. John Child, *Organization: A Guide to Problems and Practice*, Harper & Row, London, 1984.

51. Dyan Machan, "DEC's Democracy," *Forbes*, Mar. 23, 1987, pp. 154–156.

52. John Child, *Organization: A Guide to Problems and Practice*, Harper & Row, London, 1984.

53. W. Jack Duncan, *Great Ideas in Management*, Jossey-Bass, San Francisco, 1989.

54. For an interesting treatment of lessons to be learned about delegation from U.S. presidents, see Edward J. Mayo and Lance P. Jarvis, "Delegation 101: Lessons from the White House," *Business Horizons*, September–October 1988, pp. 2–12.

55. Carrie R. Leana, "Predictors and Consequences of Delegation," *Academy of Management Journal*, vol. 29, 1986, pp. 754–774.

56. Rosabeth Moss Kanter and Barry A. Stein, "Unloading Overload," *Management Review*, November 1987, pp. 22–23.

57. Morgan W. McCall, Jr., and Michael M. Lombardo, "What Makes a Top Executive?" *Psychology Today*, February 1983, pp. 26–31.

58. Adapted from Laurie Baum, "Delegating Your Way to Job Survival," *Business Week*, Nov. 2, 1987, p. 206.

59. Vivian Nossiter, "A New Approach toward Resolving the Line and Staff Dilemma," *Academy of Management Review*, vol. 4, 1979, pp. 103–106.

60. "The Shrinking of Middle Management," *Business Week*, Apr. 25, 1983, pp. 53–54.

61. B. J. Hodge and William P. Anthony, *Organization Theory*, 3d ed., Allyn and Bacon, Boston, 1988.

62. Edward C. Schleh, "Using Central Staff to Boost Line Initiative," *Management Review*, May 1976, pp. 17–23.

63. Thomas Moore, "Goodbye, Corporate Staff," *Fortune*, Dec. 21, 1987, pp. 65–76.

64. Jay R. Galbraith, *Organization Design*, Addison-Wesley, Reading, Mass., 1977.

65. Lucien Rodes, "At the Crossroads," *INC.*, February 1988, pp. 66–76.

66. Michael Tushman and David Nadler, "Organizing for Innovation," *California Management Review*, vol. 28, 1986, pp. 74–92; Andrew H. Van de Ven, "Central Problems in the Management of Innovation," *Management Science*, vol. 32, 1966, pp. 590–607; Rosabeth Moss Kanter, "When a Thousand Flowers Bloom: Structural, Collective, and Social Conditions for Innovation in Organizations," *Research in Organizational Behavior*, vol. 10, 1988, pp. 169–211.

67. Rosabeth Moss Kanter, "When a Thousand Flowers Bloom: Structural, Collective, and Social Conditions for Innovation in Organizations," *Research in Organizational Behavior*, vol. 10, 1988, pp. 169–211.

68. This section relies heavily on Jay R. Galbraith, *Organization Design*, Addison-Wesley, Reading, Mass., 1977.

69. L. J. Bourgeois, "On the Measurement of Organizational Slack," *Academy of Management Review*, vol. 6, 1981, pp. 29–39.

70. Ibid.

71. Thomas J. Peters and Robert H. Waterman, Jr., *In Search of Excellence: Lessons from America's Best-Run Companies*, Harper & Row, New York, 1982.

72. Henry C. Mishkoff, "The Network Nation Emerges," *Management Review*, August 1986, pp. 29–31.

73. The material in this section is largely based on Jay R. Galbraith, *Organization Design*, Addison-Wesley, Reading, Mass., 1977.

74. Elizabeth V. Reynolds and J. David Johnson, "Liaison Emergence: Relating Theoretical Perspectives," *Academy of Management Review*, vol. 7, 1982, pp. 551–559.

75. Jerry Flint with William Heuslein, "An Urge to Service," *Forbes*, Sept. 18, 1989, pp. 172–176.

76. Ibid.

77. David E. Whiteside, "Roger Smith's Campaign to Change the GM Culture," *Business Week*, Apr. 7, 1986, pp. 85–85.

78. John R. Adams and Nicki S. Kirchof, "The Practice of Matrix Management," in David I. Cleland (ed.), *Matrix Management Systems Handbook*, Van Nostrand Reinhold, New York, 1984, p. 21.

79. Ralph Katz and Thomas J. Allen, "Project Performance and the Locus of Influence in the R&D Matrix," *Academy of Management Journal*, vol. 28, 1985, pp. 67–87; see also Robert J. Might and William A. Fischer, "The Role of Structural Factors in Determining Project Management Success," *IEEE Transactions on Engineering Management*, May 1985, pp. 71–77.

80. Tom Nicholson, James C. Jones, and Erik Ipsen, "GM Plans a Great Divide," *Newsweek*, Jan. 9, 1984, pp. 68–69; Urban C. Lehner and Robert L. Simpson, "GM Unveils Plan for Realigning Auto Making," *The Wall Street Journal*, Jan. 11, 1984, p. 3; Michael Brody, "Can GM Manage It All?" *Fortune*, July 8, 1985, pp. 22–28; David E. Whiteside, "Roger Smith's Campaign to Change the GM Culture," *Business Week*, Apr. 7, 1986, pp. 84–85; Todd Mason, Russell Mitchell, William J. Hampton, Marc Frons, "Ross Perot's Crusade," *Business Week*, Oct. 6, 1986, pp. 60–65; David Maraniss, "Silence Can Be Golden for Perot," *The Washington Post*, Dec. 2, 1986, p. C1; Roger Smith, "The U.S. Must Do as GM Has Done,'" *Fortune*, Feb. 13, 1989, pp. 70–73; Paul Ingrassia and Jacob M. Schlesinger, "GM's Market Share Declined Last Year Even as Net Set a Mark," *The Wall Street Journal*, Feb. 15, 1989, pp. A1, A7; Jerry Flint, "'1990 Will Be the Year of the General,'" *Forbes*, Nov. 27, 1989, pp. 40–41; Warren Brown, "If You Were at the Helm of GM," *The Washington Post*, Jan. 14, 1990, pp. H1, H4; Paul Ingrassia, "GM Is to Name Stempel Today Chairman, Chief," *The Wall Street Journal*, Apr. 3, 1990, p. A3.

CHAPTER 11

1. Based on materials in P. Ranganath Nayak and John M. Ketteringham, *Break-Throughs*, Rawson Associates, New York, 1986; Alicia Johnson, "3M Organized to Innovate," *Management Review*, July 1986, pp. 38–39; Christopher Knowlton, "Keeping the Fires Lit under the Innovators," *Fortune*, Mar. 28, 1988, p. 45; Russell Mitchell, "Mining the Work Force for Ideas," *Business Week*, Innovation 1989 issue, June 16, 1989, p. 121.

2. Alfred D. Chandler, *Strategy and Structure*, M.I.T., Cambridge, Mass., 1962.

3. James W. Frederickson, "The Strategic Decision Process and Organizational Structure," *Academy of Management Review*, vol. 11, 1986, pp. 280–297.

4. Alex Taylor III, "The U.S. Gets Back in Fighting Shape," *Fortune*, Apr. 24, 1989, pp. 42–48.

5. David Nadler and Michael Tushman, *Strategic Organization Design*, Scott, Foresman, Glenview, Ill., 1988.

6. This section is based largely on Robert Duncan, "What Is the Right Organization Structure? Decision Tree Analysis Provides the Answer," *Organizational Dynamics*, Winter 1979, pp. 59–80; and Daniel Robey, *Designing Organizations*, Irwin, Homewood, Ill., 1986, pp. 210–213.

7. Daniel Robey, *Designing Organizations*, Irwin, Homewood, Ill., 1986.

8. John Child, *Organization: A Guide to Problems and Practice*, Harper & Row, Publishers, London, 1984.

9. Andrew Albert, "Citicorp Shuffles Units to Emphasize Management of Institutional Assets," *American Banker*, July 5, 1985, p. 1.

10. Robert Duncan, "What Is the Right Organization Structure? Decision Tree Analysis Provides the Answer," *Organizational Dynamics*, Winter 1979, pp. 59–80; Daniel Robey, *Designing Organizations*, Irwin, Homewood, Ill., 1986, pp. 219–222.

11. This section relies heavily on Richard L. Daft, *Organization Theory and Design*, 3d ed., West, St. Paul, Minn., 1989, and Daniel Robey, *Designing Organizations*, Irwin, Homewood, Ill., 1986, pp. 219–222.

12. This discussion relies heavily on

Stanley M. Davis and Paul R. Lawrence, *Matrix*, Addison-Wesley, Reading, Mass., 1977.
13. William Jerkovsky, "Functional Management in Matrix Organizations," *IEEE Transactions on Engineering Management*, May 1983, pp. 89–97.
14. Jay R. Galbraith and Robert K. Kazanjian, *Strategy Implementation*, 2d ed., West, St. Paul, Minn., 1986.
15. William C. Goggins, "How the Multidimensional Structure Works at Dow Corning," *Harvard Business Review*, January–February 1974.
16. The following sections rely on Stanley M. Davis and Paul R. Lawrence, *Matrix*, Addison-Wesley, Reading, Mass., 1977, pp. 129–154; John R. Adams and Nicki S. Kirchof, "The Practice of Matrix Management," in David I. Cleland (ed.), *Matrix Management Systems Handbook*, Van Nostrand Reinhold, New York, 1984, pp. 13–30; and Harold Kerzner, "Matrix Implementation: Obstacles, Problems, Questions, and Answers," in ibid.
17. Ann M. Morrison, "The General Mills Brand of Managers," *Fortune*, Jan. 12, 1981, pp. 99–107; Julie B. Solomon and John Bussey, "Pressed by Its Rivals, Procter & Gamble Co. Is Altering Its Ways," *The Wall Street Journal*, May 20, 1985, pp. 1, 22; Faye Rice, "The King of Suds Reigns Again," *Fortune*, Aug. 4, 1986, pp. 130–134; John Smale, "Behind the Brands at P&G," *Harvard Business Review*, November–December 1985, pp. 79–89.
18. "An About-Face in TI's Culture," *Business Week*, July 5, 1982, p. 77.
19. Stanley M. Davis and Paul R. Lawrence, *Matrix*, Addison-Wesley, Reading, Mass., 1977, pp. 11–20.
20. William F. Joyce, "Matrix Organization: A Social Experiment," *Academy of Management Journal*, vol. 29, 1986, pp. 536–561.
21. Harvey F. Kolodny, "Evolution to a Matrix Organization," *Academy of Management Review*, vol. 4, 1979, pp. 543–553, and "Managing in a Matrix," *Business Horizons*, March–April, 1981, pp. 17–24.
22. Louis W. Fry, "Technological-Structure Research: Three Critical Issues," *Academy of Management Journal*, vol. 25, 1982, pp. 532–552.
23. Joan Woodward, *Management and Technology*, Her Majesty's Stationery Office, London, 1958, and *Industrial Organizations: Theory and Practice*, Oxford University, London, 1965.
24. Joan Woodward, *Industrial Organization: Theory and Practice*, Oxford University, London, 1965.
25. Paul D. Collins and Frank Hull, "Technology and Span of Control: Woodward Revisited," *Journal of Management Studies*, March 1986, pp. 143–164.
26. Louis W. Fry, "Technological-Structure Research: Three Critical Issues," *Academy of Management Journal*, vol. 25, 1982, pp. 532–552.
27. Frank M. Hull and Paul D. Collins, "High-Technology Batch Production Systems: Woodward's Missing Type," *Academy of Management Journal*, vol. 30, 1987, pp. 786–797.
28. Louis W. Fry, "Technological-Structure Research: Three Critical Issues," *Academy of Management Journal*, vol. 25, 1982, pp. 532–552.
29. James D. Thompson, *Organizations in Action*, McGraw-Hill, New York, 1967, pp. 54–55.
30. Ibid., p. 55.
31. Dennis S. Mileti, David F. Gillespie, and J. Eugene Hass, "Size and Structure in Complex Organizations," *Social Forces*, September 1977, pp. 208–217; George A. Miller and Joseph Conaty, "Differentiation in Organizations: Replication and Culmination," *Social Forces*, September 1980, pp. 265–274; John B. Cullen, Kenneth S. Anderson, and Douglas D. Baker, "Blau's Theory of Structural Differentiation Revisited: A Theory of Structural Change or Scale?" *Academy of Management Journal*, vol. 29, 1986, pp. 203–229.

32. W. Graham Astley, "Organizational Size and Bureaucracy," *Organization Studies*, vol. 6, 1985, pp. 201–228.
33. John B. Cullen, Kenneth S. Anderson, and Douglas D. Baker, "Blau's Theory of Structural Differentiation Revisited: A Theory of Structural Change or Scale?" *Academy of Management Journal*, vol. 29, 1986, pp. 203–229.
34. William A. Rushing, "Organizational Size, Rules, and Surveillance," in Joseph A. Litterer (ed.), *Organizations: Structure and Behavior*, 3d ed., Wiley, New York, 1980, pp. 396–405.
35. Stephen P. Robbins, *Organization Theory: The Structure and Design of Organizations*, 3d ed., Prentice-Hall, Englewood Cliffs, N.J., 1990.
36. John A. Byrne, "Is Your Country TOO BIG?" *Business Week*, Mar. 27, 1989, pp. 84–94.
37. L. Rhodes, "The Un-Manager," *INC.*, August 1982, pp. 35–43.
38. Richard Z. Goodling and John A. Wagner III, "A Meta-Analytic Review of the Relationship between Size and Performance: The Productivity and Efficiency of Organizations and Their Subunits," *Administrative Science Quarterly*, vol. 30, 1985, pp. 462–481.
39. Tom Burns and G. M. Stalker, *The Management of Innovation*, Tavistock, London, 1961.
40. Jay W. Lorsch, "Contingency Theory and Organization Design: A Personal Odyssey," in Ralph H. Kilmann, Louis R. Pondy, and Dennis P. Slevin (eds.), *The Management of Organization Design: Strategies and Implementation*, vol. 1, North-Holland, New York, 1976, p. 143.
41. Paul R. Lawrence and Jay W. Lorsch, *Organization and Environment*, Irwin, Homewood, Ill., 1969, pp. 20–45.
42. Danny Miller, "Configurations of Strategy and Structure: Towards a Synthesis," *Strategic Management Journal*, vol. 7, 1986, pp. 233–249, and "Relating Porter's Business Strategies to Environment and Structure: Analysis and Performance Implications," *Academy of Management Journal*, vol. 31, 1988, pp. 280–308.
43. Kenneth Labich, "The Innovators," *Fortune*, June 6, 1988, pp. 51–64.
44. Modesto A. Maidique, "Entrepreneurs, Champions, and Technological Innovation," *Sloan Management Review*, Winter 1980, pp. 59–76.
45. Thomas J. Peters and Robert H. Waterman, *In Search of Excellence*, Harper and Row, New York, 1982.
46. Robert A. Burgelman, "Managing the New Venture Division: Research Findings and Implications for Strategic Management," *Strategic Management Journal*, vol. 6, 1985, pp. 39–54; Christopher K. Bart, "New Venture Units: Use Them Wisely to Manage Innovation," *Sloan Management Review*, Summer 1988, pp. 35–43.
47. Michael Schrage, "Bell Labs Is Long on Genius but Short in the Marketplace," *The Washington Post*, March 1, 1987, pp. H1, H4.
48. Based on Jules Arbose, "How Perstorp Persuades Its Managers to Innovate," *International Management*, June 1987, pp. 41–47.
49. This situation is based on Linda S. Ackerman, "Transition Management: An In-Depth Look at Managing Complex Change," *Organizational Dynamics*, Summer 1982, pp. 46–66.
50. Deborah Wise and Catherine Harris, "Apple's New Crusade," *Business Week*, Nov. 26, 1984, pp. 146–156; Jim Forbes, "Shuffle Could Aid Apple," *InfoWorld*, June 24, 1985, pp. 35–37; Bro Uttal, "Behind the Fall of Steve Jobs, *Fortune*, Aug. 5, 1985, pp. 20–24; Katherine M. Hafner and Geoff Lewis, "Apple's Comeback," *Business Week*, Jan. 19, 1987, pp. 84–89; Brenton R. Schlender, "Apple Computer Tries to Achieve Stability but Remain Creative," *The Wall Street Journal*, July 16, 1987, pp. A1–A10; 1988 Annual Report, Apple Computer, Inc. Cupertino, Calif.,

Jim Bartimo, "Rapid Growth at Apple Triggers Troubles," *The Washington Post*, Feb. 4, 1989, p. C1; G. Paschal Zachary, "Apple Computer Moves to Cut Its Costs by Eliminating Jobs and Slowing Hiring," *The Wall Street Journal*, Jan. 16, 1990, p. A4.

CHAPTER 12

1. Amanda Bennett, "CARE Makes a Comeback after Drive to Revamp Its Management Practices," *The Wall Street Journal*, Feb. 9, 1987, p. B1; Gwen Kinhead, "America's Best-Run Charities," *Fortune*, Nov. 9, 1987, pp. 145–150; additional information obtained from telephone interviews with Jack McBride and Al Warner of CARE, Inc., on Apr. 15 and Apr. 20, 1987, as well as written materials furnished by Mr. Warner.
2. Herbert G. Heneman III, Donald P. Schwab, John A. Fossum, and Lee D. Dyer, *Personnel/Human Resource Management*, 4th ed., Irwin, Homewood, Ill., 1989; William B. Werther, Jr., and Keith Davis, *Personnel Management and Human Resources*, 2d ed., McGraw-Hill, New York, 1985.
3. Harold L. Angle, Charles C. Manz, and Andrew H. Van de Ven, "Integrating Human Resource Management and Corporate Strategy: A Preview of the 3M Story," *Human Resource Management*, Spring 1985, pp. 51–68.
4. Randall S. Schuler and Susan E. Jackson, "Linking Competitive Strategies with Human Resource Management Practices," *Academy of Management Executive*, vol. 1, 1987, pp. 207–219; Stella M. Nkomo, "Strategic Planning for Human Resources—Let's Get Started," *Long Range Planning*, vol. 21, 1988, pp. 66–72; Cynthia A. Lengnick-Hall and Mark L. Lengnick-Hall, "Strategic Human Resources Management: A Review of the Literature and a Proposed Typology," *Academy of Management Review*, vol. 13, 1988, pp. 454–470; Lloyd Baird and Ilan Meshoulam, "Managing Two Fits of Strategic Human Resource Management," *Academy of Management Review*, vol. 13, 1988, pp. 116–128.
5. Don Rose, "Woolworth's Drive for Excellence," *Long Range Planning*, vol. 22, 1989, pp. 28–31.
6. Wayne F. Cascio, *Managing Human Resources*, 2d ed., McGraw-Hill, New York, 1989.
7. Cynthia A. Lengnick-Hall and Mark L. Lengnick-Hall, "Strategic Human Resources Management: A Review of the Literature and a Proposed Typology," *Academy of Management Review*, vol. 13, 1988, pp. 454–470.
8. Randall Schuler and Susan E. Jackson, "Linking Competitive Strategies with Human Resource Management Practices," *Academy of Management Executive*, vol. 1, 1987, pp. 207–219.
9. Thomas A. Mahoney and John R. Deckop, "Evolution of Concept and Practice in Personnel Administration/Human Resource Management (PA/HRM)," *Journal of Management*, vol. 12, 1986, pp. 223–241.
10. James W. Walker, *Human Resource Planning*, McGraw-Hill, New York, 1980; Cynthia A. Lengnick-Hall and Mark L. Lengnick-Hall, "Strategic Human Resources Management: A Review of the Literature and a Proposed Typology," *Academy of Management Review*, vol. 13, 1988, pp. 454–470.
11. Edward L. Levine, "Everything You Always Wanted to Know about Job Analysis," Mariner, Tampa, Fla.: 1983; George T. Milkovich and John W. Boudreau, *Personnel/Human Resource Management*, 5th ed., Business Publications, Plano, Tex., 1988.
12. Patrick M. Wright and Kenneth N. Wexley, "How to Choose the Kind of Job Analysis You Really Need," *Personnel*, May 1985, pp. 51–55.
13. James W. Walker, *Human Resource Plan-

ning, McGraw-Hill, New York, 1980; William B. Werther, Jr., and Keith Davis, *Personnel Management and Human Resources,* 3d ed., McGraw-Hill, New York, 1989.

14. M. J. Feuer, R. J. Niehaus, and J. A. Sheridan, "Human Resource Forecasting: A Survey of Practice and Potential," *Human Resource Planning,* vol. 7, no. 2, 1988, pp. 85–97.

15. This section is based on Douglas T. Hall and James G. Goodale, *Human Resource Management: Strategy, Design, and Implementation,* Scott, Foresman, Glenview, Ill., 1986; and Randall S. Schuler and Vandra L. Huber, *Personnel and Human Resource Management,* 4th ed., West, St. Paul, Minn., 1990.

16. Bartley A. Brennan and Nancy Kubasek, *The Legal Environment of Business,* Macmillan, New York, 1988; Randall S. Schuler and Vandra L. Huber, *Personnel and Human Resource Management,* 4th ed., West, St. Paul, Minn., 1990.

17. Wayne F. Cascio, *Managing Human Resources,* 2d ed., McGraw-Hill, New York, 1989.

18. Douglas T. Hall and James G. Goodale, *Human Resource Management: Strategy, Design, and Implementation,* Scott, Foresman, Glenview, Ill., 1986.

19. Bartley A. Brennan and Nancy Kubasek, *The Legal Environment of Business,* Macmillan, New York, 1988; David P. Twomey, *Equal Employment Opportunity Law,* South-Western, Cincinnati, Ohio, 1990.

20. William B. Werther, Jr., and Keith Davis, *Personnel Management and Human Resources,* 3d ed., McGraw-Hill, New York, 1989.

21. Randall S. Schuler and Vandra L. Huber, *Personnel and Human Resource Management,* 4th ed., West, St. Paul, Minn., 1990.

22. Wayne F. Cascio, *Managing Human Resources,* 2d ed., McGraw-Hill, New York, 1989.

23. Joel Dreyfuss, "Get Ready for the New Work Force," *Fortune,* Apr. 23, 1990, pp. 165–181.

24. Daniel C. Feldman, "Reconceptualizing the Nature and Consequences of Part-Time Work," *Academy of Management Review,* vol. 15, 1990, pp. 103–112; Jolie Solomon and Gilbert Fuchsberg, "Great Number of Older Americans Seen Ready to Work," *The Wall Street Journal,* Jan. 26, 1990, p. B1.

25. William B. Werther, Jr., and Keith Davis, *Personnel Management and Human Resources,* 3d ed., McGraw-Hill, New York, 1989; Randall S. Schuler and Vandra L. Huber, *Personnel and Human Resource Management,* 4th ed., West, St. Paul, Minn., 1990.

26. Benjamin Schneider and Neal Schmitt, *Staffing Organizations,* 2d ed., Scott, Foresman, Glenview, Ill., 1986.

27. Ibid.

28. Douglas T. Hall and James G. Goodale, *Human Resource Management: Strategy, Design, and Implementation,* Scott, Foresman, Glenview, Ill., 1986.

29. M. Susan Taylor and Donald W. Schmidt, "A Process-Oriented Investigation of Recruitment Source Effectiveness," *Personnel Psychology,* vol. 36, 1983, pp. 343–354; Benjamin Schneider and Neal Schmitt, *Staffing Organizations,* 2d ed., Scott, Foresman, Glenview, Ill., 1986.

30. Philip G. Swaroff, Lizabeth A. Barclay, and Alan R. Bass, "Recruiting Sources: Another Look," *Journal of Applied Psychology,* vol. 70, 1985, pp. 720–728.

31. Bruce M. Meglino, Angelo S. DeNisi, Stuart A. Youngblood, and Kevin J. Williams, "Effects of Realistic Job Previews: A Comparison Using an Enhancement and a Reduction Preview," *Journal of Applied Psychology,* vol. 73, 1988, pp. 259–266.

32. Steven L. Premack and John P. Wanous, "A Meta-Analysis of Realistic Job Preview Experiments," *Journal of Applied Psychology,* vol. 70, 1985, pp. 706–719.

33. Jolie Solomon, "The New Job Interview: Show Thyself," *The Wall Street Journal,* Dec. 4, 1989, p. B1.

34. Vida Gulbinas Scarpello and James Ledvinka, *Personnel/Human Resource Management,* PWS-Kent, Boston, 1988; Randall S. Schuler and Vandra L. Huber, *Personnel and Human Resource Management,* 4th ed., West, St. Paul, Minn., 1990.

35. Vida Gulbinas Scarpello and James Ledvinka, *Personnel/Human Resource Management,* PWS-Kent, Boston, 1988; Wayne F. Cascio, *Managing Human Resources,* 2d ed., McGraw-Hill, New York, 1989; Robert D. Gatewood and Hubert S. Feild, *Human Resource Selection,* 2d ed., Dryden, Chicago, 1990.

36. Robert D. Gatewood and Hubert S. Feild, *Human Resource Selection,* 2d ed., Dryden, Chicago, 1990.

37. Ibid.

38. Randall S. Schuler and Vandra L. Huber, *Personnel and Human Resource Management,* 4th ed., West, St. Paul, Minn., 1990.

39. Robert D. Gatewood and Hubert S. Feild, *Human Resource Selection,* 2d ed., Dryden, Chicago, 1990.

40. Ibid.

41. William B. Werther, Jr., and Keith Davis, *Personnel Management and Human Resources,* 3d ed., McGraw-Hill, New York, 1989; Robert D. Gatewood and Hubert S. Feild, *Human Resource Selection,* 2d ed., Dryden, Chicago, 1990.

42. *Personnel Policies Forum,* Survey No. 146— Recruiting and Selection Procedures, Bureau of National Affairs, Washington, D.C., May 1988.

43. *Personnel Policies Forum,* Survey No. 114, Bureau of National Affairs, Washington, D.C., September 1976; Milton Hakel, "Employment Interview," in K. Rowland and G. Ferris (eds.), *Personnel Management: New Perspectives,* Allyn and Bacon, Boston, 1982.

44. This section on types of interviews is based heavily on William B. Werther, Jr., and Keith Davis, *Personnel Management and Human Resources,* 3d ed., McGraw-Hill, New York, 1989.

45. Based on Tom Janz, Lowell Hellervik, and David C. Gilmore, *Behavior Description Interviewing,* Allyn and Bacon, Boston, 1986; James M. Jenks, and Brian L. P. Zevnik, "ABCs of Job Interviewing," *Harvard Business Review,* July–August 1989, pp. 38–42; and Robert D. Gatewood and Hubert S. Feild, *Human Resource Selection,* 2d ed., Dryden, Chicago, 1990.

46. This section is based on Robert D. Gatewood and Hubert S. Feild, *Human Resource Selection,* 2d ed., Dryden, Chicago, 1990.

47. Abby Brown, "Employment Tests: Issues without Clear Answers," *Personnel Administrator,* vol. 30, 1985, pp. 43–56.

48. Vida Gulbinas Scarpello and James Ledvinka, *Personnel/Human Resource Management,* PWS-Kent, Boston, 1988.

49. Barbara B. Gaugler, Douglas B. Rosenthal, George C. Thornton III, and Cynthia Bentson, "Meta-Analysis of Assessment Center Validity," *Journal of Applied Psychology,* vol. 72, 1987, pp. 493–511; Glenn M. McEvoy and Richard W. Beatty, "Assessment Centers and Subordinates Appraisals of Managers: A Seven-Year Examination of Predictive Validity," *Personnel Psychology,* vol. 42, 1989, pp. 37–52.

50. Randall B. Dunham, "Organizational Practice," *Industrial Organizational Psychologist,* February 1984.

51. R. L. LoPresto, D. E. Mitcham, and D. E. Ripley, *Reference Checking Handbook,* American Society for Personnel Administration, Alexandria, Va., 1986.

52. Mark Memmott, "More Firms Stop Giving References," *USA Today,* Dec. 5, 1989, p. 1B.

53. For an extensive discussion of this issue, see David C. Martin and Kathryn M. Bartol, "Potential Libel and Slander Issues Involving Discharged Employees," *Employee Relations Law Journal,* Summer 1987, pp. 600–609.

54. Kenneth N. Wexley and Gary P. Latham, *Developing and Training Human Resources in Organizations,* Scott, Foresman, Glenview, Ill., 1981; Douglas T. Hall and James G. Goodale, *Human Resource Management,* Scott, Foresman, Glenview, Ill., 1986.

55. Randall S. Schuler and Vandra L. Huber, *Personnel and Human Resource Management,* 4th ed., West, St. Paul, Minn., 1990.

56. Another interpretation sometimes used is that training applies to facilitating learning for lower-level jobs, while development is more indicative of a broader learning orientation for higher-level jobs; Wayne F. Cascio, *Managing Human Resources,* 2d ed., McGraw-Hill, New York, 1989.

57. E. B. Fiske, "Booming Corporate Education Efforts Rival College Programs, Study Says," *The New York Times,* Jan. 28, 1985, p. A10.

58. Wayne F. Cascio, *Managing Human Resources,* 2d ed., McGraw-Hill, New York, 1989.

59. Kenneth N. Wexley and Gary P. Latham, *Developing and Training Human Resources in Organizations,* Scott, Foresman, Glenview, Ill., 1981.

60. John P. Campbell, Marvin D. Dunnette, Edward E. Lawler, and Karl E. Weick, *Managerial Behavior, Performance, and Effectiveness,* McGraw-Hill, New York, 1970; Vida Gulbinas Scarpello and James Ledvinka, *Personnel/Human Resource Management,* PWS-Kent, Boston, 1988.

61. D. L. Kilpatrick, "Evaluation of Training," in R. L. Craig and L. R. Bittel (eds.), *Training and Development,* McGraw-Hill, New York, 1967.

62. Vida Gulbinas Scarpello and James Ledvinka, *Personnel/Human Resource Management,* PWS-Kent, Boston, 1988.

63. Arnold H. Wensky and Robin J. Legendre, "Incentive Training at First Service Bank," *Personnel Journal,* April 1989, pp. 102–110.

64. Allan M. Mohrman, Jr., Susan M. Resnick-West, and Edward E. Lawler III, *Designing Performance Appraisal Systems,* Jossey-Bass, San Francisco, 1989.

65. C. A. Peck, *Pay and Performance: The Interaction of Compensation and Performance Appraisal,* Research Bulletin No. 155, Conference Board, New York, 1984.

66. Wayne F. Cascio, *Managing Human Resources,* 2d ed., McGraw-Hill, New York, 1989.

67. H. John Bernardin and Richard W. Beatty, *Performance Appraisal: Assessing Human Behavior at Work,* Kent, Boston, 1984.

68. Frank J. Landy, James L. Farr, Frank E. Saal, and Walter R. Freytag, "Behaviorally Anchored Sales for Rating the Performance of Police Officers," *Journal of Applied Psychology,* vol. 61, 1976, pp. 750–758.

69. Robert Giles and Christine Landauer, "Setting Specific Standards for Appraising Creative Staffs," *Personnel Administrator,* March 1984, pp. 35–47.

70. H. John Bernardin and Richard W. Beatty, *Performance Appraisal: Assessing Human Behavior at Work,* Kent, Boston, 1984; Stephen J. Carroll, Jr., and Craig Eric Schneier, *Performance Appraisal and Review Systems,* Scott, Foresman, Glenview, Ill., 1982.

71. David E. Smith, "Training Programs for Performance Appraisal: A Review," *Academy of Management Review,* vol. 11, 1986, pp. 22–40; David C. Martin and Kathryn M. Bartol, "Training the Raters: A Key to Effective Performance Appraisal," *Public Personnel Management,* vol. 15, 1986, pp. 101–110.

72. H. H. Meyer, "Self-Appraisal of Job Performance," *Personnel Psychology,* vol. 33, 1980, pp. 291–296.

73. David C. Martin, "Performance Appraisal: Improving the Rater's Effectiveness," *Personnel,* August 1986, pp. 28–33.

74. Clinton O. Longenecker, Dennis A. Gioia,

and Henry P. Sims, Jr., "Behind the Mask: The Politics of Employee Appraisal," *Academy of Management Executive*, August 1987, pp. 183–193.

75. David C. Martin, Kathryn M. Bartol, and Marvin J. Levine, "The Legal Ramifications of Performance Appraisal," *Employee Relations Law Journal*, vol. 12, Winter 1986–1987, pp. 370–396.

76. This section is based largely on Robert M. McCaffery, *Employee Benefit Programs*, PWS-Kent, Boston, 1988; Charles H. Fay, *Glossary of Compensation & Benefits Terms*, 2d ed., American Compensation Association, Scottsdale, Ariz., 1989; and George T. Milkovich and Jerry M. Newman, *Compensation*, 3d ed., BPI/Irwin, Homewood, Ill., 1990.

77. Marc J. Wallace, Jr., and Charles H. Fay, *Compensation Theory and Practice*, 2d ed., PWS-Kent, Boston, 1988. Wallace and Fay identify a fourth type of equity, process equity, the extent to which the procedures used in determining and distributing pay are fair. Recent evidence suggests that process equity also influences employees' satisfaction with the compensation that they receive.

78. Richard L. Bunning, "Skill-Based Pay," *Personnel Administrator*, June 1989, pp. 65–68; Henry Tosi and Lisa Tosi, "What Managers Need to Know about Knowledge-Based Pay," *Organizational Dynamics*, Winter 1986, pp. 52–64.

79. Roy Merrills, "How Northern Telecom Competes on Time," *Harvard Business Review*, July–August 1989, pp. 108–114.

80. Henry Tosi and Lisa Tosi, "What Managers Need to Know about Knowledge-Based Pay," *Organizational Dynamics*, Winter 1986, pp. 52–64; R. J. Bullock and Edward E. Lawler, "Gainsharing: A Few Questions, and Fewer Answers," *Human Resource Management*, Spring 1984, pp. 23–40; Christopher S. Miller and Michael H. Schuster, "Gainsharing Plans: A Comparative Analysis," *Organizational Dynamics*, Summer, 1987, pp. 44–67.

81. Pamela Goett, "DuPont Fibers Weaves an Incentive Pay Plan in a Bold New Design," *Human Resources Professional*, March–April 1989.

82. This section is based mainly on Jay R. Galbraith, "Designing the Innovating Organization," *Organizational Dynamics*, Winter 1982, pp. 5–25; and Kirkland Ropp, "Bringing Up Baby: Nurturing Intrapreneurs," *Personnel Administrator*, June 1987, pp. 92–96.

83. Robert A. Burgelman and Leonard R. Sayles, *Inside Corporate Innovation*, Free Press, New York, 1986; Randall S. Schuler, "Fostering and Facilitating Entrepreneurship in Organizations: Implications for Organization Structure and Human Resource Management Practices," *Human Resource Management*, Winter 1986, pp. 607–629.

84. Robert M. McCaffery, *Employee Benefit Programs*, PWS-Kent, Boston, 1988.

85. Ibid.; George T. Milkovich and Jerry M. Newman, *Compensation*, 3d ed., BPI/Irwin, Homewood, Ill., 1990.

86. Robert M. McCaffery, *Employee Benefit Programs*, PWS-Kent, Boston, 1988.

87. Walter Roessing, "High Marks for Hallmark," *Compass Readings*, March 1990, pp. 32–39.

88. *Employee Benefit Plan Review*, October 1984, pp. 46–47, cited in Robert M. McCaffery, *Employee Benefit Programs*, PWS-Kent, Boston, Mass., 1988, p. 3; see also George F. Dreher, Ronald A. Ash, and Robert D. Bretz, "Benefit Coverage and Employee Cost: Critical Factors in Explaining Compensation Satisfaction," *Personnel Psychology*, vol. 41, 1988, pp. 237–254.

89. Tim Chauran, "Benefits Communication," *Personnel Journal*, January 1989, pp. 70–77.

90. Vida Gulbinas Scarpello and James Ledvinka, *Personnel/Human Resource Management*, PWS-Kent, Boston, 1988.

91. Jeanne M. Brett, "Why Employees Want Unions," *Organizational Dynamics*, Spring 1980, pp. 47–59; Wayne F. Cascio, *Managing Human Resources*, 2d ed., McGraw-Hill, New York, 1989; George T. Milkovich and John W. Boudreau, *Personnel/Human Resource Management*, 5th ed., Business Publications, Plano, Tex., 1988.

92. The method for determining the number of employees belonging to unions changed in 1979 from annual dues–paying members to union members who are employed wage and salary workers; based on information from the Bureau of Labor Statistics, Industrial Relations Research Division, Washington, D.C., May 1989.

93. Vida Gulbinas Scarpello and James Ledvinka, *Personnel/Human Resource Management*, PWS-Kent, Boston, 1988.

94. This section is based largely on Wayne F. Cascio, *Managing Human Resources*, 2d ed., McGraw-Hill, New York, 1989.

95. Dean Foust, "The UAW vs. Japan: It's Showdown Time in Tennessee," *Business Week*, July 24, 1989, pp. 64–65; Gregory A. Patterson, "The UAW's Chances at Japanese Plants Hinge on Nissan Vote," *The Wall Street Journal*, July 25, 1989, pp. A1, A12; Warren Brown, "UAW Loses Key Battle at Nissan Plant," *The Washington Post*, July 18, 1989, pp. A1, A14; Warren Brown, "Behind the UAW's Defeat in Tennessee," *The Washington Post*, July 30, 1989, p. H3.

96. Information obtained from the National Labor Relations Board Research Department.

97. This section is based largely on Ira Michael Shepard, Robert L. Duston, and Karen S. Russell, *Workplace Privacy*, Bureau of National Affairs, Washington, D.C., 1989.

98. Milo Geyelin, "Fired Managers Winning More Lawsuits," *The Wall Street Journal*, Sept. 7, 1989, pp. B1, B2.

99. *Alcohol & Drugs in the Workplace: Costs, Controls and Controversies*, Bureau of National Affairs, Washington, D.C., 1986.

100. H. W. French, "Helping the Addicted Worker," *The New York Times*, Mar. 26, 1987, pp. 29, 34.

101. "Labor Letter," *The Wall Street Journal*, Dec. 2, 1986, p. 1.

102. Judy D. Olian, "Genetic Screening for Employment Purposes," *Personnel Psychology*, vol. 37, 1984, pp. 423–438.

103. Cindy Skrzycki, "Family-Issues Experts See Rising Demand," *The Washington Post*, Jan. 7, 1990, p. H3.

104. George Gendron, "Steel Man: Ken Iverson," *INC.*, April 1986, pp. 41–48; John Ortman, "Nucor's Ken Iverson on Productivity and Pay," *Personnel Administrator*, October 1986, pp. 46–108; Ruth Simon, "Nucor's Boldest Gamble," *Forbes*, Apr. 3, 1989, pp. 122–124; Jonathan P. Hicks, "Steelmakers' Inferiority Syndrome," *The New York Times*, Aug. 7, 1989, pp. D1, D7; Clare Ansberry, "Steel Industry Is on the Verge of David vs. Goliath Test," *The Wall Street Journal*, Oct. 17, 1989, p. A8.

Sources for Part Ending Case for Part 3: Based on Joseph J. Fucini and Suzy Fucini, *Entrepreneurs*, Hall, Boston, 1985, p. 209; John Hein, "Mercedes Remembered," *Across the Board*, October 1983, pp. 5–7; "Daimler-Benz and the Family Feud," *Fortune*, May 27, 1985, p. 111; Graham Turner, "Inside Europe's Giant Companies Daimler-Benz Goes Top of the League," *Long Range Planning*, vol. 19, no. 5, 1986, pp. 12–17; Rosemary Brady, "Quality before Quantity," *Forbes*, July 16, 1984, pp. 58–59; Peter Fuhrman, "Herr Reuter Takes to the Skies," *Forbes*, Mar. 20, 1989, pp. 90–94; Louis S. Richman, "Daimler-Benz Conglomerates," *Fortune*, Oct. 27, 1986, pp. 84–86; Phyllis Berman, "We Are Still Saying Hello to Each Other," *Forbes*, May 18, 1987, pp. 94–102; "Daimler: The Giant May Turn into a Behemoth," *Business Week*, Nov. 14, 1987, pp.

80–81; Terence Roth, "Daimler-Benz Names Reuter Chairman and Sets Management Course for 1990's," *The Wall Street Journal*, July 23, 1987, p. 27; John Templeman and Mark Maremont, "The Even Bigger Shadow Daimler Could Cast," *Business Week*, May 22, 1989, pp. 54–55; Steven Greenhouse, "Daimler on a New Road," *The New York Times*, Apr. 9, 1989, pp. F1, F10; Ferdinand Protzman, "Daimler Forgoes Song and Dance," *The New York Times*, May 10, 1989, p. C1; John Templeman, "Daimler's Drive to Become a High-Tech Speedster," *Business Week*, Feb. 12, 1990, pp. 55–58; Fred Hiatt, "Mitsubishi, Daimler Discuss Alliance," *The Washington Post*, Mar. 7, 1990, pp. C1, C4; and "Daimler-Benz AG, Japan's Mitsubishi Discuss More Links," *The Wall Street Journal*, Mar. 7, 1990, p. A14.

CHAPTER 13

1. Based on Kathleen A. Hughes, "Balancing Act," *The Wall Street Journal*, Nov. 10, 1986, p. 14D; Andrew Pollack, "Taking the Crucial Next Step at Genentech," *The New York Times*, Jan. 28, 1990, sec. 3, pp. 1, 6; and Joan O'C. Hamilton, "Why Genentech Ditched the Dream of Independence," *Business Week*, Feb. 19, 1990, pp. 36–37.

2. Richard M. Steers and Lyman W. Porter (eds.), *Motivation and Work Behavior*, 4th ed., McGraw-Hill, New York, 1987, pp. 5–6.

3. John P. Campbell and Richard D. Prichard, "Motivation Theory in Industrial and Organizational Psychology," in Marvin D. Dunnette (ed.), *Handbook of Industrial and Organizational Psychology*, Rand McNally, Chicago, 1976, pp. 62–130; Terence R. Mitchell, "Motivation: New Directions for Theory, Research, and Practice," in Richard M. Steers and Lyman W. Porter (eds.), *Motivation and Work Behavior*, 4th ed., McGraw-Hill, New York, 1987, pp. 27–40.

4. Richard M. Steers and Lyman W. Porter (eds.), *Motivation and Work Behavior*, 4th ed., McGraw-Hill, New York, 1987, pp. 14–19.

5. Ibid.

6. Reva B. Tooley, "Turning Trials into Triumph," *Working Woman*, January 1987, pp. 66–70.

7. Dean Foust, "Innkeepers, Beware: Kemmons Wilson Is Checking In Again," *Business Week*, Feb. 1, 1988, pp. 79–80.

8. Mahmoud A. Wahba and Lawrence G. Bridwell, "Maslow Reconsidered: A Review of Research on the Need Hierarchy Theory," *Organizational Behavior and Human Performance*, vol. 16, 1976, pp. 212–240; Vance F. Mitchell and Pravin Moudgill, "Measurement of Maslow's Need Hierarchy," *Organizational Behavior and Human Performance*, vol. 16, 1976, pp. 334–349.

9. Clayton P. Alderfer, *Existence, Relatedness, and Growth: Human Needs in Organizational Settings*, Free Press, New York, 1972.

10. P. Ranganath Nayak and John M. Ketteringam, *Breakthroughs*, Rawson Associates, New York, 1986.

11. Clayton P. Alderfer, *Existence, Relatedness, and Growth: Human Needs in Organizational Settings*, Free Press, New York, 1972; Benjamin Schneider and Clayton P. Alderfer, "Three Studies of Measures of Need Satisfaction in Organizations," *Administrative Science Quarterly*, vol. 18, 1973, pp. 498–505; Clayton P. Alderfer, Robert E. Kaplan, and Ken K. Smith, "The Effect of Relatedness Need Satisfaction on Relatedness Desires," *Administrative Science Quarterly*, vol. 19, 1974, pp. 507–532; John P. Wanous and Abram Zwany, "A Cross-Sectional Test of Need Hierarchy Theory," *Organizational Behavior and Human Performance*, vol. 18, 1977, pp. 78–97.

12. Robert A. Mamis, "Details, Details," *INC.*, March 1988, pp. 96–98.

13. Richard M. Steers and Lyman W. Porter (eds.), *Motivation and Work Behavior*, 4th ed., McGraw-Hill, New York, 1987, pp. 463–465.

14. For articles on this controversy, see F. Herzberg, *Work and the Nature of Man*, World Publishing, Cleveland, 1966; F. Herzberg, "One More Time: How Do You Motivate Employees?" *Harvard Business Review*, January–February, 1968, pp. 53–62; R. J. House and L. A. Wigdor, "Herzberg's Dual-Factor Theory of Job Satisfaction and Motivation: A Review of the Evidence and a Criticism," *Personnel Psychology*, vol. 20, 1967, pp. 369–389; and D. A. Whitsett and E. K. Winslow, "An Analysis of Studies Critical of the Motivator-Hygiene Theory," *Personnel Psychology*, vol. 20, 1967, pp. 391–415.

15. Terence R. Mitchell, "Motivation: New Directions for Theory, Research, and Practice," in Richard M. Steers and Lyman W. Porter (eds.), *Motivation and Work Behavior*, 4th ed., McGraw-Hill, New York, 1987, pp. 27–39.

16. J. Richard Hackman and Greg R. Oldham, *Work Redesign*, Addison-Wesley, Reading, Mass., 1980.

17. Jaclyn Fierman, "The Entrepreneurs: The Best of Their Class," *Fortune*, Oct. 12, 1987, p. 144.

18. David C. McClelland, *Human Motivation*, Scott, Foresman, Glenview, Ill., 1985.

19. Richard M. Steers, "Murray's Manifest Needs Theory," in Richard M. Steers and Lyman W. Porter (eds.), *Motivation and Work Behavior*, 4th ed., McGraw-Hill, New York, 1987, pp. 59–67.

20. David C. McClelland, "Power Is the Great Motivator," *Harvard Business Review*, March–April 1976, pp. 100–110, and *Human Motivation*, Scott, Foresman, Glenview, Ill., 1985.

21. Richard M. Steers, "Murray's Manifest Needs Theory," in Richard M. Steers and Lyman W. Porter (eds.), *Motivation and Work Behavior*, 4th ed., McGraw-Hill, New York, 1987, pp. 59–67.

22. David C. McClelland, "Power Is the Great Motivator," *Harvard Business Review*, March–April 1976, pp. 100–110, and *Human Motivation*, Scott, Foresman, Glenview, Ill., 1985.

23. Brett Duval Fromson, "The Slow Death of E. F. Hutton," *Fortune*, Feb. 29, 1988, pp. 82–87.

24. David C. McClelland, *Human Motivation*, Scott, Foresman, Glenview, Ill., 1985.

25. David C. McClelland and Richard E. Boyatzis, "Leadership Motive Pattern and Long-Term Success in Management," *Journal of Applied Psychology*, vol. 67, 1982 pp. 737–743.

26. J. D. W. Andrews, "The Achievement Motive and Advancement in Two Types of Organizations," *Journal of Personality and Social Psychology*, vol. 6, 1967, pp. 163–168.

27. Richard M. Steers, "Murray's Manifest Needs Theory," in Richard M. Steers and Lyman W. Porter (eds.), *Motivation and Work Behavior*, 4th ed., McGraw-Hill, New York, 1987, pp. 59–67.

28. David C. McClelland, "Achievement Motivation Can Be Developed," *Harvard Business Review*, November–December 1965, pp. 6–25; John G. Nicholls, "Achievement Motivation: Conceptions of Authority, Subjective Experience, Task Choice, and Performance," *Psychological Review*, July 1984, pp. 328–346.

29. David C. McClelland and David H. Burnham, "Power Is the Great Motivator," *Harvard Business Review*, March–April 1976, pp. 100–110; David C. McClelland, *Human Motivation*, Scott, Foresman, Glenview, Ill., 1985, pp. 547–586.

30. Louis S. Richman, "Tomorrow's Jobs: Plentiful, But . . . ," *Fortune*, Apr. 11, 1988, pp. 42–56.

31. Barry M. Staw, "Organizational Behavior: A Review and Reformulation of the Field's Outcome Variables," *Annual Review of Psychology*, vol. 35, 1984, pp. 627–666.

32. Craig C. Pinder, *Work Motivation: Theory, Issues, and Applications*, Scott, Foresman, Glenview, Ill., 1984, pp. 144–147.

33. Frank J. Landy and Wendy S. Becker, "Motivation Theory Reconsidered," *Research in Organizational Behavior*, vol. 9, 1987, pp. 1–38.

34. D. F. Parker and L. Dyer, "Expectancy Theory as a Within Person Behavioral Choice Model: An Empirical Test of Some Conceptual and Methodological Refinements," *Organizational Behavior and Human Performance*, vol. 17, 1976, pp. 97–117; H. J. Arnold, "A Test of the Validity of the Multiplicative Hypothesis of Expectancy-Valence Theories of Work Motivation," *Academy of Management Journal*, vol. 24, 1981, pp. 128–141; John P. Wanous, Thomas L. Keon, and Janina C. Latack, "Expectancy Theory and Occupational/Organizational Choices: A Review and Test," *Organizational Behavior and Human Performance*, vol. 32, 1983, pp. 66–86.

35. David Remnick, "Revolutionary Idea for Soviet Workers: Owning Shares," *The Washington Post*, Feb. 5, 1989.

36. David A. Nadler and Edward E. Lawler III, "Motivation: A Diagnostic Approach," in J. Richard Hackman, Edward E. Lawler III, and Lyman W. Porter (eds.), *Perspectives on Behavior in Organizations*, McGraw-Hill, New York, 1983, pp. 67–78.

37. Amanda Bennett, "Salary Rules Aim at New Middle Manager," *The Wall Street Journal*, Apr. 10, 1987, p. 25.

38. Albert R. Karr, "Incentive Pay Is Extended Deeper to Lower Management and 'Key' Workers," *The Wall Street Journal*, June 23, 1987, p. 1; Frank McCoy, "Sbarro's Juicy Slice of the Fast-Food Market," *Business Week*, Sept. 7, 1987, pp. 72–73.

39. Peter Applebome, "Workers Return to Slaying Scene," *The New York Times*, Aug. 22, 1986, pp. A1, A8.

40. J. Stacy Adams, "Inequity in Social Exchange," in L. Berkowitz (ed.), *Advances in Experimental Social Psychology*, vol. 2, Academic, New York, 1965, pp. 267–299.

41. Edwin A. Locke, "The Nature and Causes of Job Satisfaction," in M. Dunnette (ed.), *Handbook of Industrial and Organizational Psychology*, Rand McNally, Chicago, 1976, pp. 1297–1349; Richard T. Mowday, "Equity Theory Predictions of Behavior in Organizations," in Richard M. Steers and Lyman W Porter (eds.), *Motivation and Work Behavior*, 4th ed., McGraw-Hill, New York, 1987, pp. 89–110.

42. Robert G. Lord and Jeffrey A. Hohenfeld, "Longitudinal Field Assessment of Equity Effects on the Performance of Major League Baseball Players," *Journal of Applied Psychology*, vol. 64, 1979, pp. 19–26.

43. Richard A. Cosier and Dan R. Dalton, "Equity Theory and Time: A Reformulation," *Academy of Management Review*, vol. 8, 1983, pp. 311–319.

44. Edwin A. Locke and Gary P. Latham, *Goal Setting: A Motivational Technique That Works!* Prentice-Hall, Englewood Cliffs, N.J., 1984; Edwin A. Locke, Karyll N. Shaw, Lise M. Saari, and Gary P. Latham, "Goal Setting and Task Performance: 1969–1980," *Psychological Bulletin*, vol. 90, 1981, pp. 125–152.

45. Richard Brandt, "It Takes More Than a Good Idea," *Business Week*, Innovation 1989 issue, June 16, 1989, p. 123.

46. Edwin A. Locke, Gary P. Latham, and Miriam Erez, "The Determinants of Goal Commitment," working paper, University of Maryland, 1986.

47. Howard Garland, "Relation of Effort Performance Expectancy to Performance in Goal-Setting Experiments," *Journal of Applied Psychology*, vol. 69, 1984, pp. 79–84.

48. Edwin A. Locke, Karyll N. Shaw, Lise M. Saari, and Gary P. Latham, "Goal Setting and Task Performance: 1969–1980," *Psychological Bulletin*, vol. 90, 1981, pp. 125–152.

49. Fred Luthans and Robert Kreitner, *Organizational Behavior Modification*, Scott, Foresman, Glenview, Ill., 1975.

50. This concept was originally articulated by E. L. Thorndike, *Animal Intelligence*, Macmillan, New York, 1911.

51. Richard D. Arvey and John M. Ivancevich, "Punishment in Organizations: A Review, Propositions, and Research Suggestions," *Academy of Management Review*, vol. 5, 1980, pp. 123–132; Janice M. Beyer and Harrison M. Trice, "A Field Study of the Use and Perceived Effects of Discipline in Controlling Work Performance," *Academy of Management Journal*, vol. 27, 1984, pp. 743–764.

52. Janice M. Beyer and Harrison M. Trice, "A Field Study of the Use and Perceived Effects of Discipline in Controlling Work Performance," *Academy of Management Journal*, vol. 27, 1984, pp. 743–764; W. Clay Hamner, "Reinforcement Theory and Contingency Management in Organizational Settings," reprinted in Richard M. Steers and Lyman W. Porter (eds.), *Motivation and Work Behavior*, 4th ed., McGraw-Hill, New York, 1987, pp. 139–165.

53. Wayne Dierks and Kathleen McNally, "Incentives You Can Bank On," *Personnel Administrator*, March 1987, pp. 60–65.

54. Albert Bandura, *Social Learning Theory*, Prentice-Hall, Englewood Cliffs, N.J., 1977, and *Social Foundations of Thought and Action: A Social Cognitive Theory*, Prentice-Hall, Englewood Cliffs, N.J., 1986; Robert Krietner and Fred Luthans, "A Social Learning Approach to Behavioral Management: Radical Behaviorists 'Mellowing Out,'" in Richard M. Steers and Lyman W. Porter (eds.), *Motivation and Work Behavior*, 4th ed., McGraw-Hill, New York, 1987, pp. 184–199.

55. J. Barling and R. Beattie, "Self-Efficacy Beliefs and Sales Performance," *Journal of Organizational Behavior Management*, vol. 5, 1983, pp. 41–51; M. Susan Taylor, Edwin A. Locke, Cynthia Lee, and Marilyn Gist, "Type A Behavior and Faculty Research Productivity: What Are the Mechanisms?" *Organizational Behavior and Human Performance*, vol. 34, 1984, pp. 402–418; Marilyn E. Gist, "Self-Efficacy: Implications for Organizational Behavior and Human Resource Management," *Academy of Management Review*, vol. 12, 1987, pp. 472–485.

56. Albert Bandura, *Social Learning Theory*, Prentice-Hall, Englewood Cliffs, N.J., 1977, pp. 128–131.

57. Tim R. V. Davis and Fred Luthans, "A Social Learning Approach to Organizational Behavior," *Academy of Management Review*, vol. 5, 1980, pp. 281–290; Charles C. Manz and Henry P. Sims, Jr., "Vicarious Learning: The Influence of Modeling on Organizational Behavior," *Academy of Management Review*, vol. 6, 1981, pp. 105–113; Martin G. Evans, "Organizational Behavior: The Central Role of Motivation," *Journal of Management*, vol. 12, 1986, pp. 203–222.

58. Based on Susan Ager, "An Appetite for More than Pizza," *Nation's Business*, February 1986, pp. 81–83; Aimee Stern, "Domino's: A Unique Concept Pays Off," *Dun's Business Month*, May 1986, pp. 50–51; Dale Feuer, "Training for Fast Times," *Training*, July 1987, pp. 25–30; John Duggleby, "The Domino's Recipe for Making Dough," *Business Week Careers*, February 1988, p. 81; Wendy Zellner, "Tom Monaghan: The Fun-Loving Prince of Pizza," *Business Week*, Feb. 8, 1988, pp. 90–93; and Martha T. Moore, "Monaghan at Crossroads, Picks Church," *USA Today*, Sept. 14, 1989, pp. 1B–2B.

59. Albert Bandura, *Social Learning Theory*, Prentice-Hall, Englewood Cliffs, N.J., 1977, pp. 48–49.

60. Ibid., pp. 154, 207.

61. Susan Ager, "An Appetite for More Than

Pizza," *Nation's Business*, February 1986, pp. 81–83.
62. "Lessons from a Successful Intrapreneur," *Journal of Business Strategy*, March–April, 1988, pp. 20–24.
63. Based on Bruce G. Posner and Bo Burlingham, "The Hottest Entrepreneur in America," *INC.*, January 1988, pp. 44–58.

CHAPTER 14

1. Based on Deborah C. Wise and Geoff Lewis, "Apple, Part 2: The No-Nonsense Era of John Sculley," *Business Week*, Jan. 27, 1986, pp. 96–98; Carol Hymowitz, "Five Future No. 1s," *The Wall Street Journal*, Mar. 20, 1987, pp. 18D–19D; Mark Potts, "Rebellious Apple Finally Grows Up," *The Washington Post*, June 14, 1987, pp. D1–D6; Brenton R. Schlender, "Apple Computer Tries to Achieve Stability but Remain Creative," *The Wall Street Journal*, July 16, 1987, pp. 1, 10; John Sculley, "Sculley's Lessons from Inside Apple," *Fortune*, Sept. 14, 1987, pp. 108–118; Katherine M. Hafner, "The World According to John Sculley," *Business Week*, Sept. 28, 1987, pp. 71–72; "Corporate Antihero John Sculley," *INC.*, October 1987, pp. 49–59; F. Milene Henley, "Good, Better, Best," *Working Woman*, December 1987, pp. 86–89; Brian O'Reilly, "Apple Computer's Risky Revolution," *Fortune*, May 8, 1989, pp. 75–80; G. Pascal Zachary, "Apple's Coleman, Refreshed, Resumes Career after a Five-Month Breather," *The Wall Street Journal*, July 13, 1989, p. B7; Andrew Pollack, "Apple Strays from Mass Appeal," *The New York Times*, Dec. 27, 1989, pp. D1, D3; and G. Pascal Zachary, "Computer Firm's Chief Faces Slowing Growth, Discord in the Ranks," *The Wall Street Journal*, Feb. 15, 1990, pp. A1, A8.
2. "The Top 25," *Forbes*, June 15, 1987, p. 151.
3. Henry Mintzberg, *Power in and around Organizations*, Prentice-Hall, Englewood Cliffs, N.J., 1983, pp. 4–5; Jeffrey Pfeffer, *Power in Organizations*, Pittman, Boston, 1981, pp. 2–4.
4. J. R. P. French and B. Raven, "The Bases of Social Power," in D. Cartwright (ed.), *Studies in Social Power*, Institute for Social Research, Ann Arbor, Mich. 1959.
5. Information power was added in later work on important power bases; see B. H. Raven and A. W. Kruglanski, "Conflict and Power," in P. Swingle (ed.), *The Structure of Conflict*, Academic, New York, 1970.
6. James R. Norman, "A Hardheaded Takeover by McLouth's Hardhats," *Business Week*, June 6, 1988, pp. 90–91; Luther Jackson, "Steel Zeal," *Detroit Free Press*, Mar. 12, 1990, pp. 1E, 5E.
7. Ronald Bailey, "Not Power but Empower," *Forbes*, May 30, 1988, pp. 120–123.
8. Resa W. King, "How Government Groomed Jim Lynn for Aetna," *Business Week*, June 2, 1986, pp. 54–55.
9. Ralph M. Stogdill, *Handbook of Leadership*, Free Press, New York, 1974, p. 72.
10. This section is based heavily on Arthur G. Jago, "Leadership: Perspectives in Theory and Research," *Management Science*, vol. 28, 1982, pp. 315–336.
11. Ibid.
12. Ralph M. Stogdill, "Personal Factors Associated with Leadership: A Survey of the Literature," *Journal of Psychology*, vol. 25, 1948, pp. 35–71; R. D. Mann, "A Review of the Relationships between Personality and Performance in Small Groups," *Psychological Bulletin*, vol. 56, 1959, pp. 241–270.
13. Ralph M. Stogdill, *Handbook of Leadership*, Free Press, New York, 1974.
14. Robert G. Lord, Christy L. De Vader, and George M. Alliger, "A Meta-Analysis of the Relation between Personality Traits and Leadership Perceptions: An Application of Validity

Generalization Procedures," *Journal of Applied Psychology*, vol. 71, 1986, pp. 402–410. For another recent study supporting the possible existence of leadership traits, see David A. Kenny and Stephen J. Zaccaro, "An Estimate of Variance Due to Traits in Leadership," *Journal of Applied Psychology*, vol. 68, 1983, pp. 678–685.
15. Mann actually used the term "masculinity-feminity" to denote this latter trait associated with aggressiveness and decisiveness. Mann's work found that leaders were more likely to be aggressive and decisive—i.e., fit the "masculinity" end of the scale. More recently, researchers have been attempting to use descriptive terms for such traits that avoid the disadvantage of possibly encouraging gender stereotypes.
16. Robert J. House and Mary L. Baetz, "Leadership: Some Empirical Generalizations and New Research Directions," *Research in Organizational Behavior*, vol. 1, 1979, pp. 341–423.
17. D. W. Bray, R. J. Campbell, and D. L. Grant, *Formative Years in Business: A Long Term AT&T Study of Managerial Lives*, Wiley, New York, 1974. See Paul R. Sackett, "Assessment Centers and Content Validity: Some Neglected Issues," *Personnel Psychology*, vol. 40, 1987, pp. 13–25, for some recent issues regarding establishing the validity of assessment centers.
18. Tom Richman, "In the Black," *INC.*, May 1988, pp. 116–120.
19. K. Lewin and R. Lippitt, "An Experimental Approach to the Study of Autocracy and Democracy: A Preliminary Note," *Sociometry*, vol. 1, 1938, pp. 292–300; K. Lewin, R. Lippitt, and R. K. White, "Patterns of Aggressive Behavior in Experimentally Created Social Climates," *Journal of Social Psychology*, vol. 10, 1939, pp. 271–301; R. Lippitt, "An Experimental Study of the Effect of Democratic and Authoritarian Group Atmospheres," *University of Iowa Studies in Child Welfare*, vol. 16, 1940, pp. 43–95.
20. Bernard M. Bass, *Stogdill's Handbook of Leadership*, Free Press, New York, 1981, pp. 289–299.
21. Robert Tannenbaum and Warren H. Schmidt, "How to Choose a Leadership Pattern," *Harvard Business Review*, vol. 51, May–June 1973, pp. 162–180.
22. Bernard M. Bass, *Stogdill's Handbook of Leadership*, Free Press, New York, 1981.
23. Rensis Likert, *New Patterns of Management*, McGraw-Hill, New York, 1961.
24. Rensis Likert, "From Production- and Employee-Centeredness to Systems 1–4," *Journal of Management*, vol. 5, 1979, pp. 147–156.
25. Mary Rowland, "Creating a Plan to Reshape a Business," *Working Woman*, August 1988, pp. 70–74.
26. Stephan Wilkinson, "The Keeping (and Stoker) of the Company Flame," *Working Woman*, October 1987, pp. 70–76.
27. Chester A. Schriesheim and Barbara J. Bird, "Contributions of the Ohio State Studies to the Field of Leadership," *Journal of Management*, vol. 5, 1979, pp. 135–145.
28. Stephan Wilkinson, "The Keeping (and Stoker) of the Company Flame," *Working Woman*, October 1987, pp. 70–76; Mary Rowland, "Creating a Plan to Reshape a Business," *Working Woman*, August 1988, pp. 70–74.
29. L. L. Larson, J. G. Hunt, and R. N. Osborn. "The Great Hi-Hi Leader Behavior Myth: A Lesson from Occam's Razor," *Academy of Management Journal*, vol. 19, 1976, pp. 628–641; Paul C. Nystrom, "Managers and the Hi-Hi Leader Myth," *Academy of Management Journal*, vol. 21, 1978, pp. 325–331.
30. Steven Kerr, Chester A. Schriesheim, Charles J. Murphy, and Ralph Stogdill, "Toward a Contingency Theory of Leadership Based on the Consideration and Initiating

Structure Literature," *Organizational Behavior and Human Performance*, May 1975, pp. 62–82; Charles N. Greene, "The Reciprocal Nature of Influence between Leader and Subordinate," *Journal of Applied Psychology*, vol. 60, 1975, pp. 187–193; Charles N. Greene, "Questions of Causation in the Path-Goal Theory of Leadership," *Academy of Management Journal*, vol. 22, 1979, pp. 22–41.
31. Robert R. Blake and Jane S. Mouton, *The Managerial Grid® III*, Gulf, Houston, 1985.
32. B. M. Bass, J. Krusell, and R. A. Alexander, "Male Managers' Attitudes toward Working Women," *American Behavioral Scientist*, vol. 15, 1971, pp. 221–236; B. Rosen and T. H. Jerdee, "Perceived Sex Differences in Managerially Relevant Characteristics," *Sex Roles*, vol. 4, 1978, pp. 837–843.
33. Kathryn M. Bartol and David C. Martin, "Women and Men in Task Groups," in R. D. Ashmore and F. K. Del Boca (eds.), *The Social Psychology of Female-Male Relations*, Academic, Orlando, Fla., 1986, pp. 259–310; Gregory H. Dobbins and Stephanie J. Platz, "Sex Differences in Leadership: How Real Are They?" *Academy of Management Review*, vol. 11, 1986, pp. 118–127.
34. Fred E. Fiedler, *A Theory of Leadership Effectiveness*, McGraw-Hill, New York, 1967. Much of our description of the contingency model is based on recent information provided in Fred E. Fiedler and Joseph E. Garcia, *New Approaches to Effective Leadership: Cognitive Resources and Organizational Performance*, Wiley, New York, 1987.
35. Fred E. Fiedler and Joseph E. Garcia, *New Approaches to Effective Leadership: Cognitive Resources and Organizational Performance*, Wiley, New York, 1987.
36. See Fred E. Fiedler and Martin M. Chemers, *Improving Leadership Effectiveness: The Leader Match Concepts*, rev. ed., Wiley, New York, 1976, pp. 134–137.
37. Seth H. Lubove, "Dravo Seeks Leadership to Pursue Turnaround Strategy," *The Wall Street Journal*, Feb. 24, 1987, p. 6.
38. See, for example, George Graen, Kenneth Alvares, James Burdeane Orris, and Joseph A. Martella, "Contingency Model of Leadership Effectiveness: Antecedent and Evidential Results," *Psychological Bulletin*, vol. 74, 1970, pp. 285–296; Robert P. Vecchio, "An Empirical Examination of the Validity of Fiedler's Model of Leadership Effectiveness," *Organizational Behavior and Human Performance*, vol. 19, 1977, pp. 180–206; and Dian-Marie Hosking, "A Critical Evaluation of Fiedler's Contingency Hypothesis," *Progress in Applied Psychology*, vol. 1, 1981, pp. 103–154.
39. M. Strube and J. Garcia, "A Meta-Analysis Investigation of Fiedler's Contingency Model of Leadership Effectiveness," *Psychological Bulletin*, vol. 90, 1981, pp. 307–321; Lawrence H. Peters, Darrell D. Hartke, and John T. Pohlmann, "Fiedler's Contingency Theory of Leadership: An Application of the Meta-Analysis Procedures of Schmidt and Hunter," *Psychological Bulletin*, vol. 97, 1985, pp. 274–285.
40. Fred E. Fiedler, "The Contribution of Cognitive Resources to Leadership Performance," *Journal of Applied Social Psychology*, vol. 16, 1986, pp. 532–548; Fred E. Fiedler and Joseph E. Garcia, *New Approaches to Effective Leadership: Cognitive Resources and Organizational Performance*, Wiley, New York, 1987.
41. Bernard M. Bass, *Stogdill's Handbook of Leadership*, Free Press, New York, 1981, pp. 97–101.
42. Fred E. Fiedler, "When to Lead, When to Stand Back," *Psychology Today*, September 1987, pp. 26–27.
43. Ibid.
44. Based on "Hyundai's Chung Ju-Yung: From Rags to Richest Man in Town," *Business Week*, Dec. 23, 1985; Laxmi Nakarmi, "Daewoo vs. Hyundai: Battle of the Korean Giants," *Business Week*, Dec. 15, 1986, pp. 72–

73; Michael Kublin, "Hyundai's Success and Mark Twain's Obituary," *Industrial Management*, November–December 1987, pp. 12–18; and Philip Glouchevitch, "Chung Ju-Yung and Family," *Forbes*, July 24, 1989, p. 206.

45. Laxmi Nakarmi, "Daewoo vs. Hyundai: Battle of the Korean Giants," *Business Week*, Dec. 15, 1986; Andrew Tanzer, "Samsung: South Korea Marches to Its Own Drummer," *Forbes*, May 16, 1988, pp. 84–89.

46. This discussion of situational leadership theory is based on Paul Hersey and Kenneth H. Blanchard, *Management of Organizational Behavior: Utilizing Human Resources*, 5th ed., Prentice-Hall, Englewood Cliffs, N.J., 1988. Some of the variable names and/or definitions have changed somewhat from previous delineations.

47. Ibid.

48. In previous editions of their book, *Management of Organizational Behavior: Utilizing Human Resources*, Hersey and Blanchard used the term "maturity" rather than "readiness." They explain in the fifth edition (1988) that they believe "readiness" is more descriptive of a person's ability and willingness to perform a specific task.

49. Claude L. Graeff, "The Situational Leadership Theory: A Critical View," *Academy of Management Review*, vol. 8, 1983, pp. 285–291.

50. Gary A. Yukl, *Leadership in Organizations*, 2d ed., Prentice-Hall, Englewood Cliffs, N.J., 1989.

51. Robert P. Vecchio, "Situational Leadership Theory: An Examination of a Prescriptive Theory," *Journal of Applied Psychology*, vol. 72, 1987, pp. 444–451.

52. Andrew S. Grove, *High Output Management*, Random House, New York, 1983, pp. 172–177.

53. Victor H. Vroom and Philip W. Yetton, *Leadership and Decision-Making*, University of Pittsburgh, Pittsburgh, 1973; Victor H. Vroom and Arthur G. Jago, "On the Validity of the Vroom-Yetton Model," *Journal of Applied Psychology*, vol. 63, 1978, pp. 151–162; Dean Tjosvold, William C. Wedley, and Richard H. G. Field, "Constructive Controversy, the Vroom-Yetton Model, and Managerial Decision-Making," *Journal of Occupational Behaviour*, vol. 7, 1986, pp. 125–138.

54. Victor H. Vroom and Arthur G. Jago, *The New Leadership: Managing Participation in Organizations*, Prentice-Hall, Englewood Cliffs, N.J., 1988.

55. Jack Stack, "Crisis Management by Committee," *INC.*, May 1988, p. 26.

56. Gary A. Yukl, *Leadership in Organizations*, 2d ed., Prentice-Hall, Englewood Cliffs, N.J., 1989.

57. The basic foundations of the theory are contained in Martin G. Evans, "The Effects of Supervisory Behavior on the Path-Goal Relationship," *Organizational Behavior and Human Performance*, vol. 5, 1970, pp. 277–298; Robert J. House, "A Path Goal Theory of Leader Effectiveness," *Administrative Science Quarterly*, vol. 16, 1971, pp. 321–338; Robert J. House and Gary Dessler, "The Path Goal Theory of Leadership: Some Post Hoc and A Priori Tests," in J. Hunt and L. Larson (eds.), *Contingency Approaches to Leadership*, Southern Illinois University, Carbondale, 1974; and Robert A. House and Terence R. Mitchell, "Path-Goal Theory of Leadership," *Journal of Contemporary Business*, vol. 3, 1974, pp. 81–97.

58. Bro Uttal, "Companies That Serve You Best," *Fortune*, Dec. 7, 1987, pp. 98–116.

59. Alan C. Filley, Robert J. House, and Steven Kerr, *Managerial Process and Organizational Behavior*, Scott, Foresman, Glenview, Ill., 1976; Charles A. Schriesheim and M. A. Von Glinow, "The Path-Goal Theory of Leadership: A Theoretical and Empirical Analysis," *Academy of Management Journal*, vol. 20, 1977, pp. 398–405; Charles Greene, "Questions of Causation in the Path-Goal Theory of Leadership," *Academy of Management Journal*,

vol. 22, 1979, pp. 22–41; Julie Indvik, "Path-Goal Theory of Leadership: A Meta-Analysis," in John A. Pearce II and Richard B. Robinson, Jr. (eds.), *Best Paper Proceedings*, Academy of Management, Chicago, 1986, pp. 189–192.

60. Gary A. Yukl, *Leadership in Organizations*, 2d ed., Prentice-Hall, Englewood Cliffs, N.J., 1989.

61. F. Milene Henley, "Good, Better, Best," *Working Woman*, December 1987, pp. 86–89.

62. Abraham Zaleznik, "The Leadership Gap," *Academy of Management Executive*, vol. 4, 1990, pp. 7–22.

63. Charles R. Holloman, "Leadership and Head: There Is a Difference," *Personnel Administration*, July–August 1968; Abraham Zaleznik, "Managers and Leaders: Are They Different?" *Harvard Business Review*, May–June, 1977.

64. This distinction was first made by James McGregor Burns, *Leadership*, Harper & Row, New York, 1978; see also Bernard M. Bass, *Leadership and Performance beyond Expectations*, Free Press, New York, 1985; Bruce J. Avolio and Bernard M. Bass, "Transformational Leadership, Charisma, and Beyond," in James Gerald Hunt, B. Rajaram Baliga, H. Peter Dachler, and Chester A. Schriesheim (eds.), *Emerging Leadership Vistas*, Heath, Boston, 1987, pp. 29–50; Bernard M. Bass, Bruce J. Avolio, and Laurie Goodheim, "Biography and the Assessment of Transformational Leadership at the World-Class Level," *Journal of Management*, vol. 13, 1987, pp. 7–19; and John J. Hater and Bernard M. Bass, "Superiors' Evaluations and Subordinates' Perceptions of Transformational and Transactional Leadership," *Journal of Applied Psychology*, vol. 73, 1988, pp. 695–702.

65. Robert J. House and Jetendra V. Singh, "Organizational Behavior: Some New Directions for I/O Psychology," *Annual Review of Psychology*, vol. 38, 1987, pp. 669–718. For related views of leader charisma, see Robert J. House, "A 1976 Theory of Charismatic Leadership," in J. G. Hunt and L. L. Larson (eds.), *Leadership: The Cutting Edge*, Southern Illinois University, Carbondale, pp. 189–207; and Kimberly B. Boal and John M. Bryson, "Charismatic Leadership: A Phenomenological and Structural Approach," in James Gerald Hunt, B. Rajaram Baliga, H. Peter Dachler, and Chester A. Schriesheim (eds.), *Emerging Leadership Vistas*, Heath, Boston, 1987, pp. 11–28.

66. Jay A. Conger and Rabindra N. Kanungo, "Toward a Behavioral Theory of Charismatic Leadership in Organizational Settings," *Academy of Management Review*, vol. 12, 1987, pp. 637–647.

67. Jane M. Howell and Peter J. Frost, "A Laboratory Study of Charismatic Leadership," *Organizational Behavior and Human Decision Processes*, vol. 43, 1989, pp. 243–269.

68. Noel M. Tichy and David O. Ulrich, "The Leadership Challenge—A Call for the Transformational Leader," *Sloan Management Review*, Fall 1984, pp. 59–68.

69. F. Milene Henley, "Good, Better, Best," *Working Woman*, December 1987, pp. 86–89.

70. Jeremy Main, "Wanted: Leaders Who Can Make a Difference," *Fortune*, Sept. 28, 1987, pp. 92–101; Abraham Zaleznik, "The Leadership Gap," *Academy of Management Executive*, vol. 4, 1990, pp. 7–22.

71. Gary Yukl, "Managerial Leadership: A Review of Theory and Research," *Journal of Management*, vol. 15, 1989, pp. 251–289.

72. Bobby J. Calder, "An Attribution Theory of Leadership," in Barry M. Staw and Gerald R. Salancik (eds.), *New Directions in Organizational Behavior*, St. Clair, Chicago, 1977, pp. 179–204; Jeffrey Pfeffer, "The Ambiguity of Leadership," *Academy of Management Review*, vol. 2, 1977, pp. 104–112.

73. James R. Meindl, Sanford B. Ehrlich, and Janet M. Dukerich, "The Romance of Leadership," *Administrative Science Quarterly*, vol. 30,

1985, pp. 78–102.

74. Bernard M. Bass, *Stogdill's Handbook of Leadership*, Free Press, New York, 1981; Jonathan E. Smith, Kenneth P. Carson, and Ralph A. Alexander, "Leadership: It Can Make a Difference," *Academy of Management Journal*, vol. 27, 1984, pp. 765–776; James R. Meindl and Sanford B. Ehrlich, "The Romance of Leadership and the Evaluation of Organizational Performance," *Academy of Management Journal*, vol. 30, 1987, pp. 91–109.

75. This section is based on Steven Kerr and John M. Jermier, "Substitutes for Leadership: Their Meaning and Measurement," *Organizational Behavior and Human Performance*, vol. 22, 1978, pp. 375–403.

76. Kathleen Brady, "The Power of Positive Stress," *Working Woman*, July 1987, pp. 74–77.

77. Jon P. Howell and Peter W. Dorfman, "Substitutes for Leadership: Test of a Construct," *Academy of Management Journal*, vol. 24, 1981, pp. 714–728; John E. Sheridan, Donald J. Vredenburgh, and Michael A. Abelson, "Contextual Model of Leadership Influence in Hospital Units," *Academy of Management Journal*, vol. 27, 1984, pp. 57–78; Jon P. Howell and Peter W. Dorfman, "Leadership and Substitutes for Leadership among Professional and Nonprofessional Workers," *Journal of Applied Behavioral Science*, vol. 22, 1986, pp. 29–46; Jon P. Howell, Peter W. Dorfman, and Steven Kerr, "Moderator Variables in Leadership Research," *Academy of Management Review*, vol. 11, 1986, pp. 88–102.

78. See B. R. Baliga and James G. Hunt, "An Organizational Life Cycle Approach to Leadership," in James Gerald Hunt, B. Rajaram Baliga, H. Peter Dachler, and Chester A. Schriesheim (eds.), *Emerging Leadership Vistas*, Heath, Boston, 1987, pp. 129–149.

79. These two case examples are reprinted from Victor H. Vroom and Arthur G. Jago, *The New Leadership: Managing Participation in Organizations*, Prentice-Hall, Englewood Cliffs, N.J., 1988, pp. 163, 166–167.

80. Aaron Bernstein and Zachary Schiller, "Jack Welch: How Good a Manager?" *Business Week*, Dec. 14, 1987, pp. 92–103; Edwin A. Finn, Jr., "General Electric," *Forbes*, Mar. 23, 1987, pp. 74–80; L. J. Davis, "They Call Him Neutron," *Business Month*, March 1988, pp. 25–29; Mark Potts, "GE's Management Mission," *The Washington Post*, May 22, 1988, pp. H1, H4; Janet Guyon, "GE Chairman Welch, Though Much Praised, Starts to Draw Critics," *The Wall Street Journal*, Aug. 4, 1988, pp. 1, 8; Stratford P. Sherman, "The Mind of Jack Welch," *Fortune*, Mar. 27, 1989, pp. 39–50.

CHAPTER 15

1. Based on Nelson W. Aldrich, Jr., "Lines of Communication," *INC.*, June 1986, pp. 140–144; Joanne Kaufman, "In the Moo: Shopping at Stew Leonard's," *The Wall Street Journal*, Sept. 17, 1987, p. 32; and Stew Leonard, "Love That Customer!" *Management Review*, October 1987, pp. 36–39.

2. Gerald M. Goldhaber, *Organizational Communication*, 4th ed., Brown, Dubuque, Iowa, 1986, pp. 4–33.

3. O. W. Baskin and Craig E. Aronoff, *Interpersonal Communication in Organizations*, Scott, Foresman, Santa Monica, Calif., 1980, p. 4.

4. Roger Smith, " 'The U.S. Must Do as GM Has Done'," *Fortune*, Feb. 13, 1989, pp. 70–73.

5. J. Thomas and P. Sireno, "Assessing Management Competency Needs," *Training and Development Journal*, vol. 34, 1980, pp. 47–51; H. W. Hildebrant, F. A. Bon, E. L. Miller, and A. W. Swinyard, "An Executive Appraisal of Courses Which Best Prepare One for General Management," *The Journal of Business Communication*, Winter 1982, pp. 5–15.

6. Robert R. Max, "Wording It Correctly," *Training and Development Journal*, March 1985, pp. 50–51; Joy Van Skiver, quoted in Neil Chesanow, "Quick, Take This Memo," *The Washington Post*, Sept. 7, 1987, p. C5.

7. For a description of the study and some suggested solutions, see Skip Swerdlow, Edward H. Goodin, and William J. Quain, "Business Letters: 43 Problems and 16 Solutions," *Cornell Hotel and Restaurant Quarterly*, August 1986, pp. 29–34.

8. Walter Kiechel III, "The Big Presentation," *Fortune*, July 26, 1982, pp. 98–100.

9. Phillip V. Lewis, *Organizational Communication: The Essence of Effective Management*, 2d ed., Prentice-Hall, Englewood Cliffs, N.J., 1980, p. 11.

10. Ibid.

11. R. Birdwhistell, *Kenesics and Context*, University of Pennsylvania, Philadelphia, 1970; A. Mehrabian, *Silent Messages*, Wadsworth, Belmont, Calif., 1972.

12. Otis W. Baskin and Craig E. Aronoff, *Interpersonal Communication in Organizations*, Scott, Foresman, Santa Monica, Calif., 1980.

13. Henry Mintzberg, *The Nature of Managerial Work*, Prentice-Hall, Englewood Cliffs, N.J., 1973; Lance B. Kurke and Howard E. Alrich, "Mintzberg Was Right! A Replication and Extension of the Nature of Managerial Work," *Management Science*, vol. 29, 1983, pp. 975–984.

14. Henry Mintzberg, *The Nature of Managerial Work*, Prentice-Hall, Englewood Cliffs, 1973.

15. Ibid.; Phillip V. Lewis, *Organizational Communication: The Essence of Effective Management*, 2d ed., Prentice-Hall, Englewood Cliffs, N.J., 1980; Larry R. Smeltzer and Gail L. Fann, "Comparison of Managerial Communication Patterns in Small, Entrepreneurial Organizations and Large, Mature Organizations," *Group & Organization Studies*, vol. 14, 1989, pp. 198–215.

16. Jan Carlzon, *Moments of Truth*, Ballinger, Cambridge, Mass, 1987; Amanda Bennett, "SAS's 'Nice Guy' Aiming to Finish First," *The Wall Street Journal*, Mar. 2, 1989, p. B12; Jonathan Kapstein, "Can SAS Keep Flying with the Big Birds?" *Business Week*, Nov. 27, 1989, pp. 142–146.

17. For a discussion of different theoretical perspectives on communication, see Kathleen J. Krone, Fredric M. Jablin, and Linda L. Putnam, "Communication Theory and Organizational Communication: Multiple Perspectives," in Fredric M. Jablin, Linda L. Putnam, Karlene H. Roberts, and Lyman W. Porter (eds.), *Handbook of Organizational Communication: An Interdisciplinary Perspective*, Sage Publications, Newbury Park, Calif., 1987, pp. 18–40.

18. Don Oldenburg, "What Do You Say?" *The Washington Post*, Aug. 23, 1989, p. C5.

19. Charles A. O'Reilly III and Karlene H. Roberts, "Information Filtration in Organizations: Three Experiments," *Organizational Behavior and Human Performance*, 1974, vol. 11, pp. 253–265; Robert E. Kaplan, Wilfred H. Drath, and Joan R. Kofodimos, "Power and Getting Criticism," *Center for Creative Leadership Issues & Observations*, August 1984, pp. 1–6.

20. Based on Clare Ansberry, "Oil Spill in the Midwest Provides Case Study in Crisis Management," *The Wall Street Journal*, Jan. 8, 1988, p. 21.

21. Fred Luthans, *Organizational Behavior*, 5th ed., McGraw-Hill, New York, 1989.

22. Judith R. Gordon, *A Diagnostic Approach to Organizational Behavior*, 2d ed., Allyn and Bacon, Boston, 1987; Fred Luthans, *Organizational Behavior*, 5th ed., McGraw-Hill, New York, 1989.

23. William Mathewson, "Shop Talk," *The Wall Street Journal*, Sept. 30, 1988, p. 29.

24. Wendell L. French, *The Personnel Management Process*, 6th ed., Houghton Mifflin, Boston, 1987, p. 256.

25. Fred Luthans, *Organizational Behavior*, 4th ed., McGraw-Hill, New York, 1985, pp. 172–174.

26. Henry L. Tosi, John R. Rizzo, and Stephen J. Carroll, *Managing Organizational Behavior*, Pitman, Marshfield, Mass., 1986; Gary Johns, *Organizational Behavior*, 2d ed., Scott, Foresman, Glenview, Ill., 1987.

27. C. S. Carver, E. DeGregoria, and R. Gillis, "Field-Study Evidence of an Attribution among Two Categories of Observers," *Personality and Social Psychology Bulletin*, vol. 6, 1980, pp. 44–50; D. G. Myers, *Social Psychology*, McGraw-Hill, New York, 1983.

28. Phillip V. Lewis, *Organizational Communication: The Essence of Effective Management*, 2d ed., Prentice-Hall, Englewood Cliffs, N.J., Ohio, 1980, p. 54.

29. Mary Munter, *Business Communication: Strategy and Skill*, Prentice-Hall, Englewood Cliffs, N.J., 1987, p. 15.

30. Stephen R. Axley, "Managerial and Organizational Communication in Terms of the Conduit Metaphor," *Academy of Management Review*, vol. 9, 1984, pp. 428–437.

31. Ernest G. Bormann, "Symbolic Convergence: Organizational Communication and Culture," in Linda Putnam and Michael E. Pacanowsky (eds.), *Communication and Organizations: An Interpretive Approach*, Sage Publications, Beverly Hills, Calif., 1983, pp. 99–122.

32. Based on Michael W. Miller, "At Many Firms, Employees Speak a Language That's All Their Own," *The Wall Street Journal*, Dec. 29, 1987, p. 17.

33. Ron Scherer, "America's Factory Workers: Immigrants Turn the Shop Floor into a 'Mini-UN,'" *The Christian Science Monitor*, June 1, 1988, pp. 1, 6.

34. Mark Knapp, *Nonverbal Communication in Human Interaction*, Holt, New York, 1972; Phillip V. Lewis, *Organizational Communication: The Essence of Effective Management*, 2d ed., Prentice-Hall, Englewood Cliffs, N.J., 1980.

35. M. A. Hayes, "Nonverbal Communication: Expression without Word," in R. C. Huseman, C. M. Logue, and D. L. Freshley (eds.), *Readings in Interpersonal and Organizational Communication*, Holbrook, Boston, 1973; Otis W. Baskin and Craig E. Aronoff, *Interpersonal Communication in Organizations*, Goodyear, Santa Monica, Calif., 1980.

36. Frederick H. Katayama, "How to Act Once You Get There," *Fortune*, Pacific Rim 1989 issue, Fall, 1987, pp. 87–88.

37. Reprinted from Judith R. Gordon, *A Diagnostic Approach to Organizational Behavior*, 2d ed., Allyn and Bacon, Boston, 1987, p. 230.

38. Marilyn H. Lewis and N. L. Reinsch, Jr., "Listening in Organizational Environments," *Journal of Business Communication*, Summer 1988, pp. 49–67.

39. Judith R. Gordon, *A Diagnostic Approach to Organizational Behavior*, 2d ed., Allyn and Bacon, Boston, 1987.

40. Walter Kiechel III, "Learn How to Listen," *Fortune*, Aug. 17, 1987, pp. 107–108.

41. Robert E. Kaplan, Wilfred H. Drath, and Joan R. Kofodimos, "Power and Getting Criticism," *Center for Creative Leadership Issues & Observations*, August 1984, pp. 1–8.

42. Ibid.

43. "Essentials of Feedback," *A Seven-Day Leadership Development Course*, Center for Creative Leadership, Greensboro, N.C., 1976, pp. 77–78, as cited in Phillip V. Lewis, *Organizational Communication: The Essence of Effective Management*, 2d ed., Prentice-Hall, Englewood Cliffs, N.J., 1980, pp. 157–158.

44. Patricia Sellers, "How to Handle Customers' Gripes," *Fortune*, Oct. 24, 1988, pp. 88–100.

45. Marvin E. Shaw, *Group Dynamics: The Psychology of Small Group Behavior*, McGraw-Hill, New York, 1981, pp. 150–157.

46. Lyman W. Porter and Karlene Roberts, "Communication in Organizations," in Mar-

vin D. Dunnette (ed.), *Handbook of Industrial and Organization Psychology*, Rand McNally, Chicago, 1976, pp. 1553–1589.

47. David Katz and Robert Kahn, *The Social Psychology of Organizations*, Wiley, New York, 1966.

48. Otis W. Baskin and Craig E. Aronoff, *Interpersonal Communication in Organizations*, Scott, Foresman, Santa Monica, Calif., 1980, pp. 92–93; Phillip V. Lewis, *Organizational Communication: The Essence of Effective Management*, 2d ed., Prentice-Hall, Englewood Cliffs, N.J., 1980, pp. 62–63.

49. Bro Uttal, "Companies That Serve You Best," *Fortune*, Dec. 7, 1987, pp. 98–116.

50. Earl Planty and William Machaver, "Upward Communications: A Project in Executive Development," *Personnel*, vol. 28, 1952, pp. 304–318; J. R. Cranwell, "How to Have a Well-Informed Boss," *Supervisory Management*, May 1969, pp. 5–6; Gerald M. Goldhaber, Organizational Communication, 4th ed., Brown, Dubuque, Iowa, 1986, pp. 170–173.

51. Charles A. O'Reilly III and Karlene H. Roberts, "Information Filtration in Organizations: Three Experiments," *Organizational Behavior and Human Performance*, vol. 11, 1974, pp. 253–265.

52. "Trainers Gauge Organizational Communication," *Training*, June 1984, p. 72.

53. Robert E. Kaplan, Wilfred H. Drath, and Joan R. Kofodimos, "Power and Getting Criticism," *Center for Creative Leadership Issues & Observations*, August 1984, pp. 1–7; Thomas J. Murray, "How to Stay Lean and Mean," *Business Month*, August 1987, pp. 29–32.

54. Nelson W. Aldrich, Jr., "Lines of Communication," *INC.*, June 1986, pp. 140–144.

55. T. J. Peters and R. H. Waterman, *In Search of Excellence: Lessons from America's Best-Run Companies*, Harper & Row, New York, 1982; Peter R. Monge, Lynda White Rothman, Eric M. Eisenberg, Katherine I. Miller, and Kenneth K. Kirste, "The Dynamics of Organizational Proximity," *Management Science*, vol. 31, 1985, pp. 1129–1141.

56. "Listen, Listen, Listen," *Business Week*, Sept. 14, 1987, p. 108.

57. Lyman W. Porter and Karlene Roberts, "Communication in Organizations," in Marvin D. Dunnette (ed.), *Handbook of Industrial and Organization Psychology*, Rand McNally, Chicago, 1976, pp. 1553–1589.

58. R. Wayne Pace, *Organizational Communication: Foundations for Human Resource Development*, Prentice-Hall, Englewood Cliffs, N.J., 1983, pp. 53–54.

59. Gerald M. Goldhaber, *Organizational Communication*, 4th ed., Brown, Dubuque, Iowa, 1986, pp. 174–175.

60. R. Wayne Pace, *Organizational Communication: Foundations for Human Resource Development*, Prentice-Hall, Englewood Cliffs, N.J., 1983, pp. 56–57.

61. Keith Davis, *Human Behavior at Work*, McGraw-Hill, New York, 1972.

62. Keith Davis, "Management Communication and the Grapevine," in Stewart Ferguson and Sherry Devereaux Ferguson (eds.), *Intercom: Readings in Organizational Communication*, Hayden, Rochelle Park, N.J., 1980, pp. 55–66.

63. S. Friedman, "Where Employees Go for Information: Some Surprises," *Administrative Management*, vol. 42, 1981, pp. 72–73; Gerald M. Goldhaber, *Organizational Communication*, 4th ed., Brown, Dubuque, Iowa, 1986, pp. 176–177; Alan Zaremba, "Working with the Organizational Grapevine," *Personnel Journal*, July 1988, pp. 38–42.

64. R. Wayne Pace, *Organizational Communication: Foundations for Human Resource Development*, Prentice-Hall, Englewood Cliffs, N.J., 1983, pp. 57–58.

65. "Out of Sight, Not Out of Mind," *The Wall Street Journal*, June 20, 1989, p. B1.

66. J. G. March and G. Sevon, "Gossip, Information, and Decision Making," in L. S.

Sproull and P. D. Larkey (eds.), *Advances in Information Processing in Organizations*, vol. 1, JAI, Greenwich, Conn., 1984, pp. 95–107; Karl E. Weick and Larry D. Browning, "Argument and Narration in Organizational Communication," *Journal of Management*, vol. 12, 1986, pp. 243–259.

67. H. B. Vickery III, "Tapping into the Employee Grapevine," *Association Management*, January 1984, pp. 59–63.

68. This section relies heavily on Rosabeth Moss Kanter, "When a Thousand Flowers Bloom: Structural, Collective, and Social Conditions for Innovation in Organizations," *Research in Organizational Behavior*, vol. 10, 1988, pp. 169–211.

69. Alan Farnham, "The Trust Gap," *Fortune*, Dec. 4, 1989, pp. 56–78.

70. See also Terrance L. Albrecht and Vickie A. Ropp, "Communicating about Innovation in Networks of Three U.S. Organizations," *Journal of Communication*, vol. 34, 1984, pp. 78–91.

71. Leslie Brennan, "McKesson Takes to Meeting Monthly," *S&MM* (Sales and Marketing Management), July 1986, pp. 102ff.

72. D. G. Marquis and S. Myers, *Successful Industrial Innovations*, National Science Foundation, Washington, D.C., 1969.

73. Tom Richman, "Seducing the Customer: Dale Ballard's Perfect Selling Machine," *INC.*, April 1988, pp. 96–104.

74. Based on Nelson W. Aldrich, Jr., "Lines of Communication," *INC.*, June 1986, pp. 140–144.

75. Lee Sproull and Sara Kiesler, "Reducing Social Context Cues: Electronic Mail in Organizational Communication," *Management Science*, vol. 32, 1986, pp. 1492–1512.

76. David Churbuck, "Prepare for E-Mail Attack," *Forbes*, Jan. 23, 1989, pp. 82–87.

77. Albert B. Crawford, "Corporate Electronic Mail—A Communication-Intensive Application of Information Technology," *MIS Quarterly*, vol. 6, 1982, pp. 1–14.

78. Edward H. Nyce and Richard Groppa, "Electronic Mail at MHT," *Management Technology*, May 1983, pp. 65–72.

79. Lee Sproull and Sara Kiesler, "Reducing Social Context Cues: Electronic Mail in Organizational Communication," *Management Science*, vol. 32, 1986, pp. 1492–1512.

80. R. E. Rice and D. Case, "Electronic Message Systems in the University: A Description of Use and Utility," *Journal of Communication*, vol. 33, 1983, pp. 131–152; Lee Sproull and Sara Kiesler, "Reducing Social Context Cues: Electronic Mail in Organizational Communication," *Management Science*, vol. 32, 1986, pp. 1492–1512.

81. Richard C. Huseman and Edward W. Miles, "Organizational Communication in the Information Age: Implications of Computer-Based Systems," *Journal of Management*, vol. 14, 1988, pp. 181–204.

82. David Churbuck, "Prepare for E-Mail Attack," *Forbes*, Jan. 23, 1989, pp. 82–87.

83. Gerald M. Goldhaber, *Organizational Communication*, 4th ed., Brown, Dubuque, Iowa, 1986, pp. 150–155.

84. Susan Hellweg, Kevin Freiberg, and Anthony Smith, "The Pervasiveness and Impact of Electronic Communication Technologies in Organizations: A Survey of Major American Corporations," paper presented at the Speech Communication Association meeting, Chicago, 1984.

85. Nelson W. Aldrich, Jr., "Lines of Communication," *INC.*, June 1986, p. 140.

86. Fleming Meeks, "Live from Dallas," *Forbes*, Dec. 26, 1988, pp. 112–113.

87. The Haney Test of Uncritical Inferences is reprinted with permission from William V. Haney (ed.), *Communication and Interpersonal Relations*, 5th ed., Irwin, Homewood, Ill., 1986, pp. 214–222.

88. Steve Coll and David A. Vise, "Chairman's Cost-Cutting Humor," *The Washington Post*, Oct. 18, 1987, pp. H1, H20.

CHAPTER 16

1. Based on Joel Kotkin, ". . . The 'Smart Team' at Compaq Computer," *INC.*, February 1986, pp. 48–56; F. Lisa Beebe, "Rod Canion: Charting the Compaq Course," *American Way*, Jan. 1, 1987, pp. 19–23; Jo Ellen Davis, "Who's Afraid of IBM?" *Business Week*, June 29, 1987, pp. 68–74; John Burgess, "Compaq Announces Expansion," *The Washington Post*, July 14, 1988, p. F1; Paul Duke, Jr., "Compaq Enters First Machine in Laptop Race," *The Wall Street Journal*, Oct. 17, 1988, p. B5; Mark Ivey, "How Compaq Gets There Firstest with the Mostest," *Business Week*, June 26, 1989, pp. 146–150; Norm Alster, "Soft Dollars, Hard Choices," *Forbes*, Sept. 4, 1989, pp. 106–110; "Compaq Computer Entry Joins a Swarm of Notebook-Sized PCs," *The Wall Street Journal*, Oct. 16, 1989, p. B4; Andy Zipser, "Compaq Rolls Out Personal Computers, Claims They Challenge Minicomputers," *The Wall Street Journal*, Nov. 7, 1989, p. B4; and Pascal Zachary and Andy Zipser, "Businessland Is Compaq's Land Yet Once Again," *The Wall Street Journal*, Mar. 8, 1990, p. B1.

2. Based on Marvin E. Shaw, *Group Dynamics: The Psychology of Small Group Behavior*, 3d ed., McGraw-Hill, New York, 1981; and Clayton P. Alderfer, "An Intergroup Perspective on Group Dynamics," in Jay W. Lorsch (ed.), *Handbook of Organizational Behavior*, Prentice-Hall, Englewood Cliffs, N.J., 1987.

3. Myron Magnet, "The Resurrection of the Rust Belt," *Fortune*, Aug. 15, 1988, pp. 40–48.

4. Bill Saporito, "Heinz Pushes to Be the Low Cost Producer," *Fortune*, June 24, 1985, pp. 44–54.

5. Ernest Stech and Sharon A. Ratliffe, *Effective Group Communication: How to Get Action by Working in Groups*, National Textbook, Lincolnwood, Ill., 1985.

6. Chress Welles and James R. Norman, "The Case of the Purloined Magazines," *Business Week*, Aug. 15, 1988, pp. 40–44.

7. Gary Weiss, "There's Already a Divorce at Ranieri Wilson," *Business Week*, Aug. 1, 1988, p. 83.

8. George Homans, *The Human Group*, Harcourt, Brace, New York, 1950.

9. P. Ranganath Nayak and John M. Ketteringham, *Breakthroughs!* Rawson Associates, New York, 1986.

10. Ibid; see also Robert A. Sigafoos, *Absolutely Positively Overnight!* St. Luke's Press, Memphis, Tenn., 1988.

11. F. Lisa Beebe, "Rod Canion: Charting the Compaq Course," *American Way*, Jan. 1, 1987, pp. 19–23.

12. J. Richard Hackman and Richard E. Walton, "Leading Groups in Organizations," in Paul S. Goodman and Associates (eds.), *Designing Effective Work Groups*, Jossey-Bass, San Francisco, 1986, pp. 72–119.

13. J. Richard Hackman, "The Design of Work Teams," in Jay W. Lorsch (ed.), *Handbook of Organizational Behavior*, Prentice-Hall, Englewood Cliffs, N.J., 1987, pp. 315–342.

14. Preston C. Bottger and Philip W. Yetton, "Improving Group Performance by Training in Individual Problem Solving," *Journal of Applied Psychology*, vol. 72, 1987, pp. 651–657.

15. Paul S. Goodman, Elizabeth C. Ravlin, and Linda Argote, "Current Thinking about Groups: Setting the Stage for New Ideas," in Paul S. Goodman and Associates (eds.), *Designing Effective Work Groups*, Jossey-Bass, San Francisco, 1986, pp. 1–33.

16. Irving S. Shapiro, "Executive Forum: Managerial Communication: The View from Inside," *California Management Review*, Fall 1984, pp. 157–172.

17. Marvin E. Shaw, *Group Dynamics: The Psychology of Small Group Behavior*, 3d ed., McGraw-Hill, New York, 1981.

18. Pete Engardio, "The Peace Corps' New Frontier," *Business Week*, Aug. 22, 1988, pp. 62–63.

19. This section is based largely on Kenneth Benne and P. H. Sheats, "Functional Roles of Group Members," *Journal of Social Issues*, vol. 4, 1948, pp. 41–49; and Seth Allcorn, "What Makes Groups Tick," *Personnel*, September 1985, pp. 52–58.

20. B. Aubrey Fisher, *Small Group Decision Making: Communication and the Group Process*, 2d ed., McGraw-Hill, New York, 1980; William B. Eddy, *The Manager and the Working Group*, Praeger, New York, 1985.

21. Bernard M. Bass, *Stogdill's Handbook of Leadership*, Free Press, New York, 1981.

22. William B. Eddy, *The Manager and the Working Group*, Praeger, New York, 1985.

23. This section is based on Fremont A. Shull, Jr., Andre L. Delbecq, and L. L. Cummings, *Organizational Decision Making*, McGraw-Hill, New York, 1970; and Marvin E. Shaw, *Group Dynamics: The Psychology of Small Group Behavior*, 3d ed., McGraw-Hill, New York, 1981.

24. William J. Altier, "SMR Forum: Task Forces—An Effective Management Tool," *Sloan Management Review*, Spring 1986, pp. 69–76.

25. Zachary Schiller, "The Marketing Revolution at Procter & Gamble," *Business Week*, July 25, 1988, pp. 72–76.

26. L. L. Cummings, George P. Huber, and Eugene Arendt, "Effects of Size and Spatial Arrangements on Group Decision Making," *Academy of Management Journal*, vol. 17, 1974, pp. 460–475; George E. Manners, Jr., "Another Look at Group Size, Group Problem Solving, and Member Consensus," *Academy of Management Journal*, vol. 18, 1975, pp. 715–724; Paul S. Goodman, Elizabeth C. Ravlin, and Linda Argote, "Current Thinking about Groups: Setting the Stage for New Ideas," in Paul S. Goodman and Associates (eds.), *Designing Effective Work Groups*, Jossey-Bass, San Francisco, 1986, pp. 1–33.

27. Richard Z. Gooding and John A. Wagner III, "A Meta-Analytic Review of the Relationship between Size and Performance: The Productivity and Efficiency of Organizations and Their Subunits," *Administrative Science Quarterly*, vol. 30, 1985, pp. 462–481; Jeffrey M. Jackson and Stephen G. Harkins, "Equity in Effort: An Explanation of the Social Loafing Effect," *Journal of Personality and Social Psychology*, vol. 49, 1985, pp. 1199–1206; Bibb Latane, "Responsibility and Effort in Organizations," in Paul S. Goodman and Associates (eds.), *Designing Effective Work Groups*, Jossey-Bass, San Francisco, 1986, pp. 277–304.

28. Study conducted by Ringelmann as cited in I. D. Steiner, *Group Process and Productivity*, Academic, New York, 1972.

29. Jeffrey M. Jackson and Stephen G. Harkins, "Equity in Effort: An Explanation of the Social Loafing Effect," *Journal of Personality and Social Psychology*, vol. 49, 1985, pp. 1199–1206.

30. Kate Szymanski and Stephen G. Harkins, "Social Loafing and Self-Evaluation with a Social Standard," *Journal of Personality and Social Psychology*, vol. 53, 1987, pp. 891–897.

31. Robert Alabanese and David D. Van Fleet, "Rational Behavior in Groups: The Free-Riding Tendency," *Academy of Management Review*, vol. 10, 1985, pp. 244–255.

32. Ibid.; Jeffrey M. Jackson and Stephen G. Harkins, "Equity in Effort: An Explanation of the Social Loafing Effect," *Journal of Personality and Social Psychology*, vol. 49, 1985, pp. 1199–1206; Stephen J. Zaccaro, "Social Loafing: The Role of Task Attractiveness," *Personality and Social Psychology Bulletin*, vol. 10, 1984, pp. 99–106.

33. Norbert L. Kerr and Steven E. Bruun,

"Dispensibility of Member Effort and Group Motivation Losses: Free Rider Effects," *Journal of Personality and Social Psychology*, vol. 44, 1983, pp. 78–94.

34. I. D. Steiner, *Group Process and Productivity*, Academic, New York, 1972.

35. This discussion of synergy is based on J. Richard Hackman, "The Design of Work Teams," in Jay W. Lorsch (ed.), *Handbook of Organizational Behavior*, Prentice-Hall, Englewood Cliffs, N.J., 1987.

36. Bill Saporito, "Luv That Market," *Fortune*, Aug. 3, 1987, p. 56.

37. Patrick E. Cole, "SCS May Have Defeated Its Worst Enemy—Itself," *Business Week*, June 27, 1988, p. 88D.

38. Paul S. Goodman, Elizabeth Ravlin, and Marshall Schminke, "Understanding Groups in Organizations," *Research in Organizational Behavior*, vol. 9, 1987, pp. 121–173.

39. Ibid.

40. Daniel C. Feldman, "The Development and Enforcement of Group Norms," *Academy of Management Review*, vol. 9, 1984, pp. 47–53.

41. The information regarding American Steel & Wire in this section is from Myron Magnet, "The Resurrection of the Rust Belt," *Fortune*, Aug. 15, 1988, pp. 40–48.

42. Kenneth Bettenhausen and J. Keith Murnighan, "The Emergence of Norms in Competitive Decision-Making Groups," *Administrative Science Quarterly*, vol. 30, 1985, pp. 350–372.

43. This section relies heavily on Hugh J. Arnold and Daniel C. Feldman, *Organizational Behavior*, McGraw-Hill, New York, 1986; and H. Joseph Reitz, *Behavior in Organizations*, 3d ed., Irwin, Homewood, Ill., 1987. See also A. V. Lott and B. E. Lott, "Group Cohesiveness as Interpersonal Attraction: A Review of Relationships with Antecedent and Consequent Variables," *Psychological Bulletin*, vol. 64, 1965, pp. 259–302; and Nancy J. Evans and Paul A. Jarvis, "Group Cohesion: A Review and Reevaluation," *Small Group Behavior*, vol. 11, 1980, pp. 359–370.

44. Gregory H. Dobbins and Stephen J. Zaccaro, "The Effects of Group Cohesion and Leader Behavior on Subordinate Satisfaction," *Group and Organizational Studies*, vol. 11, 1986, pp. 203–219.

45. Myron Magnet, "The Resurrection of the Rust Belt," *Fortune*, Aug. 15, 1988, pp. 40–48.

46. Stanley Seashore, *Group Cohesiveness in the Industrial Work Group*, Institute for Social Research, Ann Arbor, Mich., 1954; Ralph M. Stogdill, "Group Productivity, Drive, and Cohesiveness," *Organizational Behavior and Human Performance*, vol. 8, 1972, pp. 26–43.

47. Paul B. Brown, "The Anti-Marketers," *INC.*, March 1988, pp. 62–72; Fleming Meeks, "The Man Is the Message," *Forbes*, Apr. 17, 1989, pp. 148–152.

48. Bruce W. Tuckman, "Developmental Sequence in Small Groups," *Psychological Bulletin*, vol. 63, 1965, pp. 384–399; Bruce W. Tuckman and Mary Ann C. Jensen, "Stages of Small-Group Development Revisited," *Group and Organization Studies*, vol. 2, 1977, pp. 419–427.

49. John A. Seeger, "No Innate Phases in Group Problem Solving," *Academy of Management Review*, vol. 8, 1983, pp. 683–689.

50. Study by Wharton Center for Applied Research cited in Carol Hymowitz, "A Survival Guide to the Office Meeting," *The Wall Street Journal*, June 21, 1988, p. 41.

51. Helen B. Schwartzman, "The Meeting as a Neglected Social Form in Organizational Studies," *Research in Organizational Behavior*, vol. 8, 1986, pp. 233–258.

52. This section is based on Anthony Jay, "How to Run a Meeting," *Harvard Business Review*, March–April 1976, pp. 120–134; George Huber, *Managerial Decision Making*, Scott, Foresman, Glenview, Ill., 1980; David A. Whetten and Kim S. Cameron, *Developing Management Skills*, Scott, Foresman,

Glenview, Ill., 1984; and Julie Bailey, "The Fine Art of Leading a Meeting," *Working Woman*, August 1987, pp. 68–70, 103.

53. William J. Altier, "SMR Forum: Task Forces—An Effective Management Tool," *Sloan Management Review*, Spring 1986, pp. 69–75.

54. Ernest Stech and Sharon A. Ratliffe, *Effective Group Communication: How to Get Action by Working in Groups*, National Textbook, Lincolnwood, Ill., 1985.

55. Rober B. Reich, "Entrepreneurship Reconsidered: The Team as Hero," *Harvard Business Review*, May–June 1987, pp. 77–83.

56. Jerome M. Rosow, *World of Work Report*, cited in Jeffrey P. Davidson, "A Way to Work in Concert," *Management World*, March 1986, pp. 9–12.

57. Russell Mitchell, "How Ford Hit the Bull's-Eye with Taurus," *Business Week*, June 30, 1986, pp. 69–70.

58. Jerome M. Rosow, *World of Work Report*, cited in Jeffrey P. Davidson, "A Way to Work in Concert," *Management World*, March 1986, pp. 9–12.

59. Steve Lohr, "Manufacturing Cars the Volvo Way," *The New York Times*, June 23, 1987, pp. D1, D5.

60. Brian Dumaine, "Who Needs a Boss?" *Fortune*, May 7, 1990, pp. 52–60.

61. Maralyn Edid, "How Power Will Be Balanced on Saturn's Shop Floor," *Business Week*, pp. 65–66; Charles C. Manz and Henry P. Sims, Jr., "Leading Workers to Lead Themselves: The External Leadership of Self-Managing Work Teams," *Administrative Science Quarterly*, vol. 32, 1987, pp. 106–128.

62. Barbara Anne Solomon, "A Plant That Proves That Team Management Works," *Personnel*, June 1985, pp. 6–8; Patricia Galagan, "Work Teams That Work," *Training and Development Journal*, November 1986, pp. 33–35.

63. J. Richard Hackman, "The Design of Work Teams," in Jay W. Lorsch (ed.), *Handbook of Organizational Behavior*, Prentice-Hall, Englewood Cliffs, N.J., 1987, pp. 315–342.

64. Based on Ricardo Semler, "Managing without Managers," *Harvard Business Review*, September–October 1989, pp. 76–84.

65. Steven P. Robbins, *Managing Organizational Conflict: A Nontraditional Approach*, Prentice-Hall, Englewood Cliffs, N.J., 1974.

66. Dean Tjosvold, "Making Conflict Productive," *Personnel Administrator*, June 1984, pp. 121–130.

67. Ibid.

68. This section is based largely on Richard E. Walton and John M. Dutton, "The Management of Interdepartmental Conflict: A Model and Review," *Administrative Science Quarterly*, March 1969, pp. 73–84; and Stephen P. Robbins, *Organizational Theory: The Structure and Design of Organizations*, Prentice-Hall, Englewood Cliffs, N.J., 1983.

69. George Strauss, "Work Flow Frictions, Interfunctional Rivalry, and Professionalism: A Case Study of Purchasing Agents," *Human Organization*, vol. 23, 1964, pp. 137–149.

70. Noah E. Friedkin and Michael J. Simpson, "Effect of Competition on Members' Identification with Their Subunits," *Administrative Science Quarterly*, vol. 30, 1985, pp. 377–394.

71. Julia Flynn Siler, "The Slippery Ladder at Abbott Labs," *Business Week*, Oct. 30, 1989, pp. 136–137.

72. Alfie Kohn, *No Contest: The Case against Competition*, Houghton Mifflin, Boston, 1986; Alfie Kohn, "It's Hard to Get Left Out of a Pair," *Psychology Today*, Oct. 1987, pp. 53–57.

73. Bruce G. Posner, "If at First You Don't Succeed," *INC.*, May 1989, pp. 132–134.

74. This section is based on Stephen P. Robbins, *Organizational Theory: The Structure and Design of Organizations*, Prentice-Hall, Englewood Cliffs, N.J., 1983.

75. Christopher Knowlton, "Making It Right the First Time," *Fortune*, Mar. 28, 1988, p. 48.

76. Kenneth W. Thomas, "Toward Multi-

Dimensional Values in Teaching: The Example of Conflict Behaviors," *Academy of Management Review*, vol. 2, 1977, pp. 484–490; H. Joseph Reitz, *Behavior in Organizations*, 3d ed., Irwin, Homewood, Ill., 1987.

77. Stephen P. Robbins, *Organizational Theory: The Structure and Design of Organizations*, Prentice-Hall, Englewood Cliffs, N.J., 1983.

78. Kathleen K. Wiegner, "Nice Guys Finish Last," *Forbes*, June 26, 1989, p. 142.

79. Tom Peters, "Letter to the Editor," *INC.*, April 1988, pp. 80–82.

80. This exercise is adapted from John E. Jones and J. William Pfeiffer, *The 1975 Annual Handbook for Group Facilitators*, University Associates, La Jolla, Calif., 1975, pp. 28–34.

81. Based on Erik Larson, "Forever Young," *INC.*, July 1988, pp. 50–62; N. R. Kleinfield, "Wntd: C.F.O. with 'Flair for Funk,'" *The New York Times*, Mar. 26, 1989; Joe Queenan, "Purveying Yuppie Porn," *Forbes*, Nov. 13, 1989, pp. 60–64; Howard Kurtz, "Ben & Jerry: Premium Ice Cream Spinkled with Liberal Ideology," *The Washington Post*, Nov. 29, 1989, p. A3; and "Ben & Jerry's Chief to Quit at Year End; Lacy to Be President," *The Wall Street Journal*, Feb. 7, 1990, p. B5.

Sources for Part Ending Case for Part 4: Based on Robert J. McClory, "The Creative Process at Herman Miller," *Across the Board*, May 1985; Hugh DePree, *Business as Usual*, Herman Miller, Inc., 1986; *The Silver Parachute*, Herman Miller, Inc., 1986; Max DePree, *Leadership Is An Art*, Michigan State University Press, East Lansing, Mich., 1987; "Herman Miller: Where Innovation Is the Watchword," *Designers West Magazine*, Oct. 10, 1987, pp. 167–170; Beverly Geber, "Herman Miller: Where Profits and Participation Meet," *Training*, November 1987, pp. 62–66; Andrew Tanzer, "I Want to Be the Toyota of Furniture," *Forbes*, May 16, 1988, pp. 92–96; *Annual Reports—1988 & 1989 Herman Miller Inc.*; *Renewal-Abridged Edition*, Herman Miller Inc., 1988; George Melloan, "Herman Miller's Secrets of Corporate Creativity," *The Wall Street Journal*, May 3, 1988, p. 31; Kenneth Labich, "Hot Company, Warm Culture," *Fortune*, Feb. 27, 1989, pp. 74–78; *Corporate Values*, Herman Miller, Inc., 1989; *Participative Management at Herman Miller*, Herman Miller, Inc., 1989; Karen Maru File, "The 1989 Business Ethics Awards for Excellence in Ethics," *Business Ethics*, November/December, 1989, pp. 20–25; and *Corporate Critics Confidential—Furniture*, The Wall Street Transcript, Jan. 8, 1990; Memorandum—*Herman Miller Honors Outstanding Suggesters at Annual Idea Club Dinner*, Herman Miller, Inc. 1990.

CHAPTER 17

1. Kathleen Deveny, "McWorld?" *Business Week*, Oct. 13, 1986, pp. 79–86; "Big Mac Strikes Back," *Time*, Apr. 13, 1987; John Case, "Hamburger Heaven," *INC.*, September 1987, pp. 26, 28; Penny Moser, "The McDonald's Mystique," *Fortune*, July 4, 1988, pp. 112–116; Richard Phalon, "Japan's Great Burger War," *Forbes*, Oct. 17, 1988, pp. 64–65; Richard Gibson, "McDonald's Makes a Fast Pitch to Pizza Buffs Who Hate to Wait," *The Wall Street Journal*, Aug. 28, 1989, p. B5; Brian Bremner, "McDonald's Stoops to Conquer," *Business Week*, Oct. 30, 1989, pp. 120–124; Robert J. Samuelson, "In Praise of McDonald's," *The Washington Post*, Nov. 1, 1989, p. A25.

2. Robert J. Samuelson, "In Praise of McDonald's," *The Washington Post*, Nov. 1, 1989, p. A25.

3. William H. Newman, *Constructive Control*, Prentice-Hall, Englewood Cliffs, N.J., 1975.

4. Kenneth A. Merchant, *Control in Business Organizations*, Pitman, Boston, 1985, p. 4.

5. Barbara Marsh, "Going for the Golden Arches," *The Wall Street Journal*, May 1, 1989, p. B1.

6. Margaret K. Webb, "At McDonald's, Learning to Break Down Barriers," *The Washington Post*, Jan. 28, 1990, Business section, p. 9.

7. Eric Flamholtz, "Behavorial Aspects of Accounting/Control Systems," in Steven Kerr (ed.), *Organizational Behavior*, Grid Publishing, Columbus, Ohio, 1979, p. 290.

8. Kathleen Deveny, "Bag Those Fries, Squirt That Ketchup, Fry That Fish," *Business Week*, Oct. 13, 1986, p. 86.

9. Richard Brandt, Susan Benway, and Dori Jones Yang, "Worlds of Wonder: From Wall Street Charmer to Chapter 11," *Business Week*, Mar. 21, 1988, pp. 74–78.

10. Joan O'C. Hamilton, "How Levi Strauss Is Getting the Lead Out of Its Pipeline," *Business Week*, Dec. 21, 1987, p. 92.

11. Peter F. Drucker, "A Prescription for Entrepreneurial Management," *Industry Week*, Apr. 29, 1985, pp. 33–34.

12 Amy Dunkin and Michael Oneal, "Power Retailers," *Business Week*, Dec. 21, 1987, pp. 86–92.

13. Edward E. Lawler III and John Grant Rhodes, *Information and Control in Organizations*, Goodyear, Pacific Palisades, Calif., 1976.

14. Steve Weiner, "Low Marks, Few Sparks," *Forbes*, Sept. 18, 1989, pp. 146–147.

15. Alfred P. Sloan, Jr., *My Years with General Motors*, Doubleday, New York, 1964.

16. This section relies heavily on Peter Lorange, Michael F. Scott Morton, and Sumantra Ghoshal, *Strategic Control Systems*, West, St. Paul, Minn., 1986; and Georg Schreyoff and Horst Steinmann, "Strategic Control: A New Perspective," *Academy of Management Review*, vol. 12, 1987, pp. 91–103.

17. Cynthia Crossen, "Waldenbooks Peddles Books a Bit Like Soap, Transforming Market," *The Wall Street Journal*, Oct. 10, 1988, pp. A1, A6; Meg Cox, "Waldenbooks' Big-Buyer Lure May Mean War," Feb. 27, 1990, pp. B1, B7.

18. James Cook, "We Are the Market," *Forbes*, Apr. 7, 1986, pp. 54–55.

19. Joan O'C. Hamilton, "Why Rivals Are Quaking as Nordstrom Heads East," *Business Week*, June 15, 1987, pp. 99–100.

20. Kenneth A. Merchant, *Control in Business Organizations*, Pitman, Boston, 1985, p. 20.

21. Richard D. Hollinger and John P. Clark, *Theft by Employees*, Lexington Books, Lexington, Mass., 1983.

22. Richard Behar, "How the Rich Get Richer," *Forbes*, Oct. 31, 1988, p. 70.

23. Donal W. Caudill, "How to Recognize and Deter Employee Theft," *Personnel Administrator*, July 1988, pp. 86–90; see also Mark Lipman, *Stealing: How America's Employees Are Stealing Their Companies Blind*, Harper's Magazine Press, New York, 1973.

24. Bro Uttal, "Companies That Serve You Best," *Fortune*, Dec. 7, 1987, pp. 98–116.

25. Ibid.

26. Ibid.

27. William H. Newman, *Constructive Control*, Prentice-Hall, Englewood Cliffs, N.J., 1975.

28. Amy Dunkin, "Power Retailers," *Business Week*, Dec. 21, 1987, pp. 86–92.

29. Joan O'C. Hamilton, "Why Rivals Are Quaking as Nordstrom Heads East," *Business Week*, June 15, 1987, pp. 99–100.

30. Stephen G. Green and M. Ann Welsh, "Cybernetics and Dependence: Reframing the Control Concept," *Academy of Management Review*, vol. 13, 1988, pp. 287–301.

31. Richard Phalon, "Japan's Great Burger War," *Forbes*, Oct. 17, 1988, pp. 64–65.

32. Kathleen Deveny, "McWorld?" *Business Week*, Oct. 13, 1986, pp. 78–86.

33. Ibid.

34. John Lippert and Nunzio Lupo, "A Not-So Happy Birthday," *Detroit Free Press*, Aug. 28, 1988, pp. F1, F2.

35. W. G. Ouchi and M. A. Maguire, "Organizational Control: Two Functions," *Administrative Science Quarterly*, vol. 20, 1975, pp. 559–569.

36. John Lippert and Nunzio Lupo, "A Not-So Happy Birthday," *Detroit Free Press*, Aug. 28, 1988, pp. F1, F2.

37. Ibid.

38. "Teaching Discipline to Six-Year-Old-Lotus," *Business Week*, July 4, 1988, pp. 100–102; "Business Software: The Top Ten," *1988 Inc. Office Guide*, September, 1988, p. 7; William M. Bulkeley, "After Years of Glory, Lotus Is Stumbling in Software Market," *The Wall Street Journal*, Aug. 30, 1988, pp. 1, 11, and "Long Delayed New Lotus 1-2-3 Is Testing Well," *The Wall Street Journal*, May 26, 1989, pp. B1, B4; Evelyn Richards, "Lagging Lotus Releases Its New Version of 1-2-3, *The Wall Street Journal*, June 21, 1989, pp. D1, D4; John R. Wilke, "Lotus Set Back in Developing 1-2-3 for Apple," *The Wall Street Journal*, Jan. 15, 1990, pp. B1, B2.

39. Luther Jackson, "Suppliers Like Masco See Their Own Profits in Auto Firms' Cuts," *Detroit Free Press*, Mar. 2, 1987, pp. 1, 5; James B. Treece, "GM'S Bumpy Ride on the Long Road Back," *Business Week*, Feb. 13, 1989, pp. 74–78.

40. Richard E. Walton, "From Control to Commitment in the Workplace," *Harvard Business Review*, March–April 1985, pp. 77–84.

41. John Hoerr, "Work Teams Can Rev Up Paper-Pushers, Too," *Business Week*, Nov. 28, 1988, pp. 64–72, and "The Payoff from Teamwork," *Business Week*, July 10, 1989, pp. 56–62.

42. Larry Reibstein, "Federal Express Faces Challenges to Its Grip on Overnight Delivery," *The Wall Street Journal*, Jan. 6, 1988, p. 1; Kenneth Labich, "Big Changes at Big Brown," *Fortune*, Jan. 18, 1988, pp. 56–64; Resa W. King, "UPS Gets a Big Package—of Computers," *Business Week*, July 25, 1988, p. 66A, and "UPS Isn't about to Be Left Holding the Parcel," *Business Week*, Feb. 13, 1989, p. 69; "Can UPS Deliver the Goods in a New World?" *Business Week*, June 4, 1990, pp. 80–82.

43. Cortlandt Cammann and David A. Nadler, "Fit Control Systems to Your Managerial Style," *Harvard Business Review*, January–February 1976, pp. 65–72.

44. This section is based on James Brian Quinn, "Technological Innovation, Entrepreneurship, and Strategy," *Sloan Management Review*, Spring 1979, pp. 19–30, and "Managing Innovation: Controlled Chaos," *Harvard Business Review*, May–June 1985, pp. 73–84.

45. James Brian Quinn, "Managing Innovation: Controlled Chaos," *Harvard Business Review*, May–June 1985, pp. 73–84.

46. P. Ranganath Nayak and John M. Ketteringham, *Break-Throughs*, Rawson Associates, New York, 1986.

47. This section is based on Kenneth A. Merchant, *Control in Business Organizations*, Pitman, Boston, 1985.

48. John P. Kotter, Leonard A. Schlesinger, and Vijay Sathe, *Organization: Test, Cases, and Readings on the Management of Organizational Design and Change*, Irwin, Homewood, Ill., 1979.

49. Kenneth A. Merchant, "The Effects of Organizational Controls," working paper, Harvard University, Graduate School of Business Administration, 1984, cited in Kenneth A. Merchant, *Control in Business Organizations*, Pitman, Boston, 1985, p. 82.

50. David B. Greenberger and Stephen Strasser, "Development and Application of a Model of Personal Control in Organizations," *Academy of Management Review*, vol. 11, 1986, pp. 164–177.

51. Walecia Konrad and Richard A. Melcher, "So Far, JWT Has Been Turned Only Halfway Around," *Business Week*, Mar. 28, 1988, pp. 90–94.

52. Kenneth A. Merchant, "The Control Function of Management," *Sloan Management Review*, Summer 1982, pp. 43–55.

53. Kenneth A. Merchant, *Control in Business Organizations*, Pitman, Boston, 1985, pp. 10–11; James A. F. Stoner and Charles Wankel, *Management*, 3d ed., Prentice-Hall, Englewood Cliffs, N.J., 1986, pp. 586–587.

54. Penny Moser, "The McDonald's Mystique," *Fortune*, July 4, 1988, pp. 112–116.

55. Based on Roy Rowan, "E. F. Hutton's New Man on the Hot Seat," *Fortune*, Nov. 11, 1985, pp. 130–136; Elliott D. Lee, "E. F. Hutton Reports Profit for 2nd Quarter," *The Wall Street Journal*, July 17, 1987, p. 4; Brett Duvall Fromson, "The Slow Death of E. F. Hutton," *Fortune*, Feb. 29, 1988, pp. 82–88; Matthew Winkler, "American Express Plans Huge Shearson Recapitalization," *The Wall Street Journal*, Dec. 7, 1989, p. C1; Linda Sandler, "American Express Dismantles Its Eighties' Superstore," *The Wall Street Journal*, Jan. 9, 1990, p. 1C; David A. Vise, "American Express Replaces Shearson Lehman Chairman," *The Washington Post*, Jan. 31, 1990, p. 10; and William Power, "Shearson Gets Cash Infusion," *The Wall Street Journal*, Feb. 27, 1990, p. C1.

CHAPTER 18

1. William E. Sheeline, "Making Them Rich Down Home," *Fortune*, Aug. 15, 1988, pp. 51–55; Richard W. Anderson, "That Roar You Hear Is Food Lion," *Business Week*, Aug. 24, 1987, pp. 65–66.

2. Eric G. Flamholtz, "Accounting, Budgeting and Control Systems in Their Organizational Context: Theoretical and Empirical Perspectives," *Accounting, Organizations and Society*, vol. 8, 1983, pp. 253–269; Robert N. Anthony, John Dearden, and Norton M. Bedford, *Management Control Systems*, 5th ed., Irwin, Homewood, Ill., 1984; Everett E. Adam, Jr., and Ronald J. Ebert, *Production and Operations Management*, 3d ed., Prentice-Hall, Englewood Cliffs, N.J., 1986.

3. John J. Pringle and Robert S. Harris, 2d ed., *Essentials of Managerial Finance*, Scott, Foresman, Glenview, Ill., 1987. For a discussion of financial statements for not-for-profit organizations, see Robert N. Anthony, "Making Sense of Nonbusiness Accounting," *Harvard Business Review*, May–June 1980, pp. 83–93.

4. George E. Pinches, *Essentials of Financial Management*, 3d ed., Harper & Row, New York, 1990.

5. The definitions of financial control measures and related examples involving the Eagle Manufacturing Company are based on information from H. Kent Baker, *Financial Management*, Harcourt Brace Jovanovich, San Diego, Calif., 1987, pp. 88–122.

6. Jerry A. Viscione and Gordon S. Roberts, *Contemporary Financial Managment*, Merrill, Columbus, Ohio, 1987.

7. This formula is based on John J. Pringle and Robert S. Harris, *Essentials of Managerial Finance*, 2d ed., Scott, Foresman, Glenview, Ill., 1987; and Jerry A. Viscione and Gordon S. Roberts, *Contemporary Financial Management*, Merrill, Columbus, Ohio, 1987.

8. Jerry A. Viscione and Gordon S. Roberts, *Contemporary Financial Management*, Merrill, Columbus, Ohio, 1987.

9. Based on Bill Saporito, "The Tough Cookie at RJR Nabisco," *Fortune*, July 18, 1988, pp. 32–46; Scott Ticer, "The Boss at RJR Likes to Keep 'Em Guessing," *Business Week*, May 23, 1988, pp. 175–182; Peter Waldman, "New RJR Chief Faces a Daunting Challenge at Debt-Heavy Firm," *The Wall Street Journal*, Mar. 14, 1989, pp. 1, 19; Bill Saporito, "How Ross Johnson Blew the Buyout," *Fortune*, Apr. 24,

1989, pp. 296–317; Judith H. Dobrzynski, "Running the Biggest LBO," *Business Week,* Oct. 2, 1989, pp. 72–79; and Bryan Burrough and John Helyar, "Secret Scenes from the RJR Wars," *The Wall Street Journal,* Jan. 4, 1990, pp. B1, B4–B5.

10. The major sources are *Annual Statement Studies,* Robert Morris Associates, Philadelphia; *Key Business Ratios,* Dun & Bradstreet, New York; *Almanac of Business and Industrial Financial Ratios,* Prentice-Hall, Englewood Cliffs, N.J.; *Quarterly Financial Report for Manufacturing Corporations,* Federal Trade Commission and Securities and Exchange Commission, Washington, D.C.; and data from various trade associations.

11. David S. Vise, "The World According to Rupert Murdoch," *The Washington Post,* Aug. 14, 1988; Chris Welles, "Even Rupert Murdoch Has His Limits," *Business Week,* Oct. 2, 1989, pp. 34–35.

12. Walter B. Meigs and Robert F. Meigs, *Accounting: The Basis for Business Decisions,* 7th ed., McGraw-Hill, New York, 1987.

13. Wanda J. Wallace, "Internal Auditors Can Cut Outside CPA Costs," *Harvard Business Review,* March–April 1984, p. 16, 20.

14. "GE Whiz," *Fortune,* Mar. 27, 1989, p. 151.

15. Scott S. Cowen and J. Kendall Middaugh II, "Designing an Effective Financial Planning and Control System," *Long Range Planning,* vol. 21, 1988, pp. 83–92.

16. Stratford P. Sherman, "Inside the Mind of Jack Welch," *Fortune,* Mar. 27, 1988, pp. 39–50.

17. This section is based heavily on Joseph A. Maciariello, *Management Control Systems,* Prentice-Hall, Englewood Cliffs, N.J., 1984.

18. Peter Waldman, "New RJR Chief Faces a Daunting Challenge at Debt-Heavy Firm," *The Wall Street Journal,* Mar. 14, 1989, pp. A1–A19.

19. Bill Saporito, "The Tough Cookie at RJR Nabisco," *Fortune,* July 18, 1988, pp. 32–46.

20. Ibid.

21. Stratford P. Sherman, "Inside the Mind of Jack Welch," *Fortune,* Mar. 27, 1989, pp. 39–50.

22. Joseph A. Maciariello, *Management Control Systems,* Prentice-Hall, Englewood Cliffs, N.J. 1984.

23. Based on John A. Burne, "Hanson: The Dangers of Living by Takeover Alone," *Business Week,* Aug. 15, 1988, pp. 62–64; see also Sir Gordon White, "'How I Turned $3,000 into $10 Billion,'" *Fortune,* Nov. 7, 1988, pp. 80–89; and Joann S. Lublin, "Hanson Seeks Consolidated Gold Fields," *The Wall Street Journal,* June 23, 1989, p. A3.

24. Walter B. Meigs and Robert F. Meigs, *Accounting: The Basis for Business Decisions,* 7th ed., McGraw-Hill, New York, 1987.

25. Joseph A. Maciariello, *Management Control Systems,* Prentice-Hall, Englewood Cliffs, N.J., 1984; H. Kent Baker, *Financial Management,* Harcourt Brace Jovanovich, San Diego, Calif., 1987.

26. Robert N. Anthony, John Dearden, and Norton M. Bedford, *Management Control Systems,* 5th ed., Irwin, Homewood, Ill., 1984.

27. Jerry A. Viscione and Gordon S. Roberts, *Contemporary Financial Management,* Merrill, Columbus, Ohio, 1987.

28. Robert N. Anthony, John C. Dearden, and Norton M. Bedford, *Management Control Systems,* 5th ed., Irwin, Homewood, Ill., 1984.

29. Jerry A. Viscione and Gordon S. Roberts, *Contemporary Financial Management,* Merrill, Columbus, Ohio, 1987. For a thorough discussion of the capital budgeting process and its relationship to decision support systems, see Lawrence A. Gordon and George E. Pinches, *Improving Capital Budgeting: A Decision Support System Approach,* Addison-Wesley, Reading, Mass., 1984.

30. H. Kent Baker, *Financial Management,* Harcourt Brace Jovanovich, San Diego, Calif., 1987.

31. James C. Van Horne, *Financial Management and Policy,* Prentice-Hall, Englewood Cliffs, N.J., 1989.

32. Jerry A. Viscione and Gordon S. Roberts, *Contemporary Financial Management,* Merrill, Columbus, Ohio, 1987.

33. James C. Van Horne, *Financial Management and Policy,* Prentice-Hall, Englewood Cliffs, N.J., 1989.

34. This section is based mainly on Neil C. Churchill, "Budget Choice: Planning vs. Control," *Harvard Business Review,* July–August 1984, p. 154.

35. Adapted from ibid.

36. Peter A. Pyhrr, "Zero-Base Budgeting," *Harvard Business Review,* November–December 1970, pp. 111–121.

37. "What It Means to Build a Budget from Zero," *Business Week,* Apr. 18, 1977, p. 160.

38. Lawrence A. Gordon, Susan Haka, and Allen G. Schick, "Strategies for Information Systems Implementation: The Case of Zero Base Budgeting," *Accounting, Organizations and Society,* vol. 9, 1984, pp. 111–123.

39. Mark W. Dirsmith and Stephen F. Jablonsky, "Zero-Base Budgeting as a Management Technique and Political Strategy," *Academy of Management Review,* vol. 4, 1979, pp. 555–565.

40. Lawrence A. Gordon, Susan Haka, and Allen G. Schick, "Strategies for Information Systems Implementation: The Case of Zero Base Budgeting," *Accounting, Organizations and Society,* vol. 9, 1984, pp. 111–123.

41. V. Bruce Irvine, "Budgeting: Functional Analysis and Behavioral Implications," *Cost and Management,* March–April 1970, pp. 6–16; Henry L. Tosi, Jr., "The Human Effects of Budgeting Systems on Management," *MSU Business Topics,* Autumn 1974, pp. 53–63.

42. Cindy Skrzycki, "Making Quality a Priority," *The Washington Post,* Oct. 11, 1987.

43. Note to Principles of Management Textbook Authors provided by the American Society for Quality Control, Milwaukee, 1987.

44. David A. Garvin, "Competing on the Eight Dimensions of Quality," *Harvard Business Review,* November–December 1987, pp. 101–119.

45. G. M. Hostage, "Quality Control in a Service Business," *Harvard Business Review,* July–August 1975, pp. 98–106; William A. Sherden, "Gaining the Service Quality Advantage," *Journal of Business Strategy,* March–April 1988, pp. 45–48.

46. Zachary Schiller, "The Refrigerator That Has GE Feeling the Heat," *Business Week,* Apr. 25, 1988; Ira C. Magaziner and Mark Patinkin, "Cold Competition: GE Wages the Refrigerator War," *Harvard Business Review,* March–April 1989, pp. 114–124; Thomas F. O'Boyle, "GE Refrigerator Woes Illustrate the Hazards in Changing a Product," *The Wall Street Journal,* May 7, 1990, pp. A1, A5.

47. Joseph B. White, "U.S. Car-Parts Firms Form Japanese Ties," *The Wall Street Journal,* Apr. 12, 1988, p. 6.

48. Roger B. Yepsen, Jr. (ed.), *The Durability Factor,* Rodale, Emmaus, Penn., 1982, cited in Garvin, "Competing on the Eight Dimensions of Quality," *Harvard Business Review,* November–December 1987, pp. 101–109.

49. Antonio N. Fins, "A Utility That's All Charged Up over Quality," *Business Week,* Feb. 13, 1989, pp. 94A–94D.

50. Kenneth Labich, "Hot Company, Warm Culture," *Fortune,* Feb. 27, 1989, pp. 74–78.

51. David A. Garvin, "Competing on the Eight Dimensions of Quality," *Harvard Business Review,* November–December, 1987, pp. 101–109.

52. Ibid.

53. Otis Port, "The Push for Quality," *Business Week,* June 8, 1987, pp. 130–135; Roger G. Schroeder, *Operations Management,* 3d ed., McGraw-Hill, New York, 1989.

54. Adapted from W. Edwards Deming, *Out of the Crisis,* M.I.T., Center for Advanced Engineering Study, Cambridge, Mass., 1986.

55. Joseph B. White, "U.S. Car-Parts Firms Form Japanese Ties," *The Wall Street Journal,* Apr. 12, 1988, p. 6.

56. Roger G. Schroeder, *Operations Management,* 3d ed., McGraw-Hill, New York, 1989.

57. Building on the work of Juran, Armand Feigenbaum, another American quality expert, actually coined the term "total quality control" in 1956; David A. Garvin, "Competing on the Eight Dimensions of Quality," *Harvard Business Review,* November–December 1987, pp. 101–109. See also J. M. Juran, *Juran on Planning for Quality,* Free Press, New York, 1988.

58. Joseph G. Monks, *Operations Management,* 3d ed., McGraw-Hill, New York, 1987.

59. Otis Port, "The Push for Quality," *Business Week,* June 8, 1987, pp. 130–136.

60. Ellen Goldbaum, "How Quality Programs Win Respect and Get Results," *Chemical Week,* Oct. 5, 1988, pp. 30–33.

61. James Houghton, "For Better Quality, Listen to the Workers," *The New York Times,* Forum, Oct. 18, 1987. For more examples, see also Joel Dreyfus, "Victories in the Quality Crusade," *Fortune,* Oct. 10, 1988, pp. 80–88.

62. Based on Craig R. Waters, "Quality Begins at Home," *INC.,* August 1985, pp. 68–71.

63. Beverly Geber, "Quality Circles: The Second Generation," *Training,* December 1986, pp. 54–61; Joseph G. Monks, *Operations Management,* 3d ed., McGraw-Hill, New York, 1987; Roger G. Schroeder, *Operations Management,* 3d ed., McGraw-Hill, New York, 1989.

64. Mitchell Lee Marks, "The Question of Quality Circles," *Psychology Today,* March 1986, pp. 36–46.

65. Ibid.

66. Beverly Geber, "Quality Circles: The Second Generation," *Training,* December 1986, pp. 54–61.

67. Mitchell Lee Marks, "The Question of Quality Circles," *Psychology Today,* March 1986, pp. 36–46; Beverly Geber, "Quality Circles: The Second Generation," *Training,* December 1986, pp. 54–61.

68. Mitchell Lee Marks, Philip H. Mirvis, Edward J. Hackett, and James F. Grady, Jr., "Employee Participation in a Quality Circle Program: Impact on Quality of Work Life, Productivity, and Absenteeism," *Journal of Applied Psychology,* vol. 71, 1986, pp. 61–69; Murray R. Barrick and Ralph A. Alexander, "A Review of Quality Circle Efficacy and the Existence of Positive-Findings Bias," *Personnel Psychology,* vol. 40, 1987, pp. 579–592.

69. Ricky W. Griffin, "Consequences of Quality Circles in an Industrial Setting: A Longitudinal Assessment," *Academy of Management Journal,* vol. 31, 1988, pp. 338–358.

70. Global C. Pati, Robert Salitore, and Sandra Brady, "What Went Wrong with Quality Circles?" *Personnel Journal,* December 1987, pp. 83–87.

71. Beverly Geber, "Quality Circles: The Second Generation," *Training,* December 1986, pp. 54–61.

72. Ellen Goldbaum, "How Quality Programs Win Respect—And Get Results," *Chemical Week,* Oct. 5, 1988, pp. 30–33.

73. Roger G. Schroeder, *Operations Management,* 3d ed., McGraw-Hill, New York, 1989.

74. This discussion of inventory control is based largely on ibid.

75. Ibid.

76. Richard Brandt, "Worlds of Wonder: From Wall Street Charmer to Chapter 11," *Business Week,* Mar. 21, 1988, pp. 74–75.

77. Brenton R. Schlender, "Apple Slips as Result of Hoarding Chips," *The Wall Street Journal,* Jan. 30, 1989, p. A6.

78. Dennis W. McLeavey and Seetharama L. Narasimhan, *Production Planning and Inventory Control,* Allyn and Bacon, Boston, 1985.

79. This discussion is based largely on Roger G. Schroeder, *Operations Management,* 3d ed., McGraw-Hill, New York, 1989.

80. Charles G. Burck, "Can Detroit Catch Up?" *Fortune*, Feb. 8, 1982, pp. 34–39.
81. Richard J. Schonberger, "An Assessment of Just-in-Time Implementation," in *Readings in Zero Inventory* (APICS 27th Annual International Conference proceedings, Las Vegas, October 9–12, 1984), p. 57.
82. Martha E. Mangelsdorf, "Beyond Just-in-Time," *INC.*, February 1989, p. 21.
83. Andrea Rothman, "High Return Rate for Regina Vacuums May Have Added to Financial Problems," *The Wall Street Journal*, Sept. 29, 1988, p. 4, and "Judge's Opinion Says Regina Had Product Problems," *The Wall Street Journal*, Oct. 5, 1988, p. 5; Robin G. Blumenthal, "Regina Accepts Bid of Electrolux, a Georgia Firm," *The Wall Street Journal*, May 22, 1989, p. A8.

CHAPTER 19

1. "The Big Chill," *Fortune*, Jan. 7, 1985, pp. 56–65; David E. Whiteside and James B. Treece, "GM and Fanuc: An Unlikely Pair— But a Winner," *Business Week*, July 21, 1986, p. 105; Gene Bylinsky, "Japan's Robot King Wins Again," *Fortune*, May 25, 1987, pp. 53–58; "GMF Robotics Expands European Operations," *Robotics World*, September–October 1988, pp. 14, 19; Fred Hiatt, "Japanese Robots Reproducing Like Rabbits," *The Washington Post*, Jan. 2, 1990, pp. A1, A13.
2. Richard B. Chase and Eric L. Prentis, "Operations Management: A Field Rediscovered," *Journal of Management*, vol. 13, 1987, pp. 351–366.
3. Thomas A. Mahoney, "Productivity Defined: The Relativity of Efficiency, Effectiveness, and Change," in John P. Campbell, Richard J. Campbell and Associates, *Productivity in Organizations*, Jossey-Bass, San Francisco, 1988, pp. 13–39.
4. John Merwin, "A Tale of Two Worlds," *Forbes*, June 16, 1986, pp. 101–106.
5. Richard E. Kopelman, *Managing Productivity in Organizations*, McGraw-Hill, New York, 1986.
6. John W. Kendrick, *Improving Company Productivity*, Johns Hopkins, Baltimore, 1984.
7. "How to Regain the Productivity Edge," *Fortune*, May 22, 1989, pp. 92–104.
8. David Wessel, "With Labor Scarce, Service Firms Strive to Raise Productivity," *The Wall Street Journal*, June 1, 1989, pp. A1, A16.
9. This section is based heavily on Roger G. Schroeder, *Operations Management*, 3d ed., McGraw-Hill, New York, 1989.
10. Richard B. Chase, "Where Does the Customer Fit in a Service Operation?" *Harvard Business Review*, November–December 1978.
11. Ibid.
12. Richard B. Chase and Eric L. Prentis, "Operations Management: A Field Rediscovered," *Journal of Management*, vol. 13, 1987, pp. 351–366.
13. Steven Greenhouse, "Revving Up the American Factory," *The New York Times*, Jan. 11, 1987, sec. 3, pp. 1, 8.
14. Stephen C. Wheelwright and Robert H. Hayes, "Competing through Manufacturing," *Harvard Business Review*, January–February 1985, pp. 99–109.
15. Based on William J. Hampton, "What Is Motorola Making at This Factory? History," *Business Week*, Dec. 5, 1988, pp. 168D–168H; and Ronald Henkoff, "What Motorola Learns from Japan," *Fortune*, Apr. 24, 1989, pp. 157–168.
16. Ronald Henkoff, "What Motorola Learns from Japan," *Fortune*, Apr. 24, 1989, pp. 157–168.
17. John Paul Newport, Jr., "American Express: Service That Sells," *Fortune*, Nov. 20, 1989, pp. 80–94.
18. Michael Oneal, "ServiceMaster: Looking for New Worlds to Clean," *Business Week*, Jan. 19, 1987, pp. 60–61; Charles Siler, "Cleanliness, Godliness, and Business," *Business Week*, Nov. 28, 1988, pp. 219–220.
19. Richard B. Barrett and David J. Kistka, "Forecasting System at Rubbermaid," *Journal of Business Forecasting*, Spring 1987, pp. 7–9.
20. Stewart Toy, "When J. D. Power Talks, Carmakers Listen," *Business Week*, Sept. 26, 1988, p. 134.
21. Dennis W. McLeavey and Seetharama L. Narasimhan, *Production Planning and Inventory Control*, Allyn and Bacon, Boston, 1985.
22. Joseph G. Monks, *Operations Management*, 3d ed., McGraw-Hill, New York, 1987; Roger G. Schroeder, *Operations Management*, 3d ed., McGraw-Hill, New York, 1989.
23. This section is based mainly on Joseph G. Monks, *Operations Management*, 3d ed., McGraw-Hill, New York, 1987.
24. Stephanie vL. Henkel, "GMF Retrenches," *Robotics Engineering*, September 1986, p. 26.
25. "Manufacturing: The Key to Growth," *Business Week*, Jan. 11, 1988, pp. 70–73.
26. Richard B. Chase and Eric L. Prentis, "Operations Management: A Field Rediscovered," *Journal of Management*, vol. 13, 1987, pp. 351–366.
27. Ibid.
28. Roger G. Schroeder, *Operations Management*, 3d ed., McGraw-Hill, New York, 1989.
29. Byron J. Finch and James F. Cox, "Process-Oriented Production Planning and Control: Factors That Influence System Design," *Academy of Management Journal*, vol. 31, 1988, pp. 123–153.
30. Roger G. Schroeder, *Operations Management*, 3d ed., McGraw-Hill, New York, 1989.
31. Sumer C. Aggarwal, "MRP, JIT, OPT, FMS?" *Harvard Business Review*, September–October 1985, pp. 8–16; Angelo J. Kinicki, Jeff E. Heyl, and Thomas E. Callarman, "Assessing the Validity of the Cox, Zmud, and Clark Material-Requirements-Planning Audit Instrument," *Academy of Management Journal*, vol. 29, 1986, pp. 633–641.
32. Edna M. White, John C. Anderson, Roger G. Schroeder, and Sharon E. Tupy, "A Study of the MRP Implementation Process," *Journal of Operations Management*, May 1982, pp. 145–153.
33. Roger G. Schroeder, John C. Anderson, Sharon E. Tupy, and Edna M. White. "A Study of MRP Benefits and Costs," *Journal of Operations Management*, October, 1981, pp. 1–9.
34. Roger G. Schroeder, *Operations Management*, 3d ed., McGraw-Hill, New York, 1989.
35. V. Chopra, "Productivity Improvement through Closed Loop MRP (Part One)," *Production and Inventory Management Review and APCIS News*, March 1982, pp. 18–21, and "Productivity Improvement through Closed Loop MRP (Part Two)," *Production and Inventory Management Review and APCIS News*, April 1982, pp. 49–51.
36. Everett E. Adam, Jr., and Ronald J. Ebert, *Production and Operations Management*, 3d ed., Prentice-Hall, Englewood Cliffs, N.J., 1986.
37. Bryan Cockel, "Textronix," *Distribution*, August 1986, p. 54.
38. Mary Jo Foley, "Post-MRPII: What Comes Next?" *Datamation*, Dec. 1, 1988, pp. 24–36.
39. Joseph G. Monks, *Operations Management*, 3d ed., McGraw-Hill, New York, 1987.
40. This section relies heavily on David N. Burt and William I. Soukup, "Purchasing's Role in New Product Development," *Harvard Business Review*, September–October 1985, pp. 90–97.
41. This section is based partially on Elwood S. Buffa, *Modern Production/Operations Management*, 7th ed., Wiley, New York, 1983.
42. "Man in the Hot Seat," *Time*, Nov. 14, 1988, p. 49.
43. Robert H. Hayes and Steven C. Wheelwright, *Restoring Our Competitive Edge: Competing through Manufacturing*, Wiley, New York, 1984.
44. Laura R. Walbert, "Service Is Our Most Important Product," *Forbes*, Apr. 6, 1987, pp. 48–50.
45. Paul Ingrassia and Bradley A. Stertz, "Ford's Strong Sales Raise Agonizing Issue of Additional Plants," *The Wall Street Journal*, Oct. 26, 1988, pp. A1, A10.
46. See, for example, Gerald G. Brown, Glenn W. Graves, and Maria D. Honczarenko, "Design and Operation of a Multicommodity Production/Distribution System Using Primal Goal Decomposition," *Management Science*, vol. 33, 1987, pp. 1469–1480.
47. Howard Rudnitsky, "How Sam Walton Does It," *Forbes*, Aug. 16, 1982, pp. 42–44, and "Play It Again, Sam," *Forbes*, Aug. 10, 1987, p. 48.
48. Donald Dawson, "Place for a Store," *Marketing*, Apr. 7, 1988, pp. 35–36, see also Walter Weart, "OPTISITE," *Distribution*, February 1988, pp. 66–67; Terry G. Meyer, "Site Selection vs. Site Evaluation: Techniques for Locating Retail Outlets," *Real Estate Issues*, Spring–Summer 1988, pp. 25–28; Kenneth Chelst, James Schultz, and Nirupama Sanghvi, "Issues and Decision Aids for Designing Branch Networks," *Journal of Retail Banking*, Summer 1988, pp. 5–17; and Donald B. Rosenfield, "The Retailer Facility Location Problem: A Case Study," *Journal of Business Logistics*, vol. 8, 1988, pp. 95–114.
49. This section is based on Everett E. Adam, Jr., and Ronald J. Ebert, *Production and Operations Management*, 3d ed., Prentice-Hall, Englewood Cliffs, N.J., 1986; and Elwood S. Buffa, *Modern Production/Operations Management*, 7th ed., Wiley, New York, 1983.
50. Jeff Bailey and Robert L. Rose, "Maybe Winnebago Just Wasn't Ready for Big-City Bosses," *The Wall Street Journal*, Oct. 17, 1988, pp. A1, A12; Rick Reiff, "Bad News, Good Prospects," *Forbes*, Oct. 31, 1988, p. 39; Robert L. Rose, "Winnebago Dismisses Conner as Chief, as Founder Again Is Tough to Please," *The Wall Street Journal*, Apr. 13, 1990, p. A3.
51. Roger G. Schroeder, *Operations Management*, 3d ed., McGraw-Hill, New York, 1989.
52. William J. Hampton, "GM Bets an Arm and a Leg on a People-Free Plant," *Business Week*, Sept. 12, 1988, pp. 72–73.
53. Peter J. Mullins, "Cassino: Factory of the Future," *Automotive Industries*, November 1988, pp. 150–152.
54. Patricia Nemetz and Louis W. Fry, "Flexible Manufacturing Organizations: Implications for Strategy Formulation and Organizational Design," *Academy of Management Review*, vol. 13, 1988, pp. 627–638.
55. Bernard Avishai, "A CEO's Common Sense of CIM: An Interview with J. Tracy O'Rourke," *Harvard Business Review*, January–February 1989, pp. 110–117.
56. This section is based on Carol A. Beatty and John R. M. Gordon, "Barriers to the Implementation of CAD/CAM Systems," *Sloan Management Review*, Summer 1988, pp. 25–33.
57. Timothy D. Schellhardt and Carol Humowitz, "U.S. Manufacturers Face Big Changes in Years Ahead," *The Wall Street Journal*, May 2, 1989, pp. A3, A8.
58. Barnaby J. Feder, "The Drive to Speed Automation" and "How the System Works at a GM Plant," *The New York Times*, June 15, 1988, pp. D1, D8.
59. Their position is supported by Paul S. Adler, "Managing Flexible Automation," *California Management Review*, Spring 1988, pp. 35–56; and Frederick C. Weston, Jr., "Computer Integrated Manufacturing Systems: Fact or Fantasy," *Business Horizons*, July–August 1988, pp. 64–68.
60. This section is based largely on James L. Heskett, *Managing in the Service Economy*, Harvard Business School, Boston, 1986.
61. William H. Davidow and Bro Uttal, "Service Companies: Focus or Falter," *Harvard*

Business Review, July–August 1989, pp. 77–85.

62. Jaclyn Fierman, "Fidelity's Secret: Faithful Service," *Fortune*, May 7, 1990, pp. 86–92.

63. John Halusha, "Ailing Robot Industry Is Turning to Services," *The New York Times*, Feb. 14, 1989, pp. 27–28.

64. K. F. Curley, "Are There Any Real Benefits from Office Automation?" *Business Horizons*, July–August 1984, pp. 37–42.

65. Catherine L. Harris, "Office Automation: Making It Pay Off," *Business Week*, Oct. 12, 1987, pp. 134–146.

66. John Hoerr, "Work Teams Can Rev Up Paper-Pushers, Too," *Business Week*, Nov. 28, 1988, pp. 64–72.

67. Richard A. Guzzo, "Productivity Research: Reviewing Psychological and Economic Perspectives," in John P. Campbell, Richard J. Campbell and Associates, *Productivity in Organizations*, Jossey-Bass, San Francisco, 1988; Daniel R. Ilgen and Howard J. Klein, "Individual Motivation and Performance: Cognitive Influences on Effort and Choice," in ibid.

68. Wickham Skinner, "The Productivity Paradox," *Harvard Business Review*, July–August 1986, pp. 55–59.

69. "No Trend Lasts Forever," *Forbes*, Dec. 1, 1986, pp. 108–109; "The Job Cutters," *Forbes*, July 13, 1987, p. 117; Ronald Henkoff, "The Cat Is Acting Like a Tiger," *Fortune*, Dec. 19, 1988, pp. 69–76; Kathleen Deveny, "For Caterpillar, the Metamorphosis Isn't Over," *Business Week*, Aug. 31, 1987, pp. 72–74; Kathleen Deveny, Corie Brown, William J. Hampton, and James B. Treece, "Going for the Lion's Share," *Business Week*, July 18, 1988, pp. 70–72; Jeremy Main, "Manufacturing the Right Way," *Fortune*, May 21, 1990, pp. 54–64.

CHAPTER 20

1. Based on Tom Richman, "Mrs. Fields' Secret Ingredient," *INC.*, October 1987, pp. 65–72; Kevin Kennedy, "Centralizing MIS Implements Corporate Vision," *Tech Exec*, June 1989, pp. 16–18; Richard Brandt and Deidre A. Depke, "The Personal Computer Finds Its Missing Link," *Business Week*, June 5, 1989, pp. 120–128; and literature on ROI systems from the Fields Software Group, a subsidiary of Mrs. Fields Cookies.

2. Joel Dreyfuss, "Catching the Computer Wave," *Fortune*, Sept. 26, 1988, pp. 78–82.

3. Gordon B. Davis and Margrethe H. Olson, *Management Information Systems: Conceptual Foundations, Structure, and Development*, 2d ed., McGraw-Hill, New York, 1985.

4. Ralph Emmett Carlyle, "Managing IS at Multinations," *Datamation*, Mar. 1, 1988, pp. 54–66.

5. Kenneth C. Laudon and Jane Price Laudon, *Management Information Systems*, Macmillan, New York, 1988.

6. Donald H. Sanders, *Computer Concepts and Applications*, McGraw-Hill, New York, 1987.

7. These definitions related to data bases are based on Kenneth C. Laudon and Jane Price Laudon, *Management Information Systems: A Contemporary Perspective*, Macmillan, New York, 1988; and Donald H. Sanders, *Computer Concepts and Applications*, McGraw-Hill, New York, 1987.

8. Karen Gullo and Willie Schatz, "The Supercomputer Breaks Through," *Datamation*, May 1, 1988, pp. 50–63.

9. Reprinted from Michael R. Leibowitz, "Clash of the High Speed Titans," *High Technology Business*, July 1988, pp. 50–51.

10. Cited in Paul Tate, "Risk! The Third Factor," *Datamation*, Apr. 15, 1988, pp. 58–64.

11. Lee L. Gremillion and Philip J. Pyburn, *Computers and Information Systems in Business: An Introduction*, McGraw-Hill, New York, 1988.

12. Ibid.

13. This section is largely based on Kenneth C. Laudon and Jane Price Laudon, *Management Information Systems: A Contemporary Perspective*, Macmillan, New York, 1988.

14. Catherine L. Harris and Dean Foust, "An Electronic Pipeline That's Changing the Way America Does Business," *Business Week*, Aug. 3, 1987, pp. 80–82.

15. Raymond McLeod, Jr., *Management Information Systems*, Science Research Associates, Chicago, 1986; Kenneth C. Laudon and Jane Price Laudon, *Management Information Systems: A Contemporary Perspective*, Macmillan, New York, 1988.

16. Nancy B. Finn, *The Electronic Office*, Prentice-Hall, Englewood Cliffs, N.J., 1983; Raymond McLeod, Jr., *Management Information Systems*, Science Research Associates, Chicago, 1986.

17. Marsha J. Fisher, "Airport Gate System Is Ready for Arrival," *Datamation*, July 1, 1988, pp. 21–25.

18. Ron S. Dembo, Angel Chiarri, Jesus Gomez Martin, and Luis Paradinas, "Managing Hidroeléctrica Española's Hydroelectric Power System," *Interfaces*, January–February 1990, pp. 115–135.

19. Efraim Turban and Paul R. Watkins, "Integrating Expert Systems and Decision Support Systems," *MIS Quarterly*, June 1986, pp. 121–138; John C. Henderson, "Finding Synergy between Decision Support Systems and Expert Systems Research," *Decision Sciences*, vol. 18, 1987, pp. 333–349.

20. Fred L. Luconi, Thomas W. Malone, and Michael S. Scott Morton, "Expert Systems: The Next Challenge for Managers," *Sloan Management Review*, Summer 1986, pp. 3–14; Dorothy Leonard-Barton and John J. Sviokla, "Putting Expert Systems to Work," *Harvard Business Review*, March–April 1988, pp. 91–98.

21. Dorothy Leonard-Barton and John J. Sviokla, "Putting Expert Systems to Work," *Harvard Business Review*, March–April 1988, pp. 91–98.

22. Kenneth C. Laudon and Jane Price Laudon, *Management Information Systems: A Contemporary Perspective*, Macmillan, New York, 1988.

23. Daniel G. Bobrow, Sanjay Mittal, and Mark J. Stefik, "Expert Systems: Perils and Promise," *Communications of the ACM*, September 1986, pp. 880–894.

24. Ruth Simon, "The Morning After," *Forbes*, Oct. 19, 1987, pp. 164–168.

25. Susan M. Gelfond, "The Computer Age Dawns in the Corner Office," *Business Week*, June 27, 1988, pp. 84–86.

26. For example, Gregory L. Parsons, "Information Technology: A New Competitive Weapon," *Sloan Management Review*, Fall 1983, pp. 3–14; Robert I. Benjamin, John F. Rockart, Michael S. Scott Morton, and John Wyman, "Information Technology: A Strategic Opportunity," *Sloan Management Review*, Spring 1984, pp. 3–10; Michael E. Porter and Victor E. Millar, "How Information Gives You Competitive Advantage," *Harvard Business Review*, July–August 1985, pp. 149–160; and Marc Gerstein and Heather Reisman, "Creating Competitive Advantage with Computer Technology," *Journal of Business Strategy*, Summer 1987, pp. 53–60.

27. "SABRE Gives the Edge to American Airlines," *Information Week*, May 26, 1986; "American's Crandall Proves DP Profit Potential," *Computerworld*, June 9, 1986; Kenneth Labich, "Bob Crandall Sours by Flying Solo," *Fortune*, Sept. 29, 1986, pp. 118–124; Howard Banks, "Calmness Itself," *Forbes*, Mar. 21, 1988, pp. 39–40.

28. This section is based largely on Charles Wiseman and Ian C. MacMillan, "Creating Competitive Weapons from Information Systems," *Journal of Business Strategy*, Fall 1984, pp. 42–49.

29. Ibid.

30. Ibid.; Charles Wiseman, "Strategic Vision," *Computerworld*, May 20, 1985, pp. ID1–ID16.

31. Tom McCusker, "Success Stories at HP," *Datamation*, Nov. 21, 1988, p. 14.

32. Ibid., "Ocean Freighters Turn to High Tech on the High Seas," *Datamation*, Mar. 1, 1988, pp. 25–26.

33. David Wessel, "Computer Finds a Role in Buying and Selling, Reshaping Business," *The Wall Street Journal*, Mar. 8, 1987, pp. 1, 10; Warren Brown, "Electronic Pulses Replacing Paper in Workplace," *The Washington Post*, Sept. 2, 1988, pp. F1, F2.

34. Reprinted from David Wessel, "Computer Finds a Role in Buying and Selling, Reshaping Businesses," *The Wall Street Journal*, Mar. 8, 1987, p. 1.

35. Tom McCusker, "IS Drives Distribution," *Datamation*, Nov. 21, 1988, p. 20.

36. Cited in Jeffrey Rothfeder, "It's Late, Costly, Incompetent—But Try Firing a Computer System," *Business Week*, Nov. 7, 1988, pp. 164–165.

37. Ibid.

38. Otis Port, "The Software Trap: Automate—Or Else," *Business Week*, May 9, 1988, pp. 142–154.

39. Lee L. Gremillion and Philip J. Pyburn, *Computers and Information Systems in Business: An Introduction*, McGraw-Hill, New York, 1988.

40. Donald H. Sanders, *Computer Concepts and Applications*, McGraw-Hill, New York, 1987.

41. James D. McKeen, "Successful Development Strategies for Business Application Systems," *MIS Quarterly*, September 1983, pp. 47–65.

42. Kenneth C. Laudon and Jane Price Laudon, *Management Information Systems: A Contemporary Perspective*, Macmillan, New York, 1988.

43. Lee L. Gremillion and Philip J. Pyburn, *Computers and Information Systems in Business: An Introduction*, McGraw-Hill, New York, 1988.

44. Paul S. Licker, *The Art of Managing Software Development People*, Wiley, New York, 1985; Peter Tait and Iris Vessey, "The Effect of User Involvement on System Success: A Contingency Approach," *MIS Quarterly*, March 1988, pp. 91–108.

45. This section is based heavily on Lee L. Gremillion and Philip J. Pyburn, *Computers and Information Systems in Business: An Introduction*, McGraw-Hill, New York, 1988.

46. Henry C. Lucas, Jr., "Utilizing Information Technology: Guidelines for Managers," *Sloan Management Review*, Fall 1986, pp. 39–47.

47. G. Pascal Zachary, "How Ashton-Tate Lost Its Leadership in PC Software Arena," *The Wall Street Journal*, Apr. 11, 1990, pp. A1, A6.

48. Lee L. Gremillion and Philip J. Pyburn, *Computers and Information Systems in Business: An Introduction*, McGraw-Hill, New York, 1988.

49. R. I. Benjamin, "Information Technology in the 1990s: A Long-Range Planning Scenario," *MIS Quarterly*, June 1982, pp. 11–31.

50. Thomas P. Gerrity and John F. Rockart, "End-User Computing: Are You a Leader or a Laggard?" *Sloan Management Review*, Summer 1986, pp. 25–34.

51. Lee L. Gremillion and Philip J. Pyburn, *Computers and Information Systems in Business: An Introduction*, McGraw-Hill, New York, 1988.

52. Ibid.

53. Ibid.

54. This section is based largely on Raymond McLeod, Jr., *Management Information Systems*, Science Research Associates, Chicago, 1986.

55. Lee L. Gremillion and Philip J. Pyburn, *Computers and Information Systems in Business: An Introduction*, McGraw-Hill, New York, 1988.

56. John F. Rockart, ''The Line Takes the Leadership—IS Management in a Wired Society,'' *Sloan Management Review*, Summer 1988, pp. 57–64.

57. Thomas P. Gerrity and John F. Rockart, ''End-User Computing: Are You a Leader or a Laggard?'' *Sloan Management Review*, Summer 1986, pp. 25–34.

58. Laton McCartney, ''Information Centers: A Great Resource If Run Properly,'' *Dun's Business Month*, October 1985, pp. 109–110; Thomas P. Gerrity and John F. Rockart, ''End-User Computing: Are You a Leader or a Laggard?'' *Sloan Management Review*, Summer 1986, pp. 25–34.

59. John P. Murray, ''How an Information Center Improved Productivity,'' *Management Accounting*, March 1984, pp. 38–44.

60. This section is based in part on Gordon B. Davis and Margreth H. Olson, *Management Information Systems: Conceptual Foundations, Structure, and Development*, 2d ed., McGraw-Hill, New York, 1985.

61. Harold J. Leavitt and Thomas L. Whisler, ''Management in the 1980s,'' *Harvard Business Review*, Nov.–Dec. 1958, pp. 41–48.

62. Lynda M. Applegate, James I. Cash, Jr., and D. Quinn Mills, ''Information Technology and Tomorrow's Manager,'' *Harvard Business Review*, November–December 1988, pp. 128–136.

63. Ron Weber, ''Computer Technology and Jobs: An Impact Assessment Model,'' *Communications of the ACM*, January 1988, pp. 68–77.

64. P. Attewell and J. Rule, ''Computing and Organizations: What We Know and What We Don't Know,'' *Communications of the ACM*, December 1984, pp. 1184–1192.

65. Ross Gelbspan, ''Keeping a Close Watch on Electronic Work Monitoring,'' *The Washington Post*, Dec. 13, 1987, p. H4.

66. Rebecca A. Grant, Christopher A. Higgins, and Richard H. Irving, ''Computerized Performance Monitors: Are They Costing You Customers?'' *Sloan Management Review*, Spring, 1988, pp. 39–45.

67. Willie Schatz, ''Suffolk Law, New Studies Reinvigorate VDT Debate,'' *Datamation*, Aug. 15, 1988, pp. 39–41.

68. Ilan Salomon and Meira Salomon, ''Telecommuting: The Employee's Perspective,'' *Technological Forecasting and Social Change*, vol. 25, 1984, pp. 15–28; Franklin D. Becker, ''Loosely-Coupled Settings: A Strategy for Computer-Aided Work Decentralization,'' *Research in Organizational Behavior*, vol. 8, 1986, pp. 199–231.

69. Alex Kotlowitz, ''Working at Home While Caring for a Child Sounds Fine—in Theory,'' *The Wall Street Journal*, Mar. 30, 1987, p. 21.

70. Geoff Lewis, ''The Portable Executive,'' *Business Week*, Oct. 10, 1988, pp. 102–112.

71. William M. Bulkeley, ''When Laptop Computers Go on the Road, the Hassles Can Cancel Out the Benefits,'' *The Wall Street Journal*, May 16, 1990, pp. B1, B4.

72. John J. Keller, ''Software Glitch at AT&T Cuts Off Phone Service for Millions,'' *The Wall Street Journal*, Jan. 16, 1990, pp. B1, B4.

73. Katherine M. Hafner, ''Is Your Computer Secure?'' *Business Week*, Aug. 1, 1988, pp. 64–72.

74. Ibid.; John Burgess, ''Searching for a Better Computer Shield,'' *The Washington Post*, Nov. 13, 1988, p. H1.

75. Katherine M. Hafner, ''Is Your Computer Secure?'' *Business Week*, Aug. 1, 1988, pp. 64–72.

76. John Burgess, ''Searching for a Better Computer Shield,'' *The Washington Post*, Nov. 13, 1988, p. H1.

77. John Burgess, ''Prankster's Christmas Greeting Generates Few Ho-Ho-Hos at IBM,'' *The Washington Post*, Dec. 18, 1987, pp. F1, F10; Katherine M. Hafner, ''Is Your Computer Secure?'' *Business Week*, Aug. 1, 1988, pp. 64–72.

78. Katherine M. Hafner, ''Is Your Computer Secure?'' *Business Week*, Aug. 1, 1988, pp. 64–72.

79. William M. Bulkeley, ''Special Systems Make Computing Less Traumatic for Top Executives,'' *The Wall Street Journal*, June 26, 1988, p. 17; Paul B. Carroll, ''The Tough Job of Training Computerphobic Managers,'' *The Wall Street Journal*, June 26, 1988, p. 17.

80. Based on David Wessel, ''First, Ask the Right Questions,'' *The Wall Street Journal*, June 12, 1987, pp. 11D–13D; and discussions with Thomas Holmes and Ed Mahler of Du Pont on June 6, 1990.

Sources for Part Ending Case for Part 5: Based on Amanda C. Hixson, ''Creative Solutions with Everyday Systems,'' *Personal Computing*, September 1987, pp. 138–145; James Don Edwards, Cynthia D. Heagy, and Harold W. Rakes, ''How Milliken Stays on Top,'' *Journal of Accountancy*, April 1989, pp. 63–74; Alyssa A. Lappen, ''Can Roger Milliken Emulate William Randolph Hearst?,'' *Forbes*, May 29, 1989, pp. 52–64; Gary Forger, ''Slashing Lead Times with Quick Response,'' *Modern Materials Handling*, July 1989, pp. 77–78; Alyssa A. Lappen, ''Clink in the Armor,'' *Forbes*, Nov. 13, 1989, pp. 84–87; Brad Stratton, ''Xerox and Milliken Receive Malcolm Baldridge National Quality Awards,'' *Quality Progress*, Dec. 1989, pp. 17–20; John Hillkirk, ''Everyone Weaves Ideas into Milliken,'' *USA Today*, December 26, 1989; *Malcolm Baldridge National Quality Award—Milliken & Company*, Information Sheet, 1989, pp. 1–2; Meg Whittemore, ''Prize Achievements,'' *Nation's Business*, January 1990, p. 29.

CHAPTER 21

1. Based on ''How a Binational Troika Manages the World's Most Multinational Group,'' *International Management*, March 1985, pp. 38–42; ''How Unilever Moves the Earth,'' *Across the Board*, September 1985, pp. 38–48; Andrew C. Brown, ''Unilever Fights Back in the U.S.,'' *Fortune* May 26, 1986, pp. 32–38; Resa W. King, ''Unilever-Chesebrough: Why $3 Billion Looked Like a Song,'' *Business Week*, Dec. 15, 1986, pp. 32–33; and Walecia Konrad, ''The New, Improved Unilever Aims to Clean Up in the U.S.,'' *Business Week*, Nov. 27, 1989, pp. 102–106.

2. Jeremy Main, ''How to Go Global—and Why,'' *Fortune*, Aug. 28, 1989, pp. 70–76.

3. Stefan H. Robock and Kenneth Simmonds, *International Business and Multinational Enterprises*, 4th ed., Irwin, Homewood, Ill., 1989.

4. Richard M. Steers and Edwin L. Miller, ''Management in the 1990s: The International Challenge,'' *Academy of Management Executive*, vol. 11, 1988, pp. 21–22.

5. Stuart Auerbach, ''America, the 'Diminished Giant,''' *The Washington Post*, Apr. 15, 1987, pp. A1, A18.

6. Blanca Riemer, ''America's New Rush to Europe,'' *Business Week*, Mar. 26, 1990, pp. 48–49.

7. ''Perestroika in the Factory,'' *The Economist*, June 9, 1990, p. 70; Mark Maremont, ''Fields of Dreams: The West Gets a Crack at Soviet Oil,'' *Business Week*, June 11, 1990, pp. 36–38; Richard I. Kirkland, Jr., ''Can Capitalism Save Perestroika?'' *Fortune*, July 30, 1990, pp. 137–144.

8. Anthony Spaeth, ''India Beckons—and Frustrates,'' *The Wall Street Journal*, Sept. 22, 1989, pp. R23–R25.

9. William J. Holstein and Amy Borrus, ''Inching toward a North American Market,'' *Business Week*, June 25, 1990, pp. 40–41.

10. Rose Brady and Peter Galuszka, ''The Market Is Coming!'' *Business Week*, June 4, 1990, pp. 60–61.

11. Michael Weisskopf, ''The Crackdown's Cost,'' *The Washington Post*, July 9, 1989, pp. H1, H6.

12. Robert L. Rose, ''Brazil's Moves to Curb Its Inflation Also Curb U.S. Concerns' Profits,'' *The Wall Street Journal*, July 25, 1990, pp. A1, A9.

13. Franklin R. Root, *International Trade & Investment*, 5th ed., South-Western, Cincinnati, 1984, pp. 426–427.

14. Ibid.

15. Cindy Skyzycki, ''How Some Firms Become Foreign Success Stories,'' *The Washington Post*, Nov. 15, 1987, pp. H1, H6.

16. Christopher Knowlton, ''The New Export Entrepreneurs,'' *Fortune*, June 6, 1988, pp. 87–102.

17. Stefan H. Robock and Kenneth Simmonds, *International Business and Multinational Enterprises*, 4th ed., Irwin, Homewood, Ill., 1989; Betty Jane Punnett, *Experiencing International Management*, PWS-Kent, Boston, 1989.

18. This section relies heavily on the work of Howard V. Perlmutter, ''The Tortuous Evolution of the Multinational Corporation,'' *Columbia Journal of World Business*, January–February 1969, pp. 9–18.

19. Jeffrey A. Trachtenberg, ''They Didn't Listen to Anybody,'' *Forbes*, Dec. 15, 1986, pp. 168–169.

20. Howard V. Perlmutter, ''The Tortuous Evolution of the Multinational Corporation,'' *Columbia Journal of World Business*, January–February 1969, p. 13.

21. Andrew Kupfer, ''How to Be a Global Manager,'' *Fortune*, Mar. 14, 1988, pp. 52–58.

22. Anant R. Negandhi, *International Management*, Allyn and Bacon, Boston, 1987, p. 15.

23. Jeffrey Ryser and Robert Neff, ''Boiling Heat, Isolation—and 300 Multinationals,'' *Business Week*, Feb. 22, 1988, pp. 22D, 22H.

24. Christopher Knowlton, ''The New Export Entrepreneurs,'' *Fortune*, June 6, 1988, pp. 89–102.

25. Peter Gumbel, ''American Pizza Purveyors in Moscow Say It's Just a Slice of Things to Come,'' *The Wall Street Journal*, Apr. 13, 1988, p. 24.

26. ''How Unilever Moves the Earth,'' *Across the Board*, September 1985, pp. 38–48.

27. Rose Brady, ''U.S. Exporters That Aren't American,'' *Business Week*, Feb. 29, 1988, p. 71; George Melloan, ''Caterpillar Rides the Economic Policy Bumps,'' *The Wall Street Journal*, Apr. 5, 1988, p. 37.

28. Joseph V. Micallef, ''Political Risk Assessment,'' *Columbia Journal of World Business*, Summer 1981, pp. 47–52.

29. For a discussion of various alternative definitions of political risk, see Mark Fitzpatrick, ''The Definition and Assessment of Political Risk in International Business: A Review of the Literature,'' *Academy of Management Review*, vol. 8, 1983, p. 249.

30. David A. Jodice, ''Sources of Change in Third World Regimes for Direct Investment,'' *International Organization*, Spring 1980, pp. 177–206.

31. Louis Kraar, ''The Multinationals Get Smart about Political Risks,'' *Fortune*, Mar. 24, 1980, p. 88.

32. This section relies heavily on Martin C. Schnitzer, Marilyn L. Liebrenz, and Konrad W. Kubin, *International Business*, South-Western, Cincinnati, 1985, pp. 197–212.

33. Robert Kuttner, ''Gephardt Is Asking the Right Questions about Trade,'' *Business Week*, Feb. 22, 1988, p. 18.

34. John D. Daniels and Lee H. Radebaugh, *International Business*, Addison-Wesley, Reading, Mass., 1989.

35. ''Japan to Curb VCR Exports,'' *The New York Times*, Nov. 21, 1983, p. D5.

36. Martin Tolchin and Susan Tolchin, ''Cultivating Japan: How Tennessee Hustled a Harvest of Investment," *The Washington Post,* Mar. 6, 1988, p. C1.

37. Robert Weigand, "International Investments: Weighing the Incentives," *Harvard Business Review,* July–August 1983, p. C1.

38. This section is based heavily on the interpretation of Hofstede's work for organizations contained in Ellen F. Jackofsky, John W. Slocum, Jr., and Sara J. McQuaid, "Cultural Values and the CEO: Alluring Companions?" *Academy of Management Executive,* vol. 11, 1988, pp. 39–49; see also Geert Hofstede, "Motivation, Leadership, and Organization: Do American Theories Apply Abroad?" *Organizational Dynamics,* Summer 1980, pp. 42–63, and "The Cultural Relativity of the Quality of Life Concept," *Academy of Management Review,* vol. 9, 1984, pp. 389–398.

39. Ellen F. Jackofsky, John W. Slocum, Jr., and Sara J. McQuaid, "Cultural Values and the CEO: Alluring Companions?" *Academy of Management Executive,* vol. 11, 1988, pp. 39–49.

40. Joanne Lipman, "Marketers Turn Sour on Global Sales Pitch Harvard Guru Makes," *The Wall Street Journal,* May 12, 1988, pp. 1, 13.

41. Jonathan B. Levine, "GE Carves Out a Road East," *Business Week,* July 30, 1990, pp. 32–33.

42. J. Davidson Frame, *International Business and Global Technology,* Lexington Books, Lexington, Mass., 1983, p. 88.

43. Joel Dreyfuss, "How Japan Picks America's Brains," *Fortune,* Dec. 21, 1987, pp. 79–89; Robert J. Samuelson, "The Messy, Misunderstood Business of Innovation," *The Washington Post,* June 8, 1988, pp. D1, D5.

44. Michael E. Porter, "The Competitive Advantage of Nations," *Harvard Business Review,* March–April 1990, pp. 73–93, and *The Competitive Advantage of Nations,* Free Press, New York, 1990.

45. Cindy Skrzycki, "How Some Firms Become Foreign Success Stories," *The Washington Post,* Nov. 15, 1987, p. H1.

46. George Steiner and Warren M. Cannon, *Multinational Corporate Planning,* Macmillan, New York, 1966, pp. 295–314; Anant R. Negandhi and Martin K. Welge, *Beyond Theory Z,* JAI, Greenwich, Conn., 1984, pp. 47–53.

47. This section relies heavily on Martin C. Schnitzer, Marilyn L. Liebrenz, and Konrad W. Kubin, *International Business,* South-Western, Cincinnati, 1985, pp. 55–73.

48. John Rossant, "Why Pernod Didn't Go Better with Coke," *Business Week,* June 20, 1988, p. 64; Patricia Sellers, "Coke Gets Off Its Can in Europe," *Fortune,* Aug. 13, 1990, pp. 68–73.

49. Kathryn Rudie Harrigan, "Joint Ventures and Global Strategies," *Columbia Journal of World Business,* Summer 1984, p. 7, and "Strategic Alliances: Their New Role in Global Competition," *Columbia Journal of World Business,* Summer 1987, pp. 67–69; Constance Mitchell, "Westinghouse and Siemens Plan Venture to Make Factory Automation Products," *The Wall Street Journal,* Apr. 1, 1988, p. 16.

50. Dorothy B. Christelow, "International Joint Ventures: How Important Are They?" *Columbia Journal of World Business,* Summer 1987, pp. 7–13.

51. Jim Mann, "One Company's China Debacle," *Fortune,* Nov. 6, 1989, pp. 145–149.

52. Martin C. Schnitzer, Marilyn L. Liebrenz, and Konrad W. Kubin, *International Business,* South-Western, Cincinnati, 1985, p. 69; Cheryl Debes, "The Mouse That Roared at Pepsi," *Business Week,* Sept. 7, 1987, p. 42.

53. Based on Rose Brady, "McSweater, the Benettoning of America," *Working Woman,* May 1986, pp. 114–117; William C. Symonds and Amy Dunkin, "Benetton Is Betting on More of Everything," *Business Week,* Mar. 23, 1987, p. 93; Amy Dunkin, "Why Some Benetton Shopkeepers Are Losing Their Shirts,"

Business Week, Mar. 14, 1988, pp. 78–79; Warren Brown, "Bitterness at Benetton," *The Washington Post,* July 30, 1989, pp. H1, H4; and "FTC Drops Probe of Benetton," *The Washington Post,* Feb. 28, 1990, p. D11.

54. Warren Brown, "Japanese Capturing Another Segment of U.S. Auto Market: Parts," *The Washington Post,* May 8, 1988, pp. H1, H4–H5.

55. Theodore Levitt, "The Globalization of Markets," *Harvard Business Review,* May–June 1983, p. 96.

56. Joanne Lipman, "Marketers Turn Sour on Global Sales Pitch Harvard Guru Makes," *The Wall Street Journal,* May 12, 1988, pp. 1, 13.

57. Sarah Bartlett, "Is This Any Way to Run an Investment Bank? Citicorp Thinks So," *Business Week,* July 28, 1986, pp. 56–58.

58. Based on Andrew Kupfer, "The Long Arm of Jerry Junkins," *Fortune,* Mar. 14, 1988, p. 48.

59. Stefan H. Robock and Kenneth Simmonds, *International Business and Multinational Enterprises,* 4th ed., Irwin, Homewood, Ill., 1989.

60. John D. Daniels, Robert A. Pitts, and Marietta J. Tretter, "Organizing for Dual Strategies of Product Diversity and International Expansion," *Strategic Management Journal,* vol. 6, 1985, p. 301.

61. Ibid., pp. 223–237.

62. Ibid., pp. 302–303.

63. C. K. Prahalad and Yves L. Doz, *The Multinational Mission: Balancing Local Demands and Global Vision,* Free Press, New York, 1987, pp. 175–177. For a similar argument, see James C. Leontiades, *Multinational Corporate Strategy: Planning for World Markets,* Lexington Books, Lexington, Mass., 1985, pp. 198–200.

64. Robert A. Pitts and John D. Daniels, "Aftermath of the Matrix Mania," *Columbia Journal of World Business,* Summer 1984, pp. 48–54.

65. "Global Report," *The Wall Street Journal,* July 11, 1977, p. 6.

66. Cindy Scrzycki, "How Some Firms Become Foreign Success Stories," *The Washington Post,* Nov. 15, 1987, pp. H1, H6.

67. Rosalie L. Tung, "Strategic Management of Human Resources in the Multinational Enterprise," *Human Resource Management,* vol. 23, 1984, pp. 129–143.

68. Nancy J. Adler, "Expecting International Success: Female Managers Overseas," *Columbia Journal of World Business,* Fall 1984, pp. 79–85.

69. Mariann Jelinek and Nancy J. Adler, "Women: World-Class Managers for Global Competition," *Academy of Management Executive,* vol. 11, 1988, pp. 11–19.

70. Mark Mendenhall and Gary Oddou, "The Dimensions of Expatriate Acculturation: A Review," *Academy of Management Review,* vol. 10, 1985, pp. 39–47.

71. Ibid.

72. Jeremy Main, "How to Go Global—And Why," *Fortune,* Aug. 28, 1989, pp. 70–76.

73. Rosalie L. Tung, "Selection and Training of Personnel for Overseas Assignments," *Columbia Journal of World Business,* Spring 1981, pp. 68–78.

74. Mark Mendenhall and Gary Oddou, "The Dimensions of Expatriate Acculturation: A Review," *Academy of Management Review,* vol. 10, 1985, pp. 39–47.

75. Rosalie L. Tung, "Selection and Training Procedures of U.S., European, and Japanese Multinationals," *California Management Review,* vol. 25, 1982, pp. 57–71.

76. Lennie Copeland and Lewis Griggs, "Getting the Best from Foreign Employees," *Management Review,* June 1986, pp. 19–26.

77. Nancy J. Adler, Robert Dokter, and S. Gordon Redding, "From the Atlantic to the Pacific Century: Cross-Cultural Management Reviewed," *Journal of Management,* vol. 12, 1986, pp. 295–318; Lane Kelley, Arthur Whatley, and Reginald Worthley, "Assessing the

Effects of Culture on Managerial Attitudes: A Three-Culture Test," *Journal of International Business Studies,* Summer 1987, pp. 17–31.

78. Geert Hofstede, "Motivation, Leadership, and Organization: Do American Theories Apply Abroad?" *Organizational Dynamics,* Summer 1980, pp. 42–63.

79. Ellen F. Jackofsky, John W. Slocum, Jr., and Sara J. McQuaid, "Cultural Values and the CEO: Alluring Companions?" *Academy of Management Executive,* vol. 11, 1988, pp. 39–49.

80. Paul Streeten, "Multinational Revisited," *Finance & Development,* June 1979, pp. 39–42.

81. Karen Paul and Robert Barbato, "The Multinational Corporation in the Less Developed Country: The Economic Development Model versus the North-South Model," *Academy of Management Review,* 1985, vol. 10, pp. 8–14.

82. William C. Frederick, Keith Davis, and James E. Post, *Business and Society: Corporate Strategy, Public Policy, Ethics,* 6th ed., McGraw-Hill, New York, 1988, pp. 457–458.

83. This section relies heavily on William C. Frederick, Keith Davis, and James E. Post, *Business and Society: Corporate Strategy, Public Policy, Ethics,* 6th ed., McGraw-Hill, New York, 1988, pp. 458–461.

84. "The Antibribery Act Splits Executives," *Business Week,* Sept. 19, 1983, p. 16; Ford S. Worthy, "When Somebody Wants a Payoff," *Fortune,* Pacific Rim issue, Fall, 1989, pp. 117–122.

85. Andrew Kupfer, "How to Be a Global Manager," *Fortune,* Mar. 14, 1988, pp. 52–58; Resa A. King, "You Don't Have to Be a Giant to Score Big Overseas," *Business Week,* Apr. 13, 1987, p. 63; Cindy Skrzycki, "How Some Firms Become Foreign Success Stories," *The Washington Post,* Nov. 15, 1987, pp. H1, H6; "Loctite Corp. Expects Increase in Profit for Fiscal 4th Period," *The Wall Street Journal,* June 13, 1988, p. 5F.

CHAPTER 22

1. Sherrie Brammall, "Romano Unveils His Macaroni Masterpiece," *San Antonio Business Journal,* June 13–19, 1988, pp. 1, 16–17; Charles Boisseau, "Execs Go Back to the Future after Fuddruckers Success," *San Antonio Light,* May 10, 1987, pp. E1, E5; "Fuddruckers: A New Generation of Fast Food," *Restaurant Hospitality,* December 1984; Curtis Hartman, "Home Inc.," *INC.,* July 1987, pp. 62–67; Marina Pisano, "Hamburger King's Home Is His Romanoland Castle," *The San Antonio Sunday Express-News,* Mar. 15, 1988, pp. 1G–4G; Daniel Benedict, "Judge Sets $3 Million Bond for Taco Cabana's Lawsuit Award," *San Antonio Business Journal,* Apr. 10–16, 1987, pp. 1B–4B; Sherrie Brammall, "Romano Focuses on Restaurant Financing," *San Antonio Business Journal,* June 6–12, 1988, pp. 1, 2, 12, 21; Tom Richman, "Love 'Em and Leave 'Em," *INC.,* May 1986, pp. 124–130; Chuck McCollough, "Starting Anew Ends Boredom," *San Antonio Sunday Express-News,* Mar. 9, 1986, pp. 1K, 10K; Charles Boisseau, "Unlikely Duo Gets Going at DocuCon," *San Antonio Light,* May 13, 1989, pp. C1, C4, C5; "Stock to Go," *INC.,* July 1989, p. 17; interview with David C. Martin, Mar. 18, 1989; Tracey Taylor Woodard, "Mangia, Amigos! Chili's Acquires Italian Dinnerhouse," *Restaurant News,* Dec. 11, 1989, pp. 1, 77; Marj Charlier, "Romano Varies Menu to Cook Up Another Restaurant," *The Wall Street Journal,* Apr. 11, 1990, p. B2.

2. This section is based on Robert D. Hisrich and Michael P. Peters, *Entrepreneurship,* BPI/Irwin, Homewood, Ill., 1989.

3. Max S. Wortman, Jr., "Entrepreneurship: An Integrating Typology and Evaluation of the Empirical Research in the Field," *Journal of Management,* vol. 13, 1987, pp. 259–279.

4. William B. Gartner, "'Who Is an Entrepreneur?' Is the Wrong Question,'" *American Journal of Small Business,* Spring 1988, pp. 11–39; Murray B. Low and Ian C. MacMillan, "Entrepreneurship: Past Research and Future Challenges," *Journal of Management,* vol. 14, 1988, pp. 139–161.

5. Murray B. Low and Ian C. MacMillan, "Entrepreneurship: Past Research and Future Challenges," *Journal of Management,* vol. 14, 1988, pp. 139–161.

6. Joseph J. Fucini and Suzy Fucini, *Entrepreneurs,* Hall, Boston, 1985.

7. *The State of Small Business: A Report to the President,* GPO, Washington, D.C., 1985; Charles R. Kuehl and Peggy A. Lambing, *Small Business,* 2d ed., Dryden, Chicago, 1990.

8. Peter F. Drucker, *Innovation and Entrepreneurship,* Harper & Row, New York, 1985, p. 19.

9. John G. Burch, *Entrepreneurship,* Wiley, New York, 1986.

10. *The State of Small Business—1988: A Report to the President,* GPO, Washington, D.C., 1988, p. 22.

11. For a compilation of some recent statistics relating to failure rates, see Barbara J. Bird, *Entrepreneurial Behavior,* Scott, Foresman, Glenview, Ill., 1989.

12. John Case, "The Disciples of David Birch," *INC.,* January 1989, pp. 39–45.

13. Joseph J. Fucini and Suzy Fucini, *Entrepreneurs,* Hall, Boston, 1985, p. 240.

14. Howard Aldrich and Ellen R. Auster, "Even Dwarfs Started Small: Liabilities of Age and Size and Their Strategic Implications," *Research in Organizational Behavior,* vol. 8, 1986, pp. 165–198.

15. David L. Birch, *The Job Generation Process,* M.I.T. Program on Neighborhood and Regional Change, Cambridge, Mass., 1979.

16. *The State of Small Business—1988: A Report to the President,* GPO, Washington, D.C., 1988, p. 33.

17. John Case, "The Disciples of David Birch," *INC.,* January 1989, pp. 39–45; Gene Koretz, "Small Businesses Tend to Stay Pint-Size," *Business Week,* July 31, 1989, p. 20.

18. Lois A. Stevenson, "Against All Odds: The Entrepreneurship of Women," *Journal of Small Business Management,* October 1986, pp. 30–36.

19. *The State of Small Business—1989: A Report to the President,* GPO, Washington, D.C., 1989.

20. Donald D. Bowen and Robert D. Hisrich, "The Female Entrepreneur: A Career Development Perspective," *Academy of Management Review,* vol. 11, 1986, pp. 393–407.

21. Robert D. Hisrich and Candida Brush, "Characteristics of the Minority Entrepreneur," *Journal of Small Business Management,* October 1986, pp. 1–8; U.S. Department of Commerce, *Statistical Abstract of the United States,* GPO, Washington, D.C., 1989.

22. Janice Castro, "She Calls All the Shots," *Time,* July 4, 1988, pp. 54–57.

23. Andrew H. Van de Ven, Roger Hudson, and Dean M. Schroeder, "Designing New Business Startups: Entrepreneurial, Organizational, and Ecological Considerations," *Journal of Management,* vol. 10, 1984, pp. 87–107; William B. Gartner, "A Conceptual Framework for Describing the Phenomenon of New Venture Creation," *Academy of Management Review,* vol. 10, 1985, pp. 696–706; Albert Shapero and Lisa Sokol, "The Social Dimensions of Entrepreneurship," in Calvin A. Kent, Donald L. Sexton, and Karl H. Vesper (eds.), *Encyclopedia of Entrepreneurship,* Prentice-Hall, Englewood Cliffs, N.J., 1982, pp. 72–90; Robert D. Hisrich and Michael P. Peters, *Entrepreneurship,* BPI/Irwin, Homewood, Ill., 1989.

24. This section relies extensively on Murray B. Low and Ian C. MacMillan, "Entrepreneurship: Past Research and Future Challenges," *Journal of Management,* vol. 14, 1988, pp. 139–

161; Robert H. Brockhaus, Sr., and Pamela S. Horwitz, "The Psychology of the Entrepreneur," in Donald L. Sexton and Raymond W. Smilor, *The Art and Science of Entrepreneurship,* Ballinger, Cambridge, Mass., 1986, pp. 25–48; Robert H. Brockhaus, Sr., "The Psychology of the Entrepreneur," in Calvin A. Kent, Donald L. Sexton, and Karl H. Vesper (eds.), *Encyclopedia of Entrepreneurship,* Prentice-Hall, Englewood Cliffs, N.J., 1982; and Yvon Gasse, "Elaboration on the Psychology of the Entrepreneur," in ibid.

25. David C. McClelland, *Human Motivation,* Scott, Foresman, Glenview, Ill., 1985.

26. Robert H. Brockhaus, Sr., "The Psychology of the Entrepreneur," in Calvin A. Kent, Donald L. Sexton, and Karl H. Vesper (eds.), *Encyclopedia of Entrepreneurship,* Prentice-Hall, Englewood Cliffs, N.J., 1982.

27. Bernard M. Bass, *Stogdill's Handbook of Leadership,* Free Press, New York, 1981; D. L. Sexton and N. Bowman, "The Entrepreneur: A Capable Executive and More," *Journal of Business Venturing,* vol. 1, 1985, pp. 129–140.

28. This section relies heavily on Yvon Gasse, "Elaboration on the Psychology of the Entrepreneur," in Calvin A. Kent, Donald L. Sexton, and Karl H. Vesper (eds.), *Encyclopedia of Entrepreneurship,* Prentice-Hall, Englewood Cliffs, N.J., 1982; and Robert D. Hisrich and Michael P. Peters, *Entrepreneurship,* BPI/Irwin, Homewood, Ill., 1989.

29. Robert D. Hisrich and Candida G. Bruch, "The Woman Entrepreneur: Management Skills and Business Problems," *Journal of Small Business Management,* vol. 22, 1984, pp. 30–37.

30. A. C. Cooper and W. C. Dunkelberg, "Entrepreneurial Research: Old Questions, New Answers, and Methodological Issues," *American Journal of Small Business,* vol. 11, no. 3, 1987, pp. 1–20.

31. Ibid.

32. Donald D. Bowen and Robert D. Hisrich, "The Female Entrepreneur: A Career Development Perspective," *Academy of Management Review,* vol. 11, 1986, pp. 393–407.

33. Jeffry A. Timmons, Leonard E. Smollen, and Alexander L. M. Dingee, Jr., *New Venture Creation,* 2d ed., Irwin, Homewood, Ill., 1985.

34. Robert Ronstadt, "The Corridor Principle," *Journal of Business Venturing,* vol. 3, 1988, pp. 31–40.

35. Albert Shapero and Lisa Sokol, "The Social Dimensions of Entrepreneurship," in Calvin A. Kent, Donald L. Sexton, and Karl H. Vesper (eds.), *Encyclopedia of Entrepreneurship,* Prentice-Hall, Englewood Cliffs, N.J., 1982, pp. 72–90. This section also relies heavily on Robert D. Hisrich and Michael P. Peters, *Entrepreneurship,* BPI/Irwin, Homewood, Ill., 1989.

36. Robert H. Brockhaus, Sr., "The Psychology of the Entrepreneur," in Calvin A. Kent, Donald L. Sexton, and Karl H. Vesper (eds.), *Encyclopedia of Entrepreneurship,* Prentice-Hall, Englewood Cliffs, N.J., 1982.

37. Bo Burlingham and Curtis Hartman, "Cowboy Capitalist," *INC.,* January 1989, pp. 54–69.

38. David J. Jefferson, "Land of Opportunity," *The Wall Street Journal,* June 10, 1988, p. 29R.

39. Denie S. Weil, "Doing Business in the Burbs," *Working Woman,* August 1989, pp. 58–66.

40. Mark Lewyn, "Scott McNealy," *USA Today,* Jan. 19, 1988, p. 7B.

41. Barbara J. Bird, *Entrepreneurial Behavior,* Scott, Foresman, Glenview, Ill., 1989.

42. Martha T. Moore, "Fledgling Firms Learn to Fly in Incubators," *USA Today,* May 8, 1989, p. 3E.

43. Albert Shapero and Lisa Sokol, "The Social Dimensions of Entrepreneurship," in Calvin A. Kent, Donald L. Sexton, and Karl H. Vesper (eds.), *Encyclopedia of Entrepreneurship,* Prentice-Hall, Englewood Cliffs, N.J., 1982, pp. 72–90; Robert Hisrich and Michael P.

Peters, *Entrepreneurship,* BPI/Irwin, Homewood, Ill., 1989.

44. Based on Elizabeth A. Conlin and Louise Washer, "'They Tried to Steal My Business . . .'" *Working Woman,* Oct. 1988, pp. 43–46.

45. Robert D. Hisrich and Michael P. Peters, *Entrepreneurship,* BPI/Irwin, Homewood, Ill., 1989.

46. William B. Gartner, Terrence R. Mitchell, and Karl H. Vespers, "A Taxonomy of New Business Ventures," *Journal of Business Venturing,* vol. 4, 1989, pp. 169–186.

47. Based on Richard I. Kirkland, Jr., "Pile 'Em High and Sell 'Em Cheap," *Fortune,* Aug. 29, 1988, pp. 91–92; Richard Evans, "Alan Sugar Shoots for the Stars," *International Management,* March 1989, pp. 42–44.

48. Jeffry A. Timmons, Leonard E. Smollen, and Alexander L. M. Dingee, Jr., *New Venture Creation,* 2d ed., Irwin, Homewood, Ill., 1985.

49. Lena H. Sun, "Cuisinarts's Finances Dicey; It Seeks Bankruptcy Protection," *The Washington Post,* Aug. 4, 1989, p. D1.

50. Nicholas C. Siropolis, *Small Business Management,* 4th ed., Houghton Mifflin, Boston, 1990.

51. Ibid.; D. D. Seltz, *The Complete Handbook of Franchising,* Addison-Wesley, Reading, Mass., 1982.

52. Robert D. Hisrich and Michael P. Peters, *Entrepreneurship,* BPI/Irwin, Homewood, Ill., 1989.

53. Nicholas C. Siropolis, *Small Business Management,* 4th ed., Houghton Mifflin, Boston, 1990.

54. Ibid.

55. John G. Burch, *Entrepreneurship,* Wiley, New York, 1986.

56. Carson R. Kennedy, "Thinking of Opening Your Own Business? Be Prepared," *Business Horizons,* Sept.–Oct. 1985, pp. 38–42.

57. Jeffry A. Timmons, Leonard E. Smollen, and Alexander L. M. Dingee, Jr., *New Venture Creation,* 2d ed., Irwin, Homewood, Ill., 1985; John G. Burch, *Entrepreneurship,* Wiley, New York, 1986.

58. Adapted from Nicholas C. Siropolis, *Small Business Management,* 4th ed., Houghton Mifflin, Boston, 1990, pp. 164–165.

59. Zenas Block and Ian C. MacMillan, "Milestones for Successful Venture Planning," *Harvard Business Review,* September–October 1985, pp. 184–190.

60. This section relies heavily on Jeffry A. Timmons, Leonard E. Smollen, and Alexander L. M. Dingee, Jr., *New Venture Creation,* 2d ed., Irwin, Homewood, Ill., 1985; and Robert D. Hisrich and Michael P. Peters, *Entrepreneurship,* BPI/Irwin, Homewood, Ill., 1989.

61. Albert V. Bruno and Tyzoon T. Tyebjee, "The Entrepreneur's Search for Capital," *Journal of Business Venturing,* vol. 1, 1985, pp. 61–74.

62. Steven Greenhouse, "In Poland, a Small Capitalist Miracle," *The New York Times,* Dec. 19, 1989, pp. D1, D13.

63. Arnold C. Cooper and Albert V. Bruno, "Success among High Technology Firms," *Business Horizons,* April 1970, pp. 16–22; Albert V. Bruno and Tyzoon T. Tyebjee, "The Entrepreneur's Search for Capital," *Journal of Business Venturing,* vol. 1, 1985, pp. 61–74.

64. Jeffry A. Timmons, Leonard E. Smollen, and Alexander L. M. Dingee, Jr., *New Venture Creation,* 2d ed., Irwin, Homewood, Ill., 1985.

65. Robert D. Gatewood and Hubert S. Field, "A Personnel Selection Program for Small Business," *Journal of Small Business Management,* October 1987, pp. 16–25.

66. Thomas F. Jones, *Entrepreneurism,* Donald L. Fine Inc., New York, 1987.

67. This section is based on Charles R. Kuehl and Peggy A. Lambing, *Small Business,* 2d ed., Dryden, Chicago, 1990.

68. Neil C. Churchill and Virginia L. Lewis, "The Five Stages of Small Business Growth," *Harvard Business Review,* May–June 1983, pp. 30–50.

69. Information obtained from the Government Relations Office, BDM International, McLean, Va., Jan. 2, 1990.
70. Buck Brown, "James Bildner's Spectacular Rise and Fall," *The Wall Street Journal*, Oct. 24, 1988, p. B1.
71. Manfred F. R. Kets de Vries, "The Dark Side of Entrepreneurship," *Harvard Business Review*, Nov.–Dec. 1985, pp. 160–167.
72. Mark Robichaux, "Business First, Family Second," *The Wall Street Journal*, May 12, 1989, p. B1.
73. Richard B. Robinson, Jr., "The Importance of Outsiders in Small Firm Planning and Performance," *Academy of Management Journal*, vol. 25, 1982, pp. 80–93; James J. Chrisman and John Leslie, "Strategic, Administrative, and Operating Problems: The Impact of Outsiders on Small Firm Performance," *Entrepreneurship Theory and Practice*, Spring 1989, pp. 37–51.
74. Charles R. Kuehl and Peggy A. Lambing, *Small Business*, 2d ed., Dryden, Chicago, 1990; see also Justin G. Longnecker, Joseph A. McKinney, and Carlos W. Moore, "Ethics in Small Business," *Journal of Small Business Management*, January 1989, pp. 27–31.
75. Based on Barbara Wright, "How to Beat Out Big-Name Competition," *Working Woman*, May 1988, pp. 55–57.

Sources for Part Ending Case for Part 6: Based on Jill A. Fraser, "Soda with a Twist," *Profiles, Inc.*, May 1988, pp. 19–20; Richard L. Stern, "Soda War," *Forbes*, May 4, 1987, pp. 82–83; Nancy Arnott, "It's Only Natural," *Executive Female*, September–October 1987, pp. 28–30, 69; Mary Rowland, "Tales of Triumph," *Working Woman*, February 1988, pp. 76–79; Alix M. Freeman, "Seagram Takes Plunge into Soft Drinks; Assets of Maker of Soho Acquired," *The Wall Street Journal*, Mar. 28, 1989, p. B7; interview with Connie Best, by David C. Martin, Apr. 10, 1989; and written comments from Connie Best, Aug. 17, 1989.

APPENDIX

1. "New CFO at Merck Thrives on Competition," *USA Today*, June 1, 1990, p. 2B; Joseph Weber, "'I Am Intense, Aggressive, and Hard-Charging,'" *Business Week*, Apr. 30, 1990, p. 58; information obtained from Merck & Company.
2. Jeffrey H. Greenhaus, *Career Management*, Dryden, Chicago, 1987.
3. David Kirkpatrick, "Is Your Career on Track?" *Fortune*, July 2, 1990, pp. 38–48.
4. Douglas T. Hall, *Careers in Organizations*, Goodyear, Santa Monica, Calif., 1976, and "Career Development Theory in Organizations," in Duane Brown, Linda Brooks, and Associates, *Career Choice and Development*, 2d ed., Jossey-Bass, San Francisco, 1990, pp. 422–454.
5. Jeffrey H. Greenhaus, *Career Management*, Dryden, Chicago, 1987; Thomas G. Gutteridge, "Organizational Career Development Systems: The State of the Practice," in Douglas T. Hall and Associates, *Career Development in Organizations*, Jossey-Bass, San Francisco, 1986, pp. 50–94; Thomas G. Gutteridge and F. L. Otte, "Organizational Career Development: What's Going on Out There?" *Training and Development Journal*, vol. 27, no. 2, 1983, pp. 22–26.
6. This section is adapted mainly from materials in Jeffrey H. Greenhaus, *Career Management*, Dryden, Chicago, 1987.
7. Joseph Weber, "'I Am Intense, Aggressive, and Hard-Charging,'" *Business Week*, Apr. 30, 1990, p. 58.
8. Ronald Bailey, "From Hamburgers to the Airwaves," *Forbes*, Mar. 5, 1990, pp. 110–112.
9. Reported in "Job Stress Affects Nearly 50 Percent of America's Workers," *Manpower Argus*, March 1990, p. 2.
10. Howard N. Fullerton, Jr., "New Labor Force Projections, Spanning 1988 to 2000," *Monthly Labor Review*, November 1989, pp. 5–12; Louis S. Richman, "The Coming World Labor Shortage," *Fortune*, Apr. 9, 1990, pp. 70–77.
11. James W. Walker and Thomas G. Gutteridge, *Career Planning Practice: An AMA Survey Report*, AMACOM (a division of the American Management Association), New York, 1979.
12. Douglas T. Hall and James G. Goodale, *Human Resource Management*, Scott, Foresman, Glenview, Ill., 1986.
13. Richard Bolles, *What Color Is Your Parachute? A Practical Manual for Job Hunters and Career Changers*, Ten Speed Press, Berkeley, Calif., 1990.
14. For an interesting review of the career development of women, see Joan V. Gallos, "Exploring Women's Development: Implications for Career Theory, Practice, and Research," in Michael B. Arthur, Douglas T. Hall, and Barbara S. Lawrence (eds.), *Handbook of Career Theory*, Cambridge University, Cambridge, Mass., 1989, pp. 110–132. Similarly, for a review of the career development of minorities, see David A. Thomas and Clayton P. Alderfer, "The Influence of Race on Career Dynamics: Theory and Research on Minority Career Experiences," in ibid., pp. 133–158. See also Jeffrey H. Greenhaus, Saroj Parasuraman, and Wayne M. Wormley, "Effects of Race on Organizational Experiences, Job Performance Evaluations, and Career Outcomes," *Academy of Management Journal*, vol. 33, 1990, pp. 64–86; and Julia Lawlor, "Experience, Demographics in Their Favor," *USA Today*, June 1, 1990, pp. B1, B2.
15. Howard V. Hayghe, "Family Members in the Work Force," *Monthly Labor Review*, March 1990, pp. 14–19.
16. Douglas T. Hall and James G. Goodale, *Human Resource Management*, Scott, Foresman, Ill., 1986.
17. Anastasia Toufexis, "Dual Careers, Doleful Dilemmas," *Time*, Nov. 16, 1987, p. 90.
18. Uma Sekaran and Douglas T. Hall, "Asynchronism in Dual-Career and Family Linkages," in Michael B. Arthur, Douglas T. Hall, and Barbara S. Lawrence (eds.), *Handbook of Career Theory*, Cambridge University, Cambridge, Mass., 1989, pp. 159–180.
19. Joy A. Schneer and Fieda Reitman, "Effects of Employment Gaps on the Careers of M.B.A.'s: More Damaging for Men Than for Women?" *Academy of Management Journal*, vol. 33, 1990, pp. 391–406.
20. Anastasia Toufexis, "Dual Careers, Doleful Dilemmas," *Time*, Nov. 16, 1987, p. 90.
21. Carol B. Gilmore and William R. Fannin, "The Dual Career Couple: A Challenge to Personnel in the Eighties," *Business Horizons*, May–June 1982, pp. 36–41.
22. Kathy E. Kram and Lynn A. Isabella, "Mentoring Alternatives: The Role of Peer Relationships in Career Development," *Academy of Management Journal*, vol. 28, 1985, pp. 110–132.
23. Thomas P. Ference, James A. Stoner, and E. Kirby Warren, "Managing the Career Plateau," *Academy of Management Review*, vol. 2, 1977, pp. 602–612.
24. David Kirkpatrick, "Is Your Career on Track?" *Fortune*, July 2, 1990, pp. 38–48.

CHAPTER 1

Quotation in Text

Pages 15–16: Reprinted by permission of *Harvard Business Review.* "What Effective General Managers Really Do," by John P. Kotter, November–December 1982. Copyright © 1982 by the President and Fellows of Harvard College; all rights reserved.

Tables

Table 1-1: Henry Mintzberg, *The Nature of Managerial Work.* Copyright © 1973 by Henry Mintzberg. Reprinted by permission of Harper & Row, Publishers, Inc.
Table 1-2: Morgan W. McCall, Jr., and Michael M. Lombardo, "What Makes a Top Executive?" *Psychology Today* magazine, February 1983. Copyright © 1983 (PT Partners, L.P.). Reprinted by permission.
Table 1-3: *The Wall Street Journal,* Mar. 20, 1987, p. 22D. Copyright © Dow Jones & Company, Inc., 1987. Reprinted by permission of *The Wall Street Journal.* All rights reserved worldwide.

Figures

Figure 1-2: Stephen J. Carroll and Dennis J. Gillen, "Are the Classical Management Functions Useful in Describing Managerial Work?" *Academy of Management Review,* vol. 12, 1987, pp. 38–51. Adapted by permission of the Academy of Management and the authors.
Figure 1-6: Louis E. Boone, David L. Kurtz, and C. Patrick Fleenor, "CEOs: Early Signs of a Business Career." Copyright © 1988 by the Foundation for the School of Business at Indiana University. Reprinted from *Business Horizons,* (31-5) by permission.

CHAPTER 2

Table

Table 2-4: Henry Fayol, *General and Industrial Management,* trans. Constance Storrs, Sir Isaac Pitman and Sons, Ltd., 1949. Copyright © 1949 by Pitman Publishing Corporation. Reprinted by permission of Pitman Learning, Inc.

Figure

Figure 2-5: William G. Ouchi and Alfred M. Jaeger, "Theory Z Organizations: Stability in the Midst of Mobility," *Academy of Management Review,* vol. 3, 1978, pp. 308, 311. Adapted by permission of the Academy of Management and the authors.

CHAPTER 3

Tables

Table 3-1: Fred R. David, *Concepts of Strategic Management,* 2d ed., table 4-4. Copyright © 1989 Merrill Publishing Company, Columbus, Ohio. Reprinted by permission of Merrill, an imprint of Macmillan Publishing Company.
Table 3-2: Otis Port, "Back to Basics." Copyright © 1989 by McGraw-Hill, Inc. Reprinted from June 16, 1989, issue of *Business Week* by special permission.
Table 3-4: Adapted by permission of *Harvard Business Review.* "The Heart of Entrepreneurship" by Howard H. Stevenson and David E. Gumpert, March/April 1985. Copyright © 1985 by the President and Fellows of Harvard College; all rights reserved.

Figures

Figure 3-4: Robert Duncan, "What Is the Right Organizational Structure? Decision Tree Analysis Provides the Answer," *Organizational Dynamics,* Winter 1979. Copyright © 1979 American Management Association, New York. Reprinted by permission of publisher. All rights reserved.
Figure 3-5: Reprinted by permission of *Harvard Business Review.* "The Heart of Entrepreneurship" by Howard H. Stevenson and David E. Gumpert, March/April 1985. Copyright © 1985 by the President and Fellows of Harvard College; all rights reserved.

CHAPTER 4

Quotations in Text

Pages 113–114: Reprinted by permission of Johnson & Johnson.
Page 138: Reprinted by permission of *Harvard Business Review.* An exhibit from "Ethics without the Sermon," by Laura L. Nash, November–December 1981. Copyright © 1981 by the President and Fellows of Harvard College; all rights reserved.
Page 146: *National Business Employment Weekly,* Spring, 1987, p. 4. Copyright © Dow Jones & Company, Inc. 1987. Reprinted by permission of *Managing Your Career,* Spring 1987, Dow Jones and Company, Inc. All rights reserved worldwide.
Page 147: Arvind Bhambri and Jeffrey Sonnenfeld, "The Man Who Stands Alone," *New Management,* Spring, 1987, pp. 30–31. Reprinted by permission.

Tables

Table 4-1: Angelo Kinicki, Jeffrey Bracker, Robert Kreitner, Chris Lockwood, and David Lemak, "Socially Responsible Plant Closings," *Personnel Administrator,* published by the Society for Human Resource Management, Alexandria, Va. Reprinted by permission.
Table 4-2: Milton Moskowitz, "Lessons from the Best Companies to Work For." Copyright © 1985 by the Regents of the University of California. Condensed from the *California Management Review,* vol. 27, no. 2., by permission of the Regents.
Table 4-3: "Test Your Principles," *USA Today,* July 15, 1987, p. 4D. Copyright © 1987 USA Today. Reprinted by permission.
Table 4-4: *The Wall Street Journal,* Nov. 3, 1983, p. 33. Copyright © Dow Jones & Company, Inc., 1983. Reprinted by permission of *The Wall Street Journal.* All rights reserved worldwide.

Figures

Figure 4-1: Archie B. Carroll, "A Three-Dimensional Conceptual Model of Corporate Performance," *Academy of Management Review,* vol. 4, 1979, p. 499. Adapted by permission of the Academy of Management and the author.
Figure 4-2: William C. Frederick, Keith Davis, and James E. Post, *Business and Society,* 6th ed., McGraw-Hill Book Company. Copyright © 1988 McGraw-Hill, Inc. Reprinted by permission.
Figure 4-3: Copyright © 1987 by McGraw-Hill, Inc. Reprinted from July 20, 1987, issue of *Business Week* by special permission.
Figures 4-4, 4-5: Archie B. Carroll, "In Search of the Moral Manager." Copyright © 1987 by the Foundation for the School of Business at Indiana University. Reprinted from *Business Horizons* (30-2), March–April 1987, by permission.

CHAPTER 5

Tables

Table 5-1: Fred R. David, "How Companies Define Their Mission." Copyright © 1989 Pergamon Press plc. Reprinted by permission from *Long Range Planning,* February 1989.
Table 5-2: Peter F. Drucker, *Management: Tasks, Responsibilities, Practices,* Harper & Row, Publishers, Inc., 1974, pp. 100–117. Adapted by permission of the author.
Table 5-3: Edwin A. Locke and Gary P. Latham, *Goal Setting: A Motivational Technique That Works!* pp. 171–172. Copyright © 1984. Adapted by permission of Prentice-Hall, Inc., Englewood Cliffs, N.J.

Figures

Figure 5-3: *Managing in the Tradition of Partnership* (J. C. Penney Company publication). Reprinted by permission of J. C. Penney Company, Inc.
Figure 5-4: Thomas W. Lee, Edwin A. Locke, and Gary P. Latham, "Goal Setting Theory and Job Performance," in Lawrence A. Pervin (ed.), *Goal Concepts in Personality and Social Psychology,* Lawrence Erlbaum Associates, Publishers, Hillsdale, N.J., 1989. Adapted by permission of the publisher and authors.

CHAPTER 6

Tables

Table 6-1: Frank T. Paine and Carl R. Anderson, *Strategic Management,* 1983, table 12-3.

Copyright © The Dryden Press, a division of Holt, Rinehart and Winston, Inc. Reprinted by permission of the publisher.
Table 6-2: Arthur A. Thompson, Jr., and A. J. Strickland III, *Strategic Management: Concepts and Cases*, 5th ed., BPI/Irwin, 1990. Reprinted by permission of the publisher.
Tables 6-3, 6-4: Michael E. Porter, *Competitive Strategy: Techniques for Analyzing Industries and Competitors*. Copyright © 1980 by The Free Press. Reprinted by permission of The Free Press, a division of Macmillan, Inc.

Figures
Figure 6-2: John A. Pierce II and Richard B. Robinson, Jr., *Strategic Management: Strategy Formulation and Implementation*, 3d ed., Irwin, 1988. Adapted by permission of the publisher.
Figures 6-4, 6-5, 6-6: John A. Pierce II and Richard B. Robinson, Jr., *Strategic Management: Strategy Formulation and Implementation*, 3d ed., Irwin, 1988. Adapted by permission of the publisher.

CHAPTER 7

Tables
Table 7-2: Kim S. Cameron, David A. Whetton, and Myung U. Kim, "Organizational Dysfunctions of Decline," *Academy of Management Journal*, vol. 30, p. 128. Adapted by permission of the Academy of Management and the authors.
Table 7-3: *The Washington Post*, Mar. 27, 1987, p. F2. Reprinted by permission.
Table 7-4: Reprinted by permission of *Harvard Business Review*. "Choosing Strategies for Change" by John P. Kotter and Leonard A. Schlesinger, March/April 1979. Copyright © 1979 by the President and Fellows of Harvard College; all rights reserved.
Table 7-5: Judith R. Gordon, *A Diagnostic Approach to Organizational Behavior*, 2d ed., p. 695. Copyright © 1987 by Allyn and Bacon. Reprinted by permission.

Figures
Figure 7-2: Richard L. Daft and Richard M. Steers, *Organizations: A Micro/Macro Approach*. Copyright © 1986 by Scott, Foresman and Company. Reprinted by permission.
Figure 7-4: Harold J. Leavitt, "Applied Organization Change in Industry: Technical and Human Approaches," in W. W. Cooper, H. J. Leavitt, and M. W. Shelly II (eds.), *New Perspectives in Organizational Research*, John Wiley & Sons, Inc., 1964, p. 56. Adapted by permission of Carnegie Mellon University.

CHAPTER 8

Quotation in Text
Page 284: Diane E. Papalia and Sally Wendkos Olds, *Psychology*, 2d ed., McGraw-Hill Book Company. Copyright © 1988 McGraw-Hill, Inc. Reprinted by permission.

Table
Table 8-3: Daniel D. Wheeler and Irving L. Janis, *A Practical Guide for Making Decisions*. Copyright © 1980 by The Free Press. Adapted by permission of The Free Press, a division of Macmillan, Inc.

Figures
Figure 8-1: George P. Huber, *Managerial Decision Making*, Scott, Foresman and Company. Copyright © 1980 by Scott, Foresman and Company. Reprinted by permission.

Figure 8-2: Richard L. Daft and Richard M. Steers, *Organizations: A Micro/Macro Approach*. Copyright © 1986 by Scott, Foresman and Company. Reprinted by permission.
Figure 8-3: Frank Harrison, *The Managerial Decision Making Process*, 2d ed. Copyright © 1981 by Houghton Mifflin Company. Adapted by permission.
Figure 8-5: James L. Adams, *Conceptual Blockbusting: A Guide to Better Ideas*. Copyright © 1974, 1976, 1979, 1986 by James L. Adams. Used by permission of the Stanford Alumni Association and James L. Adams.

CHAPTER 9

Tables
Table 9-1: William C. Miller, *The Creative Edge*. Copyright © 1987 by William C. Miller. Reprinted by permission of Addison-Wesley Publishing Co., Inc., Reading, Mass.
Table 9-2: Spyrous Makridakis and Steven C. Wheelwright, "Forecasting an Organization's Futures," in Paul Nystrom and William H. Starbuck (eds.), *Handbook of Organizational Design*. Copyright © 1981 Oxford University Press. Adapted by permission.
Table 9-3: Everett E. Adam, Jr., and Ronald J. Ebert, *Production and Operations Management: Concepts, Models, and Behavior*, 3d ed. Copyright © 1986. Adapted by permission of Prentice-Hall, Inc., Englewood Cliffs, N.J.
Table 9-4: Elwood S. Buffa, *Modern Production/Operations Management*. Copyright © 1983 by John Wiley & Sons, Inc. Adapted by permission of John Wiley & Sons, Inc.
Table 9-5: Frank Harrison, *The Managerial Decision Making Process*, 2d ed. Copyright © 1981 by Houghton Mifflin Company. Adapted by permission.
Table 9-6: Elwood S. Buffa, *Modern Production/Operations Management*. Copyright © 1983 by John Wiley & Sons, Inc. Adapted by permission of John Wiley & Sons, Inc.

Figures
Figure 9-1: Charles A. Gallagher and Hugh J. Watson, *Quantitative Methods for Business Decisions*, McGraw-Hill Book Company. Copyright © 1980 McGraw-Hill, Inc. Adapted by permission.
Figure 9-2: Courtesy Toro Company. Reprinted by permission.
Figure 9-3: Charles A. Gallagher and Hugh J. Watson, *Quantitative Methods for Business Decisions*, McGraw-Hill Book Company. Copyright © 1980 McGraw-Hill, Inc. Adapted by permission.
Figure 9-5: Everett E. Adam and Ronald J. Ebert, *Production and Operations Management: Concepts, Models and Behavior*, 3d ed., pp. 535, 537. Copyright © 1986. Adapted by permission of Prentice-Hall, Inc., Englewood Cliffs, N.J.
Figure 9-6: Elwood S. Buffa, *Modern Production/Operations Management*. Copyright © 1983 John Wiley & Sons, Inc. Reprinted by permission of John Wiley & Sons, Inc.

CHAPTER 10

Figures
Figure 10-3: J. R. Hackman and G. R. Oldham, *Work Redesign*, fig. 4.6, p. 90. Copyright © 1980 Addison-Wesley Publishing Co., Inc., Reading, Mass. Reprinted by permission of the publisher.
Figure 10-4: Stephen P. Robbins, *Organization Theory: Structure, Design, and Applications*, 3d ed., p. 88. Copyright © 1990. Reprinted by permission of Prentice-Hall, Inc., Englewood Cliffs, N.J.

CHAPTER 11

Tables
Table 11-5: Joan Woodward, *Industrial Organization: Theory and Practice*. Copyright © 1965 Oxford University Press. Reprinted by permission.
Table 11-6: T. Burns and G. M. Stalker, *The Management of Innovation*, Tavistock Publications, London, 1961. Reprinted by permission.
Table 11-7: Adapted, in part, from Henry Mintzberg, *Structure in Fives: Designing Effective Organizations*, pp. 11, 280, 281. Copyright © 1983. Adapted by permission of Prentice-Hall, Inc., Englewood Cliffs, N.J. Also adapted, in part, from Danny Miller, "Configurations of Strategy and Structure: Towards a Synthesis," *Strategic Management Journal*, vol. 7, 1986. Adapted by permission of John Wiley & Sons, Ltd.

Tables
Table 11-8 Adapted, in part, from Danny Miller, "Configurations of Strategies and Structure: Towards a Synthesis," *Strategic Management Journal*, vol. 7, 1986. Copyright © 1986 John Wiley & Sons, Ltd. by permission of John Wiley & Sons, Ltd. Also adapted, in part, from Danny Miller, "Relating Porter's Business Strategies to Environment and Structure: Analysis and Performance Implications," *Academy of Management Journal*, vol. 31, p. 280–308, by permission of the Academy of Management and the author.

Figure
Figure 11-8: Jay R. Galbraith, "Designing the Innovating Organization," *Organizational Dynamics*, vol. 10, 1982, p. 12. Reprinted by permission of the author.

CHAPTER 12

Tables
Table 12-1: David J. Rachman, Michael H. Mescon, Courtland L. Bovée, and John V. Thill, *Business Today*, 6th ed., McGraw-Hill Book Company. Copyright © 1990 McGraw-Hill, Inc. Reprinted by permission.
Table 12-3: Marc J. Wallace, Jr., and Charles H. Fay, *Compensation Theory and Practice*, 2d ed., PWS-KENT Publishing Company, Boston, 1988, p. 214. PWS-KENT Publishing Company is a division of Wadsworth, Inc. Adapted by permission.

Figures
Figures 12-3, 12-4: Wayne F. Cascio, *Managing Human Resources*, 2d ed., McGraw-Hill Book Company. Copyright © 1989 McGraw-Hill, Inc. Reprinted by permission.
Figure 12-5: George T. Milkovich and Jerry M. Newman, *Compensation*. Copyright © 1990 BPI/Irwin, Inc. Adapted by permission.

CHAPTER 13

Figures
Figure 13-5: Judith R. Gordon, *A Diagnostic Approach to Organizational Behavior*, 2d ed., p. 92. Copyright © 1987 by Allyn and Bacon. Adapted by permission.
Figure 13-7: Lyman W. Porter and Edward E. Lawler III, *Managerial Attitudes and Performance*, Richard D. Irwin, Inc., 1968. Adapted by permission of the publisher.
Figure 13-9: Hugh J. Arnold and Daniel C. Feldman, *Organizational Behavior*, McGraw-

Hill Book Company. Copyright © 1986 McGraw-Hill, Inc. Adapted by permission.
Figure 13-10: Robert Kreitner and Fred Luthans, "A Social Learning Approach to Behavioral Management: Radical Behaviorists 'Mellowing Out,'" *Organizational Dynamics*, Autumn 1984. Copyright © 1984 American Management Association, New York. Reprinted by permission of the publisher. All rights reserved.

CHAPTER 14

Quotation in Text
Page 512: Victor H. Vroom and Arthur G. Jago, *The New Leadership: Managing Participation in Organizations*, pp. 163, 166–167. Copyright © 1988. Reprinted by permission of Prentice-Hall, Inc., Englewood Cliffs, N.J.

Tables
Table 14-1: Gary A. Yukl, *Leadership in Organizations*, 2d ed., pp. 44, 101, 102. Copyright © 1989. Adapted by permission of Prentice-Hall, Inc., Englewood Cliffs, N.J.
Table 14-2: Victor H. Vroom and Philip W. Yetton, *Leadership and Decision Making*. Copyright © 1973 by the University of Pittsburgh Press. Reprinted by permission of the University of Pittsburgh Press.

Figures
Figure 14-1: Reprinted by permission of *Harvard Business Review*. "How to Choose a Leadership Pattern" by Robert Tannenbaum and Warren H. Schmidt, May/June 1973. Copyright © 1973 by the President and Fellows of Harvard College; all rights reserved.
Figure 14-3: Robert A. Blake and Jane S. Mouton, *The Managerial Grid® III: The Key to Leadership Excellence*. Copyright © 1985 Gulf Publishing Company, Houston. Reprinted by permission of Dr. Blake and the publisher.
Figure 14-4: Arthur G. Jago, "Leadership: Perspectives in Theory and Research," *Management Science*, vol. 28, no. 3, March 1982. Copyright © 1982 The Institute of Management Science. Reprinted by permission of *Management Science* and the author.
Figure 14-5: Fred E. Fiedler and Joseph E. Garcia, *New Approaches to Effective Leadership: Cognitive Resources and Organizational Performance*. Copyright © 1987 John Wiley & Sons, Inc. Reprinted by permission of John Wiley & Sons, Inc.
Figure 14-6: Paul Hersey and Kenneth Blanchard, *Management of Organizational Behavior: Utilizing Human Resources*, 5th ed., p. 188. Copyright © 1988. Adapted by permission of Prentice-Hall, Inc., Englewood Cliffs, N.J.
Figure 14-7: Victor H. Vroom and Arthur G. Jago, *The New Leadership: Managing Participation in Organizations*, 1988, Prentice-Hall, Englewood Cliffs, N.J. Copyright © 1987 by V. H. Vroom and A. G. Jago. Reprinted by permission of the authors.
Figure 14-8: Gary A. Yukl, *Leadership in Organizations*, 2d ed., pp. 44, 101, 102. Copyright © 1989. Adapted by permission of Prentice-Hall, Inc., Englewood Cliffs, N.J.
Figure 14-9: Bernard M. Bass, *Leadership and Performance beyond Expectations*. Copyright © 1985 by The Free Press. Reprinted by permission of The Free Press, a division of Macmillan, Inc.

CHAPTER 15

Quotations in Text
Page 533: Judith R. Gordon, *A Diagnostic Approach to Organizational Behavior*, 2d ed., p. 230. Copyright © 1987 by Allyn and Bacon. Reprinted by permission.

Page 543: Reprinted by permission of Interstate Van Lines, Inc., Springfield, Va.
Page 546: William V. Haney, *Communication and Interpersonal Relations*, 5th ed., Richard D. Irwin, Inc., 1986, pp. 214–222. Reprinted by permission of the author and publisher.
Pages 547–548: Steve Coll and David A. Vise, "Chairman's Cost-Cutting Humor," *The Washington Post*, Oct. 18, 1987, pp. H1, H20. Reprinted by permission.

Tables
Table 15-1: Phillip V. Lewis, *Organizational Communication: The Essence of Effective Management*. Copyright © 1987. Reprinted by permission of Prentice-Hall, Inc., Englewood Cliffs, N.J.
Table 15-2: Richard M. Hodgetts and Steven Altman, *Organizational Behavior*, W. B. Saunders, 1979. Reprinted by permission.

Figures
Figure 15-1: Lance B. Kurke and Howard Aldrich, "Mintzberg Was Right! A Replication and Extension of *The Nature of Managerial Work*," *Management Science*, vol. 29, no. 8, August 1983. Copyright © 1983 The Institute of Management Science. Reprinted by permission of *Management Science* and the authors.
Figure 15-2: Phillip V. Lewis, *Organizational Communication: The Essence of Effective Management*. Copyright © 1987. Reprinted by permission of Prentice-Hall, Inc., Englewood Cliffs, N.J.
Figure 15-3: Otis W. Baskin and Craig E. Aronoff, *Interpersonal Communication in Organizations*. Scott, Foresman and Company, 1980, p. 77. Adapted by permission of the authors.
Figure 15-4: R. Wayne Pace, *Organizational Communication: Foundations for Human Resource Development*, p. 40. Copyright © 1983. Adapted by permission of Prentice-Hall, Inc., Englewood Cliffs, N.J.
Figure 15-5: Phillip V. Lewis, *Organizational Communication: The Essence of Effective Management*. Copyright © 1987. Reprinted by permission of Prentice-Hall, Inc., Englewood Cliffs, N.J. Edward E. Scannell, *Communication for Leadership*, McGraw-Hill Book Company, 1970. Reprinted by permission.
Figure 15-6: Keith Davis and John W. Newstrom, *Human Behavior at Work: Organizational Behavior*, 8th ed., McGraw-Hill Book Company, 1989, p. 373. Reprinted by permission.
Figure 15-7: *The Washington Post*, Oct. 18, 1987, p. H1. Reprinted by permission of Richard Thompson for *The Washington Post*.

CHAPTER 16

Quotation in Text
Pages 583–584 (Management Exercise): J. William Pfeiffer and John E. Johns (eds.), *The 1975 Annual Handbook for Group Facilitators*, San Diego, Calif., University Associates, Inc., 1975. Reprinted by permission.

Table
Table 16-1: Kenneth W. Thomas, "Toward Multi-Dimensional Values in Teaching: The Example of Conflict Behaviors," *Academy of Management Review*, vol. 2, 1977, p. 487. Reprinted by permission of the Academy of Management and the author.

Figures
Figure 16-2: Rensis Likert, *New Patterns of Management*, McGraw-Hill Book Company. Copyright © 1961 McGraw-Hill, Inc. Reprinted by permission.

Figure 16-9: J. Richard Hackman, "The Design of Work Teams," in Jay W. Lorsch (ed.), *Handbook of Organizational Behavior*, p. 331. Copyright © 1987. Reprinted by permission of Prentice-Hall, Inc., Englewood Cliffs, N.J.

CHAPTER 17

Tables
Table 17-1: Adapted by permission of *Harvard Business Review*. "From Control to Commitment in the Workplace" by Richard E. Walton, March/April 1985. Copyright © 1985 by the President and Fellows of Harvard College; all rights reserved.
Table 17-2: Reprinted by permission of *Harvard Business Review*. "Fit Control Systems to Your Management Style" by Cortland Cammann and David Nadler, January/February 1976. Copyright © 1976 by the President and Fellows of Harvard College; all rights reserved.

Figures
Figure 17-2: Peter Lorange, Michael F. Scott Morton, and Somanthra Ghoshal, *Strategic Control Systems*, p. 12. Copyright © 1986 by West Publishing Company. All rights reserved. Reprinted by permission.
Figure 17-4: Stephen G. Green and M. Ann Welsh, "Cybernetics and Dependence: Reframing the Control Concept," *Academy of Management Review*, vol. 13, pp. 287–301. Adapted by permission of the Academy of Management and the authors.
Figure 17-6: Adapted by permission of *Harvard Business Review*. "Fit Control Systems to Your Management Style" by Cortland Cammann and David Nadler, January/February 1976. Copyright © 1976 by the President and Fellows of Harvard College; all rights reserved.

CHAPTER 18

Quotation in Text
Page 649: W. Edwards Deming, *Out of the Crisis*. Copyright © 1987 by W. Edwards Deming. Published by M.I.T., Center for Advanced Engineering Study, Cambridge, Mass. 02139. Reprinted by permission.

Tables
Tables 18-1, 18-2, 18-3: H. Kent Baker, *Financial Management*, figs. 6-2, 6-8, and 6-9. Copyright © 1987 by Books for Professionals. Adapted by permission of Harcourt Brace Jovanovich, Inc.

Figures
Figure 18-3: H. Kent Baker, *Financial Management*, fig. 6-1. Copyright © 1987 by Books for Professionals. Reprinted by permission of Harcourt Brace Jovanovich, Inc.
Figure 18-5: Reprinted by permission of *Harvard Business Review*. "Budget Choice: Planning vs. Control" by Neil C. Churchill, July/August 1984. Copyright © 1984 by the President and Fellows of Harvard College; all rights reserved.
Figure 18-6: Roger G. Schroeder, *Operations Management*, 3d ed., McGraw-Hill Book Company. Copyright © 1989 McGraw-Hill, Inc. Adapted by permission.

CHAPTER 19

Tables
Table 19-1: Elwood S. Buffa, *Modern Production/Operations Management*. Copyright © 1983

CHAPTER 20

CHAPTER 21

CHAPTER 22

APPENDIX

Horan; **756** Danny Turner; **769** Donald Hamerman.

CHAPTER 22
Page 770 Jay Dickman; **772** Courtesy of Phil Romano; **778** Steven Pumphrey; **779** Mitch

Kezar/Black Star; **783** Will Crockett; **790** Michael L. Abramson; **795** Nick Kelsh; **801** Jay Dickman.

Part Ending Case for Part 6
Page 803 (*top*) Courtesy of Constance Best; **803** (*bottom*) Steven W. Lewis; **804** Courtesy of Constance Best.

APPENDIX
Page 807 Stephen Lefkovits/USA Today; **812** John S. Abbott.

Adams, J. Stacy, 461
Adler, Nancy J., 762
Ain, Mark, 164
Alderfer, Clayton, 449, 450
Aldikacti, Hulki, 244
Amabile, Teresa M., 175, 281, 282
Araskog, Rand, 30
Armacost, Samuel H., 256, 257
Arron, Judith, 19, 20
Ash, Mary Kay, 105

Babbage, Charles, 43–44
Badger, Milly, 586
Baer, Bill, 20
Bakker, Jim, 131
Bandura, Albert, 469
Baosheng Xu, 769
Barnard, Charles, 51–53
Barocci, Nancy, 780
Bass, Bernard M., 506, 507
Baxter, Gordon, 213–215
Bayley, Bjorn, 86
Bazerman, Max H., 278
Beals, Vaugh, 102
Bednarek, Jan, 791
Beman, Deane, 201
Benetton, Giulianna, 753
Bennett, William, 278
Benton, Philip, 74
Bernstein, Leonard, 20
Berreth, Richard, 685, 686
Best, Connie, 803–806
Bienek, Robert, 451
Bildner, James, 796–797
Birch, David L., 776
Blake, Robert, 489
Blanchard, Ken, 490, 496
Boesky, Ivan, 131
Bolcom, William, 19
Bolle, Richard, 812
Bos, Linda, 542
Bostic, Steven, 156, 178
Boyd, J. Mitchell, 194
Bozic, Michael, 330
Bradley, Milton, 131
Brennan, Edward A., 330
Bricker, William H., 6, 7, 8, 9
Bristol, Ron, 322
Brooks, Henry Sands, 774
Budoff, Penny Wise, 87–88
Buettner, Lawrence F., 343
Burke, James E., 113, 235
Burleson, Gene, 528
Burns, Tom, 387
Bush, George, 731
Butterworth, Kenneth W., 769

Cairns, Raymond E., 730
Caldwell, Philip, 73
Canion, Robert, 550, 551, 557
Carlson, Chester F., 110
Carlzon, Jan, 522–523, 532
Carnegie, Andrew, 115, 334
Carroll, Archie B., 134, 135
Carroll, Steven J., 9
Carter, Jimmy, 646
Chandler, Alfred D., 369
Chandler, Colby, 370
Chatwal, Sant Singh, 266
Chazen, Jerome, 76
Chen, Steve, 221, 222
Chiang Kai-shek, 232
Chung Ju-Yung, 494, 495
Claiborne, Liz, 76–77, 87
Claire, David R., 113
Clausen, A. W. "Tom," 256, 257
Cohen, Ben, 585, 586
Coleman, Deborah A., 479–480, 506, 508
Collier, Sophia, 803–806
Conant, Howard, 115
Cooley, Edward, 264
Cornwell, Bernard, 599
Crain, Gertrude, 487–488
Crandall, Robert, 713
Cray, Seymour, 221, 222
Curley, John J., 291
Cusimano, Joe, 783

Daly, Michael J., 559
Dammerman, Dennis, 638
Danner, Raymond L., 194
Darvin, Robert, 538
Davis, Stanley M., 379
Dell, Michael, 778
De Mello, Fernado Collor, 739
Deming, W. Edwards, 649
DePree, D. J., 587–588
DePree, Hugh, 587, 588
DePree, Max, 587
Diddel, Katha, 781–782, 790
Disney, Roy, 188
Disney, Walt, 188, 194, 516
Dodge, Phil, 15
Doland, Beverly F., 32
Drucker, Peter, 20, 21, 41, 157, 162, 179,
    225, 235, 270, 774
Dudley, Mary, 550
Dutt, James, 53
Dylan, Bob, 129

Eames, Charles, 587
Edison, Thomas A., 100

Eisner, Michael D., 188, 189, 190
Eklund, Stig, 398
Ellington, Kevin, 550–551
Ellison, Caryn, 348
Evans, Raymond F., 8

Faught, Thomas F., Jr., 492
Faulkner, Richard, 810, 811
Fayol, Henri, 51, 55, 67, 383
Feinblum, Barnet, 348
Feldman, Hervey, 505–506
Fiedler, Fred, 490, 491, 492, 493, 494, 495
Fields, Debbi, 697, 698
Fields, Randi, 697, 698, 699
Fischer, Burt K., 140
Flaherty, Gerald, 695
Follett, Mary Parker, 53, 54–55
Fomon, Robert, 454, 624
Forbes, Malcolm, 102
Ford, Benson, 65
Ford, Edsel, 65
Ford, Henry, 39–40, 334, 775
Ford, Henry, II, 65, 73
Ford, William Clay, 65
Frazier, Walt, 77
Frechette, Yvonne, 36
Friedman, Milton, 116–117
Fry, Arthur, 245, 368
Fugere, George T., 700

Galbraith, Jay R., 357, 393
Galvin, Robert, 30, 126
Gandhi, Mahatma, 507
Gantt, Henry L., 305–306
Garcia, Joseph E., 493, 494
Garrett, William A., 110
Gartner, William B., 782, 785
Garvin, David A., 647
Garzarelli, Elaine, 299
Gault, Stanley C., 6, 8, 541
Gerber, Dan, 774
Gerstner, Louis V., Jr., 32, 635
Giannini, A. P., 256, 257
Gibson, Verna K., 204
Gilbert, Gerald, 685, 686
Gilbreth, Frank, 47–49
Gilbreth, Lillian, 47–49
Gillen, Dennis J., 9
Gillette, King, 775
Gin, Sue Ling, 790
Gittler, Harvey, 271
Goizueta, Roberto C., 259–261, 297
Golisano, B. Thomas, 237
Gomez, José L., 139–140
Goodale, Bob, 626

Note: A comprehensive chapter-by-chapter listing of the names and sources cited in the text can be found on pages R-1 to R-31.

Gordon, Harry, 518
Gordon, William J., 288
Gorman, Leon, 164
Graham, Katharine, 480
Greco, Rosemarie, 174
Greenberg, Alan C., 547–548
Greenfield, Jerry, 585, 586
Greenhaus, Jeffrey H., 810
Grogan, Barbara, 801–802
Grove, Andrew S., 498
Gucci, Guccio, 774
Gueridon, Pierre, 694
Gumpert, David E., 105

Hackman, J. Richard, 341, 574, 575–576
Hall, John R., 526–527
Hall, Joyce, 775
Hammurabi, 41
Handler, Barbara, 774
Hansen, David A., 104
Hanson, John K., 685, 686
Harris, Jim, 557
Hartley, Mariette, 348
Harvey, Robert, 588
Hay, Wyck, 347
Hayes, Robert H., 667
Head, Howard, 229
Heinz, Henry J., 774
Henry, O. Lee, 96
Herrman, Jack, 531
Hersey, Paul, 490, 496
Herzberg, Frederick, 341, 452–453
Hewlett, Bill, 396
Hixon, Raymond L., 484
Hofer, Charles W., 210
Hofstede, Geert, 746, 747
Hogberg, David, 813
Holmes, Thomas F., 730
Homans, George, 556, 557
Hood, Edward E., Jr., 514
Houghton, James R., 4, 5, 29
Hounsfield, Godfrey, 285–286, 450
House, Robert J., 502
Hummel, Berta, 774
Hupe, Donald J., 237
Huston, Glen, 566

Iacocca, Lee, 481, 747
Ibuka, Masaru, 618
Imperiali, Leo, 792
Inaba, Seiuemon, 661, 662
Ishikawa, Akira, 756
Iverson, F. Kenneth, 357, 436–437

Jacobson, Allen F., 177
Jago, Arthur, 498
Janis, Irving, 272
Jellinek, Emil, 438
Jenkins, Ted, 16
Jobs, Steven P., 93, 396, 401, 479, 480
Johnson, General Robert Wood, 113
Johnson, Ross, 31–32
Johnston, Philip, 403
Jones, Reginald, 513, 638
Junkins, Jerry R., 755–756
Juran, J. M., 649

Kahneman, Daniel, 275
Kamprad, Ingvar, 86
Kanter, Rosabeth Moss, 23, 226–227, 541
Kapor, Mitchell, 543
Kearns, David T., 110
Kennedy, John F., 507
Keough, Donald, 259
Ketner, Ralph, 626, 627

Khomeini, Ayatollah, 745
Khosia, Vinod, 780
Kieffer, Jarold, 524
Kilman, Ralph H., 106
Kim Woo-Choong, 495
Kincaid, Nita, 406, 689
King, Martin Luther, Jr., 507
King, Susan B., 4–5, 11, 29
King, W. Frank, III, 609–610, 614
Kinsley, Michael, 117
Klein, Calvin, 774
Kotter, John, 14, 15, 18
Kram, Kathy E., 813
Kroc, Ray, 592–593, 779
Kusumoto, Sadahei, 128–129

Lamson, Joan, 552
Larson, Bill, 16
Latham, Gary P., 160, 463
Lauder, Estee, 453
Laudon, Jane Price, 709
Laudon, Kenneth C., 709
Lawler, Edward E., III, 460
Lawrence, Paul R., 379, 388
LeGrand, Teresa M., 637
Lenin, Nikolai, 459
Leofsky, Ed, 650
Leonard, Stew, Jr., 516, 517, 518
Leonard, Stew, Sr., 516, 517
Levey, Paula, 204
Lewent, Judy C., 807, 809
Lewin, Kurt, 484–485, 486
Lincoln, Lillian, 776
Llewellyn, J. Bruce, 795
Lochtenberg, Ben, 763
Locke, Edwin A., 61, 160, 164, 463
Lord, Judge Miles, 114
Lorsch, Jay W., 388
Loucks, Vernon R., Jr., 142
Low, Murray, 773–774
Luthans, Fred, 32
Lynn, Jim, 483

MacMillan, Ian C., 714, 774
Mahler, Edward G., 730
Malden, Karl, 271
Malone, Thomas J., 731
Mann, Richard D., 483–484
Manoogian, John A., 572
Marriott, Alice, 148
Marriott, J. Willard "Bill", Jr., 148–149, 150, 151
Marriott, J. Willard, Sr., 148, 149
Marriott, Richard, 151
Marshall, Wilber, 462
Martin, David W., Jr., 444–445
Maslow, Abraham, 58, 59, 448–449, 450
Masolia, George, 16
Matsushita, Konosuke, 28
Mayo, George Elton, 58
McClelland, David C., 453, 454–455, 456, 559, 777
McColough, C. Peter, 110
McCorkindale, Douglas H., 291, 292
McCormack, John, 477
McCormack, Maryanne, 477
McDonald, James F., 268
McGovern, Gordon, 236
McGowan, William, 32
McGregor, Douglas, 58, 59–60
McNealy, Scott, 780
Miller, Danny, 391, 392
Miller, Herman, 587
Miller, J., 64
Miller, Richard W., 232–233, 513

Milliken, Gerrish, 731, 732
Milliken, Roger, 708, 731, 732
Milliken, Seth, 731, 732
Minard, Sally, 509
Mintzberg, Henry, 10, 11, 14, 15, 16, 25, 389, 391, 392, 393, 521
Mitchell, Gerry, 539
Mitchell, Terence R., 782, 785
Monaghan, Tom, 471, 472, 473
Morrissette, Arthur E., 542
Mouton, Jane Srygley, 489
Münsterberg, Hugo, 54
Murdoch, Rupert, 636, 784
Murton, Bill, 557
Musgrave, Sir Richard, 8

Nash, Laura, 158
Neuharth, Allen H., 291, 292
Nicholson, Geoffrey, 368
Nobuto, Osamu, 649
Nunley, Roger, 534

Oldham, Greg, 341
Oliveira, Robert, 368
Olsen, Kenneth, 334, 335, 353
Olson, Kenneth, 540
Olson, Roy, 222
Ortenberg, Arthur, 76, 77, 87
Osborn, Alex F., 287
O'Toole, James, 125
Otte, Ruth L., 725
Ouchi, William, 68
Owen, Robert, 42–43, 49

Pace, Stan, 11
Palmquist, Phil, 244
Perlman, Itzhak, 20
Perot, H. Ross, 100, 365, 747, 779
Peters, Tom, 514
Petersen, Donald E., 73, 74, 320
Pinchot, Gifford, III, 244
Poling, Harold, 74
Porter, Lyman W., 460
Porter, Michael E., 196, 197, 198, 200, 211, 392, 714, 748, 750
Portman, John C., Jr., 151
Post, Charles W., 774
Potter, Mike, 16
Prichard, Peter, 291, 292
Pulsifer, Alzada, 124
Pyle, Judith, 191
Pyle, Thomas, 191

Quinn, James Brian, 617

Reagan, Ronald, 102
Reed, John, 483
Ritchie, Paul, 626
Rittereiser, Robert, 624
Robert, Henry Martyn, 44–45
Robinson, James D., III, 538
Rockefeller, John D., 115, 334
Roderick, David, 30
Rodgers, Dr. Thurman John, 154, 155, 156
Roebuck, Alvah Curtis, 328
Roethlisberger, Fritz J., 58
Rogers, John W., 615
Rohde, Gilbert, 587
Rollwagen, John A., 221, 222
Romano, Libby, 771
Romano, Phil, 770–772, 779, 788, 790
Romano, Rosalie, 771
Romano, Rose, 771
Roosevelt, Franklin D., 507
Rosenberg, Martin, 394

Rosenberg, Richard M., 257
Rosenwald, Julius, 328
Ross, Paula, 124
Rostropovich, Mistislav, 20
Roux, Annette, 264
Ruch, Richard, 588
Russo, Ralph R., 480

Safra, Edmond J., 142
Sahlberg, Karl-Erik, 397
Samuelson, Robert J., 593
Santino, Tony, 147
Schaefer, George, 694
Schmidt, Warren H., 485
Schnittke, Alfred, 19
Schoellhorn, Robert A., 579
Schuenke, Donald, 10
Schulman, Steve, 297
Schumpeter, Joseph, 773
Sculley, John, 24, 320, 401, 479, 480, 508
Sears, Richard Warren, 328
Seiden, Philip, 808
Semler, Richard, 577
Serrano, Tony, 518
Shea, Richard, 237–238
Sherill, Patrick Henry, 461
Shields, Jack, 540
Shields, Lytton J., 267
Shiraishi, Yuma, 27, 28
Shostack, Lynn, 487, 488
Shulman, Yankelovich Clancy, 132
Sidell, Bob, 204
Siegel, Mo, 347
Silas, C. J., 31
Silver, Spence, 368
Simon, Herbert, 265
Singer, Isaac, 775
Skinner, B. F., 464, 466
Skinner, Wickham, 690
Sloan, Alfred, 598
Smith, Adam, 43, 116, 339
Smith, Jud, 15
Smith, Richard, 585

Smith, Roger B., 104, 365, 366, 518–519
Smith, Tom, 627
Smith, Willie, 565
Stack, Jack, 166, 501–502
Stalker, G. M., 387
Stempel, Robert C., 366
Stevenson, Howard H., 105
Stewart, Rosemary, 17
Stogdill, Ralph M., 483–484
Stranahan, Duane, Jr., 96
Stucky, Steven, 19
Sugar, Alan Michael, 784–785
Sullovan, Barry, 17
Sutherland, Joan, 20

Takano, Shizuo, 27, 28
Takayanagi, Kenjiro, 27, 28
Tang, Cyrus, 482
Tannenbaum, Robert, 485
Taylor, Elizabeth, 102, 736
Taylor, Frederick, 39, 44, 45–47, 54, 55, 67, 339, 446
Telling, Edward, 329, 330
Thompson, James D., 96
Thompson, John, 15–16, 17
Thompson, John P., 326
Tolmich, Herbert, 238
Towne, Henry R., 44, 45
Trani, John M., 514
Treybeg, James, 544
Tuckman, Bruce W., 567
Tuleja, Thaddeus, 121
Tung, Rosalie, 761
Turner, Mark, 790
Tversky, Amos, 275
Tyler, Charles, 130
Tyrrell, Thomas, 564

Vagelos, P. Roy, 224–225, 806
Valente, Benita, 20
Vanderbilt, Cornelius, 115
Venable, Thomas L., 650
Veraldi, Lewis C., 572

Vesper, Karl H., 782, 785
Vetrone, Nancy, 451
Vologzhin, Valentin, 459
Vroom, Victor H., 456, 498

Wachner, Linda, 448
Wade, Marion, 670
Wallace, Robert G., 712
Walton, Samuel Moore, 185, 508, 603, 747
Wang, Dr. An, 231–233, 508
Wang, Fred, 232
Wang, Lorraine, 232
Watson, Thomas, Jr., 137, 531
Weber, Max, 49–51, 53, 346, 383
Wee-kiat, 697, 698
Welch, John F., Jr., 178–179, 513, 514
Wells, Frank G., 188, 189, 190
Wexner, Leslie, 203
Wheeler, David, 272
Wheelwright, Steven C., 667
Whitman, Marina vonNeumann, 98
Whitwam, David, 754
Wiles, Q. T., 182
Wilkins, Jerry, 16
Williams, Earle, 795
Williams, Marjorie, 779
Wilson, Joseph C., 110
Wiseman, Charles, 714
Wong-Gillmore, Marjorie, 36–37
Wood, Robert E., 115, 328–329
Woodhull, Nancy, 13, 14
Woodside, William, 269, 270
Woodward, Joan, 67, 384, 385
Woolworth, Frank, 92
Wozniak, Steven, 396
Wurlitzer, Rudolph, 774

Yetton, Philip, 498
Ylvisaker, William T., 267

Zwerner, Carl R., 798
Zwicky, Frank, 303

Ability:
  in situational leadership theory, 496
  tests of, 416
Acceptable quality level (AQL), 652
Acceptance sampling, 652
Acceptance theory of authority, 53
Accommodation, 580
Accountability, 353
Accounting, 371
Achievement-oriented leader behavior, 503
Acquired-needs theory, 453–455
Acquisition, 204, 233, 234
Action research, 251
Active listening, 533
Activity, 307
Activity ratios, 633–634
Ad hoc committees, 554, 571
Adaptive mode, 194–195
Adhocracy, 391
Adjourning stage of groups, 569
Administrative management, 51–53
Administrative protections, 745
Adverse impact, 414
Advertising, 99, 121
Aesthetics in quality control, 648
Affirmative action, 410
Affirmative action plan, 410
Age Discrimination in Employment Act, 409
Agency for International Development, 374
Aggregate production planning, 673–675
Aggressor role, 560
Agreement, change and, 242
Alcohol abuse, 432
Alternative solutions, 269–275
Alternative work schedules, 343–344
American Society for Quality Control, 646
Amoral management, 135, 136
Anchoring and adjustment, 276
Antifreeloader argument, 123
Application blank, 414
Applications software packages, 719
Artificial intelligence, 322
Assessment center, 418
Assessment phase in training, 419
Asset management ratios, 633–634
Assets, 630
  return on, 634
Attention stage of modeling, 470
Audits:
  external, 637
  financial, 636–637
  functional, 200–201
  internal, 637
Authority, 353
  acceptance theory of, 53
  control and decentralization of, 598
  functional, 356
  line, 355
Autocratic leaders, 485
Autonomous work groups, 573
Autonomy, 341

Availability, decision making and, 276
Average collection period, 634
Avoidance, 580

Back orders, 675
Backward integration, 201
Balance of payments, 744
Balance of trade, 744
Balance sheet, 630
  pro forma (projected), 644
Balance sheet budget, 644
Bankruptcy, 205, 233
  of small business, 797–798
Batch processing, computer, 701
BCG growth-share matrix, 206–208
Behavior modification, 464
Behavioral displacement, control and, 619
Behavioral science, 61
Behavioral viewpoint on management, 53–61
Behaviorally anchored rating scales, 422
Behaviorism, 464–469
Behaviors:
  carryover, 565
  emergent, 557
Belongingness needs, 449
Benchmark jobs, 426
Benefits, 424
Bill of materials (BOM), 677
Blocker role, 561
Bottom line, 632
Bottom-up budgeting, 644
Boundary spanning, 99
Bounded rationality, 265
Brainstorming, 287
Brand managers, 361
Break-even analysis, 319–320
Budget(s), 174
  types of, 642–644
Budgetary control, 638–646
  process of, 644–645, 646
  responsibility centers, 639–641
  zero-base, 645–646
Budgeting, 638
  bottom-up and top-down, 644
  zero-base (ZBB), 645–646
Buffering, 97
Bureau of Labor Statistics, 410, 411
Bureaucracy, 390
  as barrier to innovation, 617–618
Bureaucratic control, 612–613
Bureaucratic management, 49–51
Business, small (see Small business)
Business-level strategy, 193, 211–215
Business plan, developing a, 787–790

Capacity, 672
  current, 680
  equilibrium with demand, 681
  expansion options, 681
  measures of, 673

Capacity argument, 123
Capacity-lags-demand policy, 681
Capacity-leads-demand policy, 681
Capacity planning, 672–673
Capacity requirements planning, 673
Capital, 790
Capital expenditures budget, 643
Capital investments, 643
Capitalist economy, 82
Career, 807
  dual-career couples, 812–813
  ethical issues in, 138–139
  mentors and mentoring, 813
  plateaus and lateral moves, 813
  strategies for, 809
Career development:
  organizational programs and, 811–812
  stages in, 810–811
Career management, 807–813
  definition of, 808
  engaging in, 808–812
  nature of, 807–808
Carrying costs, 312, 654
Carryover behaviors, 565
Cash budget, 644
Cash cow, 207
Categorization stage of problems, 269
Causal models, 298–300
Central processing unit (CPU), computer, 701
Centralization, 352–353
Ceremonial, 104
Certification process, 430
Chain network, 535
Chain of command, 337–338
Chamber of Commerce, 428, 774
Change, 226
  forces for, 227–228
  innovation vs., 226
  key components for, 246–249
  low tolerance for, 240
  managing, 223–258
  managing resistance to, 239–243
  nature of, 225–228
  planned, 235
  reactive, 234
  six-step model of process, 235–237
Change agent, 250–251
Changing, 240
Charisma, 507
Circle network, 535
Civil Rights Act of 1964, Title VII, 410
Clan control, 612, 613
Classical viewpoint of management, 45–53
Clients, 87–88
Closed system, 64
Co-opting, 100
Coercion, change and, 242
Coercive power, 481, 482
Cognitive resource theory, 494–495
Cognitive resources, 494

Cognitive theories, 456–464
Collaboration, 580
Collectivity stage, 228, 229–230
Command (functional) group, 553
Committees, permanent, 130
Communication:
  basic components of process, 523–527
  and change, 240
  common methods of, 525
  consistency and, 531–532
  definition of, 518
  downward, 536–538
  formal, 539
  horizontal, 539, 541–542
  impeding or enhancing, 527–535
  informal, 539–541
  managerial, 515–548
    (See also Managerial communication)
  nonverbal, 520
  one-way, 526
  skills in, 532–535
  two-way, 526
  types of, 519–520
  upward, 538
  verbal, 519–520
  vertical, 536–539, 541
Communication channels, 536–544
Communication network, 535–536
Community, social responsibility and, 121–123
Compensable factors, 425
Compensation, 424–429
Competence, distinctive, 200
Competition, 580
  achieving parity with, 667–668
Competitive advantage, 191
  of nations, 748–750
Competitive analysis, 196–201
Competitive forces model, five (Porter), 196–200
Competitive strategies (Porter), 211–215
Competitors, 88–90
  keeping tabs on, 89
  as target of information systems, 714–715
  threat of new, 199
Complacency, decision making and, 272–273
Complex environments, 94
Compressed workweek, 344
Compromise, 580
Computer(s):
  centralization vs. decentralization, 721–722
  components of information systems, 701–703
  effects on jobs, 723–725
  errors in, 725
  mainframe, 703, 704
  minicomputers, 703, 704
  personal (micro), 703, 704
  sabotage and security breaches, 726
  super, 703, 704
  theft and, 725–726
Computer-aided design (CAD), 687
Computer-aided manufacturing (CAM), 687
Computer-based information systems:
  definition of, 701
  developing, 717–721
  overview of, 699–706
Computer-integrated manufacturing (CIM), 687–689
Computer virus, 726
Concentration, 201
  ethnocentric, 741
  geocentric, 742
  polycentric, 741

Concentric diversification, 203
Conceptual skills, 18
Concurrent control, 607–608, 629
Conflict management, 578–581
Conformance, quality control and, 647
Conglomerate diversification, 203
Conglomerates, 203
Consideration, 487
Constraints, 309
Consumer Product Safety Commission, 136
Contingency planning, 179
Contingency theory, 67–68
  of leadership, 490–493
Continuous-process production, 384
Contracts, negotiating, 100
Contrast error, 423
Control:
  acceptability of, 621
  accuracy of, 621
  alternatives to, 606
  behavioral displacement and, 619
  bureaucratic, 612–613
  choosing a managerial style for, 615–617
  clan, 612, 613
  concurrent, 607–608, 629
  conditions for, 604–606
  cost-effectiveness of, 621
  determining areas to, 600, 604–606
  establishing standards, 601–602
  feedback, 608, 629
  feedforward, 607, 629
  financial, 629–638
  flexibility of, 621–622
  future orientation of, 620
  and game playing, 619
  incrementalist approach to, 618–619
  in information processing, 701
  and innovation, 618–619
  levels of, 598–599
  as management process, 594–599
  managerial implementation, 611–619
  market, 611–612
  measuring performance, 602–603
  monitorability of, 621
  multidimensionality of, 620–621
  negative attitudes and, 620
  and operating delays, 619
  operational, 598
  overcontrol vs. undercontrol, 620
  performance vs. standards, 603
  postaction (output), 608
  process feasibility, 605
  process of, 600–606
  quality, 646–652
  realistic expectations and, 621
  role of, 595–598
  screening (yes-no), 608
  significance of process, 594–595
  span of, 348–350
  statistical process, 652
  strategic, 598
  systems of (see Control systems)
  tactical, 598
  timeliness and, 621
  types of, 606–611
Control models, 305–306
Control systems, 594–595
  assessing, 619–622
  budgetary, 628, 638–646
  characteristics of effective, 620–621
  cybernetic, 610
  financial, 629–638
  major, 627–629
  managerial level and, 628–629
  multiple, 609
  noncybernetic, 610–611

Control systems (Cont.):
  potential dysfunctional aspects of, 619–620
  quality, 628
  timing emphasis of, 629
Controlling, 8–9, 590–731
  definition of, 594
  information systems for management, 696–731
  managerial methods, 625–659
  operations management, 660–695
  the organization, 591–623
Convergent thinking, 282
Cooptation, change and, 242
Coordination:
  horizontal, 357–358
  vertical, 345–357
Coordinator role, 560
Corporate culture, 103
Corporate-level strategy, 192–193
  formulating, 201–211
Corporate philanthropy, 124
Corporate social responsibility, 115
Corridor principle, 779
Cost(s):
  approach to information systems, 715
  carrying, 654
  discretionary, 643
  fixed, 319, 643
  holding, 312, 654
  of inventory, 653–654
  item, 653–654
  ordering, 312–313, 654
  stockout, 654
  sunk, 278
  variable, 319, 643
Cost acceptability, 606
Cost leadership, 392
Cost leadership strategy, 211–213
Countries:
  developed, 743
  less developed (LDCs), 743
  newly industrialized (NICs), 743
Creativity:
  in decision making, 281–288
  enhancing group, 286–288
  stages of, 285
Creativity-relevant skills, 284
Crisis problem, 262
Critical events, 564
Critical path, 308
Critical Path Method (CPM), 306
Cross-sectional analysis, 636
Cross-training, 339
Cultural differences, adapting to, 761–764
Culture:
  and change, 247–248
  corporate, 103
  entrepreneurial, 105–106
  organizational, 78, 103–107
Current assets, 630
Current liabilities, 630
Customer divisions, 375–376
Customers, 87–88
  bargaining power of, 198
  and social responsibility, 120–121
  as target of information systems, 714–715
Cybernetic control systems, 610

Data, 699
Data base, 702
Data-base management system, 702
Data storage in information processing, 701
Debt capital, 790
Debt management ratios, 634
Debt ratio, 634

Decentralization, 352–353
Deciding to decide, 273
Decision(s), 263–265
Decision making, 258–292
    aids in, 293–327
    alternative solutions in, 269–275
    biases in, 275–277
    creativity in, 281–288
    defining, 261
    escalation phenomenon in, 277–278
    group, 279–281
    models of, 265–268
    nature of, 261–265
    overcoming barriers to, 272–279
    quantitative aids for, 316–321
    situations in, 262–265
    steps in effective, 268–272
    in strategy implementation, 217
    types of problems in, 262
Decision matrix, 316
Decision support systems, 321, 709–710, 711
Decision trees, 317–319
Decoding in communication, 524
Defensive avoidance, decision making and,
    273
Defensive strategies, 204–205
Delegation, 353–354
    ethics and, 142
    guidelines for effective, 355
    in situational leadership theory, 497
Delphi method, 301–303
Democratic leaders, 485
Denominator role, 561
Departmentalization, 345
Departments, permanent, 130
Dependency, extreme, ethics and, 141
Dependent demand inventory, 676
Descriptive decision-making models, 268
Developed countries, 743
Developing countries, 743
Development of employees, 418–424
Devil's advocates, 281
Diagnosis stage of problems, 269
Dialectical inquiry, 281
Differentiation, 66
    approach to information systems, 715
    and organization structure, 388
Differentiation paradox, 396
Differentiation strategy, 213
Direct analogies, 288
Direct contact, 359
Direct interlock, 100
Direct investment, 752
Directive leader behavior, 503
Discretionary costs, 643
Discretionary expense center, 639
Dismissal, protection from arbitrary, 431–
    432
Dissatisfiers, 452
Disseminator role, 13
Distinctive competence, 200
Distributed processing, 722
Distribution models, 313
Disturbance handler role, 13, 14
Divergent thinking, 282
Diversification, 203
Divestiture, 205
Divisional structure, 345, 373–377
    forms of, 374–376
    functional vs., 373
Divisionalized form, 390–391
Dog, 207
Domain-relevant skills, creativity and, 282
Domain shifts, 101
Downsizing, 349
Downward communication, 536–538

Driving forces, 243
Drug abuse and testing, 432
Dual-career couples, 812–813
Durability, quality control and, 647
Dynamic environments, 94

Econometric models, 300
Economic element, 82–83
Economic order quantity (EOQ), 654
Economy, 82
Education:
    change and, 240
    of entrepreneur, 778
Effectiveness, 20
Efficiency, 20–21
Effort-performance expectancy, 456–457,
    458, 463
Elaboration of structure stage, 228, 230–231
Electronic data processing (EDP), 700
Electronic mail systems, 543–544, 708
Electronic monitoring, 724
Emergent behaviors, 557
Emergent interactions, 557
Emergent sentiments, 557
Employee(s):
    hiring and laying off, 674
    issues affecting, 431–433
    and social responsibility, 118–120
Employee assistance program (EAP), 432
Employee benefits, 428–429
Employee-centered leadership, 486
Employee development, 418–424
Employee evaluation, 418–424
Employee involvement teams, 652
Employee Polygraph Protection Act, 433
Employment at will, 431–432
Encoding in communication, 523–524
Encourager role, 560
End user, 720
End-user computing, 720, 722–723
Energizer role, 560
Engineered expense center, 639
Enlightened self-interest argument, 123
Entrepreneur, 778–780
Entrepreneur role, 13, 14, 26–29, 774
Entrepreneurial culture, 105–106
Entrepreneurial mode, 194
Entrepreneurial stage, 228, 229
Entrepreneurial team, 571, 573
Entrepreneurship, 770–802
    assessing opportunities, 774–775
    buying an existing business, 785
    defining, 773–774
    desirability and feasibility, 781
    economic growth and, 775
    employment opportunities and, 776
    environmental conditions for, 780
    factors influencing, 776–782
    intrapreneurship vs., 797
    major issues and problems of, 797–799
    nature of, 773–776
    purchasing a franchise, 785–787
    starting a new firm, 782–783
Entropy, 66
Environmental complexity, 94
Environmental dynamism, 94
Environmental munificence, 95, 141
Environmental uncertainty, 94
Environments:
    assessment of, 196–200
    characteristics of, 503–504
    competitiveness of, 141
    external, 77, 78–91
    and human resources, 408
    internal, 77, 103–107

Environments (Cont.):
    international, assessing, 742–750
    mega-, 78–85
    and organization design, 353, 387–389
    task, 87–91
Equal Employment Opportunity Act, 410
Equal Pay Act, 116
Equity:
    return on (ROE), 634–635
    types of, 424–425
Equity capital, 790
Equity theory, 461–463
ERG theory, 449–451, 455–456
Error, 423
Escalation phenomenon, 278
Escalation situations, 277
Esteem needs, 449
Ethical organization, managing an, 140–144
Ethics, 115
Ethics in management, 112–147
    career issues, 138–139
    guidelines for, 137–138
    principles for, 142–144
    small business and, 798–799
Ethnocentric orientation, 741
Evaluation of employees, 418–424
Evaluation phase in training, 419
Event (node), 307
Exchange rate, 744
Executive support systems, 712–713
Executives, 129
Existence needs, 449
Existence stage of small business, 794
Expatriates, 762
Expectancy theory, 456–461
Expected (average) time, 308
Expected value, 317
Expense budget, 643
Expenses, 631
Expert power, 481, 482
Expert systems (ES), 321–322, 711
Explanatory (causal) models, 298–300
Explicit statements, 564
Expo 86, 278–279
Exporting, 751
Expropriation, 745
External audit, 637
External environment, 77
    adaptation to, 97–98
    analyzing conditions of, 91–96
    characteristics of, 93–95
    favorability influence approach to, 99–101
    types of, 78–91
External equity, 425
External information, sources of, 81–82
Extinction, 466
Extrinsic rewards, 457

Facilitation, change and, 241
Facilities:
    competitive retail outlets, 682
    designing and utilizing, 666, 680–686
    emergency services, 682
    expansion and contraction, 680–681
    layout of, 682–685
    location of, 681–682
    multiple factories and warehouses, 682
    single location, 682
Family issues:
    in employment, 433
    small business and entrepreneurship, 798
Fantasy analogies, 288
Feasibility space, 310
Features, quality control and, 647
Federal Bankruptcy Act, 205
Federal Trade Commission, 121

Feedback, 64
    in communication, 525–526, 534–535
    in jobs, 341
Feedback control, 608, 629
Feedforward control, 607, 629
Fiedler's contingency model, 490
Figurehead role, 11, 13
Finance:
    and functional structure, 370–371
    for small business, 790
Financial analysis, comparative, 636
Financial audits, 636–637
Financial budget, 644
Financial control, 629–638
    avoiding pitfalls, 637–638
    ratio analysis, 632–635
Financial standards, 636
Financial statements, 639–632
Finished-goods inventory, 653
First-line managers/supervisors, 22
Five competitive forces model (Porter), 196–
    200
Fixed assets, 630
Fixed costs, 319, 643
Fixed-interval schedule of reinforcement,
    467–468
Fixed-position layout, 686
Fixed-ratio schedule of reinforcement, 468
Flat structure, 349
Flexible manufacturing systems (FMS), 688
Flextime, 344
Fluctuation stock, 654
Focus strategy, 213
Follower role, 560
Food and Drug Administration, 141
Force-field analysis, 243
Forecasting, 97–98, 296–305
    choosing method of, 304–305
    demand for human resources, 408
    judgmental, 304
    operations management and, 672
    qualitative, 301–303
    quantitative, 297–301
Foreign Corrupt Practices Act, 765
Foreign sales representatives, 751
Formal communication, 539
Formalization, 346–347
Formalization and control stage, 228, 230
Forming stage of groups, 567–568
Forward integration, 202
Framing in decision making, 275
Franchise, 785–787
Franchisee, 786
Franchiser, 785–786
Free riders, 563
Friendship group, 555–556
Frustration-regression principle, 450
Functional approach to management, 51
Functional audit, 200–201
Functional authority, 356
Functional-level strategy, 193, 215–216
Functional managers, 29
Functional structure, 345, 370–373
Futurists, 126

Gainsharing, 428
Game playing, control and, 619
Game theory, 320–321
Gantt charts, 305
Garbage-can model of decision making, 267
Gatekeeper role, 560
GE business screen, 208–210
General managers, 29
Genetic screening, 432
Geocentric concentration, 742
Geographic divisions, 374

Geographic regions structure, 759
Geography, organization structure and, 353
Given sentiments, 556
Global matrix structure, 759–760
Globalization, 754
Goal incongruence, 601
Goal-setting theory, 463
Goals, 156–157
    attainable, 164
    benefits of, 158–161
    career, setting, 809
    challenging, 164
    commitment to, 166–168, 463
    content of, 164–166
    feedback and, 169
    hierarchy of, 163
    job knowledge and, 169
    levels of, 161–163
    management financial, 636
    nature of, 158–163
    official, 161
    operational, 162
    performance facilitation by, 164–172
    planning linked to, 172–179
    potential problems with, 171–172
    qualitative, 165
    quantitative, 165
    relevant, 165–166
    setting, 167
    situational constraints and, 169
    specific and measurable, 165
    strategic, 161–162
    superordinate, 580
    tactical, 162
    task complexity and, 169
    time-limited, 165
    work behavior and, 168–169
Gossip chain, 540
Government agencies, 91
Grand strategy, 201
Grapevine, 539–541
Graphic rating scales, 421
Group(s):
    cohesiveness of, 565–567
    command (functional), 553
    conflict management, 578–581
    definition of, 552
    development of, 567–569
    formal, 552–554
    friendship, 555–556
    informal, 554–557
    interest, 554
    norms of, 564–565
    project, 554
    size of, 561–563
    stages of, 567–569
    task, 553
    (See also Work groups)
Group cohesiveness, 565–567
Group decision making, 279–281
Group effectiveness model, 574–578
Group maintenance roles, 560
Group management, 549–589
    (See also Work groups)
Group observer role, 560
Group processes, 563–569
Group task roles, 560
Group technology, 688
Groupthink, 280
Growth-need strength, 342
Growth needs, 449
Growth strategy, 201

Hackers, 726
Halo effect, 423
    and communication, 528–529

Hand of government, 116
Hand of management, 116–118
Hardware, computer, 701
Harmonizer role, 560
Harvest, 205
Hawthorne effect, 57
Hawthorne studies, 55–58, 446
Hierarchy of needs theory, 448–449, 455
Historical financial standards, 636
Holding costs, 312, 654
Home country, 741
Horizontal communication, 539, 541–542
Horizontal coordination, 357–358
Horizontal integration, 201
Host country, 741
Human relations movement, 58–60
Human resource management, 402–441
    definition of, 404–405
    process of, 405–406
Human resource planning, 406–411
Human resources:
    and change, 247
    demand for, 408, 410–411
    and functional structure, 370
    managing international, 761–764
    for small business, 791
    in strategy implementation, 217
    supply of, 408–411
Human skills, 18
Hybrid structure, 345, 377–379
Hygiene factors, 452

Idea champion, 26–27, 243, 394
Immoral management, 134–136
Import quota, 745
Income statement, 631–632
Incremental model of decision making, 266–
    267
Incrementalist approach to control, 618–619
Independent demand inventory, 676
Indirect interlock, 100
Individual consideration, leadership and,
    508
Individual equity, 425
Individualism-collectivism, 746–747, 764
Industry financial standards, 636
Inequity, reducing or eliminating, 462–463
Informal communication, 539–541
Informal leader, 561
Information, 699–700
    characteristics of useful, 703–705
    presentation methods, 419
Information center, 723
Information giver role, 560
Information needs, 705–707
Information power, 481, 482
Information processing, 700–701
Information seeker role, 560
Information systems, 359
    centralization vs. decentralization, 721–
        722
    computer components of, 701–703
        [See also Computer(s)]
    definition of, 701
    developing computer-based, 717–721
    impact on organizations, 723–727
    for management, 696–730
    management (MIS), 62–63, 709, 710
    nature of, 699–701
    overview of, 699–706
    resource management, 721–723
    strategic implications of, 713–715
    types of, 706–713
Infrastructure, 743
Initiating structure, 487
Initiator-contributor role, 560

Innovation, 26, 226
approach to information systems, 715–716
bureaucracy as barrier to, 617–618
change vs., 226, 234
communication channels and, 541–543
competitive advantage of nations, 748–750
control and, 618–619
differentiation paradox and, 396
entrepreneurship and, 26–29, 105–106, 774–776
ethics and, 142
forces for, 227–228
horizontal coordination and, 357–362
information systems and, 713–715
managing, 223–258
nature of, 225–228
nontraditional compensation approaches, 427–428
organization structure and, 393–398
planning process and, 175–176
process technology, 687–689
quality circles and, 651–652
reservations and, 396–397
six-step model of process, 235–237
social learning perspective on, 472–473
social responsibility and, 125–126
special applications of work groups, 569–574
strategic management and, 194–195
technological forecasting and, 301–303
transfer process and, 397
transformational leadership, 506–508
Innovative differentiation, 392
Inputs, 63
in information processing, 701
Institutional power, 454
Integration, 55
backward/forward, 201–202
horizontal/vertical, 201
and organization structure, 388–389
Integrative unity, 55
Intellectual stimulation, 508
Intelligence, artificial, 322
Interactions:
emergent, 557
required, 556
Interest group, 554
Interlocking directorates, 100
Internal audit, 637
Internal environment, 77, 79
Internal equity, 425
International business, 738
geographic regions structure, 759
global matrix structure, 759–760
international divisions structure, 758
organizing, 756–760
worldwide functional divisions structure, 756–757
worldwide product divisions structure, 757–758
International divisions structure, 758
International element, 84–85
International human resources:
assignment policies, 761–762
expatriates, 762
international option, 761–762
leadership styles, 763–764
local option, 761
managing, 761–764
parent company option, 761
recruitment, 762
relational skills, 763
selection and training, 762–763
International management, 735–769
adapting to cultural differences, 761–764

International management (Cont.):
competitive advantage of nations, 748–750
definition of, 738
entry methods, 751–753
environment assessment, 742–750
ethical issues, 764–766
gauging strategic issues, 750–756
nature of, 738–742
organizations engaging in, 739–741
orientations toward, 741–742
questionable-payments issue, 765–766
social responsibility, 764–765
value conflicts, 765
Interpersonal roles, 11, 13
Interventions, 250
Interview:
conducting an effective, 416–417
performance appraisal, 423–424
selection, 414
structure of, 415
Intrapreneurial ideas, 245
Intrapreneurial roles, 243
Intrapreneurs, 26
Intrapreneurship, 26, 243–246
entrepreneurship vs., 797
Intrinsic rewards, 457
Inventory, 653
anticipation, 675
building up, as planning strategy, 674–675
costs of, 653–654
dependent demand, 676
finished-goods, 653
independent demand, 676
raw materials, 653
seasonal, 675
significance of, 653
work-in-process, 653
Inventory control, 653–656
just-in-time (JIT), 655–656
Inventory models, 312–313
Inventory turnover, 633
Investment:
capital, 643
direct, 752
return on (ROI), 634
Investment center, 640
Invisible hand, 115–116
Involvement, change and, 241
Iowa studies on leadership, 484–485
Iron law of responsibility, 123
Irregularities, control of, 596
Issues management, 127–128
Item cost, 653–654

Japanese management, 68
Jargon, professional, 530
Job(s):
information technology and, 723–725
key, 426
Job analysis, 407–408
Job-centered leadership, 486
Job characteristic model, 341
Job choices, 17
Job constraints, 17
Job demands, 17
Job depth, 341
Job description, 407
Job design, 338–344
Job enlargement, 340–341
Job enrichment, 341, 342–343, 453
Job evaluation, 425
Job posting, 412
Job rotation, 339–340
Job scope, 341

Job sharing, 344
Job simplification, 339
Job specification, 407
Joint ventures, 100, 752
Judgmental forecasting, 304
Jury of executive opinion, 304
Just-in-time inventory control (JIT), 655–656

Kanban, 656
Key jobs, 426
Kinesic behavior, 520
Knowledge base in management, 18
Knowledge-intensive systems, 711

La Prospective, 303
Labor dissatisfaction, ethics and, 142
Labor-management relations, 429–431
Labor supply, 90, 408–409, 410
Laissez-faire leaders, 485
Large-batch production, 384
Lateral relations, 359–362
Law of effect, 464
Layout:
of facilities, 682–685
fixed-position, 686
process, 683–684
product, 684–685
Lead time, 654
Leader-member relations, 491
Leaders:
autocratic, 485
behaviors of, 503, 504–505
democratic, 485
employee-centered, 486
female vs. male behaviors, 489–490
influence of, 480–483
informal, 561
job-centered, 486
laissez-faire, 485
role of, 13
sources of power for, 481–482
transactional, 506
Leadership, 478–514
adjusting to cultural differences, 763–764
behavior in, 484–490, 503
charisma and, 507
cognitive resource theory of, 494–495
definition of, 480
individual consideration and, 508
intellectual stimulation and, 508
normative model of, 498–502
and organizational life cycle, 510
path-goal theory of, 502–506
romance of, 508–509
searching for traits of, 483–484
situational theories of, 490–506
substitutes for, 509–510
transformational, 506–508
Leading, 8
a meeting, 570
Leading indicators, 300
Legal function, 371
Legal-political element, 83–84
Legitimate power, 481, 482
Leniency error, 423
Less developed countries (LDCs), 743
Leverage ratios, 634
Liabilities, 630
Liaison role, 13
and horizontal coordination, 359–360
Licensing, 751
for small business, 793
Life-cycle portfolio matrix, 210
Life cycles, 228
stages of, 228–231
Line authority, 355

Line position, 354–357
Linear programming (LP), 309–311
Linking pin, 553
Liquidation, 205, 233
Liquidity ratios, 632–633
Listening, 533
Local area networks (LANs), 722
Logical office, 725
Long-term liabilities, 630
LPC orientation, 490

Machine bureaucracy, 390
Management:
    administrative, 51–53
    amoral, 135, 136
    behavioral viewpoint on, 53–61, 69
    birth of ideas in, 41–42
    bureaucratic, 49–51
    challenge of, 3–37
    classical theories of, 45–53, 69
    of conflict, 578–581
    contemporary viewpoints of, 63–69
    contingency theory of, 67–68, 69
    control as process of, 594–599
    decision making in, 258–292
    defining, 6–9
    early innovative practices, 41
    ethics in, 112–147
    functional approach to, 51
    functions of, 23–24
    of groups, 549–589
        (See also Group management)
    Hawthorne studies of, 55–58
    human relations approach to, 58–60
    immoral, 134–136
    information needs of, 705–706
    international, 735–769
        (See also International management)
    issues, 127–128
    Japanese, 68
    moral, 135, 136
    operations, 62, 660–695
        (See also Operations management)
    overview of, 6–10
    pioneering ideas in, 38–74
    preclassical theories of, 42–45
    process of, 9–10
    quantitative viewpoint of, 61–63, 69
    scientific, 45–49
    of small business, 792–799
    social responsibility in, 112–147
    span of, 348–350
    strategic, 187–222
    systems theory of, 63–67, 69
    theories of (outline), 42
Management by exception, 603
Management by objectives (MBO), 179–183,
    422
Management by wandering about (MBWA),
    538–539
Management development programs, 420
Management financial goals, 636
Management information system (MIS), 62–
    63, 709, 710
Management science, 62, 294
Management skills, 18
Manager(s):
    activities and responsibilites of, 10–17
    brand, 361
    as decision makers, 265–268
    decisional roles of, 14
    education of, 30–31
    effectiveness training for, 30–33
    ethical, 131–140
    ethical guidelines for, 137–138
    experience of, 31–32

Manager(s) (Cont.):
    first-line, 22
    functional, 29
    general, 29
    informational roles of, 13–14
    interpersonal roles of, 11, 13
    knowledge base of, 18
    middle, 22–23
    product, 361
    project, 29, 361
    reasons for derailment of, 26
    roles of, 11–14, 25–26
    top, 23
    work methods of, 10–11
Managerial communication, 515–548
    nature of, 518–527
    preferences in, 520–521
Managerial control methods, 625–659
    budgetary, 638–646
    financial, 629–638
    inventory, 653–656
    major systems, 627–629
    quality, 646–652
Managerial ethics, 115
    types of, 134–136
Managerial Grid, 489
Managerial integrator, 361–362
Managerial job types, 21–30
    hierarchical levels, 21–23, 23–26
    promoting innovation, 26–29
    responsibility areas, 29–30
Managerial work agendas, 15–17
Manipulation and change, 242
Manufacturing:
    computer-aided (CAM), 687
    computer-integrated (CIM), 687–688
Manufacturing organizations, 664–666
Manufacturing resource planning (MRP II),
    679
Market control, 611–612
Market development, 201
Market differentiation, 392
Marketing and functional structure, 370
Masculinity-femininity, 747, 764
Mass production, 384
Master production schedule (MPS), 675
Master strategy, 201
Materials requirements planning (MRP),
    676–679
    benefits from, 678–679
    inputs to, 677–678
Matrix stages, 379
Matrix structure, 345, 379–383
Means-end chain, 163
Mechanistic characteristics of organizations,
    387–388
Medium in communication, 524
Mega-environment, 78–85
Mentors and mentoring, 813
Merger, 204, 233
Message:
    in communication, 524
    consistency and, 532
Michigan studies on leadership, 486, 488
Middle managers, 22–23
Mission, 157
Mission statement, 157
    components of, 159
Modeling, 470
Monitor role, 13
Monitoring methods, 300–301
Moral management, 135, 136
Morphological analysis, 303
Motivation, 443–477
    cognitive theories and, 456–464
    definition of, 445

Motivation (Cont.):
    early approaches to, 446–447
    model of, 447–448
    nature of, 445–448
    need theories and, 448–456
    reinforcement theory and, 464–469
    social learning theory and, 469–473
Motivation stage of modeling, 470
Motivators, 452
Multifocal strategy, 755
Multinational corporation (MNC), 739
    strategies for, 754–756
Multiple control systems, 609
Multiple-server queues, 312
Munificent environments, 95

National Aeronautics and Space Adminis-
    tration (NASA), 280
National Federation of Independent Busi-
    nesses, 798
National Labor Relations Board, 429, 430
National responsiveness strategy, 754–755
Natural selection model, 91
Need for achievement (nAch), 453, 777
Need for affiliation (nAff), 454
Need for power (nPow), 454
Need theories, 448–456
Needs analysis, 419
Negative entropy, 66
Negative reinforcement, 465–466
Negative synergy, 563
Negotiating contracts, 100
Negotiation, change and, 242
Negotiator role, 13, 14
Net profit margin, 634
Network(s), 11
    building, 12
    local area (LANs), 722
    wide area, 723
Network diagram, 307
Network optimization analysis, 313
Neutralizers, 509
New venture, 774
New venture teams, 396
New venture units, 396
Newly industrialized countries (NICs), 743
Niche differentiation, 392
Node, 307
Noise in communication, 525
Nominal group technique (NGT), 287
Noncrisis problem, 262
Noncybernetic control systems, 610–611
Nonprogrammed decisions, 263–265
Nonrational escalation, 278
Nonrational models of decision making, 265
Nonverbal communication, 520
Nonverbal consistency, 531–532
Normative decision-making models, 268
Normative leadership model, 498–502
Norming stage of groups, 568–569
Norms, 564
Not-for-profit organization, 9

Object language, 520
Objective function, 309
Office automation system (OAS), 708–709
Office of Federal Control Compliance Pro-
    grams, 410
Official goals, 161
Ohio State studies on leadership, 487, 488,
    489, 496, 502
Ombudsperson, 144
On-line processing, computer, 701
On-the-job training (OJT) methods, 419
One-way communication, 526
Open system, 64

Operant conditioning theory, 464–469
Operating budget, 643
Operating systems, 666
  aggregate production planning, 673–675
  capacity planning, 672–673
  developing and implementing, 666, 671–680
  forecasting, 672
  materials requirements planning, 676–679
  purchasing, 679–680
  scheduling and, 675–676
Operational control, 598
Operational goals, 162
Operational plans, 173
Operations, functional structure and, 370
Operations management, 62, 660–695
  defining, 663–666
  facilities design and utilization, 666, 680–686
  improving productivity, 690–691
  manufacturing vs.service organizations, 664–666
  process of, 666
  process technology, 666, 687–689
  productivity and, 663–664
  strategy formulation, 666–671
  systems development, 666, 671–680
Operations research, 62, 294
Operations strategy, 666, 667–670
Opinion surveys, 126
Opportunities, control and, 596
Opportunity problem, 262
Orchestrator, 27, 394
Ordering costs, 312–313, 654
Organic characteristics of organizations, 387–388
Organization, 6
  controlling the, 591–623
  not-for-profit, 9
Organization chart, 336, 337
Organization design, 336, 345
  contingency factors in, 383–391
  factors influencing, 370
  strategic, 367–401
Organization structure:
  adhocracy, 391
  alternatives assessment, 370–383
  basic elements of, 333–366
  bureaucratic, 390
  contingency factors in, 383–391
  definition of, 336
  designing, 369–370
  divisional, 345, 373–377, 390–391
  environment and, 353, 387–389
  flat, 349
  functional, 345, 370–373
  hybrid, 345, 377–379
  information technology and, 723
  matching strategy and, 391–393
  matrix, 345, 379–383
  mechanistic, 387–388
  nature of, 335–338
  organic, 387–388
  simple, 390
  size and, 386–387
  in strategy implementation, 217
  tall, 349
  technology and, 353, 383–386
Organizational assessment, strategy formulation and, 200–201
Organizational culture, 78, 103–107
  changing, 106–107, 247–248, 252–253
  manifestations of, 104–105
  nature of, 103–104
Organizational culture change, 252
Organizational development (OD), 249–253

Organizational life cycles, 228–234
Organizational problems, 268–269
Organizational requirements, human resources and, 408
Organizational social responsibility, 115
Organizational social responsiveness, 126–131
Organizational termination, 228, 233–234
Organizing, 7–8, 332–441
Organizing drive, 430
Orientation training, 420
Orienter role, 560
Ossification, 797
Output control, 608
Outputs, 64
  in information processing, 701
Overconfidence, decision making and, 276–277
Overcontrol, 620
Overtime, planning strategy and, 674

Panic, decision making and, 273
Paralanguage, 520
Partial-factor productivity, 663
Participation:
  and change, 241
  in situational leadership theory, 496–497
Participative leader behavior, 503
Path-goal theory, 502–506
Pay, skill-based, 428
Pay structure, designing a, 425–427
Pay survey, 426–427
Payoff, 316
Payoff tables, 316–317
Perception in communication, 527–528
Perceptual defense in communication, 529
Performance:
  dimensions of, 20–21
  measuring, control and, 602–603
  poor financial, ethics and, 142
  pressure for high, ethics and, 141
  and quality control, 647
Performance appraisal, 421–424
  interview, 423–424
Performance-outcome expectancy, 457, 458, 460–461, 463
Performance rating methods, 421–422
  errors in, 423
Performance tests, 417
Performing stage of groups, 569
Personal analogies, 288
Personal power, 454
Personality:
  entrepreneurship and, 777–778
  tests of, 417
PERT, 306–308
Philanthropy, corporate, 124
Physiological needs, 448
Plan(s), 157
  levels of, 172–173
  operational, 173
  recurring use and, 173–175
  single-use, 174
  standing, 174–175
  strategic, 172
  tactical, 173
Planned change, 235
Planning, 7, 153–186
  aids in, 293–327
  components of, 156–157
  contingency, 179
  goals linked to, 172–179
  manufacturing resource (MRP II), 679
  materials requirement (MRP), 676–679
  overall process of, 156–158

Planning (Cont.):
  potential obstacles to, 178–179
  project, 305–306
  replacement, 409
  succession, 409
Planning mode, 195
Planning staff, 178
Plant Closing Act of 1988, 116
Plant closings, 119
Point factor method, 425
Policy, 174
Political activity by organizations, 101
Political risk, 745
Polycentric orientation, 741
Polygraphs, 433
Pooled interdependence, 386
Population ecology model, 91–92
Population trends, labor supply and, 411
Porter's competitive strategies, 211–215
Porter's five competitive forces model, 196–200
Portfolio strategy approaches, 205–211
Position power in contingency theory, 491
Positive reinforcement, 465
Positive synergy, 563
Postaction (output) control, 608
Power:
  effective use of, 481
  institutional, 454
  of leaders, 481
  need for (nPow), 454
  position, 491
Power distance, 746
  and leadership styles, 764
Preclassical theories of management, 42–45
Preemptive ad, 121
Primacy, 564–565
Privacy rights in employment, 432–433
Pro forma (projected) balance sheet, 644
Probability, 317
Probability cluster chain, 540
Problem child, 206
Problems:
  in decision making, 262
  organizational, 268–269
  stages of, 269
Procedure, 174
Process consultation, 252
Process layout, 683–684
Process technology, 666, 687–689
  computer-integrated manufacturing, 687–689
  services applications, 689
Process theories, 456–464
Processing:
  batch, 701
  distributed, 722
  in information processing, 701
  on-line, 701
Product development, 201
Product divisions, 374
Product layout, 684–685
Product managers, 361
Product/market evolution matrix, 210–211
Production, functional structure and, 370
Production-centered leadership, 486
Production-operations management, 663
Productivity, 663
  improving, 690–691
  and operations management, 663–664
  partial-factor, 663
  total-factor, 663
Professional bureaucracy, 390
Professional jargon, 530
Profit budget, 643
Profit center, 640

Profitability ratios, 634
Program, 174
Program Evaluation and Review Technique (PERT), 306–308
Programmed decisions, 263
Project, 174, 305–306
Project group, 554
Project managers, 29
Projection in communication, 529
Prospect theory in decision making, 275
Prototyping, 719–720
Proxemics, 520
Public affairs department, 130
Public Health Service, 410
Public relations, 99
Punishment, 466
Purchasing, 679–680

Qualitative forecasting, 301–303
Qualitative goals, 165
Quality, 646
    competing on, 648
    perceived, 648
    strategic implications of, 647–648
Quality circle (QC), 651–652
Quality control, 646–652
    total (TQC), 648–650
Quantitative forecasting, 297–301
Quantitative goals, 165
Quantitative management viewpoint, 61–63
Quantum change, 246–247
Question mark, 206
Questionable payments, 765–766
Queuing (waiting-line) models, 311–312

Ratio analysis, 632–635
Rational model of decision making, 265
Rationalization, 754
Rationing, 98
Ratios:
    asset management (activity), 633–634
    current, 632–633
    debt, 634
    debt management (leverage), 634
    liquidity, 632–633
    profitability, 634–635
Raw materials inventory, 653
Reactive change, 234
Realistic job preview, 413
Receiver in communication, 524
Recency error, 423
Reciprocal interdependence, 386
Recognition seeker role, 561
Recruiting, 99
Recruitment, 412–413
    external/internal, 412–413
    in international business, 762
    selection methods, 413–414
Reference checks, 418
Reference power, 481, 482
Refreezing, 240
Regression models, 299
Rehabilitation Act of 1973, 410
Reinforcement:
    schedules of, 467–468
    types of, 464–466
Reinforcement theory, 464–469
Relatedness needs, 449
Relational skills, 763
Relationship power, 496
Reliability, quality control and, 647
Reorder point (ROP), 654
Replacement chart, 409
Replacement planning, 409
Representativeness, 276
Reproduction stage of modeling, 470

Required activities, 556
Required interactions, 556
Required sentiments, 556
Research and development, 371
Reservations, innovation and, 396–397
Resource allocator role, 13, 14
Resource dependence, 604
Resource dependence model, 92–93
Resource maturity stage of small business, 797
Resources:
    managing information system, 721–723
    slack, 359
    for small business, 790–791
Responsibility, 353
Responsibility centers, 639–641
Restraining forces, 243
Restructuring, 350
Retention stage of modeling, 470
Retrenchment strategies, 204
Return on assets, 634
Return on equity (ROE), 634–635
Return on investment (ROI), 634
Revenue budget, 643
Revenue center, 639
Revenues, 631
Revitalization, 231
Reward power, 481, 482
Reward systems in strategy implementation, 217
Rewards in expectancy theory, 457–458
Risk, 264
Rite, 104
Rivalry, competition and, 196
Robert's Rules of Order, 44–45
Robinson-Patman Law, 147
Roles:
    definition of, 560
    entrepreneurial, 13, 14, 26–29, 774
    group maintenance, 560
    group task, 560
    intrapreneurial, 243
    liaison, 13, 359–360
    of managers, 11–14, 25–26
    self-oriented, 560–561
    work group, 559–561
Romance of leadership, 508–509
Routing (distribution) models, 313
Rule, 175

SABRE system, 713
Safety needs, 449
Safety stock, 654
Sales budget, 643
Sales-force composite, 304
Sample tests, 417
Sampling, acceptance, 652
Satisfaction-progression principle, 450
Satisficing model of decision making, 265–266
Satisfiers, 452
Scalar principle, 338
Scanning stage of problems, 269
Scenarios, 303
Schedule, master production (MPS), 675–676
Schedules of reinforcement, 467–468
Scheduling, as planning strategy, 675–676
Science research, 61
Scientific management, 45–49, 62
Screening (yes-no) control, 608
Seasonal pattern, 297
Selection, 413–414
    of international personnel, 762–763
Selection interview, 414
Selective ad, 121

Self-actualization needs, 449
Self-control, 471
Self-efficacy, 469
Self-interest, resistance to change and, 239
Self-managing team, 573
Self-oriented roles, 560–561
Self-serving bias, 423, 529
Selling in situational leadership theory, 496
Semantic blocks, 529–530
Semantic net, 529
Semantics, 529–530
Sender in communication, 523
Sentiments:
    emergent, 557
    given, 556
    required, 556
Sequential interdependence, 386
Service organizations, 664–666
Serviceability, quality control and, 647–648
Severity error, 423
Shaping, 465
Shareholders, social responsibility and, 118
Shareholders' equity, 630
Sherman Antitrust Law, 147
Simple structure, 390
Simulation models, 313–314
Simulation training methods, 419
Single-server queues, 312
Single-strand chain grapevine, 540
Single-use plans, 174
Situational leadership theory, 496–498
Size, organization design and, 386–387
Skill-based pay, 428
Skill variety, 341
Skills:
    communication, 532–535
    management, 18, 24–25
Skills inventory, 409
Slack, 308
Slack resources, 358–359
Small-batch production, 384
Small business, 770–802
    bankruptcies and failures, 797–798
    financing, 790–791
    growth stages, 792–797
    human resources for, 791
    managing a, 793–799
    operating a, 787–793
    selecting site for, 792–793
    (See also Entrepreneurship)
Small Business Administration, 788, 790
Smoothing, 97
Social audit, 127
Social forecasting, 126
Social information-processing approach, 343
Social learning theory, 469–473
Social loafing, 563
Social response mechanisms, internal, 129–130
Social responsibility:
    international, 764–765
    organizational, 112–126
Social responsiveness:
    corporate, 126
    organizational, 126–131
Social scanning, 128
Socialist economy, 82
Society, social responsibility and, 123
Sociocultural element, 84
Software, 702
Soldiering, 45
Span of management (control), 348–350
Spokesperson role, 13
Sponsor, 27, 394
Spreadsheets, 702
Stability strategy, 204

Staff position, 354–357
Staffing, 411–418
Standard cost centers, 639
Standard operating procedures (SOPs), 174
Standard setter, 560
Standards, control and, 601–604
Standing committee, 553
Standing plans, 174–175
Star, 206
Star network, 535
Start-up, 782
Statement:
    financial, 630–632
    income, 631–632
Station Manpower Planning System
    (SMPS), 295
Statistical process control, 652
Statistical proof ad, 121
Stereotyping, 528
Stockout cost, 654
Stockouts, 312
Storming stage of groups, 568
Story, 104
Strategic business unit, 193
Strategic control, 598
Strategic control points, 604
Strategic goals, 161–162
Strategic management, 187–222
    concept of, 190–194
    importance of, 191–192
    modes of, 194–195
    process of, 190
Strategic plans, 172
    carrying out, 216–217
Strategy(ies), 190
    business-level, 193, 211–215
    career, developing and implementing, 809
    corporate-level, 192–193, 201–211
    cost leadership, 211–213
    defensive, 204–205
    differentiation, 213
    focus, 213
    functional-level, 193, 215–216
    grand (master), 201
    growth, 201
    implementation of, 216–218
    for informations systems, 714–715
    international issues, 750–756
    levels of, 192–194
    multinational corporation, 754–756
    and organization structure, 391–393
    portfolio approaches, 205–211
    retrenchment, 204
    stability, 204
Strategy formulation, 190, 196–201
Strategy implementation, 190
Structural configurations (Minzberg), 389–
    391
Structure:
    divisional, 345, 373–377
    flat, 349
    functional, 345, 370–373
    hybrid, 345, 377–379
    matching strategy and, 391–393
    matrix, 345, 379–383
    Minzberg configurations, 389–391
    simple, 390
    tall, 349
Subcontracting, 675
Subordinate characteristics in path-goal
    theory, 503
Substitutes, 509
    for leadership, 509–510
    threat of product, 199
Success stage of small business, 795
Succession planning, 409

Suggestive ad, 121
Sunk costs, 278
Superordinate goals, 580
Supervisors, first-line, 22
Suppliers, 90
    bargaining power of, 198–199
    as target of information systems, 714
Support, change and, 241
Supportive leader behavior, 503
Survival stage of small business, 794–795
SWOT analysis, 196, 197
Symbol, 104
Symbolic analogies, 288
Symbolic processes, 469
Synectics, 288
Synergy, 66, 200
    group, 575–576
    negative, 563
    positive, 563
System, 63
Systems development life cycle, 717–719
Systems theory, 63–67

Tactical control, 598
Tactical goals, 162
Tactical plans, 173
Taft-Hartley Act of 1947, 429
Takeoff stage of small business, 795
Takeover, 234
Tall structure, 349
Tariff, 745
Task behavior, 496
Task environment, 87–91
Task forces, 554, 571
    and horizontal coordination, 360–361
    as social response mechanism, 129–130
Task group, 553
Task identity, 341
Task motivation, creativity and, 284
Task significance, 341
Task structure in contingency theory, 491
Team building, 252
Teams, 553, 571
    employee involvement, 652
    entrepreneurial, 571, 573
    and horizontal coordination, 360–361
    new venture, 396
    self-managing, 573
    venture, 792
Technical skills, 18
    training, 420
Technological element, 79–80
Technological forecasting, 301–303
Technological interdependence, 386
Technological transfer, 747–748
Technology, 383–386
    and change, 247
    complexity of, 384
    group, 688
    and organization structure, 353, 383–386
    in strategy implementation, 216–217
Technostructural activities, 252
Telecommuting, 724–725
Telling in situational leadership theory, 496
Thematic Apperception Test (TAT), 453
Theory X and Theory Y, 59–60
Theory Z, 68
Thinking, 282
Third-party intervention, 252
Three Mile Island nuclear power plant, 602
Tiananmen Square, 739
Time-and-motion study, 46
Time-series analysis, 636
Time-series methods, 297–298
Top-down budgeting, 644
Top managers, 23

Total-factor productivity, 663
Total quality control (TQC), 648–650
Toxic Substances Control Act of 1976, 116
Tracking signal, 300
Trade associations, 100–101
Training and development, 419–420
Training design and implementation phase,
    419
Training process, phases of, 419
Training programs, types of, 419–420
Traits, 483
Transaction-processing systems (TPS), 706–
    707
Transactional leaders, 506
Transfer process, innovation and, 397
Transformation processes, 64
Transformational leadership, 506–508
Trend, 297
Turnaround, 205
Two-factor theory, 452–453, 455
Two-way communication, 526

Uncertain environments, 94
Uncertainty, 264
    control and, 596
Uncertainty avoidance, 746
Undercontrol, 620
Unfreezing, 240
Unions, 429, 431
Unit production, 384
Unity of command, 337
Upward communication, 538
User, 720

Valence in expectancy theory, 458
Validity, 413–414
Vanguard companies, 125–126
Variable costs, 319, 643
Variable-interval schedule of reinforcement,
    468
Variable-ratio schedule of reinforcement,
    468
Venture team, 792
Verbal communication, 519–520
Verbal consistency, 531–532
Vertical communication, 536–539, 541
Vertical coordination, methods of, 345–357
Vertical integration, 201
Vicarious learning, 469–470
Video display terminal (VDT), 724
Video teleconferencing, 544
Vroom-Yetton model, 498

Wage-and-salary survey, 426–427
Wagner Act of 1935, 429
Waiting-line models, 311–312
War Labor Board, 428
Wheel network, 535
Whistle-blower, 144
White-collar crime, 132
Wholly owned subsidiary, 752
Wide area networks, 723
Willingness, 496
Word processing, 702, 708
Work agendas, 15–17
Work behavior, goals and, 168–169
Work-force changes, human resources and,
    408
Work-force relations, 429–433
Work groups:
    attraction to, 559
    autonomous, 573
    cohesiveness of, 565–567
    command (functional), 553
    composition of, 558–559
    conflict management, 578–581

Work groups (Cont.):
development of, 567–569
formal, 552–554
foundations of, 552–558
informal, 554–556
inputs, 558–563
member characteristics, 559
member roles, 559–561
model of, 558
norms of, 564
operation of, 557–558
processes of, 563–569
size of, 561–563
special applications, 569–574
task, 553

Work groups (Cont.):
types of, 552–556
[*See also* Group(s)]
Work-in-process inventory, 653
Work sample tests, 417
Work schedules, alternative, 343–344
Work specialization, 43, 338
Workstations, 704
Workweek, compressed, 344
Worldwide functional divisions structure,
756–757
Worldwide integration strategy, 754

Worldwide product divisions structure, 757–
758

XCON, 712

Y network, 535
Yes-no control, 608

Zero-base budgeting (ZBB), 645–646
Zero defects, 649
Zoning, 793

Abbott Laboratories, 579
ABC Publishing, 198
ABC Radio Network, 14
Acacia Mutual Life Insurance Company, 336, 337
Acmat Corporation, 101
AEG, 438, 439
Aetna Life & Casualty Company, 322, 483
Afterthoughts, 92
A. H. Robins Company, 83, 233
Aid Association for Lutherans (AAL), 690
Albany International, 429
Albertson's, Inc., 217
Alcoa, 577
Alexander Grant & Company, 140
Allen-Bradley, 688
Allied, 234
Allied Chemical Corporation, 277
Allied-Signal, 234
Allied Stores Corporation, 205
Allie's (restaurant chain), 150
Allstate Insurance Company, 328, 329, 717
A. L. Williams Insurance, 544
Amalgamated Clothing and Textile Workers Union, 243
American Airlines, 294, 311, 713, 725
American Business Corporation (ABC), 740
American Can Company, 269, 270, 271
American Cyanamid, 750
American Express, 125, 142, 271, 534, 538, 602, 624, 627, 669, 706
American Home Products Corporation, 114, 233
American Hospital Supply, 542
American Institute of Architecture, 587
American International Group, 322
American Management Association, 142, 535
American Medical International, Inc., 528
American Microsystems, 156
American Motors Corporation, 752
American Natural Beverage Corporation, 803–806
American Photo Group, 156, 178
American President Company (APC), 715
American President Lines, 715
American Society of Mechanical Engineers, 44
American Steel & Wire, 564
Ames Department Stores, Inc., 228
AMF, Inc., 101
Amoco Corporation, 117
Ampex Corporation, 27, 28, 226
Amstrad, 784
Anderson Company, 96
Anheuser-Busch Company, 114, 298, 805
Apple Computer, Inc., 24, 230, 320, 401, 479–480, 506, 508, 653
Apple Europe, 401

Apple Pacific, 401
ARCO Transportation Company, 130
Aquitaine, 234
Armco, 436
Arthur Andersen & Company, 132
Arthur D. Little, 288
Asahi Glass Company, 32
Ashland Oil, Inc., 526–527
Ashton-Tate Corporation, 719
Associated Merchandising Corporation (AMC), 781
Atlantic Gulf & West Indies Steam Ship Lines, 92, 93
Atlantic Richfield, 125, 127
AT&T (American Telephone & Telegraph), 56, 92, 111, 162, 248, 397, 406, 418, 455, 484, 639, 648, 650, 709, 723, 725, 726, 802
Automobile Association of America, 90
Avon Products, Inc., 62, 117

Baker, 213
Baldwin Locomotive, 92, 93
Ballard Medical Products, Inc., 542
BankAmerica Corporation, 256–257
Bank of America, 256, 717
Baroni, 771, 772
Barren, Barton, Durstine & Osborn, 287
Baxer Travenol Laboratories, Inc., 142
Baxters of Speyside, 213–215
BDM International, 795
Bear, Stearns & Company, 547–548
Beech Nut Nutrition Corporation, 141
Beefsteak Charlie's, 266
Bell Atlantic Corporation, 374
Bell Labs, 397, 520
Benetton Group, 752, 753, 754
Benetton USA, 682, 753
Ben Franklin stores, 185
Ben & Jerry's Foundation, Inc., 585
Ben & Jerry's Homemade, Inc., 127, 585–586
Bethlehem Steel, 46, 47, 49, 436, 700
Bharat Heavy Electrics, Ltd., 302–303
Bic Corporation, 121
Bickford's (restaurant chain), 150
BIF Korea, 589
Big Boy, 592
Birmingham Steel Corporation, 344
Black and Decker, 179
Blue Cross of Washington and Alaska, 651
Boeing, 179, 742
Bombay Palace Restaurants, Inc., 266
Bonneville Pacific Corporation, 484
Borg-Warner Corporation, 206, 513
Boston Consulting Group, 206–208
Briggs & Stratton, 600
British Airways, 535
British Petroleum, 740

Brooks Brothers, 597, 774
Brunswick Corporation, 240, 300
Burger King, 195, 592, 665, 666
Burroughs Corporation, 233, 234
Business Radio Network, 810

Cadillac Company, 39
California Cosmetics, 204
Calvin Klein Cosmetics, 736, 737
Campbell Soup Company, 84–85, 215, 236, 237, 238, 320
Campeau Corporation, 205, 597
Canadian National Railway, 314–315
CARE, Inc. (Cooperative for American Relief Everywhere), 403–404, 405, 412, 422, 425
Carnation, 215
Carnegie Hall, 10, 18, 19–20
Carteret Savings and Loan Association, 159
Castite, 552
Catalyst Energy, 484
Caterpillar, 694–695, 744
Celestial Seasonings, 346–348
Centennial One, 776
Center for Creative Leadership, 25, 354
Cessna, 686
Chain Saw Manufacturers Association, 136
Champion Spark Plug Company, 95, 96, 97
Chantiers Bénéteau, 264
Chase Econometric Association, 300
Chem-Dry, 788
Chemed Corporation, 207
Chesebrough-Pond's, Inc., 234, 737
Chevron, 234
Chili's, Inc., 772
Chrysler Corporation, 64, 242, 320, 430, 481, 508, 740, 745, 747, 752
Ciba-Geigy, 750
Cigna, 234, 322
Citgo Petroleum Corporation, 326, 327
Citicorp, 131, 239, 359, 483, 755
Citicorp Investment Management, Inc., 376
Citizens Bank of Maryland, 413
Clean Sites, Inc., 128
Cleveland Track Materials, 565
Clorox Company, 750
Coca-Cola Company, 199, 259–261, 262, 270, 279, 297, 347, 534, 751, 752, 765, 795, 803
Coca-Cola Enterprises, Inc., 259
Coldwell Banker Real Estate Group, 328, 330, 331
Coleman, 213
Colgate-Palmolive, 215
Columbia Pictures, 259
Commentary-Fourchambault Company, 51
Compaq Computer Corporation, 550–551, 557, 571, 773
Con Edison, 724

Connecticut General, 234
Conoco, 234
Control Data, 125, 221, 685
Convex Computer, 222
Convitato Italiano, 780
Cooper Industries, 96, 112
Coopers & Lybrand, 100
Corning, Inc., 4–6, 9, 29, 32, 100, 104, 241, 301, 638, 648, 688, 752
Council on Economic Priorities, 117
Courtyard (hotels), 150
Coustic-Glo, 788
Coverall, 788
Crain Communications, Inc., 487–488
Cray Computer Corporation, 222
Cray Research, Inc., 221–222, 648
Crouse-Hinds, 122
Crown Cork and Seal, 213
Crown Zellerbach, 159
Cuisinarts, Inc., 785
Cummings Engine, 137, 613
Current, Inc., 287
Cypress Semiconductor Corporation, 154–156, 161, 162, 163, 164, 172, 173, 176, 181

Daewoo, 495
Daimler-Benz AG, 208, 438–441, 740
Dairy Queen, 592
D'Allaird's, 597
Dana Corporation, 352, 539
Data General Corporation, 550
Data Resources, 98
Dayton Hudson Corporation, 52, 101, 124, 125, 659, 779
Dean Witter Financial Services, 328, 330, 331
Delacre, 238
Delta Airlines, 294
Detroit Edison, 39
Detroit Illuminating Company, 39
Deutsche Aerospace, 438, 441
Deutsche Bank, 440
DeVilbiss, 96
Diamandis Communications, 198
Diamond Shamrock, 6, 7, 8, 9
Digital Equipment Corporation, 137, 230, 232, 248, 249, 334, 335, 340, 353, 411, 540, 543, 574, 712
Dillard's, 300, 301
Discovery Channel, 725
DocuCon, 772
Domino's Pizza, Inc., 373, 471–472, 473
Dornier, 438
Dot Discount Drug stores, 185
Dow Chemical USA, 650
Dow-Corning, 380, 759
Dun & Bradstreet, 636
Dunkin' Donuts, 741
Du Pont, 27, 92, 159, 234, 277, 306, 369, 428, 433, 730, 732, 740
Duraclean, 788

Eagle Manufacturing Company, 630–635, 636
East Lansing State Bank, 689
Eastman Kodak, 92, 110, 111, 156, 370, 727, 765
Echlin, 213, 681
Econo Lodge, 788
Economy Color Card Company, 531
EDS, 747
E. F. Hutton, 141, 454, 624
E. F. Hutton Insurance Group, Inc., 624
Electrolux, 659
Electronic Account Systems, Inc., 237

Electronic Data Services, 779
Electronic Data Systems, 233
Electro Rent Corporation, 750
Eli Lilly and Company, 159, 680
Elizabeth Arden, 780
Embassy Suites Hotels, 505–506
EMI, Ltd., 285–286, 450
Employers Reinsurance Company, 513
Enoch, 771
Equitable Life Assurance, 714
Ernst & Whinney, 725
E.S.M. Government Securities, Inc., 139, 140
ETA Systems, Inc., 221
Ethics Resource Center, 143
Eureka Corporation, 659
Exxon, 114, 740, 745
Eye Care Centers of America, Inc., 330

Fabergé, 737
Fanuc, 661–662, 664
Federal Express, 544, 556, 557, 615
Federated Department Stores, Inc., 205
Fiat, 687, 688, 740
Fidelity Bank, 174
Fidelity Investments, 406
Field's Software Group, 698
Film Recovery Systems, Inc., 120
Fireman's Fund Insurance Company, 322
First Chicago, 17
First Issue, 202
First National Bank of Chicago, 342–343
First Service Bank, 420–421
Florida Power & Light Company, 647
Flour-Daniel, 406
Food Lion, 626–627, 633–634, 639, 653
Foot Locker, 92
Ford Motor Company, 39–40, 64–66, 69, 73–74, 92, 117, 252, 320, 350, 366, 430–431, 461, 544, 571, 572, 578, 645, 652, 665, 681, 715, 740, 795, 812
Ford of Europe, Inc., 74
Fortnum & Mason, 214
Fuddruckers, 771, 779, 790
Fuji Photo, 370
Fujitsu, 162, 221, 752
Fuji Xerox, 110
Fuller Company, H. B., 122

GAF, 226
Gannett Company, Inc., 291–292, 422
Gap stores, 374
Gavilan Computer Corporation, 550
GE Fanuc Automation Corporation, 662
Gencorp Automotive, 279
Genentech, Inc., 444–445
General Dynamics, 686
General Electric Company, 55, 92, 114, 179, 205, 206, 207, 208, 209, 210, 225, 234, 288, 300, 461, 513, 514, 637, 638, 640, 647, 662, 740, 752
General Foods, 215, 234, 503, 765
General Mills, Inc., 117, 215, 382
General Motors Corporation, 22, 55, 64, 69, 74, 92, 96, 104, 135, 162, 230, 233, 234, 320, 361, 365–366, 369, 386, 425, 430, 431, 501, 518, 552, 571, 573, 577, 608, 609, 611–612, 620, 656, 662, 665, 674, 680, 687, 689, 715, 731, 740, 765
General Telephone Company, 689
Getty, 234
Gino (restaurant chain), 149
Gladieux Corporation, 150
Glass, Inc., 798
GMFanuc Robotics Corporation, 662, 674
Good Care, Inc., 307

Goodwill Industries, Inc., 115
Goodyear, 301
Gould, Inc., 267–269
Grand Metropolitan PLC, 195
Grant Thornton, 139, 140
Greater Philadelphia International Network, Inc., 86
Great Steak Escape, 790
GTEL, 689
Gulf Oil Company, 234, 277, 812

Hallmark Cards, Inc., 317, 429
Hampton Inn, 788
Hanson PLC, 641–642
Hardees Food Systems, 151, 788
Harley-Davidson, Inc., 101–102, 103, 650
Harrods, 214
Hartford Steam Boiler Inspection and Insurance Company, 322
Hartmarx Corporation, 252
Hasboro, Inc., 741
Hazleton Laboratories America, Inc., 553
Hechinger Company, 174
Heinz Company, H. J., 137, 212, 215
Heinz USA, 553
Henry Ford Company, 39
Herman Miller, Inc., 587–589, 648
Hertz Rent a Car, 651
Hewlett-Packard, 69, 200, 213, 236, 248, 396, 461, 650, 715
Hidroeléctrica Española, 710–711
Hillside Coffee, Inc., 297
Hitachi, 162, 221, 740
Hoechst Celanese, 732
Hoffman-La Roache, 750
Holiday Corporation, 505
Holiday Inn, 150
Holiday Rambler, 102
Home State Savings Bank, 140
Honda Motor Company, 102, 247, 351, 360, 406, 438, 572, 648, 664, 737, 754, 765, 769
Honeywell, 125, 542, 651
Hoover Company, 659
Host International, 149
Hot Shoppes, 148, 151
Howard Johnson, 149, 150
Hughes Aircraft Corporation, 162, 234, 366
Humana, Inc., 212
Hunt-Wesson, 320
Hyatt hotels, 151
Hypermart USA, 186
Hyundai, 494, 495

IBM Corporation, 92–93, 110, 111, 117, 137, 207, 213, 232, 247, 248, 249, 252, 301, 377, 378, 401, 531, 544, 550, 627, 650, 666–667, 676, 700, 726, 740, 765, 776, 779, 784, 802
ICL, 301
IKEA, 85–87, 98
Illinois Bell, 725
Illinois Health Care Associations, 182
Illinois Institute of Technology, 587
Imperial Chemical Industries (ICI), 763
INA, 234
Inland, 436
Intel Corporation, 52, 120, 463, 498
Intelstat, 114
Intermedics, Inc., 602
International Harvester, 428, 501
Interstate Van Lines, Inc., 542–543
IRI, 740
ITT, 802

Jack in the Box, 788
Jaguar PLC, 74
Jani-King, 788
J. Bildner & Sons, Inc., 346, 796–797
J. C. Penney, 163, 248, 544
J. D. Power & Associates, 672
Jeep, 664
John Deere, 125
John Hancock Mutual Life Insurance Company, 461
Johnson & Johnson, 113–114, 117, 143–144, 234, 235, 387, 429, 542, 772
Joyce Beverages, 313
Joyce International, 487, 488
J. P. Industries, Inc., 226
J. Sainsbury, 214
JVC (Victor Company of Japan, Ltd.), 27–28
JWT Group, Inc., 620

Kaiser Cement, 242
Katha Diddel Home Collection, 782
Kawasaki Heavy Industries, Ltd., 102, 655
Keebler, 238
Kellogg Company, 237
Kentucky Fried Chicken, 592, 786
Kerr-McGee Corporation, 200
Kia, 74
Kidder, Peabody & Company, 114, 513
Kings Super Markets, 597
K Mart, 92, 329, 331, 659
Kohlberg Kravis Roberts & Company, 32, 53, 208, 635
Komatsu, Ltd., 694, 744
Konveyer Industrial Amalgamation, 459
Kraft, Inc., 315, 347–348
Kronus, Inc., 164

Lake Financial Corporation, 652
Lands End, 703
Lane Bryant, 203
La Petite Boulangerie, 698
Laura Caspari, Ltd.—SHE, Inc., 779
Laurent-Perrier, 199
LeCreusot-Loire, 51
Lever Brothers, Ltd., 736, 737, 742
Levi Strauss, 125, 130, 131, 230, 596
Libby's, 215
Lifestyle Restaurants, Inc., 266
Limited, The, Inc., 203, 204, 329
Little Tikes Company, 8
Liz Claiborne, Inc., 76–78, 84, 87, 202, 675
L. L. Bean, 164
Lockheed Aircraft Corporation, 651, 761
Loctite Corporation, 769
London Brick, 641
Lotas Minard Patton McIver, Inc., 509
Lotus Development Corporation, 543, 609–610, 614
LTV, 436

Macaroni Grill, 772
Macy's, 338
Manor Care, 690
Manufacturers Hanover Trust, 543, 559
Manville Corporation, 83, 801
Mapcast (GE), 300
Marathon Oil, 234
Marks & Spencer, PLC, 596–598
Marks & Spencer Canada, 597
Marriott Corporation, 148–151
Marshall Field & Company, 601, 603
Martin Marietta, 813
Marty's Wine and Food Emporium, 227
Mary Kay Cosmetics, 104–105, 159

Matsushita Electric Industrial Company, Ltd. (MEIC), 27–28, 29, 170–171, 226, 281, 740
Max Factor & Company, 448
May Department Stores, 596
Mayo Clinic, 10
Maytag, 341, 647
Mazda Motor Corporation, 74, 351, 607, 608, 649, 754
McCulloch Corporation, 136
McDonald's Corporation, 84, 90, 100, 103, 330, 468, 592–594, 595, 602, 604, 605–606, 621, 653, 731, 747, 779, 786, 788, 810
McDonnell Douglas, 742
McGraw-Hill, 159
MCI Communications Corporation, 32, 723
McKesson Corporation, 542, 716
McKinsey & Company, 100, 208, 740
McLouth Steel Products Corporation, 482
Merck & Company, 117, 224, 225, 237, 807, 809
Meredith Corporation, 556
Merrill Lynch, 544
Messerschmitt-Boelkow-Blohm, 438
Metpath, 714–715
Michelin, Groupe, 201, 731, 737
Microsoft Corporation, 92–93
Midvale Steel, 45, 49
Miller Brewing, 298
Milliken & Company, 213, 708, 731–733
Millipore Corporation, 740
Miniscribe, 182
Minnetonka, Inc., 737
Minolta Corporation, 128–129
Mitsubishi Corporation, 441
Mitsubishi Heavy Industries, Ltd., 695
Mobil, 234, 740
Moët & Chandon, 199
Monsanto Company, 128, 360–361, 650, 652
Moog, Inc., 120
Morgan Guaranty, 340
Morton Thiokol, 280
Motorola Corporation, 125, 126, 159, 162, 261, 668–669, 680, 725
Mrs. Fields Bakeries, 698
Mrs. Fields Cookies, 697–699, 701, 703, 706, 723
MTU, 438
Muscular Dystrophy Association, 102
Museum of Modern Art, New York, 587

Nabisco Brands, 635, 802
National Aeronautics and Space Administration (NASA), 280
National Cancer Institute, 237
National Coffee Service Association, 100–101
National Steel, 436
National Tire Dealers and Retreaders Association, 101
Natomas, 7
NBC, 640
NEC (Nippon Electric Company), 221, 281, 737
Nestlé, 136, 737, 740
New England Telephone, 415
New Jersey Bell Telephone Company, 52
News Corporation, Ltd., 198, 636
Newsweek, 531
New York State Electric & Gas Corporation, 124–125, 711
Nippon Mining, 268
Nissan Motor Corporation, 74, 120, 351, 430–431, 740, 754, 769
Nixdorf Computer Corp, 385

Nordstrom, Inc., 20, 21, 168, 182, 213, 346
Northern Telecom, 428
Northwest Airlines, 294
Northwestern Mutual Life Insurance Co., 120, 556
Novus Windshield Repair, 788
Nucor Corporation, 357, 436–437

Occidental Petroleum Corporation, 326
Odetics, 450
Office Club, 88
Office Depot, 88
Opinion Research Corporation, 143, 429
Original Copy Centers, Inc., 451–452

Pacific Bell, 25
Pacific Gas & Electric, 92
Pacific Southwest Airlines, 724
Pacific Southwest Cable, 272
Parisian, Inc., 21
Parker Pen, Ltd., 754–755
Parky the Shipper, 788
Patagonia, Inc., 567
Paul Revere Insurance, 203
Paychex, 237
Pay 'n Save, 263
Peat Marwick Mitchell & Company, 717
Pepperidge Farm, 237–239
PepsiCo, 479, 698, 747
Pepsi-Cola, 260, 347, 479, 803
Pernod Ricard, 751
Pernovo AB, 398
Perstorp AB, 397–398
Petroleos de Venezuela, 327
PGA Tour, Inc., 201–202
Philip Morris, 234
Philips, N. V., 248–249, 740
Phillips Petroleum Corporation, 712
Phillips 66 Company, 712
Pillsbury, 195
Pinstripes Petites, 330
Pioneer/Eclipse Corporation, 357
Pitney Bowes, 812
Pitney Bowes's Data Documents, Inc., 300
Plaza Bank, 36
Polaroid Corporation, 117, 120
Polycom Hunstman, Inc., 656
Pommery et Greno, 199
Ponderosa Steakhouses, 788
Precision Castparts Corporation, 264
Primerica Corporation, 271
Procter & Gamble Company, 92, 117, 120, 238, 288, 381–382, 534, 535, 562, 563, 741
Public Service and Gas Company, 159
Purex, 179

Quaker Oats, 813
Quality Inns Intl., 788

Ragu Foods, 320, 737
Ralph Lauren, 213
Ralston Purina, 802
Ramada Inn, 150
Ranieri Wilson & Co., 556
Rayovac Corporation, 191–192, 723
Raytheon, 358
RCA Corporation, 226, 234, 513
R. C. Bigelow, Inc., 348
Reader's Digest, 120
Regina Company, 659
Remington-Rand, 306
Renault, 740
Residence Inns, 150
Reynolds Tobacco USA, 640
Rich's Shoe Store, 233

R. J. Reynolds, 31, 635, 745
RJR Nabisco, 31, 208, 215, 627, 629, 635, 639, 640
Roadway Package Systems, 215
Robert Morris Associates, 636
Robins Company, A. H., 114
Roche Holding, Ltd., 444
Rockefeller Foundation, 52
Rockwell International, 688
Roto-Rooter, Inc., 207
Round Table Pizza, 788
Royal Dutch/Shell, 234, 277, 740
Roy Rogers, 149, 150, 151, 788
R. R. Donnelly & Sons, 554
R. Stevens Corporation, 178
Rubbermaid, Inc., 6, 7, 8, 9, 165
R. W. Sears Watch Company, 328

Saab, 577
Saga Corp., 150
Samsung, 740
Sam's Wholesale Clubs, 185
San Diego Gas & Electric, 263
Sandoz, 750
Santa Fe, 234
Santa Fe Southern Pacific, 234
Sara Lee Corporation, 117, 159
Saturn Corporation, 425
Sbarro, Inc., 461
Scandinavian Airlines System (SAS), 521, 522–523, 532
Scandinavian Design, Inc., 538
Scarbrough's Department Store, 338
Schloeman-Siemag A.G., 436
Scientific Computer Systems, 564
SCM, 642
Sea Containers Ltd., 601
Seagram Beverage Company, 806
Sears, Roebuck and Company, 92, 185, 252, 328–331, 369, 587, 706
Sears Canada, 330
Sears Financial Network, 328, 330
Sears Merchandise Group, 330
Security Pacific National Bank, 36
Seeq Technology, 62
Semco S/A, 576, 577–578
Seminole Manufacturing Company, 708
Senior Employment Resources, 524
ServiceMaster, 670
Service System Corp., 150
Shaw Industries, 361
Shawmut Bank, 90
Shearson Lehman Brothers, 454, 624
Shearson Lehman Hutton Holdings, Inc., 624
Shell, 234
Sheraton Corporation, 195
Shih's Flowers, Inc., 780
Shoney's, Inc., 194
Shuckers A Real Seafood Place, 771
Siemens AG, 249, 740, 752
Sigmor Corporation, 7
Signal, 234
Sleep Inn, 690
Smith Corona, 641, 642
SmithKline Beckman, 394
Smuckers, 347
Solar Press, Inc., 579
Sony Corporation, 28, 259, 315, 618, 648, 737
Southern California Edison, 92
Southern Pacific, 234

Southland Corporation, 326–327
Southwestern Bell, 248
Spectrum Control, Inc., 650–651
Sperry Corporation, 233, 234
Springfield Remanufacturing Corporation, 166, 500–501
Springs Industries, 732
Standard Oil, 369
Standard Oil California, 234
Staples, 88
Steelcase, 589
Steuben Glass, 4–5
Steve's Homemade, 585
Stew Leonard's, 516–518, 538, 542
Stix, 771
STK, 724
Stork News, 788
Sun Microsystems, 780
Sunshine Polishing Company, 788
Supercomputer Systems, Inc., 221
Super 8 Motels, 788
Superior Oil, 234
Super Value, 689
Swarkovski, 213
Synectics, Inc., 288

Tandem Computers, 544
Tennant Company, 580
Tenneco, 179
Tesco Stores, 214
Texaco, 234, 740
Texas Air, 294, 710
Texasgulf, 234
Texas Instruments, 179, 382, 550, 645, 755–756
Texas Tortilla Bakery Incorporated, 772
Textron, Inc., 203
Textronix, 581, 679
Third Class Mail Association, 101
Thomas J. Lipton, Inc., 347, 348
Thompson S.A., 207, 513
Thorneburg Hosiery, 741
3M Corporation, 104, 176–178, 236, 244, 245, 359, 368–369, 405, 406, 428, 473, 542, 618
Tile World, 792
Time-Warner, Inc., 120
Toro Company, 298
Toshiba Corporation, 144, 162
Toyota Motor Corporation, 350–351, 438, 572, 573, 580, 647, 655, 737, 740
Toys 'R' Us, 100
Trans Union Corporation, 83
Travelers Corporation, 41, 321, 322
TRW, 301
Tungsram Co., 747
Twin Panda, Inc., 782
Tyco Toys, 595

Unie, 736
Unilever, 234, 736–738, 740, 742
Unilever NV, 736
Unilever Personal Products Group, USA, 737
Unilever PLC, 736
Union Carbide, 226, 385
Union National Bank, Little Rock, Arkansas, 468
Uniroyal Goodrich Tire Company, 201
Unisys, 233, 234
United Airlines, 294, 295–296, 703, 713
United Auto Workers, 135, 430

United Coastal Insurance, 101
United Parcel Service (UPS), 215, 614–615
United Technologies, 122, 745
United Way, 10, 556
USA Today, 13, 14, 62, 291–292
USPA & IRA Company, 726
U.S. Shoe, 341
U.S. Sprint, 174, 723
U.S. Steel, 234
USX, 234, 436, 564

Valspar Corporation, 115
Van den Bergh Foods, 737
Van Dresser Corporation, 647
Veuve Clicquot, 199
Victoria's Secret, 203
Video Data Services, 788
Visible Changes, 477
Volkswagen, 737, 740
Volvo, A. B., 573, 737

Wags (restaurant chain), 150
Waitrose Supermarkets, 214
Waldenbooks, 599
Walker Art Center, 587
Walker's, 597
Wal-Mart Stores, Inc., 92, 185–186, 331, 456, 508, 603, 682, 747
Walt Disney Company, 188–190, 191, 192, 194, 195, 530, 531
Walt Disney Productions, 188–190
Wang Laboratories, 231–233, 508
Warnaco, Inc., 448
Warner-Lambert, 121
Warren Featherborne Company, 78
Waterford Glass Group PLC, 351
Wells Fargo Bank, 179, 689
Wells Fargo & Company, 257
Western Auto Supply Company, 330
Western Electric Company, 55, 56, 205, 446
Western Industrial Contractors, Inc. (WIC), 801–802
Westinghouse Electric Corporation, 92, 179, 205, 211, 248, 752, 776
Westin Hotel Company, 195, 723
Weyerhaeuser, 125
Wharton School, 300
Whirlpool Corporation, 225, 754
Winchester Hospital, 390
Winn Dixie, 312
Winnebago Industries, Inc., 685–686
Wistom, 791
W. L. Gore & Associates, 387, 559
Woolworth, F. W., 92, 93, 405, 682
Worlds of Wonder, 595, 653
Worthington Industries, Inc., 387
WPP Group, PLC, 620
W. R. Grace, 226, 311
W. W. Granger, Inc., 159, 160

Xerox Corporation, 22, 79, 80, 87, 90, 110–111, 213, 243, 356, 544, 637, 638, 645, 648, 745, 812

Yale and Towne Manufacturing Company, 44
Yamaha Motor, 247

Zayre Corporation, 228
Zebco, 240

AEG, 438, 439
American Business Conference (ABC), 740
American Cyanamid, 750
American Express, 142, 271
American Motors Corporation, 752
American Natural Beverage, 806
Amstrad, 784–785
Apple Europe, 401
Apple Pacific, 401
Asahi Glass Company, 32
Associated Merchandising Corporation
    (AMC), 781

Baxters of Speyside, 213–215
Benetton Group, 682, 752, 753
Bharat Heavy Electricals, Ltd. (BHEL), 302
BIF Korea, 589
Boeing, 742
British Airways, 535, 740
British Petroleum, 740

Campbell Soup Company, 84–85, 215
Campeau Corporation, 205, 597
Canadian National Railway (CN), 314–315
CARE, Inc., 403
Carnation, 215
Caterpillar, 694, 695
Chantiers Bénéteau, 264
Chrysler Corporation, 740, 745, 752
Ciba-Geigy, 750
Citgo Petroleum Corporation, 327
Citicorp, 239, 359, 755
Clorox Company, 750
Coca-Cola Company, 260, 751, 752, 754, 765
Colgate-Palmolive, 215
Commentary-Fourchambault Company, 51
Corning, Inc., 4, 5, 32, 752
Cray Research, Inc., 221
Cummings Engine, 137

Daewoo, 495
Daimler-Benz AG, 208, 438–441, 740
Delacre, 238
Deutsche Aerospace, 438, 441
Deutsche Bank, 440
Diamond Shamrock, 8
Digital Equipment Corporation, 249
Dornier, 438
Dow-Corning, 759
Du Pont, 740

Eastman Kodak, 727, 765
Electro Rent Corporation, 750
EMI, Ltd., 285–286, 450
Exxon, 740

Fabergé, 737
Fanuc, 661–662, 664
Fiat, 687, 688, 737, 740
Ford Motor Company, 73, 740
Ford of Europe, Inc., 74
Fortnum & Mason, 214
Fuji Photo, 370
Fujitsu, 162, 221, 752
Fuji Xerox, 110

GE Fanuc Automation Corporation, 662
General Electric Company, 207, 637, 740,
    747, 752
General Foods, 215
General Mills, 215
General Motors Corporation, 740, 765
GMFanuc Robotics Corporation, 662, 674
Grand Metropolitan PLC, 195

Hanson PLC, 641–642
Harley-Davidson, Inc., 101
Harrods, 214
Hasbro, Inc., 741
Heinz, 215
Hidroeléctrica Española, 710–711
Hitachi, 162, 221, 740
Hoffman-La Roache, 750
Honda Motor Company, 102, 247, 351, 360,
    406, 438, 572, 648, 664, 737, 754, 765,
    769
Host International, 149
Hyundai, 494, 495

IBM (International Business Machines), 249,
    726, 740, 765, 784
ICL, 301
IKEA, 85–87, 98
Imperial Chemical Industries (ICI), 763
IRI, 740

J. Sainsbury, 214
Jaguar PLC, 74
JVC (Victor Company of Japan, Ltd.), 27–28

Katha Diddel Home Collection, 782
Kawasaki Heavy Industries, Ltd., 102, 655
Kia, 74
Komatsu, Ltd., 694, 744
Konveyer Industrial Amalgamation, 459

Laurent-Perrier, 199
LeCreusot-Loire, 51
Lever Brothers, Ltd., 736, 737, 742
Levi Strauss, 131
Libby's, 215

Lockheed Aircraft Corporation, 651, 761
Loctite Corporation, 769

Manville Corporation, 801
Marks & Spencer Canada, 597
Marks & Spencer PLC, 596, 598
Marriott Corporation, 148–151
Matsushita Electric Industrial Company,
    Ltd. (MEIC), 27–28, 29, 170–171, 226,
    281, 740
Mazda Motor Corporation, 74, 351, 607,
    608, 649, 754
McDonald's Corporation, 84, 593, 605, 606
McDonnell Douglas, 742
McKinsey & Company, 740
Messerschmitt-Boelkow-Blohm, 438
Michelin, Groupe, 201, 731, 737
Milliken & Company, 732
Millipore Corporation, 740
Minolta Corporation, 128–129
Mitsubishi Corporation, 441
Mitsubishi Heavy Industries, Ltd., 695
Mobil, 740
Moët & Chandon, 199
Motorola Corporation, 261, 669
MTU, 438

NEC (Nippon Electric Company), 221, 281,
    737
Nestlé, 136, 737, 740
News Corporation, Ltd., 636
Nippon Mining, 268
Nissan Motor Corporation, 74, 120, 351,
    430–431, 740, 754, 769
Nixdorf Computer Corporation, 385

Parker Pen, Ltd., 754–755
Pernod Ricard, 751
Pernovo AB, 398
Pertsorp AB, 397–398
Petroleos de Venezuela, 327
Philips, N. V., 248–249, 740
Pommery et Greno, 199
Procter & Gamble Company, 741

Renault, 740
R. J. Reynolds, 745
RJR Nabisco, 215
Roche Holding, Ltd., 444
Royal Dutch/Shell, 234, 277, 740
Rubbermaid, Inc., 8

Saab, 577
Samsung, 740
Sandoz, 750

Scandinavian Airlines System (SAS), 521, 522–523, 532
Schloeman-Siemag A. G., 436
Sea Containers Ltd. of London, 601
Semco S/A, 576, 577–578
Shell, 234
Siemens A.G., 249, 740, 752
Sony Corporation, 28, 259, 315, 618, 648, 737
Southland Corporation, 327
Springfield Remanufacturing Corporation, 166
STK, 724

Tennant Company, 580
Tesco Stores, 214

Texaco, 740
Texas Instruments, 755–756
Thompson S.A., 207, 513
Thorneburg Hosiery, 741
Toshiba Corporation, 144, 162
Toyota Motor Corporation, 350–351, 438, 572, 573, 580, 647, 655, 737, 740
Tungsram Co., 747

Unie, 736
Unilever, 234, 736–738, 740, 742
Unilever NV, 736–738
Unilever PLC, 736, 737
Union Carbide, 385
United Technologies, 122, 745
U.S. Shoe, 341

Veuve Clicquot, 199
Volkswagen, 737, 740
Volvo, A. B., 573, 737

Waitrose Supermarkets, 214
Walt Disney Productions, 188, 189
Waterford Glass Group PLC, 351
Whirlpool Corp., 754
Wistom, 791
Woolworth, F. W., 405
WPP Group, PLC, 620

Xerox Company, 90, 110, 745

Yamaha Motor Company, 247

Zebco, 240